Oracle®

UNLEASHED

SAMS PUBLISHING

201 West 103rd Street
Indianapolis, IN 46290

FIRST EDITION

International Standard Book Number: 0-672-30872-X

Library of Congress Catalog Card Number: 95-72326

99 98 97 96   4 3 2 1

Interpretation of the printing code: the rightmost double-digit number is the year of the book's printing; the rightmost single-digit, the number of the book's printing. For example, a printing code of 96-1 shows that the first printing of the book occurred in 1996.

Composed in Agaramond and MCPdigital by Macmillan Computer Publishing

Printed in the United States of America

Publisher and President   *Richard K. Swadley*

Acquisitions Manager   *Greg Wiegand*

Development Manager   *Dean Miller*

Managing Editor   *Cindy Morrow*

Marketing Manager   *Gregg Bushyeager*

Acquisitions Editor
Rosemarie Graham

Development Editor
Todd Bumbalough

Software Development Specialist
Steve Straiger

Production Editors
Mary Inderstrodt,
Kris Simmons

Copy Editors
Margeret Berson, David Bradford, Susan Christophersen, Mary Ann Faughnan, Greg Horman, Christine Prakel, Carla Randolph, Marla Reece, Elaine Sands, Tonya Simpson, Heather Stith, Joe Williams

Technical Reviewers
James Farmer, P. Eng Valcom Ltd., Jeffrey W. George, Dr. Robert J. Goshen, David Kennedy, Thomas J. Luers, Len Sterrett

Editorial Coordinator
Bill Whitmer

Technical Edit Coordinator
Lynette Quinn

Formatter
Frank Sinclair

Editorial Assistants
Sharon Cox, Andi Richter Rhonda Tinch-Mize

Cover Designer
Tim Amrhein

Book Designer
Alyssa Yesh

Production Team Supervisor
Brad Chinn

Production
Mona Brown, Michael Brumitt, Jeanne Clark, Michael Dietsche, Judy Everly, Jason Hand, Michael Henry, Aleata Howard, Ayanna Lacey, Kevin Laseau, Cheryl Moore, Casey Price, Brian-Kent Proffitt, Beth Rago, Bobbi Satterfield, Laura A. Smith, SA Springer, Josette Starks, Andrew Stone, Susan Van Ness, Mark Walchle, Colleen Williams

Indexer
Charlotte Clapp

Overview

Part V Designer/2000

Part VI Developer/2000

Part VII Oracle Power Objects

Contents

Part III Database Administration

Part VII Oracle Power Objects

Part VIII   Oracle Objects for OLE

Part IX   Advanced Topics

Acknowledgments

Sams Publishing wishes to thank Hugo Toledo, Dave McCutcheon, John Moss, and Michelle Trapani of the Oracle Legal Department for their assistance with the book.

AIS wishes to thank the editors at Sams Publishing and all of the authors for their contributions. We offer our special thanks to the following authors: Lori Pleiness, Andrea Sprague, Hari Sankar, Steve Faris, and the folks from G2 Technologies. Special thanks to Brett Mark for providing technical research and overseeing the project. Our extra special thanks to Dr. Frederick Lenz, author of *Surfing the Himalayas*.

Michael Richards CEO
Advanced Information Systems, Inc.
(800) 327-9725

About the Authors

ADVANCED INFORMATION SYSTEMS, Inc. Michael Richards is the CEO of Advanced Information Systems (AIS), Inc. AIS is a professional software development and consulting firm that offers a range of products and services specializing in Oracle development. A primary objective of AIS is to provide technical solutions in the form of Management Consulting, Project Staffing, Independent Consultants, and Training Services.

AIS offers a popular approach to client/server development called Rapid Application Foundation (RAF). RAF is a set of predeveloped code libraries coupled with skills transfer. RAF is offered as a one-or two-week training system that is tailored to develop an in-house application system. AIS clients receive a well-crafted client/server system that takes advantage of today's premier development systems including Oracle and Visual Basic. Oracle and these tools can be purchased at a discount from AIS. AIS can be reached at (800) 327-9725.

Rachel Becker is a software consultant who has been developing administrative business applications since 1985. She has worked primarily with Oracle Tools since 1989, using Oracle's CASE tool since 1991. Her project experience up and down the east coast includes university, insurance, utilities, and medical environments. She is currently living in the Charlotte, NC area. Reach her via e-mail at wbecker709@aol.com.

Matthew Bennett is a Senior Technical Marketing Manager in the Web/Workgroup Systems Division at Oracle Corporation. He is currently responsible for a team of application developers working on creating World Wide Web applications using Oracle's newest Web technologies. Before working at Oracle, he was the founder of Data Smiths, a Provo, Utah-based systems integration firm. At Data Smiths, he was responsible for publishing articles in Network Computing, Software Development, and numerous technical journals.

Winnie In-Kuan Cheang (B.S., M.S., M.B.A.) is currently a Senior Technical Analyst in Oracle Corporation's Worldwide Support. She provides mission-critical support to database administrators and developers of Oracle products on a wide variety of systems and networks. She is also the NetWare administrator and DBA for the Desktop Support Group production system at Oracle. Winnie is an ECNE and has many years of computer networking and relational database experience as a programmer, technical analyst, instructor, and consultant. She has presented and published papers on relational database applications for the Human Genome Project in the IEEE proceedings.

Mike Conklin, an independent consultant working in Rochester, New York, has more than 17 years experience—the past six working with Oracle-specific applications. Mike and his wife Pam have enjoyed 21 years of marriage. Together, they home-educate their three children, studying along with them. By God's grace they have chosen to build their relationships and values upon Biblical principles. Renovating an 1800's farm house where they welcome frequent (and flexible!) guests is an added challenge.

Patrick Connors is the CASE analyst for the Arizona Department of Health Services. He is responsible for administering the Designer/2000 tool and acts as a consultant on Oracle CASE projects. He has been an Oracle programmer since 1990 and a computer professional since 1980, working on a variety of projects from accounting systems to video games. In his spare time, he is a cartoonist and kayaker. Patrick is single and resides in Phoenix.

Joe Greene has worked in a variety of fields, from driving submarines to spacecraft design. Along the way, he began to implement computer systems to meet various business needs. This has lead to a career as a computer consultant with a number of assignments working with Oracle databases. His experience ranges from very large data warehouses (with more than 100 gigabytes of data) to small scientific data collection systems, with a wide variety of databases in between. He is the author of *Oracle DBA Survival Guide*, also from Sams Publishing.

Scott Hillegas is a senior consultant with Integrated Systems Consulting Group, located in Wayne, Pa. He has more than 10 years of Oracle DBA experience and more than 20 years of MIS experience on various platforms. His area of experience is the design, development, and implementation of relational database and client/server technologies, and most notably, Oracle on the UNIX platform. He began his Oracle career with version 5.1, building OLTP systems, and today is working with version 7.2, building DSS data warehousing systems.

Dan Hotka has 17 years in the computer business, 10 of those with the Oracle products. He first worked with Oracle products in the Version 4 days, when SQL*Plus was called UFI (User Friendly Interface) and when Oracle Forms was nothing more than a product called Fastforms, which generated a basic INP file that was compiled with IAG and interpreted by IAP. There was also a neat little report writer called RPT. He worked with Oracle (including Oracle Corp) as a marketing presales support representative (more than four years) and in various consulting, development, and DBA roles (more than six years). He has written language source code filters that have converted entire applications written in other languages into the Oracle languages. These filters include both data and program conversions. He has worked extensively with each of the Oracle releases since Oracle 4, including the current Oracle 7.1 release.

Steve Hughes has been in data processing for more than 10 years. With a strong applications development background in Xbase languages, primarily using FoxPro with TRO as an application foundation, he has recently turned his experience and enthusiasm to Oracle. Recently promoted to the position of Oracle DBA at CMS Therapies in Charlotte, NC, his responsibilities include installing and upgrading client/server software, data backup and recovery, user access maintenance, and performance tuning. His experience includes Oracle running on Novell NetWare 3.12 and a DEC Alpha running DEC OSF/1. He can be reached via CompuServe at 74133,1327.

Dave Kinchen has been involved with Oracle for most of his professional career, spanning development, database administration, and design on many different platforms. On the rare occasions Dave is not working, you might find him with his family doing something fun in the Rockies.

Bruce Kostival holds a BSEE degree from Pennsylvania State University and an MBA in Information Systems from the University of Colorado. Having been in the field of software development for more than 16 years, he has written software in many areas from real-time data acquisitions to Oracle RDBMS database development. He has developed Oracle software in both the VMS and UNIX environments. Currently, he is employed with a direct marketing company in private industry as a Senior Programmer/Analyst. His real-life interests are his two (going on three) children, and his lovely and talented wife Ruthann. In his little spare time, he enjoys Colorado's fabulous skiing, *on-* or *off-piste!*

Ronnie Lashaw has more than 10 years of experience developing and deploying client/server database applications for clients including the U.S. Air Force, NASA, Veterans Administration, U.S. Dept. of Education, Unisys, Boeing, and Lockheed Martin. He has a B.S. in Computer Science and a minor in Industrial Engineering from North Carolina State University. He has extensive knowledge of Oracle products with emphasis on Oracle Power Objects. His primary objective is to provide intuitive, visually appealing, user-friendly, graphical client/server applications. He can be reached on CompuServe at 74513,1076 or on the Internet at rlashaw@us.oracle.com for discussions about Power Objects.

Kelly Leigh, with more than eight years' experience in the systems administration world, made the jump into database administration over three years ago. Starting out with Informix and moving to Oracle, he has had experience in everything from product installation to database layout to implementing custom applications. Currently working for a small company in Longmont, Colorado, he is also co-owner of Colorado Business Solutions, a company created to provide small and mid-range business consulting in a wide range of areas including office automation, network installation, database installation, and software training. Outside of work, Kelly is an avid hiker and camper, spending much of his free time in the foothills of the Rocky mountains.

Keith Majkut is a Senior Software Engineer in the Workgroup Solutions Division of Oracle Corporation. He has been with Oracle for five years, and in that time has worked on a variety of products including Oracle Reports, the Oracle Workgroup Server, Oracle Objects for OLE, and currently Personal Oracle7 for Windows 95. Keith grew up in Milford, Connecticut and graduated from Northeastern University of Boston, Massachusettes in 1990 with a Bachelor of Science in Computer Science. When he's not working or spending time with his wife Karen, he can be found riding his motorcycle around the San Francisco Bay area, where he currently resides. Keith can also be found roaming the Oracle groups on the Internet and CompuServe, or you can contact him directly at kmajkut@netcom.com or on CompuServe at 74343,1566.

Byron Pearce is the Database Administrator for Nokia Mobile Phones U.S.-based operations in Fort Worth, Texas, where he has the dual capacity as the MIS Operations Supervisor. He is responsible for ensuring the availability and overall health of all UNIX and Oracle RDBMS Systems that support Nokia's U.S.-based manufacturing and distribution systems. Byron has worked in a multi-functional capacity in the MIS Departments for several companies, including SONAT and Tandy Corporation, working as a systems operator, applications developer, systems analyst, project leader, database administrator, and UNIX system administrator. Recently, he completed technical editing of the *Oracle DBA Survival Guide* by Sams. He lives in Arlington, Texas with his wife, Cherie, and can be reached via Internet at Bpearce163@aol.com.

Lave Singh (BSc, ACGI, MBCS), is founder and head of Titanium Computers Ltd., a training and consulting firm, which over the last eight years has provided Oracle training and consulting services to organizations in Europe, North America, and the Middle East. They specialize in DBA, Tuning, Forms 4.5, and Short-Term Technical Consulting, as well as running training courses for a number of blue-chip clients. More than 13 years ago, Lave began at Imperial College on a Computational Science course and since then has been working in the computing field. His wife Permjit and three young children (Benisha, Taejen, and Kashmir) provide a semblance (only just) of sanity away from machines. He can be reached on e-mail at 100135.1773@compuserve.com or by phone on +44(181) 692 5204.

Vic Stambaugh is a principal and Director of Technology Marketing for Integrated Systems Consulting Group, Inc. (ISCG), a Pennsylvania-based consulting firm that develops and integrates client/server systems for the pharmaceutical, health care, and life sciences industries. He has more than 16 years of software development experience, in both full life cycle applications development and database administration, and has worked exclusively with Oracle-based systems since 1986. Vic has designed and taught numerous database and Oracle courses, and is active in the Oracle community as a frequent presenter at international and regional user conferences. He currently serves on the Board of Directors for the Oracle CASE SIG and also served on the Board of Advisors for the Oracle Consultants Alliance.

Brian Twidt has been developing client/server database applications for five years. His experience includes applications designed for such clients as Oracle, NASA, FDA, US DOE, Boeing, and Lockheed Martin. The majority of his experience is related to using desktop development tools such as Oracle Power Objects, Microsoft Visual Basic, C++, and Oracle Card. He has a B.S. in Computer Science and a minor in Graphic Communications from North Carolina State University. His primary objective is to develop applications that are graphical, intuitive, innovative, and compelling. Any comments regarding Oracle Power Objects can be directed to Brian via the Internet at btwidt@us.oracle.com.

Gigi Wadley has been involved with Oracle for approximately five years. Her experience has been obtained through government and private industries. The majority of the work she has done consists of Pro*C and SQL*Forms. She has been married for 13 years and has a 12-year-old daughter. Most of their lives have been spent in Colorado where they enjoy the lifestyle that the state provides.

Chester "Chet" West began his computer career nine years ago as a computer operator in the U.S. Air Force. He later cross-trained into the computer programming career field where he developed and maintained real-time communications system software at both Offutt AFB and Tinker AFB. There he gained his first exposure to database programming, though home-grown. He also began development of an office configuration management system using FoxPro as his database engine. Upon completion of his B.S. in Computer Science, he went to work for Threads

USA in Gastonia, NC, where he helped develop and maintain FoxPro applications. From there, he became a consultant for The Registry and was contracted by CMS Therapies, where he developed both FoxPro and Oracle systems. He is the senior programmer, leading all new Oracle development and assisting in the maintenance of legacy FoxPro systems. He can be reached by sending e-mail to 102046,517@compuserve.com.

Kevin Whitley has worked on everything from mainframe Fortran to micro assembler over the last 15 years. He is currently a lead architect at BBN Domain and uses C++ to develop client/server applications for the pharmaceutical and manufacturing industries.

Joe Zafian III has been working full-time in Information Systems since graduation from New Jersey Institute of Technology with a B.S. in Computer Science in 1981. Currently a consultant specializing in Oracle database applications, he has been working with all versions of the RDBMS and its associated tools since 1986. As a consultant, he has worked with a number of Fortune 500 clients in several industries across a vast array of hardware platforms. This experience qualified him to speak at the international Oracle Users' Week Conference in 1994 (Predicting Storage Requirements for Large, Dynamic Oracle Databases and Advanced Techniques for Dynamic, User-Driven Applications in SQL*Forms 3.0) and 1995 (Quality Assurance for Oracle Projects and Advanced Techniques for Oracle Forms 4.5 Applications). When not striving to deliver quality Oracle systems (or writing about it), Joe enjoys sports, fishing and other outdoor activities with his wife, Ruth. He can be contacted via CompuServe at 73744,2713.

Ken Zimmerman received his Bachelor of Science in Geology from Duke University in 1982. However, his interest in computers dates back as far as 1975 when he became intrigued with what was then that era's "Information Highway," available through his preparatory school's newly acquired Digital PDP-11/70 system. His work with computers, and especially with database management systems, continued through his undergraduate years as well as during his graduate work in Petrology as an ARCO fellow at USC. In 1985, Ken founded Chateaux Software Development, Inc., a company specializing in PowerBuilder, Oracle, Lotus Notes, and Progress solutions on UNIX, VMS, MS-Windows, Windows-NT Advanced Server, and Novel platforms. His company's primary goal has been to develop high-performance applications on a variety of platforms, ranging from low-end 80x86-based DOS and UNIX systems to midrange HP-9000 HP/UX, IBM AIX, and DEC VAX systems. His firm's strengths are especially geared toward producing highly efficient systems, primarily by developing compact code, well-designed data structures, and a user-oriented architecture. Chateaux is building on these strengths and provides enterprise-quality solutions to WWW/RDBMS integration problems. Ken Zimmerman and Chateaux can be reached at 9 Tierney Lane, Greens Farms CT 06436, by phone at (203) 259-9665, and through CompuServe at 74404,1401.

Introduction

When I first started using Oracle many years ago, it was possible to *know* the database and the tools available. With the rash of recent releases of different options for the database and the spate of new tools, only people who wear their underpants over their trousers will be able to know everything there is to know about the Oracle products. If you were an experienced Oracle developer three years ago and since then have been locked away—not able to see the new Oracle versions of the database and tools—there will be very little that you will recognize today. Along with changes in other computing technologies, the rate of change with Oracle is constantly increasing, which is all the more interesting for us who get turned on by the software. You'll get a running start with the pages that follow.

Oracle Unleashed is one of the most comprehensive books on Oracle and its tools available today. It's written by authors who have real-life experience using the Oracle tools (most of whom are members of the Oracle Business Alliance Program). We will show you what's important, the pitfalls, tips from real-life experiences, and code examples—the kind of information that can give you the cumulative experience of many years of expertise.

It's a Database, Jim, But Not As We Know It

Oracle Corporation, headquartered in Redwood Shores, California, was best known for being a database company that also provided its own tools for working with the database. Many sites used the power of the Oracle database but used better third-party tools as their interface to the database.

Today, the Oracle tools are among the best and most powerful development tools available; if you want it, Oracle can do it. Oracle now provides the database, multiple choices of tools, and utilities to connect to the Oracle database from third-party products, applications (the best known of which is Financials), and a host of other products. In the next year Oracle will release an Internet machine, making the scope of Oracle products mushroom. Not just a database provider but a tools company, software house writing applications, hardware manufacturer, and Internet service provider? (Just give them time.)

SELECT * FROM book

The beginning of the book lays the foundation on top of which all the tools will be built—the architecture of the database and the two languages used in most tools, SQL and PL/SQL. If you don't (yet) want to know how the electricity works but just want to switch on the light, skip over the architecture section.

For database administrators and others who need to know how to keep the database humming, the database administration section will detail the most common functions of looking after the database and traps to watch out for. The remaining sections look at the tools of most interest to developers.

But how is Oracle going to be useful in producing your system? It gives you a multitude of choices to work with; in fact, at times it seems like too many choices. You have choices with the database itself about which database options you want to use. There are choices about which Oracle tools to use: Forms, Reports, Graphics, Power Objects, and more. If you don't want to use the Oracle tools, you can connect PowerBuilder, SQLWindows, Visual Basic, Delphi, and other third-party tools. You can even use the Oracle tools with non-Oracle data sources using ODBC, User Exits written in third-generation languages, or the gateway database products. Whatever you want to do, you can do it in one way or another. Choices, choices, and even more choices.

In addition to using the database and tools, you'll want to manage the development life cycle right from the strategy stage through to implementation and maintenance. What better tool to use than the Designer/2000 product. You can even generate your programs from this tool. Check out the Designer/2000 and Developing Applications sections of the book for designing and developing applications using Designer/2000.

Today, for any application development project, making the right selection of tools and database is even harder and more important. Pick the wrong options, and the time and effort needed can be vastly increased. The information available in this book will make sifting through the plethora of choices easier.

"But I've Used Oracle Before"

If you've used previous versions of Oracle products, you'll find it easier to get a grip on the pertinent points of the new tools and components, and to add more background to areas such as the architecture, database administration, Designer/2000, and the other tool options available. If you already have experience with the newer products, then discover how the authors are using the newest tools and options now available.

Is This Book for Me?

Now that you know what's going to be covered in the book, the next question you'll probably be asking is whether it's the right book for you.

This book is aimed at

- Experienced Oracle Developers
- Database administrators
- Intermediate developers, especially those who have used previous versions of the products
- Those who have used similar technologies and want to quickly get a grip on Oracle and its tools
- Technical managers who want to know about the available options

The book covers SQL and PL/SQL in enough detail to allow you to get up and running quickly with developing with Oracle. Because it is geared toward an intermediate to advanced audience, however, this book quickly covers the essential basics of these two languages and shows you how to start producing real-life applications.

Take a while to play around with the products while you're reading the book. Look at the examples, try them out, and explore. You'll gain a far deeper understanding by using the products while reading.

Open your mind, open the book, and get ready to unleash the power of Oracle!

Lave Singh
December, 1995

Oracle® Concepts

PART

I

What Is an RDBMS?

1

*by Victor
Stambaugh*

IN THIS CHAPTER

In recent years, database management systems (DBMS) have established themselves as the primary means of data storage for information systems ranging from large commercial transaction processing applications to PC-based desktop applications. At the heart of most of today's information systems is a relational database management system (RDBMS). RDBMSs have been the workhorse for data management operations for over a decade and continue to evolve and mature, providing sophisticated storage, retrieval, and distribution functions to enterprise-wide data processing and information management systems. Compared to the file systems, relational database management systems provide organizations with the capability to easily integrate and leverage the massive amounts of operational data into meaningful information systems. The evolution of high-powered database engines such as Oracle7™ has fostered the development of advanced "enabling" technologies including client/server, data warehousing, and online analytical processing, all of which comprise the core of today's state-of-the-art information management systems.

Examine the components of the term *relational database management system*. First, a *database* is an integrated collection of related data. Given a specific data item, the structure of a database facilitates the access to data related to it, such as a student and all of his registered courses or an employee and his dependents. Next, a *relational database* is a type of database based in the relational model; nonrelational databases commonly use a *hierarchical, network,* or *object-oriented* model as their basis. Finally, a *relational database management system* is the software that manages a relational database. These systems come in several varieties, ranging from single-user desktop systems to full-featured, global, enterprise-wide systems, such as Oracle7.

This chapter discusses the basic elements of a relational database management system, the relational database, and the software systems that manage it. Also included is a discussion of nonprocedural data access. If you are a new user to relational database technology, you'll have to change your thinking somewhat when it comes to referencing data nonprocedurally.

The Relational Database Model

Most of the database management systems used by commercial applications today are based on one of three basic models: the hierarchical model, the network model, or the relational model. The following sections describe the various differences and similarities of the models.

Hierarchical and Network Models

The first commercially available database management systems were of the CODASYL type, and many of them are still in use with mainframe-based, COBOL applications. Both network and hierarchical databases are quite complex in that they rely on the use of permanent internal *pointers* to relate records to each other. For example, in an accounts payable application, a vendor record might contain a physical pointer in its record structure that points to purchase order records. Each purchase order record in turn contains pointers to purchase order line item records.

The process of inserting, updating, and deleting records using these types of databases requires synchronization of the pointers, a task that must be performed by the application. As you might imagine, this pointer maintenance requires a significant amount of application code (usually written in COBOL) that at times can be quite cumbersome.

Elements of the Relational Model

Relational databases rely on the actual attribute values as opposed to internal pointers to link records. Instead of using an internal pointer from the vendor record to purchase order records, you would link the purchase order record to the vendor record using a common attribute from each record, such as the vendor identification number.

Although the concepts of academic theory underlying the relational model are somewhat complex, you should be familiar with some basic concepts and terminology. Essentially, there are three basic components of the relational model: relational data structures, constraints that govern the organization of the data structures, and operations that are performed on the data structures.

Relational Data Structures

The relational model supports a single, "logical" structure called a *relation*, a two-dimensional data structure commonly called a *table* in the "physical" database. *Attributes* represent the atomic data elements that are related by the relation. For example, the Customer relation might contain such attributes about a customer as the customer number, customer name, region, credit status, and so on.

> **NOTE**
>
> In relational database design literature, you might see a relation denoted as
> `Relation(attribute1, attribute2, . . .)` with the name of the relation followed by
> the attribute list enclosed in parentheses.
>
> `Customer(Customer_ID, Customer_Name, Region, . . .)`

The actual data values for the attributes of a relation are stored in *tuples*, or rows, of the table. It is not necessary for a relation to have rows in order to be a relation; even if no data exists for the relation, the relation remains defined with its set of attributes. Figure 1.1 illustrates the basic elements of the Customer relation.

FIGURE 1.1.

The basic components of a relation.

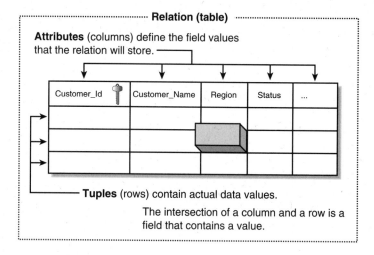

Relation (table)

Attributes (columns) define the field values that the relation will store.

Customer_Id 🔑	Customer_Name	Region	Status	...

Tuples (rows) contain actual data values.

The intersection of a column and a row is a field that contains a value.

Key Values and Referential Integrity

Attributes are grouped with other attributes based on their dependency on a *primary key* value. A primary key is an attribute or group of attributes that uniquely identifies a row in a table. A table has only one primary key, and as a rule, every table has one. Because primary key values are used as identifiers, they cannot be null. Using the conventional notation for relations, an attribute is underlined to indicate that it is the primary key of the relation. If a primary key consists of several attributes, each attribute is underlined.

You can have additional attributes in a relation with values that you define as *unique* to the relation. Unlike primary keys, unique keys can contain null values. In practice, unique keys are used to prevent duplication in the table rather than identify rows. Consider a relation that contains the attribute, United States Social Security Number (SSN). In some rows, this attribute might be null since not every person has a SSN; however, for a row that contains a non-null value for the SSN attribute, the value must be unique to the relation.

Linking one relation to another typically involves an attribute that is common to both relations. The common attributes are usually a primary key from one table and a *foreign key* from the other. *Referential integrity* rules dictate that foreign key values in one relation reference the primary key values in another relation. Foreign keys might also reference the primary key of the same relation. Figure 1.2 illustrates two foreign key relationships.

NOTE

Many database design tools use underlines to denote primary keys in diagram and report views. Depending on the tool that you use, you might also see (PK) and (FK) next to attributes to denote primary and foreign keys, respectively.

FIGURE 1.2.

Foreign keys that reference a primary key in another table as well as a primary key in the same table.

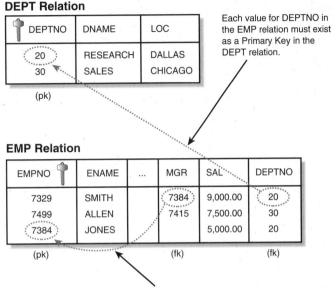

DEPT Relation

DEPTNO	DNAME	LOC
20	RESEARCH	DALLAS
30	SALES	CHICAGO

(pk)

Each value for DEPTNO in the EMP relation must exist as a Primary Key in the DEPT relation.

EMP Relation

EMPNO	ENAME	...	MGR	SAL	DEPTNO
7329	SMITH		7384	9,000.00	20
7499	ALLEN		7415	7,500.00	30
7384	JONES			5,000.00	20

(pk)   (fk)   (fk)

The MGR attribute is a self-referencing Foreign Key.

> **NOTE**
>
> You will notice frequent references to the DEPT and EMP sample tables throughout Oracle® documentation. You can find these tables along with other sample database objects in Oracle's standard demonstration account. You usually access the account with the username/password combination `scott`/`tiger`.

You typically design a relational database using the *rules of normalization* that dictate which attributes belong in which relations. There are five levels (or forms) of normalization to which a data model can comply. Of the five, most database designs minimally conform to the *third normal form*. This form serves to alleviate redundancy in the data model, requiring each atomic data element to appear once in the data model and be dependent on one and only one primary key. Employing a normalized data model protects against insert, update, and delete anomalies that can arise as a result of incorrectly defined relations.

Relational Algebra

The relational model defines the operations that are permitted on a relation or group of relations. There are *unary* and *binary* relational operators, each of which result in another relation. You should find these operations somewhat intuitive and very similar to those used with set operations. Table 1.1 describes the seven operators used to manipulate relational structures.

Binary operator types indicate that the operation uses two relations as operands; unary operators require a single relation as an operand.

Table 1.1. Algebra operations of the relational model.

Operation	Type	Resulting Relation
Union	Binary	Rows from the two relations are combined, eliminating duplicate rows.
Intersection	Binary	Rows common to two relations.
Difference	Binary	Rows that exist in the first relation but not in the second.
Projection	Unary	Rows that contain some of the columns from the source relation.
Selection	Unary	Rows from the source relation that meet query criteria.
Product	Binary	Concatenation of every row in one relation with every row in another.
Join	Binary	Concatenation of rows from one relation and related rows from another.

NOTE

The source relations used by UNION, INTERSECTION, and DIFFERENCE must have attribute lists that match in number and data type.

RDBMS Components

Two important pieces of an RDBMS architecture are the *kernel*, which is the software, and the *data dictionary*, which consists of the system-level data structures used by the kernel to manage the database.

The RDBMS Kernel

You might think of an RDBMS as an operating system (or set of subsystems), designed specifically for controlling data access; its primary functions are storing, retrieving, and securing data. Like an operating system, Oracle7 manages and controls access to a given set of resources for concurrent database users. The subsystems of an RDBMS closely resemble those of a host operating system and tightly integrate with the host's services for machine-level access to resources such as memory, CPU, devices, and file structures. An RDBMS such as Oracle7 maintains its own list of authorized users and their associated privileges; manages memory caches and paging; controls locking for concurrent resource usage; dispatches and schedules user requests; and manages space usage within its tablespace structures. Figure 1.3 illustrates the primary subsystems of the Oracle7 kernel that manage the database.

FIGURE 1.3.

An RDBMS and its multiple subsystems.

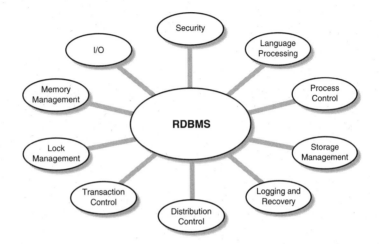

The Data Dictionary

A fundamental difference between an RDBMS and other database and file systems is in the way that they access data. An RDBMS enables you to reference physical data in a more abstract, logical fashion, providing ease and flexibility in developing application code. Programs using an RDBMS access data through a database engine, creating independence from the actual data source and insulating applications from the details of the underlying physical data structures. Rather than accessing a customer number as bytes 1 through 10 of the customer record, an application simply refers to the attribute Customer Number. The RDBMS takes care of where the field is stored in the database. Consider the amount of programming modifications that you must make if you change a record structure in a file system-based application. For example, if you move the customer number from bytes 1 through 10 to bytes 11 through 20 to accommodate an additional field, all the programs that use the customer number would require modification. However, using an RDBMS, the application code would continue to reference the attribute by name rather than by record position, alleviating the need for any modifications.

This data independence is possible because of the RDBMS's data dictionary. The data dictionary stores meta-data (data about data) for all the objects that reside in the database. Oracle7's data dictionary is a set of tables and database objects that is stored in a special area of the database and maintained exclusively by the Oracle7 kernel. As shown in Figure 1.4, requests to read or update the database are processed by the Oracle7 kernel using the information in the data dictionary. The information in the data dictionary validates the existence of the objects, provides access to them, and maps the actual physical storage location.

FIGURE 1.4.

Access to application data through the Oracle7 Kernel and Data Dictionary.

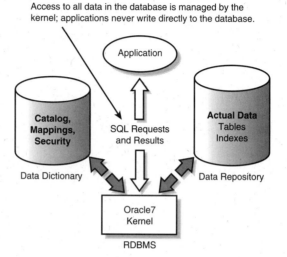

Access to all data in the database is managed by the kernel; applications never write directly to the database.

Not only does the RDBMS take care of locating data, it also determines an optimal access path to store or retrieve the data. Oracle7 uses sophisticated algorithms that enable you to retrieve information either for the best response for the first set of rows, or for total throughput of all rows to be retrieved.

Nonprocedural Data Access (SQL)

An RDBMS differentiates itself with its capability to process a set of data; other file systems and database models process data in a record-by-record fashion. You communicate with an RDBMS using Structured Query Language (SQL, pronounced sequel). SQL is a nonprocedural language that is designed specifically for data access operations on normalized relational database structures. The primary difference between SQL and other conventional programming languages is that SQL statements specify *what* data operations should be performed rather than *how* to perform them. For example, consider a procedure to give a salary increase to a particular department for each employee who had not received a raise within the past six months. The code segments in Figure 1.5 illustrate the solution to the problem using both procedural and nonprocedural methods.

Although the example in Figure 1.5 illustrates a simplistic scenario, consider a more complex application and the amount of programming that is alleviated by using SQL for data access. By reducing the amount of programming required for data access, the costs to develop and maintain the data access portions of an application are also reduced.

#### Chapter 1

FIGURE 1.5.

SQL programming versus traditional procedural programming methods.

```
Procedural method (pseudo code)

raise_date_cuttoff:= get_delta_date
(get_sysdate(),-6,"month") open/read_write
employee_file
while not EOF
 read employee_record
 if employee_record(20:2)=:target_department then
  last_raise:=convert_date(employee_rec (43:7))
  if last_raise>raise_date_cuttoff then
   salary:=decimal_unpack(employee_rec(31:4))
   salary:=salary*1.06
   employee_rec(31:4):=decimal_pack(salary)
   rewrite employee
  end if
 end if
end while
close employee_file
```

```
Nonprocedural method (SQL)

update employee
 set salary=salary*1.06
 wheredeptno=:target_department
 and last_raise>add_months(sysdate,-6)
```

Summary

This chapter describes two aspects of a relational database management system: the relational database model and the database management system. The relational model defines relations, which are the underlying database structures; constraints, which are the rules that govern their relationships to one another; and the relational algebra operations that you can perform on relations. Relational database management systems work on sets of data and employ many of the concepts of basic set theory.

A full-featured management system for a relational database is a sophisticated, complex piece of software that functions very much like an operating system. One of the reasons that Oracle has been so successful and widely used is that it has been able to implement the same "logical" database operating system on a variety of host operating systems. User access to objects in the database is controlled by the RDBMS kernel and the meta-data stored in the data dictionary. Applications never access the data in the actual operating system data files directly; instead, all access is provided through the RDBMS.

Access to RDBMS data is accomplished through nonprocedural requests using SQL. Compared to conventional file system access, SQL provides "set-at-a-time" as opposed to "row-by-row" processing. The language elements and usage of SQL are covered in Chapter 4, "SQL."

Oracle® and Client/Server

2

*by
Victor
Stambaugh*

IN THIS CHAPTER

Oracle Corporation's reputation as a database company is firmly established in its full-featured, high-performance RDBMS server. With the database as the cornerstone of its product line, Oracle has evolved into more than just a database company, complementing its RDBMS server with a rich offering of well-integrated products that are designed specifically for distributed processing and client/server applications. As Oracle's database server has evolved to support large-scale enterprise systems for transaction processing and decision support, so too have its other products, to the extent that Oracle can provide a complete solution for client/server application development and deployment. This chapter presents an overview of client/server database systems and the Oracle product architectures that support their implementation.

An Overview of Client/Server Computing

The premise of client/server computing is to distribute the execution of a task among multiple processors in a network. Each processor is dedicated to a specific, focused set of subtasks that it performs best, and the end result is increased overall efficiency and effectiveness of the system as a whole. Splitting the execution of tasks between processors is done through a protocol of service requests; one processor, the *client*, requests a service from another processor, the *server*. The most prevalent implementation of client/server processing involves separating the user interface portion of an application from the data access portion.

On the client, or *front end*, of the typical client/server configuration is a user workstation operating with a Graphical User Interface (GUI) platform, usually Microsoft Windows, Macintosh, or Motif. At the *back end* of the configuration is a database server, often managed by a UNIX, Netware, Windows NT, or VMS operating system.

Client/server architecture also takes the form of a *server-to-server* configuration. In this arrangement, one server plays the role of a client, requesting database services from another server. Multiple database servers can look like a single logical database, providing transparent access to data that is spread around the network.

Designing an efficient client/server application is somewhat of a balancing act, the goal of which is to evenly distribute execution of tasks among processors while making optimal use of available resources. Given the increased complexity and processing power required to manage a graphical user interface (GUI) and the increased demands for throughput on database servers and networks, achieving the proper distribution of tasks is challenging. Client/server systems are inherently more difficult to develop and manage than traditional host-based application systems because of the following challenges:

- The components of a client/server system are distributed across more varied types of processors. There are many more software components that manage client, network, and server functions, as well as an array of infrastructure layers, all of which must be in place and configured to be compatible with each other.

■ The complexity of GUI applications far outweighs that of their character-based predecessors. GUIs are capable of presenting much more information to the user and providing many additional navigation paths to elements of the interface.

■ Troubleshooting performance problems and errors is more difficult because of the increased number of components and layers in the system.

Databases in a Client/Server Architecture

Client/server technologies have changed the look and architecture of application systems in two ways. Not only has the supporting hardware architecture undergone substantial changes, but there have also been significant changes in the approach to designing the application logic of the system.

Prior to the advent of client/server technology, most Oracle applications ran on a single node. Typically, a character-based SQL*Forms application would access a database instance on the same machine with the application and the RDBMS competing for the same CPU and memory resources. Not only was the system responsible for supporting all the database processing, but it was also responsible for executing the application logic. In addition, the system was burdened with all the I/O processing for each terminal on the system; each keystroke and display attribute was controlled by the same processor that processed database requests and application logic.

Client/server systems change this architecture considerably by splitting all of the interface management and much of the application processing from the host system processor and distributing it to the client processor.

Combined with the advances in hardware infrastructure, the increased capabilities of RDBMS servers have also contributed to changes in the application architecture. Prior to the release of Oracle7, Oracle's RDBMS was less sophisticated in its capability to support the processing logic necessary to maintain the integrity of data in the database. For example, primary and foreign key checking and enforcement was performed by the application. As a result, the database was highly reliant on application code for enforcement of business rules and integrity, making application code bulkier and more complex. Figure 2.1 illustrates the differences between traditional host-based applications and client/server applications. Client/server database applications can take advantage of the Oracle7 Server™ features for implementation of some of the application logic.

The pre-Oracle7 databases provided little more than data-type checking at the kernel level; but with Oracle7, much of the application logic processing can be performed by the database kernel. Oracle7 contains features such as stored procedures, integrity constraint enforcement, user-defined functions, and database triggers, all of which enable the application to store more of its business rules (or semantics of the data model) at the database level. As a result, the application is freed to do more sophisticated, complex processing tasks such as GUI interface management and integration to other client-based productivity tools. As shown in Figure 2.1, the database is much more robust; no longer is it reliant on application code to maintain its integrity.

FIGURE 2.1.

Host-based applications versus client/server applications.

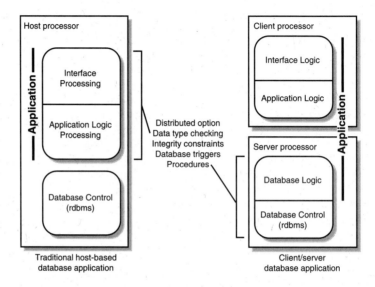

Interface Processing

Application Logic Processing

Database Control (rdbms)

Traditional host-based database application

Distributed option
Data type checking
Integrity constraints
Database triggers
Procedures

Client processor

Interface Logic

Application Logic

Server processor

Database Logic

Database Control (rdbms)

Client/server database application

Oracle and Client/Server Computing

Oracle Corporation has been a leader in introducing advanced client/server database technologies, directing its product development specifically to support the design, implementation, and management of client/server database systems. Oracle has designed products to support each of the three primary components of a client/server architecture:

- A full-featured, high-performance RDBMS server, scaleable from laptops to mainframes
- Client development and run-time products that support multiple GUI environments
- Database connectivity middleware that provides efficient and secure communications over a wide variety of network protocols

Oracle's product offerings in each area are highly scaleable, providing complete client/server solutions for application environments ranging from small workgroup to global enterprise-wide environments. Figure 2.2 illustrates some of the Oracle products used in client/server and distributed systems.

The following sections describe several of the primary components of Oracle's client/server architecture, the Oracle7 RDBMS kernel, SQL*Net, and GUI development tools, all designed specifically for client/server application systems.

FIGURE 2.2.

Oracle's client/server products.

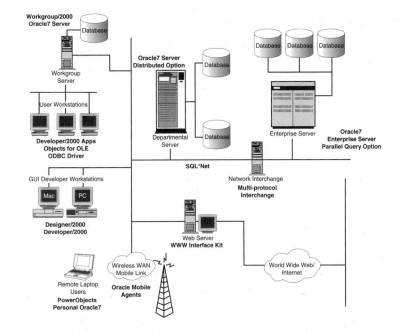

The Oracle7 RDBMS Server

The Oracle7 server is a full-featured RDBMS that is ideally suited to support sophisticated client/server environments. Many features of the Oracle7 internal architecture are designed to provide high availability, maximum throughput, security, and efficient use of its host's resources. Although all these features are important architecturally for a database server, Oracle7 also contains the following language-based features that accelerate development and improve the performance of server-side application components.

- **PL/SQL language**—A major component of the Oracle7 server is its PL/SQL processing engine. (The PL stands for Procedural Language.) PL/SQL is Oracle's fourth generation language that incorporates structured procedural language elements with the SQL language. PL/SQL is designed specifically for client/server processing in that it enables a PL/SQL program block containing application logic as well as SQL statements to be submitted to the server with a single request.

  By using PL/SQL, you can significantly reduce the amount of processing required by the client portion of an application and the network traffic required to execute the logic. For example, you might want to execute different sets of SQL statements based on the results of a query. The query, the subsequent SQL statements, and the conditional logic to execute them can all be incorporated into one PL/SQL block and submitted to the server in one network trip.

Not only can PL/SQL be processed by the Oracle7 server, but it can also be processed by SQL*Forms and Oracle Forms. PL/SQL is used extensively by these tools for client-based procedures and event trigger routines. In a client/server environment, PL/SQL is extremely flexible because the language used by client is interchangeable with that used by the server. Some extensions in the client language syntax allow for control of interface components, reference to form objects, and navigation. Figure 2.3 shows the difference between submitting an "anonymous" PL/SQL block and calling a stored procedure.

FIGURE 2.3.

Minimizing network traffic and application code by using PL/SQL.

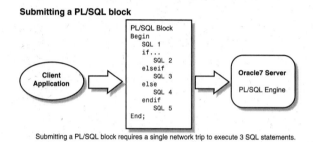

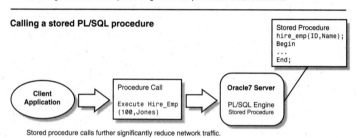

- **Stored procedures**—Although version 6 of Oracle supported server-based PL/SQL, Oracle7 provides the capability to store PL/SQL blocks as database objects in the form of stored procedures, functions, and database packages. Now, portions of the application logic, especially those requiring database access, can reside where they are processed—on the server. Using stored procedures significantly increases the efficiency of a client/server system for several reasons:

  - Calling a stored procedure from a client application generates minimal network traffic. Rather than the application submitting an entire PL/SQL program block from the client, all that is required is a single call to the procedure or function with an optional parameter list.

  - Stored procedures provide a convenient and effective security mechanism. One of the characteristics of stored PL/SQL is that it always executes with the privilege domain of the procedure owner. This enables non-privileged users to have controlled access (through the procedure code) to privileged objects.

This feature usually serves to reduce the amount of grant administration that the DBA must do.

- Both the compiled and textual forms of stored procedures are maintained in the database. Because the compiled form of the procedure is available and readily executable, the need to parse and compile the PL/SQL at run-time is alleviated.

■ **Database triggers**—Database triggers resemble stored procedures in that they are database-resident PL/SQL blocks; the difference between the two is that triggers are fired automatically by the RDBMS kernel in response to a commit time event (such as an insert, update, or delete operation). You can use triggers to enforce complex integrity checking, perform complex auditing and security functions, and implement application alerts and monitors. Like stored procedures, database triggers greatly reduce the amount of code and processing that is necessary in the client portion of an application.

Oracle7's implementation of database triggers is slightly different from that of other vendors. Although most databases support statement-level triggers, Oracle7 also includes functionality to fire triggers at the row level. Consider an UPDATE statement that affects values in a set of 100 rows. The kernel would fire a statement-level trigger once—for the UPDATE statement (either before and/or after the statement executes). Row-level triggers, on the other hand, are fired by the kernel for each row that the statement affects—in this case, 100 times. Oracle7 enables statement-level and row-level triggers to be used in conjunction with one another.

■ **Declarative integrity**—When you define a table in Oracle7, you might include integrity constraints as part of your table definition. Constraints are enforced by the server whenever records are inserted, updated, or deleted. In addition to using referential integrity constraints that enforce primary and foreign key relationships, you can also define your own constraints to control the value domains of individual columns within a table.

Server-enforced integrity reduces some of the code required for validation by the client and also increases the robustness of the business model defined within the database. With constraints, you can often improve performance and provide the flexibility to support multiple front-end interfaces.

■ **User-defined functions**—You'll also find PL/SQL blocks in user-defined functions. User-defined functions are similar to stored procedures and also reduce the amount of application code in the client portion of an application. Not only can you call these functions from PL/SQL, but you can also use them to extend the set of standard Oracle SQL functions. You can place user-defined functions in SQL statements just as you would any other Oracle SQL function.

Designing your Oracle application to make use of these server-based features not only improves the performance of a client/server system but also makes the task of developing and deploying an application easier.

Networking Products

If you're developing an Oracle-based client/server system, you'll probably use Oracle's database networking software to implement connectivity between the nodes in the network. Oracle offers a variety of products and tools that simplify the task of connecting client applications to database servers in a network.

■ **SQL*Net**—SQL*Net is database messaging software that provides optimal, reliable database messaging over every popular network protocol. SQL*Net is designed to provide server location transparency to any node within an application network and uses components that reside on both the client and server sides of an application.

In addition to providing connectivity between workstations and servers in a client/server environment, servers also use SQL*Net to communicate with other servers for distributed transactions, remote procedure calls, and table replication. Servers reference other servers using *database links* that define the names of remote databases, the network nodes where the databases are serviced, and the network protocol used to access the remote nodes. Database links simplify distributed processing by providing transparent access to remote objects such as tables and procedures, enabling an application to reference them just as if they were resident in the application's local database.

■ **Oracle Names**—With release 7.1 of Oracle7, you can make available database link and network node information to all the nodes in a network using the Oracle Names common global dictionary. This feature is particularly useful for large application networks encompassing multiple locations to simplify the administration of database link and network information.

■ **Multi-Protocol Interchange**—Whereas Version 1 of SQL*Net supports connectivity between nodes in a single network protocol, Version 2 of SQL*Net enables database communication between nodes in different network communities running different network protocols. The Multi-Protocol Interchange (MPI) provides a communications bridge over heterogeneous protocols by translating SQL*Net messages from one protocol to another. For example, a client workstation in a Token-Ring LAN can transparently access a server in a DECnet or TCP/IP network, insulating the application from the complexities of the underlying network infrastructure. In addition to providing multi-protocol communications, the MPI also provides cost-based message routing functions and uses alternate routes in the event that least-cost paths of a network are unavailable. Figure 2.4 illustrates the use of the MPI between clients and servers in SPX/IPX and TCP/IP networks.

■ **Oracle Network Manager**—The complex task of configuring and managing a distributed database network topology is made easier with the Network Manager, a GUI-based administrative interface for SQL*Net. The Network Manager is used not only to manage the Oracle Names dictionary but also to generate configuration files for client and server-side SQL*Net components and define connection routes for Multi-Protocol Interchange nodes.

FIGURE 2.4.

Transparent database access over multiple network protocols with the Multi-Protocol Interchange.

Client 1 can access Server B just as though it were in Community A.

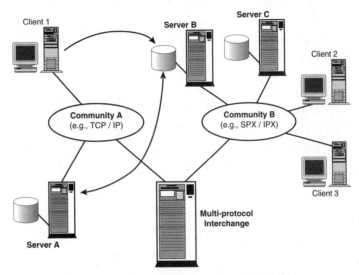

Servers can also communicate across the MPI.

Client/Server Development Tools

In addition to its server and networking products, Oracle includes a variety of client-side GUI offerings that complete its integrated client/server architecture. These product suites include full-featured Computer Assisted Software Engineering (CASE) tools, object-oriented development environments, and run-time components that are capable of operating with the Oracle7 server as well as other SQL databases.

- **Designer/2000**—For developing sophisticated Oracle client/server applications, the Designer/2000 CASE environment provides a comprehensive repository and powerful tool set that enables you to systematically analyze, model, design, and generate both client and server components of an application. Designer/2000's repository is similar in most respects to its predecessor's, Oracle*CASE; however, its user interface and functionality are significantly enhanced, and it supports graphical business process reengineering as well as Oracle7 server and Developer/2000 features. As shown in Figure 2.5, the Designer/2000's repository stores analysis, design, and generation data.

  Designer/2000 is a complex tool with many features. Once you've mastered it, you'll find that the task of developing sophisticated applications from start to finish is faster and much more efficient than it is with traditional development methods. Information collected through its graphical diagrammers for data and application modeling is used to generate sophisticated, bug-free data definition language and application code. Designer/2000 generates full-featured, full-functioning applications for Developer/2000 tools, complete with menus, security, transaction control, and extensibility for OLE containers. Application generators are also in the works for Visual Basic and Power Objects.

FIGURE 2.5.

The Repository Object Navigator of the Designer/2000 interface.

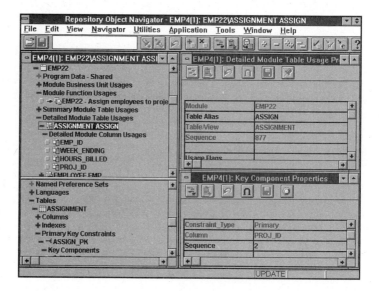

- **Developer/2000**—The Developer/2000 suite packages Oracle Forms, Oracle Reports, Oracle Graphics, and Oracle Book into a single integrated development environment. You can build your applications using just these tools or use them in conjunction with Designer/2000 to produce generated forms and reports.

  As with their character-based predecessors, SQL*Forms and SQL*ReportWriter, the Developer/2000 tools use PL/SQL as their underlying scripting language. Applications developed on one type of workstation platform can be deployed on other platforms such as Microsoft Windows, Macintosh, and Motif. Figure 2.6 illustrates a portion of the Oracle Forms Designer interface.

- **Power Objects**—In addition to the Designer/2000 and Developer/2000 tools, the Oracle GUI product suite includes another object-oriented, GUI application environment that is designed to compete with the likes of PowerBuilder and Visual Basic. Power Objects provides a rapid application development environment with lots of drag-and-drop features plus automatic database transaction management. Instead of using the PL/SQL language used by Developer/2000, Power Objects uses a Basic-style scripting language that is similar in most respects to Microsoft Visual Basic and is well suited for small to mid-sized applications. The object-oriented nature of Power Object's design interface is illustrated in Figure 2.7.

FIGURE 2.6.

The Developer/2000 Forms Designer interface.

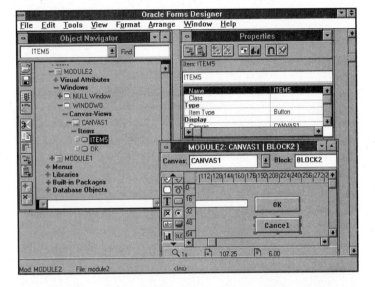

FIGURE 2.7.

Power Objects object-oriented application design interface.

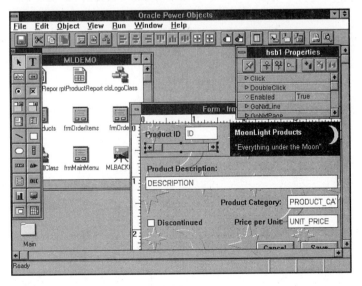

Oracle Directions

Oracle Corporation continues to be a forward-thinking leader in the technology sector, introducing new technologies that provide extended functionality and better management, development capability, connectivity, and performance for scaleable client/server database systems. Some of the new technologies introduced as of this writing include the following:

■ **Wireless client/server**—Oracle has recently introduced connectivity and messaging technologies that support remote client/server computing. This technology, which operates over cellular data networks, is particularly useful for laptop and palmtop users. A slightly more advanced form of client/server computing, *Oracle Mobile Agents* uses a *client-agent-server* architecture that enables a client to work offline and connect periodically to the network to submit requests and receive results from the server. The *agent* component of this architecture functions on behalf of the client in its absence from the network.

■ **Internet/World Wide Web interface**—Oracle's Web Interface Kit is used to integrate World Wide Web servers to Oracle7 databases. The kit provides utilities to create Web pages and interface Oracle7 data to them, enabling both storage and retrieval of Oracle data by Web users.

■ **Multimedia server**—As applications use more different types of data, especially multimedia data, database server technologies will also improve to manage them. In future releases of the Oracle server, you'll see increased support for text and document data, audio and video data, and object-oriented data access. Oracle began work on its multimedia server several years ago and leads its competitors in the development of storage and retrieval technologies. This high-throughput, high-speed server technology delivers video on demand to consumers, using set-top, "smart TV" processors as clients.

Summary

This chapter provided an overview of client/server computing (as it applies to database systems) and discussed the role of Oracle products in client/server environments. Oracle has a well-designed approach throughout its product line to support applications running in global, enterprise-wide client/server systems. Although Oracle Corporation is most famous for its database server, it has many other sophisticated, mature front-end and network products that complement and extend the functionality of the server.

There are many features about the Oracle7 server that are well suited to client/server systems and provide a complete solution in its RDBMS server, products, and client development tools. As the scope and functionality of client/server systems evolve, Oracle continues to introduce products that support new infrastructure technologies and make the task of designing, developing, and implementing complex systems manageable and efficient.

Overview of the Oracle® Architecture

3

by Lave Singh

This chapter describes the components of the Oracle database software that are present (in one form or another) on all machines on which the Oracle database can run. I describe the various components (including memory, process, hardware, and network components) and discuss the interaction between them. In addition, I discuss some of the internal objects (such as rollback segments) so you can have a greater understanding of the inner functioning and setup of the database.

Computer Architecture Fundamentals

In this section, I give a very brief overview of the architecture present in all computers; keep in mind, however, that a stand-alone machine might not have any network connections.

Memory

Memory is a storage device in a computer chip into which instructions and data are entered and retrieved when needed for processing. It is thousands, if not hundreds of thousands, times faster to read information from memory rather than directly from disk; however, there must be an initial load of information into memory from disk. The larger the memory available for a machine, the quicker it will run.

As far as Oracle is concerned, the instructions are the Oracle programs, and the data is the data read from the Oracle database files.

Processes/Programs

A process or program is a set of instructions to a computer that are run on the machine's processor. These instructions, or programs, are stored on the file system of the machine. Before you can run a program, the instructions for it are read into the machine's memory from the file system.

For Oracle, the processes are the Oracle system (background) processes that look after the database or the user processes that perform work for the user accessing the database.

File Systems

Data and programs for the computer are stored on the machine's file system, which typically consists of one or more hard disks. Programs and data, when required, are loaded from the hard disk into the machine's memory before the program or data is used.

Oracle uses the file system for the sets of the files that make up the database and the software programs that enable you to access the database.

Network

A network is a system of connections between machines that enables one machine to communicate with another and share resources. As well as the physical wires and components, you need to establish a set of rules for communication; this is known as a protocol.

Oracle can support many different types of networks and protocols. If you require communication between machines running Oracle software, you must install the Oracle SQL*Net software on all machines requiring network access.

Global View of the Oracle Architecture

The Oracle architecture described in this section is the generic architecture that applies to all platforms on which Oracle runs. There might be differences in the architecture between different platforms, but the fundamentals are the same.

What Is a Database?

A database is a collection of related data that is used and retrieved together for one or more application systems. The physical location and implementation of the database is transparent to the application programs; and in fact, you could move and restructure the physical database without affecting the programs.

Figure 3.1 illustrates the concept of a database holding data for many different (possibly unrelated) applications.

FIGURE 3.1.

Database with data for many applications.

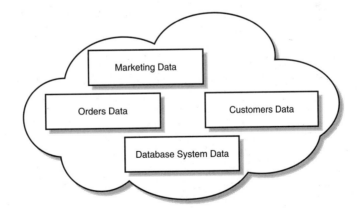

Physically, in its simplest form, an Oracle database is nothing more than a set of files somewhere on disk. The physical location of these files is irrelevant to the function (although important for the performance) of the database. The files are binary files that you can only access using the Oracle kernel software. Querying data in the database files is typically done with one of the Oracle tools (such as SQL*Plus) using the Structured Query Language (SQL).

Logically, the database is divided into a set of Oracle user accounts (schemas), each of which is identified by a username and password unique to that database. Tables and other objects are owned by one of these Oracle users, and access to the data is only available by logging into the database using an Oracle username and password. Without a valid username and password for the database, you are denied access to anything on the database. The Oracle username and password is different from the operating system username and password. For example, a database residing on a UNIX machine requires that I log in to the UNIX machine using my UNIX operating system username and password and then log in again to Oracle before I can use the database objects. (The UNIX login would not be required for a client/server setup.) This process of logging in, or connecting to, the database is required whether you're using an Oracle or non-Oracle tool.

The same table name can coexist in two separate Oracle user accounts; although the tables might have the same name, they are different tables. Sometimes, the same database (same set of physical database files) is used for holding different versions of tables (in separate Oracle accounts) for the developers, system testing, or user testing, or the same table name is used in different application systems.

Often, people refer to an Oracle user account as a database, but this is not strictly correct. You could use two Oracle user accounts to hold data for two entirely different application systems; you would have two logical databases implemented in the same physical database using two Oracle user accounts.

In addition to physical files, Oracle processes and memory structures must also be present before you can use the database.

Figure 3.2 shows the basic Oracle architecture that I discuss throughout this chapter.

Oracle Files

There are three major sets of files on disk that compose a database.

- Database files
- Control files
- Redo logs

The most important of these are the database files where the actual data resides. The control files and the redo logs support the functioning of the architecture itself.

FIGURE 3.2.

The basic Oracle architecture.

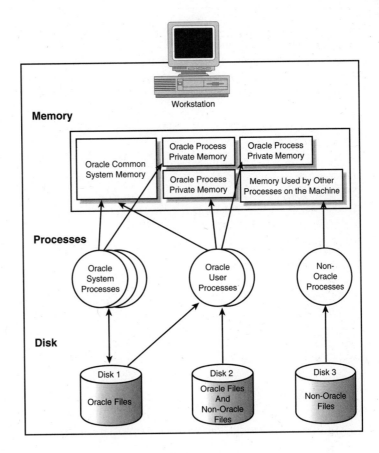

All three sets of files must be present, open, and available to Oracle for any data on the database to be useable. Without these files, you cannot access the database, and the database administrator might have to recover some or all of the database using a backup, if there is one! All the files are binary.

System and User Processes

For the database files to be useable, you must have the Oracle system processes and one or more user processes running on the machine. The Oracle system processes, also known as Oracle background processes, provide functions for the user processes—functions that would otherwise be done by the user processes themselves. There are many background processes that you can initiate, but as a minimum, only PMON, SMON, DBWR, and LGWR (all described later in the chapter) must be up and running for the database to be useable. Other background processes support optional additions to the way the database runs.

In addition to the Oracle background processes, there is one user process per connection to the database in its simplest setup. The user must make a connection to the database before he can access any of the objects. If one user logs into Oracle using SQL*Plus, another user chooses Oracle Forms, and yet another user employs the Excel spreadsheet, then you have three user processes against the database—one for each connection.

Memory

Oracle uses the memory (either real or virtual) of the system to run the user processes and the system software itself and to cache data objects. There are two major memory areas used by Oracle: memory that is shared and used by all processes running against the database and memory that is local to each individual user process.

System Memory

Oracle database-wide system memory is known as the SGA, the system global area or shared global area. The data and control structures in the SGA are shareable, and all the Oracle background processes and user processes can use them.

> **NOTE**
>
> The combination of the SGA and the Oracle background processes is known as an Oracle *instance*, a term that you'll encounter often with Oracle. Although there is typically one instance for each database, it is common to find many instances (running on different processors or even on different machines) all running against the same set of database files.

User Process Memory

For each connection to the database, Oracle allocates a PGA (process global area or program global area) in the machine's memory. Oracle also allocates a PGA for the background processes. This memory area contains data and control information for one process and is not shareable between processes.

Network Software and SQL*Net

A simple configuration for an Oracle database has the database files, memory structures, and Oracle background and user processes all running on the same machine without any networking involved. However, much more common is the configuration that implements the database on a server machine and the Oracle tools on a different machine (such as a PC with Microsoft Windows). For this type of client/server configuration, the machines are connected with some non-Oracle networking software that enables the two machines to communicate. Also, you might want two databases running on different machines to talk to each other—perhaps you're accessing tables from both databases in the same transaction or even in the same SQL statements. Again, the two machines need some non-Oracle networking software to communicate.

Whatever type of networking software and protocols you use to connect the machines (such as TCP/IP) for either the client/server or server-server setup mentioned previously, you must have the Oracle SQL*Net product to enable Oracle to interface with the networking protocol. SQL*Net supports most of the major networking protocols for both PC LANs (such as IPX/SPX) and the largest mainframes (such as SNA). Essentially, SQL*Net provides the software layer between Oracle and the networking software, providing seamless communication between an Oracle client machine (running SQL*Plus) and the database server or from one database server to another.

You must install the SQL*Net software on both machines on top of the underlying networking software for both sides to talk to each other. SQL*Net software options enable a client machine supporting one networking protocol to communicate with another supporting a different protocol.

You do not need to change the application system software itself if the networking protocols or underlying networking software changes. You can make the changes transparently with the Database Administrator, installing a different version of SQL*Net for the new network protocol.

Figure 3.3 shows the role of SQL*Net in a client/server environment with two server database machines.

FIGURE 3.3.
*SQL*Net diagram in a
client/server environment
with two server databases.*

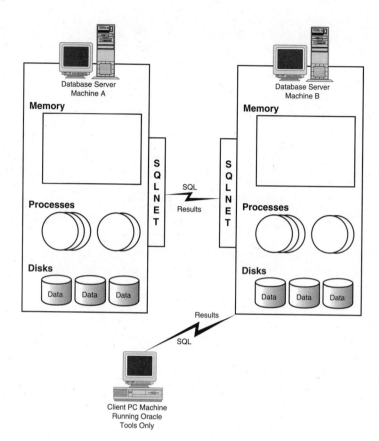

Oracle Files

In this part, I discuss the different types of files that Oracle uses on the hard disk drive of any machine.

Database Files

The database files hold the actual data and are typically the largest in size (from a few megabytes to many gigabytes). The other files (control files and redo logs) support the rest of the architecture. Depending on their sizes, the tables (and other objects) for all the user accounts can obviously go in one database file—but that's not an ideal situation because it does not make the database structure very flexible for controlling access to storage for different Oracle users, putting the database on different disk drives, or backing up and restoring just part of the database.

You must have at least one database file (adequate for a small or testing database), but usually, you have many more than one. In terms of accessing and using the data in the tables and other objects, the number (or location) of the files is immaterial.

The database files are fixed in size and never grow bigger than the size at which they were created.

Control Files

Any database must have at least one control file, although you typically have more than one to guard against loss. The control file records the name of the database, the date and time it was created, the location of the database and redo logs, and the synchronization information to ensure that all three sets of files are always in step. Every time you add a new database or redo log file to the database, the information is recorded in the control files.

Redo Logs

Any database must have at least two redo logs. These are the journals for the database; the redo logs record all changes to the user objects or system objects. If any type of failure occurs, such as loss of one or more database files, you can use the changes recorded in the redo logs to bring the database to a consistent state without losing any committed transactions. In the case of non-data loss failure, such as a machine crash, Oracle can apply the information in the redo logs automatically without intervention from the database administrator (DBA). The SMON background process automatically reapplies the committed changes in the redo logs to the database files.

Like the other files used by Oracle, the redo log files are fixed in size and never grow dynamically from the size at which they were created.

Online Redo Logs

The online redo logs are the two or more redo log files that are always in use while the Oracle instance is up and running. Changes you make are recorded to each of the redo logs in turn. When one is full, the other is written to; when that becomes full, the first is overwritten and the cycle continues.

Offline/Archived Redo Logs

The offline or archived redo logs are exact copies of the online redo logs that have been filled; it is optional whether you ask Oracle to create these. Oracle creates them only when the database is running in ARCHIVELOG mode. If the database is running in ARCHIVELOG mode, the ARCH background process wakes up and copies the online redo log to the offline destination (typically another disk drive) once it becomes full. While this copying is in progress, Oracle uses the other online redo log. If you have a complete set of offline redo logs since the database was last backed up, you have a complete record of changes that have been made. You could then use this record to reapply the changes to the backup copy of the database files if one or more online database files are lost.

Other Supporting Files

When you start an Oracle instance (in other words, when the Oracle background processes are initiated and the memory structures allocated), the instance parameter file determines the sizes and modes of the database. This parameter file is known as the INIT.ORA file. (The actual name of the file has the Oracle instance identifier appended to the filename.) This is an ordinary text file containing parameters for which you can override the default settings. The DBA is responsible for creating and modifying the contents of this parameter file.

On some Oracle platforms, an SGAPAD file is also created, which contains the starting memory address of the Oracle SGA.

System and User Processes

In this section, I discuss some of the Oracle system processes that must be running for the database to be useable, including the optional processes and the processes that are created for users connecting to the Oracle database.

Mandatory System Processes

The four Oracle system processes that must always be up and running for the database to be useable include DBWR (database writer), LGWR (log writer), SMON (system monitor), and PMON (process monitor).

DBWR (Database Writer)

The database writer background process writes modified database blocks in the SGA to the database files. It reads only the blocks that have changed (for example, if the block contains a new record, a deleted record, or a changed record). These blocks are also called *dirty* blocks. The database writer writes out the least recently used blocks first. These blocks are not necessarily written to the database when the transaction commits; the only thing that always happens on a commit is that the changes are recorded and written to the online redo log files. The database blocks will be written out later when there are not enough buffers free in the SGA to read in a new block.

LGWR (Log Writer)

The log writer process writes the entries in the SGA's redo buffer for one or more transactions to the online redo log files. For example, when a transaction commits, the log writer must write out the entries in the redo log buffer to the redo log files on disk before the process receives a message indicating that the commit was successful. Once committed, the changes are safe on disk even though the modified database blocks are still in the SGA's database buffer area waiting to be written out by DBWR. The SMON can always reapply the changes from the redo logs if the memory's most up-to-date copy of the database blocks is lost.

SMON (System Monitor)

The system monitor process looks after the instance. If two transactions are waiting for each other to release locks and neither of them can continue (known as a *deadlock* or *deadly embrace*), SMON detects the situation and one of the processes receives an error message indicating that a deadlock has occurred.

SMON also releases temporary segments that are no longer in use by the user processes which caused them to be created.

During idle periods, SMON compacts the free-space fragments in the database files, making it easier and simpler for Oracle to allocate storage for new database objects or for existing database objects to grow.

In addition, SMON automatically performs recovery when the Oracle instance is first started up (if none of the files have been lost). You won't see a message indicating that instance recovery is occurring, but the instance might take longer to come up.

PMON (Process Monitor)

The process monitor monitors the user processes. If any failure occurs with the user processes (for example, if the process is killed in the middle of a transaction), PMON automatically rolls back the work of the user process since the transaction started (anything since the last COMMIT or ROLLBACK). It releases any locks taken out and other system resources taken up by the failed process.

PMON also monitors the dispatcher and shared server processes, which are part of the multi-threaded server setup, and restarts them if they have died.

Optional System Processes

As well as the four mandatory system processes, there are a number of optional system processes that you can initiate.

ARCH (Archiver)

When the database is running in ARCHIVELOG mode and you've started the Archiver background process, it makes a copy of one of the online redo log files to the archive destination (the exact location is specified in an INIT.ORA parameter). In this way, you can have a complete history of changes made to the database files recorded in the offline and the online redo logs.

There is no point in keeping the Archiver background process running if the database is not running in ARCHIVELOG mode.

CKPT (Checkpoint Process)

A checkpoint occurs when one of the online redo log files fills; it will be overwritten when one of the other online redo logs fills. If the redo log file is overwritten, the changes recorded in that file are not available for reapplying in case of system failure. At a checkpoint, the modified database buffer blocks are written down to the relative safety of the database files on disk by the database writer background process. This means that you won't need the record of changes in the event of system failure with lost memory areas. After a checkpoint occurs, the redo log can be reused.

At a checkpoint, all the database file headers and redo log file headers are updated to record the fact that a checkpoint has occurred. The LGWR background process performs the updating task, which could be significant if there are a large number of database and redo log files. The entire database might have to wait for the checkpoint to complete before the redo logs can record further database changes. To reduce the time it takes for LGWR to update the database and redo log file headers, you can initiate the checkpoint process.

A checkpoint can occur at other times, such as when the entries in the redo log files reach a limit defined by the database administrator.

> **NOTE**
>
> Whether or not the CKPT background process is initiated, checkpointing still occurs when one of the redo log files fills.

RECO (Recoverer)

You use the recoverer background process when there is a failure in a distributed transaction (a transaction where two or more databases are updated), and one or more of the databases involved need to either commit or roll back their changes. If initiated, the recoverer attempts to automatically commit or roll back the transaction on the local database at timed intervals in synchronization with the recoverer processes on the other Oracle databases.

There is no point in keeping the recoverer background process running if you're not using distributed transactions on the database.

LCK (Lock)

You use the lock background process in the parallel server setup of Oracle where more than one instance is running against the same set of database files. The LCK processes running on all instances will synchronize locking between the instances. If a user connects to one instance and locks a row, the row remains locked for a user attempting to make a change on another instance. Other users can always query the rows regardless of how the rows are locked by other users.

You can initiate up to 10 LCK background processes to reduce the bottleneck of synchronizing locking, but one is usually more than enough.

You should not initiate the LCK background processes unless you're implementing a parallel server (multi-instance) setup of Oracle.

SQL*Net Listener

The SQL*Net listener is a process running on the machine that routes requests coming in from client machines through to the correct Oracle instance. It communicates with the underlying networking software to route requests to and from the database server and the client machine (whether that client machine is a machine running an Oracle tool or even another database server).

For example, the communications between a client machine running Oracle Forms on a PC with DOS and Windows and a database server on a UNIX machine with TCP/IP as the networking protocol would involve the following major steps:

1. The client machine sends the SQL statement execution request to the UNIX database server machine.
2. The non-Oracle TCP/IP listener process picks up the request and recognizes it as a request for Oracle.
3. The request is sent to the Oracle SQL*Net listener, which routes the request to the correct instance on the machine. (The machine might be running many instances for many different databases.)
4. A process on the instance executes the statement.
5. The results are then sent back up the communications link to the client machine.

The SQL*Net listener is not related to the instance itself but is system wide and will process requests for all instances running on the machine. You can initiate more than one SQL*Net listener, but this is uncommon.

User Processes

User processes logically consist of two halves: the Oracle server code, which translates and executes SQL statements and reads the database files and memory areas, and the tool-specific code, which is the executable code for the tool that is used. The server code is the same regardless of the tool that is executing the SQL statement; the same steps are involved. The server code is sometimes known as the Oracle kernel code.

You can configure the user processes in Oracle three different ways, all of which could coexist for the same instance. These three configurations are single task, dedicated server, or multi-threaded server.

Single Task

In the single-task configuration, the tool-specific code and database server code are both configured into one process running on the machine. Each connection to the database has one user process running on the machine. This is common on VAX VMS platforms without a client/server environment.

Dedicated Server Processes

In the dedicated server configuration (also known as *two-task* or running with *shadow* processes), the two parts of a user process are implemented as two separate processes running on the machine. They communicate with each other using the machine's interprocess communication mechanisms. Each connection to the database has two processes running on the machine. The Oracle kernel software in one process is sometimes called the shadow process.

This configuration is common for UNIX platforms because the operating system cannot (in some implementations of UNIX) protect the Oracle code and memory areas from the application code. It is also common for client/server configurations where the server code resides on the server machine and the tool-specific code runs on the client machine with communication over a network. The way the two component parts of one logical process communicate is fundamentally the same as if one process were implemented on the same machine—except that the two halves of the logical process happen to reside on two machines and communicate over the network using SQL*Net rather than the interprocess communication mechanisms of the operating system.

The dedicated server configuration can be wasteful because memory is allocated to the shadow process and the number of processes that must be serviced on the machine increases, even when the user is not making any database requests. The dedicated server (shadow process) will only process requests from one associated client process.

MTS—The Multi-Threaded Server

The multi-threaded server configuration enables one Oracle server process to perform work for many user processes. This overcomes the drawbacks of the dedicated server configuration. It reduces the number of processes running and the amount of memory used on the machine and can improve system performance. The multi-threaded server introduces two new types of system processes that support this part of the architecture.

Using one of the shared server processes that comes as part of the multi-threaded server configuration is not appropriate when a user process is making many database requests (such as an export backup of the database); for that process, you could use a dedicated server. A mixture of both configurations can coexist.

Dispatchers

One or more dispatcher processes retrieves requests for the client processes from the SQL*Net listener and routes the request to one of the shared server processes. The SQL*Net listener is required for the multi-threaded server configuration even if no networking is involved.

You must configure at least one dispatcher for each network protocol that is used to route requests to the instance. The number of dispatchers configured does not increase if the system load increases because the dispatchers are only providing the routing. The actual work is done by the shared servers.

> **NOTE**
>
> The multi-threaded server requires SQL*Net Version 2 or later, even if both the dispatcher and the user process are running on the same machine.

Shared Servers

The shared servers provide the same functionality as the dedicated server processes and contain the Oracle server code that performs the work for the client. They can service requests from many different user processes. The actual shared server used might differ from one call to another so that no user process can monopolize any one particular shared server process. Oracle uses an area in the SGA for messaging between the different processes involved.

The number of shared server processes is automatically increased (or decreased to an initial number defined by the database administrator) according to the system activity.

> **NOTE**
>
> The number of shared servers is increased or decreased automatically, but the number of dispatchers is not.

Oracle Memory

In this part, I discuss how Oracle uses the machine's memory. Generally, the greater the real memory available to Oracle, the quicker the system runs.

System Global Area (SGA)

The system global area, sometimes known as the shared global area, is for data and control structures in memory that can be shared by all the Oracle background and user processes running on that instance. Each Oracle instance has its own SGA; in fact, the SGA and background processes are what define an instance. The SGA memory area is allocated when the instance is started, and it's flushed and deallocated when the instance is shut down.

The contents of the SGA are divided into three main areas: the database buffer cache, the shared pool area, and the redo cache. The size of each of these areas is controlled by parameters in the INIT.ORA file. The bigger you can make the SGA and the more of it that can fit into the machine's real memory (as opposed to virtual memory), the quicker your instance will run. Figure 3.4 shows the Oracle SGA in memory.

FIGURE 3.4.

The Oracle SGA in memory.

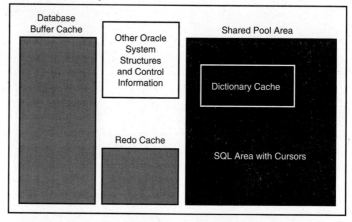

Database Buffer Cache

The database buffer cache of the SGA holds Oracle blocks that have been read in from the database files. When one process reads the blocks for a table into memory, all the processes for that instance can access those blocks.

If a process needs to access some data, Oracle checks to see if the block is already in this cache (thereby avoiding a disk read). If the Oracle block is not in the buffer, it must be read from the database files into the buffer cache. The buffer cache must have a free block available before the data block can be read from the database files.

The Oracle blocks in the database buffer cache in memory are arranged with the most recently used at one end and the least recently used at the other. This list is constantly changing as the database is used. If data must be read from the database files into memory, the blocks at the least recently used end are written back to the database files first (if they've been modified). The DBWR process is the only process that writes the blocks from the database buffer cache to the database files.

The more database blocks you can hold in real memory, the quicker an instance will run.

Redo Cache

The online redo log files record all the changes made to user objects and system objects. Before the changes are written out to the redo logs, Oracle stores them in the redo cache memory area. For example, the entries in the redo log cache are written down to the online redo logs when the cache becomes full or when a transaction issues a commit. The entries for more than one transaction can be included together in the same disk write to the redo log files.

The LGWR background process is the only process that writes out entries from this redo cache to the online redo log files.

Shared Pool Area

The shared pool area of the SGA has two main components: the SQL area and the dictionary cache. You can alter the size of these two components only by changing the size of the entire shared pool area.

SQL Area

A SQL statement sent for execution to the database server must be parsed before it can execute. The SQL area of the SGA contains the binding information, run-time buffers, parse tree, and execution plan for all the SQL statements sent to the database server. Because the shared pool area is a fixed size, you might not see the entire set of statements that have been executed since the instance first came up; Oracle might have flushed out some statements to make room for others.

If a user executes a SQL statement, that statement takes up memory in the SQL area. If another user executes exactly the same statement on the same objects, Oracle doesn't need to reparse the second statement because the parse tree and execution plan is already in the SQL area. This part of the architecture saves on reparsing overhead. The SQL area is also used to hold the parsed, compiled form of PL/SQL blocks, which can also be shared between user processes on the same instance.

> **TIP**
>
> Make SQL statements exactly the same in application code (using procedures) to avoid reparsing overhead.

Dictionary Cache

The dictionary cache in the shared pool area holds entries retrieved from the Oracle system tables, otherwise known as the Oracle data dictionary. The data dictionary is a set of tables located in the database files, and because Oracle accesses these files often, it sets aside a separate area of memory to avoid disk I/O.

The cache itself holds a subset of the data from the data dictionary. It is loaded with an initial set of entries when the instance is first started and then populated from the database data dictionary as further information is required. The cache holds information about all the users, the tables and other objects, the structure, security, storage, and so on.

The data dictionary cache grows to occupy a larger proportion of memory within the shared pool area as needed, but the size of the shared pool area remains fixed.

Process Global Area

The process global area, sometimes called the program global area or PGA, contains data and control structures for one user or server process. There is one PGA for each user process (connection) to the database.

The actual contents of the PGA depend on whether the multi-threaded server configuration is implemented, but it typically contains memory to hold the session's variables, arrays, some row results, and other information. If you're using the multi-threaded server, some of the information that is usually held in the PGA is instead held in the common SGA.

The size of the PGA depends on the operating system used to run the Oracle instance, and once allocated, it remains the same. Memory used in the PGA does not increase according to the amount of processing performed in the user process. The database administrator can control the size of the PGA by modifying some of the parameters in the instance parameter file INIT.ORA; one parameter that DBAs often change is the SORT_AREA_SIZE.

The Oracle Programs

The Oracle server code mentioned previously is code that performs the same function regardless of which tool the front-end programs are using (such as SQL*Plus, Oracle Forms, Reports, and Excel). On some platforms, the server code is loaded only once into the machine's memory, and all the processes using the instance can share it—even across instances (as long as you are running the same version of Oracle for both instances). This kernel code, also known as reentrant code, saves memory because it requires that only one copy of the code be loaded into memory.

Storage

In this section, I discuss the organization of the database files themselves. You have already learned that the database files are binary, fixed-size files on disk. I do not discuss the control and redo log files in this section.

Tablespaces and Database Files

For management, security, and performance reasons, the database is *logically* divided into one or more tablespaces that each comprise one or more database files. A database file is always associated with only one tablespace.

> **NOTE**
>
> A tablespace is a logical division of a database comprising one or more physical database files.

Every Oracle database has a tablespace named SYSTEM that has the very first file of the database allocated to it. The SYSTEM tablespace is the default location of all objects when a database is first created. The simplest database setup is one database file in the SYSTEM tablespace (simple, but not recommended).

Typically, you create many tablespaces to partition the different parts of the database. For example, you might have one tablespace for tables, another to hold indexes, and so on, and each of these tablespaces would have one or more database files associated to them.

When you create objects (such as tables) that use storage in the database, you should specify the tablespace location of the object as part of the CREATE statement for the object. Only system tables should occupy storage in the SYSTEM tablespace. The system tables are tables such as tab$, col$, ind$, and fet$.

Objects such as synonyms and views do not take up storage within the database other than the storage in the data dictionary table for their definitions, along with the definitions for all other types of objects.

Tablespaces can be added, dropped, taken offline and online, and associated with additional database files. By adding another file to a tablespace, you increase the size of the tablespace and therefore the database itself.

You cannot drop the SYSTEM tablespace; this would destroy the database because the system tables are there. You also cannot take the SYSTEM tablespace offline.

Segments

A *segment* is a generic name given to any object that occupies storage in the database files. Some examples of segments are table segments (data segments), index segments, rollback segments, temporary segments, and the cache (bootstrap) segment. A segment uses a number of Oracle blocks that are in the same tablespace (although the blocks themselves can be in different files that make up the tablespace).

Extents

The storage for any object on the database is allocated in a number of blocks that must be contiguous in the database files. These contiguous blocks are known as *extents*. For example, when a table is first created using default settings, five Oracle blocks are allocated to the table for the very first extent (otherwise known as the initial extent). As rows are inserted and updated into the table, the five blocks fill with data. When the last block has filled and new rows are inserted, the database automatically allocates another set of blocks (five blocks) for the table and the new rows are inserted into the new set of blocks. This allocating of additional storage (additional extents) continues until there is no more free space in the tablespace. The table starts with the one initial extent and is then allocated other secondary (or next) extents. The blocks for an extent must be contiguous within the database files.

Once an extent is allocated to a segment (table), those blocks cannot be used by another database object, even if all the rows in the table are deleted. The table must be dropped or truncated to release the storage allocated to the table. The exception to this is rollback segments, which can dynamically release storage that was allocated to them.

Oracle Blocks

Oracle "formats" the database files into a number of Oracle blocks when they're first created—making it easier for the RDBMS software to manage the files and easier to read data into the memory areas.

These blocks are usually 1 KB (the default for PC-DOS systems), 2 KB (the default for most UNIX machines and VAX VMS), 4 KB (the default for IBM mainframes), or larger. For a 50 MB database file, there would be 25,600 Oracle blocks assuming a block size of 2 KB (50 MB/2 KB).

The block size should be a multiple of the operating system block size. Regardless of the block size, not all of the block is available for holding data; Oracle takes up some space to manage the contents of the block. This block header has a minimum size, but it can grow. ·

These Oracle blocks are the smallest unit of storage. Increasing the Oracle block size can improve performance, but you should do this only when the database is first created.

When you first create a database, it uses some of the blocks within the first file, and the rest of the blocks are free. In the data dictionary, Oracle maintains a list of the free blocks for each data file in each tablespace.

Each Oracle block is numbered sequentially for each database file, starting at 1. Two blocks can have the same block address if they are in different database files.

CAUTION

Do not modify the Oracle block size once you've created the database.

ROWID

The ROWID is a unique database-wide physical address for every row on every table. Once assigned (when the row is first inserted into the database), it never changes until the row is deleted or the table is dropped.

The ROWID consists of the following three components, the combination of which uniquely identifies the physical storage location of the row.

- Oracle database file number, which contains the block with the row
- Oracle block address, which contains the row
- The row within the block (because each block can hold many rows)

The ROWID is used internally in indexes as a quick means of retrieving rows with a particular key value. Application developers also use it in SQL statements as a quick way to access a row once they know the ROWID.

Free Space and Automatic Compaction

When a database file is first created or added to a tablespace, all the blocks within that file are empty blocks that have never been used. As time goes by, the blocks within a database file are used by a segment (table), or they remain free blocks. Oracle tracks the file's free blocks in a list in the data dictionary. As you create and drop tables, the free space becomes fragmented, with free space in different parts of the database file. When the free blocks are scattered in this way, Oracle has no way to automatically bring the free storage together.

When two fragments of free space are physically next to each other in the database file, the two smaller fragments can be compacted together into one larger fragment, which is recorded in the free space list. This compacting reduces the overhead when Oracle actually needs the free space (when a table wants to allocate another extent of a certain size, for example). The SMON background process performs this automatic compaction.

System Database Objects

In this part, I discuss some of the system objects that support the workings of the architecture and give information about the structure of the database.

The Data Dictionary

The first tables created on any database are the system tables, also known as the Oracle data dictionary. These tables are owned by the first Oracle user account that is created automatically—by the user SYS. The system tables record information about the structure of the database and the objects within it, and Oracle accesses them when it needs information about the database or every time it executes a DDL statement (Data Definition Language) or DML statement (Data Manipulation Language). These tables are never directly updated; however, updates to them occur in the background whenever a DDL statement is executed.

The core data dictionary tables hold normalized information that is cryptic to understand, so Oracle provides a set of views to make the information in the core system tables more meaningful. You can access the names of over 170 of the views in the data dictionary with the following command:

```
SELECT * FROM DICT;
```

Oracle requires the information in the data dictionary tables to parse any SQL statement. The information is cached in the data dictionary area of the shared pool in the SGA.

Because the very first tablespace created is the SYSTEM tablespace, the data dictionary tables use storage in the database files associated with the SYSTEM tablespaces.

Rollback Segments

Whenever you change data in Oracle, the change must be either committed or reversed. If a change is reversed or *rolled back*, the contents of the data block are restored back to the original state before the change. Rollback segments are system-type objects that support this reversing process. Whenever you make any kind of change to either application tables or system tables, a rollback segment automatically holds the previous version of the data that is being modified, so the old version of the data is available if a rollback is required.

If other users want to see the data while the change is pending, they always have access to the previous version from the rollback segment. They are provided with a *read-consistent* version of the data. Once the change is committed, the modified version of the data is available.

Rollback segments are always owned by the user SYS, and no Oracle user can access them for viewing.

Rollback segments use storage in the same way as other segments in terms of extents. With a rollback segment, however, you must initially allocate a minimum of two extents instead of only one.

The first rollback segment is created automatically when the database is first created and has a name of SYSTEM, and it uses storage in the first tablespace, which also has a name of SYSTEM.

CAUTION

It can get confusing that Oracle uses the same name for three different types of objects; the first tablespace is called SYSTEM, the first rollback segment is called SYSTEM, and one of the first Oracle accounts created is called SYSTEM. They are different types of objects, so do not confuse them.

Temporary Segments

Temporary segments use storage in the database files to provide a temporary work area for intermediate stages of SQL processing and for large sort operations.

Oracle creates temporary segments on the fly, and they are automatically deleted when the SMON background process no longer needs them. If only a small working area is required, Oracle does not create a temporary segment but instead uses a part of the PGA (the program global area) memory as a temporary work area.

The following operations might cause Oracle to create a temporary segment:

- Creating an index
- Using the ORDER BY, DISTINCT, or GROUP BY clauses in a SELECT statement
- Using the set operators UNION, INTERSECT, MINUS
- Creating joins between tables
- Using some subqueries

The database administrator can control which tablespaces contain the temporary segments on a user-by-user basis.

Bootstrap/Cache Segment

A bootstrap or cache segment is a special type of object on the database that is used to perform an initial load of the data dictionary cache in the shared pool area of the SGA.

Oracle uses the cache segment only when the instance first starts and does not use it again until the instance restarts. Once the segment is used to perform the initial load of the data dictionary cache, the remainder of the cache in memory is steadily populated as statements are executed against the database.

Protecting Your Data

In this part, I discuss the idea of saving or reversing out changes made—committing and rolling back.

Transactions, Commit, and Rollback

Database changes are not saved until the user explicitly decides that the insert, update, and delete statements should be made permanent. Up until that point, the changes are in a pending status, and any failures, such as a machine crash, will reverse the changes.

A transaction is an atomic unit of work comprising one or more SQL statements; it begins when the user first connects to the database and ends when a COMMIT or ROLLBACK statement is issued. Upon a COMMIT or ROLLBACK, the next transaction automatically begins. All the statements within a transaction are either all saved (committed) or all reversed (rolled back).

Committing a transaction makes changes permanent in the entire transaction to the database, and once committed, the changes cannot then be reversed. Rolling back reverses all the inserts, updates, deletes in the transaction; again, once rolled back, those changes cannot then be committed. Internally, the process of committing means writing out the changes recorded in the SGA's redo log buffer cache to the online redo log files on disk. If this disk I/O succeeds, the application receives a message indicating a successful commit. (The text of the message changes from one tool to another.) The DBWR background process can write out the actual Oracle data blocks in the SGA's database buffer cache at a later time. If the system should crash, Oracle can automatically reapply the changes from the redo logs files, even if the Oracle data blocks were not written back to the database files before the failure.

> **CAUTION**
>
> DDL (Data Definition Language) statements such as CREATE TABLE will automatically issue a COMMIT, even if the DDL statement itself fails.

Oracle also implements the idea of statement-level rollback. If a single statement fails during a transaction, the entire statement will fail. In other words, an INSERT statement for 1,000 rows will insert either all 1,000 rows or none at all; the entire statement works, or nothing happens. If a statement does fail within a transaction, the rest of the statements in the transaction are still in a pending state and must be committed or rolled back.

If a user process terminates abnormally (the process is killed, for example), the PMON background process automatically rolls back changes. Any changes that the process had committed up to the point of failure remain committed, and only those changes for the current transaction are rolled back.

All locks held by the transaction are automatically released when the transaction commits or rolls back or when the PMON background process rolls back the transaction. In addition, other system resources (such as rollback segments) are released for other transactions to use.

Savepoints enable you to set up markers within a transaction so that you have the option of rolling back just part of the work performed in the transaction. You can use savepoints in long and complex transactions to provide the reversing option for certain statements. However, this causes extra overhead on the system to perform the work for a statement and then reverse the changes; usually, changes in the logic can produce a more optimal solution. When Oracle performs a rollback to a savepoint, the rest of the statements in the transaction remain in a pending state and must be committed or rolled back. Oracle releases the locks taken by those statements that were rolled back.

Data Integrity

Data integrity is about enforcing data validation rules—such as checking that a percentage amount is between 0 and 100—to ensure that invalid data does not get into your tables. Historically, these rules were enforced by the application programs themselves (and the same rules were checked repeatedly in different programs). Oracle, however, enables you to define and store these rules against the database objects to which they relate so that you need to code them only once so they are enforced whenever any kind of change is made to the table, regardless of which tool issues the insert, update, or delete statement. This checking takes the form of integrity constraints and database triggers.

Integrity Constraints

Integrity constraints enforce business rules at the database level by defining a set of checks for the tables in your system. These checks are automatically enforced whenever you issue an insert, update, or delete statement against the table. If any of the constraints are violated, the insert, update, or delete statement is rolled back. The other statements within the transaction remain in a pending state and can be committed or rolled back according to application logic.

Because integrity constraints are checked at the database level, they are performed regardless of where the insert, update, delete statement originated—whether it was an Oracle or a non-Oracle tool. Defining checks using these constraints is also quicker than performing the same checks using SQL. In addition, the information provided by declaring constraints is used by the Oracle optimizer to make better decisions about how to run a statement against the table. The Oracle Forms product can also use constraints to automatically generate code in the front-end programs to provide an early warning to the user of any errors.

The types of integrity constraints that you can set up on a table are NOT NULL, PRIMARY KEY, UNIQUE, FOREIGN KEY, CHECK, and indexes.

NOT NULL Constraints

You set the NOT NULL constraint against a column to specify that the column must always have a value on every row; it can never be null. By default, all the columns in a table are nullable. For example, using a NOT NULL constraint on an orders table, you can specify that there must always be an order amount.

PRIMARY KEY

The PRIMARY KEY constraint defines a column or a set of columns that you can use to uniquely identify a single row. No two rows in the table can have the same values for the primary key columns. In addition, the columns for a primary key constraint must always have a value—in other words, they are NOT NULL. If you add a constraint to a table after it has been created, any columns that make up the PRIMARY KEY constraint are modified to NOT NULL. Only one PRIMARY KEY constraint can exist for any table. For example, using a PRIMARY KEY constraint on an orders table, you can specify that a table cannot have two records with the same order number.

UNIQUE

The UNIQUE constraint defines a secondary key for the table. This is a column or set of columns that you can use as another way of uniquely identifying a row. No two rows can have the same values for the UNIQUE key column or columns. Although it is not possible for a table to have more than one primary key, a table can have more than one UNIQUE constraint.

The columns for a UNIQUE constraint do not have to be identified as NOT NULL (although they usually are). If the values for any of the columns that form the unique constraint are null, the constraint is not checked. For example, using a PRIMARY KEY and UNIQUE constraint on a customers table, you can specify that the customer number is a primary key and that the customer name is a unique key (which would mean that you could not have two customers with the same name on your table—a rare situation).

> **CAUTION**
>
> The UNIQUE constraint is not checked if the values in the column are null.

FOREIGN KEY

The FOREIGN KEY, or referential integrity constraint, enforces relationship integrity between tables. It dictates that a column or set of columns on the table match a PRIMARY KEY or UNIQUE constraint on a different table. For example, you could set up a FOREIGN KEY constraint on the orders table to specify that whenever an order record is inserted or updated, the customer number must also exist in the customers table. This ensures that you don't get orders for nonexistent customers.

You use FOREIGN KEY constraints to enforce parent/child relationships between tables. You can even use them to enforce self-referential constraints, usually in situations where a hierarchical structure is set up with all the rows held in the same table. If any of the columns of the foreign key are null, the constraint is not checked at all. Foreign key columns are usually declared as NOT NULL.

It is possible to specify that when the parent row is deleted, the delete should automatically cascade and delete the child rows—a dangerous situation. The user is informed only about the master rows that were removed, and he might not be aware of the additional rows that were deleted automatically in the background because he is not told that this cascading deletion has happened.

Only this automatic deletion of child rows is supported by specifying the ON DELETE CASCADE clause to the end of the foreign key creation statement. If you change the master table's key value, however, the child rows are not updated automatically to reflect the new key; you can implement this update cascade requirement using database triggers.

> **CAUTION**
>
> FOREIGN KEY constraints are not checked at all if any of the columns in the foreign key are null.

CHECK

A CHECK constraint specifies additional logic that must be true for the insert, update, or delete statement to work on the table. The additional logic returns a Boolean result, and in the check constraint, you ensure the values in the row being modified satisfy a set of validation checks that you specify. The syntax of a CHECK constraint is very similar to the syntax found in the WHERE clause of a SELECT statement; however, you cannot use subqueries or other columns that vary over time (such as SYSDATE). You can use database triggers to perform this additional processing that you cannot put into constraints. For example, using a CHECK constraint on the orders table, you can specify that the order amount must be greater than zero and the salesman's commission cannot be greater than 10 percent of the order total.

Indexes

PRIMARY KEY and UNIQUE constraints automatically create an index on the columns they're defined against if the constraint is enabled upon creation. If an index already exists on the columns that form the PRIMARY KEY or UNIQUE constraint, that index is used, and Oracle cannot create a new one. Oracle creates indexes when the constraint is enabled (which is the default when the constraint is first added to the table). Oracle drops the indexes from the table when the constraint is disabled. Enabling and disabling constraints can take significant time and system overhead due to the index creation and removal.

When you set up a FOREIGN KEY constraint, the columns are not indexed automatically. Because the foreign key columns are usually involved in joining tables together, you manually create indexes on those columns.

> **CAUTION**
>
> Disabling a PRIMARY KEY or UNIQUE constraint drops the index for the constraint.

Database Triggers

A database trigger is a PL/SQL block that you can define to automatically execute for insert, update, and delete statements against a table. You can define the trigger to execute once for the entire statement or once for every row that is inserted, updated, or deleted. For any one table, there are 12 events for which you can define database triggers. For each of the 12 events, you can define many database triggers for the same event.

A database trigger can call database procedures that are also written in PL/SQL. Unlike database triggers, procedures on the database are stored in a compiled form. For this reason, you should put the longer code segments into a procedure and then call the procedure from the database trigger.

In addition to implementing complex business rules, checking, and defaulting, you can use database triggers to insert, update, and delete other tables. An example of this use is providing an auditing facility where an audit trail is automatically created in an audit table whenever a row is changed on a table. Without database triggers, this function would be implemented in the front-end programs that make the change to the database; however, someone bypassing the code in the front-end programs (using SQL*Plus, for example) would not go through the checks and processing defined.

Database triggers differ from constraints in that they enable you to embed SQL statements within them, whereas constraints do not.

> **TIP**
>
> If possible, use constraints for checking; they are quicker than using database triggers.

System-Level Privileges

Each Oracle user defined on the database can have one or more of over 80 system-level privileges. These privileges control on a very fine level the right to execute SQL commands. The database administrator assigns system privileges either directly to Oracle user accounts or to roles. The roles are then assigned to the Oracle user accounts.

For example, before I can create a trigger on a table (even if I own the table as an Oracle user), I must have a system privilege called CREATE TRIGGER either assigned to my Oracle user account or assigned to a role given to the user account.

The CREATE SESSION privilege is another frequently used system-level privilege. In order to make a connection to the database, an Oracle account must have the CREATE SESSION system-level privilege assigned to it. This gives the account the privilege to make connections to the database.

Object-Level Privileges

Object-level privileges provide the capability to perform a particular type of action (select, insert, update, delete, and so on) on a specific object. The owner of the object has full control over the object and can perform any action on it; he doesn't need to have object-level privileges assigned to him. In fact, the owner of the object is the Oracle user who grants object-level privileges to others.

For example, if the user who owns a table wants another user to select and insert rows from his table (but not update or delete), he grants the select and insert object-level privileges on that table to the other user.

You can assign object-level privileges either directly to users or to roles that are then assigned to one or more Oracle user accounts.

Users and Roles

A role is a type of object that you can use to simplify the administration of system and object-level privileges. Instead of assigning privileges directly to user accounts, you can assign the privileges to roles that are then assigned to users.

Roles are essentially groupings of system and object-level privileges. They make the administration of privileges much easier because you can configure the privileges for a particular type of user once and assign those privileges to a role. When a user needs that set of privileges, you can use a single role assignment command to set that user up. Without the use of roles, you'd need to issue many commands for each of the different privileges required.

In addition, you can set up different roles with the correct privileges even though you don't yet have Oracle user accounts that require those assignments. You can assign a role to another role, building hierarchies of roles. Also, you can protect a role with a password that the user must supply when he wants to enable the role.

As already discussed, a physical database could contain many Oracle user accounts that are protected by passwords. You must supply the username and password regardless of which tool you use to gain access to the database. Roles are not the same as Oracle users; you cannot connect to the database by supplying a role name and password.

Auditing

Oracle's auditing mechanism provides three types of audit trails. One audit trail tracks which system privileges are used. Statement auditing keeps track of which SQL statements are used without regard to specific objects. Object-level auditing audits access to specific objects. You can initiate these audit trails to track when the statements succeed, when they fail, or both, so that all accesses are audited. You can use auditing to keep track of anyone attempting to break into the system.

In addition, you can set up how all the different types of auditing record the entries. The audit trail can record one entry per operation regardless of how many attempts are made on the operation during the connection session. Alternatively, request one entry in the audit trail for every attempt (successful or not) on the operation during the session.

If it's set up and enabled, the audit trail keeps the audit information in a data dictionary table owned by the user SYS. This table indicates the operation being audited, the user performing the operation, and the date and time of the operation. Oracle provides a set of data dictionary views to make the information in the dictionary audit table more meaningful. Although the audit trail is implemented in a data dictionary table, it keeps the insertion of rows in the audit trail even if the user rolls back his transaction.

The database administrator can clear out or archive the audit trail periodically.

Backup and Recovery

In this part, I discuss some of the options that the architecture gives you when it comes to backing up and recovering your database. See Chapter 14, "Backup and Recovery," for more detail.

Backup and Recovery Options

This section outlines at a high level some of the options available for backing up and restoring your database. I discuss the types of failure that can occur and the actions to take. The major part of this section describes preventive action to guard against loss of your database files.

This section discusses in theory the available options. The backup and recovery options mentioned here, along with other available options, are discussed in greater detail in Chapter 14.

Different Types of Failure

The major types of failure that can occur are statement failure, user process failure, machine failure, distributed transaction failure, instance failure, and disk failure/file loss.

Statement Failure

In Oracle, a DML statement such as UPDATE operates on either all the rows satisfying its where clause or none at all.

Failure with a statement occurs for a myriad of reasons. For example, when you insert rows into a table, the table might require more storage; if the database software discovers that no more free storage is available, it returns an error message to the user. Oracle does not leave only half the rows updated. Even if the failure occurs halfway through the statement, the rows already modified are "unmodified." This is known as statement-level rollback.

Note that other DML statements in the transaction remain in a pending state ready for a commit or rollback.

User Process Failure

A user process failure occurs when the user process making the connection to the database terminates abnormally during execution. For example, the system administrator could have killed the user process. If this does occur, the Oracle background process PMON automatically rolls back any changes for the current transaction. All changes already committed by the user process are saved, but inserts, updates, and deletes since the last commit or rollback are reversed.

Also, the PMON background process releases any locks, rollback segments, and other system resources acquired by the user process when it was alive. No database administrator involvement is necessary. The database continues to function as usual, and the tables are accessible to other users. (A slight delay could occur before the locks are released.)

Machine Failure

When the machine on which the database server is running fails and shuts down (the power is turned off, for example), the Oracle instance stops running. As long as no database files are lost, the only action required of the database administrator is restarting the Oracle instance. When you do this, the SMON background process reads the online redo log files and reapplies any changes for committed transactions. Any changes that had not been committed are rolled back.

Remember that a COMMIT statement writes only the changes to the redo log files; it does not write the database blocks back to disk at the point at which the commit was issued. If the database blocks with committed changes were written to the database files before the machine failure, the SMON background process obviously does not need to reapply the changes for those blocks.

Instance Failure

Instance failure occurs when the machine is still up and running but the Oracle instance itself fails (perhaps one of the background processes was killed). This situation is very similar to machine failure in that the database administrator needs only to restart the instance; the SMON process reapplies any changes. When restarting the instance after this kind of failure, you will notice no difference from when the instance is started after a normal shutdown.

Distributed Transaction Failure

A distributed transaction is one that involves changes to more than one database. If a failure occurs during a distributed transaction, the RECO background process (if it's running) automatically synchronizes the rollbacks of the transaction's changes across all the databases involved. Again, no manual intervention is required in all but the most serious cases. The database administrators of the instances involved in the distributed transaction can manually force the commit or rollback of the changes on their databases, but I recommend that you leave the recovery to the RECO background process if possible. This might not be possible if the links between the databases are not available for the RECO processes on all the instances to communicate.

Disk Failure/File Loss

The only time you really need to concern yourself with recovery is when you lose one or more of the files making up the database—the database files themselves, the control file, and the redo logs. Some type of manual recovery is necessary.

If you lose one or more of the files (database, redo, control), you have available the options highlighted in the following sections. In every situation, you must work with a previous backup of the database.

Cold Backup

A cold backup is when you copy the three sets of files (database files, redo logs, and control file) when the instance is shut down. This is a straight file copy, usually from the disk directly to tape. You must shut down the instance to guarantee a consistent copy. (It is possible to back up the files without bringing the instance down; see the section titled "Hot Backups.")

If you only perform a cold backup, the only option available in the event of data file loss is restoring all the files from the latest backup. All work performed on the database since the last backup is lost.

Archiving

If you've set up the database to run in ARCHIVELOG mode (easily done by the DBA), the database changes recorded in the redo logs are archived to an archive destination whenever the redo logs fill. Using this option, you have a complete record of changes made to the database files in the offline and online redo log files.

If you lose one or more of the database files, you could restore them from the last backup and reapply the changes since the last backup from the online and offline redo log files. You must have some kind of backup of the files and the complete set of online and offline redo logs from which to reapply all the changes made to the database.

With the archiving option, you lose no changes in the database if the complete set of redo logs is available. All the changes committed before the file was lost are reapplied. It is also possible to perform recovery if the control or redo log files are lost.

Hot Backups

Some sites (such as worldwide airline reservations systems) cannot shut down the database while making a backup copy of the files. The cold backup is not an available option.

You can use a different means of backing up your database—the hot backup. Issue a SQL command to indicate to Oracle, on a tablespace-by-tablespace basis, that you want to back up the files of the tablespace. The users can continue to make full use of the files, including making changes to the data. Once you have indicated that you want to back up the tablespace files, you can use your operating system to copy those files to your backup destination.

The database must be running in ARCHIVELOG mode for the hot backup option.

If a data loss failure does occur, you can restore the lost database files using the hot backup and the online and offline redo logs created since the backup was done. The database is restored to the most consistent state without any loss of committed transactions.

Export and Import

Along with the RDBMS software, Oracle provides two utilities that you can use to back up and restore the database. These utilities are useful to database administrators for system-wide backups and recoveries and also application developers for temporary backups of their own data and object recovery into their own user accounts.

The Export utility dumps the definitions and data for the specified part of the database to an operating system binary file. The Import utility reads the file produced by an export, recreates the definitions of objects, and inserts the data.

For a full database import, you must have an existing template database already created.

If you use Export and Import as a means of backing up and recovering the database, you cannot recover all the changes made to the database since the export was performed. This is similar to the situation with the cold backup. The best you can do is recover the database to the time when the export was last performed.

On large, data-filled databases, the Export and Import utilities can take a long time to run; many hours is not unusual. However, the utilities do provide an option to selectively export and import different user accounts and even objects within an Oracle user account.

Multiplexing

In this part, I discuss the options available for Oracle to duplicate data to provide an extra level of protection in the event of data loss.

Control Files

To protect against control file loss, the Oracle RDBMS software can maintain more than one copy of the control file. You do this by making a consistent copy of the existing control file and modifying an INIT.ORA parameter. This does not significantly impact the performance of the database. If all copies of the control file are lost, you can manually re-create them using the `CREATE CONTROLFILE` command.

Redo Logs

Redo logs record all the changes made to data blocks on the database. If the database is running in ARCHIVELOG mode and only the offline redo logs are lost, you should shut down the database and make another backup of the three sets of files for the database.

If the online redo logs are lost, however, you could lose some work because some of the information required to reapply changes to the database files is in the online redo log files. To guard against this, you can multiplex (mirror) the online redo log files in the same way as the control files. When the RDBMS software writes changes to one redo log, the exact same information is written to an exact copy of the redo log.

Distributed Databases

A distributed database is one logical database that is implemented as two or more physical databases on either the same machine or separate machines thousands of miles away. The system's designers decide where the tables should physically reside.

Each physical database has its own instance and sets of files, and the machines on which the databases reside are connected over a network. The location of tables can be made transparent to the application using database links and synonyms.

Oracle enables a transaction and even a single statement to access tables on two or more distributed databases. This does not necessitate any more coding by the application developers.

A distributed transaction is a transaction that modifies tables on more than one database and then expects all the changes to be committed. If there is any kind of failure, all the changes on all the databases are rolled back. A distributed transaction can involve many Oracle databases and only one non-Oracle database. The Oracle two-phase commit mechanism controls the synchronization of commits across all databases and can automatically roll back changes on all the databases if any kind of failure should occur. The RECO background process synchronizes this operation.

In addition to the this functionality, Oracle also provides the capability to replicate tables from one database to others. This is called creating a snapshot of the table.

You create a snapshot with the CREATE SNAPSHOT command on the database where you want to have the copy of the data. The Oracle RDBMS software automatically sends down any changes made to the master copy of the table to each of the snapshot copies at user-defined intervals without any manual intervention.

The snapshot mechanism enables you to make updates to the snapshot copy of the table, in which case the changes are sent from the copy table back to the master table.

Chapter 53, "Networking Oracle," discusses distributed databases in greater detail.

National Language Support

Oracle's national language support (NLS) enables users to use the database in their own languages. It provides the following functions:

◼ Support for different encoding schemes, so that data created with an encoding scheme on one machine can be processed and displayed on another. You define the character set to be used for storing data on the database as part of the CREATE DATABASE statement. For example, data created on a database with the 7-bit U.S. ASCII standard character set can be displayed on a machine connected to the same database using the Chinese GB2312-8 character set. Translation tables within the national language support provide this support.

◼ Control over the language used for server error and informational messages, numbers, dates, currency formats, and the starting day of the week.

◼ Support for linguistic sort to ensure the characters appear in the correct order next to each other in a sort.

◼ Definition of an NLS language either for the database as a whole or at the session level. With changes to the session parameters but without any changes to the Oracle user account, you could run some sessions with English, others German, others French, and so on, if the same Oracle username is connected to the database with many different sessions.

You can add support for new languages using the NLS*WorkBench product, which essentially maintains translation tables for interpreting input from the user and for displaying output.

When it comes to delivering application systems in different languages, the most important part of the user interface is the different prompts, boilerplate, and messages from the application. Currently, the application developers themselves define how the boilerplate, prompts, and messages from the application system change from one language to another. Oracle is working on a translation product to make this task easier.

Following a SQL Statement Through the Architecture

In this section, I bring together major parts of the Oracle architecture and follow the steps a typical SQL statement might go through to be executed. I use a simple scenario with both the Oracle SQL*Plus tool and the Oracle database server machine on a UNIX box without any networking involved. Using a single task configuration, the Oracle instance has just started.

The following shows some of the steps involved in executing SQL statements:

1. The user executes the SQL*Plus tool and enters the Oracle username and password.

2. Oracle validates the username and password against the data dictionary and sends a response to the user process to indicate connection.

3. The user enters a SELECT statement.

4. Oracle must translate the SELECT before it executes it so the Oracle parser and optimizer is called. If any user has issued *exactly* the same statement before, the parsed version might be in the shared pool area in memory. Oracle uses the parsed version, so no extra parsing is done for this statement.

5. To translate the SELECT statement, Oracle must obtain the names of the objects, privileges, and other information from the data dictionary. The data dictionary cache area in the shared pool in the SGA does not have the information on the tables, so parsing of the SELECT statement is suspended while the information is read in.

6. Oracle runs a recursive SQL statement (a system-generated statement) to load information about the objects from the data dictionary tables in the database files into the data dictionary cache in memory.

7. Parsing of the original user SELECT statement resumes, and Oracle constructs an optimization plan to control the way the statement runs.

8. The statement accesses a table. Assume the Oracle blocks for the table are not in the database buffer cache in the SGA. The required Oracle blocks are read in from the database files and held in the cache area of the SGA.

9. Oracle runs the statement and returns the results to the user.

10. The user issues an UPDATE statement to modify some of the fields on the rows he's just selected. Because the data dictionary cache already has the information about the table in memory, no more recursive SQL is generated (assuming that the information has not been flushed out by another process requiring space in the cache area). Also, the Oracle blocks for the table are in the database buffer cache, so you won't do another disk I/O to read these blocks in.

11. Oracle locks the rows to be updated.

12. Before Oracle makes the UPDATE, information about the old state of the blocks is recorded in a rollback segment and the original version of the values is also recorded in the redo buffers cache.

13. Oracle updates the rows and records the new version of the values in the redo buffer cache in the SGA.

14. The user issues the COMMIT command to make the change permanent to the database.

15. Oracle records an entry indicating a commit in the redo buffer cache, and the old, new, and the commit entry are all flushed down to the online redo log (whichever one is the current one in use).

16. The rollback segment is released (but not overwritten) for other processes to use.

17. Oracle releases the locks on the table.

18. The user receives a commit successful message (the exact wording of this message varies from tool to tool).

19. If the user issues a rollback instead of a commit, the old versions of the values changed are restored back to the Oracle data blocks from the rollback segment. Oracle also writes to the redo buffer cache an entry indicating that a rollback was performed.

Summary

In this chapter, I covered the major parts of the Oracle architecture—the architecture used by all the tools and commands against the database. Even though familiarity with the intricate workings of the architecture is not necessary for you to use the database and tools, it provides valuable background information in helping to work out why the database is not functioning as it should. Knowledge of the architecture also lends more meaning to some of the more cryptic error and information messages.

PART

Oracle® Tools and Utilities

SQL

4

by
Mike Conklin

IN THIS CHAPTER

Oracle's SQL: An Overview

Structured Query Language (SQL) was introduced by IBM as the language to interface with its prototype relational database management system, System R. The first commercially available SQL relational database management system was introduced in 1979 by Oracle Corporation. Today, SQL has become an industry standard, and Oracle Corporation clearly leads the world in relational database management system technology.

Because SQL is a non-procedural language, sets of records can be manipulated instead of one record at a time. The syntax is free-flowing, enabling you to concentrate on the data presentation. Oracle has two optimizers (cost- and rule-based) that will parse the syntax and format it into an efficient statement before the database engine receives it for processing. The database administrator (DBA) determines which optimizer is in effect for each database instance.

SQL—The Standard

The American National Standards Institute (ANSI) has declared SQL as the standard language for relational database management systems. Most companies that produce relational database management systems support SQL and tend to comply with the ANSI SQL89 standard.

Data Types

This chapter does not give a lesson on data modeling and creating a proper database schema. In order to write proper SQL statements, familiarity with database objects (tables, views, constraints) are essential.

One general rule to follow when you are writing SQL statements is that data types cannot be mixed. Conversion utilities are available to convert from one type to another. These conversion functions are covered later in this chapter.

Numeric

The NUMBER data type is used to store zero, negative, positive, fixed, and floating point numbers with up to 38 digits of precision. Numbers range between 1.0×10^{-130} and 1.0×10^{126}.

Numbers can be defined in one of three ways:

NUMBER(p,s)

where p is the precision up to 38 digits and s is the scale (number of digits to the right of the decimal point). The scale can range from −84 to 127.

NUMBER (p)

This is a fixed-point number with a scale of zero and a precision of p.

NUMBER

This is a floating-point number with a precision of 38.

The following table shows how Oracle stores different scales and precisions:

Actual Data	Defined as	Stored as
123456.789	NUMBER(6,2)	123456.79
123456.789	NUMBER(6)	123457
123456.789	NUMBER(6,−2)	123400
123456.789	NUMBER	123456.789

Date

Instead of storing date and time information in a character or numeric format, IBM created a separate data type. For each DATE data type, the following information is stored:

Century

Year

Month

Day

Hour

Minute

Second

You can easily retrieve the current date and time by using the function SYSDATE.

Date arithmetic is possible using number constants or other dates. Only addition and subtraction are supported. For example, SYSDATE + 7 will return one week from today.

Every database system has a default date format that is defined by the initialization parameter NLS_DATE_FORMAT. This parameter is usually set to *DD-MON-YY*, where *DD* is the day of the month (the first day of the month is 01), *MON* is the abbreviated month name, and *YY* is a two-digit year designation.

If you do not specify a time, the default time is 12:00:00 a.m. If only the time component is captured, the default date will be the first day of the current month.

Character

Four character types are available:

1. The CHAR data type is used where fixed-length fields are necessary. Any length up to 255 characters can be specified. The default length is 1. When data is entered, any space left over will be filled with blanks. All alpha-numeric characters are allowed.

2. The VARCHAR2 is used for variable-length fields. A length component must be supplied when you use this data type. The maximum length is 2,000 characters. All alpha-numeric characters are allowed.

3. The LONG data type is used to store large amounts of variable-length text. Any length up to 2 GB can be specified. Be aware that there are some restrictions to using this data type, such as:

   Only one column per table can be defined as LONG.

   A LONG column cannot be indexed.

   A LONG column cannot be passed as an argument to a procedure.

   A function cannot be used to return a LONG column.

   A LONG column cannot be used in `where`, `order by`, `group by`, or `connect by` clauses.

4. The VARCHAR data type is synonymous with VARCHAR2. Oracle Corporation is reserving this for future use. Do not use this data type.

Binary

Two data types, RAW and LONGRAW, are available for storing binary type data such as digitized sound and images. These data types take on similar characteristics as the VARCHAR2 and LONG data types already mentioned.

Use the RAW data type to store binary data up to 2,000 characters and use the LONGRAW data type to store binary data up to 2 GB.

Oracle only stores and retrieves binary data; no string manipulations are allowed. Data is retrieved as hexadecimal character values.

Others

Every row in the database has an address. You can retrieve this address by using the `ROWID` function. The format of the `ROWID` is as follows:

```
BLOCK.ROW.FILE
```

`BLOCK` is the data block of the data `FILE` containing the `ROW`. The data is in hexadecimal format and has the data type `ROWID`.

`MLSLABEL` is a data type used to store the binary format of a label used on a secure operating system.

The *CREATE* Statement

The CREATE statement opens the world to the user. Whether a simple temporary table is to be created or a complex database schema, you will repeatedly use the CREATE statement. Only a few of the more common CREATE statements are covered here.

Tables

Every database designer will have to create a table sometime. The CREATE TABLE system privilege is needed to execute this command. The DBA is responsible for administering these privileges. The syntax to create a table is

```
CREATE TABLE schema.TABLE (COLUMN DATATYPE default expression
   ➥ column constraint) table constraint
PCTFREE x PCTUSED x INITRANS x MAXTRANS x
   ➥TABLESPACE name STORAGE clause CLUSTER cluster clause
ENABLE clause DISABLE clause AS subquery
```

In this syntax, SCHEMA is an optional parameter to identify which database schema to place this table in. The default is your own.

TABLE is mandatory and is the name of your table.

COLUMN DATATYPE is required to identify each column in the table. Separate the columns with commas. There is a maximum of 254 columns per table.

The DEFAULT expression is optional and is used to assign a default value to a column when a subsequent insert statement fails to assign a value.

COLUMN CONSTRAINT is optional. It is used to define an integrity constraint such as not null.

TABLE CONSTRAINT is optional and is used to define an integrity constraint as part of the table, such as the primary key.

PCTFREE is optional but has a default of 10. This indicates that 10 percent for each data block will be reserved for future updates to the table's rows. Integers from 1 to 99 are allowed.

PCTUSED is optional but has a default of 40. This indicates the minimum percentage of space used that Oracle maintains before a data block becomes a candidate for row insertion. Integers from 1 to 99 are allowed. The sum of PCTFREE and PCTUSED must be less than 100.

INITRANS is optional but has a default of 1. Integers from 1 to 255 are allowed. It is recommended that you leave this alone. This is an allocation of the number of transaction entries assigned within the data block for the table.

MAXTRANS is optional but has a default that is a function of the data block size. This is used to identify the maximum number of concurrent transactions that can update a data block for your table. It is recommended that this parameter not be changed.

TABLESPACE is optional but has a default value as the tablespace name of the owner of the schema. A different tablespace name than the default can be used. Tablespace names are usually application-dependent. The DBA will be able to give proper recommendations.

STORAGE is optional and has default characteristics defined by the DBA.

CLUSTER is optional and specifies that a table is to be part of a cluster. You must identify the columns from the table that need to be clustered. Typically, the cluster columns are columns that comprise the primary key.

ENABLE is optional and turns on an integrity constraint.

DISABLE is optional and turns off an integrity constraint.

AS SUBQUERY is optional and inserts the rows returned by the subquery into the table upon creation.

Once the table is created, you can use the ALTER TABLE command to make alterations to the table. To modify an integrity constraint, DROP the constraint first, and then re-create it.

Let's look at two examples on creating tables:

```
CREATE TABLE ADDRESSES (ADRS_ID        NUMBER(6),
                        ACTIVE_DATE    DATE,
                        BOX_NUMBER     NUMBER(6),
                        ADDRS_1        VARCHAR2(40),
                        ADDRS_2        VARCHAR2(40),
                        CITY           VARCHAR2(40),
                        STATE          VARCHAR2(2),
                        ZIP            VARCHAR2(10));
```

This is the simplest form of a table create using all of the default capabilities. The second example follows:

```
CREATE TABLE ADDRESSES    (ADRS_ID      NUMBER(6)
   ➡CONSTRAINT PK_ADRS PRIMARY KEY,
ACTIVE_DATE    DATE          DEFAULT SYSDATE,
                        BOX_NUMBER    NUMBER(6)     DEFAULT NULL,
                        ADDRS_1       VARCHAR2(40)  NOT NULL,
                        ADDRS_2       VARCHAR2(40)  DEFAULT NULL,
                        CITY          VARCHAR2(40)  DEFAULT NULL,
                        STATE         VARCHAR2(2)   DEFAULT 'NY',
                        ZIP           VARCHAR2(10))
    PCTFREE 5
    PCTUSED 65
    TABLESPACE adrs_data
    STORAGE (INITIAL 5140
            NEXT       5140
            MINEXTENTS  1
            MAXEXTENTS 10
            PCTINCREASE 10);
```

In this example, data constraints are being utilized and certain storage parameters will be in effect. Using PCTFREE and PCTUSED is a good idea if your data is relatively static.

Indexes

Indexes are used to increase performance of the database. An index is created on one or more columns of a table or cluster. Multiple indexes per table are allowed. The CREATE INDEX system privilege is needed to execute this command. The DBA is responsible for administering these privileges. The syntax to create an index is

```
CREATE INDEX schema.index ON schema.table (COLUMN  ASC/DESC)
CLUSTER schema.cluster  INITRANS x MAXTRANS x TABLESPACE name
   ➥STORAGE  clause PCTFREE x NOSORT
```

In this syntax, SCHEMA is an optional parameter to identify which database schema to place this table in. The default is your own.

INDEX is mandatory and is the name of the index.

ON is a mandatory reserved word.

TABLE is a mandatory table name upon which the index will be built.

COLUMN is the column name to be indexed. If there is more than one column, make sure they are in order of priority.

ASC/DESC are optional parameters. Indexes are built in ascending order by default. Use DESC for descending order.

CLUSTER is needed only if this index is for a cluster.

INITRANS is optional but has a default of 1. Integers from 1 to 255 are allowed. It is recommended that this parameter not be changed. This is an allocation of the number of transaction entries assigned within the data block for the index.

MAXTRANS is optional but has a default that is a function of the data block size. It is used to identify the maximum number of concurrent transactions that can update a data block for the index. It is recommended that this parameter not be changed.

TABLESPACE is optional but has a default value as the tablespace name of the owner of the schema. A different tablespace name than the default might be needed. The DBA will be able to give some recommendations.

STORAGE is optional and has default characteristics defined by the DBA.

PCTFREE is optional but has a default of 10. This indicates that 10 percent for each data block will be reserved for future updates to the index. Integers from 1 to 99 are allowed.

NOSORT is an optional parameter that will save time when creating the index if the table data is already stored in ascending order. This cannot be used if a clustered index is being created.

Using the addresses table defined from the create table example, two indexes will be created in the next example.

```
CREATE INDEX x_adrs_id ON ADDRESSES (ADRS_ID);
```

This will create an index on the adrs_id column only.

```
CREATE INDEX x_city_state ON ADDRESSES (CITY,STATE)
TABLESPACE application_indexes;
```

This index has two columns; CITY is the primary column. In order for queries to use an index, the column names must be part of the SELECT statement. If a SELECT statement included STATE but not CITY, the index would not be used. However, if the SELECT statement contained a reference to CITY but not STATE, part of the index would be used because CITY is the first column of the index.

Sequences

Sequences are a great way to have the database automatically generate unique integer primary keys. The CREATE SEQUENCE system privilege is needed to execute this command. The DBA is responsible for administering these privileges. The syntax to create a sequence is

```
CREATE SEQUENCE schema.name
    INCREMENT BY x
    START WITH x
    MAXVALUE x      NOMAXVALUE
    MINVALUE x      NOMINVALUE
    CYCLE           NOCYCLE
    CACHE x         NOCACHE
    ORDER           NOORDER
```

In this syntax, SCHEMA is an optional parameter that identifies which database schema to place this sequence in. The default is your own.

NAME is mandatory because it is the name of the sequence.

INCREMENT BY is optional. The default is one. Zero is not allowed. If a negative integer is specified, the sequence will descend in order. A positive integer will make the sequence ascend (the default).

START WITH is an optional integer that enables the sequence to begin anywhere.

MAXVALUE is an optional integer that places a limit on the sequence.

NOMAXVALUE is optional. It causes the maximum ascending limit to be 10^{27} and -1 for descending sequences. This is the default.

MINVALUE is an optional integer that determines the minimum a sequence can be.

NOMINVALUE is optional. It causes the minimum ascending limit to be 1 and $-(10^{26})$ for descending sequences. This is the default.

CYCLE is an option that enables the sequence to continue even when the maximum has been reached. If the maximum is reached, the next sequence that will be generated is whatever the minimum value is.

NOCYCLE is an option that does not enable the sequence to generate values beyond the defined maximum or minimum. This is the default.

CACHE is an option that enables sequence numbers to be preallocated that will be stored in memory for faster access. The minimum value is 2.

NOCACHE is an option that will not enable the preallocation of sequence numbers.

ORDER is an option that ensures the sequence numbers are generated in order of request.

NOORDER is an option that does not ensure that sequence numbers are generated in the order they are requested.

If you want to create a sequence for your adrs_id column in the ADDRESSES table, it could look like the following example:

```
CREATE SEQUENCE adrs_seq
    INCREMENT BY 5
    START WITH 100;
```

To generate a new sequence number, use the pseudocolumn NEXTVAL. This needs to be preceded with your sequence name. For example, adrs_seq.nextval would return 100 for the first access and 105 for the second. If determining the current sequence number is necessary, use CURRVAL. Therefore, adrs_seq.currval will return the current value of the sequence.

Other Objects

The purpose of this chapter is not to elaborate on every SQL statement. The ones given have been covered to give an overview of the more common CREATE statements. Listed next is an alphabetical list of all objects that can be created with the CREATE statement.

CREATE *xxx*, where *xxx* is one of the following:

```
CLUSTER
CONTROLFILE
DATABASE
DATABASE LINK
DATAFILE
FUNCTION
INDEX
PACKAGE BODY
PACKAGE
PROCEDURE
PROFILE
```

```
ROLE
ROLLBACK SEGMENT
SCHEMA
SEQUENCE
SNAPSHOT
SNAPSHOT LOG
SYNONYM
TABLE
TABLESPACE
TRIGGER
USER
VIEW
```

Writing Queries

To retrieve data from the database, use the SELECT statement. Once again, proper privileges are required and are maintained by the DBA. The SELECT statement has the following format:

```
SELECT column(s)
FROM tables(s)
WHERE conditions are met
GROUP BY selected columns
ORDER BY column(s);
```

Every SQL statement ends with a semicolon (;). When you are writing scripts (disk files) that will be executed, you can also use a slash (\) to terminate the SQL statement.

When SELECT column(s) is used, it is assumed that all of the columns fitting the WHERE clause will be retrieved. It is sometimes necessary to retrieve only columns that are distinct from one another. To do this, use the reserved word DISTINCT before the column descriptions. In the following example, a SELECT statement is used to retrieve all of the cities and states from the addresses table (defined previously):

```
SELECT city, state
FROM addresses;
```

When this code run, every city and state will be retrieved from the table. If 30 people lived in Rochester, NY, the data would be displayed 30 times. To see only one occurrence for each city and state use the DISTINCT qualifier, as shown in the following example:

```
SELECT DISTINCT city, state
FROM addresses;
```

This will cause only one row to be retrieved for entries with Rochester, NY.

The FROM clause is a listing of all tables needed for the query. You can use table aliases to help simplify queries, as shown in the following example:

```
SELECT adrs.city, adrs.state
FROM addresses adrs;
```

In this example, the alias adrs has been given to the table addresses. The alias will be used to differentiate columns with the same name from different tables.

The WHERE clause is used to list the criteria necessary to restrict the output from the query or to join tables in the FROM clause. See the following example.

```
SELECT DISTINCT city, state
FROM addresses
WHERE state in ('CA','NY','CT')
    AND city is NOT NULL;
```

This example will retrieve cities and states that are in the states of California, New York, and Connecticut. The check for NOT NULL cities will not bring data back if the city field was not filled in.

The GROUP BY clause tells Oracle how to group the records together when certain functions are used.

```
SELECT dept_no, SUM(emp_salary)
FROM emp
GROUP BY dept_no;
```

The GROUP BY example will list all department numbers once with the summation of the employee salaries for that particular department.

Built-In Functions

Functions are an intrinsic part of any SQL statement. Table 4.1 shows an alphabetical list of SQL functions.

Table 4.1. SQL functions.

Name	Type	Syntax	Returns
ABS	Number	ABS(*n*)	Absolute value of *n*.
ADD_MONTHS	Date	ADD_MONTHS(*a*,*b*)	Date *a* plus *b* months.
ASCII	Character	ASCII(*c*)	Decimal representation of *c*.
AVG	Group	AVG(DISTINCT¦ALL *n*)	Average value of *n*. ALL is default.
CEIL	Number	CEIL(*n*)	Smallest integer equal to or greater than *n*.
CHARTOROWID	Conversion	CHARTOROWID(*c*)	Converts character to rowid data type.
CHR	Character	CHR(*n*)	Character having binary equivalent to *n*.

continues

Table 4.1. continued

Name	Type	Syntax	Returns
CONCAT	Character	CONCAT(1,2)	Character 1 concatenated with character 2.
CONVERT	Conversion	CONVERT(a, dest_c [,source_c])	Converts character string a from one character set to another. The source source_c to the destination character set dest_c.
COS	Number	COS(n)	Cosine of n.
COSH	Number	COSH(n)	Hyperbolic cosine of n.
COUNT	Group	COUNT(DISTINCT¦ALL e)	Number of rows in a query. ALL is default. e can be represented as * to indicate all columns.
EXP	Number	EXP(n)	e raised to the nth power.
FLOOR	Number	FLOOR(n)	Largest integer equal to or less than n.
GREATEST	Other	GREATEST(e [,e]...)	The greatest of the list of expressions e.
HEXTORAW	Conversion	HEXTORAW(c)	Converts hexadecimal character c to raw.
INITCAP	Character	INITCAP(c)	c with the first letter of each word in uppercase.
INSTR	Character	INSTR (1, 2 [, n [, m]])	Searches 1 with nth character for mth occurrence of 2 and returns the position of the occurrence.
INSTRB	Character	INSTRB(1,2[,n[,m]])	Same as INSTR except numeric parameters are in terms of bytes.
LAST_DAY	Date	LAST_DAY(a)	Last day of the month (date) containing a.
LEAST	Other	LEAST(e [,e]...)	The least of the list of expressions e.
LENGTH	Character	LENGTH(c)	Number of characters in c. If c is a fixed-length data type (char), all trailing blanks are included.

Name	*Type*	*Syntax*	*Returns*
LENGTHB	Character	LENGTHB(c)	Same as LENGTH except in bytes.
LN	Number	LN(n)	Natural logarithm if n, where n > 0.
LOG	Number	LOG(b,n)	Logarithm, base b, of n.
LOWER	Character	LOWER(c)	c with all letters in lower-case.
LPAD	Character	LPAD(1,n [,2])	Character 1 left padded to length of n. If character 2 is not omitted, use as a pattern instead of blanks.
LTRIM	Character	LTRIM(c [,set])	Removed characters from the left of c. If set is defined, remove initial characters up to the first character not in set.
MAX	Other	MAX(DISTINCT¦ALL e)	Maximum of expression e. ALL is default.
MIN	Other	MIN(DISTINCT¦ALL e)	Minimum of expression e. ALL is default.
MOD	Number	MOD(r,n)	Remainder of r divided by n.
MONTHS_BETWEEN	Date	MONTHS_BETWEEN(a,b)	Number of days between dates a and b.
NEW_TIME	Date	NEW_TIME(a, z1, z2)	Date and time in time zone z2 when date and time in time zone z1 are a.
NEXT_DAY	Date	NEXT_DAY(a, c)	Date of first weekday identified by c that is later than date a.
NLSSORT	Character	NLSSORT((c [,parm])	String of bytes to sort c.
NLS_INITCAP	Character	NLS_INITCAP (c [,parm])	c with the first letter of each word in uppercase. parm has the form of NLS_SORT = s where s is a linguistic sort or binary.

continues

Table 4.1. continued

Name	Type	Syntax	Returns
NLS_LOWER	Character	NLS_LOWER(c [,parm])	c with all letters lowercase. See parm above.
NLS_UPPER	Character	NLS_UPPER(c [,parm])	c with all letters uppercase. See parm above.
NVL	Other	NVL(e1, e2)	If e1 is null, returns e2. If e1 is not null, returns e1.
POWER	Number	POWER(m,n)	m raised to the nth power.
RAWTOHEX	Conversion	RAWTOHEX(raw)	Converts raw value to its hexadecimal equivalent.
REPLACE	Character	REPLACE(c, s1 [, r2])	Replace each occurrence of string s1 in c with r2. If r2 is omitted, all occurrences of s1 are removed.
ROUND	Date	ROUND(n [,f])	Date rounded to format model f. If f is omitted, n will be rounded to nearest day.
ROUND	Number	ROUND(n[,m])	n rounded to m places right of decimal point. If m is omitted, to 0 places.
ROWIDTOCHAR	Conversion	ROWIDTOCHAR(rowid)	Converts rowid to varchar2 format with length of 18.
RPAD	Character	RPAD(1, n [, 2])	1 right-padded to length of n with 2.
RTRIM	Character	RTRIM(c [, s])	c with characters removed after last character not in set s. If s is omitted, set defaulted to ' '.
SIGN	Number	SIGN(n)	-1 if n < 0, 0 if n = 0, 1 if n > 0.
SIN	Number	SIN(n)	Sine of n.
SINH	Number	SINH(n)	Hyperbolic sine of n.
SOUNDEX	Character	SOUNDEX(c)	A string with phonetic representation of c.

Name	*Type*	*Syntax*	*Returns*
SUBSTR	Character	SUBSTR(c, m [,n])	A portion of c beginning at character number m for n characters. If m is negative, Oracle counts backward from the end of c. If n is omitted, all characters are returned to the end of c.
SUBSTRB	Character	SUBSTRB(c, m [,n])	The same as SUBSTR except m and n are number of bytes.
SQRT	Number	SQRT(n)	Square root of n.
STDDEV	Group	STDDEV(DISTINCT¦ALL n)	Standard deviation of number n.
SUM	Group	SUM(DISTINCT¦ALL n)	Sum of numbers n.
SYSDATE	Date	SYSDATE	Current date and time.
TAN	Number	TAN(n)	Tangent of n.
TANH	Number	TANH(n)	Hyperbolic tangent of n.
TO_CHAR	Conversion	TO_CHAR (d [,f [,parm])	Converts d date to varchar2 data type with format f and nls_date_language of parm.
TO_CHAR	Conversion	TO_CHAR (n [,f [,parm])	Converts n number data type to a varchar2 equivalent and number format element parm.
TO_DATE	Conversion	TO_DATE (c [, f [, parm])	Converts varchar2¦ data type c to date data type with format f and nls date format element parm.
TO_MULTI_BYTE	Conversion	TO_MULTI_BYTE(c)	Converts c to its corresponding multibyte equivalent.
TO_NUMBER	Conversion	TO_NUMBER (c [,f [, parm]])	Converts character c to a number using format f and nls number format element parm.

continues

Table 4.1. continued

Name	Type	Syntax	Returns
TO_SINGLE_BYTE	Conversion	TO_SINGLE_BYTE(c)	Converts multibyte character c to its single byte equivalent.
TRANSLATE	Character	TRANSLATE(c, f, t)	c with each occurrences in f with each corresponding character in t.
TRUNC	Date	TRUNC(c [,f])	c with time portion truncated to format f.
TRUNC	Number	TRUNC(n[,m])	n truncated to m decimal places. If m is omitted, to 0 places.
UID	Other	UID	An integer that uniquely identifies the user.
USER	Other	USER	Current user as a varchar2.
UPPER	Character	UPPER(c)	c with all letters in uppercase.
VARIANCE	Group	VARIANCE (DISTINCT¦ALL n)	Variance of number n.
VSIZE	Other	VSIZE(e)	Number of bytes from the internal representation of e.

Now look at some examples using functions.

```
SELECT SUBSTR(addrs_1,1,30),
              city, state, zip
FROM addresses
WHERE addrs_1 is not null
     AND UPPER(city) = 'ROCHESTER'
     AND TO_NUMBER(SUBSTR(zip,1,5)) > 14525
     AND NVL(active_date,SYSDATE) > TO_DATE('01-JAN-90');
```

Notice the use of the UPPER function. When Oracle performs character string comparisons, the case (upper- and lower-) of the strings in question have to match exactly. Therefore, 'Rochester' does not equal 'ROCHESTER'. The UPPER function will ensure that the column city will be converted to uppercase prior to the comparison of the literal 'ROCHESTER'.

The SUBSTR function is also used to retrieve the characters 1 through 30 of column addrs_1. All remaining characters beyond 30 will not be seen. This function is also used in the WHERE clause to retrieve the first five characters of the zip column before converting it to a numerical value. The comparison is made after the conversion has taken place.

If the column active_date contains any nulls, they will be included in the data set because of the NVL function. If active_date is null, the current date will be returned before the comparison is made to the constant `'01-JAN-90'`. The constant `'01-JAN-90'` is converted to a date data type to ensure format compatibility. For a complete list of all date formats, see "Elements of SQL" in Oracle's *SQL Language Reference Manual*.

```
SELECT dept_no,
            SUM(emp_salary),
            AVG(emp_salary)
FROM emp
WHERE dept_no = dept_no
GROUP BY dept_no;
```

This example shows the use of the SUM and AVG functions. The retrieved data will show the summation of employee salaries and the average salary by department. Notice that the GROUP BY clause has to be used in this query.

Know Your Tables and Views

To ensure that your data contains all of the required columns and restrictions, you must be familiar with the database schema. If a schema diagram is not available, there are numerous ways to find out what tables or views might be needed for writing queries. One way is to look at some of the data dictionary tables.

To view all of the data dictionary table names, issue the following SELECT statement:

```
SELECT table_name
FROM dictionary
ORDER BY table_name;
```

Some of the tables of interest should be all_tables, all_columns, all_views and all_constraints.

To view the column names of these tables, issue `'DESC table_name'`. DESC stands for DESCribe and `'table_name'` is the name of the table in question, such as `'all_tables'`. Therefore, `'DESC all_tables'` will return all of the columns and their data types for the table `'all_tables'`.

With the help of the data dictionary tables, it is possible to determine what tables, views, and constraints are in effect for the application in question.

Joining Tables

Tables are physically joined in the FROM clause of your query. They are logically joined in the WHERE clause. Table columns that appear in the WHERE clause must have the table name listed in the FROM clause. The WHERE clause is where the tables relate one to another.

The way in which the WHERE clause is constructed greatly affects the performance of the query. A two-table join does not necessarily perform better than a ten-table join.

If there are a lot of queries that have a large number of tables joined together (more than seven tables, for example), you might need consider denormalizing certain data elements to reduce the number of table joins. This type of denormalization might be required when user productivity or system performance has significantly decreased.

Table 4.2 shows three tables that you will be working with for the examples.

Table 4.2. Table descriptions.

Table Name	Column Name	Data Type
emp	emp_id	number(6)
emp	adrs_id	number(6)
emp	first_name	varchar2(40)
emp	last_name	varchar2(40)
emp	dept_no	number(3)
emp	hire_date	date
emp	job_title	varchar2(40)
emp	salary	number(6)
emp	manager_id	number(6)
dept	dept_no	number(3)
dept	name	varchar(40)
dept	adrs_id	number(6)
addresses	adrs_id	number(6)
addresses	active_date	date
addresses	box_number	number(6)
addresses	adrs_1	varchar2(40)
addresses	adrs_2	varchar2(40)
addresses	city	varchar2(40)
addresses	state	varchar2(2)
addresses	zip	varchar2(10)

In the following example, a query is written that will list all departments with their corresponding employees and the cities in which the departments reside.

```
SELECT d.name,
       e.last_name,
       e.first_name,
       a.city
FROM emp        e,
     dept       d,
     addresses  a
WHERE d.dept_no     = e.dept_no
  AND a.adrs_id     = d.adrs_id
ORDER BY d.name,e.last_name,e.first_name;
```

If the employee city needed to be retrieved as well, the query could be written like the following:

```
SELECT d.name,
       a.city   dept_city,
       e.last_ name,
       e.first_name,
       z.city   emp_city
FROM emp        e,
     dept       d,
     addresses  a,
     addresses  z
WHERE   d.dept_no     = e.dept_no
  AND   a.adrs_id     = d.adrs_id
  AND   z.adrs_id     = e.adrs_id
ORDER BY d.name,e.last_name,e.first_name;
```

In this example the addresses table was joined twice, enabling the city column to be retrieved for both the department and employee. In order to clarify the output, aliases were assigned to the different city columns in the SELECT portion of the query.

The following example adds the employee manager's name to the query:

```
SELECT d.name,
       a.city   dept_city,
       e.last_name,
       e.first_name,
       z.city   emp_city,
       m.first_name || m.last_name manager
FROM emp        e,
     dept       d,
     addresses  a,
     addresses  z,
     emp        m
WHERE   d.dept_no     = e.dept_no
  AND   a.adrs_id     = d.adrs_id
  AND   z.adrs_id     = e.adrs_id
  AND   m.emp_id      = e.manager_id
ORDER BY    d.name,e.last_name,e.first_name;
```

The output from this query will cause the manager (alias) column to appear as one column even though it is made from two columns. The symbol (||) is used to concatenate columns together.

Avoid Cartesian Joins

A Cartesian join happens when the WHERE clause is not properly constructed. A record is returned for every occurrence in table Z and table X. See the following example:

```
SELECT X.name,
       Z.last_name,
       Z.first_name
FROM   emp          Z,
       dept         X
ORDER BY X.name, Z.last_name;
```

If the emp table had 10 employees and the department table had three departments, this query would return 30 rows. For each department name, all employees would be listed because the tables are not joined properly (not at all in this example). If the join condition WHERE X.dept_no = Z.dept_no existed, only 10 rows would be retrieved.

Outer Joins

When the columns of a table are outer joined, this tells the database to retrieve rows even if data is not found. The plus symbol (+) is used to denote an outer join condition, as shown in the following example:

```
SELECT d.name,
       a.city,
       e.last_name,
       e.first_name
FROM emp            e,
     dept           d,
     addresses      a
WHERE        d.dept_no(+)   = e.dept_no
       AND   a.adrs_id      = d.adrs_id
ORDER BY d.name,e.last_name,e.first_name;
```

If the president of the company was never assigned a department, his name would never be retrieved in previous examples because his department number would be null. The outer join would cause all rows to be retrieved even if there is not a match for dept_no.

Outer joins are effective but will make the query perform slower. You might need to rewrite the query if you need to improve performance.

Subqueries

Subqueries, or nested queries, are used to bring back a set of rows to be used by the parent query. Depending on how the subquery is written, it can be executed once for the parent query or it can be executed once for each row returned by the parent query. If the subquery is executed for each row of the parent, this is called a *correlated subquery*.

A correlated subquery can be easily identified if it contains any references to the parent subquery columns in its WHERE clause. Columns from the subquery cannot be referenced anywhere else in the parent query. The following example demonstrates a non-correlated subquery:

```
SELECT e.first_name,
       e.last_name,
       e.job_title
FROM emp  e
WHERE e.dept_no in (SELECT dept_no
                      FROM dept
                      WHERE name = 'ADMIN');
```

In this example, all employee names and job titles will be retrieved for the department 'ADMIN'. Notice the use of the operator in when referring to the subquery. The in operator is used when one or more rows might be returned by a subquery. If the equal operator (=) is used, it is assumed that only one row will be returned. If the equal operator (=) is used and more than one row is returned, Oracle will return an error.

This statement could have been written by directly joining the dept table with the emp table in the main or parent query. Subqueries are sometimes used for performance gain. If the parent query contains a lot of tables, it might be advantageous to break up the WHERE clause into subqueries.

```
SELECT d.name,
       e.first_name,
       e.last_name,
       e.job_title
FROM emp  e,
     dept d
WHERE e.dept_no = d.dept_no
  AND d.adrs_id = (SELECT adrs_id
                     FROM ADDRESSES
                     WHERE adrs_id = d.adrs_id)
ORDER BY d.name, e.job_title, e.last_name;
```

In this example, all employees with their corresponding departments will be retrieved only for departments that have a valid adrs_id in the addresses table. This is a correlated subquery because the subquery references a column in the parent query.

```
SELECT d.name,
       e.first_name,
       e.last_name,
       e.job_title
FROM emp  e,
     dept d
WHERE e.dept_no = d.dept_no
  AND not exists (SELECT 'X'
                    FROM ADDRESSES
                    WHERE city in ('ROCHESTER','NEW YORK')
                      AND adrs_id = d.adrs_id)
ORDER BY d.name, e.job_title, e.last_name;
```

This example will return all departments and employees except where departments are located in 'ROCHESTER' and 'NEW YORK'. SELECT 'X' will return a true or false type answer that will be evaluated by the not exists operator. Any constant could be used here; 'X' is only one example.

The *DECODE* Statement

One of the most powerful and overlooked SQL statements is the DECODE statement. The DECODE statement has the following syntax:

```
DECODE(val, exp1, exp2, exp3, exp4, ..., def);
```

DECODE will first evaluate the value or expression val and then compare expression *exp1* to val. If val equals *exp1*, expression exp2 will be returned. If val does not equal *exp1*, expression *exp3* will be evaluated and returns expression *exp4* if val equals *exp3*. This process continues until all expressions have been evaluated. If there are no matches, the default def will be returned.

```
SELECT e.first_name,
       e.last_name,
       e.job_title,
       DECODE(e.job_title, 'President', '******', e.salary)
FROM emp e
WHERE e.emp_id in (SELECT NVL(z.manager_id, e.emp_id)
                   FROM emp z);
```

In this example, all manager names will be retrieved with their salaries. When the row identifying the president is displayed, it shows '******' instead of his salary. Also notice the NVL function used to evaluate a null manager ID. Only the president will have a null manager ID, which would not have been retrieved without the NVL.

Also notice that DECODE is evaluating job_title and returning salary, which would normally be a data type mismatch because the job title and salary columns are different data types but is okay here.

```
SELECT e.first_name,
       e.last_name,
       e.job_title,
       e.salary
FROM emp e
WHERE DECODE(USER,'PRES',e.emp_id,
             UPPER(e.last_name),e.emp_id,  0) = e.emp_id ;
```

In this example, if the user is the president, all employees will be returned with their corresponding salaries. For all other users, only one row will be retrieved, enabling the user to see his or her own salary only.

```
SELECT e.first_name,
       e.last_name,
       e.job_title,
       DECODE(USER,'ADMIN',DECODE(e.job_title, 'PRESEDENT', '*****', e.salary),
                                   'PRES', e.salary, '******')
```

```
FROM emp e
WHERE e.emp_id in (SELECT NVL(z.manager_id, e.emp_id)
                   FROM emp z);
```

In this example, the DECODE statement is nested with another DECODE statement. If the Oracle user is 'ADMIN', show the salaries except for the president's salary. If the Oracle user is 'PRES', show all salaries and if the user is anybody else, return '******'.

Another place the DECODE statement can be used is in the ORDER BY clause. The next example will sort the output in such a way that the president is the first row returned followed by the departments 'SALES', 'ADMIN', and then 'IS' with their corresponding employees.

```
SELECT d.name,
       e.job_title,
       e.first_name,
       e.last_name
FROM emp e,
     dept d
WHERE d.dept_no = e.dept_no
ORDER BY DECODE(e.job_title,'PRESIDENT', 0,
               DECODE(d.name,'SALES',    1,
                             'ADMIN',    2, 3)), e.last_name;
```

This example does not ORDER BY e.job_title but uses this column to search for the title 'PRESIDENT' and returns a 0. For all other rows, another DECODE is used to evaluate the department name and returning numbers 1, 2, or 3 depending upon what the department name is. After the DECODEs are finished, the data is further sorted by employee last name e.last_name.

INSERTs, UPDATEs, and DELETEs

The INSERT statement is used to put new rows into the database. This can be done one row at a time using the VALUES expression or a whole set of records at a time using a subquery. The following is the syntax for an INSERT statement:

```
INSERT INTO schema.table column(s) VALUES subquery
```

where schema is an optional parameter to identify which database schema to use for the insert. The default is your own.

table is mandatory and is the name of the table.

column is a list of columns that will receive the inserted values.

VALUES is used when one row of data will be inserted. Values are represented as constants.

subquery is used when the VALUES option is not used. The columns in the subquery must match the sequence and data types of the columns in the insert list.

```
INSERT INTO dept  (dept_no,
                   name,
                   adrs_id)
```

```
VALUES (dept_seq.NEXTVAL,
        'CUSTOMER SERVICE',
        adrs_seq.NEXTVAL);
```

This example inserts one row into the table dept. Sequences dept_seq and adrs_seq are used to retrieve the next numeric values for dept_no and adrs_id.

If multiple rows need to be inserted, the INSERT EXAMPLE 1 statement would have to executed for each individual row. If a subquery can be used, multiple rows would be inserted for each row returned by the subquery.

```
INSERT INTO emp (emp_id,
                first_name,
                last_name,
                dept_no,
                hire_date,
                job_title,
                salary,
                manager_id)
    SELECT emp_seq.NEXTVAL,
           new.first_name,
           new.last_name,
           30,
           SYSDATE,
           'CUSTOMER REPRESENTATIVE',
           new.salary,
           220
    FROM candidates new
    WHERE new.accept      = 'YES'
          AND new.dept_no = 30;
```

This example will insert all rows from the candidates table that have been assigned to department number 30 and have been accepted. Because the department number and manager ID are known, they are used as constants in the subquery. The UPDATE statement is used to change existing rows in the database. The syntax for the UPDATE statement is

```
UPDATE  schema.table SET column(s) = expr sub  query  WHERE condition
```

where schema is an optional parameter to identify which database schema to use for the update. The default is your own.

table is mandatory and is the name of the table.

SET is a mandatory reserved word.

column is a list of columns that will receive the updated values.

expr is the new value to be assigned.

sub query is a SELECT statement that will retrieve the new data values.

WHERE is optional and is used to restrict which rows are to be updated.

```
UPDATE emp
   SET dept_no = 30
```

```
WHERE last_name = 'DOE'
     AND first_name = 'JOHN';
```

This example will transfer an employee named JOHN DOE to department 30. If there is more than one JOHN DOE, further restrictions will have to be made in the WHERE clause.

```
UPDATE emp
   SET salary = salary + (salary * .05);
```

This update example will give everyone in table emp a 5 percent increase in salary.

```
UPDATE emp a
   SET a.salary = (SELECT a.salary
                         + (a.salary * DECODE(d.name, 'SALES', .1,
                                                      'ADMIN', .07,
                                                              .06))
FROM dept d
                   WHERE d.dept_no = a.dept_no)
WHERE a.dept_no = (SELECT dept_no
                   FROM dept y, addresses z
                   WHERE y.adrs_id = z.adrs_id
                     AND z.city    = 'ROCHESTER');
```

This example will give raises to employees located in Rochester. The amount of the raise is handled by the DECODE statement evaluating the department name. Employees in the Sales department will receive a 10 percent raise, those in the Admin department receive a 7 percent raise, and everyone else receives a 6 percent raise.

The DELETE statement is used to remove database rows. The syntax for DELETE is

```
DELETE FROM schema.table WHERE condition
```

where SCHEMA is an optional parameter to identify which database schema to use for the delete. The default is your own.

TABLE is mandatory and is the name of the table.

WHERE restricts the delete operation.

```
DELETE FROM addresses
WHERE adrs_id = (SELECT e.adrs_id
                 FROM emp e
                 WHERE e.last_name  = 'DOE'
                   AND e.first_name = 'JOHN');

DELETE FROM emp  e
WHERE e.last_name  = 'DOE'
  AND e.first_name = 'JOHN';
```

If employee John Doe left the company, you probably would want to delete him from the database. One way to accomplish this is to delete the row containing his name from the addresses table and the emp table. In order to find John Doe in the addresses table, you must perform a subquery using the emp table. Therefore, the entry in the emp table has to be the last row to be deleted, or else there would be an orphan row in the addresses table.

```
DELETE FROM dept
WHERE adrs_id is null;
```

In this example, all rows in the dept table will be deleted if the corresponding adrs_id is null.

Deletes are permanent! Once the commit has taken place, it is impossible to get the row(s) back apart from issuing an INSERT statement. There is not an undo command available.

Master/Detail or Parent/Child SQL

Anytime a SQL statement is constructed with multiple tables, a parent/child relationship is usually in effect.

The user must be familiar with the database schema in use and the corresponding constraints in order to properly join tables. Writing poorly constructed SELECT statements will not harm the database but might decrease the system performance and possibly give a false relationship representation to the users. If there are poorly constructed INSERT, UPDATE, or DELETE statements, the effect could be disastrous.

Before you see any examples, certain assumptions need to be made.

1. An employee cannot be entered without a department number. This indicates that the emp table is a child of the dept table.

2. Addresses do not have to be entered when creating a new employee or department. Therefore, the addresses table is optional and is a child of the emp table and a child of the dept table.

If these constraints are enforced in the database, protection would be provided when a parent row is deleted but does not delete the corresponding children.

```
SELECT d.name                         dept_name,
       d.dept_no                      dept_number,
       e.first_name || e.last_name    emp_name,
       e.job_title                    title,
       e.hire_date                    start_date
FROM dept      d,
     emp       e
WHERE d.dept_no   = e.dept_no
ORDER BY d.name, e.last_name;
```

In this example, all the department names and numbers will be displayed (the parent) with all of the corresponding employees (the children) in the departments.

```
SELECT d.name                                          dept_name,
       d.dept_no                                       dept_number,
       e.first_name || e.last_name                     emp_name,
       e.job_title                                     title,
       e.hire_date                                     start_date,
       DECODE(a.box_number, NULL, a.adrs_1, a.box_number)  address,
       DECODE(a.adrs_2, NULL, NULL, a.adrs_2)          address_2,
       a.city || ', '||a.state ||'   '||a.zip          city_stat_zip
```

```
FROM dept        d,
     emp         e,
     addresses   a
WHERE d.dept_no   =  e.dept_no
  AND e.adrs_id   =  a.adrs_id (+)
ORDER BY d.name, e.last_name;
```

This example shows the addition of the optional child table, called addresses. An outer join, (+) is used so that the employee row will still be retrieved even if there is no address information available yet. The DECODEs will retrieve the box number or adrs 1 depending upon the existence of box number.

When you write INSERTs, UPDATEs, or DELETEs, be careful and make sure the proper relationships exist within the subqueries. If you must manipulate each row from the query, you must use a cursor that is part of the PL/SQL language.

Additional Tips

The following is a summary of some of the information already given in this chapter, along with some new ideas:

1. When you are comparing date data types, it might be wise to truncate the dates (TRUNC hire_date) to ensure that the time component does not cause erroneous results. If the application enables the insertion of time into the date data types, then the inserted times will also be taken into consideration when manipulating dates.

2. When writing SQL statements, null values will not be considered by the database unless they are explicitly called for.

```
SELECT e.first_name || e.last_name      emp_name,
       z.first_name || z.last_name      manager
FROM emp e,
     emp z
WHERE  z.emp_id = e.manager_id;
```

In this example, all rows for the employee table will be retrieved except for one, the row containing the president. This is because the manager_id for the president is null.

The following example shows how to retrieve the president along with the other employees.

```
SELECT e.first_name || e.last_name      emp_name,
       z.first_name || z.last_name      manager
FROM emp e,
     emp z
WHERE  z.emp_id = NVL(e.manager_id, e.emp_id);
```

This code checks for a null manager ID. If the manager ID is null, the database will return the employee ID, which will validate properly and return a row for the president.

Summary

This chapter covered the major components of the SQL language, placing emphasis on functionality that is frequently used or misunderstood (such as with the DECODE statement). The reader should have sufficient information to venture out and begin writing good SQL code.

PL/SQL—SQL Procedural Language Extension

5

by
Bruce Kostival

IN THIS CHAPTER

This chapter discusses constructs of PL/SQL that enable software developers to use this procedural language interface to the Oracle RDBMS. Constructs within PL/SQL are similar to those found in 3GL and C and provide a flexible method to manipulate database information. PL/SQL is a mainstay of SQL*Forms, but writing database procedures outside forms gives you access to common database manipulation routines by other Oracle development tools while limiting the size of forms applications.

Package Creation

Packaged Procedures

PL/SQL enables you to group all related programming in one database object called a package. A complete set of PL/SQL routines that accomplish a certain programming task is called a *packaged procedure*. Packages also help you develop an application's interface separate from internal procedure code. This concept is discussed in more detail later in this chapter.

Package Creation

Before reading about the various aspects of the PL/SQL language, examine the syntax for creating a procedure and building a script for ease of maintenance as changes occur. This code is the first step in developing a sample package for calculating dollar totals in a merchandise order—an example that is completed within this chapter. The following example illustrates some commands for creating this PL/SQL packaged procedure and script:

```
set echo on
spool order_total

CREATE OR REPLACE PACKAGE order_total
AS
      (package specifications)
END order_total

CREATE OR REPLACE PACKAGE BODY order_total
AS
      (package body specifications)
END order_total;

DROP PUBLIC SYNONYM order_total;
CREATE PUBLIC SYNONYM order_total for order_total;
GRANT EXECUTE ON order_total TO PUBLIC;

spool off

SELECT
  *
FROM
  user_errors
```

```
WHERE
  name='ORDER_TOTAL'
;
```

The first command in this script, SET ECHO ON, displays a listing of the package to the screen as it is being compiled. ECHO combined with the SPOOL *name* command creates a list file (order_total.lst) for debug purposes. This file will contain the compilation of the procedure, including errors, complete with line numbers.

CREATE OR REPLACE PACKAGE *name* is the command that starts the procedure build in the database. Declarations of objects and subroutines within the package area are visible to your applications. Think of this area as the application interface to your PL/SQL code; at the very least, you must define the procedure entry routine here. Modifications to any specifications in this area require rebuilding your applications. The END statement signifies the end of the package specification area.

CAUTION

Any declarations in the package specification area that are incompatible with Version 1.0 of PL/SQL (such as unsupported data types) cause compilation errors in SQL*Forms applications.

Next is the CREATE OR REPLACE PACKAGE BODY *name* statement that begins the specification area for declarations of PL/SQL objects and subroutines that only the procedure can "see." This area is invisible to your application but is not required in designing package procedures. However, designing procedures in this manner enables you to modify package body specifications without altering the application interface. As a result, applications do not require recompilation when these internal specifications change. Once again, the END statement marks the end of package body specifications.

NOTE

The name order_total was selected for both the package and package body names in this example, but these names need not be the same.

The next three statements work in conjunction to enable all users to access procedures defined in your package. First, any existing public synonym is dropped and subsequently re-created. The GRANT statement provides "public" access to the procedure.

NOTE

GRANT is a DDL statement that must be issued from a privileged account.

At the end of the script is the statement SPOOL OFF *name* that terminates output to the listing file. This is followed by a SELECT statement that displays any compilation errors to the terminal where the script was invoked. The *name* field in this SELECT statement identifies the name of the package being created and must be in uppercase.

> **TIP**
>
> Cross-referencing the line number from the error display to the identified line number in either the package or package body portion of the listing file will make debug sessions go much faster!

Once you create it, you can run the script using a SQL*Plus command as follows:

```
sqlplus (username/password)  @ot
```

The login specified must be a privileged account. After the @ is the name of the script that contains the package creation text. In this case, the script name is ot.sql, and because SQL is the default file extension for SQL scripts, it need not be included on the SQLPLUS command line.

Creating Package Subprograms

Creating subprograms within a package is the next step in developing a packaged procedure. You must decide which routines will be application-interface routines and which routines will be available only within the package. This determines where the subprogram specification will reside—in the package or in the package body. There are two types of subprograms in PL/SQL, procedures and functions.

Procedure Definition

To define a procedure, you must specify a routine name and the parameters to be passed in and out of the routine. In the order_total example, the following code defines the application-interface routine and resides in the package specification area:

```
PROCEDURE
  get_order_total (
    in_order_num        IN NUMBER,
    out status_code     OUT VARCHAR2,
    out_msg             OUT VARCHAR2,
    out_merch_total     OUT NUMBER,
    out_shipping        IN OUT NUMBER,
    out_taxes           IN OUT NUMBER,
    out_grand_total     OUT NUMBER
  );
```

The PROCEDURE statement begins the definition of the package application-interface routine get_order_total. Enclosed in parentheses are the parameters to be passed between the application and the order_total package. The semicolon marks the end of the procedure definition.

> **TIP**
>
> Modularity is the key to successful package design. If you limit the scope of subprograms, your code will be easier to design and debug, too!

Function Definition

Function definition is much the same as procedure definition, as illustrated by the following example:

```
FUNCTION
  calc_ship_charges (
    in_merch_total    IN NUMBER
  ) RETURN NUMBER;
```

The FUNCTION statement begins the definition of the package function calc_ship_charges. Enclosed in parentheses are the parameters to be passed to the function for calculating shipping charges. The RETURN statement identifies the data type of the calculated value to be returned. The semicolon marks the end of the function definition.

Subprogram Parameter Modes

You can define parameters as IN (the default parameter mode), IN OUT, or OUT, depending on the nature of the information to be passed. The first parameter, in_order_num, is defined as IN, which designates it as a value being passed to the subprogram. Defining a parameter as IN prevents it from being assigned a value in the routine.

Parameters out_status_code, out_msg, out_merch_total, and out_grand_total from the procedure definition example are defined as OUT—values being returned to the caller. These parameters are uninitialized upon entry to the routine and are available for assignment of a value within the routine. Designating a parameter as OUT prevents it from being used in a subprogram expression.

Parameters out_shipping and out_taxes are defined as IN OUT, the last parameter mode. Parameters designated as IN OUT are initialized variables that are available for reassignment within the subprogram.

Subprogram Specifications

After defining a subprogram and its parameters, you develop code for the packaged procedure subprogram. The following example illustrates a few basic constructs to be aware of while coding a subprogram:

```
PROCEDURE
  init_line_items
IS
  (local variables)
BEGIN
    (subprogram logic)
    EXCEPTION
      (exception handling)
END init_line_items;
```

In this example, the PROCEDURE name is init_line_items with the local variables specified after the IS statement. The BEGIN statement is the actual start of the procedure (or function) where subprogram code is developed along with any subprogram exception handling. The procedure is finished with the END *name* statement.

> **CAUTION**
>
> The procedure parameter list must exactly match the specification parameter list for the procedure being developed. This includes data types and parameter modes included in the specification.

Default Procedure Parameters

To add flexibility to procedure calls, you might specify default parameter values in your procedure definition. In this manner, you can call the procedure with all, one, or none of the specified parameters. Defaults are supplied for parameters that are not passed. The following example illustrates a procedure definition using default parameters:

```
PROCEDURE
  calc_ship_charges(
    merch_total NUMBER DEFAULT 5.95) IS
  ...
```

References to the calc_ship_charges procedure can include a merch_total or not. Calls without the merch_total parameter default to 5.95, as shown.

Stand-Alone Procedures

Procedures that are not part of a package are known as stand-alone because they are independently defined. A good example of a stand-alone procedure is one written in a SQL*Forms application. These types of procedures are not available for reference from other Oracle tools.

Another limitation of stand-alone procedures is that they are compiled at run-time, which slows execution.

Cursors

PL/SQL uses cursors for all database information access statements. The language supports the use of both implicit and explicit cursors. Implicit cursors are those established for which explicit cursors are not declared. You must use explicit cursors or cursor FOR loops in all queries that return multiple rows.

Declaring Cursors

You define cursors in the variable definition area of PL/SQL subprograms using the CURSOR *name* IS statement, as shown in the following example:

```
CURSOR c_line_item IS
(sql statement)
```

The cursor SQL statement can be any valid query statement. Subsequent to cursor initialization, you are able to control cursor actions with the OPEN, FETCH, and CLOSE statements.

Cursor Control

To use a cursor for manipulating data, you must use the statement OPEN *name* to execute the query and identify all rows that meet the select criteria. Subsequent retrieval of rows is accomplished with the FETCH statement. Once all information is processed, the CLOSE statement terminates all activity associated with the opened cursor. The following is an example of cursor control:

```
OPEN c_line_item;
  ...
   FETCH c_line_item
    INTO li_info;
  ...
  (retrieved row processing)
  ...
CLOSE c_line_item;
```

The code opens the cursor c_line_item and processes the fetched rows. After it retrieves and processes all the information, the cursor closes. Retrieved row processing is typically controlled by iterative loops as discussed later in the chapter.

Explicit Cursor Attributes

Four attributes are associated with PL/SQL cursors.

■ %NOTFOUND

■ %FOUND

■ %ROWCOUNT

■ %ISOPEN

All cursor attributes evaluate to TRUE, FALSE, or NULL, depending on the situation. The attribute %NOTFOUND evaluates to FALSE when a row is fetched, TRUE if the last FETCH did not return a row, and NULL if the cursor SELECT returned no data. Attribute %FOUND is the logical opposite of %NOTFOUND with respect to TRUE and FALSE but still evaluates to NULL if the cursor FETCH returns no data.

You can use %ROWCOUNT to determine how many rows have been selected at any point in the FETCH. This attribute increments upon successful selection of a row. In addition, %ROWCOUNT is at zero when the cursor first opens.

The final attribute, %ISOPEN, is either TRUE or FALSE, depending on whether the associated cursor is open. Before the cursor opens and after the cursor closes, %ISOPEN is FALSE. Otherwise, it evaluates to TRUE.

Cursor Parameters

You can specify parameters for cursors in the same way you do for subprograms. The following example illustrates the syntax for declaring parameter cursors:

```
CURSOR c_line_item (order_num IN NUMBER) IS
  SELECT merch_gross, recipient_num
  FROM line_item
  WHERE order_num = g_order_num;
```

The parameter mode is always IN for cursor parameters, but the data type can be any valid data type. You can reference a cursor parameter, whose value is set when the cursor opens, only during the cursor's declared SQL query.

Flexibility within cursor parameters enables the developer to pass different numbers of parameters to a cursor by using the parameter default mechanism. This is illustrated in the following example:

```
CURSOR c_line_item
  (order_num INTEGER DEFAULT 100,
   line_num INTEGER DEFAULT 1) IS ...
```

By using the INTEGER DEFAULT declaration, you can pass all, one, or none of the parameters to this cursor depending on the logic flow of your code.

Creating Cursor Packages

A cursor package is similar to a procedure package in that you specify the cursor and its return attribute, %TYPE or %ROWTYPE, in the package specification area. You then specify the cursor "body" in the package body specification area. Packaging a cursor in this manner gives you the flexibility of changing the cursor body without having to recompile applications that reference the packaged procedure. The following is a cursor package example:

```
CREATE OR REPLACE PACKAGE order_total
AS
CURSOR c_line_item RETURN line_item.merch_gross%TYPE;
  ...
END order_total;

CREATE OR REPLACE PACKAGE BODY order_total
AS
  CURSOR c_line_item RETURN line_item.merch_gross%TYPE
    SELECT merch_gross
    FROM line_item
    WHERE order_num = g_order_num;
  ...
END order_total;
```

In this example, the RETURN variable is the same as the line_item.item_merch_gross column. You can use the %ROWTYPE attribute to specify a RETURN record that mirrors a row in a database table.

Procedure Variables

The most important feature of any language is how to define variables. Once you've defined the variables, PL/SQL enables you to use them in SQL statements as well as language statements. Definition of constants within PL/SQL follows the same rules. Also, you can define variables and constants as local to one subprogram or global to the entire package you are creating.

> **CAUTION**
>
> You must declare variables and constants before referencing them in any other statement.

Variable Declaration and Assignment

Any PL/SQL or SQL data type is valid for variable definitions. The most commonly used data types are VARCHAR2, DATE, NUMBER (SQL data types), BOOLEAN, and BINARY_INTEGER (PL/SQL data types). PL/SQL scalar and composite data types are discussed in more detail later in this chapter.

Local Variables

Assume you want to declare two local variables named merch_gross and recip_count. The first, merch_gross, is to hold a ten-digit, floating-point number rounded to two decimal places; recip_count will hold an integer counter. Declare these variables as follows:

```
merch_gross       NUMBER;
recip_count       BINARY_INTEGER;
```

> **CAUTION**
>
> You can also declare merch_gross in this example as NUMBER(10,2) to explicitly show total digits and rounding. However, if it's related to a database field, a declaration of this type must change if the database definition changes.

You can use two methods to assign values to variables. The first is using an assignment operator, as follows:

```
merch_gross := 10.50;
```

The second method is to use a SQL SELECT or FETCH statement that assigns a database value, as follows:

```
SELECT merch_gross
INTO merch_gross
FROM line_item
WHERE order_num = g_order_num;
```

Local Constants

Constant declaration is similar to variable declaration except that the CONSTANT keyword must follow the variable name. You must immediately assign a value to the CONSTANT.

```
tax_rate CONSTANT NUMBER := 0.03;
```

Global Variables

Global variables are defined in the same manner as local variables, but they are defined outside of all procedure definitions. Suppose you want to define variables g_order_num and g_recip_counter to be available to all package subprograms. The following is an example of the syntax:

```
CREATE OR REPLACE PACKAGE BODY
     order_total
AS
     ...
g_order_num        NUMBER;
```

```
g_recip_counter     BINARY_INTEGER;
    ...
PROCEDURE
    ...
```

Notice that these global variables are defined in the package body specification area so as not to be "seen" by applications that call the order_total packaged procedure.

> **CAUTION**
>
> If you use variable names that are the same as database column names, results are unpredictable when performing any database operations such as SELECT or UPDATE with the variables.

DEFAULT Keyword

The DEFAULT keyword enables you to initialize variables without using the assignment operator as in the following example:

```
merch_gross    NUMBER  DEFAULT  10.50;
```

You can also use the DEFAULT keyword to initialize a subprogram's cursor parameters and fields in user-defined records.

Variable and Constant Attributes

The two attributes of PL/SQL variables and constants are %TYPE and %ROWTYPE. The %TYPE attribute enables you to declare variables similar to database columns without knowing the data type of the column. You can define merch_gross from the previous example as follows:

```
merch_gross    line_item.merch_gross%TYPE;
```

Defining a variable in this manner enables you to put database changes in effect on the next compilation of a PL/SQL procedure without changing the code.

The %ROWTYPE attribute enables you to represent a row in a table with a record type that masks the database columns. Consider the sample database information in Table 5.1.

Table 5.1. Sample of data in table LINE_ITEM.

Column Name	Data
order_num	100
line_num	1

continues

Table 5.1. continued

Column Name	Data
merch_gross	10.50
recipient_num	1000

You can define a cursor inside your procedure (see the section titled "Declaring Cursors" earlier in the chapter) to pull information from the LINE_ITEM table. Along with the cursor, define a ROWTYPE variable to store the fields in this row as follows:

```
CURSOR c_line_item IS
SELECT merch_gross, recipient_num
FROM line_item
WHERE order_num = g_ordnum;

li_info  c_line_item%ROWTYPE;
```

To retrieve the data, issue a FETCH.

```
FETCH c_line_item
INTO li_info;
```

After the FETCH, use dot notation to access the information pulled from the database.

```
g_order_merch_total := g_order_merch_total + li_info.merch_gross;
```

Scalar Data Types

PL/SQL supports a wide range of scalar data types for defining variables and constants. Unlike composite data types, scalar data types have no accessible components. These data types fall into one of the following categories:

- Boolean
- Date/time
- Character
- Number

Now, take a closer look at the data types in each category.

Boolean

The BOOLEAN data type, which takes no parameters, is used to store a binary value, TRUE or FALSE. This data type can also store the non-value NULL. You cannot insert or retrieve data from an Oracle database using this data type.

Date/Time

The data type DATE, which takes no parameters, is used to store date values. These DATE values include time when stored in a database column. Dates can range from 1/1/4712 B.C. to 12/31/4712 A.D. Defaults for the DATE data type are as follows:

- Date: first day of current month
- Time: midnight

Character

Character data types include CHAR, VARCHAR2, LONG, RAW, and LONG RAW. CHAR is for fixed-length character data, and VARCHAR2 stores variable-length character data. LONG stores variable-length character strings; RAW and LONG RAW store binary data or byte strings. The CHAR, VARCHAR2, and RAW data types take an optional parameter for specifying length.

```
datatype(max_len)
```

This length parameter, max_len, must be an integer literal, not a constant or variable. Table 5.2 shows maximum lengths and database column widths of character data types.

Table 5.2. Character data type maximum lengths and database column widths.

Data Type	Maximum Length	Maximum Database Column Width
CHAR	32767	255
VARCHAR2	32767	2000
LONG	32760	2147483647
RAW	32767	255
LONG RAW	32760	2147483647

From this table, you can see the constraint on inserting CHAR, VARCHAR2, and RAW data into database columns of the same type. The limit is the column width. However, you can insert LONG and LONG RAW data of any length into similar columns because the column width is much greater.

Number

There are two data types in the number data type category: BINARY_INTEGER and NUMBER. BINARY_INTEGER stores signed integers with a range of -2^{31} to $2^{31}-1$. The most common use for this data type is an index for PL/SQL tables.

Storage for fixed or floating-point numbers of any size is available using the NUMBER data type. For floating-point numbers, you can specify precision and scale in the following format:

```
NUMBER(10,2)
```

A variable declared in this manner has a maximum of ten digits, and rounding occurs to two decimal places. The precision default is the maximum integer supported by your system, and 0 is the default for scale. The range for precision is 1 to 38 whereas the scale range is –84 to 127.

Composite Data Types

The two composite data types in PL/SQL are TABLE and RECORD. The TABLE data type enables the user to define a PL/SQL table to be used for array processing. The RECORD data type enables the user to go beyond the %ROWTYPE variable attribute; with it, you specify user-defined fields and field data types.

Array Processing

The TABLE composite data type provides the developer a mechanism for array processing. Although it's limited to one column of information per PL/SQL table, you can store any number of rows for that column. The word from Oracle is that future versions of PL/SQL will provide more flexibility in the use of tables.

In the order_total example, define a PL/SQL table named g_recip_list (the information will be used globally). The following is an illustration of this concept:

```
TYPE RecipientTabTyp IS TABLE OF NUMBER(22)
  INDEX BY BINARY_INTEGER;
...
g_recip_list           RecipientTabTyp;
```

To initialize an array, you must first define an array name or TYPE, which in this example is RecipientTabTyp. This TABLE column is defined as NUMBER with a maximum of 22 digits. You can define the column as any valid PL/SQL data type; however, the primary key, or INDEX, must be of type BINARY_INTEGER. After defining the array structure, you can make reference for variable definition as shown with g_recip_list defined as an array of TYPE RecipientTabTyp.

Building Arrays

Arrays are available as information stores subsequent to initialization of the array. To store information in the array g_recip_list that was defined in the last example, you simply reference the array with a numeric value. This is shown in the following example:

```
g_recip_list(j) := g_recipient_num(i)
```

In this example, i and j are counters with values 1…*n*. Once information is stored in an array, you can access it, also with numeric values, as shown in the example. In this case, rows of g_recipient_num are referenced for storage in g_recip_list.

> **CAUTION**
>
> Referencing an uninitialized row in a PL/SQL array causes a NO_DATA_FOUND error. (See the section "Exception Handling" later in this chapter.)

Record Processing

The RECORD composite data type provides the developer a mechanism for record processing as described previously. Although you cannot initialize TABLEs at the time of declaration, you can with RECORDs, as illustrated in the following example:

```
TYPE LineRecTyp IS RECORD
  (merch_gross  NUMBER := 0,
    recip_num    NUMBER := 0 );
  ...
li_info LineRecTyp;
```

Defining a RECORD of TYPE LineRecTyp allows declarations such as li_info of that TYPE as shown. You can use this method of RECORD declaration in place of the li_info declaration in the previous %ROWTYPE example. As with %ROWTYPE, references to RECORD information is accomplished with dot notation.

```
g_order_merch_total := g_order_merch_total + li_info.merch_gross;
```

You can use one of three methods to assign values to records. First, you can assign a value to a record field as you would assign any variable.

```
li_info.merch_gross := 10.50;
```

A second method is to assign all fields at once by using two records that are declared with the same data type. Assume a second LineRecTyp is defined as new_li_info.

```
new_li_info := li_info;
```

This statement assigns all fields of new_li_info the values from the same fields of li_info.

> **NOTE**
>
> You cannot assign records of different types to each other.

A third method of assigning values to fields of a record is through SQL SELECT or FETCH statements.

```
OPEN c_line_item;
   ...
     FETCH c_line_item
     INTO li_info;
```

In this case, all fields of li_info are assigned values from the information retrieved by the FETCH of cursor c_line_item.

Processing Control

Every procedural language has control structures that provide processing of information in a logical manner by controlling the flow of information. Available structures within PL/SQL include IF-THEN-ELSE, LOOP, and EXIT-WHEN. These structures provide flexibility in manipulating database information.

Loop Control

Use of the LOOP statement provides iterative processing based on logical choices. The basic construct for PL/SQL LOOPs is shown in the following example:

```
<<loop_name>>
LOOP
  (repetitive processing)
END LOOP loop_name;
```

To break out of a loop such as this, you must issue an EXIT or GOTO statement based on some processing condition. If you raise a user-defined exception, the LOOP also terminates. Now, examine three types of PL/SQL loops that expressly define LOOP termination conditions.

> **TIP**
>
> You can name a loop as shown in the example by using a label such as <<loop_name>> just before the LOOP statement. Although it's not required, labeling does enable you to keep better track of nested loops.

WHILE Loops

The WHILE loop checks the status of any PL/SQL expression that evaluates to TRUE, FALSE, or NULL at the start of each processing cycle. The following is an example of the use of WHILE loops:

```
WHILE (expression) LOOP
  (loop processing)
END LOOP;
```

As stated, the program evaluates the *expression* at the start of each loop cycle. The program performs the *loop processing* if the *expression* evaluates to TRUE. A FALSE or NULL evaluation terminates the loop. Iterations through the loop are exclusively determined by the evaluation of the *expression*.

Numeric *FOR* Loops

You can control loop iterations with the use of numeric FOR loops. This mechanism enables the developer to establish a range of integers for which the loop will cycle. The following example from the order_total package illustrates numeric FOR loops:

```
<<recip_list>>
    FOR i in 1..g_line_counter LOOP
      (loop processing)
    END LOOP recip_list;
```

In this example, *loop processing* cycles over the range of integers 1 through the value of g_line_counter. The value of the loop index i is checked at the start of the loop and incremented at the end of the loop. When i is one greater than g_line_counter, the loop terminates.

Cursor *FOR* Loops

Cursor FOR loops combine cursor control and conditional control for manipulation of database information. The loop index, cursor OPEN, cursor FETCH, and cursor CLOSE are all implicit when using cursor FOR loops. Consider the following example:

```
CURSOR c_line_item IS
(sql statement)

BEGIN
  FOR li_info IN c_line_item LOOP
    (retrieved record processing)
  END LOOP;
END;
```

As shown, the program explicitly declares the c_line_item cursor before its reference in the FOR loop. When the program enters the FOR loop, the code implicitly opens c_line_item and implicitly creates the li_info record as if the following declaration were made:

```
li_info c_line_item%ROWTYPE;
```

Once inside the loop, the program can reference the fields of the li_info record that are assigned values by the implicit FETCH inside the FOR loop. Fields of li_info mirror the row retrieved by the c_line_item cursor.

When data is exhausted for the FETCH, c_line_item is implicitly closed.

> **NOTE**
>
> You cannot reference the information contained in li_info outside of the cursor FOR loop.

Iterative Control

The IF-THEN-ELSE structure provides alternative processing paths that depend on certain conditions. For example, consider merchandise orders with multiple-line items where a list of recipients is built. Using conditional and iterative control to build the recipient list, the code is as follows:

```
PROCEDURE
  init_recip_list
IS
  recipient_num  NUMBER;
  i                      BINARY_INTEGER;
  j                      BINARY_INTEGER := 1;
  k                      BINARY_INTEGER;
  BEGIN
    g_out_msg := 'init_recip_list';

    <<recip_list>>
    FOR i in 1..g_line_counter LOOP
      IF i = 1 THEN
        g_recip_list(j) := g_recipient_num(i);
        j := j + 1;
        g_recip_list(j) := 0;
      ELSE
        FOR k in 1..j LOOP
          IF g_recipient_num(i) = g_recip_list(k) THEN
            exit;
          ELSIF k = j THEN
            g_recip_list(j) := g_recipient_num(i);
            j := j + 1;
            g_recip_list(j) := 0;
          end IF;
        end LOOP;
      end IF;
    end LOOP recip_list;
END;
```

In the order_total example, the subprogram init_recip_list builds a list of unique recipient numbers for calculating additional shipping charges. There is a controlling FOR loop that cycles through each recipient number found on a particular order. The g_recip_list array is initialized with the first recipient number, and subsequent numbers are checked against all unique numbers in g_recip_list until a unique list of all recipients is compiled.

Also illustrated in this example is the IF-THEN-ELSE extension ELSIF. This statement provides further conditional control with additional constraint checks within the IF-THEN-ELSE structure. Use of ELSIF also requires a THEN statement in executing logic control.

Another example of iterative control is the use of the EXIT-WHEN statement that allows completion of a LOOP once certain conditions are met. Consider the example of exiting a cursor fetch loop:

```
open c_line_item;
  loop
    fetch c_line_item
```

```
    into li_info;
    EXIT WHEN (c_line_item%NOTFOUND) or (c_line_item%NOTFOUND is NULL);
```

In this example, the LOOP is terminated when no more data is found to satisfy the select statement of cursor c_line_item.

> **CAUTION**
>
> Use of %NOTFOUND or %FOUND can cause infinite loops if you do not check for these attributes evaluating to NULL on an EXIT-WHEN logical check.

Exception Handling

PL/SQL exception handling is a mechanism for dealing with run-time errors encountered during procedure execution. Use of this mechanism enables execution to continue if the error is not severe enough to cause procedure termination. The decision to enable a procedure to continue after an error condition is one you have to make in development as you consider possible errors that could arise.

You must define the exception handler within a subprogram specification. Errors cause the program to raise an exception with a transfer of control to the exception-handler block. After the exception handler executes, control returns to the block in which the handler was defined. If there are no more executable statements in the block, control returns to the caller.

User-Defined Exceptions

PL/SQL enables the user to define exception handlers in the declarations area of subprogram specifications. You accomplish this by naming an exception as in the following example:

```
ot_failure          EXCEPTION;
```

In this case, the exception name is ot_failure. Code associated with this handler is written in the EXCEPTION specification area as follows:

```
EXCEPTION

    when OT_FAILURE then
      out_status_code := g_out_status_code;
      out_msg         := g_out_msg;
```

This exception is defined in the order_total example to capture status and associated data for any NO_DATA_FOUND exceptions encountered in a subprogram. The following is an example of a subprogram exception:

```
EXCEPTION
    when NO_DATA_FOUND then
      g_out_status_code := 'FAIL';
      RAISE ot_failure;
```

Within this exception is the RAISE statement that transfers control back to the ot_failure exception handler. This technique of raising the exception is used to invoke all user-defined exceptions.

System-Defined Exceptions

Exceptions internal to PL/SQL are raised automatically upon error. NO_DATA_FOUND from the previous example is a system-defined exception. Table 5.3 is a complete list of internal exceptions.

Table 5.3. PL/SQL internal exceptions.

Exception Name	Oracle Error
CURSOR_ALREADY_OPEN	ORA-06511
DUP_VAL_ON_INDEX	ORA-00001
INVALID_CURSOR	ORA-01001
INVALID_NUMBER	ORA-01722
LOGIN_DENIED	ORA-01017
NO_DATA_FOUND	ORA-01403
NOT_LOGGED_ON	ORA-01012
PROGRAM_ERROR	ORA-06501
STORAGE_ERROR	ORA-06500
TIMEOUT_ON_RESOURCE	ORA-00051
TOO_MANY_ROWS	ORA-01422
TRANSACTION_BACKED_OUT	ORA-00061
VALUE_ERROR	ORA-06502
ZERO_DIVIDE	ORA-01476

In addition to this list of exceptions, there is a catch-all exception named OTHERS that traps all errors for which specific error handling has not been established. This exception is illustrated in the following example:

```
when OTHERS then
        out_status_code := 'FAIL';
        out_msg := g_out_msg || ' ' || SUBSTR(SQLERRM, 1, 60);
```

This technique is used in the order_total sample procedure to trap all procedure errors other than NO_DATA_FOUND. The information passed back to the caller in out_msg is the subprogram name contained in g_out_msg concatenated with the first 60 characters returned from the SQLERRM function by the SUBSTR function.

NOTE

Both SQLERRM and SUBSTR are internal PL/SQL functions. You can find a complete list of internal functions later in this chapter.

SQLERRM only returns a valid message when called inside an exception handler unless an argument is passed to the function that is a valid SQL error number. The Oracle error code is the first part of the message returned from SQLERRM. Next is the text associated with that Oracle error code.

In this manner, all errors encountered during procedure execution are trapped and passed back to the application for debug purposes. The following is a sample return error from the order_total procedure:

```
FAIL: init_line_items ORA-01001: invalid cursor
```

This error message (formatted by the application) reveals an illegal cursor operation in the subprogram init_line_items. The portion of the message returned from SQLERRM begins with the ORA-01001 SQL error code. Another error message is illustrated in the following example:

```
FAIL: calc_ship_charges
```

In this case, the subprogram calc_ship_charges had a NO_DATA_FOUND error. This is determined by the fact that no SQL error messages are concatenated with the message text.

Comments

Although some people think commenting code is unnecessary, there are two methods you can use to place comments within your PL/SQL procedures. The first is for commenting single lines, and the syntax is shown in the following example:

```
--*************** CREATE PACKAGE ORDER_TOTALING ***************
```

A double dash at the start of the line marks the line as a comment. The second method is used to place a sequence of comment statements in a PL/SQL package.

```
/* The following code generates a list of unique recipient
   numbers from all recipient numbers for a particular order */
```

A comment block such as this begins with the /* and ends with the */. You can place single-line and multiple-line comments in any portion of PL/SQL code.

CAUTION

PL/SQL blocks that are dynamically compiled in Oracle Precompiler applications do not support use of single-line comments.

Stored Procedures

You can store PL/SQL code in the Oracle database with the RDBMS Procedural Database Extension. Advantages of using stored procedures include easier maintenance, decreased application size, increased execution speed, and greater memory savings, to name a few. With this in mind, explore the various techniques for accessing stored procedures in the following sections.

Referencing Stored Procedures

Another big advantage to using stored procedures is the capability to reference the procedure from many different Oracle applications. You can make reference to stored procedures with other stored procedures, database triggers, applications built with Oracle Precompilers, or Oracle tools such as SQL*Forms. The following example calls the order_total procedure from another procedure:

```
order_total.get_order_total (order_num,
                                status_code,
                                message,
                                merch_gross,
                                shipping,
                                taxes,
                                grand_total);
```

The following example shows the same order_total procedure referenced from PRO*C, an Oracle Precompiler application.

```
EXEC SQL
  BEGIN
    order_total.get_order_total ( :order_num,
                                          :status_code,
                                          :message,
                                          :merch_gross,
                                          :shipping,
                                          :taxes,
                                          :grand_total);
  END;
END-EXEC;
```

All parameters in this example to the order_total procedure are Oracle bind variables that you must declare before the reference to the package. The final example illustrates a call to the order_total package from a SQL*Forms application.

```
BEGIN
  ...
  order_total.get_order_total ( order_num,
                                      status_code,
                                      message,
                                      merch_gross,
                                      shipping,
                                      taxes,
                                      grand_total);
```

```
. . .
END;
```

Once again, you must declare all variables passed as parameters before calling the procedure.

> **CAUTION**
>
> Calling stored procedures with `COMMIT`, `ROLLBACK`, or `SAVEPOINT` statements from SQL*Forms is prohibited and is discussed later in this chapter.

Stored Procedure States

After compilation, a stored procedure exists in either a *valid* or *invalid* state. If you haven't made any changes to the procedure, it is considered valid and may be referenced. If any subprogram or object referenced within a procedure changes, its state becomes invalid. Only procedures in a valid state are available for reference.

Referencing a procedure that is invalid causes Oracle to recompile any and all objects called by the referenced procedure. If the recompilation does not succeed, Oracle returns a run-time error to the caller, and the procedure remains in an invalid state. Otherwise, Oracle recompiles the referenced procedure, and if the recompilation is successful, execution continues.

> **CAUTION**
>
> Stored procedures are located in the Oracle SGA after compilation. If the SGA is too small for the user base, the procedure might be swapped out and become invalid with no indication to the caller. The first reference to the procedure after it is swapped out causes a recompilation, returning it to a valid state.

Overloading

The concept of *overloading* in PL/SQL relates to the idea that you can define procedures and functions with the same name. PL/SQL does not look only at the referenced name, however, to resolve a procedure or function call. The count and data types of formal parameters are also considered.

PL/SQL also attempts to resolve any procedure or function calls in locally defined packages before looking at globally defined packages or internal functions. To further ensure calling the proper procedure, you can use the dot notation as illustrated by previous examples on application references to stored procedures. Prefacing a procedure or function name with the package name fully qualifies any procedure or function reference.

Commits

The COMMIT statement is available to PL/SQL procedures unless you are calling the procedure from a SQL*Forms application. To enable commits within a procedure called by a SQL*Forms application, you must issue the DDL statement ALTER SESSION ENABLE COMMIT IN PROCEDURE before you invoke the PL/SQL object. Because you cannot issue this command from SQL*Forms, you must create a user exit from which you can issue the ALTER SESSION statement and subsequently call the procedure. The following is an example of calling the order_total procedure from SQL*Forms through a user exit:

```
user_exit('order_totl');
```

In this case, the order_totl routine of the SQL*Forms user exit references the order_total packaged procedure.

> **CAUTION**
>
> Issuing a COMMIT from a PL/SQL procedure that is called from SQL*Forms attempts to commit any changes from the forms application as well.

Package STANDARD

PL/SQL provides various tools in a package named STANDARD for use by developers. These tools include internal functions and internal exceptions. I previously discussed exception handling and two internal functions, SQLCODE and SQLERRM, that provide information for exception reporting and are only valid in exception handlers.

Referencing Internal Functions

Internal PL/SQL functions exemplify the concept of overloading with respect to naming procedures and functions. Remember that PL/SQL resolves a procedure or function call by matching the number and data types of formal parameters in the reference and not just by reference name. Consider the two internal functions named TO_NUMBER in the following example:

```
function TO_NUMBER (str CHAR [, fmt VARCHAR2, [, nlsparms] ]) return NUMBER
function TO_NUMBER (str VARCHAR2 [, fmt VARCHAR2 [, nlsparms] ]) return NUMBER
```

Both functions are named TO_NUMBER, but the data type of the first parameter is CHAR in the first definition and VARCHAR2 in the second. Optional parameters are the same in both cases. PL/SQL resolves a call to the TO_NUMBER function by looking at the data type of the first parameter.

You might also have a user-defined procedure or function named TO_NUMBER. In this case, the local definition takes precedence over the internal function definition. You can still access the internal function, however, by using the dot notation, as follows:

```
STANDARD.TO_NUMBER ...
```

As shown, prefacing the TO_NUMBER function call with the name of the PL/SQL package STAN-DARD references the internal function.

Internal Functions

The function TO_NUMBER is one example of a PL/SQL internal function. Table 5.4 shows a complete list of PL/SQL internal function categories along with default return values.

Table 5.4. Internal function categories and common return values.

Category	Common Return Value
Character	VARCHAR2
Conversion	None
Date	DATE
Miscellaneous	None
Number	NUMBER

Character Functions

Although most character functions return a VARCHAR2, some functions return other values. Table 5.5 lists available character functions along with a brief description, argument list, and return value if other than the most likely return value for the set of functions. Optional arguments are enclosed in square brackets. All internal character functions take the following form:

```
function ASCII (char VARCHAR2) return VARCHAR2
```

Table 5.5. Character functions.

Function	Description	Argument(s)	Return Value
ASCII	Returns standard collating code for character.	*char* VARCHAR2	NUMBER
CHR	Returns character for collating code.	*num* NUMBER	
CONCAT	Returns *str2* appended to *str1*.	*str1* VARCHAR2, *str2* VARCHAR2	

continues

Table 5.5. continued

Function	Description	Argument(s)	Return Value
INITCAP	Returns *str1* with the first letter of each word in uppercase and all others in lowercase.	*str1* VARCHAR2	
INSTR	Returns starting position of *str2* in *str1*. Search begins at *pos* for the *n*th occurrence. If *pos* is negative, the search is performed backwards. Both *pos* and *n* default to 1. The function returns 0 if *str2* is not found.	*str1* VARCHAR2, *str2* VARCHAR2 [, *pos* NUMBER [, *n* NUMBER]]	
INSTRB	Similar to INSTR except *pos* is a byte position.	*str1* VARCHAR2, *str2* VARCHAR2 [, *pos* NUMBER [, *n* NUMBER]]	
LENGTH	Returns character count in *str* and for data type CHAR; length includes trailing blanks.	*str* CHAR or *str* VARCHAR2	NUMBER
LENGTHB	Similar to LENGTH; returns byte count of *str* including trailing blanks for CHAR.	*str* CHAR or *str* VARCHAR2	NUMBER
LOWER	Returns *str* with all letters in lowercase.	*str* CHAR or *str* VARCHAR2	CHAR or VARCHAR2
LPAD	Left pads *str* to length *len* with characters in *pad*, which defaults to a single blank. Returns first *len* characters in *str* if *str* is longer than *len*.	*str* VARCHAR2 *len* NUMBER [, *pad* VARCHAR2]	
LTRIM	Returns *str* with characters removed up to first character not in *set*; *set* defaults to a single blank.	*str* VARCHAR2 [, *set* VARCHAR2]	
NLS_INITCAP	Similar to INITCAP except a sort sequence is specified by *nlsparms*.	*str* VARCHAR2 [, *nlsparms* VARCHAR2]	

Function	Description	Argument(s)	Return Value
NLS_LOWER	Similar to LOWER except a sort sequence is specified by *nlsparms*.	*str* VARCHAR2 [, *nlsparms* VARCHAR2]	
NLS_UPPER	Similar to UPPER except a sort sequence is specified by *nlsparms*.	*str* VARCHAR2 [, *nlsparms* VARCHAR2]	
NLSSORT	Returns *str* in sort sequence specified by *nlsparms*.	*str* VARCHAR2 [, *nlsparms* VARCHAR2]	RAW
REPLACE	Returns *str1* with all occurrences of *str2* replaced by *str3*. If *str3* is not specified, all occurrences of *str2* are removed.	*str1* VARCHAR2, *str2* VARCHAR2, [*str3* VARCHAR2]	
RPAD	Similar to LPAD except *str* is right padded with *len* sequence of characters in *pad*.	*str* VARCHAR2, *len* VARCHAR2, [, *pad* VARCHAR2]	NUMBER
RTRIM	Similar to LTRIM except trailing characters are removed from *str* after the first character not in *set*.	*str* VARCHAR2 [, *set* VARCHAR2]	
SOUNDEX	Returns phonetic representation of *str*.	*str* VARCHAR2	
SUBSTR	Returns substring of *str* starting at *pos* for length *len* or to the end of *str* if *len* is omitted. For *pos* < 0, SUBSTR counts backward from the end of *str*.	*str* VARCHAR2, *pos* NUMBER [, *len* NUMBER]	
SUBSTRB	Similar to SUBSTR except works on bytes, not characters.	*str* VARCHAR2, *pos* NUMBER [, *len* NUMBER]	
TRANSLATE	Replaces all occurrences of *set1* with *set2* characters in *str*.	*str* VARCHAR2, *set1* VARCHAR2, *set2* CHAR	
UPPER	Returns all letters in uppercase.	*str* CHAR or *str* VARCHAR2	

Conversion Functions

Table 5.6 lists available conversion functions along with a brief description, argument list, and return value. Optional arguments are enclosed in square brackets. All internal conversion functions are of the following form:

```
function CHARTOROWID (str VARCHAR2) return ROWID
```

Table 5.6. Conversion functions.

Function	Description	Argument(s)	Return Value
CHARTOROWID	Converts *str* to type ROWID.	*str* CHAR or *str* VARCHAR2	ROWID
CONVERT	Converts *str* from character *set1* to character *set2*. Character *set1* and *set2* can be a character set name or database column.	*str* VARCHAR2, *set1* VARCHAR2, *set2* VARCHAR2	VARCHAR2
HEXTORAW	Converts *str* from CHAR or VARCHAR2 to RAW.	*str* CHAR or *str* VARCHAR2	RAW
RAWTOHEX	Opposite of HEXTORAW.	*bin* RAW	VARCHAR2
ROWIDTOCHAR	Converts *bin* from ROWID to 18-byte hex string.	*bin* ROWID	VARCHAR2
TO_CHAR (Dates)	Converts *dte* to VARCHAR2 based on *fmt*. You can specify a language for date conversion in *nlsparms*.	*dte* DATE [, *fmt* VARCHAR2 [, *nlsparms*]]	VARCHAR2
TO_CHAR (Numbers)	Converts *num* to VARCHAR2 based on *fmt*. You can specify the following format elements in *nlsparms*: decimal character, group separator, and a symbol for local or international currency.	*num* NUMBER [, *fmt* VARCHAR2 [, *nlsparms*]]	VARCHAR2
TO_CHAR (Labels)	Converts MLSLABEL type to VARCHAR2 based on *fmt*.	*label* [, *fmt* VARCHAR2]	VARCHAR2
TO_DATE	Converts *str* or *num* to DATE value based on *fmt*. The *fmt* argument is not optional when	*str* VARCHAR2 or *num* NUMBER [,*nlsparms*]	DATE

Function	Description	Argument(s)	Return Value
	converting a number. You can specify a language for date conversion in *nlsparms*.		
TO_LABEL	Converts *str* to MLSLABEL data type. If *fmt* is omitted, *str* must be in default label format. TO_LABEL is a Trusted Oracle function.	*str* CHAR or *str* VARCHAR2 [, *fmt* VARCHAR2]	MLSLABEL
TO_MULTI_BYTE	Converts single-byte *str* to multi-byte equivalent, if it exists.	*str* CHAR *str* VARCHAR2	CHAR VARCHAR2
TO_NUMBER	Converts *str* to NUMBER value according to *fmt*. You can specify format elements in *nlsparms* as described in the TO_CHAR function.	*str* CHAR *str* VARCHAR2	NUMBER NUMBER
TO_SINGLE_BYTE	Opposite of TO_MULTI_BYTE.	*str* CHAR *str* VARCHAR2	CHAR VARCHAR2

Date Functions

All date functions return a DATE value unless otherwise specified in Table 5.7, which lists available date functions along with a brief description, argument list, and return value. Optional arguments are enclosed in square brackets. All internal date functions are of the following form:

```
function ADD_MONTHS (dte DATE, num NUMBER) return DATE
```

Table 5.7. Date functions.

Function	Description	Argument(s)	Return Value
ADD_MONTHS	Returns *dte* plus or minus *num* months.	*dte* DATE, *num* NUMBER	
LAST_DAY	Returns last day of the month for *dte*.	*dte* DATE	

continues

Table 5.7. continued

Function	Description	Argument(s)	Return Value
MONTHS_BETWEEN	Returns month count between *dte1* and *dte2*. NUMBER is < 0 if *dte1* is earlier than *dte2*.	*dte1* DATE, *dte2* DATE	NUMBER
NEW_TIME	Returns date and time in *zon2* based on *dte* date and time in time zone *zon1*.	*dte* DATE, *zon1* VARCHAR2, *zon2* VARCHAR2	
NEXT_DAY	Returns first day of the week for *day* that is later than *dte*.	*dte* DATE, *day* VARCHAR2	
ROUND	Returns *dte* rounded to specified unit in *fmt*. If no *fmt* is specified, *dte* is rounded to the nearest day.	*dte* DATE [, *fmt* VARCHAR2]	
SYSDATE	Returns current system date and time.	No arguments.	
TRUNC	Returns *dte* with the time of day truncated as specified by *fmt*.	*dte* DATE [, *fmt* VARCHAR2]	

Miscellaneous Functions

Table 5.8 lists miscellaneous functions along with a brief description, argument list, and return value. Optional arguments are enclosed in square brackets.

Table 5.8. Miscellaneous functions.

Function	Description	Argument(s)	Return Value
DUMP	Returns internal representation of *expr* based on one of the following *fmt* specifications: 8=octal 10=decimal 16=hexadecimal	*expr* DATE or *expr* NUMBER or *expr* VARCHAR2 [, *fmt* BINARY_INTEGER [, *pos* BINARY_INTEGER [, *len* BINARY_INTEGER]]]	VARCHAR2

Function	Description	Argument(s)	Return Value
	17=single character Arguments *pos* and *len* specify the portion of the representation to return.		
GREATEST	Returns greatest value of list of *exprn*. All expressions must be data-type compatible with *expr1*.	*expr1, expr2, expr3*	
GREATEST_LB	Returns greatest lower bound from list of *labels*. Each *label* must be of type MLSLABEL. GREATEST_LB is a Trusted Oracle function.	*label* [, *label*] ...	MLSLABEL
LEAST	Returns least value from list of *exprn*. All expressions must be data-type compatible with *expr1*.	*expr1, expr2, expr3* ...	
LEAST_UB	Returns least upper bound from list of *labels*. Each *label* must be of type MLSLABEL. LEAST_UB is a Trusted Oracle function.	*label* [, *label*] ...	MLSLABEL
NVL	Returns value of not null *arg1* or type of value of *arg2*. *arg1* and *arg2* must be of the *arg1* and *arg2* same data type.	*arg1, arg2*	Data
UID	Returns unique ID number of current Oracle user.	No arguments	NUMBER
USER	Returns username of current Oracle user.	No arguments	VARCHAR2
USERENV	Returns current session information based on *str*, which can be one of the following:	*str* VARCHAR2	VARCHAR2
	'ENTRYID'	audit entry identifier	
	'LABEL'	session label	

continues

Table 5.8. continued

Function	Description	Argument(s)	Return Value
	'LANGUAGE'	language, territory, and database character set	
	'SESSIONID'	auditing session identifier	
	'TERMINAL'	session terminal type	
VSIZE	Returns number of bytes in *expr*.	*expr* DATE or *expr* NUMBER or *expr* VARCHAR2	NUMBER

Number Functions

All number functions return a NUMBER value unless otherwise specified in Table 5.9, which lists available number functions along with a brief description, argument list, and return value. Optional arguments are enclosed in square brackets. All internal number functions are of the following form:

```
function ABS (n NUMBER) return NUMBER
```

Table 5.9. Number functions.

Function	Description	Argument(s)
ABS	Returns absolute value of *n*.	*n* NUMBER
CEIL	Returns smallest integer >= *n*.	*n* NUMBER
COS	Returns cosine of *a*. Angle *a* must be in radians.	*a* NUMBER
COSH	Returns hyperbolic cosine of *n*.	*n* NUMBER
EXP	Returns value of e^n.	*n* NUMBER
FLOOR	Returns largest integer <= *n*.	*n* NUMBER
LN	Returns natural log of *n* where $n > 0$.	*n* NUMBER
LOG	Returns base-*m* log of *n* where $m > 1$ and $n > 0$.	*m* NUMBER, *n* NUMBER
MOD	Returns remainder of *m/n*.	*m* NUMBER, *n* NUMBER
POWER	Returns value of m^n.	*m* NUMBER, *n* NUMBER
ROUND	Returns *m* rounded to *n* places.	*m* NUMBER, *n* NUMBER

Function	Description	Argument(s)
SIGN	Returns −1 for $n < 0$, 0 for $n=0$ and 1 for $n > 0$.	n NUMBER
SIN	Returns sine of a. Angle a must be in radians.	a NUMBER
SINH	Returns hyperbolic sine of n.	n NUMBER
SQRT	Returns square root of n.	n NUMBER
TAN	Returns tangent of a. Angle a must be in radians.	a NUMBER
TANH	Returns hyperbolic tangent of n.	n NUMBER
TRUNC	Returns m truncated to n places.	m NUMBER [, n NUMBER]

Additional Topics

There are a few more areas of PL/SQL that I would like discuss for the sake of completeness. These topics have relevance to the general understanding of the PL/SQL language and should be reviewed.

DECLARE Statement

Use of the DECLARE statement is limited to the creation of sub-blocks within PL/SQL blocks, as shown in the following example:

```
BEGIN
  ...
  <<inner>>
  DECLARE
    ...
  BEGIN
    ...
  END inner;
  ...
END;
```

This code uses DECLARE to declare cursors, variables, and constants local to the sub-block labeled inner.

Naming Conventions

PL/SQL enables you to reference all defined objects (such as variables, cursors, and packages) using simple references, qualified references, remote references, or a combination of qualified and remote references. Case is irrelevant in all object references. A simple reference to the order_total package interface takes the following form:

```
get_order_total( ... );
```

A qualified reference to the same package looks as follows:

```
order_total.get_order_total( ... );
```

A remote reference to this package is shown in the following example:

```
get_order_total@concepts( ... );
```

Finally, using a qualified and remote reference, you reference the order_total package as follows:

```
order_total.get_order_total@concepts( ... );
```

The first two instances reference the order_total procedure on the local machine. The last two instances show a remote access to the order_total procedure using the concepts database link.

Synonyms

To further simplify the reference to a procedure, you can use a synonym. You cannot use synonyms to reference PL/SQL objects contained in subprograms or packages, however. An example of synonym creation is provided in the section titled "Package Creation," which shows a sample script to build the order_total packaged procedure.

Scope of Reference

Another naming convention worth mentioning is scope of reference. This refers to the range over which you can reference a PL/SQL identifier (such as a variable or subprogram). In simple terms, the hierarchy of scope is block, local, global, and application, with respect to the range of reference. The following example illustrates this point:

```
CREATE OR REPLACE PACKAGE order_total
AS
  PROCEDURE
    get_order_total ( ... );
END order_total

CREATE OR REPLACE PACKAGE BODY order_total
AS
  ot_failure    EXCEPTION;
  ...
  PROCEDURE
    init_line_items
  IS
    i      BINARY INTEGER  := 0;
    ...
```

```
      BEGIN
        ...
        <<inner>>
        DECLARE
          j   BINARY_INTEGER  :=  0;
        BEGIN
          j = i;
          ...
        EXCEPTION
        ...
        raise ot_failure;
        END inner;
        ...
      END;
END order_total;
```

In this example, the scope of reference for variable j is the inner sub-block where it is defined. Variable i, however, is defined local to the init_line_items procedure. You can reference it in the inner sub-block as shown. The defined exception, ot_failure, is global to the package body and may be referenced by all subprograms but not by the caller. Finally, the get_order_total interface routine and associated variables are available at the application level and throughout the package.

A final note on scope of reference: You can define local identifiers in a sub-block that use the same name as global identifiers. You must then make reference to the global identifier with a qualified name that can be an enclosing block or subprogram name. You then make the qualified reference using the dot notation.

Data Type Conversion

PL/SQL supports both explicit and implicit data type conversions of specified values. Explicit conversions work through the use of an internal function, such as TO_NUMBER described previously. Implicit conversions happen at compile time where one data type is supplied and a different data type is expected. This PL/SQL feature enables you to rely on the compiler instead of using explicit conversion routines. Consider the following SQL statement:

```
SELECT SUM(grand_total)FROM order
WHERE order_date < '10-SEP-95';
```

In this case, the order_date column is stored as data type DATE, and it is being compared to '10-SEP-95', which is a literal CHAR value. PL/SQL does an implicit conversion on this literal to data type DATE when the procedure containing this SQL select is compiled.

Database Triggers

Another common use of PL/SQL procedures is the creation of database triggers. These triggers are packaged procedures that act like SQL*Forms triggers in that they "fire" automatically when a database table meets certain criteria as a result of a SQL operation. As such, database triggers are not explicitly referenced by other procedures or applications.

NOTE

You can link up to 12 database triggers to a given table.

There are three distinct pieces to consider when building a database trigger. First is the event that causes the trigger to fire. This firing leads to the action to be taken, which you can think of as the database trigger code. Finally, you must consider any optional constraints you might want to place on your trigger. Take a closer look at how database triggers are built.

Like packaged procedures, all database triggers follow a standard form in development. The following is an example of creating a database trigger:

```
CREATE TRIGGER name
  (trigger firing event)
  ...
  (optional trigger constraint)
BEGIN
  (trigger action)
END;
```

As shown by this example, all database triggers start with the CREATE TRIGGER *name* statement that is the trigger entry point for the named trigger. The *trigger firing event* code begins with a keyword to specify when the trigger is to fire. This section of code identifies the SQL operation that passes control to the *trigger action* code. Any constraints on the SQL operation are identified in the *optional trigger constraint* specification area.

NOTE

If you do not own the table where you are creating the database trigger, you must have the ALTER or ALTER ANY TABLE privilege on the table. Another privilege you need is CREATE TRIGGER, regardless of the table where you are creating the database trigger.

The following example illustrates the creation and use of a database trigger:

```
CREATE TRIGGER check_order_total
  AFTER UPDATE OF order_total ON order
  FOR EACH ROW
  WHEN (new.status = 'NEW')
BEGIN
  IF :new.order_total = 0 THEN
    INSERT INTO order_log
      values(:new.order);
    UPDATE order SET :new.status = 'ERR';
  END IF;
END;
```

This example shows that the trigger event specification begins with a keyword, AFTER in this case, that determines when the trigger should fire. The FOR EACH ROW statement has the trigger fire once for each row instead of the default of once per table. A constraint on firing is that the status of the updated order must be 'NEW'. The trigger action is to INSERT a row into the order_log table and UPDATE the order status to 'ERR'.

> **NOTE**
>
> A correlation name such as :new refers to newly updated column values. You can also reference :old values of a changing column. As shown, you do not use the colon in the *optional trigger constraint* code. You can find more information on database triggers in Chapter 20, "Enforcing Integrity."

> **CAUTION**
>
> You cannot use COMMIT, ROLLBACK, or SAVEPOINT statements in database triggers.

More on Exceptions

I previously discussed the use of exception handling within PL/SQL, but there are three more areas to consider. These areas are reraising exceptions, continuing procedure execution after an exception, and retrying a transaction.

Reraising Exceptions

I already discussed using the RAISE statement to raise exceptions within your code, but you can also use RAISE to reraise an exception. Consider the following example:

```
CREATE OR REPLACE PACKAGE order_total
AS
  ot_failure        EXCEPTION;
  ...
  BEGIN
    ...
    BEGIN
      ...
      if g_recip_counter > max_lines then
        RAISE ot_failure;
      end if;
    EXCEPTION
      when OT_FAILURE then
        ...
      RAISE;
    END;
```

```
...
EXCEPTION
   when OT_FAILURE then
      ...
   END;
END order_total;
```

In this example, the exception is raised in a sub-block with an ot_failure exception handler defined. After processing this error inside the handler, the exception is reraised for further processing in the main procedure block. This is accomplished with another ot_failure exception handler.

Continuing Execution

After an exception is raised in a PL/SQL sub-block, it is possible to continue execution before exiting the driving block. Place executable code in the driving block after the exception handler. The following is an illustration of this technique:

```
<<outer>>
BEGIN
  ...
  <<inner>>
  BEGIN
    ...
    if g_recip_counter > max_lines then
      raise ot_failure;
    end if;
  EXCEPTION
    when OT_FAILURE then
      ...
  END inner;
  UPDATE order SET status = 'SU';
  INSERT INTO suspense_queue
  VALUES (order,g_out_msg);
EXCEPTION
  ...
END outer;
```

This example shows that the exception was handled in the inner sub-block at which time control was passed to the outer driving block. As the inner exception handler ended, execution resumed with the UPDATE statement in the outer block. In this manner, execution of the procedure can continue after an otherwise fatal error is encountered.

Retrying Transactions

Another method of continuing procedure execution after an exception is raised is known as retrying a transaction. The technique is similar to continuing execution after a raised exception in that the transaction to be retried must exist in a sub-block. Using iterative loop control, you can repeat a transaction as often as you like after an exception is raised. The following example illustrates the use of this technique:

```
BEGIN
  ...
  FOR i in 1..10 LOOP
    ...
    BEGIN
      SAVEPOINT update_order
        (SQL transactions)
      COMMIT;
      EXIT;
    EXCEPTION
      WHEN ... THEN
        ROLLBACK to update_order
          (fix data problems)
      ...
    END;
  END LOOP;
END;
```

Under the control of the FOR loop, the SQL transactions can be tried a total of 10 times before procedure execution is terminated. The SAVEPOINT update_order is the point of rollback for failed transactions. If an error is encountered during the SQL transactions phase of this sub-block, control transfers to the exception handler, which tries to resolve the data problems. After execution of the error handler, control transfers to the FOR loop for another pass.

More on Control Structures

Two additional topics for discussion of the subject of PL/SQL control structures are the EXIT statement and sequential control statements. Both control structures are rarely used, but you might encounter a situation that requires the functionality.

EXIT Statement

Earlier in the chapter, I mentioned using the EXIT statement as a means to break out of a basic FOR loop. You can also use the EXIT statement in retrying transactions after raised exceptions. In this respect, EXIT provides a mechanism for unconditional transfer of control from one point of code to another and is used selectively, if at all.

Sequential Control

Using sequential control in PL/SQL is not an essential element in successful code development. However, the technique is worth mentioning for a comprehensive view of the language. Two statements are available for sequential control: GOTO and NULL.

GOTO is an unconditional branch statement that transfers control to a label defined within the scope of the branch logic. The label must precede an executable statement or define a PL/SQL block, as shown in the following example:

```
<<count_lines>>
for i in 1..g_line_counter LOOP
  ...
  if i>max_lines then
    GOTO clean_up;
  end if;
  ...
end LOOP init_lines;

<<clean_up>>
g_recip_counter = i-1;
...
```

In this example, the conditional branch transfers control to the clean_up label for further processing. Use of the GOTO statement is discouraged because it could lead to unstructured code. Other constructs within PL/SQL enable you to write code that is easier to understand and maintain.

Mainly limited to improving code readability, the NULL statement is a way to show that all possible logic choices have been considered. NULL is considered an executable statement.

```
if g_recip_counter > max_lines then
  g_recip_counter = max_lines;
else
  NULL;
end if;
```

This example uses NULL to show that there is nothing to do if g_recip_counter is within range of max_lines. Obviously, you can end this code without the ELSE clause, but using the NULL shows that other options were considered.

Summary

In this chapter, I discussed PL/SQL procedures, subprograms, and the structures associated with this procedural language extension to the Oracle database. You also saw a sample SQL script for building a packaged procedure. In the course of this chapter, I began to develop a sample packaged procedure named order_total.

I continued the development of this procedure with a discussion of error handling through the use of exceptions. Many of the examples presented during discussions of various topics came directly from the order_total procedure. As such, this procedure covers the basic elements of the PL/SQL language and is presented now in its entirety. I discuss additional topics of interest to PL/SQL developers at the end of this sample package code.

SQL*Plus

6

by Dan Hotka

IN THIS CHAPTER

Introduction

SQL*Plus (pronounced "sequel plus") is an interactive tool for the Oracle RDBMS environment. SQL*Plus can be used simply to process SQL statements one at a time, process SQL statements interactively with end users, utilize PL/SQL for procedural processing of SQL statements, list and print query results, format query results into reports, describe the contents of a given table, and copy data between databases.

This chapter concentrates on utilizing SQL*Plus to format output into a variety of reports and introduces methods of utilizing SQL*Plus to create dynamic data-driven SQL*Plus programs and operating system-specific command language programs.

History of SQL*Plus

SQL*Plus originated from the beginning of the Oracle RDBMS days as a product called User Friendly Interface (UFI). Before Version 4 of Oracle RDBMS, UFI was used primarily to administer the Oracle environment. UFI was later renamed to SQL*Plus with the advent of Oracle Version 5. There have been some improvements to SQL*Plus from the UFI days; however, most of the commands and the ease of formatting results are as easy today as they were with the UFI product. There have been additions to several of the command capabilities, additional ways of starting SQL*Plus, and a changed role for SQL*Plus through the major releases of the Oracle RDBMS kernel. For example, before Oracle Version 6, using UFI or SQL*Plus was the only way to administer the Oracle database. With Oracle Version 6 came a new tool called SQL*DBA that took over many of the database responsibilities such as backup and recovery and startup and shutdown. SQL*Plus also exists in the world of client/server and is available with all the major graphical interfaces. Specifics of these graphical interfaces are beyond the scope of this chapter.

> **NOTE**
>
> I highly recommend using SQL*DBA to create and maintain the individual Oracle databases. I would restrict SQL*Plus through the use of Oracle's PRODUCT_ USER_PROFILE Table or Oracle PROFILES to prohibit end users from performing any administrative task.

Usage and Limitations

SQL*Plus is the main *ad hoc*, character-mode interface to the Oracle RDBMS. SQL*Plus can easily be used to produce a variety of types of character mode reports. SQL*Plus can also be used to create dynamic SQL*Plus scripts or even dynamic operating system-specific command language programs. SQL*Plus can be used for some Oracle administration functions, and it can be programmed to be interactive during a specific terminal session. SQL*Plus can process ANSI SQL as well as PL/SQL blocks.

SQL*Plus has a variety of limitations; some are operating system-specific. The following list of limits or maximum values is from *Oracle SQL*Plus User's Guide and Reference*, Appendix C.

Item	Limit
Filename length	System-dependent
Username length	30 characters
User variable name length	30 characters
User variable value length	240 characters
Number of user variables	1,024
Number of variables in a SQL INSERT command INTO list	50
Number of variables per SQL command	100
Command line length	500 characters
Length of a LONG value entered through SQL*Plus	250 characters
Maximum output line size	500 characters
Minimum output line size	Five characters
Line size after variable substitution	1,000 characters (internal only)
Number of lines per SQL command	500 (assuming 80 characters per line)
Number of lines per page	50,000
Total row width	60,000 characters for VMS, otherwise 32,767 characters
Number of rows in an array fetch	5,000
Number of nested command files	20 for VMS, CMS, UNIX; otherwise, five
Page number	99,999

Platforms

SQL*Plus is typically available on any computer system that supports the Oracle RDBMS environment. In the client/server environment, SQL*Plus is available on all of the major graphical interfaces, including MS Windows and Motif.

SQL*Plus Commands

There are six types of SQL*Plus commands:

- Those that initiate the SQL*Plus environment
- SQL*Plus Execute commands
- SQL*Plus Editing commands
- SQL*Plus Formatting commands
- Miscellaneous commands
- Access commands for various databases

Those That Initiate the SQL*Plus Environment

SQL*Plus is an interactive *ad hoc* environment that can also be pre-programmed with the use of SQL*Plus commands, SQL statements, and/or PL/SQL blocks submitted via a file. Upon successful login to SQL*Plus, the user, regardless of the environment he or she is using, will receive a SQL*Plus prompt, SQL>. You can change this prompt message to any text string by changing the SQL*Plus system variable SQLPROMPT.

You can enhance the basic SQL*Plus environment for each user or group of users by utilizing a file named LOGIN.SQL. This file should be located in the directory or home environment from which SQL*Plus is initiated. Oracle and SQL*Plus run in a variety of computer environments; the method used to create files and the definition of the home environment varies greatly between types of computer operating systems. Typical contents of this file are various SET commands that alter the SQL*Plus default settings for the particular user.

> **TIP**
>
> I have set up these LOGIN.SQL files to contain column format commands for each column of the objects to which the particular user or group of users have access. This gives all *ad hoc* queries a polished appearance without the end user having to input anything but his or her *ad hoc* query.

The PRODUCT_USER_PROFILE table, owned by SYSTEM, is one way to provide product level security that enhances the security provided by the SQL GRANT and REVOKE commands. This level of security is used to disable certain SQL and SQL*Plus commands for individual users.

There are various ways to initiate the SQL*Plus environment, depending on the type of computer platform being utilized. To leave the SQL*Plus environment, simply type EXIT at the SQL> prompt and press Return or Enter. To terminate a SQL*Plus command file, make EXIT the last line of the file.

Character Mode Environments

SQL*Plus is a character-based tool that runs in both character mode and graphical environments. How the SQL*Plus environment is initiated varies greatly between the two types of environments. This section discusses the character mode environment initiation syntax and the next section, "Graphical Mode Environments," discusses the syntax required for the Windows 3.1 environment.

SQLPLUS

This syntax initiates SQL*Plus and prompts the user for a valid user name and password. Most UNIX environments implement the SQL*Plus command in lowercase. Enter a valid password and press Enter. SQL*Plus will then prompt for a password. The password does not appear on the screen.

```
SQL*Plus Version 3.1.0 - Production on Tue Aug 1 14:30:20 1995

Copyright (c) Oracle Corporation 1979, 1991.  All rights reserved.

Enter user-name:
```

The following syntax would initiate SQL*Plus but not prompt for the user ID or password.

SQLPLUS *userid/password*

If either the user ID or password is not valid, SQL*Plus will give an error and then prompt the user for a valid user ID and password.

SQLPLUS -S *userid/password*

Using the option -S or -SILENT (–S spelled out) will not display the SQL*Plus version and copyright information. This is handy when you are initiating reports written in SQL*Plus from a menu system where the appearance of a seamless application is desired.

SQLPLUS *userid/password@database*

The preceding syntax will initiate the SQL*Plus environment and connect the user to the remote database identified by the *database* name. This database name can be a SQL*Net connect string, a SQL*Net alias name, or a SQL*Net Version 2 database instance name.

SQLPLUS *userid/password @filename*

The preceding syntax will initiate the SQL*Plus environment and execute the SQL*Plus commands and the SQL (or PL/SQL blocks) contained within the file (SQL*Plus command file). The contents of this file are covered in the section "SQL*Plus Formatting Commands."

TIP

Always use operating system-dependent, fully qualified filenames with this *filename*.

```
SQLPLUS @filename
```

This syntax will initiate the SQL*Plus environment and expect the very first line of the file to contain a valid user ID and password, in this exact format. If the user ID and password are valid, then SQL*Plus will process the SQL*Plus commands and the SQL (or PL/SQL blocks) contained within the file.

```
SQLPLUS userid/password @filename param1 param2 ...
```

This syntax will initiate the SQL*Plus environment and execute the SQL*Plus commands and the SQL (or PL/SQL blocks) contained within the file. The command-line parameters will be passed to variables inside the SQL*Plus command file and be identified inside this file by &1, &2, and so on. The use of these parameters is covered in the section "Advanced Reporting Techniques."

Graphical Mode Environments

This section discusses the syntax required to initiate the SQL*Plus environment from the Windows 3.1 graphical environment.

Figure 6.1 shows the default Windows 3.1 setup that installs with Personal Oracle7 for Windows. This method prompts the user for a valid user ID, password, and host connection. (See Figure 6.2.) Once again, the password is not visible on the screen, and the host string can be a SQL*Net connect string, a SQL*Net alias name, or a SQL*Net Version 2 database instance name. (See Figure 6.3.)

FIGURE 6.1.

*Microsoft Windows SQL*Plus icon setup.*

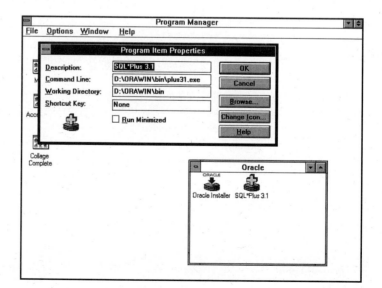

FIGURE 6.2.

*Windows SQL*Plus
login box.*

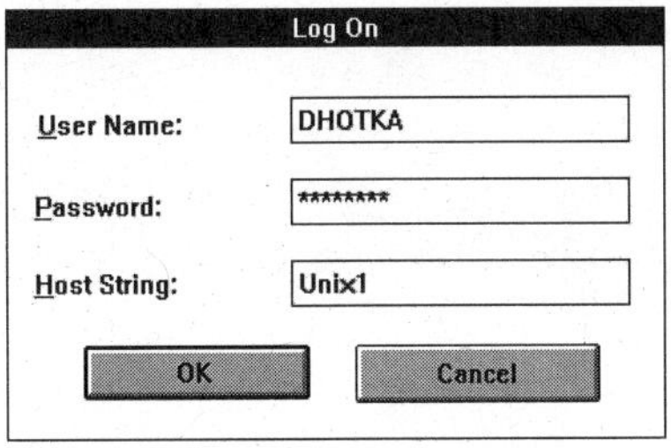

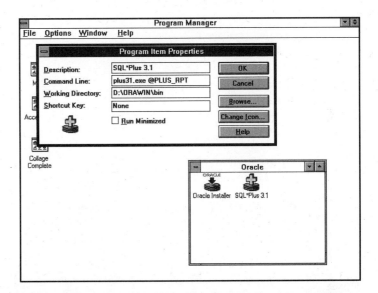

FIGURE 6.3.

*Windows SQL*Plus icon
setup to run a specific
report or program.*

TIP

For Personal Oracle7 users, use 2: for the host string to access the local Personal
Oracle7 database.

This icon would initiate the Windows SQL*Plus environment and execute the SQL*Plus commands and the SQL (or PL/SQL blocks) contained within the file. The contents of this file are
covered in the section "SQL*Plus Formatting Commands."

TIP

Always use operating system-dependent fully qualified filename with this `filename`.

SQL*Plus Execute Commands

The execute commands are used to initiate the processing of SQL statements and PL/SQL blocks, measure the processing time of SQL or PL/SQL statements, execute non-Oracle programs, execute SQL*Forms programs, or attain additional help.

/	Execute the SQL statement or PL/SQL block currently in the SQL buffer. (This is probably the most used of the SQL*Plus commands.)
HELP *topic*	Provides online assistance with SQL, PL/SQL, or SQL*Plus commands.
HOST	Execute non-Oracle commands (operating system-dependent) without leaving SQL*Plus.
RUN	Displays and executes the contents of the SQL buffer.
RUNFORM	Execute a SQL*Forms program without leaving SQL*Plus.
TIMING	Displays the system CPU time with the SQL prompt.

> **NOTE**
>
> I would not recommend this TIMING feature for tuning purposes; EXPLAIN_PLAN is a more accurate tool for gathering individual SQL statement statistics. EXPLAIN_PLAN is discussed in more detail in Chapter 15, "Performance Tuning and Optimizing."

SQL*Plus Editing Commands

The SQL buffer is a work area assigned to the SQL*Plus environment. This buffer contains only SQL or PL/SQL syntax. You can use the following commands to load, save, and manipulate the contents of this buffer:

A *new text* or APPEND *new text*	Appends text to the end of the current line of the SQL buffer.
C/*target text*/*new text*/ or CHANGE/*target text*/*new text*/	Changes the *target text* to the *new text* on the current line in the SQL buffer.
DEL	Deletes the current line in the SQL buffer.
EDIT *filename*	Utilizes an operating system-dependent text editor. To edit the SQL buffer with an operating system-dependent text editor, simply leave off the filename.

GET *filename*	Reads an operating system-dependent file into the SQL buffer.
I *text* or INPUT *text*	Adds the text after the current line in the SQL buffer.
L *number* or LIST *number*	Displays the contents of the SQL buffer. When the *number* syntax is used, LIST will display the line number and make that line the current line in the SQL buffer. SAVE *filename* saves the contents of the SQL buffer to an operating system-dependent file.

TIP

An excellent method to use when you are creating SQL*Plus command files is to utilize these editing features to arrive at the query results desired: SAVE to the operating system and then edit that file with EDIT to add the formatting and other desired features.

START *filename param1 param2 ...*	START will execute the contents of the SQL*Plus command file named in *filename* and pass any input parameters to the SQL*Plus command file.

TIP

I find it convenient to utilize this START feature when I create various database objects. It enables me to have complete control over the order in which the objects are created. I simply create a SQL*Plus command file named INSTALL.SQL, create each DDL statement in its own SQL*Plus command file, and simply add a START command in this INSTALL.SQL file for each of the DDL SQL*Plus command files.

SQL*Plus Formatting Commands

The SQL*Plus formatting commands are used to manipulate the result set from a SQL query.

BREAK ON *column_name* and options

This command controls the organization of rows returned by the query. BREAK can manipulate the appearance of the output by specifying under what conditions a BREAK should occur and what actions should be taken at the BREAK. The appearance of the output can be controlled by skipping a line or skipping to top of next page and providing totals when used in conjunction with COMPUTE. Any number of lines can be skipped at a BREAK point. BREAK points can be defined at the column level, for multiple columns, on a row, on a page, or on a report. See the COMPUTE command for BREAK examples. Entering BREAK by itself at the SQL prompt will display the current BREAK settings.

BTITLE *print_options* and/or text or variable options

BTITLE is used to place text at the bottom of each page. There are various print options that position text at various locations. BTITLE will simply center the text if no print options are specified. *print options* include BOLD, CENTER, COL, FORMAT, LEFT, RIGHT, SKIP, and TAB. BTITLE spelled out by itself will display the current text setting. Other options that can be specified are ON and OFF. BTITLE is ON by default.

CLEAR and options

CLEAR resets any of the SQL*Plus formatting commands. You can also use it to clear the screen. The options include BREAKS, BUFFER, COLUMNS, COMPUTES, SCREEN, SQL, and TIMING.

COLUMN *column_name* and options

COLUMN is used to alter the default display attributes for a given column (*column_name*) of a SQL query. There are a variety of options, but the more common ones are FORMAT, HEADING, JUSTIFY, NEWLINE, NEW_VALUE, and NOPRINT. The FORMAT option is useful in applying editing to numeric fields, date masks to date fields, and specific lengths to variable-length character fields. The HEADING option overrides the SQL*Plus default heading for the particular column. The JUSTIFY option overrides the SQL*Plus column alignment to the heading default. The NEWLINE option will print the column on the beginning of the next line. NEW_VALUE assigns the contents of the column to a SQL*Plus variable (see DEFINE, later in this section). This value can then be used in conjunction with TTITLE or to store intermediate results for master/detail type reports, and is useful to store and pass information between two or more separate SQL statements.

Examples:

```
COLUMN sal FORMAT $99,999.00 HEADING Salary
COLUMN home_dir NEW_VALUE home_path NOPRINT
```

The first SQL query would reference the *home_dir*; all other SQL queries would then reference the *home_path* for the information returned by the first SQL query.

COMPUTE *function* OF *options* ON *break options*

COMPUTE calculates and prints totals for groupings of rows defined by the BREAK command. A variety of standard *functions* can be utilized. The most common *option* is the name of the column in the query on which the total is to be calculated. The *break option* determines where the totals are to be printed and reset, as defined by the BREAK command.

Example:

```
BREAK ON sales_rep SKIP 2
BREAK ON REPORT
COMPUTE SUM OF monthly_sales ON sales_rep
COMPUTE SUM OF commissions ON sales_rep
COMPUTE SUM OF monthly_sales ON REPORT
COMPUTE SUM OF commissions ON REPORT
```

This list will produce a report with totals of monthly_sales and commissions when the sales_rep column value changes. It then skips two lines and produces monthly_sales and commissions totals at the end of the report.

> **NOTE**
>
> The COMPUTE command resets the accumulator fields back to zero after printing.

TTITLE *print_options* and/or text or variable options

> TTITLE is used to place text at the top of each page. There are various *print options* that position text at various locations. TTITLE will center the text and add date and page numbers if no *print options* are specified. *print options* include BOLD, CENTER, COL, FORMAT, LEFT, RIGHT, SKIP, and TAB. TTITLE with no options at all will display the current text setting. Other options that can be specified are ON and OFF. TTITLE is ON by default.

Miscellaneous Commands

This section presents a variety of commands that enable you to interact with the user, comment on the code, and enhance coding options.

ACCEPT *variable number* or *char PROMPT text*

> ACCEPT receives input from the terminal and places the contents in *variable*. This variable can already have been defined with the DEFINE command. If the PROMPT option is specified, then the *text* will be displayed after skipping a line. The variable attributes of *number* or *char* can be defined at this time. The variable will be a *char* if not otherwise defined.

DEFINE *variable*

> DEFINE creates a user-defined variable and assigns it to be of char (character) format. This variable can be assigned a default value at this time.

> **TIP**
>
> I find these DESC statements handy for assigning a variable name to the input parameters coming into the SQL*Plus command file. For example, DEFINE SYSTEM_NAME = &1. This line would create a character variable SYSTEM_NAME and assign it the text associated with the first input parameter. The DEFINE statement makes SQL*Plus command file code easier to follow.

DESC or DESCRIBE *database object*

> DESCRIBE displays the columns associated with a table, view, or synonym.

PAUSE *text*

> PAUSE prints the contents of *text* after skipping a line, and then waits for the Return or Enter key to be pressed.

PROMPT *text*

> PROMPT simply skips a line and prints the contents of *text*.

REM or REMARK

> SQL*Plus will ignore the contents of this line when it is used in SQL*Plus command files. REMARK enables documentation or other comments to be contained in these SQL*Plus command files.

SET *SQL*Plus System Variable*

> The SET command controls the default settings for the SQL*Plus environment. You can automatically alter these settings for each SQL*Plus session by including them in the LOGIN.SQL file, discussed earlier in this chapter. See Chapter 6 of Oracle's *SQL*Plus User's Guide and Reference* for a complete listing of the SET options.

The following are some common SET options utilized for reporting:

SET LINESIZE 80	Controls the width of the output report line
SET PAGESIZE 55	Controls the number of lines per page

The following are some common SET options that suppress various SQL*Plus output:

SET FEEDBACK OFF	Suppresses the number of query rows returned
SET VERIFY OFF	Suppresses the substitution text when using &*variables*, including command line variables
SET TERMOUT OFF	Suppresses all terminal output; this is particularly useful in conjunction with the SPOOL command
SET ECHO OFF	Suppresses the display of SQL*Plus commands

SPOOL *filename* or *options*

> The SPOOL command is used to open, close, or print an operating system-dependent file. Specifying SPOOL *filename* will create an operating system-dependent file; *filename* can contain the full pathname of the file and extension. If no file extension is given, the file suffix, LST, will be appended (*filename*.LST). Options include OFF or OUT. If OFF is specified, then the operating system-dependent file is simply closed. If OUT is specified, then the operating system-dependent file is closed and sent to the operating system-dependent printer assigned as the default printer to the user's operating system environment.

NOTE

If you issue SPOOL *filename* without issuing a SPOOL OFF or SPOOL OUT, then the current operating system-dependent file is closed and the new one as specified by the SPOOL command is opened.

TIP

I prefer to write SQL*Plus-based reports utilizing the SET variables mentioned previously in conjunction with the SPOOL command. I create the output report in the file specified by the SPOOL command and then control whether it is visually displayed to the terminal, optionally printed, or both by using operating system-dependent command language.

TIP

I always use a file suffix when specifying SPOOL *filename*. It enables me to control exactly what the entire filename is and not depend on Oracle default options (the LST suffix feature), which are subject to change without notice with newer releases of the SQL*Plus product.

UNDEFINE *variable*

> UNDEFINE removes the previously DEFINEd variable from the SQL*Plus environment.

Access Commands for Various Databases

The database access commands CONNECT, DISCONNECT, and COPY are used to connect to and share data with other Oracle databases. Discussing these commands is beyond the scope of this chapter.

SQL*Plus Reporting

You can use SQL*Plus formatting commands in a variety of combinations to create reports. This section covers reporting techniques that use control breaks, different ways to format headings, input parameters, SQL*Plus environment controls, and the SQL Union operator.

Reporting Techniques

This section covers some common SQL*Plus report formatting features. It also covers techniques for controlling the resulting output. I discuss and provide examples of simple reporting techniques and advanced reporting techniques.

The following example formats the results of a SQL query. It defines a report title and formats, assigns column headings, and applies some control breaks for intermediate and report totaling.

Listing 6.1. Simple SQL*Plus report code.

```
 1:    define ASSIGNED_ANALYST = &1
 2:    set FEEDBACK OFF
 3:    set VERIFY OFF
 4:    set TERMOUT OFF
 5:    set ECHO OFF
 6:    column APPLICATION_NAME     format a12    heading 'Application'
 7:    column PROGRAM_NAME              format a12        heading 'Program'
 8:    column PROGRAM_SIZE            format 999999      heading 'Program¦Size'
 9:    break on APPLICATION_NAME skip 2
10:    break on report skip 2
11:    compute sum of PROGRAM_SIZE on APPLICATION_NAME
12:    compute sum of PROGRAM_SIZE on report
13:    ttitle 'Programs by Application ¦ Assigned to: &&ASSIGNED_ANALYST'
14:    spool ANALYST.OUT
15:    select APPLICATION_NAME,PROGRAM_NAME,nvl(PROGRAM_SIZE,0)
16:      from APPLICATION_PROGRAMS
17:     where ASSIGNED_NAME = '&&ASSIGNED_ANALYST'
18:     order by APPLICATION_NAME,PROGRAM_NAME
19:     /
20:    spool off
21:    exit
```

The following is the output report from the code in Listing 6.1.

```
Tue Jul 13                                                      page    1
                           Programs by Application
                               Assigned to: HOTKA


                 Program
     Application  Program              Size
     -----------  -----------          -------
     COBOL        CLAIMS               10156
```

```
              HOMEOWN          22124
              PREMIUMS         10345
                              --------
    sum                        42625

    FORTRAN   ALGEBRA           6892
              MATH1             7210
              SCIENCE1         10240
                              --------
    sum                        24342

    sum                        66967
```

Listing 6.1 is a simple but common form of SQL*Plus formatting. This report passes a command-line parameter (&1 on line 1) and assigns it to the variable name ASSIGNED_ANALYST. The ASSIGNED_ANALYST variable is then used in the headings (see line 13) and again as part of the SQL query (see line 17). Lines 2, 3, 4, and 5 suspend all terminal output from the SQL*Plus environment. The && is utilized to denote substitution of an already defined variable. This report contains two breaks, one when the column APPLICATION_NAME changes (see line 9) and one at the end of the report (see line 10). Totals are also calculated for each of these breaks (see lines 11 and 12). The pipe character (¦) in the TTITLE command (see line 13) moves the following text onto its own line. Line 14 will open an operating system-dependent file named ANALYST.OUT in the current operating system-dependent directory. The order by clause of the query on line 18 ensures that the breaks occur in an orderly manner.

TIP

Always order the query output by the breaks expected by the program. The only way to guarantee the order of the rows is to use an order by clause on the query.

Advanced Reporting Techniques

The following example creates a cross-tabular report with a spreadsheet appearance.

Listing 6.2. Cross-tabular SQL*Plus report code.

```
 1:     define RPT_DATE = &1
 2:     set FEEDBACK OFF
 3:     set VERIFY OFF
 4:     set TERMOUT OFF
 5:     set ECHO OFF
 6:     column SALES_REP       format a12     heading 'Sales¦Person'
 7:     column NISSAN          format 999999 heading 'Nissan'
 8:     column TOYOTA          format 999999 heading 'Toyota'
 9:     column GM              format 999999 heading 'GM'
10:     column FORD            format 999999 heading 'Ford'
11:     column CRYSLER         format 999999 heading 'Crysler'
12:     column TOTALS          format 999999 heading 'Totals'
```

continues

Listing 6.2. continued

```
13:    break on report skip 2
14:    compute sum of NISSAN on report
15:    compute sum of TOYOTA on report
16:    compute sum of GM on report
17:    compute sum of FORD on report
18:    compute sum of CRYSLER on report
19:    compute sum of TOTALS on report
20: ttitle left '&&IN_DATE' center 'Auto Sales' RIGHT 'Page: ' format 999 -
21:         SQL.PNO skip CENTER ' by Sales Person '
22:    spool SALES.OUT
23:    select SALES_REP,
24:        sum(decode(CAR_TYPE,'N',TOTAL_SALES,0)) NISSAN,
25:        sum(decode(CAR_TYPE,'T',TOTAL_SALES,0)) TOYOTA,
26:        sum(decode(CAR_TYPE,'G',TOTAL_SALES,0)) GM,
27:        sum(decode(CAR_TYPE,'F',TOTAL_SALES,0)) FORD,
28:        sum(decode(CAR_TYPE,'C',TOTAL_SALES,0)) CRYSLER ,
29:        sum(TOTAL_SALES) TOTALS
30:    from CAR_SALES
31:    where SALES_DATE <= to_date('&&RPT_DATE')
32:    group by SALES_REP
33:    /
34:    spool off
35:    exit
```

The following code shows the output report from Listing 6.2.

```
31-AUG-95                  Auto Sales                              Page: 1
            by Sales Person

Sales
Person       Nissan    Toyota     GM       Ford     Crysler    Totals
--------    --------  --------   --------  --------  --------   ------
Elizabeth    5500      2500       0         0        4500       12500
Emily        4000      6000       4400      2000     0          16400
Thomas       2000      1000       6000      4000     1500       14500
            --------  --------   --------  --------  --------   ------
             11500     9500       10400     6000     6000       43400
```

Listing 6.2 is a cross-tabular SQL*Plus command file. This report passes a command-line parameter (&1 on line 1) and assigns it to the variable name RPT_DATE. The RPT_DATE variable is then used in the headings (see line 20) and again as part of the SQL query (see line 31). Lines 2, 3, 4, and 5 suspend all terminal output from the SQL*Plus environment. The report will be created in the operating system-dependent file SALES.OUT. Column formatting commands control the appearance of the columns (lines 6 through 12). The combination of compute commands (lines 14 through 19), the sum statements in the query (lines 24 through 29), and the group by clause in the query (line 32) give the report output the appearance of a cross-tabular report.

I utilized a different TTITLE technique in Listing 6.2 (lines 20 and 21) from that of Listing 6.1 (line 13).

The following example displays a major break field with the supporting data immediately following.

Listing 6.3. Master/detail SQL*Plus report code.

```
 1:    ttitle 'Sales Detail ¦ by Sales Rep'
 2:    set HEADINGS OFF
 3:    column DUMMY NOPRINT
 4:    select 1 DUMMY, SALES_REP_NO,'Sales Person: ' ¦¦ SALES_REP
 5:    from sales
 6:    UNION
 7:    select 2 DUMMY,SALES_REP_NO,'--------------------'
 8:    from sales
 9:    UNION
10:     select 3 DUMMY,SALES_REP_NO, rpad(CAR_MAKE,4) ¦¦ '     ' ¦¦
11:         to_char(SALE_AMT,'$999,999.99')
12:     from sales_detail
13:    UNION
14:    select 4 DUMMY,SALES_REP_NO,'          ----------'
15:    from sales
16:    UNION
17:    select 5 DUMMY,SALES_REP_NO,'Total:    ' ¦¦
18:        to_char(sum(TOTAL_SALES),'$999,999.99'))
19:    from sales
20:    UNION
21:    select 6 DUMMY,SALES_REP_NO,'            '
22:    from sales
23:    order by 2,1,3
24:    /
```

I will now only include the specific SQL*Plus commands necessary to produce the desired output in the remaining examples.

The following code shows the output report from Listing 6.3.

```
Thur Aug 31                                                   page    1
                                   Sales Detail
                      by Sales Rep


      Sales Person:  Elizabeth
      ............................
      Chrysler    $3,000
      Chrysler    $1,500
      Nissan      $2,000
      Nissan      $2,000
      Nissan      $1,500
      Toyota      $2,500
                  ----------
      Total:      $12,500

      Sales Person:  Emily
      ............................
      Ford        $1,000
      Ford        $1,000
      GM          $2,000
      GM          $2,400
      Nissan      $2,000
      Nissan      $2,000
      Toyota      $1,000
      Toyota      $2,500
      Toyota      $2,500
                  ----------
      Total:      $16,400

      Sales Person:  Thomas
      ............................
      Chrysler    $1,500
      Ford        $1,000
      Ford        $3,000
      GM          $1,400
      GM          $1,600
      GM          $3,000
      Nissan      $2,000
      Toyota      $1,000
                  ----------
      Total:      $16,400
```

Listing 6.3 creates a master/detail SQL*Plus report by utilizing the SQL UNION command. In this example, there are six distinct separate types of lines to be printed: the sales person (line 4), a line of dashes under the sales person (line 7), the detail line (line 10), a line of dashes under the detail total (line 14), a total line (line 17), and a blank line (line 21). There are six separate queries that have their output merged and sorted together by the SQL JOIN statement (see lines 6, 9, 13, 16, 19, and 23). When you use JOIN to merge the output of two or more queries, the output result set must have the same number of columns. The headings are turned off (line 2) because regular SQL*Plus column headings are not desired for this type of report. The first column of each query has an alias column name of DUMMY. This DUMMY column is used to sort the order of the six types of lines (denoted by each of the six queries). The DUMMY column's only role is to maintain the order of the lines within the major sort field (SALES_REP_NO in this example); therefor, the NOPRINT option is specified in line 3.

Listing 6.4 uses the JOIN feature to display output from two or more tables within the same report.

Listing 6.4. Multitable SQL*Plus report code.

```
 1:    column OBJECT_TYPE      format a20      heading 'Object'
 2:    column OBJECT_NAME      format a8      heading 'Name'
 3:    column COMMENT      format a8      heading 'Comments'
 4:    break on OBJECT_TYPE skip 1
 5:    ttitle 'System Summary Report
 6:    select 'Program' OBJECT_TYPE, program_name OBJECT_NAME,
 7:        program_comments  COMMENTS
 8:        from program_table
 9:    UNION
10:    select 'Command Language',cl_name, assoc_system
11:        from cl_table
12:    UNION
13:     select 'Files',file_name, 'File Size = ' ¦¦ file_size ¦¦  'Bytes'
14:        from file_table
15:     /
```

The following code shows the output report from Listing 6.4.

```
Thr Aug 31                        page    1
                           System Summary Report


Object                       Name           Comments
- - - - - - - - - - - - - - - - - - - - -    - - - - - - - -    - - - - - - - - - - - - - - - - - - - - -
Programs                     AM1            Algebra Test 1
                             AM2            Algebra Test 2
                             AM3            Algebra Test 3

Command Language             CL1            AM1
                             CL2            AM2
                             CL3            AM3

Files                        AM1.TST        File Size = 1200 Bytes
                             AM2.TST        File Size = 3000 Bytes
                             AM3.TST        File Size = 2200 Bytes
```

Listing 6.4 creates a SQL*Plus report utilizing different columns from different tables using the SQL UNION command. In this example, there are three different tables (see lines 8, 11, and 14), but there are only three columns of output. The first query contains the column names (see lines 6 and 7). This is because of the way the UNION operator works. The queries after the first query must follow the number of columns and the type of column (text or numeric) based on the column definitions of the first query. The BREAK command (line 4) causes the OBJECT_NAME to print once and creates the blank line between the groupings of records.

I will demonstrate two methods of creating reports that print with specific text in specific positions. Method 1 in Listing 6.5 utilizes the RPAD SQL function whereas Method 2 in Listing 6.6 utilizes the COLUMN formatting command. Both examples will create the same output report.

Listing 6.5. Method 1 fixed position formatting SQL*Plus report code.

```
 1:   define  TICKET_ROWID = &1
 2:   set LINESIZE 80
 3:   set  HEADING OFF
 4:   set FEEDBACK OFF
 5:   spool TICKET.OUT
 6:   select RPAD('-----------------------------------------------------' ||
 7:        null,80),
 8:   RPAD('                          Customer Contact Survey' || null,80),
 9:   RPAD('-----------------------------------------------------' || null,80),
10:   RPAD(' Customer Name: ' || CUSTOMER_NAME || ' PHONE#: ' ||
➥PHONE || null,80),
11:   RPAD(' Customer Address:  ' || CUSTOMER_ADDRESS  || null,80),
12:   RPAD('                        ' || CUSTOMER_CITY || CUSTOMER_STATE ||
13:        CUSTOMER_ZIP  || null,80),
14:   RPAD('-----------------------------------------------------' || null,80),
15:   RPAD(' ' || TO_CHAR(CONTACT_DATE,'mm/dd/yy HH:MI') ||
➥' Caller: ' || CALLER ||
16:        null,80),
17:   RPAD('-----------------------------------------------------' || null,80),
18:   RPAD(' Home Phone? ' ||  HPHONE_YN || 'Best Time to call: ' ||
➥CALL_TIME ||
19:        null,80),
20:   RPAD('    Has Catalog? ' || CATALOG_YN || 'Desire Future Calls? ' ||
➥FUTURE_YN ||
21:        null,80),
22:   RPAD('-----------------------------------------------------' || null,80),
23:   RPAD('PRINTED:  ' || TO_CHAR(SYSDATE,'mm/dd/yy HH:MI || 'BY:  ' ||
24:        OPERATOR || null,80)
25:   from CUSTOMER_TABLE
26:   where ROWID = '&&TICKET_ROWID'
27:   /
28:   set PAGESIZE 1
29:   set  NEWPAGE 0
30:   select  null from dual;
31:   set PAGESIZE 0
32:   spool OUT
33:   exit
```

Listing 6.6. Method 2 fixed position formatting SQL*Plus report code.

```
 1:     define TICKET_ROWID = &1
 2:     set PAGESIZE 55
 3:     set LINESIZE 80
 4:     set HEADING OFF
 5:     set FEEDBACK OFF
 6:     column LINE1 JUSTIFY LEFT NEWLINE
 7:     column LINE2 JUSTIFY LEFT NEWLINE
 8:     column LINE3 JUSTIFY LEFT NEWLINE
 9:     column LINE4 JUSTIFY LEFT NEWLINE
10:     column LINE5 JUSTIFY LEFT NEWLINE
11:     column LINE6 JUSTIFY LEFT NEWLINE
12:     column LINE7 JUSTIFY LEFT NEWLINE
13:     column LINE8 JUSTIFY LEFT NEWLINE
14:     column LINE9 JUSTIFY LEFT NEWLINE
15:     column LINE10 JUSTIFY LEFT NEWLINE
16:     column LINE11 JUSTIFY LEFT NEWLINE
17:     column LINE12 JUSTIFY LEFT NEWLINE
18:     column LINE13 JUSTIFY LEFT NEWLINE
19:     column LINE14 JUSTIFY LEFT NEWLINE
20:     break ON ROW SKIP PAGE
21:     SPOOL TICKET
22:     select '-----------------------------------------------' || null LINE1,
23:     '                          Customer Contact Survey' || null LINE2,
24:     '-----------------------------------------------' || null LINE3,
25:     ' Customer Name:  ' || CUSTOMER_NAME || ' PHONE#: ' ||
➡PHONE || null LINE4,
26:     ' Customer Address: ' || CUSTOMER_ADDRESS  || null LINE5,
27:     '                       ' || CUSTOMER_CITY || CUSTOMER_STATE ||
28:           CUSTOMER_ZIP  || null LINE6,
29:     '-----------------------------------------------' || null LINE7,
30:     ' ' || TO_CHAR(CONTACT_DATE,'mm/dd/yy HH:MI || '  Caller: ' ||
➡CALLER || null
31:           LINE8,
32:     '-----------------------------------------------' || null LINE9,
33:     ' Home Phone? ' ||  HPHONE_YN  || 'Best Time to call:  ' ||
➡CALL_TIME || null
34:           LINE10,
35:     '  'Has Catalog? ' || CATALOG_YN || 'Desire Future Calls? ' ||
➡FUTURE_YN || null
36:           LINE11,
37:     '-----------------------------------------------' || null LINE12,
38:     'PRINTED: ' || TO_CHAR(SYSDATE,'mm/dd/yy HH:MI || 'BY: ' ||
➡OPERATOR || null
39:           LINE13,
40:     '-----------------------------------------------' || null LINE14
41:     from CUSTOMER_TABLE
42:     where ROWID = '&&TICKET_ROWID'
43:     /
44:     spool OUT
45:     exit
```

Listings 6.5 and 6.6 both produce the same output report, as follows in Listing 6.7.

Listing 6.7. Output of Listings 6.5 and 6.6, fixed position formatting SQL*Plus report.

```
 - - - - - - - - - - - - - - - - - - - - - - - - - - - - - - - - - - - - - - - - - - - - - - -
    Customer Contact Survey
 - - - - - - - - - - - - - - - - - - - - - - - - - - - - - - - - - - - - - - - - - - - - - - -
 Customer Name:  John Smith    PHONE#: 515 123-4567
 Customer Address:  123 Oak Street
                    Anytown  VA 12345
 - - - - - - - - - - - - - - - - - - - - - - - - - - - - - - - - - - - - - - - - - - - - - - -
   31-Aug-95 10:05  Caller:  DHotka
 - - - - - - - - - - - - - - - - - - - - - - - - - - - - - - - - - - - - - - - - - - - - - - -
     Home Phone?    Y      Best Time to call:  8pm
     Has Catalog?   Y      Desire Future Calls?   N
 - - - - - - - - - - - - - - - - - - - - - - - - - - - - - - - - - - - - - - - - - - - - - - -
 PRINTED: 31-Aug-95 12:45   BY: DHotka
 - - - - - - - - - - - - - - - - - - - - - - - - - - - - - - - - - - - - - - - - - - - - - - -
```

Listings 6.5 (method 1) and 6.6 (method 2) produce the exact same output, as seen in Listing 6.7. Both of these methods will produce reports with information in fixed or predefined positions. Both of these methods could be utilized to print information on a preprinted form. These particular examples were designed to be started from inside another process, such as SQL*Forms, because the only input parameter is an Oracle ROWID used to read and process a single row from the database (see lines 1 and 26 in Listing 6.5 and lines 1 and 42 in Listing 6.6).

These examples utilize the concatenation feature of SQL (¦¦) to blend text between database fields. Each column in the SQL statement represents an individual line in the report. Both examples have the standard column headings feature turned off (line 3 of Listing 6.5, line 4 of Listing 6.6). Both examples have a one-to-one relationship between a SQL column and a line of output. The methods differ in how the columns are formatted to create the individual lines.

The main difference in these two methods is the approach used in the individual line setup. Method 1 (Listing 6.5) uses the SQL command RPAD (see line 6) in combination with LINESIZE (line 2) to create an output line. The RPAD is used to fill the line with blanks to position 80, and with LINESIZE set at 80 will cause the formatted line to appear on a line by itself. Method 2 (Listing 6.6) uses the column command with the option NEWLINE specified in conjunction with a field alias name (see lines 6 and 22). The column command with the NEWLINE option will make the formatted line appear on a line by itself.

> **NOTE**
>
> Listing 6.5 uses lines 28 through 31 to skip to the top of a new page. Listing 6.6 uses a break command to skip to a new page after each row of data from the SQL query. The entire SELECT command of each example formats one row of information from the database.

SQL*Plus Additional Functionality

The remainder of this chapter discusses a variety of ways to format SQL*Plus output to create database-driven types of output (that is, SQL code, operating system-dependent command language, and script files for other Oracle products).

SQL Creating SQL

The classic example of using SQL*Plus formatting to create other SQL statements (hence the term "SQL creating SQL") is cleaning up a table after an employee leaves a company. The Oracle data dictionary view TAB is used in this example. You can easily enter at the SQL*Plus prompt (shown here as SQL>) the steps in Listing 6.8 or adapt them to a SQL*Plus command file using features you already learned.

Listing 6.8 is an example of SQL creating SQL.

Listing 6.8. Dropping all tables owned by a particular user.

```
SQL>set headings off
SQL>set pagesize 0
SQL>set termout off
SQL>spool drop_tbl.sql
SQL>select 'DROP TABLE ' ¦¦ tname ¦¦ ';' from tab;
SQL>spool off
SQL>set termout on
SQL>start drop_tbl
```

This scenario assumes that the login ID and the owner of the table objects to be dropped are both the same. The first three commands are used to set up the SQL*Plus environment. The spool file drop_tbl.sql will capture the concatenated text and table names (tname) from the SQL query. The spool off command closes the file and the start command executes the drop table commands now inside the drop_tbl.sql file.

> **TIP**
>
> It is common practice to use this SQL-creating-SQL example to perform a variety of clean-up and monitoring tasks.

Listing 6.9 is an extension of Listing 6.8 as another example of creating useful database-driven programs. This example will add four auditing fields to the end of each table owned by the user ID that runs this particular SQL*Plus command file. This script will also create a database trigger that will automatically maintain these four added fields. I utilized the fixed position formatting discussed in Listing 6.5.

Listing 6.9. SQL creating database triggers.

```
 1:    set ECHO OFF
 2:    set TERMOUT OFF
 3:    set FEEDBACK OFF
 4:    set VERIFY OFF
 5:    set PAGESIZE 0
 6:    set LINESIZE 80
 7:    set HEADING OFF
 8:    spool cre_dbtrg.sql
 9:    select     RPAD('select '  alter table ' || TNAME || null,80),
10:      RPAD( '            add (inserted_by      varchar2(10), ' || null,80),
11:      RPAD( '                 inserted_date        date    , ' || null,80),
12:      RPAD( '                 updated_by       varchar2(10), ' || null,80),
13:      RPAD( '                 updated_date         date   ); ' || null,80)
14:    from TAB;
15:    select     RPAD(' create trigger trg_' || TNAME || null,80),
16:        RPAD(' before insert or update ' || null,80),
17:        RPAD('    on ' || TNAME || null,80),
18:        RPAD('    for each row ' || null,80),
19:        RPAD(' begin ' || null,80),
20:        RPAD('  if :old.inserted_by is null then ' || null,80),
21:        RPAD('    :new.inserted_by   := USER; ' || null,80),
22:        RPAD('    :new.inserted_date := SYSDATE; ' || null,80),
23:        RPAD('    :new.updated_by    := null; ' || null,80),
24:        RPAD('    :new.updated_date  := null; ' || null,80),
25:        RPAD('   else ' || null,80),
26:        RPAD('    :new.inserted_by   := :old.inserted_by; ' || null,80),
27:      RPAD('    :new.inserted_date := :old.inserted_date; ' || null,80),
28:        RPAD('    :new.updated_by    := USER; ' || null,80),
29:        RPAD('    :new.updated_date  := SYSDATE; ' || null,80),
30:        RPAD('   end if; ' || null,80),
31:        RPAD(' end; ' || null,80),
32:        RPAD( '/' || null,80)
33:    from TAB;
34:    spool off
35:    set FEEDBACK ON
36:    set TERMOUT ON
37:    set VERIFY ON
38:    set ECHO ON
39:    spool dbtrg.log
40:    start dbtrg.sql
41:    spool off
42:    exit
```

Lines 1 through 7 set up the SQL*Plus environment so that no extra messages appear in the cre_dbtrg.sql file (see line 8). Lines 9 through 14 create the SQL alter table statement that will add the audit fields to each table, and lines 15 through 33 create the SQL create trigger statement that will add the database triggers necessary to maintain these audit fields. Lines 35 through 38 reset the SQL*Plus environment so that all SQL commands and messages display. Line 40 then runs the SQL*Plus command file cre_dbtrg.sql that was just created.

> **TIP**
>
> In Listing 6.9, line 39 opens the file DBTRG.LOG. This file will contain the output (an audit trail) when the DBTRG.SQL statement is executed with the START command on Line 40. I like to create SQL audit trails for various DBA commands, particularly ones such as this example where the process is rather automated. The audit trails enable me to review the additions and any errors that might have occurred by simply editing the log file.

SQL Creating Command Language Scripts

SQL*Plus formatting commands are quite versatile. Besides their uses discussed previously, they can be used to create operating system-dependent command language scripts. The examples in this section apply to an MS-DOS environment; however, the scripts can easily be adapted to any operating system-dependent command language.

The example in Listing 6.10 applies the SQL creating SQL discussed in Listing 6.8 to create a DOS BAT file.

Listing 6.10. SQL creating command language scripts.

```
 1:    column HOME_DIR new_value HDIR noprint
 2:    column PROGRAM_DIR new_value PDIR noprint
 3:    column PROGRAM_SUFFIX new_value PSUF noprint
 4:    select HOME_DIR,PROGRAM_DIR,PROGRAM_SUFFIX
 5:       from APPLICATION_DEFAULTS
 6:    /
 7:    spool  LIST614.BAT
 8:    select 'CD &PDIR'
 9:       from dual
10:    /
11:    select 'DIR *.&PSUF'
12:        from dual
13:    /
14:    select 'CD &HDIR'
15:        from dual
16:    /
17:    spool off
18:    exit
```

The following code is the output created by Listing 6.10.

```
CD \COBOL\PROGRAMS
DIR *.COB
CD \
```

Listing 6.10 is a simple example of creating an MS-DOS batch file with SQL*Plus formatting commands. The important concept of this example comes in lines 1 through 3. These lines contain three column commands that contain the NEW_VALUE clause. The importance of this concept is that these variables can be loaded from the Oracle database and their values referenced again in other SQL queries. Lines 4 and 5 populate these variables as named in the column statement. Note that when the variables are referenced in other SQL queries (lines 8, 11, and 14), the reference is to the NEW_VALUE variable name.

TIP

Use the column command with the NEW_VALUE option to load variables from Oracle tables to use in other SQL queries.

SQL*Plus Creating Database-Driven Command Language Scripts

The final example, Listing 6.11, incorporates a variety of concepts discussed in this chapter. The goal of this example is to load all program names and program sizes found in a particular directory structure, along with some database information, into an Oracle database table, APPLICATION_PROGRAMS. This directory structure is stored in a different Oracle database table, APPLICATION_DEFAULTS.

Listing 6.11. MS-DOS batch command file.

```
1:   SQLPLUS -S HOTKA/DAN @LIST6_16.SQL
2:   CALL LIST6_16.BAT
3:   SED -F LIST6_19.SED LIST6_15A.DAT > LIST6_15B.DAT
4:   SQLLOAD USERID=HOTKA/DAN CONTROL=LIST6_16.CTL
```

Listing 6.10 is the actual MS-DOS bat command file that runs the four computer tasks to accomplish our goal. The SQLPLUS command on line 1 connects to the database and runs the SQL*Plus command file LIST6_16.SQL (see Listing 6.12). LIST6_16.SQL creates two files, LIST6_16.BAT (see Listing 6.12) and LIST6_16.CTL (see Listing 6.13). Line 2 executes the newly created LIST6_16.BAT file. This command creates the file, LIST6_15A.DAT, that is an MS-DOS DIR (directory) list of directory 'C:\COBOL'. Line 3 is a stream editor (SED) that deletes the first few lines and the last few lines (as directed by LIST6_19.SED; see Listing 6.15) of file LIST6_15A.DAT, creating LIST6_15B.DAT. This file is the MS-DOS DIR output without the heading and trailing text information. Line 4 then runs Oracle's SQL*Loader program, using the LIST6_16.CTL SQL*Loader control file created by line 1 and reading the datafile LIST6_15B.DAT file created by line 3.

Listing 6.12 is the LIST6_16.SQL referenced in Line 1 of Listing 6.11 and will create the LIST6_16.BAT file referenced in Line 2 of Listing 6.11.

Listing 6.12. SQL*Plus command file LIST6_16.SQL.

```
 1:    set PAGESIZE 0
 2:    column HOME_DIR new_value HDIR noprint
 3:    column PROGRAM_DIR new_value PDIR noprint
 4:    column PROGRAM_SUFFIX new_value PSUF noprint
 5:    select HOME_DIR,PROGRAM_DIR,PROGRAM_SUFFIX
 6:       from APPLICATION_DEFAULTS
 7:    /
 8:    spool  LIST6_16.BAT
 9:    select 'DIR &PDIR\*.&PSUF > &HDIR\LIST6_15A.DAT'
10:        from dual
11:    /
12:    spool off
13:    spool LIST6_16.ctl
14:    select 'load data'
15:        from dual
16:    /
17:    select 'infile ' || '''' || 'LIST6_15B.DAT' || ''''
18:          from dual
19:    /
20:    select 'append'
21:         from dual
22:    /
23:    select 'into table APPLICATION_PROGRAMS'
24:        from dual
25:    /
26:    select '(PROGRAM_NAME position(1:8) char,'
27:        from dual
28:    /
29:    select 'PROGRAM_SUFFIX constant ' || '''' || '&PSUF' || '''' || ','
30:        from dual
31:    /
32:    select 'PROGRAM_SIZE position(15:22) integer external,'
33:         from dual
34:    /
35:    select 'PROGRAM_PATH constant ' || '''' || '&PDIR' || '''' || ','
36:        from dual
37:    /
38:    select 'ASSIGNED_ANALYST constant ' || '''' || '&USER' || '''' || ')'
39:         from dual
40:    /
41:    spool off
42:    exit
```

The file in Listing 6.13, LIST6_16.BAT, was created by Listing 6.12, lines 8 and 9.

Listing 6.13. SQL creating MS-DOS batch file output.

```
DIR C:\COBOL\*.COB > C:\FILES\LIST6_15A.DAT
```

The Oracle SQL*Loader control file in Listing 6.14, LIST6_16.CTL, was created by the remainder of Listing 6.12, beginning at line 13.

Listing 6.14. SQL creating Oracle SQL*Loader control file output.

```
load data
infile 'LIST6_15B.DAT'
append
into table APPLICATION_PROGRAMS
  (PROGRAM_NAME position(1:8) char,
PROGRAM_SUFFIX constant 'COB',
PROGRAM_SIZE position(15:22) integer external,
PROGRAM_PATH constant 'C:\COBOL',
ASSIGNED_ANALYST constant 'HOTKA')
```

The file in Listing 6.15 is needed to modify the LIST16_5A.DAT file, the file created from a MS-DOS DIR command (see Listing 6.13). Remember: Listing 6.13 was created by Listing 6.12 at Line 9.

Listing 6.15. LIST6_17.SED file used in Listing 6.15, line 3.

```
1,4d
/bytes/,$d
```

Listing 6.12 expands on the Listing 6.10 example. This SQL*Plus command file reads the Oracle database, loading three user variables with default information from database table APPLICATION_DEFAULTS (lines 2 through 7). Line 8 opens the first file, LIST6_16.BAT. Simple text, in the form of MS-DOS commands, is joined with information stored in the above-mentioned variables with default information (see line 9 for syntax and Listing 6.13 to view results of this SQL query). This file is closed at line 12 and the second output file, LIST6_16.CTL, is opened. This file is the control file that tells Oracle's SQL*Loader what to do. Lines 14 through 40 are a series of select ... from dual SQL queries. Each of these SQL statements will output one line. The table DUAL (its real name is SYSTEM.DUAL) contains one column and one row and is convenient in the example when only one row of output is desired from each of these SQL queries (see lines 14 through 40). Lines 29 and 35 incorporate the default information stored in the user variables. Listing 6.14 displays the results of this series of SQL queries.

The goal here was to use information stored in the Oracle database to retrieve information from an operating system file system directory and to load this information into the Oracle database. Listing 6.11 drives this whole example, running Listing 12 to create the necessary files with information from the Oracle database, preparing the output file created for loading, and running the Oracle SQL*Loader process with the SQL*Loader control file created by Listing 6.12. The goal of this example is a simple one and used several of the concepts in this chapter.

NOTE

The table SYSTEM.DUAL, or DUAL, is a one-column, one-row table that played a major role in the programming of Oracle tools before the introduction of Oracle's PL/SQL software.

TIP

Line 9 of Listing 6.12 can easily be adapted for more complex command syntax using the SQL UNION operator discussed previously in this chapter.

Summary

In this chapter you learned the history and functional uses of SQL*Plus and saw an in-depth list of SQL*Plus commands with examples. You used these commands in a variety of ways to produce report and program output examples. Some of the features discussed in this chapter are not directly referenced in Oracle documentation.

Hopefully, you can utilize the skills and refer to the examples provided in this chapter in your application, design, and development of Oracle-based products.

SQL*DBA

7

by Kelly Leigh

IN THIS CHAPTER

The purpose of this chapter is to familiarize you with the basic, mid-level, and many advanced functions of SQL*DBA. It should also help you put that knowledge to use in your current and future environments. Although this chapter's coverage is not exhaustive, it should certainly give you all the requirements you need to forge ahead in understanding the more advanced concepts of database management with SQL*DBA.

> **NOTE**
>
> The following screen captures and sample programs come from a DG/UX Aviion 9500, 8-processor UNIX system running a DG/UX 5.4.3.10 MU02 operating system with Oracle RDBMS Version 7.1.4. The output or code could run differently on your system.

Introduction to Oracle SQL*DBA

To assist in the setup, administration, and day-to-day operations of your Oracle databases, Oracle Corporation provided a tool called SQL*DBA. Although SQL*DBA has many functions, its most obvious use is to start up and shut down local databases. If you have SQL*Net installed, SQL*DBA uses its features to start up and shut down remote databases as well. This versatility gives the database administrator great flexibility in database management.

Secondary functions of SQL*DBA include altering database and system statistics, modifying the characteristics of a database, administering users and security, restoring a database, and manipulating data files belonging to the databases. With the added capability to monitor various aspects of the database as it is running, SQL*DBA is an important and multifaceted tool.

SQL*DBA has three modes of operation:

- Line mode
- Command mode
- Menu mode

Line mode is a non-graphical interface that enables the user to interactively enter commands. The output is scrolled across the user's screen. This mode is very useful for managing portions of the database that do not require the ease of screen mode.

Command mode is identical to line mode with the exception of how it is used. Although line mode is interactive by nature, command mode is intended to run in batch mode. Generally, command mode is used to run a script, or collection of commands, created by the user.

Menu mode, also referred to as screen mode, is a graphical interface that you can use on supported ASCII terminals, including X terminals. It provides users with a menu-driven interface from which they can issue most SQL*DBA commands.

Although the menu interface is quite powerful, a handful of commands can only be executed from the command line. Table 7.1 contains a list of those commands. Screen mode supports all the commands that line mode supports in addition to a feature called monitor, which I discuss later in this chapter.

Table 7.1. SQL*DBA commands available only through the command line.

Command	Purpose
DESCRIBE	Describes tables and views
EXECUTE	Executes PL/SQL blocks
PRINT	Prints the value of a variable defined with the VARIABLE command
REMARK	Denotes a comment or remark and prevents the interpreter from executing the line
SET	Sets or modifies the characteristics of the current SQL*DBA session
SHOW	Shows characteristics of the current SQL*DBA session
VARIABLE	Defines a variable to be used within the current SQL*DBA session

Each of the modes is covered in greater detail in later sections. First, it is important to cover a few topics before proceeding to the commands.

The SQL*DBA Command Set

SQL*DBA accepts all standard SQL, PL/SQL, and SQL*DBA commands with few exceptions. Exceptions to this rule include SQL*Plus formatting commands such as set heading or set linesize. You can find a complete list of SQL*DBA specific commands in the command reference at the end of this chapter.

Before You Start SQL*DBA

There are several requirements to meet before you can run SQL*DBA. First, the user must either own the executable or be a member of the group associated with it. You can find the SQL*DBA executable in the bin directory of your ORACLE_HOME environment variable;

it's usually named sqldba (DOS-based systems might include an EXE or COM extension). If you are running Oracle on a DOS machine, the executable is located in the directory pointed to by your XBIN environment variable.

Once you can execute SQL*DBA, you must also have privileges to execute the specific commands you want to use. For instance, if you want to add a data file to a tablespace, you must have the ALTER TABLESPACE privilege.

Next, it is important to know how to connect to a database. Nearly all the commands supported by SQL*DBA require a connection to a database (especially startup and shutdown options).

Connecting to a Database

All SQL*DBA modes support the connect commands. With a username/password specification, you can connect to your default database. SQL*Net supports special connect strings to connect to remote databases on your network. You can use this option to eliminate the need for logging into every system where a database is running.

connect internal is the most typical connection using SQL*DBA. Internal, a special username viable only through SQL*DBA, is actually an alias for logging into the SYS account. Intended strictly for use with special operations such as startup and shutdown, the internal username is limited to users with the correct access to SQL*DBA (ownership and group access to the executable).

Terminating SQL*DBA Commands

SQL*DBA, like SQL*Plus, enables you to execute multiple-line commands. By default, you must terminate all commands with a semicolon (;) or forward slash (/), regardless of which mode you are using. These characters tell SQL*DBA to execute the command. Some commands might not require the terminator. If you press return while entering a command where SQL*DBA expects further input, SQL*DBA provides a continuation line for entering the next part of the command line. Entering the termination character ends the command and begins execution.

SQL*DBA Operation Modes

I mentioned the three modes of operation for SQL*DBA; only one major difference distinguishes the three modes. Screen mode is the only mode capable of running monitor programs that help you monitor various aspects of your instance. Apart from this difference, all three modes function identically. Commands that you can issue in line mode work identically when issued in either screen or command modes.

SQL*DBA in Line Mode

Line mode places the user into a line-driven, interactive interface. This mode does not support menus or additional input devices other than the keyboard. You usually use line mode for quick access to SQL*DBA commands or for automating different aspects of its functionality.

Because line and screen mode are identical in nature except for monitor commands, I limit the scope of this discussion on line mode to starting SQL*DBA in line mode, starting up and shutting down the database, and automating the startup and shutdown processes. The following section on screen mode goes into much greater depth about the commands available in SQL*DBA.

> **NOTE**
>
> Line mode is provided strictly for backward compatibility with older versions of Oracle. Oracle announced that it will not support SQL*DBA in future releases. At press time, SQL*DBA is still a supported product.

Starting SQL*DBA in Line Mode

To start SQL*DBA in line mode, you can enter one of the following commands: `sqldba mode=line` or `sqldba lmode=y`. After starting SQL*DBA, you should see a prompt that resembles `SQLDBA>`.

At this point, you can connect to the database using `connect internal` or `connect username/password`. Once you are finished with your SQL*DBA session, you can issue the `exit` command to leave.

> **NOTE**
>
> SQL*DBA is not case-sensitive unless you are dealing with the selection of data from the database. Upper- or lowercase letters are perfectly legitimate.

Startup and Shutdown with SQL*DBA in Line Mode

As stated before, the primary use for SQL*DBA is the startup and shutdown of your database. You can do this from line or screen mode, but it seems the most common way is from line mode.

> **NOTE**
>
> You cannot issue startup and shutdown commands from a connection via the Multi-Threaded Server. You must have a dedicated session to issue these commands. If running the Multi-Threaded Server, you must first disable the TWO_TASK environment variable before starting SQL*DBA.

To start up a database, use the following set of commands:

1. Start SQL*DBA by issuing the `sqldba` command.
2. Issue the CONNECT INTERNAL command to connect to the database.
3. Start the database using any of the STARTUP commands.
4. Exit SQL*DBA by typing EXIT.

You can substitute any one of the startup options for the STARTUP command listed in step 3, such as STARTUP MOUNT, or STARTUP FORCE. Later on, I discuss the startup and shutdown options in greater depth.

To shut down the database from line mode, use the following steps:

1. Start SQL*DBA by issuing the `sqldba` command.
2. Issue the CONNECT INTERNAL command to connect to the database.
3. Shut down the database using any of the SHUTDOWN commands.
4. Exit SQL*DBA by typing EXIT.

You can substitute other shutdown options for the SHUTDOWN option listed in step 3, depending on your site's needs. An example is using the SHUTDOWN IMMEDIATE command if you want to log out all processes connected to the database.

SQL*DBA in Command Mode

Command mode enables you to place a group of commands in the same file to be executed together. Various uses of command mode include starting up or shutting down an instance and collecting data for a custom report.

The format and execution of a command file for use in SQL*DBA is identical to the format of command files used in SQL*Plus. The following is a list of guidelines you can use for formatting a command file.

■ Although the SQL extension is not required, using it could help you identify the file in the future.

■ If any commands in your command file require you to be connected to the database, the first line should be CONNECT INTERNAL.

- You should terminate all single-line or multiple-line commands with ; or /. If the command is longer than a single line, only the last line of the command must have a ; or / terminating it.
- You can separate command lines with a return for readability.
- Scripts can call other scripts, but the depth of the nesting is operating-system dependent.
- The command mode does not require an EXIT command.

To call a command script while executing SQL*DBA, you can use the following command format:

```
sqldba command="@filename.sql"
```

SQL*DBA requires the quotes and the @ to execute the script properly. The following is a sample startup script:

```
REM
REM startup.sql to be used to automate the startup
REM of a database through SQL*DBA command mode
REM

connect internal;
startup;
```

With the preceding script, you can start up your database with the following command:

```
sqldba command="@startup.sql"
```

The following is a sample shutdown script:

```
REM
REM shutdown.sql to be used to automate the shutdown
REM of a database through SQL*DBA command mode

connect internal;
shutdown;
```

You can then execute this script in same way you executed startup.sql:

```
sqldba command="@shutdown.sql"
```

> **NOTE**
>
> Make sure that startup.sql and shutdown.sql reside in your current directory or somewhere within your path. If SQL*DBA cannot find your script, you are given an error and returned to a SQLDBA> prompt instead of your operating system prompt. It is a good idea to explicitly name the directory and file that you want to execute.
>
> You can further customize these scripts by adding startup and shutdown options (such as shutdown immediate) or SQL statements that show who is currently logged into the Oracle instance.

Automating the Startup and Shutdown Options

With a certain amount of operating system expertise, you can automate the startup and shut-down of your Oracle instance. This can be helpful if you have an operations staff that routinely must start and stop your database instances for basic maintenance (system reboot, offline backup, and so on).

The previous section discussed one possible way to automate startup or shutdown using command scripts. Another, more typical way is to embed these commands in a script that a system operator could run without any knowledge of Oracle commands or SQL*DBA modes. The following is a sample UNIX script for starting an Oracle instance:

```
#! /bin/sh
##########

# filename:  oracle_start.sh

#####
# As Oracle recommends, the first line is to force the script
# to run in the Bourne Shell.
#####


#####
# This script should be run from the Oracle DBA account.
# It assumes that ORACLE_HOME has been defined.  If it has not,
# this script will exit with the appropriate error message.
#
# Other assumptions include that your ORACLE_SID has been set before
# running this script.
#
#####

# If ORACLE_HOME = nothing then exit with a status of 1

if [ "${ORACLE_HOME}" = "" ]
  then
    echo "ORACLE_HOME is undefined.  It must be defined before"
    echo "continuing."
    exit 1
fi

# If ORACLE_SID is undefined, exit with a status of 2
if [ "${ORACLE_SID}" = "" ]
  then
    echo "ORACLE_SID is undefined.  It must be defined before"
    echo "continuing."
    exit 2
fi

# Check to see if the database is up
# if the sgadef(instance).dbf file is there, the instance is
# running and the startup should NOT proceed
```

```
if [ -f "${ORACLE_HOME}/dbs/${ORACLE_SID}.dbf" ]
  then
    echo "The ${ORACLE_SID} instance of Oracle is running"
    echo "You must shutdown before starting up."
    exit 3
fi

# The database is not running, so let's start it in normal mode
# using the script we defined in the preceding sections.
# If we cannot find sqldba, then we will exit with an error

if [ -f "${ORACLE_HOME}/bin/sqldba" ]
  then
    sqldba command="@startup.sql"
  else
    echo "Could not locate the sqldba executable.  Startup cannot"
    echo "proceed."
    exit 4
fi

# Now let's check to see if it came up.

if [ -f "${ORACLE_HOME}/dbs/${ORACLE_SID}.dbf" ]
  then
    echo "The instance has now started."
  else
    echo "The instance is NOT started.  Please check for errors "
    echo "before attempting to restart the database."
    exit 5
fi

exit 0

####################################
```

The following code is a sample shutdown script. This program is almost identical to the startup script except that is uses shutdown.sql and reverses the logic in checking for the sgadef (instance).dbf file.

```
#! /bin/sh
##########

# filename:  oracle_stop.sh

#####
# As Oracle recommends, the first line is to force the script
# to run in the Bourne Shell.
#####

#####
# This script should be run from the Oracle DBA account.
# It assumes that ORACLE_HOME has been defined.  If it has not,
# this script will exit with the appropriate error message.
#
# Other assumptions include that your ORACLE_SID has been set
# before running this script.
#
#####
```

```
# If ORACLE_HOME = nothing then exit with a status of 1

if [ "${ORACLE_HOME}" = "" ]
  then
    echo "ORACLE_HOME is undefined.  It must be defined before"
    echo "continuing."
    exit 1
fi

# If ORACLE_SID is undefined, exit with a status of 2
if [ "${ORACLE_SID}" = "" ]
  then
    echo "ORACLE_SID is undefined.  It must be defined before "
    echo "continuing."
    exit 2
fi

# Check to see if the database is down
# if the sgadef(instance).dbf file is not there, the instance is
# not running and the shutdown should exit

if [ ! -f "${ORACLE_HOME}/dbs/${ORACLE_SID}.dbf" ]
  then
    echo "The ${ORACLE_SID} instance of Oracle is not currently
    echo "running.  You must startup before you can shutdown."
    exit 3
fi

# The database is running, so let's do a normal shutdown
# using the script we defined in the preceding sections.
# If we cannot find sqldba, then we will exit with an error

if [ -f "${ORACLE_HOME}/bin/sqldba" ]
  then
    sqldba command="@shutdown.sql"
  else
    echo "Cannot locate sqldba.  Cannot continue the shutdown."
    exit 4
fi

# Now let's check to see if it was shut down

if [ -f "${ORACLE_HOME}/dbs/${ORACLE_SID}.dbf" ]
  then
    echo "The instance is still running, or an error"
    echo "occurred while trying to shutdown the instance."
    echo "Please refer to the alert log for any errors that"
    echo "might have occurred."
    exit 5
  else
    echo "The instance was shut down."
fi

exit 0

#########
```

SQL*DBA in Menu Mode

Although there are many arguments about whether a menu interface is faster or more efficient as opposed to an interactive line interface, there is no doubt that a menu interface is much easier to use. Otherwise, you'd have to face memorizing the myriad of commands that are available to SQL*DBA. First, I discuss the various components of the menu, and then, I discuss exactly what the menus do.

Parts of the Menu

There are four important parts of the display that are pointed out in Figure 7.1.

Menu bar   Output window

FIGURE 7.1.

SQL*DBA menu items.

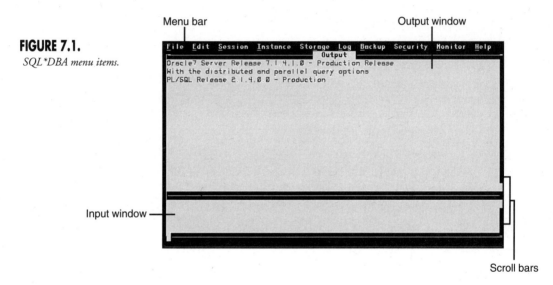

Input window

Scroll bars

On the menu bar across the top of your screen should appear ten choices: File, Edit, Session, Instance, Storage, Log, Backup, Security, Monitor, and Help. Each of these choices represents a menu or set of menus to assist in executing various SQL*DBA commands.

TIP

Notice that each option has a single underlined letter. These letters, or shortcut keys, are quick picks to the menu option. After navigating to the menu bar, you can type the underlined letter to display that menu selection. When you are familiar with the menus, this option makes menu selection much quicker.

Just below the menu bar is the output window. This window displays the output to each command you type and scrolls down as it fills.

The bottom of the screen is devoted to the input window, which is where you enter all input. The input window must be the current window to accept or display your keystrokes.

To the right of the output and input windows are two scroll bars (one for each window). These bars tell you where you are in the current windows and how much more information is left to display.

NOTE

You can tell which window is the active one by searching for your cursor. As you set your focus to different windows, your cursor follows.

Each menu could request more information, ask you to select specific options, or provide you with a list of items to choose from. In some versions of SQL*DBA and for some selections, you'll notice a keystroke command on the right of the menu option (Esc, P, for example). You can use that shortcut key as another way to reach the menu. The following lists the various types of objects associated with the different menus.

- Drop-down menus—Each menu item shown with a > to the right of the selection has a drop-down menu. The options help further define and limit the operation being performed.

- Alerts—At various times in your SQL*DBA session, an alert window might appear to caution you about the operation you are about to perform. These windows give you the chance to confirm or cancel the operation. Select the action that is appropriate.

- Dialog boxes/fields—These objects contain fields where you must enter specific data, such as role names and filenames. When the requested information is required, the word MANDATORY is displayed in the bottom-left corner. If there is a list associated with the menu item, the word LIST is displayed in the bottom-left corner as well.

- Data entry fields—Located inside dialog boxes, data entry fields enable you to enter values or select from a list of values.

- Radio buttons—A radio button is an option field indicated with ( ). You can select only one item in a list of radio buttons at a time. Use the spacebar to select or deselect the options.

- Checkboxes—A checkbox is an option field indicated with [ ]. You can check as many of these boxes as apply. As with radio buttons, you use the spacebar to select or deselect the option(s).

Navigating in SQL*DBA

If you don't know the navigational keystrokes, using SQL*DBA can be a difficult to nearly impossible task. All keys are defined through the Oracle*Terminal package and can be redefined by the user. The examples listed throughout this section use the default keystrokes for a VT-220 terminal.

Knowing how to get a complete listing of all keystrokes will put you far ahead in the game. Once in SQL*DBA, press Esc, K, or Ctrl+K. This places you in the Key Help for Text Editor window. There are two columns of data: Function and Keys. Function describes what the Keys (or keystroke) option does, and the Keys option shows the keystroke used to issue the command.

Table 7.2 contains a partial listing of the more critical commands required for navigating the menus. You can find a complete listing of Oracle's predefined functions by using the show keys command or by running Oracle*Terminal and examining the keys defined for your terminal type.

Table 7.2. Important SQL*DBA navigational keys for VT-220 terminals.

Function	Keys	Description
Cancel	PF4	Cancel the current operation (includes closing windows)
Menu	K0	Move to the menu bar (0 on your numeric keypad)
Next Group	Tab	Set focus on output or input windows (cycles through them)
Show Keys	Ctrl+K or Esc,K	Display complete table of keys and their functions
Arrow Keys	Up, Down, Left, Right	Navigate through the input, output, and menu screens

> **NOTE**
>
> The PF4 and K0 keys are VT-100 style keys. Generally, K0 is the 0 key on your numeric keypad. PF4 varies depending on the keyboard style, keyboard mapping, and terminal program, if applicable.

You use a typical navigation sequence when you start up your database. One way to accomplish this task is to issue the Menu command, use your arrow keys to move over to Instance, press Return, move your cursor over the Start Up command, press Return, and then follow the different prompts (navigating with the spacebar and tab keys), pressing Return when you reach OK.

Another quicker way is to issue the Menu command, press I (the underlined letter in Instance), press U (the underlined character in Start Up), and then navigate through the prompts until you get to OK.

Finally, you could issue the shortcut command Esc, P, navigate through the menu to choose your startup options, and select OK when finished.

As you can see, you can use many different options to navigate through the menus. The ways you choose to navigate depend on your familiarity with them and what kind of terminal you have. There is no right or wrong way, only preferred ways.

If you have a terminal that supports mouse input, one final way to use the menus is to move your cursor to the menu selection and click the mouse button.

SQL*DBA Menus

The menus in SQL*DBA provide almost the entire range of the command set. You must enter many different menus and options before a command is accepted and executed. Being familiar with these menus can greatly assist you in identifying and solving problems of all kinds. The following section explains the menus of SQL*DBA and how to use them. I also provide the actual line mode commands along with some tips on their uses.

> **TIP**
>
> Throughout all the menus, you will notice lines separating various menu options into related groups. For example, in the Security menu, you will notice lines between the User, Role, Profile, and Grant commands. These groupings are very helpful in identifying unknown menu options.

SQL*DBA File Menu

The File option, shown in Figure 7.2, has four separate options: SQL Script, Spool On, Spool Off, and Quit.

You use SQL Script to execute a SQL script file while still in SQL*DBA. After selecting this option, you are provided with a dialog box containing two options. The first is whether to Use Default File Path Name and File Extension. If you select this option, SQL*DBA searches through your path environment variable for the file. The second option is the SQL Script to Execute (Mandatory). You choose the name of the file to run. Specify the command on the line provided and select OK.

FIGURE 7.2.

*SQL*DBA File menu.*

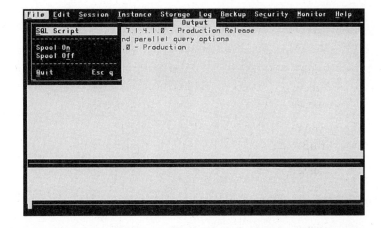

TIP

It is not necessary to place a SQL extension on the filename you specify. SQL*DBA automatically does this for you. If the file does not end with a SQL, however, you have to specify the correct extension. SQL*Plus script files do not have to end with a SQL.

After you select OK, the dialog box disappears, and the output scrolls down in the output window of your screen. Use the Next Group key to navigate to the output window to scroll through the output generated by your script.

Spool On requests a filename (mandatory) to send output to. This file is a log of all input and output generated during your SQL*DBA session with the exception of monitor output. Because the monitor output is changed every cycle, it cannot be saved to a spool file. You are limited to having only one spool file open at any time. If you attempt to spool to a second file, the first file closes before a second one opens.

> Command type: SQL*Plus
> Line mode command: SPOOL *filename*
> Required privileges: Write permissions for the current directory.

Spool Off closes the previously opened spool file (if any). SQL*DBA automatically keeps track of filenames and closes the currently open file. If you have no previously opened spool file, SQL*DBA generates an appropriate error message.

> Command type: SQL*Plus
> Line mode command: SPOOL OFF
> Required privileges: None

TIP

Use Spool On and Spool Off to log output of an interactive session and help create a command file that you can run from line mode, such as the commands generated by the SQL*DBA menus. This option is very helpful in setting up automated custom reports.

Quit, which had a shortcut of Esc, Q, brings up a caution window asking whether it is really OK to quit your session or if you want to cancel the quit session command. Selecting OK exits you to your operating system prompt.

> Command type: SQL*Plus, SQL*DBA
> Line mode command: EXIT
> QUIT
> Required privileges: None

SQL*DBA Edit Menu

The Edit menu in Figure 7.3 provides you with Cut and Paste commands, as well as Previous Command and Next Command options. Please note that there are no associated SQL*DBA commands for these options.

FIGURE 7.3.

Edit menu.

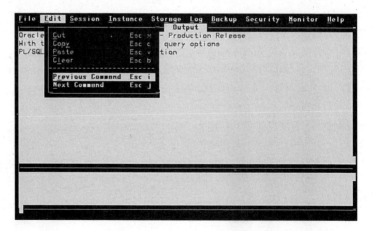

Choosing the Cut command cuts the currently selected text. Copy copies the previously selected text from the buffer to your current location in the menu. Paste copies the currently selected text into the edit buffer. Clear erases the currently selected text. It has no effect on the clipboard buffer.

Previous Command and Next Command both scroll through the last ten commands executed from the input window. Choosing these commands can be quicker than trying to retype one of your previous commands. Once you have selected the command you want to reissue, press Return to execute it.

> **TIP**
>
> The number of saved history commands is ten. You can modify this with the SET HISTORY command while in SQL*DBA. This setting is only effective for the current SQL*DBA session.

SQL*DBA Session Menu

Figure 7.4 shows the Session menu. The Connect command requests a username (mandatory) and a password in order to connect to the database. Specifying internal at the username data entry field connects you as a privileged user.

FIGURE 7.4.

Session menu.

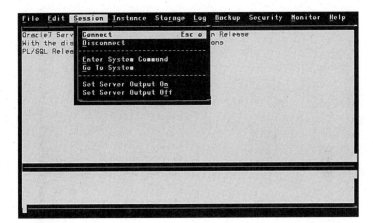

Command type: SQL*DBA
Line mode command: CONNECT
Required privileges: CREATE SESSION

Disconnect does the opposite of connect; that is, it disconnects you from the database. In this mode, you can issue only commands not requiring access to database tables.

Command type: SQL*DBA
Line mode command: DISCONNECT
Required privileges: None

Enter System Command (mandatory) enables you to execute operating system commands (or programs) from within SQL*DBA. Once this field is entered and accepted, you see an operating system window where the output from your command or program is displayed. Once the command finishes, you get a prompt to Hit Any Key to Continue. After pressing any key, you return to the SQL*DBA window.

> Command type: SQL*DBA
> Line mode command: HOST
> Required privileges: None

> **NOTE**
>
> When executing a command with the HOST option, SQL*DBA does not use any form of paging so that your output is displayed page by page. If you want this sort of option, you must add those commands, such as MORE or PG, to your host command.

Go to System takes you to an operating system window where you can enter multiple commands (as if you had exited SQL*DBA completely). It does not, however, make a complete copy of your environment, so some aliases or environment variables might not work or display correctly. You can figure this out by trial and error.

> Command type: SQL*DBA
> Line mode command: HOST
> Required privileges: None

Set Server Output On enables debugging output from stored procedures that use the DBMS_OUTPUT PUT() and PUT_LINE() commands. The size option enables you to specify, in bytes, the length of the message buffer that can be accumulated at one time. If the buffer fills before calls to get message can make more room for additional data, an error is returned to the program or procedure that is sending the message. The minimum for this buffer is 2,000 bytes.

> Command type: SQL*DBA
> Line mode command: SET SERVEROUT
> Required privileges: None

Set Server Output Off disables those messages. These two commands are very useful in coding debug information into your procedures.

> Command type: SQL*DBA
> Line mode command: SET SERVEROUT
> Required privileges: None

SQL*DBA Instance

The Instance menu options are shown in Figure 7.5. The menu enables you to start, stop, and configure various characteristics of how the instance will run. It has the following options: Start Up, Shut Down, Mount Database, Open Database, Force Checkpoint, Force Log Switch, Configure Dispatcher, Configure Shared Server, Prevent Connection, Allow Connection, and Kill Session.

FIGURE 7.5.

Instance menu.

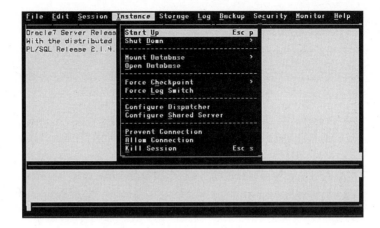

You use the Start Up option to mount and open the database for maintenance or use. You specify in the dialog box exactly how to bring this instance online.

> Command type: SQL*DBA
> Line mode command: STARTUP
> Required privileges: Capability to connect as INTERNAL

Shut Down enables you to specify one of three ways to bring your database down: Normal, Immediate, or Abort. These options are explained further in the command reference.

> Command type: SQL*DBA
> Line mode command: SHUTDOWN
> Required privileges: Capability to connect as INTERNAL

CAUTION

As mentioned throughout this chapter, you should use SHUTDOWN ABORT with *extreme* caution because it can cause data corruption!

Mount Database enables you to mount the database in either Exclusive mode (only a single instance can access the data files) or Parallel mode (multiple instances have access to the data). You must be running the Oracle Parallel Server option to make full use of the Parallel option.

> Command type: SQL*Plus
> Line mode command: ALTER DATABASE MOUNT
> Required privileges: Capability to connect as INTERNAL

The Open Database option enables you to bring the database from a mounted state to the open state. Even though the database might be mounted, the data is not accessible until it is in the open state.

Command type: SQL*Plus
Line mode command: ALTER DATABASE OPEN
Required privileges: Capability to connect as INTERNAL

You use Force Checkpoint to checkpoint either the local instance or all of the instances in your environment. If you are not running the Parallel Server option, both options work the same.

Command type: SQL*Plus
Line mode command: ALTER SYSTEM CHECKPOINT
Required privileges: ALTER SYSTEM

The Force Log Switch option forces the current instance to switch to the next available log file in the thread. Once the database has made the switch, the previous log group becomes available for archiving or maintenance.

Command type: SQL*Plus
Line mode command: ALTER SYSTEM SWITCH LOGFILE
Required privileges: ALTER SYSTEM

The next two commands are for Oracle's Multi-Threaded Server configuration (MTS).

Configure Dispatcher enables you to configure the number and type of running dispatchers. You can either add or remove dispatchers of various protocols to your system. This command effectively modifies the mts_servers parameter for the duration of the instance. It does not reset the MTS parameters in the INIT.ORA file, nor can it go beyond the value of mts_max_servers specified at startup (in the INIT.ORA file).

Command type: SQL*Plus
Line mode command: ALTER SYSTEM SET MTS_DISPATCHERS
Required privileges: ALTER SYSTEM

To configure the number of shared servers currently running, you can use the Configure Shared Server option. The dialog box that appears asks you how many shared server processes to run at one time, which must be in the range of mts_servers to mts_max_servers (found in your INIT.ORA file). You cannot go below or above these values.

Command type: SQL*Plus
Line mode command: ALTER SYSTEM SET MTS_SERVERS
Required privileges: ALTER SYSTEM

Prevent Connection enables you to limit connections to the database to only those users that have been granted the RESTRICTED SESSION privilege. Users without this privilege receive an error message stating that only specific users are permitted access.

Command type: SQL*Plus
Line mode command: ALTER SYSTEM ENABLE RESTRICTED SESSION
Required privileges: ALTER SYSTEM

Allow Connection enables all authorized users to gain access to the system again. These two commands are extremely helpful when you're doing database maintenance that requires the database to be online but unused.

> Command type: SQL*Plus
> Line mode command: ALTER SYSTEM DISABLE RESTRICTED SESSION
> Required privileges: ALTER SYSTEM

When you choose the Kill Session option, a dialog box appears listing all the current users, their session number, and their serial number. The combination of these two numbers provides a unique identification based upon a single user session, which you can use to monitor or kill the session.

> Command type: SQL*Plus
> Line mode command: ALTER SYSTEM KILL SESSION
> Required privileges: ALTER SYSTEM

SQL*DBA Storage Menu

The Storage menu enables you to manipulate all aspects of a tablespace or rollback segment, including creating and dropping them and choosing default storage options. This could be one of the most useful menus for database management.

Figure 7.6 displays the Tablespace drop-down menu under the Storage menu. The Tablespace option enables you to Create, Drop, Set Online, Set Offline, Add a Data File, Rename a Data File, and Modify Default Storage of database tablespaces.

FIGURE 7.6.

Tablespace drop-down menu.

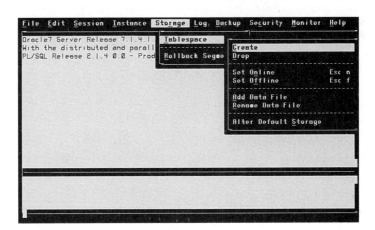

Tablespace Create creates a tablespace with the name you specify.

> Command type: SQL*Plus
> Line mode command: CREATE TABLESPACE
> Required privileges: CREATE TABLESPACE

Tablespace Drop drops the tablespace. If the tablespace is not empty (it contains tables or objects), you have to use the INCLUDING CONTENTS option.

> Command type: SQL*Plus
> Line mode command: DROP TABLESPACE
> Required privileges: DROP TABLESPACE

Set Online sets a tablespace online. This is the default, but if the instance starts up with errors or a tablespace requires recovery, the tablespace is offline.

> Command type: SQL*Plus
> Line mode command: ALTER TABLESPACE *tablespace* ONLINE
> Required privileges: ALTER TABLESPACE

Set Offline takes a tablespace offline. You use this primarily for database maintenance. There are three options in taking a tablespace offline:

- After Checkpointing—This option checks to ensure all data files belonging to the tablespace are writeable, runs the checkpointing process, and brings the tablespace offline once checkpoint is done. This corresponds to Normal mode.

- After Checkpointing Online Data Files—This option checks only the data files belonging to the tablespace that are online. Once that is finished, it begins the checkpoint process and brings the tablespace offline. This option does not wait for the checkpoint to finish, so media recovery might be necessary before you bring the tablespace back online. This corresponds to Immediate mode.

- Without Checkpointing—This option brings the tablespace offline immediately without waiting for a checkpoint. This option is helpful in beginning immediate maintenance on a tablespace. Media recovery is necessary to bring this tablespace online again. This option is only available if you are running your instance in ARCHIVELOG mode. This corresponds to Abort mode.

> Command type: SQL*Plus
> Line mode command: ALTER TABLESPACE *tablespace* OFFLINE
> Required privileges: ALTER TABLESPACE

Add Data File is useful for adding additional data to a tablespace that has grown beyond its first data file. Although it is better to have a single data file at the size you need, multiple data files are a short-term solution.

> Command type: SQL*Plus
> Line mode command: ALTER TABLESPACE *tablespace* ADD DATAFILE
> Required privileges: ALTER TABLESPACE

You use Rename Data File for relocating data files from one disk to another. This is extremely useful in tuning your database. For example, when you have several tablespaces that are active and reside on the same disk, you should move them apart to alleviate disk contention. It is important to note that this command does not rename or move the file. It only replaces the old name with the new name you specify. You must first take the tablespace offline and then use your operating system commands to relocate and rename the data file. Once you have done that, you can issue the database commands to rename the data file.

> Command type: SQL*Plus
> Line mode command: ALTER TABLESPACE *tablespace* RENAME FILE
> Required privileges: ALTER TABLESPACE and operating system privileges

Alter Default Storage modifies the storage options for the tablespace. These options include Percent Free, Percent Used, Initial Extents, and so on. If you create a table within a tablespace but do not give it any storage options, the new table gets the default storage options given to the tablespace.

> Command type: SQL*Plus
> Line mode command: ALTER TABLESPACE *tablespace* STORAGE
> Required privileges: ALTER TABLESPACE

The Rollback Segment drop-down menu, shown in Figure 7.7, enables you to manage the creation, deletion, and basic utilization of your rollback segments. The drop-down menu has the following options: Create, Drop, Set Online, Set Offline, and Alter Storage.

FIGURE 7.7.

Rollback drop-down menu.

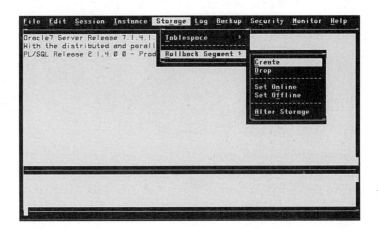

Create enables you to specify a rollback segment name, tablespace name, and storage options. You can create rollback segments as Public and Private. Public rollback segments are available to all instances sharing the database (Parallel Server option), and a Private rollback segment is used strictly for one instance.

> Command type: SQL*Plus
> Line mode command: CREATE ROLLBACK SEGMENT
> Required privileges: CREATE ROLLBACK SEGMENT

The Drop command deletes an offline rollback segment. If the rollback segment is still online, the operation fails with the following error message:

```
ORA-1545: rollback segment 'rbs01' specified not available
```

> Command type: SQL*Plus
> Line mode command: DROP ROLLBACK SEGMENT
> Required privileges: DROP ROLLBACK SEGMENT

Set Online takes an offline rollback segment and makes it available for use in the database. This operation takes effect immediately if the tablespace that the rollback segment resides in is currently usable.

> Command type: SQL*Plus
> Line mode command: ALTER ROLLBACK SEGMENT segment_name ONLINE
> Required privileges: ALTER ROLLBACK SEGMENT

Set Offline enables the DBA to take a rollback segment offline. This is very handy when you must drop and re-create a rollback segment that has reached maximum extents or when you relocate a rollback segment. If there are active transactions in the rollback segment, the database prevents new transactions from accessing the segment and waits until the current transactions are committed or rolled back before taking it offline.

> Command type: SQL*Plus
> Line mode command: ALTER ROLLBACK SEGMENT segment_name OFFLINE
> Required privileges: ALTER ROLLBACK SEGMENT

Alter Storage alters the default storage options of the rollback segment. You use this for next extents because you cannot change the initial extent once the rollback segment is created. In order to change the initial extent, you must drop the rollback segment and re-create it with the correct value.

> Command type: SQL*Plus
> Line mode command: ALTER ROLLBACK SEGMENT segment_name STORAGE
> Required privileges: ALTER ROLLBACK SEGMENT

SQL*DBA Log Menu

Figure 7.8 shows the Log menu. These log options control all aspects of the redo log files. Log files are a critical part of the online recovery method and are extremely important if you are running in ARCHIVELOG mode. In all databases, they can be a source of disk contention if your database is very active. If a redo log file is corrupted or lost and you are running in ARCHIVELOG mode, you cannot completely restore your database!

FIGURE 7.8.

Log menu.

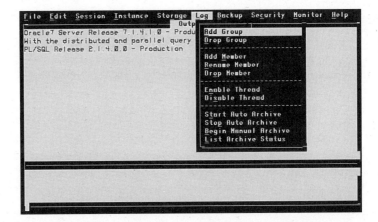

> **TIP**
>
> Split your redo log files across several disks to eliminate high amounts of disk I/O. In ARCHIVELOG mode, once a redo log fills and the log switches to another redo log file, the filled log is then written out to an archive log file. If your next redo log is on the same disk, there is added I/O while the filled log is written to disk and the new log is being written to. Alternating log files between two or more disks prevents this bottleneck from occurring.

A group is a set of mirrored redo log files that consists of one or more actual files. If you are using some form of disk mirroring or RAID technology, it is unnecessary to have more than one file per group because your system automatically employs a recovery method if you lose a disk where the redo logs reside.

The Add and Drop Group options on the Log menu enable you to add or remove groups from your currently running database. This is extremely helpful if you find that you are filling log files faster than they are written to disk.

The Add Group command enables you to add a group to your currently running database.

> Command type: SQL*Plus
> Line mode command: ALTER DATABASE ADD LOGFILE GROUP
> Required privileges: ALTER DATABASE

The Drop Group command enables you to drop an entire log file group from the database. This does not remove the files, however. The files can be reused (specifying REUSE instead of SIZE 50K in a creation statement) or deleted through your operating system commands if the files should be deleted. The Drop Group option is useful in helping to eliminate disk contention as well as increasing the number of redo log files available for a database.

Command type: SQL*Plus
Line mode command: ALTER DATABASE DROP LOGFILE GROUP
Required privileges: ALTER DATABASE

Each redo log file of a group is considered a member, and for consistency within each group, there should be an equal number of members. This is not a requirement but a suggestion. If you are running a mirrored or RAID system, it is unnecessary to have more than one member per group because the system is handling the mirroring. Adding or removing members is helpful in defining a high availability system.

> **NOTE**
>
> Creating multiple group members provides a form of failsafe should you have a disk failure. If you lose all the files in a redo log group, the database halts when trying to write to that group. If you place group members on separate disks, Oracle marks that file as offline but continues to function if one disk fails.
>
> By the nature of mirrored or RAID systems, should a single disk fail, the other members of the mirror or RAID group should still function. Because adding multiple members provides this same type of failsafe, you can eliminate the overhead of maintaining more than one redo log file without sacrificing the failsafe of a single point of failure.

To use the Add Member option, you need to decide on the name of the file and which group you want to add it to.

Command type: SQL*Plus
Line mode command: ALTER DATABASE ADD LOGFILE MEMBER
Required privileges: ALTER DATABASE

The RENAME MEMBER option is really just the RENAME DATA FILE command in disguise. As with the RENAME DATA FILE command, RENAME MEMBER only associates the name of the redo log member with a new file name inside the database. The member must be offline, and before you issue the RENAME MEMBER command, you must use your operating system commands to relocate or rename the data files in question.

Command type: SQL*Plus
Line mode command: ALTER DATABASE RENAME FILE
Required privileges: ALTER DATABASE

Using the Drop Member option is helpful if you are reconfiguring your system to use mirrored disks and want to reclaim disk space or if you are resizing your group files. The group the member is in must be offline before you can drop it.

Command type: SQL*Plus
Line mode command: ALTER DATABASE DROP LOGFILE MEMBER
Required privileges: ALTER DATABASE

A thread is a collection of two or more redo log groups. Together, these groups form a sequence of log files that the database rotates through. When one log file or group is filled, the database switches to the next group. When it reaches the last group in the thread, it cycles back to the first.

A single database that is not running in Parallel Server mode has only one thread. If a database is running in parallel, there should be one thread for each instance accessing the database. Public and Private denote the type of access for a given thread. Private means the thread is reserved for a specific instance, and Public means the thread is available for any instance to reserve at startup, if the instance does not specifically request a certain thread.

Using the Enable Thread option makes a thread available for the next instance that requests it.

Command type: SQL*Plus
Line mode command: ALTER DATABASE ENABLE THREAD
Required privileges: ALTER DATABASE

You use the Disable Thread option to take a thread offline for maintenance or to make it available for another instance. If an instance has the thread in question mounted, the command fails.

Command type: SQL*Plus
Line mode command: ALTER DATABASE DISABLE THREAD
Required privileges: ALTER DATABASE

The Start, Stop, Begin, and List Archive options refer directly to archiving redo logs to disk. Automatic archiving enables the database to write the contents of a filled (or manually switched) log file to disk and free up the redo log for use.

Start Auto Archive tells the system to automatically write data from the redo logs to disk when it's finished with the redo log. You must specify a location and the beginning part of the filename. You can do this either in the INIT file for the database or on the command line when you start Auto Archive mode.

Command type: SQL*Plus
Line mode command: ALTER SYSTEM ARCHIVE LOG START
Required privileges: ALTER SYSTEM

Stop Auto Archive disables the system from writing filled log files to disk. If you are extremely low on disk space or you're monitoring certain aspects of the database, this option can be helpful while you relocate files.

Command type: SQL*Plus
Line mode command: ALTER SYSTEM ARCHIVE LOG STOP
Required privileges: ALTER SYSTEM

Use Begin Manual Archive if you are not running in automatic archive log mode and you want to start writing redo logs to disk. The system can write redo logs according to age, change number, group and thread numbers, or all of these designations.

> Command type: SQL*Plus
> Line mode command: ALTER SYSTEM ARCHIVE LOG
> Required privileges: ALTER SYSTEM

The List Archive Status command lists the status of archiving for the current instance. Use this command to verify the status of the archive mode as well as find out current sequence numbers and the location that the archived redo logs are written to.

> Command type: SQL*Plus
> Line mode command: ARCHIVE LOG LIST
> Required privileges: Capability to connect as INTERNAL, OSOPER, or OSDBA

SQL*DBA Backup Menu

Figure 7.9 shows the Backup menu for SQL*DBA. The options on this menu include Begin Online Tablespace Backup, End Online Tablespace Backup, Recover Database, Recover Tablespace, and Recover Data File.

FIGURE 7.9.

Backup menu.

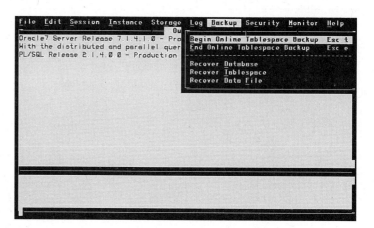

You use the backup options when you are running in ARCHIVELOG mode and you want to begin a hot backup of your data files.

To begin a tablespace backup, you must know the tablespace name. Once you issue the Begin Backup command, you can safely use your operating system commands to back up the data files that make up the tablespace.

> Command type: SQL*Plus
> Line mode command: ALTER TABLESPACE *tablespace* BEGIN BACKUP
> Required privileges: ALTER TABLESPACE

Use the End Online Tablespace Backup option when you are finished with the backup of the tablespace.

> Command type: SQL*Plus
> Line mode command: ALTER TABLESPACE *tablespace* END BACKUP
> Required privileges: ALTER TABLESPACE

CAUTION

It is usually not a good idea to set all your tablespaces to backup mode at the same time. If you have a system crash while a tablespace is in backup mode, you have to recover before you can bring the tablespace online again.

You use the Recover options to bring the database back to a usable state after some sort of database or system failure. Each option deals with a specific type of recovery. If you're running in ARCHIVELOG mode and all the archived redo log files needed for recovery are available, you can recover the database to its final state before the crash. Other recovery options provide recovery to the point where it is canceled by the operator, to a certain date and time specified by the operator, or to a specific change number. These options apply only to database and tablespace recovery. When you attempt to start an instance and recovery is required, the instance notifies you about which type of recovery is necessary.

You use Recover Database to recover the entire database. For example, you can restore all the data files and archived redo logs from tape after a serious disk failure. Once the data files and redo logs are recovered from media, you must use the recover commands to bring the database into a usable state.

> Command type: SQL*DBA
> Line mode command: RECOVER DATABASE
> Required privileges: ALTER DATABASE

You can use Recover Tablespace if you have a single disk failure and must restore all a tablespace's data files from backup. Once the files are restored to their original locations, you can issue the recover command to have the database apply redo log information to bring the tablespace online. This recovery can take place while the database is online, but all tables in the given tablespaces are unavailable for use until recovery is complete.

> Command type: SQL*DBA
> Line mode command: RECOVER TABLESPACE
> Required privileges: ALTER DATABASE

You must use Recover Data File if you have accidentally overwritten or erased a data file or if you've had a form of media failure that does not affect all the data files in a particular tablespace. Once the data file is restored, you can issue the RESTORE DATAFILE command and then bring the tablespace back online.

Command type: SQL*DBA
Line mode command: RECOVER DATAFILE
Required privileges: ALTER DATABASE

SQL*DBA Security Menu

You use the Security menu to define how and to whom you grant access to the database and its data. Through your work with user accounts, you can audit and limit data access and resource utilization. Profiles limit the amount of resources that are available to certain individuals. Roles enable you to manage table and object access by creating groups (roles), granting access to those groups, and then giving access to the group to specific users. Figure 7.10 shows the Security menu.

FIGURE 7.10.

Security menu.

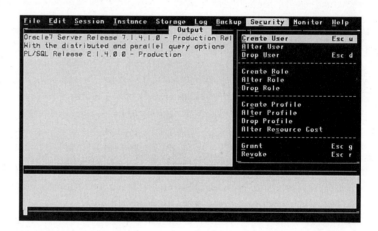

You can use the Create, Alter, and Drop User options to speed the creation or deletion of a user in the database. From these menus, you have the capability to manipulate all aspects of a user's definition.

Create User creates a database user and specifies all the parameters needed to begin working in that account. Specific information includes the user name, type of authentication, default and temporary tablespaces, quota limit, and profile (if any).

Command type: SQL*Plus
Line mode command: CREATE USER
Required privileges: CREATE USER

Alter User is nearly identical to Create User except for the Roles option. From here, you can define a default role for the user you are modifying. Use this option to change a user's characteristics.

Command type: SQL*Plus
Line mode command: ALTER USER
Required privileges: ALTER USER

You use Drop User to remove a user and possibly all tables owned by that user from the database. In order to remove a user, you must drop all the objects owned by that user either manually or with the CASCADE option.

Command type: SQL*Plus
Line mode command: DROP USER
Required privileges: DROP USER

You use the Create, Alter, and Drop Role options to define a role and how it is authenticated. You must use the grant options from the Security menu to grant table access to role names or to grant roles to users.

Command type: SQL*Plus
Line mode command: CREATE ROLE
Required privileges: CREATE ROLE

You use Alter Role to change the type of authentication for a given role. You can create roles to require passwords before a user is granted the role's access definitions.

Command type: SQL*Plus
Line mode command: ALTER ROLE
Required privileges: ALTER ANY ROLE

Using Drop Role removes the role name and all references to that role from the database. Any users who had this role granted to them will effectively have that role revoked.

Command type: SQL*Plus
Line mode command: DROP ROLE
Required privileges: DROP ANY ROLE

Profiles enable you to limit the use of specific system and database resources. There are nine limitations you can set, and a user can belong to only one profile. If a user is not defined with a profile, there are no limitations to the amount of resources available to that user. This is the default.

CREATE PROFILE creates a profile with the name and limits you specify. For resource limits not specified in the creation of the profile, the database uses its own default value, which is usually unlimited unless you change resource costs. You can modify resource costs from the Security menu by using the option Alter Resource Cost.

Command type: SQL*Plus
Line mode command: CREATE PROFILE
Required privileges: CREATE PROFILE

Alter Profile works in the same way as Create Profile, but you are given a list of the values for existing profiles. You must first select an existing profile before you can modify it.

> Command type: SQL*Plus
> Line mode command: ALTER PROFILE
> Required privileges: ALTER PROFILE

NOTE

> It is important to note that when you're altering a profile and you have selected the profile from the menu, although a list of standard values is provided, they do not reflect the current values for the profile. The only way to find the current values for the profile is to query the SYS.PROFILE table or the DBA_PROFILES view.

You use Drop Profile to remove all traces of the profile from the database. Unlike with dropping roles, you must specify the CASCADE option if a user has been assigned the profile you want to drop.

> Command type: SQL*Plus
> Line mode command: DROP PROFILE
> Required privileges: DROP PROFILE

For each resource listed in a profile, there is a resource cost associated with it. Oracle uses a formula to calculate each resource's cost in order to limit usage as defined in the profile. There are four resources that the DBA can modify: CPU Time/Session, Connect Time, Logical Reads/ Session, and Private SGA/Session. (Private SGA is for instances running in Multi-Threaded Server mode.) The default value for each resource is 0. These costs are actually weights. If a site decides that CPU should be weighted higher in resources than disk I/O, you can start the menu or enter the command from the command line and enter a higher value (5 for instance), which would weight CPU usage higher than disk I/O in resource cost. This is helpful for systems with slower CPUs or possibly slower disk access. By limiting resource usage, you can gain greater control over how the system is used.

> Command type: SQL*Plus
> Line mode command: ALTER RESOURCE COST
> Required privileges: ALTER RESOURCE COST

You use Grant and Revoke to limit access to data within the database. You can grant a role to users and grant access to objects to roles.

> Command type: SQL*Plus
> Line mode command: GRANT
> Required privileges: GRANT ANY ROLE or ADMIN access to the role being granted

---

CAUTION

Be careful with the ADMIN option. Users granted a role with the ADMIN option can grant that role to other users when you might not want to have that level of access.

Revoke removes access to the specified role or object.

> Command type: SQL*Plus
> Line mode command: REVOKE
> Required privileges: GRANT ANY ROLE or ADMIN access to the role being revoked

SQL*DBA Monitor Menu

The Monitor menu, which is shown in Figure 7.11, enables the developer or DBA (based on database privileges) to monitor various aspects of the database, such as aspects of the Multi-Threaded Server, sessions connected to the database, table access, SQL statements cached in the SGA, locks, file I/O, and so on. The Monitor option is not available in any other package supplied by Oracle (with the exception of Server Manager, Oracle's X-Window replacement for SQL*DBA).

FIGURE 7.11.

Monitor menu.

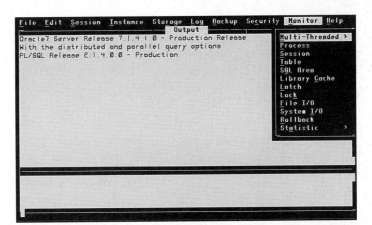

NOTE

Privileges to run the monitor commands are based on access to views created by the CATALOG.SQL file and access to various performance-based tables and views owned by SYS. If you are having problems using the monitoring commands and you have access to these tables and views, make sure that you have issued a CONNECT INTERNAL

> command and have successfully connected to the database. If you still have problems, contact Oracle support for assistance.

The Multi-Threaded option monitors shared servers, dispatchers, circuits, and queues. The options help you correctly configure the number of shared servers and dispatchers required for your environment. Too many shared servers and you are using excess memory; too few and users begin to see unnecessary wait times.

Monitoring the shared servers enables you to filter the monitor output based on server name or the status. Keep a close eye on status, total idle time, and load. If load is high and idle time is high, you might experience system bottleneck (CPU or memory).

> Command type: SQL*DBA
> Line mode command: MONITOR SHARED
> Required privileges: Access to V$SHARED_SERVER

When monitoring dispatchers, you get up-to-date information on how each dispatcher is running. Keep an eye out for load and status. If the load is too high, the dispatcher might be having trouble keeping up with the requests it has to send out to the servers. Adding more dispatchers might alleviate the problem.

> Command type: SQL*DBA
> Line mode command: MONITOR DISPATCHER
> Required privileges: Access to V$DISPATCHER

Monitoring circuits shows the virtual circuits that are related to the shared servers. These circuits are the means by which users are connected to the database. This screen links a user back to a shared server and dispatcher.

> Command type: SQL*DBA
> Line mode command: MONITOR CIRCUIT
> Required privileges: Access to V$CIRCUIT, V$DISPATCHER, V$SESSION, V$SHARED_SERVER

Monitoring queues gives you a look at the queue of requests that are handled by the Multi-Threaded Server. If the average wait time is high, you might need to add more dispatchers.

> Command type: SQL*DBA
> Line mode command: MONITOR QUEUE
> Required privileges: Access to V$QUEUE

Choosing the Process option gives you valuable information on the user and instance processes currently running. One of the key portions of this screen is Latch Waited. If a user is waiting on a latch, you could be having resource problems.

Command type: SQL*DBA
Line mode command: MONITOR PROCESS
Required privileges: Access to V$PROCESS

The Session monitor gives you information on each session connected to the database. Key points of the session output are session ID and process ID (used for kill session commands) and lock waited. If a user is waiting on a lock, his session appears to hang.

Command type: SQL*DBA
Line mode command: MONITOR SESSION
Required privileges: Access to V$PROCESS, V$SESSION

If you choose to monitor a table, you can find out the level of I/O that each table incurs. This is extremely important in alleviating disk bottlenecks. If possible, you should move I/O intensive tables to separate disks from each other.

Command type: SQL*DBA
Line mode command: MONITOR TABLE
Required privileges: Access to V$ACCESS

Monitoring the SQL Area helps you tune your custom applications. Because SQL is case-sensitive, two identical SQL statements that differ only by a single upper- or lowercase character are parsed and cached separately.

Command type: SQL*DBA
Line mode command: MONITOR SQLAREA
Required privileges: Access to V$SQLAREA

Library Cache monitoring is important because it can tell you how well your SGA is sized. It is important to keep an eye on the name space and the hit ratios associated with them. If the hit ratios are low, the database is forced to reparse and recache SQL statements back into the SGA.

Command type: SQL*DBA
Line mode command: MONITOR LCACHE
Required privileges: Access to V$LIBRARYCACHE

Latches are similar to locks, but their life spans are very short. The Latch option enables you to monitor the types of latches and their statistics.

Command type: SQL*DBA
Line mode command: MONITOR LATCH
Required privileges: Access to V$LATCH, V$LATCHHOLDER, V$LATCHNAME

Locking problems can be extremely difficult to resolve, especially in custom applications. Using the Lock monitor shows you who has locks and who is requesting them. If a process has Mode Requested listed on the right-hand side for a long period of time, you might be experiencing locking problems. It means that the user is requesting some sort of lock on the object, but the object is locked by another user. It is not uncommon for users to wait on locks, but depending on the wait time, it might warrant further investigation.

> Command type: SQL*DBA
> Line mode command: MONITOR LOCK
> Required privileges: Access to V$LOCK, V$PROCESS, V$SESSION

File I/O monitoring can be helpful in finding data files that have high I/O rates associated with them. Knowing which tablespaces and data files have the highest access rates is very helpful in eliminating disk contention.

> Command type: SQL*DBA
> Line mode command: MONITOR FILEIO
> Required privileges: Access to V$DBFILE, V$FILESTAT

If the database is running abnormally slow, it is likely that a user is running a large, I/O-intensive query. Monitoring System I/O is extremely useful in identifying users or processes with high I/O rates.

> Command type: SQL*DBA
> Line mode command: MONITOR SYSTEMIO
> Required privileges: Access to V$PROCESS, V$SESSION, V$SESSTAT

You should monitor Rollback segments to help reduce rollback segment contention. It is also important to notice the number of active transactions in each rollback segment. There is a database parameter that defines how many active transactions are allowed per rollback segment. If this limit is reached, an error can result. It is also important to see how the rollback segment is extending and shrinking and how many extents each segment has.

> Command type: SQL*DBA
> Line mode command: MONITOR ROLLBACK
> Required privileges: Access to V$ROLLNAME, V$ROLLSTAT

Session and system statistics are gathered by session ID and overall database statistics. You can do each type of monitoring on a combination of user, redo, enqueue, cache, parallel server, and SQL statistics.

Session statistics are based on each session connected to the database.

> Command type: SQL*DBA
> Line mode command: MONITOR SESSIONSTATISTIC
> Required privileges: Access to V$SESSTAT, V$SYSSTAT

System statistics are based on the current instance.

> Command type: SQL*DBA
> Line mode command: MONITOR SYSTEMSTATISTIC
> Required privileges: Access to V$SYSSTAT

SQL*DBA Help Menu

The Help menu is designed to give the user brief help on the commands and topics listed within the menu. Intended to be a brief introduction to the topics, the menu refers you to various Oracle manuals for further assistance. Figure 7.12 shows the Help menu.

FIGURE 7.12.

Help menu.

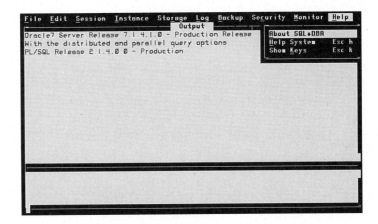

The About SQL*DBA option gives you information on version numbers of some of the products associated with your current version of the Oracle instance. There is no command associated with this option.

Show Keys gives you a menu of keys and their functions.

> Command type: SQL*DBA
> Line mode command: HELP
> Required privileges: None

SQL*DBA Command Reference

The following list contains SQL*DBA specific commands and their syntax. For more information on SQL*Plus specific commands, refer to Chapter 6, "SQL*Plus." The following commands are listed in alphabetical order.

ARCHIVE LOG

Description: The ARCHIVE LOG command controls the starting and stopping of the automatic archiving of used redo logs and displays the current status of archive logging.

Command syntax:

```
ARCHIVE LOG
     LIST
     STOP
     START     TO  filename
     NEXT      TO  filename
     ALL       TO  filename
     integer   TO  filename
```

Keywords:

LIST   Displays the current status of archive logging. The output includes log mode, automatic archival, the archive destination, the oldest online log sequence, the next sequence to archive, and the current sequence number. If the oldest online log sequence and the current log sequence numbers are different, either automatic archiving has been disabled or the previous log files have not been archived yet.

START   Enables automatic archiving, which is controlled by the ARCH process.

STOP   Disables automatic archiving.

NEXT   Manually archives the next redo groups that have not been archived.

ALL   Archives all redo groups that have not been archived.

integer   Archives the log file with the sequence number integer stored in it. If the sequence number is invalid, an error is given.

filename   Refers to the instance specific destination file or device for the log files to be written to.

Examples:

```
ARCHIVE LOG LIST;
ARCHIVE LOG START;
ARCHIVE LOG 10982 '/u01/app/oracle/admin/dev/arch/dev'
```

CONNECT

Description: You use the CONNECT command to connect to the database. Most SQL*DBA functions require that the user be connected before using them.

Command syntax:

```
CONNECT username/password
CONNECT username/password@instance
CONNECT INTERNAL
```

Keywords:

username   The user ID to connect to. It must be a valid account.

password   The password the account is identified with.

`instance`	The instance name or connect string of the destination instance. This can be either the name of a database link, an alias created in SQL*Net Version 2, or the direct connect string specifying `driver:system:instance_name`.
`INTERNAL`	A privileged login used for many higher level commands such as startup and shutdown. This login is an alias for SYS.

Example:

```
CONNECT INTERNAL;
CONNECT SYSTEM/MANAGER;
CONNECT SCOTT/TIGER;
```

DISCONNECT

Description: You use the DISCONNECT command to disconnect from the current instance without exiting SQL*DBA. It has no additional parameters. You can use this command in conjunction with SET INSTANCE to access multiple instances at your site without exiting and reentering SQL*DBA.

Command syntax:

```
DISCONNECT
```

Example:

```
DISCONNECT;
```

EXECUTE

Description: You use EXECUTE to execute a one-line PL/SQL statement. If you want to execute more than one line, you must use the BEGIN ... END format for PL/SQL. You must also be connected to a database before executing.

Command syntax:

```
EXECUTE PL/SQL statement
```

Example:

```
EXECUTE total_orders;
```

EXIT

Description: EXIT is the command you use to exit the SQL*DBA session. It automatically disconnects you from the current database if a connection has been established. This command has no parameters or keywords.

Command syntax:

```
EXIT
```

Example:

```
EXIT;
```

HOST

Description: The HOST command executes an operating system command or program while you're still in SQL*DBA. This command shells you out of SQL*DBA for the duration of the command. If issued by itself, it shells you to the operating system until you type EXIT to return to SQL*DBA.

Command syntax:

```
HOST operating system command
HOST
```

Keywords:

> `operating system command`   A valid operating system command or program.

Examples:

```
HOST who;
HOST dir;
HOST;
```

MONITOR

Description: The MONITOR command enables you to monitor various statistics and attributes of the database, processes, or users. This command is extremely helpful in analyzing and resolving database problems. You can specify any parameters that the menu requests in order on the command line.

Command syntax:

```
MONITOR    CIRCUIT
           DISPATCHER
           FILEIO
           LATCH
           LCACHE
           LOCK
           PROCESS
           QUEUE
           ROLLBACK
           SESSION
           SESSIONSTATISTIC
           SHARED
           SQLAREA
           SYSTEMIO
           SYSTEMSTATISTIC
           TABLE
```

Keywords:

CIRCUIT	Displays current information on the virtual circuits owned by each shared server in a Multi-Threaded Server environment.
DISPATCHER	Displays current information about a shared server's dispatcher processes in a Multi-Threaded Server environment.
FILEIO	Displays read/write information for every database file associated with the current instance.
LATCH	Displays information on all current latches.
LCACHE	Displays current information on the library cache.
LOCK	Lists the current processes and the locks they are waiting on. Using ALL lists all locks being held by current processes.
PROCESS	Monitors summary information for every process connected to the current instance.
QUEUE	Lists information on each shared server's message queues.
ROLLBACK	Shows activity on every active rollback segment in the instance.
SESSION	Displays active process information.
SESSIONSTATISTIC	Shows user session statistics for current user processes.
SHARED	Monitors shared server activity.
SQLAREA	Gives various statistics on the shared SQL area.
SYSTEMIO	Summarizes the read/write statistics for each Oracle process. This information is not precise but instead is representative of relative distribution of I/O.
SYSTEMSTATISTIC	Shows system statistics for the current database.
TABLE	Displays table names of tables referenced in SQL statements that have been recently parsed and reside in the shared SQL area.

Examples:

```
MONITOR PROCESS;
MONITOR LATCH;
MONITOR LOCK 10 20;
MONITOR SYSTEMSTATISTIC;
```

PRINT

Description: The PRINT command prints the value of a variable that you defined using the SQL*Plus command VARIABLE.

Command syntax:

```
PRINT variable
```

Keywords:

> `variable`   The name of the variable defined with the VARIABLE command.

Examples:

```
PRINT COUNTER;
PRINT    NAME;
```

RECOVER

Description: You use the RECOVER command to perform media recovery on data files, tablespaces, or entire databases as required. You must be connected as INTERNAL to use this command, and you must have a dedicated process. You cannot be connected through Oracle's Multi-Threaded Server.

Command syntax:

```
RECOVER DATABASE
RECOVER DATABASE UNTIL
                    CANCEL
                    CHANGE integer
                    TIME date
RECOVER DATABASE USING BACKUP CONTROLFILE
RECOVER TABLESPACE tablespace
RECOVER DATAFILE filename
```

Keywords:

DATABASE	Requests the recovery of an entire database. Will apply redo log files to all tablespaces needing media recovery.
UNTIL TIME date	Used to specify an incomplete RECOVER to a specific time. You must specify the date in the following format: `'YYYY-MM-DD:HH24:MI:SS'` YYYY is a four-digit year. MM is a two-digit month. HH24 is the time in 24-hour specification. MI is minutes. SS is seconds.
UNTIL CHANGE integer	Used to recover until a specific change number. This is very useful in restoring a tablespace where a table was accidentally dropped. integer must be a valid change number, and the redo logs must be available to Oracle.

`UNTIL CANCEL`	Specifies recovery should continue applying redo logs until the operator cancels the operation. Recovery continues redo log by redo log until canceled.
`USING BACKUP CONTROLFILE`	Tells the database to use a backup version of the control file instead of the primary one. This control file must be available to Oracle, or the command will fail.
`TABLESPACE tablespace`	Recovers the specified tablespace, or tablespaces. You can recover up to 16 of them in a single statement.
`DATAFILE filename`	Specifies a particular data file belonging to a tablespace that you want to restore. There is no limit to the number of data files you can recover in a given statement.

Examples:

```
RECOVER TABLESPACE tools;
RECOVER DATABASE;
RECOVER DATAFILE 'users_01.dbf';
RECOVER DATABASE UNTIL '1994-10-11:15:01:00';
RECOVER TABLESPACE tools, users;
```

SET

Description: The SET command sets characteristics for the current SQL*DBA session. These characteristics are not saved for future sessions.

Command syntax:

```
SET ARRAYSIZE integer
    AUTORECOVERY ON/OFF
    CHARWIDTH integer
    COMPATIBILITY V6/V7
    CYCLE integer
    DATEWIDTH integer
    ECHO ON/OFF
    FETCHROWS integer
    HISTORY integer
    INSTANCE instance-path/LOCAL
    LABWIDTH
    LINES integer
    LOGSOURCE pathname/DEFAULT
    LONGWIDTH integer
    MAXDATA integer
    NUMWIDTH integer
    RETRIES integer/INFINITE
    SERVER OUTPUT OFF/ON SIZE integer
    SPOOL filename/OFF
    STOPONERROR ON/OFF
    TERM PAGE/NOPAGE
    TERMOUT ON/OFF
    TIMING ON/OFF
```

Keywords:

ARRAYSIZE *integer*	Indicates the number of rows that are fetched from the database at one time. The default is 20, and the maximum is specific to the operating system you are running.
AUTORECOVERY	Tells the database to automatically apply all redo logs necessary to bring the database, tablespace, or data file to a usable state. When this is ON, the database begins recovery without requesting input from the operator. Log filenames are derived from the database parameters LOG_ARCHIVE_DEST and LOG_ARCHIVE_FORMAT. If the files cannot be located, operator input is requested.
CHARWIDTH *integer*	Defines the column width displayed for columns of type CHAR. The default is 80, and if no integer is specified, the parameter is reset to 80.
COMPATIBILITY V6/V7	Sets the SQL*DBA compatibility mode to either Version 6 or Version 7. This parameter affects how you specify columns of type CHAR, integrity constraint definitions, and the storage parameters for rollback segments.
CYCLE *integer*	Used for the MONITOR command, sets the time that the monitor screens cycle in gathering statistics. The default is 5 seconds. The minimum is 1 second; maximum is 3,600 seconds. The smaller the number, the higher the impact on the database.
DATEWIDTH *integer*	Sets the width for DATE data to be displayed. The default is 9, and if entered with no integer, it is reset to 9. The range of values for this parameter is operating-system specific.
ECHO ON/OFF	Enables echoing of commands that are executed from command files. The default is OFF. In this mode, only the output is displayed.
FETCHROWS *integer*	This parameter limits the number of rows that are returned by a database query. It can be very useful in returning only the first 20 or 10 rows from a database table. The default

returns all rows that match the given criteria, and as with all other parameters, entering the SET command without an *integer* resets the value to all.

HISTORY *integer*

Sets the number of SQL*DBA commands saved in the history buffer. Any commands that reside in this buffer can be recalled and reexecuted using the Previous and Next Command options in menu mode. The default is 10 commands.

INSTANCE *instance-path*/LOCAL

Sets the instance name to where all SQL*DBA commands are applied. The *instance-path* is defined by a system node name and database name separated with a hyphen. A sample connect string is my_host-my_database. Issuing the command with no database definition resets the instance back to the local default instance.

LABWIDTH

Used strictly with Oracle's Trusted Server package.

LINES *integer*

Limits the number of lines the output window of SQL*DBA can store and recall. After reaching the limit, the lines at the beginning of the buffer are erased. The default value is 1,000.

LOGSOURCE *pathname*/DEFAULT

Tells Oracle where to find archived redo logs to be used during a recovery session. Use this to set the location to a temporary location where redo logs have been restored.

LONGWIDTH *integer*

Tells SQL*DBA how to display LONG data. By default, the display is 80 characters only. Once again, the operating system defines the range of values for this parameter.

MAXDATA *integer*

Sets the maximum number of bytes that you can fetch from the database in a single SELECT statement. The default is 20,480 bytes (20KB). Your operating system defines the maximum number for this parameter.

NUMWIDTH *integer*	Defines the length in characters that data types of NUMBER are displayed in. The default is 10, and the minimum and maximum values are operating-system dependent.
RETRIES *integer*/INFINITE	Used with the STARTUP command, this specifies how many times the startup command attempts to start the database. INFINITE means it tries until it succeeds or is canceled.
SERVER OUTPUT OFF/ON SIZE *integer*	Specifies the size of the message buffer, in bytes, that can accumulate at one time. This message buffer is used by the PUT() and PUT_LINE() commands.
SPOOL *filename*/OFF	Captures commands and output from the current session to a file. Specifying OFF closes the previously opened file.
STOPONERROR ON/OFF	Tells SQL*DBA, when executing a command file, to stop if it encounters an error. If it finds one, the rest of the command file is not executed, and it returns control to the operating system.
TERM PAGE/NOPAGE	Tells SQL*DBA to display output one page at a time. The default, NOPAGE, scrolls all output to the output window. After that, you can navigate to the output window and scroll through the saved output.
TERMOUT ON/OFF	Controls the display of output from SQL commands to the output window. ON enables display of the output whereas OFF disables the output. This is helpful if you're spooling output to files. The output is sent to the spool file but not the terminal.
TIMING ON/OFF	Displays the parse, execute, and fetch times for every SQL statement executed. The default is OFF. This option is useful for establishing response times.

Examples:

```
SET INSTANCE D:DEV-PROD
SET HISTORY 50;
SET NUMWIDTH 20;
```

SHOW

Description: Using the SHOW command shows the values of all the parameters set by the SET command. Additionally, this command supports several other parameters listed in the Keywords section. For a definition of any parameter listed, refer to the previous section on SET.

Command Syntax:

```
SHOW ARRAYSIZE
        AUTORECOVERY
        CHARWIDTH
        COMPATIBILITY
        CYCLE
        DATEWIDTH
        ECHO
        FETCHROWS
        HISTORY
        INSTANCE
        LABWIDTH
        LINES
        LOGSOURCE
        LONGWIDTH
        MAXDATA
        NUMWIDTH
        RETRIES
        SERVER OUTPUT
        SPOOL
        STOPONERROR
        TERM
        TERMOUT
        TIMING
ALL
PARAMETERS
ERRORS
```

Keywords:

ALL	Shows the values of all settings. Does not show ERRORS, PARAMETERS, or SGA, which must be displayed separately.
ERRORS	Shows all errors encountered during the last compilation of a function, procedure, or package. Output includes the line, column, and error message generated.
LABEL	This is a Trusted Oracle parameter.
PARAMETERS	Shows the current values for all database parameters specified in the startup files for the current instance. Used alone, it displays all parameters. Used in conjunction with a parameter name, it shows the specific parameter. If a partial parameter name is used, the output includes all parameters that are similar.
SGA	Shows current information on the System Global Area for the connected instance.

Examples:

```
SHOW SGA;
SHOW TERMOUT;
SHOW ALL;
SHOW PARAMETERS COUNT;
SHOW ERRORS;
```

SHUTDOWN

Description: You use SHUTDOWN to stop a currently running database. Various options include closing or dismounting the database.

Command syntax:

```
SHUTDOWN  ABORT      dbname
          IMMEDIATE  dbname
          NORMAL     dbname
```

Keywords:

ABORT	Shuts down the database immediately, without checkpointing the database. This procedure immediately kills all active sessions without rolling back or committing transactions and then closes and dismounts the database. If you use this command, the database will require recovery.
IMMEDIATE	Shuts down the database by preventing new connections, terminating all existing sessions, and committing or rolling back current transactions and then checkpoints the database before dismounting and closing it. Media recovery is not required.
NORMAL	This is the default. It waits for currently connected users to disconnect, prevents new connections, checkpoints, and then closes and dismounts the database. No media recovery is required.
dbname	This is a Trusted Oracle parameter that you should not use for normal or parallel operations.

Examples:

```
SHUTDOWN;
SHUTDOWN IMMEDIATE dev;
SHUTDOWN ABORT;
```

SPOOL

Description: The SPOOL command begins or ends the spooling of command output to a specified file.

Command syntax:

```
SPOOL OFF
SPOOL filename
```

Keywords:

OFFCloses the currently opened file.

filename   The file to spool output to.

Examples:

```
SPOOL ON 'kelly.spl';
SPOOL OFF;
```

STARTUP

Description: You use STARTUP to start a database. With options, this command enables you to bring the database into various stages of use for maintenance. As with the SHUTDOWN command, you must be connected as internal, and you cannot be connected via Oracle's Multi-Threaded Server.

Command syntax:

```
STARTUP
            FORCE
            RESTRICT
            PFILE=filename
            MOUNT
            NOMOUNT
      OPEN
            RECOVER
            database
            mount options
```

Keywords:

FORCE — Issues a shutdown abort of the current instance and then attempts to start the instance again. This is sometimes required if there were shutdown errors.

RESTRICT — Same as the ALTER SYSTEM ENABLE RESTRICTED SESSION command; enables the database to start up in restricted mode and will only give access to users with the RESTRICTED SESSION role.

PFILE=filename — Enables the database to start up with a specific parameter file (INIT.ORA). Very useful if the INIT.ORA file is not in the current directory or if you are starting up a new database.

MOUNT — Mounts the database but does not open it for use.

NOMOUNT — Does not mount the database. You cannot use this option with the MOUNT, OPEN, PARALLEL, SHARED, or EXCLUSIVE options.

OPEN	Default option; mounts and opens the default database.
RECOVER	Similar to the RECOVER DATABASE command; starts the current instance and recovers the database, if required. The recovery works as if AUTORECOVERY were set to ON. If the recovery fails, the database remains mounted but does not open.
database	Starts this specific instance. If no instance is specified, startup runs on the default instance.
mount options	Specifies three types of options for the startup:

	EXCLUSIVE	Mounts and opens the database for a single instance to use.
	PARALLEL	Mounts and opens the database for parallel mode.
	SHARED	Another name for PARALLEL.
	RETRIES	Specifies the number of retries before failing.

Examples:

```
STARTUP;
STARTUP MOUNT;
STARTUP PFILE='/home/oracle/init.ora' PARALLEL;
STARTUP MOUNT RESTRICT;
STARTUP FORCE;
```

Summary

SQL*DBA is a powerful tool that is useful for creating, managing, and tuning all your Oracle instances. The flexibility to run in command, line, or menu mode gives the user a definite advantage that many other packages do not provide. The capability to automate many of the SQL*DBA commands enables the database administrator to turn over some of the database operations to secondary support personnel—which can help create a higher availability system with less down time.

Overall, this tool is valuable in the day-to-day responsibilities of every database administrator and custom developer.

SQL*Loader

8

by Scott Hillegas

IN THIS CHAPTER

Introduction

One of the many challenges DBAs face today is the problem of migrating data from external sources into the Oracle database. This task has increased in complexity with the introduction of data warehousing; the demand has gone from migrating megabytes of data to gigabytes, and in some cases, even terabytes. Oracle addresses this need with the SQL*Loader utility, a very versatile tool that loads external data into Oracle database tables. SQL*Loader is very flexible, and it is configurable to the point that you often can avoid development of 3GL procedures with embedded SQL. Whenever you face the task of converting foreign data into the Oracle format, first consider the use of SQL*Loader before resorting to other alternatives.

The purpose of this chapter is to provide an overview of SQL*Loader's functionality, highlight its capabilities, describe commonly used syntax, and provide practical examples. For additional information and in-depth reference material, refer to the *Oracle7 Server Utility User's Guide.*

Basic SQL*Loader Components

SQL*Loader requires two types of input: the *external data,* which can reside on disk or tape, and *control information* (contained in the control file), which describes the characteristics of the input data and the tables and columns to load. The outputs, some of which are optional, include the Oracle table(s), log file, bad file(s) and discard file(s). Figure 8.1 illustrates the components.

FIGURE 8.1.

*SQL*Loader components.*

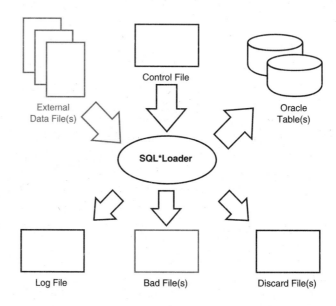

The Input Data

SQL*Loader can process practically any type of data file, and it supports native data types for almost any platform. Data is usually read from one or more data files; however, data also may be embedded in the control file, after the control information. The data file can exist as a fixed or variable format.

In *fixed format*, the data exists in fixed-length records that all have the same format. The fields for fixed-format files are defined by starting and ending positions within the record, and the fields contain the same data type and length throughout the file. (See Figure 8.2.) Binary data must be in a fixed-format file, as SQL*Loader cannot handle it in a variable format.

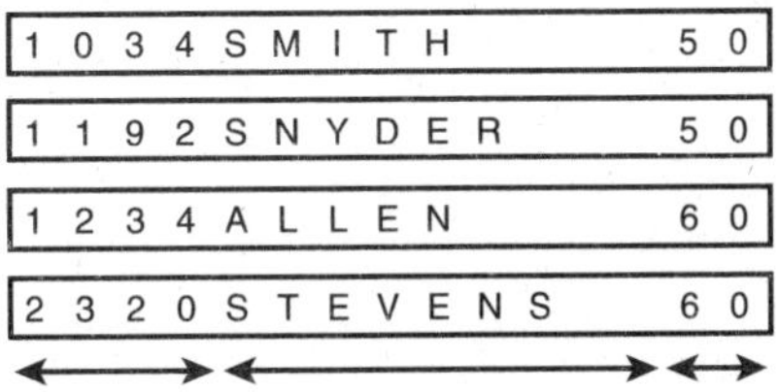

FIGURE 8.2.

Fixed-format records.

```
1 0 3 4 S M I T H          5 0

1 1 9 2 S N Y D E R        5 0

1 2 3 4 A L L E N          6 0

2 3 2 0 S T E V E N S      6 0
```

In *variable-format* files, the data exists in records that may vary in length, depending on the length of the data in the fields. The fields are only as long as necessary to contain the data. Fields in variable-format files may be separated by termination characters (such as commas or white space), enclosed by delimiter characters (such as quotation marks), or both. (See Figure 8.3.)

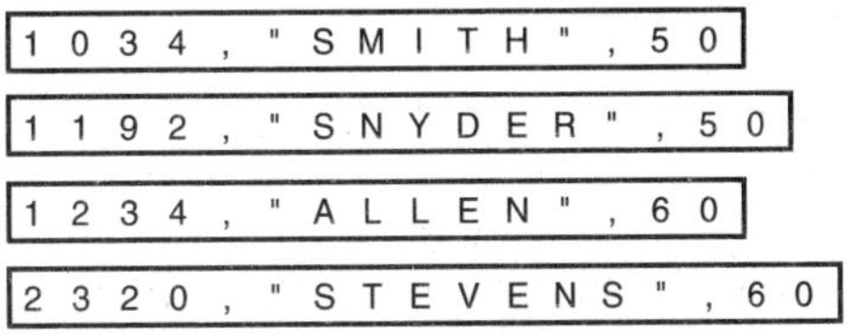

FIGURE 8.3.

Variable-format records.

```
1 0 3 4 , " S M I T H " , 5 0

1 1 9 2 , " S N Y D E R " , 5 0

1 2 3 4 , " A L L E N " , 6 0

2 3 2 0 , " S T E V E N S " , 6 0
```

NOTE

If you are using files with termination characters, make sure that any field that contains the termination character as part of the data is delimited. For example, if you are using a file with comma separation, you can use double quotes to delimit any field containing a comma.

TIP

To increase performance, use fixed-length records. Based on the tests I have done, SQL*Loader takes about 50 percent longer to process a variable-format file than a fixed-format file. I used the same amount of data for both formats and comma separation for the variable data.

Through the Oracle National Language Support (NLS), SQL*Loader has the capability to interpret and convert data with different character encoding schemes from other computer platforms and countries. For example, SQL*Loader can load an EBCDIC file into a database on an ASCII platform, or it can load an Asian character-set file into an American character-set database.

NOTE

When porting a file from one platform (like EBCDIC mainframe) to a different target platform (like ASCII UNIX) that contains binary data (like packed decimal), remember that the file is transferred in an image or binary state. For example, if you are using FTP to port the file, after you connect to the host system, be certain to put the session in an image state by typing binary at the FTP prompt. Otherwise, FTP interprets and converts the data, thereby corrupting the binary data.

The Control File

Before SQL*Loader can process the data in the data file(s), you must define the data specifications to SQL*Loader. You use the control file to define the physical data file specifications, as well as the format of the data in the file(s). The control file is a free-format file that also contains additional control data, instructing SQL*Loader how to process the data. The details concerning the control file are described in a later section.

The Log File

Upon execution, SQL*Loader creates a log file containing detailed information about the load, including these items:

- Names of the input data file(s), control file, bad file(s), and discard file(s)
- Input data and associated table specifications
- SQL*Loader errors

■ SQL*Loader results

■ Summary statistics

See Figure 8.4 for a sample log file.

FIGURE 8.4.

Sample log file.

```
SQL*Loader: Release 7.2.2.3.0 - Production on Tue Oct 10 15:20:04 1995

Copyright (c) Oracle Corporation 1979, 1994. All rights reserved.

Control File: load_unrecov_1.ctl
Data File: /data01/ORACLE/TEST/fixed_data.dat
Bad File: load_unrecov_1.bad
Discard File: load_unrecov_1.dis
(Allow all discards)

Number to load: ALL
Number to skip: 0
Errors allowed: 50
Continuation: none specified
Path used: Direct - with parallel option

Load is UNRECOVERABLE; invalidation redo is produced.

Table LOADER_TEST, loaded from every logical record.
Insert option in effect for this table: INSERT

    Column Name        Position    Len    Term Encl Datatype
    LOADER_DESC          1:30       30         CHARACTER
    LOADER_COL1         31:40       10         CHARACTER
    LOADER_COL2         41:50       10         CHARACTER
    LOADER_COL3         51:60       10         CHARACTER
    LOADER_COL4         61:70       10         CHARACTER

    LOADER_CONSTANT         CONSTANT 'A'
    LOADER_SEQUENCE         SEQUENCE(1,1)
    LOADER_RECNUM           RECNUM
    LOADER_SYSDATE          SYSDATE

Table LOADER_TEST:
778778 Rows successfully loaded.
0 Rows not loaded due to data errors.
0 Rows not loaded because all WHEN clauses were failed.
0 Rows not loaded because all fields were null.

Bind array size not used in direct path.
Space allocated for memory besides bind array: 255481 bytes

Total logical records skipped: 0
Total logical records read: 778778
Total logical records rejected: 0
Total logical records discarded: 0

Run began on Tue Oct 10 15:20:04 1995
Run ended on Tue Oct 10 15:23:33 1995

Elapsed time was: 00:03:29:01
CPU time was: 00:00:16:65
```

Discard and Bad Files

SQL*Loader has the built-in functionality, through specifications in the control file, to format the input data and include or exclude the input record based on record-selection criteria. If SQL*Loader includes the record for processing, it is passed to the Oracle kernel for insertion into the database table. Figure 8.5 shows the record-filtering process.

FIGURE 8.5.

Record-filtering process.

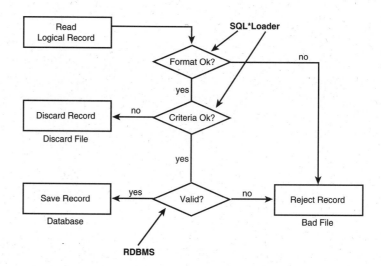

If SQL*Loader rejects the record due to a format error, or if the Oracle kernel cannot insert the record into the database table(s) for any reason, the input record is written to the BAD file, in the same format as the original input data file. If SQL*Loader rejects the record due to an exclusion based on the record-selection criteria, the input record is written to the DISCARD file (providing it was specified in the control file), also in the same format as the original input data file. Because both the BAD and DISCARD files are written in the same format as the original input data file, they can be edited, if necessary, and used as input data files to another SQL*Loader session.

Physical Versus Logical Records

Physical records are the individual lines in the input data file as they were created by the operating system on the platform from which the file originated. Physical records are terminated by a record-terminator character (like a carriage return). *Logical records* correspond to a row in a database table. A physical record can have a one-to-one association with a logical record. (See Figure 8.6.) SQL*Loader also enables you to create a many-to-one association between physical and logical records through the use of the CONCATENATE or CONTINUEIF clause in the control file. You may create a one-to-many relationship by splitting one physical record into multiple logical records.

FIGURE 8.6.

Physical versus logical records.

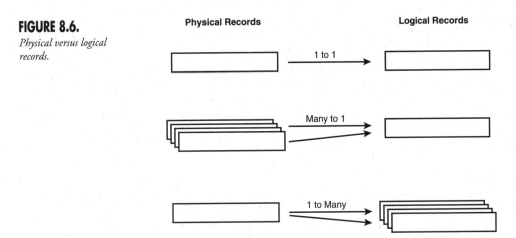

Physical Records   **Logical Records**

1 to 1

Many to 1

1 to Many

Concatenated Records

SQL*Loader can concatenate records either by specifying the number of physical records that form one logical record or by specifying conditional evaluations based on character occurrences within the data. If the number of physical records that comprise a logical record varies, then you must base the concatenation on conditional evaluations. The CONCATENATE and CONTINUEIF clauses in the control file facilitate physical record concatenation.

SQL*Loader Paths

SQL*Loader provides two paths for loading data:

- The conventional path
- The direct path

The Conventional Path

The conventional path generates a SQL INSERT command with the array processing interface to load the data into the table(s). Because of this interface, SQL*Loader competes with all other Oracle processes for buffer cache resources; Oracle looks for and tries to fill partially filled blocks on each insert. (See Figure 8.7.) If you are loading small amounts of data, this method is usually acceptable; however, with large volumes of data, this technique becomes too time consuming and resource-intensive.

These conditions exist when you load data with the conventional path:

- Other users and Oracle processes can be accessing the table concurrently with SQL*Loader.

- Indexes are updated as the rows are inserted into the table.
- All referential and integrity constraints are enforced as the data is loaded into the table.
- Database Insert triggers fire as the rows are inserted into the table.
- You can apply SQL functions to the input data as it is being loaded.
- Data can be loaded into a clustered table.
- Data can be loaded with SQL*Net.

FIGURE 8.7.

Conventional loader path.

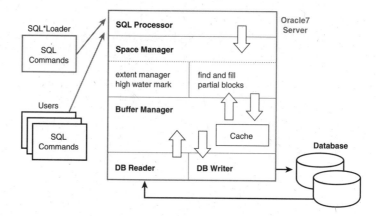

The Direct Path

In contrast to the conventional path, the direct path is optimized for bulk data loads. Instead of using the buffer cache to obtain and fill the database blocks, the direct path option uses the extent manager to get new extents and adjust the high water mark. Direct path creates formatted database blocks and writes them directly to the database. (See Figure 8.8.)

FIGURE 8.8.

Direct loader path.

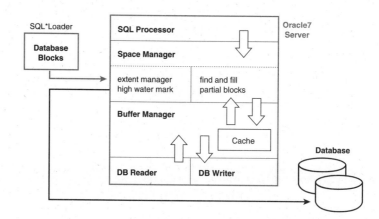

The direct path has several significant advantages:

- You can load and index large amounts of data into empty or non-empty table(s) in a relatively short period of time.

- If loading data into empty tables, you can load presorted data and eliminate the sort and merge phases of the index build, thereby significantly increasing performance.

- You can load data in parallel, which enables multiple SQL*Loader sessions to perform concurrent direct path loads into the same table.

- You can specify that a direct path load be done in an UNRECOVERABLE mode, which bypasses Oracle's redo logging activity and significantly increases performance.

Although the direct path significantly increases performance, it does have some limitations:

- The table(s) and index(es) into which you are loading data are exclusively locked at the start of the load and not released until the load is finished; the table(s) cannot have any active transactions on them and are not available to other users or processes until the load is completed.

- Indexes are put into a direct load state at the start of the load and need to be rebuilt, either automatically or manually, after the load is completed. If the SQL*Loader session does not complete successfully, the indexes are left in the direct load state and need to be rebuilt manually. Any PRIMARY KEY or UNIQUE constraints are not validated until after the load is complete and the index rebuild occurs; you may have duplicate keys and need to correct them through the use of the exceptions table before you can rebuild the index.

- The NOT NULL constraint is the only constraint checked at insertion time. All other integrity and referential constraints are re-enabled and enforced after the load is complete. If any violations exist, they are placed into the exceptions table, which you should specify when you create the constraint. The exceptions table must be created before the load session.

- Database Insert triggers do not fire. Any application functionality that relies on them must be accomplished through some other method.

- You cannot apply SQL functions to the input data as it is being loaded.

- Data cannot be loaded into a clustered table.

- Only in the case where both computer systems belong to the same family, and both are using the same character set, can data be loaded through SQL*Net. You should not use SQL*Net for direct path loads, as the direct path should be used only for large amounts of data. Network overhead offsets any performance gains associated with the direct path.

- DEFAULT column specifications are not available with the direct path.

- Synonyms that exist for the table(s) being loaded must point directly to the table; they cannot point to another synonym or view.

The main advantage to the direct path method is performance. No hard and fast rules exist to determine when to use the conventional method versus the direct path method, because the definition of "large amounts of data" varies from application to application. Other external factors vary also, such as database availability, the cleanliness of the data being loaded, and system resources. I have seen loads go from days to hours using the parallel, direct path method vs. the conventional path method, with clean data on a multi-processor system. But I have also seen cases where significant amounts of time were spent cleaning the table data so an index could rebuild after a direct path load. You need to analyze your situation, and based on all the factors, decide which method is better for your application.

Parallel Data Loading

Oracle Version 7.1 introduced the functionality of performing direct path loads in parallel. This feature gives SQL*Loader nearly linear performance gains on multi-processor systems. By using the parallel option, you can load multiple input files concurrently into separate tablespace files, with each file belonging to the tablespace in which the table resides. Maximum throughput is achieved by striping the tablespace across different devices and placing the input files on separate devices, and preferably separate controllers. (See Figure 8.9.)

FIGURE 8.9.

Striping parallel loads.

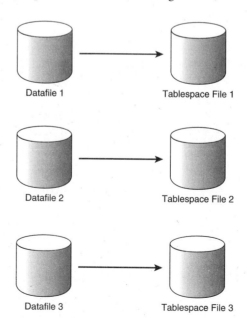

Datafile 1 → Tablespace File 1

Datafile 2 → Tablespace File 2

Datafile 3 → Tablespace File 3

When using the parallel option, SQL*Loader creates temporary segments, sized according to the NEXT storage parameter specified for the table, in the tablespace file specified in the OPTIONS clause of the control file.

> **CAUTION**
>
> The specified file *must* be in the tablespace in which the table resides, or you get a fatal error.

Upon completion of the SQL*Loader session, the temporary segments are merged (with the last extent trimmed of any free space) and added to the existing table in the database, above the high water mark for the table.

You should drop indexes, primary key constraints, and unique key constraints on the table before doing a parallel load. Oracle Version 7.1 introduced parallel index creation, but you may use it only with a CREATE INDEX statement, not within an ALTER TABLE CREATE CONSTRAINT statement. Therefore, the best method is to create the indexes first, using the parallel option, then create the primary key and unique constraints, which use the previously created indexes.

> **NOTE**
>
> Parallel SQL*Loader sessions that are interrupted normally (for example, by a Ctrl+C in UNIX) will terminate normally; they stop processing where they were interrupted. Any temporary segments created during the session are added to the table's high water mark. Any parallel session that was "killed" from an O/S command terminates abnormally; the temporary segments are dropped and not added to the table's high water mark.

> **TIP**
>
> If you are creating a very large table (which you know will be populated by the parallel option of SQL*Loader), first create a striped tablespace to hold the table, equally sizing the data files that comprise the tablespace across multiple devices. Next, create the table with the minimal initial extent size (one Oracle block), and the NEXT extent sized to fully populate the size of the stripes, less one Oracle block. Be sure to set PCTINCREASE to 0. Next, you must do some analysis of the data being loaded to determine the size of each of the input data files you want to load. You want to size the input files so that SQL*Loader fully populates (as much as possible) the striped tablespace files to minimize wasted space.

Your goal is to have concurrent SQL*Loader sessions each process an input file and place the output in a separate tablespace file, thereby maximizing throughput. Each SQL*Loader session creates one temporary segment, in its specified tablespace file, with the extent size being the size of the data file. When the session completes, SQL*Loader trims the excess space from the temporary extent (because it has only one extent) and adds it above the table's high water mark.

Using this method, you are evenly distributing the data across devices, thereby maximizing database I/O, minimizing the number of extents for the table, and maximizing SQL*Loader performance.

Control File Syntax

The control file is in free format; however, it does have a few rules:

- White space, carriage returns, tabs, and so on are allowed at any position in the file.
- As in Oracle, the contents of the file are case insensitive except for quoted (single or double) strings.
- You can include comments anywhere, except within the data (assuming the data is contained in the control file), by prefacing them with two hyphens; SQL*Loader ignores anything from the double hyphen to the end of the line.
- You may use reserved words for table or column names; however, the words must be enclosed in double quotation marks.

TIP

It is generally good practice not to use Oracle reserved words for any database object names. I have seen numerous cases in which Oracle got confused when reserved words were used as database object names (the error messages are very ambiguous). For the complete lists of reserved words for SQL*Loader, SQL*DBA, and Oracle, refer to the *Oracle7 Server Utility User's Guide* and the *SQL Language Reference Manual.*

The control file is logically organized into seven sections:

- OPTIONS clause
- UNRECOVERABLE/RECOVERABLE clause
- LOAD DATA clause
- INFILE clause
- Table loading method

- CONCATENATION clause
- INTO TABLE clause

Listings 8.1, 8.2, and 8.3 help illustrate some of the syntax described in this section.

Listing 8.1 is a sample control file for a direct path parallel load using a fixed-format input file. This control file was used to test SQL*Loader results using the direct path parallel option in an unrecoverable mode. For illustration purposes only, the SQL*Loader functions CONSTANT, SEQUENCE, SYSDATE, and RECNUM were used to populate column data.

Listing 8.1. Parallel load control file.

```
OPTIONS (direct=true, parallel=true)
UNRECOVERABLE
LOAD DATA
INFILE'/data01/ORACLE/TEST/fixed_data.dat'
BADFILE'fixed_data.bad'
DISCARDFILE'fixed_data.dis'
INSERT INTO TABLE loader_test
OPTIONS (FILE='data02/ORACLE/TEST/test1_TEST_01.dbf')
(loader_constant CONSTANT "A"
loader_sequence sequence (1,1),
loader_sysdate sysdate,
loader_recnum recnum,
loader_desc POSITION (01:30) char
loader_col1 POSITION (31:40) char,
loader_col2 POSITION (41:50) char,
loadr col3 POSITION (51:60) char,
loader_col4 POSITION (61:70) char)
```

Listing 8.2 is a sample control file for a conventional path load using a variable-format file.

Listing 8.2. Variable-format control file.

```
LOAD DATA
INFILE'data04/ORACLE/TEST/prod'
BADFILE'prod.bad'
INSERT INTO TABLE pord'
FIELDS TERMINATED BY','OPTIONALLY ENCLOSED BY ""
trailing nullcols
   (
      PROD_CODE,
      PROD_DESCR,
      PROD_CLASS,
      PROD MKTG_CODE
      terminated by whitespace)
```

Listing 8.3 is a sample control file for loading a binary EBCDIC file into a USASCII database, using the conventional path. Note that the file also is using packed decimal fields.

Listing 8.3. Foreign character set control file.

```
LOAD DATA CHARACTERSET WE8EBCDIC500
INFILE 'data01ORACLE/TEST/prod_detail'"FIX 28"
INSERT INTO TABLE prod_detail
   (
   PROD_CODE position(01:04) char,
   SALES_MTD_LY position(05:10) decimal(11,2),
   SALES_YTD_LY position(11:16) decimal(11,2),
   SALES_MTD position(17:22) decimal(11,2),
   SALES_YTD position(23:28) decimal(11,2)
   )
```

OPTIONS Clause

The OPTIONS clause, which enables you to specify some of the run-time arguments in the control file rather than on the command line, is optional. This clause is particularly useful if the length of the command line exceeds the maximum command-line length for your operating system. The arguments you can include in the OPTIONS clause are described in Table 8.1. Even if you specify the arguments in the OPTIONS clause, the command-line specifications override them.

Table 8.1. Control file OPTIONS clause arguments.

Argument	Description
SKIP = *n*	Logical records to skip
LOAD = *n*	Logical records to load (default all)
ERRORS = *n*	Errors to allow before termination
ROWS = *n*	Rows in bind array (conventional); rows between saves (direct)
BINDSIZE = *n*	Size of bind array in bytes
SILENT = {HEADER¦FEEDBACK	
ERROR¦DISCARDS¦ALL}	Messages to suppress
DIRECT = {TRUE¦FALSE}	Load path method
PARALLEL = {TRUE¦FALSE}	Multiple concurrent sessions

NOTE

When using the parallel loader, you can specify multiple input files and tables. The FILE parameter specified in the OPTIONS clause becomes the global default for all

INSERT INTO TABLE options clauses. In addition to the OPTIONS clause for the load, each INSERT INTO TABLE clause can have an OPTIONS clause, which specifies the tablespace file where the temporary segments are created. (See Listing 8.1.) If multiple input files are specified or multiple tables are being loaded, you should further qualify the options in the options section for that table.

UNRECOVERABLE/RECOVERABLE Clause

These options apply only to direct path loads; all conventional loads are by definition recoverable. When the database is in archivelog mode, if RECOVERABLE is specified, the loaded data is written to the redo logs. Specifying UNRECOVERABLE bypasses writing to the redo logs, which improves performance (by about 100 percent) but forces you to drop and re-create the loaded data if media recovery is required.

TIP

Unless you are appending data to existing data in a table, you should specify UNRE-COVERABLE for performance issues. If for some reason the instance needs recovery, recover it, and truncate the table(s) into which you were loading the data. Then start the SQL*Loader session again.

LOAD DATA Clause

The LOAD DATA clause is the main statement in the control file. Only comments, the OP-TIONS clause, and the RECOVERABLE clause can precede LOAD DATA in the control file. LOAD DATA is followed by phrases and clauses that further qualify it. For the complete syntax of the control file, refer to the *Oracle7 Server Utilities User's Guide*.

The LOAD DATA clause begins with the keyword LOAD, optionally followed by the keyword DATA. Note in Listing 8.3 that the keyword CHARACTERSET followed by the character set name is required if the input data file(s) is from a foreign character set, in this case EBCDIC. The control file may have only one LOAD DATA clause.

INFILE Clause

To specify the input file containing the data to be loaded, specify the INFILE or INDDN keyword, followed by the filename and an optional O/S-dependent file-processing specifications string. Note in Listing 8.4 that the string "FIX 28" follows the complete file pathname for a UNIX system. Listing 8.4 contains some examples of file specifications from other platforms.

228

Listing 8.4. Sample file specifications.

```
INFILE   myfile.dat
INFILE   'c\\loader\\input\\march\\sales.dat'
INFILE   '/clinical/a0004/data/clin0056.dat'
         "recsize 80 buffers 10"
         BADFILE '/clinical/a0004/logs/clin0056.bad'
         DISCARDFILE '/clinical/a004/logs/clin0056.dsc'
         DISCARDMAX 50
INFILE   'clin_a4:[data]clin0056.dat'
         DISCARDFILE 'clin_a4:[log]clin0056.dsc'
         DISCARDMAX 50
```

> **NOTE**
>
> As a rule, use single quotes around any file specification that contains punctuation marks.
>
> If the operating system uses a single backslash to specify an escape character, use a double backslash in directory structures.
>
> Filename specifications and the file-processing specifications string are generally not portable between platforms and may need to be rewritten if you are migrating to a different platform.

Following the INFILE statement is the optional bad file specification, which begins with the keyword BADFILE or BDDN followed by the filename. If no name is specified by the bad file, the name defaults to the name of the data file followed by a .BAD extension. A bad file is created only if records were rejected because of formatting errors, or the Oracle kernel returned an error while trying to insert records into the database.

Following the BADFILE statement is the optional discard file specification, which begins with the keyword DISCARDFILE or DISCARDDN and is followed by the filename. Next comes a DISCARDS or DISCARDMAX keyword, with an integer specification. SQL*Loader may create a discard file for records that do not meet any of the loading criteria specified in the WHEN clauses in the control file. If no discard file is named, and the DISCARDS and DISCARDMAX keywords are not specified, a discard file is not created even if records were discarded. However, if the DISCARDS or DISCARDMAX keyword is specified on the command line or in the control file, with no discard filename specified, a default file is created with the name of the data file followed by a .DSC extension.

The DISCARDS or DISCARDMAX clause limits the number of records to be discarded for each data file. If a limit is specified, processing for the associated data file stops when the limit is reached.

> **NOTE**
>
> For both the bad file and discard files:
> - If the file is created, it overwrites any existing files with the same name.
> - If the file is not created, and a file with the same name already exists, it remains intact.

Table Loading Methods

The table loading method keyword specifies the default global method for loading the tables. You may use one of four methods:

- INSERT
- APPEND
- REPLACE
- TRUNCATE

INSERT is the default method and requires the table to be empty before loading the data file. SQL*Loader terminates with an error if the table is not empty.

APPEND adds new rows to the table, even if the table is empty.

REPLACE uses the `SQL DELETE` command to delete all rows from the table, performs a commit, then loads the new data into the table.

TRUNCATE uses the `SQL TRUNCATE` command to remove the rows from the table, performs a commit, then loads the new data into the table. All referential constraints must be disabled before the SQL*Loader session begins, otherwise SQL*Loader terminates with an error.

> **WARNING**
>
> When you use the REPLACE method, if you specified DELETE CASCADE for the table, the cascaded deletes are also performed. Any delete triggers you have defined for the table also fire as the rows are deleted.
>
> When you use the REPLACE or TRUNCATE keyword, all rows are removed from the table before data begins loading into the table. If this result was not your intent, you may need to restore the table from a backup.

In addition to specifying a global table load method, you can specify a method for each table in the INTO TABLE clause.

CONCATENATION Clause

You can create one logical record from multiple physical records by using the CONCATENATE or the CONTINUEIF keyword.

If the number of records to combine remains constant throughout the data file, you can use the CONCATENATE keyword, followed by an integer, which indicates the number of records to combine. An example of CONCATENATE is shown in Figure 8.10.

FIGURE 8.10.

An example of CONCATENATE.

Concatenate 4 ◀——— Combine 4 sequential physical records to assemble 1 logical record

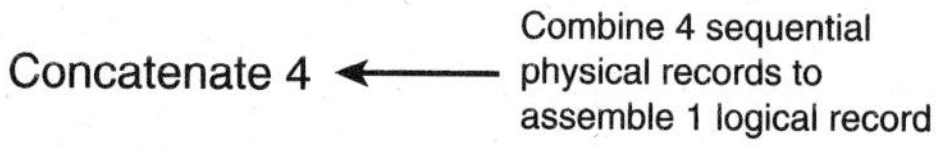

If the number of physical records varies, then you must use the CONTINUEIF keyword, followed by a condition that is evaluated for each record as it is processed.

Examples of CONTINUEIF are shown in Figure 8.11.

FIGURE 8.11.

Examples of CONTINUEIF.

```
CONTINUEIF THIS (1:2) = '_$'  ◀——— If bytes 1 through 2 of current
                                    record match pattern, combine
                                    next record

CONTINUEIF NEXT (1:2) = '_$'  ◀——— If bytes 1 through 2 of next
                                    record match pattern, combine
                                    next record

CONTINUEIF LAST ! = '#'  ◀———————— If the last non-black character
                                    of the current record is not "#",
                                    combine it with the next record
```

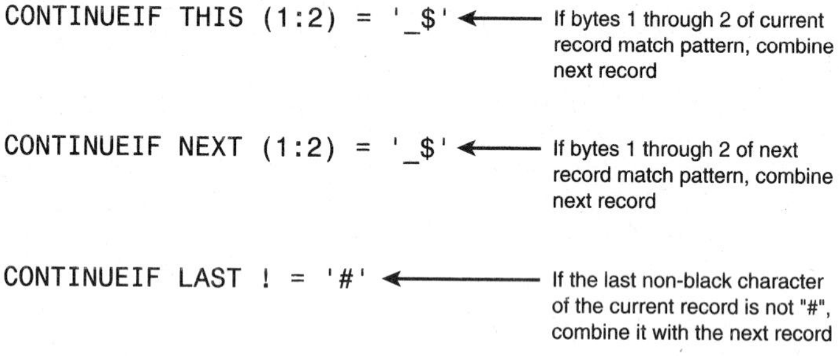

In all three cases, with the THIS, NEXT, and LAST keywords, the condition is evaluated in the current physical record. If the condition is true, SQL*Loader reads the next physical record, concatenating it to the current physical record, continuing until the condition is false. If the condition evaluates to false in the current physical record, it becomes the last physical record of the current logical record.

> **NOTE**
>
> Be aware of the following when using CONTINUEIF:
> - The continuation fields are removed from the physical records before the logical record is created when you use the THIS and NEXT keywords.
> - The continuation character is not removed from the physical record when you use the LAST keyword; it remains a part of the logical record.
> - Any trailing blanks in the physical record are part of the logical record.

INTO TABLE Clause

The INTO TABLE clause is the section of the LOAD DATA statement that contains the bulk of the control file syntax. The INTO TABLE clause contains these items:

- Table name into which the data is to be loaded
- Table-specific loading method
- Table-specific OPTIONS clause
- WHEN clause
- FIELDS clause
- TRAILING NULLCOLS clause
- Index options
- Field conditions
- Relationship between data file fields and database columns

The INTO TABLE clause begins with the keywords INTO TABLE, followed by the name of the table into which the data is to be loaded. (You must have previously created the table.)

Table-Specific Loading Method

You may include a table-specific loading method in the INTO TABLE clause. If you use the INSERT, APPEND, REPLACE, or TRUNCATE method, it overrides the global table-loading method you specified previously in the control; the override is valid only for the table referenced in the INTO TABLE clause.

Table-Specific OPTIONS Clause

You may include a table-specific OPTIONS clause in the INTO TABLE clause. The OPTIONS clause is valid only for parallel loads, and it overrides the FILE specification (the only option you can specify at the table level) in the global OPTIONS clause at the beginning of the control file.

WHEN Clause

You specify record selection criteria through the use of a WHEN clause, which is followed by field condition(s). The WHEN clause can contain multiple comparisons; they must be separated by an AND. SQL*Loader determines the values of the fields in the logical record, then evaluates the WHEN clause. The row is inserted only if the WHEN clause evaluates to true. Examples of usage of the WHEN clause are shown in Figure 8.12.

FIGURE 8.12.
*Examples of the
WHEN clause.*

```
INTO TABLE scott.emp
     WHEN (12:13) ! = '50'
```
⟵ Loads records that do not
contain 50 in positions
12 through 13

```
INTO TABLE project
     WHEN (date = '01-JAN-94')
     AND (deptno = '20')
```
⟵ Loads records for
January 1, 1994,
for department 20

Using a column reference

FIELDS Clause

Fixed-format input data file fields are usually defined by explicit byte position notation, (start:end), whereas variable-format input data file fields are usually relative to each other and separated by field termination characters. You can define the default field termination character for the file in the FIELDS clause. You can override the default at the field level by specifying the field termination character after the column name. An example of the usage of the FIELDS clause is shown in Listing 8.5.

Listing 8.5. Usage of the FIELDS clause.

```
INFO TABLE emp
    WHEN empno > 1000
    FIELDS TERMINATED BY WHITESPACE
    TRAILING NULLCOLS
    (
    emp position(1) integer external terminated by '',
    ename char terminated by whitespace,
    deptno integer external terminated by ''
    )
```

TRAILING NULLCOLS Clause

When more fields are specified in the control file than are present in the physical record, you must instruct SQL*Loader to either treat the missing fields as null columns or generate an error. When you use relative positioning, the record may end before all the fields are found. The TRAILING NULLCOLS clause instructs SQL*Loader to treat any relatively positioned columns not present in the record as null columns. See Listing 18.5 for usage of the TRAILING NULLCOLS clause.

Index Options

If you loaded the data using the direct path and the data file has been presorted on indexed columns, you can specify the SORTED INDEXES clause, followed by the name(s) of the index(es) in parentheses. The index(es) listed in the SORTED INDEXES clause must be created before you begin the direct load, or SQL*Loader returns an error. If you specify an index in the SORTED INDEXES clause and the data was not properly sorted for that index, the index is left in the direct load state at the end of the load. You must drop and re-create the index before you can use it.

Field Conditions

A field condition is an expression about a field in a logical record that evaluates to true or false. You use field conditions with the NULLIF and DEFAULTIF keywords, as well as the WHEN clause. NULLIF sets the column to null if the expression evaluates to true, whereas DEFAULTIF sets the column to zero or blank. The BLANKS keyword enables you to easily compare any length field to determine if it is entirely blank. Examples of NULLIF and DEFAULTIF are shown in Listing 18.6.

Listing 18.6. NULLIF and DEFAULTIF.

```
dept no     POISITION (1:2) integer external
                NULLIF (dept = BLANKS)

comm        POSITION (50:57) integer external
                DEFAULTIF (hiredate > '01-jan-94')
```

Column Specifications

The data type specifications in the column specification of the control file tell SQL*Loader how to interpret the data in the data file. The column definition in the data dictionary defines the data type for each column in the database. The link between the data in the data file and the database column is the column name specified in the control file.

Any number of a table's columns may be loaded, providing the unloaded columns were not created with NOT NULL constraints. Columns defined for the table, but not specified in the control file, are assigned null values when the row is inserted.

The column specification is the column name, followed by a specification for the value to be put into the column. The list of columns is enclosed by parentheses and separated by commas. Each column name must correspond to a column in the table that was named in the INTO TABLE clause. Examples of column specifications are shown in Figure 8.13.

FIGURE 8.13.

Column specifications.

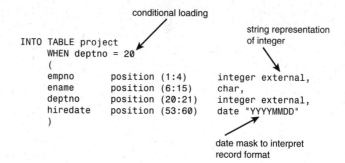

Setting the Column Values

You can set the column value in one of two ways. The value can be read from the data file by specifying either an explicit position notation (start:end) for fixed-format files, or a relative position notation for variable-format files. The second way is to generate the value using SQL*Loader functions CONSTANT, RECNUM, SYSDATE, or SEQUENCE. You can use these SQL*Loader functions for both the conventional path and the direct path. The syntax for the SQL*Loader functions is shown in Figure 8.14.

FIGURE 8.14.

*SQL*Loader functions.*

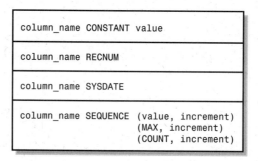

The function CONSTANT, followed by a value, generates the fixed value for every row inserted into the table. SQL*Loader interprets the value as a character, but does convert it, if necessary, to the database column type. The value may be enclosed in quotation marks.

The RECNUM function, which has no specified value associated with it, sets the column value to the number of the logical record from which the row was loaded. The records are counted sequentially from the beginning of the data file, beginning with record 1. The value is incremented for each logical record, even if the record was discarded, skipped, or rejected. If you are using the parallel option to load multiple data files concurrently, each SQL*Loader session generates duplicate values, because each session begins with 1.

The SYSDATE function gets the current system date for each array of records when using the conventional path, and for each block of records when using the direct path. The format of the date is the same as the SQL SYSDATE function. The database column must be a type of VARCHAR, CHAR, or DATE.

The SEQUENCE SQL.*Loader function (which is not the same as the database object SEQUENCE) increments, by the specified increment value specified, for each logical record that is loaded or rejected. This function does not increment for discarded or skipped records. The starting value for the SEQUENCE, based on your specification, is

- The specified integer
- COUNT, which is the number of rows in the table, plus the increment
- MAX, which is the current maximum value for the column, plus the increment

If you are using the parallel option, the SEQUENCE function is the only option available to you to in SQL*Loader to generate unique numbers; all other options require SQL functions, which you cannot use in a direct path load.

Specifying the Data Type

SQL*Loader extracts data from a field in the data file, according to the data type specification in the control file, and sends it to the RDBMS to be stored in the appropriate database column. The RDBMS automatically attempts to perform any data conversion. If the data conversion cannot be done, an error is returned and the record is rejected.

Oracle interprets both character and binary (native) data. Character data is human-readable data you can produce in a text editor, whereas binary data is usually generated programatically. SQL*Loader supports these character types:

```
CHAR
DATE
NUMERIC EXTERNAL
```

NOTE

Do not confuse the CHAR and DATE character data types in SQL*Loader with the column data types of the same names; they are *not* the same.

SQL*Loader supports these binary (native) data types:

```
INTEGER          ZONED
SMALLINT         VARCHAR
FLOAT            GRAPHIC
DOUBLE           GRAPHIC EXTERNAL
BYTEINT          VARGRAPHIC
packed DECIMAL   RAW
```

Refer to the *ORACLE7 Server Utility User's Guide* for a complete description of the various character and binary data types that SQL*Loader supports.

Using SQL Functions

You may apply SQL functions to the field data by using a SQL string. The string may contain any combination of SQL expressions that return a single value. The string appears after any other specifications for a given column and must be enclosed in double quotation marks. If the string contains a syntax error, the load terminates with an error. If the syntax in the string is correct but causes a database error, the row is rejected, but processing continues. You can reference field names in the SQL string by prefacing them with a colon. Here are some examples of the usage of SQL functions:

```
my_field position(1:18) integer external
    "TRANSLATE (RTRIM(my_field),'N/A','0')"

my_string CHAR terminated by ","
    "SUBSTR (:my_string,1,10)"

my_number position(1:9) DECIMAL EXTERNAL(8)
    ":field/1000"
```

Multiple Table Statements

You have the ability with SQL*Loader to specify multiple INTO TABLE statements. Using multiple statements, you can perform these tasks:

- Extract multiple logical records from one physical record.
- Distinguish different record formats.
- Load data into different tables.

Listing 8.7 illustrates a case where you may want to use the values from different fields to populate a column, depending on conditions within the data.

Listing 8.7. Example of using field conditions to populate columns.

```
INFO TABLE proj
  WHEN projno ! = ' '
      (empo          position(1:4) integer external,
       projno        position(29:31) integer external)

INFO TABLE proj
  WHEN PROJNO ! = ' '
      (empno         position(1:4) integer external
       projno        position(33:35) integer external)
```

Listing 8.8 illustrates a case where you may want to use the same data within a physical record to load the data into multiple tables.

Listing 8.8. Loading data from a single physical record into multiple tables.

```
INFO TABLE dept
    WHEN deptno < 100
    (deptno POSITION(1:4) INTEGER EXTERNAL
    (dname POSITION(6:19) CHAR)

INFO TABLE emp
    WHEN empno > 1000
    (empno POSITION(1:4) INTEGER EXTERNAL,
    ename POSITION(6:15) CHAR.
    deptno POSITION(17:18) INTEGER EXTERNAL)
```

Figure 8.15 illustrates a case where multiple tables are populated based on WHEN conditions.

FIGURE 8.15.
Populating multiple tables based on WHEN conditions.

```
INTO TABLE current_studies
    WHEN (status = current)
    AND (country_code = 'US')
...
INTO TABLE study_345
    WHEN (11:13) = '345'
...
INTO TABLE study_456
    WHEN (11:13) = '456'
```

Multiple tables are populated based on WHEN conditions

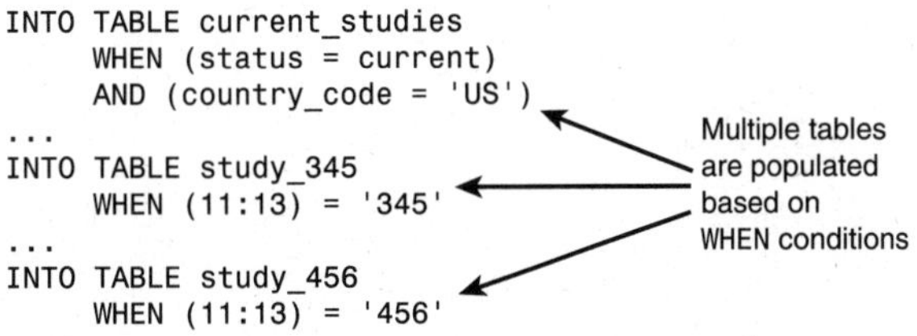

Command-Line Options and Parameter Files

The name of the SQL*Loader executable is operating-system dependent; refer to the *Installation and Configuration Guide* for your operating system to determine the executable filename.

By invoking SQL*Loader with no arguments, you see the following summary of the command-line arguments and their default values:

userid	ORACLE username/password
control	Control filename
log	Log filename
bad	Bad filename
data	Data filename
discard	Discard filename
discardmax	Number of discards to allow (Default all)
skip	Number of logical records to skip (Default 0)
load	Number of logical records to load (Default all)
errors	Number of errors to allow (Default 50)
rows	Number of rows in conventional path bind array or between direct path data saves (Default: Conventional path 64, Direct path all)

bindsize	Size of conventional path bind array in bytes (Default 65536)
silent	Suppress messages during run (header,feedback,errors,discards)
direct	Use direct path (Default FALSE)
parfile	Parameter file: name of file that contains parameter specifications
parallel	Do parallel load (Default FALSE)
file	File from which to allocate extents

For a complete description of the command-line arguments, refer to the *Oracle7 Server Utility User's Guide.*

You also can specify command-line arguments in the OPTIONS clause of the control file, or from a PARFILE, which makes arguments much easier to maintain. See Listing 8.9 for an example of using a PARFILE.

Listing 8.9. Parfile example.

```
SQLLOAD parfile=weekly.par

WEEKLY.PAR
    userid  = scott/tiger
    control = weekly.ctl
    log     = weekly.log
    errors  = 25
    direct  = true
```

Command-line arguments specified in the control file or a parfile still can be overridden from the command line.

Summary

You have probably noticed by now that SQL*Loader is a very robust utility. You can use SQL*Loader to load very small or very large amounts of data into an Oracle database. SQL*Loader supports a wide variety of external files and gives you a great deal of flexibility in loading your tables. With the parallel option, SQL*Loader is ready to support your data warehousing applications!

Import and Export

9

by
Dave Kinchen

IN THIS CHAPTER

Import and Export are two complementary utilities supplied by Oracle. You use the two utilities together primarily to back up and restore data, move data to other Oracle databases, and migrate data from an older Oracle version to a newer version. The following lists some other uses of Import and Export:

- Store data in operating system files for archiving
- Store database object definitions
- Selectively back up parts of a database
- Move data from one Oracle user's schema to another
- Move data from one hardware platform or operating system to another
- Save space and increase performance by reducing fragmentation

The operation of the Import and Export utilities is quite straightforward. Export writes information about the tables or database objects and data from Oracle tables themselves, such as table creation, index creation, table grants, sizing information, and so on. Export then saves this information to named operating system files. The operating system files that Export creates are known as dump files. The dump files, which are in Oracle binary format, are only useful to the Import utility for the most part. You can name the dump file whatever your operating system allows; if you don't specify an output filename for Export to use, it typically defaults to EXPDAT.DMP.

You can then archive the output files produced by Export to disk or offline for safe keeping, or Import can use them to re-create the exported data for recovery or maintenance purposes.

> **NOTE**
>
> Import reads only files created by Export.

Export

Sometimes you find that you desperately need something and realize that you should have never put yourself in the position of needing it in the first place. Take Import and Export, for example. If the world were perfect, you would never need to import data and therefore never need to export as well. I am certain that I would still be in hot water with a few CEOs someplace if I did not export as often as I do. I find the Export utility to be the easiest method for saving myself great pain later.

Export is a comprehensive utility supplied by Oracle. It is fairly easy to use with quite a bit of flexibility built into the utility through the use of a large parameter list. The parameter options enable Export to provide solutions to complex data management problems. On the surface, Export appears to be a simple utility, but it has the power to become an efficient backup utility for Oracle and enables the database administrator (DBA) to perform important maintenance functions for Oracle databases. Export can write out operating system files that you can move to a different operating system or a different version of Oracle.

The following code shows an example of using Export:

```
exp userid=system/manager OWNER=scott... [other options]
```

The following code shows an example of using Export with a parameter file:

```
exp userid=system/manager parfile=filename
```

Using a Parameter File

You can use a parameter file with both Export and Import. The parameter file can help with imports and exports by providing consistency and simplicity. Using a parameter file in a nightly export is a great idea. Parameter files ensure consistent exports so you can make sure you actually export all the tables that need to be exported. You can start both the command-line and the parameter methods from a shell script, but the command-line method might be too long for your operating system to accept. The export_ts script writes the parameter file that it needs. Remember that you cannot use the PARFILE parameter in the parameter file. Table 9.1 illustrates all of the parameter options.

The following code contains a sample parameter file:

```
USERID=/
LOG=../archive/export_logs/scott_export
BUFFER=64000
COMPRESS=Y
FILE=../archive/export_data/export_ts.dmp
TABLES=
SCOTT.BONUS,
SCOTT.CUSTOMER,
SCOTT.DEPT,
SCOTT.EMP,
SCOTT.EXECUTABLES,
SCOTT.FALL5,
SCOTT.ITEM,
SCOTT.ORD,
SCOTT.PRICE,
SCOTT.PRODUCT,
SCOTT.QUOTA,
SCOTT.SALES1,
SCOTT.SALES2,
SCOTT.SALGRADE
```

Table 9.1. Parameter list for Export.

Keyword	Description	Default
USERID	Username/password of the account performing the export.	
BUFFER	The size of the buffer used to fetch rows. If this is set to zero, only one row at a time is fetched. Oracle provides a good rule of thumb for estimating the buffer size: buffer = rows_in_array × max_row_size. If your table has long data types, Export must fetch one row at a time.	
FILE	Output filename created by Export.	EXPDAT.DMP
GRANTS	Indicates whether or not to export object grants.	Y
INDEXES	Indicates whether or not to export index creation statements.	Y
ROWS	Indicates whether or not to export table data.	Y
CONSTRAINTS	Indicates whether or not to export table constraints.	Y
COMPRESS	Indicates if Export should rewrite the storage parameters of the tables and indexes in the export file.	Y
FULL	Indicates whether this is a full export. If FULL=Y, then use the INCTYPE parameter to specify if the export is COMPLETE (default), CUMULATIVE, or INCREMENTAL.	N

Keyword	Description	Default
OWNER	A list of owners who will have their objects exported. OWNER=scott or OWNER=(scott,temp).	
TABLES	A list of tables to export. TABLES=emp or TABLES=(emp,dept).	
RECORDLENGTH	The length of the file record in bytes. Used to set the record length when transferring the export file to a different operating system.	
INCTYPE	Used when FULL=Y. Valid options are COMPLETE, CUMULATIVE, and INCREMENTAL. If Export is used as a backup and recovery scheme, using the INCTYPE=CUMULATIVE or INCREMENTAL parameters can provide a more efficient solution for exporting because only the changed tables are exported.	
RECORD	Indicates whether to record an incremental export in system tables.	Y
HELP	Shows the help listing.	N
PARFILE	Specifies a filename to read containing the parameter options.	
LOG	Specifies a filename to write log messages.	
CONSISTENT	Specifies if tables being exported need to be read consistent.	

continues

Table 9.1. continued

Keyword	Description	Default
	This might be necessary if you need to export related tables while in use. This is a painful option to use. Oracle needs to use a rollback segment to save the changed rows, so use this parameter during quiet times on the database to minimize impact.	N
STATISTICS	Used to collect statistics on the tables and indexes during the import. The options are ESTIMATE, COMPUTE, and NONE. I recommend using caution here. If you have an application running and tuned well in rule base optimizer, import a table with STATISTICS=COMPUTE.	
MLS	The MLS options are for Trusted Oracle only.	
MLS_LABEL_FORMAT	The MLS options are for Trusted Oracle only.	

NOTE

You can omit the keywords up to PARFILE if specified in this order. Oracle recommends using only the USERID in this manner; it provides the other parameters only for backward compatibility.

Export works in one of three modes, depending on the user exporting the data and what options are chosen. The three modes of export are full database, user, and table. Although Oracle has devised these three modes of operation, they are not actually different modes but different levels of export. In exporting owners (OWNER=scott) and tables (TABLES=emp), for example, a user might want to export only certain tables. The only mode that stands out as a true mode is full database. Export is truly in a different mode if it is run with the parameter FULL=Y. Any TABLE or OWNER parameters conflict with the full mode.

All users can export in the user and table modes, and users with the EXP_FULL_DATABASE role can export in the full database mode as well.

You invoke Export's three modes by using the proper parameter options as listed here:

User mode	`OWNER=ownerlist`
Table mode	`TABLES=tablelist`
Full database mode	`FULL=Y`

Table Mode

Use the table mode to export a single table or a list of tables rather than an entire database. The default is to export all tables that belong to the user doing the export. Users that have access to other schema can export tables from the schema by qualifying with the schema name. The following code is an example of using table mode:

```
exp USERID=scott/tiger TABLES=dept
```

You can also export from another schema:

```
exp USERID=system/manager TABLES=scott.emp
```

or

```
exp USERID=system/manager TABLES=(scott.emp,scott.dept)
```

User Mode

You primarily use the user mode to export all tables and indexes for a particular user or a list of users. This mode works well when you create a user that owns all an application's objects. For example, if I have a user named sales that owns all the tables and indexes and other objects in the sales application, the application export might resemble the following code:

```
exp USERID=system/manager OWNER=sales
```

This gives me an export file of all the objects owned by sales, independent of the tablespace.

Full Database Mode

Full database mode exports all database objects except for objects that are usually created and maintained by SYS. Only users granted the EXP_FULL_DATABASE role can use this option.

Several other nice options are worthy of noting here. By default, Oracle performs a complete export if you specify full database mode (`INCTYPE=COMPLETE`). If you specify the option `INCTYPE=INCREMENTAL`, Oracle exports only the tables that contain any rows that have changed since the last full export of any type. If you specify `INCTYPE=CUMULATIVE`, Oracle exports only tables that contain any changed rows since the last complete or cumulative export.

> **NOTE**
>
> The three modes are not very obvious, and you will find it easy to specify conflicting options. For example, specifying FULL=Y and OWNER=(scott,tom) causes the export to fail.

Command Line Versus Interactive

You can use Export in a limited interactive mode or in a command-line mode.

I usually use Export in the interactive mode when I am doing small projects that I am willing to run myself. Compressing the extents of a single table or moving a table from one tablespace to another are good candidates for the interactive method. Otherwise, I use the command-line method. You can obtain the same results either way for the most part. Use a parameter file when you need to export the same tables regularly or if the command line grows too long.

When Export starts, it prompts you for your USERID if it's not provided on the command line. Next, it prompts you for the buffer size, export filename, export mode, grants, table data, whether you want to compress, the users to export, and the tables to export.

A typical interactive export might resemble the following:

```
exp
Export: Release 7.1.4.1.0 - Production on Sun Oct  1 09:35:19 1995

Copyright (c) Oracle Corporation 1979, 1994.  All rights reserved.


Username: scott
Password:

Connected to: Oracle7 Server Release 7.1.4.1.0 - Production Release
With the distributed and parallel query options
PL/SQL Release 2.1.4.0.0 - Production
Enter array fetch buffer size: 4096 > 16384

Export file: ./expdat.dmp > scott.dmp

(2)U(sers), or (3)T(ables): (2)U > u

Export grants (yes/no): yes > y

Export table data (yes/no): yes > y

Compress extents (yes/no): yes > n
```

The equivalent command-line method resembles the following:

```
exp scott/tiger FILE=scott.dmp
```

Export responds with the following:

```
About to export SCOTT's objects ...
. exporting snapshots
. exporting snapshot logs
. exporting job queues
. exporting refresh groups and children
. exporting database links
. exporting sequence numbers
. exporting cluster definitions
. about to export SCOTT's tables ...
. exporting table                   BONUS          0 rows exported
. exporting table                CUSTOMER          9 rows exported
. exporting table                    DEPT          4 rows exported
. exporting table                   DUMMY          1 rows exported
. exporting table                     EMP         14 rows exported
. exporting table             EXECUTABLES          0 rows exported
. exporting table                   FALL5         30 rows exported
. exporting table                    ITEM         64 rows exported
. exporting table                     ORD         21 rows exported
. exporting table                   PRICE         17 rows exported
Export terminated successfully without warnings.
```

Export Parameters That Affect Performance

Export has several parameters that can affect performance during the export and also during the import. Understanding these parameters and how they impact the system resources, a user's ability to use the database, and your ability to successfully and quickly complete the export and import is quite important. Some of the parameters with the most impact on performance are discussed in this section.

COMPRESS

One of the most widely used parameters is the COMPRESS=Y option. Many people misunderstand what this does for them. Oracle writes out the export file, which contains table and index creation scripts. If COMPRESS=N, the current table storage clause remains intact, but if COMPRESS=Y, the storage clause of the table is altered to reflect one extent (whatever its size) upon importing. This is great in theory, and one extent is usually desirable.

Consider the following scenario. A 90 MB table has three equal extents of 30 MB each in a tablespace. The tablespace has three data files of 33 MB each for a total of 100 MB. Remember that an extent is a contiguous group of Oracle blocks. Because the extent must be contiguous, one extent can fit in each data file. If the table is exported using the parameter COMPRESS=Y and then imported, the import fails. The resulting import fails because extents cannot span data files, and the tablespace has three data files. The export rewrote the storage clause of the table to be one initial extent. The size of the initial extent is calculated as the sum of all existing extents at the time of the export, whether or not they contain data.

At this point, you have two options available. Re-create the tablespace with one data file of 100 MB or more, or create the table before loading the data using the original storage clause utilizing the three extents. If you precreate the table, specify the Import parameter IGNORE=Y; otherwise, Import will fail.

BUFFER

The buffer is the size of the chunk of memory claimed by Oracle to perform the export. Typically, the larger the chunk, the better (at least as far as Export is concerned). Export does not complain if you set BUFFER greater than the amount of memory that is actually available. As always, Oracle takes what it can get.

INDEXES

If you export with INDEXES=Y, you get the capability to create the required indexes without much trouble during Import—but you pay for it with time. Instead of letting Import create the indexes for you, have the import file write out the index creation scripts so that you can run the script at your leisure. This enables you to focus on the data as it is importing. You might also find that during day-to-day operation, indexes are created in the most unlikely tablespaces. Creating the indexes after the import gives you time to remap their locations.

CONSISTENT

The CONSISTENT parameter can be a killer if you are not prepared. The idea is to export the consistent data together. The consistent data refers to tables that have references to other tables. If the tables are in use, you must export them together using the CONSISTENT parameter. It's best if this is only a small number of tables. The remainder of the tables are exported in a second export. During an export, Oracle reads tables one at time. Any changes that are applied to dependent tables might not be reflected in the export file. The CONSISTENT parameter is the only way to alleviate this. During the consistent export, Oracle accumulates all of the transactions on the tables and saves them to a rollback segment. Export then saves the transactions to the export file.

Using the CONSISTENT parameter can cause the rollback segment to grow very large if there are many transactions on the consistent tables. If you must use the CONSISTENT parameter, use it when the tables to be exported have minimal inserts and updates. Your export can fail because of a rollback segment that is too small or the dreaded "snapshot too old" message.

Probably the safest move is to test the export of your consistent tables to see what happens. I know this seems crude, but you will discover what your rollback requirements are for the future.

STATISTICS

Using the STATISTICS option does not slow the export, but it dramatically slows the import while it computes or estimates statistics. I don't recommend that you use the STATISTICS parameter on any sizable tables. It is almost always better to estimate or compute the statistics after the import is complete. Your time is better spent concentrating on the import rather than gathering the statistics.

LOG

The log file creates a record of what happened during the export. When you view the log file, you notice that data in the file looks just like what was echoed to the screen during the export. If you have problems, the log file logs exactly what object failed to export and provides an error message describing why. The log file can be of great help in finding exactly what the problem was and directing you towards a possible fix. If everything goes well during the export, you don't need the log file.

Exporting Tablespaces

As you probably noticed, you can export by owner and you can export individual tables, but there is no easy way to export entire tablespaces in a database. This is one of the most needed maintenance functions of the DBA as users or applications increase their space needs. A DBA should monitor tablespaces in the database and react proactively to prevent any problems related to sizing. Unfortunately, to export a tablespace, the DBA must do quite a bit of database research to find all the tables or table owners in a tablespace.

For UNIX users, I provided a nice shell script to do just what you need. I use this shell script myself and have found it to be a big help in my maintenance efforts. It is easy enough to use that I have our night operators perform the required exports for me. The shell script has a few requirements to work properly. In short, you must be able to access DBA_TABLES, and you must have the role EXP_FULL_DATABASE. Using the script is very easy.

Enter the following from the command line of UNIX:

```
export_ts tablespace name, tablespace name, tablespace name ...
```

How It Works

The script queries the database for all the tables in the tablespace to be exported and then proceeds to build a parameter file for Export to use. The script calls exp using the parameter file as one of the export parameter options (PARFILE=export_ts.par). The parameter file script created is named export_ts.par, and the actual export file is named export_ts.dmp. The script also creates a file it uses internally, export.spl. You usually do not need to be concerned with this file.

Currently, you must run the export_ts script only once for a single tablespace. You could easily modify the script to ask for the name of the export file, thus enabling you to make multiple exports before importing any data. I will leave that modification to you.

```
EXPORT_TS
#! /bin/sh
##########

#####
#            export_ts
#
# UNIX Shell script to export all Oracle tables and indexes from a tablespace.
#            Written by Kelly Leigh and Dave Kinchen
#
#            Usage: export_ts tablespace, tablespace, tablespace
#
#            Requirements:  must be able to access DBA_TABLES
#            and must be assigned the role EXP_FULL_DATABASE
#            developed on a DGUX platform
#####

# Setup filenames that we need to create the export file


# Check to see if there are any tablespaces listed
# if not then display the usage instructions
if [ "$*" = "" ]
   then
     echo "Description:"
     echo "      export_ts is a DBA utility to export all tables in"
     echo "      one or more tablespaces. export_ts accepts a single"
     echo "      (or list) of tablespace names separated by a space."
     echo "Usage:"
     echo "      export_ts (tablespace name) (tablespace_name) "
     echo "Example:"
     echo "      export_ts users"
     exit
fi
# Create list of tablespaces to run through export

echo "Creating a list of tables in tablespaces: $*"
TSLIST=""
for TS in $*
   do
     TSLIST="$TSLIST,'$TS'"
   done
TSLIST='echo $TSLIST ¦ cut -c2-'
TSLIST='echo $TSLIST ¦ tr '[a-z]' '[A-Z]''

# Select table names from sqlplus and pipe them out to a listing file
# Send the output of the sqlplus statement to the bit bucket since
# the spool file will have it.

sqlplus -s / << EOF  > export_ts.spl
set pages 0;
set heading off;
set feed off;
```

```
SELECT owner || '.' || table_name
FROM dba_tables
WHERE tablespace_name IN (${TSLIST})
ORDER BY
  owner,
  table_name
/
EOF
# Echo the listing for the DBA to verify

echo "TABLE LISTING:"
more export_ts.spl
echo "Continue with the export? (Y/N) \c"
read CHOICE
CHOICE='echo $CHOICE | tr '[a-z]' '[A-Z]''

# If yes then first, add commas to the spool file

if [ "$CHOICE" = "Y" ]
  then
    echo "USERID=/" > $PFILE
    echo "FILE=export_ts.dmp" >> $PFILE
    echo "TABLES=" >> $PFILE
    cat export_ts.spl | sed -e "s/  *$//" -e '$!s/$/,/' >> $PFILE
    echo "\n\nStarting the export.  All export data will be written to export_ts
.dmp"
    exp parfile=export_ts.par
  else
    echo "Aborting export."
fi
```

Complete, Incremental, and Cumulative

The parameter INCTYPE tells Export to create one of three types of export files: complete, incremental, and cumulative. By using the incremental and cumulative exports, you can save space and time because only the changed tables are exported. The complete option exports the full database; it's the default for INCTYPE.

Complete

In order to use the complete parameter, the user must be able to do a full database export (FULL=Y). A full database export will export all the database objects so that the database can be recreated from the ground up. The full database export will act as the starting point for a complete import. You must already have a complete export for the incremental and cumulative exports to be of any value because you import them after you import the complete.

Incremental

Incremental exports are where you can save time by only exporting the changed tables in the database. Most databases have tables that change slowly or never at all. If your database is fairly stable, you should consider using the incremental exports. These exports are usually faster than complete exports and consume less space. The export only has tables in it that have changed since the last incremental export, or if no other incremental exports exist, it exports tables that have changed since the last cumulative export. Lastly, Export looks for tables that have changed since the last complete export if a cumulative export does not exist. To use the incremental exports, you import them after the complete and cumulative exports are finished.

Cumulative

A cumulative export, in a sense, makes all of the incremental exports unnecessary. The cumulative export will export all the tables since the last complete export, including all the tables currently exported in the incremental exports. You do not need the incremental exports once a cumulative is completed.

A Backup Strategy

You can use Import and Export as a primary backup scheme for Oracle databases. It is simple and reliable, and you can move the export file to a different platform if necessary. Incremental exports can reduce the time needed for the nightly exports. Exporting using an incremental export could decrease a system's down time during the week and increase processing time and user satisfaction at the same time. Weekly cumulative exports provide for fairly quick recoveries. Monthly complete exports are sufficient on most databases. This scenario takes a full month to repeat itself, and you can also import your data files fairly quickly, if needed.

> **NOTE**
>
> Obviously, you should not store the export files on any device that contains any Oracle data files, control files, and so on. If you were to store export files on any device that contains any Oracle data files or control files, a media failure on that device could very likely make your Oracle database unrecoverable!

Importing a database that you backed up using the incremental export is easy. You should be able to do this in your sleep. (Most DBAs work best that way, I know.) In order to re-create the database, you need the complete export along with all the cumulative exports and incremental exports since the last cumulative export. You begin the recovery by importing the complete export. Next, you import all the cumulative exports; lastly, import the incremental exports.

Import

The Import utility is the converse of the Export utility. On the surface, Import seems to be a simple utility supplied by Oracle—indeed, it functions that way—but it also has quite a few powerful features. It is responsible for reading the export files to re-create the database objects as well as whatever state they were exported in originally. Import can also convert between ASCII and EBCDIC to enable you to move data between platforms. I discuss the more common features later. Import can work interactively or from the command line. When used interactively, Import prompts the user for the necessary parameters to complete the import. It is often easier to supply the parameters on the command line or from a parameter file. Import, like Export, uses parameter files. Table 9.2 provides a full listing of the import options and their features.

Import Usage

The following code line is an example of using Import.

```
imp userid=scott/tiger file=expdat.dmp   [other options]
```

Table 9.2. Parameter list for Import.

Keyword	Description	Default
USERID	Username/password of the account performing the import.	
BUFFER	The size of the buffer used to fetch rows. Oracle provides a good rule of thumb for estimating: buffer = rows_in_array * max_row_size Set this to a large value for faster imports. If you use the COMMIT parameter, the import commits every time the buffer fills.	
FILE	The name of the Export file to import.	EXPDAT.DMP
SHOW	If show is set to Y, no import is actually performed. It just shows you what it would have done.	N
IGNORE	When you set IGNORE=Y, the Object already exists error is overlooked. Use IGNORE=Y when importing into precreated tables. If you specify IGNORE=N, the import for the object will fail if it exists in the database, and the import continues with the next object. Rows might be duplicated in a table if IGNORE=Y and if an import is attempted more than once	

continues

Table 9.2. continued

Keyword	Description	Default
	without truncating the tables or dropping them first.	N
GRANTS	Indicates whether or not to import object grants.	Y
INDEXES	Indicates whether or not to create indexes.	Y
ROWS	Indicates whether or not to import table data.	Y
FULL	Indicates if this should be considered a full Import. Must have the role IMP_FULL_DATABASE in order to import an export file created with the FULL=Y parameter. Usually used in conjunction with the same export parameter. You can use the FULL option with a USER or TABLE import also, importing all objects in the export file.	N
FROMUSER	A list of users' objects to import. This ignores all objects that are not owned by owners in the FROMUSER list. If any objects are imported into a database in which the original owner does not exist, the objects are imported into the importer's schema.	
TOUSER	This can be used to import objects from one owner to another. To use this parameter, you must have the role IMP_FULL_DATABASE.	
TABLES	A list of the tables to import. Use an asterisk (*) to specify all tables. Use the TABLES parameter to perform a table mode import. Specify one table TABLES=emp, or if you want to specify several tables, use TABLES=(emp,dept).	
RECORDLENGTH	The record length of the export file. Usually not used unless you are transferring the data to another operating system.	O/S dependent
INCTYPE	The type of Import being performed: COMPLETE, CUMULATIVE, and INCREMENTAL.	COMPLETE
COMMIT	Indicates that Import should commit after each array, as set by the BUFFER size. You will need large rollback segments if COMMIT=N. Conversely if COMMIT=Y, you need relatively small rollback segments. With COMMIT=Y you might only	

Keyword	Description	Default
	get a partial import of a table if something causes the import to fail. Import rolls back only to the last commit. If Import fails with COMMIT=Y and you have the table constraints disabled, you need to remember to truncate or drop the tables and start over to prevent duplicate rows.	N
HELP	Displays the help screen.	N
PARFILE	Indicates the name of a file to read import parameters. You can use all the parameters except PARFILE in the parameter file.	NONE
LOG	Indicates the name of a file to log all the screen information and also error messages.	
DESTROY	Indicates if the CREATE TABLESPACE commands found in a Full Export Only should be executed. Setting DESTROY=Y destroys the data files of the database being imported into.	
	I suppose that one could really hurt.	N
INDEXFILE	This is a nice option to use to write out all the CREATE and ALTER statements of the objects in the export file. All but the CREATE INDEX commands are commented out. You can import the data with INDEXFILE=*filename* and use the file created by this parameter as a basis for new table creation scripts. With a bit of editing, you can move them to a new tablespace and add more appropriate sizing and storage parameters.	
MLS	For Trusted Oracle only, to indicate if MLS labels should be imported.	N

Like Export, Import works in one of three ways, depending on the options and the user importing the data. The three modes of Import are full database, user, and table. All users can import their own objects in the user and table modes, and users with the IMP_FULL_DATABASE role can import full database exports. Users without the IMP_FULL_DATABASE can still use the FULL=Y parameter, too. When you import a table or user mode export file, you can specify FULL=Y to import the entire file without prompting for any table names or user names. You might notice that the import modes are very similar to the export modes. The modes are named the same between Import and Export. For the user mode, the parameter OWNER in Export is replaced with FROMUSER in Import.

The three modes are invoked by using the proper parameter options as listed here:

User mode	FROMUSER=*ownerlist*
Table mode	TABLES=*tablelist*
Full database mode	FULL=Y

You can import in the three modes interactively. You invoke the three modes by responding to Import's prompts. To import the entire export file, answer yes to the prompt Import entire export file (yes/no). The default for this prompt is yes. For a USER mode import, answer no. Import then asks for a username. After you enter the username, Import prompts for a list of tables. If you do not enter any table names, all the user's tables are imported one at a time. To tell Import that you are done entering table names, enter a period (.) on a new line after specifying the last table.

The following code fragments illustrate the different modes. The first example is from user mode.

```
Import entire export file (yes/no): yes > n
Username: scott
```

The following is from table mode:

```
Enter table names. Null list means all tables for user
Enter table name or . if done: emp

Enter table name or . if done: dept

Enter table name or . if done: .
```

The last example is from full database mode.

```
Import entire export file (yes/no): yes >Y
```

User Mode

The user method of Import enables you to import tables that belong to a specific user. This can also be combined with the table mode to import specific tables from a specific schema. This is important because Import attempts to create the tables in the current schema's default tablespace if the schema specified in the export file does not exist. This can work to your advantage if you need to move tables from one schema to another.

Table Mode

You usually use table mode to import a table or a list of tables, rather than all tables in the export file. If a user has access to other schema, he can import tables from other schema by qualifying with the schema name. The default is to import all tables in the schema of the user doing the import.

Full Database Mode

The full database option of Import does not quite work the same way as the full database option of Export. If you specify the full database option in Export, the entire database is exported, and to import the entire file, you must have the role IMP_FULL_DATABASE assigned to you. If the export file is a user export or table export, the entire export file is imported (whatever is in it), and you do not need to have the role IMP_FULL_DATABASE assigned to you.

Interactive Versus Command Line

Both Import and Export can operate in command-line mode and in interactive mode. Both modes have their advantages, but Oracle recommends that you use the command-line mode with a parameter file. The two modes are outlined in this section. I'm sure you will find good reasons for using both in your own situation.

Interactive Method

The interactive method is an easy way to import data from export files, but you do not have all the options of the parameter or command-line method. For example, you cannot create an index file. The interactive prompts might change depending on the response to previous prompts. The interactive prompts also have the benefit of showing the prechosen defaults. To use Import in the interactive mode, type `imp` or `imp USERID=userid/password` at the command line.

> **NOTE**
>
> The interactive method continues to exist only for backward-compatibility.

An interactive import might resemble the following:

```
/usr/local/p3016dk >  imp scott/tiger

Import: Release 7.1.4.1.0 - Production on Sun Oct  1 10:12:54 1995

Copyright (c) Oracle Corporation 1979, 1994.  All rights reserved.


Connected to: Oracle7 Server Release 7.1.4.1.0 - Production Release
With the distributed and parallel query options
PL/SQL Release 2.1.4.0.0 - Production
```

```
Import file: ./expdat.dmp > scott.dmp

Enter insert buffer size (minimum is 4096) 30720>

Export file created by EXPORT:V07.01.04
List contents of import file only (yes/no): no >

Ignore create error due to object existence (yes/no): yes > n

Import grants (yes/no): yes > y

Import table data (yes/no): yes > y

Import entire export file (yes/no): yes > y
```

Command-Line Method

The same import can be accomplished by entering the following command-line options.

```
imp USERID=scott/tiger FILE=scott.dmp ignore=N
```

Import responds with the following:

```
Import: Release 7.1.4.1.0 - Production on Sun Oct  1 10:19:12 1995

Copyright (c) Oracle Corporation 1979, 1994.  All rights reserved.


Connected to: Oracle7 Server Release 7.1.4.1.0 - Production Release
With the distributed and parallel query options
PL/SQL Release 2.1.4.0.0 - Production

Export file created by EXPORT:V07.01.04
. importing SCOTT's objects into SCOTT
. . importing table "BONUS"                         0 rows imported
. . importing table "CUSTOMER"                      9 rows imported
. . importing table "DEPT"                          4 rows imported
. . importing table "DUMMY"                         1 rows imported
. . importing table "EMP"                          14 rows imported
. . importing table "EXECUTABLES"                   0 rows imported
. . importing table "FALL5"                        30 rows imported
. . importing table "ITEM"                         64 rows imported
. . importing table "ORD"                          21 rows imported
. . importing table "PRICE"                        17 rows imported
Import terminated successfully without warnings.
```

Import Parameters That Affect Performance

As with Export, Import also has several parameters that affect performance. This section lists the parameters that affect performance the most along with an explanation of how they work and how to use them.

BUFFER

The BUFFER parameter for Import works the same way as the BUFFER parameter in Export. For the most part, you can specify a large value for best results.

COMMIT

The COMMIT parameter defaults to N, but if do not have large rollback segments to use (at least as large as the largest table), set this option to Y. If you set COMMIT to Y, Import commits every time the buffer fills and the array is inserted. The only significant performance gain you will notice is when your import fails because of a rollback issue and you must redo an import.

LOG

Quite simply, always use the LOG parameter so you can review the log file and effectively fix anything that went wrong.

How Objects Import

Objects are created in a specific order as the import progresses. The important thing to remember is that Import first creates the table and then loads the data for each table. Import creates all the indexes on the tables after it loads all the table data. Finally, Import enables all the table constraints and triggers. In some situations, the table constraints can cause interesting results (usually undesirable). If you are in the habit of precreating the tables before the import as I am, you know you'd better disable the constraints before importing. Re-enable the constraints when the import is finished. Don't forget!

Tables

Import first creates the table definitions and then loads the data. Import creates all the indexes for the table and then creates and enables the constraints and database triggers. The important thing to note is that all the tables are loaded and all of the indexes are created a table at a time. When the tables are finished, Import creates and re-enables all the table constraints.

Stored Procedures

Packages, functions, and stored procedures are imported without updating the time stamp. This enables Oracle to use the objects without recompiling them.

Snapshots

Snapshots are exported quite uneventfully. Oracle exports and imports the master table, the master table trigger, the snapshot log (if you are using one), and the snapshot itself, similar to exporting and importing tables and database triggers. If you are using a snapshot log, only the snapshot log definition is exported and imported. What this means to you is that the first fast refresh that is attempted on that snapshot will fail. Plan on a complete refresh of all of the imported snapshots after the import is complete.

Importing and Exporting with Personal Oracle7

My world has not been the same since Oracle introduced Personal Oracle7. I have been able to develop complete applications on my PC at home. Although I do not have a PC platform that compares with our Sequent, HP, or DG platforms, I can't resist the desire to develop applications on it. I haven't yet used Personal Oracle7 for any production applications, but I am sure many people have.

All of us who have had the pleasure of experiencing Personal Oracle7 will agree that the Windows front end on the Import and Export utilities is a nice addition to the old familiar utilities. I think that many Personal Oracle7 users like me are developing applications. I find myself exporting tables from the true development platforms at the job site and then importing them into my PC database so I can develop whenever and whatever I like.

Using the Personal Oracle7 version of Import and Export is quite a bit different from the old standards. Personal Oracle7 has a nice GUI interface that is hard to beat. It still works internally the same way as the character versions and outputs files that you can transfer to other Oracle instances. The main difference in Personal Oracle7 is the Windows front end. Figure 9.1 shows the Export utility in Personal Oracle7; the title bar has the caption Database Exporter. The first thing you notice is that parameters are represented by text boxes, checkboxes, or pull-down lists. Figure 9.2 shows the advanced options. The advanced options are Record Length (RECORDLENGTH), Buffer Size (BUFFER), Record Export in System Data (RECORD), Keep Components Consistent (CONSISTENT), Compress When Imported (COMPRESS), Log File (LOG) Increment Type (INCTYPE), and Statistics Type (STATISTICS). The other Export parameters follow similar translations.

Figures 9.3 and 9.4 show the Database Importer and the advanced options available. The Database Importer closely resembles the Exporter's look and feel. I do not go into detail because its functionality is fairly obvious.

FIGURE 9.1.

*Personal Oracle's
Export utility.*

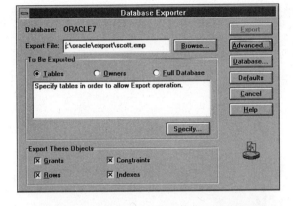

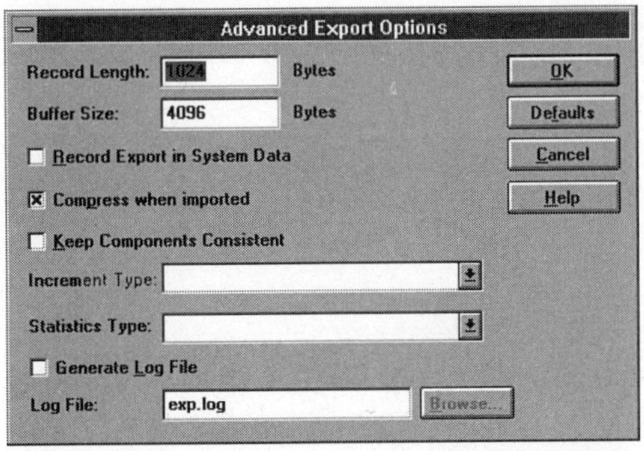

FIGURE 9.2.

*Export utility
advanced options.*

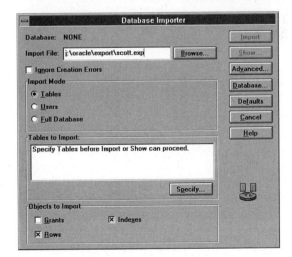

FIGURE 9.3.

The Import utility.

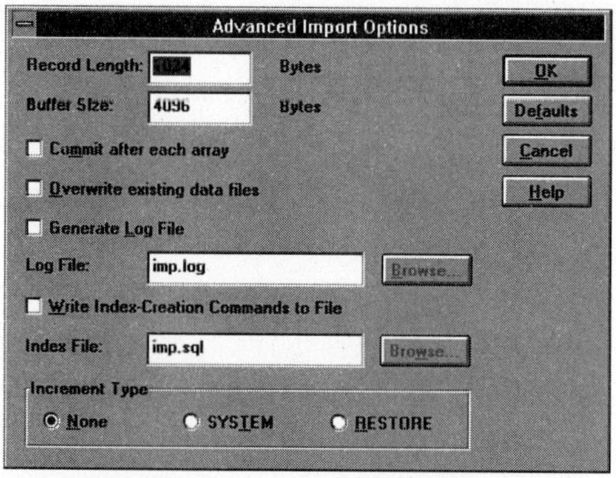

FIGURE 9.4.
*Import utility
advanced options.*

Import and Export Hints and Tips

You can use Import and Export for tasks other than just backing up data. I often use Import and Export for several other constructive reasons, and this section outlines a few of the best hints and tips.

Create an Index File

Import can create what is known as an index file. This is a SQL script of not only the creation scripts for the indexes in the export file but also creation scripts for the other database objects in the export file. All the lines in the file except for the index creation scripts are commented out. The commented-out code contains creation scripts for the remaining objects in the export file. With some editing, you can create a script that can be used to precreate all the tables and indexes and so on. This is often necessary if you use the parameter COMPRESS=Y.

Adjusting Storage Parameters

Using the parameter COMPRESS=Y rewrites the original storage parameters so that the table or index resides on one contiguous extent. Compressing the extents is a good idea as long as you actually have the contiguous extents available. I suggest precreating the tables and indexes with your edited INDEXFILE. This ensures that you can actually create the objects. Of course, if any table or index fails to create, you can adjust the initial and next extents in the INDEXFILE and attempt to create the table again. This is also a good time to adjust the PCTFREE and PCTUSED and the TABLESPACE parameters (or any of the other table parameters) in the table and index creation statements. I highly recommend that you study and adjust the size requirement if necessary at this time, especially if the storage parameters are set to their defaults. I don't go into great detail, but here are some good places to start if you have a mess of default storage parameters:

Parameter	Defaults to	Set to
PCTFREE	10%	5–20%
PCTUSED	40%	55–90%
PCTINCREASE	50%	0%
INITIAL	10240 or 2048	All data in one extent plus some growth if possible
NEXT	10240 or 20480	25% up to the size of INITIAL

There are other storage parameters, but these five are typically the most important to me.

Reorganizing Data

Users own tables, indexes, and other objects. The tables and indexes users create reside in tablespaces. If you were to export a user's tables, drop them, and then import them, they end up in the user's default tablespace again. If you need to move tables from one tablespace to another, you export the tables and change the user's default tablespace and quotas to another tablespace that you want to contain the tables. Then, when you reimport the tables, they are created in the new default tablespace.

Reducing Database Fragmentation

When a database has many small blocks of free space, you should export it with the FULL=Y parameter. Re-create the database and then do a full database import. Tablespaces also need similar help. You should plan carefully where and how many data files a tablespace has. To re-create the tablespace, export all the objects, using the nifty script provided if you like. Drop the tablespace including its contents. Re-create the tablespace and then import the fresh new tablespace.

Migrating from Version 6 to Oracle7

Import can read export files from Version 6 of Oracle. You could use this function to migrate by exporting the Version 6 database and then recreating the database in Oracle7. Some data type changes occurred after Version 6; the old Version 6 CHAR data type changed to VARCHAR2. Import handles this conversion for you. If you're wondering who is going to change all your table creation scripts from the old CHAR data type to VARCHAR2, try using the INDEXFILE parameter explained earlier. Oracle7 provides vastly expanded integrity constraints, and the SQL syntax is slightly different from Version 6. All the existing constraints are exported, but only the NOT NULL constraint is imported and enabled.

Importing Tables with *LONG* and *LONG RAW* Data Types

Did you know it is possible to export a table with extremely large columns (LONG data types can be up to 2 GB in length) only to discover that they cannot be imported? It hasn't happened to me, but Oracle reports that this could happen. The reason is that Export can break up the long data, but Import must read the data into contiguous memory to import. If you do not have enough memory, the import fails.

Summary

Import and Export not only provide data recovery, but they have quite a few database management uses as well. I am sure you will find yourself using Import and Export often to keep your database tuned well by reducing fragmentation and enabling yourself to change the storage parameters of tables and their locations or owners. Whatever task you choose for Import and Export, you will find them to be a stable pair of utilities that are easy to use.

PART

IN THIS PART

Database Administration

Installation

10

by Lave Singh

In this chapter we look at some of the issues involved in installing the Oracle software and database. However, because Oracle runs on more than 90 different platforms, we can only give an overview of the process involved here—the specifics for your operating system can be found in the *Oracle Installation and User's Guide* manual which comes with the software. In addition, the last-minute *System Release Bulletin* that comes with the software should be studied, along with the even later produced README.DOC file that is on the install media.

On most platforms, if a user process connects directly to the database server machine, two things must be known. One is the starting location of the Oracle software directory, and the other is the instance identifier to which the user process will connect. This information is provided in different ways on different operating systems, but many use an operating system command file named something such as "orauser" or "oraenv" to set up these operating system variables as soon as a user logs into the machine.

During the installation process, on most machines, an option is given to install a default database by choosing some menu options. Chapter 11, "Managing the Database," covers how to create a database if you either don't want to or cannot use the menus to give you this starting database. Usually the menus are sufficient to create a practice database, but for production and real systems, more control is needed over the choices available when creating a new database.

Installation of the Oracle tools is usually done at the same time as installation of the Oracle software. For client/server environments, an added complication is that the tools exist on a different machine than that on which the database software resides. To allow the two machines to communicate between each other, some networking software must be installed on both machines (such as TCP/IP), and on top of that both machines need a flavor of SQL*Net installed so that the Oracle software can interface to the networking software. Installing SQL*Net software for the network protocol you're using is usually done at the same time as installing the Oracle server software and tools software.

This is one of the areas where there are major differences between different operating systems due to the nature of the process itself.

Oracle Software Options

When you purchase the Oracle software, a number of additional software options are available. However, these options may not be available on all platforms at the same time (for example, at the time of this writing, the Distributed option was not yet available on the Personal Oracle 7 version of the software).

Base Product

The standard product (without the addition of the procedural, distributed, parallel, or other options) gives you the SQL language—without this not much can be done on the database. In the near future, the PL/SQL language is also to be included in the standard, base product. In addition, the database only locks those rows which are actually being modified instead of locking out the entire table. (This was an option that had to be purchased separately in Version 6 of the database server.)

The base product also includes the capability to do parallel recoveries in the case of media failure, which means that you can have more than one process running the recover tablespace command. All of these processes can run in parallel and will use whichever archived and online redo log files are required for the tablespace being recovered. Parallel tablespace backup commands can also be issued, as well as parallel loads of data from operating system files using the SQL*Loader product with the direct load path option, which is available with that product.

Procedural Option

The procedural option gives the you ability to use PL/SQL and to create procedures, functions, packages, and database triggers. At the time of this writing, this was being bundled in as part of the base product, and so was not an additional option for most platforms.

Distributed Option

The base product itself gives you the ability to write distributed queries—queries which in the same transaction or even in the same statement, query tables on one or more databases, usually by using database links (which have already been defined by the database administrator). In addition, the user can connect to a remote database and make changes to tables on that database.

However, one thing that is not possible without the distributed option is the capability to make changes to tables on more than one database within the same transaction (the same commit unit). The distributed option enables one transaction to make changes to more than one database. When the changes are committed (or rolled back), the Oracle server software ensures that either all the databases commit, or if anything goes wrong, that they all rollback the work. This is provided without requiring the developer to put in any more code than the normal commit or rollback statement.

The synchronization mechanism is provided using the 2-Phase Commit algorithm, which synchronizes all the databases involved.

In addition, with the distributed option, one non-Oracle database can take part in a distributed transaction. Usually this involves using the Oracle Gateway products that enable access to non-Oracle data sources.

If any failures do occur with a distributed transaction, the Oracle RECO background process periodically tries to either commit or to roll back the changes on the databases involved. It is better for the database administrator to allow the RECO process to recover the distributed transaction without getting involved. The Oracle data dictionary tables, DBA_2PC_NEIGHBORS and DBA_2PC_PENDING, give further information on the transactions that have been involved in a distributed failure.

The distributed option is also required if you wish to create Snapshots that are copies of tables (usually) on other databases, which are automatically replicated to your database at user defined intervals. In addition, the distributed option includes the capability to call procedures, functions, and packages, which have been defined on remote databases. So, in theory though not very practically, you can hold the database procedures, functions, and packages on one central database, and all other databases can make calls to this central copy of the code.

Parallel Server Option

The Oracle parallel server option enables more than one instance to access the same set of database files. This option ensures, for example, that if a row is locked on one instance that it is reported as locked on any other instances accessing the same database.

The parallel server option is to be used where more than one processor is available (either in the same machine or in different machines that have been clustered together).

Parallel Query Option

The parallel query option improves performance of full-table scans. This enables a large query to be executed by multiple processes so that many processes can be used to perform parts of the query, with the results being merged together automatically.

In addition, the parallel query option enables creation of indexes in parallel. This is similar in concept to the parallel query mentioned earlier, where more than one process can be used to build different parts of the index, and the results from each of these processes is merged together.

The parallel query option normally runs on those machines where more than one processor has been installed so that you can use the processing power of more than one processor to perform the heavy-load work that you require.

Trusted Oracle

Trusted Oracle provides additional security than what is available with the base product and is usually found either in military-type applications or those where a high level of security is required. This gives, for example, the ability to control which rows are accessible to which users. This is not easily done with the base product.

> **TIP**
>
> Use the v$version view, which is accessible to the system user, to see which versions of the Oracle product you have installed. In addition, the v$compatseg view shows which version of the Oracle server software introduced some of the new releases.

Installation Preparation

The actual process of installing the Oracle software and creating the first database is relatively easy on most platforms because you can follow the menu options; however, preparation before the actual install pays dividends in the long run.

One of the first things to consider is the amount of disk space required both for the software and for the database itself. In addition, the locations of the program files, database files, redo logs, and control files should be carefully considered so that disk contention does not occur.

The amount of storage required for the software varies from platform to platform—the *Oracle Installation and User's Guide* manual for your platform should be able to give you an idea for the amount of storage required.

The amount of memory required for Oracle will be split into the memory required for the Oracle software to load (much of which is re-entrant code that can be used at the same time by more than one process), the common memory areas (such as the SGA), and the private memory areas (such as the PGA for each connection to the database), as well as memory for the client programs which are executing. However, this may be on a different machine than the one on which the database server is being run.

The default memory allocations (especially for the common SGA area) are not sufficient for most databases.

In addition, some operating system specific issues need to be addressed (such as the number of semaphore sets in UNIX)—most of which will be detailed in the installation and user's guide manual.

Installing the Software

Most platforms have a menu-driven installation script or, even better, an installation program that makes the installation a one-stop point-and-click operation, such as the program for installing the Oracle software on the Microsoft Windows platform. Because dependencies exist between different components of the Oracle software, the menu first prompts for the components of software to be installed and works out the dependencies between the different components so that all required components are installed.

On some platforms, it may be necessary to create an operating system account with a high-level of privileges which will be used to install the software (usually called Oracle7).

The operations of connecting as internal, starting up the instance, shutting down the instance, and creating a database are all privileged operations. They can all be performed from within the SQL*DBA tool (or from the server manager tool if that is available on your platform). As a result, your operating system account needs to have the necessary operating system privileges in order to perform these operations (UNIX groups on UNIX, or process rights on VMS, for example). The way that Oracle determines whether these privileges are in effect is different from platform to platform.

At the time of this writing there is no check to ensure that you only install the products for which you are licensed, or that you do not exceed the number of users for which you've bought the license for.

TIP

Use the v$license view to determine whether you are exceeding the number of users for which you're licensed.

Directory Structure

For those platforms where a hierarchical directory structure exists, the Oracle default home directory has a name such as "Oracle7," and below this you'll find many subdirectories—usually one for each product being installed. Within each of these product subdirectories, further subdirectories exist for things such as the install scripts, demo files, and so on.

NOTE

The directory structure underneath the Oracle home directory should not be changed—Oracle needs to know where to find the different files for the software being installed.

For those platforms that support it, an operating system environment variable exists to define where the starting location is for the Oracle software ($ORACLE_HOME for UNIX, ORA_ROOT for VMS and the ORACLE.INI file for the MS Windows platform). After this environment variable exists, Oracle can work out the locations of the subdirectories and gain access to the files it requires.

It is also possible on some platforms to install many different versions of the Oracle software.

Operating System Specifics

In this section, we highlight some points for three of the major platforms for Oracle.

UNIX

In addition to the *Oracle Installation and User's Guide* manual provided for your platform, there is also a generic UNIX technical reference guide that applies to all UNIX platforms on which Oracle can be run. This should be read in conjunction with the installation and user's guide before starting the install.

The $ORACLE_HOME environment variable is used to locate the home directory for the Oracle software, and the $ORACLE_SID environment variable is used to determine which instance ID the user process will connect into.

The PATH environment variable should include the $ORACLE_HOME/bin directory so that you can access the various Oracle components.

One of the options available for the UNIX platform is to allow Oracle to use raw disk devices—essentially this means that the Oracle software can bypass the buffer manager for the disks and access the disk drives directly giving an increase in performance. However, you should ensure that the necessary UNIX expertise is on-hand to manage raw disk devices—something that is not to be considered for those sites new to UNIX and new to Oracle.

VMS

The ORA_ROOT logical is used to point to the location of the home directory for the Oracle software. In addition, the ORA_SID symbol is used to determine the instance identifier of the instance to which user processes will connect.

MS Windows

This is nowadays one of the easiest platforms on which to install the Oracle tools and software.

The ORACLE.INI file is used to set the various parameters used by Oracle. The parameters ending with path control where the Oracle software on the PC attempts to find the Oracle software. The default location of the database server machine, the network protocol used to connect that machine, and the instance identifier used when a connection is made to that machine, can be given by the LOCAL parameter in the INIT.ORA file.

Summary

In this chapter, you have seen an overview of some of the things to consider when installing the Oracle software. This is one of the areas where major differences exist between different platforms. As mentioned earlier, you refer to the *Oracle Installation and User's Guide* manual to learn the specifics for your platform.

Managing the Database

11

by Lave Singh

In this chapter, you learn how to perform the following tasks:

- Make a new Oracle database
- Manage the instance by bringing it up and down
- Obtain information from the Oracle system tables
- Modify the number of control and redo log files

The Parameter File: INIT.ORA

An *instance* is the set of background processes and the memory structures that Oracle uses. Every instance must have a parameter file, known as the INIT.ORA file, from which it retrieves the parameters that it uses to run and the mode of the database. This parameter file is used by the Oracle SQL*DBA tool when the instance is first started. After the instance has been started, the parameter file is not used again until the next time the instance is started. The parameter file must be on the same machine as the SQL*DBA tool.

INIT.ORA parameter files are used to specify

- Amount of storage allocated for the Oracle memory structures
- Which rollback segments to use for the instance
- National language settings
- Settings for running Oracle in parallel server mode
- Which database and control file to use
- When to issue checkpoints
- Limits for database control structures
- Which non-mandatory background processes to initialize

The file is given the generic name INIT.ORA, but the Oracle instance identifier is usually part of the filename. The name can be any filename, but it usually begins with INIT.

The parameter file is an ordinary text file, which you modify using any character-based operating system text editor. The parameters can be included in any order, and they can be specified in upper-, lower-, or mixed case.

> **NOTE**
>
> Even though the parameters can be included in mixed case, the names of operating system files must be specified according to the operating system's rules for file naming. In UNIX, for example, a filename must be specified exactly as it appears on the file system.

You specify over 130 parameters. Most of them are common to all the platforms on which Oracle runs. The number of the parameters increases from one release of the Oracle RDBMS software to the next.

An example parameter file comes with the Oracle software; its default name is INIT.ORA. You can use this file to run your instance, although you might have to adjust the parameters manually to obtain optimal performance.

It is possible to have many parameter files for the same instance, although only one is used at a time for the instance startup. If you want to use another set of parameters for the run, you must shut down and restart the instance.

Many parameters have a minimum value. If they are set below the minimum value, the Oracle instance does not start up. The values of some parameters are derived from settings in other parameters. Normally, you do not need to set them. There are even some parameters that you should not set unless the Oracle support desk instructs you to set them. Appendix A of the *Oracle7 Server Administrator's Guide* describes all the different parameters.

> **TIP**
>
> Use one parameter file for the instance for normal online operations during the day. At night, use a parameter file that optimizes performance for a batch job.

In the INIT.ORA file, the only parameter that is mandatory is the CONTROL_FILES parameter, which names one or more control files to be used for the instance. These control files are used during instance startup to determine the names and locations of the database and redo log files. Table 11.1 describes additional parameters for the INIT.ORA file.

Table 11.1. Important INIT.ORA parameters.

Parameter Name	Description
AUDIT_TRAIL	Must be set to TRUE to enable auditing rows to be inserted, even if the auditing facility has been set up by issuing the AUDIT SQL command.
BACKGROUND_ DUMP_DEST	Controls the directory location where the trace files from the Oracle background processes are written. The alert file, which records significant database events and messages, is also written to this location. You can delete the trace and alert files without affecting the performance of the database.

continues

Table 11.1. continued

Parameter Name	Description
CHECKPOINT_ PROCESS	Controls whether the Oracle CKPT background process is to be run. By running the CKPT process, load is decreased from the LGWR process in updating the database file headers whenever a checkpoint occurs.
CONTROL_FILES	Names one or more control files to be used for this instance. Control files are used during instance startup to determine the name and location of the database and redo log files.
DB_BLOCK_BUFFERS	Specifies the number of Oracle database blocks to cache in the database buffers area of the SGA. The default value of 32 is too small for all but test databases.
DB_BLOCK_SIZE	Specifies the size of each Oracle block in the database files. Set this parameter when you first create the database and then do not alter it.
DML_LOCKS	Specifies the maximum number of DML locks that can be taken out by the instance. There is one DML lock for each user for each table undergoing an INSERT, UPDATE, or DELETE operation at any time for the instance.
INIT_SQL_FILES	Specifies the name of the SQL files to be executed when the database is created. These files are typically the Oracle-supplied files used to create the data dictionary, the views on the data dictionary, and views that enable the export and import utilities to run. After these files have been run during the CREATE DATABASE operation, they are never executed again.
LICENSE_MAX_ SESSIONS	Controls the maximum number of user sessions that can be connected to the Oracle database at any time.
LOG_ARCHIVE_DEST	Controls the location to which the archived redo log files are written if the database runs in ARCHIVELOG mode.
LOG_ARCHIVE_ FORMAT	Controls the naming format of the archived files if the database is running in ARCHIVELOG mode. That way, the redo log sequence number, instance thread number, or a fixed string can be inserted into the filename.
LOG_BUFFERS	Specifies the size of the redo log buffer in the SGA into which all changes are recorded from all transactions on the instance.

Parameter Name	Description
LOG_CHECKPOINT_INTERVAL	Used to specify whether a checkpoint should occur earlier than the default time of a redo log file switch. This should not normally be set for most systems, because more frequent checkpointing incurs extra system overhead in writing out the changed database blocks in the database buffer cache in the SGA.
LOG_CHECKPOINT_TIMEOUT	Controls the amount of time to wait before issuing a check point on the database. For example, if this parameter is set to 1,800 seconds (30 minutes), a checkpoint is performed every 30 minutes, even if no activity has occurred on the system in the period.
MAX_DUMP_FILE_SIZE	Specifies the maximum size of any trace files generated. If you use the trace facility to trace large amounts of work, use this parameter to limit how much trace information can be produced.
OPTIMIZER_MODE	Specifies the default mode for the Oracle optimizer, which determines the execution plan for a SQL statement. The Oracle6 method is RULE, which means that the optimizer does not take account of any statistics that were gathered on tables by using the ANALYZE command. The default value, CHOOSE, uses statistics if they exist. Otherwise, it defaults to the rule based on the optimization method.
OS_AUTHENT_PREFIX	Specifies the proxy login. The Oracle user name defaults to the operating system user name prefixed by OPS$. You can control the password by using this parameter. The default on most platforms is OPS$, but you can change it to any prefix or even NULL.
PROCESSES	Controls the maximum number of operating system processes that can connect to the Oracle database through this instance, which includes the background processes. Four background processes are mandatory, and the instance cannot start without them.
RESOURCE_LIMIT	Must be set to TRUE to enforce checking of resource limits if system resources are controlled through database profiles assigned to Oracle users. To set this parameter online, use the ALTER SYSTEM command.

continues

Table 11.1. continued

Parameter Name	Description
ROLLBACK_SEGMENTS	Contains the names of private rollback segments that the instance should use for storing the before-image of any changes made to the database. Rollback segments not mentioned here can still be activated by using the ALTER ROLL BACK SEGMENT command. If no rollback segments are activated, the SYSTEM rollback segment—normally reserved for recording changes made to the Oracle data dictionary—is used for recording the before-image of the Oracle data blocks. If more than one instance is using the Oracle database, they cannot use the same rollback segments.
SEQUENCE_CACHE_ENTRIES	Specifies the number of sequence objects to cache in the SGA for generating unique numbers using sequences. The sequences must have been created with the CACHE parameter specified as part of the CREATE SEQUENCE statement.
SHARED_POOL_SIZE	Specifies the size of the shared pool area in the SGA that is used to hold the data dictionary cache, cursors for SQL statements, and PL/SQL code units.
SMALL_TABLE_THRESHOLD	Sets the low threshold for the data blocks in an Oracle table. Tables with Oracle data blocks below this limit are read into the SGA completely when you perform a full table scan on them. If a table has more data blocks than this limit, the full table access of the table uses only a portion of the lower part of the database buffers cache of the SGA. This ensures that active blocks in the SGA from other tables are not removed from memory when a full table scan is performed on a large table.
SQL_TRACE	Turns on the trace facility for the instance when set to TRUE. With tracing on, execution plans and statement performance can be determined by formatting the trace files produced with the TKPROF utility. Timing information is provided only if the TIMED_STATISTICS parameter is also set to TRUE.
TIMED_STATISTICS	Determines whether timing information is recorded in the trace files when tracing is enabled for the instance or for user sessions.
USER_DUMP_DEST	Determines the location of user process trace files produced when tracing is enabled for the instance or for user sessions.

Table 11.1 does not describe all the parameters in the INIT.ORA file. Refer to Appendix A of the *Oracle7 Server Administrator's Guide* for descriptions of all the parameters.

TIP

Use the IFILE parameter to name a file that contains a common set of parameters for all the instances running on the machine.

To see the parameters that the current instance is using, enter the following in SQL*DBA:

```
SQLDBA> SHOW PARAMETERS
```

You can also see only those parameters that contain a given string. For example:

```
SQLDBA>  SHOW PARAMETERS buffer
```

shows all the parameters that contain the string buffer.

To see a list of the parameters when the instance first comes up, include the word LIST in the first line of the INIT.ORA file.

To access the parameters from any Oracle tool, run a select operation against the v$parameter table, as in

```
SQLPLUS> SELECT * FROM v$parameter.
```

You must have access to the v$parameter table, which is owned by the Oracle user SYS.

The Oracle SID

The Oracle System Identifier (SID) identifies the Oracle instance on the machine. It is usually set up as an operating system variable—the $ORACLE_SID environment variable in UNIX or the ORA_SID symbol in VMS—that is used to name the Oracle background processes and to identify the SGA area in memory. Whenever a user process wants to connect to a database, the SID set up in that operating system account determines to which instance and, therefore, to which database the user will connect. The same user name can exist in different databases. For example, the Oracle system username SYS exists in all Oracle databases. With the SID, you can connect to the correct instance.

Many instances might be running on the same machine, each doing the processing for a different database. By looking at the processes running on the machine, you see many occurrences of the DBWR background process. The name of the process itself usually has the SID somewhere in it.

For client/server setups, the client machine identifies the network protocol and machine address to which the client machine wants to attach and the name of the SID of the connection. Requests are then processed against the database for which the instance is processing.

Creating a New Database

When you create a database, you create files on disk that Oracle has formatted and prepared. The structure of the database does not have to remain the same as initial structure. You can add other files later.

On some platforms, you can create a new database when the Oracle software is first installed. To create a database manually after that, follow the steps in this section. It is assumed that the software has been installed correctly on your machine. The steps provided here are general steps that apply to most platforms. Creating a database involves operating system-specific steps, of course. Refer to the *Oracle7 Installation and User's Guide* for specific information on your platform.

The crux of creating a database lies in running the CREATE DATABASE SQL statement. You must perform other steps, however, before you can run it. The syntax of the CREATE DATABASE SQL statement is

```
CREATE DATABASE mydb
  LOGFILE file1, file2 SIZE nM
  MAXLOGFILES n
  MAXLOGMEMBERS n
  MAXLOGHISTORY n
  DATAFILE file1 SIZE nM
  MAXDATAFILES n
  MAXINSTANCES n
  ARCHIVELOG ¦ NOARCHIVELOG
```

For example:

```
CREATE DATABASE mydb
    DATAFILE '/disk03/mydb/system1.dbf' SIZE 20M
    LOGFILE '/disk04/mydb/log1.log',
    'disk05/mydb/log2.log' SIZE 512K;
```

The datafile parameter will physically create the first database file on the disk specified and with the size specified. If the file already exists the command will fail (unless the REUSE option is specified as well, in which case the file will be overwritten). The same is true with the LOGFILE parameter, which creates the very first two redo log files.

CAUTION

Don't use the REUSE option of the CREATE DATABASE command, for you could accidentally overwrite a file that is being used by another database. Instead, physically delete the file. You can use REUSE on some platforms when contiguous disk space that you want to reuse has already been allocated to a file.

The default mode of the database is NOARCHIVELOG.

To specify the maximum number of data files, redo logs, and log members that can exist on the database, use the MAXDATAFILES, MAXLOGMEMBERS, and MAXLOGFILES parameters. If you specify lower limits, fewer resources are used in the SGA. The MAXINSTANCES parameter controls the maximum number of instances that can be connected to a database.

If you set these maximum limits lower than the predefined maximum as part of the CREATE DATABASE statement, you must recreate the control file manually to increase them. Instead, you should specify the limits by using the INIT.ORA parameters, which set the limits for that startup of the instance. That way, if you need to increase the limits, simply increase the INIT.ORA parameter and restart the instance.

TIP

Leave the database mode set to NOARCHIVELOG—the default—in the CREATE DATABASE command. Change the mode to ARCHIVELOG when all the application objects have been created and populated. This improves performance while the application objects and data are initially loaded.

The steps in creating a new database are

1. Plan for the creation. Make sure that there is adequate disk space for the database. It is useful to do a sizing exercise to estimate the amount of storage required to hold the data for the application system. Determine the names and locations of the database files, the control file, and the redo log files.

   Make sure that the memory on the machine is enough for the new database, including the memory for the SGA, the PGA, and the programs on the database server machine. All the Oracle memory structures should fit into the machine's real memory.

2. The operating system user account that you will use should have the INTERNAL privilege. This privilege enables your operating system account to run the CREATE DATABASE, STARTUP, and SHUTDOWN commands from the SQL*DBA tool. A lower-level form of the INTERNAL privilege is the OSOPER and OSDBA roles. INTERNAL, OSOPER, and OSDBA are assigned using operating system security mechanisms— groups on a UNIX machine or process rights on a VMS machine. Operating system administrators generally grant your account these privileges.

3. Decide what the Oracle instance identifier is going to be, and set the appropriate operating system variable names. The Oracle SID should not have the same as an existing instance on the same machine.

4. Create the INIT.ORA file for your database. The easiest way to do this is to copy an existing INIT.ORA file. Rename this file to indicate the SID used for the instance— for example, INITMYDB.ORA. Specify the name and location of the control file in the CONTROL_FILES parameter. Specify the name of the database—typically the same as the instance identifier—in the DB_NAME parameter. The name of the database must match the name given in the CREATE DATABASE command. It is recorded in all the database files, the control file, and the redo logs for the database. If you want to change the DB_BLOCK_SIZE parameter, you must do so now. It cannot be modified later.

5. Initiate the SQL*DBA tool, and make a connection to the Oracle RDBMS software by using the INTERNAL account. Although the syntax of the CONNECT command looks similar to a normal connect, no password is specified:

```
SQLDBA>  CONNECT INTERNAL
```

6. Start the Oracle background processes, and allocate memory for the SGA by starting up the Oracle instance. For example:

```
SQLDBA>  STARTUP NOMOUNT PFILE=INITMYDB.ORA
```

7. Run the CREATE DATABASE statement with the parameters specific to your requirements. For example,

```
SQLDBA>  CREATE DATABASE mydb DATAFILE '/disk03/mydb/system1.dbf' SIZE 20M
         LOGFILE '/disk04/mydb/log1.log',
                 'disk05/mydb/log2.log' SIZE 512K;
```

After the database has been created, it is immediately available for use. No further steps are necessary. At this stage, though, you have not created any objects on the database other than the ones automatically by the CATALOG.SQL file. You can now start building the structure of your application database by defining tablespaces, usernames, tables, and so on.

You might need to run additional scripts to install the objects that enable the procedural database option or to store Oracle forms and other programs on the database.

The First Objects Created

Many objects are present on the database immediately after you create it. They are

- The Oracle users SYS and SYSTEM
- A tablespace called SYSTEM
- A rollback segment called SYSTEM
- The core data dictionary tables in the user account SYS
- The CONNECT, RESOURCE, and DBA roles, which provide backward compatibility with granting privileges

SYS has the default password CHANGE_ON_INSTALL, and SYSTEM has the default password MANAGER. To test whether the database was created, try to make a connection using these user names and passwords. The default passwords should be changed. The SYS account is the Oracle user that owns the core data dictionary tables. There is usually little reason to use this account for day-to-day access to the database. The SYSTEM account does not own any of the core data dictionary tables. Instead, it uses a set of views created on them. These views help the DBA and developers obtain information on the structure of the database and its objects.

The first set of data files created as part of the CREATE DATABASE statement is allocated to the SYSTEM tablespace. Its initial contents are usually the data dictionary tables and other objects.

Additional rollback segments should be created on the database.

Along with the core data dictionary tables in the user account SYS, data dictionary views that make the information in the core tables easier to view and manage are created. Public synonyms are created for most of the data dictionary views to give Oracle users access to basic information on their user accounts.

Startup and Shutdown

Before you can use an Oracle database, an instance must be running. An *instance* is the combination of the Oracle background processes and the SGA. This section discusses how to initiate and shut down an instance.

Startup Stages

For a database to be fully open and usable, the instance must be brought through three stages of startup:

1. Starting the instance
2. Mounting the database
3. Opening the database

The first stage involves initiating the Oracle background processes and allocating memory for the SGA. During this stage, the INIT.ORA parameter file is used to determine the mode and instance initialization parameters, such as the sizes of the SGA structures in memory.

The second stage is mounting the database. It involves opening the control file—whose location is specified in the INIT.ORA parameter file used in stage 1—and determining the locations and names of the other database and redo log files.

The third stage opens the actual database files and the redo logs. After this stage has been completed, you can access and use the database objects.

> **NOTE**
>
> In MOUNT or NOMOUNT state, the database can be used only by the DBA.

In some cases, such as when recovery is to be initiated, the database might not have gone through all three stages. For example, it might be at stage 2, which means that only the control file can be accessed. The actual database files are closed, so no operations on database objects are possible.

The tool used to perform the startup and shutdown is the Oracle SQL*DBA utility, which comes with the database software. This tool has a basic menu and "fill in the blank" screens.

Before we can issue a startup or shutdown from the SQL*DBA tool, you must be connected as the INTERNAL user by means of a dedicated server connection. In other words, the multi-threaded server configuration cannot be used. This is a check whether you have operating system privileges and can perform these operations. Operating system-specific privileges, such as UNIX groups or VAX VMS process rights, determine who has access to perform these operations.

```
SQLDBA>  CONNECT INTERNAL
```

After you are connected as the INTERNAL user, you can use the STARTUP command to initiate the instance startup in whatever mode you want. During the first stage of startup, the instance parameter file must be provided. In its simplest form, the startup command brings the instance through all three stages and makes the database available for all Oracle users to access:

```
SQLDBA>  STARTUP
```

Note that the parameter file that the instance will use has not been specified. On most platforms, you can set an operating system environment variable. The default location for the parameter file on a UNIX platform is the /dbs directory under the home directory of the Oracle software.

The name of the database is assumed to have been specified in the INIT.ORA parameter file with the DB_NAME parameter. The name of the database specified is checked against the name of the database stored in the control file. If a mismatch occurs, the instance fails to start up and an error message is generated.

If you do not use this syntax, you must name the parameter file explicitly in the STARTUP command. In the following command, the DB_NAME parameter has not been specified in the INIT.ORA file. Therefore, you must specify it explicitly as part of the STARTUP command.

```
SQLDBA> STARTUP PFILE ='/disk04/initmydb.ora' db_mydbname
```

You can also use this syntax when you want to start up the instance with a set of parameters different from the default values. For example, you might want to use parameters that have been tuned to optimize batch jobs.

If you use the parallel server option, you can specify additional parameters as part of the STARTUP command. The PARALLEL and EXCLUSIVE parameters control whether other instances can access the database after the instance has started up. If you use the EXCLUSIVE parameter, any attempt to start up the instance on another processor fails.

In many cases, you might not want to take the instance through all three stages. For example, you might need to perform maintenance and recovery operations. If this is the case, specify additional parameters, depending on which stage you want.

If you use the NOMOUNT parameter, only the Oracle background processes start and the SGA area in memory is allocated. You typically use NOMOUNT only when the database is created. For example:

```
SQLDBA> STARTUP PFILE ='/disk04/initmydb.ora' NOMOUNT
```

The MOUNT option takes the instance up to the point when the control file is opened. You use MOUNT, for example, when you want to recover the database and the database files or redo logs are not present. You need to have the control file open, which is the case if the database is mounted, because it contains information that helps ensure that the files that make up the database remain in a synchronized state. For example:

```
SQLDBA> STARTUP PFILE ='/disk04/initmydb.ora' MOUNT mydbname
```

CAUTION

The next word after MOUNT or OPEN in the STARTUP command is assumed to be the name of the database. If the name of the database has already been specified in the INIT.ORA file, move the MOUNT or OPEN keyword to the end of the command.

Another option is to bring the database through all three stages but to limit access to the tables to the DBA. This is useful for performing a full export of the database, because the data will not change during the export. For example:

```
SQLDBA> STARTUP PFILE ='/disk04/initmydb.ora' RESTRICT OPEN
```

Only Oracle accounts that have been given the RESTRICTED SESSION system privilege can connect to the database after the instance is brought up with the RESTRICT keyword.

On some operating systems, a special facility is provided to databases to be started automatically when the machine is booted up. Refer to the user's guide for your platform to see how to implement this facility if it is available on your platform.

Shutdown Stages

A database is brought down in three stages:

1. Closing the database files and the redo log files
2. Dismounting the database
3. Shutting down the Oracle background processes and releasing the memory occupied for the SGA

In the first stage, the database files and the redo log files are closed. Before this happens, information in the SGA is flushed down to the database files for system and user data. Entries from the redo buffer cache in the SGA are also flushed down to the active redo log file, and a marker is made in the redo log to indicate that a shutdown has occurred.

In the second stage, the database is dismounted. This means that the control file is updated with synchronization information and closed.

In the third stage, the Oracle background processes are shut down, and the memory occupied for the SGA is released.

The SQL*DBA tool is used to perform the shutdown, and the user must be connected to the database as INTERNAL. For example,

```
SQLDBA>  CONNECT INTERNAL
```

The SHUTDOWN command takes the instance through all three shutdown stages:

```
SQLDBA>  SHUTDOWN
```

If the database is not fully open, informational messages indicate which shutdown stage is not necessary. The other stages are performed.

NOTE

If users are connected to the database, the SHUTDOWN command without any parameters waits indefinitely for them to disconnect from the database. You can disconnect users manually by using the ALTER SYSTEM KILL SESSION command or by means of the SQL*DBA menu options.

You can shut down the instance so that connected users are immediately disconnected and work in their current transactions is rolled back. Use the IMMEDIATE keyword after the SHUTDOWN command:

```
SQLDBA>  SHUTDOWN IMMEDIATE
```

You should send a message notifying all the users currently connected to disconnect from the database. There is no Oracle facility for doing this, so you must use an operating system utility. This is a problem especially for client/server setups, because the users might be running the tools on another machine.

In extreme cases, you can shut down the instance without waiting for information to be flushed from the SGA to the database and redo log files. Use the ABORT option of the SHUTDOWN command:

```
SQLDBA>  SHUTDOWN ABORT
```

Like the IMMEDIATE option, ABORT disconnects all the users currently connected, but the rollback operation is not to be performed when the instance is shut down. Instead, if a rollback is performed, it happens the next time the instance is started up. This option is quicker than the IMMEDIATE option, especially when a large update transaction has to be rolled back before the instance can be shut down. Essentially, the rollback is delayed until you next start up the instance.

A cruder way of bringing down the database on some platforms is to kill the Oracle background processes that are currently running. If the background processes are no longer running, the instance is not up. This method is not recommended, though.

Regardless of how you bring down the instance, the integrity of the database is not in any danger. The values of any changes are recorded in the redo logs; on COMMIT, they are forced to the redo log files on disk. Changes to the database blocks in the database buffer cache in the SGA that have not been written to the database files before SHUTDOWN IMMEDIATE, SHUTDOWN ABORT, or even an instance crash, are reapplied automatically the next time the instance is brought up. This is totally invisible to the user and the DBA. The only noticeable effect after SHUTDOWN IMMEDIATE or SHUTDOWN ABORT is an increase in the time taken during the opening stage of bringing up the instance.

Suppose that you started the instance in NOMOUNT or MOUNT state and need to take it from one stage of startup to another. The easy way to do this is to shut down the instance entirely and then restart it in the mode you want. Likewise, you could use the ALTER DATABASE command, which takes the database from one stage of startup to another. Refer to the *Oracle SQL Language Reference Guide* for more information on this command.

The Data Dictionary

The Oracle data dictionary is a set of tables that the Oracle software uses to record information about the structure of the database. These core system tables are owned by the Oracle user present on all Oracle databases—the SYS user. SYS is rarely used, even by DBAs, for maintenance or inquiry work. Instead, another Oracle user with high-level system privileges is used. Typically, only one other DBA account is created for the user of the DBA.

The DBA does not usually use the SYSTEM user, which is also automatically defined when the database is created. This is because product-specific tables are installed in SYSTEM, and accidental modification or deletion of these tables can interfere with the proper functioning of some of the Oracle products.

Core System Tables

The core data dictionary tables have short names, such as tab$, col$, and ind$. These core system tables are rarely referenced directly, for the information is available in more readily digestible form in the data dictionary views defined when the database is created. To obtain a complete list of the data dictionary views, query the DICT view.

Data Dictionary Views

The data dictionary views are based on the X$ and V$ tables. They make information available in a readable format. The names of these views are available by selecting from the DICT data dictionary view. Selecting all the rows from this view shows a complete list of the other accessible views.

SQL*Plus provides basic column formatting, whereas the SQL*DBA utility does not. Therefore, you use SQL*Plus for running queries on these views.

TIP

If you are not sure which data dictionary view contains the information that you want, write a query on the DICT view. Suppose, for example, that you want to find all the data dictionary views that give information about SYNONYMS—aliases for other database objects. You would write the following query:

```
SQLPLUS>  SELECT * FROM DICT WHERE TABLE_NAME LIKE '%SYNONYM%';
```

The list of views produced by this query is a list of other views that you can query.

Most views used for day-to-day access begin with USER, ALL, ROLE, or DBA.

The USER views show information on objects owned by the Oracle user running the query. Suppose, for example, that a table called FOOTBALL is owned by the Oracle user LINEKER and a table called BOXING is owned by the Oracle user BRUNO. If you log into the Oracle account LINEKER and query the USER_TABLES view, the only table that you will see is the FOOTBALL table. If you disconnect from that user and connect to the Oracle user BRUNO and then run the same query, the only table you will see is the BOXING table.

The data dictionary views beginning with ALL show information on objects owned by the current Oracle user as well as objects to which the user has been given access. Suppose, for example, that BRUNO gives SELECT access on the BOXING table to LINEKER. When you log into the Oracle database using the LINEKER account and run a query on the ALL_TABLES view, you will see information on both the FOOTBALL and BOXING tables. One is owned by the account, and the other is a table that the user can access. Note that BRUNO still sees only the BOXING table.

If you connect to the Oracle database using a more privileged account—such as SYS or SYSTEM—you can access the DBA data dictionary views. The DBA views are typically used only by the DBA. They show information for all the users of the database. The SELECT ANY TABLE system privilege enables other users to access these views. Querying the DBA_TABLES view shows the tables owned by all the Oracle user accounts on the database. If you log in as SYS and query the DBA_TABLES view, you will see that LINEKER owns the FOOTBALL table and that BRUNO owns the BOXING table.

Dynamic Performance Tables

Another set of tables often considered to be part of the data dictionary are the dynamic performance tables. They do not actually occupy storage on the database; they are in-memory tables that exist while the instance is running and disappear when the instance is shut down. Their names typically begin with X$. You rarely go directly to the X$ tables. Instead, you use views that begin with V$ to access the information in a more readable form.

The dynamic performance tables are divided into two groups: static and dynamic. Because they are held in memory, the overhead of keeping them updated is negligible.

The tables that hold static information on the instance and the database setup always show the same information while the instance is running regardless of whatever activity is occurring. For example, the V$parameter table shows the settings for the initialization parameters that have been defaulted or set in the INIT.ORA file.

The dynamic tables are updated continuously when activity occurs and provide data that is useful for tuning. For example, the v$sysstat table holds system-level statistics that show the number of Oracle blocks physically accessed from database files and the number of logical Oracle block accesses. These statistics are updated whenever a SQL command is executed on the database—whether it is user SQL or system-generated SQL.

Other Data Dictionary Views

Other data dictionary views provide the same information as the views discussed previously. These are either ANSI-standard views or views that are present for compatibility with previous versions of the Oracle database. These ANSI-standard views, such as CATALOG, show information in ANSI-standard format. Suppose, for example, that you used the ANSI-standard view names on another database. You can work with the same view names and see the same information on an Oracle database. The views, however, do not show information about the parts of the Oracle database that have surpassed the ANSI standards.

Redo Logs

The Oracle system auditing is affected by the redo logs. There must be a minimum of two redo log files for every database, and in this part, I discuss how to maintain redo log files and how they can be multiplexed.

Creating, Altering, and Dropping Redo Logs

The online redo log files are used to record changes made to the database files. They are also used in rotation. That is, when one redo log file fills, a checkpoint is performed and entries are written to the other redo log file. Once that file has filled and the checkpoint on the next has completed, the next file is used. If the checkpoint on a redo log file has not completed, it cannot be used until the checkpoint has completed. This causes the instance to hang temporarily until the checkpoint has completed. For this reason, additional redo log files can be created.

> **TIP**
>
> As a general rule, size the redo log files so that a switch from one online redo log file to another occurs roughly every 30 minutes. This ensures that not too many checkpoints occur. (Remember: At each checkpoint, the changed database blocks must be written to disk, which causes more disk I/O.) Likewise, the time needed to recover the instance if it fails is not too great; only 30 minutes of changes must be reapplied. Use the Oracle alert file or the V$ dynamic performance views to determine how often log switches occur.

You can create more than two online redo log files when you create the database or by using the ALTER DATABASE SQL command. Because you are modifying the structure of the database, you must start the instance in a mounted state. Having the instance in a mounted state means that the control file is open—the names of the redo logs are recorded in the control file.

To start up the instance in a mounted state, go into the SQL*DBA tool and issue the STARTUP MOUNT command. This assumes that the INIT.ORA parameter file is in the default location and that the name of the database is specified in the INIT.ORA file with the DB_NAME parameter. For example,

```
SQLDBA> STARTUP MOUNT
```

To add another online redo log file, enter

```
ALTER DATABASE ADD LOGFILE
    '/disk03/mydb/log3.rdo' SIZE 512K;
```

When you restart the instance, the log writer background can write to three online redo log files, which reduces the chance of having to wait for a checkpointing process to occur.

To move the redo log files, first make sure that the instance has been started in a mounted state. Use an operating system file copy command, and make a copy of the file that you want to rename or move to a new location. Then issue the following command:

```
ALTER DATABASE RENAME FILE
    '/disk03/mydb/log3.rdo' TO
    '/disk04/mydb/log4.rdo';
```

This command records the new name and location of the redo log file in the control file. Note that it is always necessary to copy the files manually to the new names or locations. Oracle does not make a copy of the files for you.

To drop an online redo log file, first make sure that the instance has been started in a mounted state. Use your operating system's file delete command to remove the file manually from disk.

To notify Oracle that the control file must be updated because the redo log file can no longer to be used, issue the following statement:

```
ALTER DATABASE DROP LOGFILE MEMBER
    '/disk04/mydb/log4.rdo';
```

TIP

The redo log files should all be the same size.

CAUTION

Make sure that there are always two or more online redo log files. Otherwise, you will not be able to restart the instance.

Multiplexing Redo Logs

The redo log files protect the database files in case of failure. If you lose the changes in the SGA, you can reapply them from the online redo log files for the committed transactions. Likewise, if the database has been set up to run in ARCHIVELOG mode, the changes made to the database file since the last backup can be reapplied automatically to a backup of the file, thereby protecting against media failure.

If the online redo log files themselves are lost, however, you run the risk of losing committed work. For this reason, it is a good idea to mirror redo log files by using redo log groups. Essentially, multiple copies of the online redo log files are kept. If one copy is lost, there is always an exact mirror copy that the instance can use. You might think that this would slow down the instance. In fact, the opposite is often the case, because the LGWR background process needs to receive a success signal from only one of the copies. If one of the copies of the redo log files in a redo log group cannot be used, the file is marked as invalid and the instance continues to run as normal.

You can mirror the redo log files when you create the database or by using the ALTER DATABASE command. A redo log group consists of one or more redo log file members, which are the redo log files. All the members of the group have the same information recorded in them—they are mirror copies of one another. The redo log groups are numbered sequentially, starting at 1. To see which group each of the existing files belongs to, access the v$log dynamic view.

In the default setup, a database has two redo log file groups, each of which has one member. This means that there are only two redo log files; the instance writes cyclically from one to the other.

When you mirror an existing redo log file, you create another redo log file member of a redo log group. The following command adds another file to redo log group 1:

```
ALTER DATABASE ADD LOGFILE MEMBER
    '/disk04/mydb/log11.rdo' TO GROUP 1;
```

The command to drop a redo log file is similar. To drop an entire group, issue the following command:

```
ALTER DATABASE DROP LOGFILE
    GROUP 3;
```

Control Files

The control file is used in the second stage of instance startup to find out the names and locations of the database files and the redo logs. Losing this file causes a major headache in recovery. Recovery options restore the control file either from a previous backup or use the CREATE CONTROL FILE SQL command to create it directly. You can set up a further level of protection by having the Oracle instance keep more than one copy of the control file always updated. This ensures that you always have another copy if one copy is lost.

Multiplexing Control Files

To make the Oracle instance update more than one copy of the control file, follow these steps:

1. Use SHUTDOWN NORMAL to bring down the instance.
2. Use an operating system utility to copy the existing control file to a different name.
3. In the CONTROL_FILES INIT.ORA parameter, specify both control files. Separate them with a comma.
4. Bring up the instance. The instance now maintains the two control files.

If you make a copy of the control file, keep the other control file on a disk different from the original to guard against losing the entire disk drive. To provide an extra level of protection, make more than two copies. The extra overhead of keeping extra copies of the control file is negligible compared to the extra protection they provide.

To ensure that more than one copy of the control file is being maintained, you can query the V$parameter table to see the names of the control files currently being updated. This table, however, often truncates the names of the control files. Another way is to put LIST on a line by itself at the start of the INIT.ORA file. When the instance starts, this parameter lists all the parameters used by the instance. The control files parameter shows the full names and locations of the control files used.

If a failure occurs with a control file—for example, if it is accidentally deleted—remove the name of the missing control file from the CONTROL_FILES parameter of the INIT.ORA file. Then shut down and restart the instance.

Trace and Alert Files

In every Oracle instance, the background processes produce trace files and an alert file. The alert file records significant events in the life of the instance, such as instance startups and shutdowns and redo log file switches. It provides information on errors that occur on the Oracle database.

The BACKGROUND_DUMP_DEST INIT.ORA parameter specifies the location of the trace files and the alert file. You can safely delete the trace and alert files, for they are recreated when the background processes need them.

In addition to the trace produced by the background processes, user processes produce trace files, which are usually used for debugging and performance optimization. These trace files are produced in different ways in the Oracle tools. For example, alter session set SQL_TRACE true is used to start tracing in a SQL*Plus or an Oracle reports module. Likewise, setting the statistics option in Oracle Forms shows the number of cursors used during the runform session and produces a trace file.

The name of the trace file is platform-dependent, and the location is given by the USER_DUMP_DEST INIT.ORA parameter. The raw trace files produced are not easy to deal with. Use the TKPROF Oracle utility to format the trace files so that they are easier to read. You can see information such as the number of logical and physical block reads, parses, executions, and fetches for the different SQL and PL/SQL statements that occurred while the trace was running. To sort the trace output, use the command line parameters of TKPROF. Show the slowest statements at the top of the trace output.

Information about the CPU and elapsed time taken by the statements appears only if the TIMED_STATISTICS INIT.ORA parameter is set to TRUE.

You can also set tracing on for the whole Oracle instance. To do this, set the SQL_TRACE INIT.ORA parameter to TRUE. The usual effect, however, is drastically reduced instance performance because all the user-generated and system-generated statements must be recorded in the trace files.

Database Modes

In this part, I discuss two modes in which the database can operate: the default, which means that redo logs are not archived when filled, and ARCHIVELOG mode, which essentially means that copies of the redo log files are made when they fill.

NOARCHIVELOG Mode

The default mode of a database is NOARCHIVELOG. When one of the online redo log files fills, a checkpoint is made and further old and new values are written to the next online redo log file. The redo log files are not archived to the archive destination. Recovery is limited to instance recovery. That is, you can protect against the instance crashing. However, if you lose the database or other files, you must restore the files to the latest backup, and all changes made to the database since the last backup cannot be reapplied. This provides the simplest setup. This setup could be applicable for a development database where losing the database is not such a big deal and where the resources to manage archiving are not available. It is also simpler to maintain because the problem of not having enough space to archive the redo logs does not occur.

ARCHIVELOG Mode

If the database runs in ARCHIVELOG mode, the redo logs are copied over to the archive destination whenever one of the online redo log files fills. The background process, ARCH, should be set up to copy the online redo log file to the archive destination automatically. Otherwise, the DBA must manually copy the files when they fill. If the online redo log files cannot be archived—either automatically by the ARCH background process or manually by the DBA—the whole database waits until the archiving is done. Setting the database in ARCHIVELOG mode obviously involves more work for the DBA, but it provides an extra level of protection. If the database, control, or redo log files is lost, they can be restored from the most recent backup, and all the changes made since the last backup can be automatically reapplied from a combination of the archived and online redo logs.

Changing the Mode of the Database

To change the mode of the database from the default mode, NOARCHIVELOG, to ARCHIVELOG so that redo log files are archived, perform the following steps in the SQL*DBA tool:

1. Shut down and restart the instance in STARTUP MOUNT mode.

2. Run the ALTER DATABASE ARCHIVELOG statement to start archiving.

3. Ensure that the ARCHIVELOG_START INIT.ORA parameter is set to TRUE to enable automatic archiving and that ARCHIVELOG_DEST is set to the destination where you want the offline redo log files copied.

4. Shut down and restart the instance normally. Check that the offline redo log files are being produced by looking at which files are produced in the archive destination or by checking the alert file.

Useful Data Dictionary Views

Table 11.2 describes the data dictionary objects. The objects are classified by purpose:

AUDIT	Views related to the Oracle audit facility
DB STRUCT	Information about the structure of the database as a whole
DUP	Information shown in other views
LOOK	Lookup tables that hold static data or data not likely to change often for the database or instance
MISC	Miscellaneous views
MON	Views that are useful in monitoring current activity in the instance
OBJ STRUCT	Information about the structure of objects within the database
PREV	Views for Oracle5 and Oracle6
SEC	Security Information, including users, roles, and privileges that have been granted or received
TUN	Views useful in tuning

NOTE

If you are not familiar with the dictionary tables and views, ignore the AUDIT, DUP, and PREV objects. Oracle auditing is rarely used. DUP views show information that is available elsewhere. PREV views are provided for compatibility with previous versions of Oracle.

Table 11.2. Data dictionary objects.

Object Purpose	Prefix	Name of Object	Description
AUDIT	USER, DBA	_AUDIT_CONNECT	Information about connections and disconnections to the database.
AUDIT	DBA	_AUDIT_DBA	Subset of DBA_AUDIT_TRAIL that lists the audit entries related to the different AUDIT statements.
AUDIT	DBA	_AUDIT_EXISTS	Subset of DBA_AUDIT_TRAIL that lists the audit entries related to the AUDIT_EXISTS and AUDIT_NOT_EXISTS statements.
AUDIT	USER	_AUDIT_OBJECT	If statement-level auditing is set up on objects, the audit trail for them can be viewed through this view. Lists the operating system user, Oracle user, terminal, and object that are affected.

Object Purpose	Prefix	Name of Object	Description
AUDIT	USER, DBA	_AUDIT_SESSION	Audit trail entries for user connections and disconnections from the database. Includes operating system user, Oracle user, time logged on/off, amount of I/O performed, and deadlocks detected during session.
AUDIT	USER, DBA	_AUDIT_STATEMENT	Audit trail records for GRANT, REVOKE, AUDIT, NOAUDIT, and ALTER SYSTEM commands, including information about which privileges were granted or revoked.
AUDIT	USER, DBA	_AUDIT_TRAIL	A complete list of everything that has been audited. This is a superset of the other audit data dictionary views.
AUDIT	ALL	_DEF_AUDIT_OPTS	If auditing is enabled, this view shows which audit options have been set up.
AUDIT	USER, DBA	_OBJ_AUDIT_OPTS	Shows which audit options have been set up for tables and views.
AUDIT	DBA	_PRIV_AUDIT_OPTS	Lists the system privileges currently being audited.
AUDIT	DBA	_STMT_AUDIT_OPTS	Lists the system auditing options currently in effect.
AUDIT	USER, DBA	_TAB_AUDIT_OPTS	Auditing options for the user's tables and views.
DB STRUCT	DBA	_DATA_FILES	The name, tablespace, and size of the database files, but not the control file or the redo logs.
DB STRUCT	ALL, USER, DBA	_DB_LINKS	Database links that enable access to other databases.
DB STRUCT	USER, DBA	_FREE_SPACE	Free space in the tablespaces, including an entry for each fragment of free space.
DB STRUCT	ALL, USER, DBA	_REFRESH	All the refresh groups that the user can touch.
DB STRUCT	ALL, USER, DBA	_REFRESH_CHILDREN	All the objects in the refresh groups that the user can touch.
DB STRUCT	DBA	_ROLLBACK_SEGS	The rollback statements that have been created in the database, including the static storage parameters and whether the rollback segment is currently in use. Use the V$rollstat dynamic view to see the current state of the rollback segment.

continues

Table 11.2. continued

Object Purpose	Prefix	Name of Object	Description
DB STRUCT	USER, DBA	_TABLESPACES	Describes the accessible tablespaces, including the default storage parameters to use if the storage parameters are not specified when objects are created in this tablespace.
DB STRUCT	USER, DBA	_TS_QUOTAS	If storage is allocated by the DBA on a tablespace by tablespace basis, this view shows how much storage the user can use in a tablespace. Information is given in terms of the number of Oracle blocks and the number of bytes.
DB STRUCT	ALL, USER, DBA	_USERS	Information about the current user or other users on the database, including the default and temporary tablespaces that are defined and encrypted passwords.
DB STRUCT		GLOBAL_NAME	Contains one row that shows the global name of the database. It is used in conjunction with database links.
DB STRUCT		NLS_DATABASE_ PARAMETERS	National language settings specified when the database was created.
DB STRUCT		NLS_INSTANCE_ PARAMETERS	National language settings specified in the INIT.ORA file for this instance.
DB STRUCT		NLS_SESSION_ PARAMETERS	National language settings currently in effect for this session.
DB STRUCT		PRODUCT_ COMPONENT_ VERSION	Version numbers for the database server products.
DB STRUCT		PUBLICSYN	Public synonyms currently defined for the database.
DUP	ALL, USER, DBA	_CATALOG	Objects—tables, views, synonyms, and sequences. This is a subset of the information shown in USER_OBJECTS.
DUP		ACCESSIBLE_ COLUMNS	Columns on all the tables accessible to the user.
DUP		CAT	Synonym for USER_CATALOG.
DUP		CATALOG	Oracle5 view that shows the objects on the database.
DUP		CLU	Synonym for USER_CLUSTERS.
DUP		COL	Oracle5 view that shows the columns on tables and views.

Object Purpose	Prefix	Name of Object	Description
DUP		COLS	Synonym for USER_TAB_COLUMNS.
DUP		COLUMN_PRIVILEGES	Oracle6 view that shows whether column-level privileges have been granted.
DUP		DB	Synonym for V_$DATABASE that shows information about the database.
DUP		DICT	Synonym for DICTIONARY.
DUP		IND	Synonym for USER_INDEXES.
DUP		OBJ	Synonym for USER_OBJECTS.
DUP		SEQ	Synonym for USER_SEQUENCES.
DUP		SYN	Synonym for USER_SYNONYMS.
DUP		SYNONYMS	Oracle5 view that shows synonym information.
DUP		SYSCATALOG	Oracle5 view that shows information about all the objects in the database.
DUP		TABLE_PRIVILEGES	Oracle6 view that shows grants on objects for which the user is the grantor, grantee, owner, or an enabled role or for which PUBLIC is the grantee.
DUP		TABS	Synonym for USER_TABLES.
LOOK		AUDIT_ACTIONS	Lookup table for the audit action codes that lists the audit action names.
LOOK		DICT_COLUMNS	Describes the columns in data dictionary tables and views. It provides information on what each column means.
LOOK		DICTIONARY	Lists all the data dictionary views and dynamic performance tables.
LOOK		RESOURCE_MAP	Lookup table that shows the name of the resource for each of the IDs in the table. The IDs are used to reference resource names in other tables.
LOOK		SYSTEM_PRIVILEGE_MAP	Shows the system privileges that can be granted to roles or directly to Oracle users.
LOOK		TABLE_PRIVILEGE_MAP	Shows the different types of table level privileges that can be granted.
LOOK		V$FIXED_TABLE	Names of all the dynamic performance tables.
LOOK		V$FIXED_VIEW_DEFINITION	Definitions of the V$ views. It shows which X$ tables are accessed by the V$ views.

continues

Table 11.2. continued

Object Purpose	Prefix	Name of Object	Description
LOOK		V$INDEXED_FIXED_COLUMN	Shows which columns of the X$ tables are indexed. It is useful in tuning SQL queries on the V$ views.
LOOK		V$LATCHNAME	Names of latches. It is used in conjunction with V$latch.
LOOK		V$NLS_VALID_VALUES	Valid values that can be set up for the national language support parameters. It is set up depending on which national language software has been installed.
LOOK		V$OPTION	Lists the options installed with the server.
LOOK		V$STATNAME	Lookup table for the names of the statistics reported in the V$sysstat table.
LOOK		V$TYPE_SIZE	Sizes of the database components. It is useful in sizing formulas used to determine the optimum initial and next extent sizes for tables and indexes.
LOOK		V$VERSION	Information about the version numbers of the components for the Oracle server software.
MISC	ALL, USER, DBA	_COL_COMMENTS	Shows the column-level comments on tables or views created using the COMMENT command.
MISC	ALL, USER, DBA	_ERRORS	Errors during the compilation of procedures, functions, packages. The SQL*Plus command SHOW ERRORS formats the contents of this table, which is cleared out automatically when the pl/sql unit has been compiled successfully.
MISC	ALL, USER, DBA	_JOBS	If the DBMS_JOB server package has been used to schedule jobs, this view lists the jobs in the job queue, including who submitted the job, when it was last executed, the next execution date, the pl/sql for the job.
MISC	ALL, USER, DBA	_TAB_COMMENTS	Lists the comments on tables created using the COMMENT command.
MISC		DEPTREE	Shows dependence between database objects. It is created by the Oracle supplied script utldtree.sql.
MISC		DUAL	The dummy table used in some SQL SELECT statements.

Object Purpose	Prefix	Name of Object	Description
MISC		V$LOADCSTAT	Statistics on SQL*Loader direct load jobs, which bypass some of the architectural overheads of Oracle by doing more on SQL*Loader. It is not useful because the table cannot be accessed during load or afterward—the data disappears.
MISC		V$LOADTSTAT	Used by SQL*Loader direct load jobs. No useful access can be made. See V$LOADCSTAT.
MISC		V$TIMER	The current time in hundredths of a second since midnight.
MON	DBA	_2PC_NEIGHBORS	Lists the transactions that are involved in a distributed transaction if the distributed option is installed for the database server. It is useful for the DBA when he must do a manual recovery of a failed distributed transaction.
MON	DBA	_2PC_PENDING	Lists the transactions that failed during a distributed update operation if the distributed database option is installed. It includes a column that advises the DBA whether a commit or rollback should be forced.
MON	DBA	_EXP_FILES	Information about full, cumulative, or incremental exports that have been performed against the database, including the name of the export file, the user doing the export, and the time of the export.
MON	DBA	_EXP_OBJECTS	Lists the objects taken by an incremental export.
MON	DBA	_EXP_VERSION	Version number of the latest export.
MON	DBA	_JOBS_RUNNING	Information about the jobs currently running that use the DBMS_JOB package, including the date when the job last run and the time when it started to run for the current execution.
MON	USER, DBA	_OBJECT_SIZE	Sizes, in bytes, of various pl/sql objects, including the source and the parsed version.
MON		V$ACCESS	Objects that are currently locked and by which sessions.

continues

Table 11.2. continued

Object Purpose	Prefix	Name of Object	Description
MON		V$ARCHIVE	Information about the archived redo log files for each thread of the database.
MON		V$BACKUP	Information about which database files have been backed up using online tablespace backup commands to do hot backups. It includes the time and the SCN when the backup started.
MON		V$BGPROCESS	Describes the background processes and the latest error to have been encountered with the background process.
MON		V$CIRCUIT	Information about which server and dispatcher processes used by the user server processes when the multi-threaded server configuration is used.
MON		V$COMPATIBILITY	Information about whether a downgrade to a previous release is possible for this instance. It might change when the instance is shut down and started up again.
MON		V$COMPATSEG	Information about which release of the software introduced the new features of the database. It is used in conjunction with V$compatibility.
MON		V$CONTROLFILE	Lists the names and statuses of the control files.
MON		V$DATABASE	The name, creation date, database mode, and information about the last SCN archived and checkpointed. This information is gathered from the control file during instance startup.
MON		V$DATAFILE	Information about the database files, including each data file's current status, the size and name of the data file, and the SCN at the last checkpoint.
MON		V$DB_PIPES	Information on the database pipes currently in use on this database, including the owner.
MON		V$DBLINK	Shows all the database links that are currently open.

Object Purpose	Prefix	Name of Object	Description
MON		V$DISPATCHER	Information on the status of the dispatcher processes and the amount of use when running the instance with the multi-threaded server setup. It also includes information useful in deciding whether to increase or reduce the number of dispatcher processes.
MON		V$INSTANCE	Status of the current instance, including whether it was started with RESTRICTED SESSION and whether it is currently being shut down.
MON		V$LATCHHOLDER	Lists which processes and latches are currently being held.
MON		V$LICENSE	Used to determine whether the number of concurrent user limits for your license is being breached. It also shows the maximum number of simultaneous user connections since this instance started.
MON		V$LOCK	Information about the locks currently taken out on this instance, including locks taken out by user processes and locks taken out by the system processes.
MON		V$LOG	Information about the online redo log groups that are currently defined, including the log sequence number and archive status. This information is obtained from the control file.
MON		V$LOG_HISTORY	Information about when the redo log files were archived to the archive destination and the name of the archived file. It is used to ensure that archived files are not created too frequently or infrequently. It is useful for determining which redo log files to apply during a recovery procedure.
MON		V$LOGFILE	Information about log files, including the status of the redo log file and the group to which the log file belongs.
MON		V$MTS	Information about the performance of the multi-threaded server, including how many shared server processes were started automatically.

continues

Table 11.2. continued

Object Purpose	Prefix	Name of Object	Description
MON		V$NLS_PARAMETERS	Values set for the national language support for the whole instance.
MON		V$OBJECT_DEPENDENCY	Shows dependencies on objects currently loaded in the shared pool area.
MON		V$PROCESS	Shows which processes are currently connected to the instance, including the operating system process identifier and the background processes.
MON		V$PWFILE_USERS	Lists users who have been given the SYSDBA and SYSOPER privileges.
MON		V$RECOVER_FILE	Information about files that must go through a media recovery process.
MON		V$RECOVERY_LOG	Information about the number and names of the archive logs needed to get the database files back into synchronization. It is used while a media recovery is in progress. It is a subset of the information in the V$log_history view.
MON		V$RESOURCE	Information about database resources.
MON		V$ROLLNAME	Names of the currently active rollback segments.
MON		V$SESSION	Information about each of the sessions connected to the instance.
MON		V$SQLTEXT	The SQL text of SQL statements in the shared cursors in the SGA.
MON		V$SQLTEXT_WITH_NEWLINES	Similar to V$SQLTEXT but with newline and tab characters to improve legibility.
MON		V$THREAD	Information about the threads that are using the database if it is running in parallel server mode with many instances.
OBJ STRUCT	USER, DBA	_CLU_COLUMNS	Shows which columns in tables owned by a user are part of a cluster.
OBJ STRUCT	USER, DBA	_CLUSTERS	Clusters that have been created. If the cluster has been analyzed, this table includes information used by the cost-based optimizer.
OBJ STRUCT	ALL, USER, DBA	_CONS_COLUMNS	Column-level constraint information on tables, including information about which columns make up the primary key, foreign key, and unique key constraints.

Object Purpose	Prefix	Name of Object	Description
OBJ STRUCT	ALL, USER, DBA	_CONSTRAINTS	Primary key, foreign key, unique key, check, and not null constraints on tables.
OBJ STRUCT	USER, DBA	_CROSS_REFS	Cross references for user views and synonyms.
OBJ STRUCT	ALL, USER, DBA	_DEPENDENCIES	Information on dependencies between database objects, such as tables, views, and procedures.
OBJ STRUCT	USER, DBA	_EXTENTS	Extents taken up by the segments. It shows the size and location of each extent.
OBJ STRUCT	ALL, USER, DBA	_IND_COLUMNS	Columns that make up the indexes on tables and the order in which the columns are included in the index.
OBJ STRUCT	ALL, USER, DBA	_INDEXES	Indexes that have been set up, including the current storage parameters in effect for the indexes. If the index has been analyzed, the information used by the cost-based optimizer is also available in this view.
OBJ STRUCT	ALL, USER, DBA	_OBJECTS	Objects—tables, views, synonyms, and procedures. Refer to this table first when you are not sure whether an object is a table, view, synonym, or procedure. It shows when the object structure was last modified.
OBJ STRUCT	USER, DBA	_SEGMENTS	Storage allocated for all the database segments, including the tablespace in which the storage is allocated and the number of extents taken up.
OBJ STRUCT	ALL, USER, DBA	_SEQUENCES	Sequences used to generate unique numbers using NEXTVAL and CURRVAL. It includes the last sequence number written to disk.
OBJ STRUCT	USER, DBA	_SNAPSHOT_LOGS	Snapshot logs that are used to refresh snapshots. It includes information about the table used to provide the snapshot log and the database trigger on the master table that is used to write to the log table.

continues

Table 11.2. continued

Object Purpose	Prefix	Name of Object	Description
OBJ STRUCT	ALL, USER, DBA	_SNAPSHOTS	Snapshots that are currently accessible to the user. It includes information about the master object the snapshot has been set up on, when the snapshot was last refreshed, the date of the next refresh, and the database trigger that is used to refresh the snapshot.
OBJ STRUCT	ALL, USER, DBA	_SOURCE	Source for procedures, functions, and packages.
OBJ STRUCT	ALL, USER, DBA	_SYNONYMS	Synonyms for tables, views, procedures, and so on.
OBJ STRUCT	ALL, USER, DBA	_TAB_COLUMNS	Column descriptions of tables, views, and clusters. If the table or cluster has been analyzed, information used by the cost-based optimizer is included in this data dictionary view.
OBJ STRUCT	ALL, USER, DBA	_TABLES	Tables, including the current storage parameters. If the table has been analyzed, it includes information used by the cost-based optimizer and information about the number of chained rows. The rowids of rows that have been chained can be obtained if the LIST CHAINED ROWS parameter is provided as part of the ANALYZE command.
OBJ STRUCT	ALL, USER, DBA	_TRIGGER_COLS	Lists columns used in triggers.
OBJ STRUCT	ALL, USER, DBA	_TRIGGERS	Database triggers that have been created on tables, including what event the trigger fires on and the source code for the trigger.
OBJ STRUCT	ALL, USER, DBA	_VIEWS	View definitions, including the underlying SQL statement for the view.
PREV		SYSFILES	Oracle5 view that shows the operating system files used by the database.
PREV		SYSSEGOBJ	Oracle5 view that shows information about the different segments on the database.
PREV		TAB	Oracle5 view that shows table information.
PREV		TABQUOTAS	Oracle5 view that shows information about the amount of storage that users can use.

Object Purpose	Prefix	Name of Object	Description
PREV		V$DBFILE	Redundant. Use V$datafile instead.
PREV		V$LOGHIST	Redundant. Use V$log_history instead.
SEC	ALL, USER, DBA	_COL_PRIVS	Shows which column level privileges have been granted or received if access to tables have been taken down to the column level.
SEC	ALL, USER	_COL_PRIVS_MADE	Shows which column-level privileges have granted if security has been taken down to the column level.
SEC	ALL, USER	_COL_PRIVS_RECD	Shows which column-level privileges have been received by the current user if security has been taken down to the column level.
SEC	DBA	_PROFILES	Lists the profiles created on the database when Oracle profiles are used to limit resource usage.
SEC	USER, DBA	_ROLE_PRIVS	Roles granted to the user. Indicates whether the role is a default, whether the user is allowed to administer the role, and whether the roles require operating system privileges to be enabled.
SEC	DBA	_ROLES	Lists the names of roles and whether a password is required to enable them.
SEC	USER, DBA	_SYS_PRIVS	System privileges that have been given directly to the user.
SEC	ALL, USER, DBA	_TAB_PRIVS	Superset view that lists the grants received or given on objects for which the user made the grant, received the grant, or is the owner of the object.
SEC	ALL, USER	_TAB_PRIVS_MADE	Subset of TAB_PRIVS that shows grants made on objects owned by the current user.
SEC	ALL, USER	_TAB_PRIVS_RECD	Subset of TAB_PRIVS that shows grants on objects for which the user has received the grant.
SEC		RESOURCE_COST	The cost of each resource. It is used to apply weighting factors for resources that can be limited for users with Oracle profiles. The user can change the weighting factors for each resource by using the ALTER SYSTEM SET RESOURCES COST statement.

continues

Table 11.2. continued

Object Purpose	Prefix	Name of Object	Description
SEC		ROLE_ROLE_PRIVS	Roles granted to roles. It indicates whether the role has been granted with the ADMINISTRATOR option.
SEC		ROLE_SYS_PRIVS	System privileges granted to roles. It indicates whether the role can grant the system privilege to other roles or users.
SEC		ROLE_TAB_PRIVS	Table privileges granted to roles. It indicates whether the role can grant the table-level privilege to other roles or users.
SEC		SESSION_PRIVS	System-level privileges available in this session.
SEC		SESSION_ROLES	Roles enabled in this session.
SEC		V$ENABLEDPRIVS	Privileges in effect for the session.
TUN	DBA	_ANALYZE_OBJECTS	List the tables, indexes, and clusters that have been analyzed using the ANALYZE SQL statement.
TUN	USER	_RESOURCE_LIMITS	Resource limits—such as CPU time and logical and physical I/O—that have been set up using Oracle profiles.
TUN		CHAINED_ROWS	The default table name used to report the rowids of rows where a chaining problem has been detected by using the ANALYZE TABLE LIST CHAINED ROWS statement. It is created by the utlchain.sql Oracle-supplied script.
TUN		EXCEPTIONS	Used to provide further information about why an exception could not be enabled. It is created by the utlexcpt.sql Oracle-supplied script.
TUN		INDEX_HISTOGRAM	Used with the VALIDATE INDEX command to determine how many times key values have been repeated. Instead, use the ANALYZE INDEX command and query the user_indexes table.
TUN		INDEX_STATS	Used after the VALIDATE INDEX command has been run. It shows lower-level information about how the index is currently constructed. Instead, use the ANALYZE INDEX command and query the user_indexes table.

Object Purpose	Prefix	Name of Object	Description
TUN		PLAN_TABLE	The default table that stores the results of the EXPLAIN PLAN statement, which shows the execution plan for the statement. It is created by the `utlxplan.sql` Oracle-supplied script.
TUN		V$DB_OBJECT_CACHE	Shows which object definitions are currently being cached in the shared pool area of the SGA, including which users are currently using the object and whether the object has been kept in the SGA.
TUN		V$FILESTAT	Information useful in tuning the database files, including number of physical reads from each database file.
TUN		V$LATCH	Usage and wait information on latches.
TUN		V$LIBRARYCACHE	Information about how efficiently the library cache area of the shared pool is being used in the SGA.
TUN		V$MLS_PARAMETERS	Parameters specified in the INIT.ORA file used to set up Trusted Oracle7.
TUN		V$MYSTAT	Tuning information for this session. It is a subset of the information available in V$sysstat. Use V$statname to get the name of the statistic whose ID is reported in this table.
TUN		V$OPEN_CURSOR	Information about the cursors that are currently open for each user session, including the first part of the SQL statement.
TUN		V$PARAMETER	The INIT.ORA parameters currently in effect. It indicates whether the parameter is the default or whether the default has been overridden in the INIT.ORA file.
TUN		V$QUEUE	Queues for the multi-threaded server setup, including information about items in queue.
TUN		V$REQDIST	Information about the time taken to process requests.
TUN		V$ROLLSTAT	Information about rollback segments, including how often the rollback segments have shrunk and wrapped back to the first extent, as well as the maximum size they have reached.

continues

Table 11.2. continued

Object Purpose	Prefix	Name of Object	Description
TUN		V$ROWCACHE	Provides information that can be used to monitor each row within the data dictionary cache in the shared pool area. The data dictionary caches can be tuned only by increasing the total size of the shared pool area that is shared between the data dictionary caches and the cursor area.
TUN		V$SESS_IO	The amount of logical and physical I/O performed by the currently connected session.
TUN		V$SESSION_CURSOR_CACHE	Tuning information that shows how many cursors have been opened during the session and how often they have been used.
TUN		V$SESSION_WAIT	Shows resources or events that currently connected sessions to the database are waiting for.
TUN		V$SESSTAT	A subset of the information shown in the V$sysstat table.
TUN		V$SGA	The amount of memory used by the SGA.
TUN		V$SGASTAT	More detailed information about the SGA in memory.
TUN		V$SHARED_SERVER	Statistical information about the shared server processes that form part of the multi-threaded server architecture. It includes information about how much work each shared server performs.
TUN		V$SQL	Similar to the V$SQLAREA view except that identical statements are listed as often as they occur.
TUN		V$SQLAREA	Information about the SQL statements currently in cursors in the shared pool area, including the amount of memory needed for them, the number of users executing the statements, the amount of I/O performed, and the number of times the statements were asked to be parsed.
TUN		V$SYSSTAT	Instance-level statistics that show the number of logins and physical and logical I/O since the instance was started.

Object Purpose	Prefix	Name of Object	Description
TUN		V$SYSTEM_CURSOR_CACHE	Similar to V$SESSION_CURSOR_CACHE but shows the cursors in the entire system.
TUN		V$SYSTEM_EVENT	Information about the number of waits for system events.
TUN		V$TRANSACTION	Information about current transactions, including which rollback segments are currently being used by the transactions.
TUN		V$WAITSTAT	Information useful in determining whether waiting occurs because of latches conflicts or because of inserts into a table. It is populated if the TIMED_STATISTICS INIT.ORA parameter is set.

Summary

In this chapter, you learned how to create a database, how to set the mode of the database to ARCHIVELOG, and how to bring an instance up and down. You also learned about the initialization parameters for an instance and the information available in the data dictionary. The fundamentals covered in this chapter are the same for whatever platform your Oracle server runs on. Study your installation and user's guide to see whether any specific differences exist for your platform.

Managing Disk Space

12

by Lave Singh

IN THIS CHAPTER

This chapter discusses the following topics:

- How Oracle manages storage
- The control you have over the amount and location of storage that is obtained
- System structures that use storage

How Object Storage Is Obtained

A database object that uses storage is called a *segment*. The different types of segments include

- Data segments (tables)
- Index segments
- Clusters
- Rollback segments
- Temporary segments
- Cache segments

Cache segments are a special type of object used to do the initial load of the data dictionary caches in the data dictionary area of the shared pool area in the SGA.

Objects such as synonyms, views, and database links do not use storage in their own right. They are only definitions that are stored within the Oracle data dictionary.

After storage is allocated to an object, it is not used by any other object. For example, suppose that you allocate 5MB of storage to a table. If you don't insert any rows in the table, the 5MB of storage remains allocated and empty until you drop or truncate the table. It makes no difference whether you delete rows from the table; the storage remains allocated to it.

Oracle Blocks in the Database Files

The Oracle database consists of files on disk that are grouped together into objects called *tablespaces.* A tablespace is a logical object and consists of one or more database files somewhere on disk. Whenever you want to create a segment such as a table, you can specify the tablespace in which the object uses storage. The object uses storage in the files that belong to the tablespace. In fact, a table or other object can use storage in more than one data file that belongs to a tablespace.

The storage within database files is managed in terms of *Oracle blocks,* which are the smallest units in which storage is used by any database object. The actual size of an Oracle block is determined when a database is created. After it is set, it cannot be modified. To change the default block size, set the DB_BLOCK SIZE parameter in the INIT.ORA file before you issue the CREATE database command. On a DOS platform, the default size is 1 KB. On many UNIX and VAX VMS platforms, the default size is 2 KB. On IBM MVS systems, the default size is 4 KB.

The default size is sufficient for most database implementations. Thus, on a UNIX machine with a block size of 2 KB, a 5 MB database file has 2,560 Oracle block units of storage that can be allocated. The first Oracle block is an overhead block used to keep the database file in synch with the rest of the database files and the control file; it is never to be used to store objects. Therefore, 2,559 Oracle blocks are available for storage.

Even though the size of an Oracle block might be 2 KB, the full 2 KB of storage is not used to store data. Approximately 80 bytes of the 2 KB—it varies with different storage parameters—is overhead storage used to manage the space within the block. Likewise, the first Oracle block allocated to a segment is not used to hold data. Instead, it is used to manage the segment's storage. Table, index, and cluster sizing formulas take this storage into account.

The Oracle blocks for a tablespace are allocated to segments or are free space fragments that can be allocated to segments when required. To see the list of free space fragments for a tablespace, access the dba_free_space data dictionary view.

> **NOTE**
>
> To improve the performance of reading Oracle blocks from disk, the database block size should be a multiple of the operating system block size.

Segments and Extents

When a segment such as a table is created, the storage parameters should be explicitly set for the segment. If no storage parameters are in effect, the segment uses the default storage parameters, which you can specify by each tablespace so that objects created in different tablespaces use different default storage parameters. For each user, a tablespace can be identified as a default tablespace. Therefore, if the tablespace clause is omitted from a CREATE statement, the user will use the default tablespace defined for him.

Assuming that all the default settings are used, when a segment is created, it will occupy a contiguous set of Oracle blocks in the database files when the CREATE statement succeeds. The segment has those Oracle blocks allocated to it and waits for data to occupy them. The first set of contiguous Oracle blocks allocated to the segment is called the segment's *initial extent.*

Suppose that the segment is a table. As rows are inserted into the table, they use the storage in the Oracle blocks allocated to the table in the table's initial extent until no more rows can be inserted into those Oracle blocks. After all the Oracle blocks of the first extent have no more room for any rows, the table automatically uses more Oracle blocks in the tablespace as further rows are inserted into the table. That is, it uses another extent of Oracle blocks. This happens invisibly to the user who is inserting rows—although a slight delay might occur on some systems as another extent is allocated to the segment. The process repeats until the table reaches the maximum number of extents that can be allocated or until no more free space is available to allocate to the table. Additional extents allocated to the segment after the first extent are called *next extents* for the object.

> **NOTE**
>
> The maximum number of extents that can be allocated depends on the size of the Oracle block. For a 2 KB Oracle block, the maximum number of extents that can be allocated is 121.

Growth Patterns

If you use the default settings, the first extent for a table has five Oracle blocks. The second extent allocated also has five Oracle blocks. Each additional extent, by default, is 50 percent larger than the previous one. It may, in fact, be slightly higher because the amount of storage used is rounded up to the nearest five blocks. Further rounding up occurs if a fragment smaller than five Oracle blocks remains after storage from a free space fragment has been allocated. This otherwise leftover fragment is allocated to the table, which avoids having many small fragments of free space cluttering up the list of free space fragments within a tablespace.

> **NOTE**
>
> For every table, Oracle keeps track of what the previous extent would be if no rounding had occurred.

Figure 12.1 shows a table with five extents. The storage parameters have default settings, and the block size is 2 KB.

Whenever a database segment allocates another extent, there is considerable overhead. This is because the data dictionary tables must be accessed to determine where and how much free storage is available. Likewise, the data dictionary must be updated because free storage has been used. The dictionary information about the segment that uses the storage is updated to record the fact that the segment now has another extent. This access to the data dictionary is performed by using *recursive SQL*—system-generated SQL, produced in the background for a number of reasons, including extent allocation. You can use the recursive SQL statistic in the v$sysstat dynamic performance table to determine the amount of recursive SQL being generated. There always is, however, some "background noise" on account of recursive SQL being generated as the Oracle background processes perform their work.

FIGURE 12.1.

A table with five extents.

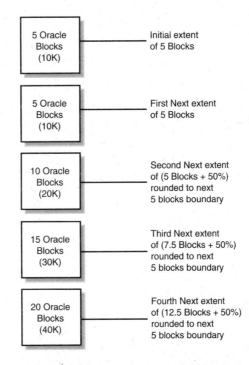

TIP

As a general rule of thumb, when a database segment uses more than 10 extents, the table should be re-created with only one extent to improve the performance of full-table scan-type accesses.

NOTE

Before you create a table, index, or cluster, you should calculate the amount of storage that the table will use. If possible, create the table with an initial extent that is capable of holding the data for it. Doing this minimizes the overhead of allocating additional extents and searching noncontiguous storage areas for data.

Forcing Additional Extents

Generally, you want to calculate the amount of storage that a table or other segment will use and to make sure that the amount of storage is allocated to the object for its initial extent. This ensures that the object has the amount of storage it requires when it is created and that the system overhead of allocating additional extents is reduced. In some cases, however, this wastes storage if it is allocated to an object but not used until some time in the future. Moreover, it might not be possible to allocate the storage required into one initial extent. The Oracle blocks for an extent must be contiguous in one datafile for the tablespace in which the object has been created.

Suppose, for example, that you have the space required, but it is not in one contiguous storage area. One solution is to modify the storage parameters for the segment when it is created so that more than one extent is allocated when the table is created. Another solution is to allocate storage manually by using the ALTER TABLE statement:

```
SQLPLUS> ALTER TABLE karam ALLOCATE EXTENT;
```

This statement allocates to the next extent. Its size is the same as what it would be if the extent were allocated automatically when more storage was required. That is, its size is larger than the previous extent by a given percentage increase parameter. The default percentage increase parameter is 50 percent.

Deleting the rows of a table does not release the storage allocated to it. The rows disappear, but the table continues to use the storage allocated. To release the storage, drop or truncate the table. Dropping the table causes all the information about its structure, the database triggers on it, and the constraints for it to be lost. The truncate command is a quick way of removing the rows of a table without modifying its structure. With the truncate SQL statement, you have the option to release all but the initial extent. The truncate command is a data definition language (DDL) statement. When it is issued successfully, it cannot be rolled back.

ROWID

The ROWID is an internal physical address for every row in every nonclustered table in the database. It is a unique identifier that is not repeated for any two rows across the whole database. The ROWID is a pseudo-column that never appears in the list of columns when a table is described. It can be selected from any table, but it can never be modified.

The ROWID is allocated for the row when the row is first inserted. It remains for the row until the row is deleted or until the table is dropped.

```
SQLPLUS> SELECT ROWID FROM karam;
```

The ROWID is composed of three number components in hexadecimal notation for each row. The last part of the ROWID gives the file number in which the row is located. The filename can be obtained from the dba_data_files dictionary view. The first part of the ROWID indicates the Oracle block within the file—each block within a database file is numbered consecutively starting at 1. The second part of the ROWID specifies the row within the block—because blocks can be many kilobytes in size, they usually hold many rows.

If you know the ROWID for a row, you can use it to access the row. In fact, using the ROWID is the quickest way to get to any row in the database. For example,

```
SQLPLUS> SELECT mycol FROM karam WHERE ROWID = '000004E.00A3.00001' FOR UPDATE OF
mycol;
```

This statement uses the ROWID to lock the row. You must always do a query to access the ROWID before you can use it. It is useful in cases when you access the row and later in the program logic need to update or lock it.

Don't assume that the ROWID remains the same across transactions. Another transaction might delete the row after one of your transactions completes.

Storage Clause

You have learned about the default storage parameters that apply to segments created in the database. Often, however, you want to have more control over the storage parameters and where the storage is allocated, especially in a production database. You can specify a generic storage clause at the end of the CREATE statements when you create the database segments.

The Storage Clause Explained

You can put a storage clause at the end of the CREATE statement for a database segment. The format is

```
STORAGE (     INITIAL xK
          NEXT      xK
          MINEXTENTS x
          MAXEXTENTS x
          PCTINCREASE x).
```

The storage clause overrides the default storage parameters that would be used for the database segment. The initial extent parameter specifies the number of bytes, kilobytes, or megabytes of storage to allocate for the first extent of the database segment. The next parameter specifies the amount of storage to allocate for the second extent for the segment. The values for the initial and next extent parameters are always specified in terms of the number of bytes, kilobytes, or megabytes rather than the number of Oracle blocks. This is because the size of an Oracle block varies from platform to platform and even from one database on a machine to another. By specifying the storage in terms of bytes, kilobytes, or megabytes, you ensure that the same amount of storage is always allocated, regardless of the size of the Oracle block.

The MINEXTENTS parameter specifies the number of extents that are allocated when the segment is created. The default is one for all segments except rollback segments, for which the default is two. The MAXEXTENTS parameter specifies the maximum number of extents that the database object can ever allocate. If this number is reached, an error message is generated and the operation that caused the segment to grab another extent fails. It is unusual, however, to enable database segments—except rollback segments—to use more than 10 extents.

You can modify the NEXT, MAXEXTENTS, and PCTINCREASE parameters after a table has been created by using the ALTER TABLE SQL statement.

You should perform a sizing estimate so that the storage parameters are correctly set for the database object, thereby minimizing the system overhead of allocating additional extents.

You can use the STORAGE parameter in the CREATE statement for database segments—tables, indexes, clusters, rollback segments, and so on. You can specify it as part of the CREATE TABLESPACE SQL statement to set the default storage parameter for objects created in that tablespace. The tablespace default storage parameter is used only where the storage parameter has not been specified as part of the segment creation command.

Other Storage Parameters

In addition to the storage parameters that you can specify in the storage clause, you can specify the TABLESPACE, PCTFREE, and PCTUSED parameters for each database segment.

The TABLESPACE parameter controls the tablespace in which the database segment is created. It assumes that the user has quota privileges to create database objects in the tablespace. Users who want to create database segments must have resource privileges to do so. For each user, you can specify the default tablespace—the default location in which his database segments are created if the TABLESPACE parameter is not specified at the end of the CREATE command for the segment.

When you create a database segment—tables, indexes, clusters, and rollback segments—you should use the TABLESPACE parameter as part of the CREATE statement so that it is explicit where storage is used for the object.

> **TIP**
>
> As a simple performance-tuning measure, put the tables and indexes into separate tablespaces and ensure that the files for the tablespaces are located on separate disk drives. This reduces the I/O bottleneck of having to read and write both table data and index data from the same disk drive.

The PCTFREE parameter for a table controls how much of each Oracle block remains free to enable the rows to expand. By default, the PCTFREE parameter is 10 percent, so that 10 percent of every Oracle block for the table is left empty so that the block's rows can expand into it. This area becomes used only when you expand rows with the UPDATE statement to increase the actual values being stored or to give values to columns that were previously null.

Oracle stores only the bytes required to store a data value. No padding out occurs. The only exception is a column that has been declared as CHAR, in which case padding with spaces occurs. CHAR declarations are not often used, however. Oracle attempts to fit as many rows as possible into an Oracle data block until the PCTFREE limit is breached. Further rows are stored in the next available block for the table. If no more blocks have enough storage free to accept a new row, another extent is allocated to the table.

For a meaningful setting for the PCTFREE parameter, you need to know something about the behavior of the table. (Ideally, this information comes from the database designers.) Suppose that rows are inserted into the table and many columns are left with null or small values. If the table will later be updated to give the columns values where they were previously null or to increase the actual amount of data held, you should set the PCTFREE parameter higher than 10 percent. The value depends on how much you expect the rows to grow.

In another table, the rows might not increase much after they are inserted. In that case, leaving the PCTFREE parameter at 10 percent wastes space that will rarely be used. Reducing the value of PCTFREE—but not to zero—improves storage utilization. Performance is improved because each Oracle block read from disk has more useful data in it.

The PCTUSED parameter is another parameter that you can set for a table. It sets a watermark level below which the amount of space used in a block must fall before new rows are accepted into the block. Take a table whose PCTUSED value is set at 40 percent. As rows are deleted from the block—or even updated where the amount of storage used by the row is reduced—the freed storage is reused until at least 60 percent of the block is empty. The amount of storage used must fall below 40 percent; in other words, more than 60 percent of the block is free. This parameter attempts to reduce the overhead of managing blocks that will accept new rows. For a static table in which not many rows are deleted or space freed within the block, you can set the PCTUSED parameter fairly high—to perhaps 80 percent. That way, storage is reused as soon as it becomes available in a block. For a busy transaction table in which many rows are inserted and deleted, you should set the PCTUSED figure lower—to perhaps 20. That way, when a block can accept new rows, you know that it is fairly empty.

TIP

It is quite common to come across the situation in which many rows are deleted from a table and the table continues to allocate additional extents. This is usually the case when the amount of storage used in a block does not fall below the PCTUSED value. Even though rows have been deleted from the table, the block does not accept new rows. Reduce the PCTUSED value so that more of the blocks are used for the new rows.

Rollback Segments

Another type of segment that uses storage on the database is the rollback segment, which is a system object that is created by the database administrator. It serves two purposes. First, for a transaction that makes changes, the old values of the changed data are kept in the rollback segment, which enables you to reverse them if the `rollback` statement is issued instead of being committed. Second, the rollback segment provides a read-consistent view of the data. This means that even though you change the data in a table and lock the rows, other users can still access the data. They see the old values of any rows until your transaction commits.

An Oracle database always has a rollback segment with the name SYSTEM and the segment type ROLLBACK. You should create additional rollback segments so that the SYSTEM rollback segment is reserved for recording the rollback information when changes are made to the data dictionary system tables—usually with DDL statements or by means of system-generated recursive SQL statements. To determine the number and sizes of the rollback segments that are required, look at the dynamic performance tables.

> **TIP**
>
> As a rule of thumb, there should be one rollback segment for every five users who are likely to make changes at any one time. There should be between 10 and 20 extents for each rollback segment.

Public and Private Rollback Segments

You can create two types of rollback segments: private and public. Private ones are more common and are the default type. A private rollback segment can be used only to record rollback information for transactions running against the instance to which the rollback segment has been associated. A public rollback segment can be used to record information for any transaction running against any instance, which assumes that the parallel server version of the software is used and that many instances are running against the same database.

Creating Additional Rollback Segments

Creating an additional rollback segment involves two steps. You first must create it, and then you must activate it. To create a rollback segment, use the following command:

```
SQLPLUS> CREATE ROLLBACK SEGMENT benisha;
```

You can specify the storage parameter and the tablespace at the end of the create statement in the same way you specified the parameters for a table. However, after you create the rollback segment, you must enable it.

A rollback segment must have a minimum of two extents when it is created. Other database segments need to have a minimum of only one. In fact, rollback segments are usually created with many extents—by using the MINEXTENTS parameter in the storage clause—because of how they are used. Each transaction making a change uses only one extent of the rollback segment, not the entire segment.

Enabling and Disabling Rollback Segments

There are two ways to enable a rollback segment. To activate a rollback segment immediately, issue the following command:

```
SQLPLUS> ALTER ROLLBACK SEGMENT benisha ONLINE;
```

This command activates the rollback segment only until the instance is brought down again (the shutdown command is used in sqldba or the shutdown option is selected in the server manager tool to close the Oracle SGA memory area and close the Oracle background processes).

The other way to activate a rollback segment is to modify the rollback_segments INIT.ORA parameter. The instance must be shut down and restarted before the init.ora parameter comes into effect. In practice, both activation methods are used so that the rollback segment comes online immediately and is reactivated whenever the instance is restarted.

> **TIP**
>
> To check which rollback segments are currently activated, query the v$rollstat dynamic performance view. It shows only the activated rollback segments. The dba_rollback_segs data dictionary view shows all the rollback segments, activated or not.

Growth and Monitoring of Rollback Segments

Like tables, rollback segments are allocated additional extents, as needed, automatically and without user intervention. For example, additional extents might be needed for a rollback segment when many users are making changes or when a batch update operation causes a large amount of redo log information to be recorded.

Unlike tables, however, rollback segments can also be set to shrink in size. You can specify the OPTIMAL clause that is part of the storage clause when you create the rollback segment. This sets a high watermark size for the rollback segment. If the rollback segment grows larger than this size, it automatically releases the additional extents that it was allocated until the amount of storage used falls below the optimal size.

Setting the optimal size is useful, for example, when you expect a monthly batch update to make the rollback segment grow and you want to reclaim the storage. Otherwise, it remains unused until the end of the next month. Don't set the optimal size too low. If you do, making the rollback segment grow when it needs and then shrinking it back to the optimal size will involve too much system overhead.

TIP

You can query the v$rollstat dynamic performance view to see how many times a rollback segment has extended and shrunk.

Rollback Segment Maintenance

All rollback segments should be created with the same extent sizes. This means that the initial and next extent parameters specified for the rollback segments are the same. The PCTINCREASE parameter cannot be specified.

You should create a tablespace just for rollback segments. One reason for this is that if a tablespace contains enabled rollback segments, it cannot be taken offline until the rollback segment is disabled.

Tablespaces

A *tablespace* is the name given to a group of one or more database files. When objects are created, you can specify in which tablespace they will occupy storage. This gives you control over where and how much storage is used. You can specify the amount of storage that users are allowed to use in each tablespace in the database.

Creating the First New Tablespace

An Oracle database always has a tablespace called SYSTEM. The first file that is created belongs to this tablespace. Because this is the first tablespace created, the data dictionary is created in this tablespace.

You can create additional tablespaces. To create tablespaces in addition to the SYSTEM tablespace, you must ensure that at least two rollback segments are enabled. One of them can be the SYSTEM rollback segment, which is automatically created. As long as at least two rollback segments are enabled rollback, you can create as many tablespaces as you want.

To create a tablespace, issue the following SQL command. It is similar to how filenames are specified with the CREATE DATABASE command.

```
SQLPLUS> CREATE TABLESPACE kashmir DATAFILE '\disk01\myfile1.dbs' SIZE 10M;
```

This command creates the tablespace and makes it immediately available. The name of the file in quotation marks is named just as you name files on the operating system—assumed in this case to be a UNIX file system. The size of the file is always given in terms of bytes, kilobytes, or megabytes. After this command is issued, you will find a file at the specified location and with the specified size. Oracle automatically formats the file into Oracle blocks, which is the smallest unit in which storage is allocated.

It is also possible to specify a default storage parameter that has the same syntax as the storage clause—for example, initial extent size, next extent size, percentage increase, and so on. This specifies the default storage that is used when an object is created in the tablespace but when no storage clause is included along with the object definition.

Creating Additional Tablespaces

You can create additional tablespaces in the same manner as described previously. You do not need to create further rollback segments as long as at least two rollback segments are still enabled.

Adding Files to a Tablespace

The filename and size given for a tablespace might eventually fill up as the free Oracle blocks are allocated to the database segments. To increase the number of files that a tablespace can use, enter the following command. It adds another file to the tablespace.

```
SQLPLUS> ALTER TABLESPACE kashmir ADD DATAFILE '\disk01\myfile2.dbs' SIZE 10M;
```

The tablespace now has another 10M of storage to use. Objects already created in the tablespace can now allocate extents from the two files that belong to the tablespace.

> **TIP**
>
> To check the amount of free space remaining in a tablespace, query the dba_free_space data dictionary view. It lists the fragments of free space for each tablespace in the database.

Dropping Tablespaces

You can drop a tablespace easily by issuing the following command:

```
SQLPLUS> DROP TABLESPACE kashmir;
```

This removes information about the tablespace from both the Oracle data dictionary and the control file. The next time the instance starts up, it will not attempt to open the file. This command, however, does not delete the file from the operating system. The database administrator must do that at the operating system level.

If any objects are still using extents in the tablespace, the DROP command shown fails. You should check which objects are using storage in the tablespace by querying the dba_segments data dictionary view. You can use the following optional clause to drop all the database objects in the tablespace before the tablespace is dropped:

```
SQLPLUS> DROP TABLESPACE kashmir INCLUDING CONTENTS;
```

This command fails if active rollback segments are still using storage in the tablespace. You must deactivate them before you remove the tablespace.

Temporary Segments

Temporary segments are database objects automatically created by Oracle when extra working space is needed. This is usually the case when large sort-type operations are performed. For example, when the order by, group by, and union clauses are run on a large table, they might cause a temporary segment to be created.

It is difficult to see the temporary segments, for they are deleted automatically by the SMON background process as soon as they are no longer required. If you suspect that a temporary segment exists, query the dba_segments data dictionary view and look for a TEMPORARY segment type. The v$sysstat dynamic performance table also shows how often temporary segments have been created since the instance was started.

To control where temporary segments are created on a user-by-user basis, issue the following command:

```
SQLPLUS> ALTER USER lave TEMPORARY TABLESPACE kashmir;
```

All users should be defined so that their temporary segments are created in the same tablespace. This ensures that free space fragmentation occurs in only one part of the database.

You can also control how the default tablespace is used. For example,

```
SQLPLUS> ALTER USER lave DEFAULT TABLESPACE kashmir;
```

means that when a user issues a CREATE statement and does not explicitly state where the object should be created, it is placed in the kashmir tablespace.

The dba_users data dictionary view shows the temporary and default tablespaces for all users.

Analyzing Storage

You often have a large amount of storage that has been allocated to a table, but you want to determine exactly how much storage the table actually uses and how much is empty. You might, for example, want to reclaim storage.

The ANALYZE command serves two purposes. By gathering statistics about the data, you can use the Oracle cost-based optimizer to make more intelligent decisions about how to run a statement against the table. Likewise, you can find out exactly how much storage a table uses.

To analyze a table, use the following command:

```
SQLPLUS> ALTER TABLE taejen COMPUTE STATISTICS;
```

This command goes through all the data for the table and gathers information about how many Oracle blocks are used or free and what percentage of them contain data. This information is available in the dba_tables and dba_indexes data dictionary tables.

It can take time to gather a complete set of statistics for a large table. You might want to gather a representative sample of statistics instead. For example,

```
SQLPLUS> ALTER TABLE taejen ESTIMATE STATISTICS SAMPLE 20 PERCENT;
```

This command produces statistics based on a random sample of 20 percent of the rows.

If you do not want the cost-based optimizer to use the statistics that you gather, you can delete the statistics by issuing the following command:

```
SQLPLUS> ALTER TABLE taejen DELETE STATISTICS;
```

After you determine how much storage is used by the table, you can use the export and import utilities to re-create the table with the optimal storage parameters.

Estimating Storage for a Table

To estimate the amount of storage that a table will use, you should know the number of rows expected in the table and their average size. In addition, you need to know the overheads that Oracle will use. The first Oracle block of each datafile is an overhead block, as is the first Oracle block of every database segment. Each block has at least 80 bytes of overhead, plus an additional 23 bytes for every increase in the MAXEXTENTS storage parameter beyond 1. There are five bytes of overhead for each row and one byte of overhead for each column that has a value. Not all the remaining space in a block is used to store your data; some of the block remains free so that the rows can expand into it. This is the PCTFREE parameter, which you can specify when you create the segment.

These overhead figures give you a rough idea of the amount of storage that you should give to a segment's initial extent. After you arrive at an estimate, add on a little more. Chapter 8 of the Oracle 7 server administrator's guide gives a more detailed example of working out the amount of storage to allocate to a segment.

Summary

In this unit, you have seen how Oracle uses the files on the file system for the database, how the storage is managed logically in terms of tablespaces, and the different types of segments that can occupy storage within a tablespace. You have also learned how storage is allocated to the segments when they are first created, when the segments need to grow, and how storage is released. You also saw the ROWID, which is the unique address for every row in a database.

Managing Users

13

by Byron Pearce

IN THIS CHAPTER

Introduction

In *The Rhyme of the Ancient Mariner*, the poet uses the phrase "water, water everywhere" to describe his plight. If this phrase were changed to "users, users everywhere" it might describe the plight of many DBAs (database administrators) throughout the world. With that analogy in mind, see if you can correctly answer the following question.

Users are

   A. Demanding
   B. Unreasonable
   C. In need of constant attention
   D. The reason for the DBA's existence
   E. All of the above

The correct answer is E. Yes, users are demanding (most of the time), unreasonable (sometimes), and in need of constant attention (at least sometimes). However, try to keep these attributes in perspective. By nature, users are typically non-technical entities who do not understand such exotic things as *tables, tablespaces, blocks,* and *buffers.* When users are having problems, they react in the manner to which they are most accustomed: they call an expert. When the sink is backed up, call the plumber; when the car is backfiring, call the mechanic; and when the database is not responding properly or an issue is unclear, call the database administrator.

Like it or not, the title of DBA makes one an expert (at least in the eyes of the user community). In fact, at some sites DBAs mystically possess the ability to diagnose applications, system administration, and network problems (which is usually untrue, but often the perception).

Many times the last thing a DBA needs is an interruption from a user ("I have a fragmented SYSTEM tablespace, two production tables at MAXEXTENTS, a full production tablespace, and a backup that didn't run properly. What do you mean you want your password reset?"). But these people are the reason the DBA can cash a monthly paycheck. As Peter Parker (the boy who would be Spider-Man) remarks in an early comic, "With great power comes great responsibility." If anyone could be a DBA, then everyone would be a DBA.

User Needs Analysis

Administering users is more complex than just having the SYS or SYSTEM password (or a similar DBA-privileged account) and creating an account. You face issues surrounding what system privileges to have (such as CREATE TABLE or CREATE VIEW), what privileges to have on what database objects, and in systems that provide application-level security (such as Oracle*Financials), what application modules a user should access. Paramount to all these issues is better understanding the needs of the user community that the DBA is supporting. Before moving on into the semantics of user creation and setup, this section briefly describes how to analyze and meet the needs of users.

To better serve users, you need to understand what users want. In short, they usually want the moon ("I need access to the Corporate General Ledger system") when they sometimes need only a telescope ("I need a copy of the report with the end-of-month sales totals"). Users often are willing to spend great lengths of time, energy, and effort telling the DBA exactly what they need. More often than not, however, the user has only a limited scope on what is occurring in the overall system; a DBA should rely on methods other than user request to determine needs. Don't ignore user requests, but take them in context of what they are trying to accomplish.

> **TIP**
>
> What a user *wants* is not always what he or she *needs*.

Although the job of the database administrator is basically, as the name implies, administrative, DBAs are often involved in the overall design process. Often, the role is of a consulting type, where the DBA evaluates data modeling in relationships or works with applications administrators to set up security roles and database access. Although a more detailed discussion of database security occurs in Chapter 16, "Database Security," this section offers a brief discussion of the procedure of evaluating needs for user roles. Then you proceed onto the syntactical elements of user management.

A DBA might pose the following questions (either rhetorically or physically) when creating a role and/or granting user access:

1. What does the user want?
2. What does the user need?
3. Is someone currently set up like this?
4. What is the minimum level of access that the user should have to do his or her job?
5. What is the maximum level of access the user should reasonably have?
6. What constraints (technical or political) exist in setting up this user?

Assume for a moment that a staff accountant approached the DBA, claiming that she required access to the sales database. Assume, also, that the corporation was a conglomerate of several different companies, each running its own database. The accountant wants access to a database instance that does not contain any of her company's data. However, she claims that the information is for a corporate-level project on which she is working. Certainly the DBA has the proper level of privileges (the power, as it were) to add the user. Should the DBA do this (the responsibility part of the equation)?

What Does the User Want?

As mentioned earlier, a user generally tells the DBA exactly what he or she needs; take this request with a grain of salt. These perceptions are important, because they do help shape and affect what the end, and overall, result will be. However, the DBA should complete a full and overall analysis (generally in cooperation with other technical and non-technical personnel) of the situation before logging into the database and complying.

Note, however, that the DBA should pay attention to what the user says (or at least give the illusion of paying attention) for a couple of reasons. First, the DBA may learn something. Often DBAs can become embroiled in the daily concerns of tuning the Shared Pool or making certain that the SORT_AREA_SIZE is properly set. Users work in their applications all day long and can often add valuable insight that the DBA, on his or her own, may not think of. In addition, listening is important, if for no other reason, to make the user feel valuable and to enhance future working relationships. It is important to stress that any organization is a team, and DBAs are not the fuhrers. Users and DBAs are both cogs (albeit cogs in different wheels) of the same corporate machine.

What Does the User Need?

This question is often trickier than "What does the user want?" (or at least trickier to answer properly). At this level, the DBA usually needs to consult with an applications administrator, manager, or someone who understands the application level of the system. In a few sites, the DBAs also serve as the applications administrators.

A user may need access to the database to run reports, view data, modify existing data, create new database rows, or just have a copy of a report (as in the earlier example). Try to identify what the user is shooting for and what means are required to accomplish that goal. Also, consider if options are available to accomplish the task without granting access. This is not to suggest that a Spanish Inquisition be conducted every time a user needs access. However, every single Oracle license costs the organization a hefty sum of cash that no one should fault the DBA for trying to save. A final factor to consider is whether or not the access needs are ongoing. If a user needs a copy of September's General Ledger, then it can be done (under most normal circumstances) by another user (or even the DBA) and passed on. However, if the same user is going to need the report every month, the same access usually would not be withheld.

> **TIP**
>
> Do not be afraid to grant a user temporary access to data unless some specific corporate policy prohibits this practice. As a rule of thumb, if it is going to take more time to produce the data than to create, and later drop, the user account, then issue the temporary account.

Is Someone Currently Set Up Like This?

A major time-saver in many organizations is to be able to set up a user like an existing user. This step limits the analysis phase to determining what the user needs and then creating the account. In these situations, you generally just need to coordinate with the appropriate applications administrator or manager to determine if this setup is correct ("Do you really want Katie to be able to do all the things Carlton can do?"). If so, then the DBA can create the account without a tremendous amount of further effort. If the setup is not correct, then you need to make determinations as with any new user situation.

What Is the Minimum Level of Access the User Should Have to Do His or Her Job?

Sometimes DBAs are perceived as minimalists by their nature. Granting user access qualifies as one of those times. In general, the level of access DBAs give to the database in terms of system and object-level privileges, as well as what applications modules the user can access, should be only what the user needs to do the job. (For more information on security, see Chapter 16.) Minimal access doesn't mean that users are incompetent, malicious people who will take advantage of every situation. However, mistakes can (and will) happen.

Take the case of Richard, a power user of an OLTP system. Richard is always making modifications to data in many tables. Because he has a working knowledge of SQL, Richard has access to the database via SQL*Plus. Instead of granting access to the specific tables, however, the DBA takes a shortcut and grants the following privileges: INSERT ANY TABLE, SELECT ANY TABLE, DELETE ANY TABLE, and UPDATE ANY TABLE. Shortly thereafter, Richard finds a book on Oracle (a book like this one) at his local bookstore and learns about the SYS-owned DBA-views. Richard begins some experimenting and one day issues the following command to see the result:

```
delete from sys.dba_users;
```

If committed, the command can cause serious problems for the DBA and everyone else using the database. This situation could have been avoided had the user account been appropriately implemented.

> **WARNING**
>
> Be very careful granting privileges that are part of the any groups (SELECT ANY TABLE, DROP ANY TABLE, and so on) because they give users a very high level of database access (more discussion on this topic in Chapter 16). As long as these privileges remain in effect, users can perform the action in question with unlimited access.

What Is the Maximum Level of Access the User Should Have?

At the opposite end of the spectrum is the concept of maximization. Where the idea of "minimum level of access" determines what a user must have to do his or her job, the idea of "maximum level of access" determines the cut-off point. For example, if a corporate policy prohibits users from changing data in certain application tables (except for a certain level, such as manager or MIS, of which the user is not a member) then no user should be granted access to perform this task.

This necessary evil must be defined in all user settings. In some settings, no upper limit may exist; users may be permitted to have any privilege short of DBA. In other environments the data may be extremely sensitive and require investigation to have access. To understand these limitations, the DBA should have an in-depth knowledge of the applications systems and the rules that drive it, or have access to someone who does.

What Constraints (Technical or Political) Exist in Setting Up This User?

At times, the DBA may not be able to do what the user asks. Perhaps granting a user access to certain tables would inadvertently give him or her access to change data that should never be changed. On the other hand, perhaps access is permissible but the comptroller does not want anyone with this access ("Not in my backyard!"). Whatever the reason, this problem falls within the realm of constraints.

Constraints (not to be confused with database constraints, which were covered in earlier chapters) take the shape of technical and political constraints. Under technical constraints, some underlying reason prevents setting up a user. Perhaps the username conflicts with an Oracle reserved word. Here, the only option is to determine another method (a workaround), perhaps giving the user another name. The other side of the constraint house is political. As mentioned earlier, no real reason exists to prevent something from being done except one or more forces in the company do not want it done. In this case, the DBA can override the users (not the best way to win friends and influence people, and upper management may then override the DBA) or work on a compromise. Of all constraints, political are by far the worst.

Although constraints may not always be a problem, they are issues you cannot ignore when setting up and managing user accounts.

User Authentication Methods

As a rule, databases do not have an open door policy that allows everyone access (of course, there are exceptions). Therefore, a database needs a way to authenticate the user, determining his or her identity and making certain that he or she has authorized access. In general, a database uses one of two proven methods: *password authentication* and *operating system authentication.*

Password Authentication

The concept behind password authentication is the same as the traditional password method used on other databases, operating systems, network servers, and the like. Under this concept, the database (in this case Oracle) issues a challenge (Password:) followed by a prompt. Each distinct user ID has an alphanumeric string associated with it that the user must enter correctly to gain database access. For example, assume a user account named CHERIE with a password of SCARLETT:

```
% sqlplus
Enter user-name: cherie
Enter password: ........
SQL> show user
user is "CHERIE"
```

Note in the preceding example that the password is not echoed to the screen. This important safety feature enables users (or even a DBA) to enter a password and not worry about others staring over his or her shoulder.

At the option of the DBA, the username and password may be passed to the application (such as SQL*Plus) on the command line. If you take this step, the password is echoed to the screen:

```
% sqlplus cherie/scarlett
SQL> show user
user is "CHERIE"
```

Operating System Authentication

In certain organizations, a person may be admitted entry if his identity is confirmed by a known person. This same tenet is true for operating system authentication; the user is allowed access to the database if he or she has a valid operating system account that shares the same username as the database account.

For example, on a UNIX-based system, a user may be set up with a user account named LANCE within UNIX (usually done by the UNIX system administrator). The DBA, in turn, creates an account called "OPS$LANCE" within the database. When Lance connects to UNIX, he need only pass nulls to the database's query for a password to gain access. The database extracts the username from UNIX (LANCE) and checks to see if an operating system authenticated account exists within the database (OPS$LANCE). If the account is found, the user is granted access; if the account is not found, the request for access is denied.

```
% sqlplus /
SQL> show user
User is "OPS$LANCE"
```

By passing a slash (/) from the command line, the DBA or user invokes this type of login. Simply put, a slash causes a null to be passed as both the username and the password. This type of authentication is enough to allow access to the database.

User Configuration Setup

After deciding on what type of authentication method to use, the DBA is still responsible for making determinations regarding how to set up the user within the database. Just like creating a UNIX user requires the UNIX system administrator to define certain things, such as the user's shell and home directory, similar things need to be defined in the database environment.

This process is known as setting up the user configuration. Although determining the number and types of privileges within the database can encompass a whole separate analysis process, the setup of the user configuration is relatively straightforward. (For more details on security, see Chapter 16.) User configuration has three basic elements:

- Profiles
- Default tablespace
- Temporary tablespace

Each of these elements serves a specific function and are discussed in more detail in the sections that follow.

Profiles

The database profile is Oracle's attempt to enable the DBA to exercise some method of resource management upon the database. According to the *Oracle7 Server Administrator's Guide*, a profile is "a named set of resource limits." To better understand this term, take a step back and try to understand where it came from.

Most of the power-user tools that exist under Oracle7 were not around in Oracle6. To a certain extent, many sites were still trapped in a mainframe mode that precluded the type of access that is now considered common. Even SQL*Plus was considered primarily a developer's tool and was not something available to users. Then, as they say, someone let the genie out of the bottle. Products were introduced that allowed for client/server access to the database data using graphical tools, and these types of tools became commonplace. However, the tools presented a problem for the DBA: how to restrict them.

Because Oracle6 used a rule-based optimizer, a change in the table order of a FROM clause or the statement order of a WHERE clause could double or triple (or more) the amount of time required to run a query. Most users were unwilling (or unable) to learn how to properly build queries, and thus were often guilty of releasing queries that could bring a production system to its knees.

Oracle7 introduced profiles, which were part of two tools to help the DBA administer an RDBMS in an ad-hoc environment (the other tool is the cost-based optimizer). Using profiles, the DBA can designate such things as how much CPU time a user can receive during a single database session or per SQL statement, how much idle time a user can accumulate, or how much time a user can be connected to the database. The DBA gives each profile a name (such as CLERK, MANAGER, or ACCOUNTANT), and certain fixed resource limits are associated with the name. This profile is then assigned to a user, who then must function within the designated profile limits.

A user with no profile assigned receives, by default, a profile named DEFAULT. The DEFAULT profile is mandatory and must be present within the database. A more complete discussion of profiles is included later in this chapter.

Default Tablespace

If you conceptually think of the Oracle database as its own operating system (as some academics have argued), then you would probably consider the *default tablespace* the "home directory" of the database world. As shown in earlier chapters of this book, you can create a table, index, or other database object using the TABLESPACE option:

```
CREATE TABLE order
    (
    orderno     NUMBER(6),
    partno      NUMBER(10),
    qty         NUMBER(3),
    cost        NUMBER(7,2)
    )
TABLESPACE users;
```

In the preceding example, the table ORDER is created in the users tablespace. However, if no tablespace is designated, as in the following example, the table is created in the tablespace designated as that user's default tablespace.

```
CREATE TABLE order
    (
    orderno     NUMBER(6),
    partno      NUMBER(10),
    qty         NUMBER(3),
    cost        NUMBER(7,2)
    );
```

The default tablespace, simply, is the tablespace where a database object is created if no other tablespace is specified.

> **WARNING**
>
> If the DBA specifies no default tablespace, a user's default tablespace is the SYSTEM tablespace. This can lead to SYSTEM tablespace, which contains the data dictionary and other information crucial to database operation, becoming fragmented or full. In some cases, the only way to correct problems is to re-create the entire database.

Temporary Tablespace

The *temporary tablespace* is also a tablespace, but it is different in function from the default tablespace. Let's continue the analogy of the database as an operating system. If the default tablespace is the home directory, then the temporary tablespace is the UNIX /tmp directory.

Fundamentally, the temporary tablespace functions as a "holding area" for SQL commands that require making sorts to the disk (as opposed to sorts in memory). Common examples of this type of operation are GROUP BY, SORT BY, and UNION ALL. When these types of operations are performed, the Oracle RDBMS takes contiguous extents on the temporary tablespace (segments) and uses this space to perform the required sorting and/or joining operations. After the operation is completed, the database releases the segments held within the tablespace.

Although a temporary tablespace is not required to be on a separate tablespace from other database objects, it is recommended. Not only does a separate tablespace reduce contention, but it also avoids fragmentation (for details on both, see Chapter 15, "Performance Tuning and Optimizing"). Separation also helps keep the tablespace from reaching capacity unexpectedly. Any user who does not have a temporary tablespace set by the DBA has a default temporary tablespace of SYSTEM.

Resource Management

As discussed earlier in this chapter, Oracle7 provides more than the capability to create user accounts within the database and constantly monitor their activity: It provides the capability to restrict activity by managing resources. To do this, Oracle7 offers two distinct features: profiles and tablespace quotas.

The primary difference between these two features is the type of resources they manage: profiles control process/memory utilization, and quotas control disk space. When implemented effectively, both features can help curtail things such as rampant, runaway queries and excessively large, unnecessary tables. Using these features, the DBA has a proactive tool to help efficiently maintain the database.

Using Profiles

As mentioned earlier in this chapter, profiles control the amount of resources a user can have. Although a list of profile resources is given below, it is important to note that you don't need to specify *every* profile resource in *every* profile. Any profile resource the DBA does not specifically set has the value of DEFAULT, corresponding to the value of the DEFAULT profile.

- SESSIONS_PER_USER
- CPU_PER_SESSION
- CPU_PER_CALL
- LOGICAL_READS_PER_SESSION
- LOGICAL_READS_PER_CALL
- IDLE_TIME
- CONNECT_TIME
- PRIVATE_SGA_PER_SESSION
- COMPOSITE_LIMIT

The database does not enforce the values of a profile unless the parameter RESOURCE_LIMIT is set in the INIT.ORA parameter file. This value is `false` by default, meaning that no profiles are enforced; the DBA should set the value to `true` if profiles are desired. In the event that a database cannot be restarted (using shutdown and startup) and profiles are needed, issue the following SQL command from Oracle Server*Manager or SQL*Plus:

```
alter system set resource_limit = true;
```

Defining Profiles

As with creating users, defining a profile is more complex than just issuing a SQL command to create it. Each individual profile is a combination of one or more resources that the database is instructed to manage. Many of these resources contain the value DEFAULT, which can change depending on the value of the default profile, or UNLIMITED, which places no upper limits on the resource.

Just as important as knowing how to create the profile, however, is knowing what to create. For example, a cost accountant and a comptroller may both work out of the accounting group; however, the comptroller may work an additional three to four hours per night above what the cost accountant works. Therefore, placing a limit of eight hours on the total connect time is not sufficient for the comptroller. In this case, you need to make the overall connect time larger (12 hours) or give the associates separate profiles. You need to understand the ramifications of the profiles and how they will impact the jobs of each user class before you implement the profiles.

The various profile resources for which limits can be set are described briefly in the following sections.

SESSIONS_PER_USER

The setting for SESSIONS_PER_USER is used to determine the maximum number of sessions (connections to the database) a user can have simultaneously. If a user has reached the limit set in the SESSIONS_PER_USER resource of his or her profile, then the next login (and any subsequent ones) produce an error condition.

For example, if a user with a SESSIONS_PER_USER of 2 pulls up an application menu via SQL*Forms and is running a report via Oracle*Reports, the user has reached his or her limit. If that user attempts to create another session via SQL*Plus (or any other application), the database denies the connection until one of the other connections is terminated.

> **WARNING**
>
> Be careful when dealing with Oracle CDE tools (such as Oracle*Forms). In many cases, if a tool makes a call to another tool, another connection is established. For example, an Oracle*Forms application that calls another Oracle*Forms application that calls an Oracle*Reports report is a total of three connections (one for each tool) and not a single connection.

CPU_PER_SESSION

Each query a user issues consumes an amount of CPU time, which varies dependent upon the query. By setting this resource item, the DBA limits the amount of CPU time a user can consume from a single database session. After reaching the CPU limit, the user can perform no further activity in that session. The user must disconnect from the database and then reconnect to reset this CPU accumulator.

The value of this parameter represents the total amount of CPU time (in minutes) that a user can consume during a single database connection.

CPU_PER_CALL

This resource, like CPU_PER_SESSION, represents the total amount of CPU time (in minutes) available to the user. However, this resource restricts the user on a per-call (SQL statement) basis rather than a per-session basis. Whenever a SQL statement reaches its limit, it ends with an error condition. Unlike CPU_PER_SESSION, however, the user has no need to disconnect from the database. When using CPU_PER_CALL, the user is free to issue another query as long as it does not exceed the total amount of time specified in CPU_PER_CALL.

LOGICAL_READS_PER_SESSION

Like CPU_PER_SESSION, this resource element is responsible for determining how much activity can take place during a given database session. In this case, the value is the total number of logical reads (in database blocks) that can be performed in a given session. If the LOGICAL_READS_PER_SESSION is exceeded, the user can still continue to function as long as he or she does not perform actions that cause reads from the database to be performed (such as a query).

To reset, the user must disconnect from the database and/or establish a new database connection.

LOGICAL_READS_PER_CALL

What CPU_PER_SESSION is to LOGICAL_READS_PER_SESSION, CPU_PER_CALL is to LOGICAL_READS_PER_CALL. The value of this parameter restricts the number of database blocks that can be read during a single CPU call (SQL statement). If the number of blocks that the database attempts to logically read exceeds the limit set, the operation is abandoned. The user may issue another SQL statement and have no problems unless the logical reads in this statement exceed the value.

IDLE_TIME

Many UNIX systems have a so-called *idle daemon*, which terminates user processes that exceed a certain amount of inactive time. The IDLE_TIME resource is an attempt by Oracle to implement such a technology at the database level.

In essence, a system (in this case) database is considered idle when it has had no activity within a certain period of time. This activity may consist of a user typing information at the keyboard or running a query. By using the IDLE_TIME resource, the DBA is able to designate how much time (in minutes) a user may allow a database connection to sit idle before terminating the connection.

NOTE

A database that is processing a long-running query is not considered idle.

A terminated connection to the database may not be readily obvious to the user, because the resource does *not* terminate any applications. The user may not realize that the database connection has been terminated until the next time he or she attempts to perform an operation (such as a query).

For example, take a user who has been sitting idle in SQL*Plus for two hours. Assuming that an IDLE_TIME value of 60 has been selected (one hour), the user's connection to the database is broken after the first hour. However, the user still sees SQL*Plus, and not until another hour passes, when he or she attempts to issue a query, does an error message inform the user of the terminated connection.

CONNECT_TIME

Limiting the amount of time for which a user can be connected to the database can sometimes be advantageous. Unlike idle time, which measures how much time a user spends performing no actions, the CONNECT_TIME resource is compared against the total amount of time the user is connected to the database. The CONNECT_TIME resource, like IDLE_TIME, is set in minutes and terminates the database connection after that limit is exceeded. This resource discriminates equally against active and idle connections.

Like IDLE_TIME, the CONNECT_TIME resource terminates only the database connection and not the applications themselves. However, any query running when the CONNECT_TIME is exceeded returns with an error message.

PRIVATE_SGA_PER_SESSION

Earlier chapters in this book described the composition of the Oracle SGA. This parameter limits the maximum size of the private SGA/SQL area for the user. The value of this parameter identifies, in database blocks, how large a user's private SQL area can be. This resource limit can be of significant importance on systems where memory is at a premium and the DBA and system administrator are working to reduce "paging" and "swapping."

Leaving this value at UNLIMITED (usually DEFAULT) is best unless circumstances warrant otherwise. Make sure the private SQL area is not too small.

COMPOSITE_LIMIT

One of the most complex and advanced resource elements is the COMPOSITE_LIMIT. Using the COMPOSITE_LIMIT, the DBA can set an overall resource limit that is a composite (as opposed to explicit) resource limit. Under this configuration, resource elements are weighted based on values called resource costs. These resource costs form a cumulative cost based on all resource elements. This cost enables the DBA to determine which resource items are more important than others when setting resource limits.

Only the following resource elements are usable when determining a resource cost:

- CPU_PER_SESSION
- LOGICAL_READS_PER_SESSION
- CONNECT_TIME
- PRIVATE_SGA

If an item has a resource cost of 0, then that resource has no cost. However, assuming that a value other than 0 exists, the DBA can set values to the resource items using the ALTER RESOURCE COST command. The syntax for this command is

```
alter resource cost connect_time 10;
```

In this example, each connection minute costs the user 10 points against the overall composite limit. Whenever the sum of the composite limit exceeds the amount set, the database connection terminates.

For example, assume the following resource costs:

■ CPU_PER_SESSION	1
■ CONNECT_TIME	0
■ LOGICAL_READS_PER_SESSION	50
■ PRIVATE_SGA_PER_SESSION	10

Now, assume the following composite limit:

■ COMPOSITE_LIMIT	15,000

The user is allowed any combination of resources that do not exceed the 15,000 COMPOSITE_LIMIT the DBA set. In this case, the user can have 15,000 CPU minutes (CPU_PER_SESSION) or 1,500 (1,500×10 = 15,000) blocks in his or her private SQL area (PRIVATE_SGA_PER_SESSION). However, the user may also have, for example, only 7,500 CPU minutes and 150 logical reads (LOGICAL_READS_PER_SESSION: 50×150 = 7,500) for a total of 15,000. The session terminates when any combination of resources triggers the limit.

Please note that the CONNECT_TIME is set to 0, which does not count against the overall COMPOSITE_LIMIT.

You may have both composite and explicit limits. Take the following example:

■ IDLE_TIME	180
■ CONNECT_TIME	600
■ CPU_PER_CALL	750
■ COMPOSITE_LIMIT	10,000

In this example, the profile causes session termination if the amount of idle time exceeds 180 minutes, the total connect time for a session exceeds 600 minutes, the amount of CPU time taken to execute a single SQL statement takes more than 750 CPU minutes, or the composite resource limit exceeds 10,000. In this case, the COMPOSITE_LIMIT is used as the termination point as long as the IDLE_TIME, CONNECT_TIME, or CPU_PER_CALL values are not exceeded. If they are, then the session disconnects despite the value of the COMPOSITE_LIMIT.

Creating Profiles

After a DBA has properly defined a profile to suit the needs of the overall database environment, the profiles need to be created. Any user (not necessarily the DBA) with adequate database privileges can create the profiles via SQL through the Oracle Server*Manager or SQL*Plus.

In the following example, the DBA creates a profile named BOSS:

```
% sqlplus system/manager
SQL> create profile boss limit
   2>    idle_time 30
   3>    cpu_per_call 600
   4>    logical_reads_per_session unlimited
   5>    composite_limit 7500;
Profile created.
```

This profile is restricted by 30 minutes of idle time, 600 minutes of CPU time per call, or an overall composite limit of 7,500. The LOGICAL_READS_PER_SESSION is set to an UNLIMITED amount. All other resource values are set to DEFAULT. Any user the DBA associates with this profile is bound by these constraints.

Modifying Profiles

As with most SQL commands, an ALTER command provides the variation on the CREATE command with which to make changes. The profiles are no different, and you may change any resource item in a profile using this command, as the following example shows:

```
% sqlplus system/manager
SQL> alter profile boss limit
   2>    sessions_per_user 3
   3>    composite_limit default
   4>    cpu_per_call unlimited;
Profile altered.
```

The resource SESSIONS_PER_USER, which was previously DEFAULT, is now set to 3. Deciding to go only with implicit profiles, the DBA also sets the COMPOSITE_LIMIT back to DEFAULT and gives the boss profile UNLIMITED CPU per call. These changes become effective for all users assigned the boss profile.

Deleting Profiles

As the roles of users evolve, you may need to remove profiles from the database. This is done, simply and effectively, by issuing the DROP PROFILE command:

```
% sqlplus system/manager
SQL> drop profile boss;
Profile dropped.
```

At this time, the boss profile is no longer available for use. If the profile is currently assigned to an existing user, an error condition occurs. You can override the error by using the CASCADE option, which will assign the DEFAULT profile to these users:

```
% sqlplus system/manager
SQL> drop profile boss cascade;
Profile dropped.
```

Using the *DEFAULT* Profile

As discussed earlier in this chapter, the DEFAULT profile is a standard part of each database. The values of each of the resource items in the DEFAULT are the values that all other profiles, by default, use unless another value is set in them. DEFAULT profile values are UNLIMITED unless otherwise changed.

You can modify the DEFAULT profile, just as you do any other profile, but you cannot drop or remove it. This profile must exist.

Quotas

What the profile does for process and resource management, the quota does for disk space management. Often, users (and developers in particular) can be pack rats when it comes to data. They tend to create tables or other database objects and leave them without ever cleaning up after themselves. Inevitably, a tablespace reaches capacity and sends a user or group of users scrambling to the DBA for more disk space. It has been said that "nature abhors a vacuum," and in many cases, the user/developer community seems insistent on proving that theorem. Despite admonishments from the DBA, users still do not remove tables created during last year's GL problem because the data "might still be needed."

Quotas provide the DBA with a way to set an upper limit on the amount of disk space that a single user can occupy. This limit prevents a single user from occupying 90 percent of a tablespace with a personal table. The database enables only a certain amount of disk space to be allocated to a user before it generates an error message. Other users can continue working normally, but the user in question cannot perform further actions until he or she removes some database objects.

The use of quotas also allows the DBA to restrict access to certain key tablespaces (such as SYSTEM) to which the users and developers should not have access. Using a quota enables the DBA to choose which tablespaces are accessible to the user/developer equation, thus possibly reducing fragmentation issues.

Enforcing Tablespace Quotas

Tablespace quotas are set in bytes, kilobytes (KB), or megabytes (MB). In general, tablespace quotas are established whenever a new user account is created or amended after the fact. If no quota is given, a user has no privilege to create tables within the database (unless he or she has the RESOURCE system privilege). The syntax for the quota portion of the user creation/modification command is as follows:

```
...
quota 1 M on tablespace users
...
```

This quota enables the user to occupy up to a single megabyte of space on the user's tablespace. The DBA should set the quota at a value that is small enough to keep the user or developer from filling up the entire tablespace but large enough to allow that same user or developer to do his or her work. This value will vary from site to site, but it can sometimes be approximated by totaling all the database objects a user would need copies of and padding it with a small amount of overhead (10 percent to 15 percent).

Assigning *UNLIMITED* Tablespace Quotas

By assigning a user an UNLIMITED quota, the DBA allows the user to occupy as much room on a tablespace as necessary. The SQL syntax is the same as it is for a regular quota:

```
...
quota unlimited on tablespace users
...
```

CAUTION

Do not confuse the UNLIMITED tablespace quota with the system privilege UNLIMITED TABLESPACE (see Chapter 16). The UNLIMITED tablespace quota grants unlimited write access to a single tablespace; the UNLIMITED TABLESPACE privilege is for the entire database.

If tablespace quotas are enforced, you should use the UNLIMITED tablespace option sparingly. In general, this option is given to the owner of the schema objects on the tablespace on which those objects reside. Additionally, this option is given to MIS/user personnel on designated tablespaces. This enables groups of users who are allowed to add/drop tables to do so, but not on tablespaces that can contain production tables.

User Database Accounts

The section you may have expected to be first in this book occurs nearly last. If this text were intended as strictly a "laundry list" of SQL syntax, then this section may have appeared earlier. However, as shown throughout the course of this chapter, creating user accounts on a database is far more than just logging in and running a script. All things considered, that task is by far one of the easiest.

User account maintenance (creating, modifying, deleting) is typically done by the DBA. However, the DBA may assign appropriate privileges to a junior administrator to handle this task. (See Chapter 16.)

Creating User Accounts

To create an account, the DBA connects to the database via Oracle Server*Manager or SQL*Plus and issues the SQL command:

```
% sqlplus system/manager
SQL> create user cherie identified by scarlett
  2>     default tablespace users
  3>     temporary tablespace temp
  4>     quota 10M on users
  5>     profile boss;
User created.
```

Please make a distinction between creating a user for password authentication and creating a user for operating system authentication. The key difference between these two methods is that of the IDENTIFIED BY portion of the SQL command. When using password authentication, IDENTIFIED BY is followed by a password (which is echoed to the screen) that identifies what password a user must enter to gain access to the database. This method differs from the operating system authentication, where a user is IDENTIFIED EXTERNALLY. This specification is a signal to the database that the user account in question will be using operating system authentication, as this example shows:

```
% sqlplus system/manager
SQL> create user ops$lance identified externally
  2>     default tablespace users
  3>     temporary tablespace temp
  4>     quota unlimited on users
  5>     profile boss;
User created.
```

Make note of this important point. The concept of operating system authentication was first created with Oracle6, when all accounts had to be prefixed with the prefix OPS$ (which designates the account as an operating system authenticated account). Under Oracle7, the DBA may tune the database so it does not require the "OPS$" prefix to authenticate. For user accounts that use a prefix other than OPS$, as described later in this section, IDENTIFIED EXTERNALLY must be used to designate an operating system authenticated account.

If an OPS$ account is created, however, and a password is specified using IDENTIFIED BY, then that user account may be authenticated in either manner. If a null password is provided from the operating system account of the user, then operating system authentication occurs and connects this person to the database. However, the user may also connect to the database using the OPS$ username and password. Currently, this method is the only one available for dual authentication.

In versions of the Oracle RDBMS that are later than 7.1, however, the IDENTIFIED BY and EXTERNALLY options are totally separate. The capability to create an account that can be authenticated by both the operating system and a password does not exist in the database for Oracle 7.2 or later versions.

> **CAUTION**
>
> If the INIT.ORA parameter LICENSE_MAX_USERS is set, the DBA cannot create any more user accounts without adjusting the parameter (which requires a shutdown and startup of the database). Although this tool is excellent for enforcing named licensing restrictions, be certain that all overhead accounts (SYS, SYSTEM, schema object accounts, non-user administrative accounts, and so on) are accounted for when determining the value for this parameter.

Modifying User Accounts

Similar to modifying profiles, you can modify user accounts using the ALTER USER command. The basic syntax is the same as for CREATE USER except that you need to specify only the value being changed.

The following syntax changes the temporary tablespace of the designated user:

```
% sqlplus system/manager
SQL> alter user cherie temporary tablespace tmptbl;
User altered.
```

Deleting User Accounts

When attempting to delete (drop) a user account, you must make a consideration similar to the one made earlier for profiles. To drop a user account, the DBA must decide what to do with all objects owned by the user (destroy the objects with the user or keep them). This situation is similar to the UNIX system administrator who is removing a UNIX account and must decide whether to remove all files owned by a user, change the ownership to another user, or leave the files alone with the same ownership.

As shown in the following example, the syntax for removing a user is far less complicated than for adding a user:

```
% sqlplus system/manager
SQL> drop user ops$lance cascade;
User dropped.
```

In the preceding example, the DBA removes the database account and, by appending the CASCADE option to the command, removes all objects owned by the database user. If you omit the CASCADE option, any existing database objects are left untouched when the user account is removed. The DBA can still access the objects.

Changing User Passwords

One of the most common tasks users ask administrators (DBA or system administrator) is to reset user passwords. Quite often, a user of the HelpDesk contacts the DBA with this request. You accomplish this task using the ALTER USER command:

```
% sqlplus system/manager
SQL> alter user cherie identified by rhett;
User altered.
```

Users can reset their own personal passwords, but they often forget how to access the account and ask the DBA to do it.

Working with INIT.ORA Parameters

A few INIT.ORA parameters deal with the creation of new user accounts, with respect to operating system authentication:

- OS_AUTHENT_PREFIX
- REMOTE_OS_AUTHENT

By setting the value of OS_AUTHENT_PREFIX, the DBA can designate a prefix other than OPS$ for operating system authenticated accounts. For example, using the following setting allows a null to be the operating system authentication prefix:

```
os_authent_prefix=""
```

This setting allows the same account name at both the operating system and database level. The user Lance may have an account, Lance, within Oracle that is operating-system authenticated.

The value of the parameter REMOTE_OS_AUTHENT is set to true or false. This parameter enables remote clients to perform authentication on the database server. If this value is not set to true, then client connections must use password authentication. The DBA should consider the sensitivity of the database information and the security of the network before setting up this type of authentication.

> **TIP**
>
> To use operating system authentication with SQL*Menu 5.0, the value of REMOTE_OS_AUTHENT in the INIT.ORA parameter file must be set to true.

Special Account Considerations

Aside from the day-to-day tasks of creating end-user accounts, the DBA should evaluate a few special account considerations. Although you may not encounter these issues in every single site (each site and environment are unique), give them some thought during early phases of database setup.

Setting Up a Generic Database Administrator

The Oracle RDBMS comes equipped with three accounts for Oracle database administration: SYS, SYSTEM, and internal. However, none of these accounts are equipped for day-to-day DBA operations.

The database user SYS is a user who stores the basic tables and views that make up the Oracle data dictionary. *Oracle7 Server Administrator's Guide* recommends not using this account except when Oracle Technical Support instructs you to do so. Some experts may argue this point, but this recommendation is sound based on the sensitivity of the database objects this user owns. Likewise, you should use SYSTEM only when installing additional software packages that require this user account. The internal connections are dangerous in that they give the DBA the ability to shut down the database and they also give unrestricted database access as SYS.

The point to remember with these accounts is that *accidents can happen anywhere*. During a late night when the DBA is working, a single typo or misplaced character can drop a data dictionary table and corrupt the entire database. Aside from this possibility, none of the accounts are flexible enough to give you a choice between operating system authentication or password authentication (they allow *only* password authentication). In addition, none of the accounts are set up to enable the creation of temporary, ad-hoc tables that the DBA may need. To this end, many sites propose a generic DBA account.

This account is set up as a user other than SYS or SYSTEM with full DBA privileges. The account generally is used by the DBA or DBAs, depending on the size of the site. The account is created to enable DBA-level access without placing data dictionary objects at risk, and to enable a choice of authentication methods.

Setting Up a Generic Applications Administrator

Along the same vein as the generic DBA account, many sites use a generic applications administrator. This type of account can be far harder to define than the DBA account because the applications environment is different between locations (every site has a DBA). The applications administrator has two distinct sides: the applications side and the database side.

On the applications side, an operating system account usually owns all programs created for the system. Any developer who wants to make changes to the programs (forms, reports, and so on) needs to have the password to the operating system applications administrator account. A database account (which is generally password-authenticated) owns the database objects. You make any changes to database objects using this account, and the password usually is known only to the DBA and the applications administrator over the applications system. In general, when setting up accounts of this nature, make an attempt to minimize traffic on the accounts that own the actual database objects. The less frequently these accounts are used, the less chance for a minor mistake (like dropping or truncating a production table).

Summary

Creating a user account for the Oracle RDBMS is one of the most common activities a DBA undertakes. During most business days, the DBA receives a user request of some type, such as creating an account, modifying an account, deleting an account, or resetting a password. However, managing users requires more than simply logging on as the DBA and entering a command.

First and foremost, you must understand the requirements of the users. If you don't, you may fail in properly setting up the user account. You also must consider things such as authentication methods (password vs. operating system) and user configuration methods (profiles and quotas), as well as basic user creation options (profiles, default tablespace, and temporary tablespace).

Only after the DBA understands all the elements surrounding creation of a user should he or she proceed with the user creation. To err on the side of prudence when creating users is to err on the proper side.

Backup and Recovery

14

by Byron Pearce

IN THIS CHAPTER

It is 3 a.m. Do you know where your data is?

The answer depends on the type of business that your Oracle RDBMS supports. Some systems, such as data warehouses and other types of decision support systems (DSS), sustain little overall activity during the day but perform database-intensive table reloading operations during off-peak hours. OLTP systems typically reserve long-running query reports or resource-intensive batch jobs for the night hours.

Of course, there is not a right or wrong answer. Every site is a unique environment and has its own business requirements. However, it is important to know what is happening on an Oracle database during typical operations so that you know how to react when the telephone rings in the middle of the night and a voice on the other end informs you that a disaster has occurred. The disaster can be anything from a database instance that has abnormally terminated to a physical disk drive failure. If you have not already planned a formal backup and recovery procedure, it would be too late to start.

Backup and recovery are among most important considerations on any system, yet they generally receive less than one percent of the total planning, developing, and testing effort. Imagine that you are a project leader. Would you allow a developer who is responsible for mission-critical corporate applications to read a few articles, kludge together a functional program, and deploy it in a production environment with only cursory testing? This is precisely the approach that most DBAs take with backup and recovery procedures.

In their defense, though, backups for the most part seem to work. Scripts are run, copies are made to tape or disk, and someone dutifully checks to make sure that nothing abnormal has happened. No one knows whether this works until the system is down and the backup is needed to restore production operations. In many cases, there are political conflicts over whose responsibility it is to make backups. At some sites, the system administrator is responsible. Other sites make each individual administrator responsible for his own database or system. A few sites rely on an operations group that assumes responsibility for backups.

Importance of Backups

In the past, when the economy was centered primarily on agriculture or manufacturing, businesses were concerned especially about production and materials. As the Information Age becomes a reality, backups become important because they safeguard the only thing that a business cannot replace—data. Data takes many different forms—customer names, part numbers, purchase orders, and so on. When businesses were mostly independent, regional companies, the loss of data was less significant. For a multinational corporation today, however, the loss of even a single hour's data can result in thousands of dollars of damage.

In the event of a catastrophe, it is imperative that the data be recovered. Two factors are critical for success: accuracy and timeliness.

If a backup does not properly record all the information necessary to recover the database, it is worthless. A backup that fails to provide a critical piece of information, such as a required database file, cannot be used to restore operations. It is essential, therefore, that all the necessary database components be part of scheduled backups. Likewise, recovery of a mission-critical database that takes several days is, in most cases, unacceptable. A backup must expeditiously and completely restore the database after a failure occurs.

Terminology

At the functional level, Oracle is simply a collection of physical data files that reside on one or more hard drives, such as the hard drive on a PC, a midrange system, or a mainframe. Thus, backing up the system becomes a matter of knowing which data files to copy to tape or disk through standard copy utilities.

Because of the large amount of processing done by the background processes that comprise an Oracle database instance, making copies of these files gets complicated. To satisfy data consistency requirements, Oracle constantly updates its database files. Most operating systems copy files in blocks, so the snapshot taken of a file when it is copied may not be the same snapshot that it finishes with. (See Figure 14.1.)

FIGURE 14.1.

Operating system backup.

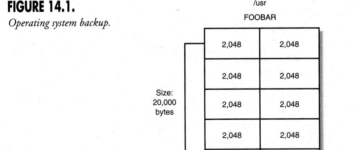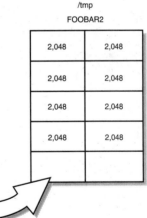

In Figure 14.1, the file FOOBAR is 20,000 bytes (a little less than 20 KB). Assuming that the operating system copies in 2,048-byte (2 KB) blocks, it can successfully copy the file in 10 packets. Compare this with Figure 14.2.

FIGURE 14.2.

Operating system backup of Oracle data file.

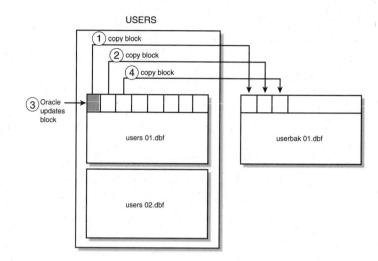

In Figure 14.2, the USERS tablespace is composed of two physical data files, each of which is 2 MB (2,048KB) in size. It takes the same operating system utility 512 separate packets to copy each file. During this time, the Oracle RDBMS continues to update the data files. Because of this, the snapshot of the database file taken by the utility is corrupt, incorrect, and unusable. Obviously, more is involved in making backups than just performing a copy with an operating system utility.

Redo Logs

Oracle maintains information concerning changes, or *transactions,* in online redo logs. These online redo logs—often called simply redo logs—are reminiscent of audit trails of information. They specify what changes were made to information within the database and in what order. In the event of an abnormal condition, such as the database instance being terminated instead of being properly shut down, the RDBMS uses information stored within the redo logs to return the database to its previous, consistent state. It uses the redo logs cyclically, as shown in Figure 14.3.

Figure 14.3 shows four 10MB redo logs. This means that the database instance can write up to 10 MB of information to each redo log, at which point it begins writing to the next online redo log in the sequence. When it reaches the final redo log, the database instance removes all the information from the first redo log and begins writing information back to it. In this way, Oracle cycles through the redo logs and keeps the most current transactions online and accessible. A recovery from an instance failure that uses only redo logs is called an *online recovery.*

FIGURE 14.3.
Oracle redo logs.

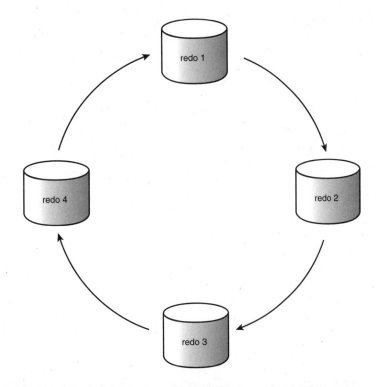

Archive Logs

Consider this disaster scenario: You encounter an internal error that causes a running Oracle RDBMS instance to terminate abnormally. While attempting to bring up the database, you discover that a media failure has occurred on the disk that contains the SYSTEM tablespace. The last backup of the system occurred over four days ago, and the redo logs have cycled several times since then. Oracle cannot do the necessary recovery from its redo logs to mount and open the database. What do you do?

Although extreme, scenarios like this one aided Oracle in developing online redo log archiving. All Oracle instances, by default or by design, run in ARCHIVELOG mode or in NOARCHIVELOG mode. (See Figure 14.4.) Each mode has its advantages and disadvantages.

FIGURE 14.4.

ARCHIVELOG mode.

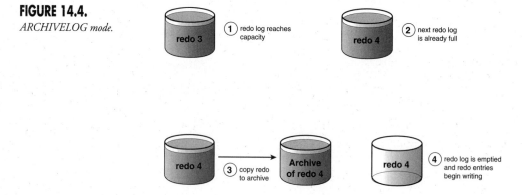

ARCHIVELOG Mode

A database running in ARCHIVELOG mode functions exactly like one in NOARCHIVELOG mode. The only exception occurs when the database completely fills one redo log and begins to write information to the next. If the redo log contains information from a previous cycle— which is true in all cases except the first cycle—an offline copy of the redo log is made. Once this copy is made, the redo log is emptied and the database resumes its normal processing by writing information to the redo log. This enables you to recover a database by using the last backup even if it precedes the earliest information in the redo logs. Note, however, that the offline redo logs must be physically accessible to the RDBMS.

Offline redo logs, commonly called *archive logs,* are simple in concept, but they involve many overhead considerations, which the administrator must decide prior to implementation. Some concerns, such as the volume of transactions processed by the database, affect others, such as how large to make the archive destination and whether to use automatic or manual archiving.

By default, the Oracle RDBMS instance runs in NOARCHIVELOG mode. To determine what mode a database instance is currently running in, issue the `archivelog list` command from within the Oracle Server*Manager. For example,

```
% svrmgrl
SVRMGR> connect internal
Connected.
SVRMGR> archive log list
Database log mode           No Archive Mode
Automatic Archival          Disabled
Automatic Destination       $ORACLE_BASE/admin//norm/arch/arch.log
Oldest online log sequence  2088
Current log sequence        2093
```

To set the archive mode of a database, the database must be mounted but not open. Once the database is in this state, the DBA needs only to issue the `alter database archivelog` or `alter database noarchivelog` command from Oracle Server*Manager. In the following code, the DBA mounts a database that has been shutdown normally, changes the database to ARCHIVELOG mode, and completes the startup by opening the database:

```
% svrmgrl
SVRMGR> connect internal
Connected to an idle instance
SVRMGR> startup mount
ORACLE instance started
Total System Global Area          95243632 bytes
Fixed Size                           46384 bytes
Variable Size                     70588480 bytes
Database Buffers                  24576000 bytes
Redo Buffers                         32768 bytes
Database mounted.
SVRMGR> alter database archivelog;
Statement processed.
SVRMGR> alter database open;
Statement processed.
```

The database runs in ARCHIVELOG mode until the DBA disables it. Even abnormal termination of the database instance or an instance shutdown or startup does not take the database out of ARCHIVELOG mode. This is because the information about whether the database is in ARCHIVELOG mode is stored in the instance's control files, along with other crucial database information.

Parameters within the INIT.ORA parameter file control various aspects of the archive process. They are

> LOG_ARCHIVE_BUFFER_SIZE
>
> LOG_ARCHIVE_BUFFERS
>
> LOG_ARCHIVE_DEST
>
> LOG_ARCHIVE_FORMAT
>
> LOG_ARCHIVE_START

The LOG_ARCHIVE_BUFFER_SIZE and LOG_ARCHIVE_BUFFERS parameters are useful primarily in database tuning.

The LOG_ARCHIVE_DEST parameter specifies the output location (such as /var/offline) or device (such as /dev/rmt/0hc) where the archive logs will be written. It must include a filename as part of the parameter—for example, /u10/admin/norm/arch/redo.

LOG_ARCHIVE_FORMAT specifies the format, or mask, used when writing archive logs to the location specified in LOG_ARCHIVE_DEST. Here is a brief list:

%s	Log sequence number
%S	Log sequence number (zero padded)

| %t | Thread number |
| %T | Thread number (zero padded) |

The value of LOG_ARCHIVE_START is either TRUE or FALSE. A value of TRUE indicates that automatic archiving should be used, while FALSE indicates manual archiving.

The values of these parameters vary among operating systems and environments. The DBA should configure the settings so that they best suit the database environment.

If archiving is not successful, the database suspends further operations, including SELECT and CONNECT, until the DBA takes corrective action. The rationale for this is simple: Because all the data is needed for recovery in ARCHIVELOG mode, Oracle stops operating until it can successfully retain the data. It is important, therefore, to address the issues of the size and availability of the archive destination before you place a database in ARCHIVELOG mode.

If users report errors from the database that deal with archiving, one of the quickest and best sources of information on the error is the ALERT.LOG file, whose location is indicated by the BACKGROUND_DUMP_DEST parameter in the INIT.ORA parameter file. The ALERT.LOG file records all major activity within the database. The following code contains several lines extracted from an actual ALERT.LOG file that a DBA might see in the event of a problem:

```
Beginning database checkpoint by background
Thread 1 advanced to log sequence 1760
    Current log# 1 seq# 1760 mem# 0: /u09/oradata/norm/redolb.log
    Current log # 1 seq# 1760 mem# 0: /u16/oradata/norm/redo1c.log
Thu Jun  8 10:21:57 1995
ARCH: Archival stopped, error occurred.  Will continue retrying
Thu Jun  8 10:21:57 1995
ORACLE instance norm - Archival Error
Thu Jun  8 10:21:57 1995
ORA-00255: error archivelog log 2 of thread 1, sequence # 1759
ORA-00312: online log 2 thread 1: '/u09/oradata/norm/redo02a.log'
ORA-00312: online log 2 thread 1: '/u16/oradata/norm/redo02b.log'
ORA-00272: error writing archive log
ARCH:
  ORA-00255: error archiving log 2 of thread 1, sequence # 1759
ORA-00312: online log 2 thread 1: '/u09/oradata/norm/redo2a.log'
ORA-00312: online log 2 thread 1: '/u16/oradata/norm/redo2b.log'
ORA-00272: error writing archive log
Thu Jun  8 10:22:07 1995
Completed database checkpoint by background
Thu Jun  8 10:24:45 1995
Beginning database checkpoint by background
```

Common problems that you might encounter when you work with archiving include

- Insufficient storage space to write the log
- Media failures or other events that render the physical device unavailable
- Conflicting archive log names
- Abnormal termination of the ARCH process that did not subsequently terminate the rest of the background processes

Conflicting archive log names are rare. They generally occur when two or more instances write to the same file system and directory with the same naming convention.

Manual Archiving

If you set the value of the LOG_ARCHIVE_START parameter to FALSE—the default value— the Oracle RDBMS instance will use manual archiving. Manual archiving places the control of, and the responsibility for, archiving redo logs in the DBA's hands. When a database runs under manual archiving, it runs unfettered until a redo log must be archived. When that occurs, the database performs no further activity until the DBA intervenes and issues the `alter system archive log all` command from Oracle Server*Manager or SQL*Plus. For example,

```
% svrmgrl
SVRMGR> connect internal
Connected.
SVRMGR> alter system archive log all;
Statement processed.
```

> **TIP**
>
> Don't use manual archiving for high-transaction databases that require a high degree of availability.

Users cannot perform any operations until the DBA takes the steps necessary to archive the redo logs manually. Therefore, adequate planning is a must for database instances that use manual archiving.

Automatic Archiving

Automatic archiving works in the same way as manual archiving, except that the database takes full responsibility for copying the archive logs to their appropriate destinations. If an error occurs during the copy—for example, a device might fail or the file system might become full—the database stops all operations until the problem is rectified. To place the database in automatic archive mode, set the value of the LOG_ARCHIVE_START parameter to TRUE.

Automatic archiving is recommended for high-transaction, high-availability systems, such as those used by OLTP, that cannot afford to have a DBA poised and ready to archive redo logs manually at a moment's notice.

Manual Archiving Versus Automatic Archiving

In manual archiving,

- The DBA controls the archiving process.
- The database must wait for the DBA to instigate archiving, which can result in database lockups.

■ Designing the size, frequency, and number of redo logs and cycles requires additional planning.

In automatic archiving,

■ The database controls the archiving process.

■ Free space and the archive destination device must be available. Otherwise, the database locks up and waits for the archive.

■ Handling the volume of continuous archive logs requires additional capacity planning and management.

NOARCHIVELOG Mode

NOARCHIVELOG mode is the default mode used by an Oracle RDBMS instance. In this mode, no archival of the redo logs is made, and no special handling is required. However, the DBA needs to guard against disaster scenarios like the one described earlier. Usually, the only databases run in NOARCHIVELOG mode are those that do not have a high volume of transactions, such as decision support databases that contain only summarized information from other applications systems. It is important to ensure that backups are made more often than the redo logs are cycled.

ARCHIVELOG Mode Versus NOARCHIVELOG Mode

In ARCHIVELOG mode:

■ Additional disk space is required.

■ Managing the archive logs entails additional administrative overhead.

■ Hot backups are available.

■ A complete database recovery can be performed in the event of a media failure.

In NOARCHIVELOG mode:

■ No additional disk space or overhead is required.

■ Only cold backups can be used.

■ All the work done since the last backup is lost in the event of a failure.

NOTE

Although you have the option to copy archive logs directly to tape (such as 4mm DAT), it is better to copy the archive to disk and to copy the disk to tape. Aside from the obvious issue of speed, disks tend to be more reliable than tapes. Copying a redo log to disk and then to tape provides a much more resilient backup method.

Requirements for Backups

In addition to ensuring that the required transactional information is available for recovery, you must make routine backups of the database. The backup procedure for an RDBMS is more complicated than simply making copies at the operating system level.

What Is a Database?

In *The Wizard of Oz*, the Wizard tells Dorothy, "Pay no attention to that man behind the curtain." The same admonishment applies to the overall functionality of the Oracle RDBMS instance.

A database is simply a collection of physical data files. The RDBMS provides a sophisticated set of programs that hide the details of the processing from the world and that enable programmers and users to view this data as tables, views, indexes, and clusters. The truth, though, is that Oracle, like the early flat-file databases that preceded it, does nothing more extravagant than store information in files. The man behind the curtain stands revealed.

Figure 14.5 shows the physical files that an Oracle instance uses. They are control files, database files, and redo log files. They must be included in the backup strategy.

FIGURE 14.5.

The physical files the make up an Oracle instance.

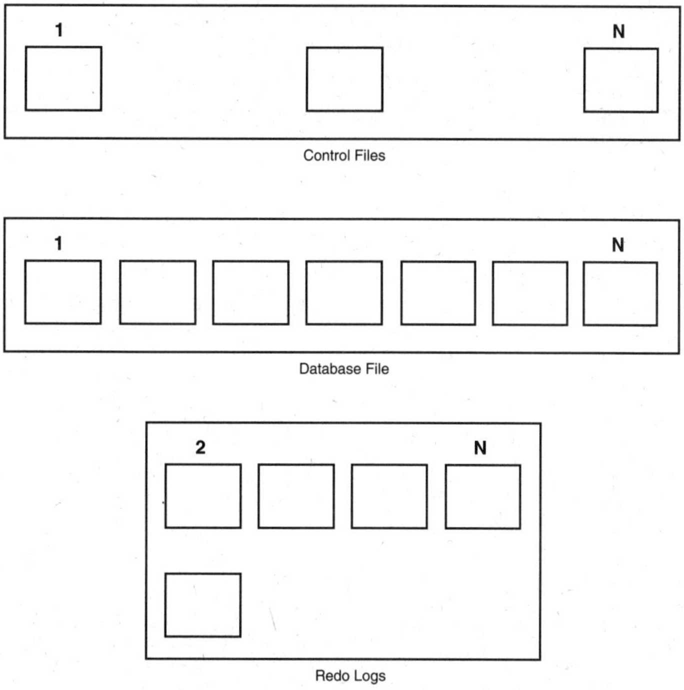

Control Files

Database File

Redo Logs

Although all the information stored by the Oracle RDBMS resides in physical data files, the information is accessible only through the tools and utilities provided by Oracle. To attempt otherwise is to risk corrupting the data within the file. There are also various kinds of files, each of which serves a different purpose and must be backed up in a specific manner. It is important to ensure that all the right files are backed up when you implement a backup strategy. Make sure that you understand the reasons why each file is backed up.

Control Files

Of all files used by the Oracle RDBMS, the control file most closely resembles the flat file of earlier databases, and each Oracle instance must contain at least one. The control file is a treasure trove of information, a great deal of which is proprietary and quite illegible. The following information "officially" exists within the control file:

- The name of the database name—the ORACLE_SID
- The name and location of all the database files
- The name and location of all the redo log files
- The system commit number (SCN), which matches the SCN in every Oracle file

Oracle users use the SCN to maintain the consistency and integrity of their databases.

The value of the control file is obvious. Without it, the database instance does not know what SCN to use, which makes it unable to tell whether all the information is in sync. The database cannot tell which database files and redo log files to mount and open as part of the database. It even suffers "database amnesia" because it does not know its own name. The control file is continuously updated while the database operates.

Database Files

The database files are the heart and soul of the database instance. They are the physical files that make up tablespaces—the logical constructs on which tables, indexes, and the like reside. Each tablespace can be made up of one or more separate physical database files. Every database instance must contain at least one database file—for the SYSTEM tablespace.

Database files tend to be the hardest type of files to make copies of. This is because the data within a database object—which lies within a tablespace and, ultimately, within a database file—is constantly updated and changed. If a database has an active user community, many INSERT, UPDATE, or DELETE operations might be running that can change the data even as it is being copied. Despite the use of the SCN, the data changes and is inconsistent with the information that the database believes is stored within the database file. (Refer to Figure 14.2.)

Redo Log Files

The redo log files hold transactions that have been applied against data within the database, including INSERT, DELETE, UPDATE, CREATE TABLE, DROP TABLE, CREATE INDEX, and DROP INDEX. Redo log files encompass online redo logs and offline redo logs, also known as archive logs. Because archive logs are simply copies of redo logs, the two are identical except for the data that they contain.

> **TIP**
>
> If an Oracle database instance's redo logs are lost and a backup is not available, you can trick the instance into believing that the archive logs are actually redo logs.

Every Oracle database instance must contain at least two online redo logs. The existence of archive logs depends on the mode in which the database is running—ARCHIVELOG or NOARCHIVELOG. Even in ARCHIVELOG mode, archive logs do not have to exist for the database to function.

Types of Backups

Each type of file that makes up an Oracle database instance has a different requirement for its individual backup. Some files can be backed up simply by using a standard operating system utility, such as the UNIX cp or cpio command. Others require you to interface directly with the database to carry out the backup. Still others require a sophisticated blend of database and operating system interfaces.

As important as knowing what to back up is knowing how to back up correctly. If a backup is not correctly made, a database recovery might not be possible.

Control File Backups

Control files resemble flat files, which means that compared to database files, they are easy to copy. Control files tend to be small, and effort needed to make copies is negligible. Control file backups are critical to being able to restore a database. Without a control file, a database cannot be brought online.

Operating System Copy

One option for making copies of database control files is to use operating system utilities. This works well, but it is not an adequate or reliable backup if the database has not first been shutdown. Because an active database—especially one with a high transaction volume—constantly updates the control file, there is the risk that the copy might not reflect the true state of the database. Some people argue that this risk is small, but it still exists.

Copying a control file at the operating system level should be done only in conjunction with a cold backup.

Mirrored Control Files

A recommended method for backing up an Oracle database control file is to mirror the control files. Unlike true disk mirroring, which is implemented at the operating system level by using technology such as RAID 0/1, this method merely designates multiple copies of the control file to which the database will write. This is done by means of the CONTROL_FILES parameter in the INIT.ORA parameter file:

```
control_files = (/u03/oradata/norm/control.ctl, /u05/oradata/norm/
control.ctl)
```

You can include additional control files by editing the INIT.ORA file, shutting down, and restarting the database instance. For example,

```
control_files = (/u03/oradata/norm/control.ctl, /u05/oradata/norm/
control.ctl, /u07/oradata/norm/control.ctl)
```

When you mirror the control files, place each control file on a separate physical disk to prevent all the copies from being lost in the event of a disk failure—the concept behind mirroring. Although an Oracle instance can function with only one control file, Oracle recommends at least two. However, you can have as many control files as there are physical disk drives. Control files are extremely cheap in terms of storage and performance cost (writing the information to the control file).

Backing Up Control Files (Online)

Although mirroring control files is useful, it is still a good idea to make actual backups of control files. In a worst case disaster scenario, all the control files could be lost and the database might need to be restored on an alternate hardware system. Mirroring is not of much use then.

Because a reliable backup of a control file is not available from the operating system, Oracle provides a method that makes a reliable backup copy of the control file while the database is running. Use the `alter database` command from Oracle Server*Manager or SQL*Plus. For example,

```
alter database backup controlfile to '/u10/admin/norm/arch/bk_control.ctl';
```

This command makes a backup control file and places it in the destination directory under the filename specified in the command. In this case, the directory is the path /u10/admin/norm/arch, and the name of the backup control file is bk_control.ctl. Here is a full script that makes backup copies of control files:

```
#!/bin/ksh
$ORACLE_HOME/bin/svrmgrl << EOF
connect internal
alter database backup controlfile to
   '/u10/admin/norm/arch/control.ctl';
exit
EOF
```

You can back up this control file to tape along with the other files. That way, you make a full recovery possible.

Backup to Trace

Suppose that during routine maintenance to extend a tablespace, you encounter an error indicating that the maximum number of database files has been reached. A low default value had been used when the instance was created. The only way to change this value is to re-create the control file. To do this, however, you must know all the data files, redo log files, and so on, that make up the instance.

With a fair amount of research, any DBA could cobble together the necessary information to perform this task. For most DBAs, though, time is a premium resource; the easier an activity can be done, the better. Oracle provides a facility that enables you to back up a control file to trace by issuing an `alter database` command from Oracle Server*Manager or SQL*Plus:

```
alter database backup controlfile to trace;
```

When you invoke this command, you create a SQL script that is capable of recreating the current control file of the Oracle instance. The destination of the script is the directory specified in the USER_DUMP_DEST parameter of the INIT.ORA parameter file. For example:

```
#!/bin/ksh
$ORACLE_HOME/bin/svrmgrl << EOF
connect internal
alter database backup controlfile to trace;
exit
EOF
```

When you execute this command, the editable SQL script shown here is produced. This script can be quickly changed and used, which ensures that all the parameters are correct. The DBA needs to worry only about scheduling, not the daunting task of checking and double-checking parameters.

```
Dump file /u01/app/oracle/admin/norm/udmp/ora_25132.trc
Oracle7 Server Release 7.1.6.2.0 - Production Release
With the distributed option
PL/SQL Release 2.1.6.2.0 - Production
ORACLE_HOME = /u07/app/oracle/product/7.1.6
ORACLE_SID = norm
```

```
Oracle process number: 9                    Unix process id: 25132
System name:      HP-UX
Node name:        testdev
Release:          A.09.00
Version:          U
Machine:          8999/867


Sat Sep  9 14:26:39 1995
Sat Sep  9 14:26:39 1995
*** SESSION ID:(6.21)
# The following commands will create a new control file and use it
# to open the database.
# No data other than log history will be lost.  Additional logs may
# be required for media recovery of offline data files.  Use this
# only if the current version of all online logs are available.
STARTUP NOMOUNT
CREATE CONTROLFILE REUSE DATABASE "NORM" NORESETLOGS NOARCHIVELOG
        MAXLOGFILES 64
        MAXLOGMEMBERS 5
        MAXDATAFILES 1022
        MAXINSTANCES 10
        MAXLOGHISTORY 100
LOGFILE
  GROUP 1 (
    '/u07/oradata/norm/redo101.log',
    '/u09/oradata/norm/redo102.log'
  ) SIZE 10M,
  GROUP 2 (
    '/u07/oradata/norm/redo201.log',
    '/u09/oradata/norm/redo202.log'
  ) SIZE 10M
DATAFILE
  '/u02/oradata/norm/system01.dbf' SIZE 80M,
  '/u04/oradata/norm/rbs01.dbf' SIZE 300M,
  '/u11/oradata/norm/temp01.dbf' SIZE 150M,
  '/u08/oradata/norm/tools01.dbf' SIZE 20M,
  '/u05/oradata/norm/users01.dbf' SIZE 10M
;
# Recovery is required if any of the datafiles are restored backups,
# or if the last shutdown was not normal or immediate.
RECOVER DATABASE
# Database can now be opened normally.
ALTER DATABASE OPEN;
```

You should periodically make a control file backup to trace, perhaps as often as you make a control file backup.

Redo Log File Backups

Although Oracle provides a concise method for making backups of control files, no such method exists for redo logs. The only option for making backups of the redo logs is the very one that you have been cautioned against—using operating system copy utilities.

Assuming that four redo logs are located on a single disk, the following code segment demonstrates various techniques for making copies:

```
cp /u01/oradata/norm/redo101.log /DB1/oradata/norm
cp /u01/oradata/norm/redo* /DB1/oradata/norm
cpio -ocvB /u01/oradata/norm/redo101* > /dev/rmt/0hc
cpio -ocvB /u01/oradata/norm/redo* > /dev/rmt/0hc
find /u*/oradata/norm/*.log ¦ cpio -ocvB > /dev/rmt/0hc
```

Some DBAs like to force the redo logs to perform a logfile switch—usually forcing an archive log to be written—before initiating a copy of the redo logs. This is done from Oracle Server*Manager or SQL*Plus by using the `alter system` command. For example,

```
alter system switch logfile;
```

Mirrored Online Redo Logs

In an attempt to preserve the data within the online redo logs in much the same way as control files, Oracle V7 introduces redo log groups. They enable redo logs to be mirrored across multiple disks. (See Figure 14.6.)

FIGURE 14.6.

Mirrored online redo logs.

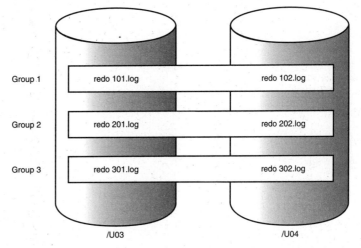

Instead of having individual redo logs, each of which contains a distinct series of transactions, the redo logs are broken down into *groups* and *members*. Each group is a set of one or more redo logs that contain the same transactions. Each member is a single redo log file within the group. The Oracle RDBMS treats all the redo logs as groups even if they contain only a single member.

You can think of redo log groups as a single redo log. There are at least two redo log groups in a database instance. Each group contains multiple members—the redo log file—which should be located on separate physical disks to benefit from the mirroring. As the Oracle RDBMS writes information to the redo log, it writes the information into each member of the group. In this way, if a single member is damaged, at least one of the other members will enable the database to continue to function. This greatly reduces the number of database failures caused by problems with redo logs.

Adding Redo Log Groups

The initial online redo log groups are created at the time of database creation. However, any number of factors can come into play that might prompt the DBA to want to add additional logfile groups. Adding a group of redo log members to the database is done by issuing the `alter database` command from within Oracle Server*Manager or SQL*Plus. For example,

```
alter database add logfile group 4 ('/u02/oradata/norm/
redo4a.log', '/u03/oradata/norm/redo4b.log') size 512K;
```

This command causes the database to create a new logfile group (group 4), which assumes that groups 1, 2, and 3 already exist and that group 4 does not. The two members of this group are 512KB files named redo4a.log and redo4b.log, which are located in /u02/oradata/norm and /u03/oradata/norm.

Adding Members to Redo Log Groups

A DBA who is not familiar with Oracle7 might have created online redo logs without mirroring the members. It would benefit him to mirror the redo logs by adding additional members to existing redo log groups. The command syntax for this is

```
alter database add logfile member '/u04/oradata/norm/redo2b.log'
to group 2;
```

This causes a logfile member named redo2b.log to be placed in the /u04/oradata/norm directory path and to be annotated as a member of redo log group 2. The new logfile member has the same size as the existing logfile members in the group to which it is added.

Renaming or Moving Members

A DBA might experience the situation in which a disk drive needs to be removed because it keeps encountering errors. Perhaps a new disk drive has been added to the system, and some of the redo log members need to be placed on the drive. Whatever the case, redo log members can be quickly renamed or moved by using `alter database` from within Oracle Server*Manager or SQL*Plus.

To move the file physically from one location to another, specify the name of the file to move and its destination. In the following example, redo1a.log is moved from its present location, /u03/oradata/norm, to its new location, /u06/oradata/norm:

```
alter database rename file '/u03/oradata/norm/redo1a.log' to '/u06/oradata/norm/
redo1a.log';
```

The same syntax is used to rename a file. Instead of specifying a new path, you specify a new filename. In the following example, redo2a.log in /u03/oradata/norm is renamed to redo3a.log. The directory path is the same.

```
alter database rename file '/u03/oradata/norm/redo2a.log' to '/u03/oradata/norm/
redo3a.log';
```

Dropping Redo Log Groups

To remove an entire group of redo log members, simply remove the group itself. After you remove the group, all the corresponding redo log members are dropped. To do this, issue the `alter database` command from within Oracle Server*Manager or SQL*Plus. The following code removes all the redo log members for redo log group 5, but it does not affect any other groups:

```
alter database drop logfile group 5;
```

Dropping Members from Redo Log Groups

If redo log files are corrupted or if you must conserve disk space, you might have to remove redo log members from a redo log group. To do this, issue the following `alter database` command from within Oracle Server*Manager or SQL*Plus:

```
alter database drop logfile member '/u07/oradata/norm/redo6a.log';
```

This command removes the specified redo log member from its associated redo log group. It does not affect the group or any other redo members.

> **NOTE**
>
> The information presented here is only for quick reference. For a more detailed discussion on adding, renaming, or removing redo log groups and members—and the restrictions associated with these tasks—consult the *Oracle7 Server Administrator's Guide.*

Cold Backups

One of the simplest backup methods, but also one of the most difficult to implement, is the cold backup. In a cold backup, the database has been totally shut down and all the physical files associated with the database are copied by means of normal operating system utilities. Because the database is not in operation, changes are not made to the physical files, and there are no conflicting integrity or consistency problems.

The difficulties in implementing this type of backup are mostly political, due largely to the amount of time required. Depending on the size of the database and the speed of the copy utility used—copies to disk are faster than copies to tape—a cold backup can take anywhere from a few minutes to several hours or even several days. Thus, a cold backup is not always an option.

Many sites supplement weekly or monthly cold backups with other backups on a nightly basis. They think that they have 24/7 operations, when in reality large windows of time are available in the evening for a cold backup. This is, of course, site-specific. It is up to the DBA to evaluate the needs of the user community versus the needs of the operations staff.

Shutting Down the Instance

To accomplish a cold backup, you must first shut down the database instance. There are three shutdown methods for an Oracle database: normal, immediate, and abort. Here is a sample shutdown:

```
% svrmgrl
SVRMGR> connect internal
Connected.
SVRMGR> shutdown
Database closed.
Database dismounted.
ORACLE instance shut down.
```

shutdown normal

When you issue a shutdown, also called a shutdown normal, from within Oracle Server*Manager, the Oracle RDBMS is very patient. In this mode, the database instance ignores further attempts to log into the database and waits for all the currently active sessions to disconnect from the database.

Using shutdown normal is not always the best option for a backup, even though it provides for the cleanest type of shutdown. If a user leaves the office with his workstation still logged in, the backup must wait until he logs out. The next morning, no one can log into the database because Oracle is still waiting to perform a shutdown, and the backup has not yet occurred.

shutdown immediate

A shutdown in the immediate mode is almost identical to a shutdown in the normal mode, with one exception: Oracle has no patience. When you issue a `shutdown immediate` command, Oracle immediately terminates all the database connections and performs rollback operations on all the outstanding transactions. Checkpoints and buffer flushing are done, and the database is brought down.

For backup operations, `shutdown immediate` works best, for it deals with users who fail to log off their workstations. Because Oracle performs all the rollback and checkpointing, the database is in a consistent, stable state when the termination occurs.

shutdown abort

The `shutdown abort` command should be used only as a last resort, and then only when all the other shutdown options have failed. By using the `shutdown abort` command, the DBA immediately terminates all the background processes that make up the Oracle database instance, but no rollback, checkpoint, or buffer flushing operations occur before the shutdown. In rare cases, this can lead to corruption of some of the data within the database.

A `shutdown abort` should not be used to stop the database before backup operations. If `shutdown abort` is required, the database should be restarted and shut down again in either immediate or normal mode to ensure a stable, consistent view of the database that is acceptable for backup operations.

> **TIP**
>
> Two utilities that come with the Oracle RDBMS are `dbshut` and `dbstart`. They are generally located in $ORACLE_HOME/bin. The `dbstart` utility starts all the database instances specified in the /etc/oratab file. The `dbshut` utility performs a `shutdown normal` operation on all the instances specified in the /etc/oratab file. These utilities are shell scripts in UNIX. You can copy and edit them to create `dbshut.immediate` and `dbshut.abort` utilities to use with backup operations.

Steps in Performing a Cold Backup

A cold backup is the simplest of all backup operations. The steps required are

1. Shutdown the Oracle database instance—either normal or immediate mode.
2. Copy all the physical files associated with the database—control files, redo log files, and database files.
3. Restart the database when you are done.

Hot Backups

Whereas a cold backup takes a backup of a database in a shutdown state, a hot backup enables you to take a backup of a database that has not been shut down. This is the most tedious backup method, but it is also the most flexible. It enables you to take backups of an active database. It ensures resource availability to end users and enables the DBA and the operations staff to recover the database.

Cold backups concentrate on copying all the physical files associated with a database instance. Hot backups, on the other hand, concentrate on the tablespace level. To do a hot backup, you must place every individual tablespace into a backup mode (by using the `alter tablespace` command), copy the physical database files that make up the tablespace, and take the tablespace out of backup mode (by using the `alter tablespace` command). You can issue these commands from Oracle Server*Manager or SQL*Plus. For example,

```
alter tablespace system begin backup;
alter tablespace system end backup;
```

When you place a tablespace in backup mode, the Oracle instance notes that a backup is being performed and internally compensates for it. As you know, it is impossible to make an authentic copy of a database file that is being written to. On receipt of the command to begin the backup, however, Oracle ceases to make direct changes to the database file. It uses a complex combination of rollback segments, buffers, redo logs, and archive logs to store the data until the end backup command is received and the database files are brought back in sync.

Simplifying a hot backup in this way is tantamount to classifying the USS *Nimitz* as a boat. The complexity of the actions taken by the Oracle RDBMS under a hot backup could consume an entire chapter and is beyond the scope of this book. What you should understand is the trade-off for taking a hot backup is increased use of rollback segments, redo logs, archive logs, and internal buffer areas within the SGA.

> **CAUTION**
>
> Don't place all the tablespaces in backup mode, perform the backup, and then take them all out of backup mode. Because of how Oracle handles hot backups, you could experience problems. Instead, you should back up each tablespace as a single unit.

When you run a hot backup, you can restore the data files that compose a single tablespace and apply all the associated redo and archive logs to bring the tablespace back in sync with the database.

> **NOTE**
>
> You must be running the database in ARCHIVELOG mode to perform a hot backup.

Steps in Performing a Hot Backup

A hot backup is a complex operation, because each tablespace involves a complete backup operation. It makes sense to break the hot backup into its component parts. The steps in a hot backup are

1. Place the tablespace in backup mode.
2. Copy all the database files associated with the tablespace.
3. Take the tablespace out of backup mode.
4. Repeat steps 1 through 3 until all the tablespaces have been backed up.
5. Copy the control file.
6. Copy the online redo logs.

Alternative Backup Methods

Cold and hot backups are not the only options available to the DBA. Other backup methods exist, but they often are unreliable and do not permit the level of recoverability that is available from cold and hot backups. These alternative backup methods are useful as supplemental backups within a backup strategy. They are not designed to replace cold and hot backups.

Tablespace Offline Copy

Of the supplemental backup methods, the tablespace offline copy method is the only one that can feasibly be used in production. It is something of a hybrid between a cold backup and a hot backup. It enables you to do essentially a cold backup of a tablespace while the database remains online.

In the tablespace offline copy method, each individual tablespace is taken offline by an `alter tablespace` command issued from Oracle Server*Manager or SQL*Plus:

```
alter tablespace users offline;
alter tablespace users online;
```

The steps in a tablespace offline copy backup are

1. Alter the tablespace offline.
2. Perform operating system copy of the database files associated with the tablespace.
3. Alter the tablespace online.
4. Repeat steps 1 through 3 until all the tablespaces have been backed up.
5. Back up the control files.
6. Back up the online redo logs.

This method permits a complete hot-style backup of the individual tablespaces but without the additional activity within the redo logs, rollback segments, and so on. By using this method, you can take a backup of a tablespace and use archive logs to recover any transactions that occurred after the backup.

The tablespace offline copy backup has some drawbacks. Database objects on the tablespace are unavailable while it is being copied. This is in direct contrast to the hot backup, in which a tablespace and its objects remain online and accessible. Likewise, you cannot back up the SYSTEM tablespace with this method because it cannot be taken offline. You must use another backup method to do that.

Export

A popular method for supplemental database backup is the exp utility, which performs exports of data within the Oracle database. The exp utility can perform three types of data exports:

- **Incremental exports.** All the information that has changed since this last incremental export is exported.
- **Cumulative exports.** All the data that has changed since the last cumulative export is exported. A cumulative export is a collection of incremental exports.
- **Full exports.** All the data within the database is exported.

There are a number of options available with the exp utility. They are described in Chapter 9, "Import and Export."

If an export is used for recovery, everything in the database that has been added, deleted, or otherwise changed since the last export is lost. For this reason, exports are used only to facilitate quick, point-in-time recoveries, such as when a static reference table is truncated. They do not provide the level of recovery that most mission-critical operations require.

Here is a partial screen listing for an export:

```
% exp file=/tmp/exp.log full=y
Export: Release 7.1.6.2.0 - Production on Mon Sep 11 03:29:09 1995
Copyright (c) Oracle Corporation 1979, 1994.  All rights reserved.
```

```
Username: system
Password: .......

Connected to: Oracle7 Server Release 7.1.6.2.0 - Production Release
With the distributed option
PL/SQL Release 2.1.6.2.0 - Production

About to export the entire database ...
. exporting tablespace defintions
. exporting profiles
. exporting user definitions
. exporting roles
. exporting resource costs
. exporting rollback segment definitions
. exporting database links
. exporting sequence numbers
```

To reclaim the exported data, use the Oracle imp utility, which imports the data. Both imp and exp are found in the $ORACLE_HOME/bin directory. For a more detailed discussion of exports, refer to the *Oracle7 Server Utilities User's Guide*.

SQL*Loader Readable File

Another strategy for backups is a result of the Oracle7 direct-load path in SQL*Loader. By using SQL scripts, PL/SQL programs, or 3GL interface programs, you can create a file for each database table in which each row is in a SQL*Loader-readable format, such as comma-delimited. With this method, you can re-create and repopulate tables quickly after a failure.

The time required to administer this method neutralizes whatever benefit you might gain by it. Whenever a change is made to a database table, the change must be reflected in the appropriate program or else it is not correct. Likewise, this backup method has many of the same limitations as exp without any of its simplicity or benefits. Because of the time and physical disk storage space required, this type of backup is a heavy undertaking. It must be policed almost constantly.

WARNING

If the structure of a database table is changed—using an alter table command for example—the programs that create the SQL*Loader readable files must be changed. If this is not done, proper backups of all data within the database object will not be taken.

For some sites, however, this type of backup is practical despite the obvious constraints. For a more detailed discussion of the implementation of SQL*Loader, refer to the *Oracle7 Server Utilities User's Guide*.

Types of Database Failure

Every DBA experiences a database failure at some point. It might be a minor failure in which the users never even know that they lost service, or it might be a severe loss that lasts for several days. Most failures fall somewhere in the middle.

Most failures result primarily from the loss or corruption of a physical data file. Of course, many other factors can cause database problems. Indeed, problems can occur in the memory structures (the SGA), the system hardware, or even the Oracle software that prevent the DBA from starting up the database. The following sections describe the most common types of failures.

Tablespace

If a loss or corruption takes place in any of the database files that make up a tablespace, media recovery is required. The extent of the media recovery needed depends largely on the extent of the data file loss or corruption. The three types of recovery available for this type of recovery are

- Database recovery
- Tablespace recovery
- Data file recovery

The database recovery method is generally chosen if the SYSTEM tablespace has been damaged, in which case it syncs all the data files within the database during the recovery procedure. The tablespace recovery method is used if recovery is needed for multiple tablespaces that have become damaged, such as from the loss of a disk drive. The data file recovery method is performed if only a single database file has been damaged. The commands used to implement these methods are

```
recover database;
recover tablespace users;
recover datafile '/u03/oradata/norm/rbs01.dbf';
```

Control File

Whenever a database loses a control file, there is generally little impact on the database itself as long as the DBA has mirrored the control files. To recover the control file, follow these steps (which assume that the control file has been mirrored):

1. From Oracle Server*Manager, do `connect internal` and perform a `shutdown` (or `shutdown immediate`) on the database.

2. Copy one of the existing control files over the corrupted file. If it is not possible to do this, copy it to another location and reflect the change in the CONTROL_FILES parameter of the INIT.ORA parameter file, or remove it completely.

3. From Oracle Server*Manager, do `connect internal` and perform a `startup` on the database.

The database will bring the control file in sync with the database, and the users will experience no loss of service or downtime.

If a control file has been lost and there is no backup, Oracle continues to run until it attempts to access the control file. At that point, the Oracle instance aborts. Two options are available to the DBA:

- Create a new control file
- Restore the control file from backup

To create a control file, you must first create a SQL script that will adequately re-create the existing control file. If a backup to trace is part of regular backups, the script already exists in the USER_DUMP_DEST directory. Use `ls -lt` in UNIX to find the most recent one. Use `view` to make sure that it creates a control file and is not simply SQL*Trace output. Perform the following steps:

1. Locate or create a SQL script.

2. From Oracle Server*Manager, do `connect internal`.

3. If a new create script was created, issue the `startup nomount` command. Execute the SQL script. Then execute the commands

```
recover database;
alter system archive log all;
alter database open;
```

4. If the create control file script is from a backup to trace, execute the script from a shutdown database. It will execute all the intermediate steps and open the database.

If you choose to use a backup control file, issue the following recover command in place of the standard recover command:

```
recover database using backup controlfile;
```

Redo Logs

As with control files, there are two possible scenarios: loss of mirrored redo logs and loss of nonmirrored redo logs. If at least one member in each redo log group is usable and not corrupted, the database continues to function normally. You should determine what caused the failure or corruption of the redo log member. Then you should rectify the problem by dropping and re-creating the log member.

If all the members of a redo log group became corrupted or were lost, the scenario is entirely different. Dealing with the loss of an entire redo log group is the same as dealing with an unmirrored redo log. The two possibilities are

■ The redo logs were not the active group.

■ The redo logs were the active group.

If the redo log group was not the active group, the corrupt group and its members eventually cause the database to shut down. The trick is to recognize that damage has been done and to react before the database shuts down. Restore the online redo log from tape, or copy it from an existing redo log group if they are the same size. If the disk itself is corrupt and unavailable, rename the redo log group. If you are lucky enough to catch the database at this time, this is the best alternative. Otherwise, if the database attempts to access the corrupted redo log, the redo log must be recovered as if the active redo log was lost (see below).

The more likely scenario is that the database aborted because it lost an inactive online redo log. The recovery steps are basically the same, but they are done in an offline fashion. Recover the offending redo log group, or make a copy of an existing group if they are the same physical size. From Oracle Server*Manager, do connect internal and start up the database. The downtime involved should be minimal.

A loss of the current online redo log requires a limited recovery scenario. Although a full database recovery is not actually applied, you must to make the database think that one has occurred. Only then can processing continue. The steps are

1. From Oracle Server*Manager, do connect internal. Use shutdown, shutdown immediate, or shutdown abort to shut down the database.

2. Execute startup mount on the database instance.

3. Once the database has been mounted, issue the recover database command. At the next prompt, enter cancel.

4. Issue an alter database rename... command to move the corrupted redo logs to a new location. The new files are created automatically.

5. Execute the alter database open resetlogs; command from Oracle Server*Manager. The database is brought back online for continued operations.

Operations that require restarting an aborted Oracle database instance can be quite complex. The complications that can arise during an operation as sensitive as a recovery are numerous. If the recovery process does not seem to work properly, stop and contact Oracle technical support immediately.

Archive Logs

You have been forced to tinker with startups, shutdowns, and renaming and recovering physical database files. At least losing archive logs does not affect the continued operations of the database.

Well, almost.

Unlike losing a database file, a control file, or a redo log—which ultimately causes an Oracle database instance to abort—losing an archive log has no visible effect on the database. After all, the logs are retained offline and are accessed only when they are created as archives of the online redo logs and when they are used for database recovery.

Even though the loss of an archive log does not affect the continued operations of the database—which is why NOARCHIVELOG mode is available—if anything occurs that requires database recovery before the next backup, *it will be impossible to recover the database.*

Because archive logs facilitate recovery, their loss is often realized only when it is too late. It is a difficult position for a DBA, and there is no clear right or wrong solution. It depends on the backup schedule. It is easier to wait a few hours until the next hot backup than to wait several days for the next cold backup.

We recommend that you immediately initiate a hot backup of the database. It will slow things and cause the system to choke a little on processing, especially during peak usage time. It is far better, though, than waiting and hoping that nothing will happen.

Recovery Methods

There are several methods for performing database recovery. Each methods offers a trade-off between speed and simplicity. The following sections describe the major types of recovery available through the Oracle RDBMS.

Cold Restore

In a cold restore, all the database files, control files, and redo logs are restored from tape or disk, and the database is restarted. It is the simplest, most complete recovery operation to perform. The primary drawback is that anything done to the database since the last backup is lost.

The steps in a cold restore are

1. Make sure that the current Oracle database instance is shut down.
2. Replace all the existing database files, control files, and redo logs with earlier versions from tape or disk.

> **NOTE**
>
> The time and date stamps on all of the files from the recovery should be for the same period of time. If they are not, the database will be out of sync and will not open properly.

3. From Oracle Server*Manager, do `connect` `internal` and issue a `startup` command. The database is now ready for use.

Full Database Recovery

In a full database recovery, also called a *complete recovery,* data changed since the last backup can be restored. One or more database files are restored from backup. Archive logs are then applied to them until they are in sync with the rest of the database.

The steps in a full database recovery are

1. Make sure that the database instance is shut down.

2. Restore the data file from tape or disk.

3. From Oracle Server*Manager, do `connect` `internal` and perform `startup` `mount` on the database instance.

4. Issue the `recover` `database` `automatic` command from within Oracle Server*Manager. Oracle Server*Manager responds by applying all the required changes to the database instance. Depending on the length of time since the last backup and the size and number of the archive logs, this wait can take a few seconds or several hours.

5. After the `SVRMGR>` prompt returns, issue the `alter` `database` `open` `noresetlogs;` command. The database is now completely recovered and available for use.

> **NOTE**
>
> There are several variations of the `recover` `database` command, including `recover` `datafile` and `recover` `tablespace`.

Time-Based Recovery

Sometimes a recovery is required, but not everything in the archive logs is necessary. Suppose, for example, that an overzealous developer deploys a job that deletes every other row in a transaction processing table. In this case, a full recovery will not work. Because the transactions that corrupted the table are in the archive logs, a full recovery simply restores from the last backup and processes all the transactions, including the haphazard delete. If you know that the job ran at 2:30 p.m., you can use time-based recovery to recover until 2:29 p.m. That way, the table is exactly as it appeared before the job ran. This is also called an *incomplete recovery.*

A time-based recover is performed exactly like a full recovery, with the exception of the `recover` `database` command. The steps are

1. Make sure that the database instance is shut down.

2. Restore the data file from tape or disk.

3. From Oracle Server*Manager, do `connect internal` and perform `startup mount` on the database instance.

4. Issue the `recover database until time 'YYYY-MM-DD:HH24:MI:SS'` command from within Oracle Server*Manager. This is a mask for the time and day on which the recovery should stop. Oracle Server*Manager responds by applying all the required changes to the database instance. Depending on the length of time since the last backup and the size and number of the archive logs, this wait can take a few seconds or several hours.

5. After the `SVRMGR>` prompt returns, issue the `alter database open resetlogs;` command. The database is now completely recovered and available for use.

Cancel-Based Recovery

Even if you do not know the exact time an error occurred, you might feel reasonably certain that you can isolate when to terminate the recovery based on the thread/sequence number. Perhaps there was a break in the archive logs because you had the database out of ARCHIVELOG mode for a short time, or perhaps you want more control over what archive logs are applied as part of the recovery. The solution is cancel-based recovery.

Under cancel-based recovery, you are prompted after each archive log is applied. The recovery process continues until either the recovery is complete or you enter `cancel` at the prompt. The prompt appears within Oracle Server*Manager as

```
Specify log: [<RET> for suggested ¦ AUTO ¦ FROM logsource ¦ CANCEL]
```

Once you enter `cancel` at the prompt, the recovery stops.

The steps in a cancel-based recovery are

1. Make sure that the database instance is shut down.

2. Restore the data file from tape or disk.

3. From Oracle Server*Manager, do `connect internal` and perform `startup mount` on the database instance.

4. Issue the `recover database until cancel` command from within Oracle Server*Manager. Oracle Server*Manager responds by prompting you before each archive log is applied. The recovery ends when the database encounters the final archive log or when you enter `cancel`.

5. The SVRMGR> prompt will return. If the recovery ran until completion, issue the alter database open noresetlogs; command. If you entered cancel to end the recovery, issue the alter database open resetlogs; command. The database will be recovered until the point of completion or cancellation.

Sample Database Backup Scripts

The code examples in the following sections show you how to set up and execute hot and cold backup schemes. These are not highly intensive processing modules. There are certainly ways to make them more sophisticated. For example, you could make the Oracle data dictionary determine which files to backup. Figure 14.7 shows the sample database that scripts try to backup.

FIGURE 14.7.

Sample Oracle database layout.

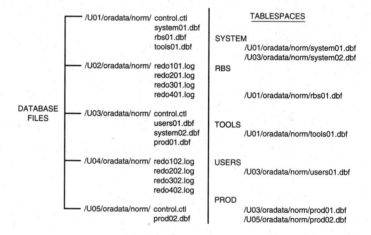

Cold Backup

This cold backup script issues a shutdown immediate command to terminate database operations. It then performs a mass copy of all the database files from the operating system to tape. When it is finished, it restarts the Oracle database instance.

```sh
#!/bin/sh
# Oracle RDBMS Cold Backup

# shutdown the database
$ORACLE_HOME/bin/svrmgrl << EOF
connect internal
shutdown immediate
exit
EOF
```

```
# make copies of all database files, control files, and redo logs
find /u*/oradata/norm/*.dbf /u*/oradata/norm/*.ctl /u*/oradata/norm/*.log ¦ cpio -
ocvB > /dev/rmt/0hc

# startup the database
$ORACLE_HOME/bin/svrmgrl << EOF
connect internal
startup
exit
EOF
```

Hot Backup

This hot backup script shows a backup that occurs to disk instead of to tape, as in the cold backup. Although the cold backup shuts down the database and does a mass file copy, the hot backup tediously copies the database files for each tablespace. The cold backup is more dynamic than the hot backup because it uses wildcards and the OFA. Whenever a new database file is added or changed, the hot backup must be changed. If it is not changed, an adequate backup is not taken.

Unlike the cold backup script, which makes its copies to tape, the hot backup script makes copies of the Oracle files to disk. Either type of copy is acceptable for either backup method.

```
#!/bin/sh
# Oracle Hot Backup Script

$ORACLE_HOME/bin/svrmgrl << EOF
connect internal

REM ** Backup System Tablespace
alter tablespace system begin backup;
!cp /u01/oradata/norm/system01.dbf /b01/oradata/norm/system01.dbf
!cp /u03/oratata/norm/system02.dbf /b03/oradata/norm/system02.dbf
alter tablespace system end backup;

REM ** Backup TOOLS tablespace
alter tablespace tools begin backup;
!cp /u01/oradata/norm/tools01.dbf /b01/oradata/norm/tools01.dbf
alter tablespace tools end backup;

REM ** Backup RBS Tablespace
alter tablespace rbs begin backup;
!cp /u01/oradata/norm/rbs01.dbf /b01/oradata/norm/rbs01.dbf
alter tablespace rbs end backup;

REM ** Backup USERS Tablespace
alter tablespace users begin backup;
!cp /u01/oradata/norm/users01.dbf /b01/oradata/norm/users01.dbf
alter tablespace users end backup;

REM ** Backup PROD Tablespace
alter tablespace prod begin backup;
!cp /u03/oradata/norm/prod01.dbf /b03/oradata/norm/prod01.dbf
!cp /u05/oradata/norm/prod02.dbf /b03/oradata/norm/prod02.dbf
alter tablespace prod end backup;
```

```
REM ** Perform Control file backup
alter database backup controlfile to '/b01/oradata/norm/control.ctl';
alter database backup controlfile to trace;

REM ** Backup OnLine Redo Logs
!cp /u03/oradata/norm/redo*.log /b03/oradata/norm
!cp /u05/oradata/norm/redo*.log /b05/oradata/norm

exit
EOF
```

Summary

This chapter discusses the resources available to an Oracle RDBMS to ensure database integrity and consistency. You learned how to implement them in a real-world backup strategy for mission-critical systems.

The information in this chapter barely scratches the surface of the backup and recovery functionality of the Oracle RDBMS. Keep in mind that an Oracle RDBMS is basically a collection of physical database files. Backup and recovery problems are most likely to occur at this level. Three types of files must be backed up: database files, control files, and online redo log files. If you omit any of these files, you have not made a successful backup of the database.

Cold backups shut down the database. Hot backups take backups while the database is functioning. There are also supplemental backup methods, such as exports. Each type of backup has its advantages and disadvantages. The major types of instance recovery are cold restore, full database recovery, time-based recovery, and cancel-based recovery.

This chapter also contains sample scripts that you can use to build your own backup scripts.

Performance Tuning and Optimizing

15

by Byron Pearce

IN THIS CHAPTER

Give a user an inch, and he wants a mile. If you change a database query so that it runs in one minute instead of five, the user will want it to work in 30 seconds. No matter how fast a database runs, there is always the need to make it go faster. Ultimately, this task falls to the DBA. A DBA really has two levels of responsibility: actual and perceived.

Actual responsibility means the tasks for which a DBA is genuinely responsible: keeping the database available for day-to-day business needs, creating new user accounts, monitoring the overall health of the database, and so on. Perceived responsibility means the responsibility incurred when there is any problem with the database—or even a conflict in the corporate IS structure. A DBA is often asked why the database is down when a link has broken in the WAN, or why the database is performing slow when a poorly written application is deployed into a production environment.

Because all database problems are perceived to be the responsibility of the DBA, it falls to him—whether he likes it or not—to validate the claims or dispel the rumors. The DBA must have a solid foundation of knowledge to base his decisions on. In many larger IS departments, the DBA may not be responsible for performance tuning. In others, the DBA may be responsible only for database—but not application—performance tuning. At some sites, the DBA is responsible for all performance-tuning functions of the database.

This chapter deals with the art of performance tuning.

> **NOTE**
>
> For more information about performance considerations while designing a database, see Chapter 17, "Designing a Database."

General Concepts in Database Tuning

When you are called on to optimize or tune a system, it is of paramount importance that you distinguish between the two levels of performance tuning: applications tuning and database tuning. They are distinct areas of expertise and are often handled by different people. The DBA should have at least an overview of the importance and functions of each type of tuning.

At the base of everything is the operating system, which drives the physical functionality—such as how to access the physical disk devices. On top of this level rests the RDBMS, which interacts with the operating system to store information physically. Applications communicate with the RDBMS to perform business tasks.

Applications Tuning

Applications tuning deals with how the various applications—forms, reports, and so on—are put together to interact with the database. Previous chapters discussed how a database is little more than a series of physical data files. Essentially, an application is nothing more than a program that issues calls to the database, which in turn are interpreted as physical reads and writes from the physical data files. Applications tuning means controlling the frequency and amount of data that the application requests from or sends to the database.

Here are some general guidelines for tuning applications:

- Generate an EXPLAIN PLAN on all the queries in the application. This helps you determine whether a query has been properly optimized. The EXPLAIN PLAN is discussed later in this chapter.

- Check the EXPLAIN PLAN of database views. This is important because views are indistinguishable from tables when they are used in queries. Because the SQL for a view is not executed until it is queried, an inefficient view can drastically slow down the performance of an otherwise efficient application. Be especially wary of joining views with other views.

- If an application that was performing acceptably begins to perform slowly, stop and determine what has changed. In many cases, queries run fine in test environments and in the first few months of production until data accumulates; an index might now be needed to expedite the database searches. In other cases, however, an index that invalidates existing EXPLAIN PLANs might have been added. This is a real danger when too many people can create indexes on production tables. The more indexes that a table has, the longer it takes to load or change data in a database table; it also impacts the speed with which the database returns query results.

- Match SQL where possible. Applications should use the same SQL statements wherever possible to take advantage of Oracle's Shared SQL Area. The SQL must match exactly to take advantage of this.

- Be as specific as possible. The more specific a database query is, the faster a query executes. For example, querying a table by a ROWID is far more specific than querying with the LIKE clause. Unless it is necessary to use less specific queries in an application, always write queries that can use the PRIMARY KEY or other indexed information.

- Be aware of how often queries are made against the database and whether they are necessary. Avoid too frequent or unnecessary calls, such calling a loop that initially queries the DUAL table for the name of the user. Each time the loop executes, the query is executed. Other types of queries are even more expensive. Whenever possible, process data in memory and refrain from querying the database.

- SQL is not a file handler. One of the most common mistakes in SQL programming is made by people who have previous programming experience using file handlers, such as BTRIEVE or ISAM. Software developers should be wary of writing two separate queries for master/detail relationships—that is, one query for the master and another for the details for that master—instead of just a single query. They involve extra processing overhead that can have a substantial overhead for applications programs.

■ Tuning does not solve the problems of poor design. This is the most essential truth in applications tuning. It emphasizes what everyone who has ever worked in systems development knows: Spend time proactively, not reactively. No matter how many indexes are created, how much optimization is done to queries, or how many caches and buffers are tweaked and tuned—if the design of a database is faulty, the performance of the overall system suffers.

These are only guidelines for applications tuning. Each site has its own specific problems and issues that affect the problems that occur in applications. More often than not, it is the duty of the developers to tune and modify their own programs without the involvement of the DBA. Because of perceived responsibility, however, the DBA must work with the applications development staff to resolve these problems.

Database Tuning

Whereas applications development addresses how a task is accomplished, tuning at the database level is more of a nuts and bolts affair. Performance tuning at the applications level relies on a methodical approach to isolating potential areas to improve. Tuning at the database level, however, is more hit and miss. It concentrates on things such as enlarging database buffers and caches by increasing INIT.ORA parameters or balancing database files to achieve optimum throughput.

Unlike applications tuning, which can be done by an applications group or the DBA depending on the environment, database tuning is the almost exclusive province of the DBA. Only in rare cases where there are multiple DBA groups, one of which specializes in performance tuning, does database tuning fall outside the domain of the DBA.

At the database level, there are three kinds of tuning:

■ Memory tuning

■ I/O tuning

■ Contention tuning

Each kind has a distinct set of areas that the DBA must examine. Memory tuning deals with optimizing the numerous caches, buffers, and shared pools that reside in memory and compose the core memory structures for the Oracle RDBMS. I/O tuning is concerned with maximizing the speed and efficiency with which the RDBMS accesses the physical data files that make up its basic storage units. Contention tuning seeks to resolve problems in which the database fights against itself for database resources.

There are only four basic steps involved in database tuning. They hold true for all three types of tuning:

1. Gather information.

2. Determine optimal changes.

3. Implement changes.

4. Monitor the database.

As with applications tuning, the more proactively the process is done, the more effective it is. The process is seldom effective when it is done on-the-fly or without the proper amount of research.

Operating System Tuning

Tuning at the operating system level is beyond the scope of this chapter. This task falls to the system administrator—only in rare cases to the DBA. However, it is often the role of the DBA to offer suggestions. Some issues to consider are

- *Paging and swapping.* At the operating system level, paging and swapping is used to transfer information from the system's memory (RAM) to disk and back again. This enables the system to manipulate more information than it normally could handle in real memory. However, excessive paging and swapping can cause system performance to degrade. The DBA and the system administrator should work together to optimize memory to reduce or eliminate paging and swapping.

- *Stripping, mirroring, and RAID.* In many cases, the disk drives write a piece of information across several disks (striping), write all the information across a pair of disks (mirroring), or write all the information across every disk in a fixed-number set (RAID). These disk drive configurations can help make I/O more efficient by distributing reads and writes across many disks. In some cases, they increase the fault-tolerance of the system itself. It is important for the DBA to be aware that many of these configurations have an impact on I/O performance. RAID drives, for example, must access each disk in the set for every read and write operation.

- *Shared memory.* Used for communication between processes, shared memory settings are usually configured within the operating system. The *Oracle Installation and Configuration Guide* gives the minimum settings for configuring shared memory for an Oracle RDBMS. These settings are the minimum required for running the RDBMS. In practice, they generally should be set higher.

- *Maximum processes.* One of the drawbacks of Oracle (or any other RDBMS) is the amount of overhead required from the system on which it runs. One of the areas that Oracle takes extended overhead is in processes. The database itself consists of background process—PMON, SMON, LGWR, DBWR, and so on—plus an additional process for each user who connects to the database. Although this value can be limited at the database level through the PROCESSES parameter in the INIT.ORA parameter file, it is important to make certain that the operating system supports the number of processes. It is also important to ensure that the number of available processes allows for growth.

■ *Maximum open files.* A particular problem in an Oracle RDBMS is the maximum number of open files that a single process can hold. The number of files is defined at the operating system and RDBMS levels. The RDBMS sets this limit with the MAXDATAFILES parameter of the create database statement. There is also a limit at the operating system level, which depends on the configuration of the operating system. In both cases, the DBA can change the value.

> **CAUTION**
>
> It is not advisable to change the operating system priority of the Oracle background processes. If these values are altered, the database might process information less efficiently. If you must modify them, set all database processes to the same value.

Performance Tools

In tuning a database, the first and most crucial step is gathering statistics on the current database performance. These tools give a benchmark of how the database is currently performing and enable the DBA to gauge progress by measuring improvement.

Viewing SGA and Parameter Settings

Use the Oracle Server*Manager to view current parameter settings for an Oracle RDBMS instance. The show sga command shows the current size and makeup of the SGA. You can also display the INIT.ORA parameters with the show parameter command. To display only a particular parameter, add it to the command. For example,

```
% svrmgrl
SVRMGR> Connect internal
Connected.
SVRMGR> show parameter block
```

All the database parameters are shown, even ones that have not been explicitly set in the INIT.ORA parameter file. Parameters that the DBA has not set are shown with their default values. By spooling this list to a data file, the DBA can get an accurate snapshot of a database's settings.

UTLBSTAT and *UTLESTAT*

To determine what needs to be fixed in an Oracle RDBMS instance, you must first determine what is broken. In some cases, performance problems occur sporadically; however, they usually have a specific pattern. Do they occur around lunchtime? At night? Early in the morning? One of the keys to performing successful performance tuning is being able to identify when the problem is occurring.

Oracle provides tools that enable you to examine in detail what the Oracle RDBMS was doing during a specific period of time. They are the begin statistics utility (`utlbstat`) and the end statistics utility (`utlestat`). These scripts enable you to take a snapshot of how the instance was performing during an interval of time. They use the Oracle dynamic performance (V$) tables to gather information.

> **CAUTION**
>
> It is important to use the `utlbstat` and `utlestat` utilities only against a database instance that has been running for a while. Because an Oracle RDBMS instance reinitializes its dynamic performance table during database startup, information gathered from a database that has not been running and had time to gather information is inconclusive.

To use `utlbstat` and `utlestat`, the database must have been started with the value of `TIMED_STATISTICS` in the INIT.ORA parameter file set to `TRUE`. Oracle does not collect some of the information required for the report if this parameter is not set to TRUE. Setting `TIMED_STATISTICS` to TRUE, however, causes the database instance to incur overhead. The amount is small—only about 4–8 percent in quantitative terms—and it is necessary to take an accurate snapshot of the database performance. Many DBAs set this parameter to `TRUE` only when they gather statistics.

Once you have set the required parameters, the database has run for a sufficient period of time, and you have identified the window, you take the snapshot by using `utlbstat`. To execute either script, you must have the ability to `connect internal` to the database. Running `utlbstat` tells the RDBMS instance to begin gathering statistics until told otherwise. It is executed as follows:

```
% svrmgrl
SVRMGR> @$ORACLE_HOME/rdbms/admin/utlbstat
```

From the moment when this script is executed, the Oracle RDBMS instance gathers performance statistics. It continues to do so until you run the `utlestat` script, which stops gathering performance statistics. It is important that the database remain active and not be shut down while `utlbstat` is running.

```
% svrmgrl
SVRMGR> @$ORACLE_HOME/rdbms/admin/utlestat
```

When you run `utlestat`, the database creates a report called REPORT.TXT in the current directory, which contains the statistical information gathered. Each report contains the following information:

- Library cache statistics
- System summary statistics
- System-wide wait event statistics

- The average length of the dirty buffer write queue
- File I/O statistics
- SGA and cache statistics
- Latch statistics
- Rollback segment statistics
- Current initialization parameter settings
- Dictionary cache statistics
- Start and stop time statistics

A sample report called REPORT.TXT is included on the CD-ROM and shows what a report produced by `utlestat` might look like.

Generating the report is simple; interpreting it is another matter entirely. The rest of this chapter looks at what this information means. The report itself gives some brief hints. When in doubt, always remember to keep hit rates high and wait times low.

EXPLAIN PLAN

Performance tuning does not always have to happen on a global, database-level view. In theory, most tuning should take place at much lower, scalable levels where the performance impact is more easily measured. A fundamental truth of database tuning and optimization is that performance tuning is not sorcery or magic. Optimizing a database will not make a poorly tuned application run faster; the reverse is also true, though less common. It is important to examine how the database handles processing at the application, or SQL, level.

To do this, Oracle provides a tool in the form of the EXPLAIN PLAN, which enables the DBA to pass a SQL statement through the Oracle optimizer and learn how the statement will be executed by the database—the *execution plan*. That way, it is possible to learn whether the database is performing as expected—for example, whether it uses an index on a table instead of scanning the entire database table.

Several factors can affect the results returned by an EXPLAIN PLAN. They include

- Changes in statistics when running the database under the Cost-Based Optimizer
- The use of HINTS under the Rule-Based Optimizer that cause the query to select a particular execution path
- The addition or deletion of new indexes on one of the tables in the SQL statement when running the database under the Rule-Based Optimizer
- Subtle changes in the WHERE or FROM clause of a SQL SELECT statement when running the database under the Rule-Based Optimizer
- The presence of database objects with the same name as the object being referenced in the schema of the user executing the query

It is important to understand that the results of an EXPLAIN PLAN are, therefore, by no means fixed and finite. The DBA must be aware of changes made to database objects—such as adding new indexes—and how fast the tables are growing.

The Oracle RDBMS uses the EXPLAIN PLAN by storing information about how a query is executing in a table within the user's schema. The table must exist for the EXPLAIN PLAN to work. To create the table, the user must execute the following script. Of course, he must have the CREATE TABLE and RESOURCE or quota privileges on his default tablespace.

```
% svrmgrl
SVRMGR> connect scott/tiger
Connected.
SVRMGR> @$ORACLE_HOME/rdbms/admin/utlxplan.sql
Statement Processed.
```

Once the table has been created, an EXPLAIN PLAN can be generated from a query by prefacing the query with the command to perform an EXPLAIN PLAN. The following script shows how to format a query for an EXPLAIN PLAN:

```
CONNECT /
EXPLAIN PLAN
SET STATEMENT_ID = 'QUERY1'
INTO PLAN_TABLE FOR
SELECT O.ORDER_DATE, O.ORDERNO, O.PARTNO, P.PART_DESC, O.QTY
FROM ORDER O, PART P
WHERE O.PARTNO = P.PARTNO
```

Note the SET STATEMENT and INTO clauses of the EXPLAIN PLAN. The value of SET STATEMENT is used to make the execution of the EXPLAIN PLAN stored within the table unique; it can be virtually any string up to 30 characters in length. Specifying a table in the INTO clause, on the other hand, tells the EXPLAIN PLAN where to place information about the query execution. In the previous example, the execution of the query is identified as QUERY1 and has its information stored in the table PLAN_TABLE.

Now that the EXPLAIN PLAN has loaded the table with information, there is the obvious question of how to retrieve and interpret the information provided. Oracle provides a script in the *Oracle7 Server Utilities Guide* that displays information in a tree-like fashion. It is

```
SELECT LPAD(' ', 2*(LEVEL-1))||operation||' '||
       options, object_name "QUERY PLAN"
FROM plan_table
START WITH id = 0 AND statement_id = 'QUERY1'
CONNECT BY PRIOR id = parent_id
/
```

By running a SQL query through the EXPLAIN PLAN, a pseudo-graph similar to the following is produced:

```
QUERY PLAN
- - - - - - - - - - - - - - - - - - - - - - - - - - - - - - - - - - - - - - - - - - -
  SORT                          ORDER BY
    NESTED LOOPS
      FILTER
```

```
NESTED LOOPS            OUTER
   TABLE ACCESS            FULL                     HEADER
   TABLE ACCESS            BY ROWID                 DETAIL
      INDEX                    RANGE SCAN           DETAIL_PK
      INDEX                    RANGE SCAN           DETAIL_PK
   TABLE ACCESS            FULL                     HEADER
   TABLE ACCESS            BY ROWID                 DETAIL
      INDEX                    RANGE SCAN           DETAIL_PK
      INDEX                    RANGE SCAN           DETAIL_PK
NESTED LOOPS            OUTER
   TABLE ACCESS            FULL                     HEADER
   TABLE ACCESS            BY ROWID                 DETAIL
      INDEX                    RANGE SCAN           DETAIL_PK
      INDEX                    RANGE SCAN           DETAIL_PK
   TABLE ACCESS            FULL                     HEADER
   TABLE ACCESS            BY ROWID                 DETAIL
      INDEX                    RANGE SCAN           DETAIL_PK
      INDEX                    RANGE SCAN           DETAIL_PK
TABLE ACCESS            BY ROWID                 DETAIL
   INDEX                RANGE SCAN               DETAIL_PK
   INDEX                RANGE SCAN               DETAIL_PK
FILTER
   TABLE ACCESS            FULL                     HEADER
   TABLE ACCESS            BY ROWID                 DETAIL°
      INDEX                    RANGE SCAN           DETAIL_PK
      INDEX                    RANGE SCAN           DETAIL_PK
   TABLE ACCESS            FULL                     HEADER
   TABLE ACCESS            BY ROWID                 DETAIL
      INDEX                    RANGE SCAN           DETAIL_PK
      INDEX                    RANGE SCAN           DETAIL_PK
NESTED LOOPS            OUTER
   TABLE ACCESS            BY ROWID                 DETAIL
      INDEX                    RANGE SCAN           DETAIL_PK
      INDEX                    RANGE SCAN           DETAIL_PK
   TABLE ACCESS            FULL                     HEADER
   TABLE ACCESS            BY ROWID                 DETAIL
      INDEX                    RANGE SCAN           DETAIL_PK
      INDEX                    RANGE SCAN           DETAIL_PK
```

When you interpret the output, it is important to understand that all operations, as reported by the EXPLAIN PLAN, are basically operation/option combinations. There is no way to discuss all these combinations or the possible interpretations of all the EXPLAIN PLAN scenarios. As with many aspects of the IS industry—especially relational databases—the only true teacher is experience. However, here are some of the more common operation/option pairs that EXPLAIN PLANs returns:

FILTER	Eliminates rows from a table by conditions specified in the WHERE clause of a SQL statement
INDEX/RANGE SCAN	Accesses information in the table via a non-unique index (specified in the object_name column)
INDEX/UNIQUE	Accesses information in the table via a unique or primary key index (specified in the object_name column)

MERGE/JOIN	Combines two sorted lists of data into a single, sorted list; used on multi-table queries
SORT/GROUP BY	Sorts table data as specified in a GROUP BY clause of the SQL statement
SORT/JOIN	Performs a sort on the data from the tables before a MERGE JOIN operation
SORT/ORDER BY	Sorts table data as specified in an ORDER BY clause of a SQL statement
SORT/UNIQUE	Performs a sort on table data being returned and eliminates duplicate rows
TABLE ACCESS/FULL	Performs a full scan of the database table to locate and return required data
TABLE ACCESS/ROWID	Locates a row in a database table by using its unique ROWID
VIEW	Returns information from a database view

The EXPLAIN PLAN is a powerful tool for software developers because it enables them to ensure that their queries are properly tuned. Of course, changes made to database objects can adversely affect the results of the EXPLAIN PLAN, but they are useful in determining where the performance drains on an application will occur.

SQL*Trace and *TKPROF*

Oracle SQL*Trace and EXPLAIN PLAN are similar in that they are both used to do performance tuning at the application level and that they both show the manner in which the Oracle RDBMS executes a query. Unlike the EXPLAIN PLAN, which simply shows how the database optimizer chooses to execute a query to return specified information, SQL*Trace reveals the quantitative numbers behind the SQL execution. In addition to an execution plan, SQL*Trace generates factors such as CPU and disk resources, in addition to an execution plan. This is often considered a lower-level view of how a database query is performing, because it shows factors at both the operating system and RDBMS levels.

To use SQL*Trace, you must first set some parameters in the INIT.ORA parameter file:

| MAX_DUMP_FILE_SIZE | Denotes the maximum size for an Oracle-generated file. This value is the number in operating system blocks (which may differ from the size in database blocks). |
| SQL_TRACE | Causes a trace file to be written for every user who connects to the database when it is set to TRUE. Because of disk space requirements and database overhead, it should be used judiciously. |

TIMED_STATISTICS	Causes the database to gather database statistics when this value is set to TRUE. It causes overhead of 4–8 percent.
USER_DUMP_DEST	The directory path where trace files will be written.

After you have set the INIT.ORA parameters, you can invoke the SQL*Trace utility manually. If the SQL_TRACE parameter is set, it is not necessary to invoke SQL*Trace manually because a trace file will be written automatically; however, it is more common to call it manually. To invoke SQL*Trace, use either SQL or PL/SQL.

Use SQL when there is a specific query to be analyzed. For example,

```
% sqlplus
SQL> ALTER SESSION SET SQL_TRACE = TRUE;
SQL> @/tmp/enter_your_query.sql
SQL> ALTER SESSION SET SQL_TRACE = FALSE;
SQL> EXIT
```

You can either type in the query at the SQL prompt or source it in from an external file that contains the query.

In many cases, especially through applications such as SQL*Forms, it is necessary to invoke the trace facility by using PL/SQL. This is especially helpful when you are dealing with a third-party application for which the SQL syntax is not readily obvious. To invoke SQL*Trace, use the following PL/SQL statement:

```
BEGIN
   DBMS_SESSION.SET_SQL_TRACE (TRUE);
   /* PL/SQL code goes here */
```

As with SQL*Plus, the trace gathers information until the session disconnects or is deactivated.

```
   /* PL/SQL code goes here */
   DBMS_SESSION.SET_SQL_TRACE (FALSE);
END;
```

After the trace file has been generated, it must be converted into a readable format. Oracle provides the TKPROF utility to accomplish this task. Using TKPROF, you can convert the raw trace file into a readable report.

TIP

Locating a trace file in the dump directory can be quite a task, especially if many other files exist. Two tricks speed this process. The first is to use the UNIX command ls -lt to list the files in date order, with the newest file listed first. The other option is to use a SELECT USERNAME FROM DUAL as part of the trace and issue a grep USERNAME *.trc to find the trace file.

Once the trace file has been located, it is necessary to run the TKPROF utility against it to produce readable output. This information is statistical and shows how queries perform at the database and operating system level. The report produced by TKPROF contains CPU usage, disk utilization, and the count of rows returned by the query (or queries) enclosed in the trace file output. You can also have TKPROF return EXPLAIN PLAN information from each query in the trace. TKPROF is invoked as follows:

```
% tkprof ora_4952.trc ora_4952.log
```

This statement takes the trace output from the ORA_4952.TRC SQL*Trace file and generates its output in the file named ORA_4952.LOG. This particular statement does not generate an EXPLAIN PLAN for any of the queries contained in the trace file. Supplemental options enable you to control a certain extent or the information that is produced. They are

EXPLAIN — Enables you to specify a username and password that will generate an EXPLAIN PLAN for each query TKPROF analyzes

INSERT — Specifies where to dump both the SQL statements in the trace file and the data contained in the insert statements

PRINT — Designates the number of queries in the trace file to examine—especially useful for trace files that contain many SQL statements

RECORD — Enables you to specify an output file that will contain all the statements in the trace file

SORT — Enables you to control the order in which the analyzed queries are displayed

SYS — Indicates whether to include queries run against the SYS tables (the data dictionary) in the trace output

TABLE — Specifies the schema.tablename to use when generating a report with the EXPLAIN option

When you run the trace file through TKPROF, it generates a report. For example,

```
************************************************************
select o.ordid, p.partid, o.qty, p.cost, (o.qty * p.cost)
from part p, order o
where o.partid = p.partid

call      count   cpu   elapsed  disk  query  current  rows
-------   -----   ----  -------- ----  -----  -------  ----
Parse         1   0.02      0.02     0      0        0     0
Execute       1   0.00      0.00     0      0        0     0
Fetch         4   0.03      0.03     1     20       10    50
-------   -----   ----  -------- ----  -----  -------  ----
total         6   0.05      0.05     1     20       10    50

Misses in library cache during parse: 0
Misses in library cache during execute: 1
Optimizer hint: CHOOSE
Parsing user id: 22  (MERLIN)
************************************************************
```

As with interpreting the `utlbstat`/`utlestat` report and the EXPLAIN PLAN, interpreting the results produced by TKPROF and SQL*Trace is more art than science. The following guidelines are helpful:

- The totals for the query and current columns represent the logical I/O (in blocks) accumulated by the query. Compare them against the total of the rows column. Except in special cases, there should be a few logical I/O blocks versus a large number of returned rows. The optimal ratio is approximately 2:1.

- In most cases, the execute value should be higher than the parse value. If the number of parses is the same as the number of executions, you should consider increasing the size of the shared pool.

- Compare the amount of physical I/O (total of the disk column) to the amount of logical I/O (sums of the totals of the query and current columns). The logical I/O should be much higher than the physical I/O.

Dynamic Performance (V$) Tables

Another useful tool for database tuning is the dynamic performance tables, also called the V$ tables (which are really views despite this name). The V$ views are views on the Oracle X$ tables, which are SGA-held memory structures created by the database at startup. These tables—and their views—are updated in real time as the database runs, and provide the DBA a good view of the current status of the database. Several third-party applications use the V$ tables to access statistical or performance monitoring data, and the views are used by the `monitor` component of the Oracle Server*Manager. After database creation, the V$ tables can be accessed only by the user SYS, who can make grants on them to other users.

> **CAUTION**
>
> Oracle Corporation has stated that it is not committed to supporting the Y$ tables in future product releases. Although that would be unlikely, given the number of market products that use these views, be aware of the possibility.

The V$ views are useful in many applications, such as backup and recovery, administrative monitoring, and performance tuning. Here are some of the more commonly used views as they apply to performance tuning:

`V$DB_OBJECT_CACHE`	Contains information about all the database objects that currently exist in the library cache of the SGA
`V$FILESTAT`	Contains the amount of physical reads and writes taking place on a specific data file associated with the database

V$LATCH	Contains a current statistical picture of all the latches within the database
V$LATCHHOLDER	Contains the name of the current latchholder of the each latch specified in V$LATCH
V$LATCHNAME	Contains the name of each latch in the V$LATCH view
V$LIBRARYCACHE	Contains statistics that represent the overall performance of the library cache area of the SGA
V$ROLLSTAT	Contains statistics on all the online rollback segments in the database
V$ROLLCACHE	Contains statistical information about the performance of the data dictionary cache of the SGA
V$SESSION_WAIT	Provides information on what sessions are waiting for other sessions if one session is waiting for another to complete a task or event
V$SESSTAT	Contains current statistical information for each active database session
V$SESS_IO	Contains current logical and physical I/O information for each active database session
V$SGASTAT	Summarizes statistical information on the overall SGA
V$SQLAREA	Contains statistical information on the cursor cache of the SGA
V$STATNAME	Contains the names of all the statistics from V$SESSTAT
V$WAITSTAT	Contains information on block contention—active only when TIMED_STATISTICS is set to TRUE

CAUTION

Because statistics are gathered over a period of time, a database that has just started up does not have sufficient statistics to provide any sort of tuning information. Statistics gathered from a newly started database are misleading and cannot pinpoint actual performance problems. As a rule of thumb, a database should run for several hours before you gather any performance statistics.

Here is a query that uses the V$ views. It displays the name and current value of each database statistic. It is useful for quickly seeing how the database is performing.

```
select n.statistic# , n.name , s.value
from v$statname n , v$sysstat s
where n.statistic# = s.statistic#
and value > 0
/
```

There are many more V$ views that are not mentioned here. Many gather I/O, cache, and buffering statistics that are invaluable for performance tuning. Consult the *Oracle7 Server Administrator's Guide* and the *Oracle7 Applications Developers Guide* for more information on these views.

SQL*DBA—the predecessor to Oracle Server*Manager—is being made obsolete in mid-1996. It contains several scripts that the monitor utility uses. Located in the $ORACLE_HOME/rdbms/sqldba directory, they give you insight into how to use some of the V$ views. They also show how many of the V$ views have relationships with other V$ views.

Tuning Database SGA

Problems with database applications often involve memory and disk drives. When the CPU runs faster than the throughput of the input/output devices (such as the disk drives), the system is called *I/O bound.* When the throughput of the input/output devices is faster than the CPU, the system is called *CPU bound.*

Most systems are I/O bound, so it is easy to dismiss poor performance as a by-product of poor throughput transfer. Many DBAs, therefore, perform load balancing and contention analysis to optimize performance. What is forgotten, however, is that poor memory management can often aggravate many performance problems. Poor use of the available memory can contribute to throughput that is less than superior. For example, sorts that could be optimized to run in memory run to disk, or the operating system pages, and swaps processes to disk.

It is important, therefore, to understand the single most memory intensive part of the Oracle RDBMS—the system global area (SGA). By definition, the SGA is simply a combination of buffers and caches stored in virtual memory that enables the database to function. To be efficient, Oracle performs many of its operations in memory, writing to disk only in bulk so as to optimize performance hits. This is good because from the standpoint of software development, accessing the disk drive is "expensive" in terms of performance cost, whereas running a process in memory is "inexpensive."

As Figure 15.1 shows, the SGA is composed of three primary units:

- The redo log buffer
- The database buffer cache
- The shared SQL area (the shared pool)

FIGURE 15.1.

Architecture of the Oracle SGA.

SGA

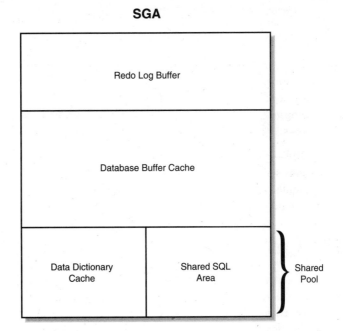

It is important to ensure that the SGA is large enough to fit comfortably into the system's existing memory. It should also be small enough to coexist with other applications and not allocate more memory than it requires. It is equally important to make certain that there is enough shared memory—*semaphores*—available to support the database instance. Like all other aspects of performance tuning, memory management means balancing available resources against needed resources and reaching an effective compromise.

Examining the Current SGA

To tune the SGA of a database instance, you must determine the current size of the SGA size. There are several ways to do this, including extracting the information from the DBA views or V$ tables or calculating it based on values in the INIT.ORA parameter file. The simplest method, however, is to issue the show sga command from Oracle Server*Manager. For example,

```
% svrmgrl
SVRMGR> connect internal
Connected.
SVRMGR> show sga
Total System Global Area        95243632 bytes
Fixed Size                         46384 bytes
Variable Size                   70588480 bytes
Database Buffers                24576000 bytes
Redo Buffers                       32768 bytes
```

The size of the SGA remains constant as long as the database is running, although the DBA can change it when the database is restarted.

Changing the SGA Size

The sum of the parts equals the whole. Sizing the SGA is no exception. Changing the size of the SGA requires that values of some INIT.ORA parameters be modified, which in turn alters the overall size of the SGA. The following parameters control the size of the SGA:

DB_BLOCK_BUFFERS	The number of database blocks (of size DB_BLOCK_SIZE) allocated to the database buffer cache
LOG_BUFFER	The size (in bytes) of the redo log buffer
SHARED_POOL_SIZE	The size (in bytes) of the Shared SQL area

> **CAUTION**
>
> Some of the parameters require their arguments in bytes, whereas others require their arguments in blocks.

After the size of an SGA buffer is set, the size of the SGA remains constant as long as the database continues to run. If the values of the these three parameters are changed and the database is restarted, they immediately take effect. You should make a backup of the INIT.ORA parameter file before you make considerable changes. For example,

```
#
# SGA Size Parameters
#

# each database block is set to 8192 (8K) bytes
db_block_size = 8192

# buffer is 25MB (8192 bytes x 3200 blocks)
db_block_buffers = 3200

# buffer is 32K
log_buffer = 32768

# buffer is 50M
shared_pool_size = 52428800
```

You should also ensure that these values are always set appropriately high, but not inordinately high. The ramifications of changing the size of the SGA are discussed later in this chapter.

Database Block Size

The "building blocks" of any database are the size of its blocks. You set this value with the DB_BLOCK_SIZE parameter, and its range is operating system-specific—approximately 512 bytes to 16MB.

This value represents how data "pieces" are transferred to and from the instance's SGA during an operation. The more data that the database can transfer in a single operation, the fewer operations that it has to perform; consequently, the overall performance of the instance improves. The value of DB_BLOCK_SIZE should be a multiple of the operating system block size. On some systems, the default operating system block size is sufficient. On other systems, the best speed is twice that value. The best way to determine this is to generate a test instance; use different sizes of blocks and conduct benchmark testing. Always keep in mind the limits imposed by the operating system when you do this. As with all other areas of performance tuning, a trade-off occurs—setting the size of the block too high can actually degrade the performance.

Once a database is created, the only way to change the value of DB_BLOCK_SIZE is to recreate the database. This makes sense. Whenever a database instance is created, Oracle physically allocates several database files of size X in which it will store various forms of information—the data dictionary, tables, indexes, and so on. These files are created with blocks of size DB_BLOCK_SIZE and are mapped so that the database can recognize each one. If the value of DB_BLOCK_SIZE is changed, the blocks no longer begin and end where the database expects. The RDBMS cannot correctly manipulate data if it cannot recognize the blocks.

To change the size of the blocks:

1. Perform a full cold backup of the database.
2. Use the exp utility to do a full database export on the database instance as the user SYS.
3. Remove all the physical data files.
4. Recreate the database with the new DB_BLOCK_SIZE.
5. Use the imp utility to import the data from the original database instance into the new database instance as the user SYS.

CAUTION

When you create a database with a new DB_BLOCK_SIZE, examine each INIT.ORA parameter for possible ramifications. Many parameters are allocated in database blocks; increasing the size of each block might adversely affect the performance of the database.

This process is time-consuming and should be done only if the performance increase will be significant.

Database Buffer Cache

The database buffer cache is the memory buffer within the SGA that holds copies of data that has been read and often changed from the physical database files. There are as many buffers in this buffer cache as the value of DB_BLOCK_BUFFERS. They include

Dirty buffers	Buffers that have been changed but not written back to disk
Pinned buffers	Buffers that are currently being accessed
Free buffers	Buffers that are available for use

Because it is desirable to have Oracle work within the SGA memory area as much as possible, the hit rate within the database buffer cache should be very high—greater than 70 percent. To determine the rate, execute the following query on the database buffer cache:

```
select name, value
from v$sysstat
where name in ('consistent gets', 'db block gets', 'physical reads')
/
```

The query returns three values, which you can plug into the following mathematical formula to obtain the current database buffer cache hit ratio:

```
hit ratio = 1 - (physical reads / (db block gets + consistent gets) )
```

If the hit ratio returned is less than 70 percent, you should seriously consider raising the number of blocks allocated to the database buffer cache of the SGA. To do that, increase the value of the INIT.ORA parameter DB_BLOCK_BUFFERS.

Shared Pool Size

The SGA shared pool area is composed primarily of two entities: the shared SQL cache and the data dictionary cache. Each one serves a distinct function. The shared SQL cache is used to retain previously executed queries, procedures, and other SQL-based operations in the SGA. Thus, frequently executed SQL statements reside in memory and do not have to be reparsed by the database before each execution. The data dictionary cache contains calls made to the data dictionary, which must be done before every single action in the database. In previous versions of Oracle, the data dictionary cache had individually tunable parameters, but they are now encompassed under the shared pool.

As with the database buffer cache, the efficiency of the shared pool cache is determined by a hit ratio that indicates how often the Oracle RDBMS can process information in memory and how often it must retrieve information from disk. The database should work as much from memory as possible without going to disk. Although that is not always practical, you should examine the various caches to ensure that their values are in acceptable ranges.

The following script compares the number of pins (how often an item was executed) to the number of reloads (how often a miss occurred):

```
select sum(pins) pins, sum(reloads) reloads
from v$librarycache
/
```

Use the following formula to determine the ratio of reloads to pins. If the result is 1 or greater, you need to tune the shared SQL area by increasing the size of the shared pool.

```
ratio = (reloads / pins) * 100
```

Similarly, the data dictionary cache determines how often the RDBMS goes to disk when it accesses information on users, privileges, tables, indexes, and so on. Most database systems reuse the same database objects repeatedly. Therefore, if a high degree of disk access takes place for operations that run the same programs, the information is likely being aged out too often. The same rule holds true for the other shared pool areas.

The following code segment enables the DBA or the user to retrieve the number of gets (information requests on an object) and getmisses (cached or missed queries).

```
select sum(gets) gets, sum(getmisses) getmisses
from v$rowcache
/
```

The formula for the ratio of gets to getmisses is

```
ratio = ( getmisses / gets) * 100
```

If the ratio is greater than 10 percent, you should consider increasing the value of the SHARED_POOL_SIZE parameter. It is usually a good idea to have a large shared pool. In a few cases, however, this can adversely affect the database.

Sort Area Size

During a single day, a database instance performs many operations that involve sorting. They include everything from an explicit command to sort (such as the SQL ORDER BY or GROUP BY option) to an implicit command (such as creating an index to a database table). Working in memory is faster than working on disk, and sorting is no exception.

Whenever an operation is undertaken that requires sorting, Oracle attempts to do it in the memory of the user process that requests the sort. Sorts are constrained by the following INIT.ORA parameters:

SORT_AREA_SIZE	The maximum amount of space (in bytes) that a user process has available to perform a sort
SORT_AREA_SIZE_RETAINED	The minimum amount of space (in bytes) that a user process will ever have available

Exceeding SORT_AREA_SIZE causes a sort to disk to occur.

To determine whether a sort is performing efficiently, you must first determine the level—memory or disk—at which the sort occurs. For example:

```
select name, value
from v$sysstat
where name like 'sort%'
/
```

produces output similar to

```
NAME                                                VALUE
--------------------------------------------------  -----
sorts (memory)                                        370
sorts (disk)                                            7
sorts (rows)                                          1997
```

Interpreting the output from the sort statistics is not as simple as calculating a hit ratio. Obviously, the lower the value of the sorts to disk, the better the sort is performing. However, many sorts to disk does not necessarily mean that the database is not sorting optimally. You should consider whether you can safely raise the value of SORT_AREA_SIZE without causing an adverse impact on the database. Likewise, these might be batch jobs, which process an inordinate amount of data. Because of the volume of data processed, it is impossible to increase the SORT_AREA_SIZE large enough to eliminate these sorts to disk.

When you deal with sorts, it is as important to know why certain results occur as it is to know that the results do occur. Watched diligently and with a knowledge about current operations, the sorts on a database are low-maintenance items.

Ramifications of SGA Changes

It is relatively easy to change the size of the buffers in the SGA, but you must consider the ramifications of making changes.

The most obvious benefit of increasing the size of the SGA is that the larger the SGA, the more information can be processed in memory. By enabling the database to have most of its data cached, physical disk I/O is minimized, which results in a system that is constrained more by the speed of the processor than by the speed of the I/O devices. The law of diminishing marginal utility applies, however. Depending on the size of the database and the amount of activity being performed, increasing the size of the SGA buffers ceases to have any positive effect after a certain point. Once this occurs, the database begins to hoard memory that could be better used by the operating system or other applications.

Another concern in tuning a database SGA is failing to consider that some parameters incur memory for every connection instead of only one. Consider, for example, the scenario in which the DBA wants to increase the size of the sort area. After some investigation, he concludes that having a 10MB sort area would greatly improve performance because many sorts are taking place to disk. This system also experiences a high level of user activity—500 users.

Instead of creating a single 10MB sort area, the DBA has actually created 500 10MB sort areas. The total memory cost is approximately 5GB—more RAM than most systems have.

Don't forget to factor in user processes and other non-Oracle applications that might reside on the system. DBAs often think that they are the only people on a hardware platform. The *Oracle Installation and Configuration Guide* has charts that enable you to calculate memory requirements based on the products being used. It is far better to make adjustments before you create an instance. Otherwise, you must expend the time and frustration of tracking down SGA settings that artificially induce paging and swapping onto the system.

Consider the following guidelines when you adjust the SGA and its associated buffers:

- Always make certain that the SGA fits comfortably in available memory, not overall system memory.
- Never make buffers larger than they need to be. Allow, of course, for growth. However, if you are actively monitoring the system, you can increase the values as needed without wasting space in memory.
- Watch out for database parameters such as SORT_AREA_SIZE, that incur use for every user. Don't set them so high that they cause the system to begin paging and swapping.
- Adequately plan changes. Remember the proverb, "An ounce of prevention is worth a pound of cure."
- Be wary of changes that affect other parameters. Changing the database block size, for example, can affect the values of several other INIT.ORA parameters and cause a database instance to consume more memory than expected.

Database instances require more disk space as they grow larger. The same is true with memory. A growing database will eventually outstrip the memory available on the system. Don't make the mistake of ignoring possible memory problems when you do a performance analysis.

Contention Issues

DBAs often ignore the physical aspects of a system. With all the logical structures that a DBA must deal with on a day-to-day basis, it is easy to forget about the physical elements that support them, such as SCSCI cards, bandwidth, or an I/O bus. Whenever you fail to consider the physical elements, *contention* can occur within the database.

Like spoiled children, database elements fight over resources. This is the most basic definition of contention. When contention happens, the database must wait for an event to occur. This event—such as writing a block of data to a physical device or locking a row inside a database table—causes an appreciable slowdown in database performance. It is the responsibility of the DBA and others, such as the system administrator, to work with the database to minimize contention. When you minimize contention, the database performs at consistent, efficient speeds.

I/O Contention and Load Balancing

Contention among physical storage devices is the most common type of contention. Each disk drive has heads that travel back and forth across the magnetic medium (the disk) to read and write information. A database is made up of several physical data files, many of which reside on the same physical disk, so it is easy to see how contention can occur. If the database requests access to several data files on the same disk, the result is contention as the drive head moves across the disk to the first location and accesses the file, moves to the second location and accesses the file, and so on. Fortunately, you can minimize I/O contention.

It is important to understand types of database files and the types of operations performed on them. Figure 15.2 compares the types of files and operations.

FIGURE 15.2.

File and access.

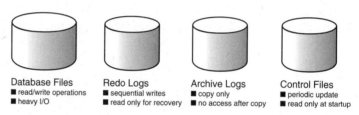

Database Files	Redo Logs	Archive Logs	Control Files
■ read/write operations	■ sequential writes	■ copy only	■ periodic update
■ heavy I/O	■ read only for recovery	■ no access after copy	■ read only at startup

In a perfect world, you could place each database file on a separate disk. On smaller database instances, this might even be possible, but they are the exception. In practice, most databases have multiple files and a limited number of disks on which to place them—generally just the amount of space that is needed. So it becomes important to work with the system administrator to determine the optimal layout of the physical database files.

As Figure 15.2 shows, each database file has specific operations. Redo logs, for example, handle straightforward, sequential output. Database files handle intensive read and write operations. You should put the following files on a physical disk separate from the other database files:

- Rollback segments
- Redo logs
- Archive logs

The files are separated so that access to these areas is not in contention with access to other files, such as database files and the control file. It is important to optimize the physical layout so that contention is minimized between the ARCH, DBWR, and LGWR processes. Because of the information generated for each transaction, it is usually best to place rollback segments on their own disk.

TIP

Some sites that use heavy OLTP create separate tablespaces for each rollback segment and spread them across disks similarly to how control files are distributed. This minimizes the I/O on a single disk and provides for less I/O contention when rollback segments are accessed.

One of the most important things that you can do to achieve I/O balancing is to put table and index data on separate physical devices, as shown in Figure 15.3. If table and index data exist on the same disk drive, any type of table access that uses indexes doubles the I/O operations on a single disk device. Take, for example, a SELECT operation. The index must be accessed to determine the fastest way to access table information, and then the table itself is accessed. This causes all the operations to wait on the access to the table or the index, and it drastically cuts throughput on all operations, especially those with many users who access data in the same tables simultaneously. By splitting the tables and the indexes across disk drives, the disk drive heads can work in tandem with the database to quickly access table data and return it to users.

FIGURE 15.3.

Table and index splitting.

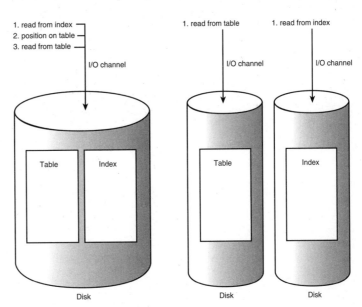

Splitting tables and indexes is the first step in setting up efficient throughput and minimizing I/O contention, but it is hardly enough to ensure optimal performance. You must pinpoint which database files are accessed most heavily and spread them across disks to balance the load. By issuing the following query as the SYS user or as another user who has access to the V$

views, you can determine the current I/O load on the database files. It is important to take these readings several times over a span of time to ensure accurate statistics. For example:

```
SQL> select d.name, f.phyrds, f.phywrts
  2  from v$datafile d, v$filestat f
  3  where d.file# = f.file#
  4  /

NAME                                            PHYRDS      PHYWRTS
---------------------------------------------   ----------  ----------
/u04/oradata/norm/system01.dbf                    383336       23257
/u20/oradata/norm/rbs01.dbf                        13740      332604
/u05/oradata/norm/temp01.dbf                        3037      147963
/u08/oradata/norm/tools01.dbf                       5338         243
/u05/oradata/norm/users01.dbf                          0           0
/u03/oradata/norm/aold01.dbf                      133879       63698
/u06/oradata/norm/aolx01.dbf                       59108       91757
/u06/oradata/norm/apd01.dbf                        68733        8119
/u09/oradata/norm/apx01.dbf                        34358       29941
/u06/oradata/norm/ard01.dbf                       107335       21018
/u09/oradata/norm/arx01.dbf                        28967       13770
```

Unfortunately, it is difficult to know what the load on the disks will be before the database is implemented. For this reason, once you determine that a significant degree of contention is occurring on a single disk, move the database file. Use the alter database rename command on a mounted—but not started—database instance. That way, you can ensure that the load on the disk drives is optimal.

There are also situations in which key database files take the brunt of the I/O. Moving them to another disk might not be possible or might not provide the best solution. For situations like these, Oracle provides *striping*—taking a single, large database file and splitting it into smaller pieces that can be distributed across multiple disks. For example:

```
SVRMGR> create tablespace dba_ts
   2>    datafile '/u03/oradata/norm/dbats01.dbf' size 50M,
   3>             '/u05/oradata/norm/dbats02.dbf' size 50M,
   4>             '/u07/oradata/norm/dbats03.dbf' size 50M,
   5>             '/u09/oradata/norm/dbats04.dbf' size 50M
   6>  /
Statement processed.
```

When you distribute a tablespace across several database files on several disks, you *stripe* it—there is a 50MB stripe of data on each disk. Striping enables the database to distribute its data across the disks, and it speeds I/O access by minimizing contention against disk drives.

Rollback Segment Contention

One of the features of an Oracle7 database is the ability to undo, or rollback, uncommitted changes to the database. In short, a transaction that physically changes database data—INSERT, UPDATE, or DELETE SQL statements—produces information that Oracle writes to its online rollback segments. Many DBAs fail to realize that because Oracle attempts to provide data consistency when a query is issued, SELECT statements use rollback segments when they access data.

When a query is issued, if a row has been changed but not committed, the Oracle RDBMS returns information from rollback segments to provide read consistency. Rollback segments are also used when an instance is forced down or ended with an abnormal termination.

Rollback segment contention can occur whenever a transaction accesses a block within a rollback segment that another rollback segment needs. Use the following query to determine the amount of contention being experienced within the rollback segments.

```
select r.name, s.gets, s.waits
from v$rollstat s, v$rollname r
where s.usn = r.usn
/
```

The following ratio compares how often a rollback segment was accessed with how often the database waited to access information with a rollback segment:

```
ratio = ( waits/gets ) * 100
```

If the result is 2 or greater, there is contention within the rollback segments. Create more rollback segments, which reduces the chance that transactions hit the same rollback segment blocks at the same time. This reduces contention, but it cannot eliminate it entirely. Here are some guidelines for the number of rollback segments that you should use:

- If the number of concurrent transactions is less than 16, use four rollback segments.
- If the number of concurrent transactions is less than 32 but at least 16, use eight rollback segments.
- If the number of concurrent transactions is 32 or more, use one rollback segment for every four transactions, up to a maximum of 50.

There is also the question of how large to make rollback segments. This is less complicated because you need to consider only two environments: OLTP and non-OLTP. OLTP environments (On-Line Transaction Processing) are those in which a large volume of database transactions are being processed by users, such as with an order entry system. The OLTP environments do better with a large number of smaller rollback segments. For non-OLTP environments, assign larger rollback segments so that data is retained longer for long transactions and long queries. It is acceptable to mix large and short rollback segments and to select explicitly which rollback segments to use.

TIP

When you use the SET TRANSACTION USE ROLLBACK SEGMENT statement, the rollback segment specified is used only for the life of the transaction. The lifetime of a transaction lasts until a commit or a rollback is issued, at which time the rollback segment is randomly selected. If you need to use the same rollback segment after a commit or rollback transaction, you must execute the SET TRANSACTION USE ROLLBACK SEGMENT statement again.

Like tables, rollback segments are constrained by the maximum extent size to which they can grow and by the amount of physical space available in a tablespace. Once these limits are reached, the database does not use a new rollback segment. Therefore, if a rollback segment or its tablespace is sized incorrectly, it is possible that the amount of rollback space needed will exceed the total size of the rollback segment.

Redo Log Contention

There is a buffer cache area in the SGA for redo information. This information is stored in memory and regulated through the use of two latches, or RAM-level locks. The *redo allocation latch* controls the allocation of space for writing redo information to the buffer. The *redo copy latch* is used to copy information to the buffer.

The `wait` latch requests wait to make a request, sleep, and then make the request again until it acquires the latch. Conversely, the `immediate` latch requests do not wait; instead, they continue processing. Use the following query to determine the status of both types of latches:

```
select name, gets, misses, sleeps, immediate_gets, immediate_misses
from v$latch
where name in ('redo allocation', 'redo copy')
/
```

Information about `wait` requests appears on the left, `immediate` requests on the right. After you execute this query—as SYS or another user with access to the V$ views—calculate the contention values:

```
immediate contention = ( immediate_misses / (immediate_gets + immediate_misses) ) *
100
wait contention = ( misses / (gets + misses) ) * 100
```

If the either value is greater than 1, contention is occurring for that latch. To alleviate contention for a redo allocation latch, reduce the amount of time that a latch is held by a process by lowering the value of the `LOG_SMALL_ENTRY_MAX_SIZE` parameter in the INIT.ORA parameter file. To alleviate contention for a redo copy latch, increase the number of latches by raising the value of the `LOG_SIMULTANEOUS_COPIES` parameter.

Checkpoints

A checkpoint is an event that occurs within the database whenever information is written from the caches within the SGA to disk. This occurs periodically to bring the database and control files in sync with the SGA. Disk I/O slows down processing time, which holds true for checkpoints. The database must synchronize the contents of its memory and data files, but too frequent synchronizing can reduce overall performance.

Checkpoints generally occur at various intervals that the DBA can control, as a result of certain events that the DBA cannot control, or when the DBA forces them.

Checkpoints occur based on one of two intervals: quantity or time. The value of the `LOG_CHECKPOINT_INTERVAL` parameter in the INIT.ORA parameter files specifies the number of redo blocks that the database will fill. When this value is reached, a checkpoint occurs. Likewise, when the amount of time specified in the `LOG_CHECKPOINT_TIMEOUT` parameter since the last checkpoint elapses, a checkpoint occurs. These values should usually be set to minimize checkpoints. In other words, set `LOG_CHECKPOINT_INTERVAL` to a value greater than the size of the largest redo log, and set `LOG_CHECKPOINT_TIMEOUT` to zero, which disables it.

Checkpoints continue to occur whenever the database is shut down (`normal` or `immediate`) or when a redo log switch occurs. The only thing that you can do to tune at this level is to make larger redo logs so that redo log switches occur less frequently.

To force a checkpoint, issue the following SQL command:

```
alter system switch logfile;
```

You might have to force a log switch when you perform maintenance on redo logs, such as when you relocate them from one physical disk to another.

Database Objects

Performance tuning does not stop with checking buffer caches and adjusting parameters in the INIT.ORA file. You also need to optimize the database's objects. This includes monitoring the objects for changes in condition, such as fragmentation, that can adversely impact performance. Unlike memory and contention problems, which generally remain stable unless a change in the database occurs, many database objects must be tuned on a regular basis.

Tables and Indexes

The database objects that cause the most problems are tables and indexes. Because transactions are constantly extracted from and inserted into database tables and indexes, problems such as chaining, migration, dynamic extension, and fragmentation can occur regularly. Because they occur often, most DBAs wait until these problems exceed a threshold, or they follow a maintenance schedule.

Migrated and Chained Rows

After the Oracle RDBMS places information in a row, it remains in that row—and utilizes its allocated space—until a change occurs. For example, an UPDATE that causes the row not to fit in a single database block might occur. The RDBMS searches for a free block in which it will fit. If it locates one, it moves the row to the new database block. The row is said to have been *migrated*. On the other hand, if a single database row is too large to fit in a single database block, the Oracle RDBMS stores the pieces of the row across several database blocks. This is called *chaining*.

Migrated and chained rows reduce performance for input and output operations. This is because the data spans multiple blocks. Instead of being able to return a single row in a single I/O operation, the database must perform multiple reads to return one row. Depending on the number of rows being returned and the number of rows that are chained or migrated, this can double or even triple the number of reads in a database operation.

Oracle provides a tool for detecting chaining and migration within the database. The SQL command analyze—used in the Cost-Based Optimizer—searches for chained rows. Before you run this query, however, you must run the utlchain.sql script provided with the database. The analyze command looks for a table called chained_rows, in which it stores the information returned. The query cannot run unless chained_rows exists. The utlchain.sql script creates this table:

```
SQL> @$ORACLE_HOME/rdbms/admin/utlchain
SQL> analyze table table_name list chained rows;
```

You must perform this operation on every table that you want checked for chaining or migration. If any rows appear in the chained_rows table, you should remove them. To remove chained or migrated rows:

1. Create a copy of the table in which chained or migrated rows occur, and place the chained or migrated rows into the new table.

   ```
   create table new_table as
   select * from table
   where rowid in
   ( select head_rowid
   from chained_rows
   where table_name = 'TABLE' );
   ```

2. Delete the chained or migrated rows from the original table.

   ```
   delete from table
   where rowid in
   ( select head_rowid
   from chained_rows
   where table_name = 'TABLE');
   ```

3. Transfer the rows in the new table back to the original table.

   ```
   insert into table
   select * from new_table;
   ```

4. Drop the new table.

   ```
   drop table new_table;
   ```

You should now analyze the table again. Rows that remain are chained rows; rows that were removed are migrated rows. To remove the chained rows, recreate the table with a higher pctfree value. The steps are

1. Perform an export on the database table.

```
exp file=/tmp/filename compress=y indexes=y grants=y constraints=y
tables=sample userid=user/password
```

2. Drop the current database table with the `drop table` command.

3. Recreate the database table with a higher `pctfree` value.

```
create table sample
  ( first_column  VARCHAR2(10),
    second_column VARCHAR2(10),
    . . .
  )
storage (initial 1024K next 1024K minextents 1
        maxextents 249 pctfree 90);
```

4. Import the data into the recreated table with the `imp` utility.

```
imp file=/tmp/filename full=y ignore=y userid=name/password
```

> **TIP**
>
> Always be sure and take a database backup before performing operations that require you to make changes to database objects.

Analyze the table again. If chained rows still exist, they might be impossible to eliminate without recreating the database with a new database block size. It is sometimes impossible to eliminate all chaining from a database, especially in databases that store information in LONG or RAW column types.

Dynamic Extension

Whenever you create a table, you must decide how large it should be, how fast it should grow, and how often its data will change. Unfortunately, the only way to gauge a table's growth is to rely on experience and trends. For that reason, you must deal with dynamic extension.

Every database object is created with an initial size. Information is added to the table or index until there is no more room left in the initial space allocation. Then the size of the table is incremented by a fixed amount. This is called *dynamic extension.*

> **NOTE**
>
> Increases in table or index size through dynamic extension do not usually occur in contiguous segments of storage.

Allocation is based on the arguments passed in the `storage` clause of the `create table` or `create index` SQL commands. If no storage clause is specified, the `default storage` parameters defined in the tablespace definition are used. Consider the following statement:

```
storage (initial x next y minextents a maxextents b pctincrease m)
```

The arguments control how large each extension is and the size that the object is capable of extending. To determine the initial size of the database object, multiply the size of initial extent by `minextents`. When the amount of data in the table and the index exceeds the initial allocation, another extent—of size next—is allocated. This process continues until the amount of free space in the tablespace is exceeded or until the number of extents is exceeded.

Dynamic extension causes problems with database performance, for recursive calls are generated because of requests from the data dictionary that are not currently in cache. Use the following query to determine whether excessive dynamic extension is occurring:

```
select owner, segment_name, sum(extents)
from dba_segments
where segment_type in ('TABLE', 'INDEX')
group by owner, segment_name
order by owner, segment_name
/
```

Monitor the extents closely to ensure that the number of extents is not too close to the value set in `maxextents`. It is necessary to recreate the table periodically with a single extent. The steps are

1. Export the database table with the `exp` utility. Don't forget to export indexes and constraints.

   ```
   exp file=/tmp/filename compress=y indexes=y grants=y constraints=y
    tables=sample userid=user/password
   ```

2. Drop the database table with the `drop table` command.

3. Recreate the table with an initial extent that is large enough to hold the entire table.

   ```
   create table sample
    ( first_column  VARCHAR2(10),
      second_column VARCHAR2(10),
      . . .
     )
   storage (initial 50M next 1024K minextents 1
           maxextents 249);
   ```

4. Import the data with the `imp` utility:

   ```
   imp file=/tmp/filename full=y ignore=y userid=name/password
   ```

Indexes are much simpler. The steps are

1. Drop the index with the `drop index` command.

2. Recreate the index with the `create index` command. Make sure that the initial extent is large enough to accommodate the entire index.

If you do not resize tables and indexes periodically—and correctly—a table can "max out," meaning it has extended to the size dictated by the `maxextents` storage parameter. To fix it, issue the following SQL command:

```
alter table table_name (storage maxextents extent_size);
```

The maximum extent for a database object is determined by the block size and the operating system. Consult the *Oracle Installation and Configuration Guide* to determine what limits are imposed. Not knowing the maximum extension of a database object and not adequately monitoring database objects as they approach this size can effectively shut down the database for production users.

Fragmentation

Fragmentation of the tablespaces on which the database objects reside also reduces performance. Tablespaces are initially allocated as contiguous units of storage. Likewise, database objects are created within the tablespaces as contiguous units of storage. As objects extend these blocks, however, they are generally not contiguous with the previous blocks of data.

As tables are created, dropped, and extended, the number of contiguous blocks of free space can increase. For example, a tablespace might have 1MB of free space—but all in 1KB blocks. If you issue a `create table` command with an initial extent of 50KB, it fails because it cannot allocate a contiguous amount of data in which to create the table. This is an especially common scenario in environments in which tables or indexes are frequently added and dropped.

To check the amount of free space available and the level of fragmentation on a tablespace, issue the following query:

```
select tablespace_name, sum(bytes), max(bytes), count(tablespace_name)
from dba_free_space
group by tablespace_name
order by tablespace_name
/
```

The results of this query tell how much free space is available within a tablespace (`sum`), what the size of the largest contiguous extent size is (`max`), and how many extents of free space make up the tablespace (`count`). If the number of contiguous blocks is greater than 10 to 15, you should defragment the tablespace. The steps are

1. Export data from all the tables in the tablespace with the exp utility. For indexes, capture the SQL required to recreate them.

2. Drop all the objects in the tablespace with the `drop table` and/or `drop index` commands.

3. Drop the tablespace with the `drop tablespace` command.

4. Recreate the tablespace with the `create tablespace` command.

5. Import the data back into the tablespace with the `imp` utility. The import recreates the database tables. Manually recreate indexes by using their SQL scripts.

Just as chained and migrated rows reduce database performance, fragmentation reduces performance by causing the disk drive head to move excessively when it queries a database table. Obviously, fragmented tablespaces should be defragmented whenever possible. To minimize fragmentation, create and drop new tables and indexes (especially those used as temporary or development tables) only on restricted tablespaces.

Views

Views are SQL statements that are treated as virtual tables. This enables you to hide the details of complex table joins and filters so that the code does not have to be used in every statement that performs a similar operation. It is important, however, to keep in mind that the statement is not issued until a SQL statement is executed against the view.

The best performance tuning that can be done on a view is preventative in nature. Run each view that you create through an EXPLAIN PLAN, and analyze it for performance. Except in rare circumstances, views that are inefficient and take a long time to return data should not be used. If a view that previously performed acceptably suddenly begins to act sluggish, you should perform another EXPLAIN PLAN or execute SQL*Trace against a query on the view.

Usually, views fail to perform as expected when changes are made—such as adding or removing indexes—or when the query is not properly optimized for a large amount of data.

Triggers

Another new feature of Oracle7 that presents a tuning challenge is database triggers. If you have worked with SQL*Forms/Oracle*Forms or other event-driven processing, you are familiar with triggers. If you have not, they can be difficult to understand.

A trigger occurs when a certain event happens—such as before or after a database table is modified—at which time a section of PL/SQL code is executed. If the SQL code contained within the PL/SQL segment is tuned—based on an EXPLAIN PLAN—triggers work well. Triggers can cause unexpected problems, however. This is generally the case when they are used by an inexperienced developer or have not been tested adequately.

A common problem with triggers is an infinite loop. One trigger activates another trigger, which activates another trigger, and so forth, until one of the triggers causes a change that sets off the original trigger—starting the process again. These errors are difficult to find and can create phantom problems. Adequate research and testing before implementing new triggers goes a long way toward heading off trigger problems.

Database Locking

Database locking is important to the DBA, because locks can slow a database. This is a frustrating performance problem to locate because it is often not obvious.

Locks within the database prevent database users in a multi-user environment from changing the same data simultaneously. Database locks ensure the integrity of the data within a database by enforcing concurrency and consistency. Concurrency means that the database ensures that users can read data from a database block without worrying whether the data is currently being written to the database block; a user writing data must wait for the write operations that precede it to complete. Consistency means that a database query returns data exactly as it appeared when the query was originally executed; changes made after the query was issued are not returned.

Types and Classes of Locks

An Oracle7 database has two types of locks: data dictionary locks (DDL) and data manipulation locks (DML). A DDL ensures that the layout of a database object—its definition—does not change while it is used within a database query. A DML protects data that multiple users are trying to access simultaneously.

All transactions fall into one of two categories: exclusive or shared. *Exclusive transactions* do not enable other users to access the data. *Shared transactions* enable data to be shared with other users, although they cannot change it. Locks are released whenever a commit or a rollback occurs.

Whenever a SQL statement accesses data within a table, a DDL is acquired on the table. The lock prevents the DBA from making changes to a table while it is in use.

DML locks, on the other, are employed against database tables. The five types of DML locks are

RS   Locks a specific row in a database table in shared mode, enabling other database queries to access the information—for example, a SELECT...FOR UPDATE OF... operation

RX   Locks a specific row in a database table in exclusive mode, restricting access to the row to the database session that acquired the lock—for example, an UPDATE operation

S   Locks a table in shared mode and prohibits activities other than queries against the table—for example, a LOCK TABLE...IN SHARE MODE operation

SRX   Locks a table in shared mode and provides row-level locks as required to modify and update data—for example, a LOCK TABLE...IN SHARE ROW EXCLUSIVE MODE operation

X   Locks an entire table, preventing access to the table by any session except the current one—for example, a LOCK TABLE...IN EXCLUSIVE MODE operation

Unresolved Locking Issues

A common database locking situation is unresolved locking, also called a *deadlock*. In a deadlock, two database operations wait for each another to release a lock.

Oracle7 is designed to detect deadlocks, but it is not always successful. You might encounter transactions that have acquired locks and are waiting on each another to free their locks so that they can proceed. Unfortunately, the only sure way to resolve this problem is to detect them as they occur and to deal with them individually. Oracle recommends two ways to avoid deadlocks:

- Applications should acquire locks in the same order.
- Always use the lowest necessary lock. For example, don't lock an entire table when only a row needs to be updated.

To resolve a deadlock, you must kill one of the processes—or both—at either the database or operating system level.

Checking Locking Situation

Oracle provides a utility script that checks the current lock state of the database. This script, `utllockt.sql`, provides a tree that shows what locks are held and what processes are waiting. It is

```
SQL> @$ORACLE_HOME/rdbms/admin/utllockt
```

You can perform a query on the DBA_WAITERS to determine which sessions are waiting on locks and the sessions that hold them. It does not show all the sessions holding locks—only the ones that cause wait states. This query enables you to view only the sessions that might cause locking problems:

```
select waiting_session, holding_session, lock_type, mode_held, mode_requested
from dba_waiters
/
```

Other views provide additional locking information. The information that each one shows is

DBA_BLOCKERS	Sessions that have another session waiting on a lock and are not in a wait status themselves
DBA_DDL_LOCKS	DDL locks held and requested within the database
DBA_DML_LOCKS	DML locks held and requested within the database
DBA_LOCKS	All locks held or requested within the database
DBA_WAITERS	Sessions that are waiting for database locks and what session is currently holding the lock
V$ACCESS	Locked database objects and the sessions that are accessing them

V$LOCK	Database locks
V$SESSION_WAIT	Database sessions that are waiting

Unlike other performance tuning and optimizing operations, monitoring locks is usually reactive. Locks are not a problem until a deadlock or similar event occurs. Locking is generally stable and requires less DBA interaction than other performance tuning tasks.

Summary

Performance tuning is the art of balancing raw statistics with intuition and experience to arrive at the best possible solution. Entire volumes of books have been written on this topic.

In this chapter, you learned some of the fundamental concepts of performance tuning. You learned how to extract and analyze memory and disk space to resolve contention. You saw guidelines and scripts that you can use to check the performance of a database.

Oracle responds differently on each platform, and the examples presented in this chapter are configured for a UNIX environment. You must determine how much of this material applies to your own site.

Database Security

16

by Byron Pearce

IN THIS CHAPTER

"Good morning, Jim. Your mission, should you choose to accept it...." So began the television series *Mission: Impossible.* This chapter begins with that sound bite in a sense of homage. Like the character in that show, database security is a mission that ultimately the DBA must accept. There are some sites where database security is simply not done—virtually everyone has access to virtually everything. The assumption is that everyone knows what he is doing, so nothing should be restricted. Other sites put a premium on security and regularly use exotic designations, such as B1 and C2—it takes what seems like an act of Congress for anyone to accomplish anything. Most Oracle sites, though, fall comfortably in the middle.

As the industry—Oracle in particular—moves toward open systems such as UNIX, there is a greater need to configure and monitor an adequate database security plan. Many users do not care a great deal about how the security for the database is configured. Their burning desire is to be able to do their jobs. The "power" users, however, want to push the envelope to see exactly what they can do. They might be motivated by their technical knowledge or even by sheer ego—they think that they should have more power than other users.

Most of the conflict comes from software developers, analysts, and management. In an age when MIS departments are constantly trying to justify their existence against the threat of outsourcing, it is far simpler for managers to authorize everyone in the organization to have privileged access than to invest the time in a proper setup. Developers and analysts vocally proclaim that they are being handcuffed and cannot do their jobs unless they are given access. In many cases, they simply need information that is contained in a table or a view owned by SYS or SYSTEM—the DBA-level views, for example—that makes them "need" DBA access.

Implementing a security plan, therefore, involves theory more than many other topics do, including the backup and recovery plan or user management. If a DBA undertakes a security plan, he accepts responsibility for enforcing the plan and determining the level of security that best suits the needs of his organization. Some organizations have groups of security administrators dedicated to this task. In practice, this becomes yet another task appended to the great DBA Job Description in the Sky.

This chapter focuses on the core ideas associated with implementing a security plan. It offers suggestions for a common security methodology.

Authentication

As discussed in Chapter 13, "Managing Users," there are two distinct methods of database authentication: *password authentication* and *operating system authentication.* With password authentication, the user must enter a unique word or character sequence to gain access. With operating system authentication, the Oracle database permits access to the database based on whether a corresponding user account exists for the current operating system account. When implementing either method, the DBA needs to be aware of various security concerns and constraints.

Password Authentication

Password authentication is the more traditional method of user authentication. Although passwords are relatively secure, they have shortcomings that can make them more vulnerable to breach or attack.

In most cases, each user creates his own password. People usually like to keep things simple, which can make password authentication vulnerable to attack. Users who have access to multiple databases often use the same password repeatedly. This creates a massive security breach if a user's password is compromised, enabling the offending party to access all the databases that share the password. Oracle has no mechanism that forces a password change. Oracle8, though, supposedly will offer this feature.

Passwords should conform to the following general standards:

- They should be at least six characters in length.
- They should contain a combination of characters and numbers or special characters that represent the actual spelling of words (such as `s1ckle` for `sickle`). Oracle database passwords, however, cannot contain spaces.
- They should not contain obvious passwords.
- They should be changed frequently.

There are only two ways to enforce this level of database password security: user education and third-party products. Neither is an easy solution. A few products on the market, such as SQL<>Secure by BrainTree Technology, give the DBA the latitude to set rules for passwords. Most sites, though, must simply try to educate users about how to set passwords properly. Unless a custom interface is used, it is impossible to prevent users from selecting simple passwords.

A number of public domain programs available on the Internet attempt to break into passwords that use common types of passwords. Using the password standards helps minimize the potential that these programs will break in—although it cannot eliminate the possibility. Some of the more common passwords that programs of this nature scan for are

- Name of user—first, middle, last, or account name
- Name of spouse, children, or pets (more often tried by coworkers or hackers than security programs)
- Colors
- Simple words that many password cracking programs contain in their data dictionaries

This list is by no means exhaustive, but it should provide a basis for judging the effectiveness of a given password. The bottom line on password authentication, however, is training users to use good passwords. Some DBAs use a program that attempts to crack a user's passwords and sends an e-mail to the user indicating that his password has been cracked. This should either induce a sense of paranoia among users or cause them to think seriously about password security.

Operating System Authentication

Operating system authentication methods require an underlying password at the operating system level, so it is important to keep in mind the security ramifications of the use of accounts that are authenticated at the operating system level. This means that the Oracle database confirms whether an account—usually prefixed by OPS$—exists within the database that corresponds to an operating system account. In this way, the operating system vouches for the user to the database. If the match is successful, the user is allowed access.

If used properly, operating system authentication is reasonably secure. No passwords need to be changed under this method. Connecting to the database is as simple as issuing a null user name and password. For example:

```
sqlplus /
```

There is a price, however. Anyone with access to the operating system account also has access to the database account. This can take a variety of forms. Aside from someone guessing or learning a user's password, there are other considerations. The system administrator, who has the root password (on a UNIX system), can switch between user accounts without the password. This is generally not a security issue, because the system administrator is considered privileged. Even so, the DBA should be aware of this capability and that the system administrator can switch to other non-root privileged accounts, such as oracle.

Under UNIX, it is possible that a user might access another user's account by means of rlogin. Essentially, a file called .rhosts is optionally located in the user's home directory. This file contains the host machine and the user name, thereby enabling a specified user on a specified machine to perform rlogin without needing the password. For example:

```
% hostname
sandbox
% whoami
natashia
% cd /users/boris
% ls .rhosts
.rhosts
% cat .rhosts
sandbox natashia
% rlogin sandbox -l boris
% whoami
boris
```

An account that is authenticated by the operating system is only as secure as the password that protects the operating system account. If proper precautions are taken, though, this method is highly reliable and often more secure than password authentication.

Why Protect Passwords?

With all the discussion about authentication methods and protecting accounts, it is common to wonder why it is necessary. Depending on the environment in which the database operates, this might be a moot issue. At many sites, the concept of security is taken very seriously. Other sites, especially ones that are not traditional IS organizations, question the necessity. There are three basic reasons for limiting database access: control, protection, and integrity.

Control

Control is a heavy-handed word that evokes images of mainframe shops that required users to file paperwork several times every hour. Although the DBA should not interfere with day-to-day operations and impose undue restrictions, neither should he throw up his hands and cry out, "Why bother?" Unfortunately, either by accident or malicious intent, a database can be easily corrupted by someone who has too much power in the database.

Consider the following scenario: A tablespace needs additional space, and an ambitious user adds a database file to the tablespace instead of calling the DBA. This action goes unnoticed for several weeks. Then the disk drive that contains the database files for this tablespace crashes. The DBA never made changes to the backup script, so there is no way to recover the data.

This is, of course, a doomsday scenario, but it could still happen. In some organizations, every developer is considered a mini-DBA and possesses all the rights and privileges of a DBA. This introduces two key concepts: *accountability* and *responsibility*. Accountability means that a user is permitted the authority that comes with being a privileged user. Think of accountability as the list of everyone who has a specified level of access to the database. Responsibility, on the other hand, means that a user has the ultimate duty to keep the database functioning. He is the one who gets telephone calls at 3:00 in the morning.

Control is a tricky issue. It can also be highly political. In a situation with multiple database instances, the manager of each department that has information in the database feels that he needs to have DBA access. This level of access should be limited to people who actually perform DBA functions.

Determining the level of access and which users are considered privileged happens on a site-by-site basis. It is generally best to give too little access at first and to add privileges as needed.

Protection

Aside from the control issues, limiting database access is one of the most effective methods for protecting the data within a database and the database itself. Although most users would not maliciously harm a database, an accident can be just as devastating as sabotage.

At the operating system level, all database files are owned by the `oracle` account. Oracle advises against using this account except for performing startups and shutdowns of the database, software installations, and the like. If a delete is issued from the operating system, any of the physical files—database files, control files, redo logs, and archive logs—can be removed. This can cause a crash of the database instance. From the database level, users who have access to certain system privileges can modify the database and its objects irrespective of their operating system account ID or who owns the database object. It is far too easy to drop a production table and cripple an entire production system.

Privileges to make modifications to a production database or database objects within a production database should be limited. In most cases, the responsibility for maintaining the database falls on the DBA. There are gray areas, however, such as sites at which maintenance of the database objects is the domain of a project manager or applications manager. In these cases, it is important that the DBA and the other responsible parties work together to control changes to database objects and to ensure that up-to-date build scripts exist.

Integrity

The final consideration for protecting passwords is the integrity of the data within the database objects. Many privileges within the database enable users to manipulate database data indiscriminately. These privileges include system-level privileges such as UPDATE ANY TABLE and DELETE ANY TABLE. With these privileges, a user can override object-level security and modify the data in any database table.

> **WARNING**
>
> Be very careful when granting the ANY class of privileges, because they extend to internal database tables and user-owned objects. It is easy to cause database corruption.

Making changes to data within database objects is one of the most difficult issues to control. After all, the users must be able to access database data. Oracle provides a means for simplifying this, such as roles. As with controlling access and protecting the physical database itself, protecting the data within the database objects should be of paramount concern when you design and implement a security plan.

Privileged Accounts

Privileged accounts for the Oracle RDBMS take a number of forms. Some are traditional password authenticated accounts, whereas others are derived from operating system groups that grant special database privileges. Each site can have its own custom-defined DBA or privileged-access accounts. This discusses users found on all Oracle installations.

SYS

The database user SYS is the owner of all base tables, user views, and data dictionary views. At the time of database creation, these tables and views are created through internal mechanisms and scripts that reside in $ORACLE_HOME/rdbms/admin, such as catalog.sql, catproc.sql, and catexp.sql.

Because this owner is the table/view owner and because this account has full system privileges within the database, it should be restricted. Improper use of this account can lead to corruption of the database.

At the time of database creation, the default password for this account is change_on_install. It should be changed immediately. For example,

```
% sqlplus sys
Password: ...............
SQL> alter user sys identified by more_secure_password;
```

In general, this account should be used only by the DBA when he changes the core database views and only at the instructions of Oracle. Moreover, no tables other than those created by the Oracle RDBMS should be owned by SYS. Other accounts that can perform the same functions as SYS without the risk to the data dictionary are available.

SYSTEM

Like SYS, the SYSTEM account is created when the database is created. Whereas the SYS user owns tables and views that reference internal database information, the SYSTEM account owns tables that are owned by Oracle tools, such as SQL*Menu. This schema is used to install software products for most third-party tools.

SYSTEM has the initial password manager. Many textbooks (such as this one), in fact, show examples that use SYSTEM/MANAGER as the user name and password. As with SYS, this password should be changed immediately after installation.

Although it is generally acceptable to use the SYSTEM account for day-to-day DBA operations, many DBAs do not. The SYSTEM account owns a number of important tables that drive some of the Oracle tools, applications, and so on.

Operating System Group: *dba*

Oracle provides a third method of authentication. It is very specific in nature. It provides certain privileges and must be carefully monitored.

If a user is a member of the dba group, specified in the UNIX /etc/group file, he can do connect internal to the database. This is a privilege level used by the DBA that enables him to connect to the database as SYS with special privileges. The dba group is typically the default group of the user oracle. It is necessary to do connect internal to perform startup and shutdown operations on the database.

> **WARNING**
>
> The umask of the UNIX /etc/group file should be at most 644—read/write owner, read group, read world—and it should be owned by the root user. If anyone other than root can edit this file, he can set himself up as a privileged database user by placing his UNIX account in the dba group and issuing a connect internal.

A connect internal can be done only from within Oracle Server*Manager or the soon-to-be-obsolete SQL*DBA. This feature is not available from within other tools, such as SQL*Plus or SQL*Forms. As a member of this group, the DBA always has access to the database even if a co-DBA makes changes to the SYS or SYSTEM passwords. Although it is not so designed, the dba group ensures that the DBA can never be locked out of the database. For example,

```
% cat /etc/groups
sys::3:root,uucp
adm::4:root,adm
daemon::5:root,daemon
mail::6:root
lp::7:root,lp
tty::10:
nuucp::11:nuucp
users::20:
nogroup:*:-2:
dba::100:oracle
% whoami
oracle
% svrmgrl
SVRMGR> connect internal
Connected.
```

It is also possible to password protect the internal connections. The specifics on this are covered later in this chapter.

Object Versus System Security

At the heart of database security lies the concept that someone in a position to grant authority—the DBA—gives a user the specific ability to perform certain operations within the database. These privileges can be granted explicitly by issuing a grant command or implicitly by granting privileges to a role. According to Oracle, privileges fall into two distinct categories: *system privileges* and *object privileges*.

Object Security

Object security is responsible for defining the specific rights that a user has on a specific database object. The Oracle database itself implements a method of default security. A database user has full privileges on the database object that he owns. This user, in turn, can grant any and all privileges on these objects to another database user. Any user who attempts to access a database object to which he has not been granted access receives an error message. For example,

```
% sqlplus susan
Password: ......
SQL> select * from cat;

TABLE_NAME                        TABLE_TYPE
----------------------------      ----------
PAYROLL                           TABLE
POLICY                            TABLE

SQL> select count(*) from policy;

   COUNT(*)
- - - - -
        100

SQL> grant select on policy to mike;

Grant succeeded.

SQL> connect mike
Enter password: ......
Connected.
SQL> select * from cat;

TABLE_NAME                        TABLE_TYPE
----------------------------      ----------
POLICY                            TABLE

SQL> select count(*) from mike.policy;

   COUNT(*)
----------
        500

SQL> select count(*) from susan.policy;

   COUNT(*)
----------
        100

SQL> select count(*) from policy;

   COUNT(*)
----------
        500

SQL> delete from susan.policy;

ERROR at line 1:
ORA-01031: insufficient privileges

SQL> delete from policy;

500 rows deleted.
```

It is important to prefix the name of the table with the name of the database user who owns the table—the *schema*. If this is not done, the database assumes that the table is owned by the current user's account.

Access Rights

One of the key aspects of understanding object privileges is to understand what privileges are available to the database user. There are nine Oracle object privileges:

ALTER enables the user to alter a database table, including adjusting storage constraints, adding columns, and performing similar operations.

DELETE enables the user to remove rows from database objects by using the DELETE command from SQL.

EXECUTE enables the user to execute a stored procedure or package within the database.

INDEX enables the user to create a new index or to modify an existing index on a database table.

INSERT enables the user to create new rows in a database table.

REFERENCES enables the user to create a table that references characteristic information, by means of a foreign key, within another table.

SELECT enables the user to view rows of information within a database object.

UPDATE enables the user to modify existing rows within a database object.

ALL gives the user all the previous privileges on a database object.

It is possible to combine multiple database privileges within a single grant option. For example,

```
% sqlplus ashley
Password: ........
SQL> grant select, insert, update on treat_table to frisko;

Grant succeeded.
```

These privileges are valid only for the lifetime of a single database object. Even if a database object is re-created with the same object name, the privileges are not recovered. For example,

```
% sqlplus rhett
Password: ........
SQL> create table bonnie
  2>    (
  3>       pony_column varchar2(15)
  4>    )
  5> tablespace users;
```

```
Table created.

SQL> grant select, insert, update on bonnie to scarlett;

Grant succeeded.

SQL> connect scarlett
Enter password: ......

SQL> select count(*) from rhett.bonnie;

  COUNT(*)
----------
         0

SQL> connect rhett
Enter password: ........
Connected.

SQL> drop table bonnie;

Table dropped.

SQL> create table bonnie
  2>    (
  3>       pony_column varchar2(15)
  4>    )
  5> tablespace users;

Table created.

SQL> connect scarlett
Enter password: ......
Connected.

SQL> select count(*) from rhett.bonnie;
Error at line 1:
ORA-00942: table or view does not exist
```

RHETT owns the table BONNIE, and he has granted SCARLETT access to the table. If BONNIE is dropped by RHETT and re-created with the same object name, SCARLETT no longer has access to the table. This is true until RHETT makes the grant again. If there were multiple grants, each grant must be made for each user on each database object. This can be quite cumbersome.

The *WITH GRANT OPTION* Option

In many environments, it is beneficial to have users other than the DBA perform grants. For example, the DBA might want to allow a project leader to grant rights on database objects to people working on his project. Thus, the DBA has to do the grants only once; then it falls to the project leader to make further grants as necessary.

Oracle provides a mechanism for doing this: GRANT OPTION of the grant SQL command. With it, a user can issue grant commands just as though he were the actual owner of the database object. For example:

```
% sqlplus aimee
Password: ........
Connected.

SQL> grant select on order to jason with grant option;

Grant succeeded.

SQL> connect jason
Enter password: ........
Connected.

SQL> grant select on aimee.order to lucinda;

Grant succeeded.
```

A database user who has received a grant with the ALL privilege does not receive GRANT OPTION automatically; it must be explicitly granted. As specified with object privileges above, GRANT OPTION remains in effect only until an object is dropped.

> **NOTE**
>
> SCARLETT owns a view of another database view called GEORGIA. This view is based on a table owned by another user, RHETT, and is called CHARLESTON. SCARLETT must have WITH GRANT OPTION on GEORGIA. If this is not done, grants of this view to other users will not work properly.

Resolving Object Synonyms

A synonym is simply a designation for a database object that enables it to be referenced by another name. There are two types of these synonyms: private and public. A *private synonym* is a synonym created by the user that only he uses; no one other than the user who created the synonym can use it. A *public synonym* is accessible to all users in the database.

Suppose, for example, that a user, TAL, has a table named HOCKEY for which two synonyms exist—ICE, a private synonym, and SPORT, a public synonym. This gives five distinct methods for accessing this particular table:

- As TAL, using the actual table name, HOCKEY.
- As TAL, using the private synonym name, ICE.
- As TAL, using the public synonym name, SPORT.
- As another user, using the database object owner and object name, TAL.HOCKEY.
- As another user, using the public synonym name, SPORT.

This example assumes that the appropriate grants have been made on the HOCKEY table to permit access. In dealing with synonyms, it is important to understand the order in which the database resolves naming. This is important when you test programs for which there is a global table and a local table. Consider the following SQL statement:

```
select * from emp;
```

When it attempts to resolve this statement, the database first checks whether a database object—such as a table, view, or database link—exists and is owned by the current database user. If it finds a match, it stops. If a match does not exist, it checks for a private synonym that will direct it to a specific database object. If no private synonym exists, it checks for a public synonym that will point it toward an existing database object. If no resolution is found, if the database objects referenced by the synonyms do not exist, or if the user has no privileges on the object in question, an error condition occurs.

System Security

Whereas object privilege deals with what a user can do to database objects, system privilege deals with what actions a user can perform against the database itself. The actions include connecting to the database, creating database tables, and dropping an entire tablespace (with all the database objects in it). The functionality of Oracle7 makes the system privileges far more scaleable than in Oracle6.

Under Oracle6, the Oracle RDBMS resembled UNIX in its overall security scheme. UNIX maintains that an account is either the root user or a regular user. Admittedly, UNIX has evolved to enable a greater deal of scalability by using things such as access control lists (ACLs) and root set userid (suid) programs. Oracle6 is set up so that all users are either the DBA or not the DBA. With the release of Oracle7, Oracle moves away from this methodology. It is possible now to grant specific privileges to non-DBA users, thereby enabling them to perform certain applications without giving them full DBA access.

Defined System Privileges

In Oracle6, three system privileges are available. More than 80 system privileges are available in Oracle7. The following is a partial list of the database system privileges. The information comes from the *Oracle7 Server Administrator's Guide,* an excellent reference that describes the capabilities of each privilege.

    ALTER DATABASE
    ALTER PROFILE
    ALTER RESOURCE COST
    ALTER ROLLBACK SEGMENT
    ALTER SESSION

ALTER SYSTEM
ALTER TABLESPACE
ALTER USER
AUDIT SYSTEM
BECOME USER
CREATE CLUSTER
CREATE DATABASE LINK
CREATE PROCEDURE
CREATE PROFILE
CREATE PUBLIC DATABASE LINK
CREATE PUBLIC SYNONYM
CREATE ROLE
CREATE ROLLBACK SEGMENT
CREATE SEQUENCE
CREATE SESSION
CREATE SNAPSHOT
CREATE SYNONYM
CREATE TABLE
CREATE TABLESPACE
CREATE TRIGGER
CREATE USER
CREATE VIEW
DROP PROFILE
DROP PUBLIC DATABASE LINK
DROP PUBLIC SYNONYM
DROP ROLLBACK SEGMENT
DROP TABLESPACE
DROP USER
FORCE TRANSACTION
MANAGE TABLESPACE
READUP
RESTRICTED SESSION
UNLIMITED TABLESPACE

Like object privileges, system privileges are given to users through the grant SQL command. The following code segment demonstrates how a system privilege grant is done:

```
% sqlplus system
Password: ........
Connected.

SQL> grant create session, alter session to anna;

Grant succeeded.
```

The revoke SQL command takes away system or object privileges that were given through the grant command. It is important to note that revoking a privilege does not destroy a database object. In the following example, the table remains even though the privilege to create new tables has been revoked:

```
% sqlplus fred
Password: ......
Connected.

SQL> select * from cat;

TABLE_NAME                          TABLE_TYPE
------------------------------      ----------
SPORTS                              TABLE

1 rows selected.

SQL> connect system
Enter password: ........
Connected.

SQL> revoke create table from fred;

Revoke succeeded.

SQL> connect fred
Enter password: ........
Connected.

SQL> select * from cat;

TABLE_NAME                          TABLE_TYPE
------------------------------      ----------
SPORTS                              TABLE

1 rows selected.
```

The *WITH ADMIN OPTION* Option

WITH ADMIN OPTION is to database system privileges what WITH GRANT OPTION is to database object privileges. By making a grant WITH ADMIN OPTION, the DBA enables a user to grant the system privilege to another user. For example,

```
% sqlplus system
Password: ........

SQL> grant create user to helpdesk with admin option;
Grant succeeded.
```

ANY Privileges

The ANY privileges are a special class of privileges within the database system privileges. They are enhanced system privileges that grant the user the ability to perform specified actions without restrictions. If a user has these system privileges, he can override normal default security. Therefore, he has access to other database objects, regardless of whether an object-level grant is made. The following is a list of the ANY privileges. They are described in detail in the *Oracle7 Server Administrator's Guide*.

> ALTER ANY CLUSTER
> ALTER ANY INDEX
> ALTER ANY PROCEDURE
> ALTER ANY ROLE
> ALTER ANY SEQUENCE
> ALTER ANY SNAPSHOT
> ALTER ANY TABLE
> ALTER ANY TRIGGER
> BACKUP ANY TABLE
> COMMENT ANY TABLE
> CREATE ANY CLUSTER
> CREATE ANY INDEX
> CREATE ANY PROCEDURE
> CREATE ANY SEQUENCE
> CREATE ANY SNAPSHOT
> CREATE ANY SYNONYM
> CREATE ANY TABLE
> CREATE ANY TRIGGER
> CREATE ANY VIEW
> DELETE ANY TABLE
> DROP ANY CLUSTER
> DROP ANY INDEX
> DROP ANY PROCEDURE
> DROP ANY ROLE

DROP ANY SEQUENCE

DROP ANY SNAPSHOT

DROP ANY SYNONYM

DROP ANY TABLE

DROP ANY TRIGGER

DROP ANY VIEW

EXECUTE ANY PROCEDURE

FORCE ANY TRANSACTION

GRANT ANY PRIVILEGE

GRANT ANY ROLE

INSERT ANY TABLE

LOCK ANY TABLE

SELECT ANY SEQUENCE

SELECT ANY TABLE

UPDATE ANY TABLE

The DBA should be careful when granting system privileges, especially the ANY class of privileges. Some of them are not meant for public use. They put too much power in the hands of users if they are not adequately managed. Although the privileges are more scaleable than under previous Oracle versions, the DBA should treat them as mini-DBA privileges when determining who should receive them.

A final issue regarding protecting system privileges is what effect these privileges have within a secure database. In most databases, some tables contain information that should not be distributed to the general public, such as payroll information. A user with some of the ANY privileges, such as SELECT ANY or UPDATE ANY, has access to the tables even without an explicit grant.

Grants to PUBLIC

It is possible to make grants on both system and object privileges to PUBLIC. This is a special Oracle account to which all other accounts have access. Any grant made to PUBLIC is accessible by any database user. For example,

```
% sqlplus system
Password: ........
Connected.

SQL> grant select on hr.emp_name to public;
Grant succeeded.
```

The DBA can use the PUBLIC account to set up a common set of grants—such as the CREATE SESSION privilege, which permits connection to the database—and grant them to PUBLIC. In doing this, the DBA removes the need to make explicit grants to every user when a new account is added.

TIP

The DBA can use PUBLIC to lock groups of users out of the database without having to restart the instance in RESTRICT mode. For example, he can grant CREATE SESSION to PUBLIC and make explicit CREATE SESSION grants to key users, such as IS personnel. In the event that activity needs to be done on the database, the following command can be executed from SQL*Plus or Oracle Server*Manager:

```
revoke create session from public;
```

This command effectively locks out everyone except the IS users after all the users have logged off the database. The grants can be reinstated as follows:

```
grant create session to public;
```

Object Security Model

The DBA must consider other factors when setting up a security plan. Not only should the setup of the database users be considered, but also the ownership of the database objects. Although there is no right or wrong way to go about this, the following sections outline some of the concerns faced by the DBA when setting up object ownership models.

Protected Object Ownership Schema

One security model implemented by many sites is the *protected schema*—sometimes called the *pure schema*. Under this model, the DBA sets up an account that is not associated with any specific database user. This account is used as an ownership account for all the database objects—tables, views, and so on. Public synonyms are set up for each database object, and grants are made to each user for each database object. Therefore, a single user owns the objects, but the account can be restricted by not issuing passwords to any users except those who perform database object maintenance.

There is nothing incredibly mystical about this setup. The object owner exists as just another account within the database. Depending on the environment, the DBA can configure the database to have only connection or resource privileges during maintenance windows and then revoke those privileges when completed. Thus, access to the object owner account can be given to other users—who might, for example, want to look at the contents of the CAT or USER_TABLES table—without enabling them to make changes to the database objects themselves.

One important note here is that the DBA or person responsible for database object maintenance should maintain a build script for the object. Although this information can be obtained from the Oracle Data Dictionary, it is important to have this information accessible in emergency situations.

Capacity Planning Requirements

In dealing with database objects, one of the key elements for which the DBA is responsible is the capacity planning requirements of the database. Many sites hold to the philosophy that the creation and maintenance of the database objects are responsibilities separate from overall database maintenance; most of these sites still agree that capacity planning is a responsibility of the DBA. Everything in the database is stored physically in database files.

Volumes have been written concerning the best ways to optimize the capacity planning of database objects within tablespaces. The main concern of capacity planning in this chapter is on security. Because users other than the DBA might be involved in creating database objects, he should stay abreast of modifications as they occur. For example, it takes only a typographical error in the STORAGE clause to inadvertently fill up a tablespace—1,000 KB and 10,000 KB are different by just one zero. When no further space is available to expand the tablespace, this can bring production databases to a screeching halt. By the same token, if the next extent sizes are set wrong—forgetting the KB in 512 KB makes it 512 bytes—a database object can quickly reach its MAXEXTENTS. When this happens, the only option is to rebuild the object with proper extent sizes. Depending on how much data is stored, this might be no small feat.

The bottom line on capacity planning requirements from a database security standpoint is to be certain that accountability exists. Object creations should generally be limited to developers or analysts who have the technical knowledge to understand what object creation entails. It should not be necessary to hold anyone's hand. Likewise, they should not be given a blank check.

Avoiding Tablespace Fragmentation Issues

Given the prevalence of tools like Defrag by ARIS and TSReorg by Platinum Technology, tablespace fragmentation is an obvious problem for most DBAs. Tablespace fragmentation, illustrated in Figure 16.1, occurs when free space is available in a tablespace, but when the blocks of free space are not grouped in contiguous blocks. That is, they are not together. Although the amount of fragmentation in Oracle7 is much better than in Oracle6, it remains a persistent

FIGURE 16.1.

Tablespace fragmentation.

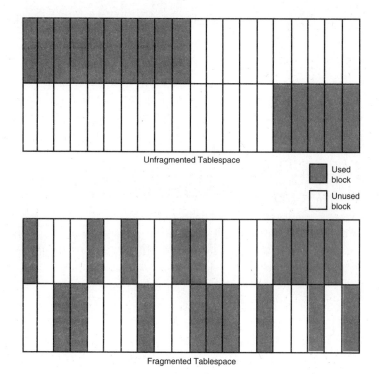

Unfragmented Tablespace

Used block

Unused block

Fragmented Tablespace

problem.

Many DBAs might wonder what tablespace fragmentation has to do with database security. The answer is simple: Steps that can be built into the security plan of the database that help minimize some of the main causes of database fragmentation.

Suppose, for example, that a developer calls and complains that he cannot create a new table in tablespace XYZ. Whenever he tries to issue the CREATE TABLE command from SQL, he receives this error message:

```
cannot allocate extent of size 99 in tablespace XYZ
```

A quick check of the view DBA_FREE_SPACE shows the amount of free space available in the tablespace, so it is possible to calculate the total amount of free space capable of holding the table. The first question that the DBA should pose to the developer is, "How often are you dropping tables and indexes?" This is the most common cause of tablespace fragmentation, especially for tablespaces to which developers have access. As a rule, developers perform CREATE TABLE/INDEX and DROP TABLE/INDEX operations on a regular basis, which inevitably leads to problems.

It is a good idea to limit or eliminate access to the tablespaces on which production objects reside. You can do this by using tablespace quotas and by not giving anyone other than the protected schema access to the tablespaces. Generally, a special work tablespace called WORK or MISC is created. Developers can perform adds and drops on it. If this tablespace fragments, it can be defragmented at the DBA's discretion. If many people have access to the schema ownership account, it is often a good idea to revoke quotas on the tablespace from the schema until such a time as needed. This depends largely on the user community that is using the account.

By limiting the amount of access to production tablespaces, the DBA can help reduce—although not eliminate—tablespace fragmentation. This helps eliminate the amount of crisis mode management that a DBA must undertake.

Defining Database Roles

In versions of Oracle prior to Oracle7, explicit grants from the system and the object privilege level are the rule. At first, this was not much of a hindrance because of the size of most databases. Large databases were the exception; small databases were the rule. As databases grew in size, many DBAs began to see how cumbersome and difficult that method of access grants was. For example, in a database system with 40 database tables and views and 100 database users, more than 4,000 separate grants must be processed. This is a relatively small database, so it is easy to see the cumulative effects of adding users and objects on larger databases systems. Likewise, if a change in privilege needs to be made or a table is re-created, all the privileges must be made again.

Most DBAs found avenues around this problem by creating SQL scripts or by writing programs that handle the cumbersome grant process. Oracle responded to this problem by providing its user community with database roles.

At the simplest level, roles are simply groups of system or object privileges that can be assigned to database users. Grants on the desired privileges, such as CREATE SESSION or SELECT ON SCOTT.EMP, are made to a role. This role is then granted to a user. The database user has all the privileges that have been assigned to the role. There is no limit to the number of people who can have the role assigned to them, and changes are replicated to all the database users by making a change in the grants to the role.

Creating Roles

Aside from defining the privileges necessary for each role and selecting appropriately descriptive names, the process of creating a role is simple. The syntax is similar to creating a database user. For example,

```
% sqlplus system
Password: ........
Connected.

SQL> create role global_mis;
Role created.
```

Modifying Roles

Making changes to database roles consists of changing the database privileges—object or system—to which the role has access. This is done through standard SQL grant and revoke statements. For example,

```
% sqlplus system
Password: ........
Connected.

SQL> alter role global_mis identified by universe;
Role altered.
```

It is not necessary to replicate the change for each database user. After the grant or revoke is successfully performed on the role, it immediately takes effect for all the database users who have the role assigned to them. There are no special steps or cumbersome processes. In the example database, only 100 grants—the total number of users—must be performed, unless multiple roles are assigned to a single user. For example, if the DBA needs to change access on a table from UPDATE to SELECT, he would issue the appropriate revoke command on the role. The change takes effect on all the database users with that role.

> **CAUTION**
>
> Although it is possible to grant roles to other roles—which is called *nesting*—there is a limit to the number of active roles that can be in effect for a single user at any one time. This is determined by the value of the INIT.ORA parameter MAX_ENABLED_ROLES. The database does not permit more than the limit set by this value to be enabled.

Deleting Roles

The DBA can delete a role from the database. This operation removes information pertaining to the role from all the users and roles currently in existence. As with revoking a system privilege, deleting a role does not affect existing database objects. For example:

```
% sqlplus system
Password: ........
Connected.

SQL> drop role admin;
Role dropped.
```

Setting and Changing the Default Role

Whenever a role is granted to a user, the privileges within the role do not take effect until the role has been set as the *default role*. The default role tells the database that it is the role whose privileges are currently being used. The default role determines which database role the user uses when he first connects to the database. For example:

```
% sqlplus system
Password: .......
Connected.

SQL> alter user amy default role admin;
Statement processed.
```

The user or the DBA can also change the current default role. At the discretion of the DBA, every role assigned to a user can be set as the default role. In this way, a user does not have to switch between roles. Instead, he can benefit from the system and object privileges of all of the active roles at a given time without being forced to change default roles each time. For example:

```
% sqlplus system
Password: .......
Connected.

SQL> alter user logan default role all;
Statement processed.
```

The DBA should carefully evaluate the ramifications of setting all the roles as default roles before he institutes this option.

Password Protecting Roles

At some sites, users are grouped into different privilege levels that require a decision before they perform a certain task. Take, for example, a user in an OLTP system who has three roles—ORD_ENTRY, MANAGER, and SUPERUSER. Each level might have different levels of privileges. MANAGER might have SELECT, INSERT, UPDATE, and DELETE capabilities on key tables that are not accessible to ORD_ENTR. MANAGER might lack certain system privileges that belong to SUPERUSER. Whatever the case, the DBA might require a password for each level.

This password helps protect the privilege levels by keeping others out of the role, and it also forces the user to know what role he is currently using. In theory, he would remember which password he most recently entered. Likewise, the password enables the DBA to keep users out of certain privilege groups by changing the password associated with the role.

Switching between roles is the same as switching between roles that have no passwords. The sole difference is that a correct password must be given before Oracle will accept the role change. For example:

```
% sqlplus jordan
Password: ........
Connected.

SQL> set role lawyer;
Enter password: ........
Statement processed.
```

Defining Roles at Operating System Level

It is possible to grant roles dynamically at the operating system level. For this to take place, a few additional steps must be performed when the roles are created. The benefit is that roles are always identified at the operating system level—in /etc/groups in UNIX, for example. They can easily be changed by someone who has the privilege to make modifications—usually the system administrator.

> **CAUTION**
>
> Using operating system authenticated roles should be considered only at sites where the DBA can make changes to the appropriate file. If the DBA lacks this authority, the entire process entails too much overhead to be useful. Grants should be performed at the database level instead.

One of the first steps in creating an operating system authenticated role is to make certain that the parameter OS_ROLES in the INIT.ORA parameter file is set to TRUE. This parameter enables the DBA to enable or disable the use of operating system authenticated roles.

> **CAUTION**
>
> To prevent possible breaches of security, a default role cannot be authenticated at the operating system level when Oracle's Multi-Thread Server is running. If breaches of security are not a concern, you can enable them for multi-thread sites by setting the value of REMOTE_OS_ROLES to TRUE. Consider this carefully.

Operating system authenticated roles, like operating system authenticated accounts, must be created at the database level. As with user accounts, this is done by identifying them EXTERNALLY. For example,

```
% sqlplus system
Password: ........
Connected.

SQL> create role manager identified externally;
Role created.
```

Each role to be used by the Oracle database instance must be defined as being identified externally in the database. It must also be defined at the operating system. The role always has the prefix ora_, followed by the Oracle SID of the instance and the name of the role. It can also have the suffix d (if it is a default role) or a (if the user has ADMIN OPTION on the role).

In the following example, a role named manager is set up in the norm instance:

```
ora_norm_manager_ad:*:512:larry,daryl,o_daryl
```

The users larry, daryl, and o_daryl have manager as their default role, with ADMIN OPTION on it. Assuming that the role has been created—that is, identified externally—within the database and that the database has been restarted with OS_ROLES set to TRUE, this is all that is required to authenticate an account at the operating system level. Modifying this role is a matter of simply adding a user to the group at the UNIX level. Note that operating system authentication is not available on all platforms.

System Privilege Roles

Oracle6 has only three system privileges. The privileges are

- connect, which enables the user to connect to the database
- resource, which enables the user to create objects in database tablespaces
- dba, which gives the user full system rights on the database

Oracle7 provides for backward compatibility by giving combination privileges that simulate the same functionality as their Oracle6 counterparts. It uses roles of system privileges to accomplish this task.

The Oracle7 CONNECT privileges that are assigned to a user by means of system privilege roles are

> ALTER SESSION
> CREATE CLUSTER
> CREATE DATABASE LINK
> CREATE SEQUENCE
> CREATE SESSION
> CREATE SYNONYM
> CREATE TABLE
> CREATE VIEW

The Oracle7 RESOURCE privileges that are assigned to a user by means of system privilege roles are

> CREATE CLUSTER
> CREATE PROCEDURE

CREATE SEQUENCE

CREATE TABLE

CREATE TRIGGER

UNLIMITED TABLESPACE

UNLIMITED TABLESPACE is normally not available as part of a role. Oracle enables it specifically to deal with backward compatibility.

The Oracle7 EXP_FULL_DATABASE privileges that are assigned to a user by means of system privilege roles are

SELECT ANY TABLE

BACKUP ANY TABLE

INSERT, UPDATE, and DELETE on SYS.INCEXP

INSERT, UPDATE, and DELETE on SYS.INCVID

INSERT, UPDATE, and DELETE on SYS.INCFIL

The Oracle7 IMP_FULL_DATABASE privilege that is assigned to a user by means of system privilege roles is

BECOME USER

The Oracle7 DBA privileges that are assigned to a user by means of system privilege roles are

ALL PRIVILEGES WITH ADMIN OPTION

EXP_FULL_DATABASE

IMP_FULL_DATABASE

There have been rumors that these system roles have been provided only for backward compatibility with previous versions of Oracle and that future releases will not support them. Although this seems unlikely given the amount of software that relies on these privileges, you should be aware of it. After all, Oracle undertook drastic changes when it moved from Oracle6 to Oracle7.

Database Auditing

This section on database auditing is the one that really causes the *Mission: Impossible* soundtrack to play louder. Auditing gives the DBA the ability to track information within the database. It provides information on who performed a certain operation and when it was performed. This is a powerful security feature of the Oracle RDBMS, but it comes with a price.

Auditing is a reactive function. It gives the DBA information about an activity only after it has already occurred. This reactive information provides a snapshot of what occurred, depending on the level of detail being audited. It gives the DBA a basis for tracking changes within the database.

Because auditing causes additional rows to be added to the database for each operation, it is important to balance the auditing being done against constraints such as performance overhead and physical storage requirements. Unless site-specific reasons require otherwise, the DBA should limit the amount of information being audited. It is not uncommon for DBAs to run continuous high-level audit trails that track which users are connecting to the database, for example. It is much more uncommon for the database to track all SQL statements being issued by all users at all times. As a rule of thumb, the DBA should introduce only lower levels of auditing when he suspects inappropriate activity, and he should be specific about whom the audit is directed against.

To activate auditing for a database instance, the DBA must make certain that the AUDIT_TRAIL parameter of the INIT.ORA parameter file is set to DB or OS to indicate where the audit trail should be written. The default value for this parameter is NONE.

Statement Level Auditing

Auditing that occurs at the statement level—sometimes called the privilege level—has a wide scope. With this level of auditing, an audit record is written for each specific SQL statement that is issued. It is possible to limit it to a specific user—such as all CREATE TABLE commands issued by DAVE—or to all users—such as any ALTER TABLE command issued by any user. Depending on how specific the DBA makes this level of auditing, the audit information generated can be substantial.

In the following example, two audit options are set. One option logs CREATE TABLE activity within the database. The other option logs all CREATE SESSION activity done by BETO.

```
% sqlplus system
Password: ........
Connected.

SQL> audit create table by access whenever successful;

Statement processed.

SQL> audit create session by beto by access whenever successful;
Statement processed.
```

Two important parameters appear in every SQL audit command:

- BY SESSION/BY ACCESS
- WHENEVER SUCCESSFUL/WHENEVER NOT SUCCESSFUL

BY SESSION/BY ACCESS determines how often audit records should be written. In a BY SESSION audit, the database writes a single audit record that sums all the times that an action took place during a given session. In a BY ACCESS audit, the database writes a single audit record for each SQL statement that was issued.

WHENEVER SUCCESSFUL/WHENEVER NOT SUCCESSFUL determines the conditions under which the audit records should be written. Audits that are WHENEVER SUCCESSFUL have information written only if they succeed. WHENEVER NOT SUCCESSFUL audits are written only if they do not succeed.

System-level roles can be used to implement auditing, so that only a single SQL statement is required to audit several different operations. Consult the *Oracle7 Server Administrator's Guide* for more information.

The CLUSTER statement audits

> CREATE CLUSTER
> ALTER CLUSTER
> DROP CLUSTER
> TRUNCATE CLUSTER

The DATABASE LINK statement audits

> CREATE DATABASE LINK
> DROP DATABASE LINK

The INDEX statement audits

> CREATE INDEX
> ALTER INDEX
> DROP INDEX

The EXISTS statement indicates a failure because a value currently exists in the database. This is a feature of Trusted Oracle7 only.

The NOT EXISTS statement indicates a failure because database objects do not exist.

The PROCEDURE statement audits

> CREATE FUNCTION
> CREATE PACKAGE
> CREATE PACKAGE BODY
> CREATE PROCEDURE
> DROP FUNCTION
> DROP PACKAGE
> DROP PROCEDURE

The PROFILE statement audits

> CREATE PROFILE
> ALTER PROFILE
> DROP PROFILE

The PUBLIC DATABASE LINK statement audits

> CREATE PUBLIC DATABASE LINK
> DROP PUBLIC DATABASE LINK

The PUBLIC SYNONYM statement audits

> CREATE PUBLIC SYNONYM
> DROP PUBLIC SYNONYM

The ROLE statement audits

> CREATE ROLE
> ALTER ROLE
> DROP ROLE
> SET ROLE

The ROLLBACK SEGMENT statement audits

> CREATE ROLLBACK SEGMENT
> ALTER ROLLBACK SEGMENT
> DROP ROLLBACK SEGMENT

The SEQUENCE statement audits

> CREATE SEQUENCE
> DROP SEQUENCE

The SESSION statement audits database connections and disconnections.

The SYNONYM statement audits

> CREATE SYNONYM
> DROP SYNONYM

The SYSTEM AUDIT statement audits

> AUDIT
> NOAUDIT

The SYSTEM GRANT statement audits

> GRANT on system privileges and roles
>
> REVOKE on system privileges and roles

The TABLE statement audits

> CREATE TABLE
>
> DROP TABLE
>
> TRUNCATE TABLE

The TABLESPACE statement audits

> CREATE TABLESPACE
>
> ALTER TABLESPACE
>
> DROP TABLESPACE

The TRIGGER statement audits

> CREATE TRIGGER
>
> ALTER TRIGGER ENABLE/DISABLE
>
> DROP TRIGGER
>
> ALTER TABLE with the ENABLE/DISABLE option

The USER statement audits

> CREATE USER
>
> ALTER USER
>
> DROP USER

The VIEW statement audits

> CREATE VIEW
>
> DROP VIEW

Object Level Auditing

It is possible to audit database information at the database object level, which enables you to trap operations done on a specific database object. The syntax is essentially the same as that for a statement level audit:

```
% sqlplus system
Password: ........
Connected.

SQL> audit delete on hr.payroll;
Statement processed.
```

The statement audit specifies a class of statements and, optionally, which user to audit for these statements. The object audit, on the other hand, points to a type of object operation and the name of an object.

The types of object level operations that can be performed are

ALTER

AUDIT

COMMENT

DELETE

EXECUTE

GRANT

INDEX

INSERT

LOCK

RENAME

SELECT

UPDATE

These object level operations can be performed on any of the following types of database objects:

- Tables
- Views
- Sequences
- Stored procedures, functions, or packages
- Snapshots

Consult the *Oracle7 Server Administrator's Guide* for more information.

To deactivate object or privilege level auditing, bounce the database and set AUDIT_TRAIL to NONE, or specify the current audit options with the NOAUDIT command. For example:

```
% sqlplus system
Password: ........
Connected.

SQL> noaudit all;
Statement processed.
```

Audit Trail Location

The audit trails from Oracle's AUDIT option can be stored in either the database or the operating system. The location is determined at database startup, based on the value of the INIT.ORA parameter AUDIT_TRAIL.

Database

All audit information stored within the database is stored in the table SYS.AUD$, which by default is stored in the SYSTEM tablespace. You should move this table into a separate tablespace to prevent undue fragmentation of SYSTEM.

There are two methods for performing this operation:

- Before you turn on auditing, extract the SQL for this table creation from `sql.bsq`—do a `describe` of the table from SQL*Plus to get the exact sizes of the columns. Drop the table and re-create it in the new tablespace. Make sure that all the relevant grants on the table are made.

- Export the table. Generate a copy of the creation SQL by means of the `imp` utility. Create the table, and import it with the `IGNORE=Y` flag set.

In an audited database, it is important to make sure that audit trail information is not erased. To prevent that from happening, the DBA should limit the users who can actually write information to this table to SYS. This is difficult to do, however, if users have been granted the DELETE ANY TABLE system privilege. The following code segment illustrates a simple way to trap users who attempt to modify the SYS.AUD$ table:

```
% sqlplus system
Password: ......
Connected.

SQL> audit insert, update, delete
 2> on sys.aud$
 3> by access;

Statement processed.
```

Although this technique cannot prevent a more experienced user from circumventing auditing, it should keep cursory pilferings at bay, especially if the users lack the ability to modify the audit status.

The database stops processing, however, if the SYS.AUD$ table reaches its maximum capacity. This problem is easily resolved. As a DBA user, do `connect internal` from Oracle Server*Manager. From Oracle Server*Manager, do `truncate sys.aud$`. This returns the database to its full operational capacity.

Operating System

By directing the database to archive its information at the operating system level, the DBA enables Oracle to store its audit trail information in the same location as the audit information generated by the operating system. This provides a consolidated source of information for DBAs who fill the dual roles DBA and system administrator.

There are a few drawbacks to consider, though. Because the data is no longer in a table, non-database utilities are needed to access it. Likewise, depending on the amount of information being audited, the database can produce double, triple, or even further increase the amount of information that the operating system currently produces.

Summary

Setting up a security plan for a site can be a challenge for any Oracle DBA. Aside from the development issues involved in defining requirements and developing an overall plan, he is faced with political issues that are often insurmountable in creating the security plan.

It is important to understand that there are two types of privileges: system privileges and object privileges. They are the basis of anything that a user can do while he is connected to an Oracle database. These also form the building blocks of database roles, which provide a means for the DBA to group together sets of similar privileges and to grant them to a single user or a group of users.

The idea of a security policy is not an easy thing to implement, especially in environments in which one has never existed. Even so, it is a crucial piece of the database setup that should not be overlooked.

IV

PART

Developing Applications

Designing a Database

17

*by Advanced
Information
Systems, Inc.*

There are several steps involved in developing an effective database design. As with all types of applications, the process begins with requirements analysis. In terms of relational database design, this phase answers questions regarding what data elements must be stored, who will access them, and how.

The second step is to define the logical database. This phase does not deal with how the data will be stored physically, but with how information is grouped logically. The requirements are translated into a model that provides a level of abstraction from the physical database, representing data in terms of business entities and relationships, rather than in terms of tables and columns.

Physical design is the final phase, in which individual data elements are given attributes and defined as columns in tables. This phase also deals with performance considerations relating to the creation of indexes, rollback segments, temporary segments, and the physical layout of data files on disk. DDL (Data Definition Language) scripts are written to create database objects and to be used for capacity planning.

A simple contact manager will be used as a sample application throughout this chapter, illustrating the concepts and techniques presented for each phase of the design process.

Requirements Definition

System requirements are typically gathered through a series of interviews with the end users. This is an iterative process in which systems designers provide structure to the ongoing dialog, document findings, and solicit feedback from the users. Although requirements definition is not normally considered part of the design process, the design is driven by the requirements, and the two processes often overlap. For example, the logical model may bring out new requirements that were not recognized in the earlier phases of analysis. It is important, however, to identify all requirements before developing a physical design, because capacity planning and hardware purchasing decisions are ineffective without a full understanding of system requirements.

A common technique used to define and document database requirements is to develop a data dictionary. As the name implies, a data dictionary simply enumerates and defines the individual data elements that must be stored. An initial draft of the data dictionary for a simple contact manager might look like Table 17.1.

Table 17.1. Data dictionary for the contact manager sample application.

Item	Description
Last Name	The individual contact's last name
First Name	The individual's first name
Middle Initial	The individual's middle initial

Item	Description
Contact Type	Standardized description indicating whether this individual represents a client, a prospect, a vendor, or some other type of contact
Individual Notes	Additional information related to the individual
Company	The name of thecompany that the individual represents
Company Notes	Additional information related to the individual's company
Address Line 1	Line 1 of the individual's street address
Address Line 2	Line 2 of the individual's street address
Address Line 3	Line 3 of the individual's street address
City	City name of the individual's mailing address
State	State name for the individual's mailing address
Zip Code	Zip code for the individual's mailing address
Address Type	Standardized description indicating whether this is a work, home, or some other type of address
Phone Number	The individual's area code and phone number
Phone Type	Standardized description indicating whether this is a home, office, or other type of phone number
Date Contacted	The date that this individual was contacted
Contacted By	The name of the salesperson or employee who contacted this individual
Contact Method	Standardized description indicating whether the individual was contacted by phone, mail, fax, or some other method
Contact Reason	Standardized description of the reason that the individual was contacted
Contact Notes	Additional information related to this specific contact

Although this is a good way to start defining database requirements, there are obvious short-comings. The data dictionary does not describe how these individual items are related. It also lacks information regarding how the data is created, updated, and retrieved, among other things.

A functional specification documents the system requirements in plain English and should fill in details concerning who will be using the system, when, and how. Information concerning the number of concurrent users accessing the system, how frequently records are inserted and updated, and how information will be retrieved are particularly important topics to be covered in the functional specification. These factors will help determine hardware and software licensing requirements, and have a significant impact on issues relating to performance, security, and database integrity.

The functional description for the sample contact manager might include a summary similar to the text that follows:

> The system will be available to 40 sales representatives, 5 sales managers, 26 sales assistants, 6 purchasing agents, 1 purchasing department manager, and 2 purchasing assistants, for a total of 80 users. Of these 80 possible users, it is expected that a maximum of 20 would be actively using the system at any given time. Purchasing department personnel should have access only to purchasing department contacts, and sales department personnel should have access only to sales contacts.

> All users may add information regarding a specific contact at any time, but whereas sales representatives and purchasing agents can add new prospects, only assistants can add new vendors and clients (after obtaining proper approval from a manager). Sales representatives and purchasing agents should have access only to their accounts and prospects, whereas managers should have full access to the entire database for their specific departments.

> One assistant from each department will be designated as a system administrator. Only the system administrators will be able to add and modify address, phone, contact types, contact methods, and contact reasons. With the approval of a manager, a system administrator will be able to reassign a vendor or client to a new purchasing agent or sales representative.

> For audit purposes, every time information is added or modified, the individual who made the modification and the date and time that the information was modified should be recorded.

In the preceding example, the functional specification added several new data elements to the requirements, in addition to pertinent information regarding access and security. The functional specification and data dictionary are often developed simultaneously, as one document may provide relevant information that should be reflected in the other.

An important part of requirements analysis is to anticipate the needs of the users, because they will not always be able to fully explain the system requirements on their own. Based on information from the previous examples, the system designers may have these follow-up questions:

- Will a contact have only one address and phone number? One company? One type?
- How does a prospect become a client or vendor?
- How are client and vendor accounts assigned to sales representatives and purchasing agents initially?
- How are client and vendor account numbers assigned?
- Can contact and audit information be archived? If so, after how many months?

These are obviously just a few of the questions that come to mind. In practice, the functional description should describe the system to the fullest extent and detail possible. The importance of thorough requirements analysis and documentation is often underestimated. Put simply, poor requirements definition will most likely result in poor or inadequate design, because these requirements provide the foundation for the later phases of design, including the logical and physical data models.

The Logical Model

A common way to represent the logical model is through an Entity-Relationship (E-R) diagram. For the purposes of this type of model, an *entity* is defined as a discrete object for which items of data are being stored, and a *relationship* refers to an association between two entities.

In the contact manager example, there are five main entities for which data is being stored:

- Individuals (with whom contacts are made)
- Addresses
- Phone Numbers
- Contacts (communications with individuals)
- Employees

The relationships between these entities can be summarized in plain terms:

- Employees have access to zero, one, or many Individuals
- Individuals have one or many Addresses
- Individuals have one or many Phone Numbers
- Employees make zero, one, or many Contacts
- Individuals have zero, one, or many Contacts

These entities and their relationships can be represented graphically by an E-R diagram, as shown in Figure 17.1.

FIGURE 17.1.

E-R diagram for the contact manager sample application.

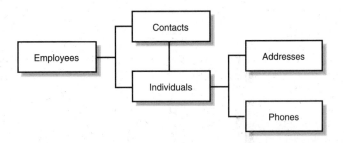

NOTE

Observe how the one-to-one-or-many and one-to-zero-one-or-many relationships are represented. One-to-one and one-to-zero-or-one relationships can be represented using similar notation.

This may seem to be a simplistic approach to modeling the application's data, but it is often a good first step. In larger applications with hundreds of entities, these models can become extremely complex.

This model can be taken a step further by defining attributes for each entity. An entity's attributes are the individual items of data to be stored that relate specifically to the object. The attributes for each entity in the example are listed in Table 17.2.

Table 17.2. Simple entity and attribute definitions.

Employees	*Individuals*	*Contacts*
Employee Number	Last Name	Contact Date
User ID	First Name	Contacted By
	Middle Initial	Contact Reason
	Company	Contact Method
	Individual Notes	Contact Type
	Company Notes	Contact Notes

Addresses	*Phone Numbers*
Address Line 1	Phone Number
Address Line 2	Phone Type
Address Line 3	
City	
State	
Zip Code	
Address Type	

Note that several items of information are missing. The audit information mentioned in the functional specification is omitted. This can be handled by adding a Last Update User ID and Last Update Date/Time Stamp attribute to each entity. More important, there are attributes missing that are required to relate entities to each other. These data items will be handled somewhat differently because they are not "natural" attributes belonging to a specific entity.

This is a highly abstract view of the data, concerned only with broad categories of data (entities) and the logical relationships between them. The E-R model, although good at representing basic data concepts, is not of much use when it comes to physical implementation. The relational model helps bridge this gap.

The relational model is characterized by its use of keys and relations, among other things. The term *relation* in the context of relational database theory should not be confused with a relationship. A relation can be viewed as an unordered, two-dimensional table, where each row is distinct. Relationships are built between relations (tables) through common attributes. These common attributes are called *keys*.

There are several types of keys, and they sometimes differ only in terms of their relationships to other attributes and relations. A primary key uniquely identifies a row in a relation and each relation can have only one primary key, even if more than one attribute is unique. In some cases, it takes more than one attribute to uniquely identify each row in a relation. The aggregate of these attributes is called a concatenated key, or a composite key. In other cases, a primary key must be generated. The entity Individuals in the preceding example illustrates this point. Although it may be likely, there is no guarantee that the combination of the entity's attributes will be unique. A new attribute should be created based on generated values to make Individuals a relation. This can be accomplished in Oracle through the use of a sequence.

Another type of key, called a *foreign key*, exists only in terms of the relationship between two relations. A foreign key in a relation is a nonkey attribute that is a primary key (or part of the primary key) in another relation. This is the shared attribute that forms a relationship between two relations (tables). Primary and foreign key relationships are illustrated in Table 17.3.

Referring back to the example, the entities' attributes can be extended to fulfill the audit requirements and make the model relational. Note that the ID attribute is a generated primary key in each relation in which it appears. The reasons for this will be explained in further detail in the following section on performance considerations.

Table 17.3. Entity attributes (relational model).

Employees	*Individuals*
Employee Number (PK)	ID (PK)
User ID	Last Name
Last Update User ID	First Name
Last Update Date/Time	Middle Initial
	Company
	Contact Type
	Assigned Employee (FK)
	Individual Notes

continues

Table 17.3. continued

Employees	Individuals
	Company Notes
	Last Update User ID
	Last Update Date/Time

Addresses	Phone Numbers
ID (PK)	ID (PK)
Individual ID (FK)	Individual ID (FK)
Address Line 1	Phone Number
Address Line 2	Phone Type
Address Line 3	Last Update User ID
City	Last Update Date/Time
State	
Zip Code	
Address Type	
Last Update User ID	
Last Update Date/Time	

Contacts
ID (PK)
Individual ID (FK)
Contacted By (FK)
Contact Date
Contact Reason
Contact Method
Contact Notes
Last Update User ID
Last Update Date/Time

NOTE

(PK) indicates that the attribute is the primary key of the relation. (FK) indicates that the attribute is a foreign key.

There are numerous limitations and redundancies in this model. For example, if one individual works for more than one company, he or she must be stored as two separate individuals to be associated with both companies. Redundancies are also introduced when multiple contacts share the same address and phone number.

The Normalization Process

A process known as normalization is a technique used to group attributes in ways that eliminate these types of problems. More specifically, the goals of normalization are to minimize redundancy and functional dependency. Functional dependencies occur when the value of one attribute can be determined from the value of another attribute. The attribute that can be determined is said to be functionally dependent on the attribute that is the determinant. By definition, then, all nonkey attributes will be functionally dependent on the primary key in every relation (because the primary key uniquely defines each row). When one attribute of a relation does not uniquely define another attribute, but limits it to a set of predefined values, this is called a multivalued dependency. A partial dependency exists when an attribute of a relation is functionally dependent on only one attribute of a concatenated key. Transitive dependencies occur when a nonkey attribute is functionally dependent on one or more other nonkey attributes in the relation.

Normalization is measured in terms of normal forms, and the process of normalization consists of taking appropriate steps to reach the next normal form:

- First normal form is very easy to achieve. The only requirement is that each "cell" in the table has a single value. In other words, first normal form will be violated only if multiple values are being stored in a single row and column combination of a table.

- Second normal form is achieved when all partial dependencies are removed. If there are no composite keys in the relations, this level of normalization is very easy to achieve also.

- Third normal form requires that all transitive dependencies are removed. In the sample relations presented previously, there are at least two transitive dependencies. In the Addresses relation, both city and state are dependent on zip code. (It could also be said that there is a multivalued dependency between zip code and city and state.)

- Fourth normal form is reached when all multivalued dependencies are removed.

(There are other normal forms, but they are beyond the scope of this discussion.)

Third normal form can be reached in the example by removing the transitive dependencies that exist in the Address relation. This can be achieved by removing city and state from the Address relation and creating two new relations, as you will note in Table 17.4.

Table 17.4. Third normal form of States and Cities tables.

Cities	*States*
Zip Code (PK)	Zip Code (PK)
City (PK)	State

NOTE

The (PK) next to both Zip Code and City in the Cities relation indicates that the attributes make up the concatenated primary key. It would be very unusual to have such a relation, where all attributes are part of the primary key.

This makes both the zip code and city attributes in the Address relation foreign keys. (Note that City is made part of the key because, in rural areas, one zip code may have more than one city.) The model can be further normalized by eliminating several of the multivalued dependencies, as you will note in Table 17.5.

Table 17.5. Tables defined with identifying primary keys.

Address Type	*Phone Type*	*Contact Type*
ID (PK)	ID (PK)	ID (PK)
Type	Type	Type

Contact Method	*Contact Reason*	
ID (PK)	ID (PK)	
Method	Reason	

Where these attributes exist in the previously defined relations, they will remain as foreign keys. As these examples illustrate, the dependencies are not eliminated, but their nature is changed so that dependencies exist on key attributes rather than nonkey attributes. In this example, however, fourth normal form is still not achieved. In the Individual relation, Company has a multivalued dependency (at best) on the Last Name, First Name, and Middle Initial.

Separating Company from Individuals brings the model to fourth normal form. Additional relations allow addresses and phones to be associated with either companies or individuals, and allow individuals to be related to more than one company, as you will note in Table 17.6.

Table 17.6. Fourth normal form.

Individuals	Individual-Company Relation
ID (PK)	Individual ID (FK)
Last Name	Company ID (FK)
First Name	
Middle Initial	
Contact Type (FK)	
Assigned Employee (FK)	
Individual Notes	
Last Update User ID	
Last Update Date/Time	

Companies	Entity Type
ID (PK)	ID (PK)
Company	Type
Company Notes	

Addresses	Phone Numbers
ID (PK)	ID (PK)
Entity Type (FK)	Entity Type (FK)
Entity ID (FK)	Entity ID (FK)
Address Line 1	Phone Number
Address Line 2	Phone Type (FK)
Address Line 3	Last Update User ID
City (FK)	Last Update Date/Time
Zip Code (FK)	
Address Type (FK)	
Last Update User ID	
Last Update Date/Time	

An additional aspect of the logical model is the design of tablespaces. A *tablespace* consists of one or more data files and, as the name implies, a tablespace houses one or more database objects. Before proceeding to the physical design, designers should consider how they may want to use tablespaces to group database objects along logical boundaries.

One tablespace is always created when Oracle is installed. This tablespace, called SYSTEM, houses all system tables and other system objects used by Oracle itself. Although this tablespace can be used to house additional tables, it is preferable to create separate tablespaces for application-specific objects. In many cases, it is desirable to create several tablespaces to house different types of database objects. A common logical division is to create separate tablespaces for roll-back segments, indexes, tables, and temporary segments. This topic will be discussed in greater detail in the following section, but these logical design issues are worthy of some consideration before proceeding to the physical design.

The Physical Model

The physical database consists of data files, tablespaces, rollback segments, tables, columns, and indexes. There are dependencies between these elements that impose an order on the design process. The process often starts with designing the smallest units of physical storage (the column) and proceeds, in order, to each successively larger unit of storage. Overall capacity and performance considerations provide constraints to the design, and should be considered at every step. As with logical modeling, developing a physical design can be a somewhat iterative process.

Column Attributes and DDL

Designing the physical database begins with assigning column attributes. The attributes of a column determine how it will be physically stored in the database by defining its data type and maximum length. The data type and length of a column should be carefully chosen at design time, because it is sometimes difficult to change these attributes after data has been loaded. Consider the following summarizations of each of the Oracle data types:

CHAR(*SIZE*)	Used to store fixed-length alphanumeric data. The (*SIZE*) determines the number of characters that will be stored for each value in the column. If a value is inserted into the column that is shorter than (*SIZE*), it will be padded with spaces on the right until it reaches (*SIZE*) characters in length. The maximum length of this data type is 255 bytes. If (*SIZE*) is omitted, the default is 1 byte.
VARCHAR2(*SIZE*)	Used to store variable-length alphanumeric data. This data type differs from CHAR in that inserted values will not be padded with spaces, and the maximum (*SIZE*) for this type is 2000 bytes.
NUMBER(*P*, *S*)	Used to store positive or negative, fixed or floating-point numeric values. The precision, (*P*), determines the maximum length of the data, whereas the scale, (*S*), determines the number of places to the right of the decimal. If scale is omitted, the default is 0. If precision is omitted, values are stored with their original precision up to the maximum of 38 digits.

DATE	Used to store dates and times. Oracle uses its own internal format to store 7 bytes each for day, month, century, year, hour, minute and second. This is important because it illustrates the point that dates are fairly expensive to store—49 bytes per record, even if only a portion of the information is used. The default representation for dates in Oracle is DD-MON-YY. For example, 01-JAN-95 is used to represent January 1, 1995.
LONG	Used to store up to 2 gigabytes of alphanumeric data. As with VARCHAR2, values are stored at their actual lengths. LONG values cannot be indexed, and the normal character functions such as SUBSTR cannot be applied to LONG values.
RAW	Used to store binary data with no character set conversion. RAW data cannot exceed 255 bytes. RAW data can be indexed, but no functions can be performed on RAW values.
LONG RAW	Used to store large binary objects such as whole documents, video, and graphics or entire compiled programs. LONG RAW can store up to 2 gigabytes of information, but cannot be indexed.
ROWID	Used to represent a row's physical address. Every table has a ROWID pseudo-column, which is not evident when describing the table or issuing SELECT * FROM *table_name*. This address will remain unchanged unless the table is exported and imported, or otherwise physically moved on disk. In practice, this value is rarely used.

You should consider additional factors besides the nature of the data and its length when selecting a data type for a column. For example, one might assume that it is always better to use VARCHAR2 instead of CHAR, so that only the actual number of bytes present in the data will be stored. There are differences, however, in how comparisons are handled with these data types. Two VARCHAR2 values must be the same length to be considered equal, where two CHAR values are compared without consideration of trailing spaces. As a result, if the values 'WORD' and 'WORD' are being compared, they will compare as equal if they are CHAR values, but will be not be considered equal if they are VARCHAR2 values because of the trailing spaces in the second value.

When using the NUMBER data type, the declared precision and scale greatly affect how the data is stored. If not fully understood, these values may not behave as intended. For example, assume that a column has been declared NUMBER(10,4). One might conclude this means that up to 10 digits can be stored in this column, as many as four of which may be to the right of the decimal. This is not necessarily the case, however. An attempt to insert a value of 1234567 into this column will fail, with an error code of ORA-01438 (value larger than specified precision allows for this column). The declaration of NUMBER(10,4) does allow up to 10 digits of precision, but only 6 of these may be to the left of the decimal.

The default DATE format can be changed for the database instance, or for a particular session. If you wish to store times in a column declared as DATE, you must alter the default date format to include the time, or all values inserted will have the default time of 12:00 A.M. (with the exception of the SYSDATE system variable). To insert date values from an application using the default date format, a statement such as:

```
INSERT INTO table_name (column_name) VALUES ('01-JAN-95')
```

must be issued. Because there is no way to specify time using the default data format, Oracle will store the default value of 12:00 A.M. If this statement is changed to:

```
INSERT INTO table_name (column_name) VALUES(SYSDATE)
```

the time is inserted accurately because SYSDATE shares the same internal representation. The date format can be altered for a session by issuing a statement such as:

```
ALTER SESSION SET NLS_DATE_FORMAT = 'MM-DD-YYYY HH:MI A.M.'
```

After this statement has been issued, times can be inserted accurately using the new format:

```
INSERT INTO table_name (column_name) VALUES('12-31-1994 11:59 P.M.')
```

Note that this format is valid only for the session. In any subsequent sessions, the statement:

```
SELECT column_name FROM table_name
```

will return 31-DEC-94 for the previously inserted value until the session is altered again.

> **TIP**
>
> The NLS_DATE_FORMAT can be set for the database instance by including it in the initialization file.

Using the contact manager application example, the column attributes for the Addresses table might be defined as in Table 17.7.

Table 17.7. Definition of the column attributes of the Addresses relation in the contact manager sample application.

Column	Attribute
ID	NUMBER(10)
Entity Type	NUMBER(10)
Entity ID	NUMBER(10)
Address Line 1	VARCHAR2(40)
Address Line 2	VARCHAR2(40)
Address Line 3	VARCHAR2(40)

Column	Attribute
City	VARCHAR2(30)
Zip Code	NUMBER(5)
Address Type	NUMBER(10)
Last Update User ID	VARCHAR2(20)
Last Update Date/Time	DATE

Defining the column attributes is an important step in capacity planning. From this information, the maximum record size for each table can be determined. This combined with an estimate of the total number of rows helps determine the amount of storage required to house the data.

The next step is to begin creating Data Definition Language (DDL) scripts that will be used to create the tables. This may seem like a step toward implementation, but DDL can be used as a tool for capacity planning and the design of tablespaces and data file layout. The DDL for creating tables consists of defining column attributes and constraints, storage specification, table constraints, and rules. Constraints and rules are discussed in detail in the chapter on enforcing integrity; therefore, for now, the description of DDL focuses on column attributes and storage specification.

Referring back to the sample application, assume that it is estimated that 5,000 address records will be stored initially, and that the number of records is expected to double in the next several years. From the definition of the column attributes for the address table, it is apparent that the maximum size of any single record is 264 bytes. (Remember that DATE columns require 49 bytes always.) Assume further that the primary and foreign key IDs will be sequenced starting with 1, and that Address Line 2 and Address Line 3 are rarely populated. Based on this additional information, a conservative estimate would be that the average record size will be 200 bytes. The total size of the table can then be estimated at 1 MB initially. The script in Listing 17.1 can then be written with an appropriate storage specification.

Listing 17.1. DDL script that illustrates the use of the STORAGE clause.

```
CREATE TABLE Addresses (
        Address_ID              NUMBER(10)      PRIMARY KEY
        ,Address_Type_ID        NUMBER(10)      NOT NULL
        ,Entity_ID              NUMBER(10)      NOT NULL
        ,Entity_Type_ID         NUMBER(10)      NOT NULL
        ,Address_Line1          VARCHAR2(40)    NOT NULL
        ,Address_Line2          VARCHAR2(40)
        ,Address_Line3          VARCHAR2(40)
        ,City                   VARCHAR2(30)    NOT NULL
        ,Zip_Code               NUMBER(5)       NOT NULL
        ,Last_Updt_User         VARCHAR2(20)        NOT NULL
```

continues

Listing 17.1. continued

```
        ,Last_Updt_Timestamp     DATE              NOT NULL
    )
    TABLESPACE Contact_Main
    STORAGE (    INITIAL            1M
                 NEXT             100K
                 MINEXTENTS          1
                 MAXEXTENTS        100
                 PCTINCREASE        10  );
```

Note that, although the columns have been rearranged and renamed, the physical table still reflects the logical relation, with a few exceptions. The foreign key constraints have been omitted. There are a number of ways to enforce the foreign key constraints, through column constraints, table constraints, or other means. The issue of enforcing integrity through table and column constraints is revisited briefly later in this chapter, and all options will be discussed in full detail in the chapter on enforcing database integrity.

The primary key constraint is an important consideration for a number of reasons. At this point, it is important to recognize that Oracle will automatically generate a unique index for this column. This should not be overlooked in capacity planning.

The tablespace Contact_Main does not exist yet, but scripts referencing the tablespace help determine its size. The STORAGE specification indicates that 1 megabyte will be allocated initially, that additional extents will start at 100 kilobytes, that there will be a minimum of 1 extent and a maximum of 10 extents, and that each extent will be 10 percent larger than the previous extent. Obviously, this specification will allow the table to grow to well over 2 megabytes, which is the planned maximum. Although storage specifications can be modified using ALTER TABLE, in the additional design phase and for capacity planning purposes, it is usually best to allow for the maximum estimated size or more. This is based on the assumption that it is better to overestimate storage requirements than to underestimate them.

After DDL scripts have been created for each of the tables, scripts can be written for the tablespaces that will house them. Assume that the sample application will store all application tables in the tablespace named Contact_Main. The data file(s) created with the tablespace should be sufficiently large to contain all tables at their full size (this can be calculated based on the INITIAL, NEXT, and PCTINCREASE parameters in the STORAGE clause of each table). The script to create Contact_Main might look like Listing 17.2.

Listing 17.2. DDL script that creates a tablespace in a single data file.

```
    CREATE TABLESPACE Contact_Main
        DATAFILE '/oradata/tables/main1.dat' SIZE 10M REUSE
        DEFAULT STORAGE (   INITIAL           2K
                            NEXT              2K
                            MAXEXTENTS      100
                            PCTINCREASE       0  );
```

The DEFAULT STORAGE clause of CREATE TABLESPACE determines how space for tables will be allocated when tables are created without a STORAGE specification. Lookup tables are typically numerous and very small, so it may be desirable to create a default storage that will be sufficient to handle all lookup tables. The STORAGE clause can then be omitted from those CREATE TABLE scripts.

Performance Considerations

When designing the physical database, performance is an important consideration. There are numerous factors related to the design that will affect the overall performance of the database. These factors include the data model itself, indexing, rollback and temporary segments, and the physical location of the data on the disks.

> **NOTE**
>
> For more on performance tuning issues, see Chapter 15, "Performance Tuning and Optimizing."

A factor that can heavily impact overall performance stems from the logical model. The degree of normalization in the model often comes down to a trade-off between flexibility and performance. In the example of normalization presented in the section on the logical model, several relations were created that improved the flexibility of the model, as shown in Table 17.8.

Table 17.8. Junction table used to relate Individuals to Companies.

Individual-Company Relation	*Companies*
Individual ID (FK)	ID (PK)
Company ID (FK)	Company
	Company Notes

Entity Type
ID (PK)
Type

Separating company information from the Individuals relation added a considerable amount of flexibility. This allowed individuals to be related to more than one company, and it allowed addresses and phones to be related to either an individual or a company. Another nice feature of the normalized model is that it allows any number of phones and addresses to be related to an individual or a company as in Table 17.9.

Table 17.9. One-to-many relationships.

Addresses	Phone Numbers
ID (PK)	ID (PK)
Entity Type (FK)	Individual ID (FK)
Entity ID (FK)	Phone Number
Address Line 1	Phone Type (FK)
Address Line 2	Last Update User ID
Address Line 3	Last Update Date/Time
City (FK)	
Zip Code (FK)	
Address Type (FK)	
Last Update User ID	
Last Update Date/Time	

Address Type	Phone Type
ID (PK)	ID (PK)
Type	Type

A less useful feature of the normalized model is the separation of city and state as in Table 17.10.

Table 17.10. Separation of City and State.

Cities	States
Zip Code (PK)	Zip Code (PK)
City (CK)	State

The end result is a very flexible (but possibly overly complex) data model. Assume, for example, that one of the primary uses of the database is to generate a listing of the names of contacts and their companies, addresses, and phone numbers. This is a fairly complex query and illustrates a potential flaw in the model: Although addresses and phones can be related to either companies or individuals, there is nothing in the model that allows phones and addresses to be related to an individual at a company. Assume that, as a workaround, a third entity type is created for an individual at a company, and a rule is imposed that the Individual ID is used for that entity where an entity's ID is required as a foreign key. The phone list can be generated under this scenario, but it requires joining nine tables. Individuals must be joined to Addresses, Phone Numbers, and Individual-Company Relation, which must be joined to Companies to get the company name, and Addresses must be joined to Cities and States. In addition, Phone

Numbers and Addresses must be joined to Phone Types and Address Types to get their respective standardized type descriptions. Although joining nine tables is not a particularly difficult task, if the database contains millions of Individuals, the number of joins can have a very significant impact on performance. If this report is generated up-to-the-minute online, and the database has a high volume of transactions, the impact is further magnified.

Denormalization, the opposite of normalization, can be used to improve performance under these circumstances. By combining some of the relations, the number of joins can be reduced without sacrificing flexibility. In Table 17.11, the listed denormalizations may be appropriate.

Table 17.11. Denormalization of City and State information.

Addresses	*Phone Numbers*
ID (PK)	ID (PK)
Individual ID	Individual ID
Company ID	Company ID
Address Line 1	Phone Number
Address Line 2	Phone Type
Address Line 3	Last Update User ID
City	Last Update Date/Time
State	
Zip Code	
Address Type	
Last Update User ID	
Last Update Date/Time	

Individual-Company Relation	*Companies*
Individual ID (FK)	ID (PK)
Company ID (FK)	Company

With this model, only seven tables must be joined to generate the list, and no flexibility is lost. Note that the foreign key constraints must be removed from Individual ID and Company ID on the Addresses and Phone Numbers tables because one or the other might be NULL. Listing 17.3 demonstrates the SQL used to create the report after this denormalization.

Listing 17.3. SQL script that generates an address and phone list.

```
SELECT First_Name, Middle_Init, Last_Name, Company_Name,
       F.Type, Address_Line1, Address_Line2,
```

continues

Listing 17.3. continued

```
        Address_Line3, City, State, Zip, G.Type,
        Phone_Number
FROM    Individuals A, Individual_Company_Relation B,
        Companies C, Addresses D, Phones_Numbers E,
        Address_Types F, Phone_Types G
WHERE   A.ID = B.Individual_ID
        AND B.Company_ID = C.ID
        AND B.Individual_ID = D.Individual_ID
        AND B.Company_ID = D.Company_ID
        AND B.Individual_ID = E.Individual_ID
        AND B.Company_ID = E.Company_ID
        AND D.Address_Type = F.ID
        AND E.Phone_Type = G.ID
```

TIP

Aliasing table names with a single letter can save a lot of typing.

Additional denormalization could improve performance further, but probably at the cost of flexibility.

The previous example can also be used to illustrate the importance of indexes. Indexes can be created on single or multiple columns, and may or may not be unique. When creating an index on multiple columns, the order in which the columns are declared is particularly important, because Oracle treats the values of such an index as an aggregate. The column that will be used the most should be declared first in a multicolumn index. In the previous example, the Employee_Company_Relation table is a prime candidate for an index. If both columns are indexed in aggregate, the table itself should never be read. Individual_ID should be declared as the first column in the index because it is used for one more join. The DDL to create this column and its index might look like the script in Listing 17.4.

Listing 17.4. DDL script that creates a table and an aggregate index.

```
CREATE TABLE Individual_Company_Relation (
    Individual_ID          NUMBER(10)     NOT NULL
   ,Company_ID             NUMBER(10)     NOT NULL
)
TABLESPACE Contact_Main
STORAGE (INITIAL      50K
         NEXT              10K
         MAXEXTENTS    10  );


CREATE INDEX Indiv_Co
    ON Individual_Company_Relation (Individual_ID, Company_ID)
```

```
TABLESPACE Contact_Index
STORAGE (INITIAL        50K
         NEXT           10K
         MAXEXTENTS      10);
```

Note that the MINEXTENTS parameter to the STORAGE clause was not used. The default value of 1 is acceptable in most circumstances.

The creation of indexes should be planned very carefully, because improper use of indexes can have a damaging effect on performance. Even where indexes improve the performance of SELECT statements, they have a negative impact on INSERTs and UPDATEs, because the indexes must be modified in addition to the tables.

The column attributes themselves play a role in performance as well. Wherever possible, integers should be used as keys because they can be compared faster than any other data type. Column and table constraints should be avoided because they must be checked whenever a value is inserted or updated. Although these constraints are often necessary, integrity should be enforced by other means when it is possible to do so safely.

Rollback segments also play an important role in the overall performance of the database. As the name would imply, Oracle uses rollback segments as temporary storage for data needed to reverse a transaction. This data must be stored until the transaction is committed. Rollback segments must be sufficiently large to store this data for all transactions occurring at a given time. If rollback segments are not large enough, transactions will fail.

To properly estimate the size of the rollback segments needed, the designer must know how many users will be submitting transactions, and the maximum size of the rows affected by a single transaction. In many large databases, transactions are initiated by batch processes used to load and update data from external sources, or to create summary tables. These batch processes often generate much larger transactions than the user community, and should be considered when planning rollback segments. A rollback segment, like other database objects, can be created with a script, as demonstrated in Listing 17.5.

Listing 17.5. DDL script that creates a rollback segment and brings it online.

```
CREATE PUBLIC ROLLBACK SEGMENT contact_rbs1
    TABLESPACE contact_rb_segs
    STORAGE (INITIAL         100K
             NEXT            100K
             OPTIMAL         500K
             MAXEXTENTS      100);

ALTER ROLLBACK SEGMENT contact_rbs1 ONLINE;
```

> **NOTE**
>
> When a rollback segment is created, it is not immediately available for use. The ALTER ROLLBACK SEGMENT command must be issued to bring the rollback segment ONLINE before it can be used.

The OPTIMAL parameter to the STORAGE clause indicates that when extents have been created, they will not be deallocated below this value. This, in effect, sets the minimum size of the rollback segment after that threshold is reached.

Rollback segments are typically created in a separate tablespace. The size of the data files in this tablespace should be sufficient to hold the rollback segments at their maximum extents.

Another performance consideration relates to the creation of temporary segments. Temporary segments are similar to rollback segments, except that they are used to store result sets rather than transaction information. When a SELECT statement produces a result set that is too large to be stored in memory, a temporary table is created to store the results until the cursor is closed. Temporary tables may also be created by Oracle to store temporary result sets for complex joins or unions. As with rollback segments, these temporary segments must be sufficiently large to store this data, or SELECT statements may fail.

Temporary segments must be assigned to users explicitly. If no temporary segment is assigned, the SYSTEM tablespace is used by default. It is preferable to create a separate tablespace for these temporary segments, and assign it to users using the TEMPORARY TABLESPACE clause of the CREATE USER command. When designing temporary tablespaces, keep in mind any batch processes that may create large cursors. These, too, will require the use of temporary segments.

It may be preferable to create separate segments (both temporary and rollback) for different groups of users, based on the transactions and result sets generated by different groups of users.

Other performance considerations relate to the physical layout of files on disk. Proper use of multiple disks and controllers, clustering, and striping can improve performance greatly in certain situations.

In the example on the creation of indexes (see Listing 17.4), notice that the table and the index were created in separate tablespaces. The example assumes that the tablespaces were created on separate disks, using separate controllers. Keeping indexes on separate physical devices with separate controllers allows the index and the tables to be read almost simultaneously, and minimizes the movement of the read/write heads. In the sample SQL statement, this would allow the read/write head of one drive to continue reading the index while a separate controller reads the Addresses and Phones tables to find the corresponding values. If the index were on the same disk, either the whole index would have to be read into memory before the table, or the heads would have to move back and forth, reading part of the index and part of the table.

The use of separate controllers and disks also applies to rollback and temporary segments. In an ideal configuration, tables, indexes, rollback segments, and temporary segments would all be on separate disks using separate controllers. This configuration would greatly improve overall performance, particularly for batch processes such as the creation of summary tables. In practice, however, this configuration is rarely possible. Regardless of the actual hardware configuration, the designer should carefully consider how these data files will be accessed. The design should attempt to minimize the movement of read/write heads for the most common or mission-critical database operations.

Clustering is another way to improve performance through physical layout on the disk. It is sometimes advantageous to create an indexed cluster for a group of tables that are frequently joined. The index used to join the tables in the cluster must be declared as part of the cluster. Tables created in the cluster must specify this index in the CLUSTER clause of the CREATE TABLE statement. When an indexed cluster is created, each value for the cluster index (or cluster key) is stored only once. The rows of the tables that contain the clustered key value are physically stored together, as if already joined. This method minimizes the movement of read/write heads when accessing these tables and conserves disk space by storing the key value only once.

In the contact manager example, assume that the users will typically be contacting individuals by telephone, and that they will be retrieving this information much more frequently than they will be updating it. Clustering the Individuals and Phone Numbers relations should be considered in this case. The DDL script in Listing 17.6 illustrates how this cluster might be created.

Listing 17.6. DDL script that creates an indexed cluster.

```
CREATE CLUSTER Individual_Phone_Numbers

(Individual_ID      NUMBER(10))

SIZE    256

STORAGE (INITIAL        1M
         NEXT           1M
         MAXEXTENTS     100
         PCTINCREASE    10);


CREATE TABLE Individuals (
        Individual_ID         NUMBER(10)    PRIMARY KEY
        ,Last_Name            VARCHAR2(30)  NOT NULL
        ,First_Name           VARCHAR2(20)  NOT NULL
        ,Middle_Initial       CHAR(1)
        ,Last_Updt_User       VARCHAR2(20)  NOT NULL
        ,Last_Updt_Timestamp  DATE          NOT NULL
)
CLUSTER Individual_Phone_Numbers(Individual_ID);


CREATE TABLE Phone_Numbers (
        Phone_ID              NUMBER(10)    PRIMARY KEY
        ,Individual_ID        NUMBER(10)    NOT NULL
        ,Company_ID           NUMBER(10)    NOT NULL
        ,Phone_Number         NUMBER(10)    NOT NULL
```

continues

Listing 17.6. continued

```
        ,Phone_Type_ID         NUMBER(10)    NOT NULL
        ,Last_Updt_User        VARCHAR2(20)  NOT NULL
        ,Last_Updt_Timestamp   DATE          NOT NULL
)
CLUSTER Individual_Phone_Numbers(Individual_ID);


CREATE INDEX Indiv_Phone on CLUSTER Individual_Phone_Numbers;
```

> **NOTE**
>
> The storage specification is not needed for the individual tables. Their rows will be stored in the cluster, and the storage specification for the cluster will be used by all objects that it will contain.

In Listing 17.6, the SIZE keyword indicates the size in bytes needed to store the rows corresponding to one key value. The size is always rounded up to the nearest block size. In the example, because the cluster key is stored only once, it will take only 245 bytes to store the rows for each cluster key. The example assumes that 256 bytes is the closest block size.

A second type of cluster, known as a hash key cluster, can also be utilized to improve performance. Rather than store rows based on a common indexed key, rows are stored together based on a common hash value, which is not physically stored in the database. The hash value is calculated at run-time, using either a user-defined function or Oracle's internal hashing function. Although this reduces physical disk accesses, hash key clustering should be used only on small tables, or tables that will have a maximum size that is known at design time. This is because the number of hash keys is fixed at design time, and resolving collisions requires additional reads.

Clustering should not be overused because there can be a negative impact on performance when clustered tables are accessed separately. Insert, update, and delete operations on clustered tables will typically be slower as well. For these reasons, the designer should carefully consider how tables will be used before creating a cluster.

Striping is a technique that consists of spreading a large database object over multiple disks. Performance can be greatly improved by striping, particularly when large tables are accessed by full table scans. The striping of a particular table can be forced by creating a tablespace with multiple data files on separate disks, each of which is smaller than the table itself. To provide maximum control over how the table is striped, it should be the only object in the tablespace. Listing 17.7 provides one example of how striping can be accomplished in Oracle.

Listing 17.7. An example of striping.

```
CREATE TABLESPACE Individual_Stripes
    DATAFILE 'disk1/oradata/stripe1.dat' SIZE 100K REUSE,
```

```
                        'disk2/oradata/stripe2.dat' SIZE 100K REUSE
         DEFAULT STORAGE (  INITIAL          200K
                            NEXT             200K
                            MAXEXTENTS       100
                            PCTINCREASE        0  );

    CREATE TABLE Individuals (
            Individual_ID          NUMBER(10)    PRIMARY KEY
           ,Last_Name              VARCHAR2(30)  NOT NULL
           ,First_Name             VARCHAR2(20)  NOT NULL
           ,Middle_Initial         CHAR(1)
           ,Last_Updt_User         VARCHAR2(20)  NOT NULL
           ,Last_Updt_Timestamp    DATE          NOT NULL
    )
    TABLESPACE Individual_Stripes
         STORAGE (INITIAL          90K
                  NEXT             90K
                  MINEXTENTS        2
                  MAXEXTENTS      100
                  PCTINCREASE       0  );
```

Obviously, a third extent will not be able to be allocated for this table, making this approach to striping a high maintenance proposition. The size of the table must be continually monitored, and new data files must be added to the tablespace when needed, using the ALTER TABLESPACE command with ADD DATAFILE. Although this approach requires additional maintenance, performance gains can be very significant, particularly if the disks have separate controllers. The designer should consider the trade-offs carefully before recommending that a table be striped.

Capacity Planning

Capacity planning is important in ensuring that adequate storage is available for future growth. The DDL scripts for each database object are invaluable in determining the overall storage required by the database. In fact, the process of capacity planning actually begins with the DDL scripts.

It starts with defining the column attributes. These column attributes, in turn, determine the size of each row in the table. The column attributes also determine the size of each row in indexes created on the columns. These attributes, combined with the estimated total number of rows (including provisions for future growth), are used in defining the storage clause for tables and indexes. For purposes of capacity planning, it should be assumed that all objects will reach their maximum extents.

CAUTION

The MAXEXTENTS parameter to the STORAGE clause has an upper limit that is determined by the operating system and file system environment in which the database resides. It is a bad practice to set MAXEXTENTS equal to the maximum allowable value. If the object grows more than expected, the NEXT parameter can be changed using ALTER *object_type*. If the maximum extents have already been allocated, however, this will have no effect. In this situation, the size of the object cannot be extended unless MAXEXTENTS can be increased.

The next step is creating DDL for tablespaces. The data file(s) created by these scripts should be sufficiently large to contain all objects that they will contain. When determining the size of the data files, it should be assumed that all objects within the tablespace will reach their maximum size, as defined by the STORAGE clause in the DDL script for each object.

The total size of the database can then be determined by simply adding the sizes of the data files. Never assume, however, that this estimate is accurate and complete. Also, there are a number of additional considerations to be made.

TIP

Remember to consider the sizes of log files. These are defined when the database is created.

In capacity planning, the designer must accommodate for unexpected growth. As a general rule of thumb, at least 25 percent (preferably 50 percent) of each disk should be free after the initial installation. This will allow additional data files to be created wherever necessary if tables grow larger than expected. It is common to experience unanticipated growth, and it is even more common to underestimate the requirements for temporary and rollback segments, or to identify the need for additional indexes after the initial design is complete.

The initial hardware configuration and data file layout should accommodate these possibilities. Capacity limitations can be crippling in the event that additional rollback segments or temporary segments cannot be created when needed.

For this reason, the importance of capacity planning should not be underestimated.

Summary

Designing a database is a methodical process. It begins with defining the requirements of the application. Entities and attributes are grouped into a logical data model that meets the business needs. The logical data model can be represented graphically as an Entity-Relationship diagram. These entities and attributes are then translated into a physical model. The physical model is when data types and column constraints are defined. The normalization process is used to eliminate redundancy of data. Denormalization is a process of breaking the normalization rules to gain performance increases. A well-designed database is important for future expansion as well as yielding ease of application programming.

Object-Oriented Programming with Packages

18

by Advanced Information Systems, Inc.

Although Oracle is a relational database, (as opposed to an object-oriented database), it provides a very powerful object-oriented feature in its implementation of packages. An Oracle package is a group of procedures, functions, variables, constants, cursors, and type declarations that function as a logical unit. Packages provide many of the characteristics typically associated with object-oriented languages, including encapsulation, information hiding, and function overloading.

Packages can also provide improved performance because when a packaged object is referenced, the entire package is loaded into memory. This reduces or eliminates disk I/O for subsequent calls to objects in the package. As a result, these calls execute more quickly than similar calls to stand-alone functions and procedures, which must be read from disk as requested.

There are two parts to a package: the package specification and the package body. The *package specification* provides the interface through which applications and other subprograms access packaged objects. The *package body* contains the actual code for objects in the specification, as well as any declarations and subprograms that are private to the package.

If a package specification has only variables, constants, and type declarations, it need not have a body at all. This independence from the body of the package enables the specification to be compiled separately, even when a body is required. This can improve the development process by enabling developers to define the application interface before writing the underlying code. Objects referencing the package are dependent only on the specification. Therefore, the package body can also be compiled independently from the specification without affecting any external references, provided that there are no changes to the interface.

The following sections demonstrate the creation of package specifications and bodies, highlighting key features. In addition to PL/SQL, an example is provided in C++ to illustrate the use of Oracle packages in object-oriented client applications.

The Package Specification

The package specification must contain all objects that will be accessed by external subprograms or applications. It can be viewed as the public declarations section of the package. You can construct packages to perform all operations on an underlying database object or to perform operations on groups of similar objects. Any logical grouping of data and subprograms is an acceptable candidate for a package, as dictated by the application or applications that will be accessing the database.

Listing 18.1 shows an example of a package specification that encapsulates methods for maintaining lookup tables in the database.

Listing 18.1. This package specification contains functions used to maintain lookup tables.

```
CREATE OR REPLACE PACKAGE lookup_admin AS
    FUNCTION add_address_type(description VARCHAR2) RETURN NUMBER;
    FUNCTION add_phone_type(description VARCHAR2) RETURN NUMBER;
    FUNCTION add_contact_type(description VARCHAR2) RETURN NUMBER;
    FUNCTION add_contact_method(description VARCHAR2)
            RETURN NUMBER;
    FUNCTION add_contact_reason(description VARCHAR2)
            RETURN NUMBER;

    /* add update and delete functions here */

END lookup_admin;
```

In addition to functions and procedures, the package specification can contain variables, constants, and user-defined exceptions and data types. The code example in Listing 18.2 includes a user-defined data type based on an underlying table and provides functions to operate on the table.

Listing 18.2. This package specification contains a user-defined data type.

```
CREATE OR REPLACE PACKAGE manage_individuals AS
    TYPE indiv_rec IS RECORD(
        ID              NUMBER(10)
        ,last_name      VARCHAR2(30)
        ,first_name     VARCHAR2(30)
        ,notes          VARCHAR2(255)
        ,date_of_birth  DATE
        ,last_updt_user VARCHAR2(20)
        ,last_updt_date DATE
    );
    FUNCTION insert_individual(indiv_in INDIV_REC) RETURN NUMBER;
    FUNCTION update_individual(indiv_in INDIV_REC) RETURN NUMBER;
    FUNCTION delete_individual(indiv_in INDIV_REC) RETURN NUMBER;
END manage_individuals;
```

Perhaps the most powerful feature of packaged functions and procedures is *overloading*. Overloading enables a single function or procedure to accept different sets of parameters. To overload a packaged subprogram in Oracle, simply declare it separately for each desired parameter list, as shown in Listing 18.3.

Listing 18.3. This package specification demonstrates function overloading.

```
CREATE OR REPLACE PACKAGE manage_individuals AS
    FUNCTION insert_individual(last_in VARCHAR2, first_in VARCHAR2)
            RETURN NUMBER;
    FUNCTION insert_individual(last_in VARCHAR2, first_in VARCHAR2,
```

continues

Listing 18.3. continued

```
            notes_in VARCHAR2) RETURN NUMBER;
    FUNCTION insert_individual(last_in VARCHAR2, first_in VARCHAR2,
            d_o_b DATE, notes_in VARCHAR2) RETURN NUMBER;
    FUNCTION insert_individual(last_in VARCHAR2, first_in VARCHAR2,
            d_o_b DATE) RETURN NUMBER;

    /* add update and delete functions here */

END manage_individuals;
```

> **CAUTION**
>
> Be careful to avoid ambiguous parameter lists. For example, if the *d_o_b* parameter in the fourth function declaration of Listing 18.3 was defined as type VARCHAR2, it would become indistinguishable from the second function declaration. In the context of Listing 18.3, that would result in values being inserted into the wrong columns.

You should recompile the package specification as infrequently as possible. Other packaged and stand-alone subprograms that reference objects in the package specification will be invalidated when it is recompiled. As a result, objects referencing the package specification must also be recompiled every time the specification is recompiled.

The Package Body

The package body contains the code for all subprograms defined in the specification, as well as any private variables, constants, cursors, data types, or subprograms. Objects declared within the package body are accessible only by other objects within the body. This enables you to use the package body to hide information and encapsulate subprograms within the package. However, objects within the package body can reference objects in other package specifications, as well as stand-alone objects.

A package body cannot exist without a package declaration. If the body does not contain all subprograms and cursors declared in the specification, or if declarations in the body are in conflict with declarations in the specification, compilation errors result. However, you can compile the body separately from the specification, which is extremely useful when you are debugging packaged subprograms.

Packaged subprograms that contain explicit commits and rollbacks cannot be accessed by triggers or other subprograms that apply transactions. You should keep this in mind when you are designing packages, along with the effects of any implicit commits and rollbacks that might occur. Transactions applied within a packaged subprogram are rolled back implicitly when an unhandled exception occurs. An implicit commit occurs for all uncommitted transactions when the current session is terminated. In general, packaged subprograms involving transactions should not participate in transactions with other subprograms and should not be referenced by triggers. It is usually preferable to explicitly commit or roll back transactions that occur within packaged subprograms.

Package Variables and Initialization

The first time a packaged object is referenced, the entire package is loaded into memory. It is important to note that each session gets its own instance of package variables. Packaged data cannot be shared across sessions, and all values stored for a particular session are lost when the session ends.

Variables declared within the package body, but outside of subprograms, hold their values for the life of the session. As with stand-alone functions and procedures, variables declared within packaged subprograms persist only within the scope of the subprograms in which they are declared.

Variables and cursors declared at the package level can be accessed by all subprograms within the package body. Any code in the body of the package itself is executed only once, when the package is first loaded. For this reason, package code is typically used only to initialize package variables. Listing 18.4, which is a portion of the package body for the specification in Listing 18.1, uses only one statement in the package body.

Listing 18.4. This package body provides functions to insert records into lookup tables.

```
CREATE OR REPLACE PACKAGE BODY lookup_admin AS
    user_id VARCHAR2(20);

    FUNCTION add_address_type(description VARCHAR2) RETURN NUMBER
    IS
    BEGIN
        INSERT INTO address_type VALUES(address_type_ids.nextval,
                    description, user_id, sysdate);
        COMMIT;
        RETURN(0);
    EXCEPTION
        WHEN OTHERS THEN
            ROLLBACK;
            RETURN(-1);
    END add_address_type;

    /* all functions in the specification must be defined in the body */

BEGIN
    SELECT user INTO user_id FROM dual;
END lookup_admin;
```

Packaged subprograms and data are accessed using *owner.package_name.object_name* notation. You can create public synonyms for packages, as with other objects, to eliminate the need for the owner prefix.

Note that the SELECT statement in the package body is executed only once, which is somewhat of an optimization when multiple transactions are applied using the functions in the package. For example, the SELECT statement stores the user_id upon package instantiation (first function call). All subsequent calls do not execute the SELECT statement.

To this point, the code listings in this chapter have included functions in preference to procedures. Each of these functions returns a value that indicates the success or failure of the operation it performs. The same result can be achieved by using an output parameter in a procedure, as illustrated by the package specification in Listing 18.5, which simply redefines the functions declared in Listing 18.3 as procedures.

Listing 18.5. This package specification demonstrates the use of an output parameter in an overloaded procedure.

```
CREATE OR REPLACE PACKAGE manage_individuals AS
    PROCEDURE insert_individual(ret_code OUT NUMBER,
            last_in IN VARCHAR2, first_in IN VARCHAR2);
    PROCEDURE insert_individual(ret_code OUT NUMBER,
            last_in IN VARCHAR2, first_in IN VARCHAR2,
            notes_in IN VARCHAR2);
    PROCEDURE insert_individual(ret_code OUT NUMBER,
            last_in IN VARCHAR2, first_in IN VARCHAR2,
            d_o_b IN DATE, notes_in IN VARCHAR2);
    PROCEDURE insert_individual(ret_code OUT NUMBER,
            last_in IN VARCHAR2, first_in IN VARCHAR2,
            d_o_b IN DATE);

    /* add update and delete functions here */

END manage_individuals;
```

The use of functions instead of procedures is merely a design consideration based on the assumption that it is better to clearly distinguish return codes from actual data.

Overloading

The capability to overload a subprogram is one of the primary advantages of packages. This feature is not available to stand-alone procedures and functions. Overloading is particularly useful when you are inserting records into tables with optional fields, or when you are updating existing records. When overloading is implemented correctly, you can minimize the data passed between the application and the database and reduce the possibility of error. Listing 18.6 shows an example of function overloading in the package body, based on the package specification in Listing 18.3.

Listing 18.6. This package demonstrates function overloading.

```
CREATE OR REPLACE PACKAGE BODY manage_individuals AS
    user_id VARCHAR2(20);

    FUNCTION insert_individual(last_in VARCHAR2, first_in VARCHAR2)
            RETURN NUMBER
    IS
        new_id NUMBER;
    BEGIN
        SELECT individual_ids.nextval INTO new_id FROM dual;
        INSERT INTO individual (id, last_name, first_name,
                                last_updt_user, last_updt_date)
            VALUES (new_id, last_in, first_in, user_id, sysdate);
      COMMIT;
    RETURN(new_id);
    EXCEPTION
        WHEN OTHERS THEN
            ROLLBACK;
            RETURN(-1);
    END insert_individual;

    FUNCTION insert_individual(last_in VARCHAR2, first_in VARCHAR2,
            notes_in VARCHAR2) RETURN NUMBER
    IS
        new_id NUMBER;
    BEGIN
        SELECT individual_ids.nextval INTO new_id FROM dual;
        INSERT INTO individual (id, last_name, first_name, notes,
                                last_updt_user, last_updt_date)
            VALUES (new_id, last_in, first_in, notes_in, user_id,
                    sysdate);
      COMMIT;
      RETURN(new_id);
    EXCEPTION
        WHEN OTHERS THEN
            ROLLBACK;
            RETURN(-1);
    END insert_individual;

    FUNCTION insert_individual(last_in VARCHAR2, first_in VARCHAR2,
            d_o_b DATE, notes_in VARCHAR2) RETURN NUMBER
    IS
        new_id NUMBER;
    BEGIN
        SELECT individual_ids.nextval INTO new_id FROM dual;
        INSERT INTO individual (id, last_name, first_name,
            date_of_birth, notes, last_updt_user, last_updt_date)
        VALUES (new_id, last_in, first_in, d_o_b, notes_in,
                user_id, sysdate);
        COMMIT;
      RETURN(new_id);
    EXCEPTION
      WHEN OTHERS THEN
            ROLLBACK;
            RETURN(-1);
    END insert_individual;
```

continues

Listing 18.6. continued

```
FUNCTION insert_individual(last_in VARCHAR2, first_in VARCHAR2,
        d_o_b DATE) RETURN NUMBER
IS
    new_id NUMBER;
BEGIN
    SELECT individual_ids.nextval INTO new_id FROM dual;
    INSERT INTO individual (id, last_name, first_name,
                date_of_birth, last_updt_user, last_updt_date)
        VALUES (new_id, last_in, first_in, d_o_b, user_id,
                sysdate);
  COMMIT;
 RETURN(new_id);
EXCEPTION
    WHEN OTHERS THEN
        ROLLBACK;
        RETURN(-1);
END insert_individual;

BEGIN
    SELECT user INTO user_id FROM dual;
END manage_individuals;
```

Consider how you might accomplish this insert by using a user-defined record type or a single function that accepts all values. Using either alternative, applications calling the packaged insert function would have to ensure that null values are supplied for the fields for which no data exists. It is a much better programming practice to encapsulate all default values within the packaged routines rather than in various calling routines.

The potential for problems is magnified for update operations. In update operations, the function would need logic to determine which fields are actually being updated or would have to update all columns in the table. In the latter case, the application would then be responsible for supplying all values accurately to avoid accidental column updates. Function overloading simplifies application development by enabling applications to supply only the values required for each transaction. Passing only the values needed to perform the update can improve performance through minimizing disk writes of unnecessary data.

Retrieving Results

Oracle stored procedures and functions currently do not support the retrieval of result sets. However, you can overcome this limitation by using a packaged subprogram. Remember that cursors declared at the package level persist for the duration of the session. This enables a set of functions to open a cursor and perform operations on it, maintaining the current position within the cursor from one call to the next. Output parameters can be used to pass data from packaged functions to the calling application. Listing 18.7 shows an example of how these features can be used to return result sets to an application from a packaged subprogram.

Listing 18.7. This code example uses a packaged cursor and functions to retrieve a result set.

```
CREATE OR REPLACE PACKAGE address_type_info AS
    FUNCTION get_next_address_type(id_out OUT NUMBER,
        description_out OUT VARCHAR2) RETURN NUMBER;
    FUNCTION close_address_type RETURN NUMBER;
    FUNCTION reopen_address_type RETURN NUMBER;
END address_type_info;

CREATE OR REPLACE PACKAGE BODY address_type_info AS
    last_id NUMBER(10);
    CURSOR c1 IS SELECT id, description FROM address_type;

    FUNCTION get_next_address_type(id_out OUT NUMBER,
            description_out OUT VARCHAR2) RETURN NUMBER
    IS
        end_of_cursor EXCEPTION;
        temp_id       NUMBER(10);
        temp_desc     VARCHAR2(40);
    BEGIN
    FETCH c1 INTO temp_id, temp_desc;
        IF (temp_id = last_id) THEN
            RAISE end_of_cursor;
        ELSE
            last_id := temp_id;
            id_out := temp_id;
            description_out := temp_desc;
        END IF;
        RETURN(0);
    EXCEPTION
        WHEN end_of_cursor THEN
            RETURN(1);
        WHEN OTHERS THEN
            RETURN(-1);
    END get_next_address_type;

    FUNCTION close_address_type RETURN NUMBER
    IS
    BEGIN
        CLOSE c1;
        RETURN(0);
    EXCEPTION
        WHEN OTHERS THEN
            RETURN(-1);
    END close_address_type;

    FUNCTION reopen_address_type RETURN NUMBER
    IS
    BEGIN
        OPEN c1;
        RETURN(0);
    EXCEPTION
        WHEN OTHERS THEN
            RETURN(-1);
    END reopen_address_type;
BEGIN
    OPEN c1;
END address_type_info;
```

Note that the cursor is opened in the body of the package itself. To retrieve the first row, an application need only call address_type_info.get_next_address_type to retrieve the first row. When this function returns 1, it informs the calling application that the end of the cursor has been reached. The application should then call address_type_info.close_address_type. The OPEN c1 statement in the body of the cursor will be executed only once, when the package is first loaded. In order to access the cursor a second time, the application must first call address_type_info.reopen_address_type. Subsequent calls to address_type_info. get_next_address_type can then be used to retrieve rows.

Although this approach might be somewhat cumbersome, it might be acceptable for retrieving small result sets. This method could also be useful in producing reports that require breaks and subtotals. You could employ additional package-level variables to determine breakpoints and hold summary information as each row is returned to the application. This is just one example of how packages can be used to overcome many of the limitations of PL/SQL.

Exception Handling

Oracle provides many predefined exceptions, and a number of functions and procedures that can be used to handle them. Oracle implicitly raises predefined exceptions when they occur in PL/SQL blocks. Among these, the OTHERS exception is extremely valuable because it can be used as a catch-all (all other exceptions that are not explicitly handled), which in many cases is all that is needed. Even when specific handlers are used, using the OTHERS exception is a good idea. Using this exception prevents an application from bombing because of an unhandled error in a subprogram.

In some cases, defining an exception that does not exist in Oracle might be useful. User-defined exceptions are declared in much the same way as variables. For example, in Listing 18.7, the user-defined exception end_of_cursor is declared in the get_next_address_type function. Control is passed to the exception handler using the RAISE statement. User-defined exceptions are particularly useful in performing sanity checks within PL/SQL blocks. You can use a package variable to associate user-defined text with an exception, which can be accessed by the application through an additional packaged subprogram. Listing 18.8 demonstrates how packaged constructs can be used to give an application additional information concerning a user-defined error.

Listing 18.8. A demonstration of user-defined exception handling.

```
CREATE OR REPLACE PACKAGE manage_individuals AS
    FUNCTION insert_individual(last_in VARCHAR2, first_in VARCHAR2,
            d_o_b DATE, notes_in VARCHAR2) RETURN NUMBER;
    FUNCTION get_error_text(text_out OUT VARCHAR2) RETURN NUMBER;
END manage_individuals;

CREATE OR REPLACE PACKAGE BODY manage_individuals AS
    user_id         VARCHAR2(20);
```

```
    invalid_b_day  EXCEPTION;
    error_text     VARCHAR2(255);

    FUNCTION insert_individual(last_in VARCHAR2, first_in VARCHAR2,
            d_o_b DATE, notes_in VARCHAR2) RETURN NUMBER
    IS
        new_id          NUMBER;
        temp_bd         VARCHAR2(20);
        temp_today      VARCHAR2(20);
    BEGIN
        temp_bd:=TO_CHAR(d_o_b, 'MM-DD-YYYY',
                            'nls_date_language = American');
        SELECT TO_CHAR(sysdate, 'MM-DD-YYYY',
                    'nls_date_language = American')
            INTO temp_today FROM dual;
        IF ((to_date(temp_bd, 'MM-DD-YYYY',
            'nls_date_language = American')  >
            to_date(temp_today, 'MM-DD-YYYY',
            'nls_date_language = American')) OR
            ((SUBSTR(temp_today, 7, 4) - SUBSTR(temp_bd, 7, 4))
            > 100)) THEN
            RAISE invalid_b_day;
        ELSE
            SELECT individual_ids.nextval INTO new_id FROM dual;
            INSERT INTO individual (id, last_name, first_name,
                        date_of_birth, notes, last_updt_user,
                        last_updt_date) VALUES (new_id, last_in,
                        first_in, d_o_b, notes_in, user_id,
                        sysdate);
            error_text:= ' ';
            RETURN(new_id);
        END IF;
    EXCEPTION
        WHEN invalid_b_day THEN
            error_text:= 'Date of birth outside normal range.';
            RETURN(-11);
        WHEN OTHERS THEN
            error_text:=SUBSTR(SQLERRM, 1, 255);
            RETURN(-1);
    END insert_individual;

    FUNCTION get_error_text(text_out OUT VARCHAR2) RETURN NUMBER
    IS
    BEGIN
        text_out:=error_text;
        RETURN(0);
    EXCEPTION
        WHEN OTHERS THEN
            text_out:='Unable to retrieve error information.';
            RETURN(-1);
    END get_error_text;

BEGIN
    SELECT user INTO user_id FROM dual;
END manage_individuals;
```

The example in Listing 18.8 uses a package-level variable to store error text and provides a function to retrieve error text. Note the use of the predefined function SQLERRM in the OTHERS handler. In this context, SQLERRM is used to copy the Oracle error message into the package variable.

The example in Listing 18.8 is just one way to deal with exceptions in packages. Oracle includes many other predefined functions used to handle exceptions, including SQLCODE, EXCEPTION_INIT, and RAISE_APPLICATION_ERROR. SQLCODE returns the Oracle error number associated with an exception; EXCEPTION_INIT enables the developer to associate a name with an Oracle error number; and RAISE_APPLICATION_ERROR raises a user-defined exception, accepting an error number and error text as parameters. The way in which exceptions are handled depends entirely on the nature of the application. What is most important is that all exceptions are handled. As a general rule, the OTHERS handler should always be used to trap all exceptions that do not have specific handlers.

Package Privileges

Using packages can greatly simplify the process of granting rights to users and roles. When you grant a user the EXECUTE privilege for a package, the user can access any data and subprograms in the package specification. In the package body, subprograms can access other packaged or stand-alone subprograms and other database objects. The user to whom EXECUTE is granted does not need to have any rights to the external objects referenced in the package body. This is another way in which packages can be used for information hiding. In Listing 18.9, the lookup_admin package from Listing 18.4 is redefined to hide the implementation of address_type_info from Listing 18.7.

Listing 18.9. A demonstration of indirect function calling.

```
CREATE OR REPLACE PACKAGE lookup_admin AS
    FUNCTION get_next_address_type(id_out OUT NUMBER,
            description_out OUT VARCHAR2) RETURN NUMBER;
    FUNCTION close_address_type RETURN NUMBER;
    FUNCTION reopen_address_type RETURN NUMBER;

    /* add get_next, close, and reopen functions */
    /* for other lookups here                    */

    FUNCTION add_address_type(description VARCHAR2) RETURN NUMBER;
    FUNCTION add_phone_type(description VARCHAR2) RETURN NUMBER;
    FUNCTION add_contact_type(description VARCHAR2) RETURN NUMBER;
    FUNCTION add_contact_method(description VARCHAR2) RETURN NUMBER;
    FUNCTION add_contact_reason(description VARCHAR2) RETURN NUMBER;

    /* add update and delete functions here */

END lookup_admin;

/
```

```
CREATE OR REPLACE PACKAGE BODY lookup_admin AS
    user_id VARCHAR2(40);
    temp_id NUMBER(10);
    temp_desc VARCHAR2(40);

    FUNCTION get_next_address_type(id_out OUT NUMBER,
            description_out OUT VARCHAR2) RETURN NUMBER
    IS
        ret NUMBER(10);
    BEGIN
        ret:=address_type_info.get_next_address_type(id_out, description_out);
        RETURN(ret);
    EXCEPTION
        WHEN OTHERS THEN
            RETURN(-1);
    END get_next_address_type;

    FUNCTION close_address_type RETURN NUMBER
    IS
        ret NUMBER(10);
    BEGIN
        ret:=address_type_info.close_address_type;
        RETURN(ret);
    EXCEPTION
        WHEN OTHERS THEN
            RETURN(-1);
    END close_address_type;

    FUNCTION reopen_address_type RETURN NUMBER
    IS
        ret NUMBER(10);
    BEGIN
        ret:=address_type_info.reopen_address_type;
        RETURN(ret);
    EXCEPTION
        WHEN OTHERS THEN
            RETURN(-1);
    END reopen_address_type;


BEGIN
    SELECT USER INTO user_id FROM dual;
END lookup_admin;
```

When a user is granted the EXECUTE privilege on `lookup_admin`, as defined in Listing 18.9, the user gains indirect access to `address_type_info`, as well as the sequences and lookup tables referenced in the insert functions. Unless other privileges have been granted, however, the user will not be able to access the objects directly. For example, the user can read a row from the address_type table using `lookup_admin.get_next_address_type` but will not be able to access `address_type_info.get_next_address_type` directly, or even use SELECT * FROM address_type. This is an example of how packages can be used to abstract the details of implementation from users and application interfaces.

Granting privileges at the package level has the additional advantage of simplifying the entire process of granting rights to users and roles. This should be taken into consideration when you design packages. For example, if a particular role should have read-only access to the lookup tables referenced in Listing 18.9, you should create a separate package that does not include the insert functions.

Accessing Oracle Packages from Client Applications

Oracle's implementation of the package fits the object model used in C++ particularly well, and using packages exclusively can simplify the process of designing the client application. The development of the client application, in many cases, can begin with the duplication of the structures and subprograms defined in the database packages.

Listing 18.9 provides an example of a C++ class that is based on database objects, including packaged constructs. The data members of the class correspond to the columns in a table, and the Insert() member function of the Individual class is mapped to the overloaded insert functions in the manage_individuals package from Listing 18.6. The code example in Listing 18.10 is intended to demonstrate how overloaded C++ member functions can be mapped directly to overloaded functions in Oracle packages, not to illustrate good C++ programming technique.

Listing 18.10. A C++ class illustrating overloading using a host language.

```
class Individual
{
    public:
        long ID;
        char LastName[30];
        char FirstName[30];
        char DateOfBirth[10];    /* DD-MON-YY */
        char Notes[255];
        char LastUpdateUser[20];
        char LastUpdateTS[20];    /* DD-MM-YYYY HH:MI:SS */

        int  Insert(OSession SessionHandle, char* Last, char* First);
        int  Insert(OSession SessionHandle, char* Last, char* First,
                char* Notes_Or_DOB);
        int  Insert(OSession SessionHandle, char* Last, char* First,
                char* DateOfBirth, char* Notes);
};
```

The data members of the Individual class are identical to the columns of the Individual table in Oracle, with one exception. The date of birth is stored as a string, requiring the overloaded form Individual::Insert(char*, char*, char*) to be able to distinguish a date from ordinary text in order to call the proper function in Oracle.

Perhaps a better implementation of the Individual class would include an overloaded constructor to perform the insertion so that the data members could be protected. Declaring the data members as public is analogous to declaring variables in an Oracle package specification.

Despite the shortcomings of the example in Listing 18.10, it demonstrates the point that if Oracle packages are designed properly they can be replicated in the client application. This can simplify the design of the client application, as well as ensure consistency in the object models being used throughout the system.

Many Windows development tools use ODBC to communicate with the database. Unfortunately, the current Oracle ODBC driver does not support the access of packaged objects through ODBC. In order to access packaged objects, you must create stand-alone functions and subprograms to call the packaged objects from within Oracle. Listing 18.10 is an example of a stub that can be used to access packaged functions. Because overloading is not allowed in stand-alone functions and procedures, you must create separate subprograms to access each form of the overloaded packaged subprogram.

When you are developing ODBC applications, you should carefully consider this limitation in the design process. The necessity of external stubs might nullify many of the advantages to using packages. User-defined data types and exceptions, variables, and cursors cannot be accessed from package specifications, and overloading is nullified by the requirement of separate external stubs corresponding to each form of the overloaded function. In addition, you must grant rights to each external stub that accesses the package. In some cases, there is no advantage to using packages when the database is being accessed through ODBC. The exception is when the application needs user-defined types or persistent variables. These can be packaged and accessed indirectly through the external stubs, such as the example in Listing 18.11.

Listing 18.11. This stand-alone function is needed to access a packaged function through ODBC.

```
CREATE OR REPLACE FUNCTION ins_indiv_stub1
(last_in   IN VARCHAR2
,first_in IN VARCHAR2)
RETURN NUMBER

IS
    ret NUMBER;
BEGIN
    ret:=manage_individuals.insert_individual(last_in, first_in, SYSDATE, 'new
    individual');
    RETURN(ret);
END ins_indiv_stub1;
```

Products that communicate with SQL*Net and the Oracle Call Interface directly can be used to overcome this ODBC-specific limitation. Using packages in an ODBC application is also inconsistent with one of the primary goals of ODBC, which is to provide database independence.

Object-Oriented Concepts

As mentioned previously, Oracle packages provide several features that are typically associated with object-oriented programming. Among these are encapsulation, information hiding, and function overloading. In this section you will learn additional object-oriented features that apply not to the database itself, but to several of Oracle's newest development tools. C++, in particular, is used to illustrate these concepts.

Encapsulation is simply the grouping of related data, procedures, and functions to form a collection. An *object*, or a package, is simply a name for this encapsulated data and methods for operating on it. In C++, an object is implemented as a class or an instance of a class. The class itself defines the object's data and methods, whereas an *instance* contains the data specific to one particular object belonging to the class. In terms of Oracle packages, the package specification and package body make up the class, whereas each session gets a specific instance of the class.

In C++ terminology, objects are created and destroyed using constructors and destructors. A constructor allocates memory for the new instance of the object and loads it, whereas a destructor unloads the object and frees memory allocated to it. You have the option of placing code in the constructor and destructor of an object. In Oracle, an instance of a package is constructed when it is first referenced in a session and destructed when the session ends. Code in the body of the package itself is fired when an instance is constructed. No code can be specified for the destructor of a package.

Listing 18.12 provides a simple example of an object in C++, with a single constructor and a single destructor. Note that in C++ the constructor has the same name as the class and returns a pointer to an instance of an object belonging to the class. Although the arguments to the constructor can be redefined, the return type cannot be. If no constructor is specified, the compiler creates a default constructor that simply allocates memory for the new instance and loads it. Similar rules apply to the destructor, which always has the name of the class preceded by a tilde and returns void, (nothing). In Listing 18.12, the destructor is named ~Car().

Listing 18.12. A simple class, with a constructor and destructor as the only member functions.

```
class Car {
    public:
        char      *Make;
        char      *Model;
        unsigned  Year;

        Car(char* CarMake, char* CarModel, unsigned CarYear);
        ~Car();
};

Car::Car(char* CarMake, char* CarModel, unsigned CarYear)
{
```

```
      Make = strdup(CarMake);
      Model = strdup(CarModel);
      Year = CarYear;
}

Car::~Car()
{
      free(Make);
      free(Model);
}
```

NOTE

The `free` statements in the destructor are very important. When the class is instantiated, additional memory is allocated for these data members. The default destructor will only free memory allocated for the object itself, which includes only the pointers.

To create an instance of car, declare a pointer to `Car`, which will receive the return value of the constructor:

```
Car *MyCar;
MyCar = new Car("Ford", "Mustang", 1967);
// To destroy the object, use the delete operator:
delete MyCar;
```

This simple example illustrates the encapsulation of data and methods in an object and the instantiation and destruction of an instance of the object. These concepts are the very foundation of object-oriented programming techniques.

Information hiding is a form of encapsulation in which data elements or methods can be accessed only by the methods of the object. This point was illustrated in the context of Oracle packages in several ways. In Listing 18.6, the user who last updated a record and the timestamp indicating when the record was last updated were inserted by a function, without any intervention by the user or the calling application. Tables, functions, procedures, and other database objects can also be hidden by Oracle packages as illustrated in Listing 18.9. In general, variables and constructs declared in the package specification are visible, or public. Variables and constructs declared within the package only are hidden, or private.

In C++, variables and functions can be declared as `public`, `private`, or `protected` in the class definition. Public constructs can be accessed anywhere in a program, whereas private and protected data and methods can be accessed only through member functions and member functions of `friend` classes. These subjects are discussed in greater detail in the explanation of Listing 18.14. At this point, it is only important to recognize that this is how C++ hides information. For example, if the `Car` class from Listing 18.12 were redefined as in Listing 18.13, the Mileage data member could only be accessed by the constructor and the member functions `GetMileage` and `IncrementMileage`.

Listing 18.13. A redefinition of the `Car` class, illustrating the use of the `protected` keyword.

```
class Car {
    public:
        char      *Make;
        char      *Model;
        unsigned  Year;

        Car(char* CarMake, char* CarModel, unsigned CarYear
            ,unsigned long Mileage);
        ~Car();

        unsigned long GetMileage();
        void IncrementMileage(unsigned Miles);

    protected:
        unsigned long Mileage;
};
```

If this were the extent of the implementation of the `Car` class, `Mileage` could only be increased after the instance is constructed. If `Mileage` were declared as public, however, it could be modified at any time through an assignment, such as

```
MyCar->Mileage = 10;
```

Protected data and functions can also be used to abstract implementation details, such as database transactions. The SQL used to insert a car could be declared protected, parameterized, and initialized when an instance is constructed. The application could then add a car to the database by accessing a public member function without knowing the SQL syntax, or that it even exists.

An extremely important feature of the object-oriented model is the concept of *inheritance*. Inheritance defines a class hierarchy in which a descendant class receives the member functions and data elements of the parent class to which it belongs. For example, you can create a base class without any intention of constructing the object. Base classes are often created only to be inherited from. Listing 18.14 illustrates this point in the context of the simple example of the `Car` class.

Listing 18.14. This implementation of the `Car` class illustrates the concept of inheritance.

```
class Vehicle {
    public:
        char      *Make;
        char      *Model;
        unsigned  Year;
};

class Car : public Vehicle {
```

```
public:
    Car(char* CarMake, char* CarModel, unsigned CarYear
        ,unsigned long Mileage);
    ~Car();

    unsigned long GetMileage();
    void IncrementMileage(unsigned Miles);

protected:
    unsigned long Mileage;
};
```

Note that the base class `Vehicle` enables the compiler to generate the default constructor and destructor, and that it now contains the public data members. They still exist in the `Car` class because they are inherited from `Vehicle`. The keywords `private` and `protected` are important to the behavior of inheritance. Although protected member functions can be accessed by derived classes, private members cannot be. A `friend` class can access both private and protected members. Friend classes do not inherit from the base class but have full access rights to member functions of the base class.

The `virtual` keyword is also important to inheritance. Class functions declared as `virtual` can be redefined by descendants, without changing the call interface (overloading the function). If the function is redefined in the descendant with different arguments or return types, the `virtual` keyword is ignored, and the function is, in effect, overloaded.

Base classes commonly contain virtual functions, with the intention of enabling descendants to override them rather than overload them. Although descendants can override base class functions without the `virtual` keyword, pure virtual functions can be used to force descendants to redefine functions. A pure virtual function has a void return type and no arguments. Listing 18.15 is an example of a base class with pure virtual functions and two derived classes that override the virtual functions, or redeclare them.

Listing 18.15. These class definitions illustrate the use of virtual functions.

```
class Transaction {
    public:
        virtual void Insert();
        virtual void Update();
        virtual void Delete();

    protected:
        int GetConnection();
};

class AddressHistoryTrans : public Transaction
{
    public:
        int Insert(Address* last);
```

continues

Listing 18.15. continued

```
        void Update(); /* Overrides base class */
        void Delete(); /* Overrides base class */

};

class AddressTrans : public Transaction
{
    public:
        int Insert(Address* last);
        /* int Update(); ILLEGAL—only return type is different */
        int Update(Address* last);
        int Delete(unsigned long OldID);

};
```

In Listing 18.15, the protected member function GetConnection is inherited normally by the derived classes. However, the functions declared as virtual must be redefined in the derived classes. In both derived classes, the Insert function is treated as overloaded because it differs in arguments and return type from the base class's Insert function. However, the redeclaration of Update and Delete in AddressHistoryTrans completely hides the base class implementations of these functions because they match exactly in terms of arguments and return type. Note that the arguments must change in the derived class to overload a base class function. It is illegal to change only the return type of a pure virtual function, except when the base class function returns a pointer to the base class and the derived class function returns a pointer to the derived class. In this case, the compiler will cause the derived classes function to override the base classes function.

Class objects can also inherit from multiple bases. For example, the previously defined classes can be used as bases to derive a Transaction class for the Car class, as illustrated in Listing 18.16.

Listing 18.16. An illustration of multiple inheritance and overriding virtual base functions.

```
class CarTransaction : public Car, public Transaction {
    public:
        virtual void Insert();
        virtual void Update();
        virtual void Delete();
    protected:
        void Commit();
        void Rollback();
};
```

The class CarTransaction provides only two new member functions: Commit and Rollback. It inherits all of the data and methods of the Car class, overrides Delete, inherits GetConnection, and overloads the Insert and Update member functions of the Transaction class. The technique of inheriting from multiple bases and overriding base class implementations in derived classes is often referred to as *polymorphism*, which combines many of the features of object-oriented programming.

Inheritance is an extremely powerful, yet dangerous, feature of object-oriented programming. Changes made to a base class are proliferated to all descendants that inherit from the base. This is very powerful when you are fixing a bug in a base class or adding new data or methods that should apply to all descendants. However, you should always be very careful when you make changes to base classes. If a bug is introduced in a base class member function, it will affect every descendant that relies on the member function. Also, removing data and member functions from base classes is very difficult. When a data member is removed from a base class, it invalidates references to that data member in every member function of the base class and every member function of descendant classes where it is referenced.

Always remember that when you inherit from a class to derive a new one, all data members are inherited whether they are used or not. When you define base classes think small, and use inheritance carefully. As critics of C++ often point out, poor design of class hierarchies and over-use of inheritance results in bloated code.

Although C++ was used in this chapter to illustrate the concepts presented in this section, an increasing number of development tools are embracing the object-oriented model. The implementation of object-oriented features varies greatly among these tools, but the basic concepts are essentially the same. Visual Basic, PowerBuilder, SQLWindows, and more recently, Delphi, have all implemented the object-oriented paradigm with varying degrees of success. Regardless of which development tool you use, you need to understand the basic concepts of the object-oriented model.

Summary

Although Oracle is a relational database, the Oracle package provides the object-oriented capabilities of encapsulation, information hiding, and function overloading. Inheritance is not supported in version 7.1, but because Oracle seems to be moving in an object-oriented direction, it cannot be ruled out as a possibility in version 8. The newest of the Oracle development tools, including Oracle Power Objects™ and Oracle Objects™ for OLE, provide true object-oriented capabilities for developing Oracle client applications. However, the capabilities of the object model will not be fully exploited until there are more object-oriented features in the database itself. This will simplify the process of designing database applications and provide consistency by enabling a single object model to exist in both sides of the application.

Transaction Processing

19

by Kelly Leigh

IN THIS CHAPTER

Understanding how a transaction begins, executes, and ends, and knowing what happens along each step of the way are vital parts of making Oracle work for you. This knowledge is helpful not only to system and database administrators, but to Oracle developers as well. Knowing when a transaction is issued a rollback segment, or how locking occurs in the database can drastically change the strategy of creating applications or nightly processes.

This chapter covers, from start to finish:

- The difference between a session and a transaction
- What happens when a transaction is started
- How rollback segments are assigned
- How the database handles multiple and concurrent transactions
- Locking techniques used to ensure data integrity
- Execution of SQL and PL/SQL statements
- In-doubt and distributed transactions
- Commits, setpoints, and rollbacks
- Behind-the-scenes processes that comprise a session and transaction
- Database parameters that affect the execution of a transaction

Sessions Versus Transactions

A transaction is directly related to a session, but it is still considered a separate entity. A *session*, simply stated, is a single connection to a database instance based upon a username and, optionally, a password. All sessions in a database instance are unique, which means that they have a unique identifier setting them apart from the other users and processes accessing the database. This unique identifier, called a SID, is assigned by the instance and can be reused after a session is ended. The combination of the SID and a session serial number guarantees that each no session, even if the number is reused, is identical.

> **NOTE**
>
> The serial number is used to uniquely identify the objects being manipulated in a given session, and the combination of the SID and serial number guarantees uniqueness. The serial number is used to ensure that any session-level commands are applied to the correct object in the event that a session is terminated and the SID is reassigned.

A *transaction*, also in simplified terms, is a specific task, or set of tasks, to be executed against the database. Transactions start with an executable DML statement and end when the statement or multiple statements are all either rolled back or committed to the database, or when a DDL (Data Definition Language) statement is issued during the transaction.

If COMMIT or ROLLBACK statements are issued from the command line, the transaction is said to have been explicitly ended. However, if you issue a DDL command (DROP TABLE, ALTER TABLE, and so on), the previous statements in your transaction will be committed (or rolled back if unable to commit), the transaction will be implicitly ended, and a new transaction will begin and then end.

> **NOTE**
>
> A DDL statement constitutes an entire transaction, due to the nature of the statements. When a DDL statement that begins your previous transaction is implicitly ended, a new transaction begins and then the transaction is ended.

To illustrate these rules, assume that you log into your database to update and modify your customer tables. What you would like to do is enter 100 new customers to your database. You do this by creating a temporary table to hold that customer information, search your customer table for duplicates, and update those records if they do not exist. Though this is unlikely, assume that you must update customer table *before* checking for duplicate entries. The sequence would look like the steps listed in the following sequence of session and transaction begins and ends without savepoints.

1. Connect to SQL*Plus (begin session #1).
2. Create temporary customer table (begin *and* end transaction #1).
3. Insert new customer information into temporary table (begin transaction #2).
4. Step through entries in temporary table (continue transaction #2).
5. Update customer table (continue transaction #2).
6. Check for duplicate entries (continue transaction #2).

   If duplicates exist, roll back entire transaction (end transaction #2).
7. Repeat steps 4-7 until complete or duplicates are found.
8. Drop temporary table (end transaction #2, begin *and* end transaction #3).
9. Exit from SQL*Plus (end session #1).

Notice how the create-table and drop-table steps (2 and 8) begin and end a transaction. If you found duplicate entries in your tables, step 8 would actually end transaction #3 and begin and end transaction #4. Also note that the DDL command in step 5 implicitly ended transaction #2 by committing any changes made before beginning transaction #3. Finally, it is important to realize that if you had done another update between steps 5 and 6, the exit from SQL*Plus would have implicitly ended transaction #4 (started by the update) by issuing a commit before exiting.

> **NOTE**
>
> The relationship between tables is irrelevant when discussing transaction begins and ends. For example, if you update a set of related tables and then attempt to issue a DDL statement against another set of tables from within the same session, the DDL statement attempts to commit the previous set of changes (your previous transaction), if they have not already been committed or rolled back, and then executes the DDL statement as yet another transaction.

One other form of implicitly ending a transaction includes terminating a session either normally or abnormally. When these situations arise, the instance automatically attempts to commit the current transaction. If that is not possible, the transaction will be rolled back.

Commits, Rollbacks, and Savepoints

Although these topics are discussed elsewhere in this book, it is important to note how they affect a given transaction. As mentioned earlier, commits and rollbacks both end a transaction. Commit makes all changes made to the data permanent. Rollback reverses all changes made during the transaction by restoring the previous state of all modified data. With the use of savepoints, the ROLLBACK command can also be used to roll back only a portion of a transaction.

Savepoints were designed to be used as logical stopping points from within a single transaction. They are helpful in splitting up extremely long transactions into smaller portions, and they provide points of recovery along the way. Using savepoints within a transaction enables you to roll back the transaction to any given savepoint as long as a commit has not been issued (which immediately commits all data, erases all savepoints, and ends the transaction). Refer to Chapter 6, "SQL*Plus," to learn more about the SAVEPOINT command as well as how to use ROLLBACK to roll the current transaction back to a specified savepoint.

The following list is an update to the previously shown sequence with the addition of savepoints. Refer to this example to show how savepoints affect the transaction.

1. Connect to SQL*Plus (begin session #1).
2. Create temporary customer table (begin *and* end transaction #1).
3. Insert new customer information into temporary table (begin transaction #2).
4. Step through each entry in the temporary table (continue transaction #2).
5. Create unique savepoint (continue transaction #2).
6. Update customer table with information from temporary table (continue transaction #2).

7. If duplicate customer is found, roll back to savepoint (continue transaction #2).

8. Repeat steps 4-7 until finished.

9. Issue commit (end transaction #2).

10. Drop temporary table (begin *and* end transaction #3).

11. Exit from SQL*Plus (end session #1).

Notice how the savepoint enables you to roll back to a point within your current transaction without affecting the previous updates before the savepoint. Anywhere within your procedure, you can roll back to any savepoint or you can roll back the entire transaction. By using the savepoints, you are providing a collection of recovery points that are available to you until you end that transaction. Once the transaction is ended, all savepoints are erased.

TIP

Use savepoints to logically break up large commits. For example, if you have a situation in which you must update a large history table before checking for inaccurate data, you could:

1. Complete previous processing.

2. Issue savepoint.

3. Update the history table.

4. Check for inaccurate data.

5. Roll back to the savepoint (if required).

6. Commit and continue with processing if possible.

Multiple savepoints give you even greater flexibility in rolling back portions of long or complex transactions if an error occurs before the completion of the process.

There is no limit to the number of savepoints you can create during any given transaction, but be careful that the ones you do create are logically named in case you must roll back to them.

CAUTION

Once a transaction is ended (that is, commit or rollback), it is impossible to roll back to a savepoint. At that point, all savepoints are deleted and can be reused. If you specify a duplicate name for a savepoint, the previous savepoint will be deleted and a new one set at the current point in the transaction.

Transaction Control Statements

Transaction control statements are statements that affect the execution or properties of a transaction, whether it is the management of data or characteristics of how the transaction executes. The family of transaction control statements include:

- COMMIT
- SAVEPOINT
- ROLLBACK
- SET TRANSACTION

Types of Transactions

Several names are used to identify transactions and their states. Knowing these terms is helpful in understanding the terms mentioned by Oracle and interpreting Oracle errors returned during a transaction. These terms cover types of transactions as well as other terms used in identifying them.

Concurrent Transactions

Concurrent transactions are transactions that are executed in the same general time. These transactions, because they have started so close to each other, generally do not see the changes made by the other transactions. Any data that has been updated by a concurrent transaction and requested by another concurrently running transaction must be read from rollback segments until the transaction requesting the data has completed. This has the potential of leading to the error message Snapshot too old, which is discussed in more detail under the "Assigning Rollback Segments" section of this chapter.

Discreet Transactions

A *discreet* transaction is used to improve the performance of short transactions. For developers creating custom applications, the procedure BEGIN_DISCREET_TRANSACTION() changes the steps followed during the duration of a session in order to speed its processing. The main differences are as follows:

- All changes are held until the transaction ends.
- Other transactions cannot see uncommitted changes.
- Redo information is stored in a separate location in the SGA.
- No rollback information is written because all changes are held until a commit and then applied directly to the data block(s).

Because the overhead associated with redo and rollback segments is bypassed by storing information directly in the SGA, these transactions bypass a goodly amount of processing overhead. At first this sounds more like a flaw than a feature, but on second thought, most changes can be made in a very short amount of time because these transactions are short in nature.

> **NOTE**
>
> Discreet transactions will not work as distributed transactions due to the changes in transaction processing.

Distributed Transactions

Distributed transactions are transactions in which one or more statements manipulate data on two or more nodes, or remote systems, of a distributed database. If a transaction manipulates data on only one node, it is considered a remote transaction. As in a remote transaction, none of the redo information is stored locally.

In-Doubt Transactions

An *in-doubt transaction* is actually a state of a transaction instead of a type and refers to transactions within a distributed database environment. One situation that causes this state is if an instance involved in a currently running transaction fails, that transaction must be either rolled back or committed. It is difficult, however, to do either without knowing the state of the transaction in the affected database. In this case, all other instances in the distributed environment mark this transaction as in-doubt. Once the instance is restarted, the transaction can be analyzed and all instances can either commit or rollback.

It is possible to force the commit or rollback of a distributed transaction by using either SQL*DBA and doing a Recover In-Doubt Transaction, or the command COMMIT WORK ... FORCE with the local or global transaction ID of the in-doubt transaction. Refer to Chapter 7, "SQL*DBA," or Chapter 6, "SQL*Plus," for further information on how to roll back or commit this transaction.

Normal Transactions

Normal transaction is a term used to refer to a local (non-remote) transaction. All redo information is stored in the local database, and all data manipulation is done to the same database. This type of transaction is the focus for the discussion on transaction processing.

Read-Only Transactions

Read-only refers to the type of read consistency that is set or defaulted to for a given transaction. By default, the level of read consistency is statement level, which is also known as read-write. This means that each consecutive statement in your transaction will see the changes made to the database by any previous statements regardless of which transaction has committed the changes.

By changing the read consistency from statement level to transaction level, you force the current transaction to ignore any changes made to the database during this transaction and view the data as it existed immediately before the transaction started. This mode is helpful if you are executing long running reports against tables that might change during the duration of the report.

When you are creating a read-only transaction, two major changes take effect. First, the number of commands available to the read-only transaction is limited. Second, because the process is literally read-only, it does not require additional locks against tables and does not acquire a rollback segment or redo log. This is helpful because it limits the processing overhead from the database associated with normal transactions.

Please refer to the command reference at the end of this chapter for a list of commands to which read-only transactions are limited.

Remote Transactions

Remote transactions are transactions containing single or multiple statement(s) to be executed against a non-local database. These statements all reference the same node. If they do not, they are considered separate remote transactions and the instance will split them up. One of the major differences between remote and normal transactions is that redo and rollback information against a remote transaction is stored on the remote database. None of this information is transferred to your local database to be used for recovery.

Read-Consistency

Read-consistency is not a difficult concept to grasp. In short, *read-consistency* guarantees that the data you are viewing while executing a transaction does not change during that transaction. With read-consistency, if two users are updating the same table at the same time, user1 will not see the changes made by the other user during their transaction. User2, likewise, cannot see any changes committed by user1 until both transactions are complete. If they happen to be working on the same row in the table, this becomes a locking issue instead of read-consistency. A later section in this chapter discusses locking.

Read-consistency is the major building block that enables multiple users to update, select, and delete from the same tables without having to keep a private copy for each user. When combined with locking techniques, read-consistency provides the foundation for a multi-user database in which users can do similar or identical operations without difficulty.

Take a look at an example of the way read-consistency works in a theoretical telemarketing department. User1 is entering an order for a customer, while user2 is changing customer information. Both users have concurrent transactions (they are executing at the same time), but user1 began his or her transaction first. Suppose that user2 makes a mistake and changes the phone number for the same customer whose order is being entered. Because user1 began their transaction first, they will always be looking at the "before picture" of the customer data and will see the customer's previous phone number when querying the user's data. This is true even if user2 commits his or her changes. Why? Because it is possible that user1's transaction is solely dependent on the data that existed when his or her transaction began. Imagine the confusion that would result if data could be changed while an already executing query were making changes based on that data! It would be nearly impossible to guarantee the coordination and functioning of all processing within the application.

Read-consistency is also a secondary function of rollback segments. Aside from being able to undo changes from a transaction, they also provide other users with a "before picture" of the data being modified by any process. If a transaction must review data that has been modified by a concurrent uncommitted transaction, it must look in the rollback segments to find that data. You can find more information in the section on rollback segments within this chapter.

Steps to Processing a Transaction

Understanding the steps followed during the execution of a transaction can be quite helpful in planning and implementing custom applications. It is also important for the database administrator to know these steps because they can help in understanding and tuning the database parameters and processes. This discussion covers normal transactions. Other transactions, such as distributed, remote, and discreet, are treated a bit differently, because these transactions are short in nature, and those differences are documented throughout this chapter. The processing steps follow.

1. DML/DDL statement is entered.
2. Rollback segment is assigned or requested.
3. Statement is optimized.
4. Optimizer generates an execution plan.
5. The execution plan is followed to manipulate/return data.
7. Transaction loops through steps 1-5 until commit, rollback or session termination.

The following sections examine each step individually.

Entering DML/DDL Statements

The issuing of DML or DDL statements can take place through a number of ways, including SQL*Forms, SQL*Plus, and custom C programs. The rules governing the start and end of transactions are the same no matter which way a SQL statement is issued.

Assigning Rollback Segments

Rollback segments are assigned randomly by Oracle at the beginning of each transaction (not session) when the first DML statement is issued, and they are used to roll back the transaction to a specified savepoint or to the beginning of a transaction. The selection of a rollback segment is based on which rollback segments are currently available and how busy each segment is. By default, DDL statements are not issued rollback segments due to the nature of DDL commands. They are, however, issued redo entries so that the modifications can be reapplied if the database must be recovered.

> **TIP**
>
> In an Oracle7 database, you can examine the number of times a particular rollback segment was requested and was waited for. Check the data dictionary view STATS$ROLL for the column TRANS_TBL_WAITS and TRANS_TBL_GETS. If the ratio of GETS to WAITS is high, you may need to increase the number of rollback segments in your database.

Two types of transactions do not acquire rollback segments. These are read-only transactions and remote transactions. Read-only transactions, by their nature, do not modify data, so they do not require a rollback segment. Remote transactions actually do acquire rollback segments, but these rollback segments are allocated on the remote database that the transaction is executed on. Distributed transactions are really a form of remote transactions and follow the same rule.

There is no limit to the number of rollback segments a user can access throughout a given session, but only one rollback segment will be used at any given time for any transaction. In other words, a transaction will acquire one and only one rollback segment to be used for the duration of the transaction. Once the transaction is complete, the rollback segment is released. Space used in that rollback segment is dictated by the amount of data that is modified.

Long-Running Transactions and Rollback Segment Allocation

Transactions that modify large amounts of data require larger rollback segments. By using the SET TRANSACTION command, you can specify a specific rollback segment to be used by a given transaction. Reference the section on SET TRANSACTION for a further explanation of how to do this. It is important to note, however, that a SET TRANSACTION command must be the very first command issued in a transaction. If it is not, an error message will be returned.

Once a transaction is completed, the rollback segment is released. This does not mean that the segment's data is overwritten immediately, though. Sometimes other transactions that started before this transaction finished need access to the unmodified data for read-consistency. In this case, the rollback segment containing the "before picture" will be used. Unfortunately, Oracle does not lock this data into the rollback segment to prevent the data blocks from being reused if needed. If your rollback segments are too small, you may encounter the error rollback seg-ment too old. If this error occurs, the transaction that received the error is forced to rollback. This error implies two things:

- A rollback segment's extent was reused for a new transaction
- A transaction that started before the other transaction ended required access to the previously unmodified data for read-consistency

In either situation, a transaction was accessing the before picture of some data that was still in a rollback segment when the system was forced to reclaim that extent to use for a currently executing transaction. Because this before picture is no longer available, the executing transaction cannot continue. You can use three steps (separately or in conjunction with each other) to alleviate this problem:

1. Increase the size of your rollback segments.
2. Increase the OPTIMAL size of your rollback segments.
3. Reschedule your processing so that no two processes are updating and/or reading from updated tables while the other is running.

> **TIP**
>
> Make sure that your rollback segments are sized according to the largest common transaction that takes place. Create a large rollback segment to accommodate unusually large updates, and use the SET TRANSACTION command to force that transaction to use the larger rollback segment.

Using the Optimizer

Oracle's optimizer is a critical part in the execution of a transaction. The optimizer is responsible for taking a SQL statement, identifying the most efficient way of executing the statement, and then returning the data requested. There is a high likelihood that a SQL statement can be executed in more than one way. The optimizer is responsible for identifying the most efficient means of executing that statement.

Optimization can take many steps to complete, depending on the SQL statement. The steps used to execute the SQL statement are called an *execution plan*. Once the execution plan is completed, it is then followed to provide the desired results (updated or returned data).

Many factors govern how the optimizer creates an execution plan. These factors are based on the type of optimization method the database uses. At the database level, you have two types of optimization: cost-based and rule-based. The database parameter OPTIMIZER_MODE, located in the init.ora parameter file, determines which type of optimization mode your instance will use. The parameter has two possible values:

- Cost: Use cost-based analysis
- Rule: Use rule-based analysis

CAUTION

Two words of wisdom: First, with each version of Oracle that is released, there are more modifications to the way the optimizer makes a statement more efficient. With this in mind, it is important to note that the optimizer in each version may function differently, and each statement passed to the optimizer may perform differently.

Second, although the optimizer makes every attempt to create an execution plan that is optimal in performance, the Developer has the true knowledge of the data and its purpose. In some situations, the Developer may be able to choose a more efficient means of executing the statement than the optimizer can. Whenever possible, the developer should use the EXPLAIN PLAN option of the database to examine the execution plan provided by the optimizer.

Cost-Based Analysis

Cost-based analysis is a mode of analyzing SQL statements to provide the most efficient way of execution. When the optimizer is running in cost-based mode, it follows these steps to decide which plan is the best way to execute the statement unless the developer has provided a hint to use in the execution.

1. Generate a set of execution plans based on available access paths.
2. Rank each plan based on estimated elapsed time to complete.
3. Choose the plan with the lowest ranking (shortest elapsed time).

Cost-based analysis uses statistics generated by the ANALYZE command for tables, indexes, and clusters to estimate the total I/O, CPU, and memory requirements required to run each execution plan. Because the goal of the cost-based approach is to provide maximum throughput, the execution plan with the lowest ranking or lowest estimated I/O, CPU, and memory requirements will be used.

The analysis used to provide the final cost of an execution plan is based on the following data dictionary views:

- USER_TABLES, USER_TAB_COLUMNS, USER_INDEXES, USER_CLUSTERS
- ALL_TABLES, ALL_TAB_COLUMNS, ALL_INDEXES, ALL_CLUSTERS
- DBA_TABLES, DBA_TAB_COLUMNS, DBA_INDEXES, DBA_CLUSTERS

Rule-Based Analysis

Rule-based analysis rates the execution plans according to the access paths available and the information in Table 19.1. The rule-based approach uses those rankings to provide an overall rating on the execution plan and uses the plan with the lowest ranking. Generally speaking, the lower the rating, the shorter the execution time—though this is not always the case.

Table 19.1. Access type ratings.

Ranking	Type of Access
1	Single row by ROWID
2	Single row by cluster join
3	Single row by hash cluster key with unique or primary key
4	Single row by unique or primary key
5	Cluster join
6	Hash cluster key
7	Indexed cluster key
8	Composite index
9	Single-column index
10	Bounded range search on indexed columns
11	Unbounded range search on indexed columns
12	Sort-merge join
13	MAX() or MIN() of indexed column
14	ORDER BY on indexed columns
15	Full table scan

Overriding the *OPTIMIZER_MODE* Parameter

Because the developer can sometimes optimize code more efficiently than the optimizer can, various directives, called *hints*, can be issued from within the SQL statement to force the optimizer to choose a different method of optimization. This method works at the statement level from within the transaction and affects only the current statement.

To affect all statements at the transaction level, the SQL command ALTER SESSION SET OPTIMIZER_GOAL can be used. This command overrides the OPTIMIZER_MODE initialization parameter and forces all statements within the current transaction to be optimized according to this value. This parameter has four possible values:

- CHOOSE. Tells the optimizer to search the data dictionary views for data on at least one related table (referenced in the SQL statement). If the data exists, the optimizer will optimize the statement according to the cost-based approach. If no data exists for any tables being referenced, the optimizer will use rule-based analysis.
- ALL_ROWS. Chooses cost-based analysis with the goal of best throughput.
- FIRST_ROWS. Chooses cost-based analysis with the goal of best response time.
- RULE. Chooses rule-based analysis regardless of the presence of data in the data dictionary views related to the tables being referenced.

This parameter affects all SQL statements issued from within the transaction, including functions and stored procedures that are called. OPTIMIZER_MODE is still used for any recursive SQL calls issued by Oracle on behalf of the transaction, though.

Parsing Statements

A parsed statement is not to be confused with an execution plan of a statement. Whereas an execution plan examines the most efficient way to execute a statement, parsing the statement creates the actual executable statements to be used in retrieving the data. Parsing a statement is a one-step process by the optimizer to do the following:

- Check semantics and syntax
- Verify that the user has the appropriate privileges to execute this statement
- Allocate private SQL space to store the statement
- Check for duplicate statements in the shared SQL area
- Generate an executable version of parsed SQL if necessary
- Allocate and stores SQL in shared library cache if it does not already exist

When checking the syntax and semantics, the instance is verifying that no key words or necessary parameters are missing. If the statement is in correct form, the instance then verifies that the user has the correct privileges required to carry out the execution of the statement. Once these have been verified, space is allocated in the private SQL area for the user's statement. This statement is saved until either it is needed again or the memory space is required to store another parsed statement.

After allocating space in the private SQL area, the instance searches through the shared SQL area for any duplicate statements. If a duplicate statement is found, the executable version of the statement is retrieved from memory and executed by the process, and the private SQL area is pointed to the statement in the shared area. If it is not found, an executable version is created and stored in the private SQL area only.

TIP

When parsing a SQL statement, all characters are not treated equally. Uppercase and lowercase letters are considered different characters. Two SQL statements, identical in nature but differing in case (even if by only one character) will be treated as a separate statement. The "different" statement will be parsed and placed in the private SQL area as would a completely different SQL statement.

The following two statements are completely different statements, according to the parser:

```
SELECT * FROM V$LOCK
SELECT * FROM v$lock
```

This is a major reasoning behind packaged procedures. There is only one procedure to maintain, and all users execute that same code.

Handling Locks

The locking of data rows and/or tables is completely automated and transparent to the user. Once the executable version of the SQL statement is run, Oracle automatically attempts to lock data at the lowest level required. This means that if possible, a row will be locked instead of the entire table. This is dependent solely on how the SQL statement was written and what types of access are required (full table scan versus single rows).

A form of manual, or explicit, locking can take place by using the LOCK TABLE command. By default, these commands are not necessary in day-to-day processing. Oracle recommends that you allow the database to handle all locking of data whenever possible.

TIP

One of the most overlooked causes of locking problems in a database is failing to create indexes on the columns you have used as foreign keys. If the foreign keys are unindexed and you attempt to modify the child table (the table where the foreign keys reside), the database may require a shared lock on the parent table, or the table where the keys reference in order to modify the child table. When the foreign keys have corresponding indexes, the database can do row-level locking on the parent table.

> **TIP**
>
> One other overlooked cause of locking problems is the PCTFREE parameter on the table. If the value of PCTFREE is set too low, many concurrent transactions are executing DML statements against the table, and the data blocks are filled, a shared lock may be requested on the entire table. This transaction is not waiting for a lock, but instead is either waiting on free space or a release of an INITRANS within the transaction layer of the data block.

Generating Redo Logs

Each transaction that is committed has a corresponding redo log entry generated. This entry records just the changes applied to the database files, as well as rollback segment information. These entries in the redo logs are not traceable to a user process. Should the database be brought offline by a system or database failure, you can use these redo logs to reconstruct the database files to a usable state.

Redo log entries are written to the redo log buffer in the SGA. These entries are then written to the online redo logs by the LGWR process. If the instance is running in archive log mode, the redo log files, once filled, are then written to corresponding archived redo log files, which are separate from the data files that hold tables and data. These archived redo logs are the primary recovery method when the online redo logs have been cycled through or corrupted and no longer hold the data needed for recovery.

> **CAUTION**
>
> Although the results of a DDL statement, DROP TABLE for example, have associated redo logs generated for them, they have no rollback segments. Therefore, it is not easy to recover from an accidentally dropped table. To recover from a dropped table or tablespace that contains data, the tablespace in question must be brought offline, an older version of the data file(s) must be restored from a previous backup, and then archived redo logs must be used to recover the tablespace to a specific point in time just before the drop command was issued.

Stepping Through the Transaction

From this point, there are several paths that a transaction can take to completion. Most commonly, the transaction is committed. Still, handling must be taken into account for transactions that are rolled back. Following are the steps taken during a commit.

1. Instance's transaction table marks transaction as complete.
2. A unique SCN (system change number) is generated.
3. Redo log entries are written to disk.
4. Any acquired locks are released.
5. Transaction is marked as having completed.

If any of these steps fail, the transaction cannot be committed. Depending on the nature of the error, the transaction will either wait for the problem to be fixed so it can complete the transaction, or it will be rolled back.

> **NOTE**
>
> The DBWR process is responsible for writing updated data from the buffer cache in the SGA back to the database. It is possible that even though a transaction has not been committed, its data has been written to disk. Uncommitted data is written to prevent all of the buffers in the SGA from filling up. Should the buffers fill, the database cannot continue modifying data until they are freed. The writing of uncommitted data is not a problem, however. Should a process be rolled back, its data is taken from the rollback segment and reapplied to the modified table(s).

The following steps illustrate what must take place if a transaction is rolled back.

1. All changes are rolled back to previous savepoint and savepoint is preserved (or beginning of transaction if no savepoints have been specified).
2. If savepoint is not the last specified savepoint, all savepoints after this one are erased.
3. Acquired locks are released.
4. Transaction continues (if no savepoints were specified then the transaction is ended).
5. If transaction is ended, rollback segments are released as well, though no SCN is recorded.

Processing a Remote or Distributed Transaction

The steps required to process remote and distributed transactions are nearly identical to the way normal transactions are processed. The biggest difference is where the statement is parsed, and the instance whose resources are used for processing. The following steps add the logic required for remote and distributed transaction processing.

> **NOTE**
>
> In order for a remote transaction to work, you *must* have a networking package, such as SQL*Net Version 1 or 2, installed on all systems holding a database that you want to retrieve or update information on. If all databases reside on the same physical system, that system must have SQL*Net installed.
>
> Distributed transactions require SQL*Net as well as Oracle's distributed option installed and working.
>
> Once all of these requirements are met, standard SQL connection strings can be used to access the remote database(s). Refer to Chapter 6, "SQL*Plus," for further information regarding SQL*Net connection strings.

1. DML/DDL statement is entered.

2. If transaction modifies data in current instance, a rollback segment is assigned.

3. Statement is broken down into separate statements by references to remote database(s).

4. Any statements that modify local data are optimized.

5. Statements referencing remote databases are forwarded to the remote database to be optimized.

6. On the remote databases, statements that require rollback segments or redo information to be stored acquire those resources from themselves.

7. The optimizer on each remote database generates an execution plan for received statements.

8. The execution plans are followed to return data to the database that originally started the remote or distributed transaction.

9. The local database collects all data returned and sorts through data and finishes processing like joins.

10. Transaction loops through steps 1-9 until commit, rollback, or session termination.

Once again, look at each step individually in the following sections.

Entering DDL/DML Statements

All statements for remote and distributed transactions are entered on a local database, or a database where local data resides. It is not necessary to log in to a database where data will be manipulated in order to issue queries against that database, because that is essentially what a remote or distributed transaction is.

Assigning Rollback Segments

Just as in a normal transaction, if any part of the transaction's statements modify data on the local database, a rollback segment is assigned to track any changes made to the data.

Breaking Down Statements

Oracle must break down all statements that query or modify remote data in order to send them as a group to the remote database(s). Once they are grouped according to remote database, the statements are sent, via SQL*Net, to their intended destination.

Optimizing Local Statements

Just as in a normal transaction, the local statements are optimized, based on either the database parameter OPTIMIZER_MODE or the transaction-level parameter OPTIMIZER_GOAL. Once the desired explain plan is created and executed, data is returned and held until all data from remote transactions has been received.

Forwarding Remote Commands

All remote commands are forwarded to the intended database before they are optimized or parsed. Once the remote database has received the information, it acts just as it would on a local database: The statement is parsed, the shared SQL area is searched in order to find an identical parsed representation of the statement, the statement is optimized if necessary, and then the statement is executed.

At this point, all data is returned to the local database user or application. If data is to be compared with other data from the local or another remote database, that action takes place on the local database. The local database is responsible for correlating all returned data to provide the final desired output.

> **NOTE**
>
> DDL statements (such as DROP TABLE or ALTER TABLE) are not allowed on remote database. To execute this family of commands, you must log into the database as a local connection or issue a CONNECT command to access the remote database.

Assigning Remote Rollback Segments and Writing Redo Logs

All statements that are sent to remote databases to update/manipulate data are assigned a rollback segment on the remote database as they would if manipulating data. The remote database is then responsible for all recovery operations should the database fail or should the transaction require a rollback. Remote transactions function like normal transactions when a commit or rollback statement is issued.

Optimizing Remote Statements

Statements that are sent to remote databases are not parsed by the local database. This is so that the remote database's shared SQL area can be searched for identical statements. Once the statement is parsed, it is either optimized or the optimized execution plan for the identical statement is used. Data is then returned to the local database.

Returning Data to the Local Database

As stated earlier, it is the responsibility of the local database, or the database from where the transaction was initiated, to receive data from all remote databases, correlate it, and return only the data that the original statement requested. This can include joins, WHERE and IN clauses, and GROUP BY statements.

Summarizing Remote and Distributed Transactions

Despite the differences in where the bulk of the transaction processing resides, the steps are much the same. When working in a distributed environment, though, you need to take into account quite a few other steps when dealing with complex updates and error handling. Should a transaction be abnormally terminated or an instance in the distributed environment go down, there are quite a few extra steps needed to help decide whether a distributed transaction should be committed or rolled back. It is better to refer to more in-depth documentation to learn more about two-phase commits and exactly how Oracle deals with the problems resulting from a downed instance or terminated session from within a distributed environment.

The *SET TRANSACTION* Command Reference

SET TRANSACTION is used to alter the current transaction's properties. There are three options available, and the command *must* be the first command in your transaction. If you have already issued commands in the current transaction, you must either issue a COMMIT or ROLL-BACK before the SET TRANSACTION command will be accepted.

SET TRANSACTION has the following options:

■ READ ONLY   Sets the current transaction to read only

■ READ WRITE   The default

■ USE ROLLBACK SEGMENT *rollback_segment_name*   Explicitly selects a rollback segment

READ ONLY Option

READ ONLY refers to a read-only process where no updates can be performed on any tables in the database. It also sets the read-consistency level to transaction level, where all data viewed is a snapshot of the data as it existed when the transaction first started. This option is helpful for sessions that will only query data because the processing overhead for this type of transaction is smaller than that of a normal transaction. It is also helpful for transactions, such as reports, that require a snapshot in time of the current data. For these types of queries, though, processing overhead may be higher because other transactions that modify data will force the reporting transaction to search through rollback segments for the original unmodified data.

In a read-only transaction, the command set is limited to five groups of commands:

■ ALTER SESSION

■ ALTER SYSTEM

■ LOCK TABLE

■ SELECT (with the exception of SELECT FOR UPDATE)

■ SET ROLE

READ WRITE Option

This type of transaction is the default, where the user has the ability to update and delete as well as query tables if they have the appropriate database privileges, and the read consistency is set to statement level. No SET TRANSACTION command must take place for this option to be in effect because it is the default.

USE ROLLBACK SEGMENT Option

This option is used to set the rollback segment for transactions that update large amounts of data and therefore create larger than normal rollback segments. This rollback segment may have been created with larger initial and next extents to prevent the maximum number of extents being reached in the rollback segment. The OPTIMAL parameter may also have been set higher, or not used, to prevent extents from being reclaimed and causing a read-consistency error for other concurrent transactions.

Transaction Space

Three parameters affect how transactions can work with objects. These parameters affect snapshots, clusters, indexes and tables. These parameters are

- PCTFREE. Controls the amount of free space in each block set aside for the expansion of columns
- INITRANS. Sets aside space for each transaction that will concurrently access this table
- MAXTRANS. Specifies the maximum number of concurrent processes that can update a table (does not affect SELECT statements)

The PCTFREE parameter is used to set aside a percentage of a data block for work space in the object. This space is usually used for extending columns (such as VARCHAR2 data types). If this value is set too high, the result is wasted space in your data file that cannot be reclaimed without extra work by the database administrator. If the value is too low, the result is either relocated or chained rows. Chained rows are rows that span more than one data block. This creates a problem in that the database must do an additional seek to read the second data block for the row.

INITRANS specifies initial transactions, or the average number of concurrent transactions. For each transaction that will concurrently update a given object, 23 bytes of space are set aside for each data block to keep track of each transaction against the row(s) located within that block. If this value is set too low, the database must dynamically allocate space from the free space in the object's data blocks to use as temporary storage. Dynamically allocating this space can slow down the execution time of a transaction. If no free space can be allocated, the transaction will hang until free space can be allocated. The process may time-out if the wait is long enough.

MAXTRANS is the maximum number concurrent processes that can update a data block in use by the object. If this value is reached, further transactions cannot continue until other transactions have completed.

Summary

As you can see, knowing the steps that must be taken to process a transaction can greatly affect how a custom application is developed. If a transaction is querying data only, using a read-only transaction can greatly reduce the amount of processing overhead required to run an application. If many users are running the same read-only query, this savings on overhead can be a considerable amount.

Likewise, knowing more about how statements are optimized can save a great deal of time in reaching the goals set for a new application. Because optimization methods take a critical role in meeting those goals, it is imperative that you take this into account.

Overall, knowing transaction processing steps is just plain helpful for administrators and developers alike.

Enforcing Integrity

20

*by Advanced
Information
Systems, Inc.*

IN THIS CHAPTER

Referential integrity is a condition in which all references to external objects within each database object are valid. Enforcing referential integrity is a critical task in ensuring that data is accurate and complete. Referential integrity problems can result in data loss, wasted storage, and inaccurate data. Overall database integrity is a broader issue, relating to the values stored within a single object. Non-referential problems with integrity are typically somewhat less serious, resulting in inaccuracies and the storage of unwanted values.

Oracle provides many ways to enforce integrity, including column constraints, table constraints, sequences, and triggers. Each of these methods will be examined in this chapter, through the use of a common example.

A Common Integrity Problem

Many different types of applications need to store information regarding individuals, companies, phone numbers, and addresses. This same information has been stored in databases in many different ways, with varying degrees of success. Assume, for the sake of example, that the following rules apply to the storage of this information.

- Individuals, Companies, Addresses, and Phones should not be stored redundantly.
- An individual may be related to zero, one, or many companies.
- Addresses and Phones may be related to an individual, a company, or an individual at a company.
- Addresses and Phones will have standard descriptions, such as Home and Office.
- A phone may or may not be related to an address.
- The current user and timestamp will be stored for each record when it is inserted or updated, and the application will use an optimistic locking scheme.

The DDL in Listing 20.1 provides an example of one possible physical model that will accommodate these rules.

Listing 20.1. This DDL contains the column attributes for the sample application that will be used to demonstrate integrity constraints.

```
CREATE TABLE individual (
     ID               NUMBER(10)
    ,last_name        VARCHAR2(30)
    ,first_name       VARCHAR2(30)
    ,notes            VARCHAR2(255)
    ,date_of_birth    DATE
    ,last_updt_user   VARCHAR2(20)
    ,last_updt_date   DATE
);

CREATE TABLE company (
     ID               NUMBER(10)
    ,name             VARCHAR2(30)
```

```
     ,notes           VARCHAR2(255)
     ,last_updt_user  VARCHAR2(20)
     ,last_updt_date  DATE
);

CREATE TABLE ind_co_rel (
     individual_id    NUMBER(10)
     ,company_id      NUMBER(10)
     ,title           VARCHAR2(80)
     ,last_updt_user  VARCHAR2(20)
     ,last_updt_date  DATE
);

CREATE TABLE address (
     ID               NUMBER(10)
     ,address_type_id NUMBER(10)
     ,address_line1   VARCHAR2(40)
     ,address_line2   VARCHAR2(40)
     ,address_line3   VARCHAR2(40)
     ,city            VARCHAR2(40)
     ,state           CHAR(2)
     ,zip             NUMBER(5)
     ,zip_4           NUMBER(4)
     ,last_updt_user  VARCHAR2(20)
     ,last_updt_date  DATE
);

CREATE TABLE phone (
     ID               NUMBER(10)
     ,phone_type_id   NUMBER(10)
     ,area_code       CHAR(3)
     ,prefix          CHAR(3)
     ,line            CHAR(4)
     ,extension       VARCHAR2(6)
     ,last_updt_user  VARCHAR2(20)
     ,last_updt_date  DATE
);

CREATE TABLE address_rel (
     address_id       NUMBER(10)
     ,individual_id   NUMBER(10)
     ,company_id      NUMBER(10)
     ,last_updt_user  VARCHAR2(20)
     ,last_updt_date  DATE
);

CREATE TABLE phone_rel (
     phone_id         NUMBER(10)
     ,address_id      NUMBER(10)
     ,individual_id   NUMBER(10)
     ,company_id      NUMBER(10)
     ,last_updt_user  VARCHAR2(20)
     ,last_updt_date  DATE
);

CREATE TABLE address_type (
     ID               NUMBER(10)
     ,description     VARCHAR2(40)
```

continues

Listing 20.1. continued

```
     ,last_updt_user  VARCHAR2(40)
     ,last_updt_date  DATE
);

CREATE TABLE phone_type (
     ID               NUMBER(10)
     ,description      VARCHAR2(40)
     ,last_updt_user   VARCHAR2(40)
     ,last_updt_date   DATE
);
```

Although this data typically makes up only a small portion of a real application's data model, the many relationships among these tables present great potential for referential integrity problems. In the sections that follow, issues relating to the integrity of these objects are used to illustrate the various means of enforcing integrity in Oracle databases.

Column Constraints

Column constraints are probably the most widely used means of enforcing integrity. Of these, PRIMARY KEY is the most significant. It is used to ensure that each row in the table is unique. When a column is declared as the PRIMARY KEY, an index on this column is automatically created and assigned a unique name by Oracle. The additional constraints UNIQUE and NOT NULL are implied by the PRIMARY KEY constraint.

In the sample application, the ID column is used as the PRIMARY KEY in each table in which it occurs. This column contains unique numeric values generated by an Oracle sequence. Listing 20.2 contains the DDL for the individual table with the column constraint PRIMARY KEY enabled. Assume that the ID column is declared identically in each table where it is used.

Listing 20.2. This DDL contains a PRIMARY KEY column constraint.

```
CREATE TABLE individual (
     ID               NUMBER(10)    PRIMARY KEY
     ,last_name        VARCHAR2(30)
     ,first_name       VARCHAR2(30)
     ,notes            VARCHAR2(255)
     ,date_of_birth    DATE
     ,last_updt_user   VARCHAR2(20)
     ,last_updt_date   DATE
);
```

The generated column, ID, is necessary to create a primary key for the individual table, because no combination of columns is guaranteed to be unique. Although it is highly unlikely, two individuals with the same name and the same date of birth could exist in the database.

A common mistake in developing database applications relates to lookup tables, which are sometimes created almost as an afterthought. The PRIMARY KEY constraint is particularly important to lookups because of the way in which they are used. If two rows of the lookup have the same value in the column that is used in joins, unwanted duplicates will be returned in the result set. This point may seem obvious, but a simple oversight can cause this error to go unnoticed until long after a duplicate is inserted, when SQL statements joining to the lookup produce results that are visibly erroneous.

The UNIQUE constraint, which is implied by PRIMARY KEY, can be used on a different column to designate a secondary key. A UNIQUE constraint, like PRIMARY KEY, causes Oracle to automatically create an index and assign it a unique name.

Listing 20.3 creates a unique index on the description column in the address_type lookup table. Although this guarantees uniqueness for each row in the table, it is still preferable to use ID as the primary key. The primary key will be stored in another table, and because the description can be fairly long, using an ID (which will start at 1) conserves disk space. Another advantage to using the generated value as the primary key is that joins are typically faster on numeric values.

Listing 20.3. This DDL contains both a primary key and a unique constraint.

```
CREATE TABLE address_type (
    ID              NUMBER(10)     PRIMARY KEY
    ,description     VARCHAR2(40) UNIQUE
    ,last_updt_user  VARCHAR2(40)
    ,last_updt_date  DATE
);
```

> **TIP**
>
> The CONSTRAINT keyword can be used to assign a name to a constraint and its corresponding index. See Listing 20.4 for an example of the CONSTRAINT syntax for column constraints.

Listing 20.4. This DDL script demonstrates the use of the CONSTRAINT keyword.

```
CREATE TABLE address_type (
    ID                  NUMBER(10)
                        CONSTRAINT addr_type_pk    PRIMARY KEY
    ,description         VARCHAR2(40)
                        CONSTRAINT addr_type_desc UNIQUE
    ,last_updt_id        VARCHAR2(40)
    ,last_updt_date      DATE
);
```

The UNIQUE constraint does not prevent null values from being inserted. For this reason, it is often used for columns that should be unique but do not necessarily need to be populated. For example, an application may need to store the Social Security number for individuals if it is known, while allowing individuals to be inserted before their Social Security numbers are known. If a duplicate were to exist in this column, it would obviously be in error. However, the column cannot be defined as the primary key, because null values must be allowed.

The NOT NULL column constraint ensures that null values are not inserted into a column, and they can be used in conjunction with the UNIQUE constraint. Listing 20.5 demonstrates the use of NOT NULL as the sole constraint on a column, as well as its use in conjunction with a UNIQUE constraint.

Listing 20.5. This DDL script illustrates the uses of NOT NULL column constraints.

```
CREATE TABLE address_type (
    ID                  NUMBER(10)
                        CONSTRAINT addr_type_pk       PRIMARY KEY
    ,description        VARCHAR2(40)
                        CONSTRAINT addr_type_desc_u   UNIQUE
                        CONSTRAINT addr_type_desc_nn  NOT NULL
    ,last_updt_id       VARCHAR2(40)
                        CONSTRAINT addr_type_lu_id    NOT NULL
    ,last_updt_date     DATE
                        CONSTRAINT addr_type_lu_dt    NOT NULL
);
```

The NOT NULL constraint is used to simply define required columns, which may or may not be unique. For example, first and last name may be required to add an individual to the database. Specifying these columns with a NOT NULL constraint ensures that records missing either of these fields will not be inserted.

The most flexible column constraint is the CHECK constraint. A CHECK constraint can reference any column in the table, but it cannot reference any external objects, system variables, or system constants. When a CHECK constraint references columns, the conditions are always applied to the current row. In order to insert or update a column with the CHECK constraint, the specified condition must evaluate to TRUE or unknown (when a NULL value is being inserted into one of the columns referenced by the CHECK condition). CHECK constraints can be used in conjunction with other column constraints.

CHECK constraints, as the name implies, are particularly useful in sanity checking. Listing 20.6 demonstrates the use of a CHECK constraint on the individual table, which ensures that no individual can be inserted who is over 150 years old.

Listing 20.6. This DDL script features a CHECK constraint.

```
CREATE TABLE individual (
    ID                  NUMBER(10)
                        CONSTRAINT indiv_pk          PRIMARY KEY
    ,last_name          VARCHAR2(30)
                        CONSTRAINT indiv_l_name      NOT NULL
    ,first_name         VARCHAR2(30)
                        CONSTRAINT indiv_f_name      NOT NULL
    ,notes              VARCHAR2(255)
    ,date_of_birth      DATE
                        CONSTRAINT indiv_chk_bday
                        CHECK (date_of_birth > TO_DATE('01-JAN-1845',
                               'DD-MON-YYYY',
                               'nls_date_language = American'))
    ,last_updt_user     VARCHAR2(20)
                        CONSTRAINT indiv_lu_id NOT NULL
    ,last_updt_date     DATE
                        CONSTRAINT indiv_lu_dt NOT NULL
);
```

When used as a column constraint, only one column can be referenced in the CHECK condition, and only one CHECK constraint is allowed per column.

To use the Social Security number as an example again, an application may want to store the dashes for easy reporting. You can use a CHECK constraint to ensure that the Social Security number is the correct length and that the dashes are in the correct positions.

TIP

The system catalog tables, user_indexes and user_constraints, contain all information regarding indexes and constraints. Listing 20.7 contains two simple SQL scripts that query these tables. The scripts can be executed in SQL*Plus or SQL*DBA to produce the output shown in Figure 20.1.

Listing 20.7. These simple SQL scripts query catalog tables to display information on existing indexes and constraints.

```
/* INDEXES.SQL */
select table_name, index_name, uniqueness
from user_indexes
order by 1, 2

/

/* CONST.SQL */
select table_name, constraint_name, constraint_type
from user_constraints
order by 1, 2

/
```

FIGURE 20.1.

*This output was generated by running the SQL scripts from Listing 20.7 in SQL*Plus.*

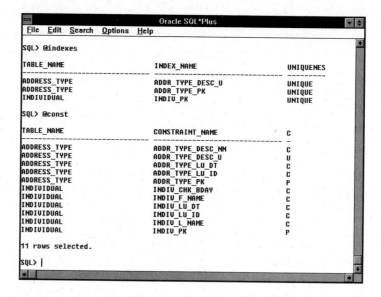

Column constraints can be employed to enforce referential integrity for foreign keys using the REFERENCES keyword. The table and column specified in the REFERENCES clause must already exist, and the referenced column must be defined as a unique or PRIMARY KEY. Listing 20.9 demonstrates the use of two foreign keys in a table used only to join the referenced objects. Note that the script in Listing 20.8 must be run first, or the second REFERENCES constraint in Listing 20.9 will produce an error.

Listing 20.8. This DDL script creates the company table which is referenced by a foreign key constraint in Listing 20.9.

```
CREATE TABLE company (
    ID              NUMBER(10)
                    CONSTRAINT company_pk PRIMARY KEY
    ,name           VARCHAR2(30)
                    CONSTRAINT co_name_u   UNIQUE
                    CONSTRAINT co_name_nn NOT NULL
    ,notes          VARCHAR2(255)
    ,last_updt_user VARCHAR2(20)
                    CONSTRAINT co_lu_id    NOT NULL
    ,last_updt_date DATE
                    CONSTRAINT co_lu_dt    NOT NULL
);
```

Listing 20.9. This DDL script contains two REFERENCES column constraints.

```
CREATE TABLE ind_co_rel (
    individual_id   NUMBER(10)
                    CONSTRAINT indco_ind_fk
                        REFERENCES individual(ID)
                        ON DELETE CASCADE
                    CONSTRAINT indco_ind_nn NOT NULL
    ,company_id     NUMBER(10)
                    CONSTRAINT indco_co_fk
                        REFERENCES company(ID)
                        ON DELETE CASCADE
                    CONSTRAINT indco_co_nn  NOT NULL
    ,title          VARCHAR2(80)
    ,last_updt_user VARCHAR2(20)
                    CONSTRAINT indco_lu_id  NOT NULL
    ,last_updt_date DATE
                    CONSTRAINT indco_lu_dt  NOT NULL
);
```

The REFERENCES column constraint does not imply NOT NULL, but NOT NULL can be used in conjunction with a REFERENCES constraint on a column. As a result of the REFERENCES clauses in Listing 20.8, an application cannot insert a row into this table, unless both the individual_id and company_id values exist in their respective tables.

> **NOTE**
>
> The data type is unnecessary for columns containing a REFERENCES constraint. The column will automatically be defined with the data type of the column it references.

The ON DELETE CASCADE option is a very significant feature of the REFERENCES column constraint. If it is not specified, rows with key values in the parent table cannot be deleted until all corresponding rows in the table containing the REFERENCES constraint are deleted. When ON DELETE CASCADE is specified, deletions in the parent table cause all references in the child table to be deleted automatically. In this respect, using ON DELETE CASCADE is similar to creating a DELETE trigger on the referenced table. This is an extremely powerful option and should be used with caution. If it is not properly understood, unwanted automatic deletions could result.

Although they are ideally suited to enforcing referential integrity, REFERENCES constraints may not be desirable in certain situations. For example, if a table has a high volume of transactions and contains several foreign keys that are simple lookups, performance can be adversely affected by using the REFERENCES constraint. Each time a row is inserted or updated, the referenced tables must be checked to ensure that each foreign key being inserted exists in the referenced tables. Depending on the nature of the data and the importance of performance, it may be preferable to enforce the foreign keys through the application itself.

Table Constraints

Each of the column constraints described in the previous section can also be applied as table constraints, with the exception of NOT NULL. Table constraints have the additional advantage of being able to operate on multiple columns.

Refer to the CHECK constraint in Listing 20.6. This provides a sanity check on the lower bounds of date_of_birth, but it would be better to check the upper bounds as well. Listing 20.10 illustrates how you can accomplish this using a table constraint.

Listing 20.10. This DDL script, containing a CHECK table constraint, is an improvement on the column constraint used in Listing 20.6.

```
CREATE TABLE individual (
    ID                  NUMBER(10)
                        CONSTRAINT indiv_pk         PRIMARY KEY
    ,last_name          VARCHAR2(30)
                        CONSTRAINT indiv_l_name     NOT NULL
    ,first_name         VARCHAR2(30)
                        CONSTRAINT indiv_f_name     NOT NULL
    ,notes              VARCHAR2(255)
    ,date_of_birth      DATE
    ,last_updt_user     VARCHAR2(20)
                        CONSTRAINT indiv_lu_id NOT NULL
    ,last_updt_date     DATE
                        CONSTRAINT indiv_lu_dt NOT NULL
    ,CONSTRAINT indiv_chk_bday
        CHECK (date_of_birth BETWEEN (TO_DATE('01-JAN-1845',
            'DD-MON-YYYY', 'nls_date_language = American'))
            AND last_updt_date)
);
```

The syntax of table constraints is nearly identical to that of column constraints, except that the CONSTRAINT clause comes at the end of the column list.

Another advantage to using a table constraint applies only to constraints that result in the creation of an index. The table constraint syntax allows the designation of a tablespace and storage specification for the corresponding index. When indexes are created automatically for column constraints, they are created in the default tablespace using the default storage specification. The script in Listing 20.11 adds a UNIQUE constraint to the ind_co_rel table, enforcing uniqueness in the combination of individual_id and company_id. It also implements the USING INDEX clause to designate a tablespace and storage specification for the index that will be created.

Listing 20.11. This DDL script uses the ALTER TABLE syntax to create a UNIQUE table constraint and a storage specification for the corresponding index.

```
ALTER TABLE ind_co_rel
ADD CONSTRAINT ind_co_rel_u UNIQUE(individual_id, company_id)
    USING INDEX
    TABLESPACE oracle_unleashed
    STORAGE (INITIAL    10K
             NEXT       10K
             MAXEXTENTS 100
             PCTINCREASE 10);
```

The syntax for tablespace and storage specification following the USING INDEX keyword is identical to that for the CREATE INDEX statement. The USING INDEX clause can also be used in a PRIMARY KEY constraint, as illustrated in Listing 20.12.

Listing 20.12. This DDL script removes the UNIQUE constraint created in Listing 20.11 and re-creates it as a PRIMARY KEY.

```
ALTER TABLE ind_co_rel
DROP CONSTRAINT ind_co_rel_u

/

ALTER TABLE ind_co_rel
DROP CONSTRAINT indco_ind_nn

/

ALTER TABLE ind_co_rel
DROP CONSTRAINT indco_co_nn

/

ALTER TABLE ind_co_rel
ADD CONSTRAINT ind_co_rel_pk PRIMARY KEY(individual_id, company_id)
    USING INDEX
    TABLESPACE oracle_unleashed
    STORAGE (INITIAL    10K
             NEXT       10K
             MAXEXTENTS 100
             PCTINCREASE 10)

/
```

Notice that the NOT NULL constraints on the individual_id and company_id columns were also dropped. To keep them would be redundant, because columns included in a PRIMARY KEY constraint cannot have null values.

Foreign key table constraints are implemented in much the same way as REFERENCING column constraints. If necessary, multiple columns can be included in a FOREIGN KEY table constraint. This is not the case with the column constraint implementation. Note also that the FOREIGN KEY keyword is only available for the table constraint syntax. Listing 20.13, the final script for ind_co_rel, also defines temporary tables into which exceptions are logged.

Listing 20.13. The final ind_co_rel script uses the FOREIGN KEY table constraint syntax and logs exceptions into temporary tables.

```
CREATE TABLE ind_co_rel (
    individual_id   NUMBER(10)
   ,company_id      NUMBER(10)
   ,title           VARCHAR2(80)
   ,last_updt_user  VARCHAR2(20)
                    CONSTRAINT indco_lu_id  NOT NULL
                    EXCEPTIONS INTO ind_co_err_1
   ,last_updt_date  DATE
                    CONSTRAINT indco_lu_dt  NOT NULL
                    EXCEPTIONS INTO ind_co_err_2
   ,CONSTRAINT indco_ind_fk FOREIGN KEY (individual_id)
        REFERENCES individual(ID)
        ON DELETE CASCADE
        EXCEPTIONS INTO ind_co_err_3
   ,CONSTRAINT indco_co_fk  FOREIGN KEY (company_id)
        REFERENCES company(ID)
        ON DELETE CASCADE
        EXCEPTIONS INTO ind_co_err_4
   ,CONSTRAINT ind_co_rel_pk PRIMARY KEY(individual_id, company_id)
        USING INDEX
        TABLESPACE oracle_unleashed
        STORAGE (INITIAL     10K
                 NEXT        10K
                 MAXEXTENTS  100
                 PCTINCREASE 10)
        EXCEPTIONS INTO ind_co_err_5
)
TABLESPACE oracle_unleashed;
```

Each type of exception is logged into a different temporary table in Listing 20.13, which is helpful in debugging and resolving integrity problems. The tables into which exceptions are logged should be identical to the ind_co_rel table, except that they should have no constraints, for obvious reasons. The EXCEPTIONS INTO clause can be used for any type of column or table constraint. If the table referenced by EXCEPTIONS INTO does not exist, using the clause will produce an error.

The EXCEPTIONS INTO clause is particularly useful in applications where frequent and timely bulk loads are required. In order to use SQL*Loader with the direct path option to maximize its performance, constraints must be disabled. When the constraints are re-enabled, the EXCEPTIONS INTO clause can be used to categorize problem records by inserting them in separate tables based on the constraint that was violated. This minimizes the negative impact constraints have on performance, while maintaining integrity and providing a means of identifying and resolving problems with the data being loaded.

As shown by these examples, Oracle provides a wide variety of options for enforcing integrity through column and table constraints. Constraints are powerful tools for enforcing integrity, but they should be used with care. Overuse of constraints can add significantly to long-term maintenance requirements, and misuse can create unwanted dependencies or unnecessary exceptions. The possible trade-offs involving constraints and performance will be discussed in greater detail later in this chapter.

Using Sequences

Oracle sequences are ideally suited to the task of generating unique key values. A sequence is a stored object that simply generates a sequence of numbers. Listing 20.14 illustrates the syntax for creating a sequence.

Listing 20.14. This sequence is used to generate primary keys for the individual table.

```
CREATE SEQUENCE individual_ids
    START WITH 1
    INCREMENT BY 1
    NOMAXVALUE;
```

The values specified for the START WITH and INCREMENT BY parameters in Listing 20.14 are the defaults. NOMAXVALUE is the default as well. The script in Listing 20.13 will produce the same result as the following:

```
CREATE SEQUENCE individual_ids;
```

It is a good practice to explicitly declare these defaults for documentation purposes, if nothing else. The implementation is fairly self-explanatory. The START WITH parameter indicates the first number that will be generated, INCREMENT BY specifies a number to be added to the current value to generate the next value, and NOMAXVALUE indicates that there is no maximum to the numbers it will generate, (practically no maximum, although there is an upper limit).

The MINVALUE parameter is used only by descending sequences. (Specifying a negative value for INCREMENT BY produces a descending sequence.) CYCLE, when used in conjunction with MAXVALUE or MINVALUE, indicates that the sequence should start from the beginning when the minimum or maximum value is reached. The default for this option is NOCYCLE.

The CACHE parameter indicates the number of values that should be pre-generated and cached by the sequence. The default value for CACHE is 20. Raising this parameter can improve performance in high transaction volume environments.

ORDER ensures that sequences are used in the order generated. Regardless of the setting of this option, the same value will never be returned twice. If an application uses a sequence in a transaction that is rolled back, the value is simply discarded. NORDER, the default for this option, is acceptable unless the sequence is being used like a timestamp to indicate the order of events over time.

A sequence has two pseudocolumns, currval and nextval. Currval returns the current value of the sequence, while nextval increments the sequence and returns the new value. Listing 20.15 demonstrates how a sequence can be used in an Oracle function to generate new keys when inserting records.

Listing 20.15. This function accesses a sequence to fetch a new key when inserting a record.

```
CREATE OR REPLACE FUNCTION insert_indiv (last CHAR, first CHAR,
                           notes CHAR, dob DATE) RETURN NUMBER
IS
    new_id NUMBER;
BEGIN
    SELECT individual_ids.nextval INTO new_id FROM dual;
    INSERT INTO individual VALUES (new_id, last, first, notes,
                              dob, user, sysdate);
    COMMIT;
    RETURN(new_id);
EXCEPTION
    WHEN OTHERS THEN
        ROLLBACK;
        RETURN(-1);
END insert_indiv;
```

It is a common practice to use sequences for generating unique primary keys. One sequence can be used for many tables, or a separate sequence can be created for each table requiring generated keys. Either option is preferable to any key that requires user intervention, because typographical errors are bound to occur. It is typically preferable to generate unique keys even when one exists naturally in the data (Social Security number, for example).

Using a sequence to generate primary keys can improve performance in certain situations, as well. As mentioned previously, integer joins are typically faster than character-based joins, and even when a natural integer primary key exists, a sequence is often a better choice. To use Social Security number as an example, 10 bytes must be stored for each key. If a sequence is used, starting with 1, a considerable amount of disk space can be conserved, and a much smaller index produced, which will result in less I/O. Perhaps a less important consideration is the order in which values are inserted. Depending on how inserts are handled by applications accessing the sequence, the index on a sequence-generated primary key may be created in ascending order naturally, which is somewhat of an optimization in terms of I/O performance. If the sequence is created with the ORDER option, and inserts are handled using Oracle subprograms similar to Listing 20.15, this will always be true.

Using Triggers

Triggers are stored procedures associated with a specific operation on a specific table. A trigger is automatically fired when the operation with which it is associated is performed on the table with which it is associated. Triggers can perform many of the same tasks as constraints, and in most cases, they can go beyond what constraints can do. For example, a NOT NULL constraint can only ensure that a value is present in a column, but it does nothing to ensure the accuracy of the data. Listing 20.16 provides an example of how you can use triggers to enforce a NOT NULL constraint and ensure the accuracy of the data being inserted.

Listing 20.16. This trigger ensures that the columns last_updt_user and last_updt_date are inserted and updated accurately.

```
CREATE OR REPLACE TRIGGER indiv_timestamp
BEFORE INSERT OR UPDATE ON individual FOR EACH ROW
BEGIN
     :new.last_updt_user := user;
     :new.last_updt_date := sysdate;
END indiv_timestamp;
```

The simple trigger in Listing 20.16 ensures that the last_updt_user and last_updt_date are being inserted and updated accurately in the individual table. In effect, the trigger intercepts the actual values being inserted and replaces them with user and sysdate. Using the NOT NULL constraint for these columns is no longer necessary, and the trigger goes far beyond what the constraint could do.

> **NOTE**
>
> The trigger in Listing 20.16 also relieves the application of the burden of supplying values for the last_updt_user and last_updt_date columns when inserting and updating records.

INSERT and UPDATE triggers are commonly used for customized transaction logging, or to generate statistical summaries to be accessed by a different group of users than those applying the transactions. For example, a large order entry system might use an INSERT trigger to write only the date, the order amount, and the salesperson to a separate table to be used only for management reporting.

The syntax for creating triggers is very similar to the creation of procedures, with a few notable exceptions. The BEFORE or AFTER keyword must follow the name of the trigger, indicating whether it should be fired before or after the operation that causes it is fired.

> **NOTE**
>
> Although it may not seem logical to do so, this trigger had to be created with the BEFORE option. Trying to implement this trigger with the AFTER option produces the following error:
>
> ```
> ORA-04091: table SCOTTY.INDIVIDUAL is mutating, trigger/function may not see
> it
> ```
>
> Because the trigger is being executed by a process that is currently involved in a transaction on the same row, it cannot be created with the AFTER option. This would, in effect, invalidate the *old* correlation of the trigger.

Immediately following the BEFORE or AFTER keyword is the action (or actions) with which the trigger is associated. This can be INSERT, UPDATE, or DELETE, or any combination of these separated by OR. The FOR EACH ROW keyword defines the behavior of the trigger when it is fired by statements affecting multiple rows. The default behavior is to fire the trigger only once, regardless of the number of rows affected. A trigger may also include a WHEN clause, which limits the conditions under which it will fire.

The WHEN clause can be used for specialized reporting, or to draw attention to a value that may seem to be out of range. For example, an accounts payable system might use an INSERT trigger to log all payments of greater than $10,000 to a temporary table, which can then be used to generate a report for management's review and approval. This could be an alternative to a CHECK condition, which might prove to be overly restrictive. In most circumstances, it would not be acceptable to reject a valid payment simply because it is unusually high. On the other hand, management may be interested in reviewing or auditing these payments. In this respect, a trigger can be used in a way that is analogous to passively enforcing a CHECK constraint.

Note that in Listing 20.16, the variable *new* is never declared. This is the default correlation name associated with the new row (which is valid for inserts and updates only). The name *old* is associated with the old row by default, and is valid for updates and deletes only. These default names can be reassigned using a REFERENCING clause. The REFERENCING clause should be placed immediately before the FOR EACH ROW keyword (if it is used), as in Listing 20.17.

Listing 20.17. This trigger uses a REFERENCING clause to rename new.

```
CREATE OR REPLACE TRIGGER indiv_timestamp
BEFORE INSERT OR UPDATE ON individual
REFERENCING new AS new_row FOR EACH ROW
BEGIN
    :new_row.last_updt_user := user;
    :new_row.last_updt_date := sysdate;
END indiv_timestamp;
```

The REFERENCING clause is rarely used, but it is provided in order to allow the use of *new* and *old* as regular program variables.

Triggers, when used with sequences, can also be used to enforce primary key constraints. Listing 20.18 creates a trigger that ensures that new rows in the individual table are assigned unique primary key values. The trigger also ensures that the sequence is used, by overriding any value specified in an insert statement with the next value in the sequence.

Listing 20.18. This trigger enforces the primary key on the individual table.

```
CREATE OR REPLACE TRIGGER indiv_get_key
BEFORE INSERT ON individual FOR EACH ROW
DECLARE
    new_id NUMBER;
BEGIN
    SELECT individual_ids.nextval INTO new_id FROM dual;
    :new.id := new_id;
END indiv_get_key;
```

Unfortunately, this trigger cannot coexist with the trigger in Listing 20.17. For each table, only one trigger can exist for each operation. Listing 20.19 demonstrates how these can be implemented together, replacing the CHECK constraint on date_of_birth in the process.

Listing 20.19. These triggers can be used to enforce several constraints on the individual table.

```
CREATE OR REPLACE TRIGGER indiv_ins_trg
BEFORE INSERT ON individual FOR EACH ROW
DECLARE
    new_id NUMBER;
BEGIN
    IF ((:new.date_of_birth < TO_DATE('01-JAN-1845', 'DD-MON-YYYY',
        'nls_date_language = American'))
OR (:new.date_of_birth > sysdate)) THEN
        RAISE_APPLICATION_ERROR(-20001, 'Invalid birth date.');
    ELSE
        SELECT individual_ids.nextval INTO new_id FROM dual;
        :new.id := new_id;
        :new.last_updt_user := user;
        :new.last_updt_date := sysdate;
    END IF;
END indiv_ins_trg;

CREATE OR REPLACE TRIGGER indiv_updt_trg
BEFORE UPDATE ON individual FOR EACH ROW
BEGIN
    IF ((:new.date_of_birth < TO_DATE('01-JAN-1845',
        'DD-MON-YYYY', 'nls_date_language = American'))
        OR (:new.date_of_birth > sysdate)) THEN
        RAISE_APPLICATION_ERROR(-20001, 'Invalid birth date.');
```

continues

Listing 20.19. continued

```
    ELSE
        :new.id := :old.id;
        :new.last_updt_user := user;
        :new.last_updt_date := sysdate;
    END IF;
END indiv_updt_trg;
```

In Listing 20.19, the PRIMARY KEY constraint is enforced for both inserts and updates. The UPDATE trigger completely prevents an ID from being changed, which might not be acceptable if this were not a generated key. The triggers also enforce a CHECK constraint on date_of_birth and the NOT NULL constraints on last_updt_user and last_updt_date.

Triggers can be used to enforce foreign key constraints, as well. Refer to Listing 20.9. The REFERENCES constraints in the example both contained the ON DELETE CASCADE option. If the foreign keys integrity constraints are enforced by the triggers in Listing 20.20, the REFERENCES column constraints could be removed.

Listing 20.20. These triggers can be used to enforce foreign key constraints.

```
CREATE OR REPLACE TRIGGER indiv_del_trg
BEFORE DELETE ON individual FOR EACH ROW
BEGIN
    DELETE FROM ind_co_rel WHERE individual_id = :old.id;
END indiv_del_trg;


CREATE OR REPLACE TRIGGER co_del_trg
BEFORE DELETE ON company FOR EACH ROW
BEGIN
    DELETE FROM ind_co_rel WHERE company_id = :old.id;
END co_del_trg;

CREATE OR REPLACE TRIGGER ind_co_trg
BEFORE INSERT OR UPDATE ON ind_co_rel FOR EACH ROW
DECLARE
    co_id    NUMBER;
    indiv_id NUMBER;
BEGIN
    SELECT ID INTO co_id FROM company WHERE ID = :new.company_id;
    SELECT ID INTO indiv_id FROM individual
            WHERE ID = :new.individual_id;
    EXCEPTION
        WHEN OTHERS THEN
            RAISE_APPLICATION_ERROR(-20002, 'Invalid id.');
END ind_co_trg;
```

As these examples demonstrate, triggers can be used to perform the same tasks as table and column constraints. In many cases, it may be preferable to use triggers because they are likely to provide better performance. This is particularly true in distributed environments, where it may not be possible to enforce foreign key constraints at all.

When designing triggers, you should pay special attention to cascading triggers. Cascading occurs when a trigger on one table causes a trigger on another table to be fired. Codependencies, in particular, can be a problem.

Note that in Listing 20.20, the individual and company tables both have DELETE triggers that delete corresponding rows from ind_co_rel. For the sake of example, assume that ind_co_rel has a DELETE trigger that deletes corresponding rows in address_rel and phone_rel, and that individual and company also include these deletions in their DELETE triggers.

This presents numerous integrity problems. If a relationship between an individual and a company is deleted, records in address_rel and phone_rel that are related to both should be deleted. Also, if an individual or company is deleted entirely, all address_rel and phone_rel records related to the specific individual or company should be deleted. When an individual or company is deleted, the ind_co_rel record is deleted, which causes its trigger to be fired, resulting in deletions from the address_rel and phone_rel tables. If these records are also to be deleted by the trigger that was originally fired by the deletion of the individual or company, the mutating table problem described earlier will occur. In this case, the ind_co_rel should probably not have a DELETE trigger at all. Meaningless records in address_rel and phone_rel exist only until the corresponding individual or company is deleted. This is just one example of how cascading triggers can produce unexpected results.

Application and Performance Considerations

Regardless of how integrity is enforced in the database, the application must have knowledge of the constraints. The application must be able to submit transaction statements in the proper order, and it must know how to respond to exceptions resulting from integrity problems. This point is best illustrated through the use of an example. Assume that the application needs to perform a single transaction based on the objects created in Listing 20.21.

Listing 20.21. These objects participate in a single transaction.

```
CREATE SEQUENCE individual_ids
    START WITH 1
    INCREMENT BY 1
    NOMAXVALUE;


CREATE TABLE individual (
    ID              NUMBER(10)
                    CONSTRAINT indiv_pk        PRIMARY KEY
    ,last_name      VARCHAR2(30)
```

continues

Listing 20.21. continued

```
                        CONSTRAINT indiv_l_name      NOT NULL
    ,first_name         VARCHAR2(30)
                        CONSTRAINT indiv_f_name      NOT NULL
    ,notes              VARCHAR2(255)
    ,date_of_birth      DATE
    ,last_updt_user     VARCHAR2(20)
                        CONSTRAINT indiv_lu_id NOT NULL
    ,last_updt_date     DATE
                        CONSTRAINT indiv_lu_dt NOT NULL
    ,CONSTRAINT indiv_chk_bday
        CHECK (date_of_birth BETWEEN (TO_DATE('01-JAN-1845',
                'DD-MON-YYYY', 'nls_date_language = American'))
                AND last_updt_date)
);

CREATE SEQUENCE company_ids
    START WITH 1
    INCREMENT BY 1
    NOMAXVALUE;

CREATE TABLE company (
    ID                  NUMBER(10)
                        CONSTRAINT company_pk PRIMARY KEY
    ,name               VARCHAR2(30)
                        CONSTRAINT co_name_u   UNIQUE
                        CONSTRAINT co_name_nn NOT NULL
    ,notes              VARCHAR2(255)
    ,last_updt_user     VARCHAR2(20)
                        CONSTRAINT co_lu_id    NOT NULL
    ,last_updt_date     DATE
                        CONSTRAINT co_lu_dt    NOT NULL
);

CREATE TABLE ind_co_rel (
    individual_id    NUMBER(10)
    ,company_id      NUMBER(10)
    ,title           VARCHAR2(80)
    ,last_updt_user  VARCHAR2(20)
                     CONSTRAINT indco_lu_id  NOT NULL
                     EXCEPTIONS INTO ind_co_err_1
    ,last_updt_date  DATE
                     CONSTRAINT indco_lu_dt  NOT NULL
                     EXCEPTIONS INTO ind_co_err_2
    ,CONSTRAINT indco_ind_fk FOREIGN KEY (individual_id)
        REFERENCES individual(ID)
        ON DELETE CASCADE
        EXCEPTIONS INTO ind_co_err_3
    ,CONSTRAINT indco_co_fk  FOREIGN KEY (company_id)
        REFERENCES company(ID)
        ON DELETE CASCADE
        EXCEPTIONS INTO ind_co_err_4
    ,CONSTRAINT ind_co_rel_pk PRIMARY KEY(individual_id, company_id)
        USING INDEX
        TABLESPACE oracle_unleashed
        STORAGE (INITIAL     10K
                 NEXT        10K
                 MAXEXTENTS  100
```

```
                    PCTINCREASE  10)
          EXCEPTIONS INTO ind_co_err_5
);
```

It would be useful if the application could insert an individual, a company, and a record relating the two in one transaction. The foreign key constraints on ind_co_rel dictate that this record must be inserted last. In designing a process to complete this transaction, you should also consider that the application will need to insert an individual and a company separately, as well. Listing 20.22 provides three functions to accomplish these tasks.

Listing 20.22. These three functions guarantee that integrity constraints are satisfied for inserts into the objects in Listing 20.21.

```
CREATE OR REPLACE FUNCTION insert_indiv (last CHAR, first CHAR,
                          notes CHAR, dob DATE)
RETURN NUMBER
IS
    invalid_name EXCEPTION;
    new_id       NUMBER;
BEGIN
    IF ((LENGTH(RTRIM(last)) > 0) AND
        (LENGTH(RTRIM(first)) > 0)) THEN
        SELECT individual_ids.nextval INTO new_id FROM dual;
        INSERT INTO individual VALUES (new_id, last, first,
                    notes, dob, user, sysdate);
        RETURN(new_id);
    ELSE
        RAISE invalid_name;
    END IF;
EXCEPTION
    WHEN invalid_name THEN
        ROLLBACK;
        RETURN(-20001);
    WHEN OTHERS THEN
        ROLLBACK;
        RETURN(-1);
END insert_indiv;

CREATE OR REPLACE FUNCTION insert_company (name CHAR, notes CHAR)
RETURN NUMBER
IS
    invalid_name EXCEPTION;
    new_id       NUMBER;
BEGIN
    IF (LENGTH(RTRIM(name)) > 0) THEN
        SELECT company_ids.nextval INTO new_id FROM dual;
        INSERT INTO company VALUES (new_id, name, notes, user,
                                    sysdate);
        RETURN(new_id);
    ELSE
        RAISE invalid_name;
    END IF;
EXCEPTION
```

continues

Listing 20.22. continued

```
            WHEN invalid_name THEN
                ROLLBACK;
                RETURN(-20001);
            WHEN OTHERS THEN
                ROLLBACK;
                RETURN(-1);
        END insert_company;


        CREATE OR REPLACE FUNCTION insert_ind_co(last CHAR, first CHAR,
                                    notes CHAR, dob DATE, co_name CHAR,
                                    co_notes CHAR, title CHAR)
        RETURN NUMBER
        IS
            ret             NUMBER;
            ind_id          NUMBER;
            co_id           NUMBER;
        BEGIN
            ret:=insert_indiv(last, first, notes, dob);
            IF (ret > 0) THEN
                ind_id:=ret;
                ret:=insert_company(co_name, co_notes);
                IF (ret > 0) THEN
                    co_id:=ret;
                    INSERT INTO ind_co_rel VALUES (ind_id, co_id, title,
                                    user, sysdate);
                    RETURN(ind_id);
                ELSE
                    ROLLBACK;
                    RETURN(ret);
                END IF;
            ELSE
                ROLLBACK;
                RETURN(ret);
            END IF;
        EXCEPTION
            WHEN OTHERS THEN
                ROLLBACK;
                RETURN(-1);
        END insert_ind_co;
```

The transaction ensures that all constraints are being met, with the exception of the check constraint on individual, which could easily be added to the insert_indiv function. Sequences are used to generate primary keys, the functions check for null values, and the foreign key constraints in ind_co_rel are enforced by the order in which inserts occur. If an error occurs in any of the transactions, a rollback is issued, but commits are left out altogether. This is to ensure that an individual or company is not committed as part of the transaction that establishes their relationship. It is up to the calling application to commit the transaction as a whole.

These functions illustrate the point that in some cases, it may be a good solution to allow the client application to enforce integrity. Column and table constraints can be costly, especially foreign key constraints, which require an additional read. In an environment with a high volume of transactions and users, these constraints can have a significant negative impact on performance, possibly resulting in unnecessary contention, snapshot problems, and other bottlenecks.

When using the application itself to enforce referential integrity, you can run batch processes periodically to ensure that the application is enforcing integrity. You can create temporary tables to store exceptions for further analysis and resolution, and you can use simple SQL to identify problem records. For example, you can use a statement like the one following to identify invalid references to individuals in the ind_co_rel table.

```
SELECT * FROM ind_co_rel INTO temp_no_ind WHERE individual_id NOT IN
        (SELECT ID FROM individual)
```

If the application is properly designed, batch processes should not identify exceptions and would need to be run very infrequently.

Primary key constraints, on the other hand, typically improve performance, especially if they are defined as a single small column. This constraint causes an index to be built, and primary key values are often stored as foreign keys in other tables. In these cases, declaring the primary key usually results in faster joins.

In general, however, constraints have a negative impact on overall performance. Depending on the nature of the data, security considerations, and standards of acceptable performance, you can rely upon the application itself to enforce many of the required integrity constraints.

Summary

Column constraints, table constraints, triggers, and PL/SQL are all useful in enforcing integrity, but each approach also has limitations. The best way to combine these elements to enforce integrity depends entirely on the application. Most designs use a combination of all of these methods and attempt to strike a balance between pure performance and the strict enforcement of integrity.

Application Security

21

*by Advanced
Information
Systems, Inc.*

IN THIS CHAPTER

Application security limits database access from the client side of the system. Database security limits access to specific database objects, whereas application security limits access to specific interface objects. In a broader sense, application security also includes the use of any application-specific database objects that are created to enhance security.

There are several reasons why you should use application security in addition to database security. These reasons are discussed in the following section. This chapter also covers the use of application-specific database objects and table-driven user interfaces, as well as application and performance considerations relating to the use of application security.

Reasons for Using Application Security

In general, application security is used to enhance and supplement database security. However, it would be dangerous to rely only on application security because there is no guarantee that users will access the database only through a single application.

Application security can enhance database security by further limiting access to database objects and by providing an additional layer of abstraction (hiding the details of available database objects). If you limit access to application-specific stored procedures and functions and create application-specific roles, you can hide objects based on the specific user or the role of the user accessing the system. On the same basis, the application can limit access of specific columns or make specific columns read-only by using different views for different roles or users.

In a typical database application, the interface enables the user to communicate with the database by using menus and forms related to business processes and objects rather than tables and columns. This is a convenient layer that prevents users from having to know the names of the tables and columns being accessed.

In many cases, information in the database is used to control the behavior of the interface, based on the role of the user. System tables contain security information used by the application to drive what capabilities are available to the interface. Menu options and forms to which the user has privileges to access are made visible, while others are hidden.

For example, if an application has an administration menu containing options specific to database administration functions, the entire menu is hidden from users who do not have the administrator role. Any forms relating to these specific functions are inaccessible as well. This method of using application security is obviously preferable to providing a homogenous interface that enables users to try to perform operations on tables to which they have no privileges. If the application allowed the user to access a database object that they did not have privileges to, the resulting errors would have to be trapped and displayed to the user, which can result in misunderstanding and frustration on the users' part. Using the database to drive application security is also preferable to hard-coding rules into the client application. Table-driven application security makes it easy to update a user's privileges without having to reprogram the application.

Another reason for using application security relates to databases that are accessed by multiple applications. In this case, a single user might have multiple roles, of which only one applies to the specific application. Use an Oracle table when there are different application roles that could apply. For example, an order entry system might have three different roles: one for order entry, one for management reporting, and one for system administration. A billing system and an accounts receivable system might share common tables and be used by many of the same users. These users may have slightly different role definitions for each application. A simple Oracle table containing a user ID and a corresponding role can be used to determine the correct role to be used for the application at runtime. The privileges of the appropriate role can then be used to limit the user's view of the database to the scope that was intended for the particular application.

Using Application-Specific Database Objects

The distinction between application security and database security is sometimes blurred, as is the case when you use application-specific database objects. As illustrated by the previous example, different applications often access a common database. When you create objects to be used only by a specific application, application-level security is common. Although the objects exist in the database and database security is used, if the object exists only to service a specific application, it is "owned" by the application. The argument can be made that rights granted to the stored object fall under the category of application security.

In the definition of overall systems security, the "base" objects (clusters, tables, indexes, and sequences) and rights granted to these objects are categorized as database security issues. Views, procedures, and functions are considered application-specific objects, and rights granted to them are categorized as application security issues.

Typically, in large database environments the primary DBA will not be responsible for creating and maintaining all application-specific objects. One possible way to handle security for a large database accessed by multiple applications is to grant rights to sequences and views of the tables to lead developers or administrators who serve as DBAs for the individual applications. To do this, use the WITH GRANT OPTION clause. Listing 21.1 follows the example of the database shared by order entry and billing/accounts receivable applications. It demonstrates how the WITH GRANT OPTION might be used on a subset of the database objects.

Listing 21.1. This script grants limited rights to the common database objects.

```
/* SEQUENCE */
CREATE PUBLIC SYNONYM account_no FOR account_no;

CREATE OR REPLACE VIEW accounts AS
   SELECT * FROM account;
```

continues

Listing 21.1. continued

```
CREATE PUBLIC SYNONYM accounts FOR accounts;

/* SEQUENCE */
CREATE PUBLIC SYNONYM order_no FOR order_no;

CREATE OR REPLACE VIEW orders AS
    SELECT * FROM order_on_acct;
CREATE PUBLIC SYNONYM orders FOR orders;

/* Billing-AR System DBA & rights */
GRANT CONNECT
    ,RESOURCE
    ,CREATE USER
    ,CREATE ROLE
    ,CREATE PUBLIC SYNONYM
TO bardba IDENTIFIED BY billing;

GRANT SELECT ON account_no TO bardba
    WITH GRANT OPTION;
GRANT SELECT, INSERT, UPDATE ON accounts TO bardba
    WITH GRANT OPTION;
GRANT SELECT ON orders TO bardba
    WITH GRANT OPTION;


/* Order Entry System DBA & rights */
GRANT CONNECT
    ,RESOURCE
    ,CREATE USER
    ,CREATE ROLE
    ,CREATE PUBLIC SYNONYM
TO oedba IDENTIFIED BY entry;

GRANT SELECT ON order_no TO oedba
    WITH GRANT OPTION;
GRANT SELECT, INSERT, UPDATE ON orders TO oedba
    WITH GRANT OPTION;
GRANT SELECT ON accounts TO oedba
    WITH GRANT OPTION;
```

According to the previously described model of security, the script in Listing 21.1 is where database security ends and application security begins; enforcement responsibilities are delegated to the administrators of the specific applications. Note that public synonyms were created to hide the system ID of the DBA, and that limited rights were granted to each application "super-user." The bardba and oedba users will create application-specific objects, roles, and users, and grant rights based on the individual application—within the database security restrictions enforced by the DBA by the limited rights granted to them.

Note that the bardba user received read-only access to the orders view, and that the oedba user received read-only access to the accounts view, while neither user received the delete privilege to either view. This will limit the objects they can create, as well as the rights that they can grant to additional roles and users. For example, the bardba user will not be able to create a procedure to insert records into orders, or grant the insert privilege on orders to other roles and users.

Application-specific objects include procedures, functions, packages, and views.

Stored procedures and functions are typically used to insert, update, and delete records. In many cases, these subprograms will operate only on views, and not on the underlying tables themselves. This makes it easier for administrators to change the underlying structures as needed, without affecting the applications that access them. Views are also used to present separate tables as one logical business object or to limit access to specific columns.

You should use procedures and functions to perform all transactions for several reasons. One reason to use database subroutines is that they can be used to enforce integrity. For example, if a sequence is used to generate unique primary key values for a particular table, encapsulating the insert into a procedure or function can ensure that the sequence is always used. When user IDs or timestamps are being stored, the values for the user IDs and timestamps can be supplied from within the stored procedure or function as well. This ensures the integrity of these values, simplifies transaction processing for the client-side application, and helps reduce the amount of data being passed between the client and the server.

Using procedures and functions can also enhance database security. By granting only EXECUTE privileges on subprograms, the views and tables on which the subprograms operate remain unavailable. This prevents users from accessing them through SQL*Plus or one of the many desktop database or reporting tools that might enable them to modify the subprograms.

There are additional advantages to using packages. An Oracle package encapsulates a group of variables, constants, cursors, and subprograms into a single logical unit. This can greatly simplify the process of granting privileges, and improve overall performance. When EXECUTE is granted on a package, the user receives the execute privilege for each subprogram contained in the package specification. The entire package is loaded into memory when a packaged object is first referenced by the application, which reduces I/O and improves performance for subsequent calls to subprograms within the package.

You should always use views to present result sets to the application. As mentioned previously, using views can help insulate the application from structural changes to the underlying tables and limit access to specific columns. Views can also simplify embedded SQL in the application by completely eliminating the need for joins. If all joins are handled by the views, the application can treat the result set as if it were a single table. This can also simplify the process of granting privileges. For example, if a view is created that joins seven tables, the user need only have the SELECT privilege to the view, not the underlying seven tables. The user will then be able to access the view. If the join were accomplished within SQL embedded in the application, the user would need the SELECT privilege for each of the seven tables. Through column aliasing, views can also present result sets in terms of business lingo rather than column names, which are often very different.

Ideally, application-specific stored procedures and functions are used for all transactions and operate only on views, whereas all result sets are retrieved through application-specific views. Such a configuration greatly enhances overall security and can completely insulate the client application from changes to the structure of the underlying tables. The procedures, functions, and views can be used to present a consistent database interface, regardless of the underlying structures on which they operate. By granting only EXECUTE on subprograms and SELECT on views, the users cannot perform any transactions or SELECTs from outside the application-specific objects to which these privileges are granted. Exclusive use of procedures, functions, and views places a layer of abstraction between the users and the database, hiding the actual implementations of the tables. This is becoming an increasingly important security consideration as users become more sophisticated and generic reporting tools become more powerful.

Public synonyms are a method of making a database object available to all users of the database. You can use public synonyms to hide the ID of the owner of application objects and prevent an application from having to specify a schema. Granting privileges to the public synonyms rather than the objects themselves also provides an additional layer of abstraction. The diagram in Figure 21.1 provides a visual representation of the model of application security that has been presented in this section.

FIGURE 21.1.

This diagram represents the role of database objects in application security.

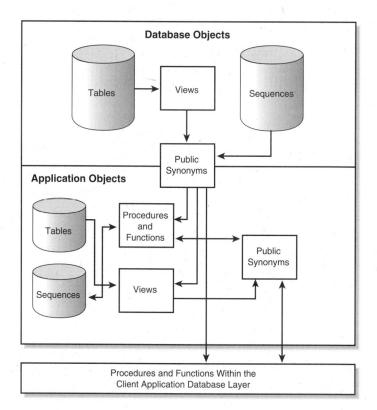

The application itself communicates with application-specific objects in the database through public synonyms. Stored procedures and functions operating on views are used exclusively for transaction processing, and views are used to retrieve all result sets. This method of communicating with the database provides the highest degree of abstraction and security and simplifies the process of developing the client application.

Table-Driven Application Security

You can use information stored in Oracle tables to drive application security. This solution is particularly useful when security restrictions are likely to change and flexibility is required. As mentioned in the previous section, you can use a table in Oracle to determine the default application role of the current user. The role can then be used as the basis for determining which menu options, forms, and controls are available to the user.

First, you must construct a table to store the application role of each user. This can be a simple two-column table made up of the user ID and application role. Each user should have only one role. If a particular user should have access to more than one role, you should create a new role and grant the privileges of the required roles. For example, if a user should have the privileges of the roles oe_user, oe_management, and oe_admin, a fourth role should be created as shown following:

```
CREATE ROLE oe_superuser;
GRANT oe_user, oe_management, oe_admin TO oe_superuser;
GRANT CONNECT, oe_superuser TO scotty IDENTIFIED BY tiger;
```

The user's role should be determined by the application immediately after the connection is established so that it can be used to enable, disable, or hide menu options as needed. The code that will alter the main window's menu should be placed in the window's constructor so that all changes are made before the window is instantiated. This will prevent the hidden options from being momentarily visible, before the menu is repainted. One possible table definition for controlling menu behavior appears in Listing 21.2.

Listing 21.2. One possible way to store application security information related to menus.

```
CREATE TABLE oe_menu_privileges (
     app_role        VARCHAR2(20)
    ,menu_item_id    VARCHAR2(10)
    ,visible         NUMBER(1)     NOT NULL
    ,enabled         NUMBER(1)     NOT NULL
    ,CONSTRAINT menu_priv_pk PRIMARY KEY (app_role, menu_item_id)
);
```

Defining the menu item identifier as a numeric value might be preferable to a character data type, depending on the tool you used to develop the client application. Many popular Windows development tools provide the Tag property as the only possible way to identify a particular control at runtime (besides the actual text of the menu item). This property is typically a string data type and should be stored as such in the database. Be careful to prevent trailing spaces from being stored in this column. Trailing spaces are easily overlooked, and might cause comparison problems.

The visible and enabled columns in Listing 21.2 should contain the numeric representations of the boolean values TRUE and FALSE so that they can be used to set the corresponding properties directly. For example, a Delphi application might use a method like the following one to directly enable or disable a menu option from a TTable object:

```
mnuAdmin.Enabled := tblMenuSecurity.FieldByName("ENABLED").AsBoolean;
```

One difficulty in dynamically altering menu options based on tabled information is in determining which menu option is referenced in the table. Depending on the tool being used, a menu item can be identified by an integer ID or by a string value assigned to the Tag property. Regardless of the means by which a menu option is identified, the application must be able to iterate through menu options to find a match for a menu ID read from the database. In some cases, the only available means of accomplishing this is to provide a switch statement, with a separate case for each possible menu item identifier. Consider this when you design menu security. If only a few items will be disabled or hidden for any given role, the number of items that must be checked against values read from the database will be minimized. This, in turn, will make the code required to accomplish these tasks smaller and easier to maintain. Listing 21.3 presents a sample implementation of these concepts in Visual Basic.

Listing 21.3. This Visual Basic subroutine uses a control array to alter a form's menu at run-time.

```
Sub SetMenuOptions(dsMenuOptions() As Dynaset)

    Dim i As Integer

    While Not dsMenuOptions(0).EOF
        For i = 0 To MAX_MENU_OPTIONS
            If (mnuTop(i).Tag =
                dsMenuOptions(0).Fields("MENU_OPTION")) Then

                mnuTop(i).Enabled =
                    dsMenuOptions(0).Fields("ENABLED")

                mnuTop(i).Visible =
                    dsMenuOptions(0).Fields("VISIBLE")
```

```
            Exit For
        End If
    Next i

    dsMenuOptions(0).MoveNext
Wend

End Sub
```

Note that Visual Basic's implementation of the control array provides a generic way to match a menu's identifier with values read from the database. However, this approach has its limitations. A menu control array can contain options only at the same level. Also, when controls are part of an array in Visual Basic, they share the same event code. Each event receives the index of the array to which the event currently applies as a parameter. This requires additional logic in event handlers for control arrays.

Many development tools do not provide control arrays as an option, so the code to match a menu item with a database value becomes more application-specific. The problem inherent to this method of using tables to control menu options is that the hard-coded menu identifiers must exactly match the values stored for them in the database. A change to either the identifier within the client application or to the value of the identifier in the table will cause this means of enforcing application security to fail. In most cases, if a menu option can possibly be disabled by the application security mechanism, it should be disabled by default. This is based on the assumption that if there are problems in properly matching values from the database, erring on the side of increased security is usually better.

Maintaining application security for menu options can be simplified by the design of the menus. Options that can potentially be disabled or hidden should be top-level menu items, and where groups of options can be disabled, they should be grouped together under the same top-level menu item wherever possible. Limiting the number of items that will need to be stored in the database and checked at runtime will improve performance and limit the possible points of failure.

Using the previously described order entry subsystem as an example, assume that only users with the role oe_admin will have access to update and insert records into lookup tables and to add new users to the system. These two operations can be logically grouped into a top-level menu category, Admin. Using this design, the application need only set the state for the top-level menu item. The Admin menu option should probably be made invisible (rather than disabled) for users who do not have access to it, because the options it contains will not be available to these users under any circumstances. Figures 21.2 and 21.3 show examples of what the main application window might look like to oe_admin and non-oe_admin users, respectively.

FIGURE 21.2.

This main window has all top-level menus visible and enabled.

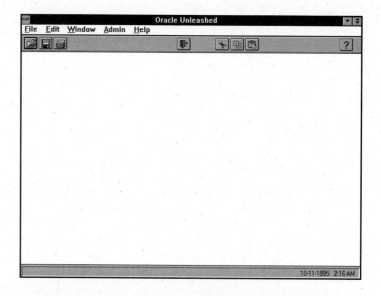

FIGURE 21.3.

In this main window, the top-level menu item Admin is completely hidden from a user who does not have the oe_admin role.

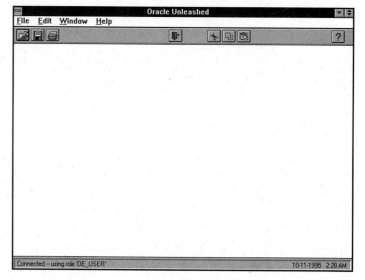

In some cases, it might be necessary to enable access to a subset of options in a drop-down menu. For example, a second role, oe_manager, might have privileges to add a new user, but not to modify lookup tables. For this user, the application's main menu can appear as in Figure 21.4.

FIGURE 21.4.

In this main window, the menu option Look-Ups is disabled for a user who has the oe_manager role.

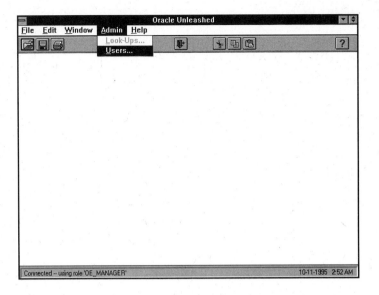

Whether you make menu options invisible or disabled is a matter of design preference. In most cases, it makes more sense to completely hide an option that is unavailable to the current user. Simply disabling a menu option implies that there are circumstances under which it will be enabled. However, when the menu option is part of a drop-down, making it invisible can leave only a single option, which is inconsistent with the standard uses of drop-down menus. Regardless of the way you enforce application security for menus, you should apply it consistently throughout the application.

You can apply similar methods and principles to enforce application security for windows and specific controls. In some cases, disabling or hiding a menu option prevents access to a particular form. Under these circumstances, no additional security should be required to prevent a user from accessing the form. However, it is more common for a particular form to be read-only for a specific application role or group of roles. In some cases, specific controls must be made read-only or disabled based on the role of the user.

As with menu options, you can design tables to drive application security for access to forms and specific controls. Listing 21.4 demonstrates one possible implementation of data-driven window and control-based application security.

Listing 21.4. This DDL script creates tables that can be used to dynamically alter the states of windows and controls at run-time.

```
CREATE TABLE oe_window_privileges (
    app_role        VARCHAR2(20)
    ,window_id       VARCHAR2(10)
```

continues

Listing 21.4. continued

```
     ,read_only       NUMBER(1)      NOT NULL
     ,CONSTRAINT window_priv_pk PRIMARY KEY (app_role, window_id)
);

CREATE TABLE oe_control_privileges (
     app_role         VARCHAR2(20)
    ,window_id        VARCHAR2(10)
    ,control_id       VARCHAR2(10)
    ,visible          NUMBER(1)      NOT NULL
    ,read_only        NUMBER(1)      NOT NULL
    ,CONSTRAINT cntrl_priv_pk PRIMARY KEY
               (app_role, window_id, control_id)
);
```

The same potential problems that apply to data-driven menu security apply to data-driven window and control security. First, there must be a method of determining the application role for a specific user. If application security is being applied to menu options, the same application role should apply to window and control-based security for a specific user. The user's role would then need to be read only once and stored in a global variable to be used whenever security restrictions must be checked. Within the table being used to determine which windows and controls can be accessed for a particular role, there must be a way to uniquely identify a window as well as individual controls within a window. Again, the problem with this approach is that the identifiers must exactly match those being used by the client application. As is the case with menu options, many development tools have only a Tag property available to use as this identifier. Any mismatch between identifiers in the application and the identifiers being stored in the table will result in a breakdown of application security.

Code used to retrieve security information from the database and alter the states for windows and controls should be placed in the appropriate constructors. Depending on the development tool, this can be a potential problem because objects that need to be referenced might not be instantiated at the time the window is constructed. For example, in C or C++, the constructors for a window's controls are typically called from within the constructor of the window itself. The application should retrieve values from the database before calling the constructors for any controls that might be affected by application security. The controls themselves can then be disabled or hidden as needed.

In MFC applications, for example, the Create member function is used to position and set the style for most interface objects. An application can set the style constants dynamically at runtime by calling Create with style constants read from the database. For example, in Windows 3.1, the ES_READONLY style constant can be passed to the Create member function of an edit control to make it read-only, and any control object that inherits from CWnd can use the WS_DISABLED style constant to disable a control. If the objects are constructed as part of a dialog resource, messages can be sent that will have the same effect. For example, EM_SETREADONLY can be sent to an edit box to make it read-only at any time after it is constructed.

In some cases, an application will need to hide controls based on the current user. In this case, the objects themselves should simply not be constructed, if possible. Note that the oe_control_privileges table in Listing 21.4 contains the columns visible and read_only. The read_only column should be redefined for C and C++ applications to accept style constants instead of the numeric representations of the boolean values TRUE and FALSE. If a control will not be visible, no values need be supplied for the style constant.

The order in which objects are constructed is not as much of a concern with most Windows GUI design tools, such as PowerBuilder and Visual Basic, unless controls are being placed dynamically at runtime. In Visual Basic, for example, all controls that were placed on a form at design time can be referenced in the load event (constructor) of a form. Unfortunately, Visual Basic controls do not provide all of the flexibility of the analogous MFC objects. The Visual Basic text box, which is roughly equivalent to the MFC CEdit class, does not provide a read-only property. However, the Windows API can be used to set a Visual Basic text box read-only at runtime, using the SendMessage function and the hWnd property of the text box.

The development tool being used will have an impact on the structure of the tables being used to drive application security. Tables such as those in Listing 21.4 will fit most situations, with minor modifications. Because the application must interpret the values in the tables based on the columns in which the values appear, the actual implementation is not important as long as it is applied consistently. For example, the oe_control_privileges table does not have an enabled column. However, the application will set the control as enabled rather than read-only based on the data in the control. As mentioned previously, if the application is being developed using C or C++, it might be preferable to replace the read_only column with a style column, used to store a style constant, or a combination of style constants to be applied to the control.

Regardless of the development tool or data structures you use to drive the interface, follow the same basic steps to enforce application security for windows and controls. First, in the constructor of a window, security information pertaining to the window is read from the database. This information must then be interpreted by the application through a process that maps values from the database to controls and properties. Finally, the properties of controls must be set based on this information. The entire process can become more complicated when a particular window serves more than one purpose. For example, in many cases the same form that is used to add a record is used to edit a record.

Typically, different rules or security restrictions will apply to adding a record versus editing an existing record. In these cases, the tables provided as an example in Listing 21.4 will not suffice. One possible solution is to define a constant to be used by the application to determine whether the window is being used to add a record or to edit one. You could add an additional column to the tables in Listing 21.4 to differentiate these modes. This column would also have to be part of the primary key. The application will now be required to prepare a different select statement based on whether the window is in add mode or edit mode.

Listing 21.5, which applies to the Order Item form shown in Figure 21.5, provides a simple example of how these concepts can be applied to application security using Visual Basic. The example is based on an order detail entry form that is used to add records by all salespeople. The example assumes that the date shipped field is updated by another process (such as the shipping department filling the order and creating a packing slip). It also assumes that only a manager can override the default price read from the database, and can do so only after the item has been added to the order. Although this simple example might seem a bit contrived, these types of rules are sometimes enforced to provide an additional audit trail for unusual transactions.

Listing 21.5. An example of enforcing application security for windows and controls in Visual Basic.

```
Sub SetSecurityStates(dsControlSecurity() As Dynaset)

    Dim iControlID As Integer
    Dim bVal      As Integer
    Dim iRet      As Integer

    While Not dsMenuOptions(0).EOF

        iControlID = dsControlSecurity(0).Fields("control_id")
        bVal = dsControlSecurity(0).Fields("read_only")

        Select Case iControlID
            Case Val(txtPrice.Tag)
                If (bVal = False) Then
                    lblPrice.ForeColor = COLOR_BLACK
                    iRet = SendMessage(txtPrice.hWnd,
                        EM_SETREADONLY, False, NILL)
                End If
            Case Val(txtDateShipped.Tag)
                If (bVal = False) Then
                    lblDateShipped.ForeColor = COLOR_BLACK
                    iRet = SendMessage(txtDateShipped.hWnd,
                        EM_SETREADONLY, False, NILL)
                End If
        dsControlSecurity(0).MoveNext
    Wend

End Sub
```

In the example, security restrictions apply to only two fields; therefore, only two fields are checked. Note that the Listing 21.5 assumes that the fields were set read-only by default in the constructor for the window. Where security restrictions apply, the default behavior of windows and controls should be to assume that the current user does not have privileges, so that if there is any problem with the data (other than valid, but inaccurate values), the application will err on the side of increased, rather than reduced, security.

FIGURE 21.5.

This window uses application security to make the price and date shipped for a particular role read-only.

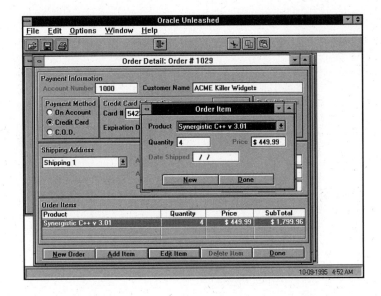

The example in Listing 21.5 points out one of the powerful uses of application security, as opposed to database security. The mechanism by which the default price is changed would be very difficult to implement in the database. For example, if the table that stores order details defines the ID of the item ordered as a foreign key to a product table, the price can never be changed. On the other hand, if price is simply defined as a column in the table that stores order details, there is no way to enforce the default prices. In cases such as these, using application security is the only way to enforce the rule. Separate procedures or functions to perform inserts and updates for each role; however, in that case, the client application would still be enforcing security by determining which procedure to call based on the role of the user. This is just one example of how you can use application security to enforce rules that would be difficult, if not impossible, to enforce through database security alone.

Another way in which application security is used is to filter result sets being returned from the database. For example, an order entry system might enable salespersons to view and edit only their own orders. Filtering is best accomplished through the use of views. A view to create a list of a specific salesperson's accounts can be as simple as the following statement:

```
CREATE OR REPLACE VIEW saleperson_orders AS
    SELECT * FROM orders WHERE salesperson = user;
```

In most cases, the same filter will not be applied to all users. Create a separate view to apply different filters. Managers using the sample order entry system might use a view that applies no filter, whereas the shipping department might access the system through a view similar to the following one:

```
CREATE OR REPLACE VIEW shipping_orders AS
    SELECT * FROM orders WHERE status = 'OPEN';
```

The application will need to determine which view to use for each particular role. As with other means of enforcing application security, this process can be table-driven. In order to use table-driven filtering, the application must have some way to assign a unique identifier to each result set for which a filter is to be applied. Again, potential problems exist in tying this information to the database. Duplicate IDs, or mismatches between IDs used in the application and IDs stored in the database, will result in database errors or incorrect result sets being returned.

Once unique identifiers have been assigned to the result sets, you can use a simple table consisting of a role name, a result-set identifier, and a view name to apply a filter to a particular application role. To implement filtering based on information in the database, an application must retrieve the data used to apply the filter before retrieving the result set. Using views as the filter mechanism keeps the size of the security table to a minimum, which will help limit the negative impact on performance caused by the additional read required. Using views also simplifies the process of building dynamic SQL in the application. You can construct the views in such a way that no additional information is required by the client application. In this case, the only thing dynamic about the SQL is the name of the view. The SQL in the client application would look like the following:

```
SELECT * FROM view_name
```

In the preceding SQL statement, the `view_name` is the value read from the database for the particular role and result-set identifier. Simply concatenating two strings is a simple task in any programming language. Using views to apply filters makes this task of application security the easiest to implement.

Application and Performance Considerations

If application security is not implemented properly, the result will be a less intuitive interface that requires more error handling. For example, if users who do not have the insert privilege for a particular table are allowed to enter data into a form that inserts values into the table, the users will not know that they do not have access until they try to save. At that point, the application must deal with the resulting database error and display some message to the user. Users will be frustrated by these efforts, and in many cases will interpret the resulting message as a bug. In this respect, application security should be used to hide the fact that database security exists. Generally, users should not see menu options, forms, and controls that they can never use. Hiding inaccessible menu options and controls will result in a less cluttered and more intuitive interface.

However, as the previous section illustrated, the task of enforcing application security can be somewhat complicated, particularly when you use the database to control it. If the rules governing application security are relatively static, it usually preferable to enforce them without using the database. Although this type of "hard-coding" is generally viewed as unsavory, it can be implemented in a way that is much cleaner than using the database to drive application security. The methods for altering menus and controls can be completely encapsulated in the windows to which they apply. The application need only retrieve the role of the current user from the database. Using values stored in the database to enforce application security, in some respects, amounts to an even less acceptable means of hard-coding. The identifiers used for menus, forms, and controls in the application must exactly match the identifiers being stored in the database, which introduces otherwise unnecessary dependencies. Also, the additional database reads required by this method will have some negative impact on performance. The degree to which performance is affected depends on the network and hardware environments and the size of the records and tables being used to drive application security.

In addition to the likelihood of changes in security restrictions, consider the number of users and their locations when you determine how to enforce application security. In general, unless security will be changed frequently and there are many users at remote sites, the improved performance and encapsulation of client-side enforcement will outweigh the benefits of table-driven application security. Even if it is known that security restrictions will change frequently, if there are very few users at a single site, coding security into the client application might be preferable because it would not be difficult to release and install a new version. Also, even if there are a large number of users at remote sites, if security restrictions are expected to remain static, client-side enforcement might be preferable for performance reasons. This is particularly true if there are a large number of restrictions, which will increase the amount of data that must be stored and read to enforce them, as well as increase the likelihood of errors in the data.

If application security must be table-driven, the design of the application interface and security tables should aim to minimize the negative impact on performance. On the client side, you do this by designing menus and forms in a way that minimizes the number of rules that must be applied. On the server side, design the tables to minimize the size of each record. Applying to both, the identifiers used for forms, windows, and controls should be as small as possible, and the values stored in the database should be of the same type as what is used in the application. This will minimize the number of conversions that are required and simplify the code and reduce the possibility of errors. In most cases, you can use a single integer value to represent the desired state of a control.

The client application should use appropriate defaults, and data should only be stored for those cases in which the default behavior must be overridden. For example, if the defaults apply to a specific role in all cases, that role will have no records in tables used to drive menu, window, and control-level security. Check the security tables as windows are constructed and, if possible, buffer the data locally so that it is read from the database only once. In general, the design of the application and the required tables should try to minimize the amount of data required to enforce application security, and try to minimize the negative impact on performance.

Summary

Application security is not a substitute for database security, but it can be used to enhance database security and enforce rules that cannot be enforced through integrity constraints. Using application-specific stored procedures, functions, and views will enhance security and performance, while simplifying the process of developing the client application. Enforcing application security through the application will result in a more intuitive and user-friendly interface.

PART

IN THIS PART

Designer/2000

Designer/2000

22

by Steve Hughes

Introduction

Designer/2000 is a revolutionary second-generation client/server tool for developing and prototyping enterprise-wide information systems solutions. For software developers of enterprise-wide information solutions, the techniques and technologies to perform these tasks are constantly changing. As soon as one promising solution to providing rapid development of information systems solutions appears and accumulates a following, the technology and tools seem to change almost overnight. As professional developers, we are constantly being asked to change methods, tools, and technologies when confronted with a new solution to developing and maintaining enterprise information systems.

Although the profession of designing and deploying information systems is in a state of constant change, we are often reminded that our customers are in need of solutions. Whether our customers dwell in corner offices and have personalized parking spaces, process payroll registers, or perform data entry for the majority of the day, all of their efforts contribute to the performance, progress, and success of the company. Strangely enough, those in corner offices often have their information system needs put ahead of others, for whatever reason.

Designing, developing, and implementing the solutions needed by these groups or individuals is often a task not often completed by information system departments. Often, the solution is implemented too late to be effective. Internal or external changes may have changed the flow or importance of information since the initiation of the project. Other times, what the customer needed is not exactly what was delivered. And, at other times, we as professionals fail to consider how a solution developed for one group will impact another related group or division. All these aspects are of dire importance when developing information system solutions.

Successful information systems often share common properties. These properties can be defined as

1. Rapid Application Development. Most business climates change at least once a year. Responding to those quickly changing environments often requires utilizing tools that assist in the rapid development of information systems. A federal tax package program is able to process your checkbook register, dial into your broker's computer and access your stock portfolio, dial your mortgage holder and gather mortgage interest payments, and gather additional related tax information at the push of a button. To prepare an accurate return, the program must have up-to-date tax information, which changes from year to year. Information systems must be to be effective.

2. Flexibility. As mentioned previously, business climates are in a constant state of fluctuation. Too many times, the scope of the project changes from week to week, depending on the needs of the customer. Any tool used to develop information systems must also be able to change as the complexity and/or scope of the project changes. Internal as well as external business forces may require radical changes to a project already in a development cycle.

3. Dependable. As simple or complex as the information system becomes, it must work and perform as the customer expects. During the design of the system, the customer should be involved in how the system will interact with the end user. Users should know what to expect from the system once implemented.

4. End-user driven. This involves getting the user involved as much as possible in the development and implementation of an information system. This may even involve divisional, or possibly corporate management involvement in the design of the system. Any divisions or department even slightly affected in the implementation of the information system should also be included in the development cycle.

Although successful information systems often contain common attributes, the approaches to attain the end results have been changing radically throughout the past several years. New approaches are being developed, and old tried and true approaches are still being utilized because of their past successes. While no single approach is suitable for every situation, Designer/2000's objective is to support a wide range of approaches in delivering information systems. It is the responsibility of the developers to match the proper approach with the need of each project. Let's discuss each approach tightly integrated into Designer/2000, and when you should use each of the four approaches.

Business Process Reengineering (BPR)

It's the 1990s. Businesses are downsizing, integrating, merging, and expanding—all seemingly in a single step. This often leads to smaller departments, yet increased visibility and responsibility within the enterprise. At the other end of the spectrum, small businesses can grow from two employees to several hundred within a very short amount of time.

Both of the above situations may need to investigate Business Process Reengineering, or BPR, in developing an information system. BPR often starts with the notion that something is wrong with the integration of the enterprise. This could be caused by downsizing, or rapid growth, as described above.

This approach often involves integrating multiple departments, each with complex information systems needs. The overall integration of the enterprise is often revealed when BPR is utilized. While BPR might resemble more traditional approaches, this methodology incorporates an emphasis on redesign of processes within the enterprise, and how those processes interact with each other.

Once the diagnosis has been completed, you must act upon that diagnosis. Knowing that you have a cold based on a runny nose, coughing, and congestion does nothing to help you until you actually do something, like take some medication. Once the processes have (possibly) been redesigned, the process model is of little significance unless acted upon. To achieve a successful implementation using BPR, the redesigned processes and procedures must be implemented. New procedures may be required, or old ones changed radically, as well as an information system to support those new procedures and processes.

BPR utilizes the following portions of Designer/2000:

1. Process Modeller. The Process Modeller is used to capture how activities flow through an enterprise. A unique capability of the Process Modeller is the Ability to use multimedia in presenting this information. For example, you can attach an icon of a dollar sign to represent a revenue-generating processes. You can even attach sound and multimedia clips to strengthen the concept of how processes integrate, and how information flows through the enterprise. Another capability of the Process Modeller is its capability to capture process time requirements and turnaround time, and its capability to deal with staffing and expenditure requirements. This critical information can even be exported to popular spreadsheet programs for further analysis. The Process Modeller, showing flow of information through a sample application, is shown in Figure 22.1.

FIGURE 22.1.

The Process Modeller in action, displaying the flow of information through a single department.

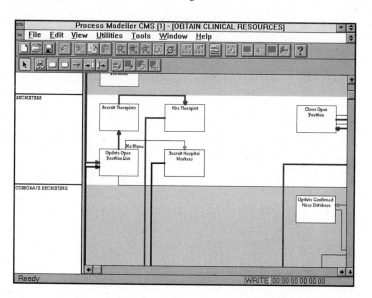

2. System Modeller. The System Modeller, comprised of the Entity Relationship Diagrammer, Function Hierarchy Diagrammer, and the Dataflow Diagrammer, is the next step in implementing a BPR information system solution. During this stage of the process, you enter the analysis phase, where relationships are mapped and additional details are added. The Function Hierarchy Diagrammer uses the information from the Process Modeller to view processes as functions, showing their organization via a hierarchy diagram. The Dataflow Diagrammer shows how data flows within each process, possibly giving a more visual and concise representation of the model.

3. System Designer. The System Designer encompasses the Data Diagrammer, Module Logic Navigator, Module Data Diagrammer, Preferences Diagrammer, and Module Structure Diagrammer. During use of these tools, the processes are brought into more detail. The Data Diagrammer gives you an initial database design that can be further

polished as necessary. The Preferences Navigator is used to initiate programming standards. This ensures that the applications generated will have a consistent user interface and processing style.

4. Generators. The Server Generator, Forms Generator, and Reports Generator comprise the final step in implementing a BPR information system. The Server Generator produces SQL commands that create the server tables. The Forms Generator creates a fully functional application, complete with insert, update, delete, and query functionality. The Report Generator generates reporting applications. All the above are combined to create a fully functional, client/server application.

TIP

Business Process Reengineering takes a lot of involvement from management within each affected process. Be aware that with the involvement of numerous separate processes, you must juggle personalities, conflicts, and differences within each department or division.

Information Engineering

"He who controls the data controls the world." Although not entirely true, that is the concept behind information engineering. This approach to information systems development considers data as one of the most valuable resources of an enterprise. By analysis of information, and how that information impacts the divisions within the enterprise, future plans to implement information systems can be derived. The steps and processes utilized within Designer/2000 to implement an information engineering approach to an information system are as follows:

1. System Modeller. The suite of tools within the System Modeller (Entity Relationship Diagrammer, Function Hierarchy Diagrammer, and Data Flow Diagrammer) can prepare stand-alone business models. The Entity Relationship Diagrammer (ERD) lies at the center in deployment of an information engineering information system. The ERD shows the important data elements, and how they are associated with one another.

2. Systems Designer. The tools within the Systems Designer (Data Diagrammer, Module Logic Navigator, Module Data Diagrammer, Preference Navigator, and Module Structure Diagrammer) are then used to refine, cultivate, and enrich the findings from the System Modeller. The Application Design Wizard helps in the creation of modules from your defined business functions. At a later step, you can use the Module Structure Diagrammer to refine the relationships between the models.

3. Generators. The Server Generator, Forms Generator, and Reports Generator are the final step. The Server Generator produces SQL commands that create the server

tables. The Forms Generator creates a fully functional application, complete with insert, update, delete, and query functionality. The Report Generator generates reporting applications.

Rapid Application Development

As you can derive from the name, Rapid Application Development (RAD) attempts to provide quick, useful, and effective information systems. Through use of specialized tools, developers can quickly prototype and generate entire applications. In this approach, the end user is very aware of what is needed for a successful information system. Other than verifying what the user is requesting, you also verify what will be delivered and the impact, or lack of impact, on other divisions or departments. Delivering a working application is not impossible. Using Designer/2000, developers can quickly prototype an information system, and deliver a working application in a relatively short amount of time. The steps and processes utilized within Designer/2000 to implement an RAD approach to an information system are as follows:

1. Systems Designer. The tools within the Systems Designer (Data Diagrammer, Module Logic Navigator, Module Data Diagrammer, Preference Navigator, and Module Structure Diagrammer) are used to define, cultivate, and verify information gathered from the end user. Use the Data Diagrammer to design the layout of your databases, and how the information should behave with an application. You can then use the Module Structure Diagrammer to form the links between your modules. The Preferences Navigator is used to initiate programming standards. This ensures that the application to be generated will have a consistent user interface and processing methodology.

2. Generators. The Server Generator, Forms Generator, and Reports Generator are the second and final step. As you can see, only two steps are involved in using the RAD approach to developing information systems. The Server Generator produces SQL commands that create the server tables. The Forms Generator creates fully functional applications, complete with insert, update, delete, and query functionality. The Report Generator generates reporting applications.

TIP

The RAD approach to implementing an information system is best used when the end user is well aware of what is needed, and when the scope of the project is not likely to fluctuate to a great degree. Another advantage to using the RAD approach is that the information system will not greatly affect, either directly or indirectly, the operation of other divisions or departments.

Legacy Led Development

In using the legacy led approach, an existing system is being replaced, upgraded, or added to. As the enterprise grows, expands, and possibly broadens its business horizon, information systems already in place may outlive their usefulness. If a previous analysis of the process is available, you are one step ahead of the process. This should allow analysis of how the new additions will impact the system, or what processes the replacement must perform. If the system was developed using the predecessor to Designer/2000, Oracle CASE, its design will be readily available to Designer/2000.

Using the legacy led development approach, existing processes are reverse engineered into Designer/2000. These definitions are stored in the Designer/2000 Repository, where they are available as the central source of redesign. The processes utilized within Designer/2000 to implement a legacy led development approach to an information system are as follows:

1. Systems Designer. The tools within the Systems Designer (Data Diagrammer, Module Logic Navigator, Module Data Diagrammer, Preference Navigator, and Module Structure Diagrammer) are used once the existing definitions have been reverse engineered into the Repository. Fields, columns, and even column characteristics can then be modified through use of the Data Diagrammer. You can then use the Module Data Diagrammer to refine the definitions.

2. Generators. The Server Generator, Forms Generator, and Reports Generator are the final step. As with all final steps, these Designer/2000 tools produce the applicable server code, forms, and reports for the information system.

Summary

With Designer/2000's capability to support multiple approaches to developing information systems, its common repository, entity reusability, and its consistency of application development, Designer/2000 is a tool that every professional system developer can utilize.

Installing Designer/2000

23

by Steve Hughes

Before you utilize the full potential, power, and design tools of Designer/2000, you must install the product. Because Designer/2000 is a client/server product, you need to perform some tasks on the client (often an IBM PC or compatible) and perform server-specific tasks on the server (possibly a Windows NT server, a Dec Alpha, or other platform supporting Oracle).

One of the most popular platforms on which to run the client side of Designer/2000 is Microsoft Windows. In this chapter, you'll learn how to install Designer/2000 for Microsoft Windows. As of this writing, Designer/2000 is at release 1.1. Enhancements over release 1.0 include remarkable increases in speed, some taming of previous "untamed enhancements" (some people call them bugs), and minor enhancements to the software.

The following table indicates where components of Designer/2000 reside.

Client	Server
Repository Administrator	Remote database
Forms Generator	Designer/2000 Repository
Process Modeller	Application Program Interface
Report Generator	
Server Generator	
System Designer	
System Modeller	

System Requirements

For Designer/2000 to execute properly, certain minimum system requirements must be met. The following list explains the minimum system requirements for the client and server sides of Designer/2000 version 1.1. Remember, these are the minimum requirements. Often, when manufacturers state the minimum requirements they state the base minimum for the product to function. And even though the product will function under the minimum requirements, additional horsepower, such as a speedy hard disk, additional processing power (Pentium-level processor), plenty of RAM, and a finely tuned Oracle server will make the software run much more efficiently.

Client

For the client side of your installation, the following is a list of the minimum requirements:

- IBM PC, or 100-percent compatible, with at least 486/25 processing power.
- CD-ROM drive that can be assigned to a logical drive letter, often D: or E:.

- Available disk space of 350 MB if all options are installed, 300 MB for a typical installation. Also, at least 40 MB of swap space. (Use a permanent swap file when you allocate this space.)
- RAM requirements: a hefty 16 MB available, with a recommendation of 32.

NOTE

Acquire as much RAM as possible; try to match or better the 32 MB. Additional RAM, especially above the 16MB minimum, will gain the most increase in performance within Designer/2000, with the exception of installing a faster processor.

- At least 400 KB of conventional RAM (memory below 640 KB) available before starting Windows.
- Microsoft Windows, version 3.1 or higher, in enhanced mode.

NOTE

Although Designer/2000 has not been specifically engineered for Windows 95, it seems to run well under the new operating system.

- MS-DOS, version 5.0 or greater.
- SQL*Net, version 1.1 or 2.0 for Windows, both of which are supplied on the Designer/2000 CD-ROM. If you are planning to use SQL*Plus, it must be version 3.1.3.5.5 or 3.1.3.7.2C; the latest version will be included on the Designer/2000 CD-ROM.

Server

On the server side of the installation, the following list is a list of minimum requirements:

- Oracle7 Server, with the procedural option installed. Ask your Oracle database administrator (DBA) if all procedural option packages have been installed on the server.
- A minimum of 35 MB in the system tablespace is needed for the repository PL/SQL packages, procedures, and views that comprise Designer/2000.

NOTE

Remember, 35 MB is the minimum. In actuality, if sufficient disk space is available, allocate at least 65 MB of additional space to the SYSTEM tablespace. Also, try to make sure the available SYSTEM tablespace is fairly contiguous.

■ If you plan to utilize the legacy-driven approach to information systems, using the reverse engineering tools, you must configure the Oracle server with distributed options.

Back Up, Back Up, Back Up

Although the Designer/2000 product has been tested thoroughly by Oracle, as well as numerous current users of Designer/2000, always protect your current system by performing a complete backup of your machine. During the installation process, entries will be made to your WIN.INI file. The installation process might include coordination with your DBA to ensure all data on the Oracle server has also been backed up. If any problems occur after the installation, you will be able to return your system to its original state before the installation if you have backed it up.

Upgrading to Designer/2000

Which Oracle CASE product you have already installed on your client impacts how you begin to install Designer/2000. The following scenarios will help you determine which steps to perform to upgrade to Designer/2000.

Oracle CASE 5.1

Here, a functional Oracle CASE version 5.1 resides on the client PC. To upgrade to Designer/2000, remove CASE 5.1 from the client PC, and proceed to Client Installation. On the server side, you will need to upgrade the repository.

Designer/2000 version 6.0.0 to 6.0.4

A previous, early version of Designer/2000 resides on the client. To upgrade to the current release of Designer/2000, uninstall the old version and proceed to Client Installation. On the server side, you will need to upgrade the server repository.

Designer/2000 6.0.5 to 6.06

Although a previous version of Designer/2000 exists on the client, you will not have to uninstall it before upgrading to the latest release of Designer/2000. Proceed to Client Installation, which will overwrite the current version of Designer/2000. On the server side, you will need to upgrade the server repository.

Client Installation

To install the client side of Designer/2000, a Windows-based product developed by Oracle called Oracle Installer is utilized. This installation program is located on the CD-ROM and performs the following steps during installation of Designer/2000:

1. Creates the Oracle home directory (usually ORAWIN), and appropriate subdirectories.
2. Copies installation-specific files to the appropriate subdirectory.
3. Creates a Designer/2000 program group.
4. Installs selected components of Designer/2000.
5. Installs Designer/2000, online documentation, and appropriate icons within the Designer/2000 program group.

Before you start Oracle Installer, make sure that no other Windows tasks are currently running.

> **CAUTION**
>
> When you make sure that no other Windows tasks are currently running, you also should disable all screen savers and incoming/outgoing fax management software, because the installation process can be a time-consuming process that should not be interrupted after it is initiated.

After Windows is running, insert the CD-ROM into the available CD-ROM drive.

> **NOTE**
>
> In the following examples, [CD-ROM Drive Letter] refers to the drive letter associated with your CD-ROM drive. This is often drive D: or E:. Substitute the proper drive letter whenever you encounter [CD-ROM Drive Letter].

With the CD-ROM properly inserted in the CD-ROM driver, start the installation process by selecting File | Run from the Windows Program Manager. When prompted to enter the command line to execute, enter the following:

```
[CD-Rom Drive Letter]:\INSTALL\ORAINST.EXE
```

Alternatively, you can use the Windows File Manager to view the contents of the CD-ROM and execute the preceding program.

The remaining steps of installing the Designer/2000 client portion are numbered in the order they should be processed.

1. After the installation loads into memory and performs a few initialization steps, the first screen of the Oracle Installer will appear. This window enables you to select the language to be used during the installation process. (See Figure 23.1.)

FIGURE 23.1.

The Language selection menu.

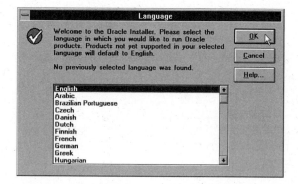

2. Next, you will be prompted for some license information, as well as the Oracle Home directory. Enter the name of your company, and move to the Oracle Home directory field. Change the value displayed or accept the default, C:\ORAWIN. (See Figure 23.2.)

FIGURE 23.2.

License information and the Oracle Home directory.

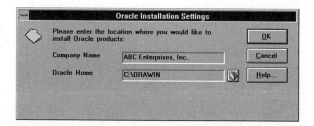

TIP

Take a minute to jot down the Oracle Home directory because it is a very important piece of information. This location is where all information concerning Designer/2000 and all subsequent Oracle Products is installed.

3. If the Oracle Home directory, specified in the previous step, is not part of your PATH statement, the Oracle Installer will ask you if your AUTOEXEC.BAT file should be modified to include the Oracle Home path. Unless you intend to add the path

yourself, let Oracle Installer add Oracle Home to your PATH statement in the
AUTOEXEC.BAT file by selecting the Yes button. (See Figure 23.3.)

> **NOTE**
>
> If you select Yes in step 3, you will need to reboot your computer before the changes
> will take effect.

FIGURE 23.3.

*The Oracle Installer asking
if the Oracle Home
subdirectory should be
added to the PATH
statement in your
AUTOEXEC.BAT.*

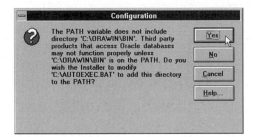

4. Designer/2000 can be installed one of three ways. Each method of installation
   requires different amounts of disk space, and takes more or less installation time,
   depending on the number of components selected to install. (See Figure 23.4.)

FIGURE 23.4.

*The three methods of
installing Designer/2000.*

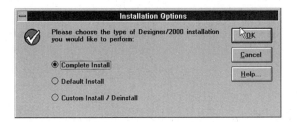

Complete Installation

As the name implies, a complete install will install all components of Designer/2000, including the option to install SQL*Net products. The Oracle Installer is pretty smart. If the user has
an older version of SQL*Net, it will ask if he wants to upgrade. Also, a custom install or complete install asks about SQL*Net. To perform a complete installation, select Complete Install.
The following lists the components for a Complete Install.

1. SQL*Net installation. Select the version of SQL*Net you plan to run by selecting the
   appropriate version. (See Figure 23.5.) If you do not make a selection for SQL*Net at
   this point, you can install SQL*Net later by performing a custom installation/
   deinstallation.

FIGURE 23.5.

Available SQL*Net options that can be installed during a custom installation.

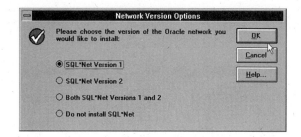

2. If you chose to install SQL*Net in step 1, you will then be presented with a list of SQL*Net products to install. (See Figure 23.6.) Select the proper SQL*Net option.

FIGURE 23.6.

List of SQL*Net products available for installation.

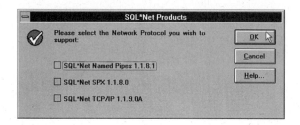

3. The actual install process will begin after you select OK. If you have a previous version of Designer/2000, you might be prompted on whether to rename the old files (previous versions of a new file), or simply overwrite them. Always select the option to rename the previous files if sufficient disk space is available. See Figure 23.7, which appears right before the installation process begins.

FIGURE 23.7.

The Oracle Installer screen before the actual Designer/2000 installation begins.

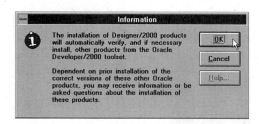

4. Certain Oracle files, called executables, are stored in a special area, as defined by [Oracle Home]\BIN. Each additional component of Designer/2000 should have its own specific subdirectory. This enables patches and upgrades to be implemented more easily. You will next be prompted to enter the location where the common Designer/2000 files should reside. (See Figure 23.8.)

FIGURE 23.8.

Prompt for the location of the Designer/2000 files.

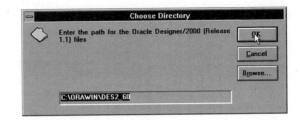

5. Because Oracle applications being developed in Designer/2000 can take advantage of OLE2, some of your Windows system files might need to be updated. You will be prompted as to whether or not you want Oracle Installer to update these files. (See Figure 23.9.) You should not encounter any problems when you upgrade to newer versions of these files. Select Yes to continue.

WARNING

You cannot remove these files by using the Deinstall utility. After they are installed, you will have to manually remove them.

FIGURE 23.9.

The prompt denoting additional system support files might be required.

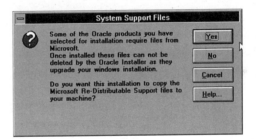

6. Your next prompt is for the location of SQL*Plus. (See Figure 23.10.) This is where the SQL*Plus files, and future versions of SQL*Plus, will reside. Change the value displayed, or accept the default.

FIGURE 23.10.

*The prompt for the location of the SQL*Plus files.*

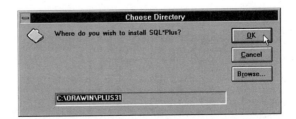

7. The next prompt will determine where the Developer/2000 Forms runtime files are to be located. (See Figure 23.11.) Change the value displayed, or accept the default.

FIGURE 23.11.

The prompt for the location of the Developer/2000 Forms runtime files.

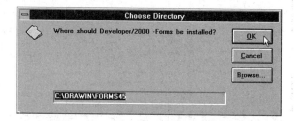

8. In this step, you will resolve the location of the Developer/2000 Reports runtime files. (See Figure 23.12.) Change the value displayed, or accept the default.

FIGURE 23.12.

The prompt for the location of the Developer/2000 Reports runtime files.

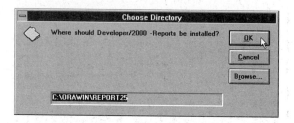

9. Next, define the location of the Designer/2000 Repository Administrator files. (See Figure 23.13.) Change the value displayed, or accept the default.

FIGURE 23.13.

Select the location of the Designer/2000 Repository Administrator files.

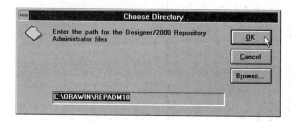

10. A single client should be assigned to initiate and configure the Oracle Repository on the Oracle server. (See Figure 23.14.) If this client PC is going to be designated as such, select Yes. Make the appropriate selection, and continue.

NOTE

If the client is selected, an additional 10 MB of disk space will be needed for additional files.

FIGURE 23.14.

The selection menu for determining if this client is assigned to configure the Oracle Repository on the Oracle server.

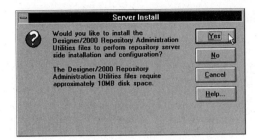

11. Next, specify where the Designer/2000 Systems Designer files will reside. (See Figure 23.15.) Change the value displayed, or accept the default

FIGURE 23.15.

Selection for the destination of the Designer/2000 Systems Designer files.

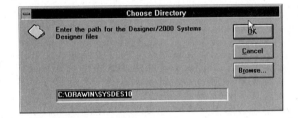

12. After step 11, you are asked where the Designer/2000 Reports Generator files should dwell. (See Figure 23.16.) Change the value displayed, or accept the default.

FIGURE 23.16.

Selection for the location of the Designer/2000 Reports Generator files.

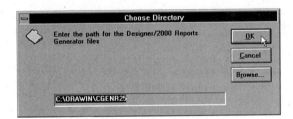

13. Next, you determine the location of the Designer/2000 Server Generator files. (See Figure 23.17.) Change the value displayed, or accept the default.

FIGURE 23.17.

The location of the Designer/2000 Server Generator files.

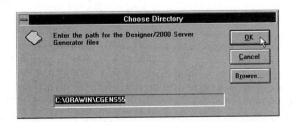

14. Subsequently, the Oracle Installer prompts you for the location of the Designer/2000 Forms Generator files. (See Figure 23.18.) Change the value displayed, or accept the default.

FIGURE 23.18.

The prompt for the location of the Designer/2000 Forms Generator files.

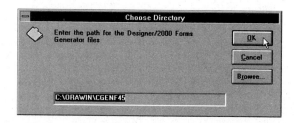

15. In the next-to-last prompt for the location of a Designer/2000 component, define the location of the Designer/2000 Process Modeller files. (See Figure 23.19.) Change the value displayed, or accept the default.

FIGURE 23.19.

The location of the Designer/2000 Process Modeller files.

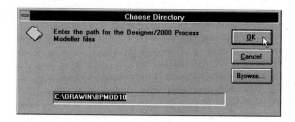

16. The final prompt defines the location of the Designer/2000 Systems Modeller files. (See Figure 23.20.) Change the value displayed, or accept the default.

FIGURE 23.20.

The location of the Designer/2000 Systems Modeller files.

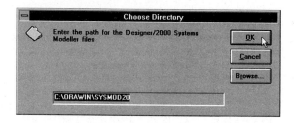

17. Oracle Installer will now show you all the products you have selected for installation. (See Figure 23.21.) All of the selected components will now be copied to their selected destination.

FIGURE 23.21.

Version information associated with each component selected for installation.

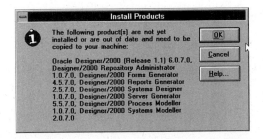

> **TIP**
>
> Take a minute to write down the information displayed, especially the version numbers associated with each component. If you ever need to call Oracle support, they will need this information in order to serve you better and assist you with any problems you might encounter.

18. Oracle Installer now lists any additional files it has determined it needs to install. (See Figure 23.22.) Once again, take a minute to record this information for future reference. After you have captured this information, continue the installation process.

FIGURE 23.22.

Additional files Oracle Installer has determined it needs to install.

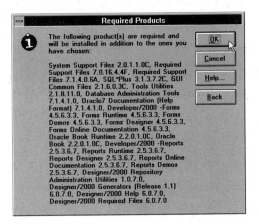

Oracle Installer will now compute the disk space requirements and make sure sufficient space is available on the destination drive. After space requirements have been met, the actual components will be copied to the destination drive. Oracle Installer will display a progress indicator and update the progress while files are being copied. When the progress indicator reaches 100 percent, the installation of Designer/2000 for the client is complete. Proceed to the section titled "Server Installation" to complete the necessary steps on the Designer/2000 server.

Default Installation

When installing Designer/2000, most sites select default installation. The main difference between a custom installation (described previously) and a default installation is your ability to change the location of the Designer/2000 files. This process copies a default configuration, complete with default file locations. The following are the steps involved:

1. SQL*Net installation. Select the version of SQL*Net you plan to run by selecting the appropriate version (refer to Figure 23.6). If you do not make a selection for SQL*Net now, you can install SQL*Net later by performing a custom installation/ deinstallation.

2. If you chose to install SQL*Net in step 1, you will be presented with a list of SQL*Net products to install (refer to Figure 23.7). Select the proper SQL*Net option.

3. Because Oracle applications being developed in Designer/2000 can take advantage of OLE2, some of your Windows system files might need to be updated. You will be prompted as to whether or not you want Oracle Installer to update these files (refer to Figure 23.8). You should not encounter any problems when you upgrade to newer versions of these files. Select Yes to continue.

WARNING

You cannot remove these files by using the Deinstall utility. After they are installed, you will have to manually remove them.

4. Oracle Installer will now show you all the products you have selected for installation (refer to Figure 23.22). All of the selected components will now be copied to their selected destination.

TIP

Take a minute to write down the information displayed, especially the version numbers associated with each component. If you ever need to call Oracle support, they will need this information in order to serve you better and assist you with any problems you might encounter.

5. Any additional files Oracle Installer has determined need to be installed will now be listed. Once again, take a minute to record this information for future reference.

Oracle Installer will now compute the disk space requirements and make sure sufficient space is available on the destination drive. After space requirements have been met, the actual components will be copied to the destination drive. Oracle Installer will display a progress indicator and update the progress while files are being copied. When the progress indicator reaches 100 percent, the installation of Designer/2000 for the client is complete. Please proceed to the section titled "Server Installation" to complete the necessary steps on the Designer/2000 server.

Custom Installation/Deinstallation

During a complete install, you can install or deinstall a list of selectable Designer/2000 components. A window to the left indicates components that can be installed, and a window on the right indicates components of Designer/2000 that can be deinstalled.

Installing Designer/2000 on a client is a fairly simple process. Using the Oracle Installer is an intuitive process; it automatically determines which components of Designer/2000 are dependent upon others and gathers necessary information quickly and easily.

Server Installation

After you have installed the client portion of Designer/2000, a series of steps is necessary to set up the server side of Designer/2000. The series of steps performed in this section must be performed by an Oracle DBA who has specific privileges to the system areas of your Oracle server.

> **WARNING**
>
> Designer/2000 needs the Oracle Server procedural option to be installed. Your DBA can do this by executing the CATPROC script.

During this setup process, you will create additional tablespaces on your Oracle server and allocate space to these tablespaces. You will also create a repository owner, who is granted special Oracle system privileges needed by Designer/2000. You will also confirm that your Oracle server meets the minimum requirements in several areas, including SYSTEM tablespace, SGA shared pool size, and other parameters. The following are the steps involved:

1. Start the server process by creating a new tablespace and an accompanying tablespace for the Designer/2000 indexes.

> **CAUTION**
>
> Do not install the Designer/2000 tables in the SYSTEM tablespace. Designer/2000 enables you to specify another tablespace, so please do. Keep your SYSTEM tablespace as clean and clutter-free as possible.

It is recommended that the tablespace be called DES2, and the tablespace for the indexes be called DES2_I. The size of these tablespaces should be 13 MB and 11 MB, respectively. As the Oracle DBA, don't forget to assign quota limits (or an unlimited quota) to these newly created tablespaces.

2. Large rollback segments are a necessity for proper use of Designer/2000. Although most rollback segments within an Oracle installation are often the same size, you might need to increase their size if you are receiving errors because of the size of insufficient rollback segments. Designer 2000 does not commit the changes made to the Oracle instance frequently, so it requires large rollback segments. These large rollback segments are only needed during the installation of Designer/2000. After it's successfully installed, you can alter the size of the rollback segments.

> **TIP**
>
> You can create a very large, single rollback segment. Take all other rollback segments offline, and the installation process will be forced to use the large rollback segment. After the large rollback segment is successfully installed, you can drop it and return your system to its normal state.

3. In addition to adding data in the previously created DES and DES_I tablespaces, the installation process will add data to the SYSTEM tablespace. Designer/2000 will need a minimum of 35 MB of additional space in the SYSTEM tablespace. Although this is the minimum, experience has shown that typically about 60 MB of space is needed. If possible, the space available should be as contiguous as possible. Fragmentation within the SYSTEM tablespace can lead to extremely poor performance.

4. Create a repository owner/user for the installation process. Define the DES tablespace as the default and temporary tablespace. Also, allow this user an unlimited quota on DES and DES_I tablespaces. You will need to assign special system privileges to this user. These are as follows:

```
CREATE SESSION
ALTER SESSION
CREATE TABLE
CREATE VIEW
CREATE SEQUENCE
CREATE PROCEDURE
CREATE TRIGGER
CREATE CLUSTER
CREATE SYNONYM
CREATE ANY SYNONYM
DROP ANY SYNONYM
CREATE DATABASE LINK
CREATE ROLE
CREATE SNAPSHOT
```

5. Create a role, possibly called DES2000_OWNER, that contains the privileges listed in step 4. A script is available for performing these actions, and is located in [Oracle home]\REPADM10\UTL. This SQL script, CKROROLE.SQL, can be run from the SYS (not the SYSTEM) account. After the role has been created, the DBA can assign the created role to the owner.

6. Some parameters within the Oracle server INIT.ORA file might need modification. The parameters that might need to be modified, and their minimum values (or required values) are

Parameter	Minimum/Proper Setting
shared_pool_size	18000000
db_block_buffers	1000
open_cursors	200
processes	20
global_names	False

Remember, these are minimum settings. If your Oracle instance contains larger values than those references here, no changes are necessary. If changes are made to any of the preceding parameters, you must shut down your Oracle database, and then restart your database for the new parameters to take effect.

7. During the installation process, the Import utility is needed. For the Import utility to function properly, your ORACLE.INI must contain a LOCAL parameter setting. This specifies which Oracle server and database to connect to. The connect string, if a TCP/IP connection is being used, might resemble the following:

LOCAL=t:*server*:*database*

where *server* is the name of the Oracle server, and *database* is the name of the database to which to connect. Use an ASCII text editor to add this LOCAL parameter to your ORACLE.INI file.

8. You are now ready to start the Repository Administration Utility and install a new repository instance. From Windows, open the Designer/2000 program group if it is not already open. Start the process by double-clicking the Repository Administration Utility. A connection prompt will appear, asking for a user name and password. These were set up by your DBA, probably as OWNER1. Enter the information, and select Connect to continue.

9. Select the proper tablespaces where the Designer/2000 repository information will reside. Your DBA has probably defined these tablespaces as DES for the table tablespace, and DES_I for the indexes tablespace.

10. To make sure enough system resources are available and the proper system privileges have been assigned, select the Pre-Check button to ensure an error-free installation.

> **CAUTION**
>
> The installation process can often take several hours to complete. Always run the Pre-Check process to ensure the proper steps have been completed before the Designer/2000 repository has been installed.

11. Begin the long installation process by selecting Execute. Be patient during the installation process. At two separate times during the install, the Import function will be summoned. After each import of data, you will be required to close the import message box when the import is complete. Simply select Close when it becomes available for selection.

> **TIP**
>
> Move the mouse occasionally because the mouse icon is not properly updated from an hourglass to a normal mouse pointer after the import utility has completed its task.

Remember, the process might take some time to complete, based on the quickness with which your server can process information. Don't be alarmed if the process seems to have locked up your computer. Give the process at least six to seven hours to process before concluding that the computer has locked. Before rebooting the client, contact your DBA, and ask if any activity is being performed on the server. If activity is detected, do not reboot—things are still running.

After the installation processes have completed, the Designer/2000 is ready for use.

Summary

The installation process is a somewhat lengthy process. If at all possible, you might want to schedule the installation for a weekend. Also, don't forget to have complete backups of both the client and server data before you install Designer/2000.

Repository Administration

24

by Chet West

What Is Repository Administration?

Just as there are duties required to maintain a database system, usually designated to one or more database administrators, there are also maintenance duties required to ensure the proper performance and use of the Designer/2000 repository. The repository itself is a large enough and important enough entity in a database system to require its own level of security, general administrative maintenance, and tuning. There are four utilities in the Designer/2000 suite to provide for this administration. Theses utilities are commonly known as

- The Repository Administration Utility
- The Matrix Diagrammer
- The Repository Object Navigator
- Repository Reports

These administration utilities can provide complete access to every aspect of maintaining the Designer/2000 repository internally. When assigning the duties of repository management, it's wise to separate these duties from the database administrator's duties. The person(s) performing these duties should be the more experienced designers that have an understanding of case methodologies. The duties will include two distinct types of repository administration, which are External Database issues and Internal Repository issues. The persons performing repository administration will work directly with the database administrator in working out repository installation, sizing, performance, and security issues. Not to mention that the repository will provide an excellent place for the database administrator to document exactly how each instance he administrates is setup. These same tools will also be used in managing all the internal objects of the repository.

The Repository Administration Utility

As seen in the previous discussion of Designer/2000 installation, the first utility that will be used is the Repository Administration Utility. This utility will perform all installations and upgrades of the repository. It will also provide for easy recreation and backup of the repository's objects, as well as some tuning. This will also be the utility to use when providing users access to the repository and extending the capabilities of the repository to meet the needs and requirements of the application and corporate policies. The tool can only be used by the repository owner. The repository owner user id should be independent, only for repository administration, and not a database administrator.

> **NOTE**
>
> An attempt to use this tool as SYS, SYSTEM, or any other subordinate, no matter what their security level is, will fail.

The repository administration utility will provide a dialog box with the following screen's accessible view tabs:

- Repository Management
- Privileges
- Tablespace
- Maintain User*
- User Extensibility*
- UE Utilities*

> **NOTE**
>
> Items marked with an asterisk are not available during repository installation.

There will also be a button always visible at the bottom of the dialog box labeled Disconnect. This button will allow the termination of the current repository owner session.

Repository Management Tab

When the repository administration utility is started, this will be the first tab screen open. During the initialization process, the utility will determine if the repository already exists. Based on this determination, it will automatically set the Install or Upgrade as the active radio button. There will also be some system information at the top of the screen showing the user id and Repository Release if an upgrade should be performed. Figure 24.1 shows the Repository Management tab in install mode, and Figure 24.2 shows the tab in upgrade mode.

If performing an upgrade, the version may be displayed in two different ways. Upgrading from CASE Designer 5.0 or 5.1, or any Designer/2000 Beta or Pre-Production versions, will cause the upgrade radio button label to read TO version. Upgrading from production releases of Designer/2000 will cause the upgrade radio button label to read TO version Inter-Release.

FIGURE 24.1.

Repository Management tab screen (install mode).

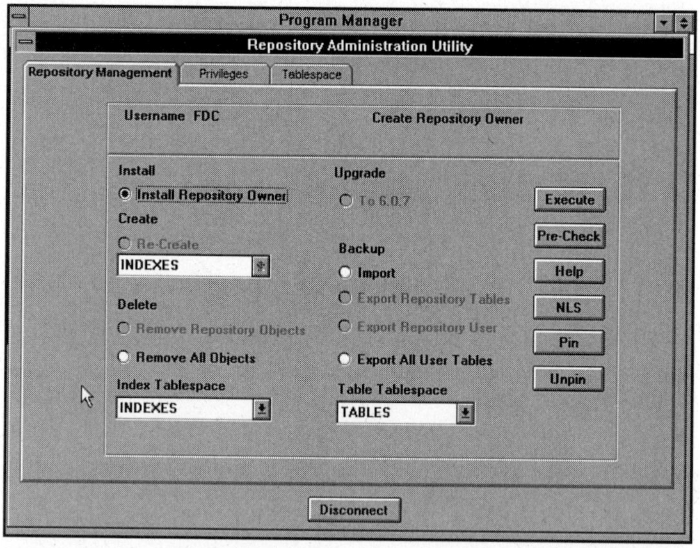

FIGURE 24.2.

Repository Management tab screen (upgrade mode).

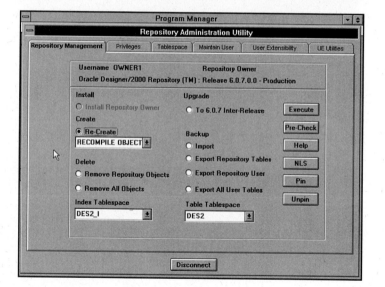

Create Section

The Create section of the screen is only available to current installed versions of Designer/2000. Choosing the Re-Create radio button in this section will turn off the Upgrade radio button and allow the repository administrator to re-create specific objects of the repository instance to correct problems. This may be a quicker solution to fixing problems, rather than running the entire upgrade process again. The options that can be selected from the Re-Create drop-down list box are

- INDEXES
- VIEWS
- TRIGGERS
- PACKAGES
- RECOMPILE OBJECTS
- RECONCILE OWNER

Delete Section

This section can be very dangerous! The first option here is Remove Repository Objects. This will drop all database objects created for the repository instance. The second option is Remove All Objects. This option will drop ALL objects owned by the repository owner. Again, be aware that objects will be gone after executing one of these two options.

> **NOTE**
>
> The Remove All Objects option is available when a new install option is detected. This could be useful in ensuring the repository owner owns nothing prior to repository installation. It is recommended that the database administrator ensure that objects to be dropped are indeed dropped.

Backup Section

This section provides for repository-specific backup capabilities, outside of the backups performed by the database administrator. The repository manager has the capability of exporting and importing in the following ways:

- Import: This will use the Oracle IMPORT utility to import tables, views, and packages that belong to the repository from a previously created export file.
- Export Repository Tables: This will create an export file of all repository tables. (Only the tables!)
- Export Repository User: This will create an export file of ALL objects owned by the repository owner.
- Export All User Tables: This will create an export file of ALL TABLES owned by the repository owner.

Tablespace Selections

There are two tablespace selection drop-down list boxes. They are included to allow the repository manager to select tablespaces other than the default tablespace setup for the repository owner. It will also allow for separation of the repository indexes from the repository tables for tuning purposes. This is highly recommended.

Buttons

The buttons actually initiate actions from the repository management tab screen. The buttons initiate the following actions:

■ Execute: This tells the utility to perform whatever action has been selected.

■ Pre-Check: This tells the utility to check the repository owner's privileges and check the selected tablespaces for the proper amount of space required for the repository to be installed or upgraded.

■ Help: Brings up the online help.

■ NLS: Allows for the setting of a new language used in the Designer/2000 screens and reports. It also allows for additions to the list of languages available.

■ Pin: This will tell the database to keep frequently used packages, used by Designer/2000, in memory for quicker access. This will take up more of the database's SGA, though.

■ Unpin: Enables for package swapping in the SGA. (DEFAULT)

Privileges Tab

This tab screen, as seen in Figure 24.3, is primarily a display of the necessary privileges needed to be a repository owner. If any privilege does not have x in it, the DBA will need to be notified prior to installation or upgrade.

FIGURE 24.3.

Repository Administration Privileges summary tab screen.

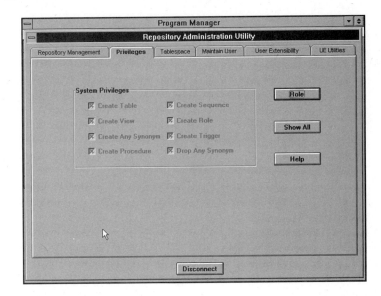

There are three buttons available in this tab screen also. These buttons are as follows.

- Role: Database roles assigned to the repository owner.
- Show All: Shows all database privileges assigned to the repository owner.
- Help: Initiates the online help.

If the DBA has created specific roles for repository owners and users, this can then be easily seen here.

Tablespace Tab

This tab screen, as seen in Figure 24.4, shows an overview of the tablespaces the repository owner has access to. This will be an important place for the repository manager to monitor the space requirements of the repository. The utility also identifies the repository owner's default, temporary tablespaces, and user quota.

FIGURE 24.4.

*Repository Administration
Tablespace Analysis tab
screen.*

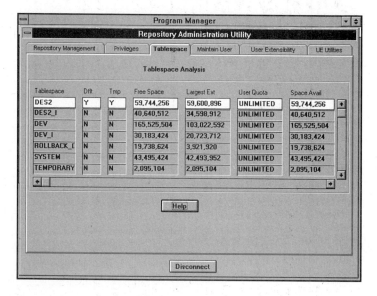

Maintain User Tab

This tab screen, as shown in Figure 24.5, is where the internal security is managed for the
Designer/2000 products. It does not correspond to database security equivalency in any way.
Thus, a user with read-only privileges here could still access the repository tables via such prod-
ucts as SQL*Plus.

FIGURE 24.5.

*Repository Administration
Maintain User tab screen.*

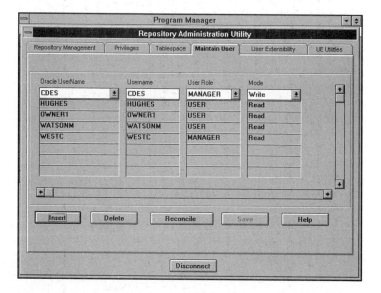

User Spread Table Items

The Oracle UserName can be selected via the drop-down list box. This will list all users on the database instance.

There are two Designer/2000 roles, USER and MANAGER. The USER role is the default and gives access to all Designer/2000. The exception is that a USER cannot access the Application menu option in the Repository Object Navigator. The MANAGER role has access to all Designer/2000 tools except for Repository Administration Utility. This is only accessible by the repository owner. A MANAGER is also the only user type that can be an application system owner.

There are also two modes that can be assigned to users, READ and WRITE. The READ mode gives read-only access to the repository via the Designer/2000 tools. The WRITE mode gives full read and write access to the repository via the Designer/2000 tools.

> **CAUTION**
>
> The READ and WRITE modes only affect the Designer/2000 tools internally and do not correspond to user database privileges!

Scrolling the user spread table horizontally also shows an editable Description field. Here, the repository manager can put in some meaningful text to identify the repository user.

The final item in this spread table is the repository user creation date. This is not directly editable.

> **NOTE**
>
> Privileges will still need to be granted for each application by the application owner. This can be done in the Repository Object Navigator under the Application | Grant Access menu option.

Buttons

The buttons for this tab screen provide the following actions:

- Insert: Inserts a new record into the spread table.
- Delete: Deletes a record from the spread table.
- Reconcile: Performs the additions, deletions, and changes saved in the spread table. Reconciliation must be initiated for changes to take affect.

614

\

- Save: Saves the current spread table. Only available after an insert, delete, or modification.
- Help: Brings up the online help.

User Extensibility Tab

User extensibility allows organizations to add Element, Association, and Text Types to the repository. These extensions allow organizations to add items that are not currently included. An example would be to add a text type that identifies a contractor or project number. This text type then could be added to the Application System element type. An example of the User Extensibility tab can be seen in Figure 24.6.

FIGURE 24.6.

User Extensibility tab screen.

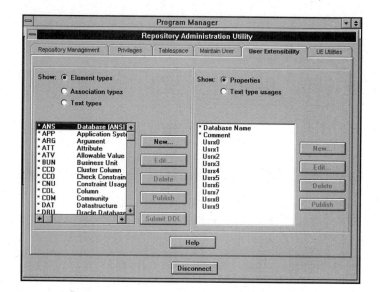

Element Type

An element type would be a top level object in an application system. User extensions for the element type can have a short name of E0 - E99. Elements that come as a default for an application in Designer/2000 would be things like

- Events
- Entities
- Tables
- Modules

Chapter 24

615

Association Type

An association type defines the meta-model association between elements. User extensions for the association type can have a short name of A0 - A99. An example of a Designer/2000-supplied association would be such things as:

- Application Document: Links Application Systems to Documents.
- Trigger Column Usage: Links Database Triggers to Columns.
- Module Function Usage: Links Functions to Modules.

Text Type

A text type is basically any object best defined in a textual mode. These text items can be anything needed to better document your system. An example of Designer/2000-provided text items would be

- Description
- PL/SQL Block
- Where/Validation Condition

Extending the Repository

The extensions can be added in two ways, which are creating new types or modifying existing types. To add a new type:

- Select one of the type radio buttons on the left.
- Fill in the information in the dialog box for that type.
- Add any properties or text-type usages required.
- Publish the new type by selecting the Publish button.
- Submit the DDL (actually updates the Repository Meta-Model).

> **CAUTION**
>
> Once an extension has been published, it cannot be edited or deleted.

The second way to extend the repository is to add new properties or text-type usages to existing types. To do this either edit one of the Usrx objects and edit the properties or select the New button and select an existing type to add. Once this has been completed, publish the changes.

UE Utilities Tab

This tab, as seen in Figure 24.7, provides three options for user extensions.

FIGURE 24.7.

UE Utilities tab screen.

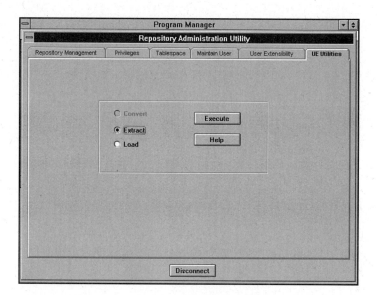

■ Convert: Used to convert Case Dictionary 5.0, 5.1, and early releases of Designer/2000 user extensions for use in the Designer/2000 repository.

■ Extract: Used to export user extensions.

■ Load: Used to append previously extracted extensions to the repository definition tables.

The Matrix Diagrammer

The matrix diagrammer is a designer/project leader tool. It is nothing more than a repository reporting tool that will display in a GUI format or provide printed output. Per its name, the reporting done is a matrix style. Thus, there will be rows, columns, and a condition to report on. These reports are used to show completion or missing items in the application design process. An example of a matrix diagram is seen in Figure 24.8.

FIGURE 24.8.

A matrix diagram.

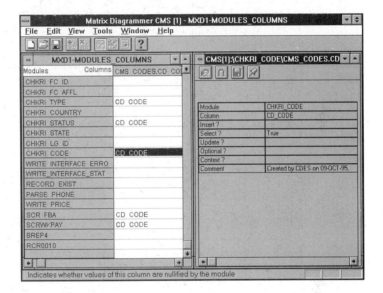

Matrix items for the rows and columns are in a list box of choices, and are the same initially in the new matrix dialog box. Once something is chosen in either list box, the other list-box elements will only show those items that can be reported against. The items that will be shown in the two list boxes are as follows:

- Assumptions
- Attributes
- Business Functions
- Business Units
- Columns
- Critical Success Factors
- Entities
- Key Performance Indicators

- Locations
- Modules
- Nodes
- Objectives
- Problems
- Relations

When both row and column options are chosen, a settings dialog box will be displayed. Here is where row and column display items are chosen along with any filters and ordering conditions. Next intersection properties of the row and column are chosen. After the settings and filters are completed, the matrix diagram will be generated. Once the matrix diagram is created, row or column items can be drilled down on, bringing up the property sheet, or the matrix result can be drilled down on, bringing up its property sheet. Items in the property sheets can then be edited. The columns and rows of the matrix can be added and deleted, and three different views can be shown based on preferences set. The matrix report can also be printed out, but in some cases the matrix lines will not print.

The Repository Object Navigator

As in the previous versions of Oracle CASE Dictionary and its Main Menu, Designer/2000 also provides a tool for viewing any portion, or the entire repository, and launching any of the supplied utilities and design tools. This tool is called the Repository Object Navigator, sometimes referred to as RON. New to this tool is the use of the hierarchy tree display method and the Visual Basic–like property sheet, as seen in Figure 24.9.

FIGURE 24.9.

Repository Object Navigator.

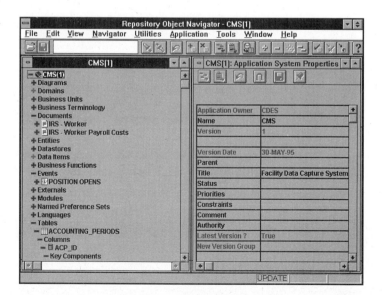

Startup

First the user will either create a new application for the repository by selecting menu option File | New, or by opening an existing application by selecting menu option File | Open.

From the initial startup of the Repository Object Navigator, the user has several choices to choose from in the Filter dialog box, as seen in Figure 24.10. This dialog will be displayed by default, but can be suppressed by editing the Repository Object Navigator preferences.

FIGURE 24.10.

Repository Object Navigator Filter dialog box.

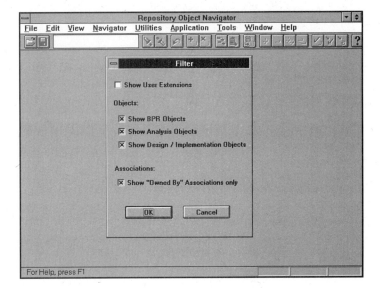

The filters shown will turn on and off the viewing of specified object types. Using these filters can help keep unnecessary information from being displayed to designers. These filters are displayed as check boxes and filter the following:

- Show User Extensions: Selecting this check box will display any user-defined repository extensions, as defined in the Repository Administration Utility.
- Show BPR Objects: Selecting this check box will cause objects defined in the Process Modelling stage to be displayed.
- Show Analysis Objects: Selecting this check box will cause objects defined in the Systems Modelling stage to be displayed.
- Show Design/Implementation Objects: Selecting this check box will cause objects defined in the Systems Design stage to be displayed.
- Show "Owned By" Associations Only: Selecting this check box will cause only ownership associations to be displayed.

Creating New Applications

The user will be placed at the top of the hierarchy tree in the Repository Object Navigator and prompted for the new application's name. The new application name can be up to fourteen characters in length. The name should be meaningful and cover the entire scope of the application. At this point, the initial application properties should be completed in the property sheet even though only the name is required.

Opening Existing Applications

The Open Application dialog is displayed and will list all applications available in the repository, application versions, and related user security assigned for the application. The user can also specify read-only mode if no changes are intended to be made. The Open Application dialog can be seen in Figure 24.11.

FIGURE 24.11.

Repository Object Navigator Open Application dialog box.

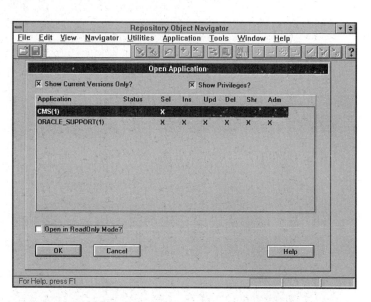

NOTE

If multiple applications are opened, each will have its own application window available.

Viewing and Preferences

There are two child windows that will be initially visible in the Repository Object Navigator's main window. The first is always available when an application is open, which is the Application

Hierarchy Tree window. The second, the Properties window, is optional. There are four different colors used to identify items as Normal items, Error/Mandatory items, Modified items, and Shared/Non-Editable items. These colors can be modified in the user preferences. Think of the hierarchy tree as being rows or records of information in the repository. Think of properties being the actual columns that make up these rows.

Navigating the Hierarchy Tree

The standard look and feel of the Designer/2000 and Developer/2000 products will use a hierarchy tree where appropriate. The Repository Object Navigator's hierarchy tree can be seen in Figure 24.12. The tree can be split into to two views by using the split bar located just above the window's vertical scroll bar.

FIGURE 24.12.

Repository Object Navigator hierarchy tree.

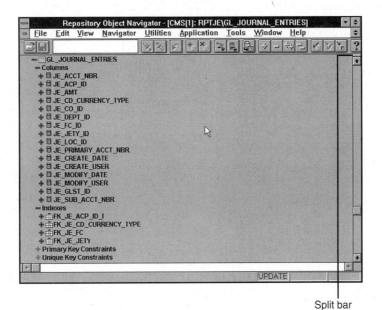

Split bar

Tree items can be expanded one at a time by either mouse click on the preceding colored +, or by selecting the object and using the Navigator | Expand menu option. Collapsing tree branches back can be done by mouse click on the preceding ·, or by selecting the object and using the Navigator | Collapse menu option.

> **NOTE**
>
> The entire hierarchy tree can be expanded or collapsed by using the Navigator | Expand All or Navigator | Collapse All menu options.

Objects can be added to the various object types selecting the object type and using the + button on the toolbar, or by using the Edit | Create menu option. Objects can be deleted from object types by selecting the object, and by using the x button on the toolbar or using the Edit | Delete menu option.

The Property Sheet

Selecting an object on the tree will cause the object's properties to be shown in the properties window, where applicable, if the properties window is open. In the properties window, the details about the object will be displayed and can be added or modified directly here. An example property sheet can be seen in Figure 24.13.

FIGURE 24.13.

Repository Object Navigator property sheet.

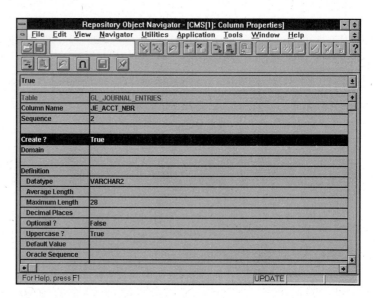

All editing will be done by selecting the property and using the supplied edit method at the top of the property sheet. The edit methods will be either a plain edit field, a list box, or an edit box with a bubble button to the right which can be selected to bring up an editor window.

A new property sheet can be opened by selecting the Window | New Property Sheet menu option. Currently, all property sheets open showing only the properties to the currently selected object. Thus, you can only compare properties using the Union/Intersect button and highlighting multiple objects.

The Toolbar

The Repository Object Navigator provides an iconic toolbar just below the menu to provide mouse shortcuts that map directly to menu items for repository actions. The toolbar can be seen in Figure 24.14.

FIGURE 24.14.

*Repository Object
Navigator Toolbar.*

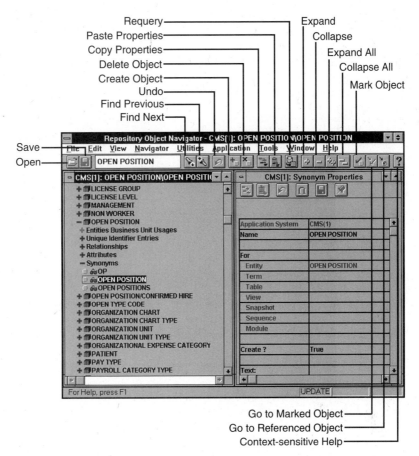

From left to right the buttons perform the following actions:

- Open an existing application.
- Save/Commit all changes to the repository.
- Find Next string occurrence in the hierarchy tree.
- Find Previous string occurrence in the hierarchy tree.
- Undo all outstanding changes.
- Create Object.

TIP

Holding the mouse cursor above the button for a short period of time will cause bubble help dialogs to appear describing the button's action.

- Delete Object.
- Copy Properties helps duplicate like properties.
- Paste Properties updates property sheet with copied properties.
- Requery the repository tables.
- Expand one.
- Collapse one.
- Expand all.
- Collapse all.
- Mark an object, such as a bookmark.
- Go to a marked object.
- Go to a referenced object.
- Context-sensitive help on next mouse-clicked item.

The Menu

The menu can provide for initiating all actions available in the Repository Object Navigator. The menu also provides a driver for initiating any of the other Designer/2000 tools.

File Menu Option

The File menu provides basic application and repository actions. The File menu options are described in Table 24.1.

Table 24.1. File menu options.

Menu Item	Action
New	Create a new application in current repository.
Open	Open an existing application in current repository.
Save	Save any application changes made to the repository.
Load	Loads object definitions from a text file into the current application hierarchy.
Unload	Creates a text file record of all owned repository entries. Also any associations or shared entries will be recorded.
Unload for Exchange	Creates an input file for Oracle*Exchange to import repository items into third-party products.
Check Out	Unloads user-defined sets and the elements in them to a text file.

Menu Item	Action
Check In	Loads a user-defined set text file into the repository. Either updating or creating new entries.
Lock Set	Locks elements in a user-defined set so they cannot be updated.
Unlock Set	Unlocks elements in a user-defined set so they can be updated.
Change Connection	Log in as a new user.
Print	Print the current hierarchy display.
Print Preview	Display what would be printed.
Print Setup	Set up print options.
Exit	Exit the Repository Object Navigator.

Edit Menu

This menu provides basic editing capabilities to the user. The Edit menu options are described in Table 24.2.

Table 24.2. Edit menu options.

Menu Item	Action
Undo	Undoes last change made, prior to a save.
Create	Create a new object under current position in the tree.
Delete	Delete the selected tree object.
Copy Properties	Copies selected properties to the clipboard.
Paste Properties	Pastes copied properties to the current property sheet.
View Copied Properties	Provides a dialog box to preview properties that have been copied prior to pasting.
Preferences	Specifies Repository Object Navigator preferences.

View Menu

This menu option provides for some repository viewing preferences. The menu options are described in Table 24.3.

Table 24.3. View menu options.

Menu Item	Action
Requery	Requeries the repository for the current definitions of all objects under the currently selected object type.
Sort by Type Sequence	Sorts the hierarchy by normal entry sequence.
Sort by Type Name	Sorts the hierarchy alphabetically.
Toolbar	Turns on and off the property sheet toolbar.
Status Bar	Turns on and off the Repository Object Navigator's status bar.

Navigator Menu

This menu option provides for all hierarchy navigation. The menu options are described in Table 24.4.

Table 24.4. Navigator menu options.

Menu Item	Action
Expand	Expand the tree object one level.
Collapse	Collapse the currently expanded object.
Expand All	Expand all objects under the currently selected object.
Collapse All	Collapse all objects under the currently selected object.
Set Mark	Mark the current object for later.
Go to Mark	Navigate to a previously set mark.
Go to Referenced Object	Navigate to the object identified as referenced.
Find	Find the next occurrence of a text string in the hierarchy.

Utilities Menu

The Utilities menu option provides for execution of all repository utilities. The menu options are described in Table 24.5.

Table 24.5. Utilities menu options.

Menu Item	Action
Database Design Wizard	Starts the database design wizard utility.
Application Design Wizard	Starts the application design wizard utility.
Generate DDL	Starts the Server DDL Generation utility.
Generate Module	Starts one of the Client Application Generation utilities for Oracle Forms or Oracle Reports modules.
Generate Module As	Generates Oracle Forms from report modules or Oracle Reports from form modules.
Regenerate Module	Regenerates a form module using new changes.
Generate Reference Tables	Creates text help tables for use by end users.
Reverse Engineer DDL	Starts the database reverse engineering utility.
Reverse Engineer Form	Starts the forms reverse engineering utility.
Reverse Engineer Report	Starts the reports reverse engineering utility.
Table Entity Retrofit	Creates entities for tables not linked to current entities.
Reconcile	Starts the Server reconciliation utility.
Create Function Attribute Matrix	Starts dialog for creating a function/attribute matrix.
Create Default Module Data Usages	Creates module data usages either from summary usages or function usages.
Update Attributes in a Domain	Updates changed attributes in a domain.
Update Columns in a Domain	Updates changed columns in a domain.
Transfer Ownership	Transfers object ownership to another user.
Share	Allows access to an object by another application.
Unshare	Revokes access to an object from other applications.
Copy	Copies elements to specified applications.
Force Delete	Deletes an object and all references to it in all applications.

Application Menu

This menu option provides a means to perform application-specific operations and maintenance. The Application menu requires the manager role to be set in the Repository Administration utility for the user. The menu options are described in Table 24.6.

Table 24.6. Application menu options.

Menu Item	Action
Freeze/Unfreeze	Will lock/unlock an application to prevent or allow modification.
Rename	Gives a new name to the application if owned by the user.
Transfer	Transfers application ownership to another user.
Grant Access	Grants, revokes, and specifies user access to defined applications.
New Version	Creates a new version of the application. The previous version is frozen.
Delete	Deletes an owned application.
Archive	Archives a specified application.
Export	Exports archive tables to a file.
Import	Imports an exported application.
Restore	Restores an archived application.
Reset	Clears archive tables.

Tools Menu

This menu option provides an easy way to directly execute all the Designer/2000 application tools. Executing from this menu will automatically create a new session using the same user id and password that is currently logged in.

Window Menu

This provides generic window manipulation and navigation.

Help Menu

This provides access to the Repository Object Navigator's online help and access to the Repository Object Navigator's about box that will not only give its version number, but also the repository version, database version, and many others that will be helpful when calling Oracle Support.

Database Design Wizard

This tool is the first part of moving from requirements definitions to design definitions. This dialog box provides a textual method of defining and maintaining entity-to-table or attribute-to-column links. This wizard is used in creating initial table designs from the requirements defined. Will also use your designs to create foreign keys, subtype tables, and so on.

> **NOTE**
>
> This utility must be run prior to running the Application Design Wizard so that modules can properly reference tables.

Application Design Wizard

This tool is the second part of moving from requirements definitions to design definitions. It will be used once all of the business requirement models are complete and you are ready to migrate to the actual physical design models. It basically creates a rough draft of what it thinks you want and need on the physical-application side in the form of PL/SQL, Form, and Report modules. This is done using the rules and definitions created and the options set in the Application Design Wizard.

> **NOTE**
>
> Ensure that the Database Design Wizard has been run and Quality Checked prior to running this tool for optimum results.

Repository Reports

The Repository Reports module provides a way to run all of the predefined repository reports. The reports are split into the following categories:

- Data Model Reports
- Function Model Reports
- Dataflow Model Reports
- BPR Model Reports
- System Design Reports
- Module Design Reports
- System Access Reports

- Database Design Reports
- Quality Reports
- User Extensibility Reports
- Impact Analysis Reports
- Function Point Analysis Reports
- Global Reports
- Repository Administration Reports

The actual report-definition files are located in your %ORACLE_HOME%\REPADM10\SRW directory. Thus, these reports can be copied and/or customized to meet organizational needs. The reports can be used throughout the entire life-cycle of applications and the repository itself. This is a very good tool to use when analyzing what it would take to change or add requirements. This will then translate into a quicker return in time and resource requirements being reported to end users requesting changes. It is also a good tool to use when looking for gaps or flaws in a current application design.

> **NOTE**
>
> Depending on Repository and Application size, these reports may take a while to run.

Summary

The repository administration tools are the most important tools available in the Designer/ 2000 suite, but at times they are also the most underutilized. It is important also to understand that a quality application design effort will require good repository management. Without a disciplined management of the repository, or any CASE tool for that matter, it may become junk. This of course is what is hoped to be avoided when using any CASE tool. Remember that the graphical tools are provided to help in visualizing what is being designed. A tool like the Repository Object Navigator and the Repository Reports module could be used exclusively and still provide all that is needed to create an entire application. Oracle has provided lots of tools for use in maintaining its repository. All of these are not necessary for a good and complete application design, but it is good to know what is available to you.

Process Modeling

by Patrick
Connors

25

What Is Process Modeler?

The Process Modeler is the first tool used in the Designer/2000 application development cycle. This tool is used to document business processes and information flows with a minimum of data processing terminology. It can be used to perform critical-path analysis as well as to animate a process. In addition, the process animation shows the time required to complete a process. Process diagrams can also be created for individual processes, thus enabling a top-down approach to documenting processes.

All data entered in the Process Modeler is stored in the Repository. Other tools in Designer/ 2000 will use this data.

Documenting Process Flow

The Process Modeler is used beginning with high-level analysis. Once business units and processes are recorded through interviews, they are entered into the Repository using this tool. Within the Process Modeler, detailed attributes can be kept for each step of a process, down to the lowest level. Figure 25.1 shows the major features of the Process Modeler screen.

FIGURE 25.1.

Major features of the Process Modeler.

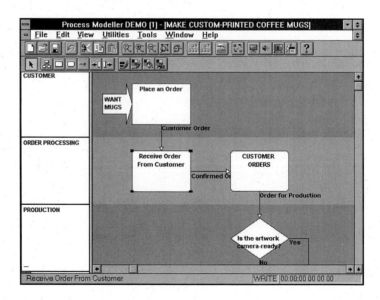

Here are the steps to create a new process flow diagram:

1. Select File | New from the menu. The New Diagram dialog box appears. (See Figure 25.2.)

FIGURE 25.2.

The New Diagram pop-up window.

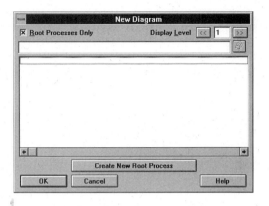

2. Select the Create New Root Function button. This calls the Create Process Step window. (See Figure 25.3.)

FIGURE 25.3.

The Create Process Step pop-up window is used to create all new process steps.

3. Enter the name of the process step.
4. Enter the short name of the process step.
5. Select OK. This function becomes the root process step of the diagram.

Organization Units

Organization units are displayed down the left side of the main Process Modeler window. To the right, each organization unit has a colored band, called a swim lane. The process steps, stores, and decision points belonging to that function are displayed in its swim lane.

When a project is first opened, there is one organization unit, Unspecified, which always exists.

To create a new organization unit:

1. Select the Organization Unit button on the toolbar.
2. Select the organization unit, which will be the parent of the unit being created. Or select Unspecified to create an organization unit without parents. This opens the Create Organization Unit dialog box. (See Figure 25.4.)

FIGURE 25.4.

Enter basic organization data in the Create Organization Unit dialog box.

3. Enter the name and short name of the organization unit.

4. Optionally, enter the cost of the organization unit. There is a drop-down list for the unit of cost.

5. Select OK. The main screen will show the new organization unit. (See Figure 25.5.)

FIGURE 25.5.

Organization units. Note the relationship between the Production and Design units.

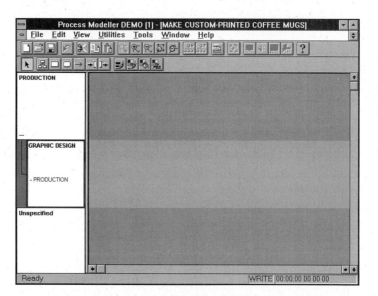

TIP

If an organization unit is entered at the wrong place in the hierarchy, its parent can be changed in the Organization dialog box.

When an organization unit is first created in the Modeler, its swim lane is tall enough for one box. (The Modeler handles most of the details of placing and connecting boxes.) This is easily adjusted. Just select the organization unit and press Shift+down arrow to make its swim lane taller.

Further details about an organization unit, including its size and description, may be entered via the Organization dialog box.

To enter further detail about an organization unit:

1. Double-click the organization unit. The Organization dialog box appears. (See Figure 25.6.)

FIGURE 25.6.

Further detail can be entered via the Organization dialog box. Organizational hierarchy can also be changed here.

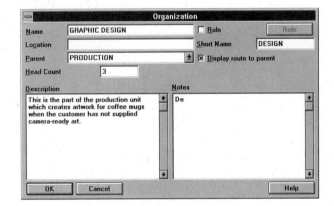

2. Edit the appropriate fields.
3. Select OK.

TIP

Organization units can be moved up and down the screen by selecting the organization unit and pressing the up or down arrows.

Process Steps

Process steps are the actual steps taken to accomplish larger tasks. In the Process Modeler, each step has a name and other data—such as completion time—associated with it.

To create a new process step:

1. Select the Create Process Step button on the Toolbar.
2. Select the spot on the swim lane for the process step. The Create Process Step dialog box appears. (See Figure 25.7.)

FIGURE 25.7.

The Create Process Step dialog box.

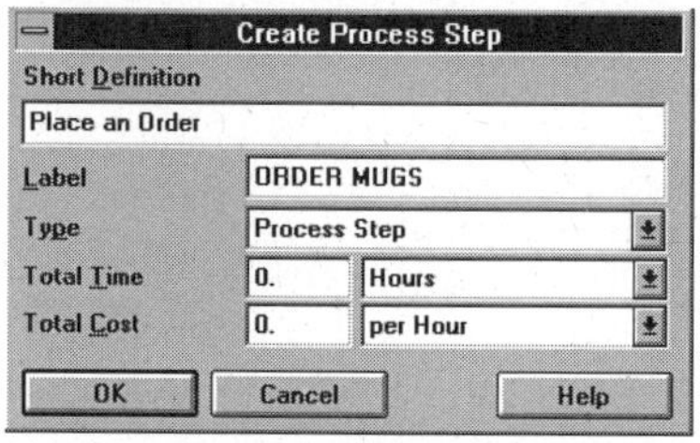

If the exact organization unit of a business function, store, or decision point is uncertain, place it in the Unspecified organization unit. It can easily be moved later, if necessary.

3. Enter the definition and label for the process step.

The label is used by the Repository as the name of the process step. It is limited to ten characters and must be unique.

4. Select the type of process step from the drop-down list.
5. Optionally, enter the total time and cost for this process step.

When you are creating a number of objects at once, Shift+click the object's button on the Toolbar. This creates a new object every time you click on a swim lane. To escape this mode, click on another object or the Selection arrow.

To move a process step, drag it to the correct spot on the diagram. Notice that the process steps are placed on a grid. This grid is maintained by the Process Modeler. You can set the size of the grid in the Preferences dialog box.

To delete an object, select it and press the Delete key. A dialog box will appear asking you to confirm the deletion.

To create a diagram that documents a process step in greater detail, select the process step, then select File | Open Down from the menu. This opens a new diagram with the selected process step as its root process step.

Once a process step has been entered, more detailed editing is possible. Double-click on a process step to open its Edit Process Step dialog box.

There are five tabs on the Edit Process Step dialog box:

- Main
- Specific
- Resources
- Multimedia
- Text

The Main tab is for detailed time and cost figures. (See Figure 25.8.)

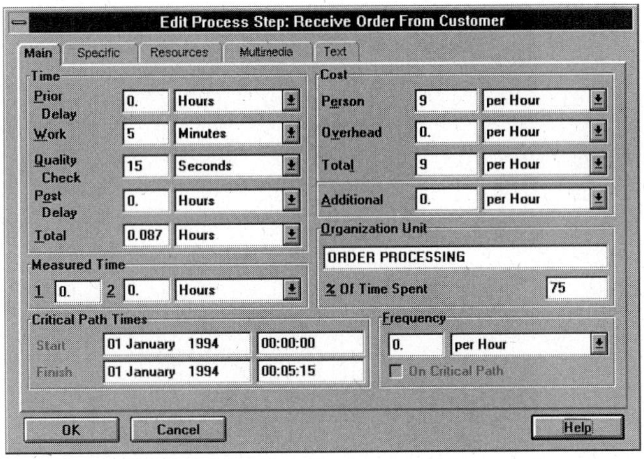

FIGURE 25.8.

Use the Main tab to track time and cost details.

In the Time area, enter either the total time for the process, or more detailed time entries for each category. Each category can be tracked by a separate unit of time.

If time is entered in the detail areas, their total will overwrite the figure in the Total box.

In the Cost area, enter either the total cost for the process, or more detailed entries under Person or Overhead. Costs can be tracked individually by time unit or by unit.

> **NOTE**
>
> If cost is entered in the detail areas, the total cost will overwrite the figure in the Total box.

The Measured Time area is to record up to two measured times for this process step. Figures entered into this area are for documentation only, and are not carried forward into other processing.

The Organization Unit box shows the organization unit associated with this process step. The percentage of time spent box is for entering the percentage of time spent on this task by the organization unit. It is used only for reporting purposes.

The times in the Critical Path box are filled in when the Critical Path Analysis function is run. They show where this process step occurs in time.

The On Critical Path checkbox is also filled in by the Critical Path Analysis function. It is checked if the current process is on the critical path.

In the Frequency box, the frequency of this function can be entered.

The Specific tab shown in Figure 25.9 is for editing specific names and descriptions of this process step.

FIGURE 25.9.

The Specific tab is used to edit the name and description of the process.

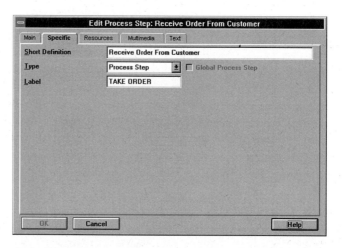

The Resources tab is for entering resources used, and for the quality yield of the process step. These are used for documentation only and do not affect anything else in the Repository. See Figure 25.10 for an example.

FIGURE 25.10.

Enter resource requirements for a process step in the Resources tab.

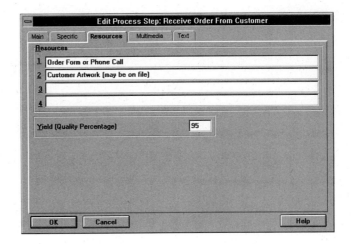

The Multimedia tab controls the various display options that are available for this process step. Figure 25.11 is a picture of the Multimedia tab. It will be addressed in detail in the "Multimedia" section of this chapter.

FIGURE 25.11.

The Multimedia tab controls display options for a process step.

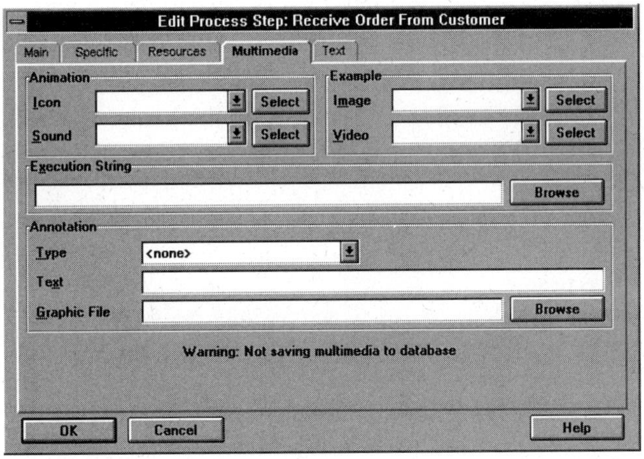

The Text tab is where text is entered to fully describe a process step. Several kinds of text are available. You can view and enter up to two different text types at the same time. (See Figure 25.12.) These are only used for documentation.

Stores

A store is a storage point for information or materials. It could be a filing cabinet, computer system, form, or any other kind of storage.

FIGURE 25.12.

Document process steps and flows with the Text tab.

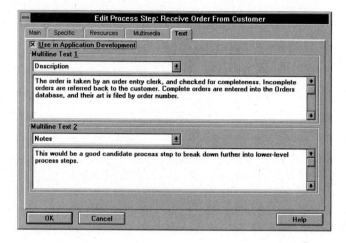

Stores are created in much the same way as process steps. There are three different kinds of stores, including data stores, material stores, and a generic store. The type of store can be changed at any time.

To create a store:

1. Select the Create Store button on the toolbar.
2. Select the spot on the swim lane for the process step. The Create Store dialog box appears. (See Figure 25.13.)

FIGURE 25.13.

The Create Store dialog box.

3. Enter the definition and label for the store.
4. Select the type of store from the drop-down list.
5. Optionally, enter the total cost for this process step.

NOTE

Data stores cannot have time entries associated with them.

6. Select OK. The store appears on the diagram in a rounded box, as shown in Figure 25.14.

FIGURE 25.14.

The new store is shown on the process diagram.

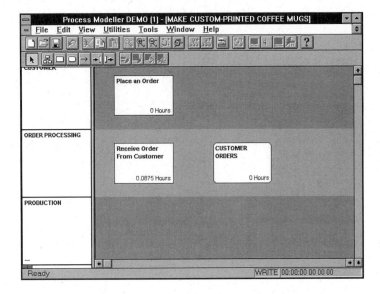

Flows

A flow is a path for information or materials. It is represented on the diagram as an arrow pointing from the origin of the information to its destination. There are four different kinds of flows: data flows, material flows, temporal flows, and the default flow, which is simply called a flow. All flows on a diagram must connect two boxes on that diagram.

To create a flow:

1. Select the Create Flow tool from the toolbar. Move the pointer to the object representing the origin of the flow, and drag it to the destination. The Create Flow dialog box (see Figure 25.15) appears.

CAUTION

Be sure you drag the cursor in the direction of the flow.

TIP

To move a flow from one item to another, select the flow and drag each end individually to the other item. To reverse a flow, drag the arrow end of the flow line temporarily to another item. Then drag the origin of the flow to its proper place. Finally, drag the arrow into its final position.

FIGURE 25.15.

Enter details about a flow in the Create Flow dialog box.

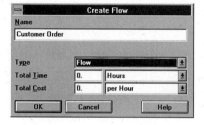

2. Select the type of flow from the drop-down list.

3. Optionally, enter the time data.

4. Select OK. The flow line is automatically routed between the two objects you connected. (See Figure 25.16.)

FIGURE 25.16.

The Process Modeler creates the arrows denoting the flow.

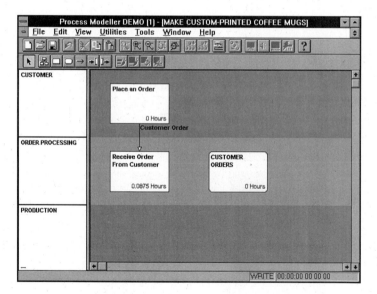

Decision Points

A decision point is a point in a process where a business decision must be made. There will usually be more than one possible outcome from a decision point.

To create a decision point:

1. Select the Create Process Step button on the toolbar.

2. Select the spot on the swim lane for the decision point. The Create Process Step dialog box appears. (See Figure 25.17.)

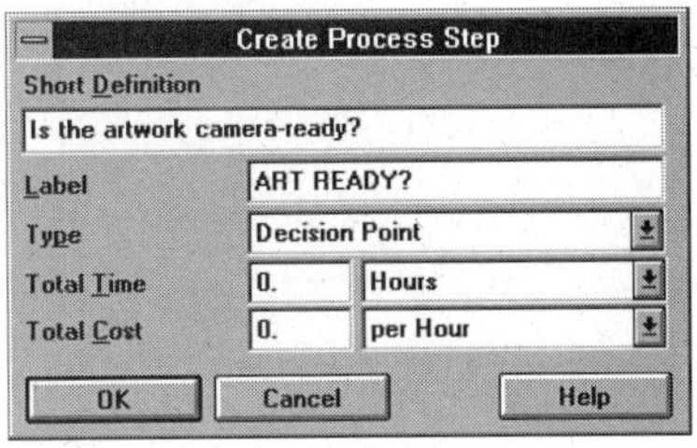

FIGURE 25.17.

A decision point is a type of process step.

3. Enter the definition and label for the process step.
4. Select Decision Point from the Type of Process Step drop-down list.
5. Optionally, enter the total time and cost for this decision point.
6. Select OK.

Triggers and Outcomes

Triggers and outcomes are quite similar. A trigger is an event at the beginning of a process that starts the process. An outcome is the result of the process. A process can have multiple triggers and outcomes.

To create a trigger:

1. Select Create Trigger from the toolbar.
2. Select the process step to which the trigger will be attached.

> **TIP**
>
> The trigger symbol is added to the left side of a process step. If the process step is immediately to the right of the organization unit heading, it will be covered by the heading. Move the process step one unit to the right to reveal the trigger.

3. Enter the text of the trigger in the Create Trigger dialog box, shown in Figure 25.18.

> **TIP**
>
> For a clean diagram, make the trigger's first two words significant and short. The tool displays as much as it can on the diagram, and it will truncate the display of long names unless you adjust the font.

FIGURE 25.18.

The Create Trigger dialog box.

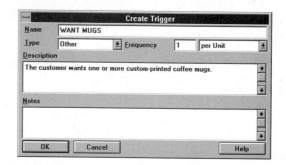

4. Select OK. The trigger appears on the diagram as shown in Figure 25.19.

FIGURE 25.19.

The completed trigger looks like this.

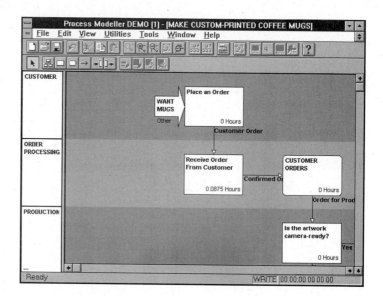

To create an outcome:

1. Select Create Outcome from the toolbar.

2. Select the process step to which the outcome will be attached.

3. Enter the text of the trigger in the Edit Outcome dialog box, shown in Figure 25.20.

4. Select OK. The outcome appears on the diagram as shown in Figure 25.21.

FIGURE 25.20.

The Edit Outcome dialog box.

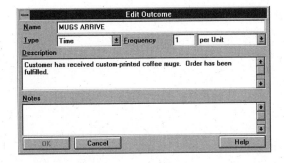

FIGURE 25.21.

The outcome from a process looks like this.

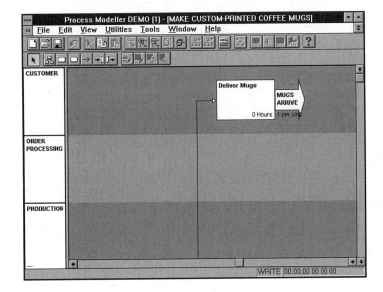

Critical Path

The Process Modeler can calculate the critical path for a process. It will take into account the times entered for each process step and flow. The critical path is shown in a contrasting color (the default is red) and may be recalculated at any time. (See Figure 25.22.)

To display the critical path:

1. Verify the time entries for each object.
2. Select one object on the process diagram.

NOTE

At least one diagram element must have time details entered before the critical path analysis is run.

FIGURE 25.22.

The Process Modeler displays the critical path of a process.

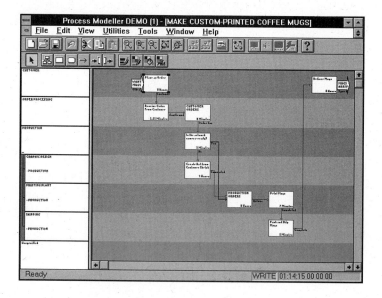

3. Select Utilities | Calculate Critical Path from the menu. The Critical Path Analysis dialog box appears. (See Figure 25.23.)

FIGURE 25.23.

The Critical Path Analysis dialog box.

4. Optionally, enter the start date and time. These default to the beginning of the current year.

5. Another dialog box appears. Enter Yes if you want the time for the critical path to appear in the Total Time attribute for the base process (this is Make Custom-Printed Coffee Mugs in this example).

6. Select OK. The critical path is displayed.

To turn off the critical path display, select Utilities | Reset Critical Path.

Exporting to Spreadsheets

The Process Modeler can export data for use in documentation, older versions of Oracle CASE, spreadsheets, or other CASE applications. It can export the entire diagram, or just export selected objects. It exports in the following five different formats:

- Oracle CASE 5.1
- Organization (Spreadsheet)
- Process (Spreadsheet)
- Proprietary
- Text

The Oracle CASE 5.1 option is for users of the older version of Oracle CASE.

The two spreadsheet options produce comma-delimited spreadsheets that can be imported as text directly into many spreadsheets, including Microsoft Excel. These files are text files, and can be edited manually if a given spreadsheet does not import comma-delimited files (such as Quattro Pro).

The Proprietary option exports to a proprietary format, which can be imported into another Process Modeler.

The Text option produces an ASCII text file describing the selected elements.

The Proprietary and Text export file types also allow the user to specify, in greater detail, which elements will be exported. This is done via a dialog box at the time of the export.

To export data from the Process Modeler:

1. Select Utilities | Export Data from the menu. The Export Data dialog box appears.
2. Select the type of export to perform.
3. Specify a file name for the export file.
4. If Proprietary or Text are selected, select the elements you wish to export.

> **NOTE**
>
> If any elements are blank, a dialog box will warn you. You may continue the export.

Preferences and Presentation Options

There are a number of preferences that can be set to control the appearance of a process flow diagram. These are set by selecting Edit | Preferences from the menu. See Figure 25.24.

FIGURE 25.24.

The Graphical Preferences dialog box.

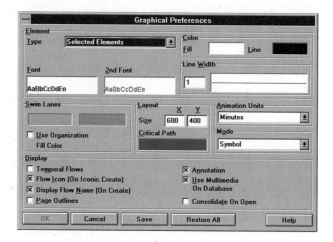

There are six major divisions of the Graphical Preferences dialog box.

Element allows you to specify colors, line width, and fonts for the selected element type, or for elements that are selected. The Type pull-down menu controls which element type is being reset.

Swim Lanes allows you to set the colors of the swim lanes. If the Use Organization Fill Color box is set, the swim lanes will be the same color as the background of the corresponding Organization Unit box.

Layout has two items. Size sets the size of the cells and boxes on the diagram. The unit of measure for this is about a tenth of a millimeter. Critical Path allows you to reset the color of the critical path.

Animation Units allows you to specify the time unit that corresponds to each second in an animation.

Mode selects the display mode.

Display contains a number of display options. Two in particular are significant because they are not display options. Use Multimedia on Database specifies whether or not to store the file names (not the contents) of multimedia files in the Repository. Consolidate on Open specifies whether or not to consolidate the diagram, which applies database changes to the diagram, when the diagram is opened.

TIP

You can select Edit | Consolidate | All from the menu at any time to consolidate a diagram.

The OK button applies preference changes for the current session only.

The Save button saves the preferences to the database.

Once your preferences are set, consider the display of the diagram itself.

There are three different ways to display a process flow diagram.

Symbol

Symbol is the default presentation type. Each element or decision point is shown as a rectangle. Stores are shown as soft boxes. The total time for each element is shown in the unit specified for that element. Select View | Symbol from the main menu, or Symbol from the Mode group of the Preferences menu to set this display mode. Figure 25.25 shows part of a diagram in Symbol mode.

FIGURE 25.25.

The Symbol view is Modeler's default.

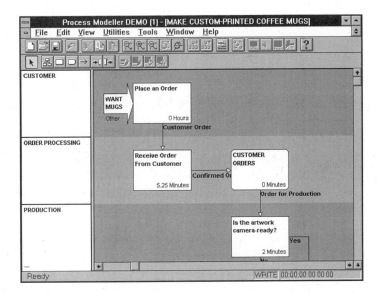

Enhanced Symbol

Enhanced Symbol mode is a different version of Symbol mode, which resembles the traditional programmer's flowchart. In this mode, elements have differing shapes based on their functions. The time for each element is not displayed. Select View | Enhanced Symbol from the main menu, or Enhanced Symbol from the Mode group of the Preferences menu to set this display mode. Figure 25.26 points out the different shapes used in Enhanced Symbol mode.

FIGURE 25.26.

This view shows the different shapes in Enhanced Symbol mode.

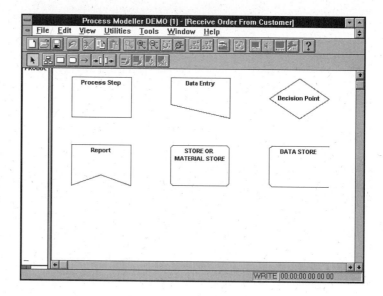

Iconic

In the iconic mode, objects are represented by icons. Each object can be associated with its own icon. The icons can be animated. This is the only view where animations are played.

When animations are played, the icons attached to each process step play for an amount of time proportional to the time they take in the overall process. The total elapsed time for the process appears at the bottom right of the main view. (See Figure 25.27.) Select View | Iconic from the main menu, or Iconic from the Mode group of the Preferences menu to set this display mode.

> **NOTE**
>
> When an animation is started, the view switches to Iconic.

Animating Icons

The icons shown in the iconic view are animated automatically by the Process Modeler. A number of icons are provided with the tool; however, it is quite easy to create custom animated icons.

When displaying an icon, the Process Modeler looks at the icon name. If the icon name is *xxx*1.bmp, it will try to load *xxx*2.bmp and *xxx*3.bmp as well. If it is successful, it will animate the icons in a loop.

FIGURE 25.27.

The iconic view is used for presentation to the user.

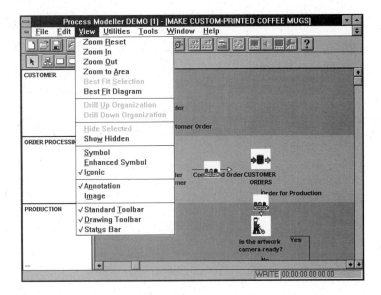

To create custom animated icons for an object:

1. Use any image editor to create a group of three icons, named *xxx*1.bmp through *xxx*3.bmp. Store them all in the same directory.

NOTE

All three image files should be the same size and color palette. Oracle recommends a maximum of 32 by 32 pixels for best performance.

2. In the Icon section of the Edit Process Step dialog box (under the Multimedia tab), store the name of the first image file.

To play an animation:

1. Select the process step where the animation is to start.
2. Press the Play Animation button on the toolbar.

Multimedia

Multimedia capabilities can be used to enhance process flow presentations. Each step in a process can have an image, sound, video, or program attached to it. Figure 25.28 shows the Configuration – Basic dialog box.

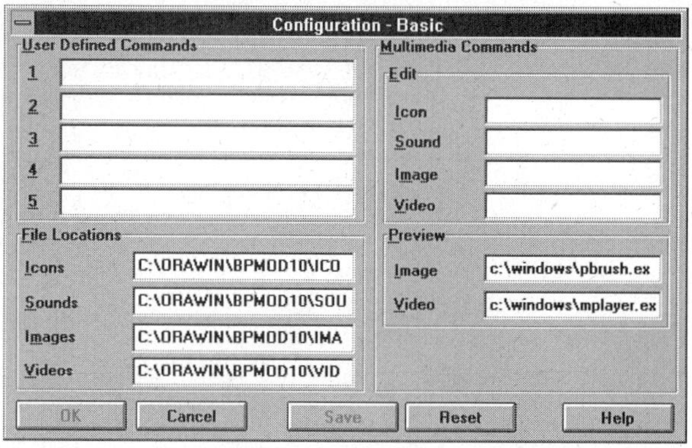

FIGURE 25.28.

The Configuration-Basic dialog box.

The User-Defined Commands section allows you to specify up to five programs. These can be run using the Tools | User Defined Command menu selection.

The File Locations section specifies directories where the Process Modeler will look for various types of files.

The Multimedia Commands section specifies commands that will be used to play or edit multimedia components.

Once this configuration is set, you attach a multimedia command to a process step by using the Multimedia tab of the Edit Process Step dialog box. Select the multimedia option you want to use by pressing its Browse button. The Multimedia Select dialog box appears. (See Figure 25.29.) When you select a file, it appears in the Preview area. Select OK to attach the multimedia file to the process step.

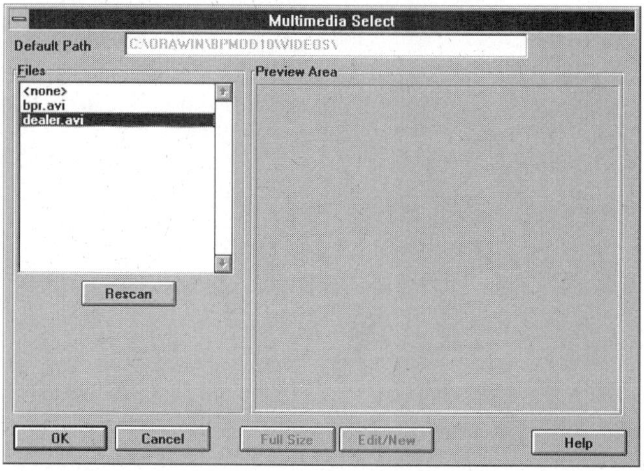

FIGURE 25.29.

The Multimedia Select dialog box.

Once you have associated multimedia files to process steps, you can play the files by selecting the process step, then selecting the appropriate play button from the toolbar.

Summary

The Process Modeler is used to document business processes, whether or not they will be automated. It is used to record organization units and their associated functions in the Designer/2000 Repository. Objects created using the Modeler are used to create data for further steps in Designer/2000. Any object in the Process Modeler can have a variety of descriptive text associated with it. Organization units may be placed in a hierarchy within the Modeler. Process steps are placed to the right of their associated organization units in graphic blocks called swim lanes. Flows of data or materials in a process are shown as arrows. Each flow and process step can have its elapsed time recorded. This enables the Modeler to perform critical path analysis on a process. For presentation purposes, the Modeler can animate the process flows with a user-defined icon at each step. In addition, each object and process step can have multimedia files attached to it.

Systems Modeling

26

by Rachel Becker

IN THIS CHAPTER

The system modeling tools are used to do a large portion of the analysis work in the life cycle of an Oracle project. The tools discussed in this chapter—the Entity Relationship Diagrammer, the Functional Hierarchy Diagrammer, and the Dataflow Diagrammer—all have a very similar screen format. On the top is a pull-down menu as well as a toolbar of icons. All of the functions that these icons perform can also be found on the menu bar under Edit, View, Utilities, and Tools. Whether the user wants to use the icons or the menu is a matter of style. For the most part, the descriptions in this chapter use the icons rather than the menu bar.

Initially you may create a new diagram either by choosing New from the File menu or by hitting the New Diagram icon. When you choose this icon or any icon from the Designer/2000 toolset, help is always available. The help message appears in a balloon to the right of the icon when you move your cursor next to the icon and do not depress it. You can also get help by selecting anything on your diagram (whether an icon or an element) and pressing the question mark icon. Finally, you can search for help on any topic from the Help menu.

Entity Relationship Diagrammer

This section provides a brief overview as to how to model information using the Entity Relationship Diagrammer. *Entities,* or things of significance in your system, can be shown graphically with this tool. Using this method, you can also show the relationships between entities.

Starting Up

You start the Entity Relationship Diagrammer by clicking on its icon and entering your user ID, password, and application. Across the top of the screen, you will see a set of icons used for designing a diagram, as shown in Figure 26.1.

Creating a Diagram

To create any entity relationship diagram you must follow certain steps. You will need to include summary information, add entities and relationships, and save the diagram in the database.

Summary Information

Initially when your diagram is started, you may want to fill in the summary information so that you can easily identify the diagram when it is printed. Under the File menu is a choice called Summary Information. A window pops up showing you all the choices for information to be included on your chart. (See Figure 26.2.)

FIGURE 26.1.

The Entity Relationship Diagrammer.

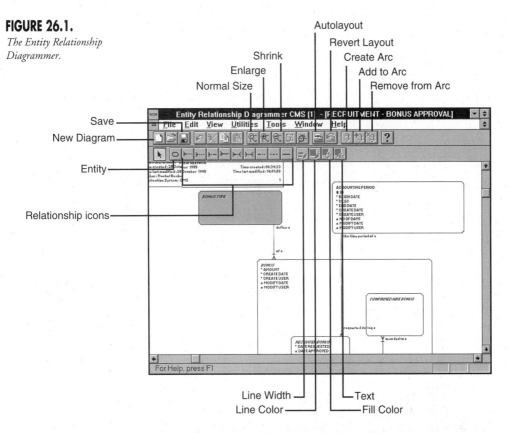

FIGURE 26.2.

The entity relationship diagram Summary Information.

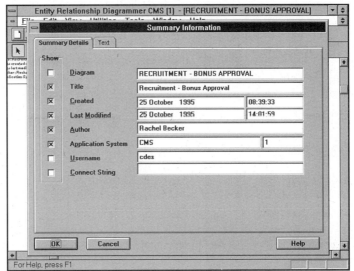

Select any information you want to display on the diagram. If you want to include your name or a diagram title, you need to fill in these items.

Adding the Entities

You are now ready to start adding information or entities to your diagram. You may have already created your entities in RON—the Repository Object Navigator—or some may have been entered by another user in RON or on another diagram. You can also create them right here in the Entity Relationship Diagrammer. If you need to create entities, select the Entity icon (refer to Figure 26.1). After you depress the icon, drag your cursor onto the diagram page. After you select a spot for the entity, you will be prompted for a name, short name, and plural for your entity. Then the entity is created. You can edit the entity by double-clicking on its shape. You can add attributes, unique keys, synonyms, and any descriptive text at this point. As long as you make the size of your entity sufficiently large on the screen, all of the attributes will be displayed. Otherwise, a set of dots signifies that more information is available about the entity. You may increase or decrease the size of the entity by selecting it and dragging it from one of its bold-faced points. After you create an entity on your diagram, the entity and any information you add or edit on it is added to RON.

> **TIP**
>
> If you want to create more than one entity without having to select the button each time, hold down the Shift key when you select the Entity button. When you are ready to move to another activity, press another button on the icon bar.

You can also select entities from RON. From the menu bar, choose Edit | Include | Entities. A list of available entities will appear. After you select an entity, the diagrammer automatically puts on the diagram the entity as well as any relationships it already has to any other entities on the diagram. You can bring in an entity with or without its relationships. To bring it in with relationships, select the With Relationships box before hitting the OK button.

> **TIP**
>
> To select multiple entities from the include list, hold down the Ctrl key and click on the entities you require or select a block of entities by holding down the Shift key. If you choose a large number, your diagram may become too difficult to follow for the initial editing, so keep this in mind when you make your selection.

Editing Attributes

You can add a great deal of information about attributes in the Entities properties screen. Just double-click on the entity and go to the Attributes Detail tab. Here you can add field type, length, a comment (which is the basis for the database comment and hint), and nullability. Go to the Attribute Values tab, and you can add allowable values or an allowable range for an attribute.

Creating Subtypes and Supertypes

You may want to divide your entity into subtypes. To add a subtype inside an entity, just create an entity and place your cursor inside the supertype when you place it on the diagram. You can also create subtypes and supertypes by dragging existing entities into the existing entity that will be the supertype.

Adding Relationships

After you have multiple entities on your diagram, you may want to show their relationships to one another. To do so, select one of the Relationship icons (refer to Figure 26.1). Select the relationship for which you are looking. Then select the From entity. Next select the To entity. When they are both selected, the system prompts you for the two relationship names. Then it places the relationship lines and the names on the diagram.

> **TIP**
>
> If you want to create more than one relationship without having to select the button each time, hold down the Shift key when you select the relationship button. When you are ready to move on to another activity, press another button on the icon bar.

If you set the property of including entities not to include relationships, you can include relationships from RON. To do so, choose Edit | Include | Relationships from the menu bar. Choose the relationship you want to include from the list, and it will appear on the diagram.

> **TIP**
>
> To select multiple relationships from the list, hold down the Ctrl key and click on the relationships you require, or select a block of relationships by holding down the Shift key. If you choose a large number, your diagram may become too difficult to follow for the initial editing, so keep this in mind when you make your selection.

Sometimes you may want to show an arc across multiple relationships. First select each relationship in the arc by selecting one and then holding down the Ctrl key while selecting the others. The Create Arc icon becomes active (refer to Figure 26.1). Click on the Create Arc icon, and the arc will appear. To remove a relationship from an arc, click on the arc and then hold down the Ctrl key while selecting the relationships to remove. Then the Remove from Arc icon becomes active. Click on the Remove from Arc icon, and the relationships will be removed from the arc. If you want to add a relationship to the arc, click on the relationship to add and hold down the Ctrl key while selecting the relationships to add. Then the Add to Arc icon will become active. Click on the Add to Arc icon, and the relationships will be added to the arc.

Using Domains

To create a domain, use Edit | Domain from the menu bar. You will find a window where you can define the attributes and allowable values of the domain. A domain cannot be depicted on an entity relationship diagram as an entity, only as an attribute of an entity. In the attribute definition, the attribute can be linked to a domain.

> **NOTE**
>
> For depiction purposes at the analysis level, it makes sense to depict domains as entities without attributes. All of these entities could have a similar title, such as Types. For example, you could use Payroll Type, Employee Type, or Status Type to represent attribute types that will become domains in your physical model.

Saving the Diagram

When you are ready to save the diagram, do so by selecting File | Save from the menu bar. You can also save by clicking the Save icon (refer to Figure 26.1). At this point you can name your diagram.

> **NOTE**
>
> It is important to save often. The Oracle client/server tools use a large amount of memory and can sometimes cause a general protection fault on the PC. Saving often decreases the risk of losing any unsaved work.

Multiple Diagrams

Often, there are multiple diagrams for one application. For example, a business may have an accounting department and a payroll department. Both departments could have separate diagrams. A third diagram could depict all of the departments in the business.

Consolidating

When you make changes to an entity or its relationships, the changes can be made in either the Entity Relationship Diagrammer or RON. The changes will not be reflected on other diagrams that use the same entities. There may be a reason for the user to keep the changes off—the changes may reflect an earlier point in time, or they may reflect the business opinions of another department. However, it is possible to take into account changes from other users and consolidate them into the current diagram. To do so, you must choose Edit | Consolidate from the menu bar. At this point you can choose whether to consolidate a specific entity, relationship, or the entire diagram.

> **NOTE**
>
> If you do not consolidate an element that has changed, you cannot edit it.

Making a Diagram Easier to Follow

In several ways you can make the diagram easier for the customer to follow.

Autolayout

As you add entities to the diagram, you will place them where they seem to fit, and the layout may become crowded. When an existing entity is chosen from Include, the entities may be placed on the diagram in a haphazard manner. If the diagram starts to look ugly, use the Autolayout icon (refer to Figure 26.1). When the icon is clicked, the entities and relationships are shifted around for readability. If you don't like the way the computer resets the layout, you can press the Autolayout icon again. You can continue to press the icon until you are happy with the outcome. You can go back to the last prior autolayout by using the Revert Layout icon.

Autolayout for a Specific Area

Sometimes you will add a number of new entities to a specific area, and the layout of these entities will become difficult to follow. To reposition these entities, you need to select just these entities and press the Autolayout button. To reposition these entities to another area on the diagram, select these entities and choose Utilities | Autolayout to New Area from the menu bar. Select where you want to reposition the entities and drag an area large enough to fit the entities. When you release the mouse, the entities will be repositioned in the new area.

Using Colors, Fonts, and Line Width

It is also possible to change the colors of entities and relationships, the fonts of words, and the line width of entity outlines and relationships. By changing these items, you can make the diagram more readable and add intelligibility. For example, all Type entities (the ones which may represent domains) can be filled in with blue.

> **NOTE**
>
> The colors on the diagram show up only if you have a color printer. If you are using a black-and-white printer, however, colors show up as different shades of gray, so one color differentiation can be used.

You can change all of the diagram or just a specific entity, relationship, or combination. To change the entire diagram, choose Edit | Select All from the menu bar. To select one or more entities or relationships, select one and hold down the Ctrl key until all the items are selected.

To change the line width, select the Line Width icon (refer to Figure 26.1). Choose a line width from the items listed. To change the line color, choose the Line Color icon. Choose a line color from the colors listed. To change the fill color of entities, choose the Fill Color icon. Choose a color from the items listed. To change the font of any text selected, choose the Text icon. The font, the font style, and the size of text all can be changed.

Working with Large Diagrams

When you work with large diagrams, you may find it difficult to keep track of where you are on the diagram. Also, the diagram can consume many pages when it is printed. There are simple ways to deal with these irritations.

Using Navigate

From Edit | Navigate on the menu bar, select either an entity or a relationship. The cursor selects the item requested, and the focus of the screen includes the item requested.

Minimizing the Number of Pages

Often, when the diagram is filled with many entities, it becomes very large, sprawling horizontally or vertically. As a result, many blank pages may fill the borders of the diagram. You can reposition the diagram to use the fewest number of pages by using the Minimize Number Of Pages icon. Pressing this icon repositions the entire diagram so that it uses the least number of pages.

Zooming In and Out

You can zoom in and out of your picture to see how an area or the entire picture looks. The magnifying glass icons enable you to perform this function. Use the Normal Size icon (refer to Figure 26.1) to return to regular screen size. Use the Enlarge icon to enlarge the view. Use the Shrink icon to shrink the view.

Functional Hierarchy Diagrammer

This section provides a brief overview of how to model information using the Functional Hierarchy Diagrammer. *Functions,* or activities in your system, can be shown graphically with this tool. Using this method, you can also show the relationships or hierarchy among functions.

Starting Up

Start the Functional Hierarchy Diagrammer by clicking on its icon and entering your user ID, password, and application. Across the top of the screen, you will see a set of icons used for designing a diagram, as shown in Figure 26.3.

Creating a Diagram

To create any functional hierarchy diagram, you must follow certain steps. You should include functions, lay out the hierarchy, and save the diagram in the database.

Adding Functions to a Diagram

You can create functions on the diagram or bring them in from RON—the Repository Object Navigator. To create a function on the diagram, select the Function icon (see Figure 26.3). After selecting the icon, click on a place on the diagram where the function should be placed. The system will prompt you for a short name and title for the function.

FIGURE 26.3.

The Functional Hierarchy Diagrammer.

Normal Size

Enlarge

Shrink

Save

Function

Reparent

Resequence

Line Width

Line Color

Fill Color

Text

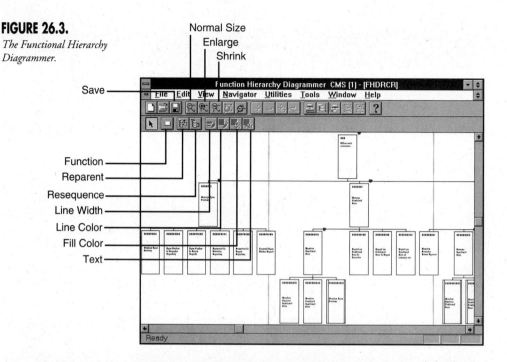

If you want to create more than one function without having to select the button each time, hold down the Shift key when you select the Function button. When you are ready to move on to another activity, press another button on the icon bar.

The short name of the function can contain information about the function—such as ACCOUNT for "Keep track of user accounts"—or it can represent the functional breakdown of the function within the hierarchy, such as REP for all reports, and REP01, REP02, and REP03 for each report.

In the Repository Reports, the Function Definition Report has an option for listing all functions on a diagram. Currently, this option does not work unless you give all functions short names that start with the same alphanumeric string. Make sure no function outside this diagram starts with this string. You can ask for the report by functions that start with the string.

NOTE

The short name of a function is the default for the short name of a module, which is the default for the name of a Windows file. Therefore, the name should be limited to eight characters to conform to Windows standards.

After you add the function, you can include other information about the function just by double-clicking on the function box. The edit function window pops up where you can edit the definition of the function, any notes to be added, the frequency of use, the entities used by the function, the attributes, the CRUD (Create, Retrieve Update, Delete usage), and triggers.

To enter or edit entities and attributes, select an entity from the list. Then select an attribute or set of attributes by holding down the Ctrl key. Next, click the down arrow to insert your choice onto the dataflow list. To remove them from the dataflow list, click the up arrow. Data items are manually entered.

In the trigger area, you can specify any functions that are triggered by completion of the current function. For example, the function of printing payroll checks may trigger the function of distributing payroll checks.

A function can also be created as a child of another function. After you press the Function icon, select the parent function from the diagram. Then continue as you normally would in creating the function. The function will now be displayed as a child.

CAUTION

All of the characteristics of a function are editable. However, if you edit the short name of a function and it is the parent of another function, when you print out the function definition, the old name of the parent function will appear on the definition of the child. This error occurs because the system has denormalized the function definition table and the original parent name is stored with the child. If you run into this problem, contact Oracle Support and they will supply you with a utility to solve this problem.

You can also include a function from the RON. Using Edit | Include | Function from the menu bar, choose the function from the available list.

Changing Diagram Layout

There are three types of diagram layout:

> Vertical—all functions are displayed vertically on the diagram (see Figure 26.4).

> Horizontal—all functions are displayed horizontally, with each level displaying vertically (see Figure 26.5).

> Hybrid—a combination of Vertical and Horizontal that seems the most appealing based on the functional breakdown (see Figure 26.6).

To choose a specific layout type, select Tools from the menu bar. Choose Vertical, Horizontal, or Hybrid from the layout choices.

FIGURE 26.4.

A vertical layout for a functional hierarchy.

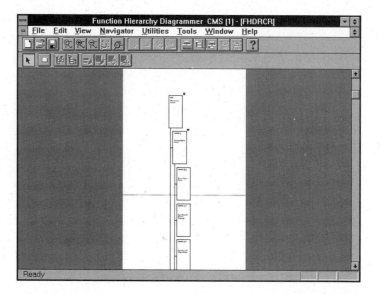

FIGURE 26.5.

A horizontal layout for a functional hierarchy.

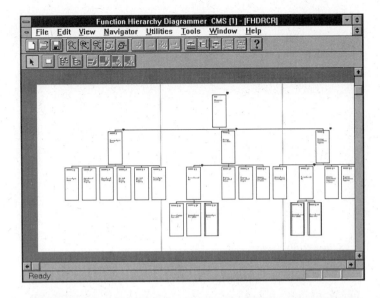

FIGURE 26.6.

A hybrid layout for a functional hierarchy.

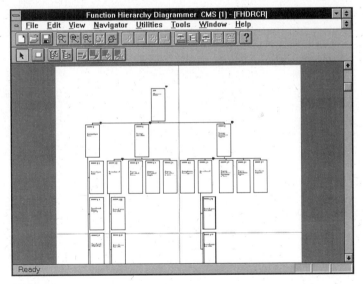

Resequencing Functions

After you have created your diagram, you may want to resequence certain functions. To do so, click on the Resequence icon (refer to Figure 26.3). Then select the function you wish to resequence. Drag it just beyond the function you want it to follow. Then release the button.

TIP

When you make a function the last function, there is no room on the function hierarchy for it at the end. Instead, make it the second-to-last function. Then move the last function in front of it.

Moving a Function to a New Parent

Sometimes it makes sense to move a function from one area of the diagram to another. To reparent a function, click on the Reparent icon (refer to Figure 26.3). Then select the function you wish to reparent. Drag the cursor to the new parent and release the button.

Sharing Functions

Sometimes a function is used more than once in an application, or a function is used in multiple applications. Rather than make a function redundant, you can refer to it multiple times or make it into a shared function. Double-click on the function that will be a copy of another function. In the common area, enter the application and the short name of the function you are copying.

CAUTION

Designer/2000 enables you to enter any information on a referencing function that you would on a regular function, such as notes, description, entity usage, and so on. However, when you are printing a function definition for a function that references another function, the only data that is displayed is the data from the common function, not any extra notes you may have added to the function referencing the information.

Saving the Diagram

When you are ready to save the diagram, do so by selecting File | Save from the menu bar. You can also save by clicking the Save icon (refer to Figure 26.3). At this point you can name your diagram.

NOTE

It is important to save often. The Oracle client/server tools use a large amount of memory and can cause a general protection fault on the PC. Saving often decreases the risk of losing any unsaved work.

Consolidating

When you make changes to a function's definition or its point in the hierarchy, you can enter the changes in either the Diagrammer or RON. The changes are reflected on other diagrams that use the same functions. There may be a reason for you to keep the changes off—they may reflect an earlier time or the business opinions of another department. However, it is possible to take into account the changes from other users and consolidate them into the current diagram. To do so, you must choose Edit | Consolidate from the menu bar. At this point you can choose whether to consolidate a specific function or the entire diagram.

NOTE

If you do not consolidate an element that has changed, you cannot edit it.

Making Diagrams Easier to Follow

When you work with large diagrams, it can become difficult to keep track of where you are on the diagram, and the diagram can consume many pages when printing. There are simple ways to deal with these irritations.

Minimizing the Number of Pages

Often, when the diagram is filled with many functions, it becomes very large, sprawling horizontally or vertically. As a result, many blank pages may fill the borders of the diagram. The diagram can be repositioned to use the fewest number of pages by using the Minimize Number Of Pages icon. Pressing this icon will reposition the entire diagram so that the least number of pages are used.

Using Colors, Fonts, and Line Width

It is also possible to change the colors of functions and the hierarchy lines, the fonts of words, and the line width of function outlines and hierarchy lines. By changing these items, you can make the diagram more readable and intelligible. For example, all payroll functions could be filled in with green.

NOTE

The colors on the diagram will only show up if you have a color printer. If you are using a black-and-white printer, colors will show up as gray, so one color differentiation can be used between gray and black.

You can change all of the diagram or just a specific function, hierarchy line, or a combination. To change the entire diagram, choose Edit | Select all from the menu bar. To select one or more function or hierarchy line, pick one and hold down the Ctrl key until all the items are selected.

To change the line width, select the Line Width icon (refer to Figure 26.3). Choose a line width from the items listed. To change the line color, choose the Line Color icon. Choose a line color from the line colors listed. To change the fill color of entities, choose the Fill Color icon. Choose a color from the items listed. To change the font of any text selected choose the Text icon. The font, font style, and size of text can all be changed.

Zooming In and Out

You can zoom in and out of your picture to see how an area or the entire picture looks. The magnifying glass icons enable you to perform this function. Use the Normal Size icon (refer to Figure 26.3) to return to normal size. Use the Enlarge icon to enlarge the view. Use the Shrink icon to shrink the view.

Dataflow Diagrammer

This section provides a brief overview of how to model information using the Dataflow Diagrammer. Data flows between functions and the world outside the business model. The Dataflow Diagrammer is used to show when the data is brought into the system, what format it is in, and where it ends up in the model being designed.

Starting Up

Start the Dataflow Diagrammer by clicking on its icon and entering your user ID, password, and application. Across the top of the screen, you will see a set of icons used for designing a diagram (see Figure 26.7).

Creating a Diagram

To create any dataflow diagram, you must follow certain steps. You should include functions, define dataflows, datastores, and external storage, and save the diagram.

FIGURE 26.7.

The Dataflow Diagrammer.

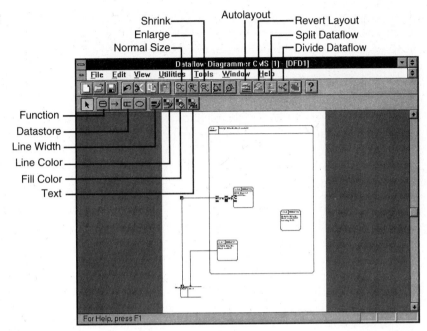

Shrink

Enlarge

Normal Size

Autolayout

Revert Layout

Split Dataflow

Divide Dataflow

Function

Datastore

Line Width

Line Color

Fill Color

Text

Using Functions

A dataflow diagram must contain functions, so you should create a functional hierarchy prior to using the tool in either RON or the Function Hierarchy Diagrammer. If you discover while using the Dataflow Diagrammer that you forgot a function, you can add it directly in the Dataflow Diagrammer. Press the Function icon (refer to Figure 26.7). You will be prompted for a short name and a description (similar to using the Function Hierarchy Diagrammer). If you need to create an entire hierarchy, it is better to use the Function Hierarchy Diagrammer.

When you create a new diagram, you will be prompted to select a function that will be the base for the diagram, generally a parent function. Next, add the children you want to depict in the diagram. To include an existing function from the application, just use Edit | Include | Function from the menu bar. Then choose where you want to place it on the diagram.

TIP

To select multiple functions from the list, hold down the Ctrl key and click on the functions you require, or select a block of functions by holding down the Shift key. If you choose a large number, your diagram may become too difficult to follow for the initial editing, so keep this in mind when you make your selection.

After adding a function, you can edit it. The entities used in this function can be defined, as well as the attributes of the entities within this function. Double-click on the function to edit it.

Adding Datastores

A *datastore* is a site where data for entities or attributes can be stored for use by a function. For example, a paper timecard is temporarily the datastore for an employee's hours until the hours are entered into the system. The datastore can be added by clicking the Datastore icon (refer to Figure 26.7). After you decide where you want the datastore on the diagram, you can add the short name and description for the datastore. If a datastore is used when performing a function, place it inside the function.

After adding the datastore, you can edit it. The entities in the datastore can be defined, as well as the attributes of the entities. Double-click on the datastore to edit it. From there you can edit the description, any notes on the datastore, and the entities, their attributes, and other data elements. Select an entity from the list. Then select an attribute or set of attributes by holding down the Ctrl key. Next, press the down arrow to insert them onto the dataflow list. To remove them from the dataflow list, hit the up arrow. Data items are just manually entered.

You can also include datastores from RON, if you entered them previously on another diagram. To select an existing datastore, select Edit | Include Datastore from the menu. Select an existing datastore from the list.

Adding Externals

Externals are repositories outside of the function where entities, attributes, or data elements are stored. To add externals to the diagram, select the External icon. Place the cursor where you want the external on the diagram. Enter the short name and description.

TIP

If you want to create more than one external without having to select the button each time, hold down the Shift key when you select the External button. When you are ready to move on to another activity, press another button on the icon bar.

After you add an external, you can edit it. To do so, double-click on the external. On the screen you can edit the short name, description, information about whether it comes from outside the application (possibly from another application), a comment, and its representation. The representation signifies whether it is an entity or business unit. You can select a specific entity or business unit from the list of values.

You can also include externals from RON, if you entered them previously on another diagram. To select an existing external, select Edit | Include Datastore from the menu. Select an existing external from the list.

Adding Dataflows

Dataflows can be added to signify the flow of data from any one element to another. To create a dataflow, select the Dataflow icon. Select the parent element for the flow and then select the child element. Now enter a description for the flow. If no description is entered, the diagrammer will list the word *none*.

> **TIP**
>
> If you want to create more than one dataflow without having to select the button each time, hold down the Shift key when you select the Dataflow button. When you are ready to move on to another activity, press another button on the icon bar.

After you add a dataflow, you can edit it by double-clicking on the item. From there you can edit the description, any notes on the dataflow, and the actual data flowing out of the parent element—the entities, their attributes, and other data elements. Select an entity from the list. Then select an attribute or set of attributes by holding down the Ctrl key. Next, hit the down arrow to insert them onto the dataflow list. To remove them from the dataflow list, hit the up arrow. Data items are manually entered.

You can also include dataflows from RON, if you entered them previously on another diagram. To select an existing dataflow, choose Edit | Include Dataflow from the menu. Select an existing dataflow from the list.

Adding Resolved Flows

Resolved flows, or dataflows at levels lower than the functions displayed, can be added to the diagram to display the flow of data below the level of your diagram. To select an existing resolved flow, select Edit | Include Resolved Flow from the menu. Select an existing dataflow from the list.

Saving the Diagram

When you are ready to save the diagram, do so by selecting File | Save from the menu bar. You can also save by depressing the Save icon. At this point, you can name your diagram.

> **NOTE**
>
> It is important to save often. The Oracle client/server tools use a large amount of memory and can cause a general protection fault on the PC. Saving often decreases the risk of losing any unsaved work.

Modifying Dataflow Structure

After a diagram has been developed, you may return to analysis and discover that one dataflow actually represents multiple dataflows. You can then split or divide the dataflow.

> **NOTE**
>
> You cannot split or divide a resolved flow.

Splitting a Dataflow

Splitting a dataflow creates an interim datastore between the two original elements of a dataflow. To split a dataflow, select the Split Dataflow icon (refer to Figure 26.7). A default name is derived from the name of the dataflow. To edit the new datastore, double-click on the item.

Dividing a Dataflow

If a dataflow contains multiple attributes or data elements, you may discover that the dataflow actually originates from different sources. To divide the dataflow, click the Divide Dataflow icon (refer to Figure 26.7). This creates an identical dataflow, with the name of the original flow followed by a number 1. Select the elements to be removed from the new dataflow (since they are identical to the original dataflow) with the down arrow. Change the name of the dataflow to a more acceptable one. Once the Dataflow Diagrammer resumes, move the new dataflow to the proper elements.

Multiple Diagrams

Often there will be multiple diagrams for one application. For example, a business may have an accounting department and a payroll department. Both departments could have separate diagrams. There could be a third diagram that depicts all of the departments in the business.

Consolidating

When you make changes to an entity or its relationships, you can make them in either the Dataflow Diagrammer or RON. The changes will not be reflected on other diagrams that use the same entities. There may be a reason for the user to keep the changes off—they may reflect an earlier time or the business opinions of another department. However, it is possible to utilize changes from other users and consolidate them into the current diagram. To do so, you must choose Edit | Consolidate from the menu bar. At this point, you can choose whether to consolidate a specific entity, relationship, or the entire diagram.

NOTE

If you do not consolidate an element that has changed, you cannot edit it.

Making a Diagram Easier to Follow

There are several ways you can make the diagram easier for the customer to follow.

Autolayout

When you add entities to the diagram, you will place them where they seem to fit. As you add entities, the layout may become crowded. When an existing function is chosen from Include, the function may be placed on the diagram in a haphazard manner. When the diagram starts to look ugly, it is time to use the Autolayout icon (refer to Figure 26.7). When the icon is clicked, the elements and their dataflows are shifted around for readability. If you don't like the way the computer resets the layout, you can press the Autolayout icon again. You can continue to press the icon until you are satisfied with the outcome. To go back to the previous layout, you can click the Revert Layout icon.

Autolayout for a Specific Area

Sometimes when you add a number of new elements to a specific area, the layout of these elements becomes difficult to follow. To reposition these entities, you need to select only these entities and press the Autolayout icon. To reposition these entities to another area on the diagram, select the entities and choose Utilities | Autolayout to New Area from the menu bar. Decide where you want to reposition the entities and drag an area large enough to fit the entities. When you release the mouse the entities will be repositioned in the new area.

Using Colors, Fonts, and Line Width

It is also possible to change the colors of functions, dataflows, datastores, and externals, the fonts of words, and the line width of element outlines and dataflows. By changing these items, you can make your diagram more readable and add intelligence. For example, all Payroll externals can be filled in with blue.

> **NOTE**
>
> The colors on the diagram will only show up if you have a color printer. However, if you are using a black-and-white printer, colors will show up grayed, so one color differentiation can be used.

You can change all of the diagram or a specific element, dataflow, or combination. To change the entire diagram choose Edit | Select All from the menu bar. To select one or more elements or dataflows, choose one and hold down the Ctrl key until all the items are selected.

To change the line width, select the Line Width icon (refer to Figure 26.7). Choose a line width from the items listed. To change the line color, choose the Line Color icon. Choose a line color from the colors listed. To change the fill color of entities, choose the Fill Color icon. Choose a color from the items listed. To change the font of any text selected, choose the Text icon. The font, font style, and size of text can all be changed.

Working with Large Diagrams

When you work with large diagrams, you may have difficulty keeping track of where you are on the diagram, and the diagram can consume many pages when printing. There are simple ways to deal with these irritations.

Minimizing the Number of Pages

Often a diagram filled with many elements becomes very large, sprawling horizontally or vertically. As a result, many blank pages may fill the borders of the diagram. You can reposition the diagram to use the fewest pages by using the Minimize Number of Pages icon. Clicking this icon will reposition the entire diagram so that fewest pages are used.

Zooming In and Out

You can zoom in and out of your picture to see how an area of the picture or the entire picture looks. The magnifying glass icons enable you to perform this function. Use the Normal Size icon (refer to Figure 26.7) to return to normal size. Use the Enlarge icon to enlarge. Use the Shrink icon to shrink.

Summary

The system modeling tools are used to do analysis work in the life cycle of an Oracle project. The Entity Relationship Diagrammer creates a diagram of the information stored in the business model. The Functional Hierarchy Diagrammer creates a diagram of the way the information is used in the business model. Once the entity relationship diagram and functional hierarchy diagrams are created, the Dataflow Diagrammer creates a diagram that shows how the information flows in and out of the business functions.

Systems Design

27

by Rachel Becker

IN THIS CHAPTER

You perform system design at the end of analysis and the beginning of design. The tools you use bring the analysis logical model of entities and relationships into the physical model of tables and foreign keys. They bring the logical model of functions into the physical model of reports, screens, and menus. The tools in system design include the following:

- Database Design Wizard—for transferring entities into table definitions
- Data Diagrammer—for editing table and column format
- Application Design Wizard—for transferring functions into modules
- Module Structure Diagrammer—for transferring module hierarchy into a menu
- Preferences Navigator—for setting up the preferences for generating reports, screens, and menus

Stand-Alone Tools

Some of the tools discussed in this chapter—the Data Diagrammer, the Module Structure Diagrammer, and the Preferences Navigator—have very similar screen formats. At the top of the screen is a pull-down menu, as well as a toolbar of icons. All the functions that these icons perform also appear on the menu bar under Edit, View, Utilities, and Tools. Whether the user wants to use the icons or the menu is simply a style choice. For the most part, the descriptions in this chapter refer to the icons rather than the menu bar.

Initially, you can create a new diagram by either choosing New from the File menu or clicking the first icon on the upper-left corner of the page. When choosing this icon or any icon from the Designer/2000 toolset, you always have help available. The help message appears in a balloon to the right of the icon when you move your cursor to it without clicking the mouse. You can also get help by selecting anything on your diagram (icon or element) and clicking the Question Mark icon. Finally, you can search for help on any topic from the help menu pick.

Database Design Wizard

You use the Database Design Wizard for generating table definitions from entity definitions. Before running the tool, make sure that your entities are properly defined. To check them, you can run the Entities With No… reports off the Repository Reports. The Matrix Diagrammer is also helpful in ensuring that all of the manipulation of entities—Create, Retrieve, Update, Delete (CRUD)—is covered under at least one function. For more information on running these reports, see Chapter 24, "Repository Administration."

Starting the Database Design Wizard

You can invoke the Database Design Wizard from either the Repository Object Navigator (RON) or Entity Relationship Diagrammer. Select Utilities | Database Design Wizard.

Initially, the tool loads all the entity and table information available in your application.

The Table Mappings Tab

The first screen that appears is the Table Mappings tab. (See Figure 27.1.) It contains all the entity names, whether they have been mapped to a table, and the table name. If you want to generate or regenerate an entire entity into a table, select the In Set box.

FIGURE 27.1.

The Table Mappings tab.

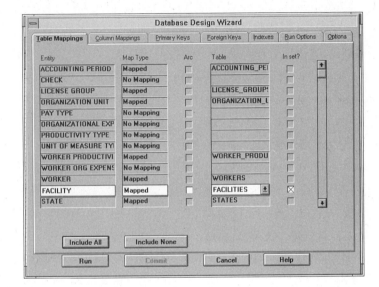

If the Design Wizard has not yet generated a table name, leave the table name blank. It is generated when the table definition is generated.

The rest of the tabs refer to information specific to each table.

The Column Mappings Tab

On the Column Mappings tab (see Figure 27.2), you can choose columns to generate initially or columns to regenerate. You might want to regenerate a table because it relates to a new entity or because you did more analysis and added new attributes to the entity. On the Column Mappings tab, you can remap attributes to existing columns, add new attributes, or add new columns. If an entity is in the set, there is no reason to add the attributes; they are included. You can select a single attribute without selecting the table. If the table does not exist, only these attributes selected generate columns in the table.

The Primary Keys Tab

On the Primary Keys tab, you can choose primary keys to generate initially or primary keys to regenerate. On the Primary Keys tab, you can remap attributes to existing unique keys or add new unique keys to the table. If an entity is in the set, there is no reason to add the keys; they are included. You can select a single key without selecting the table. If the table does not exist, only these unique IDs selected will generate unique keys in the table. The screen looks the same as the screen for the Column Mappings tab but shows unique IDs and primary keys instead of attributes and columns.

FIGURE 27.2.

The Columns Mapping tab.

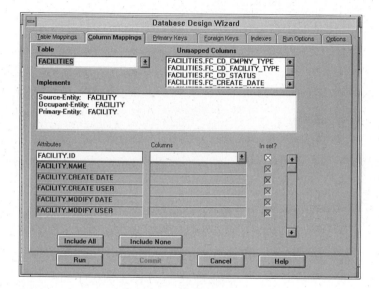

The Foreign Keys Tab

On the Foreign Keys tab, you can choose foreign keys to generate initially or foreign keys to regenerate. Here, you can remap attributes to existing foreign keys or add new ones to the table. If an entity is in the set, there is no reason to add the keys; they are included. You can select a single key however without selecting the table. If the table does not exist, only the foreign keys selected will generate foreign keys in the table. The screen looks the same as the screen for the Column Mappings tab but shows relationships and foreign keys instead of attributes and columns.

The Indexes Tab

On the Indexes tab, you can choose indexes to generate initially or indexes to regenerate. Here, you can remap relationships and unique IDs to existing indexes or add new indexes to the table. If an entity is in the set, there is no reason to add the indexes; they are included. You can select a single index without selecting the table. If the table does not exist, only the indexes selected will generate indexes in the table. The screen looks the same as the screen for the Column Mappings tab but shows foreign keys and indexes instead of attributes and columns.

The Run Options Tab

For each table definition generated, you can set the options for what types of items are created or modified. (See Figure 27.3.)

FIGURE 27.3.

The Run Options tab.

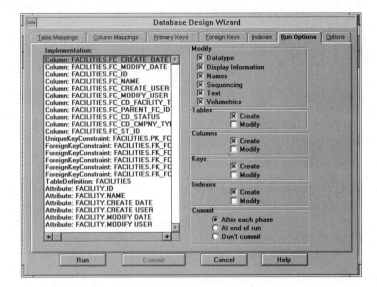

The Options Tab

For each table definition generated, you can set the options for what data storage structures store the table. If you provide no information, the Database Design Wizard uses the defaults. If you give no table prefix, the Wizard uses the short name of the entity. If you choose the Don't Commit option, the Wizard validates your choices but does not generate the tables. For the first time through, choosing this option is a good idea to ensure that your selections generate properly.

Continuing to Generate

Once you are satisfied with all your choices, you can click the Start button. The Design Wizard Output window prompts you as it generates the definitions, letting you know what steps are taken. Any warnings (such as a table is missing for a foreign key) or errors (such as a table name is too long) display on-screen. Once the generation is complete, you are returned to the Table Options tab so you can continue additional generation or leave the tool.

The Data Diagrammer

You use the Data Diagrammer to create a physical model of the database. This physical model is then used by the DDL Generator to generate the Data Definition Language (DLL) that is run to create tables, views, keys, and snapshots.

Start the Data Diagrammer by clicking its icon and entering your user ID, password, and application. Across the top of the screen, you see a set of icons used for designing a diagram. (See Figure 27.4.)

FIGURE 27.4.

The Data Diagrammer.

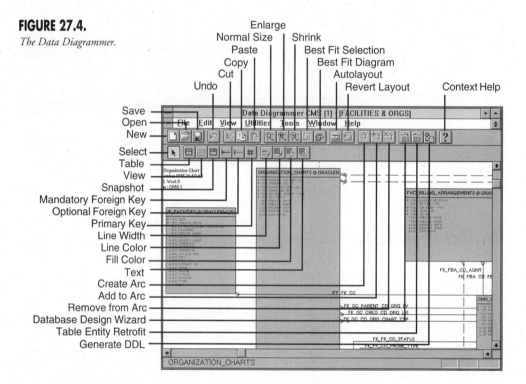

Creating a Diagram

To create a diagram, you need to create summary information, add tables, link tables together with foreign keys, add views and snapshots if necessary, and save the diagram.

Summary Information

You can enter any summary information you want to display on the top of the diagram. To edit the summary information, choose File | Summary Information. (See Figure 27.5.)

FIGURE 27.5.

The Summary screen.

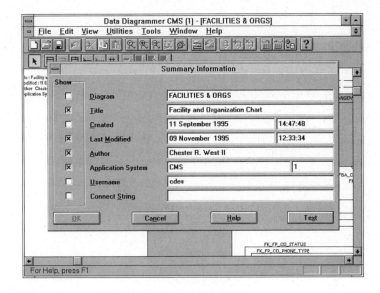

Adding Tables, Views, and Snapshots to the Diagram

If you used the Database Design Wizard, tables exist in RON, the Repository Object Navigator. You could add tables into RON directly or through another database diagram. To select an existing table or view, select Edit | Include. Select the table or view from the list available.

> **TIP**
>
> To select multiple tables or views from the include list, hold down the Ctrl key and click the modules you require, or select a block of tables by holding down the Shift key. If you choose a large number, your diagram could be too difficult to follow for the initial editing, so keep this in mind when making your selection.

When you add a table to the diagram, any existing relationships to tables already on the diagram are also added.

Creating New Tables, Views, and Snapshots

You might want to create a table because you forgot an entity in your analysis so the table you need was not generated, or you might want to simply create your system starting at the design level. To create a new table, click the Table icon (refer to Figure 27.4). Click where you want the table to appear on the diagram. The Data Diagrammer prompts you for a name, alias, and display title. To create a view, select the View icon. To create a snapshot, select the Snapshot icon.

TIP

To create multiple items, hold down the Ctrl button while you click the icon. When
you are finished creating the items, select another icon.

Editing Tables

To edit a table, double-click the table on the diagram. You see a set of tabs. The Table tab lists
the information needed for generating the table. (See Figure 27.6.)

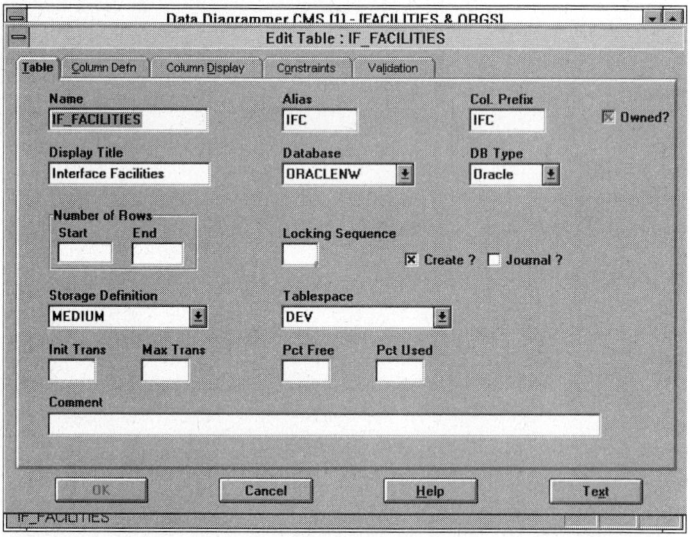

FIGURE 27.6.

The Table tab.

The Column Defn tab lists the definition information for columns. Tables generated from
entities have columns named with the table prefix joined to the attribute name. Any spaces are
replaced with underlines. Here you can edit column names, sequence, data type, length, and
so on.

The Column Display tab lists the display information about a column. The information is used
when table definitions are used in creating screen and report modules in the Application Generator. Whether or not an item should be displayed, the display type, the display length, and
the display sequence are modifiable here.

The Constraints tabs enable you to define keys and check constraints. You can define the names,
columns, and rules on these tabs. (See Figure 27.7.)

The Validation Tab enables you to enter a valid list of values for a column as well as a failure
message if the column is not filled with a valid item. (See Figure 27.8.)

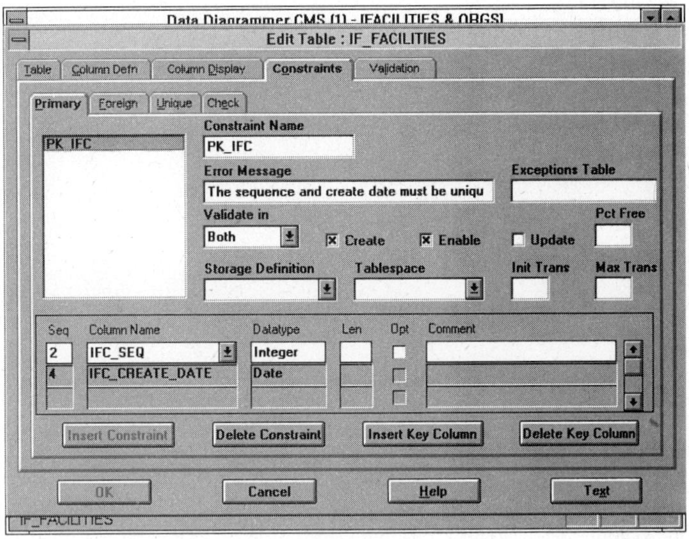

FIGURE 27.7.

The Constraints tabs.

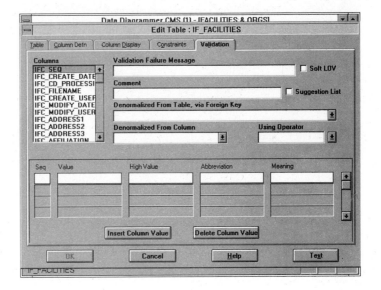

FIGURE 27.8.

The Validation tab.

Editing Views

To edit a view, double-click the view on the diagram. You see a set of tabs. The tabs are very similar to the table tabs, except for the Base Relations tab and the Base Cols tab. The Base Relations tab is where you add all the tables included in the view. You define their sequences and aliases here. The Base Cols tab is where you list the columns within the included tables. You define their aliases and sequences here.

Adding Foreign Keys

When you add a new table to the diagram, it can relate to an existing table. You also might want to add a relationship between two existing tables. To create a foreign key, you need to click one of the foreign key icons—the Mandatory Foreign Key icon or the Optional Foreign Key icon. (Refer to Figure 27.4.) After selecting the icon, select the From table and then the To table on the diagram. You are then prompted for the constraint name.

> **TIP**
>
> To create multiple keys, hold down the Ctrl button while you click the icon. When you are finished creating the keys, select another icon.

Sometimes, you might want to show an arc across multiple foreign keys. First, select each foreign key in the arc by selecting one and then holding down the Ctrl key while selecting the others. Then, select the table that they arc to. The Create Arc icon becomes active. (Refer to Figure 27.4.) Click the Create Arc icon, and the arc appears. To remove a foreign key from an arc, click the arc and then hold down the Ctrl key while selecting the foreign keys to remove. The Remove from Arc icon becomes active. Click the Remove from Arc icon, and the foreign keys are removed from the arc. If you want to add a foreign key to the arc, click the foreign key to add. The Add to Arc icon becomes active. Click the Add to Arc icon, and the foreign key is added to the arc.

Creating Primary Keys

You can create a primary key on the diagram rather than through the Constraint tab on a table or view. Select the first item in the primary key. Hold down the Ctrl key and select any other items in the key. Click the Primary Key. (Refer to Figure 27.4.)

Saving the Diagram

To save the diagram, click the Save icon. (Refer to Figure 27.4.) You can name your diagram anything you like; it probably makes sense to name it something related to the top menu level.

> **NOTE**
>
> It is important to save often. The Oracle client/server tools use a large amount of memory and can sometimes cause a general protection fault on the PC. Saving often decreases the risk of losing any unsaved work.

Multiple Diagrams

Often, you could have multiple diagrams for one application in Designer/2000. For example, a business might have an accounting department and a payroll department. Both departments could have separate diagrams, and a third diagram might depict all the departments in the business.

Consolidating

You can make changes to a table or its foreign keys in either the Data Diagrammer or RON. The changes are not reflected on other diagrams that use the same tables. The user might have a reason to keep the changes off—for example, to reflect an earlier point in time or the business opinions of another department. It is possible to take into account the changes from other users and consolidate them into the current diagram. To do so, choose Edit | Consolidate from the menu bar. At this point, you can choose whether to consolidate a specific table, foreign key, or the entire diagram.

> **NOTE**
>
> If you do not consolidate an element that has changed, you cannot edit it.

If foreign keys have been added to tables that are on your diagram, you can add them to your diagram by choosing Edit | Include | Relationship. All the relationships missing from your diagram appear on a list, and you can select the ones you want to add to your diagram.

Making a Diagram Easier to Follow

There are several ways you can make the diagram easier for the customer to follow. You can change the layout to make the table layout easier to follow, and you can change the colors and line widths.

Autolayout

When you add tables to a diagram, you place them where they seem to fit, and as you add more tables, the layout might become crowded. When the diagram starts to look ugly, it is time to use the Autolayout icon. (Refer to Figure 27.4.) When you click the icon, the tables and foreign keys shift around for readability. If you don't like the way the computer reset the layout, you can click the Autolayout icon again. You can continue to click the icon until you are happy with the outcome. You can go to the previous autolayout using the Revert Layout button.

Autolayout for a Specific Area

Sometimes, you add a number of new tables to a specific area, and the layout of these tables is difficult to follow. To reposition them, you need to select just those tables and click the Autolayout button. To reposition the tables to another area on the diagram, select the tables and choose Utilities | Autolayout to New Area. Select where you want to reposition the tables and drag an area large enough to fit them. When you release the mouse, the tables are repositioned in the new area.

Using Colors, Fonts, and Line Width

It is possible to change the colors of tables and foreign keys, the fonts of words, and the line width of table outlines and foreign keys. By changing these items, you can make the diagram more readable and add intelligence. For example, you can fill in all payroll tables with red.

> **NOTE**
>
> The colors on the diagram show up only if you have a color printer; however, if you use a black and white printer, colors show up grayed so you can use the various shades of gray for differentiation.

You can change all of the diagram or just one specific table, foreign key, or combination. To change the entire diagram, choose Edit | Select All. To select one or more tables or foreign keys, select one and hold down the Ctrl key while you select all the items.

To change the line width, select the Line Width icon. (Refer to Figure 27.4.) Choose a line width from the items listed. To change the line color, choose the Line Color icon. Choose a line color from the colors listed. To change the fill color of tables, choose the Fill Color icon. Choose a color from the items listed. To change the font of any selected text, choose the Text icon. You can change the font, the font style, and the text size.

You can also change the preferences for specific types of items. By choosing Edit | Preferences, you can set all tables to be one color, all views to be another color, and all snapshots to be yet another color.

Working with Large Diagrams

When you work with large diagrams, it can become difficult to keep track of where you are on the diagram. The diagram might take up many pages when printing. There are simple ways to deal with these irritations.

Using Navigate

Select Edit | Navigate and choose either a table, view, snapshot, or foreign key. The cursor selects the requested item, and the focus of the screen changes to include the item.

Using Minimize Number of Pages

When a diagram is filled with many tables, it often becomes very large, sprawling horizontally or vertically. As a result, many blank pages might fill the borders of the diagram. You can reposition the diagram to use the least number of pages by using the Minimize Number of Pages icon. Clicking this icon repositions the entire diagram so that it uses the least number of pages.

Zooming In and Out

You can zoom in and out of your picture to get a better idea of how an area of the picture looks or how the entire picture looks. The magnifying glass icons enable you to perform this function. Use the Normal Size icon to return to normal size (refer to Figure 27.4). Use the Enlarge icon to enlarge. Use the Shrink icon to shrink.

Generate the Tables Again

If you are not satisfied with the generation of any tables or there are new entities you want to generate as tables, you can do so from the diagrammer. Click the Database Design Wizard icon to regenerate or generate any tables from entities. (Refer to Figure 27.4.) For more information on the Database Design Wizard, see the "Database Design Wizard" section earlier in this chapter.

Retrofit

If you have made changes to a table that you want to see reflected in the entity the table was generated from, click the Table Entity Retrofit icon (refer to Figure 27.4). You can choose what tables to retrofit, what entity they return to, and what columns and constraints should be passed back.

Generating DDL

Once you are satisfied with what you have created in the Data Diagrammer, you can generate the DDL for creating the tables, views, snapshots, and constraints on your database. Make sure you save the diagram before generating. Click the Generate DDL icon. (Refer to Figure 27.4.) Select what tables, views, snapshots, and constraints you want to generate. The scripts to create the items are created at this point. The scripts receive the following names:

- *XXX*.TAB creates table code
- *XXX*.VW creates view code
- *XXX*.SS creates snapshot code
- *XXX*.CON creates constraints code
- *XXX*.IND creates index code

The *XXX* is defined as the short name for your table. You can examine the scripts and run them right from the generator. The DDL Generator also generates DBA information such as triggers, tablespaces, clusters, and so on.

The Application Design Wizard

You use the Application Design Wizard to generate modules and menus from functions. Before running the tool, you should make sure that your functions are properly defined. To check them, run the Matrix Diagrammer to ensure the functions are covering all the CRUD for the entities to be generated. For more information on running these reports, see Chapter 24, "Repository Administration." Finally, the Database Design Wizard should have already generated the table definitions so that the table usages are recognized by the Application Design Wizard.

Starting the Application Design Wizard

You can invoke the Application Design Wizard from either the Repository Object Navigator, the Function Hierarchy Diagrammer, or the Dataflow Diagrammer. Select Utilities | Database Design Wizard.

The Application Design Wizard selection screen appears. (See Figure 27.9.) You can select the start function level, the module prefix, the language options, the merge granularity, and whether to generate modules or menus.

> **NOTE**
>
> You can enter any language options you want for the module options; however, the module generator only generates Oracle Forms, Oracle Reports, and PL/SQL. Any other languages you specify are for documentation purposes only.

Merge granularity refers to the level of information coming from the functions. The transfer can be at the attribute level or only the entity level.

Once you click the Generate button, the system generates the modules from the candidate functions. You are prompted when the generation is complete. Next, you can click the Show Results button to see a Notepad file showing what functions were generated into modules.

FIGURE 27.9.

The Application Design Wizard.

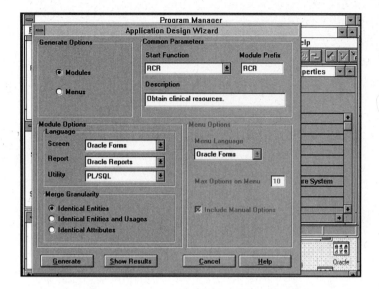

The module names take on the following format: the prefix (if any was given) 0010 (incrementing by tens from the initial elementary function through the last function). You can edit the name in RON.

> **TIP**
>
> To generate module names in system blocks, choose the parent at the top of each system (payroll, accounting, and so on) and give it a unique prefix.

Functions that are elementary generate as screen, report, or manual operation modules (if there is no entity usage). Functions that are not elementary generate as menu modules.

To regenerate a module, you must first delete it.

The Module Structure Diagrammer

You use the Module Structure Diagrammer to set up a hierarchy of modules that are generated into a menu.

Starting Up

Start the Module Structure Diagrammer by clicking its icon and entering your user ID, password, and application. Across the top of the screen, you see a set of icons used for designing a diagram. (See Figure 27.10.)

FIGURE 27.10.

The Module Structure Diagrammer.

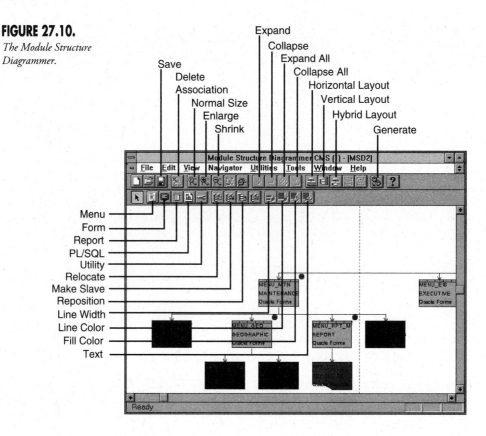

A menu consists of different menu levels and actual screens, reports, procedures, and utilities. You can start your menu at the top level and work down, or you can select groups of modules that belong together and then link them together under menu points.

Summary Information

You can enter any summary information you want to display on the top of the diagram. To edit the summary information, choose File | Summary Information. (See Figure 27.11.)

Adding Items

You can either use existing modules in your diagram or create new modules. If you forget a module or realize when you are creating your Module Structure Diagram that you should include a new module, you can add one. Otherwise, you are better off creating your module in the Module Data Diagrammer. For more information on using the Module Data Diagrammer, see Chapter 28, "Client Application Generation."

FIGURE 27.11.

The Summary screen.

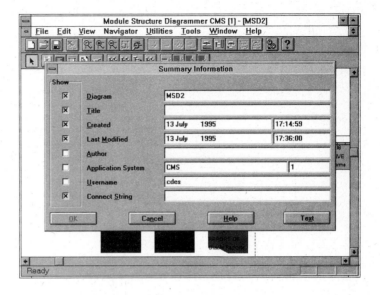

Sometimes, a module is similar to an existing module. Rather than create a new module, you can copy an old one and give the copy a new name. To copy a module, click the Copy Module icon, which is the fifth icon from the right on the bottom bar. Select the module to copy and then drag the cursor to the spot for the copied module. You are prompted to give the name and description information.

To include an existing module on the diagram, choose Edit | Include Network. A list of modules appears. You can pare down the list by selecting a type or by entering a string contained in the module's short name. Once you choose an item, it is added to the diagram.

TIP

To select multiple modules from the include list, hold down the Ctrl key and click the modules you require or select a block of modules while holding down the Shift key. If you choose a large number, your diagram could become too difficult to follow for the initial editing, so keep this in mind when making your selection.

You can also add a new module to the diagram. Decide what kind of item you want to put on the diagram and select its icon: Menu, Form, Report, PL/SQL, or Utility. (Refer to Figure 27.10.) Once you place the cursor on the diagram, you are prompted for a short name, a description, the module type, and the language the module will be generated in.

Editing a Module

If you want to edit information about any of the modules, double-click the module on the diagram. You then have a set of tabs for defining module information. The first tab, Module, defines general module information. (See Figure 27.12.)

FIGURE 27.12.

The Module tab.

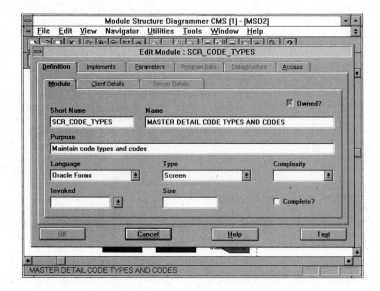

The Implements tab refers to what functions or business units are implemented by the module. If the module is new or the module implements additional functions, you can add these functions here.

The Parameters tab lists the parameters needed to run this module, their data types, and whether the parameters are input, output, or both.

The Access tab lists the users or groups that can access the menu. Groups are set up in business units to determine what roles can run certain functions. When the functions create modules, these groups get passed along to the modules. You can change or add these groups here.

For Client Tools Only

Certain tabs are only available to client modules—or screens, reports, and menus. (See Figure 27.13.) The Client Details tab contains information specific to generating a client tool.

For Server Tools Only

If you are generating a utility or PL/SQL, you have a Server Details tab. (See Figure 27.14.) The server details list items specific for generating a function or procedure—type, name, database, return type, and so on.

> **TIP**
>
> When you're making a module the last module, there is no room on the menu for it at the end. Instead, make it the second-to-last module; then, move the last module in front of it.

Moving a Module

Sometimes, it makes sense to move a module from one area of the diagram to another. To reparent a module, click the Relocate icon. (Refer to Figure 27.10.) Select the module you want to move. Drag the cursor to the new parent and release the button or drag it to empty space to make it an orphan.

Delete a Module and its Slave Modules

If you delete a parent module from the diagram, the slave modules hook up to the parent above their original parent. To delete the entire chain, use the Delete Association icon. (Refer to Figure 27.10.) Click the icon and select the parent module you want to delete. The module and all its slave modules are deleted.

Consolidating

You can make changes to a module's definition or its point in the structure in either the Module Structure Diagrammer or RON. The changes are not reflected on other diagrams that use the same modules. You might have a reason to keep the changes off—for example, to reflect an earlier point in time or the business opinions of another department. It is possible to take into account the changes from other users and consolidate them into the current diagram. To do so, choose Edit | Consolidate. At this point, you can choose whether to consolidate a specific module or the entire diagram.

> **NOTE**
>
> If you do not consolidate an element that has changed, you cannot edit it.

Making Diagrams Easier to Follow

When you work with large diagrams, it might get difficult to keep track of where you are on the diagram. The diagram can take up many pages when printing. There are simple ways to deal with these irritations.

Decompose and Recompose

As you add slaves to parent modules, they make the diagram larger and larger. Sometimes, you want to look at the diagram at a higher level and ignore the lower level. If a parent has a minus sign to the right of it, you can recompose it. If a parent has a plus sign to the right of it, you can decompose it in order to see more modules. To decompose an item, click the Collapse icon. (Refer to Figure 27.10.) To decompose an item to its lowest level, click the Collapse All icon. To recompose a decomposed item, click the Expand icon. To recompose an item and all the items below it, click the Expand All icon.

Changing Diagram Layout

There are three types of diagram layout. (See Figures 27.15, 27.16, and 27.17.)

- Vertical—all modules display vertically on the diagram.
- Horizontal—all modules display horizontally, with each level displaying vertically.
- Hybrid—a combination of vertical and horizontal that seems the most appealing based on the structure.

FIGURE 27.15.

A vertical layout for a module structure.

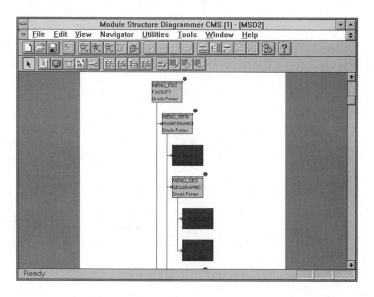

To choose a specific layout type, select the icon: Horizontal, Vertical, or Hybrid. (Refer to Figure 27.10.)

You can also choose a structure for an area of the diagram from a parent down. Select the parent of the area you want to restructure. Then, select the Horizontal icon or the Vertical icon.

FIGURE 27.16.

A horizontal layout for a module structure.

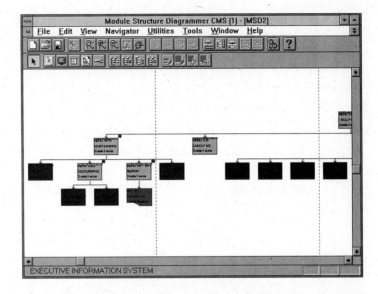

FIGURE 27.17.

A hybrid layout for a module structure.

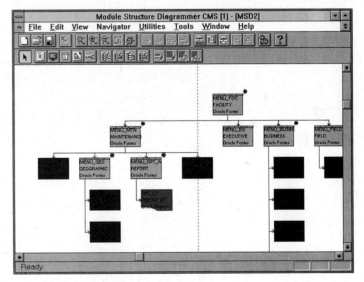

Using Colors, Fonts, and Line Width

You can change the colors of module, the fonts of words, and the line width of module outlines and breakdown lines. By changing these items, you make the diagram more readable and add intelligence. For example, you can fill in all screen modules with blue.

> **NOTE**
>
> The colors on the diagram only show up if you have a color printer; however, if you use a black and white printer, colors show up grayed, and you can use the various shades for differentiation.

You can change all of the diagram or just a specific module or connection line combination. To change the entire diagram, choose Edit | Select All. To select one or more modules or connection lines, select one and hold down the Ctrl key while you select all the items.

To change the line width, select the Line Width icon. (Refer to Figure 27.10.) Choose a line width from the items listed. To change the line color, choose the Line Color icon. Choose a line color from the colors listed. To change the fill color of modules, choose the Fill Color icon. Choose a color from the items listed. To change the font of any selected text, choose the Text icon. You can change the font, the font style, and the text size.

You can change the preferences of your diagram so that screens are always one color and menus always another color and so on. To make these global changes, select Edit | Preferences. (See Figure 27.18.)

FIGURE 27.18.

The Diagram Preferences screen.

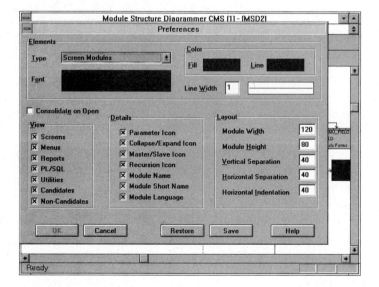

Working with Large Diagrams

When you work with large diagrams, it can be difficult to keep track of where you are on the diagram. The diagram can take up many pages when printing. There are simple ways to deal with these irritations.

Using Minimize Number of Pages

When you fill a diagram with many modules, it often becomes very large, sprawling horizontally or vertically. As a result, many blank pages might fill the borders of the diagram. You can reposition the diagram to use the least number of pages by clicking the Minimize Number of Pages icon. Clicking this icon repositions the entire diagram so that it uses the least number of pages.

Zooming In and Out

You can zoom in and out of your diagram to get a better idea of how an area of the diagram looks or how the entire diagram looks. The magnifying glass icons enable you to perform this function. Use the Normal Size icon to return to normal size (refer to Figure 27.10). Use the Enlarge icon to enlarge. Use the Shrink icon to shrink.

Ready to Generate

Once you are satisfied with your diagram, you are ready to generate. Click the Generate icon. (Refer to Figure 27.10.) You see the generate screen. For more information on using the generator, see Chapter 28, "Client Application Generation."

> **NOTE**
>
> If your diagram starts at a menu level, the generator generates a menu. You need to link this menu to an Oracle form in order to use the menu.

The Preference Navigator

You use the Preference Navigator to set up the standards for generating screens and reports for an application. You can start it from its own icon or from the Repository Object Navigator or the Module Data Diagrammer via the Tools | Preference Navigator option. Initially, you start from RON or the icon itself to set up the global preferences for the entire application. When you are generating the modules, it is good to start from the Module Data Diagrammer so that you can set specific preferences for a specific module as you generate. That way, you can perform what-if scenarios with the preferences and see the results as you generate.

Starting Up

After you decide where to start the Preference Navigator, start it up. If you are starting from the icon, you need to enter your user ID, password, and application. If you are starting from another tool, the tool passes this information. The first thing you must do is enter whether you are setting preferences for Oracle Forms, Oracle Reports, or Visual Basic.

> **NOTE**
>
> You can set preferences for Visual Basic, but you cannot generate in Visual Basic at this time.

The screen pops up a list of decomposable items. (See Figure 27.19.)

- Application Preference
- Domain
- Table
- Module

FIGURE 27.19.

The Preference Navigator.

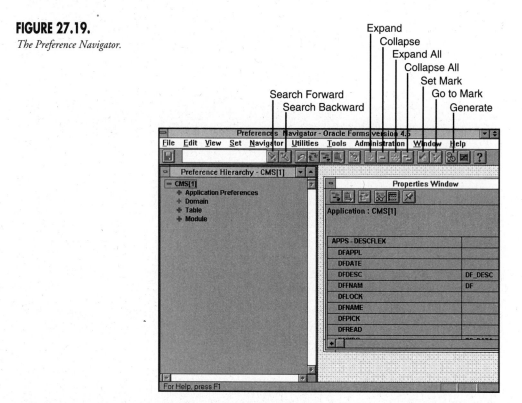

You know these items are decomposable because they each have a plus sign to the left of its name. You can set preferences at any one of these levels.

Application Level

Preferences at the application level include things such as commenting, coding style, layout, and so on. For a screen, layout includes things such as buttons, canvases, or check boxes. For a report, layout includes things such as frame style, box style, or field format. Many of the preferences for both screens and reports are the same. If you click the plus sign to the left of Application Preferences, it decomposes again.

Once you pick a preference summary level such as button layout, it decomposes again into the specific preferences. These preferences have minus signs to the left of them because they are at the lowest composition level.

When you select a preference from the list, the meaning of the preference appears on the bottom of the screen. For example, BUTMAX is the maximum number of buttons within a radio group. The properties window displays the current value for the preference. You can change it to whatever you choose.

By setting the preferences at the application level, all your reports can have the same look and feel throughout the entire application.

Working Below the Application Level

You can also set preferences at levels below the application level for any domain, table, or module. For example, assume you set the BUTMAX preference at the application level to 6, but you want it to be 3 on a specific screen. Select that module from the module list, go to the button layout preferences, and change the BUTMAX preference to 3. When that module generates, the maximum number of buttons within a radio group will be 3. If you later decide to switch the preference back to the application level, just click the Remove Properties icon, the fifth from the left on the icon bar.

Saving Your Preferences

When you are satisfied that you set your preferences to a point where you want to generate, click the Save icon, the first icon from the left.

> **NOTE**
>
> It is important to save often. The Oracle client/server tools use a large amount of memory and can sometimes cause a general protection fault on the PC. Saving often decreases the risk of losing any unsaved work.

Generating the Calling Module

If you accessed the Preference Navigator from the Module Data Diagrammer, you can generate the module by clicking the Generate icon, (refer to Figure 27.19). To learn more about generating a module, see Chapter 28, "Client Application Generation."

Moving Through the Preferences Easily

With so many preferences under so many decomposable items, it can be difficult to sift through all the preferences. There are some methods that make using Preference Navigator less difficult.

Decomposing and Recomposing

To decompose a decomposable item, click the Collapse icon (refer to Figure 27.19). To decompose an item to its lowest level, click the Collapse All icon. To recompose a decomposed item, click the Expand icon. To recompose an item and all the items below it, click the Expand All icon.

Marking a Preference

Suppose you are looking at a preference in application preferences. Then, you jump to a preference in table preferences, and you want to go back to the preference in application preferences. You either have to do a lot of scrolling back and forth on your screen, or you have to do a lot of decomposing and recomposing. To go back to a certain point fairly quickly, you can set a mark on it. To set a mark, click the Set Mark icon (refer to Figure 27.19). When you are ready to go back to that point, click the Go To Mark icon. You can mark only one item at a time.

Searching for Preferences

If you know the name of your preference or block of preferences, but you are not sure where they are on the preference hierarchy, you can find the preference or preference block with a search. Fill in the blank box to the right of the first icon on the icon bar. Then, click the Search Forward icon to look down the hierarchy for the search item, or click the Search Backward icon to look up the hierarchy for the search item. (Refer to Figure 27.19.)

Summary

Once you have completed the analysis of your application, you are ready to move on to design work. You use the Database Design Wizard initially to set up default tables from the entities created during analysis. Next, you use the Data Diagrammer for fine-tuning the table definitions created and adding new table definitions where necessary. You use the Applications Design Wizard to set up default modules from the function definitions created during analysis. You use the Module Structure Diagrammer to link the module definitions together into a proper hierarchy for an application menu. Finally, you use the Preferences Navigator to set up the preferences so that you can move on to application generation.

Client Application Generation

28

by Rachel Becker

IN THIS CHAPTER

Client application generation is the creation of screens and reports. You perform client application generation during the design and build phases of the life cycle of an Oracle project. In this chapter, you will learn the Module Data Diagrammer tool, which is used to generate both screens and reports. On the top of the screen are a pull-down menu and a toolbar of icons. All of the functions that these icons perform can also be found on the menu bar under Edit, View, Utilities, and Tools. Whether you want to use the icons or the menu is just a matter of usage style. For the most part, the descriptions in this chapter use the icons rather than the menu bar.

Start the Module Data Diagrammer by clicking its icon and entering your user ID, password, and CASE application. Across the top of the screen, you will see a set of icons used to design a diagram. (See Figure 28.1.)

FIGURE 28.1.

The Module Data Diagrammer.

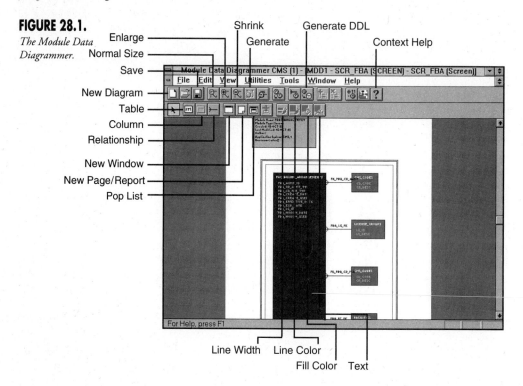

Initially, you can create a new diagram by either choosing New from the File menu or pressing the New Diagram icon. (Refer to Figure 28.1.) When you choose this icon, or any icon from the Designer/2000 toolset, help is always available. You can see the help message appear in a balloon to the right of the icon when you move your cursor to an icon without pressing the mouse button. You can also get help by pressing the Context Help icon and then selecting anything on your screen (either an icon or an element). Finally, you can search for help on any topic from the Help menu pick.

Generating Screens and Reports

You can use the Module Data Diagrammer to generate screens and reports from Designer/2000. The module basis can come from a number of sources:

- A function that generated a module when you used the Module Design Wizard
- A module that is created in the Repository Object Navigator (RON)
- A module that is created in the Module Data Diagrammer

Creating a Module Data Diagram

To create a module data diagram you need to take certain steps. You must create or select the module, add or modify the summary information, select the data usages, and generate the screen or report.

Selecting the Module

To select a module, select the Create Module icon. At this point, a list of module names appears. Select Report if you are creating a report or Screen if you are creating a screen and then select the module name from the list. If you are creating the module for the first time, click the Create Module button. Now fill in the module short name, description, language, and module type.

> **NOTE**
>
> Designer/2000 generates only the new reporting tool ORACLE Reports and not SQL*Reportwriter. You can choose SQL*Reportwriter if you are in fact writing your reports with this tool, but they will not be generated from Designer/2000.
>
> Designer/2000 generates only the new screen painting tool ORACLE Forms and not SQL*Forms. You can choose SQL*Forms if you are in fact writing your reports with this tool, but they will not be generated from Designer/2000.

Summary Information

Initially, when you start your diagram you might want to fill in the summary information so that you can easily identify the diagram when it is printed. Under the File menu is a pick called Summary Information. (See Figure 28.2.) A window will pop up showing you all the choices you have for information to be included on your chart.

Select any information you want to display on the diagram. If you want your name or a diagram title, you need to fill in these items.

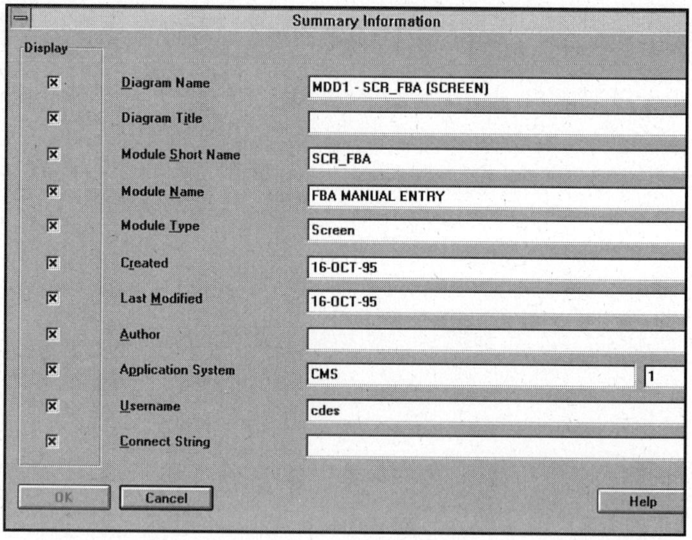

FIGURE 28.2.

The module data diagram summary information.

Table Usages

If you selected an already existing module that contains table usages, they will appear in a data diagrammer format. Parent/child relationships will display with the parent table on the top and the child on the bottom. Lookup relationships will display with the lookup to the right of the base table.

If you are creating a new module or need to add new table usages to your module you need to select the Table icon. (Refer to Figure 28.1.) Click the icon and select a table from the list of values.

> **TIP**
>
> If you want to include more than one table without having to select the button each time, hold down the Shift key when you select the table button. When you are ready to move on to another activity, press another button on the icon bar.

After you have added a table to the diagram you can edit its usage.

Editing Table Usage for a Screen

To edit table usage for a screen, double-click the item, and you can edit Table Details, Table Layout, and Table Text.

Under the Table Details tab (see Figure 28.3), you can edit the allowable actions that are on-screen: insert, update, delete, query. These usages are the default for the entire table. Next, you can change the alias, block title, and comment. These will default from what was entered in the table definition.

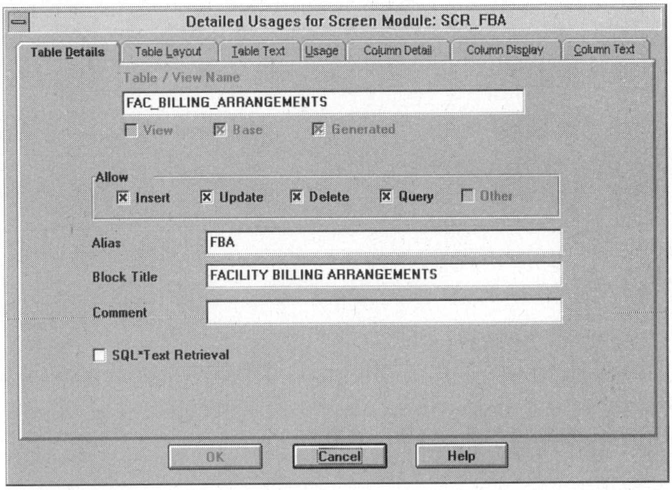

FIGURE 28.3.

The Table Details tab for a screen.

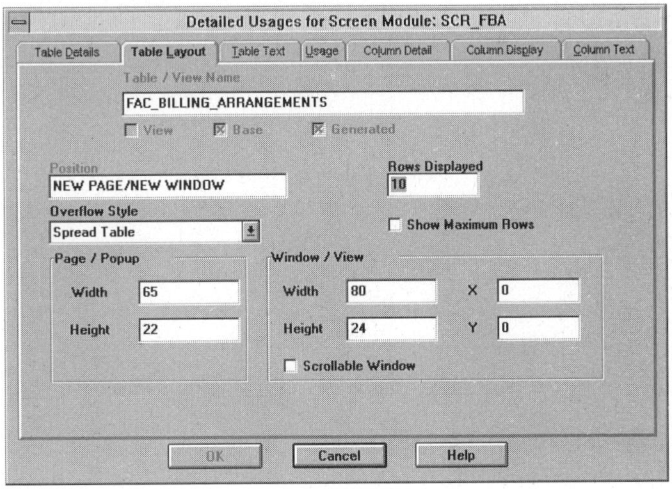

FIGURE 28.4.

The Table Layout tab for a screen.

In the Table Layout tab (see Figure 28.4), you can select the number of rows to be displayed, the overflow style (whether the window should scroll, if only the field will scroll, or if the field will truncate), and the measurements of the canvas and window.

In the Table Text tab (see Figure 28.5), you can type in any WHERE clause, any notes, and any help text that you want for online help on the screen you are designing. The WHERE clause can trim down the selection from the table based on some rule defined for the module being generated.

FIGURE 28.5.

*The Table Text tab
for a screen.*

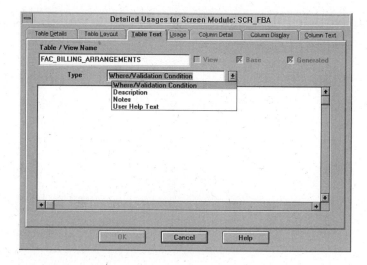

Editing Table Usage for a Report

To edit table usage for a report, double-click the item. Under the Table Details tab (see Figure 28.6), you can edit the title and alias to be displayed, add comments, and choose the layout style. You can also choose the maximum number of records that can appear on a page.

FIGURE 28.6.

*The Table Details tab
for a report.*

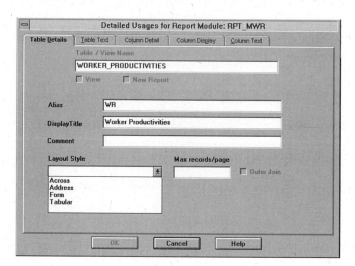

Under the Table Text tab (see Figure 28.7), you can put in any additional notes and any WHERE clause. The WHERE clause can trim down the selection from the table based on some rule for the module being generated.

FIGURE 28.7.

The Table Text tab for a report.

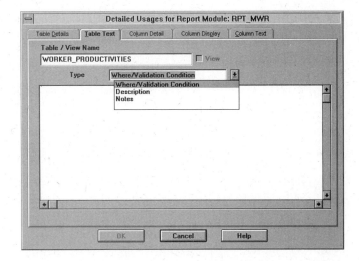

Wait to edit table usage until after you have added column usage. That way you only have to go into the edit screen once.

Relationships Between Tables

After you have added more than one table to a diagram you will want to display the relationships between the tables. Usually, when you add the second table in a relationship, the diagrammer will automatically add the relationship. Sometimes it does not. To add the relationship, select the Relationship icon. (Refer to Figure 28.1.) Next, select one of the tables in the relationship, and then the other table in the relationship. The diagrammer will automatically place the relationship on the diagram.

Sometimes the diagrammer will not accept the relationship as valid, even though the foreign key does exist in the table definition. The best way to handle this problem is to use Tools | Data Diagrammer off the menu bar. From the Data Diagrammer, find the table with which you are working and look at the foreign keys. Look up the foreign key you are trying to link to make sure it is valid. Now exit the diagrammer. Try to create the relationship again. If it still does not work, delete the lookup table from the diagram and try to add it again. If you cannot get the relationship to display, call Oracle Support.

Column Usages

If you select an already existing module that contains column usages, they will appear in a data diagrammer format. If you are creating a new module or need to add new column usages to your module, you need to select the table to which you are adding column usages. Then select the Column icon. (Refer to Figure 28.1.) Click the icon and select a column from the list of values.

> **TIP**
>
> If you want to include more than one column without having to select the button each time, hold down the Ctrl key when you select the column button. If you want to select a set of columns, use the Shift key. If you want to select all the columns press the Select All button.
>
> On a table with many columns where you want to keep most, but not all of the columns, it is easier to press the Select All button, and then deselect the columns you do not want by pressing the Ctrl key at the same time you select the unwanted column.

The columns will appear on your screen or report in the order they display on the table box. To change the order of columns, simply select the one to be moved and drag it up or down to the position in which you want it to be.

After you have added the column usages you can edit them. Double-click the table or any of the columns listed. Double-clicking the table will bring up the edit window at the Table Details tab. Double-clicking the column will bring up the edit window at the Column Details tab, displaying the selected column.

Editing Columns on a Screen

Different tabs are available for modifying the look and feel of columns on a screen on the Detail Usages For A Screen dialog box: Usage, Column Details, Column Display, and Column Text.

Editing Usages

The Usages tab enables you to view and modify the usage of a column while you look at the usages of all the columns on the screen. (See Figure 28.8.)

FIGURE 28.8.

The column Usage tab for a screen.

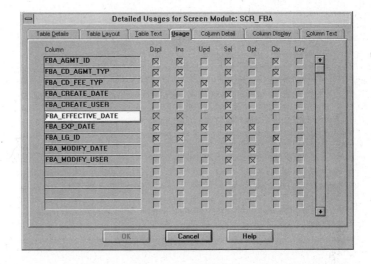

NOTE

If you enter a usage that is not available for the table usage, the form will ignore the column usage. For example, if the employee table does not allow insert in your module, any insert usage on a column will be ignored when you run the Oracle Form that the module generator creates.

Editing Column Detail

The Column Detail tab enables you to edit usage, sort order, summary information, and hints. (See Figure 28.9.)

FIGURE 28.9.

The Column Detail tab for a screen.

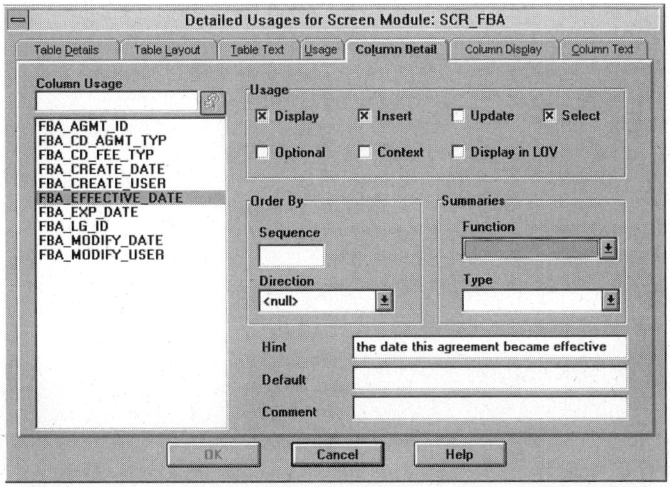

The Usage area is the same as the Usage tab; however, you can see only one column of the screen at a time.

Order By refers to how the information is ordered in the selection from the database. For example, if you place a 1 in this box for the ID column, the data will order by the ID column. In the lower drop-down list you can select in which direction the information is ordered—either ascending or descending.

In the Summaries box you list what type of summary calculation you want on a column. The Function box is a pop-up list of function types—sum or count. Type is a pop-up list of where you would want the break to be—the group. Source is a pop-up list of the columns available on the table; choose the one to be summarized.

> **NOTE**
>
> To select both the detail and summary of a column, select the column twice. In the second selection, fill in the summary information. Do the same thing to create a calculated field.

The hint area is where you enter the hint for the user. When the screen is generated, this hint appears when the user enters the field on the screen. You can also enter a default value for the column at this point.

Editing the Column Display

The Column Display tab describes how columns will be displayed on the screen. (See Figure 28.10.)

FIGURE 28.10.

The Column Display tab for a screen.

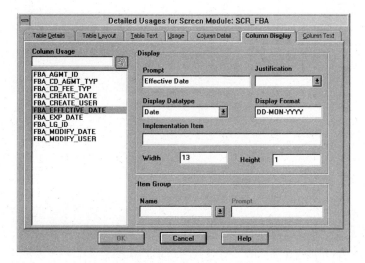

The display box contains the prompt that will appear on the screen. You can set the justification of the column—right, left, and so on—from the Justification pop-up list. You select the data type of the column—character, numeric, and so on—from the Display Datatype pop-up list. In the Display Format box you can enter a format mask. You enter the implementation item—whether the item is OLE or VBX—in the Implementation Item box. The width and height requirements can be entered for the column.

TIP

If you make the width of the column the same as the width of the field, the generated box for the field will not be wide enough to fit a value that is as wide as the maximum width. Add an additional two characters to the width of a field; it will not scroll off the screen.

CAUTION

If you enter three or four column heights, the screen will not generate. It will look as if it continues to process, but the screen will never return from generation.

The Item Group box in the Column Display tab contains the name of the item group. If you want to display blocks of columns together, enter a name in the Item Group box. Then enter the prompt for the item group. The next time you want to add a column to this group, select the name from the Item Group pop-up list.

Editing Column Text

The Column Text tab (see Figure 28.11) contains any notes you might want to have on the column, any derivation expressions or formulas for extracting the columns, any PL/SQL needed to derive the column, any user text you might want to supply online, and any conditions for highlighting (a negative number, a yes answer to a question, any date beyond 90 days from the current date, and so on).

Editing Columns on a Report

Different tabs are available for modifying the look and feel of columns on a report on the Detail Usages For A Screen dialog box: Column Details, Column Display, and Column Text.

Editing Column Details

The Column Detail tab enables you to edit order by, argument, and summary information. (See Figure 28.12.)

FIGURE 28.11.

The Column Text tab for a screen.

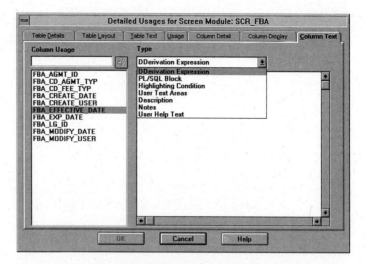

FIGURE 28.12.

The Column Detail tab for a report.

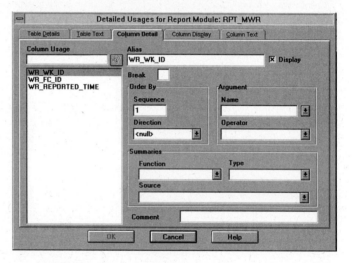

Alias refers to a nickname you want to give the column. This action is useful if it is a user-defined, summary, or duplicate selection. If you do not define an alias, the report generator might bomb out because it is trying to create a SQL query with two references to a table with the same name. Click the Display box if the column contents will be displayed on the report.

Order By refers to how the information is ordered in the selection from the database. For example if you place a 1 in this box, the data will order by this column first. In the lower drop-down list you can select the direction for the sort order: ascending or descending.

Argument refers to any paring down you might want to do in the selection of the column. The Operator drop-down list is a list of argument types: =, >, like, and so on. You enter the comparison value in the Name box.

In the Summaries box, you would list the type of summary calculation you want on a column. The Function box is a drop-down list of function types, such as sum, standard deviation, and so on. Type is a pop-up list of where you would want the break to be, such as in the item, the page, or the report. Source is a pop-up list of the columns available on the table; choose the one to be summarized.

> **NOTE**
>
> To select both the detail and summary of a column, select Column Usage twice. The second time you select it, fill in the summary information. Repeat this step to create a calculated field.

Editing the Column Display for a Report

If you select the Column Display tab (see Figure 28.13), you can edit the display and grouping characteristics. These will default from whatever was entered in the attribute definition and generated as a column, or whatever was added or edited in the column definition.

FIGURE 28.13.

The Column Display tab for a report.

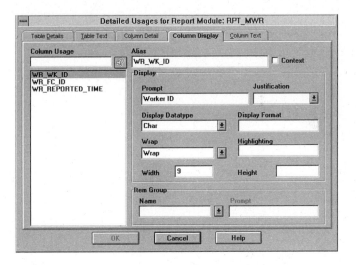

The Display box contains the prompt that will appear on the header of each breakpoint. In the Justification drop-down list, set the justification of the column—right, left, and so on. Select the data type of the columns—character, numeric, and so on—from the Display Datatype drop-down list. Select whether the column should be cut off or wrap on a page by selecting the option from the Wrap drop-down list. Finally, in the Width and Height boxes, select the width and height requirements for the column.

> **CAUTION**
>
> If you enter too many varying column heights, the report will not generate. It will look as if it continues to process, but the tool will never return from generation.

The Item Group box contains the name of the item group. If you want to display blocks of columns together, enter a name in the Item Group box. Then, enter the prompt for the item group. The next time you want to add a column to this group, select the name from the Item Group Name drop-down list.

Editing Column Text

The Column Text tab (see Figure 28.14) contains any notes you might want to include on the column, any derivation expressions or formulas for extracting the columns, and any conditions for highlighting (a negative number, a yes answer to a question, any date beyond 90 days from the current date, and so on).

FIGURE 28.14.

The Column Text tab for a report.

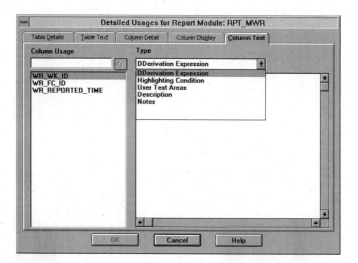

Saving Your Diagram

When you are ready to save the diagram select File | Save from the menu bar. You can also save your work by pressing the Save icon. (Refer to Figure 28.1.) At this point you can name your diagram.

> **NOTE**
>
> It is important to save often. The Oracle Client/Server tools use a large amount of memory and can sometimes cause a general protection fault on the PC. Saving often decreases the risk of losing any unsaved work.

Placing Screen Items on Different Windows or Canvases

Sometimes you will want some of your data to display on a different window or canvas than other data. For example, you might have an employee's personal information on one window and his or her address on the next window. To move an item to a different window, select the New Window icon. (Refer to Figure 28.1.) Place the cursor on the diagram and a new window will appear. You can add tables to this window or move existing tables from one window to another.

You might also want to place a table, such as a lookup table, on a pop-up list. To add a pop-up list, select the Pop List icon. (Refer to Figure 28.1.) Drag the cursor around the base table and the lookup that will be the pop-up.

Placing Report Items on Different Pages

Sometimes you will want some of your data to print on a different page than other data. For example, you might want to print summary information first, and then detail information. To move an item to a different page, select the New Page/Report icon. (Refer to Figure 28.1.) Place the cursor on the diagram and a new page will appear. You can add tables to this page or move existing tables from one page to another.

Consolidating

You can make changes to a table or its relationships in either the Data Diagrammer or RON. The changes will not be reflected on any module data diagrams that use the same tables. There might be a reason for the user to keep the changes off—to reflect an earlier point in time or reflect the business opinions of another department. However, it is possible to take into account the changes from other users and consolidate them into the current diagram. To do so, you must choose Edit | Consolidate from the menu bar. At this point, you can choose whether to consolidate a specific entity, relationship, or the entire diagram.

If new tables were added to a module definition in RON they will not be on the diagram. To add these tables or relationships to the diagram, select Edit | Include New. Any new tables or relationships will be added to the diagram.

NOTE

If you do not consolidate an element that has changed, you cannot edit the module.

Making a Diagram Easier to Follow

There are several ways in which you can make the diagram easier for the customer to follow, as explained in the following sections.

Using Colors, Fonts, and Line Width

You can change the colors of tables and relationships, the fonts of words, and the line width of table outlines and relationships. By changing these items you can make the diagram more readable and more intelligent. For example, you can fill in with blue all lookup tables. The diagrammer has default colors set up for the base table, lookup table, page, and so on. You change the defaults under Edit | Preferences off the menu bar.

NOTE

The colors on the diagram will show up only if you have a color printer. However, if you are using a black-and-white printer, colors will show up grayed, so you can use one color differentiation.

You can change the entire diagram or just a specific entity, relationship, or combination. To change the entire diagram choose Edit | Select all off the menu bar. To select one or more entities or relationships, select one and hold down the Ctrl key until all the items are selected.

To change the line width, select the Line Width icon. (Refer to Figure 28.1.) Choose a line width from the items listed. To change the line color, choose the Line Color icon. Choose a line color from the colors listed. To change the fill color of entities, choose the Fill Color icon. Choose a color from the items listed. To change the font of any text selected, choose the Text icon. You can change the font, the style of the font, and the size of text.

Working with Large Diagrams

When you work with large diagrams, keeping track of where you are on the diagram can become difficult, and the diagram can take up many pages when it prints. There are simple ways to deal with these irritations.

Using Navigate

To move from table to table on the diagram, use Edit | Navigate on the menu bar and then select a table. The cursor will select the table you request, and the focus of the screen will include the table requested.

Using Minimize Number of Pages

Often, when the diagram is filled with many entities, it becomes very large, sprawling horizontally or vertically. As a result, many blank pages can fill the borders of the diagram. You can reposition the diagram to use the least amount of pages by using the Minimize Number of Pages icon. Pressing this icon will reposition the entire diagram so that the least number of pages are used.

Zooming In and Out

You can zoom in and out of your picture to get a better idea of how an area of the picture looks or how the entire picture looks. The magnifying glass icons enable you to perform this function. Use the Normal Size icon to return to normal size. To enlarge, use the Enlarge icon. To shrink, use the Shrink icon.

Generating

When you are satisfied that your diagram represents what you want your report or screen to do, you can go ahead and generate it. First, make sure you save the diagram. Second, make sure that the tables your module uses are already generated on your database. To generate tables right from the Module Data Diagrammer, press the Generate DDL icon. (Refer to Figure 28.1.) Refer to Chapter 29, "Server Generation," on how to Generate DDL. To generate the module, press the Generate icon. The Generate Form screen will appear. (See Figure 28.15.)

The screen defaults to the current module to be generated, but you can change any of the objects to generate a different module.

Options When Generating the Screen

You can set many options when you generate a screen. The following tabs are available: Form Option, Menu Option, Compile, Run, Template, and Other.

The Form Option tab (see Figure 28.16) enables the user to select where the generated form will be located and how it will be generated.

FIGURE 28.15.

The Generate tab in the Generate Form screen.

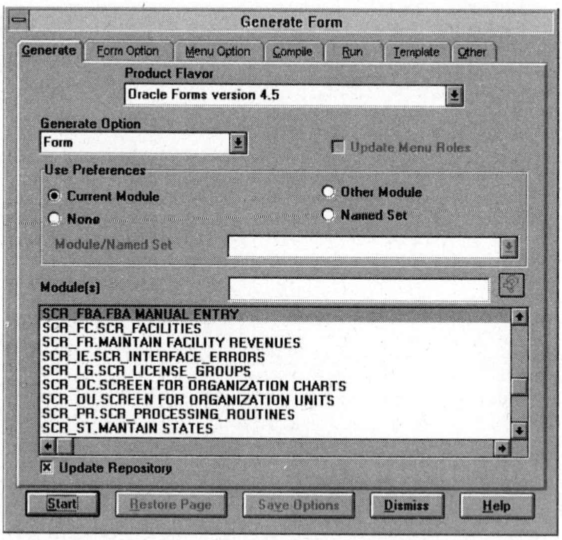

FIGURE 28.16.

The Form Option tab in the Generate Form dialog box.

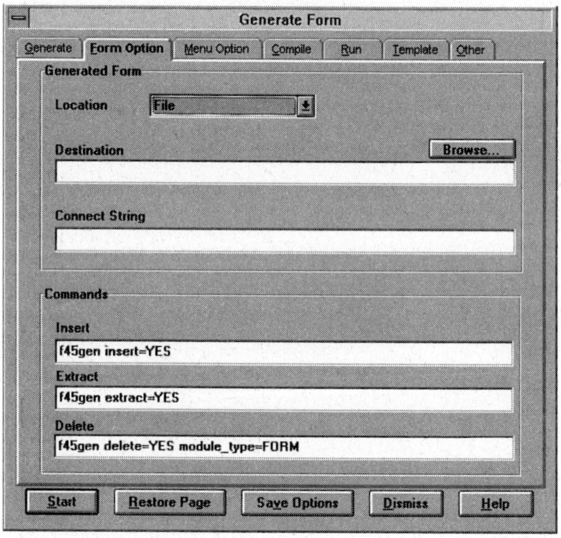

The Menu Option tab looks the same as the Form Option tab. It shows the location of the menu that needs to be generated to attach to the form, if the default menu will not be used.

The Compile tab (see Figure 28.17) lets you specify if and where compiled forms will be generated. You can choose not to generate executable code or to put it in a different place than the compiled code.

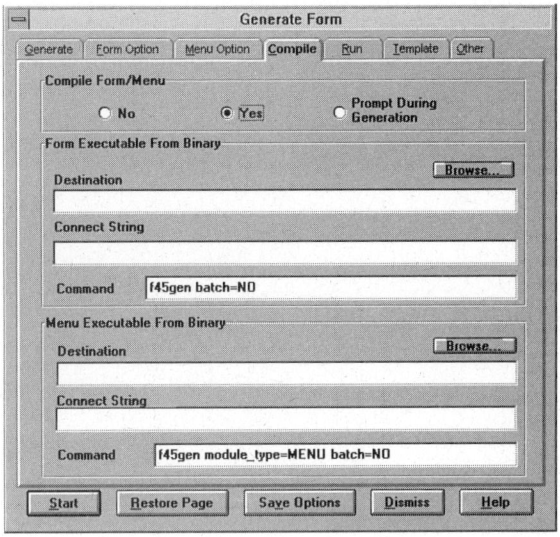

FIGURE 28.17.

The Compile tab in the Generate Form dialog box.

The Run tab (see Figure 28.18) enables you to select whether the form should be run after it is generated and the commands to run the form.

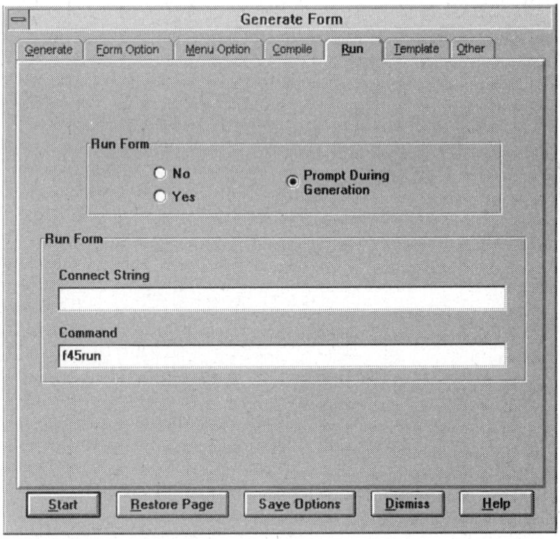

FIGURE 28.18.

The Run tab in the Generate Form dialog box.

The Template tab enables you to enter a template form and a menu template for generating the form. (See Figure 28.19.)

FIGURE 28.19.

The Template tab in the Generate Form dialog box.

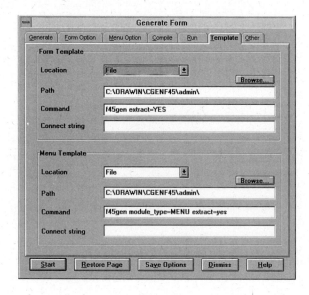

The Other tab enables you to enter any log you want to keep, any library being used, and any default terminal information needed to run the screen. (See Figure 28.20.)

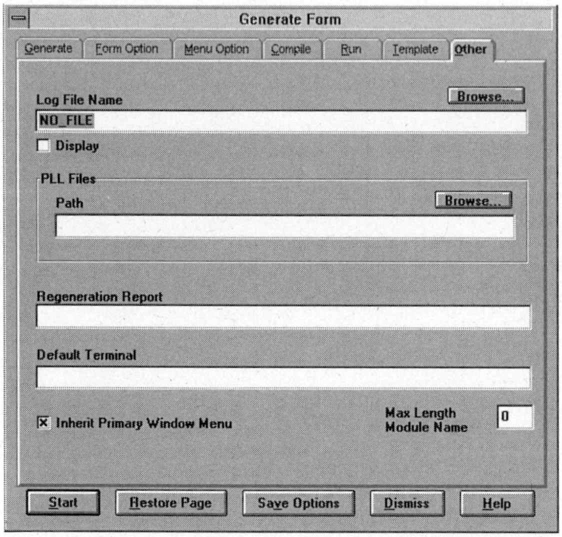

FIGURE 28.20.

The Other tab in the Generate Form dialog box.

Options When Generating the Report

The Report Options tab in the Generate Report dialog box, in which you generate report modules, lists the options you have for generating a report. (See Figure 28.21.)

FIGURE 28.21.

The Report Options tab.

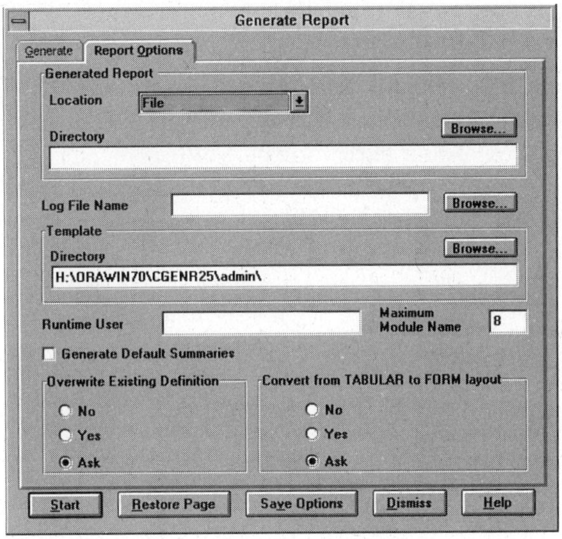

You can change and save any of the options in this tab as the default.

When you are ready to generate the report, press the Start key. As the tool generates, the cursor will turn into turning gears.

> **NOTE**
>
> If you have the minimal amount of memory, the gears will not turn.

If the generator has any question on any data you entered, it will prompt you. For example, if you did not fill in the maximum number of lines on a screen or page, the generator will suggest a default, and you will be given the opportunity to overwrite it.

If anything seems suspicious to the generator, such as a column length that displays longer than the column itself, the generator will list a warning message.

If anything will make generation impossible, the generator will list an error message and the generation will terminate. One example might be if a table that is used in your module definition does not exist.

If you want to stop generating at any time, just press the Stop button.

When the generation is complete, the application will run or prompt you, depending on which run option you chose.

Summary

Application generation is the generation of screens and reports using the Module Data Diagrammer and Module Generator. Using the Module Data Diagrammer, you can set up the look and feel of your screen or report. When you are satisfied with your module definition, you can go ahead and generate your screen or report. Your screen or report will be well documented in the module definition and created to the exact specifications defined in the Module Data Diagrammer.

Server Generation

29

by Chet West

What Is Server Generation?

Server Generation is the second half of application development. The server generator will provide two important elements in an Oracle7 application. First, it provides for the generation of the PL/SQL code for implementation of triggers, procedures, functions, and packages embedded on the server side. Second, it also provides for the generation of the SQL code necessary to create tablespaces, tables, views, snapshots, indexes, roles, and users.

Server Generation consists of three distinct tools that can be used throughout the life-cycle of an application system. These tools include the DDL Generator, the Reconciliation Utilities, and the Reverse Engineering Utilities. The first two are used to create the data definition language (DDL) necessary to create new and update existing database objects that have been added or changed in the repository. The latter will become vital in ensuring that the repository contains references to any server related objects that were not generated from Designer/2000, or that have been changed online from their original repository definition.

Generating DDL

The DDL Generation utility is to be used when system design has been completed, or when new objects have been added to the application system. The generator is intended for Oracle7 DDL generation but can also generate some Oracle V6 and ANSI compatible DDL scripts. See the Designer/2000 documentation, on-line help, and release notes for specific generator capabilities and restrictions as these may change with newer versions of the DDL generator. The DDL generation tool can be executed from any of the following Designer/2000 applications:

- Data Diagrammer
- Module Data Diagrammer
- Module Structure Diagrammer
- Module Logic Navigator
- Repository Object Navigator

Pre-Generation Quality Control

It is recommended that a quality check be performed on server objects in the repository prior to generation by running some or all of the quality control reports available for the repository. These reports provide information such as object validity, incomplete definitions, and create status checks. Also, ensure that the database being generated for has a name and version defined in the repository.

> **NOTE**
>
> Any table definition that does not have the Create Flag set will be ignored by the DDL Generator. For PL/SQL modules that are linked together, make sure that the link is appropriate. An INCLUDE link is meaningful, whereas a CALL link is for documentation only.

Generation of DDL Scripts

To generate DDL script files based on repository definitions, select the Utilities | Generate SQL DDL menu option. Figure 29.1 shows the Generate DDL dialog box that will be displayed when started. Notice the three tab selectors used in the dialog box.

FIGURE 29.1.

Generate DDL dialog box.

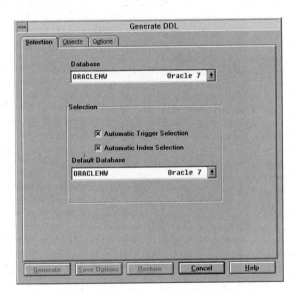

Selection Tab

In the Selection tab, a list box is available to choose the database in which the objects to create will be located. There are also selection option checkboxes to turn on and off automatic trigger and index selection. These are very helpful when generating DDL to ensure that everything defined in the repository is accounted for. Finally, there is a second list box, which a default database can be specified. Any objects selected that have not been associated with a database name will be generated for the default database identified. To save the selection options for future use, select the Save Options button. If option changes are not saved, a prompt will appear prior to exiting the Generate DDL dialog box.

Objects Tab

The Objects tab is where the designer actually picks objects that DDL scripts are to be generated for. Figure 29.2 shows an example of the Objects tab in use.

FIGURE 29.2.

Objects selection tab for DDL generation.

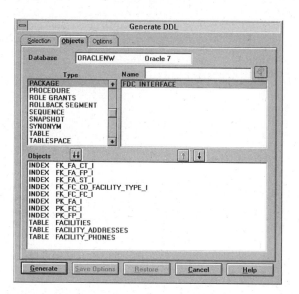

The Objects tab provides a list of object types in the Type list box, found in the upper left of this tab. Selecting an object type will cause the DDL generator to retrieve all defined objects of that type for the database being generated. These objects will then be listed, by name, in the Name list box, which is found in the upper right of this tab. Objects can be moved to the Objects list box, found at the bottom of this tab, by highlighting the object and selecting the down arrow button or all objects listed by selecting the double down-arrow button found in the objects selection tab. An object can also be removed from the Objects list box by highlighting the object and selecting the up-arrow button.

Options Tab

The Options tab provides the user with the capabilities of specifying how objects are to be generated. An example of the Options tab in use can be seen in Figure 29.3.

FIGURE 29.3.

Options selection tab for DDL generation.

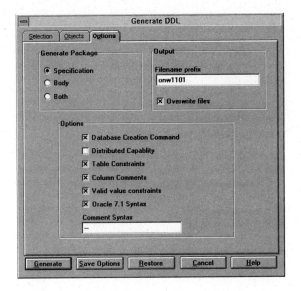

The first option group is a radio selection in which package specifications, bodies, or both can be selected for generation. Some IS departments may wish that package specification and package body DDL scripts be generated into separate files. It also provides for the black box capabilities of packages by allowing for the creation of the package specifications to be done prior to package body completion. This will help decrease the amount of time other developers have to spend waiting for database packages to be created for use in their development efforts.

Generation output options are defined in the second option group. There is a checkbox to turn on and off file overwriting. There is also an edit box where the filename prefix for each of the DDL generation scripts is defined. Each script file has this filename and has different extensions based on the type of object it generates. It is good practice to use a filenaming scheme that will identify the application system and release or generation number so that system creation history can be maintained and configuration management can be better controlled. For example, CS1129 could be used for the November 29th generation of the Customer Service application. See the operating system documentation for restrictions on filenaming conventions.

> **CAUTION**
>
> If the Overwrite files option is checked, any previous DDL scripts with that filename prefix will be lost if that object type is generated! The SQL*Plus driver script is always created and thus overwritten!

The last options group provides for an array of generation options not already defined. If a new system is being created, the database creation command option should be checked. The distributed capability is only generated for systems that have the distributed option loaded. Both table level constraint creation and column level check constraints creation can be turned on or off. The column comments places any comments on a column's repository definition into the database's data dictionary. The Oracle 7.1 syntax option tells the generator to create its DDL scripts in Oracle 7.1 format. Finally, the comment syntax is the syntax used by the generator to comment the DDL script files.

Generation and its Output

Once a database and object(s) have been selected, DDL generation can begin. To start the generation process, simply select the Generate button found at the bottom of the Generate DDL dialog box. Generation time will depend on the number of objects selected and the size of the repository. When generation has completed, a second dialogue box will be displayed showing the files that have been created. At this point, any of the files can be viewed or executed by selecting either the Browse or the Execute buttons. Figure 29.4 shows the results of DDL generation.

FIGURE 29.4.

DDL generation output dialog box.

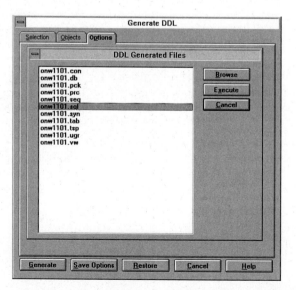

Post Generation Activities

It is best not to run the generated DDL scripts immediately. First, edit the .SQL master execution script and ensure that objects are generated in the correct order. Also, check for validity of the statements generated. Ensure that all objects that were intended to be created have scripts available. Furthermore, there will be a QUIT command at the end of the .SQL script. Removing this command will allow the executor to verify the results of the DDL execution. Table 29.1 shows the object types and their generated output filename extensions.

Table 29.1. DDL Generator output file extensions.

OBJECT	*GENERATOR EXTENSION*
MASTER EXECUTION FILE	.sql
DATABASE	.db
TABLESPACE	.tsp
ROLLBACK SEGMENT	.rgr
CLUSTER	.cls
TABLE	.tab
INDEX	.ind
CONSTRAINTS	.con
VIEW	.vw
SNAPSHOT	.ss
SYNONYM	.syn
SEQUENCE	.seq
TRIGGER	.tgr
PACKAGE	.pck
FUNCTION	.fnc
PROCEDURE	.prc
USER GRANTS	.ugr
ROLE GRANTS	.rgr

Once the generated DDL scripts have been validated, then the scripts should be turned over to the database administrator (DBA.) The DBA can execute them using the master execution file the generator created or by calling them individually from the SQL*Plus command prompt.

Reconcile Utilities

Only in a perfect world will the repository and the database stay the same at all times. Very active databases will be changing all the time, if for no other reason than database tuning. For this, Designer/2000 provides two reconciliation utilities. A cross reference report and an alter database DDL generator. Both reconciliation utilities can be started by selecting the Utilities | Reconcile menu option from any of the following Designer/2000 applications:

- Data Diagrammer
- Module Data Diagrammer
- Module Structure Diagrammer
- Module Logic Navigator
- Repository Object Navigator

Once started, the Reconcile Repository Object Definitions dialog box will be displayed as in Figure 29.5. Notice in the options group, at the bottom of the dialog box, there is a radio button group. Here is where either the cross reference report or the alter database DDL generator are selected.

The database list box will identify the Oracle database that the objects are to be reconciled in. The database must be predefined in the repository. The object owner identifies the user on the physical database that owns the objects being reconciled.

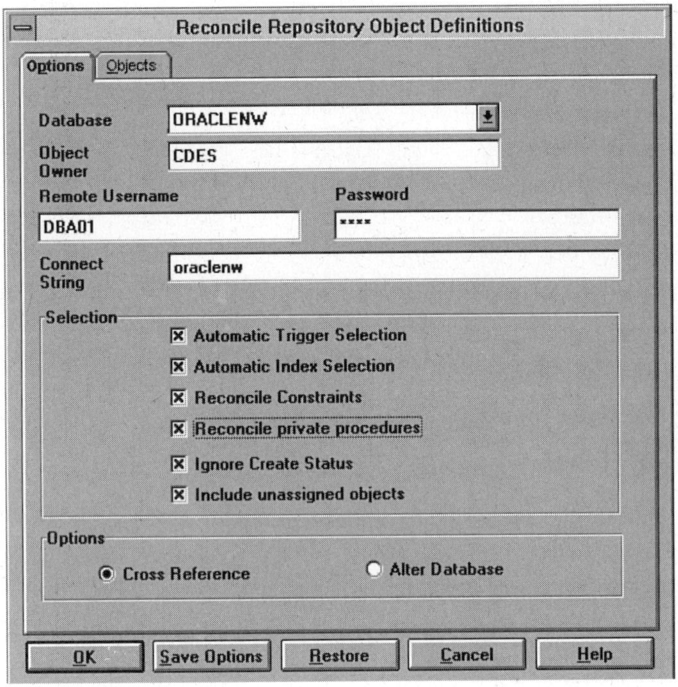

FIGURE 29.5.

Reconcile Repository Object Definitions dialog box.

The remote user, password, and connect string fields are only needed if the objects are located on a remote server. The connect string format will be determined by the SQL*Net version.

The first two selection options determine whether a table's associated trigger and index objects are selected automatically in the object's tab. The Reconcile Constraints option determines whether the declarative table level constraints will be looked at during reconciliation. The Reconcile private procedures option will allow the utility to also reconcile procedures and functions declared as private in a package. The Ignore Create Status is used to turn off checking of the repository create flag on an object. Finally, the Include unassigned objects option will attempt to reconcile repository objects that are not assigned to a database to the database being reconciled against.

CAUTION

If the Ignore Create Status option is not selected and the create status is false on the object, the reconciliation utility will ignore it even if it exists on the database.

Reconciliation Report Output

The reconciliation report is probably the most helpful of the two utilities. It provides a wide variety of information to the user. Since the inconsistencies may exist as problems, either in the repository or the data dictionary, it is best to look at the report and decide which is correct. The report will output to a preview screen. From here it can be printed. The output also is saved in a file called CDRK55.LIS, which will remain for reference if upon exit, the delete output dialog is answered NO.

The report will list some administrative information at the top. These items include the following:

- Server Generator version number
- Application name
- Usernames
- Object types

The body of the report will have four columns of the following titles:

- Database Object Name/Property
- Repository value
- Data Dictionary value
- Error

An example of the possible reported errors identified would be a column in the repository that was defined as NOT NULL, but in the data dictionary is actually NULL. The Error column would identify this error. The report also identifies sizing differences. These will more commonly be different due to database tuning. At the end of each objects listing, there is an error count total for the object.

Reconciliation DDL Output

The reconciliation DDL will be generated to the file CDRK55.SQL. While the DDL will give a starting point for methods in correcting database discrepancies, it is very likely that it will fail upon execution. Some of the reasons for failure are:

- Adding a NOT NULL column
- Modifying a column's data type when data exist in the column
- Modifying sizes below current data sizes

If tables are modified, remember to modify any VIEWS that may be using this table accordingly.

It is more likely that the repository has not been kept up to date and thus, the DDL generated would do more harm than good.

Reverse Engineer Utilities

In many situations, older applications may not have been developed using a CASE product. Server objects and client applications may also be created or modified on the fly by the DBA, or by other developers when quick development is essential to success. Reverse engineering utilities will become an important tool used to create references for legacy systems or keep the current Designer/2000 repository application definitions up to date with changes. There are three utilities available for reverse-engineering DDL objects, FORMS, and REPORTS.

Reverse Engineering DDL Objects

The most common occurrence for DDL or server objects to be changed without repository updates is from database tuning. Another possible cause is the quick fix syndrome that plagues any system without strict management controls. To start the reverse-engineering utility for DDL or server objects, select the Utilities | Reverse Engineer DDL menu option from one of the following Designer/2000 applications:

- Data Diagrammer
- Module Data Diagrammer
- Module Structure Diagrammer
- Module Logic Navigator
- Repository Object Navigator

The Reverse Engineer Database Objects dialog box will be displayed at startup. There are two tab screens for this utility, Options and Objects, as shown in Figure 29.6.

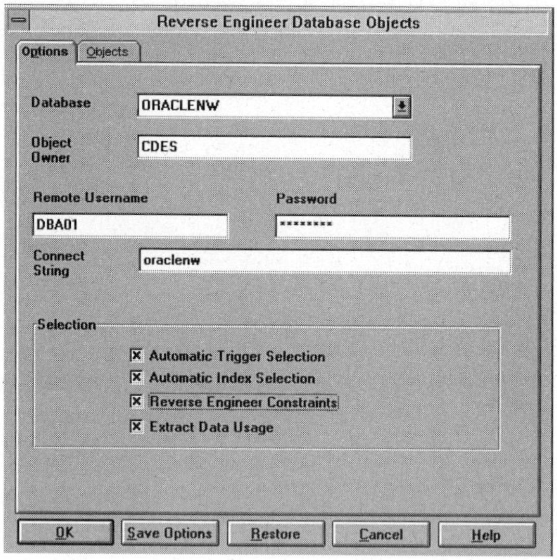

FIGURE 29.6.

Reverse Engineer Database Objects dialog box.

Options Tab

The Options tab first provides a drop-down list of known database names. This will correspond to the database that objects are being reverse engineered from. The object owner identifies the database user that the object belongs, too. This will probably not be the same as the repository owner.

> **NOTE**
>
> Any user can reverse engineer any object on a database if read access has been granted to that user for that object.

The remote username, password, and connect string fields are only needed if the object exists on a remote server. The connect string must be in SQL*Net format. As in the DDL Generator, there are checkboxes to turn on or off automatic trigger and index selection in the Objects tab. There are also checkboxes that will enable reverse engineering of declarative table level constraints and package, procedure, and function data usage. If reverse engineering is being done on objects not defined in the repository, it is best to select all of these options. If the object is already defined in the repository, the object will need to be dropped and then reverse engineered in. The utility will not overwrite existing objects.

Objects Tab

The Objects tab is used in the same manor as the Objects tab found in the DDL Generate. The up and down arrow buttons move selected objects to and from object's list box, and the double down arrow button moves all objects in the name list box to the object's list box.

> **TIP**
>
> You can move all objects of multiple types by holding down the Ctrl key and selecting the types and then selecting the double down arrow button. The objects will not appear in the name list box.

Reverse Engineering Forms

There is also a tool for reverse engineering client side objects. The first of these are forms. To start the forms reverse-engineering utility, select the Utilities | Reverse Engineer Form menu option from one of the following Designer/2000 applications:

- Data Diagrammer
- Module Data Diagrammer
- Module Structure Diagrammer
- Module Logic Navigator
- Repository Object Navigator

When this utility is started, the Reverse Engineer Form dialog box will be displayed as in Figure 29.7.

This utility is more like the Form Generator than the DDL Generator. Under the product-flavor list box, the only of the following type of form that can be reverse engineered is Oracle Forms version 4.5. Since future releases of the Forms Generator utility will be able to generate Visual Basic forms, it is likely that Visual Basic forms will be included in reverse engineering.

The location list box will default to File but can be changed to Database if the form is stored in the database. The destination list box is an editable list. Either a currently defined module can be selected, or a new object name can be typed in.

The Use-Preferences group determines where module preferences are defined. The Other Module item is used when the new module uses the same preferences identified in another module already defined in the repository. The module short name is specified in the list box. If Named Set is used, the specified named set of preferences is used.

The files group at the bottom has a name field and a list box. The Browse button can be selected to navigate directly through the directory structure to the form .fmb file, or the path and filename can be typed in. Upon entering the filename, the file's internal module name will appear in the list box. Multiple form modules can be put into the list box, but only one can be reverse engineered at a time.

FIGURE 29.7.

Reverse Engineer Form dialog box.

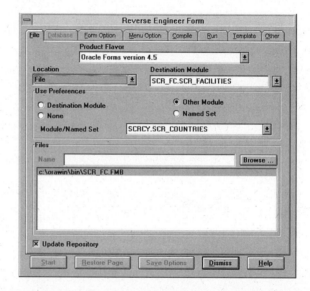

> **NOTE**
>
> The other tab option screens in this dialog box are the same as those used in the form generator and will not be discussed here.

Reverse Engineering Reports

The second of the reverse-engineering utilities for client-side objects is for reports. To start the reports reverse-engineering utility, select the Utilities | Reverse Engineer Report menu option from one of the following Designer/2000 applications:

- Data Diagrammer
- Module Data Diagrammer
- Module Structure Diagrammer
- Module Logic Navigator
- Repository Object Navigator

When this utility is started, the Reverse Engineer Report dialog box will be displayed as in Figure 29.8.

FIGURE 29.8.

Reverse Engineer Report dialog box.

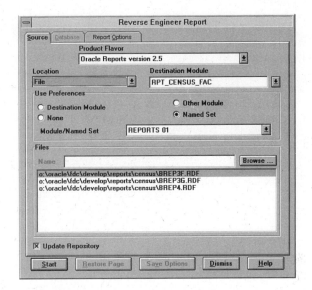

This utility is also like its counterpart, the Report Generator, rather than the DDL Generator. Under the product-flavor list box, one of the following types of reports can be reverse engineered:

- Oracle Reports version 2.5
- SQL*ReportWriter 1.1
- SQL*Plus Reports
- SQL*Reports (RPT)
- Oracle Precompiler (PRO*C)

The location list box will default to File but can be changed to Database if the form is stored in the database. The destination list box is an editable list. Either a currently defined module can be selected, or a new object name can be typed in.

The Use-Preferences group determines where module preferences are defined. The Other Module item is used when the new module is to use the same preferences identified in another module already defined in the repository. The module short name is specified in the list box. If Named Set is used, the specified named set of preferences is used.

The files group at the bottom has a name field and a list box. The Browse button can be selected to navigate directly through the directory structure to the report .rdf file, or the path and filename can be typed in. Upon entering the filename, the file's internal module name will appear in the list box. Multiple report modules can be put into the list box, but only one can be reverse engineered at a time.

> **NOTE**
>
> The other tab option screens in this dialog box are the same as those used in the report generator and will not be discussed here.

Post Reverse Engineering

After completion of the reverse-engineering process, the objects will need to be modified using the Repository Object Navigator. Identification of which entities and functions the tables and modules are fulfilling will link the new physical definitions back to the system model. There will most likely be some incomplete information in complex modules that may need to be updated.

> **TIP**
>
> If a module definition is incomplete or cannot be reverse engineered, ensure that the summary and detail table usages are defined. Then put a note in the module comment section that indicates the module should not be generated from CASE.

Summary

The tools in the Server Generation suite can be divided into two distinct categories. The first category is those that generate output to update the database. This category includes two tools: the Generate DDL utility and the Reconcile-Alter Database utility. Both of these produce DDL scripts that can be run against the database. The second category is those that update the repository tables. This category includes the Reverse Engineer DDL, the Reverse Engineer Forms, and the Reverse Engineer Reports utilities. All of these utilities look at external objects and automatically update the repository. The Reconcile-Cross Reference report utility can be considered to span both categories to a some extent. Its only output is a report, but the information provided on the report can lead to changes being made in either the repository or the database.

With Oracle's commitment to becoming an open systems solution provider, the server generation tools will most likely expand in capabilities in the future. Already, the Client Application generators are venturing into the generation of Visual Basic applications. It could be assumed that a reverse engineering tool will follow to support existing systems. Other possibilities could include capabilities to generate more ANSI-compliant DDL scripts that can be used with products like SQL Server and Sybase.

Using Designer/2000 with Developer/2000

30

by Chet West

Why Use Developer/2000, Too?

After months of analysis, modeling, and design, you finally generate the application system. You create the database and its tables. You generate and compile modules of forms, reports, and PL/SQL code. All that you need to do now is set up the client machines to run the runtime applications and give them access to the newly generated forms and reports. The client is overwhelmed and very impressed by how much you accomplished in such a short time and how close you actually came to what he wanted. Then, the requests come: "I really work better with graphs and charts such as my old spreadsheets; can my Oracle form do this?" Looking through Designer/2000, you see the Server Generation tools, the Form Generator, and the Report Generator, but no Graphics Generator. There is not even a menu, button, or toolbar available on any of the Designer/2000 diagrammers; however, you know you've seen examples of graphs being used in Oracle.

Remember what the Designer/2000 tool is supposed to do for you. As with any CASE tool, you use it to help ensure that you meet business rules and requirements and follow relational database rules. Designer/2000 provides an easy way to study the impacts of system changes and even offers some basic project management, change management, and version control capabilities. The report or form layouts might never come out exactly as intended, though. What Designer/2000 does not provide is a way to perform the debugging, tweaking, and tuning necessary to make an application development effort a complete success.

For this type of module designing and testing, the Developer/2000 tools pick up where Designer/2000 leaves off. With Developer/2000, you can actually create graphics or develop forms and reports to access legacy systems using ODBC drivers or one of Oracle's gateways. Developer/2000's other advantages include the debugging utilities and performance testing. With the new object-oriented capabilities of the tools, you can easily move a PL/SQL function that was running on the client side to the server and back again to see exactly where it runs faster. The speed at which you can create modules using the Developer/2000 tool might be a business saver, too. Any new development in Developer/2000 can be reverse engineered into the Designer/2000 repository definitions without much effort. You can find more information about using the Developer/2000 tools in Part VI, "Developer/2000."

What If I Need to Make Changes to a Module?

When you need to make any change to a form or report that has already been generated, you should use Designer/2000 first. If they are only cosmetic changes, there is no real functionality change. You need to document the changes in the repository so that when you need to make a major functionality change, you can restore the cosmetic changes.

As seen in Figure 30.1, the module properties include several documentation text fields. You can use a module generation history field to log when and why the module was regenerated from the repository. You can track module release notes along with any other documentation.

FIGURE 30.1.

Module property sheet documentation.

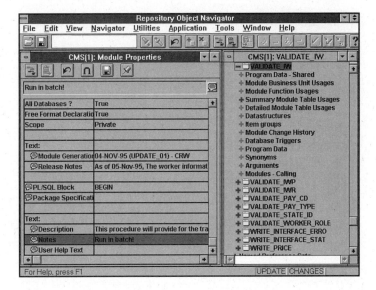

The Designer/2000 tool provides an entire subcategory for tracking module change history. This is useful in tracking dates, directories, and descriptions of the changes that you make to a module, as shown in Figure 30.2. These changes do not necessarily correspond to a module generation—for example, you made a cosmetic change.

FIGURE 30.2.

Module change history.

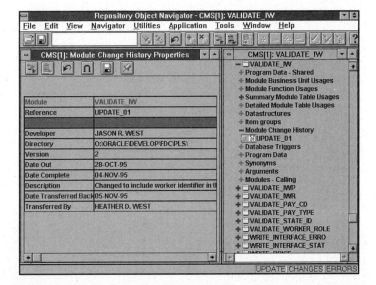

If you need more documentation items than what Designer/2000 provides, remember that you can extend the repository itself using the Repository Administration Tool. This enables you to add module subcategories and individual text fields for existing subcategories.

Creating and Tracking Module Documentation

You can also track detailed user, maintenance, interface, test, or any other documentation that you generate for the modules you create. There is actually an application category called Documents, as shown in Figure 30.3.

FIGURE 30.3.

Repository documentation category.

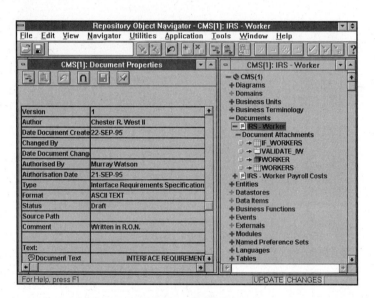

In the Documents category, you can actually store documents or provide path names for the documents' locations. You can also store information about document creation and changes. Best of all, each document has a subcategory called Document Attachments that links the document to any of the following repository categories:

Assumptions	Business Functions
Business Terminology	Business Units
Clusters	Communities
Critical Success Factors	Data Items
Databases	Databases (ANSI)

Databases (Oracle)	Datastores
Diagrams	Documents
Domains	Entities
Events	Externals
Files	Groups
Key Performance Indicators	Languages
Locations	Modules
Named Preference Sets	Nodes
Objectives	Oracle Database Users
Problems	Relations
Rollback Segments	Sequences
Snapshots	Storage Definitions
Tables	Tablespaces
User Defined Sets	Views

Any documentation you do on a system should be tracked in some way. The Designer/2000 tool provides a perfect solution for doing this by providing the beginnings of a simple document tracking system. As mentioned previously, the repository is not limited to what initially comes with the Designer/2000 product. There are always user extensions that you can add to meet your needs.

Summary

You can utilize both the Designer/2000 and Developer/2000 tools throughout the life cycle of an application, but it does require some effort. Although both tools work well together, they are still separate products that work just fine by themselves. All developers and designers should remember the effort it took to create all the definitions and specifications to model and meet the system requirements. You should also put the same effort into the entire maintenance life cycle to ensure that you meet the final goal of the repository. That goal is to provide the information systems staff with a tool to better gauge the impact of future system changes and enhancements—which also provides for an easier way to interface future applications into your existing applications.

PART

Developer/2000

Introduction to Developer/2000

31

by Joe Zafian

IN THIS CHAPTER

Oracle released the first generation of its front-end development tools with version 5.0 of its RDBMS. These products were known as SQL*Forms 2.0 and RPT. Although these tools are primitive by today's standards, they were a great advance for developers of applications to access this powerful database management system. As more features were added to the RDBMS through versions 5.1, 6.0, 7.0, 7.1, and now Oracle 7.2, the front-end tools also evolved into the product that is now called Oracle Developer/2000.

What Is Developer/2000?

Developer/2000 primarily consists of three distinct products: Oracle Forms 4.5, Oracle Reports 2.5, and Oracle Graphics 2.5. These products can all be used individually or as an integrated application development platform. Although each has a separate purpose, there are many similarities that enable you to create consistent and powerful applications.

Oracle Forms 4.5

Oracle Forms 4.5 is a tool that you can use to enter, access, change, or delete data from an Oracle database in a form-based environment. Unlike conventional third-generation programming languages, the developer does not write a program that presents and manipulates the data. Instead, you build an Oracle Forms application by creating on-screen objects that are containers representing the data elements in the database. You then place these objects on the form with a graphical layout editor.

Based on selected activities called events, you can write triggers and program units to define the process to be executed whenever the event occurs. Oracle Forms 4.5 utilizes the concepts of object-oriented programming (OOP) with object inheritance, reusability, and encapsulation, as well as modularity and polymorphism. These features enable the developer to construct high-quality, mission-critical applications in a very short time.

Oracle Reports 2.5

Oracle Reports 2.5 is used primarily to produce reports from data in the Oracle database. You, as the developer, can construct a report in the designer with a structured WYSIWYG ("what you see is what you get") layout editor based on a data model that you create. You build this data model using the data model editor by defining a related set of database queries and break levels.

You can include procedural constructs to provide additional functionality for data formatting and display filters. Additionally, this tool provides several useful functions that can be utilized to calculate summary information (such as totals or averages) at the various break levels. You can also use Oracle Reports 2.5 to execute database maintenance functions, although better tools can usually be found to perform these tasks.

Oracle Graphics 2.5

Oracle Graphics 2.5 is used to graphically display Oracle data in a chart. These charts can be any of several types (for example, pie or bar charts) and are based on the data returned from a query. Although Oracle Graphics will produce these charts in a stand-alone mode, the true power of this tool is as an OLE 2 server application that can be incorporated into OLE container applications such as Visual Basic, Excel, and, of course, Oracle Forms and Oracle Reports.

Why Use Developer/2000?

The Oracle Developer/2000 tool set requires a lot of resources! The version that runs on an IBM-compatible Windows 3.*x* PC requires at least 16 MB of RAM, with an additional permanent swap file of at least 8 MB to design any new application modules. (It is possible to run most Oracle Developer/2000 applications on a smaller machine; however, highly complex modules will still perform poorly on a lesser system.) To load all of the tools with demos and on-line documentation requires nearly 200 MB of hard disk storage. This does not include Windows, DOS, or any other software, not to mention the applications that you need to develop.

With an abundance of tools available that interface with Oracle databases (such as Power Objects, PowerBuilder, Visual Basic, and so on), why should you choose to use Developer/2000?

When you work with small tables with very few joins, a less powerful, easier-to-use tool might be acceptable. However, if application performance is a critical factor, the Oracle Developer/2000 tools provide, by far, the best mechanisms for performance tuning.

Oracle Forms provides several mechanisms that help ensure that an application provides consistently reliable data maintenance and presentation. With a few lines of code, (or in some cases, by selecting appropriate object properties), you can construct a module based on several related tables with applicable propagation of changes whenever maintenance occurs. You can use these master-detail constructs to ensure that data integrity is preserved throughout the application.

Another very important concept that is "automatic" in Oracle Forms is row-level data locking. This ensures that more than one user cannot update the data at the same time and prevents arbitrary changes from occurring. These seemingly minor features are the essential ingredients necessary for enterprise-wide database systems.

The Power Objects tool (also produced by Oracle Corporation) is powerful enough to be used for many query-only applications or for small single-table maintenance applications. This tool is syntactically compatible with Visual Basic and therefore is easy to use. However, in order to build a menu-driven integrated application with the complexity necessary for enterprise-wide data processing, Power Objects falls short. Additionally, you must explicitly code data locking and master-detail propagation to ensure proper integrity.

Visual Basic (a Microsoft product) can access Oracle databases using ODBC connectivity. Visual Basic has an advantage over Oracle Forms based on the fact that it is a more mature product and therefore offers the availability of many more add-on components. The primary disadvantage of Visual Basic is its lack of support for data integrity issues.

PowerBuilder (produced by Powersoft) has several features that are not found in the Oracle tools. The most significant of these is its capability to provide queries that can be defined dynamically at runtime. However, PowerBuilder has been written to support the Watcom SQL database engine and therefore lacks direct support for Oracle's data integrity. Another disadvantage of PowerBuilder is the fact that, in most cases, significantly fewer lines of code must be written using Developer/2000 when accessing an Oracle database.

Features of Developer/2000

What truly sets Developer/2000 ahead of the other development products for Oracle databases are its features. These features enable the knowledgeable developer to rapidly deliver powerful, complex application units that can serve the diverse needs of the users of an enterprise database system.

All of the development tools provide a similar point-and-click interface for constructing application components. This interface follows standard Windows-compliant conventions to ensure ease-of-use. By manipulating a mouse cursor, the developer can select, copy, move, and delete the elements that combine to make up an individual module. The primary common elements of this interface are

1. An object navigator that presents a hierarchical view of all the objects that combine to form an application unit. By selecting the item in the object navigator, the developer can view and update the object's properties as well as the appearance of the object on the screen.

2. A layout editor that enables the developer to place objects onto the end-user screen or report so that he or she can view the final product layout as it evolves. Functions are provided for aligning, stacking, and distributing objects, as well as defining the size and appearance of each item.

3. Various 3-D buttons that can be used to perform functions such as opening and saving application units and adding, copying, or deleting objects and object properties. Other buttons are used to run the application, toggle debugger mode, and expand or contract levels in the object navigator.

As objects are added to a unit, the Developer/2000 tools utilize intelligent defaulting to define the properties of the object based on the context in which it is used. This feature enables the developer to construct simple default modules with practically no programming. In many cases, routine database table maintenance can be performed according to predefined general rules and therefore do not require any special programming.

If you want to develop modules that do not operate according to the generalized defaults, Oracle Developer/2000 provides a feature called User Extensibility. This feature enables you to write procedural program code (using PL/SQL) to override the default operation of Oracle Forms applications. These program units and triggers can be used for data validation, secondary data retrieval, or transactional control, to name just a few of the uses of this feature.

In today's ever-changing environment of corporate and MIS right-sizing, Developer/2000 (like all prior Oracle front-end tools) features the capability to run on a vast array of computer platforms. *Portability* enables you to write and test applications on one platform and then "port" them to another system without any programming changes. Many organizations construct systems on stand-alone or networked PCs and then migrate them to an enterprise UNIX or mainframe computer. Except for minimal user interface changes, the entire migration should not require any code modifications, which enables MIS departments to free themselves from lifetime commitments to obsolescing computer environments.

Another feature of Developer/2000 is that all of its components have been designed to be integrated. A complete database system requires the capability to display and maintain data in an on-line environment accessed by many diverse users. Many times, users need reports that summarize information not available on-screen or need to provide a tremendous amount of detail that would not be practical in an on-line mode. Additionally, users sometimes need hard-copy reports for external customers or vendors. Finally, graphical displays of data help users understand the information as it is presented. Through the use of menus, module tie-ins, and other functions, Developer/2000 is a complete database management tool.

Finally, the Developer/2000 tools can be used with non-Oracle data sources. This feature is especially useful in an environment in which users can access data from a variety of sources. The Developer/2000 tools can be used to migrate data from a legacy (for example, DB2) database to the Oracle database. The Oracle tools can also access normal text files directly using some of the interface functions that have been provided.

Common Tool Set Features

In order to provide a consistent development environment, several elements of the Developer/2000 tools are universal to all three tools. By learning how to use the function within one tool, you will understand how to use it in the others.

The Object Navigator

The Object Navigator, shown in Figure 31.1, is used to present an interface to the hierarchical structure of all opened application units. The example shown is for a new Oracle Forms 4.5 module; however, all of the Developer/2000 tools use a similar Object Navigator interface.

FIGURE 31.1.

The Object Navigator.

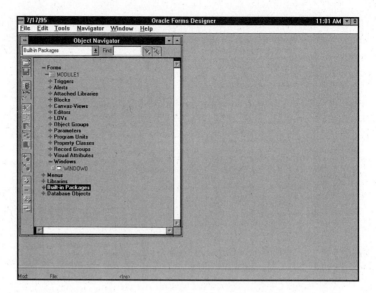

Within the Object Navigator window, the structure of all open units is displayed in either the Ownership View (shown in the figure) or the Visual View. The Ownership View displays the object structured according to the block (representing records from a single table or view) where each is found. The Visual View, on the other hand, displays objects structured according to where they appear on the end-user screen. The developer can use the Navigator menu item to select the view that he desires based on his own personal preference. Each item in the displayed structure can be preceded with an expand (+) or contract (-) icon to inform the developer that further details can be displayed for the object. By moving the mouse cursor and clicking a highlighted icon, the structure will expand to show the next lower level of detail or remove the lower level from the display, respectively.

Standard scroll bars are provided on the right and bottom of the Navigator to enable the developer to change the portion of the application structure that appears within the window. Buttons that close, minimize, and maximize windows have also been included; they operate similarly to those found in most windows applications.

Below the Navigator window title bar are two fields and two iconic buttons. The first field displays the currently selected item in a list box. (Note: The currently selected item is also highlighted in the Navigator window, but because it can be "scrolled out" of the window, this field reinforces the selection.) The second field is the Find item. The developer can type in this box and press Return to automatically navigate to the entered item. The two iconic buttons (which look like flashlights) are used to search for the item in the Find box in either the forward or reverse direction, respectively.

The last part of the Navigator to be discussed is the iconic button bar, which appears on the left side of the Navigator window. These buttons are used to perform tasks that can also usually be executed using menu picks or hot keys.

The first button appears as a partially open file folder and is used to open existing application units, which can be Forms modules, menus, or program unit libraries when used in Oracle Forms. The next button, which appears as a floppy disk, is used to save the current module to either a file or the database.

The next two buttons, a traffic light representing go, and an insect-like creature, are used to run the application module and to toggle the debugger facility on or off, respectively. If the debug facility is on, the user will be able to trace program execution and track changes to application variables when the application is run. Full details on using the debug facility are discussed in the next chapter.

The next series of buttons are cut, copy, paste, copy properties, and paste properties, respectively. The first three work like the corresponding Windows 3.1 functions, whereas the last two are used to copy the individual properties of one object to another existing object of the same type.

The next set of buttons is used to add and delete objects within the navigator. Depending on the currently selected object in the navigator, the newly added item will be created using intelligent defaulting to rapidly create application functionality. Intelligent defaulting refers to the fact that based on the context of the activity, the default properties of the items will reflect the type of item and the environment within which it is inserted.

The last set of iconic buttons are used to expand and contract the structure of the module. These buttons, in order, are expand item, contract item, expand all lower items, and contract all lower items.

Database Connectivity

One of the features of the Developer/2000 tools is that they can be used without connecting to an Oracle database. This enables you to work on an application unit while you are unable to connect to an Oracle database. However, to generate (compile) an application unit or run the module, the developer/user must connect to the database using the dialog box shown in Figure 31.2.

The first two fields in the Connect dialog box represent the user's user ID and password (Note: the password will appear as asterisks as it is typed in) and the third field is the database connectivity string. For local database access, this field can be left empty; however, for remote database access this field is required. The definition for this field can be defined in the user's oracle.ini (for Windows 3.*x*) or corresponding file. The connectivity string should be provided by your system administrator who will also set up your user ID and password.

FIGURE 31.2.

*Connecting to an Oracle
database.*

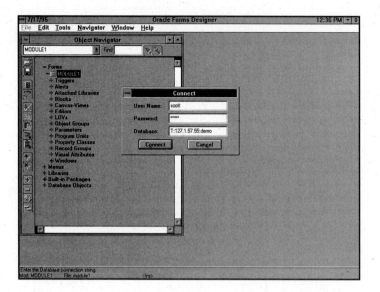

Module Access

All of the Developer/2000 components use a similar interface for loading existing application units into their respective Designer environments. Based on the tool in use, an initial option dialog box will be displayed for the user to select the location (file system or database) and the module type of the application unit to be opened. If you choose to open the program unit from the database, a second dialog box will appear that displays all stored units of the requested type in the database. If, on the other hand, you choose to open the application unit from the file system, the standard Windows 3.*x* Open dialog box will appear, enabling you to select the source drive, directory, and file that should be opened.

Summary

Oracle Developer/2000 consists of three distinct products: Oracle Forms 4.5 for on-line data maintenance and presentation, Oracle Reports 2.5 for large-volume data reporting or hard-copy report generation, and Oracle Graphics 2.5 for graphical presentation of data. These products require substantial system resources, but due to their reliable handling of integrity and transactional issues, they are superior to most other products for diverse enterprise database needs.

Developer/2000 features a point-and-click interface so it is easy to use, intelligent defaulting, user extensibility, portability, integration, and the capability to access non-Oracle databases. These features are unique among the tools available that access Oracle databases. Although some of these features might exist in other products, no other products feature all these attributes combined.

To facilitate ease-of-use between the three integrated tools, Oracle has provided several common functions such as the object navigator, database connectivity, and access to the individual application units. These units are similar between each of the tools, so that the developer who learns to use one will automatically know how to use the others.

The next three chapters explore each of these tools individually and in depth. After explaining each tool separately, the last chapter of this section explains how to integrate these tools with each other and external applications to provide a seamless application system for end users.

Although you will be looking at many advanced topics, it is not possible to fully dissect each and every option for every application component in this book section. I have been working with the Oracle tools for over ten years, and I can honestly say that most of my abilities have not been learned from a book. As far as I know, not a single major league baseball player has ever gotten where he was by reading how to play the game, but has done so by lots of dedicated practice and experience. Likewise, I hope that this section of the book can impart to you enough knowledge that you can work out the rough spots and become an adept all-star Developer/2000 programmer. Most of what I know has been gained through experimentation and observing the techniques used by other Oracle professionals. Hopefully, my experience will assist you on the road to using these development tools.

Oracle Forms

32

by Joe Zafian

As stated in the previous chapter, Oracle Forms 4.5 is a development tool that can be used to create applications to enter, access, change, or delete data from an Oracle database in an online, form-based environment. Forms has provided many objects for developing an effective application module. Coupled with the concept of user extensibility, Forms can be used to serve virtually every online need in an Oracle database environment.

This chapter will explore many of the concepts related to Oracle Forms development. The examples will start with a few baby steps and gradually add enough information so that you will be able to walk on your own. With each advance in complexity, the applications will become more powerful. By the end, you will be able to delve further into many advanced concepts and perhaps add innovations of your own.

The Oracle Forms Environment

Oracle Forms 4.5 operates in a graphical user interface (GUI) environment such as Microsoft Windows 3.x. The primary tools used to develop customized forms are the Object Navigator, the Layout Editor, and the object property sheets. In addition to online forms, Oracle Forms 4.5 is also used to create and maintain application menus and program unit libraries.

The Object Navigator

The Object Navigator (shown in Figure 32.1) presents all the elements that combine to create an Oracle Forms application module. These elements (or objects) may be manipulated using the iconic buttons and menu options. Within the Object Navigator, the application components are presented to the developer in a hierarchical outline format indicating the organization of the form elements. The individual element groupings are described in the following subsections.

FIGURE 32.1.

The Oracle Forms Object Navigator and property sheets.

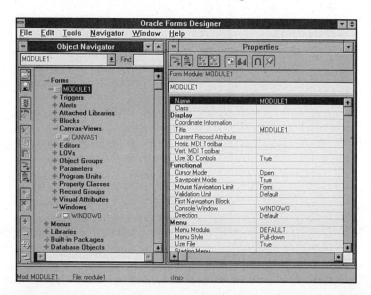

Triggers

Triggers are PL/SQL functions that will be executed based on some specific activity or condition in the form. These activities, called events, are the foundation of Oracle Forms' user extensibility feature. While many of the trigger events will perform a particular default function, a trigger can be written to disable, modify, or enhance the default processing capabilities associated with the event. Triggers can be defined at the form, block, record, or individual field level. In addition, a trigger may cause another trigger to "fire" as well as execute another related program unit.

Alerts

Alerts are used to provide additional information or other messages that require response or acknowledgment from the user. An alert may contain one to three buttons that can be used to define the action the user wants to execute based on the condition.

Attached Libraries

Libraries are special Oracle Forms modules that can be defined to contain reusable procedures and functions. By attaching program unit libraries to a form, the program code can be maintained in a single file rather than in each individual form module. Libraries help to assure the quality of an application by ensuring that all modules follow the same set of business rules.

Blocks

A block in a form generally corresponds to an individual entity (table, view, or snapshot) in the database. Additionally, blocks may be created that do not correspond to any table. These blocks, called *non-base table blocks*, are usually used to hold generic control information, such as query criteria, counters, conditional indicators, and other information that may relate to more than one record or activity. (Blocks that relate to an entity are referred to as *base table blocks*.)

Items

Items (which are not shown in Figure 32.1) are grouped in the Object Navigator within their respective blocks. An item corresponds to a single data element or field. These items may contain database columns or may be used as containers for other related data.

Relationships

Relationships (not shown in Figure 32.1) are defined according to how the separate blocks in a form relate to each other. Typically in a multiple block form, one block is usually defined as the primary or master table, and the other blocks display detail information associated with the current record in the master block. An example of a master-detail form would be a customer record application where the master block shows the customer name and address and the detail block will display the history of purchases made by the customer in multiple records.

Canvas-Views

A canvas is the virtual structure where the form objects are laid out. For the most part, canvases are defined as either content or stacked canvases. A content canvas is displayed in its entirety within the form window. Whenever a content canvas is first displayed, any other canvases will be hidden in the window. A stacked canvas, on the other hand, will display "on top" of any existing canvases within the form window. In addition to these two canvas types, a third canvas type has been included in Forms 4.5: a button bar canvas. A button bar canvas will appear on top of all displayed canvases and is usually used to contain iconic buttons for user commands. A special null canvas exists to contain objects that are not displayed.

Editor

An editor is a window for viewing and maintaining large data fields. These fields are sometimes included for the entry of user comments or other information that would not normally fit in a displayed item.

LOVs

LOVs (also called *lists of values*) provide the user with a list of valid entries for a field. A list of values presents data contained within an object called a record group whereby the user will select one value from the list to populate a form item. The list of values may also be used to validate user input to ensure that a valid value is entered.

Object Groups

An object group is a special mechanism for packaging several form objects into a container, which may then be used in other forms with a minimum of programming. Once an object group is created in a form, any of the form objects may be copied into the object group. For example, a form may contain a secondary page showing a scheduling template. The components of this submodule may be copied to the object group and other forms may reference the object group, which will behave as if it were part of the second form itself. This is another feature of Forms that promotes the object-oriented approach while assuring quality through consistency.

Parameters

Parameters may be defined for a form in order to provide a startup input for the form. Typically, parameters are used to pass values from one form to a newly called form in a multiple

The Layout Editor

The Layout Editor (shown in Figure 32.2) presents the canvas on which the form objects are laid out. This tool is operated through the use of iconic buttons and menu choices. The buttons along the left side of the Layout Editor window are used to create and manipulate the form layout objects. These buttons (top to bottom, left to right) are described in Table 32.1.

FIGURE 32.2.

Oracle Forms Layout Editor.

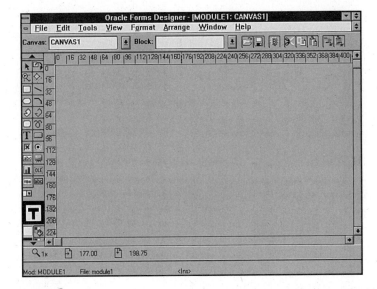

Table 32.1. Layout Editor Buttons.

Button	Usage
Select	Selects object(s) on the canvas.
Magnify	Zooms in/out on the canvas. Click within the canvas to zoom in. Click while holding the shift key to zoom out. The current magnification level is shown in the lower-left area of the Layout Editor window.
Rectangle	Draws a rectangle on the canvas.
Ellipse	Draws a circle or ellipse.
Polygon	Draws a multiple-sided object.
Rounded Rectangle	Draws a rectangle with rounded corners.
Text	Adds boilerplate text to the canvas.
Check Box	Creates a check box item.
Text Item	Creates a text item field.

continues

Table 32.1. continued

Button	Usage
Oracle Graphics	Inserts an Oracle Graphics chart item.
VBX	Creates a VBX control item.
List Item	Creates a drop down list item.
Rotate	Rotates the selected object.
Reshape	Reshapes the selected object.
Linc	Draws a line.
Arc	Draws a curved line.
Polyline	Draws a series of connected lines.
Freehand	Draws in freehand mode.
Button	Creates a button item.
Radio Button	Creates a radio button item.
Image Item	Attaches an image item to the canvas.
OLE	Creates an OLE container item.
Display Item	Creates an item for display purposes only.

The list boxes at the top of the Layout Editor allow the user to navigate between the multiple canvases and blocks in the form, while the iconic buttons are used for command control within the editor. These buttons, in order, are:

Open	Opens an existing module.
Save	Saves the current module.
Run	Runs the current module.
Cut	Cuts the selected object(s).
Copy	Copies selected object(s).
Paste	Pastes object(s) from clipboard.
Copy Properties	Copies properties to clipboard.
Paste Properties	Pastes properties from clipboard.

Customizing the Forms Environment

Oracle Forms 4.5 allows the programmer to modify the development environment using the Tool | Options menu choice. The Designer Options dialog box (shown in Figure 32.3) is used to set the behavior of the Oracle Forms Designer.

FIGURE 32.3.

Defining Oracle Forms designer options.

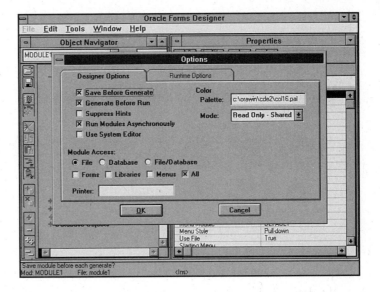

The five check boxes establish the operating mode for Oracle Forms Designer. If checked, the first box will cause the current module to be saved automatically whenever a form is generated, and the second box will cause the form to be generated (compiled) whenever it is run from the designer. (The net effect of having both boxes checked is that every form will be saved and generated by clicking the run button.)

> **NOTE**
>
> Many of the earlier versions of Oracle Forms were notorious for producing General Protection Faults, which usually resulted in work being lost. Thus, it became a common practice to use these checkboxes practically universally. Unfortunately, unless a backup of a module is saved, changes can wipe out prior versions of a form if these options are used.

By default, Oracle Forms displays a hint in the lower-left area of the screen based on the context of the designer. By selecting the next check box, these hints will be suppressed. If the next option, Run Modules Asynchronously, is checked, the Forms Designer enables the developer to run a form module and work in the designer simultaneously. Otherwise, the run-time form must be exited before using the designer further. The last check box defines the editor that should be used in the designer. Checking this box causes the designer to use an operating system editor rather than the default forms editor.

The color palette determines the colors that should be used in a form. It is recommended that the Oracle 16-color palette be used, as shown in the figure, to ensure color-matching capability between form objects. The Color Palette Mode is used to define how color palettes should be handled in Oracle Forms. The options for the list box are: Editable, Read Only - Shared, and Read Only - Private. Editable means that the color palette of the active form will replace the system color palette, causing the active form to be shown accurately, while the appearance of any inactive forms may not be accurate. Read Only - Shared means that each form's color palette will be appended to the system palette until the space reserved for the palette becomes full. If any forms are then opened which use a different color palette, they may not appear accurately. Finally, Read Only - Private operates the same as shared mode except that Oracle Forms assures that the palette used is always valid for the active form, and any inactive forms may not appear correctly because their color palettes have been cleared to make room for the new form.

The module access options define whether modules should be opened from the database or the file system (or both) and what types of files should be included in the selection. The last option defines the printer that should be used for any printing requirements in the Forms Designer.

The second tab in this window (shown in Figure 32.4) is used to define the options to be used when a module is run from within the Oracle Forms Designer. The first option, Buffer Records, will cause Forms to buffer only the minimum number of records (the number of records displayed plus three) in memory. All additional rows retrieved will be stored in a temporary file. The next option causes the form to be executed in debug mode. This option allows the developer to insert break statements in the PL/SQL segments to observe the values in form items and to trace the execution of the program code.

FIGURE 32.4.

Setting Oracle Forms run-time options.

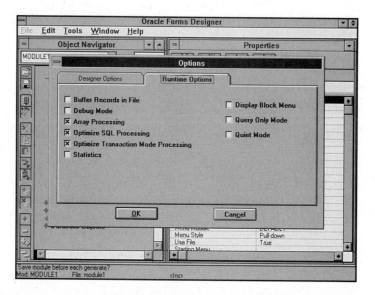

The next four options are related to performance tuning of Oracle Forms. Array processing allows the form to return multiple rows from the database in a single fetch cycle rather than one at a time. This usually causes better performance; however, fetching more than one row at a time may impact the memory usage in the form. In order to maintain backward compatibility, Oracle Forms allows the developer to use Version 2-style triggers (separate processing steps) in the form. The Optimize SQL Processing option causes these triggers to be processed using an optimization technique to take advantage of the more "modern" capabilities that have been incorporated into PL/SQL. Transaction Mode Optimization causes all implicit SQL statements (for example, posting and committing triggers) to optimize cursor usage so that the cursors may be shared within the form. The Statistics option will return statistics regarding cursors and other resource utilization when the form is run. The other effect of this option is that a SQL Trace session will be generated, which can be analyzed by TKPROF, or another performance-analysis tool, to assist with tuning.

The next option will display the block menu for a form—rather than the form itself—as soon as the form starts up. This menu will allow the developer to navigate directly to a particular block rather than to the initial default. Query-only mode disables any inserts, deletes, or updates in a form. Finally, Quiet mode "turns off" the audible beep that is played whenever a message is generated in the form.

Creating New Forms Modules

A form may be created using the File | New | Form menu choice or by using the create-form hot key (Ctrl+Y). The new form will be added to the Object Navigator. Additionally, whenever the Oracle Forms Designer is started, a new empty form is automatically created. Similarly, program-unit libraries (Ctrl+I) and menu modules (Ctrl+-E) may also be created from the menu. These modules may in turn be saved, either by running them (with the appropriate options selected) or by explicitly executing a save from the File menu or using the iconic button in the Designer windows.

Building a Simple Default Form

Oracle Forms' feature of intelligent defaulting allows the developer to create a basic form in mere minutes. As an example, the Warehouse Maintenance form (shown in Figure 32.5) can be created quickly without writing a single line of program code.

To build this form, first create a new form in the Object Navigator (log into the database if you have not already done so) and select the Blocks group within the new form. The block-definition dialog box will appear as shown in Figure 32.6. This form will be based on the WAREHOUSES table; therefore, enter it into the base table field and navigate to the next field using the Tab key. (Alternatively, the table name can be obtained using the Select button to the right of the table name field. This button will present a dialog box that may be used to list all the available tables in the database.) Notice that by default the name of the block changes to match the table name, although the name can be any value the developer desires. Hit the Tab key again to navigate to the canvas field, which has defaulted to a value such as CANVAS1. Change the name of this field to WH_CANVAS.

FIGURE 32.5.

Warehouse Maintenance form.

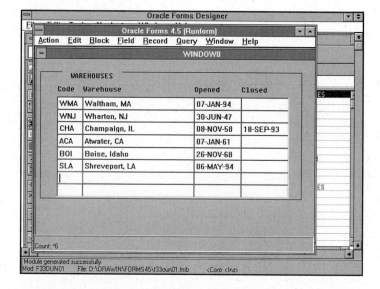

FIGURE 32.6.

Block-definition dialog box.

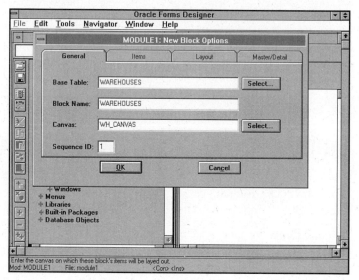

Once this box is completed, click on the Items tab to present the Item-definition dialog box shown in Figure 32.7. To obtain the columns in this table, click on the Select Columns button and all columns in the table will be listed. A plus sign preceding the column indicates that the column will be used in the form. To exclude a column, double-click on the column name in the list box. For each column listed, modify the column label and width as indicated in Table 32.2.

Table 32.2. Warehouse Maintenance Form Column Definitions.

DB Column	Label	Width
WH_CODE	Code	35
WH_NAME	Warehouse	150
WH_OPEN_DATE	Opened	60
WH_CLOSE_DATE	Closed	60

FIGURE 32.7.

Default-column definition dialog box.

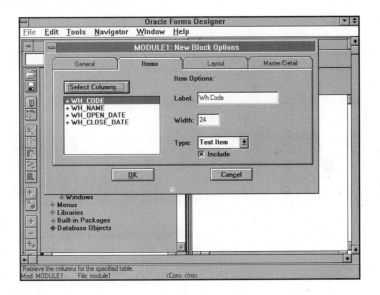

After the column definition is completed, the form layout should be defined using the Layout tab as shown in Figure 32.8. This form presents multiple rows in a tabular arrangement with the individual rows arranged vertically. The records field representing the maximum number of records displayed should be 8, and there should be no spacing between the records. Other options are used to determine whether integrity constraints should be enforced for the form and if a button palette is needed for the table. (The button palette will create a default set of iconic buttons that can be used for table maintenance.) The last checkbox will include a scrollbar in the form that can be used to navigate through the block if all records cannot be displayed at one time.

FIGURE 32.8.

Defining form style and layout.

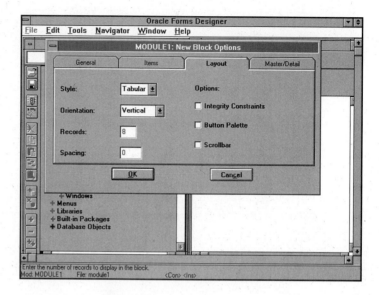

After this dialog box has been completed, click the OK box to finish constructing the form. To test the form, run it by clicking the Run icon or choose the Run option in the File menu. (Note: This chapter will assume that the Designer options Save Before Generate and Generate Before Run are selected. Otherwise these steps must be done manually prior to running the form.) The form will appear, as shown previously in Figure 32.5, with all of the data boxes empty. To list the existing data, select the Query | Execute menu choice. Data may be entered into the fields and then saved using the Action | Save menu choice, and the Action | Exit menu choice is used to close the form.

Using Boilerplate Text and Graphics to Enhance Forms Applications

The previous example does not provide the three-dimensional look and feel that is common in most Windows software. By utilizing some of Oracle Forms' graphical objects and visual effects, you can transform the previous example into a more aesthetically pleasing application, as shown in Figure 32.9.

To modify this form, first select the block title in the Layout Editor and remove it using the Delete key. Do the same with the box around the data grid. Now, using the select tool, select all of the column headings on the screen. To modify the font, choose the Format | Font menu choice to display the font selection dialog box as shown in Figure 32.10. In this case, choose the Arial font, Bold Italic style, and size 9 (a sample of the selected font will be shown within the dialog box) and click the OK button to change the fonts.

FIGURE 32.9.

Using boilerplate objects to enhance applications.

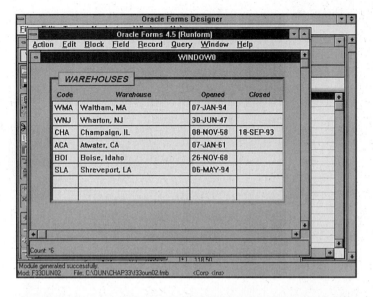

FIGURE 32.10.

Font-selection dialog box.

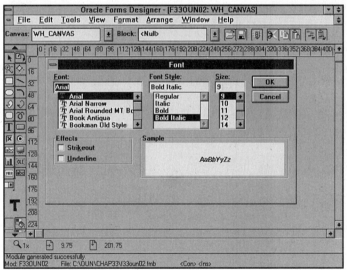

Now, position the column headings at the center above the column (defaults to left-justified) using the Align Objects tool. To do this, click on the column heading text for the Warehouse Code and then, while holding the shift key, click on the code field. Using the Arrange | Align Objects menu choice, choose the alignment options as shown in Figure 32.11. Repeat for all four columns.

FIGURE 32.11.

Align Objects dialog box.

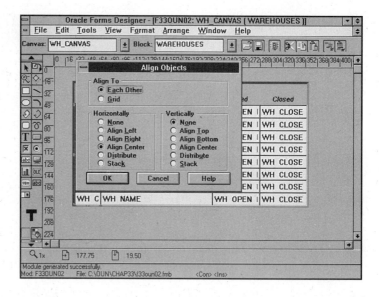

Now, select the Rectangle tool, and draw a rectangle as shown in Figure 32.9 so that it borders both sides and the bottom of the data grid. (Use the sizing anchors to resize and position the rectangle if necessary.) To create the three-dimensional effect, select the Format | Bevel menu choice and select the lowered effect to create the appearance of a lowered block on the screen. The depth may be adjusted using the Format | Line menu choice. Create another smaller rectangle overlapping the previous rectangle for the screen label. Using the Text tool, create the screen label (WAREHOUSES) using an appropriate font. Using the mouse, arrange the objects to appear on the screen as shown in the example.

NOTE

Sometimes the intelligent defaulting feature of Oracle Forms causes objects to appear differently than desired, especially regarding the fill and border-line visual attributes for the object. These can be corrected using the attribute palette buttons below the current visual-attribute display in the Layout Editor. Also, the Arrange menu provides options to move objects in front of or behind other objects.

Customizing Forms with Properties

As previously mentioned, Oracle Forms' intelligent defaulting capabilities can be used to create useful applications. In many cases, however, it is necessary to define specific characteristics for application objects. This can be done by modifying the properties of the form objects using the object property sheets.

To examine properties, again load the form from the previous section. Each object in the form (including the form itself) has an associated context-sensitive property sheet. The properties for the objects are organized in logical groups based on usage. To change a property, select the object in the Object Navigator. If the property sheet is visible in the split window arrangement, the property sheet will automatically display for the object. If the property sheet is not visible, double-click on the icon at the left of the object name in the Object Navigator to view the property sheet. Usually, only some of the properties are visible in the window and a scrollbar is available to view the other properties. To modify a property, click on the property in the property sheet. The value of the property will be copied to the top line of the property sheet window. Edit this line and press return to modify the property.

The first custom modifications to be made will affect the overall application appearance. First select the property sheet for the form window. Change the Window Title to "Warehouse Maintenance Form," then change the window width to 382 and the height to 200. To prevent a user from using the Windows function to resize the window frame or to minimize the form, update the Fixed Size property to True and the Iconifiable property to False for the form window. Additionally, repeat the sizing properties for the WH_CANVAS canvas.

Now, select the WH_CODE item and change the Update Allowed property to False. This change will protect the primary key for the Warehouses table from being changed. Finally, select the WH_OPEN_DATE and WH_CLOSE_DATE fields together. Notice that the common property sheet shows that multiple objects have been selected and that in cases where the properties are different, a set of asterisks is shown. In this case, modify the Format Mask property to be MM/DD/YY. As a final step, change the font and sizing for all of the fields in the warehouse record, by selecting all of them and displaying the common property sheet. Modify the height to equal 14 and change the font name to Arial with a size of 8 points and a weight of bold.

Upon completion of these changes, save and run the new form. The result should look like the form shown in Figure 32.12. Compare this form with the form created in the previous section to see how the property changes have affected the resulting form module.

FIGURE 32.12.

Example form demonstrating custom properties.

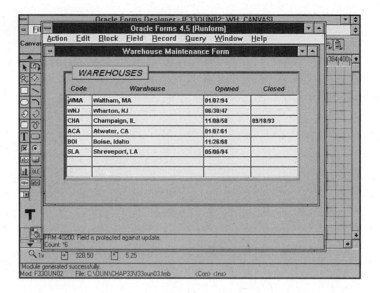

Implementing Triggers and Program Units

Oracle Forms applications can be further customized by developing PL/SQL procedures and functions called triggers. These triggers are attached to specific activities in the form called events. Events typically are defined as before (PRE-FORM, PRE-QUERY, PRE-INSERT), after (POST-FORM, POST-QUERY, POST-INSERT), or during (WHEN-NEW-FORM-INSTANCE, WHEN-BUTTON-PRESSED) common database activities. Additionally, triggers can be associated with certain keyboard activities (for backward compatibility with character-based applications), although the trend is to minimize key triggers.

The customer maintenance form shown in Figure 32.13 utilizes a pre-insert trigger to determine a unique customer number based on a sequence generator. Additionally, triggers are defined for the buttons at the bottom of the form.

To construct this form, create a block for the CUSTOMERS table using a form style in the block layout definition. Arrange the items and boilerplate objects as shown in the figure and using the button tool, create three buttons as shown on the screen. (These buttons will be labeled as PUSH_BUTTONx.) Using the Size Objects and Align Objects tools in the Arrange menu, position and size the form objects to appear as shown.

Now, define the object properties as needed by defining the window and canvas sizes and titles. Next, because the customer number should be protected from update, change the Update Allowed and Navigable properties for the CUST_NO item to False. Modify the label properties for the buttons to reflect the text that is shown in the figure.

FIGURE 32.13.

Customer Maintenance form.

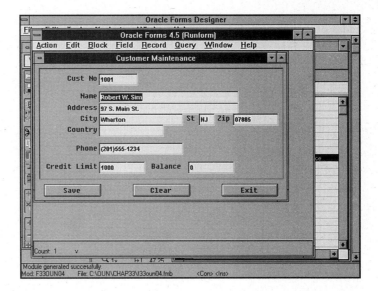

At this point, the additional processing logic may be added to the form. First, select the triggers group directly below the CUSTOMERS block in the Object Navigator. Click the Add Object button and a list will appear with the names of all allowable triggers that can be built for the form. The trigger to be built will determine the customer number for a new customer prior to insert based on the database sequence generator. While the list is displayed, either use the scroll bar to find the PRE-INSERT trigger or type the trigger name into the input box.

> **NOTE**
>
> Generally, lists in Oracle Forms use an algorithm to narrow a list as keys are typed. In this case, after typing P and R, the list will show all PRE-x triggers and the input line will type ahead because no other triggers exist that begin with those letters. Type an I and the PRE-INSERT trigger will be the only trigger in the list.

The PL/SQL editor (shown in Figure 32.14) will now appear, indicating the trigger level and the name of the trigger with an area that may be used to enter the trigger procedure as shown. Once the text has been entered, click the Compile button to make sure that there are no code errors and then click the Close button to complete the trigger definition. Note the colon used to reference form fields. Other buttons can be used to revert to the version prior as of the last close or compilation, to create a new trigger, or to delete the existing trigger.

FIGURE 32.14.

PL/SQL editor for trigger creation.

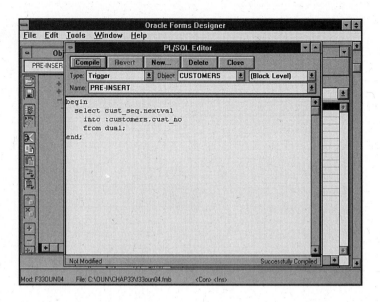

Finally, WHEN-BUTTON-PRESSED triggers should be created for the three buttons that were created on the form canvas as follows:

```
Save:      begin
             commit_form;
        end;
Clear:     begin
             clear_form;
        end;
Exit:      begin
             do_key ('EXIT_FORM');
        end;
```

The first two triggers use standard built-in procedures, while the third uses the DO_KEY built-in procedure to simulate pressing the Exit key.

NOTE

The Exit key is defined by the keyboard mapping for your display device. On the IBM PC keyboard, this normally defaults to the Esc key but may be modified using Oracle Terminal. To view the actual key mapping during Oracle Forms run-time, type Cntrl-K or select show keys from the help menu in the form.

This is generally a good practice to use when there is more than one way to perform the same function. Any special logic that needs to be performed prior to exiting the form can be coded in a KEY-EXIT trigger to ensure consistency. Additionally, a trigger can be written so that it calls a user defined program unit. For example, if the customer maintenance form changes the credit limit for a customer, an acceptance letter should be sent to the customer. The POST-COMMIT trigger should be written as follows:

```
begin
        if :customers.cust_credit_limit > 0 and :customers.old_credit is null then
            print_confirmation_letter (:customers.cust_no);
        end if;
    end;
```

The `print_confirmation_letter` procedure would then be created as a program unit in the form. The actual logic for this procedure will be discussed in Chapter 36 in the section describing integration of Oracle Forms and Oracle Reports.

Using Record Groups and Lists of Values for Data Validation

A record group is an internal structure that is analogous to a table in memory. Record groups contain columns and rows with data based on a structure defined by a query or column definition. Usages of record groups include parameters, structured arrays, and validation entities. This last usage of record groups will be demonstrated in the Item Price Maintenance form shown in Figure 32.15.

FIGURE 32.15.

Item Price Maintenance form.

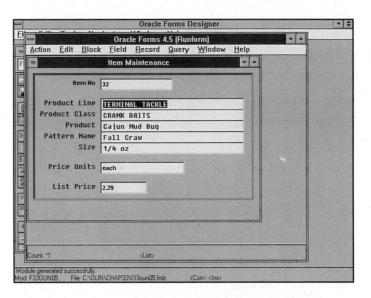

To build this form, start with a default block for the items table using the form style layout. Next, change the Displayed Canvas to <Null> and the Displayed property to False for the ITEM_PL_ID, ITEM_PC_ID, ITEM_PROD_NO, ITEM_CP_NO, and ITEM_SIZE_CODE items. These items will be hidden from view and will be updated by the List of Values validations that will be constructed for this form. Also, make the ITEM_NO field non-updatable and non-navigable.

To make this form more user-friendly, the translations for the code fields will be displayed as the input fields in the form. Using the Field tool, create five new fields as PL_NAME, PC_NAME, PROD_NAME, CP_NAME, and SIZE_DESC. The properties for these fields are shown in Table 32.3.

Table 32.3. Item maintenance description fields.

Property	Value
Canvas	ITEM_CANVAS
Displayed	True
Width	200
Height	200
Database Table Item	False

These fields will need to be populated with data whenever an ITEMS record is queried. To do this, create the POST-QUERY trigger on the ITEMS block as follows:

```
begin
    select pl.pl_name, pc.pc_name, prod.prod_name, cp.cp_name, s.size_desc
        into :items.pl_name, :items.pc_name, :items.prod_name, :items.cp_name,
            :items.size_desc
        from product_lines pl, product_classes pc, products prod,
            color_patterns cp, sizes s
    where pl.pl_id = pc.pc_pl_id
        and pc.pc_pl_id = prod.prod_pl_id
        and pc.pc_id = prod.prod_pc_id
        and prod.prod_pl_id = :items.item_pl_id
        and prod.prod_pc_id = :items.item_pc_id
        and prod.prod_no = :items.item_prod_no
        and cp.cp_no = :items.item_cp_no
        and s.size_code = :items.item_size_code;
exception
    when NO_DATA_FOUND then
        message ('Database Integrity Error. Contact your DBA.');
        bell;
        raise FORM_TRIGGER_FAILURE;
end;
```

NOTE

This trigger has been written this way because in a client/server application, a single query is much more efficient than multiple independent queries. Because each of the five fields that must be loaded can be obtained through a unique row query, they can be merged in a single query step. Another (and probably better) approach would be to create a view that retrieves these values in the initial query. A view could always be used as the base table for a block. The exception step introduces a few new concepts regarding triggers. The message built-in is used to send a message to the user screen and the bell built-in will play an audible beep from the user's terminal. Also, the FORM_TRIGGER_FAILURE exception that is raised prior to exiting the trigger will cause all processing to be aborted on failure.

Now the lists of values should be defined for each of the fields. To create a list of values, select LOVs in the Object Navigator and click the Add Object button. The new LOV dialog box will appear as shown in Figure 32.16. In the Query Text box, type in the query against the PRODUCT_LINES table as shown and click the OK button when finished. This will create a new record group and associate it with the new LOV. (Note that a list of values may also be created based on an existing record group.)

FIGURE 32.16.

Creating a new list of values.

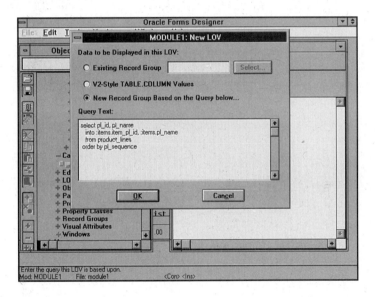

Now, select the new LOV and its property sheet. Change the name of the LOV to PRODLINE_LOV and select the Column Mapping property in the property sheet. A button will appear in the Value Edit box with the label More. Click this button to display the column mapping dialog box as shown in Figure 32.17. The column names from the query will be displayed in a table with the characteristics for the column shown below the table. To hide the ID column from the display, set the display width equal to 0. Select the PL_NAME column and set its display width to 150 and change the column title to Product Lines. Click OK to complete the column mapping. Now attach this LOV to the PL_NAME field in the ITEMS block by selecting its property sheet and scrolling towards the bottom to the Miscellaneous Properties section. Change the LOV property to PRODLINE_LOV and set the LOV X Position and

LOV Y Position to 100 and 50, respectively. Finally, set the LOV For Validation property to True. This will cause the form to make sure that the value entered is valid without having to write a validation trigger. (To ensure data integrity, a WHEN-VALIDATE-ITEM trigger may be written for this field to "null out" the Product Class and Product Name fields whenever the Product Line is changed.) Create a List of Values for each of the remaining non-database fields. (Use the POST-QUERY trigger to determine the columns and tables for the mapping.)

FIGURE 32.17.

Column mapping for a list of values.

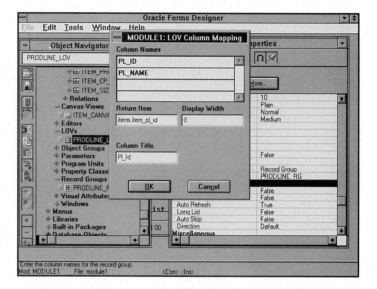

Finally, to complete the form, create a PRE-INSERT trigger on the items block to select the next ITEM_SEQ value from the sequence generator as the value for a new ITEM_NO. The form should then be saved and generated to test this concept. A couple features to note are that the list can be activated using the List Values key (F9 in most standard IBM PC configurations. To see a list of defined keys, select Help | Show Keys from the menu.) and that the validation feature allows the user to type only part of the field name to narrow the list. For example, type T into the Product Line field and then hit the tab key. The complete name, Terminal Tackle, will be filled in.

Using Relationships to Link Separate Blocks in a Form

Thus far, all of the examples discussed here have used only a single block for data. The key feature of Oracle (or other relational databases) is that the tables are related to each other by key fields. An example of the use of related tables is shown in Figure 32.18 in the Order Entry Form.

FIGURE 32.18.

Order entry form.

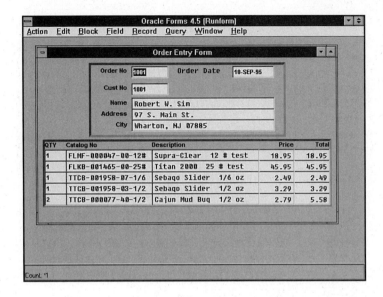

To construct this form, first create a default block for the Orders table using the form layout style. Create non-database fields for customer name, address, and city using the Display Field tool. (A display field is used to display data but does not need to provide input capability.) Also, create a list of values for the customer number field and define the order number and order date fields as non-navigable. (These fields will be populated in a pre-insert trigger.) A post-query trigger should be written to populate the customer information.

Now, create a second block for the order_items table using a vertical tabular style that will display five rows of data. Modify the properties for the OI_ITEM_NO field so that it is not displayed and is assigned to the <Null> canvas. The only field that will remain on the canvas will be OI_QTY. Create non-database fields in this block for CATALOG_NO, ITEM_DESC, LIST_PRICE, ITEM_TOTAL using the Display Field tool. Also, create a numeric, non-displayed field ITEM_PRICE on the null canvas. Create a POST-QUERY trigger for the ORDER_ITEMS block as follows:

```
begin
      select i.item_pl_id||i.item_pc_id||'-'||
            ltrim (to_char (i.item_prod_no, '099999'), ' ')||'-'||
            ltrim (to_char (i.item_cp_no, '09'), ' ')||'-'||
            i.item_size_code,
            p.prod_name||decode (cp.cp_name, 'N/A', ' ',' '||cp.cp_name||'
            ')||
            s.size_desc,
            i.item_price
      into :order_items.catalog_no, :order_items.item_desc,
        :order_items.item_price
      from items i, products p, color_patterns cp, sizes s
     where items.item_no = :order_items.oi_item_no
        and p.prod_pl_id = i.item_pl_id
        and p.prod_pc_id = i.item_pc_id
        and p.prod_no = i.item_prod_no
```

```
        and cp.cp_no = i.item_cp_no
        and s.size_code = i.item_size_code;
:order_items.list_price := ltrim(to_char(:order_items.item_price,
'990.00'), ' ');
:order_items.item_total := ltrim ( to_char
                    ((:order_items.oi_qty * :order_items.item_price),
                    '990.00'), ' ');
end;
```

> **TIP**
>
> Oracle Forms does not allow for a format mask on display items. For that reason, the fields should be defined as character fields and the item should be formatted using PL/SQL. Using right justification, the fields can be displayed so that the individual digits are properly aligned.

To complete this block, create a list of values for the catalog number field with a WHEN-VALI-DATE-ITEM trigger to display the list price and item total fields.

Finally, to complete this form, select the Relationships group under the Orders block. Click the Add Object button to display the Relation dialog box as shown in Figure 32.19. Modify the relation name to order_item_rel and define the detail block as ORDER_ITEMS. Next, define the logic that should be followed if a master record is deleted. In this case, select a cascading delete. (All detail records will be deleted if the associated master record is deleted.) The block coordination should be defined so that the detail query is immediate (Deferred is off), and the user should not be able to navigate to the detail block unless a record exists in the master block.

FIGURE 32.19.

Creating block relationships in a form.

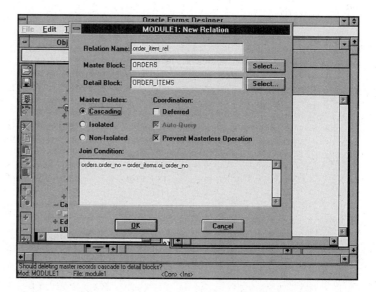

Mouse Events, Timers, and Other Advanced Widgets

The standard Windows interface uses various graphical controls and other objects to control the operation of application components. Oracle Forms provides access to many of these features through the use of mouse triggers, timers, and VBX controls. Additionally, messaging in most Windows software is through an object called an alert box that has been implemented in Oracle Forms.

Working with the Mouse

The mouse pointer is the primary user-input device for navigation and selection in most Windows applications. Triggers have been provided in Oracle Forms to detect and act on various mouse activities.

Oracle Forms 4.5 utilizes the mouse for navigation and command input. Additionally, the mouse can be used to trigger specific events. An event can be triggered when the mouse passes over an item on the screen (WHEN-MOUSE-ENTER) or when it leaves the item (WHEN-MOUSE-LEAVE). A third mouse status event can occur if the mouse moves within an item (WHEN-MOUSE-MOVE).

Additional triggers that have been added for mouse button activities are shown in Table 32.4.

Table 32.4. Mouse triggers.

Trigger Name	Event Description
WHEN-MOUSE-DOWN	Operator presses and holds the mouse button.
WHEN-MOUSE-UP	Operator releases the mouse button.
WHEN-MOUSE-CLICK	Operator quickly presses and releases button.
WHEN-MOUSE-DOUBLECLICK	Operator clicks mouse twice in succession.

When these activities occur, several system variables exist to retrieve status information for the mouse. These variables are shown in Table 32.5.

Table 32.5. Mouse system variables.

Variable	Value
MOUSE_BUTTON_PRESSED	Returns 1 for left button; 2 for middle/right.
MOUSE_BUTTON_SHIFT_STATE	Returns <Null>, Shift+, Ctrl+, or Shift+Ctrl+ depending on key pressed.

continues

Table 32.5. continued

Variable	*Value*
MOUSE_ITEM	Current item where mouse cursor is located.
MOUSE_CANVAS	Current canvas where mouse cursor is located.
MOUSE_X_POS	Current x position of mouse within item.
MOUSE_Y_POS	Current y position of mouse within item.
MOUSE_RECORD	Record within block where mouse cursor is located.
MOUSE_RECORD_OFFSET	Record where mouse cursor is located relative to first displayed record.
MOUSE_FORM	Current form where mouse cursor is located.

The sample form shown in Figure 32.20 can be constructed to test and observe the operations of the mouse triggers and variables. To construct this form, create a block, b1, that is not associated with a table. In the Layout Editor, create four fields for TRIGGER_NAME, BUTTON_NUMBER, SHIFT_STATE, and MOUSE_ITEM1, and position these fields with the appropriate caption as shown in the figure. Set the Default value property for the MOUSE_ITEM1 field as WILL TURN RED ON MOUSE ENTRY. Also, create a button object, DRAG_BUTTON, on the canvas with a Label property of Drag This Button.

FIGURE 32.20.

Mouse observation form.

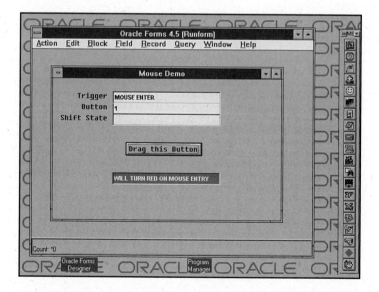

Next, select the Visual Attributes group in the Object Navigator and click the Add Objects button. In the property sheet for this object, set the font to Arial, size 8, and weight bold. Define the foreground color as BLACK and set the background to WHITE. Name this object BLACK_ON_WHITE. Create a second visual attribute, WHITE_ON_RED, with a white foreground and red background. These visual attributes will be used to define the display colors of the MOUSE_ITEM1 field using a WHEN-MOUSE-ENTER trigger as follows:

```
begin
    :b1.trigger_name := 'MOUSE ENTER';
    set_item_property ('B1.MOUSE_ITEM1', VISUAL_ATTRIBUTE,
                                 'WHITE_ON_RED');
end;
```

Similarly create a WHEN-MOUSE-LEAVE trigger to use the BLACK_ON_WHITE attribute. Now, create WHEN-MOUSE-DOWN, WHEN-MOUSE-UP, WHEN-MOUSE-CLICK, and WHEN-MOUSE-DOUBLECLICK triggers at the form level to display the status of the mouse whenever a trigger event occurs.

```
begin  -- WHEN-MOUSE-DOWN trigger
    :b1.trigger_name := 'MOUSE DOWN';
    :b1.button_number := :system.mouse_button_pressed;
    :b1.shift_state := :system.mouse_button_shift_state;
end;
```

The default installation of Oracle Forms includes several libraries and sample programs that can be used in your Forms development. One of these libraries, DRAG.PLL, provides functions that can be used for drag-and-drop functionality in Oracle Forms. To use this library, select the Attached Libraries group in the form and click the Add Object button. Select the DRAG.PLL file to attach to the form.

To implement drag-and-drop in this form, create two triggers on the DRAG BUTTON item as follows:

```
begin -- WHEN-MOUSE-DOWN trigger
    mouse.click;
end;

begin -- WHEN-MOUSE-MOVE trigger
    if :system.mouse_button_pressed = 1 then
        mouse.move;
    end if;
end;
```

These triggers that reference procedures in the mouse package in the DRAG.PLL library are all that is needed to implement drag operations in a form. A third trigger should be created for the object to define the logic associated with the drop operation (WHEN-MOUSE-UP trigger).

This completes the design of the mouse control form. Run the form to observe how it operates. A few important points should be noted at this time. First, observe the operation of passing the cursor over the MOUSE_ITEM1 field. The color of the field will change and the name of the trigger will appear in the appropriate field. Now, click anywhere on the canvas. Three triggers will actually fire with what appears to be a single action. The WHEN-MOUSE-DOWN and WHEN-MOUSE-UP triggers fired before the WHEN-MOUSE-CLICK trigger. A double-click event will fire all of these triggers before firing the WHEN-MOUSE-DOUBLECLICK trigger. Therefore when working with the mouse, care should be taken when defining multiple triggers to prevent unwanted logic to be executed.

Working with Alerts

Alerts are devices that can be included in a form to provide the user with information that requires a response. An alert can be one of three styles: Stop (usually fatal errors), Caution (warning messages), and Note (informational). Depending on the style chosen, a different icon will appear in the alert box. Additionally, the programmer may define up to three labeled buttons to determine the user response. The default setting is a two-button alert box with the captions OK and Cancel. To display the alert, a built-in function has been provided using the following syntax:

```
button_no := SHOW_ALERT (alert_name);
```

where button_no is defined as a numeric PL/SQL variable. Using the SET_ALERT_PROPERTY built-in, the ALERT_MESSAGE_TEXT property can be dynamically changed at run-time. Thus, using the standard trigger, ON-MESSAGE, an alert box can be created that will present all messages to the user in an alert box rather than on the status line, which may sometimes be missed by a user. An ON-MESSAGE that uses the MSG_ALERT dialog box (STOP, 1 button labeled OK) can be written as follows:

```
declare
   msgtext      VARCHAR(80) := message_text;
   bno          number;
begin
   set_alert_property ('MSG_ALERT', ALERT_MESSAGE_TEXT, msgtext);
   bno := show_alert ('MSG_ALERT');
end;
```

Thus, whenever the message built-in is used, the message will be displayed as shown in Figure 32.21. The form that contains this alert will be described in the next section.

FIGURE 32.21.

Alert message.

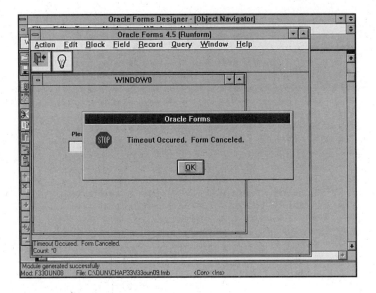

Using Timers for Event Control

Timers may be used in Oracle Forms to trigger events that are dependent on a specific time interval. These timers may be iterative (repeating) or one-time only. Examples of iterative timers are a report queue manager that looks for requests every 15 seconds or a database status form that "refreshes" the screen every two minutes. Uses for a one-time only trigger may be as a delay timer for button help or as a timeout trigger. To create a timer, the following command would be issued:

```
TIMER_ID := CREATE_TIMER (timer_name, interval, REPEAT¦NO REPEAT);
```

where TIMER_ID is a PL/SQL variable of type TIMER, TIMER_NAME is the name given to the timer by the programmer, and INTERVAL is the duration of the timer in milliseconds.

Oracle Forms supports multiple timers; however, only one WHEN_TIMER_EXPIRED trigger may be included at the form level. To determine which timer has expired, the trigger should use the GET_APPLICATION_PROPERTY (TIMER_NAME) built-in function. Then by checking against the various timer names, the appropriate program sequence may be executed. The SET_TIMER (same syntax as the CREATE_TIMER built-in) built-in may be used to restart an existing timer or to change its interval or repeat parameters. Finally, the DELETE_TIMER built-in may be used to remove a timer.

The example shown in Figure 32.22 shows how to implement multiple timers in a form using an iconic button bar. The WHEN_NEW_FORM_INSTANCE trigger creates two triggers that will be used in the form and the WHEN_TIMER_EXPIRED trigger executes the logic necessary when a timer expires. The first trigger is used to create an animated button in a form button bar by toggling the icon file used based on a time interval. The second timer is used to validate that the user enters a valid name within 30 seconds or the form will terminate. Finally, the WHEN_MOUSE_ENTER and WHEN_MOUSE_LEAVE triggers have been set up to create a timer that will display button help after the mouse has been "resting" on a button for at least one half second.

FIGURE 32.22.

Timer demo form.

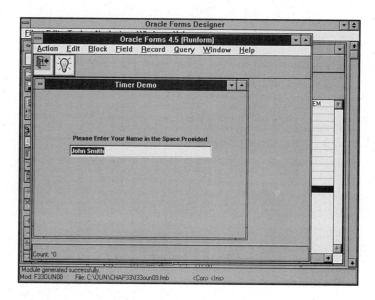

First, create a canvas called DESKTOP and a non-database block called control. The Desktop and associated window should be defined as 300 points wide by 200 high. Create the USER_NAME field as shown on the desktop with the appropriate valid condition. Now, create an alert, called TIMEOUT_ALERT, as an informational alert with one button. The message text for this alert should be

```
R E M I N D E R
    This form will terminate unless a valid user name
    is entered within 30 seconds after startup.
```

This alert will be displayed whenever the Show Note button is pressed.

Now, to create the iconic button bar, create a second canvas called BUTTON_BAR. The Canvas Type property for this canvas should be Horizontal Button Bar and it should be 300 points wide by 30 points high. Now create a button for the exit function. Properties for this button are shown below in Table 32.5.

Table 32.5. Button bar iconic button properties.

Property	Value
Name	EXIT_BUTTON
Canvas	BUTTON_BAR

Property	Value
X Position	0
Y Position	0
Width	30
Height	30
Navigable	False
Mouse Navigable	False
Label	Exit Form
Iconic	True
Icon Name	Exit

Additionally create a second button, SHOW_NOTE, adjacent to the EXIT_BUTTON that will use the lighton iconic file. (Note the icon file will change to 'blink' the light at run-time.) Now, the button bar must be defined as such to the form. To do this, change the Horiz. MDI toolbar to point to the BUTTON_BAR canvas. This will cause the button bar to appear outside the frame of the form window when the form is executed.

NOTE

At any one time, only one MDI (Multiple Document Interface) button bar will appear in a Windows application. This prevents confusion when multiple documents or forms are open at the same time. Only one document may be active at any time and the MDI button bar will show the buttons associated with the active document. This is especially useful when working with multiple forms or OLE applications.

Create triggers that will execute the proper commands when the button is pressed. The trigger for the EXIT_BUTTON item should be DO_KEY ('EXIT_FORM') and the following WHEN-BUT-TON-PRESSED trigger should be created for the SHOW_NOTE button:

```
declare
   bno      NUMBER;
begin
   bno := show_alert ('TIMEOUT_ALERT');
--
-- Note additional logic may be placed here based on the button pressed
-- by the user.
--
end;
```

Now, the timer triggers may be added to the form. First, the timeout and blink timers are set up for the form in the WHEN-NEW-FORM-INSTANCE trigger. (This trigger replaces the KEY-STARTUP trigger in Forms 3.0.) This trigger is coded as follows:

```
declare
    timeout_id          TIMER;
    blink_id            TIMER;
begin
    timeout_id := CREATE_TIMER ('TIMEOUT', 30000, NO_REPEAT);
    blink_id := CREATE_TIMER ('BLINK', 500, REPEAT);
end;
```

Additionally, triggers need to be added to provide button help as needed. This help text, which is a standard in many Windows applications, displays the value that was entered for the button Label directly below the iconic button. To add this functionality, attach the HINT.PLL library to the form and create a WHEN-MOUSE-ENTER and WHEN-MOUSE-LEAVE trigger for the form as follows:

```
begin -- WHEN-MOUSE-ENTER trigger
    HINT.ShowButtonHelp;
end;

begin -- WHEN-MOUSE-LEAVE trigger
    HINT.HideButtonHelp;
end;
```

If the user enters a valid name in the user name field, the timeout timer should be canceled. To do this, create a WHEN-VALIDATE-ITEM trigger for the USER_NAME field.

```
begin -- WHEN-VALIDATE-ITEM trigger
    if :control.user_name is not null then -- other validation logic may be
    needed.
        delete_timer ('TIMEOUT');
    end if;
end;
```

To complete this form, a WHEN-TIMER-EXPIRED trigger must be written for all timers in the form. This trigger, shown forthwith, determines the timer that caused the trigger to fire and processes the logic associated with the trigger.

```
declare -- WHEN-TIMER-EXPIRED trigger
    which_timer     VARCHAR2(50);
begin
    which_timer := get_application_property (TIMER_NAME);
    if which_timer := 'BLINK' then
        :control.message_switch := mod (:control.message_switch +1, 2);
        if :control.message_switch = 0 then
            set_item_property ('CONTROL.SHOW_NOTE', ICON_FILE, 'lightoff');
        else
            set_item_property ('CONTROL.SHOW_NOTE', ICON_FILE, 'lighton');
        end if;
    elsif which_timer = 'TIMEOUT' then
        message ('Timeout Occurred.  Form Canceled.');
        do_key ('EXIT_FORM');
    else
```

```
        HINT.ShowButtonHelpHandler;
    end if;
end;
```

A couple of important points should be noted when working with timers:

1. Only one timer can be handled by the WHEN-TIMER-EXPIRED trigger at a time. If a second timer expires while this trigger is handling the first, it will be placed on the stack until the trigger is completed.

2. The WHEN-TIMER-EXPIRED trigger will fire during transaction processing, navigation, and so on. If a second form is called by the form containing the trigger, the timer will be deferred until the user returns to the calling form.

3. A repeating trigger will not repeat until it is taken off the queue. In other words, the interval does not start up again until the first iteration is handled.

4. Any existing timers are deleted when the form is exited. If any timed activity is pending or on the queue, it will not complete if the form is exited.

5. Finally, do not use timers where precise timing is essential. Because the above conditions can delay the actual execution time of the trigger logic, the Oracle timer can not be used for industrial fail-safe operations.

Implementing VBX Controls

VBX controls were originally developed as user interface elements for Microsoft Visual Basic programs. As the Visual Basic environment became accepted as a powerful business-applications development environment, interfaces to VBX controls were added to many other popular Windows program-development products. While only a few VBX controls are included with the Visual Basic software, many third party VBX controls are available for purchase. Additionally, developers may create their own VBX controls using C++ or other programming languages.

With the advent of Oracle Forms 4.5, these elements have been incorporated into the Oracle application tools. In Oracle Forms, a VBX control may be used to either provide information to an application or to display application information in some specialized way. To demonstrate the ease with which these elements may be incorporated into a form, the simple form module shown in Figure 32.23 may be constructed.

This form utilizes two VBX controls that are connected to a text item with triggers. The first VBX control is the Spin Control, which will increase or decrease the value in the text box by 500 units depending on whether the up arrow or down arrow is clicked with the mouse. The other VBX control is a VBX gauge control, which is defined as a horizontal bar gauge. This gauge will be filled based on the value of the text item as a percentage of the maximum value of 25,000.

To create this form, create a numeric text field, VBX_VALUE, on the form as shown. The default value for this item should be 10000. Next, create a VBX control in the Layout

Designer next to the text field. This VBX control should then be attached to the VBX file for the Spin button. The properties for this object are shown in Table 32.6.

FIGURE 32.23.

VBX demonstration form.

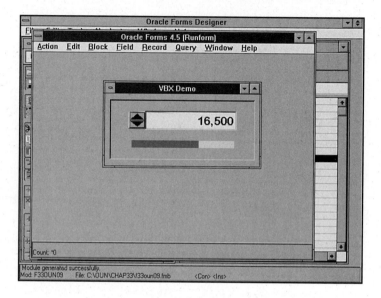

Table 32.6. Spin control properties.

Property	Value
VBX Control File	C:\WINDOWS\SYSTEM\spin.vbx
VBX Control Name	SpinButton
VBX Control Value Property	Name
Border Thickness	1
Spin Orientation	0 -Vertical

A second VBX control should be added below the other items and attached to the gauge VBX file. The properties for this control are shown in Table 32.7.

Table 32.7. Gauge control properties.

Property	Value
VBX Control File	C:\WINDOWS\SYSTEM\gauge.vbx
VBX Control Name	Gauge

Property	Value
VBX Control Value Property	Value
Max	25000
Min	0
Style	0—Horizontal Bar
Value	10000

Finally, triggers need to be created to link these three items. To establish the initial values, the WHEN_NEW_FORM_INSTANCE trigger should contain the following lines:

```
:B_VBX.VBX_VALUE := 10000;
:B_VBX.VBX_GAUGE := :B_VBX.VBX_VALUE;
```

A WHEN_CUSTOM_ITEM_EVENT trigger should then be created for the Spin Control:

```
BEGIN
   if :SYSTEM.CUSTOM_ITEM_EVENT =  'SpinUp' then
      if :B_VBX.VBX_VALUE < 24501 then
         :B_VBX.VBX_VALUE := :B_VBX.VBX_VALUE + 500;
      end if;
   elsif :SYSTEM.CUSTOM_ITEM_EVENT = 'SpinDown' then
      if :B_VBX.VBX_VALUE > 499 then
         :B_VBX.VBX_VALUE := :B_VBX.VBX_VALUE - 500;
      end if;
   end if;
   :B_VBX.VBX_GAUGE := :B_VBX.VBX_VALUE;
END;
```

A WHEN_VALIDATE_ITEM trigger should be written for the VBX_VALUE text item containing the following line:

```
:B_VBX.VBX_GAUGE := :b_VBX.VBX_VALUE;
```

Finally, triggers may be written for the cursor up and down keys so that pressing either of them will trigger the corresponding Spin Up or Spin Down events:

```
BEGIN  -- KEY-UP trigger
   VBX.FIRE_EVENT ('B_VBX.VBX_SPIN', 'SpinUp', NULL);
END;
```

Considerations for Multiple Form Applications

Oracle Forms provides three built-in procedures that enable the user to access other forms from an original calling form. These procedures are: NEW_FORM, CALL_FORM, and OPEN_FORM.

NEW_FORM terminates execution of the original form and starts up the next form. If any changes have been made to database data, the user will be asked if he wants to commit the data. If he chooses not to commit his changes, these changes will be lost. A NEW_FORM call is typically used when the user navigates to an unrelated application module.

CALL_FORM, on the other hand, passes execution to the next form, while maintaining a call stack that will return to the calling form when the called form is exited. If changes are pending in the calling form, the called form will be executed in POST-ONLY mode. If the user tries to save changes made in the called form, the changes will be posted to the database (a rollback will lose any changes) and they will be saved when the original form is committed. Typically, CALL_FORM is used when the two forms are dependent on each other and values can be passed either in global variables or as parameters. One usage of the CALL_FORM would be to add a button to the Order Entry form (discussed in the section on relationships) that can be used to create a new customer record. The second form could then be used to create the customer record, and after the new record is inserted and posted or committed, the customer number could be returned in a global variable to be used for order entry.

Finally, OPEN_FORM is used to load a second form while maintaining the functionality of the first form. The second form, by default, becomes the active form; however, the user can activate the first form by clicking within its frame. If the second form should not be made the active form, the second parameter in the procedure call can be defined as NO_ACTIVATE. Additionally, the new form will be opened in the same session as the original calling form. It is possible, however, to call the second form with a separate session by defining the third parameter in the call as SESSION. This would connect the user in a second (or third, etc.) session. The advantage of having the second session open is that changes can be made within the first form and committed without affecting pending changes in the first form. An interesting application can be developed where the first form executes a query based on a timer (for example, every two minutes). The second form could then be used to maintain records on the database and the changes would show up in the original form. (This would be a crude but effective way to pass data between two application areas.)

Techniques for Dynamic, Run-Time Applications

In its simplest form, an Oracle Forms query can be defined by the default where property for the queried block. Typically, a form will contain query criteria elements in a control block and the default where property may be defined as

```
where database_table_field = :CONTROL.control_field
```

This would work in cases where the query is based on a single required field such as customer number. In reality, however, a query form is seldom so cut-and-dried. The customer inquiry may also need to be based on the customer name. Using the above technique, the default where property would become

```
where database_field1 = :CONTROL.input_field1 or
      (:CONTROL.input_field1 is null and
           database_field2 = :CONTOL.input_field2)
```

The performance of this query is poor because the Oracle optimizer will resolve both halves of the query and then merge the result. As can be seen by this basic example, as the number of query fields increases in the control block, the where clause would become more complex and the performance of the query would degrade very quickly. Ideally, the where clause should be written to reflect only the fields that contain data.

Starting with Oracle Forms 4.0, an application may modify the where clause dynamically at run-time. Thus, in the previous example, the following PRE-QUERY trigger may be written to dynamically update the query:

```
declare
    qry_where     VARCHAR2(100);
begin
    if :control.cust_no is not null then
        qry_where := 'cust_no ='||to_char (:control.cust_no);
    elsif :control.cust_name is not null then
        qry_where := 'cust_name = '''||:control.cust_name||'''';
    else
        message ('Either customer number or name must be entered.');
        raise FORM_TRIGGER_FAILURE;
    end if;
    set_block_property ('CUSTOMERS', DEFAULT_WHERE, qry_where);
end;
```

While in many cases directly building a where clause at run-time seems to be the best way to handle dynamic queries, the techniques that have been available in prior versions of SQL*Forms may be used. In order to accomplish this, a database field is set equal to a value based on how the where clause should be created. The following table will define possible entries using the field ITEM_VALUE.

Table 32.8. Implementing dynamic queries in Oracle Forms.

Field Contents	Run-time Modification	Example	Resulting
any text value	Checks for equality to entered value.	SMITH	ITEM_VALUE = 'SMITH'
begins with <, <=, >=, >, or !=	Checks for respective inequalities.	> 47	ITEM_VALUE > 47
contains % or _	Uses pattern matching algorithm.	%SM_TH	ITEM_VALUE like '%SM_TH'
begins with # character	Inserts the text following the # directly into the where clause following the field name reference.	# between '01-JAN-95' and '31-OCT-95'	ITEM_VALUE between '01-JAN-95' and '31-OCT-95'
		# in ('01', '02', '03')	ITEM_VALUE in ('01','02', '03')

Field Contents	Run-time Modification	Example	Resulting
		# is not null	ITEM_VALUE is not null
		# = 1.10 * OTHER_VALUE	ITEM_VALUE = 1.10 * OTHER_VALUE
		# = ITEM_VALUE and exists (select 'x' from orders o where o.order_cust_no = CUSTOMERS.cust_no)	ITEM_VALUE = ITEM_VALUE and exists (select 'x' from orders o where o.order_cust_no = CUSTOMERS.cust_no)

Generally speaking, treating each column independently in the PRE-QUERY trigger will result in a more maintainable module. Given that most environments are in a constant state of change, ease of maintenance should be a determining factor.

Working with Menus

Thus far, all of the application modules that have been developed in this chapter have been completely independent of each other. While an application can be developed using iconic buttons and procedures that can be used to pass control from one form to the next, most applications are held together using menu modules. Typically, a main form is executed first, and all other forms are called from the original module. As you may have noticed in the Form property sheet, each form module may define a menu to be used within the form.

To create a menu module, use the File | New | Menu menu choice in the Oracle Forms designer. A new menu module will be created in the Object Navigator. Object groups in the menu are attached libraries, menus, object groups, parameters, program units, property classes, and visual attributes. A menu is defined as a list of options that may reference other submenus or perform tasks such as commands or processing Forms functions.

The initial menu module begins by creating a menu called MAIN_MENU. To edit the main menu, double-click on the menu icon and the menu editor will appear as shown in Figure 32.24. The initial menu contains one item called <New Item>, which can be customized by double-clicking on the item and defining its properties in the property sheet. Important properties to note for the item are Item Type, Command Type, and Command Text.

FIGURE 32.24.

Menu editor.

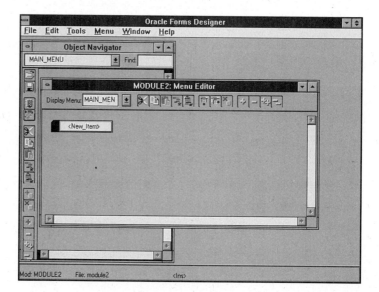

Item types are: Plain, Check, Radio, Separator, and Magic. Most items that will be defined for navigation will be of the Plain type. A Check item is used to set a user option from the menu, and a Radio type item is used to select an option from a list of valid options. A Separator item is used to draw a horizontal line in a drop down menu. Finally, a Magic item performs a default Forms function defined by the Magic item property.

The command types are Null, Menu, PL/SQL, Plus, Form, and Macro. The Null command performs no function when the menu item is selected, and a menu item will present a new submenu. A PL/SQL command type is used to execute a PL/SQL program block. Plus and Form are used to invoke SQL*Plus and Oracle Forms.

Thus, by defining a set of menus, the user will be able to create applications that can be navigated through the use of the various menu items. Figure 32.25 below shows a File Menu as it is being constructed with separators between the logical menu areas appearing similar to many Windows 3.1 applications.

FIGURE 32.25.

Sample File menu.

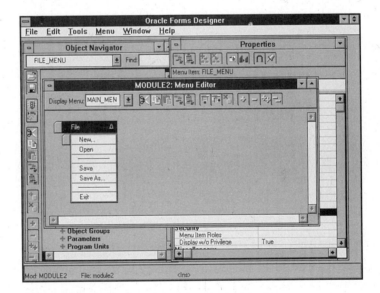

Libraries, Object Classes, and Visual Attributes

One of the major features of object-oriented programming environments is the concept of reusability. By creating reusable objects, standards can be enforced globally and applications can be developed at an unprecedented pace. Users become more comfortable with an application that appears and operates uniformly. Several objects have been included in Oracle Forms to provide this reusability.

As already discussed, libraries are repositories of reusable PL/SQL program units. To work with a library, create the library in the Object Navigator as you would a form. A library can attach other libraries and can contain PL/SQL program units. To use these program units in other forms, attach the library to the form and reference the procedures and functions as if they were part of the form itself. If changes are made to the library, each form that uses the library must be regenerated to reflect the change.

Visual attributes, on the other hand, are defined as part of the form itself. A visual attribute defines the font characteristics and the colors for the object. A special visual attribute called Default exists for every form based on the value of the FORMS45_DEFAULTFONT parameter in the oracle.ini file in your system. Visual attributes can be designed to define meaning for the item. For example, a financial application may show negative values in red or special characteristics may be needed to indicate errors or statistical extremes. Another valuable usage of a visual attribute is to indicate the current record selected. The current-record attribute is available at either the block or form level and is often used in multirow applications. Finally, the visual attribute for an instance of an item can be changed dynamically at run-time using the DISPLAY_ITEM built-in procedure.

The last feature that provides reusability within a form is a property class. A property class takes the class represented by the visual attribute and utilizes it further by defining all of the properties for a class of objects. This allows the developer to define a set of valid property classes and to use these properties throughout the application without having to define each individual property for every object.

Quality Considerations for Oracle Forms

Oracle Forms can handle a vast array of database processing functions. As with any powerful tool, there are many ways to accomplish the same task. It is the job of the developer to create applications that deliver the highest quality return for the lowest overall cost. Quality in an Oracle system can be classified according to several key attributes:

- **Reliability**: The system must deliver accurate and dependable results.
- **Performance**: The system must deliver the results quickly.
- **Features:** The system must deliver the functionality needed.
- **Durability:** The system must sustain growth.
- **Serviceability:** The system must be easily modified.
- **Conformance:** The system must adhere to standards.
- **Aesthetics:** The system must look good doing all of the above.

Oracle Forms provides many tools to ensure the quality of an Oracle application. Triggers provide the constructs necessary to ensure the reliability of a form in adhering to business rules as they have been established. By coupling these concepts with database triggers and procedures, the system development process can enforce conformance to all of the business rules. In addition, program unit libraries and reference forms with defined object classes and visual attributes can assist the developer in delivering a reliable system that conforms to the standard presentation format that has been established for the organization. These components also make a system easier to modify to reflect changes in rules or newly installed interfaces.

Such modifications are inevitable in practically every Oracle database application, and if object-oriented principals are used from the beginning, changes will be easier to make in the future.

The final concept that is absolutely key in the development of Oracle applications is performance. Unfortunately, in many cases, performance is an afterthought in application development. Many systems actually end up in production without any performance tuning. At best, most applications have received only minimal tuning effort. This is not completely the fault of the developer, although the developer should be most concerned with the performance of the system. After all, whenever a system performs poorly, the finger of blame will usually point to the developer.

What can be done by the developer to ensure optimum performance? The answer, in a word, is testing. Each SQL statement executed in the form should be checked for optimized code. To see what SQL statements are being run for a form, run the form with the STATISTICS mode on. This will create a trace file in the Oracle Home directory. (Your DBA should be able to help you find this directory.) The trace file should then be translated using the TKPROF utility (Oracle's performance tuning utility) as follows:

```
TKPROF tracefile listfile EXPLAIN=username/password
```

This utility will describe the access path for every SQL statement executed in the form. Look at the execution plans to make sure that every table access uses an index where desired and that full table scans are minimized. Generally, when using multiple table views in a query, the result should be minimized as quickly as possible. Therefore, make sure that the indexes that return the fewest result rows are used earliest. Second, a full table scan is not always a bad thing in a query, especially when most of the blocks in a table must be accessed anyway. Tuning individual statements will come with practice, and many times even a seasoned veteran will find the optimum query through trial and error.

Besides making sure that each SQL statement is efficient, there are several other "rules" that the developer can follow when building a form, especially in a client/server environment. Some of these include:

- Minimize the number of queries. A POST-QUERY trigger will be called for every row returned by the initial query. Try to create a view that contains all the information in the first query.

- Combine unrelated queries if possible. Several queries that all return one row using a unique index can be combined into a single query. This saves round-trips over the network.

■ Use database triggers and procedures where possible. These constructs ensure that all maintenance to the data uses the same business rules. Additionally, communications to the database will be minimized.

■ Finally, before rolling out to production, stress test the application with a large volume of data with many users. This testing will shake out bottlenecks and indicate where locking strategies may need to be revised.

Summary

The material presented in this chapter has defined the primary building blocks for creating Oracle Forms applications that access data in an Oracle database. Items are built into form blocks, which appear on a canvas in defined windows. Triggers and program units combine to provide a robust development system that can be customized to the specific needs of the end users. Properties, lists of values, alerts, and the various graphical objects further enhance the ability of the developer to construct useful and powerful database applications.

Unfortunately, because of the limitations of defining the entire tool in a single chapter, many of the topics were not explained in as much detail as is needed to make you an expert developer. What I hope to have provided you is a set of tools and the basic knowledge to use them. You can think of yourself now as the equivalent of an apprentice carpenter fresh out of trade school. Only with experience using the tools can the apprentice hone his skills until he can be considered a master craftsman. Likewise, the only way to learn how to use a tool set as powerful as Oracle Forms is to use the tool and try new techniques until you, too, are an expert.

Oracle Reports 2.5

33

by Joe Zafian

IN THIS CHAPTER

For many years, the predictors of the future have envisioned the concept of the paperless office wherein all correspondence and corporate records are stored online and all paper reporting has been eliminated. Reality, however, has shown that hardcopy reports continue to be required at an ever-increasing rate.

Oracle Reports is the Developer/2000 tool that has been provided to produce reports of data in the Oracle database. These reports can be previewed on the user screen before being printed or can be printed directly. Optionally, report output may also be saved in a file to be used at a later date.

This chapter explains how to set up the Oracle Reports environment and the methodology for constructing several reports. These reports will cover all aspects of report development using Oracle Reports 2.5. Finally, this chapter summarizes a set of key tips to follow when creating a report.

The Oracle Reports 2.5 Environment

Oracle Reports operates in a Graphical User Interface (GUI) environment such as Microsoft Windows. Functions may be performed by clicking iconic buttons or via menu picks. The menus used by Reports dynamically change based on the current context of the tool and are fairly intuitive as to their specific purpose. The individual menu items will be explained as needed throughout this chapter. The Oracle Reports Designer interface consists of three primary components or tools: the Object Navigator (described in Chapter 32), the Data Model Editor and the Layout Editor.

The Data Model Editor

The Data Model Editor (shown in Figure 33.1) is used to define all of the data elements that are to be included in the report. These data elements are queries, links, and miscellaneous columns that are organized into sets called *groups*. The Data Model Editor is operated using a set of iconic buttons that can be selected with the mouse.

On the left side of the window is a set of eight buttons used to create and modify the data elements. These buttons (top to bottom, left to right) are described in Table 33.1.

Table 33.1. Data Model Editor buttons.

Button	Usage
Select	Select data element(s) to be manipulated.
Query	Define report SQL queries.
Summary Column	Create column that will be computed based on a column at a lower level.

Button	Usage
Placeholder Column	Create a column that will be calculated in a PL/SQL procedure.
Magnify	Zoom in/out in the editor. Click within the editor to zoom in on an object, or click while holding the Shift key to zoom out.
Link Data	Create a logical link between separate database queries.
Formula Column	Create a column that will be calculated as the result of a PL/SQL function.
Cross Product	Define a matrix from two separate query groups. This button is used only for a special report called a matrix report.

FIGURE 33.1.

The Data Model Editor.

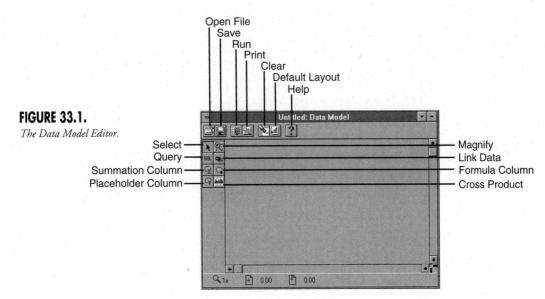

The buttons at the top of the editor window are used to perform functions that can also be found as functions in the menu. The first button is used to open an already existing report, and the next is used to save the current report. The next two buttons run the report (the user defines the output destination) and print the report directly to the default printer. The next button clears the selected objects from the editor canvas. The sixth button presents a dialog that is used to create the default layout based on the structure of the data model. Finally, the last button invokes the context-sensitive help facility within Oracle Reports.

The Layout Editor

The Layout Editor (shown in Figure 33.2) is used to construct the format for the report. The editor presents each of the layout elements exactly as it will appear on the final report. Like the Data Model Editor, the Layout Editor is controlled through a set of iconic buttons as well as from the menus. The buttons along the left side of the editor window are used to manipulate the layout objects. These buttons (top to bottom, left to right) are described in Table 33.2.

FIGURE 33.2.

The Layout Editor.

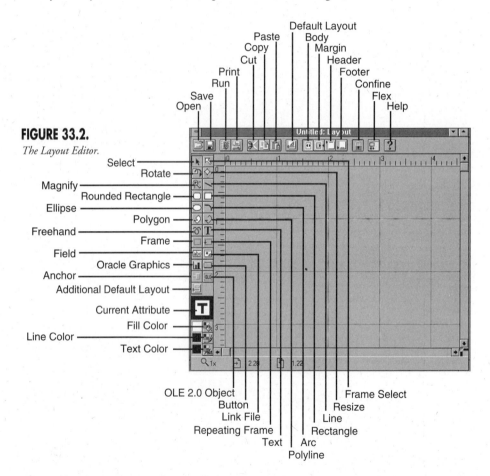

Table 33.2. Layout Editor buttons.

Button	Usage
Select	Select the object(s) to be manipulated.
Rotate	Rotate the object.

Button	Usage
Magnify	zoom in/out in the Editor. Click within the editor canvas to zoom in and click while holding the Shift key to zoom out.
Rounded Rectangle	Draw a rectangle with rounded corners.
Ellipse	Draw an ellipse or circle.
Polygon	Draw a multisided graphical object.
Freehand	Draw a freehand object while dragging the mouse.
Frame	Create a layout frame.
Field	Create a report field.
Oracle Graphics	Attach an Oracle Graphics Object to the report.
Anchor	Attach an object to another so that they will maintain the relative position from each other in the final report.
Additional Default Layout	Create an additional layout for the report.
Frame Select	Select all objects within a frame.
Reshape	Reshape object(s).
Line	Draw a line.
Rectangle	Draw a rectangle.
Arc	Draw a segment of a circle.
Polyline	Draw a series of connected lines.
Text	Insert constant text.
Repeating Frame	Create a repeating frame.
Link File	Attach an external file to the report.
Button	Create a button on the report.
OLE2 Object	Embed an OLE 2.0 object in the report.

Below the editor buttons is a square (with the letter T in the center of it) that displays the attribute characteristics of any objects on the Layout Editor canvas. This display indicates the fill color, outside line color, and the text color of the object—and can be changed with the palette selector buttons that appear directly below it.

At the top of the Layout Editor window is another series of iconic buttons for report control. The first four buttons (which are the same as the Data Model Editor) are Open File, Save File, Run Report, and Print Report. The next three buttons perform the standard Windows functions of cut, copy, and paste, whereby objects can be moved between the report and the clipboard. Next, the Default Layout button presents a dialog box for the designer to choose the data model columns to be included in the report, and based on the user-defined options and the report type selected, the default report will be created.

The next four buttons are used to select one of the four parts of the report that are to be edited. These parts in order are the body, margin, header, and footer. The body of the report is usually the main report and is the only essential part of the report that must be created. The margin is used to define items that should appear at the top or bottom of every report body page. The header is a page or set of pages that precede the report body, and the footer follows the report body. The header and footer are often used to present a summary of the information contained in the report body. Another use of these elements is to present the conditions that were used to define the report queries or to provide a banner page.

The next button in this window is used to toggle the Confine mode in the Layout Editor. By default, all objects within a frame cannot be moved outside of the parent frame unless the confine mode is off.

NOTE

The only time the confine mode should be turned off is during copy and paste operations or when the designer specifically needs to move an object to another level in the report. Otherwise, objects and frames could end up overlapping, which will cause indeterminate problems at runtime.

The next button is used to turn the Flex mode on and off. With the Flex mode on, whenever a frame is resized, all child objects within the frame will be resized accordingly. The last button is used to access the context-sensitive online help system.

Initializing the Reports Environment

Before you develop any reports, the development environment should be set up based on the individual preferences as well as any standards defined by the programming organization. Use the menu pick Tools | Options to present the Tools Options dialog box, as shown in Figure 33.3. This dialog box consists of three separate tabs, Preferences, Runtime Parameters, and Runtime Settings.

The Preferences tab is used to set the specific user preferences for the developer. These options define the parameters used by the Reports Designer. The first checkbox is used to disable PL/SQL compilation. Typically, Oracle Reports compiles each PL/SQL program unit it is closed. When you disable compilation, all program units will be compiled when the report is generated, thereby improving the performance of the tool while the report is being designed.

FIGURE 33.3.

Tools Options.

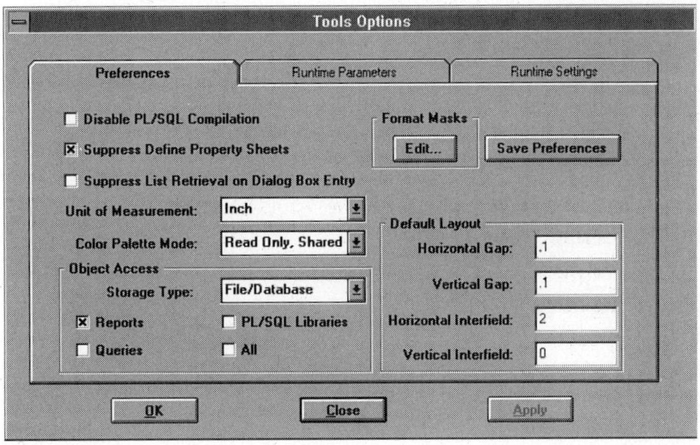

The next option, Suppress Define Property Sheets, is used to instruct the Reports Designer whether a property sheet should be automatically opened whenever an object is created. When this box is checked, the object will be created with a default name and the user must double-click the object to update the property sheet.

Next, the Suppress List Retrieval on Dialog Box Entry checkbox, prevents a list from being displayed whenever a database retrieval dialog box is selected. When suppressing the object list, the designer must know the exact name of the database object to be retrieved. This can be used as a security mechanism to prevent unauthorized access to a user's objects.

Next, a listbox is used to define the Unit of Measurement to be used in the Layout Editor. The individual options are centimeter, inch, and point. The unit of measure is used to define default sizes of the objects on the Layout Editor screen.

The Color Palette Mode is used to define how color palettes should be handled in Oracle Reports. The options for the list box are Editable, Read Only - Shared, and Read Only - Private. Editable means that the color palette of the active report will replace the system color palette causing the active report to be shown accurately while the appearance of any inactive reports may not be accurate. Read Only - Shared means that each report's color palette will be appended to the system palette until the space reserved for the palette becomes full. If any reports are then opened that use a different color palette, they might not appear accurately. Finally, Read Only - Private operates the same as shared mode except that Reports assures that the palette used is always valid for the active report and any inactive reports might not appear correctly because their color palettes have been cleared to make room for the new report. For the most part, these options are of minimal concern because reports will be printed typically in black and white or in a set of very basic colors.

The Object Access block of this form defines where report program modules will be stored. The storage may be defined as File, Database, or File/Database, and the tool may be used to access reports, PL/SQL Libraries, and/or queries.

The Preferences dialog may also be used to set up format masks that can be used to display data in the report. These format masks will then be available to the developer in the Layout Editor. The format for a field in the layout may also be defined at runtime; therefore, it is usually not necessary to define them here.

The last part of the Preferences box is the definition of the default layout parameters. The first two, Horizontal Gap and Vertical Gap, define the space between layout frames and displayed fields as defined by the value and the selected unit of measurement for the report. The most difficult aspect of working with Reports is the manipulation of frames and making sure that all elements are enclosed by the frames where they belong. A novice might want to use a relatively large gap value, whereas a more experienced user may use a smaller value.

> **NOTE**
>
> When working with character mode reports, the gap values are not used, resulting in frames and fields appearing to be exactly the same size. As a result, a complex character mode report can be very difficult to work with.

The horizontal and vertical interfield values are used to define the amount of whitespace that should appear between fields on a report. Setting these values to zero will cause the fields to be strung together with no whitespace between. Finally, these preferences can be saved by clicking the Save Preferences button next to the Format Mask edit button.

Creating a Report

To create a new report, either select File | New | Report from the menu or type Ctrl+E. This will create a report named "Untitled" in the Object Navigator. After the report is created, its properties should be defined using the Tools | Properties menu selection. The Report Properties dialog box (shown in Figure 33.4) defines the dimensions for the report. The first selection in this form is for the unit of measure for the report. Valid values are inch, centimeter, or point and represent the coordinate system to be used for the report. Next, the page height and width are defined based on the actual printable size of a page for the printer (typically 8 inches by 10.5 inches for most laser printers). The total size of the report is determined by multiplying these values by the logical page size of the report. In other words, if the report physical page size is 8 inches by 10.5 inches and the logical page size is 3 by 2 (as shown in Figure 33.5), the total logical page size would be 24 inches wide by 21 inches high.

FIGURE 33.4.

Report Properties dialog box.

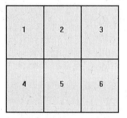

Untitled: Report Properties

| Report | Parameter Form | Character Mode | Comment |

Unit of Measurement: `Inch`

Page Width x Height: `8.5` x `11` inches

Logical Page Size: `1` x `1`

Maximum Body Pages: `10` x `10`

Maximum Header Pages: `10`

Maximum Trailer Pages: `10`

Panel Print Order: `Across/Down`

Direction: `Default`

OK   Close   Apply

FIGURE 33.5.

Logical pages versus physical pages.

1	2	3
4	5	6

TIP

To facilitate the design of a report that will use the default layout tool, you should specify the initial page width significantly wider than the actual physical size of the page. After the layout elements are properly resized and placed correctly, the page size may be adjusted to the proper values.

The remaining parameters for this form should be modified for only very special cases. The maximum pages parameters are used to define the maximum sizes of a logical page in the report. Next, the Panel Print Order is used for defining the order that multiple pages that define a logical page will be printed. A value of Across/Down would cause the physical pages in Figure 33.5 to be printed in the order 1, 2, 3, 4, 5, 6, whereas Down/Across would print in the order 1, 4, 2, 5, 3, 6. The final parameter in this form defines the direction that the layout objects are to be placed on the layout. By selecting Default, the objects will be added to the canvas according to the default direction of the NLS language being used by the developer. Other options may be selected as Left to Right or Right to Left.

Constructing a Tabular Report

The first and most basic report that can be developed using Reports is the tabular report. As shown in the example in Figure 33.6, the tabular report appears as a columnar listing of the selected rows. This report lists all of the warehouses for Down East Tackle with statistical information regarding shipments during the year 1995.

FIGURE 33.6.

Tabular report.

1995 WAREHOUSE PERFORMANCE REPORT
Down East Tackle, Inc.

W.H. Location	Total Ships	Avg Ship Delay	Max Ship Delay
Atwater, CA	26,868	4.1	9
Boise, Idaho	130,140	3.2	8
Shreveport, LA	32,563	6.7	16
Waltham, MA	31,840	3.6	12
Wharton, NJ	87,947	1.5	4

To build this report, create a new report using the menu pick File | New | Report. This will create a new report called "Untitled" in the Object Navigator. (When you initially enter Reports, a new report module is automatically opened.) After setting the development environment (set the global page width to > 20 inches using Tools | Properties), open the Data Model Editor using the Tools | Data Model Editor menu pick.

NOTE

The first step in building any report is the definition of the data elements that make up the report. In the case of this report, all data is supplied from a single query. Click the SQL icon (second from top on left side of Data Model Editor tool box) and create the query box on the canvas, as shown in Figure 33.7.

FIGURE 33.7.

Creating a query box.

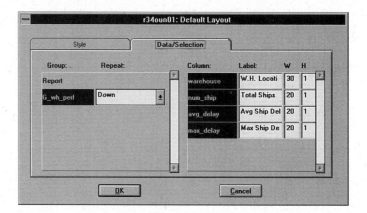

FIGURE 33.8.

Defining the query.

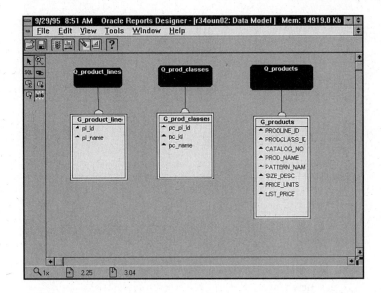

Double-click the newly created query box, thereby opening the query definition form, which can be filled in, as shown in Figure 33.8.

After you click the OK button within the Query Editor, a new box will appear in the Data Model Editor listing all of the columns that were generated by the select statement in the query. One data element will be defined for each column of the select statement, which will in turn be used to create the report columns. Double-click any of the columns to open the column definition form. For any columns that might result in null values, a default may be defined for the report (In this case, set avg_delay and max_delay equal to zero for this report.)

At this point, the report layout may be constructed using the default Layout Editor using the Tools | Default Layout menu pick. The first tab in this form displays six report types (click the Tabular report radio button), and the second is used to select which columns should be included in the report. On the second tab, make sure that all columns are selected (shown in inverse color) and modify the label and widths, as shown in Figure 33.9.

After you click the OK button in the default layout form, the Layout Editor will appear with the report shown in WYSIWYG (What You See Is What You Get) format. Note that the data columns all appear across a line with the appropriate headings above each column. Also note that the entire report is surrounded by two boxes (called *frames*). The outermost frame defines the query group belonging to the group in the data model. The inner frame is a special type called a repeating frame (designated with a downward-pointing triangle), which will repeat for every record returned by the query.

Each element can be resized and moved within the report using the mouse. For now, just make sure that all of the report columns and labels fit within a standard 8-inch wide page (allowing for margins) by dragging the item's sizing points with the mouse. Techniques for custom sizing and font selection are discussed later in this chapter.

FIGURE 33.9.
Default Report layout.

FALL 1995 PRICE LIST
Down East Tackle, Inc.

Catalog No	Product	Pattern	Size	Price Units	List Price
		FISHING LINE			
MONOFILAMENT LINES					
FLMF-000047-00-2#	Supra-Clear	N/A	2 # test	200 yds.	9.95
FLMF-000047-00-4#	Supra-Clear	N/A	4 # test	200 yds.	12.95
FLMF-000047-00-6#	Supra-Clear	N/A	6 # test	150 yds.	14.95
FLMF-000047-00-8#	Supra-Clear	N/A	8 # test	150 yds.	16.95
FLMF-000047-00-12#	Supra-Clear	N/A	12 # test	100 yds.	18.95
FLMF-000096-00-2#	Supra-Flex	N/A	2 # test	200 yds.	10.95
FLMF-000096-00-4#	Supra-Flex	N/A	4 # test	200 yds.	14.95
FLMF-000096-00-8#	Supra-Flex	N/A	8 # test	150 yds.	18.95
FLMF-000096-00-12#	Supra-Flex	N/A	12 # test	100 yds.	21.95
FLMF-008063-00-6#	Ultra-Vis	N/A	6 # test	200 yds.	9.95
FLMF-008063-00-10#	Ultra-Vis	N/A	10 # test	150 yds.	12.95
FLMF-008063-00-15#	Ultra-Vis	N/A	15 # test	100 yds.	14.95
KEVLAR BRAIDED LINES					
FLKB-001465-00-5#	Titan 2000	N/A	5 # test	100 yds.	24.95
FLKB-001465-00-10#	Titan 2000	N/A	10 # test	200 ft.	35.95
FLKB-001465-00-15#	Titan 2000	N/A	15 # test	200 ft.	40.95
FLKB-001465-00-20#	Titan 2000	N/A	20 # test	150 ft.	43.95
FLKB-001465-00-25#	Titan 2000	N/A	25 # test	150 ft.	45.95
FLKB-001465-00-30#	Titan 2000	N/A	30 # test	150 ft.	47.95
LEAD-CORE LINES					
FLLC-002311-00-12#	Deep 6	N/A	12 # test	300 yds.	24.95
FLLC-002311-00-18#	Deep 6	N/A	18 # test	250 yds.	30.95
FLLC-002311-00-25#	Deep 6	N/A	25 # test	200 yds.	35.95
FLLC-002311-00-35#	Deep 6	N/A	35 # test	150 yds.	40.95
FLLC-002311-00-45#	Deep 6	N/A	45 # test	100 yds.	45.95
		TERMINAL TACKLE			
CRANK BAITS					
TTCB-001958-03-1/6	Sebago Slider	Shad	1/6 oz	each	2.49
TTCB-001958-07-1/6	Sebago Slider	Tiger	1/6 oz	each	2.49
TTCB-001958-03-1/4	Sebago Slider	Shad	1/4 oz	each	2.79
TTCB-001958-07-1/4	Sebago Slider	Tiger	1/4 oz	each	2.79
TTCB-001958-07-1/2	Sebago Slider	Tiger	1/2 oz	each	3.29
TTCB-001958-03-1/2	Sebago Slider	Shad	1/2 oz	each	3.29
TTCB-000077-40-1/4	Cajun Mud Bug	Fall Craw	1/4 oz	each	2.29
TTCB-000077-39-1/4	Cajun Mud Bug	Spring Craw	1/4 oz	each	2.29
TTCB-000077-39-1/2	Cajun Mud Bug	Spring Craw	1/2 oz	each	2.79
TTCB-000077-40-1/2	Cajun Mud Bug	Fall Craw	1/2 oz	each	2.79
TTCB-000269-03-1/6	Harrison's Diving Plug	Shad	1/6 oz	each	2.99
TTCB-000269-03-1/4	Harrison's Diving Plug	Shad	1/4 oz	each	3.19
TTCB-000269-03-1/2	Harrison's Diving Plug	Shad	1/2 oz	each	3.49
SOFT PLASTICS					
TTPL-000843-93-3in	Slip Stick	Motor Oil	3 inches	50 pieces	1.19
TTPL-000843-44-3in	Slip Stick	Amber Glow	3 inches	50 pieces	1.19
TTPL-000843-03-3in	Slip Stick	Shad	3 inches	50 pieces	1.19

To complete the report, add the titles at the top of the page. In order to create the titles, select the Margins icon at the top of the Layout Editor page. After you click this button, the area above the report body will be visible and you will be unable to edit any of the report body. Select Format | Fonts from the menu and choose a large font for the report title. Create the title by choosing the Text icon from the Layout tool box and typing the report title at the top of the margin. To complete entry of a text item, click the mouse cursor outside of the text box. Similarly, the subtitle may be created using a slightly smaller font. Finally, position the title and subtitle at the center of the margin area and then click the report body icon to close the margin definition.

Run the report by choosing File | Run from the menu or by clicking the traffic light icon. The report may be executed directly to a printer, or be first sent to the screen or a file to be printed at a later time. Additionally, the report may be sent to another user via mail. A final destination option, Preview, should be used when the report is most likely going to be printed. This is because when a report is sent to the screen, the Windows fonts are used for display, but using preview causes the printer fonts to be used, which may be different. After you satisfied with the report, you can save it using the File | Save as menu pick.

Creating a Master-Detail Report

The Master-Detail report is a report that organizes the data according to specific break groups as shown in Figure 33.10. The price list is listed by product within a product class within a product line. Break groups are shown in the Data Model Editor as separate boxes containing the data columns belonging to the individual break group.

FIGURE 33.10.

Master-Detail Report with breaks.

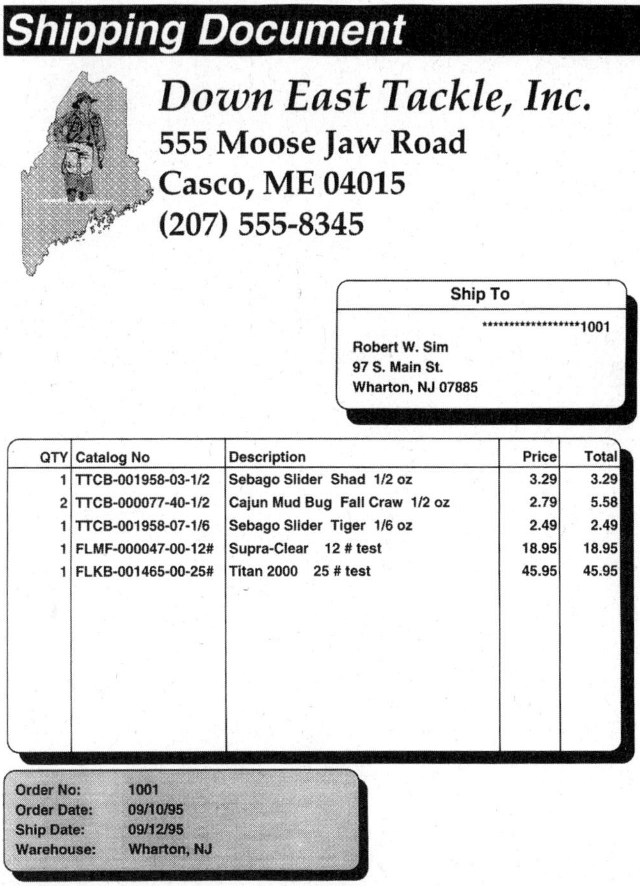

Shipping Document

Down East Tackle, Inc.
555 Moose Jaw Road
Casco, ME 04015
(207) 555-8345

Ship To
****************1001
Robert W. Sim
97 S. Main St.
Wharton, NJ 07885

QTY	Catalog No	Description	Price	Total
1	TTCB-001958-03-1/2	Sebago Slider Shad 1/2 oz	3.29	3.29
2	TTCB-000077-40-1/2	Cajun Mud Bug Fall Craw 1/2 oz	2.79	5.58
1	TTCB-001958-07-1/6	Sebago Slider Tiger 1/6 oz	2.49	2.49
1	FLMF-000047-00-12#	Supra-Clear 12 # test	18.95	18.95
1	FLKB-001465-00-25#	Titan 2000 25 # test	45.95	45.95

Order No:	1001
Order Date:	09/10/95
Ship Date:	09/12/95
Warehouse:	Wharton, NJ

Using Secondary Queries

One way to create break groups is to define secondary queries associated with the previous query so that for each record returned for a query, a second data selection will be performed to retrieve the related data. To build this report, once again create a new report and set the dimensions for the report using the Report Properties dialog box.

After the report has been created, create three separate query groups (shown in Figure 33.11).

FIGURE 33.11.

Defining multiple queries.

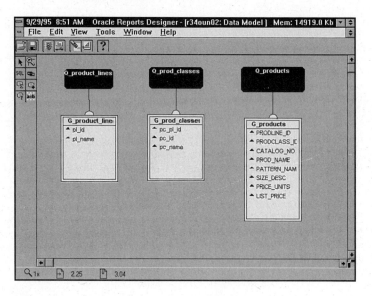

```
Query:    Q_product_lines
Text:     select pl_id, pl_name
            from product_lines
          order by pl_sequence

Query:    Q_prod_classes
Text:     select pc_pl_id, pc_id, pc_name
            from product_classes
          order by pc_sequence

Query:    Q_products
Text:     select i.item_pl_id              PRODLINE_ID,
              i.item_pc_id                 PRODCLASS_ID,
              i.item_pl_id||i.item_pc_id||
              '-'||ltrim (to_char (i.item_prod_no, '099999'), ' ')||
              '-'||ltrim (to_char (i.item_cp_no, '09'), ' ')||'-'||
              i.item_size_code             CATALOG_NO,
              p.prod_name                  PROD_NAME,
              c.cp_name                    PATTERN_NAME,
              s.size_desc                  SIZE_DESC,
              i.item_price_units           PRICE_UNITS,
              i.item_price                 LIST_PRICE
```

```
      from items i,
           products p,
           color_patterns c,
           sizes s
           where i.item_pl_id = p.prod_pl_id
             and i.item_pc_id = p.prod_pc_id
             and i.item_prod_no = p.prod_no
             and i.item_cp_no = c.cp_no
             and i.item_size_code = s.size_code
    order by p.prod_sequence, i.item_price
```

After the three queries are established as separate groups in the data model, they must be linked together to specify the relationship between each query element. To do this, select the data link tool in the Data Model Editor (appears as two overlapping ovals) and move the mouse to the pl_id column in the G_product_line group. Hold the left mouse button down, drag the mouse to the pc_pl_id column in the G_prod_classes group, and release the mouse button. A line will now appear connecting the two query groups; at runtime, the select statement for the second query will be modified to include the data relationship. Repeat the same process to connect the third query to the second by establishing links between pc_pl_id and PRODLINE_ID and between pc_id and PRODCLASS_ID. The resulting data model is now shown in Figure 33.12.

FIGURE 33.12.

Linking related secondary queries.

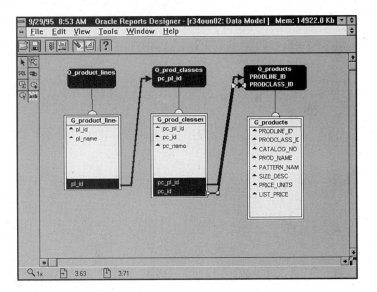

To create the Master-Detail report layout, choose Master-Detail in the Default Layout tool and select all data columns except for the ID values in the report. Click the OK button and the Layout Editor will appear with the initial Master-Detail report. As in the previous example, two frames are created for each group in the report. Also, note that an extra frame has been created representing the column headings for the G_products group.

As shown in the example, however, the column headings should appear only at the top of each page. To do this, the frame containing the headings must be moved to the outermost frame of the report. One of the key features of Reports 2.5 is that the Layout Editor does not allow the designer to move an object outside of its enclosing frame under default operation. To move the frame out of the G_products enclosing frame, first click on the Confine button (appears as a padlock) at the top of the Layout Editor window. Now, using the Frame Select tool, click on the frame containing the headings and drag it out of the report frame altogether. Now, you can resize and reposition the remaining objects toward the bottom of the report frame to make room for the column headings at the top of the outermost frame. Now, the column headings frame may be repositioned to the top of the report. The final result should look like that shown in Figure 33.13.

FIGURE 33.13.

Master-Detail report layout.

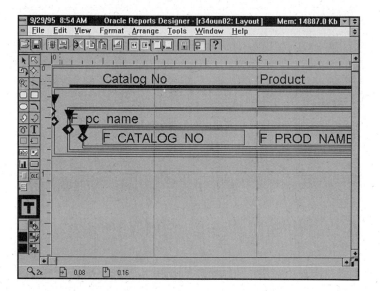

To complete the report, click the Margin icon and add the title and subtitle. This report can now be run as explained in the previous example and then saved in a file or to the database.

Adding Report Break Levels

The previous report example illustrates how to connect secondary related queries; however, it is usually preferable to retrieve all data in a single query, especially in a client/server environment.

In the previous example, suppose that the first query retrieved 10 rows of data in blocks that can hold up to 50 rows of data, and the second and third queries also retrieved the same amount of data in similar blocks. In its most simple form, 111 requests would be sent to retrieve 1110 rows of data in 111 blocks. This results in a total of 222 blocks being communicated across the network. Now, suppose that the same data can be retrieved in a single query that will return 1000 rows in blocks that can hold approximately 16 (one third of 50) rows of data each. The resulting network traffic would be a single request with 63 blocks returned with the 1000 rows of data or a total of 64 blocks across the network—a performance gain of over 70 percent! When this savings is combined with the time required to process each request, the savings can be quite substantial for a lengthy report.

To create this report based on a single query, again create a new report by first setting up the page and defining a query in the Data Model Editor. The query named Q_products should read as this:

```
select pl.pl_sequence                          LINE_SEQ,
       pl.pl_name                                LINE_NAME,
       pc.pc_sequence                            CLASS_SEQ,
       pc.pc_name                                CLASS_NAME,
       i.item_pl_id||i.item_pc_id||'-'||
       ltrim(to_char(i.item_prod_no,'099999'),' ')
       ||'-'||ltrim(to_char(i.item_cp_no, '09'),' ')||'-'||
       i.item_size_code                          CATALOG_NO,
       p.prod_name                               PROD_NAME,
       c.cp_name                                 PATTERN_NAME,
       s.size_desc                               SIZE_DESC,
       i.item_price_units                        PRICE_UNITS,
       i.item_price                              LIST_PRICE
  from product_lines pl,
       product_classes pc,
       items i,
       products p,
       color_patterns c,
       sizes s
 where pl.pl_id = pc.pc_pl_id
   and pc.pc_id = p.prod_pc_id
   and i.item_pl_id = p.prod_pl_id
   and i.item_pc_id = p.prod_pc_id
   and i.item_prod_no = p.prod_no
   and i.item_cp_no = c.cp_no
   and i.item_size_code = s.size_code
 order by p.prod_sequence, i.item_price
```

When the query is entered and accepted, a box will appear in the Data Model Editor showing all of the queried columns. Using the mouse, select the CLASS_SEQ column in the column box and then drag it to the right of the column box; then release the mouse button to create a new break box, as shown in Figure 33.14.

FIGURE 33.14.

Creating report breaks.

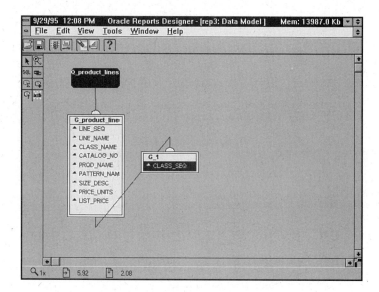

Using the mouse, drag the new box to align it with the original query columns box and then resize it to allow additional columns to be added to the box. Then, drag the other columns (except LINE_SEQ and LINE_NAME) into the new break box. Repeat the process by creating a third break box with CLASS_SEQ and CLASS_NAME remaining in the second break box. When completed, the data model will appear as shown in Figure 33.15.

The report layout can then be created with the default layout tool, as illustrated in the previous example for secondary queries.

FIGURE 33.15.

The completed break report data model.

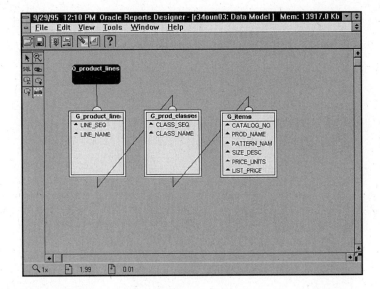

Customizing Reports with Boilerplate Text and Graphics

The reports that have been explored in this chapter thus far utilize the powerful, intelligent default capabilities of Oracle Reports 2.5. Many times, however, it becomes necessary to enhance the report with explanatory text and graphical objects. The Shipping Document report displayed in Figure 33.16 is an example of a report that has been customized with special boilerplate text and other graphical objects.

To build this report, create a new report, and this time define the page size as 8 inches wide by 10.5 inches high. Within the data model, create the query as shown here:

```
select o.order_no                                             ORDER_NO,
       c.cust_no                                              CUST_NO,
       c.cust_name                                            CUST_NAME,
       c.cust_address                                         ADDRESS,
       c.cust_city||', '||c.cust_state||' '||c.cust_postal_code  CITY,
       o.order_date                                           ORDER_DATE,
       o.order_ship_date                                      SHIP_DATE,
       wh.wh_name                                             WAREHOUSE,
       oi.oi_qty                                              QTY,
       i.item_pl_id||i.item_pc_id||'-'||
       ltrim (to_char (i.item_prod_no, '099999'), ' ')||'-'||
       ltrim (to_char (i.item_cp_no, '09'), '  ')||'-'||
       i.item_size_code                                       CATALOG_NO,
       p.prod_name||'  '||
       decode (cp.cp_name, 'N/A', null, cp.cp_name)||'  '||
       s.size_desc                                            PRODUCT,
       i.item_price                                           PRICE,
       i.item_price * oi.oi_qty                               ITEM_TOTAL
```

```
  from products p,
       sizes s,
       color_patterns cp,
       items i,
       customers c,
       warehouses wh,
       order_items oi,
       orders o
 where p.prod_pl_id = i.item_pl_id
   and p.prod_pc_id = i.item_pc_id
   and p.prod_no = i.item_prod_no
   and cp.cp_no = i.item_cp_no
   and s.size_code = i.item_size_code
   and i.item_no = oi.oi_item_no
   and oi.oi_order_no = o.order_no
   and wh.wh_code = o.order_wh_code
   and c.cust_no = o.order_cust_no
   and o.order_no = 1001
```

FIGURE 33.16.

Boilerplate text and graphics.

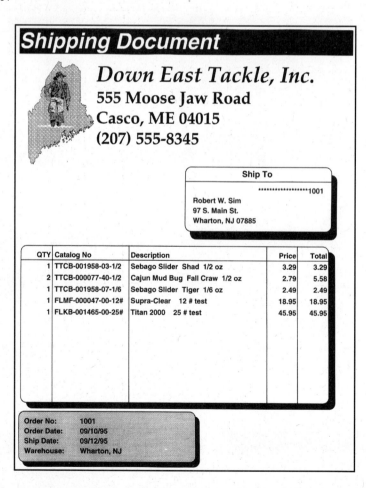

Shipping Document

Down East Tackle, Inc.
555 Moose Jaw Road
Casco, ME 04015
(207) 555-8345

Ship To

******************1001

Robert W. Sim
97 S. Main St.
Wharton, NJ 07885

QTY	Catalog No	Description	Price	Total
1	TTCB-001958-03-1/2	Sebago Slider Shad 1/2 oz	3.29	3.29
2	TTCB-000077-40-1/2	Cajun Mud Bug Fall Craw 1/2 oz	2.79	5.58
1	TTCB-001958-07-1/6	Sebago Slider Tiger 1/6 oz	2.49	2.49
1	FLMF-000047-00-12#	Supra-Clear 12 # test	18.95	18.95
1	FLKB-001465-00-25#	Titan 2000 25 # test	45.95	45.95

Order No:	1001
Order Date:	09/10/95
Ship Date:	09/12/95
Warehouse:	Wharton, NJ

Create a break at the order item level and separate the data columns as shown in Figure 33.17. At this point, select the Layout Editor from the Tools menu, and the blank canvas will be displayed. Because no margin information is needed for this report, select the margins with the Margin icon button and drag the top and bottom of the report body box to the top and bottom of the page, respectively. By resizing the margins, the report body can use the entire printable page for the report.

FIGURE 33.17.

Defining breaks for Shipping Document report.

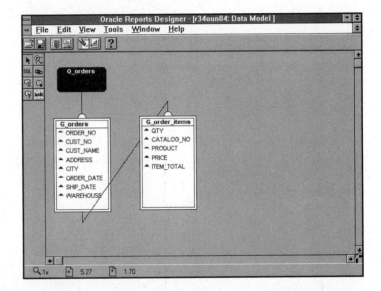

> **NOTE**
>
> For some reports, it might be necessary to construct a title area or footer area that is larger than the default ½ inch. By resizing the report body, the developer can enlarge or shrink the margins.

Once the report body has been resized, the report is laid out manually. Select the Frame tool and create a frame that is nearly the same size as the entire report body. Within this frame, create a repeating frame that is about the same size as the first frame. Double-click in the repeating frame to set its properties using the dialog box shown in Figure 33.18. Change the name of the frame to R_orders and set the source for the frame to G_orders. Also, make sure that only one order will be printed on a page by setting the maximum records per page to 1.

Next, the document title should be created at the top of the report. First, select the font to be used for the title bar using the Tools | Font menu option. Using the Font dialog box, shown in Figure 33.19, select the Arial font with the style Bold Italic and size 36 points. (Note that when a font is selected, a sample of the text appears within the dialog box, showing how the font will look.) When the font is selected, press the OK button to select the font.

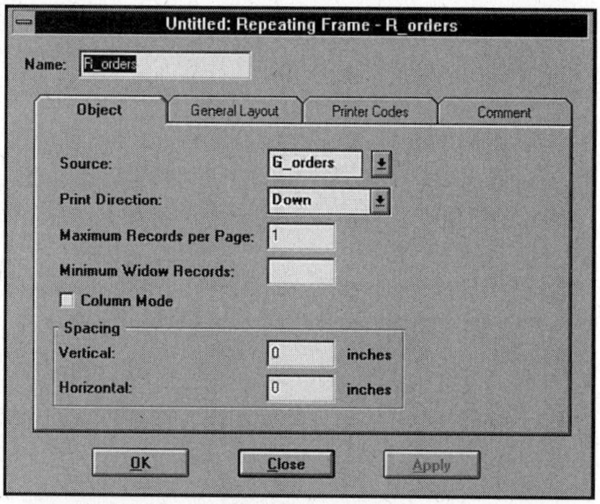

FIGURE 33.18.

The Repeating Frame dialog box.

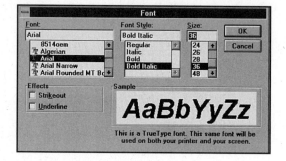

FIGURE 33.19.

The Font dialog box.

Using the Text tool, click within the Layout Editor canvas and type Shipping Document in the box that appears. After the text has been entered, click outside the textbox to complete the entry. Modify the attributes of this boilerplate text by choosing a black fill with white text. Resize the text by holding down the Shift key while clicking the mouse within the R_orders frame and then selecting the Tools | Size Objects menu option to display the dialog box. As shown in Figure 33.20, select the Largest radio button under Width to adjust the size of the text to match the enclosing frame.

FIGURE 33.20.

The Size Objects dialog box.

At this point, position the title bar by selecting the Tools | Align Objects menu option. Select to align these objects to each other as well as to align them by the horizontal center, as shown in Figure 33.21.

FIGURE 33.21.

The Align Objects dialog box.

To add the company logo, choose the Link File tool and drag a box at the appropriate position on the report. An × will appear on the canvas where the object is created. Double-click this object to present the External Boilerplate dialog box. (See Figure 33.21.) Change the name of the object to B_logo and select Image for the object format; then enter the filename for the logo image (in this case, downeast.tif). Click the OK button, and the graphics image appears on the report canvas.

FIGURE 33.22.

Linking an external graphics image file.

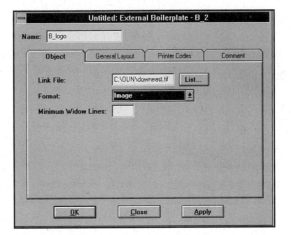

The company name and address header should then be added to the report with the Text tool and positioned next to the logo. For this example, the company name is created with a different font than the address, and the two objects can be aligned with the Align Objects tool. This heading is then joined as a single group by typing Ctrl+G or using the Arrange | Group menu option.

Next, lay out the remaining report sections by creating three frames on the report canvas as containers for the remaining report objects. These frames correspond to the boxes that appear on the report and serve as containers for the enclosed information. Therefore, the default properties for the frames do not need to be modified in any way. To create the boxes, select the Rounded Rectangle tool and drag a rectangle within the appropriate frame. When the mouse button is released, the object appears as a rectangle with rounded corners. Select the fill palette to fill the rectangle with black. Copy the rectangle to the Clipboard with Ctrl+C (or you can use the Edit | Copy menu option or the iconic button) and then paste it back to the canvas with the Ctrl+V key combination. Using the mouse, drag the new box above and to the left of the previous box and change the box's fill pattern to white (or gray for the order data). The object now appears as a rounded box with a drop shadow.

To draw the remaining graphical lines, select the Line tool and draw horizontal and vertical lines as needed. Make sure that the lines are exactly the same size as the boxes and that they are properly aligned with the edge of their respective boxes.

> **TIP**
>
> One technique that works well (and saves a lot of time and frustration) is to create the lines smaller than needed and then use the Size Objects and Align Objects dialog boxes to adjust the lines properly. When using the Align Objects tool, the alignment direction determines where the objects are located. For example, if the horizontal alignment is left, the objects will be positioned to align with the left edge of the leftmost object on the canvas, depending on the container frames and confine mode in operation. Also, the Stack and Distribute options are extremely useful for aligning the objects against each other or for spacing them evenly, respectively.

The remaining heading text and field prompts can then be added using the Text tool in the boxes as needed. Use the exhibit as a guideline to complete the boilerplate text.

The form layout is now complete, and the query data may be added to the form to finish the report. So far, all of the information that has been placed in the report is contained within the R_orders repeating frame, which is associated with the G_orders data block. Therefore, the data for this block can be added directly to the report using the Field tool. In the Order Data box at the bottom of the report, drag a box that will hold the order number field, ORDER_NO. This box will be created with an F_1 appearing within the box. Double-click this field to display the Object Properties dialog box for this object. As shown in Figure 33.23, change the name of the object to F_order_no and select ORDER_NO as the data source for this column.

FIGURE 33.23.

*The Layout Field
dialog box.*

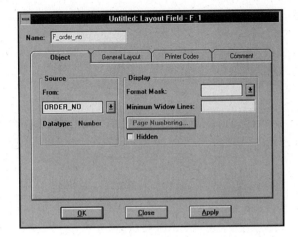

To complete the report data for this block, create fields for order_date, ship_date, and warehouse in the Order Data box, and create fields for cust_no, cust_name, address, and city in the Ship To box.

To associate data with a record group, a repeating frame must be created and associated with its appropriate data group. Unfortunately, because no boilerplate objects may intersect with a frame that does not entirely close it, five separate repeating frames need to be created within the Items box so that they do not intersect the separating lines. These frames, which should be associated with the G_order_items group, should be the same size and aligned at the top. Within each of these frames, create the appropriate layout field and set its properties as needed.

This completes the shipping document report, which may be saved as needed.

Working with Summary and Formula Columns

So far this chapter has only explored the display and manipulation of data retrieved directly as the result of a query. One of the most powerful features of Reports 2.5 is its ability to provide client-side computations to deliver added functionality to the reporting environment. An example of a report that includes these types of computations is shown in Figure 33.24.

In the previous example, the line total was calculated by the query and returned with the other report data. This value, which is the product of QTY and PRICE, can be calculated by Reports instead. In addition, it would be useful for the report to update the inventory levels for each item as it is included in the shipping document. To make this possible, the query must be modified to return the warehouse and item identifiers and to remove the item_total from the query. The resulting query is shown here:

```
select o.order_no                                              ORDER_NO,
       c.cust_no                                               CUST_NO,
       c.cust_name                                             CUST_NAME,
       c.cust_address                                          ADDRESS,
       c.cust_city||', '||c.cust_state||' '||c.cust_postal_code CITY,
       o.order_date                                            ORDER_DATE,
       o.order_ship_date                                       SHIP_DATE,
       wh.wh_code                                              WH_CODE,
       wh.wh_name                                              WAREHOUSE,
       oi.oi_qty                                               QTY,
       i.item_no                                               ITEM_NO,
       i.item_pl_id||i.item_pc_id||'-'||
       ltrim (to_char (i.item_prod_no, '099999'), ' ')||'-'||
       ltrim (to_char (i.item_cp_no, '09'), ' ')||'-'||
       i.item_size_code                                        CATALOG_NO,
       p.prod_name||' '||
       decode (cp.cp_name, 'N/A', null, cp.cp_name)||' '||
       s.size_desc                                             PRODUCT,
       i.item_price                                            PRICE
  from products p,
       sizes s,
       color_patterns cp,
       items i,
       customers c,
       warehouses wh,
       order_items oi,
       orders o
 where p.prod_pl_id = i.item_pl_id
   and p.prod_pc_id = i.item_pc_id
   and p.prod_no = i.item_prod_no
   and cp.cp_no = i.item_cp_no
   and s.size_code = i.item_size_code
   and i.item_no = oi.oi_item_no
   and oi.oi_order_no = o.order_no
   and wh.wh_code = o.order_wh_code
   and c.cust_no = o.order_cust_no
   and o.order_no = 1001
```

FIGURE 34.24.
A report with computational fields.

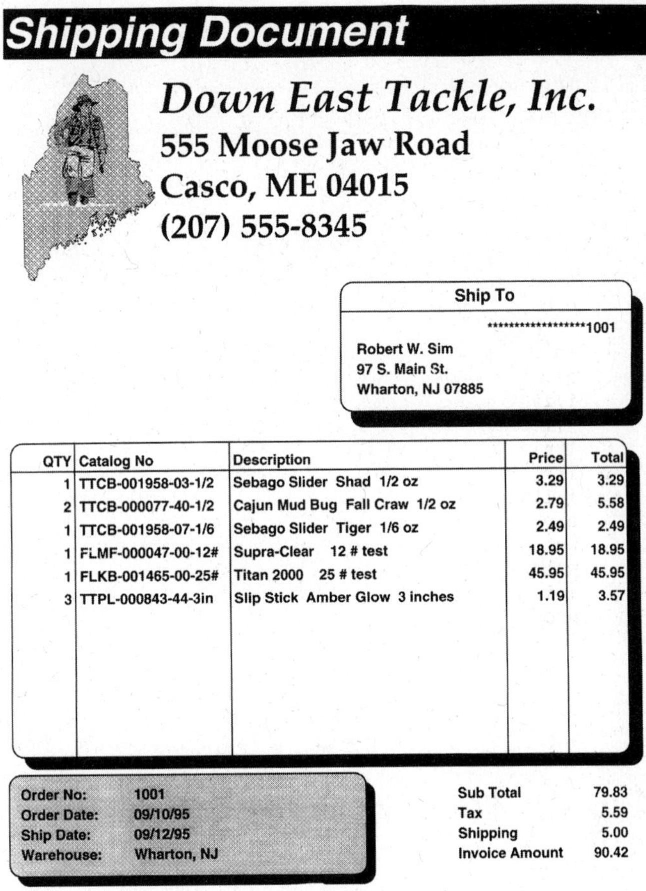

Shipping Document

Down East Tackle, Inc.
555 Moose Jaw Road
Casco, ME 04015
(207) 555-8345

Ship To
******************1001
Robert W. Sim
97 S. Main St.
Wharton, NJ 07885

QTY	Catalog No	Description	Price	Total
1	TTCB-001958-03-1/2	Sebago Slider Shad 1/2 oz	3.29	3.29
2	TTCB-000077-40-1/2	Cajun Mud Bug Fall Craw 1/2 oz	2.79	5.58
1	TTCB-001958-07-1/6	Sebago Slider Tiger 1/6 oz	2.49	2.49
1	FLMF-000047-00-12#	Supra-Clear 12 # test	18.95	18.95
1	FLKB-001465-00-25#	Titan 2000 25 # test	45.95	45.95
3	TTPL-000843-44-3in	Slip Stick Amber Glow 3 inches	1.19	3.57

Order No:	1001	Sub Total	79.83
Order Date:	09/10/95	Tax	5.59
Ship Date:	09/12/95	Shipping	5.00
Warehouse:	Wharton, NJ	Invoice Amount	90.42

To create the item_total column, open the Data Model Editor, select the Formula Column tool, and then click within the G_order_items group. A column, designated CF_1, is added to the group. Double-click the column name, and the column definition dialog box appears. Change the name of the column to item_total and define it as a numeric column with 10 character positions (digits). To set up the formula for this column, click the Edit button to open the PL/SQL Editor. In order to view the entire editor, click the OK button for the column. This editor provides an area to create PL/SQL functions and procedures for the report. For this field, enter the text as it appears in Figure 33.25. Note that references to report columns are accomplished by preceding the column name with a colon (:).

FIGURE 33.25.

Creating a formula column.

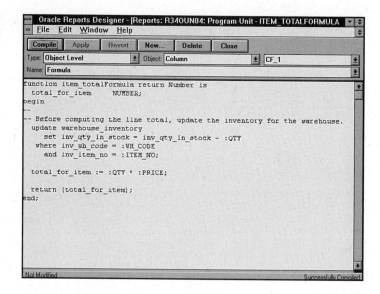

The buttons that appear across the top of the editor perform the functions outlined in Table 33.3.

Table 33.3. The PL/SQL Editor buttons.

Button	Function
Compile	Checks the syntax of the program unit.
Apply	Applies any changes to the report. This function has been included for compatibility with Reports 2.0.
Revert	Restores the program unit to its contents at the time of the last compile or apply function.
New	Creates a new program unit.
Delete	Deletes this program unit.
Close	Closes the PL/SQL Editor window.

The next field needed for this report is the subtotal, which is calculated as the sum of all the item totals. To create this column, use the Summary Column tool and click within the G_orders group. Double-click this new column to display the Summary Column dialog box, shown in Figure 33.26. Modify the name to order_total and choose the sum function (other functions include avg, min, max, and so on); then select item_total as the data source and reset at the G_orders group.

FIGURE 33.26.
Summary Column dialog box.

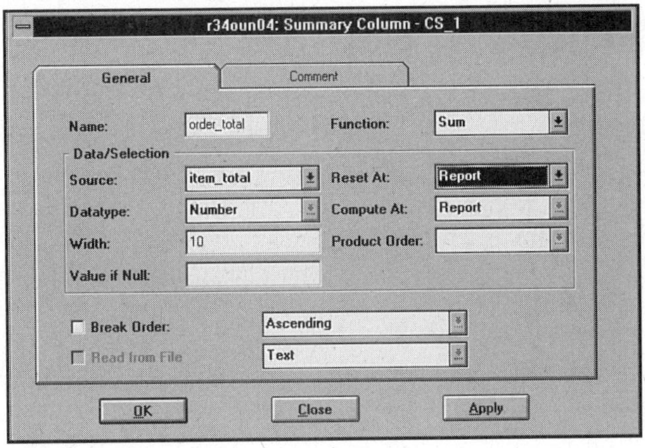

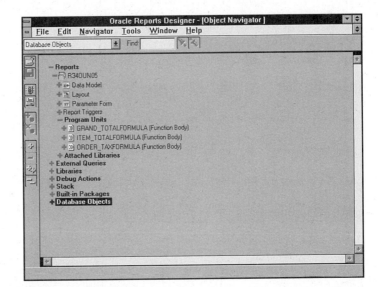

The tax is computed in a formula column as 0.07 * order_total and the invoice_amount is also calculated as order_total + tax + 5 (the shipping cost is assumed to be $5.00 for all orders). To complete the report, open the Layout Editor, double-click the F_item_total field and assign it to the new item_total data source. Create a frame at the lower right of the page to contain the summary fields, and then create the appropriate boilerplate text and fields as needed. (For the format mask for each of these fields, enter 990.00. This is explained in the following section.)

To work with existing program units for a report, expand the program units category in the Object Navigator, as shown in Figure 33.27. To edit any one of these program units, double-click the page icon to the left of each program unit name.

FIGURE 33.27.
Displaying existing program units.

Formatting Reports

The reports discussed up to this point display the data exactly as it appears in the database. Typically, however, it is necessary to apply special formatting to the individual fields or frames within a report. This type of formatting can be used to change how a field appears or whether the field or frame appears at all. Also, there may be a desire to prevent partial report groups from being split on two pages or for a report to break automatically whenever a value changes. Figure 33.28 illustrates an example of how to apply special formatting to an existing report.

FIGURE 33.28.

Report formatting techniques.

FALL 1995 PRICE LIST
Down East Tackle, Inc.

Catalog No	Product	Pattern	Size	Price Units	List Price
		FISHING LINE			
MONOFILAMENT LINES					
FLMF-000047-00-2#	Supra-Clear		2 # test	200 yds.	9.95
FLMF-000047-00-4#	Supra-Clear		4 # test	200 yds.	12.95
FLMF-000047-00-6#	Supra-Clear		6 # test	150 yds.	14.95
FLMF-000047-00-8#	Supra-Clear		8 # test	150 yds.	16.95
FLMF-000047-00-12#	Supra-Clear		12 # test	100 yds.	18.95
FLMF-000096-00-2#	Supra-Flex		2 # test	200 yds.	10.95
FLMF-000096-00-4#	Supra-Flex		4 # test	200 yds.	14.95
FLMF-000096-00-8#	Supra-Flex		8 # test	150 yds.	18.95
FLMF-000096-00-12#	Supra-Flex		12 # test	100 yds.	21.95
FLMF-008063-00-6#	Ultra-Vis		6 # test	200 yds	9.95
FLMF-008063-00-10#	Ultra-Vis		10 # test	150 yds.	12.95
FLMF-008063-00-15#	Ultra-Vis		15 # test	100 yds.	14.95
KEVLAR BRAIDED LINES					
FLKB-001465-00-5#	Titan 2000		5 # test	100 yds.	24.95
FLKB-001465-00-10#	Titan 2000		10 # test	200 ft.	35.95
FLKB-001465-00-15#	Titan 2000		15 # test	200 ft.	40.95
FLKB-001465-00-20#	Titan 2000		20 # test	150 ft.	43.95
FLKB-001465-00-25#	Titan 2000		25 # test	150 ft.	45.95
FLKB-001465-00-30#	Titan 2000		30 # test	150 ft	47.95
LEAD-CORE LINES					
FLLC-002311-00-12#	Deep 6		12 # test	300 yds.	24.95
FLLC-002311-00-18#	Deep 6		18 # test	250 yds.	30.95
FLLC-002311-00-25#	Deep 6		25 # test	200 yds.	35.95
FLLC-002311-00-35#	Deep 6		35 # test	150 yds.	40.95
FLLC-002311-00-45#	Deep 6		45 # test	100 yds.	45.95
		TERMINAL TACKLE			
CRANK BAITS					
TTCB-001958-03-1/6	Sebago Slider	Shad	1/6 oz	each	2.49
TTCB-001958-07-1/6	Sebago Slider	Tiger	1/6 oz	each	2.49
TTCB-001958-03-1/4	Sebago Slider	Shad	1/4 oz	each	2.79
TTCB-001958-07-1/4	Sebago Slider	Tiger	1/4 oz	each	2.79
TTCB-001958-07-1/2	Sebago Slider	Tiger	1/2 oz	each	3.29
TTCB-001958-03-1/2	Sebago Slider	Shad	1/2 oz	each	3.29
TTCB-000077-40-1/4	Cajun Mud Bug	Fall Craw	1/4 oz	each	2.29
TTCB-000077-39-1/4	Cajun Mud Bug	Spring Craw	1/4 oz	each	2.29
TTCB-000077-39-1/2	Cajun Mud Bug	Spring Craw	1/2 oz	each	2.79
TTCB-000077-40-1/2	Cajun Mud Bug	Fall Craw	1/2 oz	each	2.79
TTCB-000269-03-1/6	Harrison's Diving Plug	Shad	1/6 oz	each	2.99
TTCB-000269-03 1/4	Harrison's Diving Plug	Shad	1/4 oz	each	3.19
TTCB-000269-03-1/2	Harrison's Diving Plug	Shad	1/2 oz	each	3.49

To explore the techniques discussed in this section, open the report r34oun03.rdf, built during the discussion of creating break groups. The first formatting concept illustrates how to define the displayed format for a field value (this was briefly mentioned in the last section) and is shown in Figure 33.29. Double-click the LIST_PRICE field in the Layout Editor to present this box. Enter 9990.00 in the Format Mask field. This causes the number to be displayed with all leading zeroes suppressed up to and including tens. (For example, the number 3000 will be displayed as 3,000.00, while the value .63 will display as 0.63.) There are many different masks that can be applied to a field, and these can be found by selecting Help from within Reports and doing a search on *format mask*.

FIGURE 33.29.

Setting field format masks.

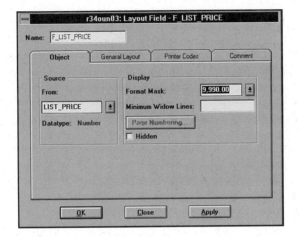

To suppress a field from displaying, the developer can create a format trigger for the field, as illustrated in Figure 33.30. This button can be accessed using the General Layout tab in the Layout Field property sheet (double-click field in Layout Editor). The illustrated example suppresses the pattern name if the value is equal to 'N/A'. The text to suppress this display is shown here:

```
function F_PATTERN_NAMEFormat_Trigger return boolean is
begin
   if :PATTERN_NAME = 'N/A' then
       return (FALSE);
   else
       return (TRUE);
   end if;
end;
```

FIGURE 33.30.

Creating a report trigger.

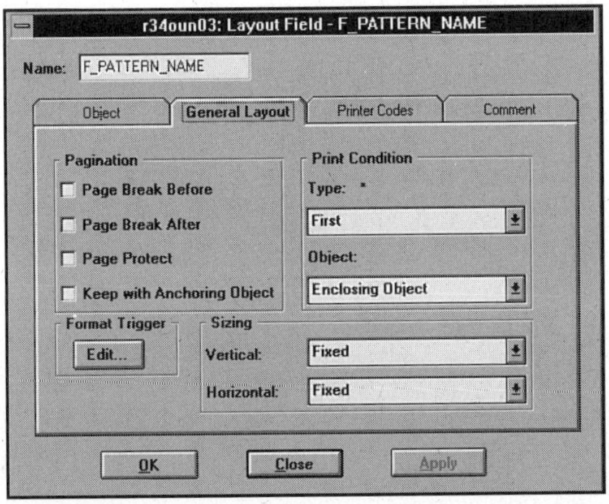

Finally, to prevent the product class groups from being split between two pages, double-click the R_prod_class repeating frame to display the property sheet, and then select the General Layout tab. (See Figure 33.31.) Select the Page Protect check box and click the OK button to cause the entire group to print on a single page.

FIGURE 33.31.

Page-protecting data groups.

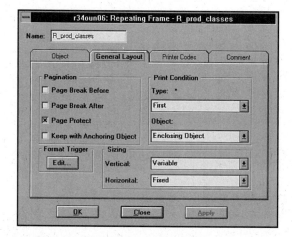

Other options are Page Break Before, Page Break After, and Keep with Anchoring Object. The first two options are fairly obvious, while the third is not. Multiple items in a report are typically implicitly anchored in that it is usually implied that an object will maintain the same relative position from its surrounding objects. When there are many objects nearby, Reports infers the position of any object using an arbitrary algorithm (which may cause any object to print improperly). To secure the position of an object, use the Anchor tool to connect a child (*dependent*) object to its parent (*fixed*) object.

Finally, to cause a report to execute a page break every time the value changes, use the Object tab of the repeating frame to set the maximum records per page to 1.

Exploring Complex Reports

In addition to the reports previously discussed, Oracle Reports provides the capability to create several special report types. These special reports include a mailing label report, form letter report, and matrix report.

The Mailing Label Report

The mailing label report (shown in Figure 33.32) is used to print address labels on special paper, which is usually perforated to print labels for multiple address records. (This particular example was printed with a report page size of 8 inches wide and 2.5 inches tall to illustrate the concepts for the report.)

FIGURE 33.32.

Mailing Label Report.

To build this report, create a new report with the proper page size for the label paper. In the Data Model Editor, create a simple query from the customers table as shown here:

```
select cust_no,
     cust_name,
     cust_address,
     cust_city||', '||nvl (cust_state, cust_country)||
          ' '||cust_postal_code   city
from customers
     order by cust_no
```

After the query has been created, select the Default Layout tool, select mailing label as the report type, delete all column headings in the Data Selection tab, and then click the OK button. The label will be formatted with all the fields within the label. Double-click the repeating frame to display the property sheet shown in Figure 33.33. Make sure that the print direction is selected as Down/Across, and then click the OK button. This causes the labels to be printed along the left side of the page until the bottom of the page; they will be continued in the next column from the top, and so on, until the page is filled.

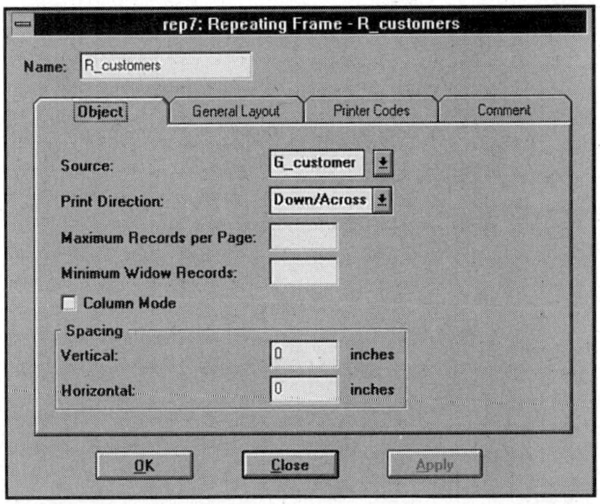

FIGURE 33.33.

A mailing label Repeating Frame property sheet.

The Form Letter Report

The form letter report (see Figure 33.34) applies database data to a specific text format.

FIGURE 33.34.

Sample form letter report.

Down East Tackle, Inc.
555 Moose Jaw Road
Casco, ME 04015

Robert W. Sim
97 S. Main St.
Wharton, NJ 07885

Dear Robert W. Sim:

We are pleased to inform you that your credit application has been accepted with Down East Tackle, Inc. As you are aware, our company is one of the leading manufacturers of quality specialty fishing equipment. We have set your initial credit limit at $1000.
This limit will be adjusted accordingly as you establish a credit history with our company.

If you have any questions regarding your account please feel free to contact Mr. O'Brien in our Credit Services department at (207)555-8632. Please refer to account number 1001 when making any inquiries.

Sincerely,

John T. O'Brien
Credit Manager

To build this report, create a new report using the following data model query:

```
select cust_no,
      cust_name,
      cust_address,
      cust_city||', '||nvl (cust_state, cust_country)||
            ' '||cust_postal_code city,
cust_credit_limit
   from customers
   where cust_no = 1001
```

After the query has been entered, select Form Letter style from the Default Layout tool and click the OK button. The resulting report layout appears in Figure 33.35. The field boxes that appear within the report frame are hidden when the report is run. The values in the fields can be displayed using the &fieldname lexical parameter embedded in the text of the letter.

To create the letter text, select the Text tool and click within the report frame. The actual letter can then be typed within the box. Any time a report column is needed in the report, it may be included by specifying the layout field name with an ampersand (&) preceding the layout name. For example, the customer number is specified as &F_cust_no.

FIGURE 33.35.
The form letter layout.

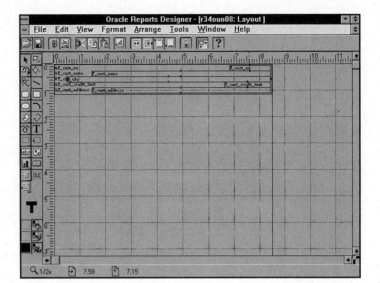

The Matrix Report

A matrix report appears like a columnar report, except that the column headings are retrieved as part of the database query. An example of a matrix report is shown in the warehouse shipments report in Figure 33.36.

FIGURE 33.36.
A sample matrix report.

Down East Tackle, Inc.
Warehouse Shipments by Month

	JAN	FEB	MAR	APR	MAY	JUN	JUL	AUG	SEP	OCT	NOV	DEC	
Atwater, CA	606	401	3,581	5,213	7,542	4,609	1,533	996	711	511	302	863	26,868
Boise, Idaho	6,083	4,219	40,626	33,842	8,503	6,768	6,873	7,681	4,925	3,551	2,536	4,533	130,140
Shreveport, LA					9,287	4,255	3,928	3,801	3,144	2,655	2,588	2,905	32,563
Waltham, MA	1,257	803	7,866	6,532	4,342	2,155	2,057	1,996	1,507	1,057	923	1,345	31,840
Wharton, NJ	4,583	2,051	17,537	14,555	10,512	8,543	7,933	6,544	4,521	4,261	2,052	4,855	87,947
	12,529	7,474	69,610	60,142	40,186	26,330	22,324	21,018	14,808	12,035	8,401	14,501	309,358

This report groups the data horizontally, based on the values in the matrix columns. In cases where no data exists (such as the Shreveport warehouse in this example), the column will appear as blank unless the developer specifies a default value if the field is null.

To create this report, modify the system parameter ORIENTATION to have a default value of Landscape and define the page as 10.5 inches wide by 8 inches high. In the Data Model Editor, define the following query:

```
select w.wh_name                    WAREHOUSE,
       h.hist_month_no              MONTHNO,
       to_char (to_date (to_char (h.hist_month_no),
                'MM'),'MON')        RPT_MONTH,
```

```
        h.hist_ord_shipped                      SHIPS
  from warehouses w,
       warehouse_history h
  where w.wh_code = h.hist_wh_code
     and h.hist_year = 1994
```

This query results in four data columns in the G_history group. Separate this group into three distinct groups and position the groups as shown in Figure 33.37. Next, select the Cross-Product tool to draw a box around the two matrix groups, as shown, and name the matrix group G_matrix.

FIGURE 33.37.

A matrix report data model.

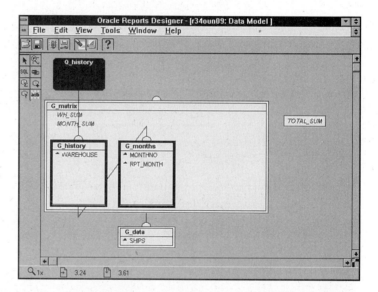

The month number has been included within the query so that the months may appear in calendar order rather than in alphabetical order (which would be the default without a sequence column).

To complete the data model, create total columns for each month and warehouse as well as a total for the entire report. The report total is created the same way as any total is created outside the data groups—by clicking in a blank area of the data model canvas. To create the matrix totals, select the Summary Column tool and click *inside the title area of the matrix group box.* The WH_SUM summary column will appear within the matrix box; its properties should be modified to summarize SHIPS, to reset at the G_history group, and to set the product order at the G_history level as well. The MONTH_SUM should be based on the G_months group.

Finally, to complete the report layout, select Matrix as the style from the Default Layout tool, delete all column headings from the data selection window, and then deselect the month_no column. To cause the month names to appear across the top of the report, change the repeat direction to Across. Click the OK button to generate the default layout, which will look similar to the one shown Figure 33.38.

FIGURE 33.38.

The matrix report layout model.

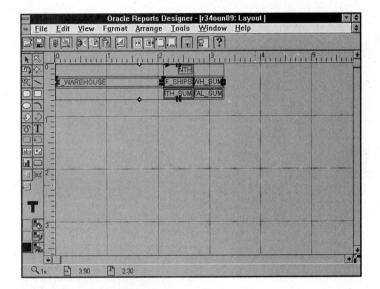

Creating Dynamic Reports

As a final concept, this chapter will describe techniques for producing reports that define their queries based on runtime selections by the operator. This feature can be used through dynamic query parameters for runtime modification of a query with lexical constructs.

Using Dynamic Query Parameters

The developer can define a user parameter for a report that defines the query. To accomplish this, open the r34oun05.rdf (shipping document with summary columns) report that was created earlier. Select the User Parameters heading in the Object Navigator and create a new user parameter using the Add Object tool at the left of the Object Navigator window. The new user parameter will appear under the User Parameters heading, as shown in Figure 33.39.

Double-click the icon to the left of this parameter to display the properties sheet for the parameter. (See Figure 33.40.) Change the name of the parameter to P_order_no and define it as numeric with a maximum width of 15 digits. To ensure that a valid entry has been made, create a validation trigger as follows:

```
function P_ordernoValidation_Trigger return boolean is
   checkval    VARCHAR2(1);
begin
   select 'x'
      into checkval
      from orders
    where order_no = :P_order_no;
   return (TRUE);
exception
   when NO_DATA_FOUND then
      srw.message (1001, 'A valid order number must be entered.');
      return (FALSE);
end;
```

FIGURE 33.39.

User parameter creation.

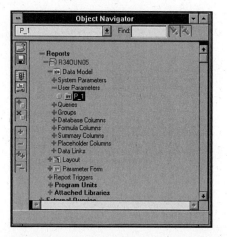

FIGURE 33.40.

The user parameter Property definition dialog box.

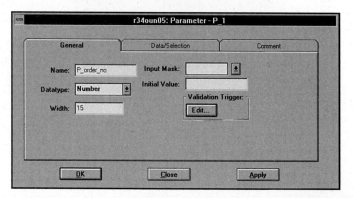

The query should then be modified to use :P_order_no instead of the hard-coded value that originally existed. The new report will present a default parameter form at run-time, where the user may enter a valid order number to produce a shipping document. If an invalid order number is entered, Oracle Reports presents the error message shown in Figure 33.41.

FIGURE 33.41.

The validation error message box.

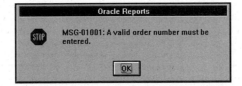

Defining Run-Time Queries with Lexical Parameters

The report query can be modified at run-time using lexical parameters. A lexical parameter is a placeholder column containing the actual text to be used in a query. To illustrate this concept, open the matrix report that was built earlier. For this report, create a parameter for the report year and a parameter for the user to enter one of the following values, depending on the data preference:

Function	Data Value
SUM	Monthly total orders shipped
AVG	Average shipping delay by month
MAX	Maximum shipping delay by month

Also, create the appropriate validation triggers for the individual parameters.

Next, create a placeholder column at the report level called SELECTION_DATA. Set this field as a character field with a width of 100 characters and assign a default value of h.hist_ord_shipped. Next, create a before report trigger as follows:

```
function Before_Report_Trigger return boolean is
begin
   if :P_REPORT_TYPE = 'SUM' then
      :SELECTION_CRITERIA := 'h.hist_ord_shipped';
   elsif :P_REPORT_TYPE = 'AVG' then
      :SELECTION_CRITERIA := 'h.hist_ship_days / h.hist_ord_shipped';
   else
      :SELECTION_CRITERIA := 'h.hist_max_days';
   end if;
end;
```

Finally, the query should be modified as this:

```
select w.wh_name              WAREHOUSE,
       h.hist_month_no    MONTHNO,
       to_char (to_date (to_char (h.hist_month_no),
                         'MM'),'MON') RPT_MONTH,
       &SELECTION_CRITERIA
from warehouses w,
       warehouse_history h
   where w.wh_code = h.hist_wh_code
     and h.hist_year = :P_year
```

The lexical parameter is referenced in the query using an ampersand before the parameter name. Lexical parameters within a query substitute the text stored in the parameter directly into the query. For this reason, when using a lexical parameter, a default value must be entered for NULL values to assist with compilation in the designer.

Top Ten Tips for Oracle Reports 2.5

Oracle Reports 2.5 is a powerful tool that can be used to generate useful reports against Oracle databases. While there are no hard and fast rules regarding how the tool should be used, experience has borne out a number of useful tips that make a developer's utilization of this tool much easier:

- Attempt to layout the report on paper. This will assist with the development of the data model as well as the final layout. Understand where subtotals should be provided to create the data breaks up front.

- When the default layout is used, define the page size to be excessively wide. The data columns can then be resized and repositioned to fit within the printable page.

- If possible, formulate the data retrieval in a single query. Experience has shown that a single, somewhat inefficient query can perform better than several dependent well-tuned queries.

- Complete the data model before attempting to finalize the layout. The addition of a single column in a query might necessitate a redesign of the layout and thus a misuse of time.

- When adding an additional break level to an existing report, 90 percent of the time it is faster to redo the default layout. Adding another intermediate level frame is one of the most difficult tasks to be done. It can be done, but is often not worth the effort.

- Rather than trying to resize or reposition objects in the Layout Editor, use the Size Objects and Align Objects tools. Several columns can be selected at once and all made the same custom size quickly, and they can be aligned and spaced with minimal effort.

- To lock the relative position of multiple objects, select them and create a group to join them together.

- Use the Magnify tool to zoom in to view the relative positions of the objects or to zoom out to view the total report structure.

- When you make a mistake in the editor, use the Edit | Undo menu option to reverse the action rather than trying to correct it with the mouse.

- Before running any report, save it in a file to make sure that it can be recovered. Also, save different versions to facilitate recovery.

Summary

This chapter explored several techniques for developing Oracle Reports. Due to the limitations of space available, some of the simpler features might have been glossed over. Also, as with any powerful application development tool, there are many ways to produce the same result. Hopefully enough material has been presented to give you a fairly extensive understanding of this product.

It has been my experience that the only way to truly learn a tool such as this is through repetitive practice and experimentation. I encourage you to expand on this material to gain the expertise necessary to use this tool knowledgeably and efficiently.

Oracle Graphics 2.5

34

by Joe Zafian

An old adage states that "A picture paints a thousand words." This adage is certainly evident in many executive information systems. By being able to view database trends graphically, an Oracle database user is better able to make decisions based on this data. Oracle Graphics 2.5 is used to graphically display database information.

You can run Oracle Graphics 2.5 to display data charts from the Oracle database; however, this tool is used primarily as a graphical server that can present Oracle data within other compatible applications such as Oracle Forms or Oracle Reports. This chapter explains how to create graphs and charts of Oracle data. These charts will encompass many of the available chart types and techniques that can be used to create highly useful displays of graphical data.

The Oracle Graphics Environment

Like Oracle Forms and Oracle Reports, Oracle Graphics is designed to operate in a graphical user interface (GUI) environment such as Microsoft Windows. You can perform functions either by selecting them from a menu or by clicking an iconic button. The Oracle Graphics Designer consists of two primary components: the Object Navigator (described in Chapter 31) and the Layout Editor.

The Layout Editor

The Layout Editor (shown in Figure 34.1) presents a canvas that will contain the charts as they are created. You operate this tool by using iconic buttons and menu picks. You use the buttons along the left side of the Layout Editor window to create and manipulate the chart layout objects. These buttons (top to bottom, left to right) are described in Table 34.1.

Table 34.1. Layout Editor buttons.

Button	Usage
Select	Select object(s) from canvas.
Magnify	Zoom in/out in Layout Editor. Click on the canvas to zoom in at the mouse location. Click while holding the Shift key to zoom out.
Rectangle	Draw a rectangle.
Ellipse	Draw an ellipse or circle.
Polygon	Draw a multi-sided object.
Rounded Rectangle	Draw a rectangle with rounded corners.
Chart	Add a new chart to the layout.
Symbol	Insert a chart symbol.
Rotate	Rotate the object.

Button	Usage
Reshape	Reshape the object.
Line	Draw a line.
Arc	Draw an arc segment.
Polyline	Draw a series of connected lines.
Freehand	Draw in freehand mode.
Text	Insert text.
Field	Insert a text field.

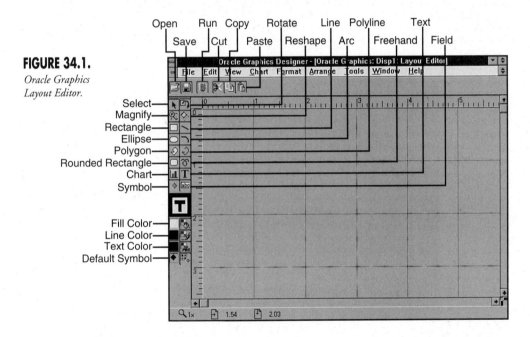

FIGURE 34.1.

Oracle Graphics Layout Editor.

Below these iconic buttons there is a square that displays the current visual attribute for the selected item (or the default, if no object is selected). This display indicates the fill color, line color, and text color for the object. Below the display is a series of three palette controls that you use to adjust the visual attribute. The fourth button in this area defines the current symbol to be used for charts that display a symbol.

At the top of the Layout Editor window is another series of iconic buttons that are used for module control. The first two buttons open an existing chart and save the current chart. The next button is used to start up the runtime simulator to test the operation of the graphics module as it would operate in production. The last three buttons are used to cut, copy, and paste layout objects between the display and the Windows clipboard.

Initializing the Graphics Environment

To utilize the features of Oracle Graphics and to ensure compatibility with other tools, Oracle Graphics enables you to initialize the designer environment based on a set of personal (and possibly departmental) preferences. To configure Oracle Graphics, select the Tools Options dialog box by selecting Tools | Tools Options from the menu.

The Oracle Graphics 2.5 options are defined in two tabs. The first tab, Defaults, defines the parameters for charts that will be created in the Graphics Designer; the first field defines the copyright message that will appear on the charts. This dialog box is shown in Figure 34.2.

FIGURE 34.2.

The Oracle Graphics default options dialog box.

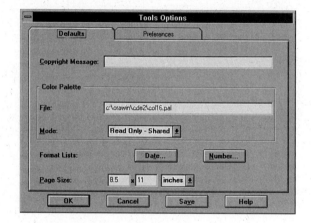

In the next field in the Defaults tab, you set the color palette file to be used for the chart. (The example shown uses Oracle's sixteen-color palette, which is the recommended setting for most applications.) You use Color Palette Mode to define how color palettes should be handled in Oracle Graphics. The options for the list box are Editable, Read Only - Shared, and Read Only - Private. Editable means that the color palette of the active chart will replace the system color palette. This shows the active chart accurately while the appearance of any inactive charts might not be accurate. Read Only - Shared means that each chart's color palette will be appended to the system palette until the space reserved for the palette becomes full. If any charts that use a different color palette are then opened, they might not appear accurately. Finally, Read Only - Private operates the same as shared mode except that Graphics ensures that the palette used is always valid for the active chart; any inactive charts might not appear correctly because their color palettes have been cleared to make room for the new chart.

The Date and Number buttons are used to establish format masks for dates and numeric fields in Oracle Graphics. You can then use these masks throughout the designer to display data.

The last set of fields on the Defaults tab define the default page width and height and the unit of measure for the chart.

The second tab in the Tools Options dialog box is used to define the user preferences in the designer (see Figure 34.3). You can set the Startup options to automatically create a new blank display, prompt for an existing display, or do nothing whenever the Graphics Designer is started. If the checkbox in this block is selected, Oracle Graphics Designer will prompt you to log in to the database whenever the Designer is started.

FIGURE 34.3.

The Oracle Graphics Preferences dialog box.

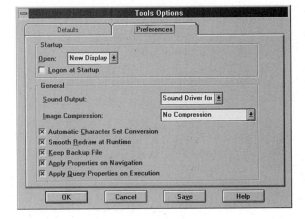

Under the General options box, the Sound Output option is based on the sound drivers that have been installed in the operating environment. (These drivers are installed in the Control Panel for Microsoft Windows 3.1.) Image Compression determines how graphical objects will be stored in the graphics file. If you select No Compression, the resulting file will be larger; however, when you select Compression, the application will run slower as the image is decompressed.

The last six options in the Preferences tab define the way Oracle Graphics will operate in the Designer and during runtime operation. Checking Automatic Character Set Conversion causes Oracle Graphics to automatically convert the character set used by Oracle Graphics to the default set based on the National Language Support (NLS) setting for the user. You would need to select this option when you develop an application for international use. Smooth Redraw at Runtime instructs Graphics to redraw any "damaged" screen areas in an internal memory buffer before the screen is updated. This option can reduce flickering and should be used unless there are memory problems.

The Keep Backup File option makes Oracle Graphics copy the graphics file to a backup (extension .bak) before saving the new version. The last two options, Apply Properties on Navigation and Apply Query Properties on Execution, instruct Oracle Graphics to apply any changes to the display whenever the developer navigates out of the object. Otherwise, the developer will be prompted to apply the changes before navigation is allowed.

Creating a New Display

As stated in the previous section, you can configure Oracle Graphics to automatically open a new blank display upon startup. However, if you need to create a new display after startup, you can do so by selecting File | New | Display from the Designer menu or using the Ctrl+N shortcut key. A new blank display will be created in the Object Navigator according to the preferences defined in the Tools Options dialog box.

Defining Displays

A *display* is the basic modular unit for Oracle Graphics. Within a display, a chart or set of charts comprises the functional module that makes up an Oracle Graphics application unit.

Creating a Pie Chart

A pie chart presents data from several sources to indicate the portion that each contributes to the total for all sources. As shown in Figure 34.4, the Warehouse Shipments chart shows the relative percentage of shipments for a single warehouse for a single year.

FIGURE 34.4.

The Warehouse Shipments pie chart.

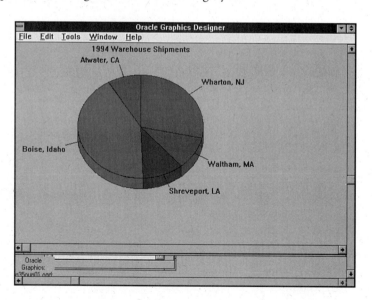

You can create a new chart in Oracle Graphics using either a one-step or two-step method. To use the one-step method, first click the mouse within the Layout Editor canvas to activate the editor and then select Chart | Create Chart from the menu. A query dialog box will appear that will enable you to name and create a new query to select data for the pie chart. Using this box, create the query, Q_performance, as shown in Figure 34.5.

FIGURE 34.5.

Creating a new chart query.

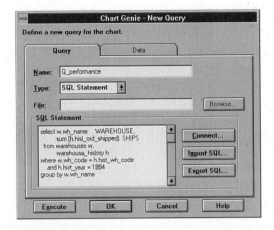

> **NOTE**
>
> In addition to creating an Oracle Graphics chart using an embedded query, you can use data from external programs such as Microsoft Excel (SYLK file format) or Lotus 1-2-3 (WKS file format), as well as from a .PRN output file. Also, an Oracle select statement stored in an operating system external SQL file can be used to retrieve data for your chart.

After you create the query, the developer can test it by clicking the Execute button at the bottom of the dialog box. (Note: You can use the Connect button to connect to the database if you have not yet done so.) The results of the query are shown in the second tab of the New Query dialog box. When you are satisfied with the query, click OK to view the Chart Properties dialog box.

The Chart Properties dialog box (shown in Figure 34.6) is used to define how the data from the query will be laid out on the presentation canvas. To create the pie chart, enter the chart name and title as shown. Define the format for the chart by selecting the type and subtype icon for the chart you want. For this chart, first select the pie chart type (second row, left), and then select the pie chart with depth subtype (far right). The format you select will be stored as a template that you can name within the display for any additional charts that might be needed (the default is template#).

After the chart layout is completed, click OK to display the chart on the Layout Editor canvas. (You might have to drag the chart from the edge of the canvas to view the entire chart.) At this point, you can save the chart to the file system (or database) by selecting File | Save As from the menu. Save this chart as g34oun01.odg.

FIGURE 34.6.

The Chart properties sheet.

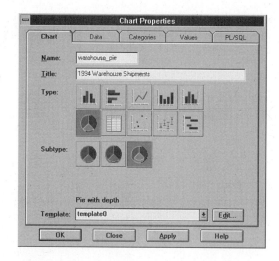

Creating a Columnar Chart

A columnar chart displays related data in a series of vertical filled bars. As shown in Figure 34.7, the Monthly Shipments chart displays the number of orders shipped each month for a warehouse.

FIGURE 34.7.

The Monthly Shipments columnar chart.

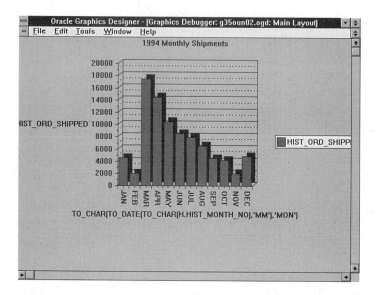

To create this chart using the two-step method, click the mouse within the Object Navigator and select the Queries category. Using the iconic buttons at the left of the Object Navigator, click the Add Object icon to create a new query. In the first tab of the Query Properties dialog box, define the new query with the name Q_mly_ships as:

```
select to_char ( to_date (to_char (hist_month_no), 'MM'), 'MON'),
          hist_ord_shipped
    from warehouse_history
    where hist_year = 1994
    and hist_wh_code = 'WNJ'
  order by hist_month_no
```

To build the columnar chart, activate the Layout Editor and select the Chart tool from the Graphics tool palette. Using this tool, drag a region for the chart on the layout canvas. This action will cause the Chart Genie dialog box to appear, enabling you to define the data source for the new chart, as shown in Figure 34.8. For this example, select the Existing Query radio button and choose the query, Q_mly_ships, that was previously defined.

FIGURE 34.8.

*Assigning a query for
a new chart.*

Define the layout for the chart using the Chart Properties dialog box as shown by selecting the Columnar Chart type (top row, left) and the Columnar Chart with Shadow subtype (top row, right). When you are satisfied with the chart, save it as g34oun02.ogd.

Other Chart Types

Oracle Graphics 2.5 provides the functionality to create ten types of charts, with further sub-type delineation, to define a total of 56 different chart formats. The first chart type is the column chart that was shown in the previous section. In its most basic form, a simple column chart consists of a series of filled rectangles indicating a value based on the height of the bar. Oracle Graphics has variations of the columnar chart for charts that present data that can be grouped in subcategories. (An example would be shipments for all warehouses for each month.) These variances include columns with stacked bars (the individual bars are stacked on top of each other to indicate the totals for the category), columns with overlapping bars (the individual bars overlap within the group), and columns with percent scaling (each segment shows the percentage that each bar contributes to the total 100 percent).

The column with baseline at zero is a chart subtype for negative data values. A column chart with shadows displays the bars in a three-dimensional background—the bar shadow shows behind the bars. A column chart with depth presents each bar as a 3-D object in a multidimensional background. The last column chart subtype, column with connecting lines, displays the bars with a solid line connecting the tops of each bar.

The next chart type is the bar chart. This chart displays the data in a series of horizontal bars. The same variations are available for the bar chart as in the case of the column chart.

The next set of chart formats is the line chart and its variations. These chart subtypes can be classified in three major subcategories.

- Line—straight lines connecting the individual data points
- Step—a horizontal line is drawn at the data point and vertical lines connect the individual point values
- Curve—a smooth curve is drawn through the data points

Within each of these subcategories, you can choose to show symbols at each data point. You also can show multiple data entities as additive values on the same chart as individual stacked lines or as stacked lines with a solid fill between the line and the horizontal axis or prior line.

The next chart type enables you to create a chart that shows two different data values as a mixture of columns and lines. Typically, this report will indicate discreet data values on each column and the line would be used to indicate summary or trend data. The standard mixed chart presents a simple column chart with a straight line chart on the same grid. You can vary the way this chart type appears by using either a straight or curved line with or without fill.

The last chart type on the top line is called the Double-Y chart. This chart provides a y-axis on both sides of the chart. Column chart variations are either a simple column or a column with overlapping bars. Line chart variances enable you to use a simple line or a line chart with symbols.

The next chart type is the pie chart, which was presented as the first chart type created. You can create either a pie chart with a shadow below it or one with depth, which appears as a 3-D object. The table chart presents the data in a tabular format with the same optional effects that exist for the pie chart.

The next type is the scatter chart, which displays data on the chart as individual points in a two-dimensional coordinate system. Typically, you can use this chart type in engineering applications to display scientific data points. Options enable you to use a regression line that approximates a straight line formula for the data. You can include a grid in the chart to facilitate reading the data values. The chart can also be displayed using a logarithmic y-axis or with both axes using a logarithmic scale. Finally, you can draw the chart with lines connecting the individual data points in the order that they are retrieved.

The next chart type, the high-low chart, is typically used to analyze data values related to values that can fluctuate within a short interval, such as stock prices over time. For each horizontal data point, there is a high value and a low value as well as (in some cases) a closing (or ending) value. The simple high-low chart indicates the high value and low value with a horizontal tick mark at each position and a vertical line connecting the two points. Variations show a closing value symbol. You can indicate the high and low value using spikes (vertical line only) rather than separate tick marks. The next subtype connects the closing values with a line. The last subtype connects consecutive data points with a fill line between the high and low values.

The final chart type is a Gantt chart. A Gantt chart is a special chart type that is used to indicate data over a specified time interval. This chart is typically used in project management to present the time schedule needed to accomplish individual tasks for the project. You can vary how this chart looks by using a background shadow or a 3-D bar to show depth.

Defining Parameters for Charts

The charts created earlier in this chapter depend on the query conditions that are defined in the query definition dialog box. In practice, however, many graphical applications need the user to execute the query based on a variable parameter that is defined at runtime. Depending on the value entered, the chart will be drawn dynamically by changing the data in the chart at runtime, based on the selection criteria entered by the user.

Using the columnar chart created earlier in module g34oun02.ogd, modify the chart to execute the query based on a user-specified parameter for the warehouse code and the chart year. To create a parameter, select Parameters within the Object Navigator to display the Parameters dialog box as shown in Figure 34.9. Define this parameter as a character field named P_WH_CODE with an initial value of WNJ. (Give the initial value as a valid value to help you develop the graphical display.) Additionally, create a numeric parameter called P_YEAR for the chart year.

FIGURE 34.9.

Creating graphics parameters.

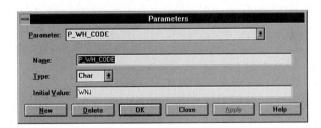

Next, modify the chart query to include the parameters as follows:

```
select to_char ( to_date (to_char (hist_month_no), 'MM'), 'MON'),
    hist_ord_shipped
from warehouse_history
where hist_year = :P_YEAR
and hist_wh_code = :P_WH_CODE
```

The chart will now use the value of the parameter at runtime to display the appropriate chart. To test the runtime capabilities of Oracle Graphics, you must first create a runtime module. (The module must be saved prior to creating the runtime module. Save this module as g34oun03.ogr.) To create the runtime module, select File | Administration | Generate, and then create the module as g34oun03.ogr. To test the interactive capability of the module, use the following command:

```
g25run module=g34oun03 userid=uid/pwd P_WH_CODE='ACA' P_YEAR=1994
```

Multiple Chart Applications

Oracle Graphics provides the capability to create individual displays that are based on multiple charts that are linked through parameters. One example of a multiple chart application is a drill-down chart, which displays a secondary chart based on data passed from one chart to the next. In other cases, a second chart can be included within the same application to display additional related data on separate chart layers.

Creating a Drill-Down Chart

A drill-down chart is a multi-chart application in which an individual chart is dependent on another linked chart. One example of this chart is shown in Figure 34.10; the two charts that were created previously are combined in a single display. By clicking on an individual pie segment, the user will make the monthly shipments chart indicate the orders shipped for the warehouse associated with the segment.

FIGURE 34.10.

A sample drill-down chart.

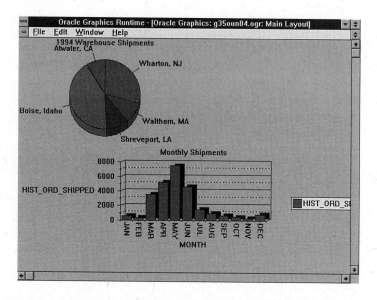

To create this chart, open the Warehouse Shipments pie chart that was created earlier in module g34oun01.ogd. Create parameters for the warehouse code and year as in the previous section and create the monthly shipments query within the Object Navigator. Modify the pie chart query to include the year parameter and to select the warehouse code from the initial query.

Navigate to the Layout Editor and use the chart drag points for the pie chart to resize the chart to provide room for the monthly shipments column chart.

Now, using the Chart tool from the Graphics tool palette, drag an area for the new column chart in a blank area of the Layout Editor. Define the column chart the same as in g34oun02, when you created the column chart.

To link the two charts in a drill-down relationship, click within the pie chart area to select the pie chart and then click one of the pie segments. This will present the object definition property sheet. Select the Drill-down tab as shown in Figure 34.11. This tab is used to define the drill-down relationship for the charts. You define the relationship by selecting the parameter that will hold the value for the query. For this chart, select the P_WH_CODE parameter and set it equal to the value of the WH_CODE. Finally, set the drill-down relationship to execute the query for the monthly shipments chart.

FIGURE 34.11.

Creating a drill-down relationship.

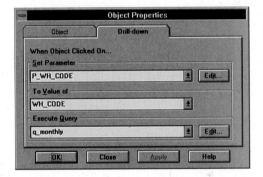

You can now test this chart by clicking the Run icon in the Layout Editor. Notice how the monthly chart changes based on the pie segment selected. You can now save this module as g34oun04.

Creating a Multilayer Chart

Another type of multichart application is operated by presenting a single chart at a time based on user interaction. To do this, you can create charts on separate layers and coordinate them through the use of buttons or other interface elements. Typically, multilayer charts are used to display different aspects of related data on separate chart layers. The example that you will create in this section displays the total shipments, average shipping delay, and maximum shipping delay for a given warehouse by month.

To create this display, define the parameters and query to retrieve the data for all three charts in a single query as follows:

```
select to_char (to_date (to_char (hist_month_no), 'MM', 'MON') "Month",
    hist_ord_shipped "Shipments",
    hist_ship_days / hist_ord_shipped "Average Delay",
```

```
        hist_max_days "Maximum Delay"
from warehouse_history
where hist_year = :P_YEAR
and hist_wh_code = :P_WH_CODE
order by hist_month_no
```

In the Layout Editor, create a chart for the total shipments by month. Define this chart as a column chart with shadow as in module g34oun02.ogd. This time, however, before you finish the chart select the Values tab from the Chart Properties dialog box, as shown in Figure 34.12. As shown in this figure, the available data columns are shown in the left box on the property sheet and the box on the right displays the columns that will be used for the chart. Use the Insert and Delete buttons to set up the selection as shown in the figure. Now the chart will display only the monthly shipments.

FIGURE 34.12.

Selecting the value column for a chart.

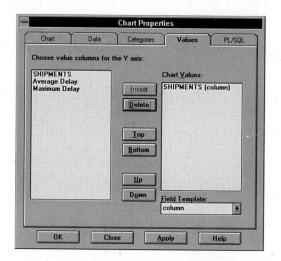

After you create the first chart, display the layers property sheet for the display by selecting the Tools | Layers menu pick. The Layer Settings dialog box (shown in Figure 34.13) manages the layers for a display. Using this dialog box, you can rename, activate, hide, and display the layer. You can also create new layers and delete existing layers.

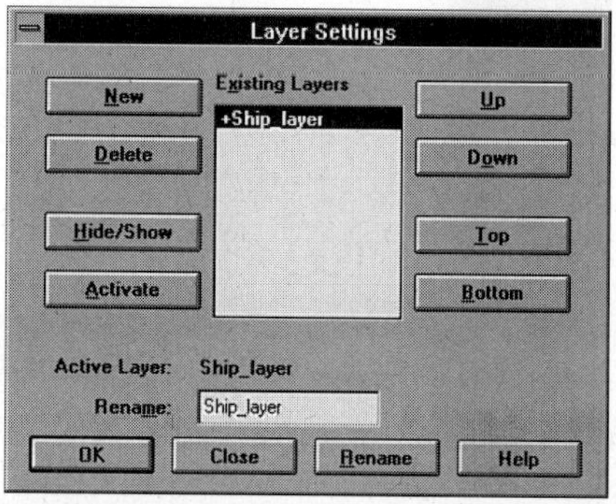

FIGURE 34.13.

The Layer Settings dialog box.

Using this dialog box, rename the first layer to Ship_layer and create a new layer named Avg_layer. The new layer will automatically be activated. Click OK to return to the Layout Editor. At this point, try to select an item from the Monthly Shipments chart on the first layer. Note that nothing from the first layer can be selected because it is not the active layer. Select the Layer Settings dialog box again and click Ship_layer in the Existing Layers box, click the Hide/Show button, and then return again to the Layout Editor. The existing chart is now hidden.

Now, create a new chart that displays the average shipping delay by month. Create this chart on the second layer. Repeat this process to create a third layer named Max_layer and a chart to display the maximum monthly shipping delay. The last step necessary to facilitate navigation between the layers of a chart is to create program units that will execute the navigation.

The program units must be assigned to an object, such as a button, in the Graphics display. The first button will navigate from the Shipments layer to the Average Delay layer. Using the Layer Settings dialog box, activate the Shipments layer and hide all other layers. To build a button, first select the text tool and click in the Layout Editor where the button should appear. In the text box, type `Average Delay` on two lines. To complete the text entry, click outside the text box. Next, select the Rounded Rectangle tool and draw a rectangle around the text box. Using the visual attribute definition buttons at the lower left of the layout editor, modify the rectangle to define the color and border that you want. Using Format | Bevel from the menu, select a raised bevel effect for the rectangle. Using the Select tool, select the rectangle and the text item and link them as a group object by typing Ctrl+G. This combined item is called a graphics button.

You should next create a procedure for the button by selecting Tools | Properties. The Object Properties dialog box that appears (shown in Figure 34.14) enables you to name the object and to assign a button procedure to the object.

FIGURE 34.14.

The button object property sheet.

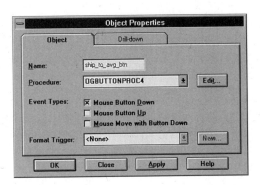

After you name the button, click the New button (displayed as Edit... in Figure 34.14) next to the button procedure field to create the button procedure. In the PL/SQL editor box, enter the text for the procedure as shown here:

```
PROCEDURE OGBUTTONPROC4 (buttonobj IN og_object,
                          hitobj IN og_object,
                          win IN og_window,
                          eventinfo IN og_event) IS
      ship_layer    OG_LAYER;
      avg_layer     OG_LAYER;
   BEGIN
      ship_layer := OG_GET_LAYER ('Ship_layer');
      avg_layer := OG_GET_LAYER ('Avg_layer');
      OG_ACTIVATE_LAYER (avg_layer);
      OG_HIDE_LAYER (ship_layer);
   END;
```

Repeat this process by creating buttons on all layers to navigate between the chart layers. When you are finished, save the display as g34oun05.ogd. To test the chart module, click the run iconic button. When the display appears, click the appropriate buttons to navigate between the separate layers and view the appropriate chart.

Formatting Charts with Text and Breaks

Oracle Graphics provides several optional functions that you can use to customize a chart. These functions include text objects and mechanisms for customizing the labels on a chart. Additionally, by grouping data in subcategories, the displays can show data from multiple data sets on the same chart.

Adding Text Items to Charts

You can add boilerplate text to a chart to provide user instructions or additional information on a chart. To demonstrate this function, open the drill-down chart that was created earlier in module g34oun04.ogd. Add a text object to this chart that will instruct the user on how to use the drill-down function of the chart.

Select the Text tool from the tool palette and click in a blank area of the Layout Editor. A text box will appear where you can enter the user instructions. Type `Click on any pie segment to view the Monthly Shipments for the selected warehouse`. After the text has been entered, click outside the text box to complete the entry.

You can further customize this text box using the palette controls to define the background fill, outside line color, and color of the text. You can also use the Format menu to define other effects such as font selection and style, text justification, border line thickness, and other attributes. By modifying these attributes, you can customize the text object to provide the effects you want.

Customizing the Chart Labels

Take a look at the shipments chart that you created as the second chart in this chapter (refer to Figure 34.7). The axis labels are based on the columns selected in the query associated with the chart. Under most circumstances, the column names are undesirable for a chart because they do not mean anything to the end user.

Oracle Graphics 2.5 provides two methods for customizing the axis labels for a chart. One way to define the labels is to use the SQL syntax method for creating a column alias directly in the select statement. (This syntax was demonstrated earlier in the multilayer chart example.)

The other way you can modify the chart labels is to explicitly define the axis labels. To do this, load the Monthly Shipments chart that was created in the "Defining Parameters for Charts" section of this chapter. Activate the chart in the Layout Editor and select Chart | Axes. You use the Axis Properties sheet (shown in Figure 34.15) to define the properties of the chart axes. In the list box at the top you select the axis to be defined, and you can define the custom label for the axis as well as other properties associated with the axis. Change the label for the X-axis to be Month and the Y1-axis to be Shipments.

FIGURE 34.15.

The axis definition property sheet.

Additionally, because there is only one data value set displayed in the chart, you can remove the legend box by selecting Chart | Frame. The Frame tab of the Frame Properties dialog box that appears (shown in Figure 34.16) defines the visual effects used for the chart. To remove the legend box, make sure that the Show Legend check box is not selected.

The last modification for this chart is to dynamically modify the chart title at runtime. Instead of displaying a generic title, the title should include the name of the warehouse being displayed. Using the PL/SQL feature of Oracle Graphics, you can change the title in a trigger which will fire when the display is first opened. To create this trigger, select Tools | Display. Click the Edit button at the right of the Open Procedure field and create the procedure as listed following:

```
PROCEDURE OGTRIGGERPROC1 IS
   chart   OG_OBJECT;
```

```
wh         VARCHAR2(3);
year       number;
whname     VARCHAR2(50);
title      VARCHAR2(100);
BEGIN
  chart := og_get_object ('wh_monthly');
  wh := og_get_char_param ('P_WH_CODE');
  year := og_get_num_param ('P_YEAR');
  select wh_name
    into whname
    from warehouses
   where wh_code = wh;
  title := to_char (year)||' Monthly Shipments for '||whname;
  og_set_title (chart, title);
exception
  when NO_DATA_FOUND then
    og_set_title (chart, 'Unknown Warehouse');
END;
```

FIGURE 34.16.

The Frame Properties dialog box.

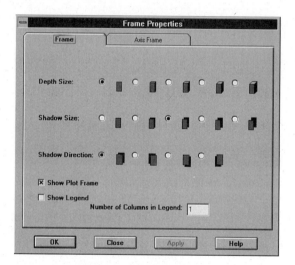

In this procedure, the chart handle must be retrieved as a parameter to the og_set_title built-in procedure. The values of the parameters are then retrieved into PL/SQL variables to be used to define the new title. The exception code is used in case the display receives an invalid warehouse code.

Creating a Break Chart

A break is a special type of chart that displays data for multiple similar entities on a single chart. An example of this chart is the monthly shipments shown in Figure 34.17. This chart shows the monthly shipments for all five warehouses plotted as separate curves on the same chart.

FIGURE 34.17.

An example of a break chart.

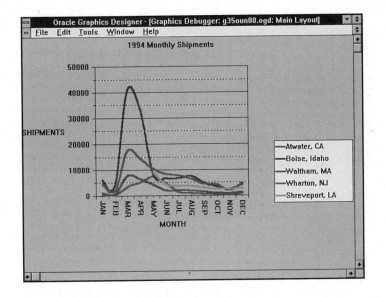

To create this chart, first define a parameter for the chart year and build the following query:

```
select to_char (to_date (to_char (h.hist_month_no), 'MM'), 'MON') Month,
       w.wh_name Warehouse,
       h.hist_ord_shipped Shipments
from warehouses w,
       warehouse_history h
where h.hist_wh_code = w.wh_code
and h.hist_year = :P_YEAR
order by h.hist_month_no, w.wh_name
```

In the Layout Editor, create a chart using the curved line chart subtype. To define the multiple lines, select the Categories tab in the Chart Properties dialog box as shown in Figure 34.18. To create a multiline chart, first define the chart category as Month and also set the Subcategory (lower right) equal to Warehouse. This will cause the X-axis to vary by month and the data within each category value will be grouped by warehouse.

Press OK to complete the chart design. Note that the five lines are presented in separate colors with a legend box at the right of the chart that can be used to translate the chart. Save the chart as g34oun08.

Advanced Formatting Techniques

As in all of the Developer/2000 products, Oracle Graphics provides facilities to enhance the application module by using PL/SQL program units. These program units can be used to modify the default processing for a chart as well as to define how data can be displayed or to determine if the data should be included in the chart at all.

FIGURE 34.18.

Defining a break chart subcategory.

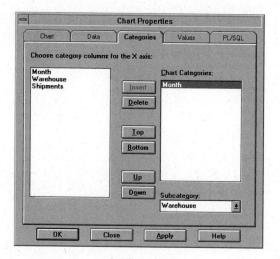

Using Format Triggers

A *format trigger* is used to modify how a chart element can be displayed. In the chart that was created in the section "Creating a Multilayer Chart," the chart on the third layer displayed the maximum shipping delay for each month. Suppose that management has set a standard that all orders must be shipped within one week of order placement. In order to emphasize substandard performance, the chart should indicate any month in which the maximum delay is greater than seven.

To demonstrate this technique, load the chart created in the "Creating a Multilayer Chart" section. In the Layout Editor, use the Layers Management tools to activate the Maximum Delay layer and chart. (Hide all other charts.) Within this chart, click any one of the tick mark labels along the X-axis. This will select all the labels as the active objects. To build the format trigger, select Tools | Properties. Next to the format trigger field, click the New button to activate the PL/SQL editor behind the property definition sheet. Click OK to close the property sheet.

In the PL/SQL editor, complete the format trigger procedure as shown following:

```
-- Chart Element Format trigger. Called for each member of a
-- specified chart element group (e.g., each bar in a group of
-- bars for a bar chart).
-- ARGUMENTS:
--   ELEM   The current chart element.
--   QUERY  The query associated with this chart. The current
--          row of the query is the one associated with ELEM.
--          Use OG_GET_xxxCELL to get at column values for the
--          current row.
PROCEDURE OGFORMATTRIG0(elem IN og_object,
                        query IN og_query) IS
   maxdel      NUMBER;
BEGIN
   maxdel := OG_GET_NUMCELL (query, OG_NEWDATA, 'Maximum Delay');
```

```
      if maxdel > 7 then
        og_set_gcolor (elem, 'red');
      end if;
   END;
```

This procedure retrieves the value from the query into a PL/SQL variable, and if this value is greater than seven, the month label will be displayed in red.

Creating Data Filters

A *data filter* is used to eliminate data retrieved by a query that should not be included in the chart. Sometimes for better performance a query will retrieve all data from a table without restricting the retrieval in the where clause.

Another use of the data filter is to retrieve all data necessary for all charts in a display and to restrict the results to the individual chart for which it is needed. This data can then be eliminated from the query using a data filter. A data filter is a PL/SQL procedure that is attached to a chart. To create a data filter, select the Data tab in the Chart Properties dialog box. Click the New button next to the filter field to create the filter function in the same way you create a format trigger. This filter is a Boolean (TRUE or FALSE) function and will be used to determine if a row should be plotted on the chart. Suppose, for example, that in the break chart created earlier only the Wharton, NJ and Boise, ID warehouses should be plotted.

This function should be created as

```
        FUNCTION OGQUERYFILTER0 (chartobj IN og_object,
                                 query IN og_query) RETURN BOOLEAN IS
whname     VARCHAR2(50);
     BEGIN
        whname := OG_GET_CHARCELLL (query, OG_NEWDATA, 'Warehouse');
        if whname in ('Wharton, NJ', 'Boise, ID') then
          RETURN TRUE;
        else
          RETURN FALSE;
        end if;
     END;
```

This filter will return a value of TRUE for all valid rows that will then be plotted on the chart.

Summary

This chapter presented many of the capabilities of Oracle Graphics 2.5 that will enable most Oracle developers to use this tool constructively. By practicing and working with the tool set you can quickly become an expert user of this powerful tool.

You can use Oracle Graphics to present graphical representations of Oracle data. The extensive options of this tool gives the Oracle developer the capability to create more than 50 different chart types that can be customized to provide the functionality needed for today's high-level executive information systems. Graphical views of data deliver the impact that cannot be achieved with mere textual views of numerical data.

Developer/2000 Integration

35

by Joe Zafian

IN THIS CHAPTER

The previous three chapters discussed the Developer/2000 components as independent, standalone tools. Based on Oracle's concept of the open-enterprise connectivity, each of the Oracle tools have been designed to be combined into a multi-faceted, integrated application. Oracle Forms can display graphics on the presentation canvas, and reports can be spawned from within the tool. Additionally, Oracle Reports can display an Oracle Graphic's chart directly in the report itself. In addition to the capability of the Developer/2000 tools to work with each other, the Oracle tools have the capability to work in an integrated environment with other compatible non-Oracle applications.

This chapter will describe the steps necessary to produce these integrated applications quickly.

Displaying Oracle Graphics in Oracle Forms

Oracle Graphics charts can be integrated into an Oracle Forms module using specific forms objects and built-in procedures and functions. An example of a module that integrates these tools is shown in Figure 35.1. In this form, the annual sales for all warehouses is shown in standard form text fields, and a pie chart that indicates the relative contribution of each warehouse is shown next to the text items. Below these text items, the monthly shipments for the current warehouse is shown in a bar chart. The user may click on any of the pie segments to select a record in the form. Additionally, if the user selects any record in the form, the bar chart will change to show data for the new warehouse.

FIGURE 35.1.

Integrated Oracle Forms and Oracle Graphics module.

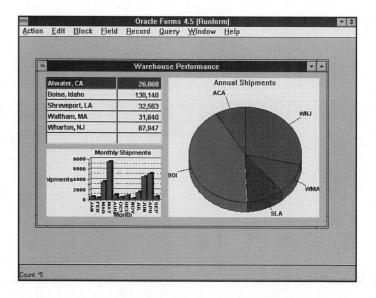

To build this module, first build the two graphics modules using the Oracle Graphics Designer. The first chart should be based on the following query:

```
select hist_wh_code,
         sum (hist_ord_shipped) Shipments,
   from warehouse_history
  where hist_year = 1994
  group by hist_wh_code;
```

Next, define a pie chart for this query using the pie with depth attribute. After the pie chart is displayed in the layout editor, double-click on one of the pie segments to present the trigger-definition form for the pie slices. Select the drill-down tab, and set this item to P_wh_code parameter equal to hist_wh_code on a mouse down trigger. (Note: Do not select a query for the drill-down trigger.)

The next chart will be a bar chart with shadow and will be based on the following query:

```
select to_char (to_date (to_char (hist_month_no), 'MM'), 'MON') Month,
         hist_ord_shipped Shipments
   from warehouse_history
  where hist_year = 1994
      and hist_wh_code = :P_wh_code;
```

The P_wh_code parameter will hold the value for the warehouse code for the chart.

Now, create the form for the WH_ANNUAL_SHIPS view displaying the warehouse name and total annual shipments for 1994. Next, create a control block to hold the chart items and using the Chart Item tool in the Layout Editor, create the two areas for the Graphics charts on the canvas. These items will be linked to the Graphics modules using PL/SQL. To use the Oracle Graphics built-in program units, the OG.PLL library must be attached to the form.

The first trigger that should be created is the WHEN-NEW-FORM-INSTANCE trigger that will set up the charts as soon as the form is started. The bar chart requires parameters to define the warehouse that should be displayed in the chart. This trigger should be defined as follows:

```
declare
   plist        ParamList;
begin
   execute_query;
   OG.Open ('g35oun01.ogd', 'CONTROL.PIE_CHART', FALSE);
   plist := Create_parameter_list ('chart_parms');
   Add_parameter (plist, 'P_wh_code',TEXT_PARAMETER,:wh_annual_ships.wh_code);
   OG.Open ('g35oun02.ogd', 'CONTROL.BAR_CHART', FALSE, TRUE, plist);
   Destroy_parameter_list (plist);
end;
```

The parameters for the OG.Open procedure are the chart module name, form display object, clip indicator, refresh indicator, and parameter list id. By defining the clip indicator in this procedure call as FALSE, the chart will be included on the form by scaling it to fit within the defined area. The default value of TRUE will cause the chart to be clipped to fit within the display. Now, the mouse down trigger interface must be built in the form. For the PIE_CHART item, create a WHEN_MOUSE_CLICK procedure as follows:

```
declare
       wh      VARCHAR2(3);
       plist   ParamList;
    begin
       OG.mouse_down ('g35oun01.ogd', 'CONTROL.PIE_CHART');
       wh := OG.GETCHARPARM ('g35oun01.ogd', 'CONTROL.PIE_CHART',
                                                    'P_wh_code');
       go_block ('WH_ANNUAL_SHIPS');
       loop
          if wh = :WH_ANNUAL_SHIPS.WH_CODE then
             exit;
           end if;
          next_record;
       end loop;
       plist := create_parameter_list ('chart_parms');
       add_parameter (plist, 'P_wh_code', TEXT_PARAMETER, wh);
       OG.REFRESH ('g35oun02.ogd', 'CONTROL.BAR_CHART', plist);
       destroy_parameter_list (plist);
    end;
```

The GETCHARPARAM function will extract the parameter from the first chart, and the OG.REFRESH procedure will pass the new parameter value to the second chart.

> **NOTE**
>
> One thing to note when working with Graphics in Oracle Forms is that the displays may look different when displayed in Forms, especially when the chart is scaled to fit within the chart area. The primary problem relates to the text labels on a chart due to the fact that Oracle Forms tries to use the closest fitting font to the defined display, often resulting in overlapping labels. The best advice is to define the chart with the smallest possible fonts, and hope for the best. Honestly, building forms where everything fits properly can be done, but it will require a significant effort. Also, when building the chart, define the chart area as approximately the same size as it will be in the integrated module.

Executing Oracle Reports from Oracle Forms

Printing an Oracle Reports 2.5 report from Oracle Forms requires the use of a single built-in procedure, RUN_PRODUCT. To demonstrate this concept, open the form that was created in Chapter 32 in the section on multi-block relationships. This form was used to enter new orders into the system. The boilerplate graphic's report that was built in Chapter 33 was a Shipping Document for an order. This two modules will be integrated using a form button with a WHEN-BUTTON-PRESSED trigger. First create a new button on the form canvas labeled Print Document, then create the trigger as

```
declare
   plist        ParamList;
begin
   plist := create_parameter_list ('print_parms');
   add_parameter (plist, 'P-order_no', TEXT_PARAMETER,
                                       to_char (:orders.order_no));
   add_parameter (plist, 'PARAMFORM, TEXT_PARAMETER, 'NO');
   add_parameter (plist, 'DESTYPE', TEXT_PARAMETER, 'PRINTER');
   add_parameter (plist, 'BATCH', TEXT_PARAMETER, 'YES');
   RUN_PRODUCT (REPORTS, 'r35oun01.rdf', ASYNCHRONOUS, BATCH,
                                       FILESYSTEM, plist);
   destroy_parameter_list (plist);
end;
```

As indicated by this module, the command-line parameters for the R25RUN command are passed to the product as part of the parameter list. This is all that is needed to run a report directly to the printer from Oracle Forms. Also, notice that the report will be run asynchronously in background, while the operator is free to execute other tasks as the report is printing. The RUN_PRODUCT built-in may also be used to invoke Oracle Graphics from Oracle Forms; however, the Graphics chart will not have the same interactive functionality as shown in the prior section.

Displaying Oracle Graphics in Oracle Reports

Oracle Graphics can be added to a Report by using the Oracle Graphics tool in the Reports Layout Editor. To demonstrate this concept, open the first report created in Chapter 33. The warehouse pie chart will be added to the report, to be displayed below the numerical data.

Select the Oracle Graphics tool from the tool palette, and drag an area for the chart below the main report layout. The new object will display a chart in the designated area. Double-click in this area to display the Chart Definition dialog box, as shown in Figure 35.2. Name this object D_performance, and define the Graphics File as g35oun01.ogd. Run the report and save the new report in a file.

Interfacing to Non-Oracle Applications

Oracle Forms 4.5 provides the capability to interface with non-Oracle applications, such as Microsoft Excel or Microsoft Word, using OLE2 protocol as defined by Microsoft Corporation. For example, the Customer Credit Maintenance Form shown in Figure 35.3 includes an Excel Spreadsheet embedded directly as part of the form. Whenever a user double-clicks the spreadsheet box, the complete functionality of Microsoft Excel will be included in the form.

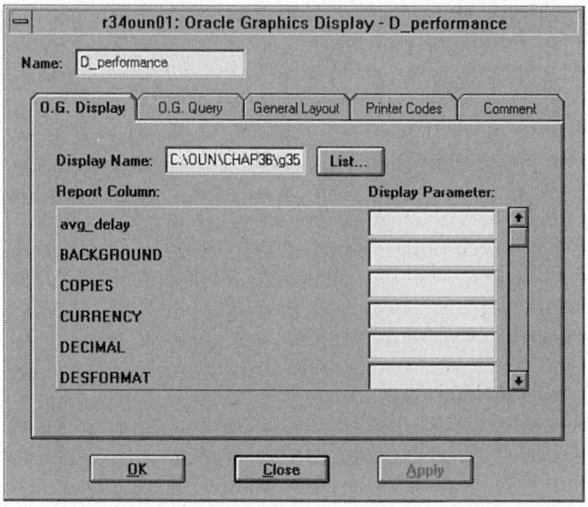

FIGURE 35.2.

*Oracle Graphics Chart
Definition dialog box.*

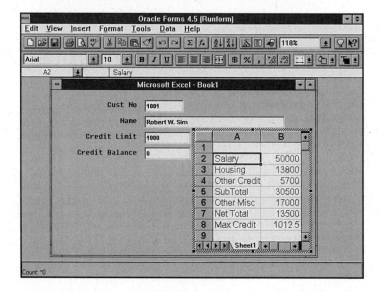

FIGURE 35.3.

*Integrating an OLE
application into Oracle
Forms.*

To construct this form module, first build the CUSTOMERS block as shown displaying the customer number, name, and the credit information fields. Now, select the OLE2 tool from the palette in the Layout Editor. Drag an area on the canvas that will hold the OLE container. (Note: When the tool is activated, the actual area for the tool will appear larger to accommodate the row and column headers, as well as the scrollbar information.)

Select the property sheet for the OLE object, and modify the properties as indicated in Table 35.1.

Table 35.1. OLE object properties.

Property	Value
OLE In-Place Activation	True
OLE Activation Style	Double-Click
OLE Resize Style	Scale
OLE Tenant Types	Embedded
Show Do In Out	True
OLE Tenant Aspect	Content

Now select the OLE object in the Layout Editor and click the right mouse button to display the OLE object menu. Select Insert Object from the menu to display the dialog box shown in Figure 35.4. Select Excel Worksheet and click on OK. (Note: The Display As Icon check box will cause the item to display as an Excel icon until it is activated.) At this point, the Excel spreadsheet is embedded into the form module. To initialize the spreadsheet, select the edit spreadsheet function from the OLE object menu (right mouse button) and create the initial spreadsheet. For more information, refer to your Excel documentation to understand the functions of this tool.

FIGURE 35.4.

OLE Object Type definition dialog box.

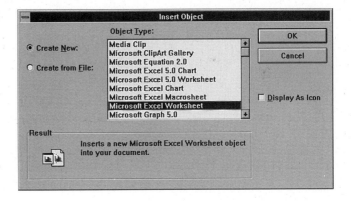

These techniques can be used to embed an OLE compliant application in an Oracle Forms module. Alternatively, instead of embedding an application in the form, OLE linking can be used. OLE linking causes the form module to link directly to an existing OLE compliant file, such as any .XLS Excel Spreadsheet. To link the file, the only differences needed would be to define the OLE Tenant Types property to Linked, and to select the existing file from the Insert Object menu pick.

> **NOTE**
>
> Linking files in Oracle Forms requires a lot of resources on the client computer. Make sure that only necessary applications are running on a machine that has been maximized with RAM. Without a very powerful machine, object linking results in frequent General Protection Faults.

Interfacing with the Windows API and Other DLLs

Oracle Forms also enables the user to interface to subprograms or routines that have been written in a third-generation programming language such as C or COBOL. These functions must be loaded into a dynamic library, such as a .DLL file in Microsoft Windows, or a shared library in UNIX systems. These functions may be Oracle Pre-Compiler foreign functions or non-Oracle functions. The method for using either type of function is the same.

In order to use a foreign function, first the dynamic library must be loaded using the ORA_FFI.LOAD_LIBRARY procedure:

```
fh_mylib := ora_ffi.load_library (path, filename);
```

After the library has been loaded, the function must be registered in FORMS (example shown for a C subprogram module):

```
fh_func := ora_ffi.register_function (fh_mylib, function_name, ora_ffi.C_STD);
```

The next step would be to register the parameters for the module in the order in which they would appear in the function definition (as shown below for a C integer value):

```
ora_ffi.register_parameter (fh_func, ORA_FFI.C_INT);
```

Finally, the last step needed to register the function is to define the return value type for the function:

```
ora_ffi.register_return (fh_func, ORA_FFI.C_INT);
```

The PL/SQL interface to this function would then be created as follows:

```
FUNCTION ff_pls_equiv_my_func (ff_handle ORA_FFI.FUNCHANDLETYPE,
                                          parm1 IN BINARY_INTEGER,
                                          parm2 IN BINARY_INTEGER)
                            RETURN BINARY_INTEGER is
   PRAGMA interface (C, ff_pls_equiv_my_func, 11265);
BEGIN
        ...
END;
```

The foreign function can then be called directly using PL/SQL IN parameters to return a value.

This interface is recommended over building user exits because libraries are only linked in as needed, and thus the form modules can be smaller. Additionally, using a user exit requires that the Oracle Forms runtime designer need to be recompiled, and all forms need to run the version of the tools with the embedded user exit. As a result, user exits tend to require more resources than may be needed for each form.

Summary

This chapter has shown how the Oracle Developer /2000 tools can be used to integrate with each other, as well as non-Oracle applications and subprograms. As one of the key features of Oracle Corporation's concept of open enterprise computing, Developer/2000 integration is highly useful for state-of-the-art powerful applications.

One thing to note in using these features is the fact that all of these tools demand a large amount of resources. When multiple application modules and tools are combined, the limited resources of a PC will quickly be consumed, resulting in applications that can perform slowly. or not at all.

I am by no means attempting to dissuade anyone from using the integrated features of these tools. I am just trying to caution you as to the pitfalls that you will surely encounter.

VII

PART

Oracle Power Objects™

Introduction to Oracle Power Objects™

36

by Ronnie Lashaw

This chapter introduces a new and exciting product, Oracle Power Objects (OPO), from Oracle Corporation. A general overview of Oracle Power Objects is presented, followed by a more detailed presentation of OPO key features. The Oracle Object Marketplace is introduced. Also, the relationship between OPO and Oracle Developer/2000 is discussed. Whenever possible, references will be made to the original sample applications that are shipped with OPO version 1.0. This is so a reader will have ready access to any code references.

Overview of Oracle Power Objects

Oracle Power Objects (OPO) is a visual, object-oriented, client/server database application development tool like no other in its class. Application developers are now able to rapidly design, prototype, develop, and deliver powerful, high quality, robust, client/server applications. These applications require less overall cycle time with significantly less code than with other widely used products such as Microsoft's Visual Basic.

Oracle Corporation has designed Oracle Power Objects from the ground up to be an object-oriented, data-centric, client/server, database application development tool. OPO is not a general purpose application development tool, unlike Microsoft Visual Basic. Oracle kept the developer in mind when choosing the programming language for Power Objects—Oracle Basic. Oracle Basic is extremely similar to Visual Basic, with the additions of object extensions and Structured Query Language (SQL) extensions. BASIC is the most commonly used programming language. Any developer familiar with any version of BASIC will be able to quickly and easily transition to writing Oracle Basic code in Power Objects.

Oracle Power Objects has multiplatform support and supports the leading database engines. OPO is available in Windows and Macintosh versions, and will soon be available for OS/2 Warp. OPO has native drivers for Oracle7 databases and for Microsoft SQL Server and Sybase. Oracle7 support extends from Personal Oracle7 all the way up through Trusted Oracle7 on massively parallel processors.

Power Objects is object-oriented. There are no class libraries to learn. There are no complex rules for developing new classes of objects or for using these new object classes. Oracle Power Objects allows a developer to visually develop a new object class by using existing objects to build the new object class. Often, little to no code is required to build a new object class. Once the class is built, it can be used in as many applications as you choose, and the rules of object-oriented programming are enforced as you would hope and should expect. OPO supports multilevel inheritance, encapsulation, and polymorphism. To assist in the development of new object classes, OPO also supports the addition of user-defined properties and methods. The developer can write new methods for processing data from the database. Yet again, Oracle has considered the developer by supplying a large number of properties and methods with each type of object. These properties and methods have been designed to maximize efficiency in developing object-oriented, data-centric, client/server database applications. The three link properties discussed next illustrate the simplicity behind the functionality of OPO's data-centric objects.

Power Objects has built-in features at the object level to manage simple and complex relational database functionality. OPO does not require any coding to achieve this. Developers can easily create master-detail relationships by setting three link properties on the property sheet for the detail object. Providing the name of the column from the database table, view, or synonym for the LinkDetailColumn and LinkMasterColumn values will set the equality condition (equi-join) defining the master-detail relationship. Providing the name of the object (the object is not required to be a form and often is not) representing the master concept for the LinkMasterForm value will finish all of the required steps for establishing a master-detail relationship. A good developer might spend two to four hours programming and debugging this type of relationship with other products where Power Objects permits the same developer to accomplish this goal within a few seconds.

To promote data integrity at the application level, Oracle Power Objects has included built-in referential integrity for master-detail relationships. OPO has three levels of built-in referential integrity control including Refuse if Children Present, Update/Delete Cascade, and Orphan Details. Refuse if Children Present is the highest level of integrity enforcement stipulating that a user can not modify any of the primary key values associated with the master-detail relationship and also stipulating that a user cannot delete a record from the master database table, view, or synonym reference if there exists any associated or related detail records. Update/Delete Cascade is the second, or most often enforced level of referential integrity that developers can use. It stipulates that a user can modify primary key values and/or delete master records if detail records exist. If the primary key values are changed, then the associated foreign key values in the detail records will be immediately updated. Orphan Details is often considered a nightmare for database administrators (DBAs) with respect to referential integrity because this forces the links between the master record and the detail records to be lost. There are times when this is a desired and valuable result of referential integrity support, but in general this will complicate the support and maintenance of your database.

Key Features

Oracle Power Objects has numerous features that set it apart from other products including its diverse database connectivity, its integrated database session manager, and its integrated development environment. For cross-platform development and deployment, OPO application source code files and compiled p-code application files are binary-portable across all supported hardware/software configurations. (P-code is code that is in a halfway state between original source code and final compiled code.)

Hardware and Software Requirements

OPO is designed to run in three different major hardware/software configurations. These include Microsoft Windows 3.1 or Microsoft Windows for Workgroups 3.11 running on a 386 or higher (486 recommended) IBM/Compaq compatible PC; Macintosh System 7.0 or 7.5

running on a 68020 or higher; and IBM OS/2 Version 3.0 running on a 386 or higher (486 recommended) IBM/Compaq compatible PC. Figure 36.1 illustrates the various platforms that OPO runs on and the various databases that OPO connect to.

FIGURE 36.1.

Cross-platform and cross-database connectivity.

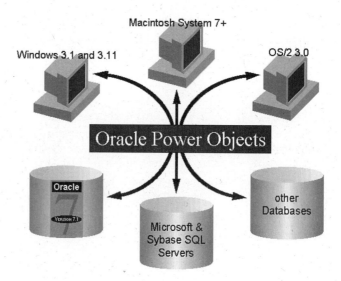

Database Connectivity

OPO provides database connectivity to the leading relational database environments. Naturally, OPO can connect to Oracle products. These include Personal Oracle7, Oracle7 Workgroup Server, and up through the massively parallel Oracle7 servers. Any Oracle 7.1 database server, local or remote, is supported. OPO provides support for Microsoft SQL Server 4.2 and Sybase SQL Server 9 through its implementation of dblib. OPO also provides a local database engine known as Blaze. Blaze is a SQL-92 compliant, single-user, single-session, relational database engine. Blaze supports computed fields, inner joins, and join expressions. Blaze provides support for long raw or BLOB (binary large objects) objects for multimedia applications and for bitmap graphic manipulation. Blaze is fully upward compatible with Oracle7. Blaze was designed for stand-alone and disconnected-client prototyping and application development and deployment.

Integrated Database Session Manager

The integrated database session manager found in OPO provides the greatest distinction between OPO and other similar products, such as Microsoft Visual Basic and Borland Delphi. The session manager allows a developer to create, modify, restructure, view, and edit tables directly while respecting the constraints and limitations placed on these database objects by the database back end. The session manager can create, modify, and delete table indexes, views, sequences, and synonyms. An index is used to improve the performance of the database by providing quicker access to the table information. A view is a combination of one or more tables with columns from each table represented in the view. Views are not editable unless they contain only one table. The session manager has a built-in view designer that is very graphical and powerful. Views can be designed by dragging and dropping relationships and columns. Conditions can be placed on the view. Also, labels can be specified for the columns in the view. A sequence is a special table construct provided whereby a number can be generated and guaranteed to be unique. A synonym is a reference to a database object by a different name. All the database privileges and constraints placed on the original database object still apply to the synonym object.

Figure 36.2 shows the sample MLDATA session in the Main folder window, with the MLDATA session database objects displayed in the MLDATA window. The MLDATA session has been connected to the Blaze database indicated in the `DesignConnect` property. Database tables, sequences, and views are shown in the MLDATA window.

FIGURE 36.2.

Session manager.

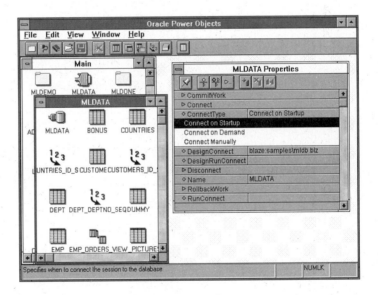

The session manager maintains all connection and session-related information including the `ConnectType` property illustrated in Figure 36.2. The `ConnectType` specifies when OPO attempts to establish the database session connection. `Connect On Startup` indicates that OPO should establish the connection when the application referencing the session is started. Data migration and upsizing can be accomplished through the drag-and-drop interface of the session manager. The session manager also provides built-in transaction processing logic and referential integrity checking. Without programming, a developer is protected from losing data without specifying that such data should be committed (saved) or rolled back (deleted). The developer has complete access to session manager operations from the object code level if they desire to override or augment some of these built-in functions.

Integrated Development Environment

The OPO integrated development environment includes a graphical application manager for displaying all application component objects. Component objects include applications, libraries, and sessions. Applications contains forms, reports, classes, OLE objects, and bitmap resources. Libraries contain reusable classes and bitmap resource objects. Sessions contain information relating to the database connection. Each of these application objects and its contained object components is represented visually in the OPO development environment.

OPO provides full support, under Microsoft Windows, for Dynamic Link Libraries (DLLs), OCX, and OLE 2.0. OpenDoc support for OS/2 and Macintosh is under development. Within the integrated development environment, a developer can create reusable objects called classes. The developer has a graphical forms designer to use in developing either these class objects or forms. Forms are the screen interface that a user will interact with. For each form and subsequently embedded object, a property sheet exists. The property sheet allows the developer to customize an object without requiring coding, simply point and click in many instances. The form designer has toolbar icons for object alignment and z-ordering (visibility layer). Standard objects on the tool palette include static text, field, button, radio button, checkbox, combo, pop-up, list box, radio frame, line, rectangle, oval, vertical and horizontal scrollbars, current row pointer, group object, OLE object, chart, bitmap, embedded form, and repeater. Many of these objects are data-aware, where several can act as containers. A container has the ability to have other objects instanced within it so they are completely within the boundaries of the containing object. The tool palette can be extended through 16-bit OCX controls. When these are registered with OPO they will show up on the tool palette. Figure 36.3 shows the form designer displaying the form, frmRegister, from the sample finance application.

FIGURE 36.3.

Form designer.

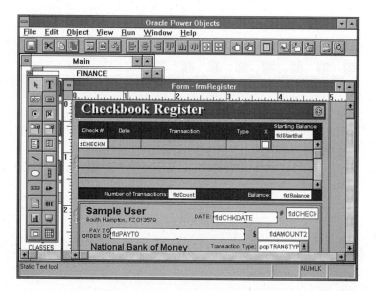

An integrated graphical banded report designer is provided for developing simplified reports. These reports can include multi-level sorting and custom-group specifications. The report designer includes on-screen preview and print-to-printer capabilities. Figure 36.4 displays the report designer with the report, rptAmortize, from the sample finance application. The form designer and report designer are very similar in structure and function. Once a developer has been exposed to either designer, the other designer will seem much easier to use and understand.

FIGURE 36.4.

Report designer.

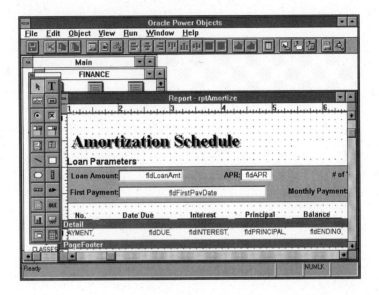

Developers will appreciate the integrated Oracle Basic runtime debugger. The debugger can be called from within Basic script, on startup of the application, or can be manually activated. The debugger provides a graphical object hierarchy diagram for selection of and navigation through the object, property, and method lists. A developer can set conditional breakpoints and watch variables. A developer can also step-through, step-into, and step-over code execution. Expressions and variables can be modified and evaluated from within the debugger. Figure 36.5 displays the sample finance application running with the debugger focused on the form, frmAmortize, inspecting the Oracle Basic code in the Click() method of the button, btnAmortize. The developer has set a breakpoint on the EXEC SQL statement.

The development environment also includes an integrated Query-by-Form capability for use during run-time. Users can specify and apply limiting conditions to the information being displayed on a form without any programming. Lastly, the development environment includes the ability to create stand-alone executable images including database connectivity without run-time fees. All the features mentioned, coupled with detailed online help documentation and extensive sample applications, and the overall Power Objects environment, form a well-rounded client/server database application development product.

FIGURE 36.5.
Run-time debugger.

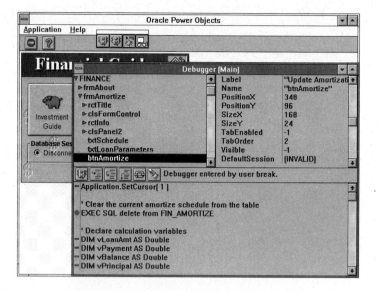

What Is Oracle's Object Marketplace?

Oracle's Object Marketplace is a shopping center for Power Objects application components. The Object Marketplace is part of the innovative Oracle Internet sales initiative, the Oracle Store, available on the World Wide Web at www.oracle.com. The Marketplace is an online store for selling and purchasing Power Objects components and applications. These components can be OCX objects or OPO objects and applications. Developers will receive royalty payments for sales of their components by Oracle on the Internet. More than 250,000 copies of Power Objects have been sold, and more than 2,000,000 visits have been made to the Oracle home page. The Object Marketplace is an exciting addition to Oracle's marketing strategy for products and services.

Goals of the Object Marketplace include providing easy access to OPO components which enhance developer productivity, providing objects that encapsulate business logic commonly in use today, and providing a common forum for the exchange of these objects. Objects will be classified by concepts such as functional area, industry affected, hardware/software requirements, platforms supported, and so on. Not all objects will run on all supported OPO platforms.

The user interface to the Object Marketplace is accessible through almost any commonly available web browser. The CompuServe NetLauncher is just one such alternative web browser environment. I was able to download the product, install the product, and connect to Oracle's home page within a total of 30 minutes (on a 486 DX4/75 24MB RAM PC running Windows for Workgroups 3.11). Other web browser products are probably just as easy to install and use.

Objects in the Marketplace will have a wide range of pricing. The prices are set by the developer of the object and approved by Oracle. Typical prices will be in the range $25–$200 per object. Support for the objects will be provided by the developer who created the object. Some support will be available through the Oracle Object Marketplace, or through Oracle's CompuServe forum.

Each object in the Marketplace has documentation provided online with the purchased object package. The objects must be developed in compliance with Oracle's coding guidelines and standards. One important guideline is the inclusion of in-line coding comments explaining the code used to support the object. Demonstration code or a sample application for each object is another required piece of the object's promotional package.

Buyers can download demo versions of objects for trying without buying. Buyers also have the option of ordering over the phone or downloading the object from the Marketplace. VISA and MasterCard charges will be accepted by phone or via electronic cash for purchasing the objects.

Oracle Power Objects and Oracle Developer/2000

Deciding which product to use is a challenging task when one or more products can give acceptable results. While at first glance, it might appear that Oracle Power Objects and Oracle Developer/2000 seem to be competing in the same application development space, this is not the case. Table 36.1 illustrates the positioning of various client/server tools.

Table 36.1. Client/server tools positioning.

Product	End User	Power User	Workgroup (< 25 Users)	Department (< 50 Users)	Enterprise (>= 50 Users)
Microsoft Access	High*	High			
Microsoft Visual Basic		High	Low		
Oracle Power Objects		High	High		
Borland Delphi		High	Medium		
Sybase PowerBuilder			High	High	Low
Gupta SQLWindows				High	Low
Oracle Developer/2000				High	High

* Low meets minimum user requirements; Medium meets average user requirements; and High meets or exceeds user requirements.

As shown above, Oracle Developer/2000 is designed for department and enterprise-wide application development. Although Developer/2000 can be used for the lower-end development areas, it's often considered to be overkill with a steep learning curve with the need for a high-end deployment environment. Oracle Power Objects is designed for workgroup and power-user development environments. Table 36.2 addresses some of the factors that can be used in deciding between using Oracle Power Objects and Oracle Developer/2000.

Table 36.2. Feature comparison.

Feature	Power Objects	Developer/2000
Logical Application Size	20 tables and 20 forms	Thousands of tables, screens/forms
Language	Oracle Basic	PL/SQL
Case Integration	None	Strong
Portability	Windows, Macintosh, OS/2	Windows, Macintosh, UNIX, character mode
Development Team Size	< 5, no direct support	Hundreds, direct support
Reporting	Business	Advanced
Charting	Business	Advanced
Oracle Integration	Strong	Very Strong
Resource Requirements	8MB RAM	12MB RAM
Local Database	Includes Blaze	Personal Oracle7

In general, if you are seriously considering using Visual Basic for departmental or enterprise-wide application development, you will be better off in the long run using Oracle Developer/2000 coupled with Oracle Designer/2000 over Power Objects. However, if you cannot use these high-end products, then you should strongly consider using Oracle Power Objects. The data-centric nature of the product will greatly improve your developer productivity as opposed to straight Visual Basic application development.

Summary

Oracle Power Objects is a visual, object-oriented, client/server database application development environment well suited to today's workgroup and power-user environments. With cross-platform support for the three dominant operating systems, Windows, Macintosh, and OS/2, and native database connectivity to Oracle and Sybase, Power Objects is a strong performer in the highly competitive, rapid application development marketplace. With Oracle's commitment to broad spectrum application development support and emerging Internet services like the Oracle Object Marketplace, Power Objects will be a strong factor in client/server application development and deployment for years to come.

Connecting to Database Sources Through Sessions

37

by Brian Twidt

One of the most integral parts of OPO application development is the session object. This chapter introduces the use of session objects and their importance within OPO. Further, sessions will be explained in terms of what they represent, their properties and methods, and how they are used to manage data and build applications.

Overview of the Session Object

A session object represents a connection between an OPO application and a database. Through this connection, OPO communicates with the database and performs all data operations. Database objects, including tables, views, indexes, sequences, and synonyms, are represented as graphical icons in the session's window. Whether a session is connected to a Blaze database, an Oracle database, or any other database, the session interacts with the database and displays the database objects identically. This is important because it enables OPO to seamlessly connect to any database through sessions. Figure 37.1 illustrates the relationship between a session object and the various database back ends that OPO can connect to.

FIGURE 37.1.

A session's graphical interface to different databases.

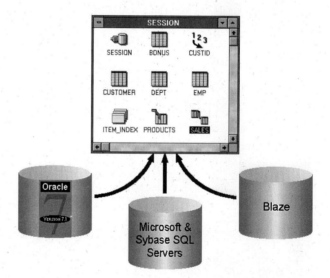

Through the session's graphical interface, developers can efficiently maintain database objects. Tables, views, indexes, sequences, and synonyms can be created, modified, deleted, or populated from a session with the ease of point-and-click. Additionally, database objects are used to automate the task of form and report building. For example, dropping a table onto a form automatically populates the form with text fields corresponding to each identified column in that table.

Another important feature of OPO is that it enables multiple active sessions. This feature permits OPO applications to interact with any number of database connections simultaneously.

On any given form of an application, data can be displayed from one or more Blaze, Oracle, and Sybase sessions. As well, master-detail or any other relationship can be made between the database objects from different databases.

OPO also provides full transaction processing for each session. From the time a session is connected, a transaction is opened recording any changes made to data through the session. The data is not actually saved to the database until the user chooses to commit the changes. Alternatively, the user can choose to rollback or revert the changes. Once the user commits or reverts the changes, a new transaction is started.

Session Properties

The properties of a session identify when a session should connect to a database and to which database the connection should be made.

ConnectType

The `ConnectType` property tells an application when to activate a session. The possible values for the `ConnectType` property include connect on startup, connect on demand, and connect manually. Table 37.1 contains possible `ConnectType` values.

Table 37.1. `ConnectType` values.

Connect Type	When an Application Activates a Session
Connect on startup	When the Application starts
Connect on demand	Not until an object references the session
Connect manually	Not until the user manually activates the session through its `Connect` method

DesignConnect

The `DesignConnect` property specifies the connect string used by the session when it attempts to connect to a database during application development from the OPO Designer.

DesignRunConnect

The `DesignRunConnect` property specifies the connect string used by the session when it attempts to connect to a database when testing or running an application from the OPO Designer. If the `DesignRunConnect` property is left empty, then the session will use the value of the `DesignConnect` property as the connect string.

Name

The Name property provides a reference to a session. Objects that require session information can refer to a session through its name. For example, a form's RecSrcSession property can be set to the name of a session. This allows a form to equate that any database activity will be done through the specified session's database connection.

RunConnect

The RunConnect property specifies the connect string used by the session when it attempts to connect to a database when the application is executed from the OPO Runtime. If the RunConnect property is left empty, then the session will use the value of the DesignConnect property as the connect string.

Session Methods on the Property Sheet

The methods of a session are used to perform session connections, status querying, and transaction processing.

CommitWork()

The CommitWork method commits or saves any changes made to data within the current transaction for the given session. After CommitWork is called, a new transaction is started.

Connect()

The Connect method attempts to connect the session to the database specified by the appropriate connect string property.

Disconnect()

The Disconnect method disconnects the session from the currently connected database.

IsConnected()

The IsConnected method evaluates whether the session is currently connected to a database. True is returned if the session is connected; otherwise, false is returned.

IsWorkPending()

The IsWorkPending method evaluates whether the session has any outstanding changes made to data. True is returned if the session has outstanding data changes; otherwise, false is returned.

RollbackWork()

The RollbackWork method rolls back or reverts the values of any changes made to data within the current transaction for the given session. After RollbackWork is called, a new transaction is started.

Creating Session Objects

New sessions are created from the OPO Designer by clicking on the toolbar's New Session button, or by selecting New Session from the File menu. The Create Session dialog appears and requests the database type and connect string for the new session, as shown in Figure 37.2.

FIGURE 37.2.

Create Session dialog box.

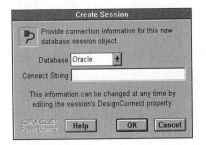

Using the stand-alone version of OPO, the database type can be Blaze or Oracle. The stand-alone version connects only to local Oracle, Personal Oracle7. For the client/server version of OPO, the database type can be Blaze, Oracle, or Sybase where Oracle is local or remote and Sybase represents Sybase SQL Server or Microsoft SQL Server. In future releases of OPO, sessions will also be able to connect to any ODBC-compliant database.

> **NOTE**
>
> If you want to create a session for a new Blaze database, you must first create the new Blaze database by selecting New Blaze Database from the File menu.

The connect string identifies database specific information such as username, password, and database/hostname. Table 37.2 illustrates possible connect strings for Blaze and Oracle.

Table 37.2. Connect string examples.

Database	Connect String
Blaze	`Blaze:[`*username*`/`*password*`@]`*filename*
	`Blaze:blazedb.blz`
	`Blaze:dba/dba@blazedb.blz`
Oracle	`Oracle:`*username*`/`*password*`[@`*host*`]`
	`Oracle:scott/tiger`
	`Oracle:scott/tiger@x:IPXServerName`
	`Oracle:scott/tiger@t:123.456.789.123`

After specifying the database type and connect string, OPO pops up a file dialog requesting a filename for the session. The filename you specify will also be the initial name of the session which can be changed through the `Name` property.

After the session has been created, a window representing the session appears. Initially, the session is disconnected and there is only a single object in the session window. This object is the session's connector icon. When the session is disconnected, the connector icon appears to be disconnected (the plug is not connected to the cylinder). Alternatively, when the session is connected, the connector icon appears to be connected. (The plug is connected to the cylinder.)

Connecting the Session Object to a Database Source

Connecting a session to a database is referred to as activating the session. When a session is activated, it attempts to connect or log in to the database specified in the connect string.

In the OPO Designer, double-clicking a session's connector icon activates a session using the value of the `DesignConnect` property as the connect string. Once connected, the session will display the database's data objects. The session is now considered active. Double-clicking an active session's connector icon will disconnect the session from the database and remove the database's data objects from display.

While running a form or application from the OPO Designer, a session will attempt to connect to the database using the value of the `DesignRunConnect` property as the connect string.

While running an application from the OPO Runtime, a session will attempt to connect to the database using the value of the `RunConnect` property as the connect string.

As shown above, OPO has maximized connectivity options by providing separate connect strings for each of its modes—designer, design run-time, and run-time. This allows development, testing and deployment to connect to different databases. However, it's not necessary to enter values for all connect properties. Both `DesignRunConnect` and `RunConnect` will default to the `DesignConnect` value if they are empty when the session attempts to connect.

Additionally, an application can change a session's connect string during run-time as long as the session is not active. A session's connect string is set during run-time either by setting the `RunConnect` property through method code, or by prompting the user for the value of the connect string. To prompt the user for the connect string during application run-time, set the value of the `RunConnect` property to ? then call the session's `Connect` method. If the session is already connected to a database, it is necessary to call the session's `Disconnect` method before calling the `Connect` method. After calling the session's `Connect` method, the Database Login dialog will appear and prompt the user for the desired connect string, as illustrated in Figure 37.3.

FIGURE 37.3.

Database Logon dialog box.

Session Object Components

Once connected, the session displays most of the database objects contained in the database. The database objects shown in the session window consist of the following: tables, views, indexes, sequences, and synonyms. Illustrated in Figure 37.4 are the database objects that appear in an active session's window.

FIGURE 37.4.

A session's database objects.

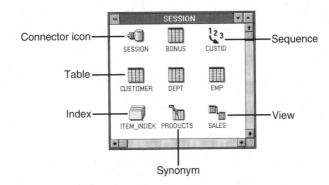

These objects can be created and deleted from the database through the session interface using toolbar or menu commands. Tables and views are editable through the Table Editor and View Editor, which are activated by double-clicking a table or view database object. Currently, sessions are unable to display public or granted privilege database objects from other database connections. In future releases, database objects with granted privileges and other database objects, such as stored procedures and triggers, should be displayed in the session window.

Migrating Data Between Database Sources

An important feature of OPO is its capability to graphically migrate data between active sessions. Through drag-and-drop, a database object can be migrated or copied from one session to another. This allows developers to easily upsize or downsize application databases by quickly moving their database objects to alternate databases.

Easily migrating data between OPO sessions is enabled through the session metaphor. By the same measure that enables OPO to display various databases seamlessly as sessions, OPO can translate database structures and data between these databases. However, some limitations or exceptions do exist. Some of these exceptions are as follows: Oracle and Sybase store dates and times in slightly different formats; Oracle permits a table to have dual primary keys where Blaze does not; Blaze does not fully support the full range of number formats supported by Oracle. If one of these exceptions is encountered while migrating data, OPO either converts the data as best it can or it notifies the developer that some rows were not migrated.

Using a Session to Generate Forms and Reports

One of the most powerful advantages of using OPO to develop database applications is its unique capability to automatically create forms and reports based on database objects. By dragging and dropping a table or view onto a form or report, OPO populates that form or report with application objects corresponding to the identified columns of the table or view. Figure 37.5 illustrates dragging and dropping a table onto a form.

Below is list of events that occur when a table is dropped onto a form and the form is generated from the tables data definition.

1. The form's RecordSource property is set to the name of the table.
2. The form's RecSrcSession property is set to the name of the session that contains the table.
3. For each column of the table, a label (static text field) and data-entry (text edit field) objects is created on the form.

4. Each of the label objects displays the name of a corresponding column.

5. Each of the data-entry objects is bound to a corresponding column by setting the `DataSize`, `DataSource`, and `DataType` properties according to the column's data definition.

FIGURE 37.5.

Generating forms through drag-and-drop.

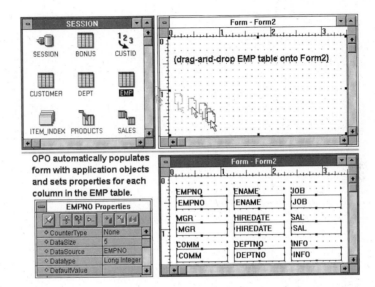

Additionally, dropping a single column from a table or view onto an object, such as a text field or pop-up list, sets the necessary properties of that object to bind it to the identified column. Sequences can also be dropped onto text fields that represent a counter for that table. Dropping a sequence onto an application object causes that object to receive the appropriate sequence number whenever a new record is created.

The ability to automatically create forms through drag-and-drop allows developers to build applications efficiently. Further, developers are able to concentrate on application design rather than the database interface.

Summary

As illustrated, sessions are one of the most powerful components of OPO. They provide a transparent interface to multiple databases simultaneously. Sessions enable developers to easily view the database objects within a database and efficiently create database applications.

Managing the Database

38

by Brian Twidt

A key feature of OPO is its built-in database management. As you would expect from Oracle, OPO provides a graphical environment where database objects can be created, modified, and deleted. The ability to manage objects within a database from the application design environment is one of OPO's major advantages over competitor products. This chapter illustrates how to manage database objects from the OPO Designer. Also discussed in this chapter are several database management limitations imposed by this initial release of OPO.

Overview of the Database Designer

Unlike most other application development tools, OPO allows the developer to manage database objects from the design environment. In OPO, database management is performed through the session object. After a session has been activated or connected to the database, objects within the database such as tables, views, indexes, sequences, and synonyms can be managed through the database designer. The database designer consists of a table editor for creating and modifying tables, a view editor for creating and modifying views, and dialogs for creating indexes, sequences, and synonyms.

Table Editor

When you create a new table within a session, by either clicking the New Table toolbar button or by selecting the File | New Table menu command, the table editor is invoked. The table editor is a spreadsheet-type window used to define a table's data structure as illustrated in Figure 38.1.

FIGURE 38.1.

The Table Editor.

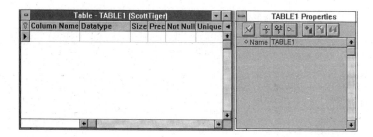

The title of the table editor indicates the name of the table and it's associated session that you are currently editing. Each row of this spreadsheet represents a data column of the table. For each of the table's columns, there are fields that define the characteristics of that column. Table 38.1 is a list of a column's characteristics:

Table 38.1. Table column characteristics.

Characteristic	Description
Column Name	The identifier used to refer to this column.

Characteristic	*Description*
Data Type	The type of data that this column will contain, such as varchar2, number, date, and so on.
Size	The largest number of digits, characters, or bytes that this column can store. A column of data type number and size 5 precision 0 can have a value with up to five digits, such as 67345.
Prec	For a column of data type number, Prec or precision indicates how many digits can be stored for the number's fractional part. A column of data type number, Size 5, and Prec 2 can have a value of three decimal digits and two fractional digits, i.e. 345.19.
Not Null	This is an on/off toggle that indicates whether null values can be stored in this column. If Not Null is checked, this column is required to have a value when sent to the database. If Not Null is not checked, specifying a value for this column is optional.
Unique	This is an on/off toggle that indicates whether duplicate values can be stored in this column. If Unique is checked, the column must have a value that is distinct from any other value in this column; if Unique is not checked, this column does not require a distinct value.

NOTE

The Blaze database does not enforce the size and prec fields for numeric data types; however, the Oracle database drivers do.

The column definitions are set by entering the column name, selecting a data type from a pop-up list and entering any other desired characteristics. Occasionally, column definition values are too large to fit in the table editor fields. Each of the fields can be resized by grabbing and moving the fields boundaries.

The table editor can also set primary keys for columns in a table (Blaze tables are limited to a single primary key per table). Setting a primary key creates an index for that column. This index is useful for searching the table against the primary key column or for establishing relational links between columns of two tables. To designate a primary key, select the desired column by clicking on the leftmost, gray portion of that column. Then, set this column as a primary key column by clicking on the primary key button in the upper left of the table editor. A primary key indicator will appear in the gray area on the left of the column. To remove a primary key, repeat the same steps used to set the primary key.

The table is given a default name, which is indicated in the property sheet's Name property. The Name will be used to label this table in the session and as an identifier in future table operations. After completing the table information and specifying the table's Name, the table can be saved using the Save toolbar button or selecting the File | Save menu command. Figure 38.2 shows a completed table named EMP which has several columns of various data types and a primary key.

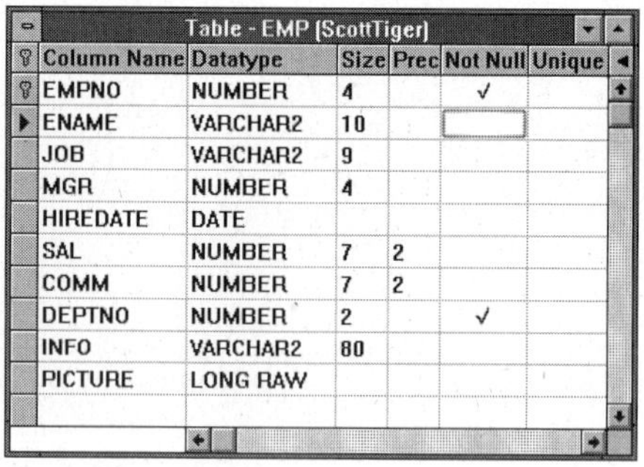

FIGURE 38.2.

A completed table definition.

Column Name	Datatype	Size	Prec	Not Null	Unique
EMPNO	NUMBER	4		√	
ENAME	VARCHAR2	10			
JOB	VARCHAR2	9			
MGR	NUMBER	4			
HIREDATE	DATE				
SAL	NUMBER	7	2		
COMM	NUMBER	7	2		
DEPTNO	NUMBER	2		√	
INFO	VARCHAR2	80			
PICTURE	LONG RAW				

Table - EMP [ScottTiger]

Modifying a Table Structure

At any time, the structure of a table can be modified. Currently, this does not apply to Blaze tables, which are not editable. Double-clicking on an existing table in a session opens the table editor with that table's information. Although the column name cannot be altered due to database restrictions, the other column characteristics can be edited. In some cases, such as changing a column's data type from varchar2 to number or setting Not Null to true, it may be necessary to delete the stored values in the database for this column before the modification can be made. After modifying the table structure, the table should be saved.

Entering Data into a Table

An extended feature of the table editor is the ability to populate a table with data from the design environment. Though most application development tools require data to be entered by running the application or using external data editors, OPO provides a built-in data editor. While the table editor window is open, clicking on the Run Table toolbar button opens the data editor, which is shown in Figure 38.3.

The data editor temporarily replaces the table editor until the data editor is closed. The data editor displays the values of all the columns for each row in a table. New rows can be inserted and other rows can be edited or deleted. When the data editor has the focus, the toolbar displays the runtime-toolbar, which has buttons for inserting and deleting rows, for requerying the database and for committing or rolling back any outstanding changes. If values are too large to fit, the display fields can be stretched by dragging the fields boundaries to the desired size. Any changes made to the data must be committed, which saves the changes, or rolled back, which reverts the changes, before the data editor can be closed. To close the data editor, simply click on the stop toolbar button.

FIGURE 38.3.

The Data Editor.

	EMPNO	ENAME	JOB	MGR	HIREDATE	SAL	COMM	DEPTNO	INFO	PICTURE
▶	7369	SMITH	CLERK	7902	12/17/80	800		20		
	7499	ALLEN	SALESMAN	7698	2/20/81	1600	300	30		
	7521	WARD	SALESMAN	7698	2/22/81	1250	500	30		
	7566	JONES	MANAGER	7839	4/2/81	2975		20		
	7654	MARTIN	SALESMAN	7698	9/28/81	1250	1400	30		
	7698	BLAKE	MANAGER	7839	5/1/81	2850		30		
	7782	CLARK	MANAGER	7839	6/9/81	2450		10		
	7788	SCOTT	ANALYST	7566	12/9/82	3000		20		
	7839	KING	PRESIDENT		11/17/81	5000		10		
	7844	TURNER	SALESMAN	7698	9/8/81	1500	0	30		
	7876	ADAMS	CLERK	7788	1/12/83	1100		20		
	7900	JAMES	CLERK	7698	12/3/81	950		30		
	7902	FORD	ANALYST	7566	12/3/81	3000		20		
	7934	MILLER	CLERK	7782	1/23/82	1300		10		

Table - EMP [ScottTiger]

View Editor

Within OPO, views can be created and modified easily through the view editor. The view editor is a graphical tool used to specify which tables and columns are represented by a view, as well as the relationships and conditions among these columns. The view editor is invoked when the New View toolbar button is clicked, when the File | New View menu command is selected, or when an existing view's icon in a session is double-clicked. Figure 38.4 is an illustration of an existing view that was opened.

FIGURE 38.4.

The View Editor.

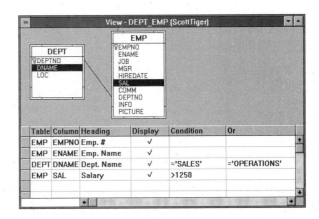

Table	Column	Heading	Display	Condition	Or
EMP	EMPNO	Emp. #	✓		
EMP	ENAME	Emp. Name	✓		
DEPT	DNAME	Dept. Name	✓	='SALES'	='OPERATIONS'
EMP	SAL	Salary	✓	>1250	

The view editor consists of two areas, which are the table display area and the column display area. The table display area illustrates the tables whose columns are used to build this view. The column display area represents which columns are represented by this view. In addition, views also have a single property on the property sheet, which is the Name property. Like tables, the Name property can be specified and used to refer to the view.

> **NOTE**
>
> The View Editor will only show a graphical representation of a view that was created using OPO. Views created using other tools or directly from SQL code cannot be graphically displayed.

The view editor is similar to the table editor, except that columns are selected from existing tables instead of defined. The first action of defining a view is to bring in any necessary tables, which are referred to as base tables. From any open session, a table can be dropped onto the view editor. The view's table display area shows all the base tables as list boxes. For each table's list box, the title indicates the table name and the list represents all the columns in that table. To specify any join relationships between tables, select a column, then drag-and-drop that column onto a column in another table. A line between these columns represents the join. To remove a join, select the join line and delete it. Currently, OPO only provides equi-join relationships. In later releases, inner and outer joins will be supported.

Double-clicking any of the columns in the tables in the table display area adds that column to the column display area. The column display area lists all the columns that have been selected and that will be represented by this view. Each column in the view has several characteristics that define how the view is displayed and what data the view contains. Table 38.2 defines the view's column characteristics.

Table 38.2. View column characteristics.

Characteristic	Description
Table	The base table that contains the column.
Column	The column from the base table that represents values that will be displayed for this column.
Heading	The label that will be used when displaying this column.
Display	This is an on/off toggle that indicates if this column is displayable. If Display is checked and this view is dropped onto a form, a field will be created to display this column.

Characteristic	Description
Condition	An expression that restricts which column values will be included in this view. If the Condition is >1000, then only the records where this column is greater than 1000 will be included in the data set for this view.
Or	An additional expression used to restrict the column values. The Or expression will be ORed (union) with the Condition expression.

The view definition in Figure 38.4, the DEPT_EMP view, demonstrates how the column characteristics define the view. The DEPT_EMP view includes the EMPNO, ENAME, and SALARY columns from the EMP table and the DNAME column from the DEPT table. Basically, this provides a view that has the key elements of the EMP table, as well as the name of the department of the employee. Without using a view, displaying this relationship would involve a database lookup to get the name of the department based on the employees' department number, DEPTNO. Additionally, this view provides column labels that are more recognizable than the column name. The EMPNO column will be given the Heading Emp. # versus the column name, EMPNO when this view is dropped onto a form. Although the developer could manually change a label from EMPNO to Emp. #, it's easier if this is done automatically, especially when multiple instances of this view will be used. The conditions for this view allow the view to contain only specific records from the base table. The DEPT_EMP view will only contain records of employees who work in Operations or Sales, and whose salary is greater than 1250.

After completing the view information and specifying the view's Name, the view can be saved using the Save toolbar button or selecting the File | Save menu command. Once saved, you can examine the view's data by clicking on the run view toolbar button, which opens the view browser window shown in Figure 38.5.

FIGURE 38.5.

The View Browser.

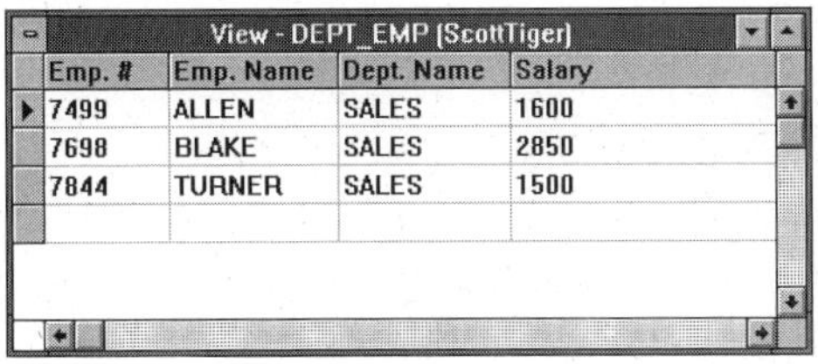

Running a view is similar to running a table. You view the values of the columns for each row in a spreadsheet-type window. However, for views with two or more base tables, the data cannot be modified. Although this would be a nice feature, it's not a likely feature, since many databases, including Oracle7, do not directly permit this action.

Synonyms

Synonyms provide public, yet limited, access to tables, views, or sequences through aliases. Within a session, clicking on the New Synonym toolbar button or selecting the File | New Synonym menu command invokes the Create Synonym Dialog Box, which is shown in Figure 38.6.

FIGURE 38.6.

The Create Synonym dialog box.

The Synonym Name is the identifier used to refer to this synonym. The For Object specifies the name of the table, view, or sequence for which the synonym is to be created. The Public button indicates whether the synonym is public. If you check the Public button, the synonym is public; otherwise, the synonym is private.

Currently, a session in OPO only displays synonyms owned by the user (objects created by the user). Later releases of OPO will provide access to objects with public and granted access, which will permit a session to display public synonyms, as well as other objects, that were not created by the user.

Sequences

Sequences generate sequential integers that are generally used to generate unique values for primary key columns. Within a session, clicking on the New Sequence toolbar button or selecting the File | New Sequence menu command invokes the Create Sequence dialog box, which is shown in Figure 38.7.

The Sequence Name is the identifier used to refer to this sequence. The Starting Value indicates the first sequential value. The Increment By specifies the amount to increment between the sequential values. The Minimum Value is the lowest value that can be generated by the sequence. The Maximum Value is the highest value that can be generated by the sequence. The Cycling button indicates whether the sequence should start the sequence over if it reaches the minimum or maximum value.

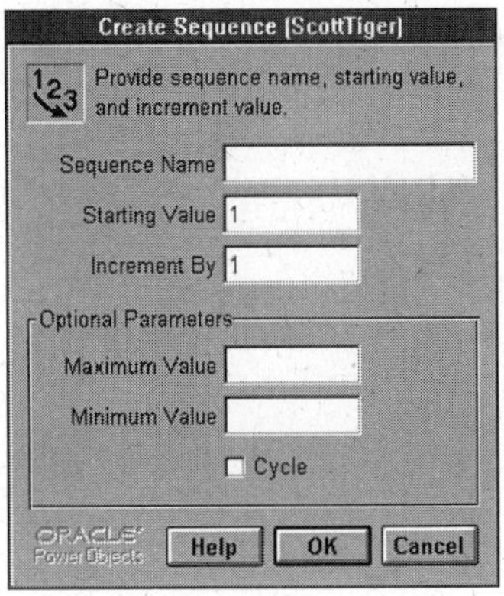

FIGURE 38.7.

The Create Sequence dialog box.

Indexes

Indexes provide fast access to tables for query and sorting operations. Within a session, clicking on the New Index toolbar button or selecting the File | New Index menu command invokes the Create Index Dialog Box, which is shown in Figure 38.8.

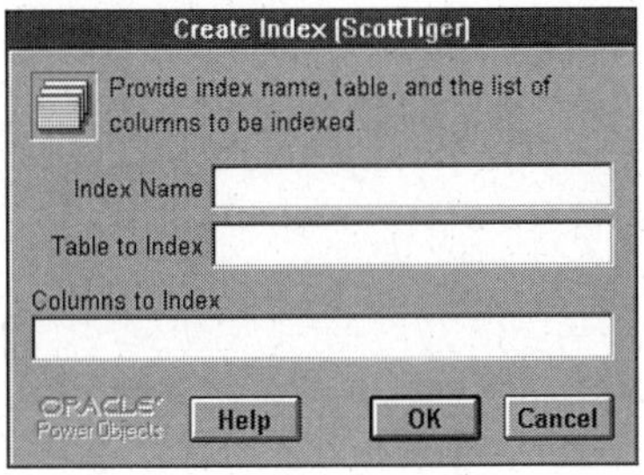

FIGURE 38.8.

The Create Index dialog box.

The Index Name is the identifier used to refer to this index. The Table to Index is the name of the table containing the columns to be indexed. The Columns to Index field is a comma-separated list of columns that will be included in the index.

> **NOTE**
>
> The Blaze database does not support indexes across multiple columns, only single columns.

Summary

Power Objects provides all the required tools to create and maintain tables, views, synonyms, sequences, and indexes. Data can be entered, deleted, and viewed through the data editor window. These visual editor windows promote simplicity in creation and maintenance of the database objects essential to the creation of database applications. The user is not limited just to this visual environment, because database objects can be created using other tools such as Oracle SQL*Plus or by using EXEC SQL calls from within an OPO application.

Understanding the Application Model

39

by Bryan Twidt

The objective of Oracle Power Objects (OPO) is database application development. At the highest level, OPO consists of the following three object types: applications, sessions, and libraries. Since application development is OPO's focus, the application object (application) is the core component of OPO. Sessions act as database interfaces for applications and libraries. Classes are used for storing reusable application resources. This chapter will provide a better understanding of the components within an application object and how they interact with the OPO environment.

Overview of Application Model

OPO organizes its components within a folder metaphor. Within a session are database objects. Within a library are reusable classes and bitmaps. This same metaphor applies to applications, as they contain other objects. An application consists of properties, methods, and objects that define the interface and actions of that application.

Applications are constructed using forms, reports, classes, bitmaps, and OLE objects. Applications interface with users through forms and reports. Each form and report is built by constructing screens that the user will see by creating and organizing objects, and controls to display information, data, and control options. The user navigates through the forms and reports accomplishing whatever tasks the application provides.

Application Properties and Methods

As with any other object in OPO, the application object has properties and methods. These properties and methods determine how the application, as a whole, interacts with the database and performs certain actions.

The properties specify the name, label, and default session for the application. Additionally, the declarations property is used to declare global variables, constants, and external functions that are used in the application. Table 39.1 is a list of the application properties.

Table 39.1. Applications properties.

Property	Description
(Declarations)	Section where global variables, constants, and external functions such as Dynamic Link Library (DLL) and Code Fragment procedures are declared.
DefaultSession	The name of the default session object to be used for database interaction. If an object does not specify a particular session, the DefaultSession will be used.

Property	Description
Label	The text you will see in the title bar of the main OPO window when the application is run.
Name	The identifier used to refer to this application.

The methods of an application provide the ability to initialize components and specify what actions occur when the application starts and ends. An application's methods also allow the developer to customize toolbar and menu bar actions. Table 39.2 is a list of the application methods.

Table 39.2. Application methods.

Method	Description
CloseApp	Use this method to call to quit the application. It can be used to ask the user if they are sure they want to quit, to complete processing, or to clean up the application before exiting.
DoCommand	This method is called when the user selects a toolbar button or menu command. It can be used to override default toolbar or menu bar processing or to perform actions for custom toolbars or menu bars elements.
Initialize	This method is the first method called when an application runs. This method is invoked for both Run App and Run Form. It can be used to initialize variables or objects.
LastWindowClosed	This method is called when the last open window is closed. It indicates that the user didn't specifically quit the application, but that the last window was closed. The developer can either allow the application to quit or continue the application by opening another window.
OnLoad	This method is called when starting the application. More precisely, it is called when the application is loaded into memory. This method is invoked by Run App, not by Run Form. It is used to initialize variables and objects specific to the application. This method should also tell the application which form(s) to open initially.
TestCommand	This method is called when the OPO draws the toolbar and menu bar. It is used to determine which toolbar buttons and menu items are enabled or disabled. It can be used to override the default system processing or to indicate the enabled/disabled status for custom toolbar or menu bar elements.

Objects Within the Application

Forms, reports, classes, bitmaps, and OLE objects are the major components that make up an application. The specific set of these objects that comprise any given applications are displayed as icons in the applications window. Figure 39.1 illustrates an application named SAMPLAPP that contains one of each of the main application objects.

FIGURE 39.1.

An application's objects.

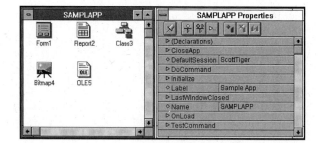

Each of these components, which are objects themselves, can be comprised of other objects. Within OPO there is a form designer, a report designer, and a class designer. These designers are used to create forms, reports, and classes that incorporate graphical and data controls that convey information to the user.

Forms are the core application object. Each form represents a screen that can be viewed by the user. This screen may display data or other information, it may require input from the user, it may provide navigational control, it may simply draw a picture, or it may do all of the above. In any sense, a form interacts with the user for displaying information and receiving feedback.

Reports display data in a presentation manner. Reports are designed and look similar to forms, so they can contain essentially the same information as a form. However, the user cannot directly interact with reports. Reports simply provide a way to view and print data from an application.

Classes are a very powerful concept within OPO. They are reusable, object-oriented components that can be incorporated into forms, reports, or other classes. A class is basically a self-contained form. Its design, look, and functions are exactly like a form. Classes are generally created to perform tasks that are used multiple times by different forms. A simple example would be an exit button. If each form of an application required the same code to be activated on the Click method of an exit button, then a class containing an exit button with the appropriate code could be created and instanced on each form. Each instance of the class can be customized, yet tied to the parent class. If the code for this button changes, only the code in the parent class would need to be changed.

Bitmaps are used to add imagery to application objects. Forms, reports, classes, and buttons can display bitmaps by setting the Bitmap property of the object to the name of the bitmap, or by dropping the bitmap onto the object. Currently, OPO only supports the Windows BMP file type. In future releases, OPO will permit Mac PICT files and other file types to be imported as bitmaps.

OLE objects are instances of another software's objects that can be embedded into a form, report, or class. Object Linking and Embedding (OLE) allows different software that are OLE-enabled to share components. For example, a Microsoft Word (Word) document and functionality can be used in an OPO form. The instanced document has the same look and feel as it does in Word, and when the instance of the document is selected, the menu bar and toolbar of Word are incorporated into OPO. There are many different products that can be included in an OPO application through OLE, including Excel, PowerPoint, Video for Windows, Sound, Paintbrush, and any other installed product that is an OLE Server.

Running a Form or an Application

Once an application is completed, the application can be run by clicking on the Run App toolbar button, or by selecting the Run | Run Application menu command. This causes OPO to compile the application objects to program code (p-code) and run the application. If any errors exist, the compiler will stop its execution, notify the developer, and highlight the error in the designer. Additionally, each form and report can be run individually for faster testing. With the form or report open, click the Run Form/Report toolbar button, or select the Run | Run Form menu command. This will quickly compile the code for just this form or report and run it. This prevents you from having to compile the entire application when working with a single form or report. Note, you cannot run a form or report by itself if it relies on other forms, nor can you navigate to other forms or reports simply because only that form or report has been compiled.

Distributing Your Application to Customers

After you run and test an application, it's ready to be distributed. The first step in distributing an application is to compile it. Clicking on the Generate Executable toolbar button invokes the Generate Runtime File Dialog Box, which is illustrated in Figure 39.2.

FIGURE 39.2.

*Generate Runtime File
dialog box.*

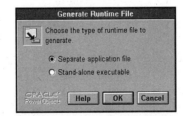

This dialog allows the application to be compiled to a separate application file, or as a stand-alone executable file. This dialog can be bypassed by selecting either the Run | Compile Application or Run | Generate Executable menu commands.

Creating a separate application file compiles the application and writes just the compiled p-code to a Power Objects (PO) file. This file can be executed using the OPO Runtime (PWRRUN.EXE). Compiling to a stand-alone executable first compiles the application to p-code, then binds it to a minimized copy of the OPO Runtime. This creates a self-sufficient executable (EXE) file. In either sense, the compiled application is executed via the OPO Runtime. Don't worry, the OPO Runtime is freely distributable, which is something new for Oracle.

The advantage of compiling separate application files is size. The PO files are small, generally 25-100 KB. The EXE files tend to be greater than 2 MB. If several applications are to be compiled and distributed together, it makes sense to compile separate application files and simply distribute them and the OPO Runtime. The user simply needs to start the OPO Runtime and specify which PO file to run. However, it's easier for the user to simply run a single executable, which is why stand-alone executables are often preferred.

If compiling separate applications files, the PO and PWRRUN.EXE files will need to be distributed. Otherwise, if compiling stand-alone executables, only the EXE file needs to be distributed. Other files that need to be distributed are database files and any external function files used by the application. If the application uses a Blaze database, the file that was created for the Blaze database file needs to be distributed. If the application runs against an Oracle, Sybase, or SQLServer database, then the corresponding Power Objects Database (POD) file needs to be distributed with the application. Additionally, if the application references any Dynamic Link Library (DLL) functions, then the associated DLL file needs to be distributed. Other files, such as session and library files, shouldn't be distributed, since they are compiled into the PO and EXE file.

Summary

Power Objects is designed to facilitate rapid application development and deployment of database applications. The application model uses three conceptual building blocks to accomplish this goal. The session object provides a connectivity layer to database back ends. The library object provides access to application-level objects to enhance standardization and to promote object reuse. Finally, the application object represents the set of related activities that make up the application. With these three conceptual objects, a developer can maintain each conceptual area independently of the others and produce database applications to meet their current and future needs.

Objects Within Oracle Power Objects™

40

by Ronnie Lashaw

This chapter provides detailed information on each of the object types within Oracle Power Objects (OPO). Many of these objects are visible during design time; some are visible only during run-time. Some objects are non-visual. This chapter defines the methods and properties associated with each object and documents which methods and properties OPO version 1.0 does not use.

Overview of Objects

The Oracle Power Objects product is completely structured around the concept of objects. The highest level of object classification consists of applications, libraries, and database sessions. Figure 40.1 illustrates the icons for these objects.

FIGURE 40.1.

OPO objects.

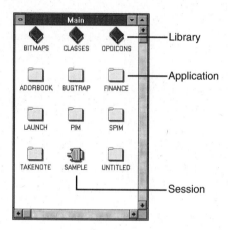

The application object is what the developer uses to interface between the user, the database, and any other peripheral devices. The application object contains the objects required to implement the level of interaction necessary for the given set of related tasks comprising the application. Library objects consist of bitmap resource objects and class objects. Each of these object types is covered in detail in the following application-level objects sections. The only difference between the objects found in a library and those found in an application is that the library objects can be shared from a library and cannot be shared from an application. For more information on database session objects, refer to Chapter 37, "Connecting to Database Sources Through Sessions."

Events, Methods, and Properties

Objects within the OPO framework have predefined behaviors and characteristics. Behaviors represent the mapping of system- and user-generated events into *methods*. These methods also represent behaviors that respond to programmatic references to themselves and that respond to previously referenced methods (a chain of sequential events). Objects within Power Objects also have characteristics that are represented by the concept of *properties*. Examples of properties are FontName, SizeX, SizeY, PositionX, PositionY, and so on. All of the properties and methods for an application are listed in alphabetical order on its *property sheet*. Figure 40.2 shows an open property sheet for the Finance sample application from OPO. A diamond object in the leftmost column denotes properties. A pointer object in the leftmost column denotes methods.

FIGURE 40.2.

An example of a property sheet.

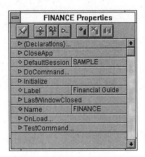

Although this chapter does not cover of all of the various properties and methods for each object in OPO, it does present a summary of the most frequently used properties and methods. If you need more detailed information, refer to OPO online documentation.

Common Properties

Many objects in OPO have the same properties. For example, a button object and a field object each have a FontName property. Although OPO has a predefined default FontName value for each of these objects, often a developer wants to change the predefined value to a new value. If you select both the field object and the button object, the property sheet is labeled Multiple Selection Properties and only displays those properties and methods that all the selected objects have in common. In Figure 40.3, button1 and field1 are selected and the FontName property has been expanded. Notice that <multiple> is the current value of the FontName property. The developer can select a name from the list, such as Arial, to change the FontName value to that name.

The following paragraphs highlight and discuss those properties that are common to most of the objects within Power Objects. Not all objects have these properties, but many objects do. These properties are those that are most likely to be changed by a developer.

The Bitmap property specifies the name of a bitmap resource object that should be displayed on the specified control. Although the online OPO help says this property has a string datatype and is readable and writeable at run-time, these statements are not entirely true. For example, reading the value of the Bitmap property should work with the following Basic statement:

```
msgbox form1.Bitmap
```

This statement works if the value is NULL, but it yields the following Basic error if the Bitmap value is specified:

```
BAS-01023: Invalid type for built-in function
```

The datatype for Bitmap is string, supposedly. The following statement works:

```
form1.Bitmap = Flowers
```

Flowers is the name of a bitmap resource object within the active application. Notice that the word Flowers is not surrounded by quotation marks. Quotation marks imply a string. Although the Bitmap property may be of a string datatype, setting its value programmatically requires a reference to an existing bitmap resource object, not a string reference.

The BitmapTiled property specifies whether the bitmap should be tiled across the control. The datatype is Boolean. This property is readable and writeable at run-time. If the value is False, the bitmap is centered across either the width and/or height of the control provided that either of these control dimensions is as large or larger than the corresponding bitmap dimensions; otherwise, it is top-left justified in the control. If the value is True, the bitmap is tiled across the control with clipping applied to the right and bottom limits of the control.

The DataSize property is the number of bytes set aside for a bound control. The datatype is integer. This property is readable at run-time. The displayed default value is zero. This value is not the actual default value, however. The long integer, double, and date datatypes ignore the DataSize setting. The DataSize for string datatypes represents the exact number of bytes or characters that the control can contain. The default value for the string datatype is 41. If the developer drags either one or more columns or the entire table onto a container, the DataSize for the string datatype is set to the actual number of characters specified in the database table, and the DataSize for the date datatype is set to 11.

Suppose that a column from a table in the database has a VarChar2 type and a size of 50. If the developer has a control bound to that column and sets the DataSize to 0, the following problem could occur. The end user of the application can enter up to 41 characters in the control. Entering more than 41 characters but less than 51 characters is valid from the perspective of the database, but is not acceptable for the OPO application. The opposite is also true. Suppose that a column from a table in the database is of the type VarChar2 and has a size of 10, and the developer binds a control to the column and sets the DataSize to 0. The user can enter more than 10 and less than 42 characters into the field, and the OPO application will accept the entry. The database will not accept the entry, however, and an error will be generated for the end user. The developer should take care to avoid both of these problems and specify the actual DataSize for the bound control that is specified in the database.

The DataSource property determines whether the control is bound to a database table column or to a derived value. The datatype is string. This property is readable at run-time. If the control is bound to a database table column, the value is the name of the column. If the database table column is using case-sensitive names, surround the DataSource value with double quotation marks. If the control is bound to a derived value, the first character of the DataSource value is an equal sign. The remainder of the value must evaluate to a valid OPO equation or literal. Finally, an empty DataSource property implies that the control is not bound to data. The user can enter data into an unbound control, the record manager can manage the data, and validation methods can be applied to the value, but the data is not stored in the database. Derived values are similar to these unbound data controls. The data specified by a derived control cannot be directly stored in the database.

The DataType property indicates the type of data that the control contains from the perspective of the application. These DataType values are independent of the database back end. The datatype is long integer. This property is readable at run-time. Values are as follows:

    3 = Long Integer
    5 = Double
    8 = String
    7 = Date

The DrawStyle property determines whether the control uses the 3-D sculpted look and feel. The datatype is long integer. This property is not readable nor writeable at run-time. The default DrawStyle for all controls in OPO is Standard Control (a 2-D display modality). In OPO version 1.0, the alternative DrawStyle setting is 3D Control. The following controls respect the DrawStyle setting: field, rectangle, frame, and button. Although many of the OPO controls respect the 3D Control DrawStyle, the following controls do not actually display in a 3-D mode: line, oval, pop-up, combo box, and list box. The following controls do not have a DrawStyle property: chart, horizontal and vertical scrollbars, embedded form, repeater, bitmap, OLE, report group, current row pointer, and static text. Scrollbars and buttons do not display in a 2-D mode.

The datatype for the Enabled property is string. This property is readable and writeable at run-time.

Text for the control is displayed using the font indicated in the FontName property. The datatype for this property is string. This property is readable and writeable at run-time. If a font specified for FontName in the OPO design environment is not available on the target client environment, OPO uses the closest matching available font based on font name and font characteristics. If no matching font is found, the default font is used. System Font is the default font for button, chart, static field, checkbox, list box, and pop-up controls. Application Font is the default font for field, combo, and frame controls.

TIP

You can set the FontName property during run-time as follows:

```
button1.FontName = "Times New Roman"
```

OPO intelligently maps the supplied name against the list of available font names and picks the closest matching name. In a Microsoft Windows environment, for example, Times New Roman, Times Roman, Times, and Roman all yield the same font, Times New Roman. Remember that this FontName change is only valid during the active run-time mode for the affected objects. When the developer returns to the design-time environment, the change is lost and the FontName property is returned to its original design-time value.

The HelpText property sets the text that is displayed in the active status line object when the cursor is moved over the object. The datatype for this property is string. This property is readable and writeable at run-time.

NOTE

OPO version 1.0 does not display the HelpText property during run-time.

The ReadOnly property determines whether the user can enter/edit the value of data in a control. The datatype is long integer. This property is readable and writeable at run-time. If the value of ReadOnly is True, the user cannot tab to the control or set the focus to the control.

The ScrollWithRow property determines whether a value specified for an unbound data control should scroll with each record in the active record manager. The datatype is long integer. This property is readable at runtime. By default, ScrollWithRow is True, which implies that the record manager has a value for the unbound data control for each record in the table. If ScrollWithRow is False, the unbound data control is acting independently of the record manager and has only one value. This property is extremely valuable for controls that are used to limit the display of data within other record manager sets. For example, a pop-up could list all of the available departments in a company. Choosing a department from the pop-up could limit the list of employees displayed in a repeater to only those employees working in that department.

The TabEnabled property determines whether the user can set the focus to the specified control using the Tab key. The datatype is long integer. This property is readable and writeable at run-time. The default value is True. If TabEnabled is True, pressing the Tab key navigates to this control in the order specified by the TabOrder property. Pushbuttons, radio buttons, and checkbox buttons are not tab-enabled on the Macintosh, although they are in the Microsoft Windows environment. If TabEnabled is False, the user cannot use the Tab key to navigate to the control. A `False` value for the `TabEnabled` property does not affect other methods or properties of the specified control.

The `TabOrder` property specifies the order in which controls will be navigated when the user uses the Tab key. The datatype is long integer. This property is readable and writeable at run-time.

The `Value` property specifies the data stored in a control. The datatype is specified by the control. This property is readable and writeable at run-time. This property does not show up on the property sheet.

The `Visible` property specifies whether the user can view the control. The datatype for this property is long integer. This property is readable and writeable at run-time. If the `Visible` property's value is `False`, the user cannot tab to the control or edit data in the control with the keyboard. Setting the `Visible` property of a container control also affects the visibility of the contained controls. Setting the `Visible` property of an embedded form, for example, hides the embedded form and all of the controls contained within the embedded form.

TIP

The `ZOrder` property is not one of the properties for OPO controls that is displayed in the property sheet. The `ZOrder` represents the graphical redraw order when OPO redraws the screen. Objects are drawn starting with the lowest `ZOrder` up through the highest `ZOrder`. The developer can manipulate the `ZOrder` property from the design environment through the Design menu, however. Under the Object menu item you will find the Further front, Bring to front, Further back, and Send to back options. These menu options, as well as the Bring to front and Send to Back toolbar icons, provide the developer with the ability to control the `ZOrder` of the currently selected controls. This property is not readable or writeable during run-time.

Common Methods

Not only do many of the OPO objects have properties in common, they also have several common methods. For example, a button and a field object each have a `Click()` method. The default action associated with the `Click()` method varies according to the type of object, but generally the object receives a mouse down event followed by a mouse up event, and then receives the focus. Often a developer will want to perform special actions associated with the `Click()` method. A simple example would be to have the object issue a `Beep` command. If you select the field object and the button object on a form, the property sheet is titled Multiple Selection Properties and only displays the properties and methods that all the selected objects have in common. In Figure 40.3, button1 and field1 are selected and the `Click()` method is visible. If the developer opens the `Click()` method script window and enters the `Beep` command, clicking in the field or on the button causes a beep to be heard when the form is run.

FIGURE 40.3.

*A Multiple Selection
Properties property sheet.*

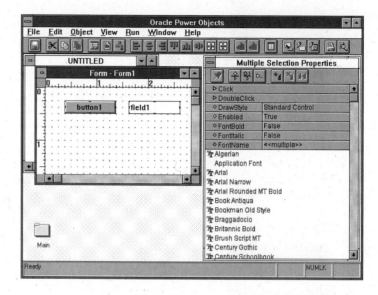

The following paragraphs highlight and discuss those methods that are common to most of the objects within Power Objects. Not all objects have these methods, but many objects do. These methods are those that are most likely to be changed by a developer.

The Click() method responds to programmatic references and a specific series of user-generated events, mouse down followed by mouse up. This method returns no data. If the developer doesn't override the Click() method, the click event propagates up the hierarchical containment to the object's container's ChildClick() method.

The DoubleClick() method responds to programmatic references and a specific series of user-generated events: mouse down, mouse up, click, mouse down, and mouse up. The datatype is long integer. If the developer specifies a non-zero return value, the Click() method is triggered after the DoubleClick() method is processed. Normally, the Click() method is not processed after the DoubleClick() method.

The MouseDown() method responds to the user-generated event of mouse down and to programmatic references. This method returns no data.

The MouseMove() method responds to user-generated events focused around changing the position of the mouse following a mouse down event. This method returns no data. The MouseMove() method fires for every position update inside and outside of the original object dimensions until the user releases the mouse, which forces a mouse up event. Visual effects are possible from within the MouseMove() method due to the inherent screen refresh after each pass through of the method code.

The MouseUp() method responds to the user-generated event of mouse up and to programmatic references. This method returns no data.

The OnLoad() method responds to an application-generated event. The event is the action of the OPO environment loading an object into active memory in order to process it or other related objects. This method returns no data. The OnLoad() method is a good place to put initialize code specific to an object. Exceptions to this rule include objects that have Initialize() or InitializeWindow() methods.

The PostChange() method responds to the event of data being changed in a control through editing and scrolling of the record manager. Programmatic changing of data in a control does not fire the PostChange() method. This method returns no data. The PostChange() method is triggered after the Validate() method returns True.

The RevertValue() method responds to the Esc key or to a programmatic reference. This method returns no data. The purpose of this method is to return the value of a control to its value prior to any editing.

The Validate() method responds to the user editing the data in a control and attempting to force the data to update. The datatype is long integer. If the Validate() method returns False, the focus remains in the control until a True result is returned for the Validate() method. The developer should take care to ensure that a True value can be returned; otherwise, an infinite loop will exist once the user edits the related control.

Application-Level Objects

The objects found within the application level form the basis for all interactions between the user, the database, and any other peripherals. These objects and their methods and properties are combined to build a series of screens and reports that approximate the set of related tasks that form the application. A form object is a screen or window. A report object can provide both a visual report and a printed report. Other application-level objects include bitmap resource objects, class objects, and OLE objects. Figure 40.4 displays the icons for each of these application-level objects.

FIGURE 40.4.

Application-level objects.

Form Objects

The form object is the object that an OPO developer uses most often. The form is the window or screen that the developer designs to interact with the user. The form is also the primary object for interfacing to the database. The form can contain other objects, except for other forms, reports, and report groups. The form is useful for displaying data, manipulating data, navigating to other forms, and linking to other applications through embedded OLE objects and OCX objects. Figure 40.5 displays a blank form with its accompanying property sheet. The remaining paragraphs within this section discuss the various properties and methods that are relevant to a form object.

FIGURE 40.5.

A form object.

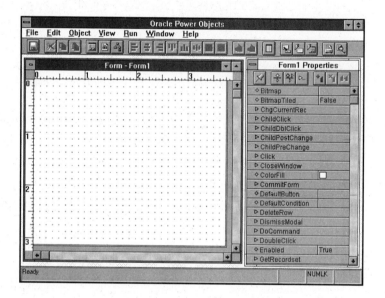

The `CloseWindow()` method responds to the action of closing a window both programmatically and through user events such as the System Menu Close menu item. This method returns no data. This method must be inherited in order for the window to close. For example, if the developer places code in the `CloseWindow()` method, the code must also include `inherited.CloseWindow()`.

The `CommitForm()` method responds to the Commit toolbar icon and to programmatic references. This method returns no data. The purpose of this method is to commit or save all outstanding changes associated with the Database Session associated with the form's RecordSource. If the developer places code in this method, then `inherited.CommitForm()` must be included or the commit action will never successfully complete for the specified form.

The `DefaultButton` method specifies the button that should accept the default behavior for a pressed Enter or Return key when the active focus is not in a field control. The datatype is string. This method is not readable or writeable at run-time.

The DefaultCondition method specifies the limiting condition to apply to the record manager for the specified form. The datatype is string. This method is readable and writeable at run-time. The DefaultCondition is synonymous to the where condition in a SQL statement.

The DefaultMenuBar() method initializes a menu bar with the system default menus and application default menus appropriate to the form or report. This method deletes any existing menus before initializing the menu bar.

The DefaultToolbar() method initializes the toolbar with the application default buttons appropriate to the form or report. This method deletes any existing buttons before initializing the toolbar.

The DoCommand() method responds to programmatic references and user-generated events of menu and toolbar selections. The datatype is long integer. DoCommand() passes the cmdCode up to the application level from the form or report level if the form or report does not process the cmdCode. The proper method for ensuring that the form- and report-level processing is completed prior to escalating to application-level processing is to assign the return value of True for the cmdCode.

The GetMenuBar() method returns a reference to the menu bar associated with the form or report. The datatype is object.

The GetRecordset() method returns a handle or pointer to the record manager of the specified control. The datatype is object. This method is readable at run-time. This method is required for processing the data within a record manager programmatically and for DBRecordsets that have no controls associated with them for point-and-click interfacing.

The GetStatusLine() method returns a handle to the status line object associated with the form. The datatype is object.

The GetToolbar() method returns a reference to the toolbar associated with the form. The datatype is object.

The InitializeWindow() method is used primarily for the creation of menus, toolbars, and status lines relevant to the active form. This method returns no data. The developer should create custom menus, toolbars, and status lines in this method.

The Label property specifies the title to display in the window frame title bar, if the WindowStyle option has a title bar. The datatype is string. This method is readable and writeable at run-time.

The LinkDetailColumn property specifies the name of the column from the detail table to use when performing master-detail linking relationships. The datatype is string. This method is readable at run-time.

The LinkMasterColumn property specifies the name of the column from the master table to use when performing master-detail linking relationships. The datatype is string. The method is readable at run-time.

The `LinkMasterDel` property specifies what the default action will be with respect to detail (foreign key) records when the master (primary key) records are deleted. The datatype is long integer. This method is readable and writeable at run-time. This property helps to ensure and enforce the application's referential integrity. The values range from `Refuse if children present`, to `Delete cascade`, to `Orphan details`.

The `LinkMasterForm` property specifies the name of the object that has the record manager for the master in the master-detail relationship. The datatype is string. This method is readable at run-time.

The `LinkMasterUpd` property specifies what the default action will be with respect to detail (foreign key) records when the master (primary key) records are updated. The datatype is long integer. This method is readable and writeable at run-time. This property helps to ensure and enforce an application's referential integrity. The values range from `Refuse if children present`, to `Update cascade`, to `Orphan details`.

The `OpenWindow()` method responds to programmatic references. This method returns no data. This method is responsible for displaying the form and its contained controls on-screen. If the developer places code in this method, the developer also needs to place `inherited.OpenWindow()` in the code so that the form draws on-screen.

The `Query()` method responds to programmatic references and to the default menu and toolbar query commands. This method returns no data. The `Query()` method is responsible for updating the set of records being managed by the record manager that the `Query()` method is attached to. `Query()` also propagates to the session associated with the record manager. If the developer places code in this method, the record manager is not updated unless `inherited.Query()` is also placed in the code. This method respects the settings specified by the `DefaultCondition` for limiting the records that are brought into the record manager.

The `QueryWhere()` method responds to programmatic references only. This method returns no data. `QueryWhere()` is very similar to the `Query()` method with the following exception. `QueryWhere()` includes the condition that is to be applied to the affected record manager in place of the `DefaultCondition`. As with many critical methods, if the developer overrides the processing of the `QueryWhere()` method by placing code in the method, the method does not execute unless `inherited.QueryWhere( condition )` is also in the method code.

The `RecordSource` property specifies the name of the database object, table, view, synonym, and so on that is being controlled by the record manager associated with the control. The datatype is string. This method is readable at run-time.

The `RecSrcSession` property specifies the name of the database session object that links to the database objects used by the container. The datatype is string. This method is not readable or writeable at run-time. If the `RecSrcSession` is empty, the application's `DefaultSession` is used.

The `RollbackForm()` method responds to the Rollback toolbar icon and to programmatic references. This method returns no data. The purpose of this method is to discard all outstanding changes associated with the database session associated with the form's `RecordSource`. If the

The OpenPrint() method must be called programmatically. This method returns no data. The printer redirection dialog box open for the user to selects among printer options. OK causes a dialog box to appear that indicates that the report or form is printing.

There are seven kinds of report objects:

- The ReportHeader Band object displays data at the top of the report that is considered global to the overall report.

- The PageHeader Band object displays data at the top of each printed page of a report. The FirstPgHdr property specifies whether the PageHeader band will be printed on the first page. The datatype is long integer. This property is neither readable nor writeable at run-time.

- The developer creates the GroupHeader Band object by dropping the Report Group control onto a report. This band is used to display data at the top of each grouped area. The GroupCol property specifies the database column that the report uses for grouping. The datatype is string. This property is neither readable nor writeable at run-time. The PageOnBreak property specifies whether the report should begin a new page with every new group. The datatype is long integer. This property is neither readable nor writeable at run-time.

- The Detail Band object displays the bulk of data related to the report. The detail band is effectively like the repeat_panel of the repeater object in that it repeats once for each record in the database object being reported on. The OrderBy property specifies the column or columns that the report should use to order the data. The datatype is string. This property is neither readable nor writeable at run-time.

- The developer creates the GroupFooter Band object by dropping the Report Group control onto a report. This band is used to display data at the bottom of each grouped area.

- The PageFooter Band object displays data at the bottom of each printed page of a report. The FirstPgFtr property specifies whether a page footer should be displayed on the first page of the report. The datatype is long integer. This property is neither readable nor writeable at run-time. The LastPgFtr property specifies whether a page footer should be displayed on the last page of the report. The datatype is long integer. This property is neither readable nor writeable at run-time.

- The ReportFooter Band object displays data at the bottom of the report that is considered global to the overall report.

Class Objects

The class object provides a mechanism for creating reusable objects. Class objects can be as simple as an OK button or as complex as the calendar class that ships with the OPO Sample Applications. Class objects are instanced into an application by dragging them from the application or library window onto the form or report. These instances are linked to the parent at the property and method level. This implies that code written for a parent method will not be shown in the instance but will be executed unless overridden. Figure 40.7 illustrates four classes that are provided with the OPO Sample Applications: the form control, the record control, the meter control, and the calendar class.

FIGURE 40.7.

Class objects.

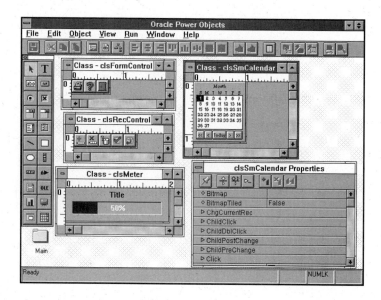

Each of the OPO Sample Application classes illustrated in Figure 40.7 is well documented in the OPO Sample Application online help. If the developer uses the class model illustrated in the OPO Sample help, the developed classes are more usable and maintainable. Class objects represent the real reusable power behind OPO. Class objects support the concepts of encapsulation, inheritance, nested instancing, and polymorphism. You can embed custom business logic and rules within class objects and then standardize them through libraries for use in corporate-wide application development and deployment. A mechanism for embedding custom logic is provided through the capability to create user-defined properties and methods. All the sample class objects provided with the OPO Sample Applications use user-defined properties and methods at various levels.

Bitmap Resource Objects

The bitmap resource object provides a mechanism for displaying graphic images on buttons, forms, embedded forms, and user-defined classes. There are no properties that can be changed or methods that execute with respect to bitmap resource objects. These objects are not editable or scaleable. Perhaps the best use of bitmap resource objects is for standardization of backgrounds and button icons in corporate-wide applications. Bitmap resource objects stored in an OPO library perform just this function. The OPO Sample Applications provide two libraries dedicated to bitmap resource objects. The Bitmaps library contains 68 bitmaps and the OPOICONS library contains 96 bitmaps. Figure 40.8 illustrates a few of the bitmap resources available from the Bitmaps library.

FIGURE 40.8.

Bitmap resource objects.

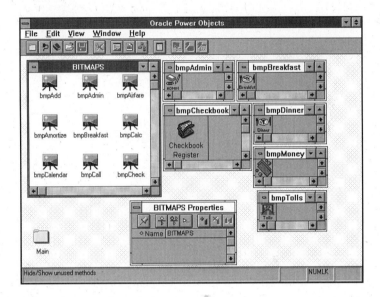

OLE Objects

OLE objects provide a mechanism for using the Object Linking and Embedding (OLE) technology developed by Microsoft. You can only use these objects in the Microsoft Windows version of OPO. You can insert the OLE object from the design-time menu or instance it from an application or a library. Figure 40.9 displays two OLE objects in the untitled OPO application and instanced onto a form. OLE5 is a PC Paintbrush object. OLE11 is a Microsoft Word 6.0 object with an embedded picture object. OLE objects permit other applications to be embedded within OPO. OPO version 1.0 doesn't have a mechanism for tying the functionality of the OLE object to the database or even to a programmatic reference from within OPO. Due to this interaction limitation, OLE objects in OPO are of minimal value.

FIGURE 40.9.

OLE objects.

Instance of
OLE5 object

Instance of OLE11 object
(Paintbrush file)

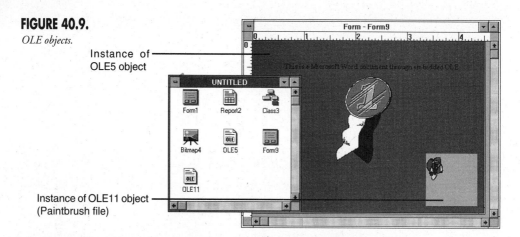

Objects for Building Applications

Objects for building applications include data-bound and graphical objects. These building blocks or objects used in conjunction with the application-level objects enable the developer to build custom database applications. Each of these objects is described in the remainder of this section. Each description lists the object's most common uses, its significant properties and methods, and any areas of concern that a developer should be aware of with respect to using the object.

Chart Object

The chart object is a bindable control for displaying data as a vertical bar, horizontal bar, line graph, or pie graph. The developer cannot drag-and-drop columns from a table onto the chart object because the object would not know whether these columns were x- or y-axis columns. The chart object is not editable in any way with respect to the data it displays. Figure 40.10 displays chart objects displaying the same employee data in various formats.

You can link the chart object to other record manager objects in master-detail relationships. The developer can make the chart object a detail view of data by setting the LinkDetailColumn, LinkMasterColumn, and LinkMasterForm properties of the chart object. One simple example to set up is to drop the familiar SCOTT/TIGER DEPT table onto a form. Create a chart object with ENAME as ChartXCol and SAL as ChartYCols, set the link properties appropriately on the chart object, and then run the form. The chart object will be the detail of employees per department. Figure 40.10 illustrates this master-detail relationship with the form as master to four detail chart objects. The chart object has many other properties similar to the form object. The following are chart-specific properties of interest:

The ChartAutoFormat property specifies whether the y-axis scales to the actual minimum and maximum values or uses the specified minimum and maximum values. The datatype is Boolean. This property is readable and writeable at run-time.

FIGURE 40.10.

Chart objects.

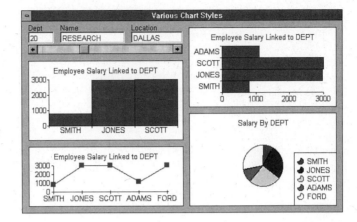

The ChartGap property specifies the gap in pixels between groups of bars in horizontal and vertical bar graphs. The datatype is long integer. This property is readable and writeable at run-time.

The ChartLabelStyle property specifies the type of labels beside each bar in a horizontal or vertical bar graph. The datatype is long integer. This property is readable and writeable at run-time. Possible values are none, values, labels, or categories.

The ChartLegendHAlign property specifies that the chart legend should be aligned on the left or right side of the chart object. The datatype is long integer. This property is readable and writeable at run-time.

The ChartLegendVAlign property specifies that the chart legend should be aligned on the top or bottom side of the chart object. The datatype is long integer. This property is readable and writeable at run-time.

The ChartLineStyle property specifies the style of line to use in drawing the chart object. The datatype is long integer. This property is readable and writeable at run-time. In OPO version 1.0, this property has no effect.

The ChartMaxValue property specifies the maximum y-axis value for a vertical bar, horizontal bar, and line graph chart object. The datatype is long integer. This property is readable and writeable at run-time. The ChartAutoFormat property must be False for this value to have meaning.

The ChartMinValue property specifies the minimum y-axis value for a vertical bar, horizontal bar, and line graph chart object. The datatype is long integer. This property is readable and writeable at run-time. The ChartAutoFormat property must be False for this value to have meaning.

The ChartOverlap property specifies the amount of overlap in pixels between the bars in the same group for horizontal and vertical bar graphs. The datatype is long integer. This property is readable and writeable at run-time.

The `ChartPieCircle` property specifies whether the chart object displays pies as circles or as ovals conforming to the dimensions of the chart object. The datatype is Boolean. This property is readable and writeable at run-time.

The `ChartRowCount` property specifies the maximum number of rows that the chart object will display. The datatype is long integer. This property is readable at run-time. The default value is zero, which implies all rows will be displayed. Any non-zero value, represented by *n*, causes the first *n* records to be displayed.

The `ChartShowGrid` property specifies the type of grid that the chart object should display. The datatype is long integer. This property is readable and writeable at run-time. Possible values are none, horizontal, vertical, or both.

The `ChartShowLegend` property specifies whether the chart object should display a legend. The datatype is Boolean. This property is readable and writeable at run-time.

The `ChartStacked` property specifies whether vertical and horizontal bar graphs should display data in groups or as a single stacked value. The datatype is Boolean. This property is readable and writeable at run-time.

The `ChartStyle` property specifies the type of chart or graph. The datatype is long integer. This property is readable and writeable at run-time. Possible values include `Vertical Bar`, `Horizontal Bar`, `Line`, or `Pie`.

The `ChartXCol` property specifies the name of the column from the database to be used for the x-axis. The datatype is string. This property is readable at run-time. You must specify this property even if the chart type does not need an x-axis variable.

The `ChartYCols` property specifies the names of the columns from the database to be used for the y-axis. The datatype is string. This property is readable at run-time.

Checkbox Object

The checkbox object is a data bound control. The checkbox is typically used to represent a toggle state of values for a particular column in the database. The checkbox is also used to represent a set of mutually exclusive values where one or more values can be chosen at a time from the set of all possible values. Checkbox-specific properties of interest are described as follows:

The `ValueOff` property specifies the value of the control when it is not selected. The datatype is set to be the same as the radio button datatype. This property is readable and writeable at run-time. The default value is null.

The `ValueOn` property specifies the value of the control when it is selected. The datatype is set to be the same as the radio button datatype. This property is readable and writeable at run-time.

Combo Box Object

The combo box object is a more versatile version of the pop-up object. Although each object allows the user to pick a value from a list, the combo box allows the user to enter values not already in the list. The combo box does not respect the 3D Control style for the DrawStyle property. Figure 40.11 displays three combo boxes; each displays a different type of data.

FIGURE 40.11.

Combo box objects.

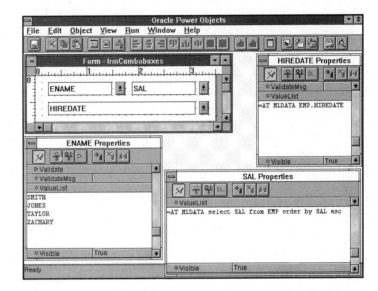

The following are combo box–specific methods and properties of interest:

The UpdateList() method must be called programmatically. This method returns no data. UpdateList() is called to update the data within a record manager for a pop-up, combo, or list box control.

The ValueList property specifies the list of values that a combo box can display. The datatype is string. This property is readable and writeable at run-time. There are three methods for setting the values in the ValueList property: 1) create a hard-coded list of one value per line; 2) use table column mapping, which selects all of the values for a specified column from the specified table; and 3) use queried values that a fully qualified SQL statement selects a column from a table using conditions and other SQL operators. In Figure 41.11, the ENAME combo box uses method 1, the HIREDATE combo box uses method 2, and the SAL combo box uses method 3 to populate the ValueList property.

Current Row Pointer Object

The current row pointer object is used to indicate the status of a record in relation to the database. A gray arrow indicates that the record is the current record, but it is not active; a white arrow indicates a separate record. A black arrow indicates that the record is the current record and is also the active record, and a lock beside the arrow indicates that the record has changed and needs to be updated to the database. The current row pointer is of great value to a database application developer because it gives a quick visual cue indicating which records have pending changes. End users, however, are not accustomed to seeing current row pointers. The developer must use care in distributing applications to users unfamiliar with the current row pointer concept. The developer should explain what the object represents or not use it at all.

DBRecordset Object

The DBRecordset object is a non-visible object. It is a method of having a record manager that is not attached to a visible object. All the actions that are valid for the record manager of a form, embedded form, or repeater are valid for the DBRecordset object. The developer has to programmatically create and delete these objects. They use memory resources and must be deleted when the developer is finished using them.

Embedded Form Object

This object has all the properties of the form object with the exception of those methods specifically related to the style of window framing, such as WindowInitPos, WindowStyle, and so on. The embedded form is generally used for displaying a single record from a table. It is also generally used in forming master-detail relationships where the detail only needs to display one record.

Field Object

The field object carries most of the programming and database interface weight for the entire OPO product. This object enables the user to edit existing data and enter new data. You can set up counters using sequences, maximum values from a table plus a specified increment, and user-generated values. Display formats are available based on the DataType of the field. The following are field-specific methods and properties of interest:

The CounterGenKey() method responds to the need to specify a user-generated sequence. The datatype is string. You must write method code to generate a sequence value. One reason for using this method over a sequence from the database is that the database may not support sequences. Another reason is to free up server-based resources.

The CounterIncBy property specifies the increment value to use in generating a new sequence value when using the Table, MAX() + CounterIncBy CounterType. The datatype is long integer. This property is readable at run-time.

The CounterSeq property specifies the name of the sequence from the database to be used for generating new values. The datatype is string. This property is readable at run-time.

The CounterTiming property determines when the counter value is to be generated. The datatype is long integer. This property is readable at run-time. Values are Immediate (upon insertion into the record manager) and Deferred (upon flushing the record to the database).

The CounterType property specifies whether the field is a counter field and how it gets its values. The datatype is long integer. This property is readable at run-time. Values include None, Sequence, Table,MAX()+CounterIncBy, and User Generated.

The HasScrollBar property specifies whether the object has a vertical scrollbar. The datatype is long integer. This property is readable at run-time. For field objects, the MultiLine property must be True for the scrollbar to display.

The MultiLine property specifies whether the object can handle multiline data. The datatype is long integer. This property is neither readable nor writeable at run-time. In the Windows version of OPO, a multiline field wraps only at carriage return linefeeds. In the Macintosh version of OPO, a field wraps when data flows beyond the right side of the field or when a linefeed is entered.

Horizontal and Vertical Scrollbar Objects

Horizontal and vertical scrollbar objects are designed to handle the scrolling of data within a record manager. Although each of these objects exists independently on the object palette, either can become visibly like the other just by changing its position and size. Each has the same methods and properties. Scrollbar-specific methods and properties of interest are described as follows:

The GoNxtLine() method responds to scrollbar requests and programmatic references. This method scrolls the record manager to the next record, if one exists, based on the ScrollAmtLine. This method returns no data.

The GoNxtPage() method responds to scrollbar requests and programmatic references. This method scrolls the record manager to the next block of records, if one exists, based on the ScrollAmtPage. This method returns no data.

The GoPos() method responds to scrollbar requests and programmatic references. This method scrolls the record manager to the next record, if one exists, based on the newpos requested. This method returns no data.

The GoPrvLine() method responds to scrollbar requests and programmatic references. This method scrolls the record manager to the previous record, if one exists, based on the ScrollAmtLine. This method returns no data.

The GoPrvPage() method responds to scrollbar requests and programmatic references. This method scrolls the record manager to the previous block of records, if one exists, based on the ScrollAmtPage. This method returns no data.

The ScrollAmtLine property specifies the amount to scroll when a GoNxtLine() or GoPrvLine() method is encountered. The datatype is long integer. This property is readable and writeable at run-time.

The ScrollAmtPage property specifies the amount to scroll when a GoNxtPage() or GoPrvPage() method is encountered. The datatype is long integer. This property is readable and writeable at run-time.

The ScrollMax property specifies the upper limit of the scrollbar for visually positioning the scrollbox. The datatype is long integer. This property is readable and writeable at run-time.

The ScrollMin property specifies the lower limit of the scrollbar for visually positioning the scrollbox. The datatype is long integer. This property is readable and writeable at run-time.

The ScrollObj property specifies the container whose record manager is to be controlled by the scrollbar. The datatype is string. This property is readable and writeable at run-time.

The ScrollPos property specifies the current record in the record manager. The datatype is long integer. This property is readable and writeable at run-time.

Line Object

The line object is a visual object. It cannot be bound to data. This object is useful for creating visual effects to enhance the user interface. The line does not respect the 3D Control style for DrawStyle. The Direction property specifies the direction of the line object. The datatype is long integer. This property is readable and writeable at run-time. Values are Upper Left to Lower Right and Lower Left to Upper Right.

List Box Object

The list box object is a version of the pop-up object where the display values are visible at all times. The list box highlights the selected value. The list box object does not respect the 3D Control style for DrawStyle. Figure 40.12 displays three list boxes; each is displaying a different type of data.

The Translation property specifies the list of values that map between what is displayed to the user and internal values. The datatype is string. This property is readable and writeable at run-time. There are three methods for setting the values in the Translation property: 1) create a hard-coded list of one display value and one internal value per line, 2) use table column mapping, which selects all the display and internal values for two specified columns from the specified table, and 3) use queried values from the display and internal value columns that a fully qualified SQL statement selects from a table using conditions and other SQL operators. In Figure 40.12, the ENAME list box uses method 1, displaying ENAME and storing ENAME; the DEPTNO list box uses method 2, displaying DNAME and storing DEPTNO; and the MGR list box uses method 3, displaying ENAME and storing MGR for populating the Translation property.

FIGURE 40.12.

List box objects.

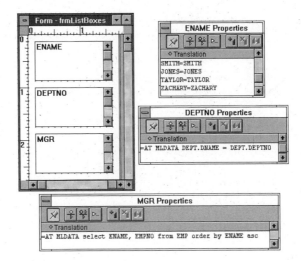

Menu Bar, Menu, and Menu Item Objects

The menu bar object contains menus, which in turn contain menu items. The menu bar is a graphical object that is not visible during design time and will not display during run-time unless the developer creates one and writes method code to cause it to display and update. Each form has its own individual menu bar object. Menu bars provide a series of menus that the user can select to perform actions that the developer has associated with the particular menu items belonging to that menu. Menu bars should work for forms and reports. In OPO Version 1.0, menu bars only work for forms. Menu bar–specific methods of interest are described as follows:

The AppendMenu() method appends a menu to the end of the menu bar. The menu is inserted before any system default menus that would normally appear at the end of the menu bar.

The ClearMenuBar() method removes all menus from the menu bar. The menu objects are not removed from memory. You must delete the menu objects individually using the DELETE menu_object command or using the DeleteAllMenus() method.

The DeleteAllMenus() method removes all menus from the menu bar and deletes the menu objects associated with the menu bar from memory.

The GetMenu() method returns a reference to the specified menu object in the menu bar. The datatype is object.

The GetMenuCount() method returns a count of all menus in the menu bar. The datatype is long integer.

The InsertMenu() method inserts a menu into the specified position in the menu bar.

The RemoveMenu() method removes a menu from the specified position in the menu bar. The menu object is not removed from memory. You must delete the menu object individually by using the DELETE menu_object command or the DeleteAllMenus() method.

The SysDefaultMenuBar() method initializes a menu bar with the system default menus. This method deletes any existing menus before initializing the menu bar.

Menus represent a grouping of related topics. A File menu has Open, Close, Save, and Save As topics, for example. These topics are referred to as menu items. Menu items represent hooks into a specific subsection of code within the TestCommand() and DoCommand() methods of the form, report, or application. A menu bar is limited to one level of menus; a menu item cannot open a subsequent menu. The following are menu-specific methods of interest:

The AppendMenuItem() method appends a menu item to the end of the menu. The developer specifies the item's label, command code, help context, and keyboard hot key.

The DeleteMenuItem() method deletes a menu item from the specified position in the menu.

The GetItemCount() method returns a count of all items in a menu. The datatype is long integer.

The GetMenuItem() method returns a specified piece of information about a specified menu item in the menu. Possible types of information include the label, command code, help context, and keyboard hot key. The datatype varies depending on the type of information requested.

The InsertMenuItem() method inserts a menu item at the specified position in a menu. The developer specifies the item's label, command code, help context, and a keyboard hot key.

The SetMenuItem() method modifies a specified piece of information about a specified item in a menu.

OCX Object

An OCX object is a custom object imported into Oracle Power Objects. OCX objects are defined by Microsoft standards. The OCX object is replacing the existing VBX object definitions. OCX objects are loaded into the OPO object palette by loading the object into the OCX register. Any OCX objects that have been registered in the developer's Windows environment automatically are appended to the OPO object palette. OCX objects are available only in the Microsoft Windows version of OPO. These objects represent fully operational, self-contained applications embedded with the host application. OPO supports the concept of embedded OCX objects, but provides no programmatic interface to an OCX and provides no support for binding the OCX object to data from the database through the OPO record manager. More in-depth support for OCX objects is planned for OPO version 1.1. If you need more information, please refer to the appropriate Microsoft documentation.

Oval Object

The oval object is a visual object. It cannot be bound to data. This object is useful for creating visual effects to enhance the user interface. The oval object does not respect the 3D Control style for DrawStyle. The oval object also has another interesting characteristic—it can contain other objects. Containing another object means that the contained object is completely within the boundaries of the container object.

Picture Object

The picture object is a data bound control. It is specifically designed to handle long raw data formatted in the BMP picture format. Note the absence of the DataSize and Datatype properties. These properties are not required because the picture object is designed to expect only long raw data.

Pop-up Object

The pop-up object is a data bound control that performs an inherent lookup operation that allows the developer to display one value while storing the same or a different value. The pop-up does not respect the 3D Control style for DrawStyle. The pop-up also performs another very important, but not so obvious, function. Because the developer specifies the values that the pop-up can display and store, the user is guaranteed that a value chosen from a pop-up is valid. The same validity concept applies to list boxes, but not to combo boxes. Combo boxes must validate their values because the user can enter a value not in the ValueList. Figure 40.13 displays three pop-ups; each displays a different type of data.

FIGURE 40.13.

Pop-up objects.

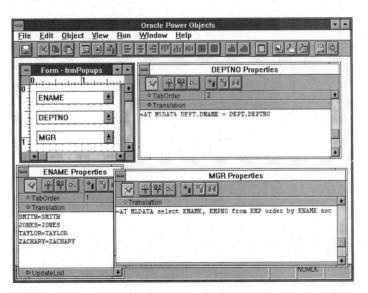

The Translation property specifies the list of values that map between what is displayed to the user and internal values. The datatype is string. This property is readable and writeable at run-time. There are three methods for setting the values in the Translation property: 1) create a hard-coded list of one display value and one internal value per line; 2) use table column mapping, which selects all the display and internal values for two specified columns from the specified table; and 3) use queried values where a fully qualified SQL statement selects the display and internal value columns from a table using conditions and other SQL operators. In Figure 40.13, the ENAME pop-up uses method 1, displaying ENAME and storing ENAME; the DEPTNO pop-up uses method 2, displaying DNAME and storing DEPTNO; and the MGR pop-up uses method 3, displaying ENAME and storing MGR for populating the Translation property.

Radio Button and Radio Button Frame Objects

The radio button object is a data bound control. The radio button is used to represent a set of dependent values from which only one value can be chosen at a time from the set of all possible values.

The ValueOff property specifies the value of the radio button when it is not selected. The datatype is set to be the same as the radio button datatype. This property is readable and writeable at run-time. The default value is null.

The ValueOn property specifies the value of the radio button when it is selected. The datatype is set to be the same as the radio button datatype. This property is readable and writeable at run-time.

The frame object is a special-purpose, data bound control. The frame object has inherent behaviors that allow it to control the mutually exclusive nature of radio buttons that are within its containment hierarchy. If the developer places a number of radio buttons within the frame object, taking care to set the ValueOn property of each radio button to a unique value, setting the value of the frame controls the behavior of the contained radio buttons. Also, clicking on a radio button within the frame sets the value of the frame and subsequently controls the behavior of the other contained radio buttons.

Rectangle Object

The rectangle object is a visual object. It cannot be bound to data. This object is useful for creating visual effects to enhance the user interface. The rectangle object also has another interesting characteristic—it can contain other objects.

Repeater and Repeat Panel Objects

The repeater object has all of the characteristics of the form object except for window-related properties. The repeater object allows the developer to design an interface in which objects are repeated. This repeating concept is implemented using the repeat_panel. The repeater is most similar to the grid control from Microsoft Visual Basic except that the repeater has built-in record-manager functionality for binding data from the database to objects within the repeat_panel. Anytime that the developer needs to display more than one record at a time, that developer should choose the repeater as the primary container for the display.

The repeat_panel object forms the basis the repeater object. The panel can contain any object that can be bound to data or that is strictly a graphical object. Objects that should not be used inside the repeat_panel include embedded forms, classes tied to record managers, and other repeaters. Although these objects can be instanced and embedded within the repeat_panel, they will not function as expected. The number of visible repeat_panels determines the maximum number of records that the user sees during run-time.

Static Text Object

The static text object is a visual object. It cannot be bound to data. This object is useful for creating labels and directions to aid the user in understanding what is being presented to them. Although the object implies an inability to change its display during run-time by using the term static, keep in mind that you can change the Label property of the static text object during run-time to reflect the message that the developer deems appropriate at the time.

Status Line Object

The status line object is a graphical object that is not visible during design time and does not display during run-time unless the developer creates one and writes method code to cause it to display and update. Each form has its own individual status line object. Status line–specific methods of interest are described as follows:

The ClearStatusLine() method deletes all panels from the status line except the summary panel. This method returns no data.

The DeleteStatusPanel() method deletes the specified status panel from the status line based on the pos parameter, an integer. You cannot delete the summary panel.

The GetStatCount() method returns the number of status panels in the specified status line. The datatype is long integer.

The GetStatPanel() method returns a specified piece of information about a specified panel in the status line. The datatype varies depending on the type of information requested. The possible types of information that you can request include panel text, width of panel in pixels, command code, "enabled" text, "checked" text, "disabled" text, and "disabled and checked" text.

The InsertStatusPanel() method inserts a new panel at the specified position pos, width wid, and maximum message length maxMsgLen. All of the parameters are integers.

The SetStatDispList() method designates a status panel on a status line to be updated. You must specify the panel's command code and the message strings associated with the panel's status.

The SetStatusPanelMsg() method sets the text displayed in a specified panel of the status line.

The SysDefaultStatusLine() method initializes a status line with the system default panels. This method deletes any existing panels before initializing the status line.

Toolbar Object

The toolbar object is a graphical object that is not visible during design time and does not display during run-time unless the developer creates one and writes method code to cause it to display and update. Each form has its own individual toolbar object. Toolbars provide a series of buttons or icons that the user can select to perform actions that the developer has associated with the particular button or icon. Toolbars should work for forms and reports. In OPO version 1.0, toolbars only work for forms. Toolbar-specific methods of interest are described as follows:

The ClearToolbar() method deletes all buttons on the toolbar.

The TBAppendButton() method appends a button to the end of the toolbar. The developer specifies the command code, a bitmap, a button style, and a help context.

TIP

The help context specified in the TBAppendButton() method is a help context id. OPO Version 1.0 doesn't have a method for the developer to indicate the help file to look in for the help context. OPO looks in PWROBJX.HLP, the default Microsoft Window Help file for Power Objects. A developer who wants to support context-based help for an application could create a help file, name it PWROBJX.HLP, and replace the original OPO help file. This solution permits the OPO environment to resolve the application-defined help contexts. Unfortunately, this solution also disables the user's ability to search for help from the original OPO help file. This oversight should be corrected in OPO Version 1.1.

The TBDeleteButton() method deletes a button from the specified position in the toolbar.

The TBGetButton() method returns a specified piece of information about a specific button in the toolbar. You can find out the button's command code, bitmap, the button style, or help context. The datatype varies depending on the type of information requested.

The TBGetCount() method returns a count of all buttons in the toolbar, including separator buttons. The datatype is long integer.

The TBInsertButton() method inserts a button at a specified position in the toolbar. The developer specifies the command code, bitmap, button style, and help context.

The TBSetButton() method modifies a specific piece of information about a specific button in a toolbar. You can set any of the button characteristics including command code, bitmap, button style, and help context.

Summary

Oracle Power Objects is a product that makes developing database applications an easier task than it has been in the past. OPO has an assortment of powerful objects. Some objects are purely graphical in nature; others are bound to data, and others handle containers and record managers. With reusable classes and libraries for storing and sharing classes, bitmaps, and OLE objects, OPO version 1.0 is a contender in today's database application development arena. The OPO Sample Applications that ship with every OPO configuration are a good place to start to explore how combining these OPO objects into forms and then combining forms into applications can effectively solve your database application development requirements.

Building an Application with the Form Designer

41

by Ronnie
Lashaw

IN THIS CHAPTER

Oracle Power Objects provides a data-centric approach to application development; the evidence is in the tight integration between the Form Designer and the supported database back ends. You can construct forms using the familiar drag-and-drop metaphor. Application-enforced referential integrity and transaction processing are also tightly integrated into the automated design environment. This chapter discusses these areas of application development using the Form Designer.

Overview of the Form Designer

In Power Objects, you construct applications with forms, reports, bitmaps, classes, and OLE objects. Building a simple data entry form is as easy as picking the columns from a table, dragging and dropping them onto a form, and then running the form. Using the CONTACT table from the SAMPLE session and the TakeNote application, both from the Oracle Power Objects 1.0 examples, look at how easy it is to create a simple data entry form in the Microsoft Windows environment.

Building a Simple Data Entry Form

A developer needs an application with a form and a session connecting to a database in order to build a data entry form. The following steps guide you through this simple procedure.

1. Create an application named UNTITLED.POA.
2. Create a form and set its name property to CONTACT.
3. Open the SAMPLE session and connect to the Blaze database by double-clicking the session icon.
4. Open the CONTACT table by double-clicking its icon in the SAMPLE database session window.
5. Using the Ctrl key and the mouse, select the columns indicated in the Figure 41.1 from the CONTACT table.
6. After selecting the columns, click and hold down the mouse on one of the columns selected. While holding down the mouse, drag the columns onto the CONTACT form. The cursor changes to a document icon.
7. Releasing the mouse over the CONTACT form creates the labels and fields shown in Figure 41.1.

You can run this form or reposition fields as you like. The downside to running the CONTACT form at this point is that you can only view the first record in the table. You do not have a method for scrolling through records.

FIGURE 41.1.

Drag-and-drop form building.

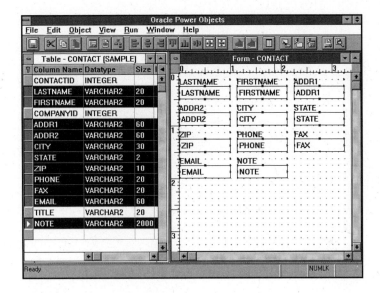

Adding Record Scrolling to the Form

Adding scrolling to a form is just one example of how Power Objects is a data-centric development tool. In Visual Basic, a scroll bar can scroll data only through extensive coding. In Power Objects, the scroll bar automatically scrolls through a record set when you set the ScrollObj property. The ScrollObj property is set automatically when you place the scroll bar object on a form or manually when the developer types a value into the ScrollObj property.

Figure 41.2 shows the horizontal scroll bar object selected from the tool palette. I placed the scroll bar onto the form named CONTACT, and the ScrollObj property was filled in automatically with the value container, which is an object identifier. container is an indirect object reference to the object containing the scroll bar.

Testing the Form

At this point, the CONTACT form is ready to test. Power Objects is equipped with a design-time test environment where a developer can test a specific form or an entire application. If the developer wants to, he can also turn on the Power Objects debugger. Because you do not expect any problems to exist at this point, simply run the form by clicking the RunForm icon on the toolbar.

Figure 41.3 shows the running form. You display the first and second records by clicking the right arrow on the scroll bar.

FIGURE 41.2.

Scrolling through records.

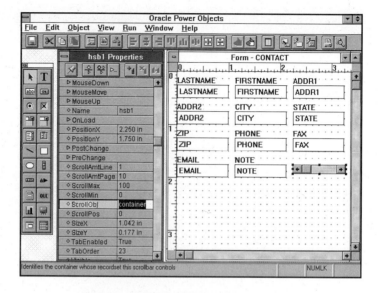

FIGURE 41.3.

Running a form.

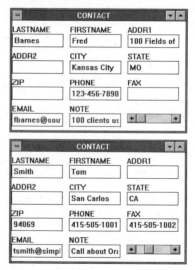

Master-Detail Relationships Made Easy

Creating master-detail relationships is one of the many strengths of Power Objects. If you drag and drop columns from the CONTACT table onto a form and give that form a scrolling capability, that form can serve as a master object. You can create a repeater object on the form and drag and drop columns from the TASKS table onto it. This would be a separate master object at this point. To make it the detail object, type in the values for three properties. The LinkDetailColumn and LinkMasterColumn properties are the database column names that form a "join" relationship between the master and detail objects. Because you set these property values on the detail form or object, you must specify what the master form or object is in the `LinkMasterForm` property. Figure 41.4 illustrates what is involved.

FIGURE 41.4.

Design-time master-detail relationships.

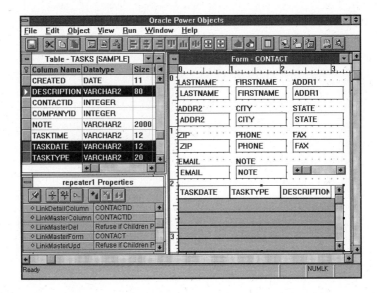

At this point, you could run the form, and you'd see that the detail data scrolls as the master data changes. The master-detail relationship has been established. Figure 41.5 displays this successful relationship.

FIGURE 41.5.

Run-time master-detail relationships.

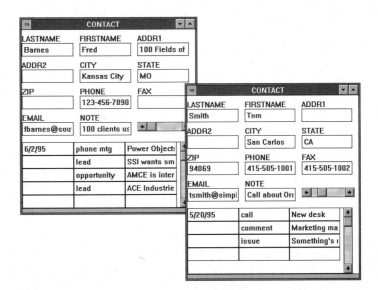

Sharing the Same Record Source

A common problem for PowerSoft's PowerBuilder is that when two or more data controls want to share the same data source; for example, they each want to manipulate values for a given record and maintain data synchronization between the various controls. Power Objects took care of this shortcoming in PowerBuilder by permitting the "sharing" of record sources. For example, you might want a master list of contacts displaying only names and a separate detail section displaying some specifics on the contact. You want to be able to edit the name in either location and have the changes reflected and posted to the database properly. Power Objects built this functionality into the product so that you don't have to add it through coding. Figure 41.6 illustrates this "shared" record source concept.

FIGURE 41.6.

A shared record source.

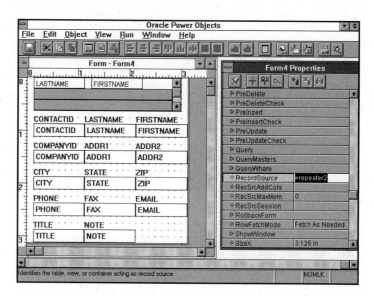

As the user scrolls through the records in the master list, the detail section updates to show a different view of the same record. Changes made in the master list are also made in the detail section. Figure 41.7 demonstrates the synchronization without any additional coding.

FIGURE 41.7.

Synchronizing data through a shared record source.

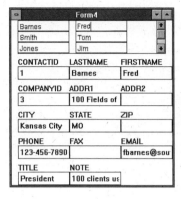

Supporting Business Rules with Application-Enforced Constraints

Although database-enforced constraints support business rules and data integrity uniformly on the back end, it is also possible to ensure data integrity with Oracle Basic method code in methods such as PreInsert() and PreUpdate() (refer to the validation-related topics later in this chapter for more on these methods). However, such business rules or *application constraints* are associated with the object containing the method and not the database object itself, so they are more difficult to support and maintain. You can reduce the maintenance and support burden by using *user-defined* methods for common business rule models—such as a user value must be between two specified values. A user-defined method could be defined as function IsBetween (*testValue, lower, upper*) as Boolean, which returns TRUE or FALSE as appropriate.

It is a good business practice to enforce business rules on the database server back end whenever possible. The advantage here is that the application developer might forget to encode application constraints everywhere they are needed, but the database applies the same constraint to a given transaction no matter where in the application it was generated. Power Objects is innovative in that it provides for application-enforced constraints so that the developer could use a database back-end server, such as dBASE, which does not have the capability to enforce constraints. Another good business practice is to encode business rules in the application layer when you consider a database back end that might not support constraints.

Validation on Data Entry

As the user enters a new value into a control, you can enforce business rules using the Validate() method and the ValidationMsg property. By entering the necessary code in the Validate() method for the control, you can set the business rule to be enforced whenever the user changes the value of the control.

As a result, you can prevent the user from entering negative values into a control by having the Validate() method return FALSE whenever it detects an internal value for the control that is less than zero. If you have entered text in the ValidationMsg property of the control, that text appears in a warning dialog box when the validation fails.

When Validate returns FALSE, the internal value of the control remains set to its original value, but the display value remains unchanged. The user can still see the mistaken value entered for the control, making it possible to enter changes without completely retyping the value. If you want the display value to automatically revert to the original value of the control, call the RevertValue() method from within the Validate() method. Figure 41.8 illustrates a Validate() method that ensures the user enters a value in the range from $0.01 to $100,000.00.

FIGURE 41.8.

Range check validation on a field.

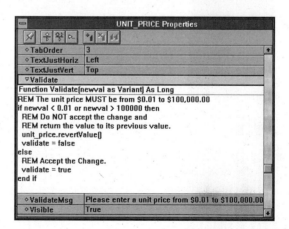

Validation When Saving Changes to an Existing Record

Validate() is useful when checking the value entered into a single control. When you want to check values entered in several controls, use the ValidateRow() method. ValidateRow() is triggered whenever the user tries to save changes to an existing record. As a result, ValidateRow() is especially useful when checking on dependencies among the values appearing in multiple controls.

The `ValidateRow()` method appears on a container, not on an individual control. When `ValidateRow()` returns FALSE, the application displays any text entered for the `ValidateRowMsg` property of the container, explaining why the validation failed.

Validation When Inserting or Deleting Records

When you want to enforce business rules before a record is inserted into or deleted from a record source, you use a different set of methods from the `Validate()` and `ValidateRow()` methods. When controlling the insertion of new records, you use the `PreInsertCheck()`, `PreInsert()`, and `PostInsert()` methods. You must add the method code controlling whether the insertion should proceed to `PreInsertCheck()`, which is triggered before the application sends the instruction to insert the new record. If you want to allow the insertion, enter the statement `PreInsertCheck = Inherited.PreInsertCheck()` (instructing the method to return TRUE) into the method code added to `PreInsertCheck()`. `PreInsert()`, on the other hand, is called immediately before the insertion but after the decision to insert the record has been made. Finally, `PostInsert()` is triggered after the record has been inserted.

When you're working with master and detail records, it is often important to capture the insertion of detail records as well as master records. If you want to control the insertion of detail records, use the `LinkPreInsertCheck()`, `LinkPreInsert()`, and `LinkPostInsert()` methods, which are triggered on the container displaying master records.

When controlling the deletion of records, you use a similar set of methods. `PreDeleteCheck()`, `PreDelete()`, and `PostDelete()` control the insertion of master records or records with no associated detail records. `LinkPreDeleteCheck()`, `LinkPreDelete()`, and `LinkPostDelete()` control the deletion of detail records. Figure 41.9 illustrates a `PreDeleteCheck()` method, which enforces that the user must okay the delete operation.

FIGURE 41.9.

Enforcing a deletion business rule.

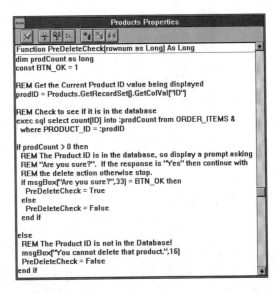

```
                  Products Properties
 X  +%+ >   * * !!

Function PreDeleteCheck(rownum as Long) As Long
dim prodCount as long
const BTN_OK = 1

REM Get the Current Product ID value being displayed
prodID = Products.GetRecordSet().GetColVal("ID")

REM Check to see if it is in the database
exec sql select count(ID) into :prodCount from ORDER_ITEMS &
  where PRODUCT_ID = :prodID

if prodCount > 0 then
  REM The Product ID is in the database, so display a prompt asking
  REM "Are you sure?".  If the response is "Yes" then continue with
  REM the delete action otherwise stop.
  if msgBox("Are you sure?",33) = BTN_OK then
    PreDeleteCheck = True
  else
    PreDeleteCheck = False
  end if

else
  REM The Product ID is not in the Database!
  msgBox("You cannot delete that product.",16)
  PreDeleteCheck = False
end if
```

Transaction-Processing Logic Without Programming

Oracle Power Objects was designed to provide significant database integrity with respect to transaction-processing logic without requiring the developer to do any coding. Whenever you have a bound container loaded into memory, the application keeps track of any inserted, deleted, or modified records through the Record Manager object. The Record Manager holds the record set queried for the container, including a record of all pending transactions to be performed on the record set. Each bound container either has its own associated record set object or shares it with another bound container. Figure 41.10 illustrates what happens when a record is updated and the user attempts to close the window without actively committing or rolling back his changes to the database.

FIGURE 41.10.

Transaction-processing logic.

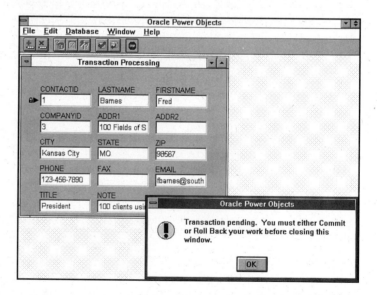

Each Record Manager object gains access to corresponding database objects through a session object. As is the case with other application objects, the session object has properties and methods associated with it, including the following transaction processing-related methods:

IsWorkPending()	Indicates whether there are any transactions pending for the session.
CommitWork()	Commits transactions pending for the session.
RollbackWork()	Rolls back the last transaction set committed for the session.

Figure 41.11 illustrates the relationship between form objects, record managers, session objects, and database servers.

FIGURE 41.11.

Relationship between forms, record managers, session objects, and database servers.

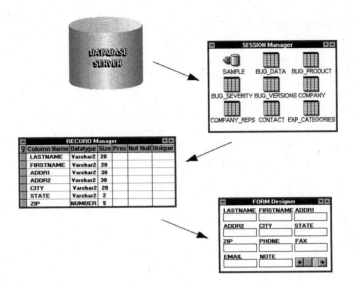

Committing and Rolling Back Transactions

The application commits any transactions whenever the following occurs:

- The user presses the Commit button on the Runtime toolbar. The application then commits all work pending on the active form, including insertions, deletions, and updates, by calling the `CommitForm()` method.

- The application calls the `CommitWork()` or `CommitForm()` method. `CommitWork()` acts on the session, committing all pending work for a session, and `CommitForm()` commits the pending transactions for all sessions represented on an individual form.

The application rolls back transactions whenever the following occurs:

- The user presses the Rollback button on the Runtime toolbar. The application then rolls back the last transaction committed on the active form.

- The application calls the `RollbackWork()` or `RollbackForm()` method. `RollbackWork()` rolls back the entire transaction set last committed for a single session, and `RollbackForm()` rolls back the work in all sessions represented on a form.

Referential Integrity Enforcement by the Application

Oracle Power Objects goes far beyond the non-datacentric capabilities of other products such as Microsoft Visual Basic, Microsoft Access, and PowerSoft PowerBuilder in enforcing multiple levels of application-based referential integrity. In Power Objects, there is no programming required to enforce application-based referential integrity; all you need to do is select among the various levels from a pull-down list. By default, Power Objects enforces the highest level of referential integrity by not permitting the deletion or update of a master (primary key) record if any detail (foreign key) records exist. Table 41.1 lists the levels of referential integrity enforcement.

Table 41.1. Client/server tools positioning.

Referential Integrity	Level	Description
Refuse if Children Present	Highest	You cannot delete or update a master record while there are detail records linked to it.
Delete Cascade or Update Cascade	Medium	The application automatically deletes or updates all detail records associated with the changed master record.
Orphan Details	Lowest	The application deletes or updates the master record but leaves all associated detail records untouched. The detail records are now *orphaned* because they do not correspond to any master record.

Figure 41.12 illustrates the actions that Power Objects takes when a user attempts to update or delete a master record when referential integrity is set to the highest level of Refuse if Children Present.

FIGURE 41.12.

Highest level of referential integrity.

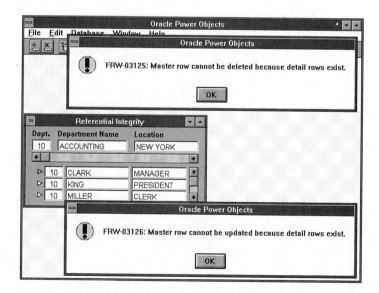

Assume that the referential integrity is set to Update Cascade and Delete Cascade, and the original DEPTNO is 10, but the user changes it to 11. The detail records acquire row-level locks and update as reflected in Figure 41.13.

FIGURE 41.13.

Cascading referential integrity.

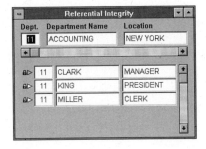

Assume that the referential integrity is set to Orphan Details, and the original DEPTNO is 10, but the user changes it to 11. The detail records are orphaned, as reflected in Figure 41.14.

FIGURE 41.14.

Orphan details referential integrity.

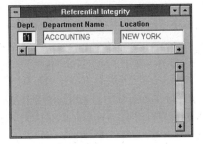

Summary

The Oracle Power Objects Form Designer coupled with the built-in transaction processing, application-enforced referential integrity support, and the overall datacentric orientation of the object model is a very capable design environment. Developers can quickly prototype their applications, knowing that the default Power Objects application environment handles scrolling data, maintaining synchronization between views of the same data, protecting against the user making changes and accidentally forgetting to save changes, and providing referential integrity. Power Objects applications have excellent data integrity and sufficient methods available so that developers can embed custom business rules.

Creating Reports

42

by Brian Twidt

Within an Oracle Power Objects (OPO) application, reports represent data or graphical screens that can be printed. Reports are fairly easy to create, yet they are far more limited than forms in the content that they can contain. This chapter introduces the components of the Report Designer, demonstrates how to effectively create reports, and highlights some limitations of building reports.

Overview of the Report Designer

The Report Designer is the graphical interface that helps the developer easily create reports. OPO's Report Designer is identical to the Form Designer with respect to how objects are created on the report, with the exception of the report's window format. The report window is sectioned into horizontal zones called bands. This type of report is referred to as a banded report, where each band represents a different section of the report. Banded reports are extremely useful for printing repetitive, columnar data such as records from a table. However, there is little freedom to design reports that are arranged similar to forms or that contain complex relationships.

The Report Designer Sections

When the Report Designer is invoked by clicking the New Report toolbar button or by selecting File | New Report from the menu, the developer is presented with a control palette, a properties window, and a report window, as illustrated in Figure 42.1.

FIGURE 42.1.

The Report Designer.

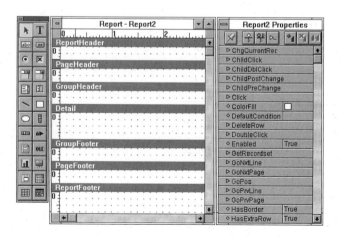

Notice this looks like the Form Designer, except for the horizontal bands separating the report. Each band corresponds to a different section of the report such as the headers, data, and footers. Objects, such as static text and text fields, are placed in these sections to create listing-type reports of database tables. The various report sections are described in Table 42.1.

Table 42.1. The report sections.

Section	Description
ReportHeader	The objects in this section appear at the top of the first page of a report. It's used primarily as a report title.
PageHeader	The objects in this section appear on the top of every page of the report. Its primary uses are to provide group overviews, or to display labels for detail column headings.
GroupHeader	The objects in this section appear on the top of every group detail. Its primary use is to provide column headings for each grouping of the detail section.
Detail	The objects in this section represent a single table record. For each record in the table or table grouping, the detail section will be repeated.
GroupFooter	The objects in this section appear after each grouping of the detail section. Its primary use is for displaying detail grouping summaries.
PageFooter	The objects in this section appear at the bottom of each page. Its primary use is to display page information such as page count.
ReportFooter	The objects in this section appear at the end of a report. Its primary use is to display aggregate functions applied over all detail groupings, and to display report summary information.

Building a Basic Report

The simplest way to create a basic report is to drop a table or several columns from a table onto the Detail section of a report. This action creates static text and text field objects for each column in the table. Next, select all of the static text objects and move them to the PageHeader section. To get the PageHeader to display on the first page of the report, it is also necessary to set the PageHeader's FirstPgHdr property to True. Additionally, give the report a title by adding a static text to the ReportHeader. Figure 42.2 illustrates this basic report.

Once the report has been designed, it can be run by clicking the Run Report toolbar button, or by selecting the Run | Run Form menu command. When this report runs, it displays a listing of the ENAME, JOB, and SALARY columns from the EMP table. The same report that was created above is shown running in Figure 42.3.

As you can see, the report runs as expected. The detail section is expanded, and each record of the EMP table is displayed. However, the Report Designer has one small error: The ReportHeader is misplaced after the PageHeader.

FIGURE 42.2.

A basic report.

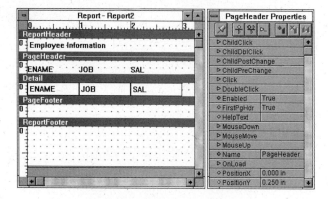

FIGURE 42.3.

Running a basic report.

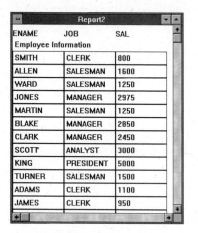

While the report is running, it can be printed by clicking the Printer toolbar button. Viewing a report from an application is accomplished by calling the report's `OpenPreview()` method. Also, the report can be sent straight to the printer by calling its `OpenPrint()` method. Although these actions enable an application to view or print reports, there are several limitations. When printing a report, there is currently no way to prevent the common printer dialog from being displayed. Thus, reports cannot be automatically printed without user interaction. Additionally, an entire report is restricted to be of the same format—there can be only one detail section for each report. Repeater controls can be used to display a different list of table records. However, repeater controls will not display their data beyond their physical boundaries, and they won't repeat themselves in order to show all their records. Lastly, only a single report can be invoked at a time, which prevents reports from being queued.

Adding Functionality to Reports

Another concept relevant to reports is grouping. A report can partition the detail section into groups by the value of one of its columns. To add a group to a report, select the Report Group control from the control palette and click the report. Adding a report group adds a GroupHeader and GroupFooter around the report's Detail section. The Detail section is grouped by selecting the GroupHeader and specifying its GroupCol property. Using the previously built report as an example, the GroupCol can be set to DEPTNO, which will cause the detail section to group the employees by their respective departments.

The report will now generate a detail section for each group. For this reason, moving the column labels from the PageHeader into the GroupHeader section allows each grouped Detail section to have its own column headings. Additionally, an identifier for the group can be attached by dropping the grouping column from the table into the GroupHeader. In the example, the detail section could be grouped by the DEPTNO column. Because DEPTNO is an integer, the displayed value may not be meaningful to the user. An additional text field object can be added to the GroupHeader to display the name of the department. This is done by setting the text field's DataType to String, and the DataSource to the following derived value:

```
=SQLLOOKUP("select dname from dept where deptno = " & DEPTNO )
```

The identifier DEPTNO in the SQLLOOKUP function refers to the name of the text field that was created when the DEPTNO column was dropped onto the GroupHeader.

Another useful concept in designing reports is adding summary information for the Detail section. A text field can be added to the GroupFooter section that will perform an aggregate function over one of the Detail section text fields. Continuing this example, a text field can be added to the GroupFooter to show the sum of the departments' salaries. The text field's DataType should be set to Double, and the DataSource should be set to the following derived value:

```
=SUM( SAL )
```

The identifier SAL in the SUM function refers to the name of the salary field in the Detail section.

Other static text objects can be added to label the department name and salary summation text fields. The example of this extended report is illustrated in Figure 42.4.

Running this report provides a look at what is effectively a master-detail report. The name of each department is displayed along with a list of employees in that department. The running report is shown in Figure 42.5.

FIGURE 42.4.

Building an extended report.

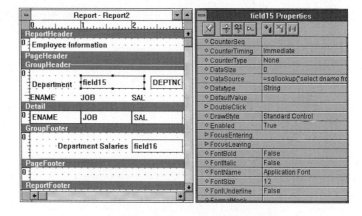

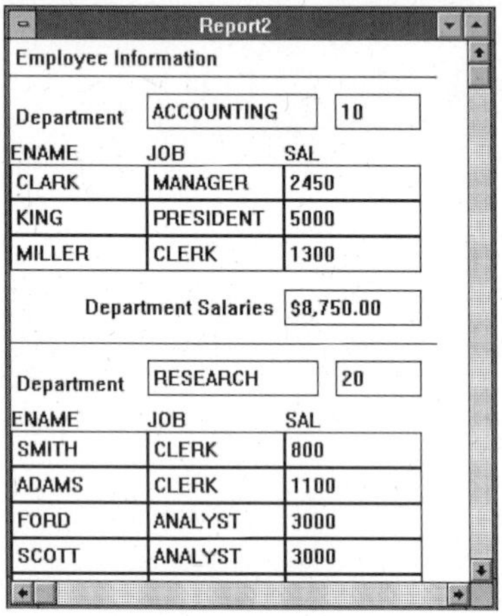

FIGURE 42.5.

Running an extended report.

Summary

As a whole, OPO provides an easy way to create efficient application reports through the Report Designer. Basic table listings, master-detail, and cross-tab reports can be built with little effort. More advanced reports that display complex data sets can also be designed by using repeaters and embedded forms. However, these types of objects don't lend themselves to correctly repeating and displaying all of their data. Reports can also display a bitmap background, dynamically set the value and text of objects through basic code, and display long raw data columns in bitmap controls. Still, reports are limited because the banded-report model doesn't fully allow the developer to create reports that display information exactly like forms. Other limitations include the following: chart objects don't function in reports, the common printer dialog box cannot be suppressed, and reports cannot be queued. Reports also display some of the following graphical problems: The ReportHeader is placed after the PageHeader, objects such as text fields always have a border, and text fields don't always wrap text correctly.

Overall, OPO's report model is extremely useful for creating reports that are simple in content and appearance. Trying to create complex reports, or replicating reports provided by other tools, may be frustrating and beyond the Report Designer's abilities. A possible alternative would be to use a third-party product such as Crystal Reports.

Using the Debugger

43

*by Ronnie
Lashaw*

IN THIS CHAPTER

Power Objects provides a full-featured, run-time debugging environment. With the debugger, a developer can set break points, watch variables, set the value of variables, and step over, around, and through code. This chapter explains how to use and take advantage of the Power Objects debugger.

Overview of the Debugger

Power Objects provides a run-time debugger so that developers can debug their applications. Syntax-related bugs are not the type of bug that a developer generally needs to track down; a syntax-related bug is caught during compilation. The typical bug is a programmer-generated logic bug. In order to pursue a bug, the developer must have a method for activating the debugger. There are three methods for initiating or activating the debugger.

Two of these methods are controlled through the design-time menu. The menu commands include Use Debugger and Debug Startup Code. The Use Debugger menu command activates the debugger palette when you're running an application, form, or report during design time. The Debug Startup Code menu command also activates the debugger palette when you're running the application, form, or report; it also stops execution at the first Basic statement of the first startup method containing Basic code. If none of the startup methods contain Basic code, execution will not be stopped. The third method is to use the STOP command. This method is documented but does not actually work in Oracle Power Objects Version 1.0. If you use the STOP command and run the application, after the run-time environment encounters the STOP command, it generates a Basic error, BAS-00322: General syntax error. This error is followed by BAS-01058: Error compiling source code.

When using the run-time debugger, the first component of the debugger that the developer encounters is the debugger palette. Figure 43.1 illustrates the four components of the debugger palette. The first component is the Continue button, which tells the debugger to resume execution of the application. The second component stops or halts execution of the application. The third component opens the debugger's main window, and the fourth component opens the debugger's expressions window.

Oracle designed Power Objects applications to respond to user input. The types of input include keyboard and mouse events. The startup condition for a Power Objects application is not affected by these types of input. Executing the startup code permits the application to achieve a steady state in which it can then begin to process the various user inputs. If a developer wants to debug the startup code, he must check the Debug Startup Code menu option. Otherwise, the debugger activates the debugger palette immediately after the startup code has been processed.

The Debug Startup Code menu option and the debugger palette's Open Debugger icon both enable you to activate the debugger palette and open the debugger main window. Figure 43.2 shows the debugger main window open for debugging the startup code for the Finance sample application.

FIGURE 43.1.

Debugger palette.

Continue —

Stop —

Open Debugger —

Open Expressions Window —

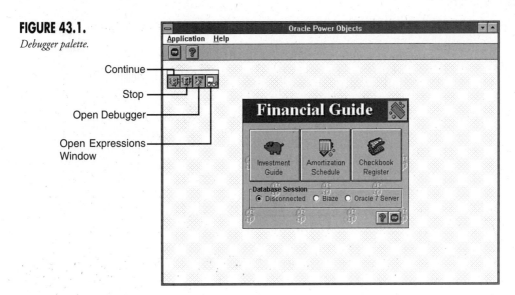

Experienced Power Objects developers will notice that the run-time debugger windows are not limited to the boundaries of the Oracle Power Objects design environment window. The debugger palette, debugger main window, and debugger expressions window are non-MDI (multiple document interface) windows, which permits their boundaries to be independent of the design environment.

FIGURE 43.2.

Debugger window.

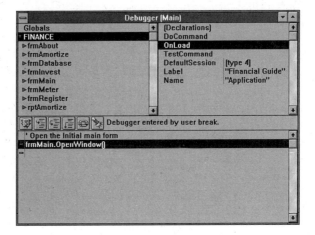

Setting and Clearing Break Points

Usually, developers have a general idea of where to begin looking for a bug. They attempt to narrow down the problem area by using break points and watching the values of variables throughout the entire application. The debugger main window enables the developer to set and clear break points within the application. To illustrate setting and clearing break points and other debugging operations, I use the Finance application. The amortization screen has a button that updates the amortization schedule. I want to set and later clear break points within the recalculation code. Figure 43.3 displays the Click() method code for the btnAmortize button.

FIGURE 43.3.

Setting a break point.

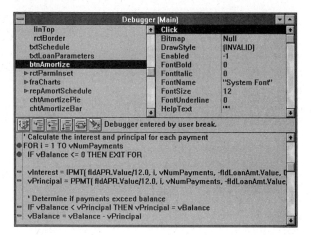

The stop sign symbol to the left of the FOR i = 1 TO vNumPayments line indicates that I set a break point. An open hyphen symbol to the left of a Basic statement indicates that you could set a break point for that line, but one has not yet been set. If there is no symbol to the left of a Basic statement, the statement cannot have a break point set. What I have done is set a break point at the beginning of the FOR loop and immediately after the completion of the FOR loop. The purpose is to determine if the loop is executing the proper number of cycles and also if the remaining balance is calculated correctly.

If the developer is through debugging a specific bug and wants to clear all break points, he can click the Debugger Window icon, which contains a pencil erasing a bug. You can clear a single break point simply by clicking the stop sign symbol; the break point is effectively a toggle condition.

Watching Values of Variables

Querying the value of variables and other application objects during run time is what enables the developer to determine where a bug exists. The debugger has a separate debugger expressions window that permits the developer to specify variables to query. Figure 43.4 illustrates the debugger expressions window with a number of variables and expressions to watch.

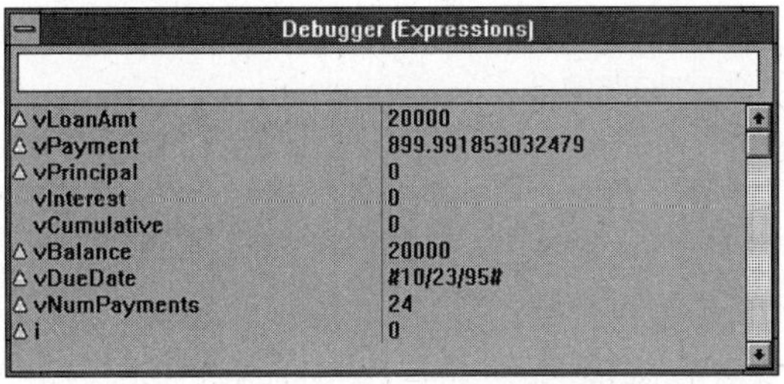

FIGURE 43.4.

Watching an expression value.

```
┌───────────────── Debugger (Expressions) ─────────────────┐
│ ▭                                                         │
│ ┌─────────────────────────────────────────────────────┐ │
│ │                                                       │ │
│ └─────────────────────────────────────────────────────┘ │
│ △ vLoanAmt              20000                          ▲  │
│ △ vPayment              899.991853032479                 │
│ △ vPrincipal            0                                 │
│    vInterest            0                                 │
│    vCumulative          0                                 │
│ △ vBalance              20000                             │
│ △ vDueDate              #10/23/95#                        │
│ △ vNumPayments          24                                │
│ △ i                     0                              ▼  │
└──────────────────────────────────────────────────────────┘
```

Many of these variables and expressions are selected to be updated at every break point or stoppage of execution within the debugging environment. Expressions are updated automatically if they have the yellow triangle to their left, but you can update them manually by selecting the expression with the mouse and pressing the Enter key. By clicking the Resume icon in the debugger main window, you can watch the expression values change on every cycle through the FOR loop. The Resume icon proceeds with execution until the next break point is encountered or until the application stops execution under programmatic control.

Stepping Into, Through, and Over Code

The run-time debugger not only provides the capability to set and clear break points and watch the value of expressions, but it also provides the capability to step into, through, and over code. When the debugger is running through the code in a method, it shows the next line to be executed in a reverse video highlight. Stepping into the code implies that if the next statement to be executed is a method attached to an object, the debugger will trace the statement to that object method and continue debugging from there. If the statement is a Basic function, stepping into it is the same as executing the statement and staying in the current object method code. Stepping through a statement results in executing the statement without the debugger tracing into it. The debugger stops on the next executable statement. Stepping over a statement executes all the remaining statements in the current method without the debugger tracing into them.

There are two other nice features of the debugger. The first is documented. The Call Chain icon displays the object hierarchy that leads to the current method being executed. For example, if a button `Click()` method calls a form `InsertRow()` method, then when the debugger is in the `InsertRow()` method, the call chain indicates that the button `Click()` method called the `InsertRow()` method. The developer can immediately jump to the `Click()` or `InsertRow()` method to interrogate values or to set break points.

The final nice feature of the run-time debugger is not documented very well, but it's one of the more valuable options. You can change the execution point during run time. All the developer needs to do is click the statement that is displayed in reverse video highlight and move the highlight to the new starting point. The only limitation is that the next starting point must be further down in the code. You cannot back up the execution point. Moving the execution point helps you avoid problematic code.

Limitations of the Run-Time Debugger

The Oracle Power Objects run-time debugger provides an object hierarchy diagram in the debugger window. The debugger window also displays methods that have code in them and the values of properties of the currently selected object. The debugger displays values of expressions in the debugger expressions window. A developer can accomplish a lot with these capabilities, but the debugger still has several shortcomings.

One of the shortcomings is that you cannot debug a class object. This applies only to the master class method code. If an instance overrides the master class method code, then you can debug the overridden code.

Another limitation is that working with modal dialog boxes causes the debugger to hang up the Microsoft Windows environment. The only method of escape is to reboot the entire machine. A final limitation of note is that looping constructs such as the FOR loop only seem to receive the execution focus once. In order to debug a FOR loop on every cycle, you must set a break point on the first statement after the FOR loop initialization statement. This is really only a nuisance because it is not critical to the overall performance of the debugger.

Summary

Oracle Power Objects has delivered a functional run-time debugger. The debugger provides the minimum set of features necessary to successfully debug an application. The object hierarchy browser provides a diagrammatic view of the application. The expressions window is reliable and updates in a fashion that does not impede run-time execution performance. The capability to move the starting execution point is very nice, and the online documentation should have discussed it more prominently. Although there are some limitations to the run-time debugger, the overall performance and capabilities of the debugger make it very useful in tracking down developer-generated logic bugs.

Oracle Basic

44

*by Ronnie
Lashaw*

IN THIS CHAPTER

Power Objects uses Oracle Basic as its programming language. Oracle Basic is fully compatible with ANSI BASIC with the additions of object extensions and Structured Query Language (SQL) extensions. Oracle chose Basic as the programming language in order to appeal to the widest range of developer experience. This chapter discusses when to use Oracle Basic; how to write, test, and compile code; and how to extend the functionality of Power Objects through Oracle Basic. Refer to the included CD-ROM for Appendix E, "Oracle Power Objects Programming Reference," for a reference on the syntax and purpose of the majority of all the commands and functions comprising Oracle Basic.

Overview of Oracle Basic

Oracle Basic is fully compatible with ANSI BASIC and is therefore also compatible with Microsoft Visual Basic. You don't have to write Basic code in order to use Power Objects effectively, but if you find that the default functionality of a method or process does not exactly meet your requirements, you can overwrite the method to modify the default behavior using Oracle Basic code.

Using Oracle Basic, you can create user-defined functions and methods. You can declare variables, external commands, and functions and obtain direct access to the data contained in visual and non-visual objects. Oracle Basic gives the developer the capability to create those features in the Oracle Power Objects product that he or she finds are missing or incomplete.

How to Write, Test, and Compile Oracle Basic Code

In order to use Oracle Basic effectively, you must understand how to write code, how to test your code, and how to compile the final application. Oracle Basic code always exists within a method definition, subroutine, or function. You expand the method where you want to place code by clicking the method name. A small editor window opens up, and you can begin typing code in the window. Looking at the btnPick object from the Oracle Power Objects Sample Launch application, you find the following code in the `Click()` method:

```
Application.SetCursor( 1 )
' This method determines which application to run based on the value of its
' Bitmap property.

DIM vResult AS Integer
DIM vDisplay AS Integer
DIM vApp AS String
DIM vMsg AS String

' If the current platform is Windows, then ...
IF SystemName() = "Windows" THEN
```

```
' Determine which application to run based on the Bitmap property value.
SELECT CASE Bitmap
   CASE BITMAPS.bmpNotepad: vApp = "notepad"
   CASE BITMAPS.bmpWrite:   vApp = "write"
   CASE BITMAPS.bmpPaint:   vApp = "pbrush"
   CASE BITMAPS.bmpCalc:    vApp = "calc"
   CASE ELSE
      vApp = NULL
END SELECT
IF IsNull( vApp ) THEN
   MSGBOX( "The Programmer has made a fundamental error! " & &
"Please check the code.", 48, Application.Label )
ELSE
   vResult = WinExec( vApp, 1 )
   vDisplay = TRUE
   SELECT CASE vResult
      CASE 0:  vMsg = "Out of Memory."
      CASE 2:  vMsg = "File not found."
      CASE 3:  vMsg = "Path not found."
      CASE 5:  vMsg = "Attempt to dynamically link to a task."
      CASE 6:  vMsg = "Library requires separate data segments for each task."
      CASE 10: vMsg = "Incorrect Windows version."
      CASE 11: vMsg = "Invalid EXE file."
      CASE 12: vMsg = "OS/2 application."
      CASE 13: vMsg = "DOS 4.0 application."
      CASE 14: vMsg = "Unknown EXE type."
      CASE 15: vMsg = "Attempt to load a Windows application " & &
"for an earlier version of Windows."
      CASE 16: vMsg = "Attempt to load an additional instance of an .EXE file."
      CASE 17: vMsg = "Attempt to load a second instance of an " & &
"application in a large-frame EMS mode."
      CASE 18: vMsg = "Attempt to load a protected-mode application in " & &
"real mode."
      CASE ELSE
         vDisplay = FALSE
   END SELECT
   IF vDisplay THEN MSGBOX( vMsg, 48, Application.Label )
END IF
ELSE
  MSGBOX( "Currently, Launching Other Applications is implemented on " & &
"Windows platforms ONLY!", 48, Application.Label )
END IF
```

If you use the default Click() method functionality, the only action that the btnPick button performs is to visually go down and up. By adding the preceding code, you enable the btnPick button to execute another Microsoft Windows program and return the resulting code for launching that program.

Testing the code is as simple as clicking the RunForm icon on the toolbar. Once the form is running, you can click the btnPick button, and the application that is displayed begins running. Compiling is just as easy. Clicking the Generate Application icon on the toolbar brings up a dialog box that asks whether you want a separate application file or a stand-alone application. After you finish this dialog box, you are asked to supply the filename for the compiled application.

Manipulating Data from a Record Manager Using Oracle Basic

The default record manager manipulation available to a user consists of insert, delete, and edit operations through the run-time menu or run-time toolbar and scroll operations through the associated scrollbar. Usually, these record managers are visually represented by objects such as the form, embedded form, repeater, class, list box, combo box, or popup.

Although the form, embedded form, or repeater require little to no actual programming, the other objects often require code. In fact, it is impossible to have data associated with a list box, combo box, or popup without using some Oracle Basic code. You place this code in either the translation or valuelist property as appropriate. For a popup to display employee names while storing employee IDs, you use the following translation for a session called OracleSession pointing to database objects owned by the Oracle database account SCOTT/TIGER:

```
=AT OracleSession SELECT ename, empno FROM emp ORDER BY ename ASC
```

A more formidable task is to have a repeater displaying employee names with a field to enter in a name to search for. The field should position the focus of the repeater to the record that most closely matches the text string entered into the field. Figure 44.1 illustrates what the repeater might display when you enter the value SH in the field.

FIGURE 44.1.

Employee name lookup field.

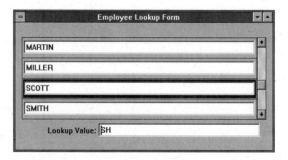

SH highlights SCOTT because there is no partial match; the next name is SMITH. You place the following code in the PostChange() method of the field to enforce the lookup.

```
Value = UCASE( Value )

DIM rec AS Object
DIM test AS String
rec = repeater1.GetRecordSet()
j = LEN( Value )
IF NOT ISNULL( Value ) THEN
  FOR i = 1 to rec.GetRowCount()
    rec.SetCurRow( i )
    whole = rec.GetColVal( "ENAME" )
    test = LEFT( whole, j )
```

```
      IF whole > Value THEN
        IF test <> Value THEN
          IF i > 1 THEN rec.SetCurRow( i - 1 )
        END IF
        EXIT FOR
      ELSEIF test = Value THEN
        EXIT FOR
      END IF
    NEXT i
END IF
```

The preceding code searches through the records in a record manager one at a time until it finds a match or the test case is greater than the search case. This code illustrates many Oracle Basic fundamentals including visual record manager manipulation, string operations, and conditional logic.

Enforcing a Limiting Condition on a Record Manager

There are five different, yet related, methods for imposing or enforcing a limiting condition on a record manager. The first method is through the master-detail linking relationship using the LinkDetailColumn, LinkMasterColumn, and LinkMasterForm properties. This method forces the detail record set to display records only where the columns specified in the LinkDetailColumn property have values that match the values of the columns specified in the LinkMasterColumn property. The second method is through a shared record source by setting the RecordSource property of a repeater2 object to the repeater1 object containing the actual record source to be shared (repeater2.RecordSource is assigned the value =repeater1). This method forces the record managers of each repeater to effectively use the single database cursor allocated to the repeater1 object.

The third method is to set the DefaultCondition property of the object having the record manager. This method is equivalent to specifying a WHERE clause in an SQL statement during design time. The fourth method is to use the built-in Query-By-Form (QBF) capability of Oracle Power Objects. This method is equivalent to specifying a DefaultCondition during run time. The fifth and final method for imposing or enforcing limitations on a record manager is to call the QueryWhere() method of the object with a limiting condition. The limiting condition is exactly like the DefaultCondition except that it is programmatically defined during run time.

Performing Validation

Power Objects performs various levels of field and row level validation by default. These validations verify that dates are valid, numeric fields contain numbers, and database constraints are enforced. If the developer wants to impose validation rules other than these defaults, he must add code to the Validation() method of the field and the ValidateRow() method of the record manager object. Figure 44.2 illustrates the code necessary to implement a business rule where a value must be less than or equal to 10. The message that is displayed is shown in the ValidationMsg property for field1 during design time and in the Oracle Power Objects modal dialog box window during run time.

FIGURE 44.2.

Enforcing a field value.

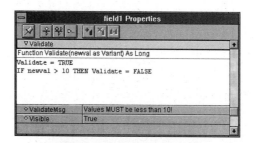

EXEC SQL Operations: *Select, Insert, Update, Delete, and Commit*

Although Power Objects provides all the functionality of the SQL operations Select, Insert, Update, Delete, and Commit for the default behavior of the application environment, a developer often wants to make changes to the database independent from the visual interface. In this section, I briefly discuss each of these commands and refer to the search terms for the online help.

Select is an operation to retrieve data from the database into local variables. Oracle Power Objects cannot select data directly into an object or a record manager. It must select data into a variable and move it into the object or existing record manager. The Select statement can retrieve multiple values from the database with one statement. For more information on the syntax of the Select statement, enter Select (SQL) as the search phrase and topic from the online help.

Insert is an operation to store data in the database from local variables. The Insert statement cannot store arrays of data with one statement; a single statement relates to a single record. For more information on the syntax of the Insert statement, enter Insert (SQL) as the search phrase and topic from the online help.

Update is an operation to change data stored in the database from local variables. The Update statement cannot change arrays of data with one statement; a single statement relates to a single record. For more information on the syntax of the Update statement, enter Update (SQL) as the search phrase and topic from the online help.

Delete is an operation to remove data from the database using local variables to specify limiting conditions. The Delete statement can delete multiple rows of data with one statement. For more information on the syntax of the Delete statement, enter Delete (SQL) as the search phrase and topic from the online help.

Commit is an operation to cause all changes made since the previous Commit to be flushed to the database, which causes the changes to take effect. The Commit statement is not related to any specific data records. For more information on the syntax of the Commit statement, enter Commit (SQL) as the search phrase and topic from the online help.

Stored Procedures, Functions, and PL/SQL Blocks

Some database environments, such as Oracle, support the concept of stored procedures and functions, which are often written using procedural language extensions (PL) to standard SQL. A serious developer can write his own stored procedures and functions. You should look up the required syntax in an appropriate manual such as the Oracle7 PL/SQL manual. The following code fragment is a PL/SQL block that builds a table and populates it with data:

```
EXEC SQL AT Oracle CREATE TABLE MyTest (EMPID NUMBER)
EXEC SQL AT Oracle BEGIN &
  FOR i IN 1..10 LOOP &
    INSERT INTO MyTest(EMPID) VALUES (i*2); &
  END LOOP; &
  COMMIT; &
END;
```

The following code fragment demonstrates how to create a stored procedure in Oracle and then reference that procedure from Oracle Basic:

```
REM Declare the DOIT() procedure.
EXEC SQL AT Oracle CREATE OR REPLACE PROCEDURE doit &
  ( t_id IN NUMBER, amount IN NUMBER ) AS &
  BEGIN &
    UPDATE MyTest SET EMPID = amount WHERE EMPID = t_id; &
  END;

REM Now Reference DOIT() with appropriate values.
EXEC SQL AT Oracle BEGIN doit( 2, 13 ); COMMIT; END;
```

Extending the Functionality of Power Objects

Oracle designed Power Objects to promote ease of use with existing standards. Power Objects can embed and interact with OCX controls in an application. It can also link to dynamic link libraries (DLLs) under Microsoft Windows and to external commands (XCMDs) and functions (XFCNs) on the Macintosh. Oracle will add OpenDoc support in a future release to promote externally reusable code resources across OS/2 Warp and Macintosh. Power Objects supports object linking and embedding (OLE 2.0) under Microsoft Windows but not OLE automation. Limited OLE automation is planned for a future release.

Oracle Power Objects has a built-in mechanism for extending its functionality through the use of classes. A developer can create a class to perform a basic function not inherent in the basic Power Objects environment. Multiple applications can share and reuse the classes.

To demonstrate its commitment to standards and extensibility, Oracle Power Objects Version 2.0 either will include bundled OCX controls or will supply information on how to obtain some off the Internet. Another reflection of Oracle's commitment to extensibility is that Oracle is placing a ObjectShop or MarketPlace on its World Wide Web site (`http://www.oracle.com`) where developers can upload or purchase and download objects for use in Power Objects. Refer to Chapter 36, "Introduction to Oracle Power Objects," for more information.

Summary

Oracle Power Objects provides a wide range of constants, commands, and functions for the application developer to use when writing custom code to solve his database application needs. The constants, commands, and functions maintain consistency with ANSI BASIC and provide the necessary object-oriented and SQL-related extensions to ensure that Power Objects is a powerful and flexible database application development environment.

Oracle Power Objects provides numerous built-in SQL and custom data-related operations. You can enhance these default behaviors through Oracle Basic. Ultimately, the strength of a visual tool is measured in the strength of the underlying programming language available to the developer. With object and SQL extensions, Oracle Basic is powerful and flexible. Through its use of dynamic link libraries, Apple Script, OCXs, and soon OpenDoc, Power Objects is truly a powerful application development environment.

Libraries, User-Defined Properties and Methods, and Classes

45

by Brian Twidt

Without a doubt, the area of Oracle Power Objects with the most potential is its user-definable, reusable components. Developers can increase their productivity through the capability to create classes that can be reused, shared in libraries, and extended beyond the normal set of properties and methods. This chapter demonstrates how to share objects across multiple applications through the use of libraries—prebuilt classes that you can easily reuse throughout applications. I also discuss how to add functionality to objects through user-defined properties and methods.

Overview of Libraries

Libraries are similar to applications in that they contain other objects. You use libraries to store user-definable classes and bitmaps that applications can share. You can reuse objects within a library in any number of forms, applications, or other classes. Sharing objects in libraries is useful for minimizing storage requirements and reducing the need to reimplement objects multiple times. For a single developer, a workgroup, or even an MIS department, libraries provide the means for standardizing object implementation within Oracle Power Objects.

Creating and Using Libraries

You create a library by clicking the New Library toolbar button or by selecting the File | New Library menu command. In the Main window, a library is represented by an icon of a book. Double-clicking a library's icon opens a library window, which is shown in Figure 45.1.

FIGURE 45.1.

The library window.

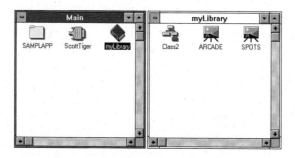

The library window displays the objects contained in the library. You can add objects to the library by creating new objects or by dropping existing objects onto the library.

You add a new bitmap object to the library by selecting the File | Import BMP menu command. This invokes the Import Bitmap dialog box, which is shown in Figure 45.2.

To specify a bitmap, locate and select the desired BMP file. A new bitmap object appears in the library window. The name of the new bitmap object is automatically set to the BMP's filename. If the name assigned to the bitmap object is a reserved word in Oracle Power Objects, such as open, the New Object Name dialog box appears, as shown in Figure 45.3. This dialog box asks you to enter a different name for the bitmap object.

FIGURE 45.2.

The Import Bitmap dialog box.

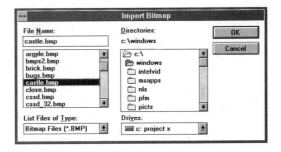

FIGURE 45.3.

The New Object Name dialog box.

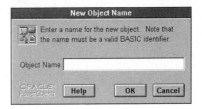

Because a bitmap object's name is usually generated automatically and cannot be changed, it's difficult to provide meaningful names for bitmap objects.

> **TIP**
>
> To get around the limitation on naming bitmaps, you can use the following trick. Before importing a bitmap, change the filename of the BMP to one of Power Objects' reserved words, such as open.bmp, or to a name such as 1mybmp.bmp (1mybmp.bmp is a valid DOS filename but not a valid OPO object name). Either of these filenames invokes the New Object Name dialog box, enabling you to enter your own name for the bitmap object when you import it.

Overview of User-Defined Properties and Methods

User-defined properties (UDP) and user-defined methods (UDM) are properties and methods that you can add to the normal set of properties and methods for any application object. You use UDPs and UDMs to extend the functionality and flexibility of Oracle Basic. You can use UDPs to globally store and track variables. UDMs provide a method where developers can program Basic code that is not directly related to any of Oracle Power Objects' event methods. UDMs also permit modular coding and method overloading. I discuss method overloading later in this section.

Using User-Defined Properties and Methods

UDPs and UDMs appear on the property sheet. You add, delete, and manage an object's UDPs and UDMs through the toolbar buttons on the property sheet. The property sheet's toolbar buttons are shown in Figure 45.4.

FIGURE 45.4.

The property sheet's toolbar.

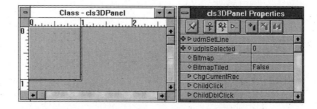

To add UDPs or UDMs, click the Add a New Property or Method toolbar button on the property sheet. This invokes the User Properties window, which is shown in Figure 45.5.

FIGURE 45.5.

The User Properties window.

Name	Type	Datatype	Arguments
udmClassDescription	Sub		
udmClassHistory	Sub		
udmClassInstancing	Sub		
udmClassUsage	Sub		
udmSetLine	Sub		pObj as Object, pX, pY, pW, pH as Integer
udmSetLine	Sub		pObj as Object,pX, pY, pW, pH, pC, pO as In
udmSetNormal	Sub		
udmSetObjRect	Sub		pObj as Object, pX, pY, pW, pH as Integer
udmSetSelected	Sub		
udmTabSelected	Sub		pValue as String
udpIsSelected	Property	Long	
udpLabel	Property	String	
udpOrientation	Property	String	
udpParentObject	Property	Object	
udpSelectStyle	Property	String	
udpSlopeSize	Property	Long	

Enter the name, type, datatype, and list of arguments that specify the method or property to be added. You create overloaded methods by specifying methods with the same name and different numbers of arguments. When you make a call to an overloaded UDM, Power Objects examines the number of arguments and references the appropriate method.

You attach UDPs and UDMs to objects by dragging and dropping them from the User Properties window to the object itself or the object's property sheet. You detach them by selecting the UDP or UDM on the property sheet and clicking the Delete Current Property or Method toolbar button on the property sheet. After you attach them to an object, you can use UDPs and UDMs just like any other property or method.

You use UDPs to associate special values with an object. You can also use them in place of globals. Unlike globals, which are single instances, a UDP has an instance associated with each object to which it is attached.

Method Overloading

Method overloading is a process whereby you can invoke a user-defined method using different parameter types or a different number of parameters. Power Objects supports the latter process using a different number of parameters. For example, you can define UDMs called udmClick() and udmClick(pMsg AS String). Create a form with a button on it and add the two new UDMs to the button. Place the following code in each respective UDM.

```
Sub udmClick()
MSGBOX( "udmClick()" )

Sub udmClick(pMsg AS String)
MSGBOX( pMsg )
```

If you place the following code in the Click() method of a button on a form and run the form, you will observe that the appropriate method gets called based on the number of parameters passed.

```
Sub Click()
udmClick()
udmClick( "This is a test" )
```

First, a message box displays udmClick(), followed by a second message box that displays This is a test.

Although you can write UDMs to overload OPO defined methods, the OPO environment does not call these; however, you can call these UDMs through Basic code from the OPO standard methods, or any method for that matter.

Overview of Classes

Classes are some of the most powerful objects within Oracle Power Objects. A class is a collection of application objects that work together to perform specific tasks. After you create a class, you can share and reuse it in other classes, forms, reports, or applications. Classes are custom controls that extend Power Objects' functionality, enable modular development, and increase productivity.

Power Objects ships with several sample class objects in the CLASSES library as examples of the flexibility, power, and productivity associated with classes. These classes include a form control class (clsFormControl) with print, help, and exit buttons; a record manager control class (clsRecControl) with insert row, delete row, query refresh, commit work, and rollback work buttons; a progress meter class (clsMeter) displaying percent complete; an Oracle Mobile Agents

(OMA) class (clsOMA) to facilitate working with OMA; a tab class (clsTab) for building applications requiring a tabbed folder look and feel; and a calendar class (clsSmCalendar) for viewing months and selecting a date. Each of these class objects is covered in detail in the OPO online documentation, and each is used in at least one of the OPO sample applications.

An important aspect of classes is that they are object-oriented. This means that you can create and then instance a single class into other forms or classes. Instancing a class creates a copy of that class that is linked back to the class definition. Each instance of the class has the same objects, properties, and methods as those of the parent class; however, you can customize the class instance by changing any of its objects, properties, or methods.

A simple example of a class is an exit button that appears on every form of an application. You could copy this button from form to form; however, editing the properties or methods of the button would require the developer to edit the button on each of the application's forms. A better solution is to create a class, clsExitBtn, that contains the exit button. Set the script of the button's Click() method to the following generic script:

```
Self.GetTopContainer().CloseWindow()
```

Instance the clsExitBtn class onto each form. Any changes you make to the clsExitBtn class—such as changing the button's label, color, or Click() method—are reflected in the instances of that class. Additionally, you can customize each of the instances. Perhaps one of the exit buttons performs specific tasks before it exits, or maybe buttons on particular screens are a different color or have a different label.

Creating Classes

To create a new class, first select the application or library that will contain the class. Next, click the New Class toolbar button or select the File | New Class menu command. When you create a new class or open an existing class, you see the Class Editor, as shown in Figure 45.6.

FIGURE 45.6.

The Class editor.

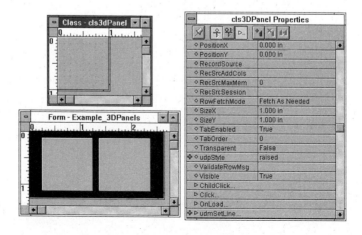

The Class Editor looks just like the Form Editor. In fact, a class is actually a modular, reusable form. Classes are designed like forms, they can contain the same objects as forms, and they have almost the same set of properties and methods as forms.

An example of a simple class to build is a 3-D panel as shown in Figure 45.6. To build this class, create a new class and set its name and label to `cls3DPanel`. Set the `ColorFill` to light gray and the `HasBorder` to `FALSE`. Also, resize the class so that it's about one inch square. Next, add four line objects, named line1 through line4, to the class. Reposition and resize each line so that it covers a different edge of the class. The lines should border the class. Set the `ColorBrdr` of the left and top lines to white. Set the `ColorBrdr` of the right and bottom lines to dark gray. After saving it, you can use this cls3DPanel to create raised panels, which is a control that is not inherent to Oracle Power Objects.

Making Dynamic Classes

Although classes are extremely useful for Rapid Application Development (RAD), they can become cumbersome when you attempt to reorient the objects within the class to fit the current form. When possible, it is best to create classes that you can dynamically change based on UDPs when they're loaded. Take the example of the cls3DPanel; although it's a time-saving control for creating raised panels, how much work is required to change the size of the panel? It would be nice if the panel could reposition its lines or change its orientation when the class was resized. You can do this during run time in the `OnLoad()` method. First, create the following user properties and attach them to the class:

```
udpStyle        Property        String

udmSetLine      Sub            pObj As Object, pX,pY,pW,pH,pC,pO As Integer
```

Set the `udpStyle` property to raised. Next, set the method `udmSetLine()` to the following code:

```
' Description:
' Given a pointer to a line object: set its x-y position, x-y size,
' color and direction.

' Parameter(s):
' pObj        Object    pointer to a line object
' pX                    Integer   new PositionX
' pY                    Integer   new PositionY
' pW                    Integer   new SizeX
' pH                    Integer   new SizeY
' pC                    Integer   new ColorBrdr
' pO                    Integer   new Direction

' Return: <nothing>

pObj.PositionX = pX
pObj.PositionY = pY
pObj.SizeX = pW
pObj.SizeY = pH
IF pC >= 0 THEN pObj.ColorBrdr = pC
IF pO >= 0 THEN pObj.Direction = pO
```

Lastly, the OnLoad() method fires when the class is first loaded into the application at run time. You can put the following code into the OnLoad() method to redraw the class' lines to respect the size and udpStyle of the class:

```
' This method is crucial to correctly drawing the Panel instance.
' This method calls the appropriate user-defined methods so the Panel
' instance will draw based on the user defined parameters.

' line1 refers to the line on the top
' line2 refers to the line on the left
' line3 refers to the line on the right
' line4 refers to the line on the bottom

vShade = 11
vHilite = 1

'Process the user-defined style parameter.
IF LCASE( udpStyle ) = "inset" THEN
  vDirection = DIRECTION_UPPER_LEFT_TO_LOWER_RIGHT
  udmSetLine( line1, 0, 0, SizeX + 1, 1, vShade, vDirection)
  udmSetLine( line2, 0, 0, 1, SizeY + 1, vShade, vDirection)
  udmSetLine( line3, SizeX - 1, 0, 1, SizeY + 1, vHilite, vDirection)
  udmSetLine( line4, 0, SizeY - 1, SizeX + 1, 1, vHilite, vDirection)
ELSE ' style is defaulted to raised
  vDirection = DIRECTION_UPPER_LEFT_TO_LOWER_RIGHT
  udmSetLine( line1, 0, 0, SizeX + 1, 1, vHilite, vDirection)
  udmSetLine( line2, 0, 0, 1, SizeY + 1, vHilite, vDirection)
  udmSetLine( line3, SizeX - 1, 0, 1, SizeY + 1, vShade, vDirection)
  udmSetLine( line4, 0, SizeY - 1, SizeX + 1, 1, vShade, vDirection)
END IF
```

Upon instancing the class, you can change the size of the class and set the udpStyle to inset or raised. When the class is drawn during run time, the lines are redrawn based on the class' size and udpStyle. This creates the appropriately sized inset or raised 3-D panel.

Making Self-Contained Classes

The real power of Oracle Power Objects classes is their capability to be self-contained modules that you can share, reuse, and even distribute. To make a class self-contained, it is often necessary to use generic object references within any of the class' Basic code. The generic object references enable the code to refer to the class itself, the class' container, the class' form, and methods for stepping through all the other forms' objects. Table 45.1 describes the generic object references available in Oracle Basic code.

Table 45.1. The Oracle Basic generic object references.

Reference	Description
Self	The object making the reference.
Container	The container of the object making this reference. Container is a keyword that is evaluated at compile time. It is useful for generically setting a scrollbar's ScrollObj property or specifying a class' RecordSource to be shared with its container's RecordSource (for example, =Container).
TopContainer	The highest level container, the form of class, that contains the object making this reference. TopContainer is a keyword that is evaluated at compile time.
GetContainer()	The container of the object making this reference. GetContainer() is a method that is evaluated at run time.
GetTopContainer()	The highest level container, the form, that contains the object making this reference. GetTopContainer() is a method that is evaluated at run time.
FirstChild()	This method returns a reference to the first object contained within the object that calls this method.
NextControl()	Subsequent calls to this method return a reference to each of the objects contained within the object that calls this method.
GetFirstForm()	This method returns a reference to the first form within an application.
GetNextForm()	Subsequent calls to this method return a reference to each of the forms within an application.

You can use each of these generic object references to create Basic code that does not rely on specific object identifiers. This type of coding should enable you to distribute a class to other developers, who could then drop the class into their applications without any modifications. Using generic object references is good; however, sometimes it is more efficient to create a UDP of data type object and set its value to the container or form. You can use this UDP in the code to refer to the parent object or objects contained in the parent.

Using some of the generic object references also makes it easy to tie several objects on the same form together. You could use several cls3DPanels on the same form like a set of radio buttons. When a raised panel is clicked, any panels that are inset are redrawn as raised and the selected panel is redrawn as inset. Adding ChildClick(Self) to the Click() method of the cls3DPanel, and the following code to the ChildClick() method of the cls3DPanel enables a group of cls3DPanels at the same object containment level to act as radio buttons:

```
DIM vAnyObj AS Object

' Initialize to the first object within the same containment level.
vAnyObj = Self.GetContainer().FirstChild()

' Process all of the objects at the same containment level.
DO
  ' If the Object is a User-defined Class.
  IF vAnyObj.ControlType = 10 THEN
    ' If the Object is a 3dpanel class
    IF INSTR( LCASE( vAnyObj.Label ), "cls3dpanel" ) <> 0 THEN
      IF vAnyObj.udpStyle = "inset" THEN
        vAnyObj.udpStyle = "raised"
        vAnyObj.OnLoad()
        EXIT DO
      END IF
    END IF
  END IF

  ' Determine if all objects have been tested.
  IF IsNull( vAnyObj.NextControl() ) THEN
    EXIT DO

  ' Get the next control
  ELSE
    vAnyObj = vAnyObj.NextControl()
  END IF
LOOP
' Redraw self as inset
Self.udpStyle = "inset"
Self.OnLoad()
```

Summary

Classes provide a powerful way to extend application development in Oracle Power Objects. They enable you to create, reuse, share, and easily redistribute new objects. Classes, in conjunction with libraries and user-defined methods and properties, are useful RAD tools within the Power Objects environment. Classes provide a way to create an object once, use it many times, and customize each instance of the class.

PART

VIII

Oracle Objects™ for OLE

Introduction to Oracle Objects™ for OLE

46

by Keith Majkut

This chapter introduces a new and exciting product, Oracle Objects for OLE, from Oracle Corporation. This chapter contains general information about Oracle Objects for OLE such as components and architecture, plus important issues such as performance and deployment considerations. The following three chapters each discuss one of these major components of Oracle Objects for OLE: Oracle In Process Server, Oracle Data Control, and Oracle Objects C++ Class Library. These chapters are designed to go beyond the reference model of the product documentation by providing important information about how all the pieces of Oracle Objects for OLE interact with each other and with Oracle7.

To get the most from these chapters, you should read the Oracle Objects for OLE documentation to gain a reasonable understanding of the product. You also should create at least one application with Oracle Objects for OLE. Code snippets and screen shots are provided where appropriate within these chapters.

The information documented in Chapters 46 through 49 is accurate for Oracle Objects for OLE 1.0 (patch level 55). Because Oracle periodically releases patches and upgrades, please contact Oracle for information about future releases.

Overview of Oracle Objects for OLE

Oracle Objects for OLE (OO4O) consists of three distinct components. The first and most important element is the Oracle OLE Automation Server used to communicate with an Oracle7 database. Although the OLE Automation Server is very powerful by itself, OO4O also contains the Oracle Data Control and a C++ Class Library to make using the OLE Server within those environments even easier.

If your application development environment can support VBXs, OLE Automation, or C++, and only connects to Oracle7, then Oracle Objects for OLE may be the right product for your task. Oracle Objects for OLE does not replace ODBC or the Oracle Call Interface, but it does provide excellent alternatives. Keep in mind that Oracle Objects for OLE has a basis in these other interfaces, but it's not a clone.

Oracle OLE Automation Server

An OLE Automation Server is an OLE object (which may or may not expose some GUI interface) that exposes a set of methods and properties which other applications can query and invoke. Each method can accept any number of parameters of different types, just as each property can return values of different types. Applications that support OLE Automation can query the OLE Server, and it returns information on all its available methods and properties, plus their parameters and return types. By implementing an OLE Server, you can automatically extend the macro language of OLE-enabled applications to support your interface.

The Oracle OLE Automation Server implements a number of objects and interfaces to Oracle7 that are similar to the Data Access Objects (DAO) implemented by the Microsoft JET SQL engine and often used in Microsoft Access and Visual Basic. The Oracle objects and interfaces were designed with DAO in mind but are implemented from an Oracle7 point of view. The objects and interfaces favor "true" client/server development by allowing Oracle7 to perform much of the processing while allowing the local OLE Server to perform the bookkeeping and interaction with the application.

Oracle Data Control

A Visual Basic Extension (VBX) is used to add functionality to various applications, most notably Microsoft Visual Basic 3.0. A VBX is actually a Dynamic Link Library (DLL) with a standard interface and the .VBX file extension. A VBX may be graphical in nature or may provide its functionality just using properties and methods. A VBX generally encapsulates what would have taken a large amount of development and presents to the user a property palette where you can alter the control's appearance or operation with a few mouse clicks and maybe some typing. (This explanation is an over-simplification in some cases, but it generally describes the situation.)

The data control in Visual Basic 3.0 is not actually a VBX (it is built into the product), but it does function like one. The data control provides three important features:

- A user interface for record movement
- Access to the DAO in the Microsoft JET SQL engine
- An interface to which other controls can bind

The binding is probably the most important. Binding enables other controls to "attach" themselves to the data control in order to query, process, and/or present data in some manner. These controls are called *data aware* or *bound controls*. Data aware controls are available to present data in grid format (rows and columns), drop-down lists, radio buttons, and many other ways too numerous to mention. Bound controls aid development because they can simplify the data querying, processing, and/or presenting step to filling in a property palette item with the name of a control.

The Oracle Data Control (ODC) is a Visual Basic 3.0 extension (VBX), implemented as level III custom control. The ODC is the only control that, for the most part, is a drop-in replacement for the Microsoft Visual Basic 3.0 data control when your application only needs to access Oracle7. Other data controls are available, but they require the purchase of specialized bound controls that work only with that particular data control. The ODC is designed to provide the same interface that the Visual Basic 3.0 data control provides so any standard bound control can work with it. The ODC is not a complete clone, but it does implement enough of the standard data control interface to work with many of the most popular controls available. See Chapter 48, "The Oracle Data Control," for more information.

Oracle C++ Class Library

The Oracle Objects for OLE C++ Class Library uses the Oracle OLE Automation Server to implement a set of flexible, powerful, and easy-to-use classes. These classes provide a C++ developer with object-oriented access to the relational data stored in an Oracle database. The class library offers classes that implement all the objects available to the Visual Basic user, as well as some additional functionality. The class library also supports the idea of bound objects, giving the C++ developer the ease of use that the Visual Basic programmer gets when using bound controls with the Oracle Data Control.

Architecture of Oracle Objects for OLE

Oracle Objects for OLE version 1.x is a 16-bit Windows product. Therefore, the OLE Server, the Oracle Data Control, and the C++ class library are 16-bit Windows components. The OLE Server requires Microsoft OLE 2.0 to operate and can communicate only with an Oracle7 database (either local or remote). Figure 46.1 illustrates the various software layers used to communicate with an Oracle database using Oracle Objects for OLE.

FIGURE 46.1.

Architecture of Oracle Objects for OLE.

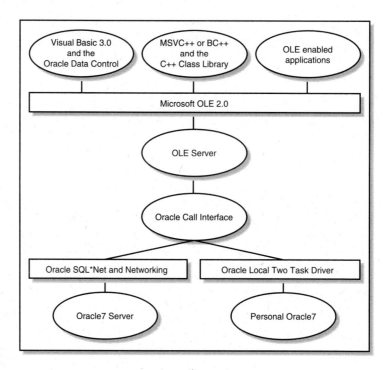

These components are 16-bit and generally cannot be used with a 32-bit host application or development environment. Specifically, the Oracle Data Control was designed for Visual Basic 3.0, although it should work with any application that can support level III custom controls. The Oracle OLE In Process (Automation) Server and C++ Class Library were designed for use with 16-bit host applications and development environments such as Microsoft Visual Basic 3.0, Microsoft Visual C++ 1.5x, and Borland C++ 4.x.

These designs do not mean, however, that Oracle objects used with a 16-bit application or development environment *cannot* run under a 32-bit environment. For example, a 16-bit Visual Basic application developed using Oracle Objects for OLE can run on Windows NT within its 16-bit subsystem.

Although Oracle Objects for OLE contains an OLE Automation Server, it does not contain an OLE Custom Control (OCX). The OCX is the successor to the VBX and would be an obvious progression of the product.

> **NOTE**
>
> The word *object* used in this chapter and in the name of the product is not meant to suggest a totally object-oriented interface to Oracle, although the C++ class library does provide a form of one.

Implementing Objects on the Basis of DAO/JET

The objects of Oracle Objects for OLE have their basis in the Data Access Objects (DAO) of the Microsoft JET SQL engine. JET parses queries and contains its own SQL syntax. JET performs query joins locally; using ODBC, JET might not be able to make full use of features available in a particular database.

JET implements a number of objects used to represent and manipulate the objects of a database. The DAO concepts are good, but their implementation is poor and they suffer from having to represent data in the form of flat files up to relational database.

Oracle Objects implements some, but not all, of the DAO but does so from a client/server point of view and does so realizing the potential size and organization of Oracle7.

Oracle Objects for OLE does not contain its own SQL engine and relies on Oracle7 to parse all queries using its syntax. If an application only needs to communicate with Oracle7, why introduce an intermediate SQL engine with its own syntax? Oracle Objects for OLE does not perform local query joins and can access practically all SQL and PL/SQL (Oracle Procedural Language SQL) features. Because Oracle7 can potentially contain millions of rows and because a server is generally more powerful than a client, how could you and why would you perform joins locally? Finally, why not make use of Oracle-specific features and functionality such as PL/SQL?

A larger comparison of the Oracle objects and DAO is done in the following chapter, but a brief summary is appropriate here. Discussion of three objects shows the most overlap. These objects are the database, the dynaset, and the field.

Within DAO, a database object is used to represent an open database file and a connection to a database, as well as to control database-wide permissions and functionality. A dynaset object is used to represent the return set from a SQL select statement. (A snapshot object also exists, which is basically a read-only dynaset.) A field object is used to represent a single column of a query that has been returned as a dynaset.

Using Oracle Objects for OLE, an OraDatabase object is used to represent Oracle7 and to provide options on row locking and column defaulting. An OraDynaset object is used to represent the return set from a SQL select statement and to implement backward scrolling cursors, which Oracle7 does not natively support. (Instead of implementing a snapshot object, you can mark the dynaset as read-only.) An OraField is used to represent a single column of a query that has been returned as a dynaset.

In addition to those objects, DAO has a tabledef object that represents the definition of a table—columns and their data types. Oracle Objects for OLE does not have any such object, although it would be an interesting addition. Adding this type of object would not necessarily violate Oracle Objects client/server model because you still could store the actual table definition in Oracle7, and use the local object to manipulate it.

DAO also contains a querydef object, used to save a query for easy reuse. Oracle Objects does not contain such an object, but Oracle7 does have views that are an excellent equivalent. This way, code is stored on the server and can be used by an even wider range of users and does not need to be stored with the application. Again, Oracle Objects relies on Oracle7 to provide functionality where appropriate.

Data Access Using OLE

Although the acronym OLE (Object Linking and Embedding) does not mention it, OLE Automation may be the most important feature of that technology. OLE Automation enables the implementation of an interface that is registered with the Windows system and is instantly available to any application capable of being an OLE (Automation) client. This means that the objects, methods, and properties of OO4O are presented consistently across applications such as Microsoft Visual Basic 3.0, Access 2.0, and Excel 5.0. Code written using OO4O for accessing Oracle7 can be run unchanged in any of those and other environments.

Why OO4O Uses OLE (and Not Other Methods)

OO4O provides an interface that can be used unchanged in multiple environments, as just described. The amount of code you can reuse is large and the learning curve small.

Dynamic Link Libraries (DLL) also provide extensibility, but they do not have a specification for registering and querying their interface. Having no standards has led many applications to implement DLL interfaces differently so that even if the DLL can be used, code is not very portable.

OLE 2.0 is still a developing technology with Microsoft adding feature support (distributed objects) and more vendors adding application support. Eventually, OLE will become the basis of Microsoft's next-generation operating systems.

How to Use OLE Automation

Using OLE Automation in the products that currently support Oracle Objects is quite easy. OLE objects are declared just like integers or strings and can be manipulated using whatever methods or properties are available with a dot notation. The following code shows how to create an OraDynaset and loop through records:

```
Dim OraSession as Object
Dim OraDatabase as Object
Dim OraDynaset as Object
Set OraSession = CreateObject("OracleInProcServer.XOraSession")
Set OraDatabase = OraSession.OpenDatabase("Oracle7","scott/tiger", 0&)
Set OraDynaset = OraDatabase.CreateDynaset("select name, address from addrbook",0&)
While Not (OraDynaset.EOF)
 MsgBox "Name = " & OraDynaset.Fields("Address").value & " Address = " &
  OraDynaset.Fields("name").value
  OraDynaset.MoveNext
Wend
```

The dot is used to append a property or method name to an object. If the next-level method or property returns another object or collection of objects (like OraDynaset.Fields), then further clarification may be needed to identify a particular object (in the case of a collection) or the desired property of the object (the value).

Performance Overview

Common questions are "How fast is it?" and "How does it compare to X?" and "Why is it slower than Z?". This section provides no easy answers, just recommendations to help you make the correct decision based on the correct information.

Making an Accurate Comparison

Although Oracle Objects for OLE is based on DAO, its implementation is significantly different. For example, an OraDynaset has a local data cache that stores all fetched rows locally to implement backward scrollable cursors. A DAO dynaset only stores a window for data locally and refetches based on a primary key when rows are needed. An OraDynaset provides read consistency and a DAO dynaset does not.

You can create an OraDynaset with three calls. Internally, using OCI, the implementation requires much more code.

Many database access methods and products are available, and none are implemented exactly the same as Oracle Objects for OLE. A fair comparison, and one that is done often, is to DAO/JET in non-SQLPASSTHROUGH mode. These two methods are related most closely in terms of functionality; just make sure you understand the implementations of both methods before making comparisons.

Considering Oracle Tips

Although database tuning and SQL optimizations are beyond the scope of this documentation, you should remember a few basic tips when performance is an issue:

- Don't select any more rows or columns than necessary. Oracle Objects for OLE fetches rows as needed and caches all rows locally.
- Moving the processing from a flat file or single-user system to a remote multiuser database causes the network involved to play a major part in performance.
- Oracle has documentation on query optimizing or database optimizing. If performance is very important, maybe your table needs an index or maybe the database parameters need tuning.

Whatever the situation, remember that Oracle Objects for OLE is mostly a piece of middleware that uses the server for processing. The performance of all components (hardware locally, network, database, hardware remotely) is important.

Development Issues

Oracle Objects for OLE development requirements are minimal when compared to those of the additional software required. OO4O has all the typical development requirements (environment, disk, memory) plus it needs a host application to drive it. If your current hardware/software already supports connecting to Oracle7 and can run an appropriate host application for Oracle Objects, then you should have no problem adding Oracle Objects to the equation.

You can find Oracle Objects for OLE typically packaged by itself or bundled with various versions of Personal Oracle7 and the Oracle Workgroup Server. Because you may not have Oracle7 or you may want to run it on your own system, these bundles are excellent values. Don't assume Oracle Objects is included in all similar and future bundles of these products, because the bundling changes at Oracle's discretion.

Oracle Objects for OLE also is available as a 90-day trial product on Oracle's World Wide Web site at http:\\www.oracle.com. Again, this offering is subject to change by Oracle.

Software Requirements

Oracle Objects for OLE is not a complete development environment but a development aid. OO4O requires a host application or development environment with which to build one, plus access to Oracle7.

Oracle Objects basically requires a system capable of running 16-bit Windows applications that can also connect to Oracle7. These systems include but are not limited to Windows 3.1, Windows for Workgroups, and Windows NT 3.x.

Host Environments

The Oracle Data Control can theoretically work in any environment that supports level III custom controls, but it is documented to work only within Visual Basic 3.0.

> **NOTE**
>
> Microsoft Visual C++ 1.5x supports level I custom controls only and cannot load other higher-level controls.

The Oracle In Process Server requires any application that can support scripting to an OLE Automation Server. These programs are Visual Basic 3.0 (Standard or Professional), Access 2.0, and Excel 5.0. Word 6.0 can act as an OLE Server, but it does not support scripting to an OLE Server.

You could use C or C++ to write your own OLE scripting client, but you probably should not because no help is offered in the product documentation. If you want to try, C++ is easier because of the automatic code-generation tools shipped with most popular development environments.

Even easier than writing an OLE client yourself is to use the Oracle Objects C++ Class Library. The class library provides the same objects that the OLE Server does and takes care of various OLE initialization tasks and some memory management. The C++ class library also contains a class that enables dynaset-to-data widget binding much like the Oracle Data Control.

The Oracle C++ Class Library contains two components and is built in two flavors. The first component contains classes that are implemented as a DLL over the objects found in the OLE Server. The second component contains classes to enable the dynaset-to-data widget binding. The dynaset-to-data widget binding functionality is implemented as a static library and implementations are provided for MFC (Microsoft Foundation Classes) and OWL (Object Windows Library).

Each of the components has been built for use with Microsoft Visual C++ 1.5x and Borland C++ 4.x. These two formats are necessary because of differences in C++ name-mangling that affects how classes are exported from a DLL.

The documentation says that no other compiler is supported, although others may work if they follow the calling conventions and C++ name-mangling conventions of MSVC++ or BC++.

> **NOTE**
>
> The first production release of OO4O (1.0.42) did not work properly with Borland C++ 4.5 (you received the error `Undefined symbol: v_U_U_W_Dispatch` when linking). This problem was fixed in a later patch (1.0.55).

Remote Database Access

If your database is a remote server, Oracle SQL*Net for 16-bit Windows is required. Some of the original packaging may have suggested that Oracle SQL*Net was built into the product, but this is not the case.

Oracle Objects for OLE does not depend on any particular protocol, version (V1 versus V2), or patch level of Oracle SQL*Net. You can use any valid combination of SQL*Net client to SQL*Net server that is available.

Local Database Access

If your database is local, you probably don't need any additional software to connect to the database. For example, although Personal Oracle7 for Windows 3.1 is Win32s-based, it contains a layer to communicate locally from 16-bit applications to the 32-bit database.

The exception is if you are developing on the same machine as the server. For example, if you are developing on Windows NT, you are still accessing Oracle7 in a client/server mode and you still need Oracle SQL*Net as just mentioned.

Memory Requirements

OO4O is actually a very small piece of software. In terms of size, the Oracle Data Control is only about 64K, the Oracle In Process Server is about 239K, and the C++ Class Libraries for Borland and Microsoft are 74K and 137K respectively. Does this mean that the memory requirement for OO4O is no more than 300K? No, unfortunately it doesn't.

Although OO4O is not a large amount of code, it does store data in memory per the settings of its cache parameters in ORAOLE.INI (discussed in more detail in Chapter 47, "Oracle OLE Automation Server"). You can tune these settings so that data is swapped to disk, but performance suffers. An exact number is not possible, because operating and bookkeeping overhead is involved. After reading the "Tuning and Customization" topic in the product documentation, I estimate that MemoryUsage = (SliceSize * PerBlock * CacheBlocks).

Because OO4O depends on other software to operate, you must take into account the memory requirements of the other software. Check the documentation of the host application you're using to determine its development memory requirements.

Disk Requirements

The complete OO4O package has typically been distributed on four high-density (1.4M) disks. Although almost all the files on the disks are compressed, a closer look reveals that most of the files are not part of OO4O proper, but either Microsoft OLE 2.0 or the Oracle Required Support Files (RSF).

A complete OO4O installation including all sample applications, Oracle Required Support Files, and Microsoft OLE 2.0 requires about 8M of disk space. You may not use that much disk space for several reasons: OLE 2.0 is most likely included with your host application or development environment; the Oracle Required Support Files are shipped with almost every Oracle Windows application (which you may have); or you may choose not to install all the sample applications (which are about 1.5M by themselves).

Considering that a typical installation of Microsoft Visual C++ 1.5 needs 45M of disk space and a Visual Basic 3.0 needs about 12M, OO4O does not require an unreasonable amount of space.

Finally, Oracle Objects for OLE swaps OraDynaset data to disk as it is fetched and cannot fit into memory. A reasonable estimate of disk space required for an OraDynaset is the size of the columns and rows of the data fetched. (This size is not necessarily the size of the entire OraDynaset if you have not reached the end.) The size of the data fetched is close to the size of the data from the first row to the farthest row reached. You don't necessarily need to add LONG and LONG RAW data, because that data is fetched only on demand. Because estimates are not easy to calculate, the best way to determine run-time disk usage is to try Oracle Objects in a simulated user environment.

Deployment Issues

Even though you have been developing with Oracle Objects and everything works fine, you need to make some extra considerations for deployment.

Software Requirements

The run-time requirements for Oracle Objects are very similar to the development requirements, except for licensing or acquiring the needed components for connecting to Oracle7 on each client.

The product documentation lists exactly what Oracle Objects for OLE files are needed and what Microsoft OLE 2.0 files are needed under the on-line documentation topic "Redistributable Files."

Oracle Software

Although run-time distribution of specific OO4O files is free, deployment of other required Oracle software is not. OO4O requires the Oracle7 Required Support Files for 16-bit Windows. You usually can obtain this software from the Personal Oracle7 package if the end user will be connecting to a personal database. Or you can obtain the software from the Oracle SQL*Net for Windows package if the end user will be connecting to a remote database.

> **NOTE**
>
> The Oracle7 Required Support Files are numbered for the various Oracle7 releases such as 7.0, 7.1, and 7.2. Because filenames typically change between releases, you must make sure that the RSF on the deployment system matches the one required by OO4O. OO4O originally required a version 7.1 RSF (up to release 1.0.57) and in the future could require a higher version. You can find out which version of the RSF your deployment system has by checking the release media or running the Oracle Installer (which stores a list of installed products and their versions).

Host Environments

Again, the host environments that are supported for development are the same for deployment. Some of the supported environments do have run-time versions; some do not.

Of the known supported host environments, Visual Basic 3.0 (Standard or Professional) and Access 2.0 have run-time versions. Excel 5.0 does not. Microsoft Visual C++ 1.5 and Borland C++ 4.x can obviously build an executable that you ship.

Always consult the particular host product documentation as to which files are needed and which are distributable because this information can change between versions.

> **CAUTION**
>
> Visual Basic 3.0 does not ship with a complete set of OLE 2.0 run-time files. The file TYPELIB.DLL is missing. This point is mentioned briefly in the "Troubleshooting" topic of the on-line documentation and is well worth mentioning here.
>
> Check the on-line documentation topic "Redistributable Files" for complete details.

Remote Database Access

If your deployment system will be accessing Oracle7 remotely, then a copy (license) of Oracle SQL*Net is necessary. Even though this product may have been included with the bundle you purchased for development, Oracle SQL*Net has historically not been licensed for free distribution. The same requirements listed earlier in "Remote Database Access" for development also apply here.

Local Database Access

If your deployment system will be accessing Oracle7 locally, then a copy of that database (typically a Personal Oracle7 bundle) is necessary. Even though this database may have been included with the bundle you purchased for development, the Oracle database has historically not been licensed for free distribution. The same requirements and exceptions listed earlier in "Local Database Access" for development also apply here.

Memory Requirements

As noted earlier in "Memory Requirements" for development, OO4O by itself has a very small code base and is highly dependent on the cache settings in ORAOLE.INI and the amount of data fetched. All other requirements listed in that section are valid at run-time because the OO4O code is the same for both.

Disk Requirements

As with almost every other deployment issue, disk requirements are mostly dependent on the host application and on the other required files. The complete set of run-time files for Oracle Objects is roughly about 400K, but the other needed files can run into multi-megabytes. Again, check the documentation of the host application and other software required because this information may change between releases.

Summary

Oracle Objects for OLE provides excellent access to Oracle7 from many popular applications. The interface is designed to resemble the Microsoft Data Access Objects, but it should not be judged strictly on its duplication of the DAO interface. Oracle Objects for OLE provides better integration with Oracle7, leverages more of the power of Oracle7, and uses one of the newest and most popular Windows technologies (OLE 2.0) to do so.

A natural progression of this product would be to add more of the DAO interface and provide easier access to Oracle7 features. Oracle has made improvements even in the small patch releases and will presumably continue developing Oracle Objects for OLE for use on 32-bit platforms using OLE controls. This product is small but provides formidable competition to similar interfaces.

Oracle OLE Automation Server

47

by Keith Majkut

IN THIS CHAPTER

The Oracle OLE Automation Server implements a number of objects used to represent the Oracle7 database and objects within it. The objects are high level and do not require the user to understand SQL processing steps such as parse, bind, define, execute, and fetch. The user must be able to provide database connection information and a SQL statement, then he or she can edit data using familiar methods such as Add(), Edit(), and Delete().

Background

The objects of the Oracle OLE Automation Server are based on the Data Access Objects (DAO) of the Microsoft JET SQL engine. The concepts of DAO are good, but the implementation does not provide very smooth integration with Oracle and Oracle-specific features. The Oracle OLE Automation Server and its objects were designed for an Oracle database and provide tighter integration than DAO.

What Is an OLE Automation Server?

An OLE Automation Server is an OLE object (application) with exposed methods and properties you use to manipulate the object. After the methods and properties become available, you can manipulate the objects within the OLE Server from any OLE Automation client.

What Is an OLE Automation Object?

An OLE Automation object is an instance of a class of your application for which you have exposed methods and properties, which you use to manipulate the object.

A useful feature of OLE Automation objects is a reference count. A *reference count* is kept so an OLE Automation Server can destroy an object when it is no longer used. For this reason, the Oracle OLE Automation Server has no Close() methods. When an object goes out of scope and is no longer used, the OLE Automation Server automatically destroys it.

What Is an OLE Automation Collection?

You use a collection object to manage other objects. A collection object can contain zero or more objects. By specification, a collection should support iterating through its objects and a count property to determine the number of objects in it. A collection also should support some form of indexing so you can access individual objects in the collection. You can index the various collections in the Oracle OLE Automation Server by name or number (0 to Count - 1).

Object Hierarchy

The relationship between all the Oracle objects is hierarchical and rather straightforward, as shown in Figure 47.1.

FIGURE 47.1.

Object hierarchy of OLE objects.

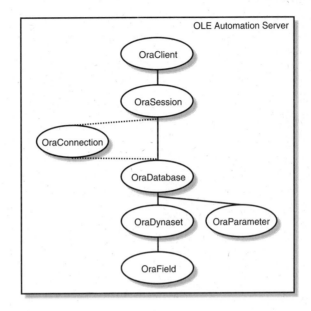

Only one OraClient object exists for all applications in the system. OraClient is created implicitly when the first OraSession is created. The OraClient object exists only as a root for all the other objects.

One default OraSession exists per OraClient, but you can create other named OraSession objects. Database transactions are normally affected at the OraSession level.

An OraConnection represents an actual connection to Oracle and may be shared by multiple OraDatabase objects. An OraConnection cannot be explicitly created, only implicitly, by creating an OraDatabase object. Database transactions can be committed at the OraConnection level, but it is not recommended.

An OraDatabase object is created using a username, password, and database name. The OraDatabase object is used to control the connection (which can be shared among OraDatabase objects), to create dynasets, and to execute any other SQL statements.

An OraDynaset represents the return set from a SQL select statement and contains one or more OraField objects.

An OraField object represents one column of the return set of a SQL select statement.

An OraParameter represents a SQL or PL/SQL bind variable and is valid for all dynasets under its parent OraDatabase.

Types of Oracle Objects

The product documentation is well-written as a reference guide, but it lacks discussion of the relationship that the following objects have with each other and with Oracle7.

OraClient

The OraClient object is more important to the OLE Server than to the developer. This object is the root of all objects on a given client system and is created implicitly by the OLE Server when the first OraSession in any Oracle Objects for OLE (OO4O) application is created.

The OraClient object is accessible only from an OraSession object. The OraClient contains a collection of all the OraSessions of a particular application, but it does not enable one application to use for accessing the objects of another.

The OraClient has only one method, `CreateSession()`, which has been duplicated as `CreateNamedSession()` and added as a helper method to the OraSession object.

OraSession

The OraSession object has much more importance to the developer than the OraClient. This object is the one that the developer most likely sees as the root of all objects in an application. An OraSession must be created first, and the initial one is the only object created directly by an OLE interface; the rest are created by methods of other objects. An OraSession is created with a call to `CreateObject()`, as this example shows:

```
Dim OraSession as Object
Set OraSession = CreateObject("OracleInProcServer.XOraSession")
```

The OraSession has three important roles. The first is to be a point of Oracle error handling; the second is to be a point to begin, commit, or roll back database transactions; and the third is to enable creation of an OraDatabase. The OraSession also owns the OraConnections collection and the OraDatabase objects created from it.

The OraSession receives only errors relating to Oracle connections, the OraConnections collection, or OraDatabase creation.

Because an OraSession may be managing many connections to Oracle via the OraConnections collection, transactions are actually only guaranteed at the Oracle connection (not OraConnection) level.

NOTE

The original product documentation stated that one application could share an Oracle connection (login) of another application by using `ConnectSession()` and passing in the name of the desired OraSession. This feature would be very powerful, because making a connection to Oracle is more expensive than using an existing one. Unfortunately, this feature did not work and was removed from the product. In the current product, `ConnectSession()` does not recognize OraSessions of other applications at all.

OraConnection

An OraConnection object is created implicitly when an OraDatabase is created (OraDatabase has one-to-one mapping). An OraConnection may represent an actual Oracle connection (login) or a shared one. Try to share Oracle connections when possible, because the server requires more overhead to manage connections than it does to manage extra cursors created within a connection.

A shared OraConnection is created when the username, password, and database name of an existing OraDatabase match those of a new OraDatabase being created. Also, the existing OraDatabase must have been created under the same OraSession. Connection sharing is not possible across different OraSessions.

The most important item to remember is that Oracle transactions are accomplished at the Oracle connection level, while OO4O transactions are done at the OraSession and then the OraConnection level. Therefore, committing a transaction that is making use of a shared OraConnection will commit all other outstanding transactions within the actual Oracle connection. Unfortunately, `OpenDatabase()` doesn't have an option to not attempt to share connections. The workaround is to create a different OraSession (using OraClient.`CreateSession()` or OraSession.`CreateNamedSession()`, which are exactly the same) and then create an OraDatabase using that new OraSession.

No method or property exists to tell whether an OraConnection is sharing an Oracle connection, but there is a way to tell. Oracle connections are shared based on username, password, and database name. The username and database name are available as properties of an OraDatabase and of an OraConnection. Comparing these two properties is enough because a database cannot have more than one user with the same username.

OraDatabase

An OraDatabase initiates connections (when an OraConnection is created) and security to Oracle7. The OraDatabase also handles another layer of error reporting, the execution of SQL and PL/SQL statements, OraDynaset creation, and the behavior of database-wide settings.

The OraDatabase receives errors relating to the execution of SQL and PL/SQL statements using `CreateDynaset()` and `ExecuteSQL()`. These errors will also include any encountered while processing any SQL statement executed on behalf of the user to support adding, editing, or deleting of rows or the manipulating of binary data (LONG or LONG RAW columns) of an OraDynaset.

Although many OraDatabase objects may be created within an OraSession, these objects are not kept as part of a formal collection available to the developer.

The `OpenDatabase()` method of the OraSession object is used to create an OraDatabase. The connection information to the database is needed, and you can set some options that affect database-wide behavior. Building on the OraSession example, an OraDatabase is created like this:

```
Dim OraSession as Object
Dim OraDatabase as Object

Set OraSession = CreateObject("OracleInProcServer.XOraSession")
Set OraDatabase = OraSession.OpenDatabase("t:prod:orcl", "scott/tiger", 0&)
```

OraParameter

An OraParameter is used to represent a scalar value for bind variable replacement in a SQL or PL/SQL statement. Using an OraParameter object allows for better Oracle integration with SQL and PL/SQL, and for better code reuse. Without the OraParameter object, all SQL and PL/SQL statements would need to use literal values and need to be rebuilt to change WHERE clause values and (stored procedure) parameters.

Using an OraParameter may require some initial coding, but it never impacts performance negatively because Oracle bind variable (which an OraParameter represents) operations do not cause trips to the Oracle server (including setting and getting values).

Consider a case where you would like to query the name and address from a table named ADDRESSBOOK:

```
...
'build my sql query
query$="select name, number from addressbook where name = 'SMITH'"
'create the dynaset
dyn = CreateDynaset(query$, ... )
'OK, now I can do something with SMITH
```

```
'rebuild my sql query
query$="select name, number from addressbook where name = 'JONES'"
'recreate the dynaset
dyn = CreateDynaset(query$, ... )
'OK, now I can do something with JONES
...
```

You could modify the preceding code to use a string variable for the name, and you could move the recreation to a helper function, but that's not the point. The point is that you must rebuild the query manually, every time, and resubmit it to Oracle. Using a SQL bind variable (:NAME) with an OraParameter makes this task much easier and can improve performance.

```
...
'build my sql query
query$="select name, number from addressbook where name = :NAME"
'set the parameter value
parameters("NAME").value = 'SMITH'
'create the dynaset
dyn = CreateDynaset(query$, ... )
'reset the parameter value
parameters("NAME").value = 'JONES'
'refresh the dynaset
dyn.refresh
...
```

OraDynaset

An OraDynaset represents the return set (columns and rows) of a SQL select statement. Although an OraDynaset seems to map directly to an Oracle cursor, that is not the case. The initial processing (parse, describe, bind, define, execute, fetch) of a SQL select statement only requires one cursor, but subsequent adding, editing, or deleting of rows or the manipulating of binary data (LONG or LONG RAW columns) requires extra cursors.

The OraDynaset object internally implements a data cache of fetched rows to provide the appearance of backward scrolling cursors, which Oracle (as of Oracle7.2) does not support. The data cache also provides read-consistency because rows are not refetched.

You create an OraDynaset object using the CreateDynaset() method of the OraDatabase object. A SQL select statement is needed, and you can set some options that affect dynaset-wide behavior. Building on the OraDatabase example, an OraDynaset is created like this:

```
Dim OraSession as Object
Dim OraDatabase as Object
Dim OraDynaset as Object

Set OraSession = CreateObject("OracleInProcServer.XOraSession")
Set OraDatabase = OraSession.OpenDatabase("t:prod:orcl", "scott/tiger", 0&)
Set OraDynaset = OraDatabase.CreateDynaset("select * from addressbook", 0&)
```

OraField

An OraField represents a single column of the return set (columns and rows) of a SQL select statement. All column data of a row is fetched on demand except for binary data stored in LONG or LONG RAW columns. Those columns can hold up to a maximum of two gigabytes of data, and retrieving even one column of that size would exhaust the storage of most PCs.

The OraField object contains properties to determine the data type and methods to operate on binary data.

Collections

Think of a collection as an array of objects you can access by subscripting (using ordinal integers) or by using the name the object was given at its creation. A collection should support a Count property that returns the number of items in the collection, and the indices of the collection should go from 0 (zero) to Count - 1.

OraSessions

One OraSessions collection exists per application and is owned by the OraClient. This collection does not provide any other information other than the OraSession objects contained in it.

OraConnections

One OraConnections collection exists per OraSession. This collection does not provide any information other than the OraConnection objects contained in it.

The Count property is the only property available to the OraConnections collection. No methods are available because OraConnection objects are created automatically upon OraDatabase creation and cannot be added or removed programmatically.

OraParameters

One OraParameters collection exists per OraDatabase. All OraParameter objects within the collection are available to use with any CreateDynaset() or ExecuteSQL() call made from the OraDatabase. This practice causes a problem only if the code was written to use two parameters of different types but the same name. You can fix this dilemma easily because bind variables (implemented using OraParameter objects) can have any name; the name is used for a substitution marker when the call is made.

The Count property is the only property available to the OraParameters collection. You can add and remove OraParameter objects by using the Add() and Remove() methods, respectively.

OraFields

One OraFields collection exists per OraDynaset. The OraFields collection represents all the columns returned in the select list.

The Count property is the only property available to the OraFields collection. No methods are available because OraField objects are automatically created upon OraDynaset creation and cannot be added or removed programmatically.

Dynaset Data Issues

Generally speaking, most applications want to create an OraDynaset and also view, add, edit, or delete data. In addition to the options available with OpenDatabase(), the following options are available with CreateDynaset():

- The *NoAutoBind* option stops the binding of any OraParameters to the SQL statement. Binding does not affect performance because it does not cause a round trip. This option is not very useful but is probably available for completeness.

- The *NoBlankStrip* option is important, especially when using CHAR columns that are padded to the column length. By default, trailing blanks are stripped from character data returned from the database.

- The *ReadOnly* option causes the dynaset to be read-only regardless of the updatability of the SQL statement. This condition does not affect performance much, except that each row retrieved is slightly smaller because it doesn't contain a ROWID.

- The *NoCache* option stops the saving of rows fetched to a local data cache. System resources are saved, but backward record movement is no longer possible. You should use this option when an application needs to make a single pass through a large number of rows.

Using Valid SQL Select Statements

You may use any valid SQL select statement, including but not limited to statements using unions, joins, subqueries, and the FOR UPDATE clause.

Whenever data is updated, the OLE Automation Server must do a SELECT...FOR UPDATE to lock the row in question, causing a trip to the Oracle database. Within a transaction, you can use the FOR UPDATE clause to eliminate these extra per-row trips. Use caution when taking this step because although all rows may not be returned to the dynaset, they are all locked during the life of the dynaset.

Selecting Data

When selecting data, keep in mind the `OpenDatabase()` and `CreateDynaset()` settings as well as the definition of the table from which you are selecting. All of these criteria can affect updatability and performance.

Editing Rows

An OraDynaset is updatable if the select statement used to create it selects only from one table, does not include column aliases or functions in the select list, and allows the Oracle ROWID to be selected. You can edit rows if they are uniquely identifiable. The Oracle ROWID is used to identify each row.

When you invoke `Edit()`, the row cached locally is compared to the original row stored in the database. If the rows match, the row is locked for update and the edit can proceed. If the rows do not match, an error is generated. The comparison is not done for LONG or LONG RAW columns because they can hold up to two gigabytes of data and most likely could not be fetched and stored locally if filled.

When editing, the same column defaulting issues listed in the following "Adding Rows" section apply to editing as well.

Adding Rows

When you add rows, the most important issue to consider may be default column values. You have two options for default column values. This behavior is set at the OraDatabase level when `OpenDatabase()` is called.

In the default mode, the OLE Server sets to NULL any columns that are represented in the OraFields collection but have not been explicitly set. A SQL insert statement is then created and the new row is added to the database. Only columns that were selected into the OraDynaset are inserted, so Oracle still defaults any column values that were not specified. Also, you can set database triggers to execute, which may change column values. This change causes problems with the OraDynaset if you attempt to edit the row again, because the OraDynaset selects the row from the database to see if the currently cached copy matches the one in the database. If any of the previously mentioned conditions were true, the rows do not match and an error occurs.

To prevent that type of error, use the ORAMODE flag when calling `OpenDatabase()`. This flag causes the OLE Server to immediately reselect rows added (or updated) to the database. Oracle defaults any column values and executes any triggers. The row stored in the local cache now should match the one in the database (unless another user changes or removes it).

Deleting Data

You delete data using the `Delete()` method of the OraDynaset object. The current row is removed from the OraDynaset and a delete statement is issued to the database. The current row position does not change, although the current row is invalid (cannot be accessed) after `Delete()` is called. When record movement occurs after a delete, the deleted row no longer appears in the OraDynaset.

SQL Parameters

You can use an OraParameter in SQL statements to represent a scalar bind variable. If you use an OraParameter in a WHERE clause, for example, you can change the OraParameter value and refresh the OraDynaset. Refreshing an OraDynaset is preferable over re-creating it because the query needs to be re-executed only with the new OraParameter value (instead of with all the steps: parse, describe, bind, define, execute, fetch).

Binary (LONG/LONG RAW) Columns

Operating on binary data stored in a LONG or LONG RAW column of the database is different than using any other data type, mostly because of the potential size of one of these columns.

The normal behavior of an OraDynaset is to fetch all column data and cache locally. This technique works fine for most data types, even strings (column of type VARCHAR) that can hold up to 2048 bytes. This behavior does not work well for binary (column of type LONG or LONG RAW) data because the columns in Oracle7 can hold up to two gigabytes of data. Most PCs don't have two gigabytes of disk space to hold one column of one row, never mind multiple rows.

To overcome this problem, the `GetChunk()` and `AppendChunk()` methods of the OraField object are available. `GetChunk()` enables fetching of a piece of binary data and `AppendChunk()` enables putting of a piece of binary data. `GetChunk()` normally causes a trip to the server to retrieve the requested piece.

`AppendChunk()` does not immediately cause a trip to the server to update the column, but it updates a locally stored item. After the `Update()` method is called, the whole column is updated at once. This type of update occurs because the Oracle Call Interface does not have a method for piece-wise updating of LONG or LONG RAW columns.

Because the basis of row identification in Oracle Objects is the Oracle ROWID and because binary data must be fetched separately, a ROWID is necessary to fetch LONG or LONG RAW columns. Therefore, you must give careful consideration to a SQL select statement with a LONG or LONG RAW column in it.

Transactions

You can begin database transactions only at the OraSession level, although transactions can be committed, rolled back, or reset (rolled back without events) at both the OraSession and OraConnection level. Rollback savepoints are not supported.

Although you could conceivably begin/end transactions using ExecuteSQL, this method is not recommended because it undermines the OraDynaset operations. The OraDynaset would not know when a rollback occurred, so it could not refresh data. You definitely should not start a transaction with OraSession.Begin Trans() and then end it with an OraDatabase.ExecuteSQL(), because the internal flag will think a transaction is still in progress.

When transactions are committed at the OraSession level, the OraConnections collection is traversed, and each connection is committed individually. No verification or two-phase commit behavior takes place, so if an error occurs, some connections can be left uncommitted.

Remember that DDL SQL statements made on the same connection as a dynaset with open transactions will cause the pending dynaset changes to be committed, which you probably don't want. For less confusion and errors, creating two OraSession objects is best—one for OraDynaset operations and one for ExecuteSQL() operations.

ExecuteSQL() Method

ExecuteSQL() is a very useful method because it allows the execution of any non-select SQL statement or PL/SQL block. These statements include Data Definition Language (DDL), Data Manipulation Language (DML), Session Control, and System Control statements.

Transactional control statements such as COMMIT and ROLLBACK are possible but discouraged. Embedded SQL is not supported.

Data Definition Language (DDL)

You can use any valid DDL statement with ExecuteSQL(), but use caution when using a statement that may undermine any internal operations of the OLE Server, such as committing transactions.

CAUTION

Issuing DDL statements within the same OraSession and OraDatabase using the same actual Oracle connection (login) causes any pending transactions in an OraDynaset to be committed. The best way to avoid this problem is to create separate OraSession and OraDatabase objects for DDL and for OraDynaset operations. This step is easy using the OraSession.`CreateNamedSession()` method, as shown in the following code. Do not simply call `CreateObject()` again, because it will return the same default OraSession.

```
...
Dim OraSession as Object
Dim OraSessionDDL as Object
Dim OraDatabase as Object
Dim OraDatabaseDDL as Object

'Create the default OraSession and a second named one
Set OraSession = CreateObject("OracleInProcServer.XOraSession")
Set OraSessionDDL = OraSession.CreateNamedSession("DDL")

'Create two OraDatabase objects, one for each set of operations
'These will not share a connection because they are using
' different OraSession objects
Set OraDatabase = OraSession.OpenDatabase("Oracle7", "scott/tiger", 0&)
Set OraDatabaseDDL = OraSessionDDL.OpenDatabase("Oracle7", "scott/tiger", 0&)

...
```

Data Manipulation Language (DML)

You can use any valid DML statement with ExecuteSQL(). These statements include but are not limited to ALTER, CREATE, DROP, and GRANT.

Stored Procedures/Functions

Calling a stored procedure is slightly different than executing SQL statements. When calling a stored procedure or function, you must place a begin and end around the call, as shown in this example:

```
...
OraParameters(":oldnum").value = '555-1234'
OraParameters(":newnum").value = '555-7890'
sp$="begin AddrBook.NumberChange(:oldnum, :newnum); end;"
OraDatabase.ExecuteSQL(sp$, 0&)
...
```

The OraParameter object can represent any scalar data type available to a PL/SQL stored procedure or function. Like SQL statements, using parameters means better code reuse. Using parameters does not mean better performance because after a call to a stored procedure is made, no object in the OLE Server is created to represent the code and save it for reuse. An OraParameter can also have values returned into it.

Some More Properties

You should remember these few useful miscellaneous properties.

The RecordCount property of the OraDynaset is useful but has one side effect to note. Accessing RecordCount forces all rows in the OraDynaset to be traversed. The rows are fetched and stored locally if you are in default mode, but not if you are in NoCache mode. In normal mode, you potentially could fetch thousands or more rows. In NoCache mode, the rows aren't all stored locally, but they also are no longer available (a new OraDynaset must be created).

The RecordCount property works this way for two reasons. First, the OLE Server does not have a SQL parser to decompose the SQL statement such that the OLE Server could create a new statement with the same conditions to issue a count. Second, even if the OLE Server could process the SQL statement to obtain a record count, this behavior would violate the read consistency model on the OraDynaset. If a second Oracle cursor needs to be opened, you have no guarantee that the OraDynaset created will be equal to the first. This is because the first OraDynaset does not cause all rows to be locked, and another user may have added, removed, or updated some rows.

You can use the Bookmark property to save a pointer to a row and immediately jump back to the row later without having to execute multiple move operations. Bookmarks are valid between an OraDynaset and its clone. You can use this feature to perform record movement on a clone (possibly to find a certain record) and then move the current row of the original OraDynaset directly to that row.

Portability of Source Code

The idea of implementing an OLE Server is to present the same interface to many applications. If the applications implement OLE client scripting per the specification, then the code to access the OLE Server is absolutely portable between host environments.

Unfortunately, though, none of these applications allow saving an external file format understood by them all so the code would be easily reusable.

Host Environments

Of the three known supported OLE scripting environments, only one provides true OLE client scripting support. Excel 5.0, Visual Basic 3.0, and Access 2.0 each have a number of reserved words that those applications interpret to be internal commands and not OLE interface methods. These words are listed in the product documentation, and the list contains practically every method of the OLE Server. To work around this limitation, the OLE Server enables all of its method names to be prefixed by "Db" if necessary.

Performance

Because performance is always an issue, you should consider at least three areas of performance—Database, OLE Server, and OLE. You can manipulate some tuning capabilities of each area when you are trying to improve performance.

Database Performance

Oracle documentation contains a large amount of information about tuning the database, database schemas, and SQL queries. Review this documentation.

As far as the OLE Server is concerned, the object that most affects performance is the OraParameter used with SQL select statements. You must perform a number of steps before rows can be fetched from a query—parse, describe, bind, define, execute, fetch. When using parameters, you skip the parse, describe, bind, and define steps, and you simply re-execute the query. In addition, the query may still be available in the Oracle shared SQL pool, which also improves performance. If the query did not use an OraParameter, you would need to do all steps, and the query would not match the previous query in the shared SQL pool, which would degrade performance.

OLE Server Performance

The OLE Server fetches and caches rows so that backward scrolling is possible. The data fetching and caching have some tunable parameters. These parameters should be set in ORAOLE.INI, normally located in the WINDOWS directory. If the file does not exist, create one with a text editor.

The section named FetchParameters has two settings: FetchLimit and FetchSize. Set FetchLimit to the number of rows to fetch in one single call. The higher the FetchLimit, the more memory required for the fetch. Set FetchSize to the size of the initial chunk to fetch from a LONG or LONG RAW column. Again, the higher the FetchSize, the more memory required to fetch. Also, remember that in addition to the other column data, the number of FetchSize * FetchLimit bytes will be allocated just for the LONG or LONG RAW columns.

The section named CacheParameters has three settings: SliceSize, PerBlock, and CacheBlocks. SliceSize represents the smallest data block allocated for any data item (column). PerBlock represents how many Slices of SliceSize will be in each Block. CacheBlocks represents how many Blocks will be kept in memory before swapping to disk. SliceSize * PerBlock * CacheBlocks is the total amount of memory used by the data cache.

Most importantly, don't make any of the settings so high that Windows needs to swap just to meet your memory needs. This causes double swapping in the case of the data cache and decreases performance. The best advice is to experiment with your particular OraDynaset needs.

The only problem with the cache and fetch settings is that they are per system and not per OraDynaset. OraDynasets that are very different in the data types and number of rows fetched may perform better with very different fetch and cache settings. Through testing, you can find a medium.

OLE Performance

OLE Automation is not without overhead. Every time you reference a method, property, or sub-object, you are making an object reference. Reducing the number of these references can greatly improve performance. If you are referencing some object many times, you should create a temporary object and set it to the object you are referencing too often. The product documentation describes this issue in detail in the topic "Coding Techniques."

Error Handling

The known supported applications handle errors with an ON ERROR GOTO statement that enables jumping to a label in the code when an error occurs. After this step, the application must determine if the error was an application or an Oracle error.

Application Errors

Application errors are generally all raised via one error variable. A number of errors that normally occur have predefined error numbers. For the OLE Server, only one error number is formally raised: 440, OLE Automation Error. When this error occurs, the application must check for an Oracle error to see if more information is available.

Oracle Errors

After an error is raised, you can query Oracle errors from the LastServerErr properties of the corresponding OraDatabase or OraSession object. Errors are set at either the OraDatabase or OraSession, but never both. Error codes are not automatically cleared, so you must use the

`LastServerErrReset` property to set the error code to zero. This point is important to the developer but not the OLE Server, because the OLE Server only sets that error number; the OLE Server doesn't use the number to determine whether an error has occurred. The following code fragment demonstrates how to trap errors on either the OraSession or OraDatabase objects, depending on what methods are being called.

```
...
Dim OraSession as Object
Dim OraDatabase as Object
Dim OraDynaset as Object

'Set a handler for OraSession creation
on error goto OraSessionErr
'Generic OLE error could occur, especially ones related to
'installation and configuration of needed Oracle and OLE files
Set OraSession = CreateObject("OracleInProcServer.XOraSession")

on error goto OraDatabaseErr
'The only error that could occur here is a connection problem.
Set OraDatabase = OraSession.OpenDatabase("Oracle7", "scott/tiger", 0&)

on error goto OraSessionErr
'Notice that "select" is spelled wrong
Set OraDynaset = OraDatabase.CreateDynaset("seletc * from houses", 0&)
exit sub

OraSessionErr:
'Process OraSession Errors
MsgBox "Error creating an OraSession"
exit sub

OraDatabaseErr:
'Process OraDatabase Errors
MsgBox "Error creating an OraDatabase"
If OraSession.LastServerErr <> 0 Then
 MsgBox OraSession.LastServerErrText
 OraSession.LastServerErrReset
Else
 MsgBox Error$
End If
exit sub

OraDynasetErr:
'Process OraDynaset Errors
MsgBox "Error creating an OraDynaset"
If OraDatabase.LastServerErr <> 0 Then
 MsgBox OraDatabase.LastServerErrText
 OraDatabase.LastServerErrReset
Else
 MsgBox Error$
End If
exit sub
...
```

Comparison with DAO/JET

Although the Oracle objects are conceptually close to the Microsoft Data Access Objects (implemented using the JET SQL engine), the Oracle implementation has a number of fundamental differences. These differences affect, among other things, data access, data updatability, and Oracle feature access.

DAO can make use of a local SQL engine, called JET, to process queries and data from flat files or ODBC data sources. You can bypass this engine (using SQLPASSTHROUGH mode), but all the built-in data updatability of DAO is lost and must be coded manually.

Differences Between Oracle Objects and DAO

Microsoft's DAO are conceptually sound. A number of database objects are represented at a high level. The interface is simple, requiring only a few lines to open a database, create a dynaset, and edit or add data. Unfortunately, the implementation using JET may not be very desirable. Instead of operating in a client/server mode, JET (a database engine) turns the implementation into client-server/server mode. Instead of letting Oracle7 process requests, JET first processes the request locally; then JET passes the request to Oracle7 (remotely), and again locally, and then returns it to the application. Too much processing is involved if your application is going to work only with Oracle7.

Oracle Objects for OLE was designed by taking some of the DAO objects and concepts and building them into a product that operated with less overhead and in more environments, communicated directly with Oracle, and could access Oracle-specific features.

Oracle-Specific Features

The JET SQL engine understands its own SQL variant and is not necessarily compatible with the Oracle SQL engine that you ultimately want to process your query. Queries are routinely parsed and reconstructed so the JET engine can understand them. Therefore, the Oracle SQL you have created may look nothing like the query that is submitted to Oracle. OO4O does not contain a SQL engine, and as a rule, does not reconstruct the queries provided to it. The OO4O model is to pass the query to Oracle, let Oracle parse it, and then ask Oracle for the query description.

Oracle SQL and PL/SQL allow for the embedding of bind variables (parameters), which enables code reuse and improved performance. DAOs do not contain an object to make use of bind variables. OO4O contains the OraParameters collection so that SQL and PL/SQL statements can be reused.

Data Updatability

Ideally, you should control data updatability by the rules of the database and the privileges you have been granted. This is not the case with JET, which requires that a table have a primary key (unique index) to be updatable. The key is used to identify a particular row; you may need to modify the table definition to accommodate JET users. OO4O does not have this requirement because it uses the native Oracle ROWID to identify a particular row. OO4O does not place any extra restrictions on data updatability.

A database may have many large tables cryptically named or tables containing large amounts of information that not every user needs to access. Database views and synonyms are frequently used to provide simpler or restricted access to database objects. Using views and synonyms with JET automatically causes your dynaset to be read-only. OO4O does not automatically cause a dynaset to be read-only, and the data is updatable if Oracle normally allows it.

Data Access

Column aliases and schema references make queries more readable and qualify object access. You can use these techniques only with the SQLPASSTHROUGH mode of JET, which means the data is read-only. OO4O freely accepts those references, and the data is updatable if Oracle normally allows it.

References to object names (tables, views, synonyms, and so on) in Oracle are normally not case-sensitive, but JET, by default, uses uppercase unless you are in SQLPASSTHROUGH mode. This situation can cause problems when Oracle database objects are defined case-sensitively. OO4O does not modify the case of any object's reference.

Implementation of the OLE Server

JET performs a large amount of processing locally, such as table joins. JET provides updatability of joins (which Oracle does not allow), but what if the Oracle database contained millions of rows? Would the JET engine be able to retrieve and process that much data on your local PC? OO4O does not contain its own SQL engine and does not perform that type of processing locally—it lets Oracle do it.

JET fetches data, as needed, and stores a "window" of rows locally while the dynaset is traversed. This method means that data must be continually fetched using multiple trips to the server to keep the "window" fresh. Because the data is not locked, the data also could change during the time you're selecting it (no read consistency). OO4O fetches rows as needed and stores them all locally as the dynaset is traversed. Admittedly, this method can lead to a large amount of local storage, but it does provide read consistency.

JET requires `Close()` methods on objects, but Oracle Objects does not. The OLE objects keep a reference count and are automatically destroyed when they go out of scope and the count reaches zero.

Performance of the OLE Server

Because their implementations are different, OO4O and DAO/JET are not easy to compare directly. Because their features are similar, this comparison is frequently made. OO4O ships with a sample application called Object Test. This application's main purpose is to show that using OO4O to access and update Oracle database objects is much easier than using DAO/JET. Object Test also performs some timing, but the small amount of sample data cannot provide relevant performance data.

If you modify this application to use a larger data set, OO4O becomes faster. The main reason is that OLE Automation has overhead, and while fetching a small amount of data, that overhead is a large percentage of the time.

After the data of a dynaset has been entirely fetched, OO4O is simply accessing a disk cache while JET may need to refetch the data. This situation is a benefit in performance, but it may cause a large amount of temporary disk space to be used.

Again, as with memory and disk usage, testing your particular application is the only way to determine if it will meet your performance needs. You should consider hardware, software, and networking.

JET/DAO Migration Issues

Apart from understanding the different objects and error handling, you should consider a few important migration issues when moving from DAO/JET to Oracle Objects.

One of the fundamental migration issues is data types. DAOs are declared as some native data type (dynaset, database, etc.), and the Oracle objects are always declared as type "object." Also, you cannot compare data of type objects to zero or null or empty as easily as you can with other data types.

As mentioned earlier, the OLE Server objects do not provide all the same objects, methods, and properties as DAO/JET.

One of the most popular sets of methods of the dynaset object is the FIND method set (FindFirst, FindNext, FindLast, FindPrevious). The OraDynaset does not provide these methods, because the OLE Server would need to decompose the SQL statement, add a new WHERE clause, and reprocess it. Oracle Objects does not have a local SQL engine and cannot easily complete that task. Implementing this feature, although helpful, would defeat the current client/server mode that OO4O tries very hard to maintain.

The best workaround for the "missing" FIND methods is to use an OraParameter within the WHERE clause. You then can change the OraParameter value and refresh the OraDynaset. This workaround is limited. A second choice workaround is to make use of dynaset clones and bookmarks. Because bookmarks are valid between a dynaset and its clone, you could create a clone, search it for the desired record, set a bookmark, and then set the current row of the original dynaset to the bookmark. Again, this workaround is not complete for all cases.

Summary

The Oracle OLE Automation Server is a very complex tool. When developing an application, you must consider the relationship of objects to each other and to Oracle because some operations can cause side effects. Make sure to use built-in functionality and don't try to undermine features implemented in the OLE Server, even if they are not complete. You usually cause more trouble than it's worth. Try to make use of the OLE Server and its features without comparing the OLE Server to its design basis DAO. The OLE Server's features (data caching, read consistency) and unique objects (OraParameters) and its tight integration with Oracle7 make it a very powerful interface you should thoroughly consider when choosing a database connectivity layer.

The Oracle Data Control

48

by Keith Majkut

IN THIS CHAPTER

The Oracle Data Control (ODC) is a level III Visual Basic Extension (VBX) designed to be compatible with the Visual Basic 3.0 data control. The ODC uses the OLE Server to access an Oracle7 database. Unlike some data controls, the ODC does not ship with its own controls such as a text box, list box, combo box, grid, and so on. The ODC theoretically can have any other third-party controls bound to it.

Understanding ODC

Oracle Objects for OLE (OO4O) provides an OLE Server for programmatic development. Because Visual Basic 3.0 is a popular environment and because data-aware controls make development even easier, the Oracle Data Control is an excellent helper tool and logical addition to Oracle Objects for OLE. The inclusion of the Oracle Data Control makes Oracle Objects for OLE a reasonable replacement for the native database access in Visual Basic 3.0.

What Is a VBX?

VBX is short for Visual Basic Extension and is basically a Windows Dynamic Link Library (DLL) with a specific interface. Visual Basic 3.0 contains a control development kit that specifies the various interfaces a VBX must support. A VBX is used to extend the functionality of Visual Basic (and possibly other applications) by adding functionality not contained in the original product.

What Type of VBX Is the Oracle Data Control?

The Oracle Data Control is a level III custom control. Although the Oracle Data Control appears to be a data control, it is not. The control development kit has no specification for writing a data control. The control development kit explains how to write a data aware control (a control that uses a data control) so the kit does discuss the behavior of the Microsoft data control and therefore implies how to write a data control.

Reviewing the Relationship Between the ODC and the OLE Server

The Oracle Data Control provides an easy way to create an OraDynaset and all other needed objects. After you refresh the data control, all objects are available using properties of the data control.

Object Creation

Refreshing the Oracle Data Control, assuming you have set certain properties correctly, causes an OraDynaset to be created. Examining the programmatic interface shows that an OraSession and OraDatabase must be created before an OraDynaset. This rule is consistent with the Oracle Data Control having Database (OraDatabase) and Session (OraSession) properties. All objects used to refresh the data control are then available as properties of it. One drawback is that the OraSession created or used by any data control is the default OraSession; you can never change the default. Along the same lines, all the object properties of the data control are read-only; you cannot assign a particular OraSession, OraDatabase, OraDynaset, and so on, to a data control.

After you have refreshed the Oracle Data Control successfully, you can use all the objects it creates to mix and match usage of the data control with the programmatic interface. The following example demonstrates this procedure:

```
Dim OraSession as Object
Dim OraDatabase as Object

'Set properties needed to create the OraSession, OraDatabase
' and OraDynaset objects.
OraData1.Connect = "scott/tiger"
OraData1.Databasename = "t:prod:orcl"
OraData1.RecordSource = "select name, number from addressbook"
OraData1.Refresh

'Use the OraSession object of the data control to create a
' second named OraSession to be used for DDL statements. Remember
' that DDL executed within the same OraSession and using the same
' Oracle Connection will commit pending transactions.
Set OraSession = OraData1.Session.CreateNamedSession("DDLSession")
Set OraDatabase = OraSession.OpenDatabase("scott/tiger@t:prod:orcl",0&)
OraDatabase.DbExecuteSQL("create table temp (col1 number)")...
...
```

Using SQL Parameters

The OraParameters collection is a property of the OraDatabase object. You must create an OraParameter after the OraDatabase but before an OraDynaset. At first you may think you cannot use OraParameters with the data control, but you can. You can refresh the Oracle Data Control after you set the Connect and DatabaseName properties. If those properties are valid, the OraSession and OraDatabase objects that the data control needs are created. Again, this practice is consistent with the programmatic interface in that those values are the only ones needed to create an OraSession and OraDatabase.

After these objects have been created, you can add OraParameters to the OraDatabase object before creating the OraDynaset. After the OraParameters have been created, set the RecordSource property and refresh the data control again. This step causes the OraDynaset to be created. Just as with the programmatic interface, you can change an OraParameters value and refresh the OraDynaset. If this explanation sounds confusing, review this example:

```
'Set properties needed to create the OraSession and OraDatabase
OraData1.Connect = "scott/tiger"
OraData1.Databasename = "t:prod:orcl"
OraData1.Refresh

'Add an OraParamter
OraData1.Database.Parameters.Add "NAME", "SMITH", 1

'Set the RecordSource so I can create the OraDynaset
OraData1.RecordSource = "select name, number from addressbook where name = :NAME"
OraData1.Refresh

'Change the value of the OraParameter and refresh the data control
OraData1.Database.Parameters("NAME").value = "JONES"
OraData1.RecordSet.Refresh
...
```

Controlling Transactions

You initiate transactions using the OraSession object, and you need to initiate them before creating the OraDynaset. At first you may think that you cannot use transactions with the data control, but you can. You can refresh the Oracle Data Control after setting the Connect and DatabaseName properties. If those properties are valid, the OraSession and OraDatabase objects that the data control needs are created. Again, this practice is consistent with the programmatic interface in that those values are the only ones needed to create an OraSession and OraDatabase. After these objects are created, you can start a transaction. After the transaction is started, set the RecordSource property and refresh the data control again. This step causes the OraDynaset to be created. Just as with the programmatic interface, you can change, commit, or roll back data. If this explanation sounds confusing, review this example:

```
'Set properties needed to create the OraSession and OraDatabase
OraData1.Connect = "scott/tiger"
OraData1.Databasename = "t:prod:orcl"
OraData1.Refresh

'Add an OraParamter
OraData1.Database.Parameters.Add "NAME", "SMITH", 1

'Begin a transaction
OraData1.Session.BeginTrans

'Set the RecordSource so I can create the OraDynaset
OraData1.RecordSource = "select name, number from addressbook where name = :NAME"
OraData1.Refresh

'Update any data here.
...

'Commit the changes
OraData1.Session.CommitTrans
```

```
'Roll back the changes
'OraData1.Session.Rollback
...
```

Using ODC in Visual Basic

Using the Oracle Data Control in Visual Basic 3.0 is just like using any other VBX. Choose the File, Add File menu option and add the file ORADC.VBX (normally installed in \WINDOWS\SYSTEM).

Using ODC in a New Project

Using the Oracle Data Control is almost as easy as using the Microsoft data control or any other custom control. Follow these steps:

1. Start Visual Basic 3.0 and begin a new project (File | New Project).
2. Add the Oracle Data Control to this project (File | Add File). The Oracle Data Control is named ORADC.VBX and is normally located in the \WINDOWS\SYSTEM directory. After adding ODC, the tool palette looks something like Figure 48.1.

FIGURE 48.1.

The tool palette.

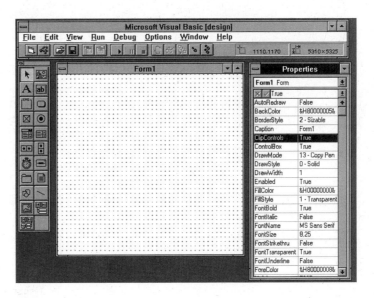

3. Click on the Oracle Data Control and proceed to draw the control on a new form as you would with any other control.

4. After you draw the control, click it so the property palette is displayed. (See Figure 48.2.)

FIGURE 48.2.

Oracle Data Control and property palette.

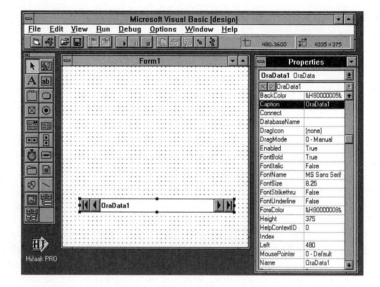

5. Set the Connect, DatabaseName, and RecordSource properties of the Oracle Data Control to valid values such as "scott/tiger," "AddressDb," and "select name from addressbook."

6. Click the text edit control icon on the tool palette and draw the control on the form.

7. Click the text edit, and then go to the property palette and set the DataSource property to be the same as the Name property of the Oracle Data Control ("oradata1" by default). Set the DataFields property to be "Name," the name of the column to bind to this control. Your form should look something like Figure 48.3.

8. Run the project (Run | Start).

If you properly set the necessary properties of the Oracle Data Control and the text edit, then data appears in the text edit. Notice that the arrows on the control move the records forward and backward and that you can edit the data to update the database (assuming the table is updatable). You can stop the application using Run | End.

FIGURE 48.3.

Oracle Data Control and text edit on a form.

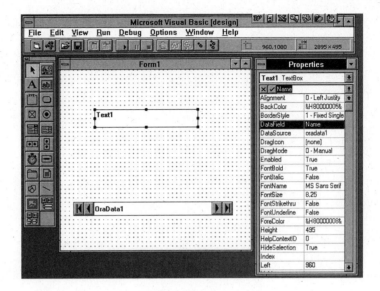

Using ODC with a Third-Party Data Aware Control

Using the Oracle Data Control with a third-party data aware control is almost as easy as using that control with the Microsoft data control. Follow these steps:

1. Start Visual Basic 3.0 and begin a new project (File | New Project).

2. Add the Oracle Data Control and the data aware control to the project (File | Add File).

   The Oracle Data Control is named ORADC.VBX and is normally located in the \WINDOWS\SYSTEM directory. This example uses a data-aware control named TRUEGRID.VBX developed by Apex Software Corporation. After you have added both controls, the tool palette looks something like Figure 48.4.

3. Set the Connect, DatabaseName, and RecordSource properties of the Oracle Data Control to valid values such as "scott/tiger," "AddressDb," and "select name from addressbook."

4. Click the TrueGrid control icon on the tool palette and draw this control on the form.

5. Click the TrueGrid, and then go to the property palette and set the DataSource property to be the same as the Name property of the Oracle Data Control ("oradata1" by default). The form should resemble Figure 48.5.

FIGURE 48.4.

Oracle Data Control, TrueGrid, and the tool palette.

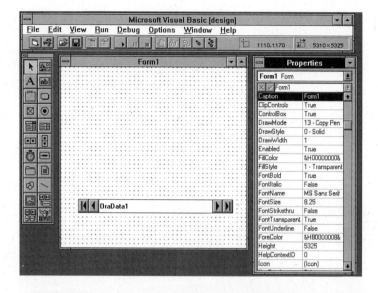

FIGURE 48.5.

Oracle Data Control and TrueGrid on a form.

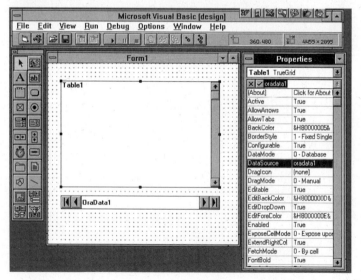

6. Run the project (Run | Start).

If you properly set the necessary properties of the Oracle Data Control and the TrueGrid, then rows and columns appear in the TrueGrid. You can stop the application using Run | End.

Comparing ODC with the Visual Basic Data Control

The Oracle Data Control is designed to be a replacement for the Microsoft data control in Visual Basic 3.0. The Oracle Data Control provides basically the same properties and methods as the Microsoft data control.

Functionality

The Oracle Data Control provides a number of extra properties not found in the Microsoft data control.

ODC Properties Not Found in Visual Basic

The AllowMoveLast property determines whether the user can click the rightmost (MoveLast) button of the data control when running an application. When a MoveLast() is executed, all the records satisfying the query are fetched and stored locally, and the operation cannot be interrupted. This operation could potentially involve a large amount of data and take a long time, so the application designer can use this property to disable that button. This feature is useful only for the user, because a developer can still execute a MoveLast(). Also, disabling the MoveLast button does not prevent the user from repeatedly clicking the MoveNext button.

The AutoBinding property is the same as the NoAutoBind flag of the options parameters in the CreateDynaset() method.

The TrailingBlanks property is the same as the NoTrailBlanks flag of the options parameters in the CreateDynaset() method.

The HelpContextID property is used to set a help context ID number that is accessed (in the application's help file) when the user presses F1 and the Oracle Data Control has focus.

The Session and Database properties of the Oracle Data Control refer to the OraSession and OraDatabase objects used to create the OraDynaset object that the RecordSet property refers to.

The DatabaseName and Connect properties are similar in nature to those of the Microsoft data control, but they have a much different syntax. For the Oracle Data Control, set the Connect property to the username, a forward slash, and the password (as in "scott/tiger"). Set the DatabaseName to the Oracle SQL*Net connect string for that database. This identifier varies depending on the version of Oracle SQL*Net you are using (V1 or V2), so consult the Oracle documentation for more details (a V1 example is something like "t:prod:orcl"). When using DAO/JET/ODBC, the Microsoft data control uses the Connect property to specify all the connection information using a keyword equal value (keyword = value) format.

Limitations of the ODC

Although the Oracle Data Control works like a data control, it does not (nor could it) support every detail or unsupported feature that the Microsoft data control does. The Control Developer's Kit has no specification of a data control; you find only information on what to expect from the data control given certain situations.

The Oracle Data Control doesn't appear as a data control to Visual Basic so you cannot autoselect it from the drop-down list of data sources that some data aware controls have.

The Oracle Data Control does not support getting its Hwnd (Window Handle) property so that you can access it from another form, nor does the ODC work with controls that rely on undocumented features of the Microsoft data control.

As far as features go, the Oracle Data Control can only read images, not write them. This point is not mentioned in the product documentation, but you can easily test the feature by setting a bitmap to a picture control and then trying to update.

The product documentation lists a number of differences between the Oracle Data Control and the Microsoft data control as well as problems that some data aware controls have when trying to use the Oracle Data Control.

Migrating from the MS Data Control/ODBC to the ODC/OLE Server

Moving from the Microsoft data control to the Oracle Data Control requires a small number of steps, but some of those steps could cause code redesign. Before moving, make sure to see whether the Oracle Data Control is compatible with any data aware controls your application requires.

You should consider all of the following items when migrating from the Microsoft data control to the Oracle Data Control:

- After adding the Oracle Data Control to the project, modify property values that are similar but have different values, such as the Options property, AllowMoveLast, TrailingBlanks, AutoBinding, Connect, and DatabaseName. You may need to modify the RecordSource property if the SQL your application is using contains JET-specific syntax.

- You need to rewrite any code that uses dynaset Find*() methods because Oracle Objects does not support these methods. Remove any Close() methods because Oracle Objects doesn't need them.

- Declare the objects of Oracle Objects for OLE as type "object" and not as native Visual Basic data types such as database, dynaset, and so on.

- You may need to prefix some method names with "Db" because Visual Basic considers names invalid if you use them from an object that is not a native data type. Review the product documentation topic called "Method and Property Name Conflicts."

- Review your application's use of the FieldSize(), GetChunk(), and AppendChunk() methods because these methods are implemented differently than in DAO/JET. Again, consult the product documentation on these methods' behavior.

- Error handling is significantly different when using Oracle Objects. The product documentation contains a topic describing error handling.

- Read the product documentation topics entitled "Coding Techniques" and "Tuning and Customization" to enhance performance.

Summary

The ODC is a good replacement for the Microsoft data control of Visual Basic 3.0. Unlike other similar controls, the Oracle Data Control is designed to work with any third-party data-aware control.

Unfortunately, though, some fundamental differences exist that may require modifications to third-party controls. The product documentation concedes that testing of third-party controls was not thorough, because many data aware controls are available. Some testing was done, and the Oracle Data Control does appear to work with a variety of popular controls.

The best advice is to test the Oracle Data Control with any data aware controls that your application may require, because compatibility is not guaranteed.

OLE C++ Class Library

49

by Kevin Whitley

In the last several chapters, you have seen what Oracle Objects is and how to use it from Visual Basic. The same power is available to C++ developers through the Oracle Objects for OLE C++ class library.

Because this class library is based on the Oracle Objects for OLE product, it shares many of the same concepts and techniques. Before reading this chapter, you should read the preceding chapters on Oracle Objects for OLE. Those chapters discuss the basic ideas of Oracle Objects for OLE and provide details such as software requirements.

This chapter takes a quick overview of the class library and then looks at how to use the class library to build some simple routines. The emphasis is more on how to use the library rather than on details about what each method does. A few code snippets are provided, and the full source code is provided on the accompanying CD-ROM.

The information documented here is accurate for Oracle Objects for OLE 1.0 (patch level 55). Oracle does periodically release patches and upgrades, so please contact Oracle for information about future releases.

A Quick Demonstration

To give you a flavor of the class library, look very quickly at a snippet of code. You will write a function to look at Oracle's standard demonstration schema and extract the maximum salary paid to any employee. What kind of code would you have to write to do this with existing C++ tools? You would have to declare working areas, open a database connection, create a cursor, parse SQL statements, fetch data, and perform various bookkeeping tasks. Here is the function written in the Oracle Objects for OLE class library:

```
double GetMaxSalary()
{
    /* connect to the database */
    ODatabase dbref("t:123.4.5.67:ORCL", "scott", "tiger");

    /* open a dynaset with the SQL query */
    ODynaset dynref(dbref, "select max(sal) from emp");

    /* get the data */
    double maxsal;
    dynref.GetFieldValue(1, &maxsal);   // get value of column 1

    /* return the value */
    return(maxsal);
}
```

This code does all those previously mentioned tasks in only five lines of C++ code, three of which are declarations! The Oracle Objects for OLE C++ class library gives you methods that enable you to work with your SQL statements without having to worry about all of the book-keeping code that you would have to write if you were working directly with Oracle's call interface, or ODBC. Later in the chapter, you'll go through this example line by line to understand what it is doing.

Overview

The Oracle Objects for OLE class library is a C++ class library that provides object-oriented access to data stored in an Oracle relational database. It uses the Oracle Objects automation server DLL to perform most of its tasks.

The Parts of the Product

The class library portion of the Oracle Objects for OLE product has several major components. They are

- The class library
- Sample bound classes for MFC widgets
- Sample bound classes for OWL widgets
- Documentation for the class library
- A workbook
- Source code for the class library

The class library provides some basic classes that correspond to the objects in the Oracle Automation Server. It also provides some extra classes for dealing with bound objects. These bound object classes give functionality in C++ that roughly corresponds to the functionality of data controls and bound objects in Visual Basic. You'll learn about these very powerful bound object classes toward the end of the chapter.

The class library consists of a library file that you link against and a DLL that you use at run time. Versions of the library file are available for both Microsoft and Borland compilers, as are both debug and non-debug versions of the DLLs (for both Microsoft and Borland). The Microsoft files have names ending in "m", and the Borland files have names ending in "b".

The sample bound classes are provided in both MFC and OWL versions. These are provided as libraries rather than as DLLs. These libraries enable you to use the user interface widgets of the application frameworks as bound objects in your database application.

The documentation for the class library consists mostly of a single help file, which is more of a reference than a learning guide. An icon for this document was installed in the Oracle Objects for OLE program group. There are also write files for the MFC and OWL bound widget libraries.

The class library comes with a workbook, which is the piece of documentation that is intended to teach you how to use the library. This workbook works through several examples in detail. Source code is provided.

A complete set of source code for the library itself is also provided. You need the header files to compile your code, of course, but the source code is very handy when it comes time to debug your program. Source code is also provided, in separate directories, for the MFC and OWL bound widgets.

Relationship to Oracle Objects for OLE

The interface of the class library has a great deal in common with the objects that you saw in the preceding chapters. There are session, database, dynaset, field, and parameter objects. The objects in Oracle Objects mostly become classes in the class library. Many of the methods have similar names and behavior. The class library also implements a number of additional classes.

The class library is implemented using the Oracle Objects for OLE automation DLL. Instead of using the OLE automation interfaces that are so useful for Visual Basic, however, the class library uses custom OLE interfaces that the DLL makes available. This is important because it means that the performance of the class library will be better than an equivalent program written in Visual Basic.

In fact, you could consider the class library's dependence on Oracle Objects for OLE to be strictly an implementation detail. For all that you can see in the library's interface, it could have been implemented a number of different ways. It isn't until it comes time to distribute your product that you will need to remember the Oracle Objects automation DLL.

The Use of OLE

The class library uses OLE. Does that mean that you will need to learn OLE to use it? Absolutely not. In fact, you will not even need to include OLE header files in your source code to use the class library. Like the Oracle Objects for OLE layer, OLE is used strictly as an implementation device. You will only need to link against the OLE libraries.

A Comparison with MFC

Users of Microsoft's Visual C++ development environment know that its Microsoft Foundation Classes (MFC) library has database classes in it. Because they are part of MFC, they are nicely integrated into the development environment. The Application Wizard helps you build an application that supports databases, and the Class Wizard makes it easy for you to create C++ classes that correspond to database tables. For an application that is working with a known, fixed schema, the MFC database classes are very convenient and powerful. How does the Oracle Objects for OLE class library compare to the MFC database classes?

The two libraries take very different approaches. MFC uses a CRecordset class as a base class that handles the database interaction. You then subclass this class for your particular query, constructing a class that has member variables corresponding to the columns in your result set. This means two things: First, the set of columns that you are working with is determined at compile time; and second, you create a new class for every different query. The benefit to this approach is that it makes nice tools like the Class Wizard possible. And you never have to see any SQL.

Oracle Objects for OLE has an ODatabase class that handles the database connection and an ODynaset class that handles the SQL query result set. The SQL statement is handed to the ODynaset instance at run time, rather than compile time. This means that you can create the SQL statement dynamically in your program. However, because the details of the result set aren't known until run-time, it is not possible to have a class with column values as member variables. Instead, you call methods such as ODynaset::GetFieldValue() to get column values. It is a slightly more complicated approach but one that is more flexible.

Which one should you use? If your application only has a few queries, and they are running against a fixed schema, it will probably be easier to use MFC's classes. On the other hand, if your schema is changing or not known until run time, or if you have many small queries (would you have wanted to create a new class for the trivial query of our simple example at the beginning of the chapter?), you are probably better off using the Oracle Objects for OLE class library.

Dependencies

The requirements for using the class library are basically the same as the requirements for using the Visual Basic part of Oracle Objects. You need access to an Oracle database, either locally (such as Personal Oracle7) or remotely via SQL*Net. The OO4O DLL is 16-bit, so if you use SQL*Net you will need a 16-bit version of SQL*Net.

The class library is a 16-bit library, so you can only use it to build 16-bit applications. This means that to use Visual C++, you will need a 1.x version (1.0 to 1.5). For Borland compilers, you will need a 4.x version.

The Library's Classes

This section looks at the classes in the library. These classes are very similar to the objects in the rest of Oracle Objects for OLE, so in many cases, you will simply be noting differences.

The most important classes are ODatabase, which gives you a database connection, and ODynaset, which allows you to execute SQL statements. OValue, which will hold an arbitrary value, and OParameter, which lets you parameterize your SQL statements, are also important.

> **CAUTION**
>
> Instances of all of the classes (with the exception of OValue, ODynasetMark, and OAdvise) are actually surrogate objects. The class library uses a reference-counted surrogate-master architecture. This means that copying something like an ODatabase instance is

> very cheap and that the copy will refer to the same master object. It is important to keep track of which operations affect the surrogate and which affect the master. Most affect the master.

The Basic Classes

Many of the classes in the class library can be called "basic" both because they are the simple foundations of the library, but also because they correspond very closely to the objects used in the Visual Basic version of Oracle Objects for OLE. These classes are OClient, OSession, ODatabase, ODynaset, OParameter, OField, and the collection classes OSessionCollection, OConnectionCollection, OFieldCollection, and OParameterCollection. These classes correspond to the automation objects OraClient, OraSession, and so on. You can consult both Chapter 47 and the product documentation to learn about the corresponding automation objects.

For the most part, you can expect these classes to work the way their similarly named object counterparts work (just change "Ora" to "O").

There are a few general differences:

- The C++ methods return error codes.
- Whereas the automation objects have both properties and methods, the classes only have methods. The object properties have been replaced with C++ methods that get values.
- In some cases, the method names have been changed to be more similar to the names of methods in the MFC database classes rather than Visual Basic names.
- Derived objects are not created by calling a method on their parent. They are created by calling a constructor for the object. The constructor will have an argument for the parent object. For instance, the OLE automation object OraDatabase has a CreateDynaset method. ODatabase has no CreateDynaset method. Instead, ODynaset has an Open() method that takes an ODatabase as an argument.

Let's quickly go over some of the bigger differences between the objects and the classes. Classes that aren't mentioned have minor differences.

OSession

The ConnectSession and CreateNamedSession automation object methods don't exist. The class library implements the same functionality with overloadings of the Open method.

ODynaset

A few of the changes are some simple renamings, for instance EOF() becomes IsEOF() and Transactions() becomes CanTransact(). Settable properties become Set() methods; for instance, setting the SQL property becomes SetSQL().

The way bookmarks are handled is somewhat different. In C++, a bookmark is an instance of another class: ODynasetMark. When you retrieve a bookmark, you are handed an instance of this class. Instead of setting the bookmark property, you call the MoveToMark() method with an ODynasetMark instance as an argument. Also, you can retrieve a mark from the last modified record, as opposed to the current record, using GetLastModifiedMark().

A number of additional methods exist. IsValidRecord() checks whether the current record is valid. CancelEdit() cancels an edit operation on the current record, which is useful to undo an edit on a record without rolling back the database transaction. DuplicateRecord() is a handy helper function that copies the column values of the current record to a newly added record.

The biggest addition to ODynaset is that you can directly access field information from the result set, rather than having to obtain a field collection first. You can get field values, set field values, get the number of fields, and so on all through methods such as ODynaset::GetFieldValue().

OConnection

The CommitTrans() and Rollback() methods are not supported in C++. Oracle recommends against using them anyway.

OField and OParameter

In addition to the GetValue() methods, which are overloaded for various types, there are also overloaded cast operators. This means that when you have an OField instance, you can simply assign it to a native C++ type. For instance:

```
OField  fsalary;
double dsalary;
fsalary = someDynaset.GetField("mycolumn");  // get a field
dsalary = fsalary;  // works because of overloaded cast
```

OOracleObject

OOracleObject does not correspond to any automation object. It is the base class for most of the rest of the objects in the class library. You will never need to instantiate OOracleObject. The most important thing to notice about OOracleObject is that it contains the methods for error handling, which are then available to all its subclasses.

OOracleCollection

OOracleCollection is a subclass of OOracleObject, and like OOracleObject, it is only used as a base class. You will never want to create an instance of OOracleCollection. The only important method of OOracleCollection is OOracleCollection::Count(), which returns the number of objects in the collection.

The classes OSessionCollection, OConnectionCollection, and OFieldCollection are all collections that the class library will create internally. You can open such a collection, but you cannot create a new collection. You will use these classes when you have asked the library for information, for instance about all connections. OParameterCollection is a little different in that you can assemble a new collection yourself, using OParameterCollection::Add().

> **CAUTION**
>
> The OParameterCollection object gives you a list of parameters attached to an ODatabase's master object. When the OParameterCollection is destroyed, the parameters in the collection are not destroyed because they are still attached to the database object. To delete a parameter, you need to explicitly call OParameterCollection::Remove().

ODynasetMark

In the OLE Automation Server, the bookmark that is returned by OraDynaset is a string. In the C++ class library, this has been replaced by a separate class, ODynasetMark. Instances of ODynasetMark are returned to you by the ODynaset methods GetMark() and GetLastModifiedMark(). ODynasetMarks can be copied and compared for equality. You can return to a marked record with ODynaset::MoveToMark().

A very typical use for an ODynasetMark is for a drop-down list. You get a set of records from the database with an ODynaset and then place the values of one of the columns in the drop-down list. You can get an ODynasetMark for each record and associate it with its corresponding line in the drop-down list. Then, when the user chooses the item, you can use the ODynasetMark to set the current record in the ODynaset to the record that corresponds to the chosen item.

OValue

Because the columns of your query are run-time bound, it is not possible for either you or the compiler to always determine the type of "column 3." What you need is a variable that can accommodate any data type. The OValue class fills that need. You can place many different types of data into an OValue and ask for many different types as output. The OValue instance will make an effort to convert the data if needed.

OValue takes a conservative approach to your data. It remembers the original data and type of data that it was set to. Consider the case where you set a VARIANT to a value of 1.3, a value of type double. Then you ask for its value as an int, and receive the value 1. If you then ask for the value as a double again, you do not want to be told 1.0; you want 1.3. OValue is "driftless." The data does not drift depending on what types of values you ask it for.

> **TIP**
>
> An OValue object is a remarkably easy way to do data conversions. It does string-to-number and number-to-string conversions using OLE's VARIANT functionality. All you need to do is to construct an OValue with the type you have, and then cast it to the type that you want.

OAdvise

Occasionally you will create an ODynaset and keep it open, allowing the user to navigate through the result set and make changes to the data it refers to. The navigation and data changes affect the ODynaset's master object. Perhaps because of the processing you are doing, you want to know about what's going on with the master dynaset object. You could add some notification code at all the places in your program that edit and navigate using the ODynaset. This scattered code, however, would be a maintenance headache.

An alternative is to let the dynaset tell you when something is done to it. That's what OAdvise is about. It is essentially a method for registering callbacks. You create a subclass of OAdvise, overriding methods that pertain to actions you are interested in. You then hand an instance of your OAdvise subclass to an ODynaset, and you will get callbacks when things happen.

Handling Errors

There are a host of reasons why something can go wrong in your database application. You will need to detect and handle any error conditions.

Closed Objects

If you look at one of the surrogate objects, say an ODatabase instance, you can ask the question: is this instance connected to a master or not? In the Oracle Objects class library, this is what is meant by whether an object is open or not. An open object is connected to a master, and a closed object is not. You can't do much with closed objects except to ask them whether they're closed, or to obtain error information.

You can make a closed object yourself, either with the default constructor or by calling the `Close()` method on an already open object. But the most important way to get a closed object is in case of an error.

If you attempt to create or get an object and an error occurs, the object that is returned to you is closed. Or if you use one of the constructors that does some real work, perhaps the `ODatabase` constructor that opens a connection to the database, and some problem occurs, the constructed object will be closed instead of open. Because a constructor can't return an error condition, the only way that you can tell that the constructor failed is that the resulting object is closed.

In either case, the closed object will have error information attached to it. You can query the closed object to find out what went wrong—why it couldn't be created open.

Error Reporting

Oracle Objects has two levels of errors that you need to worry about: standard Oracle errors and Oracle Objects errors.

The standard Oracle errors occur for all the reasons that you might get an error from Oracle. For instance, your SQL statement tries to delete records in a table where you only have read privileges.

The Oracle Objects errors are internal library errors. Perhaps you tried to use an object that is closed, or your program has run out of memory.

The Oracle Objects for OLE C++ class library does not throw exceptions. All error handling is done through return values and error-reporting methods.

Most of the methods return a result of type `oresult`. A return of `oresult` can have two values: `OSUCCESS` or `OFAILURE`. All this tells you is whether the routine worked or not. If the routine did not work, you want to call the routine `OOracleObject::ErrorNumber()` to get an internal `OracleObject` error number. These numbers are listed in the `oracl.h` header file, with comments indicating what the errors mean.

To get an Oracle error, call `ServerErrorNumber()` for the Oracle error number or `GetServerErrorText()` to get the error message text.

An Explanation of the Example

This section goes through the example at the beginning of the chapter in some detail so that you know what it is doing. This will illustrate a lot of the power of the class library.

The first line of the example constructs and opens an `ODatabase` instance, creating a connection to the database in the process:

```
ODatabase dbref("t:123.4.5.67:ORCL", "scott", "tiger");
```

This form of the `ODatabase` constructor does not take an `OSession` instance as an argument. Therefore, it uses the default session for this connection, which is what you usually want. If the default session hasn't been created yet, this `ODatabase` constructor makes it for you. The three arguments to the constructor are the database connection, the username, and password. These are used to make a connection to an Oracle database instance. As a side effect, it creates a connection automation object to keep track of the connection. If you had already used this connection elsewhere in your program, that connection would be shared here.

If you wanted to write your code correctly and check for error conditions, you could call `ODatabase::IsOpen()` here to check if the `ODatabase` instance was opened. If it is open, then everything worked correctly.

The second line of code constructs an `ODynaset`:

```
ODynaset dynref(dbref, "select max(sal) from emp");
```

The first argument is the database you want to fetch data from. The second argument is the SQL statement. This line of code takes care of all the SQL parsing and executing, as well as running a data cache, so that you can have a client-side scrollable cursor. It also fetches the first row of data. Again, robust code would check for an error condition by checking whether the `ODynaset` has been properly opened. In a real program, it is often the case that the SQL statement is created dynamically, rather than using a static string.

The fourth line declares a C++ double variable that will hold our return value.

The fifth line fetches the desired value out of the result set:

```
dynref.GetFieldValue(1, &maxsal); // get value of column 1
```

The first argument is a field index. You are getting the value of the first column, which in this case is the only column. The value is placed into `maxsal`. It is possible that some data conversion may have to be done, for example, if for some crazy reason the database schema is representing salaries with character strings. The `GetFieldValue()` method will do type conversions for you so that, in this case, you end up with a good `double` value.

At this point, the function returns its value and the listing ends. But is that the end of the function? No, it is not. The C++ run-time engine will call the destructors of the `ODatabase` and `ODynaset` instances for you. Those destructors will take care of doing all the necessary bookkeeping for you: freeing memory caches, dropping database connections, and so forth. Because of the reference-counting mechanisms, the order of the destructors is not important.

Building a Program

This section walks through the steps you need to take to actually build a working program with the class library.

Initializations

In addition to the code that you will be writing, you need to initialize and uninitialize the class library. Initialization is done with a call to OStartup(), and deinitialization is done with a call to OShutdown(). These should only be called once in your program. It is easiest if you place calls to these routines in the application initialization and shutdown code. For instance, if you are working with an application framework that has an object for the application, you can make these calls in the constructor and destructor of that object.

> **NOTE**
>
> This is for those of you writing applications that call OLE directly. One of the things that OStartup() and OShutdown() do is to call OleInitialize() and OleUninitialize(). You can either call OleInitialize() yourself or let OStartup() call it for you. If you call OleInitialize() before OStartup(), you will be responsible for calling OleUninitialize(), because OStartup() notes whether it was the first initializer.

Compiling

To compile your code, you will need to access the header files for the class library. These were placed in the oo4o\cpp\include directory when you installed the product. You will always need to include oracl.h. If you are using the OBound and OBinder classes, you will also need obound.h.

If you are using one of the bound widget libraries, you will need its header file, located in either oo4o\cpp\mfc\include or oo4o\cpp\owl\include.

Two other details require your attention. The class library assumes that you are working with the large memory model. So you will need to compile your calling code with the large memory model. And you may need to increase the stack size of your program.

Linking

Your program will need to link against one of the provided export libs. There is a different version for Microsoft and Borland compilers. These files are in the oo4o\cpp\lib directory, oraclm.lib for Microsoft, and oraclb.lib for Borland. You do not have to worry about linking against OLE libraries.

If you are using the bound widget libraries, you'll need to link against them. There are different versions for MFC (Microsoft) and OWL (Borland).

Running

You will need either the file oraclm.dll or oraclb.dll, which are the Microsoft and Borland versions respectively, in either the debug or non-debug flavor, depending on how you built your application.

> **CAUTION**
>
> The class library's DLL is not installed into your path. You will need to copy the appropriate DLL to somewhere on your path, or change your path variable to point to oo4o\cpp\bin or oo4o\cpp\bin\dbg before your program will run.

Debugging

The complete source code for the class library has been provided to help developers debug their applications. The source code is available in oo4o\cpp\src, and the debug DLLs have been built with symbols properly referring to the source. Stepping into the code and watching it work (or fail) is straightforward.

Basic Example

An example of a working program has been provided with this book as the program SeeStock. It is a simple program that looks at stock holdings. The program was written in Visual C++ 1.5, but developers using other environments should have little difficulty adapting the code.

The program assumes the existence of a user "stock" (with password "ticker"). The example comes with an SQL script named stock.sql that should be run in the "stock" account to set up the database.

This section won't go over the source of the program line by line. We'll just cover the high points here. You can examine the sample source code at your leisure.

The *StockHolding* Class

The heart of this program is the class StockHolding. Its declaration is

```
class StockHolding
{
public:
    StockHolding(ODatabase odb, const char *stockname);

    oresult GetInformation(double *price, long *nshares);
    oresult BuyShares(long nbuy);
    oresult SellShares(long nsell);
```

```
private:
    ODatabase m_db;
    OValue m_stockname;
};
```

An instance of StockHolding enables you to manipulate information about stock in one company. Having a class like this isolates your application from the details of the database. Although in this case the stock information is all taken out of a single trivial table, in a real application the stock holdings would probably be in one table and the stock pricing information would be in another table, which would be getting up-to-date price information in real time. All that would change in the test program is the StockHolding class.

The Database Connection

To create an instance of StockHolding, you pass in the name of the stock as well as an ODatabase instance. That ODatabase instance is assumed to be open; the connection to the Oracle database has already been established. The StockHolding instance then keeps a copy of that ODatabase. As long as the StockHolding object exists, the connection to the database will be kept open. What's really happening is that the StockHolding instance has, as a member variable, a surrogate database object. As long as that object is open, the master database object will stay open, and so the connection will stay open.

You can imagine that you connect to the database in one part of your program and then create several StockHolding objects, corresponding to the different stocks owned by the user of the program. All of the StockHolding objects use different surrogate databases (different ODatabase instances), but they all refer to the same master database object. When all the StockHolding objects are destroyed, for instance when your program is shutting down, the connection is finally closed when the reference count on the master object goes to zero.

> **CAUTION**
>
> When you have independent objects sharing a database connection, you need to think carefully about database transactions. A commit executed by any one object commits for all objects on the same connection. The same is true for rollbacks. You also need to be careful when one object is writing to a table that another object is reading, because the reading object may see some old records and some new records, leading to inconsistencies.

SQL and Parameters

The query that you need to execute to obtain the stock information is always the same; all that changes is the name of the company. There are two ways you could create an SQL statement that gets the desired data for a particular company. You could construct the selection statement dynamically, including a WHERE clause that explicitly selected a company:

```
select * from stockinfo where s_name = 'NullBits'
```

You can take such an approach with this class library because it works with dynamically generated SQL. Because each StockHolding instance will only work with a particular company, it could generate its SQL SELECT statement in its constructor.

Another approach is to use an SQL statement that has a parameter in it, and change the value of the parameter. In this case, the SELECT statement would be:

```
select * from stockinfo where s_name = :stockname
```

In this case, the SQL statement is the same for all instances. This enables you to manage the SQL statement string better. Instead of writing code that generates the SQL string, you can read it out of a resource or file. This means that if the database schema changes, all you need to do is to change the SQL statement, instead of your code.

The StockHolding class uses the second approach. The SQL statement is implemented as a static string. The StockHolding constructor guarantees the existence of the named parameter in the database object so that later selections can just set the value of the parameter and then execute the selection. Note that parameters are attached to the database, which means that all of the StockHolding objects share the same parameters because they are sharing the same database. The parameters are never destroyed. They go away when the database is destroyed.

Editing the Data

The StockHolding class has two different methods for changing data in the database: StockHolding::BuyShares() and StockHolding::SellShares(). For demonstration purposes, these two routines have been implemented with different techniques.

The routine StockHolding::BuyShares() updates the database directly with an SQL update statement. A static SQL string with a parameter is used, similar to the SQL string used for selection. Executing an SQL statement directly like this gives you the most power, if you want to use SQL. Note, however, that if you have any open dynasets that have read from the updated table, they will not immediately see the new data.

The routine StockHolding::SellShares() uses another technique. It creates a dynaset and then uses it to update the database. If your program holds onto the dynaset, either for later reading or for more updating, this method is easier to use. It also guarantees that you see the changes that you have made in the dynaset that was used to make the change.

The Bound Object Classes

The ODynaset object is very useful for interacting with an Oracle database. It reads data. It will let you edit data. It lets you write that edited data back to the database.

Now consider how you would use it to set the text in an edittext control to the value of a column in your query result and make it write any changes back to the database. Whenever your code navigated to a new record, you would get the new column value and put it into the edit column. You want to notice if any changes are made to the text in the control. And when the user or your programs navigates to the next record, you want to save any changes (if there were any changes) back to the database. It is a fair amount of tedious work. And that tedious work is pretty much the same for all columns, whether they are displayed as edittext controls or check boxes or exist simply as a variable in your program.

This is the problem that the bound object classes are built to solve. They take care of the tedious work, giving you hooks so that you can intervene when you want to.

The OBound class is a base class that lets you build *bound objects*. These are objects whose values are bound to the value of a particular column in a query result. As your program or user navigates through the result set, the value of the bound object automatically changes. Typically there are several bound objects per result set, for instance one per column. The OBound class also keeps track of whether the object's value has changed.

The OBinder class is a dynaset manager. An OBinder instance will manage a single dynaset, keeping track of all the bound objects attached to the dynaset, giving them their new values as dynaset navigation occurs. The OBinder instance also watches all the attached bound objects for value changes. Before the dynaset is allowed to navigate away from the current record, the OBinder class saves any changes in the current record back to the database.

Using *OBound*

OBinder is a useful class as it stands, because its default functionality gives the simple behavior described. But you will use a subclass of OBound, overriding at least two of its methods. You need to override OBound::Refresh(), which is the method that transfers data from the dynaset to the bound object. And you need to override OBound::SaveChange(), which is the method that transfers data from the bound object to the dynaset. Because you implement these data transfer methods, your object can be anything you like: an edit control, a slider, or simply a variable.

Trigger Methods

Overriding OBound::Refresh() and OBound::SaveChange() will give you useful functionality, but you have even more power available to you if you are willing to override the trigger methods of OBinder and OBound.

A *trigger* is a piece of code that is executed when a specific event happens. In the application framework world, you would probably call it an event handler. In the database world, you see the term triggers when talking about procedures stored in an Oracle database, or code in 4GL environments such as Oracle Forms. For instance, there may be a trigger that is run before inserts are performed on a table. Another trigger may run after records are deleted from a table.

Both OBinder and OBound have triggers that are run both before and after the operations of adding (inserting), deleting, and updating records. Other events supported are navigating, querying, and the special startup and shutdown triggers. All the same triggers exist for OBinder and OBound. The difference is that the OBinder triggers are appropriate for record-level processing, while the OBound triggers are appropriate for field-level processing.

The Bound Objects for MFC

Libraries of bound user-interface widgets are supplied with the Oracle Objects for OLE C++ class library. There are two separate libraries, one for Microsoft's MFC environment and another for Borland's OWL. These widgets make it incredibly easy to implement a database application with a simple user interface. This section looks quickly at the MFC library and then examines a sample application built with the MFC widgets.

Available Objects

The OMFC library contains bound classes for several of the most important user interface elements. It provides OBound subclass implementations for the following kinds of widgets:

- Text edit control (OBoundEdit)
- Static text (OBoundStatic)
- Check box (OBoundCheckBox)
- Radio button set (OBoundGroupButton)
- Slider (OBoundSlider)

In all cases, it is helpful to remember that the OBound subclass is not the widget itself, but an object that is managing the widget.

The widget that you will use most often is the text edit control. This control can be used to display the value of a column in the current record and edit the value of the column by editing the text in the control.

The static text is useful for displaying read-only values.

The check box control is useful for displaying a column that is expected to have one of two values. One value is assigned to the checked state, and the other is assigned to the unchecked state.

There is no bound control for controlling a single radio button. Instead, OBoundGroupButton is used to control a set of radio buttons. A group of radio buttons is useful for displaying a column whose values are expected to be one of a small number of discrete possibilities. Each radio button corresponds to a single value.

The slider is used to directly display and manipulate a numeric value.

Using the Bound Widgets

There are three setup steps to get an OBinder record block going:

1. The OBinder must be set up with a database connection and an SQL SELECT statement. This creates a dynaset that will be used to fetch and edit the data.

2. Each OBound instance must be attached to a column in the result set. This is done with the OBound::BindToBinder() routine.

3. Each OBound instance must be attached to the user interface widget that it is controlling. This is done with the BindToControl() routine in the bound widget classes.

Once you have performed this setup, there is little else you need to do. When the program runs, the user's changes will be automatically entered into the database. The OBinder class has navigation methods, such as MoveNext(), that you will want to use for moving through your result set.

A Sample Bound Control Application

The SeeStock application in the previous example was fine as long as you only wanted to display your stock holdings. It would be much more interesting, however, if you could actually edit your stock holdings. Writing all the code to note changes and then saving them back to the database would be a lot of work with the basic classes, but with the bound control classes, it is easy.

The EdtStock application takes advantage of the bound controls. The application displays information about one stock at a time. It uses static text controls to display the name of the current stock and its price. And it uses a text edit control to display and edit the number of shares currently owned.

The full Visual C++ 1.5 source for this application is provided on the example disk, in the directory SeeStock, ready to compile and run. Those of you who work with other development environments will still be able to read and understand the source code.

Like the SeeStock example, this program expects to connect to an account named "scott" (with password "ticker") on a Personal Oracle7 database. The account should be initialized with the stock.sql SQL script. This application will work with the following query:

```
select s_name, s_price, s_shares from stockinfo;
```

This query gives you the records of the result set.

Building the Application

To build the application, you first have to do the usual tasks required for the Oracle Objects for OLE class library. You need to get access to the include files oracl.h, obound.h, and omfc.h.

You need to link against the `oraclm.lib` and `omfc.lib` libraries. And the program needs to call `OStartup()` and `OShutdown()` at its beginning and end.

The user interface is easy to construct. It is simply a standard MFC dialog-based application. In this case, the single window is a formview. The form is constructed using the standard tools in Visual C++: the AppStudio resource editor and the ClassWizard. All of the controls are created with the resource editor using the dialog editor. They do not have to be given member variables. The navigation buttons are given methods.

The form view class, which is declared in `edtstvw.h`, defines a single `OBinder` instance variable and several variables that are subclasses of `OBound`:

```
// part of the CEdtstockView class declaration
class CEdtstockView : public CFormView
{
/*
    Most of the declaration has been removed...
*/
private:
    // bind objects
    OBinder m_stockrec;
    OBoundStatic m_name;
    OBoundStatic m_price;
    OBoundEdit m_nshares;
};
```

The portion of the class declaration shown here is added to the code that the AppWizard and ClassWizard generated.

The `OBinder` instance replaces both the `ODatabase` and `ODynaset` of the previous example. In fact, an `OBinder` instance contains both an `ODatabase` and an `ODynaset` as members. You have a single `OBinder` instance because this application is working with a single result set.

You have a separate `OBound` instance for each bound control, in this case two `OBoundStatics` and a single `OBoundEdit`.

Examining the Sample Application

To make the bound controls work, you have to get them connected up with all the other objects they need to communicate with. As you saw earlier, each bound control needs to connect to a column in a query, which is controlled by the `OBinder` instance, and with a user interface widget. Here are the two relevant lines of code for the edit text control:

```
m_nshares.BindToBinder(&m_stockrec, "s_shares");
m_nshares.BindToControl(this, IDC_NSHARES);
```

The first line connects the `OBound` object to an `OBinder` object, specifying that the column that it is displaying and edited is named `s_shares`. The second line connects the `OBound` object to a particular user interface widget, whose id is `IDC_NSHARES`. The first argument to `OMFCBound.BindToControl()` is `this`, which refers to the `CFormView` instance. It enables the widgets to get information about their containing window.

Because the binding between user interface widgets and controlling objects is made at run time via method calls, it could be done dynamically. You could create widgets on the fly and bind them to columns in dynamically created SQL statements if you so desired. This example uses AppStudio for convenience.

When the application starts, it is not connected to a database. The user presses the Connect button to connect to a database. In this example, the connection is hard-coded. In a real program, the user would be given some sort of login dialog. The program will then connect to the database and display the information for the first record in the query result set.

To display and edit other records from the result set, you need to navigate to those other records. EdtStock only implements single record forward and backward scrolling. This is done with the Next and Previous buttons. The code for the routines that implement these is very simple. Here is the code for the Next button:

```
void CEdtstockView::OnNext()
{
    m_stockrec.MoveNext();
}
```

You call OBinder::MoveNext(), and it takes care of the bookkeeping, updating the database if necessary, fetching another row, and updating the widgets with new values. Notice that you did not have to write any code that set the values of the widgets or read the current values of the widgets and put them back into the database. The OBinder class, with the help of the MFC bound widget classes, takes care of all that for you.

This application gives you a little taste of the power available to you when using the class library's bound object classes. Overriding the various trigger methods of OBinder and OBound is outside the scope of this book. One thing you can do with a trigger is to perform an additional calculation. For instance, you might want to display a field showing the total value of the shares of stock, which would be calculated automatically whenever the application moves to a new record. Or you could use triggers to validate the values of columns before entering them into the database, for instance, making sure that the control which is displaying the number of shares owned contains a valid number.

Summary

The Oracle Objects for OLE C++ class library is a powerful tool for C++ programmers who want access to data stored in Oracle databases.

The class library shares many features with the rest of the Oracle Objects for OLE. It is dynamic, meaning that it can work with SQL statements generated at run time. It requires very little bookkeeping by the developer using the product. And it has a rich set of operations available.

You saw how the basic classes work, and how they differ from their analogs in Oracle Objects for OLE. You also explored the bound objects classes, which is an important extension to the Oracle Objects product.

Applications are easy to build with these class libraries, as shown by some of the examples. If you are building an application with a complex user interface, you may want to consider using the MFC or OWL user interface widget bound objects.

PART

Advanced Topics

Oracle Precompilers

50

by Gigi Wadley

Extracting and manipulating data from a relational database would be very difficult if not for tools such as precompilers. The precompiler allows SQL statements to be embedded within procedural languages. Applications developed with this tool can use the best features of SQL, combined with the best features of the procedural language, creating a powerful module. This chapter discusses Oracle precompilers, creating a source program and some of the new features that Version 1.4 precompilers have.

Oracle Precompilers

The precompiler is a mechanism that allows SQL statements to be embedded within procedural languages. This tool provides the programmer with unlimited capabilities. So you fully understand all the benefits of this tool, this chapter will focus on why we precompile, general features of the precompiler, what languages source code can be written in, how standardized are the precompilers, what options do they have, how to precompile your source code, and what conditional precompiling is.

Why Precompile Source Code?

Embedded SQL statements are not something a high-level language understands. The precompiler must therefore take the SQL statements and translate them into something the high-level language will understand. Libraries contain data structures that help guide the translation process for consistency. This general concept will help in understanding the precompiler features.

General Precompiler Features

One of the primary reasons to use a precompiler is to have the capability of utilizing SQL statements in a high-level language. Oracle precompilers offer many benefits and features that can help in this development. These features include the following:

- Source code can be written in six different high-level languages, which all have ANSI/ISO precompilers.

- Using a precompiler enables a user to take advantage of dynamic SQL, which allows for a more highly customized application.

- Precompilers enable a user to process PL/SQL transaction blocks and use host arrays to process large amounts of data quickly; both dramatically improve performance.

- Precompilers make conversions between Oracle internal datatypes and language datatypes, and check syntax and semantics.

- Precompilers may also include conditional parameters to enable the program to be executed in different environments.
- Direct interfaces with SQL*Forms can be done using user exits.
- Precompilers provide variables to handle warning and error conditions, which are included in the ORACLE Communication Area (ORACA).

Each of these features will be discussed in further detail later in the chapter. But you should know how many precompilers Oracle has before too much more detail is given.

Precompiler Languages

There are six procedural languages for which Oracle has precompilers available. During installation of Oracle, the host language is determined and the appropriate compiler is installed. The six languages include the following:

- Ada
- C
- COBOL
- FORTRAN
- Pascal
- PL/I

With Oracle precompilers, you have the capabilities of precompiling and compiling several host programs, then linking them together into one module. Each program does not need to be written in the same language to be linked together, so standardization is a must. Oracle precompilers do meet national standards and will be discussed in the next section.

ANSI/IO Standards

Because SQL has become the standard language for relational databases, standardization has become an important issue. Oracle precompilers have taken exceptional efforts to meet standards set by the following organizations:

- American National Standards Institute (ANSI)
- International Standards Organization (ISO)
- U.S. National Institute of Standards and Technology (NIST)

Compliance for these requirements is measured by NIST, which uses over 300 test programs. Oracle precompilers have conformed to these standards by checking the SQL statements that are being embedded for standard syntax and semantics. But there is much more to precompiler function than syntax checking.

Precompiler Options

To increase flexibility among applications, Oracle precompilers have options that can be manipulated by the programmer to allow for certain conditions. For example, if a line of the source program exceeds 80 characters, an error occurs while precompiling. There is a precompiler option that allows the programmer to extend that line to 132 characters. These controls, along with others, are outlined in Table 50.1. The * character next to an item indicates that it can be entered inline.

Table 50.1. Precompiler options.

Syntax	Default	Specifies
COMMON_NAME=block_name		Name of FORTRAN-common blocks
DEFINE=symbol		Symbol used in conditional precompilation
ERRORS=YES¦NO*	YES	Whether errors are sent to the terminal
FORMAT=ANSI¦TERMINAL	ANSI	Format of COBOL or FORTRAN input line
HOLD_CURSOR=YES¦NO*	NO	How a cursor cache handles SQL statements
HOST=C		
COB74		Host language
COBOL		
FORTRAN		
PASCAL		
PLI		
INAME=path and filename		Name of input file
INCLUDE=path *		Directory path for the INCLUDEd files
IRECLEN=integer	80	Record length of input file
LINES=YES¦NO	NO	Whether C #line directives are generated
LITDELIM=APOSTQUOTE*	QUOTE	Delimiter for COBOL strings
LNAME=path and filename		Name of listing file

Syntax	Default	Specifies
LRECLEN=integer	132	Record length of listing file
LTYPE=LONG	LONG	Type of listing
SHORT		
NONE		
MAXLITERAL=integer*		Maximum length of string
MAXOPENCURSORS=integer*	10	Maximum number of cursors cached
MODE=ORACLE	ORACLE	Compliance with ANSI/ISO
ASNI		standard
ANSI13		
ANSI14		
ISO		
ISO13		
ISO14		
ONAME=path and filename		Name of output file
ORACA=YES¦NO	NO	Whether the ORACA is used
ORECLEN=integer	80	Record length of output file
PAGELEN=integer	66	Lines per page in listing
RELEASE_CURSOR=YES¦NO*	NO	How cursor cache handles SQL statements
SELECT_ERROR=YES¦NO*	YES	How SELECT errors are handled
SQLCHECK=SEMANTICS	SYNTAX	Extent of syntax and/ or semantic checking
FULL		
SYNTAX		
LIMITED		
NONE *		
USERID=username/password		Valid Oracle username and password
XREF=YES¦NO*	YES	Cross-reference section in listing

A precompiler command line might look something like the following:

```
proc iname=example.pc include=ora_pcc: include=clib: ireclen=132
```

There is only one required argument, `iname`. This argument tells the precompiler what the input filename is. So the minimum requirements for any precompiler command line could look like the following:

```
proc iname=example.pc
```

All of these precompiler options can be accessed online. Just enter the precompiler option without any argument at your operating system prompt. This help feature will display the name, syntax, default value and purpose of each option.

There are some general guidelines to follow when setting options for precompiling:

■ When you precompile the program module that CONNECTs to Oracle, specify a value for MAXOPENCURSORS that is high enough for any of the program modules that will be linked together.

■ If you want to use just one SQLCA, you must declare it as a global in one of the program modules and as an external in the other modules. In C, for example, this is done by using the external storage class, which tells the precompiler to look for the SQLCA in another program module. Unless you declare the SQLCA as external, each program module will use its own local SQLCA.

■ You *cannot* DECLARE a cursor in one file and reference it in another.

All these options can be utilized in several ways when precompiling your program, but what is the best way to precompile, compile, and link your source program?

How to Precompile a Program

In Version 1.4 of the precompilers, executables exist for each of the six languages previously mentioned. So each host language has a different command to run the precompiler. Table 50.2 shows which command to use for a specific language.

Table 50.2. Precompiler commands.

Host Language	Precompiler Command
C	PROC
COBOL	PROCOB
FORTRAN	PROFOR
Pascal	PROPAS
PL/I	PROPLI

There are several ways an embedded SQL program can be precompiled, compiled, and linked. Compiling multiple embedded SQL programs can become very time consuming if each step is done per program. This approach of issuing individual commands can lead to inconsistency between program modules. Executing each step of the compilation process should probably be used when it doesn't matter if standardization is met. For example, it doesn't matter if a common library is linked into your program but all other programs for this system depend on it. Therefore, utilizing a control file simplifies compiling your source program. This control file will evaluate what tasks need to be accomplished while adhering to company standards. Depending upon the platform that you are working on an executable file such as a .BAT or .COM can be created to accept parameters. The following example shows what a command line using a control file might look like.

```
@PCL   TEST   TEST100   PCL.
```

```
Control Filename:   @PCL
System Name:        TEST
Host Program:       TEST100
Options:            P(recompile)
                    C(compile)
                    L(ink)
```

After receiving the parameters to evaluate, the control file can determine what needs to be done. This approach helps keep all the programs consistent with others in terms of linking current libraries, objects, or other files. The following PCL.COM file is an example taken from a VAX platform to show how executable files can be created to control precompiling, compiling, and linking host programs.

```
$ write sys$output "PCL.COM Version 2.3"
$
$ write sys$output " "
$       set noverify
$ assign $disk7:[vaxprod.com.ccom],$disk7:[vaxprod.'P1'.c'P1'] clib
$ if "''P1'" .eqs "" then goto USAGE
$ if "''P2'" .eqs "" then goto USAGE
$!
$ if "''P3'" .eqs "" then goto precompile
$ if "''P3'" .eqs "P" then goto precompile
$ if "''P3'" .eqs "p" then goto precompile
$ if "''P3'" .eqs "PC" then goto precompile
$ if "''P3'" .eqs "pc" then goto precompile
$ if "''P3'" .eqs "PCL" then goto precompile
$ if "''P3'" .eqs "pcl" then goto precompile
$ if "''P3'" .eqs "PCLR" then goto precompile
$ if "''P3'" .eqs "pclr" then goto precompile
$!
$ if "''P3'" .eqs "c" then goto compile
$ if "''P3'" .eqs "C" then goto compile
$ if "''P3'" .eqs "cl" then goto compile
$ if "''P3'" .eqs "CL" then goto compile
$ if "''P3'" .eqs "clr" then goto compile
$ if "''P3'" .eqs "CLR" then goto compile
$!
```

```
$ if "''P3'" .eqs "l" then goto link
$ if "''P3'" .eqs "L" then goto link
$ if "''P3'" .eqs "lr" then goto link
$ if "''P3'" .eqs "LR" then goto link
$!
$ if "''P3'" .eqs "r" then goto run
$ if "''P3'" .eqs "R" then goto run
$ goto USAGE
$!
$!
$! ***********************************************************************
$! *************************** Precompile ****************************
$! ***********************************************************************
$ precompile:
$   proc iname='P2'.pc include=ora_pcc: include=clib: ireclen=132
$
$ if "''P3'" .eqs "p" then goto continue
$ if "''P3'" .eqs "P" then goto continue
$
$
$! ***********************************************************************
$! *************************** Compile *****************************
$! ***********************************************************************
$ compile:
$ write sys$output "Compiling ''P2'.C"
$ cc/noopt/include_directory=clib:/define=VMS 'P2'
$!
$ if "''P3'" .eqs "pc" then goto continue
$ if "''P3'" .eqs "PC" then goto continue
$ if "''P3'" .eqs "c" then goto continue
$ if "''P3'" .eqs "C" then goto continue
$!
$!
$! ***********************************************************************
$! *************************** Link *****************************
$! ***********************************************************************
$ link:
$!
$ @ora_rdbms:loutl 'P2' 'P2''P4',clib:c'P1'.olb/lib,clib:ccom.olb/lib-
,ora_util:sqllib.olb/lib,ora_rdbms:oci/lib/include=(ocicee) 'P2' s
$!
$ endlink:
$ if "''P3'" .eqs "PCL" then goto continue
$ if "''P3'" .eqs "pcl" then goto continue
$ if "''P3'" .eqs "cl" then goto continue
$ if "''P3'" .eqs "CL" then goto continue
$ if "''P3'" .eqs "l" then goto continue
$ if "''P3'" .eqs "L" then goto continue
$!
$!
$! ***********************************************************************
$! *************************** Run *****************************
$! ***********************************************************************
$ run:
```

```
$ P2 P1/P1
$!
$!
$! **********************************************************************
$! ************************      continue      ************************
$! **********************************************************************
$ continue:
$ goto exit
$!
$! **********************************************************************
$! ***************************      USAGE      ************************
$! **********************************************************************
$ USAGE:
$ write sys$output " "
$ write sys$output " "
$ write sys$output "Usage: @PCL [SYSTEM] [PROGRAM NAME] [options] [d] [libinfo]
$ write sys$output " "
$ write sys$output "Where: APPLICATION - Application system: (TEST, etc)
$ write sys$output "                     Used to link the system library
(ie.LTEST.OLB/LIB)
$ write sys$output "     PROGRAM NAME - (TEST100, TEST200, etc)
$ write sys$output "          options - Options (PCLR): P = precompile
$ write sys$output "                                    C = compile
$ write sys$output "                                    L = link
$ write sys$output "                                    R = run
$ write sys$output "                                 PCLR = all the above
(default)
$ write sys$output "                         Options entered must appear in above
order.
$ write sys$output "                        valid: P PC C CL PCL    not valid: CP
LC PL
$ write sys$output "                        d - Compile with #define DEBUG   (default is
nodebug)
$ write sys$output "                   libinfo - Additional User link libraries:
,mydir:mylib.olb/lib
$ write sys$output " "
$ write sys$output "*Note: Upper case are REQUIRED, Lower case are optional
$ write sys$output " "
$ write sys$output "Example: @PCL TEST TEST100 PCL
$ write sys$output "          (compile TEST100.C, nodebug, links TEST200.OBJ including
MYLIB.OLB)
$ write sys$output " "
$ goto exit
$
$
$ exit:
$ deassign clib
```

Compiling using a control file such as PCL.COM can be used even if you don't have embedded SQL in your program. This keeps all applications created by your shop consistent with each other.

A programmer can do still more to control how and what is precompiled in his or her source. The next section of the chapter discusses conditional precompiling.

Conditional Precompiling

The precompiler also allows for conditional precompiling. This gives you the ability to write a program for several different platforms. For example, you might want to include some section of your program for a UNIX platform but not for a VMS platform. Oracle precompilers recognize conditional sections of code. These sections are indicated by statements that define the environment and what actions to take. In this section, procedural and embedded SQL statements can be used to perform platform specific operations.

CAUTION

Remember that conditional statements must be included in your source code, not the control file that will compile your code.

The following Oracle statements are utilized when creating a conditional section.

Statement	Meaning
EXEC ORACLE DEFINE symbol	Define a symbol
EXEC ORACLE IFDEF symbol	If symbol is defined
EXEC ORACLE IFNDEF symbol	If symbol is not defined
EXEC ORACLE ELSE	Otherwise
EXEC ORACLE ENDIF	End this control block

Some symbols are port-specific and predefined for you when the Oracle precompilers are installed. Predefined operating-system symbols include CMS, MVS, DOS, UNIX, and VMS. In the following example, conditional precompiling is shown using a predefined symbol.

```
#include <stdio.h>
#include <string.h>
#include <stdlib.h>
#ifdef DOS
   #include <dos.h>
#endif

/* DECLARE AREA */
EXEC SQL BEGIN DECLARE SECTION;
  VARCHAR user_id[20];
  VARCHAR passwd[20]
EXEC SQL END DECLARE SECTION;

/* INCLUDE AREA */
EXEC SQL INCLUDE SQLCA;

/* FILE DECLARATIONS */
FILE *t_file;
main()
{
```

```
        printf("/n What is your User ID: ");
        scanf("%s",user_id.arr);
        printf("\nEnter Password: ");
        scanf("%s",passwd.arr);

        user_id.len = strlen(user_id.arr);
        passwd.len = strlen(passwrd.arr);

/* CONNECTS TO DATABASE */
        EXEC SQL CONNECT :userid IDENTIFIED BY :passwd;

        if (sqlca.sqlcode < 0)
        {
            printf("\n%s",sqlca.sqlerrm.sqlerrmc);
            EXEC SQL ROLLBACK WORK RELEASE;
            exit(1);
        }
        else
        {
            printf("\nSuccessfully connected to Oracle.");
            #ifdef DOS
                t_file = fopen("\\login.lst","w");
                fprintf(t_file,"log in by %s",:userid);
                fclose(t_file);
            #end if;
            EXEC SQL COMMIT WORK RELEASE;
            exit(0);
        }
    }
```

Now that you have an understanding of what the precompiler does and what you can control, creating a embedded SQL program will take front stage. The next section of this chapter focuses just on an embedded SQL program. This section will look at the basics of a source program, program requirements and how to handle errors.

Embedded SQL Host Program

Creating a host program that utilizes embedded SQL statements can be very beneficial. There are some specific guidelines and requirements that must be included in an embedded SQL program. This section of the chapter focuses on the basics of a precompiled program, program requirements, handling errors, host arrays, dynamic SQL, user exits, and performance tuning. As each topic is introduced, code examples will be provided in C for that section which will build into a completed program by chapter's end. You then can precompile, compile, link, and execute it. This section begins with some basic concepts.

Basics of a Host Program

Three basic concepts must be discussed to ensure an understanding of the material that will be presented later in this chapter. These concepts are naming conventions, embedding SQL, and using PL/SQL blocks.

Naming Conventions

All embedded SQL programs must have the appropriate extension for the host language. This notifies the precompiler that embedded SQL is included and the program must be translated (precompiled) into the host language format. Table 50.3 indicates what extension should be used for the host language.

Table 50.3. Host language file extensions.

Host Language	Standard File Extension
C	PC
COBOL	PCO
FORTRAN	PFO
Pascal	PPA
PL/I	PPL

After your program has been precompiled, a new file is created with a different extension; normal compiling and linking can then continue.

CAUTION

When you modify your source code, remember to change the original file. In C, for example, the .PC file should be modified and not the .C file; otherwise your changes will not go into effect.

The second basic concept, which is the focus of these programs, is embedded SQL statements.

Embedded SQL

Embedded SQL refers to SQL statements that are placed within an application program. The program itself is referred to as the host program. All standard SQL commands can be used in the embedded statement. There are two types of embedded SQL statements: executable and declarative.

CAUTION

Any SQL command can be embedded within a high-level language, but not the extended SQL commands that are included in SQL*PLUS. These include report formatting, editing SQL statements, and environment-setting commands.

Executable Statements

Executable statements are used to connect to Oracle; query, manipulate and control access to Oracle data; and to process data. These statements result in calls to and return codes from Oracle. There are four types of executable embedded SQL statements: data definition, data control, data manipulation, and data retrieval. Later in the chapter each of these statements will be discussed in detail.

Declarative Statements

Declarative statements are used to declare Oracle objects, communication areas, and SQL variables. These statements do not result in Oracle calls or return codes and do not operate on Oracle data. Now that you know there are two sections involved in writing an embedded SQL host program, we should look at exactly what is required.

The last concept is utilizing PL/SQL blocks. The next section will cover how PL/SQL blocks are included into your source program.

PL/SQL Blocks

Oracle precompilers treat PL/SQL blocks as a single SQL statement. This can greatly enhance the performance of your program.

Benefits of PL/SQL Blocks

Using PL/SQL blocks can drastically reduce processing overhead, improve performance, and increase productivity. For example, each SQL statement that is executed generates a certain amount of communication and processing overhead. Depending upon what type of environment you are working in, this could create an enormous amount of traffic—simply slowing everything down to a crawl. If you use a PL/SQL block, you can pack multiple SQL statements into a section of code and execute the entire block. Because Oracle treats the entire block as a single statement, you can reduce overhead multiple times.

Including PL/SQL Blocks

To include PL/SQL in your host program, you need to first DECLARE the host variables that you want to use in the PL/SQL block. Next, you need to bracket the SQL statement that will be included in the PL/SQL blocks with the keywords EXEC SQL EXECUTE and END-EXEC. The following code example shows how a PL/SQL block is incorporated into your program:

```
#include <stdio.h>

/* DECLARE AREA */
EXEC SQL BEGIN DECLARE SECTION;
  VARCHAR   user_id[20];
```

```
    VARCHAR    passwd[20]
     int                 emp_number;
     VARCHAR  job_title[20];
     VARCHAR  hire_date[10];
     real                salary;
EXEC SQL END DECLARE SECTION;

/* INCLUDE AREA */
EXEC SQL INCLUDE SQLCA;

/* FUNCTION DECLARATIONS */
void get_employee_data();

main()
{
    printf("/n What is your User ID: ");
    scanf("%s",user_id.arr);
    printf("\nEnter Password: ");
    scanf("%s",passwd.arr);

    user_id.len = strlen(user_id.arr);
    passwd.len = strlen(passwd.arr);

/* CONNECTS TO DATABASE */
    EXEC SQL CONNECT :userid IDENTIFIED BY :passwd;

    if (sqlca.sqlcode < 0)
    {
       printf("\n%s",sqlca.sqlerrm.sqlerrmc);
       EXEC SQL ROLLBACK WORK RELEASE;
       exit(1);
    }
    else
    {
      printf("\nSuccessfully connected to Oracle.");
     EXEC SQL COMMIT WORK RELEASE;
     get_employee_data();
    }
exit(0);
  }

void get_employee_data()
{
    printf("\nEmployee Number? ");
    scanf("%d\n",empl_number);

/* BEGIN OF PL/SQL BLOCK */
  EXEC SQL EXECUTE
    BEGIN
      SELECT JOB, HIREDATE, SAL
           INTO :job_title, :hire_date, :salary
          FROM EMP
         WHERE EMPNO = :emp_number;
    END;
  END-EXEC;
/* END OF PL/SQL BLOCK */

  printf("%s %s %d\n",:job_title.arr,:hire_date.arr,:salary);
}
```

If you are working with a system that is database-intensive, utilizing PL/SQL blocks will improve performance.

Host Program Requirements

Being able to pass data between Oracle and your application requires a variety of tasks to be completed successfully. There are two primary parts of an embedded SQL program that must be included: the data declaration area (which involves the declarative statements) and the data manipulation area (which involves the executable statements). Before you can execute anything in your program, you must make your program aware of the players.

Data Declaration Area

This area is used to define all host variables, include extra files, and establish a connection to the database. Sometimes this area is referred to as the *program prologue*. There are three required sections within the data declaration area: the DECLARE section, SQL Include section, and the SQL connect area.

Declare Section

All host language variables referenced in a SQL statement must be declared to Oracle; otherwise, an error message will be issued at precompile time. These variables are declared in the DECLARE section. Most host languages will allow multiple DECLARE sections per precompiled unit, but you must have at least one. These sections can be defined locally or globally. Host variables within this section can be of any length, but only the first 31 characters are evaluated. These variables can consist of letters, digits, and underscores, but they must begin with an alpha character. To store a datatype, Oracle must know the format and valid range of values. Oracle recognizes only two kinds of datatypes: internal and external. Internal datatypes indicate how Oracle will store the data, and external specifies how the data is stored in the host variable. Table 50.4 shows the internal datatypes.

Table 50.4. Internal datatypes.

Name	Code	Description
CHAR	1	< 255-byte, fixed-length character string
NUMBER	2	Fixed or floating point number
LONG	8	< 65535-byte, fixed-length character string
ROWID	11	Fixed-length binary number
DATE	12	7-byte, fixed-length date/time value
RAW	23	< 255-byte, fixed-length binary data
LONGRAW	24	< 65535-byte, fixed-length binary data

Table 50.5 shows the external datatypes.

Table 50.5. External datatypes.

Name	Code	Description
VARCHAR2	1	< 255-byte, fixed-length character string
CHAR	1	< 255-byte, fixed-length character string
NUMBER	2	Fixed or floating point number
INTEGER	3	2-byte or 4-byte signed integer
FLOAT	4	4-byte or 8-byte floating-point number
STRING	5	Null-terminated character string
VARNUM	6	Variable-length binary number
DECIMAL	7	COBOL or PL/I packed decimal
LONG	8	< 65535-byte, fixed-length character string
VARCHAR	9	< 65535-byte, fixed-length character string
ROWID	11	Fixed-length binary number
DATE	12	7-byte, fixed-length date/time value
VARRAW	15	< 65533-byte, fixed-length binary data
RAW	23	< 255-byte, fixed-length binary data
LONGRAW	24	< 65535-byte, fixed-length binary data
UNSIGNED	68	2-byte or 4-byte unsigned integer
DISPLAY	91	COBOL numeric-character data

It is important that the host variables (external) within the DECLARE section match the database datatype (internal). For example, if you declare a host variable such as receipt_date a character string and the database has it declared as a DATE type, you will receive an error. The following guidelines are recommended when declaring and referencing host variables. A host variable must be

- Explicitly declared in the DECLARE section
- Referenced with a colon(:) in all SQL statements and PL/SQL blocks
- Of a datatype supported by the host language
- Of a datatype compatible with that of its source or target database column

A host variable must not be

- Subscripted
- Prefixed with a colon in the host language statement

- Used to identify a column, table, or other Oracle object
- Used in data definition statements such as ALTER, CREATE, and DROP

A host variable can be

- Used anywhere an expression can be used in a SQL statement

At precompile time, an association is made between variables declared and the database column type. If there is a discrepancy, a runtime error will occur; otherwise, the datatype is converted. VARCHAR variables are converted into the following structure:

```
struct {
  unsigned short    len;
  unsigned char     arr[20];
} username;
This structure helps eliminate character-counting algorithms. You can reference
each element of the structure and manipulate it. The following example shows the
syntax for the DECLARE section and how the elements of a VARCHAR can be used.


#include <stdio.h>

/* DECLARE SECTION */
EXEC SQL BEGIN DECLARE SECTION;
  VARCHAR user_id[15];
EXEC SQL END DECLARE SECTION;

main()
{
    printf("/n What is your User ID: ");
    scanf("%s",user_id.arr);                      /* referencing the character
string element */
    user_id.len = strlen(user_id.arr);       /* referencing the length element */
}
```

After declaring a variety of host variables communication between the host program and Oracle needs to be established to monitor successes and failures. This communication is made by utilizing the SQL Include area.

SQL Include Area

This section of the program enables the user to include copies of files into the host program. Any file can be included if it contains embedded SQL statements. The most common include file is the SQL Communication Area file (SQLCA).

> **TIP**
>
> When MODE=ORACLE (the default for the precompiler) or MODE=ANSI13, you must declare the SQLCA by hardcoding it, or by copying it into your program with the INCLUDE statement. If MODE=ANSI14 declaring the SQLCA is optional, however, you must declare the status variable SQLCODE.

The SQLCA is a data structure that handles certain events and provides diagnostic checking between the Oracle RDMBS and the host program. SQLCA variables maintain valuable run-time statistics such as warning codes with text, Oracle error codes, and number of rows processed that are convenient for handling special conditions within the host program. The following examples shows the syntax for including this file in the host program:

```
-- declare section --
#include <stdio.h>

EXEC SQL BEGIN DECLARE SECTION;
  VARCHAR user_id[15];
EXEC SQL END DECLARE SECTION;

/* SQL INCLUDE AREA */
EXEC SQL INCLUDE SQLCA;

main()
{
    printf("/n What is your User ID: ");
    scanf("%s",user_id.arr);
    user_id.len = strlen(user_id.arr);
}
```

After establishing communication capabilities, the program must connect to the database to actually start communicating.

SQL Connect Area

The host program must log onto Oracle before you will be able to manipulate data. A CONNECT statement must be issued and be the first statement to be executed. The userID and password must be host-language variables and cannot exceed 20 characters. SQL*Net will allow you to concurrently access any combination of local and remote databases, or you can make multiple connections to the same database. You should contact your network manager for specific connect guidelines. The following example shows how to connect to Oracle.

```
#include <stdio.h>

/* DECLARE AREA */
EXEC SQL BEGIN DECLARE SECTION;
  VARCHAR user_id[20];
  VARCHAR passwd[20]
EXEC SQL END DECLARE SECTION;

/* INCLUDE AREA */
EXEC SQL INCLUDE SQLCA;

main()
{
    printf("/n What is your User ID: ");
    scanf("%s",user_id.arr);
    printf("\nEnter Password: ");
    scanf("%s",passwd.arr);
```

```
   user_id.len = strlen(user_id.arr);
   passwd.len = strlen(passwrd.arr);

/* CONNECTS TO DATABASE */
   EXEC SQL CONNECT :userid IDENTIFIED BY :passwd;

   if (sqlca.sqlcode < 0)
   {
      printf("\n%s",sqlca.sqlerrm.sqlerrmc);
      EXEC SQL ROLLBACK WORK RELEASE;
      exit(1);
   }
   else
   {
      printf("\nSuccessfully connected to Oracle.");
      EXEC SQL COMMIT WORK RELEASE;
      exit(0);
   }
}
```

TIP

To take advantage of the automatic logon feature, assign / to a variable and simply pass the variable to the precompiler.

Now that you have declared host variables, established a communication channel and connected to the database, you can start to manipulate data.

Data Manipulation Area

The data manipulation area is where SQL statements are executed. This section is often referred to as the *program body*. This section of the chapter focuses on the types of SQL statements, the logical unit of work, controlling transactions, locking data, and the EXIT command.

Types of Executable SQL Statements

Several different types of SQL statements can be executed in the data manipulation area: data manipulation statements, data definition statements, and data control statements.

Data manipulation (DML) statements are used to change the data. The following is a list of commands that are considered DML statements:

- UPDATE column values in existing rows
- DELETE rows from a table
- COMMIT WORK writes data to the table
- ROLLBACK WORK removes any changes made to the data
- LOCK reserves the row or table exclusively for the user

Data definition (DDL) statements are used to define and maintain database objects. Some common uses of the DDL statements are to create tables or views. The following is a list of commands that are considered DDL:

- CREATE TABLE
- CREATE VIEW
- ALTER table or view
- DROP table, view, grant, or sequence number

Data control (DCL) statements are used to access tables and the data associated with them. There are two types of access that these statements will control. The first type is connecting to the database; the CONNECT and GRANT commands enable a user to do this. The second type of control is access to the data; the GRANT SELECT and REVOKE DELETE commands are examples of this.

Pulling together a combination of all three of these statements creates what is known as a *logical unit of work.*

Logical Unit of Work

A logical unit of work is defined as a group of SQL statements treated as a single transaction to the Oracle kernel. This unit of work begins with any valid SQL DML statement and ends with either an implicit or explicit release of work. An implicit commit release is performed by the execution of any DDL statement, whereas an implicit rollback release is performed upon abnormal termination of your program. A program may explicitly release the logical unit of work, which is discussed in the following section "Controlling Transactions."

Controlling Transactions

Because Oracle is transaction oriented and processes information in logical units of work, controlling these statements is essential to data integrity. A transaction begins with the first EXEC SQL statement issued in your program. When one transaction ends, the next begins. You can end a transaction in one of two means: COMMIT or ROLLBACK. If you do not subdivide your program with a COMMIT or ROLLBACK statement, Oracle will treat the whole program as one transaction.

CAUTION

Remember to commit what you are not willing to re-create. Losing one large transaction could be dangerous; smaller transaction losses are easier to recover from.

To make changes to the database permanent, use the COMMIT command. The COMMIT command does the following:

- Makes permanent all changes to the databases during the current transactions
- Makes these changes visible to other users
- Erases all savepoints
- Releases all row and table locks, but not parse locks
- Closes cursors referenced in a CURRENT OF clause
- Ends the transaction

The COMMIT statement has no effect on the values of host variables or on the flow of control in your program. This statement should be placed in the main path through your program. The following example shows the syntax of the COMMIT command:

```
EXEC SQL COMMIT WORK RELEASE;
```

The RELEASE option on COMMIT or ROLLBACK releases all process resources and provides a clean exit from Oracle. After the release, there is no further access to the Oracle database until another connect is issued.

CAUTION

An explicit COMMIT or ROLLBACK with RELEASE should always be done at the end of your program. If the RELEASE option is not specified, any locks or resources obtained will not be released until Oracle recognizes that the process is no longer active.

NOTE

The keyword WORK provides ANSI compatibility, whereas the optional RELEASE parameter frees all Oracle resources.

To undo pending changes, use the ROLLBACK statement. This statement lets you return to the starting point, so the database is not left in an inconsistent state. The ROLLBACK statement does the following:

- Undoes all changes made to the database during the current transaction
- Erases all savepoints
- Ends the transaction
- Releases all row and table locks, but not parse locks
- Closes cursors referenced in a CURRENT OF clause

The ROLLBACK statement has no effect on the values of host variables or on the flow of control in your program. The following example shows the syntax for the ROLLBACK statement.

```
EXEC SQL ROLLBACK WORK RELEASE;
```

> **TIP**
>
> The ROLLBACK statement is useful when you accidentally delete rows from the table. Do a ROLLBACK before the COMMIT.

Committing and releasing changes that have been made to the database gives the program enormous control over data, but what happens when someone else executes a program and it tries to manipulate the same data? Oracle has provided a mechanism that enables you to reserve the data just for your use.

Locking

Oracle uses locks (sometimes called enqueues) to control access to the data. When a row of data is being sought, Oracle will lock the row until the user has completed the current transaction. A user can get hung up in an application when two or more sources are trying to access the data at the same time. Because of data-integrity constraints, Oracle will give temporary ownership of a row to whomever has completed the most amount of work or got to the row first. The following guidelines should be followed when using locks:

- Unless specified, any DML operation will acquire a table-level lock.
- A DML lock can be bypassed by explicitly requesting a row-level lock. See the following code example:

```
/* LOCKS ALL ROWS */
EXEC SQL LOCK TABLE STUDENT
    IN SHARE UPDATE MODE[NOWAIT];

/*   IN THE FOLLOWING SELECT STATE THE [NOWAIT] */
/* PARAMETER TELLS ORACLE  NOT TO WAIT FOR THE TABLE IF IT HAS BEEN */
/*LOCKED BY ANOTHER USER */
EXEC SQL SELECT FNMAE
    FROM STUDENT
    WHERE BIRTHDATE < '01-JAN-60'
    FOR UPDATE OF LNAME[NOWAIT];
```

Exit Command

The last statement in a Pro*C program should be the EXIT command. This command has the option of returning a status check—especially useful when used as a SQL*Forms user exit. Table 50.6 shows the return code.

Table 50.6. Return codes.

Return Code	Description
exit(0);	Successful termination
exit(1);	Unsuccessful termination

Error Handling

What can be done if a program does exit with a value of 1 (unsuccessful termination)? There are many types of errors that your program may encounter. Error handling should be a major part of every application, in order to anticipate when errors will occur. Because errors can occur from a variety of sources—design fault, coding mistakes, hardware failure, and invalid user input—it is advisable to try and handle them. This section will look at some general guidelines for error handling and three ways of handling errors: SQLCA variables, WHENEVER statements, and indicator variables.

General Guidelines

The following guidelines will help avoid some common pitfalls:

- Code a WHENEVER statement before your first executable statement. This will ensure that all ensuing errors are trapped, because WHENEVER statements stay in effect to the end of the file.

- When using a cursor to fetch rows of data, your program should be able to handle an end-of-data condition.

- Try to avoid branching to error routines with GOTOs.

Oracle has provided variables that help monitor when one of these guidelines has not been followed or some other type of error has occurred. These variables are included in the SQLCA file.

SQLCA Variables

The SQLCA is a data structure that is updated after every executable SQL statement. SQLCA variables can be implicitly or explicitly checked. Some of the components that can be checked are described in the Table 50.7.

Table 50.7. SQLCA processing static variables.

Name	Type	Description
SQLAID[8]	char	"SQLCA"
SQLABC	long	Length of SQLCA
SQLCODE	long	Oracle Error code
		0: Successful execution
		<0: Abnormal termination with error code
		>0: Successful execution with status code
		+1403: No data found
SQLERRM	struct	Error code & message text
SQLERRML	short	Code
SQLERRMC[70]	char	Message text
SQLERRP[8]	char	(not currently used)
SQLERRD[6]	long	Third cell is # rows processed
SQLWARN[8]	char	Array of warning flags
[0]		Warning
[1]		Truncation
[2]		NULL ignored
[3]		SELECT list INTO list
[4]		N. WHERE Clause on DELETE or UPDATE
[5]		(Not currently used)
[6]		Implied COMMIT or ROLLBACK
[7]		Modified since query began
SQLEXT[9]	char	(Not currently used)

TIP

Warning flags are set to null if not set and W if set. If SQLCODE is a negative number, you will want to check SQLERRD[5].

The following code demonstrates how SQLCA variables can be used to detect errors:

```c
#include <stdio.h>


/* DECLARE AREA */
EXEC SQL BEGIN DECLARE SECTION;
  VARCHAR user_id[20];
  VARCHAR passwd[20];
   char           pssn[9];
   char           pfname[12], plname[20];
   char           pmajor[4], pdegree_program[1];
   char           pccode[4], pcname[30];
EXEC SQL END DECLARE SECTION;

/* INCLUDE AREA */
EXEC SQL INCLUDE SQLCA;

main()
{
    printf("/n What is your User ID: ");
    scanf("%s",user_id.arr);
    printf("\nEnter Password: ");
    scanf("%s",passwd.arr);

    user_id.len = strlen(user_id.arr);
    passwd.len = strlen(passwrd.arr);

    EXEC SQL CONNECT :userid IDENTIFIED BY :passwd;

    if (sqlca.sqlcode < 0)
    {
        printf("\n%s",sqlca.sqlerrm.sqlerrmc);
        EXEC SQL ROLLBACK WORK RELEASE;
        exit(1);
    }
    else
        printf("\nSuccessfully connected to Oracle.");

  printf("\nEnter data for new student -- 'Q' to quit");
  printf("\nSSN: ");
  scanf("%s",pssn);
  while (*pssn != 'Q')
  {
     printf("\n First Name: ");
     scanf("%s",pfname);
     printf("\n Last Name: ");
     scanf("%s",plname);
     printf("\n Major: ");
     scanf("%s",pmajor);
     printf("\nDegree Program: ");
     scanf("%s",pdegree_program);

/* INSERT NEW RECORD INTO DATABASE */
     EXEC SQL INSERT INTO STUDENT
       (SSN,FNAME,LNAME,MAJOR,DEGREE_PROGRAM)
        VALUES
        (:pssn,:pfname,:plname,:initcap(:pmajor),:pdegree_program);
```

```
    if (sqlca.sqlcode < 0)
    {
        printf("\n%s",sqlca.sqlerrm.sqlerrmc);
        EXEC SQL ROLLBACK WORK RELEASE;
        exit(1);
    }
    else
        printf("\nSuccessfully inserted record.");

/* VERIFY MAJOR IS VALID */
  EXEC SQL SELECT DEPT FROM DEPT WHERE DEPT= initcap(:pmajor);

 if (sqlca.sqlcode == 1403)
{
    printf("\nInvalid Major");
    EXEC SQL ROLLBACK WORK;
}

/* ENROLL STUDENT IN ALL ENTRY LEVEL CLASSES */
  EXEC SQL INSERT INTO GRADE (SSN,CCODE)
    SELECT :pssn, CCODE
    FROM CLASS
    WHERE PREREQ IS NULL;

if (sqlca.sqlcode < 0)
    {
        printf("\n%s",sqlca.sqlerrm.sqlerrmc);
        EXEC SQL ROLLBACK WORK RELEASE;
        exit(1);
    }
    else
        printf("\Student %s is now enrolled in %d
classes.",plname,sqlca.sqlerrd[2]);
} /* END WHILE */

EXEC SQL COMMIT WORK RELEASE;
exit(0);
}
```

If you need more Oracle-specific diagnostic information, you can include the ORACA file. This file contains additional system statistics, option settings, and extended diagnostic variables. ORACA is declared just as the SQLCA file is. The following example shows the syntax for declaring ORACA:

```
EXEC SQL INCLUDE oraca;
```

To enable the ORACA file, you must set the precompiler option to YES. The following example shows two ways to set this option:

```
/* OFF LINE */
ORACA = YES

/* IN LINE */
EXEC ORACLE OPTION (ORACA=YES)
```

Certain flags need to be set for the runtime options. By setting these flags to a non-zero value, you are able to do the following:

- Save the text of SQL statements
- Enable DEBUG operations
- Check cursor cache consistency
- Check heap consistency
- Gather cursor statistics

Some of the flags are shown here:

Flag Name	Description
ORACAID	Character string "ORACA"
ORACABC	Length of ORACA data structure in bytes
ORACCHF	Cursor cache consistency flag
ORADBGF	Master debug flag
ORAHCHF	Heap consistency flag
ORASTXTF	Save-SQL-statement flag
ORASTXT	Subrecord for storing SQL statements
ORASFNM	Subrecord for storing filename
ORASLNR	Line in file at or near current SQL statement
ORAHOC	Highest MAXOPENCURSORS requested
ORAMOC	Maximum open cursors required
ORACOC	Current number of cursors used
ORANOR	Number of cursor cache reassignments
ORANPR	Number of SQL statement parses
ORANEX	Number of SQL statement executions

WHENEVER Statement

WHENEVER statements are declarative in nature; therefore, their scope is positional—not logical. These statements test all executable SQL statements that follow it until another WHENEVER statement is encountered. This type of error detection is preferable because it is easier, more portable, and ANSI-compliant. These statements are used to direct a program's execution whenever an error or warning condition occurs. Some of the conditions that this statement can detect are Oracle errors, Oracle warnings, and no data found. If a WHENEVER statement is omitted, the process will continue. The following example shows the syntax of the WHENEVER statement.

```
EXEC SQL WHENEVER <condition> <action>
```

> **CAUTION**
>
> Careless use of WHENEVER statements may cause problems such as infinite looping.

All the possible error conditions are described in following list:

- SQLERROR   Sqlcode is negative
- SQLWARNING Sqlwarn[0] is set to "W"
- NOT FOUND   Sqlcode is +1403

Several different actions can be taken when one of the error conditions is encountered. The following list describes those actions:

- Continue
- Do function_call() | break
- Goto statement_label
- Stop

> **TIP**
>
> When using a WHENEVER-DO statement, parameters may not be passed to or from the function being called.

Indicator Variables

An indicator variable is associated with a host variable. Each time the host variable is used in an executable SQL statement, a return code is assigned to the indicator variable. This enables the user to monitor the host variables. There are two primary uses for indicator variables: detecting null values or truncated data values with the SELECT INTO clause, and setting columns to null values without explicitly hard-coding them for use with the UPDATE and INSERT statements. Indicator variables must be explicitly declared in the DECLARE section as a 2-byte integer (short), and it is good practice to declare them after the host variable. The following example shows how to declare these variables.

```
EXEC SQL BEGIN DECLARE SECTION;
  int    emp_number;
  float salary;
  short sal_ind;   /* indicator variable */
EXEC SQL END DECLARE SECTION;
```

Indicator variables can be used in VALUES, INTO, and SET clauses in executable SQL statements. To reference these variables, you must prefix them with a colon and append them to their associate host variables; they cannot be referenced by themselves. See the following syntax guideline.

```
:host_variable:indicator_variable
```

> **TIP**
>
> You cannot use indicator variables in WHERE clauses.

Some of the possible values for indicator variables are outlined in the following list:

- Return codes for SELECTs (output)

    0: Successful return of value into host variable

    -1: Returned value of null

    >0: Returned value was truncated

- Return codes for UPDATE or DELETE (input)

    >=0: Value of host variable will be used

    -1: Null value will be used in place of host variable

The following example shows how indicator variables can be used:

```
-- declare section --
#include <stdio.h>

EXEC SQL BEGIN DECLARE SECTION;
  VARCHAR user_id[20];
  VARCHAR passwd[20];
   char            pssn[9];
   char            pfname[12], plname[20];
   char            pmajor[4], pdegree_program[1];
   char            pccode[4], pcname[30];
    short          imajor;
EXEC SQL END DECLARE SECTION;

-- SQL include section --
EXEC SQL INCLUDE SQLCA;

main()
{
    printf("/n What is your User ID: ");
    scanf("%s",user_id.arr);
    printf("\nEnter Password: ");
    scanf("%s",passwd.arr);

    user_id.len = strlen(user_id.arr);
    passwd.len = strlen(passwrd.arr);

    EXEC SQL CONNECT :userid IDENTIFIED BY :passwd;
```

```
    if (sqlca.sqlcode < 0)
    {
        printf("\n%s",sqlca.sqlerrm.sqlerrmc);
        EXEC SQL ROLLBACK WORK RELEASE;
        exit(1);
    }
    else
        printf("\nSuccessfully connected to Oracle.");

  printf("\nEnter data for new student -- 'Q' to quit");
  printf("\nSSN: ");
  scanf("%s",pssn);
  while (*pssn != 'Q')
  {
      printf("\n First Name: ");
      scanf("%s",pfname);
      printf("\n Last Name: ");
      scanf("%s",plname);
      printf("\n Major: ");
      scanf("%s",pmajor);
      printf("\nDegree Program: ");
      scanf("%s",pdegree_program);

/* INSERT NEW RECORD INTO DATABASE */
      EXEC SQL INSERT INTO STUDENT
         (SSN,FNAME,LNAME,MAJOR,DEGREE_PROGRAM)
          VALUES
          (:pssn,:pfname,:plname,:initcap(:pmajor),:pdegree_program);
      if (sqlca.sqlcode < 0)
      {
          printf("\n%s",sqlca.sqlerrm.sqlerrmc);
          EXEC SQL ROLLBACK WORK RELEASE;
          exit(1);
      }
      else
          printf("\nSuccessfully inserted record.");

/* VERIFY MAJOR IS VALID */
  EXEC SQL SELECT DEPT FROM DEPT WHERE DEPT= initcap(:pmajor);

/* The indicator variable is set after each select for :pmajor */
switch (imajor)
{
    case 0:  printf("\nMajor is valid");
                  break;
     case -1: printf("\nMajor is invalid");
                  break;
    default:  printf("\nMajor is truncated");
                  break;
}

/* ENROLL STUDENT IN ALL ENTRY LEVEL CLASSES */
  EXEC SQL INSERT INTO GRADE (SSN,CCODE)
    SELECT :pssn, CCODE
    FROM CLASS
    WHERE PREREQ IS NULL;

if (sqlca.sqlcode < 0)
    {
```

```
            printf("\n%s",sqlca.sqlerrm.sqlerrmc);
            EXEC SQL ROLLBACK WORK RELEASE;
            exit(1);
    }
    else
        printf("\Student %s is now enrolled in %d
classes.",plname,sqlca.sqlerrd[2]);
} /* END WHILE */

EXEC SQL COMMIT WORK RELEASE;
exit(0);
}
```

Host Arrays

A host array is a collection of related data items, called elements, that is associated with a single variable name. Arrays ease programming and improve performance, because large amounts of data can be manipulated at one time with a single Oracle statement. You declare arrays in the DECLARE section just as you do for simple variables, except you must set the size of the array. The maximum dimension of a host array is 32,767 elements. The following example shows the DECLARE section for host arrays:

```
EXEC SQL BEGIN DECLARE SECTION;
    int    emp_number[50];
    char emp_name[50];
    float salary[50];
EXEC SQL END DECLARE SECTION;
```

CAUTION

If you exceed the maximum dimension of a host array, you will receive the "parameter out of range" run-time error. Also, IF you use multiple host arrays in a single SQL statement, then all the arrays must be of the same dimension; otherwise, you will receive a run-time error of "array size mismatched."

Some of the restrictions that are imposed include not declaring a two-dimensional array or not declaring an array of pointers.

Arrays can be used as input variables in the INSERT, UPDATE, and DELETE statements, and as output variables in the INTO clause of SELECT and FETCH statements. When using the arrays as an output variable, if you know the exact number of rows that will be returned, you will want to dimension the array to that number. You need not process host arrays in a loop, unless you are batching. Simply use the unsubscripted array names in your SQL statement. The following example shows the syntax for array processing:

```
EXEC SQL BEGIN DECLARE SECTION;
```

```
    int    emp_number[50];
    char emp_name[50];
    float salary[50];
EXEC SQL END DECLARE SECTION;

/* POPULATE HOST ARRAY HERE */
EXEC SQL INSERT INTO EMP (EMPNO, ENAME, DEPTNO)
    VALUES (:emp_number, :emp_name, :dept_number);
```

If you are unsure of the number of rows that will be returned, you should do batch FETCHes. Batch FETCHes within a loop will allow you to retrieve a large amount of data without knowing exactly how many rows you will be retrieving. Each FETCH returns the next batch of rows from the current active set. The maximum rows returned is dependent on the array size. Fewer rows are returned under the following conditions:

■ The end of the active set is reached

■ Fewer than a full batch of rows remain to be FETCHed

■ An error is detected while processing a row

> **TIP**
>
> For INSERT, UPDATE, DELETE, and SELECT INTO statements, SQLERRD[3] records the number of rows processed. For FETCH statements, it records the cumulative sum of rows processed.

Dynamic SQL

Dynamic SQL is nothing more than SQL statements that are not known at compile time. Unlike static SQL statements, dynamic SQL statements are not embedded in your source program. These statements are stored in a character string or built by the program at runtime. Dynamic SQL statements can be built interactively or read from a file. The primary advantage of dynamic SQL is that it is much more versatile than plain embedded SQL. One of the disadvantages of dynamic SQL is it requires added processing time. Dynamic SQL should be utilized when one of the following is unknown:

■ Text of the SQL statement

■ The number of host variables

■ The datatypes of host variables

■ References to database objects such as columns, indexes, sequences, tables, usernames, and views

In order to represent a dynamic SQL statement, a character string must contain the required text of a valid SQL statement, without the EXEC SQL clause, host-language delimiters or statement terminators, or any of the following embedded SQL commands:

■ CLOSE

■ DECLARE

■ DESCRIBE

■ EXECUTE

■ FETCH

■ INCLUDE

■ OPEN

■ PREPARE

■ WHENEVER

TIP

Initialize your character string before you use or reuse it, and do not null terminate the string.

These character strings are manipulated by Oracle via cursors. Cursors are areas of memory used for processing SQL statements. The scope of the cursors is the entire Pro*C program. There are no limits to the number of cursors a Pro*C program can have, but there is a maximum number on how many cursors can be open at one time. The INIT.ORA file contains a parameter that will set how many open cursors are allowed at one time. There are two types of cursors: implicit and explicit. Implicit cursors are automatically declared and can be used for all SQL statements. Explicit cursors are required to manipulate multi-rowed SELECTs. They are also used to keep track of the current set or row. Four Oracle statements are associated with cursors.

■ DECLARE: Associate SQL statement with cursor

■ OPEN: Execute SQL statement

■ FETCH: Retrieve next row and store in buffer

■ CLOSE: Release cursor area back to Oracle.

The DECLARE statement defines the cursor by giving it a name which is associated with the SQL statement. This name is used by the precompiler and should not be defined in the DECLARE section. Cursor names should not be hyphenated and can be any length, but only the first 31 characters are evaluated. Because this statement is a declarative statement, it must precede all other SQL statements and must be declared only once.

TIP

For ANSI compatibility, use cursor names no longer than 18 characters.

The following example shows how to DECLARE a cursor:

```
EXEC SQL DECLARE Class_Students CURSOR FOR
                SELECT FNAME, LNAME, GRADE
                FROM STUDENT S, GRADE G
                WHERE S.SSN = G.SSN
                AND G.CCODE = :class_code
                ORDER BY LNAME;
```

NOTE

When using explicit cursors, the INTO clause must be omitted.

After declaring a cursor, it must be opened so that Oracle can parse it, replace variables and parameters, and execute the query. The OPEN command positions the cursor just before the first row that will be retrieved from the active set. It also zeroes the row-processed count kept by the third element of the SQLERRD in the SQLCA. Remember that rows have not been retrieved at this point. After a cursor has been opened, the variables are not reexamined until it is opened again; therefore, if you want a different active set, you must reopen the cursor. The amount of work done by the OPEN command depends on the values of three precompiler options: HOLD_CURSOR, RELEASE_CURSOR, and MAXOPENCURSORS. The following example shows the syntax of the OPEN command.

```
EXEC SQL OPEN Class_Students;
```

After the cursor has been opened, data can be retrieved using the FETCH command. The FETCH command requires that you specify the output host variables that will contain the results from the query by using the INTO clause. The first time you execute the FETCH command the cursor moves to the first row in the active set. With each execution of FETCH the cursor advances one row until it encounters no rows to retrieve. The cursor can only move forward. If you want a previous row you must reOPEN the cursor. After the last row has been retrieved, SQLCODE in the SQLCA has a value of 1403. Only one FETCH statement can be associated with an open cursor. The following example shows the syntax for the FETCH command:

```
EXEC SQL FETCH Class_Students
                INTO :first, :last, :grade;
```

NOTE

The SQLWARN[3] flag is set when the number of columns in the SELECT does not match the number of INTO host variables.

The last statement used is the `CLOSE` command. This command releases all cursor resources back to Oracle. The active set will become undefined and an invalid cursor error will occur if a `FETCH` is executed against a closed cursor. A cursor can be closed multiple times, but it usually is closed only when there is no further need for the SQL statement. The following example shows the syntax for the `CLOSE` command:

```
EXEC SQL CLOSE Class_Students;
```

There are four methods for programming a dynamic SQL statement. With all four methods you must store dynamic SQL statements in a character string, which must be a quoted literal or a host variable. Choosing the right method can be confusing, but Figure 50.1 will help make this decision.

FIGURE 50.1.

This logic flow chart will help decide what method is appropriate for your statement.

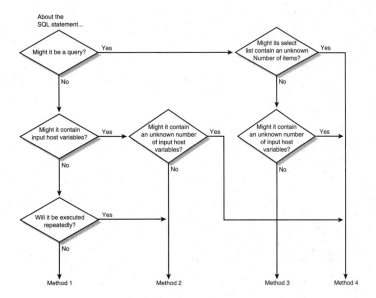

After deciding what method is appropriate for your situation, try to avoid some of the common errors described in the following list:

- When using a character array to store the dynamic SQL, blank-pad the array before starting.

- Do not null-terminate the host string. Oracle does not recognize the null terminator as an end-of-string; instead it treats it as part of the SQL statement.

- If you use a `VARCHAR` variable to store the dynamic SQL statement, make sure the length of the `VARCHAR` is set correctly before you execute the `PREPARE` or `EXECUTE IMMEDIATE` command.

Coding Methods for Dynamic SQL Statements

Now let's look at the four different methods that can be used to code dynamic SQL statements.

Method One

Method one lets you build a dynamic SQL statement and immediately execute it using the EXECUTE IMMEDIATE command. This method results in success or failure and uses no host variables. Statements in method one are parsed every time they are executed. These statements do not allow SELECTs. The following example shows a method-one statement:

```
#include <stdio.h>

EXEC SQL BEGIN DECLARE SECTION;
    VARCHAR   sql_statement[300];
    VARCHAR   username[20];
    VARCHAR   password[20];
EXEC SQL END DELCAR SECTION;

search_cond      char[40];

EXEC SQL INCLUDE SQLCA;

main()
{
    printf("\nUsername: ");
    scanf("%s\n",username.arr);
    printf("\n"Password: ");
    scanf("%s\n"password.arr);

  EXEC SQL CONNECT :username IDENTIFIED BY :password;

  if (sqlca.sqlcode < 0)
  {
      printf("\n%s",sqlca.sqlerrm.sqlerrmc);
      EXEC SQL ROLLBACK WORK RELEASE;
      exit(1);
   }
   else
      printf("\nSuccessfully connected to Oracle.");
}
  strcpy(sql_statement.arr,"UPDATE EMP SET COMM = 500 WHERE ");
  printf("\nEnter a search condition for the following statement: ");
  printf("\n%s",sql_statement.arr);
  scanf("%s\n",search_cond);
  strcat(sql_statement.arr,search_cond);

  EXEC SQL EXECUTE IMMEDIATE :sql_statment;
  EXEC SQL COMMIT WORK RELEASE;
  exit(0);
}
```

Method Two

Method two is identical to method one except that you may use host variables, which need to be known at precompile time. With method two, the SQL is parsed just once but can be executed many times. This method enables the user to use the USING clause. Every placeholder in the prepared dynamic SQL statement must match a corresponding host variable in the USING clause. The following examples shows a method-two statement:

```c
#include <stdio.h>

EXEC SQL BEGIN DECLARE SECTION;
    VARCHAR  sql_statement[300];
    VARCHAR  username[20];
    VARCHAR  password[20];
     REAL           commission;
EXEC SQL END DELCAR SECTION;

search_cond    char[40];

EXEC SQL INCLUDE SQLCA;

main()
{
    printf("\nUsername: ");
    scanf("%s\n",username.arr);
    printf("\n"Password: ");
    scanf("%s\n"password.arr);

  EXEC SQL CONNECT :username IDENTIFIED BY :password;

  if (sqlca.sqlcode < 0)
  {
      printf("\n%s",sqlca.sqlerrm.sqlerrmc);
      EXEC SQL ROLLBACK WORK RELEASE;
      exit(1);
  }
  else
      printf("\nSuccessfully connected to Oracle.");
}
  strcpy(sql_statement.arr,"UPDATE EMP SET COMM = :c WHERE ";
  printf("\nEnter a search condition for the following statement: ");
  printf("\n%s",sql_statement.arr);
  scanf("%s\n",search_cond);
  strcat(sql_statement.arr,search_cond);

EXEC SQL C1 FROM :sql_statment;

printf("\nCommission: ");
scanf("%d\n",commission);

EXEC SQL EXECUTE C1 USING :commission;

EXEC SQL COMMIT WORK RELEASE;
exit(0);
}
```

TIP

If one host variable is an array, all the variables must be arrays.

Method Three

Method three allows your program to accept or build a dynamic query, then process it using PREPARE command with the DECLARE, OPEN, FETCH and CLOSE cursor commands. At precompile time the following need to be known: select-list items, number of placeholders and datatypes of host variables. Method three is used for dynamic SQL with a known select list, giving the programmer more flexibility to build SQL statements on the fly. The following example shows a method-three statement:

```c
#include <stdio.h>

EXEC SQL BEGIN DECLARE SECTION;
  VARCHAR userid[20]
  VARCHAR passwd[20];
  VARCHAR student_id[10];
  VARCHAR student_name[30];
  VARCHAR classes[30];
  VARCHAR sql_statement[600];
EXEC SQL END DECLARE SECTION;

/* PROGRAM VARIABLES */
int employee_number;

/* PROCEDURE DECLARATION */
void log_on();
void build_select();

main()
{
  char    where_clause[80];
/* LOG ONTO DATABASE */
  log_on();
  build_select();
  EXEC SQL PREPARE C1 FROM :sql_statement.arr;
  EXEC SQL DECLARE C1 CURSOR FOR S1;
  sql_statement.len := length(sql_statement.arr);
  EXEC SQL OPEN C1 USING employee_number;
  EXEC SQL FETCH C1 INTO :student_name;
  if (sqlca.sqlcode < 0)
  {
    printf("\n%s",sqlca.sqlerrm.sqlerrmc);
    EXEC SQL ROLLBACK WORK RELEASE;
    exit(1);
  }
  else
    printf("\n%s\n",:student_name.arr);

    EXEC SQL CLOSE C1;
```

```
      exit(0);
}

void log_on()
{
    printf("/n What is your User ID: ");
    scanf("%s",user_id.arr);
    printf("\nEnter Password: ");
    scanf("%s",passwd.arr);

    user_id.len = strlen(user_id.arr);
    passwd.len = strlen(passwrd.arr);

    EXEC SQL CONNECT :userid IDENTIFIED BY :passwd;

    if (sqlca.sqlcode < 0)
    {
        printf("\n%s",sqlca.sqlerrm.sqlerrmc);
        EXEC SQL ROLLBACK WORK RELEASE;
        exit(1);
    }
    else
        printf("\nSuccessfully connected to Oracle.");
}


void build_select()
{
    strcpy(sql_statement.arr,"SELECT FIRST_NAME ¦¦ ' '¦¦ LAST_NAME, ");
    strcat(sql_statement.arr,"FROM EMP ");
    strcat(sql_statement.arr,"WHERE EMPNO = ");
    printf("\nEnter employee number: ");
    scanf("%d",employee_number);
    strcat(sql_statement.arr,employee_number);
}
```

Method Four

Method four is probably the most complex of the four methods, but it is very diverse in its use. It allows the program to accept or build a dynamic SQL statement, then process it using descriptors. At precompile time, the following are unknown: select-list items, number of placeholders, and datatypes of host variables. To process this type of dynamic query, you must be able to use the DESCRIBE SELECT LIST command and be able to declare a data structure called the SQL descriptor area (SQLDA). Descriptors are a segment of memory used by the computer and Oracle to hold a complete description of the variables in a dynamic SQL statement. Descriptor variables are defined as a data structure containing the following information:

- Maximum number of columns that can be evaluated
- Actual number of columns in the SELECT list
- Array of pointers to column names
- Array of maximum lengths of columns

- Array of actual column lengths
- Array of data types for each column
- Array of pointers to data values
- Array of pointers to indicator variables

To process the dynamic SQL statement, your program must issue the DESCRIBE BIND VARIABLES command and declare another kind of SQLDA, called a bind descriptor, to hold descriptions of the placeholders for input. If you have more than one method for SQL statements, each statement will require its own SQLDA(s); nonconcurrent cursors, however, can reuse SQLDAs. There is no set limit on the number of SQLDAs in a program.

The DESCRIBE command is useful in determining what the SQL statement contains. DESCRIBE instructs Oracle to provide the host variables for any select statement. It examines the select statement to determine the number of columns and type of each in the select list. Oracle must define a storage area to hold fetched rows from the database, and actual data returned from the select is stored in descriptor variables.

The following are steps in coding for method four:

1. Define a descriptor variable:

   ```
   SQLDA *descr_var
   ```

2. Place a SQL SELECT statement into a host variable:

   ```
   scanf("%[^\n",sql_statement);
   ```

3. Prepare the SQL statement:

   ```
   EXEC SQL PREPARE S1 FROM sql_statement;
   ```

4. Declare a cursor area for the SELECT statement:

   ```
   EXECSQL DECLARE C1 CURSOR FOR S1
   ```

5. Execute the query and create an active set:

   ```
   EXEC SQL OPEN C1 USING DESCRIPTOR descr_var;
   ```

6. DESCRIBE the SELECT into the descriptor variable:

   ```
   EXEC SQL DESCRIBE SELECT LIST FOR S1 INTO desc_var
   ```

7. FETCH rows from active set:

   ```
   EXEC SQL FETCH C1 USING DESCRIPTOR descr_var;
   ```

8. CLOSE the cursor:

   ```
   EXEC SQL CLOSE C1;
   ```

But is it possible to write a program that can be used by other Oracle tools, such as SQL*Forms? The answer is yes, and user exits provide this functionality.

User Exits

A user exit is a host-language subroutine that is called by SQL*Forms to do special processing. Sometimes SQL*Forms triggers are unable to perform complex calculations or field validations. Embedded SQL commands and PL/SQL blocks are allowed in user exits. User exits are invoked in the form but execute outside the SQL*Form. Usually, user exits are faster than SQL commands but their down side is that they are more difficult to debug and are more complicated to write. Some of the common uses of user exits include the following: controlling real time devices or processes, data manipulations that need extended procedural capabilities, or special file I/O operations. The following list is some general rules and guidelines to use when writing user exits:

- User exits are written in a third-generation language, with SQL commands embedded inside. This code is precompiled in order to translate the SQL commands into host-language statements.
- Third-generation language statements (host-language statements) are written as an ordinary host-language program. Upper- and lowercase are used as normal.
- SQL commands are customarily written entirely in uppercase.
- User-exit variables must be written according to the rules of the host language.
- Connecting to the database via EXEC SQL CONNECT is not necessary as in the Pro*USE. Connection is made through SQL*Forms.
- Any user-exit variables that receive/write values from/to SQL*Forms or data tables must be declared in the DECLARE section of the user exit.
- The name of the user exit should not be a reserved word in Oracle. Also, avoid names that conflict with SQL*Forms commands, function codes, and externally defined names. SQL*Forms will convert the name of the user exit to uppercase before searching for the exit; therefore, the EXIT command must be in uppercase.
- Sometimes SQL*Forms I/O calls interfere with printer I/O routines. If they do, the user exit will be unable to utilize the printer. This restriction does not apply to user exits written in C.
- A user exit should not UPDATE a database table that is associated with a form; when the form COMMITs the data, it could overwrite what the user exit has saved.

It is possible to pass values to a user exit and receive a value in return. When a SQL*Forms trigger calls a user exit, it passes the following information:

- A character string that contains the exit name and specified parameters
- The trigger step failure message, if one is defined
- A flag indicating whether the user exit was called in normal or query mode

Global values can also be passed to a user exit by using IAF GETS.

The returning values from a user exit indicate whether it succeeded or failed. The return code is an integer constant, which is defined in SQL*Forms. There are three possible return values, which are outlined in Table 50.8.

Table 50.8. User-exit return values.

Return Type	Description
Success	No errors were encountered. SQL*Forms can continue to the next step.
Failure	The user exit detected an error. A message will be displayed.
Fatal error	The user exit detected an error that will not let the process continue.

To incorporate a user exit into a form, take the following steps:

1. Write the user exit in a supported host language.
2. Precompile the source code.
3. Compile the modified source code.
4. Use the GENXTB utility to add an entry to the IAP program table IAPXTB in the module IAPXIT. (IAP is the component of SQL*Forms that runs a form).
5. Create a new IAP by linking the standard IAP modules, the modified IAPXIT module, and the new user-exit module.
6. In the form, define a trigger step to call the user exit.
7. Instruct operators to use the new IAP when running the form.

The following example shows a user exit that calculates an order total:

```
/********************************************************************/
int
order_totl( void )
/********************************************************************/
{
    EXEC SQL BEGIN DECLARE SECTION;
        int    order_num;
        ASCIZ_8 status_code;
        ASCIZ_80  msg;
        float merch_gross;
        float mult_prod_disc;
        float cust_disc;
        float merch_total;
        float reg_shipping;
        float upg_shipping;
        float frgn_shipping;
        float taxes;
        float grand_total;
```

```
EXEC SQL END DECLARE SECTION;
EXEC SQL WHENEVER SQLERROR CONTINUE;

EXEC IAF GET GLOBAL.OT_ORDER_NUM INTO :order_num;
EXEC SQL ALTER SESSION ENABLE COMMIT IN PROCEDURE;
EXEC SQL EXECUTE
  BEGIN
    order_totaling.get_order_total( :order_num,
                                    :status_code,
                                    :msg,
                                    :merch_gross,
                                    :mult_prod_disc,
                                    :cust_disc,
                                    :merch_total,
                                    :reg_shipping,
                                    :upg_shipping,
                                    :frgn_shipping,
                                    :taxes,
                                    :grand_total
                                  );
  END;
END-EXEC;

if (sqlca.sqlcode != 0){
  sprintf(sql_errmsg,"order total: procedure call failed");
  sql_errlen=strlen(sql_errmsg);
  sqliem(sql_errmsg,&sql_errlen);
  return(IAPFAIL);
}

EXEC IAF PUT GLOBAL.OT_STATUS_CODE VALUES ( :status_code );
EXEC IAF PUT GLOBAL.OT_MSG VALUES ( :msg );

if (sqlca.sqlcode != 0){
  sprintf(sql_errmsg,"order total: procedure call failed");
  sql_errlen=strlen(sql_errmsg);
  sqliem(sql_errmsg,&sql_errlen);
  return(IAPFAIL);
} else {

EXEC IAF PUT GLOBAL.OT_MERCH_GROSS VALUES ( :merch_gross );
EXEC IAF PUT GLOBAL.OT_MULT_PROD_DISC VALUES ( :mult_prod_disc );
EXEC IAF PUT GLOBAL.OT_CUST_DISC VALUES ( :cust_disc );
EXEC IAF PUT GLOBAL.OT_MERCH_TOTAL VALUES ( :merch_total );
EXEC IAF PUT GLOBAL.OT_REG_SHIPPING VALUES ( :reg_shipping );
EXEC IAF PUT GLOBAL.OT_UPG_SHIPPING VALUES ( :upg_shipping );
EXEC IAF PUT GLOBAL.OT_FRGN_SHIPPING VALUES ( :frgn_shipping );
EXEC IAF PUT GLOBAL.OT_TAXES VALUES ( :taxes );
EXEC IAF PUT GLOBAL.OT_GRAND_TOTAL VALUES ( :grand_total );

  return(IAPSUCC);
  }
}
```

To call this user exit from a SQL*Forms trigger, you insert the following code:

```
user_exit('order_total');
```

Utilizing dynamic SQL or user exits can create problems with performance, and if your program is in a high-demand system this could become very undesirable. The next section of this chapter will look how to tune your SQL to improve performance.

Performance Tuning

When developing applications with embedded SQL, performance can become a major issue depending on what type of platform you may be using. This section provides easy-to-apply methods for improving the performance of your applications. It looks at what causes poor performance and how performance can be improved.

> **NOTE**
>
> See Chapter 15, "Performance Tuning and Optimizing," for more information about performance tuning.

Poor Performance

One of the first causes of poor performance is high Oracle communication overhead. Oracle processes each SQL statement one at a time, which results in numerous calls to Oracle. If you are operating in a network environment, each call creates additional traffic on the network. The more traffic you have, the slower the performance will become.

The second cause of poor performance is inefficient SQL statements. Just because SQL statements can be written in several different ways and still get the same results, this does not mean that every statement is running efficiently. In some cases, full table scans will be occurring (which is time consuming if the table is large); in other cases, using indexes greatly speeds up the search.

The third cause of poor performance is managing cursors inefficiently. The result of not managing cursors correctly is additional parsing and binding, which adds noticeable processing overhead for Oracle.

These problems can be improved by reducing Oracle communication overhead or reducing processing overhead. The next section provides methods that will help reduce overhead and improve performance.

Improving Performance

Improving performance can make a dramatic difference in the way your application functions under normal or high usage. Two areas always should be considered when writing an SQL statement: Oracle communications and processing overhead.

Reducing Oracle Communication Overhead

There are two methods that can be used to reduce Oracle communication overhead: host arrays and PL/SQL blocks.

Using host arrays can dramatically boost your applications performance. You can issue one SQL statement to manipulate numerous rows, instead of issuing a SQL statement for each row. For example, if you wanted to update 1,200 student grades, you could issue one SQL statement with a host array instead of 1,200 with just a host variable. For more information, see the section on host arrays.

The second method to reducing Oracle communication overhead is to use embedded PL/SQL. If your application is database intensive, you can utilize PL/SQL blocks to group SQL statements together and then send the block to Oracle for processing.

After reducing the Oracle communication overhead, your next step should be to reduce processing overhead.

Reducing Processing Overhead

In order to reduce processing overhead, your SQL statement should be analyzed to ensure it is using the appropriate indexes, it is using row-locking properly, and it is managing cursors effectively. To ensure that indexes are being used properly, Oracle has provided tools that will help to identify problem areas.

The trace facility in conjunction with the EXPLAIN PLAN statement will generate statistics enabling you to identify which SQL statements are taking a lot of time to execute. This explain plan describes what database operations need to be carried out by Oracle to complete processing of the SQL statement that you have written. One of the most common problems with SQL statements is that full table scans are being done instead of indexes being utilized. The explain plan indicates if full table scans are being done; from this you can alter the SQL statements to utilize indexes.

Another area that can improve performance is how the database is locking data. To increase performance you want to lock only at the row level. This will enable many users (instead of just one) to access the table. Applications that do online transactions can drastically benefit from row locking versus table locking. The default value is different depending on what version of Oracle you are using. In Oracle Version 6, row-locking is the default.

Managing cursors can create an enormous amount of processing overhead. The easiest way to manage cursors is to declare them explicitly. This gives you the flexibility to control them as you need resources. Remember that you need to PREPARE, DECLARE, OPEN, and CLOSE explicit cursors in dynamic SQL—especially with methods three and four. After a cursor has been PREPAREd (which does the parsing), it can be used multiple times until it is CLOSEd. This can drastically reduce the parsing and binding that is done with each cursor.

Now that you have stepped through each part of creating an embedded SQL host program, it would be advisable to stay current on what new features the precompilers have. Oracle has taken extra effort in improving its tools with each step; as a programmer, you should capitalize on these features.

New Features in Version 1.4

The new features in Version 1.4 precompilers help meet the needs of professional software developers. Some of the features are as follows:

- *New debugging aid.* The SQLCA stores additional runtime information about the outcome of SQL operations.
- *Enhanced WHENEVER statement.* The improved WHENEVER statement now lets you take actions when an error or warning is detected. With previous versions you only had three choices: GOTO, CONTINUE, or STOP. Added to Version 1.4 is the DO statement, which allows for procedural functions to be taken.
- *Revised HOST option.* With previous versions of precompilers, the HOST parameter indicated what host language was being used. Version 1.4 uses separate precompilers executables each designed for a specify language.
- In previous versions of Oracle precompilers, options for setting the area size (which is initially set for cursor) had to be specified. With the current version of precompilers, resizing is automatically done. This feature makes the AREASIZE and REBIND options obsolete.
- Previous versions of precompilers generated several database calls per embedded SQL statement. In Version 1.4, precompilers generate only one (bundled) database call per embedded SQL statement.

Remember to try and keep current on the new features Oracle includes in its precompilers. This could make a dramatic difference in the performance and functionality of your program.

Summary

ORACLE precompilers provide an excellent tool for programmers to create dynamic applications. This chapter provided information on what a precompiler does, the benefits of being able to embed SQL statements, how to use a precompiler, and how to create a host program.

This concludes the section on precompilers. I hope that the information has been beneficial to you and has given you some quick tips to enhance performance.

ODBC

51

by Advanced Information Systems, Inc.

IN THIS CHAPTER

ODBC (Open Database Connectivity) is an industry standard programming interface that enables applications to access a variety of database management systems residing on many different platforms. ODBC provides a large degree of database independence through a standard SQL syntax, which can be translated by database-specific drivers to the native SQL of the DBMS.

Database independence and ease of use are the primary advantages to using ODBC. It is supported by many popular development tools, including Visual Basic, PowerBuilder, Delphi, and SQLWindows. These tools and numerous others provide their own interfaces to ODBC, making ODBC easier to use by insulating the developer from many of the complexities of the ODBC API.

Components of ODBC

ODBC software is made up of several distinct components. The Application layer contains embedded SQL and logic for data entry, preparing transactions, and displaying result sets. It calls API functions exported by the driver manager to connect to the data source, apply SQL, and retrieve results and error codes. The driver manager provides the common ODBC interface, loads database-specific drivers as requested by the application, performs call-level validations, and maps ODBC calls to functions exported by the database-specific driver. The database-specific driver processes the ODBC function calls, optionally converting SQL and data types to the native syntax of the DBMS, and formats DBMS error codes into a standard format. It also returns result sets and error codes to the driver manager. The data source consists of the DBMS itself, in addition to any network or operating system software required to connect to it. Figure 51.1 illustrates these layers.

FIGURE 51.1.

This is a visual representation of the components of ODBC.

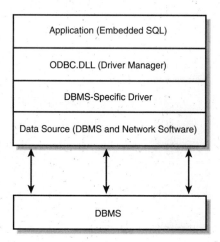

For local desktop databases, the data source might simply consist of the name of local server or database file. When the DBMS resides on a remote server, however, the data source includes any network software required to access the remote host. For example, if you attempt to access Oracle on a remote server, SQL*Net must be installed and properly configured. Although this software is not actually part of ODBC, it is considered part of the data source because it is required by ODBC to connect to the database.

Configuring an ODBC Data Source

The process of configuring an ODBC data source is simply a matter of providing some information to the driver manager and the DBMS-specific driver. The driver manager uses entries in ODBC.INI to determine what driver to load for a particular data source name. The specific driver may use ODBC.INI to determine the server name and the values of any database-specific parameters required to connect.

The ODBC administration program ships with nearly all Windows development tools that support ODBC and is typically installed as part of the Windows Control Panel applet. This program, ODBCADM.EXE, and a DLL, ODBCINST.DLL, are used to install specific drivers and configure data sources. The following instructions on how to use the driver manager are based on version 1.02 of ODBCADM.EXE. This application may vary slightly from version to version, but the functions provided are essentially the same.

> **CAUTION**
>
> Always use the ODBC administration program to install drivers and configure data sources. ODBC.INI and ODBCINST.INI should not be edited manually, unless it becomes absolutely necessary because of corruption or other extreme problems. If this situation arises, the files should be backed up prior to editing.

When the administration application is started, a list of defined data sources is presented, as shown in Figure 51.2.

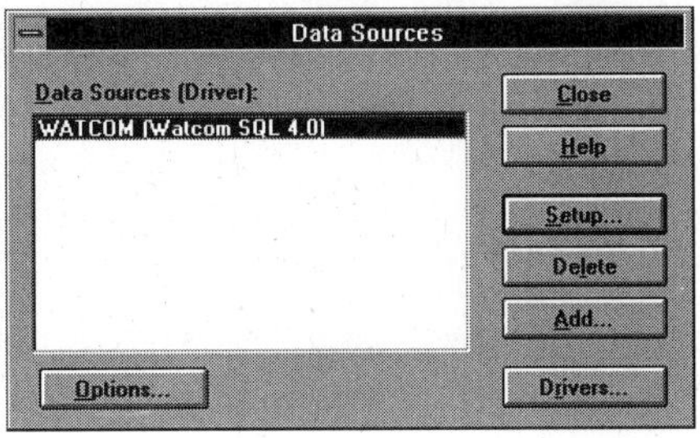

FIGURE 51.2.

The Data Sources dialog displays a list of defined data sources.

The Close and Help buttons should be self-explanatory, and the Options button will be discussed later, in the section on debugging. Add is used to define a new data source for one of the installed drivers. Delete is used to delete an existing data source, but does not delete the driver. The configuration of the selected data source can be edited by clicking on the Setup button. The Drivers button is used to install additional DBMS-specific ODBC drivers.

The following examples illustrate the installation of the Oracle ODBC driver and the configuration of an Oracle data source. This process begins with the installation of the Oracle ODBC driver. First, select Drivers from the Data Sources dialog. When this button is clicked, all installed drivers are displayed, as shown in Figure 51.3.

FIGURE 51.3.

The Drivers dialog displays a list of installed drivers.

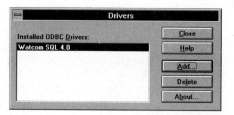

To install the Oracle ODBC driver, click the Add button. This will display a dialog requesting the location of the drivers. Select the drive and directory containing the ODBC.INF file and click OK. The dialog box shown in Figure 51.4 indicates that the Oracle ODBC driver was located.

FIGURE 51.4.

The Install Drivers dialog displays a list of drivers available for installation.

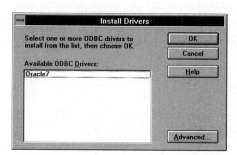

The Advanced button displays a dialog that allows the user to specify installation of the driver manager and code page translators. The Versions button in the lower-right corner brings up a second dialog that can be used to view extended version information about each component available to install. These two dialogs are shown in Figure 51.5.

FIGURE 51.5.

The Advanced Installation Options and Versions dialogs can be used to control the installation of the Oracle ODBC driver.

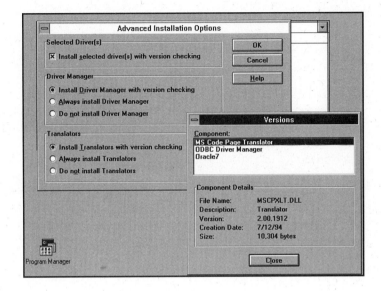

The Install selected driver(s) with version checking should be selected. This will cause the installation program to prompt before overwriting an existing driver if it is the same or a newer version of the driver being installed.

The version checking options should also be used for the installation of the Driver Manager and translators. Newer versions of these DLLs should not be overwritten if they exist.

Code page translators are used to translate between different character sets and languages. In some cases, they are used for encryption or data type conversion. Although a translator is not needed in most cases, you can install them for possible future use. After making your selections from these options, click the OK button to return to the Install Drivers dialog.

To complete the installation of the Oracle7 driver, make sure that Oracle7 is highlighted in the list box and click the OK button. The Drivers dialog should now appear as shown in Figure 51.6.

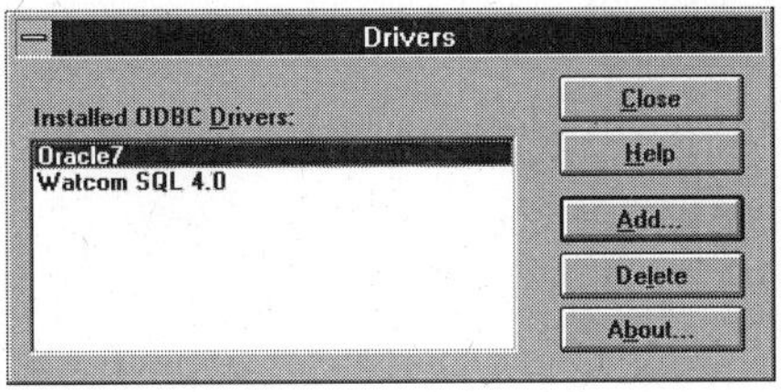

FIGURE 51.6.

The Drivers dialog shows that the Oracle ODBC driver was successfully installed.

Click the Close button to complete driver installation.

Configuring the data source is simply a matter of specifying a driver, naming the data source, and providing some additional information for the driver to use when connecting to the database. Refer to the Data Sources dialog in Figure 51.2. From this dialog, click Add to configure a new Oracle data source. The next dialog, Add Data Sources, requires the selection of an installed driver. Select Oracle7 from the list and click the OK button. Next, the Oracle7 ODBC Setup dialog prompts the user for a data source name, description, and SQL*Net connect string, as illustrated in Figure 51.7.

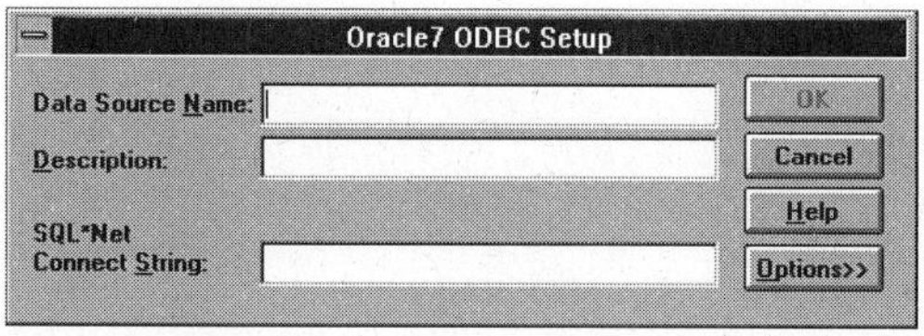

FIGURE 51.7.

This is the Oracle7 ODBC Setup dialog.

The connect string is specific to the network transport (if any), the hostname or address of the server, and the system ID of the database to be accessed (if more than one Oracle database exists on the host). The syntax of the connect string is

```
transport_code:host_name:database
```

The `transport_code` is a single character used to specify the SQL*Net driver to be used (T for TCP/IP, X for IPX/SPX, and so on). The `host_name` is the name, alias, or network address of the server. The `database` argument is necessary only if more than one Oracle database exists on the host. In this case, the argument should be the system name of the database, as specified when the database was created with the CREATE DATABASE command. Consult the Oracle ODBC driver release notes and the SQL*Net documentation for further information on the SQL*Net Connect String.

For the purposes of this example, assume that the database resides on a UNIX host and will be accessed from the Windows workstation using TCP/IP. Enter ORACLE for the data source name, Oracle 7.1 for the description, and T:ORACLE_SERVER for the SQL*Net connect string. The dialog should now look like the one shown in Figure 51.8.

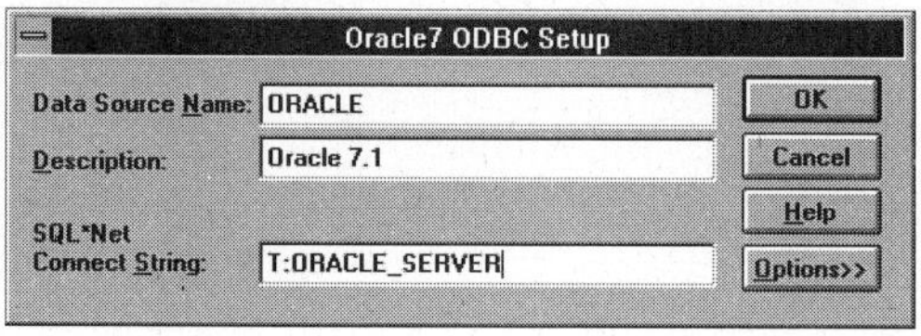

FIGURE 51.8.

*The Oracle7 ODBC Setup dialog requires a name and a SQL*Net Connect String. The description is optional.*

The Options button enables the user to select a code page translator, assuming that a translator was installed with the driver. In most cases, no translation is necessary. Click OK to complete the data source setup. The new data source should appear in the Data Sources dialog as shown in Figure 51.9.

FIGURE 51.9.

The Data Sources dialog shows that the new Oracle7 Data Source was successfully added.

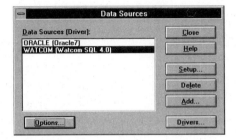

The data source is now fully configured and ready to be accessed by an application. Note that the setup routine in Figure 51.7 and Figure 51.8 is specific to the driver (Oracle 7.1 version 1.11.0002, in this case). This setup dialog will vary slightly from driver to driver, but will always require similar information.

Connecting to an ODBC Data Source Using the ODBC API

Before your application connects to the ODBC data source, some memory allocation and initialization must be performed. First, the application must call SQLAllocEnv, passing a pointer to memory allocated to store an environment handle. This handle will be used to establish connections and for transaction processing. The application might need to establish more than one environment handle, but a single environment handle is usually sufficient, except in multithreaded environments.

Next, the application should call SQLAllocConnect, passing the previously established environment handle and a pointer to storage allocated for the connection handle. The driver manager allocates storage for connection information and associates the resulting connection handle with the environment handle. Multiple connections can be established for a single environment handle, but each connection can only be associated with a single environment. The connection handle will be used to allocate statement handles and process embedded SQL transactions.

Finally, the application may call either SQLConnect or SQLDriverConnect, passing the connection handle instantiated by the call to SQLAllocConnect. The primary difference between these two functions is that SQLDriverConnect accepts a full connection string, rather than separate arguments for the data source name, userid, and password. This allows for additional database-specific parameters to be passed to the driver as part of the connection string. Additionally, `SQLDriverConnect` provides an argument used to define the behavior of the driver manager and a window handle to be used as the parent of the data sources dialog (if one will be presented). The arguments to `SQLDriverConnect` are, in order:

- An allocated connection handle.
- The handle of the parent window from the Data Sources dialog (or NULL, if no dialog will be presented).
- A connection string.
- The length of the connection string.
- A pointer to storage for the connection string actually used by the driver. (It may add information to the connection string it receives.)
- A pointer to storage to hold the length of the completed connection string.
- An integer constant used to control the behavior of the driver manager.

> **NOTE**
>
> A typical connection string looks like this:
>
> `DSN=ORACLE;UID=scotty;PWD=tiger;`
>
> Additional database-specific parameters may be provided, or the connection string may be partial, or empty, in which case the driver will provide a dialog requesting the information required to connect. If `SQL_DRIVER_NOPROMPT` is passed as the completion constant, the application must provide all required information in the connection string.

C applications should include ODBC.H (or SQL.H and SQLEXT.H, depending on the compiler), which contains all function prototypes, data types, and constants available in the ODBC API. When using other development tools, the developer must provide prototypes for all ODBC functions used by the application. Listings 51.1 and 51.2 demonstrate connecting to an ODBC data source in C and Visual Basic, in a Microsoft Windows application context.

Listing 51.1. This C function establishes a single connection to a data source.

```
int ConnectToDataSource(
HENV *hEnv,     /* used to store the environment handle */
HDBC *hDBc)     /* used to store the connection handle  */
{
    UCHAR       *szConnect;
    UCHAR       szConnectOut[SQL_MAX_MESSAGE_LENGTH];
    SWORD       iConnectOutLen;
    RETCODE     iError;
```

```
    szConnect = strdup("DSN=ORACLE;UID=scotty;PWD=tiger;");
    iError = SQLAllocEnv(hEnv);

    if (iError == SQL_SUCCESS)
        iError = SQLAllocConnect(*hEnv, hDBc);
    if (iError == SQL_SUCCESS)      iError = SQLDriverConnect(*hDBc,
                                    NULL,
                                    szConnect,
                                    SQL_NTS,
                                    szConnectOut,
                                    (SQL_MAX_MESSAGE_LENGTH - 1),
                                    &iConnectOutLen,
                                    SQL_DRIVER_NOPROMPT);
    return(iError);
}
```

Listing 51.2. This Visual Basic function establishes a connection to a data source.

```
' include these prototypes in the module:
Declare Function SQLAllocEnv
                Lib "odbc.dll" (hEnv As Long) As Integer
Declare Function SQLAllocConnect
                Lib "odbc.dll" (ByVal hEnv As Long,
                                hDBc As Long) As Integer
Declare Function SQLDriverConnect
                Lib "odbc.dll" (ByVal hDBc As Long,
                                ByVal hWnd As Integer,
                                ByVal szCSin As String,
                                ByVal iCSinLen As Integer,
                                ByVal szCSOut As String,
                                ByVal iCSOutMaxLen As Integer,
                                iCSOutLen As Integer,
                                ByVal iDriverComplete As Integer)
                                As Integer


' also define these constants:
Global Const SQL_SUCCESS = 0
Global Const SQL_SUCCESS_WITH_INFO = 1
Global Const SQL_STILL_EXECUTING = 2
Global Const SQL_NEED_DATA = 99
Global Const SQL_NO_DATA_FOUND = 100
Global Const SQL_ERROR = -1
Global Const SQL_INVALID_HANDLE = -2

Global Const SQL_NTS = -3

Global Const SQL_DRIVER_NOPROMPT = 0

Global Const SQL_MAX_MESSAGE_LENGTH = 512


Function ConnectToDataSource(hEnv As Long, hDBc As Long) As Integer

    Dim     szConnect As String
    Dim     szConnectOut As String
```

continues

Listing 51.2. continued

```
    Dim    iConnectOutLen As Integer
    Dim    iError As Integer

    szConnectOut = Space$(SQL_MAX_MESSAGE_LENGTH)

    szConnect = "DSN=ORACLE;UID=scotty;PWD=tiger;"

    iError = SQLAllocEnv(hEnv)

    If (iError = SQL_SUCCESS) Then
        iError = SQLAllocConnect(hEnv, hDBc)
    End If
    If (iError = SQL_SUCCESS) Then
        iError = SQLDriverConnect(hDBc, 0, szConnect, SQL_NTS,           szConnectOut,
                            (SQL_MAX_MESSAGE_LENGTH - 1),
                            iConnectOutLen,
                            SQL_DRIVER_NOPROMPT)
    End If

    ConnectToDataSource = iError

End Function
```

Although the preceding examples might be somewhat oversimplified, they should be sufficient to illustrate the steps necessary to connect to a data source using the ODBC API. For clarification of the data types and constants used in the examples, consult the ODBC.H header file included in the Microsoft ODBC SDK.

Setting Connection Options

After you allocate a connection, options can be set to control the behavior of statements processed by the connection, using SQLSetConnectOption. There are numerous parameters available, the most significant of which is the SQL_AUTOCOMMIT option. By default, this option is enabled, which means that transactions are committed as sent, with no possibility of rollback. This can be very dangerous if the application uses multiple statements to process one logical transaction. For DBMSs that do not support stored procedures and triggers, this situation is nearly unavoidable. The function examples in Listing 51.3 demonstrates the ODBC API call to set a connection option.

Listing 51.3. This C function disables the AUTOCOMMIT option for a connection.

```
/* not part of ODBC.H */
enum ConnectOptionValues
{
    OFF,
    ON
);

int DisableAutoCommit(
```

```
HDBC hDBc)      /* connection handle created using SQLAllocConnect */
{
    RETCODE iError;

    iError = SQLSetConnectOption(hDBc, SQL_AUTOCOMMIT, OFF);

    return(iError);
}
```

Other connection options enable connections to be made read-only, to specify a translation DLL, to specify a trace file for debugging, and to set transaction isolation levels. In addition, SQLSetConnectOption can be called using any of the SQLSetStatementOption parameters. In this case, the option applies not to a specific statement handle, but to all statement handles processed by the connection.

Applying SQL Transactions

Transaction control through ODBC is dependent on SQL_AUTOCOMMIT being set to OFF, as described in the previous section. Before applying SQL, the application must call SQLAllocStmt to create a statement handle. After allocating a statement handle, the application can then apply SQL using either prepared, or direct execution.

Prepared execution should be used when the statement to be processed is complex and will be called repeatedly. Under the prepared execution method, the statement is compiled and the access plan is bound before the SQL is executed. For each subsequent execution of the statement, the driver sends only an access plan identifier, instead of the entire statement, to the server. To implement prepared execution, the application calls SQLPrepare, passing an allocated statement handle, the SQL statement, and the length of the SQL statement. The application can then reuse the statement handle and the associated SQL statement using SQLExecute. The SQL statement can be parameterized, using ? as a placeholder for a parameter. Parameter values can be set with each execution through calls to SQLSetParam. The arguments to SQLSetParam are as follows:

- The statement handle for which the SQL will be executed.
- The number of the parameter to be set (position, starting at 1, within the prepared statement).
- The C data type of the parameter.
- The ODBC SQL data type of the parameter.
- The precision of the parameter value.
- The scale of the parameter value.
- A pointer to storage containing the parameter value.
- A pointer to storage that contains the length of the parameter value. (This might always be NULL, provided that any strings are null-terminated.)

> **NOTE**
>
> For full descriptions of C data types, ODBC SQL data types, and their corresponding precisions and scales, refer to the Microsoft ODBC SDK documentation.

If a statement will be executed only once or is fairly simple, direct execution may be preferable. It requires fewer functions calls, so it is easier to implement. It should also be faster than the prepared method for the first execution of a statement. Direct execution requires only a single call to SQLExecDirect, passing an allocated statement handle, the SQL string, and the length of the SQL string.

Regardless of the type of execution used, the application should call SQLTransact to commit or roll back transactions based on the return code of the call to SQLExecute or SQLExecDirect. If SQL_AUTOCOMMIT is set to OFF and the application calls SQLTransact with SQL_ROLLBACK, all statements processed by the connection since the last commit will be rolled back. The statement handle can then be freed using SQLFreeStmt. If the statement handle is not freed, it is available to be reused or overwritten. The second parameter to SQLFreeStmt is an integer constant used to close an open cursor, release buffers for parameters and bound columns, or free all resources associated with the statement (invalidating the handle).

Listings 51.4 and 51.5 demonstrate how an application can insert values into a table, using either the prepared or the direct execution method.

Listing 51.4. This C function inserts records into a table using prepared execution.

```
/* structure containing company information */
typedef struct
{
    long ID;
    char *Company;
    char *Notes;
}
COMPANY;

int InsertCompanyRecords(
HENV    hEnv,           /* pre-allocated environment handle */
HDBC    hDBc,           /* pre-allocated connection handle  */
COMPANY *Companies,     /* pointer to an array of COMPANYs   */
int     iNumCompanies)  /* number of COMPANYs in the array */
{
    RETCODE iError;
    int     i;
    HSTMT   hStmt;

    iError = SQLAllocStmt(hDBc, &hStmt);

    if (iError == SQL_SUCCESS)
        iError = SQLPrepare(hStmt,
```

```
                              "INSERT INTO COMPANY VALUES (
                              CompanyIDs.NextVal, ?, ?) \0",
                              SQL_NTS);

    if (iError == SQL_SUCCESS)
    {
        for (i = 0; i < iNumCompanies; i++)
        {
            SQLSetParam(hStmt, 1, SQL_C_CHAR, SQL_CHAR,
                        strlen(Companies[i].Company), 0,
                        Companies[i].Company, NULL);
            SQLSetParam(hStmt, 2, SQL_C_CHAR, SQL_C_CHAR,
                        strlen(Companies[i].Notes), 0,
                        Companies[i].Notes, NULL);

            iError = SQLExecute(hStmt);

            if (iError != SQL_SUCCESS)
                break;
        }
    }

    if (iError == SQL_SUCCESS)
        iError = SQLTransact(hEnv, hDBc, SQL_COMMIT);
    else
        iError = SQLTransact(hEnv, hDBc, SQL_ROLLBACK);

    if (iError == SQL_SUCCESS)
        iError = SQLFreeStmt(hStmt, SQL_DROP);

    return(iError);
}
```

Listing 51.5. This Visual Basic function inserts records into a table using direct execution.

```
' include these prototypes in the module:
Declare Function SQLAllocStmt Lib "odbc.dll" (ByVal hStmt As Long)
                As Integer
Declare Function SQLExecDirect Lib "odbc.dll" (ByVal hStmt As Long,
                ByVal szSQL As String, ByVal iSQLLen As Long)
                As Integer
Declare Function SQLFreeStmt Lib "odbc.dll" (ByVal hStmt As Long
                ByVal iOption As Integer) As Integer
Declare Function SQLTransact Lib "odbc.dll" (ByVal hEnv As Long,
                ByVal hDBc As Long, ByVal iType As Integer)
                As Integer

' also define these constants:
Global Const SQL_CHAR = 1
Global Const SQL_INTEGER = 4

Global Const SQL_C_CHAR = 0
Global Const SQL_C_LONG = 1
```

continues

Listing 51.5. continued

```
Global Const SQL_COMMIT = 0
Global Const SQL_ROLLBACK = 1

Global Const SQL_CLOSE = 0
Global Const SQL_DROP = 1
Global Const SQL_UNBIND = 2
Global Const SQL_RESET_PARAMS = 3

Type COMPANY
    Dim ID      As Long
    Dim Company As String
    Dim Notes   As String
End Type

Function InsertCompanyRecords(ByVal hEnv As Long,
        ByVal hDBc As Long, Companies() As COMPANY,
        ByVal iNumCompanies As Integer) As Integer

    Dim iError As Integer
    Dim i      As Integer
    Dim hStmt  As Long
    Dim szSQL  As String

    iError = SQLAllocStmt(hDBc, hStmt)

    If (iError = SQL_SUCCESS) Then
        For i = 0 To (iNumCompanies - 1)
            szSQL = "INSERT INTO COMPANY VALUES ("
            szSQL = szSQL & "CompanyIDs.NextVal, '"
            szSQL = szSQL & Companies(i).Company & "', '"
            szSQL = szSQL & Companies(i).Notes & "')"

            iError = SQLExecDirect(hStmt, szSQL, SQL_NTS)

            If (iError <> SQL_SUCCESS) Then
                Exit For
            End If
        Next i
    End If

    If (iError = SQL_SUCCESS) Then
        iError = SQLTransact(hEnv, hDBc, SQL_COMMIT)
    Else
        iError = SQLTransact(hEnv, hDBc, SQL_ROLLBACK)
    End If

    If (iError = SQL_SUCCESS) Then
        iError = SQLFreeStmt(hStmt, SQL_DROP)
    End If

    InsertCompanyRecords = iError

End Function
```

There are several variations on the prepared execution method. These include setting multiple values for each parameter, and providing parameter values after the call to SQLExecute. For information on these methods, consult the ODBC SDK documentation for the SQLParamData and SQLPutData functions.

Retrieving Result Sets

The prepared execution and direct execution methods also apply to SQL SELECT statements. The additional methods available to retrieve results through ODBC, however, are almost too numerous to mention. SQLSetStmtOption can be used to enable asynchronous processing, which allows single-threaded environments such as Windows 3.x to process multiple statements simultaneously. When used with SQLSetScrollOptions, SQLSetStmtOption can enable multiple rows to be fetched with a single call to SQLExtendedFetch. SQLSetScrollOptions and SQLExtendedFetch can also be used to create cursors that scroll in both directions; and when used with SQLSetPos, the record pointer can be placed at a specific row in the result set.

Unfortunately, these extended functions are not part of the core ODBC standard and are currently unsupported by the Oracle ODBC driver. Although third-party driver vendors might supply some of these functions, the code examples in this section will focus on bound and unbound fetches using prepared and direct execution. These examples use core functions and level 1 extensions, all of which are supported by the current Oracle ODBC driver available from Oracle Corporation.

Although the SQL to retrieve result sets can be executed in exactly the same manner as SQL to-process transactions, the application must take additional steps to bind result set columns to application variables. Columns may be prebound using SQLBindCol, or bound after execution, using SQLGetData.

In order to bind columns prior to execution, SQLBindCol must be called once for each column to be bound. The arguments to SQLBindCol are somewhat similar to those for SQLSetParam, as enumerated here:

- The statement handle for the executed SQL.
- The number of the column to be bound (position, starting at 1, within the result set).
- The C data type of the variable to be bound.
- A pointer to storage allocated for the variable.
- The maximum length of the variable, in bytes.
- A pointer for storage to receive the full length of the column in the result set. This can be used to determine if data was truncated.

Alternatively, the application can bind variables to result set columns after execution, using SQLGetData. Its arguments are identical to those for SQLBindCol. The difference between these two methods is essentially a matter of when the application variables are bound to result set columns.

> **TIP**
>
> SQLDescribeCol can be called prior to SQLGetData to obtain information about a column, including its name, data type, and length. This information can be used to ensure that no data is truncated, among other things. For example, when used with SQLNumResultCols, a result set generated by a SQL statement such as
>
> SELECT * FROM *view_name*
>
> can be completely bound to application variables dynamically at run-time.

Regardless of when the columns are bound to variables, the application calls SQLFetch, with the statement handle as the only argument. This positions the cursor at the next row in the result set. If columns are prebound, data is placed in variables at this time. Otherwise, the call to SQLFetch simply scrolls the cursor one row forward.

> **TIP**
>
> An application can use SQLFetch with SQLGetData to locate a specific row or set of rows in the result set, based on the value of one or more columns. Although this can be accomplished with bound columns, it should be more efficient to use SQLGetData to do comparisons on a single column when there are many rows and columns in the result set.

The code examples in Listings 51.6 and 51.7 demonstrate the fetching of bound and unbound columns, using direct execution.

Listing 51.6. This C function retrieves the first record in a result set using column-wise binding.

```
int GetCompanyInfo(
HENV    hEnv,         /* pre-allocated environment handle */
HDBC    hDBc,         /* pre-allocated connection handle  */
COMPANY *Company,     /* pointer to a  COMPANY            */
char    *szName)      /* Company Name to find            */
{
    RETCODE iError;
    HSTMT   hStmt;
    long    tempID;
    long    iLenOut1, iLenOut2, iLenOut3;
    char    tempName[80];
```

```
char    tempNotes[255];
char    szSQL[255];

iError = SQLAllocStmt(hDBc, &hStmt);

if (iError == SQL_SUCCESS)
{
    sprintf (szSQL,
            "SELECT ID, Company, Notes FROM Company WHERE
            Company LIKE '%");
    strcat(szSQL, szName);
    strcat(szSQL, "%'");

    iError = SQLExecDirect(hStmt, szSQL, SQL_NTS);

    if (iError == SQL_SUCCESS)
    {
        iError = SQLBindCol(hStmt, 1, SQL_C_LONG, &tempID, 0
                        , &iLenOut1);
        iError = SQLBindCol(hStmt, 2, SQL_C_CHAR, tempName
                        , 80, &iLenOut2);
        iError = SQLBindCol(hStmt, 3, SQL_C_CHAR, tempNotes
                        , 255, &iLenOut3);

        iError = SQLFetch(hStmt);

        if (iError >= SQL_SUCCESS)
        {
            Company->ID = tempID;
            Company->Company = strdup(tempName);
            Company->Notes = strdup(tempNotes);
        }
    }

    SQLFreeStmt(hStmt, SQL_CLOSE);
    SQLFreeStmt(hStmt, SQL_DROP);
}

return(iError);
}
```

Listing 51.7. This Visual Basic function retrieves multiple records with unbound columns.

```
' include these prototypes in the module:
Declare Function SQLFetch Lib "odbc.dll" (ByVal hStmt As Long)
            As Integer

Declare Function SQLGetData Lib "odbc.dll" (ByVal hStmt As Long,
            ByVal iColNum As Integer,
            ByVal iDataType As Integer, ByVal hBuffer As Any,
            ByVal iBuffLen As Long, iLenOut As Long)
            As Integer
```

continues

Listing 51.7. continued

```
Function GetCompanies (ByVal hDBc As Long, Companies() As Company,
                        iNumCoOut As Integer) As Integer

    Dim iError    As Integer
    Dim hStmt     As Long
    Dim szSQL     As String
    Dim iOut1     As Long
    Dim iOut2     As Long
    Dim iTemp     As Integer

    iNumCoOut = 0
    ReDim Companies(iNumCoOut)

    iError = SQLAllocStmt(hDBc, hStmt)

    If (iError = SQL_SUCCESS) Then
        szSQL = "SELECT COMPANY, NOTES FROM COMPANY ORDER BY 2"

        iError = SQLExecDirect(hStmt, szSQL, SQL_NTS)

        If (iError = SQL_SUCCESS) Then

            While (iError >= SQL_SUCCESS)
                ReDim Preserve Companies(iNumCoOut)
                iError = SQLFetch(hStmt)

                iError = SQLGetData(hStmt, 1, SQL_C_CHAR,
                Companies(iNumCoOut).Company,
                        80, iOut1)

iError = SQLGetData(hStmt, 2, SQL_C_CHAR,
                        Companies(iNumCoOut).Notes, 255, iOut2)

                If (iError >= SQL_SUCCESS) Then
                    iNumCoOut = iNumCoOut + 1
                End If
            Wend
        End If

    End If

    iTemp = SQLFreeStmt(hStmt, SQL_CLOSE)
    iTemp = SQLFreeStmt(hStmt, SQL_DROP)

    GetCompanies = iError

End Function
```

The examples in Listings 51.6 and 51.7 also demonstrate dynamic SQL building by the application. Although prepared execution could be used to parameterize the SQL statements, prepared execution is not always the best choice for dynamic SQL. When retrieving result sets, the SQL is typically not executed repeatedly, and in these cases, direct execution is often preferable.

Handling Errors

The return values of ODBC functions should always be checked to determine whether an error has occurred. The return code SQL_SUCCESS is defined as 0. Error codes are defined as negative numbers, whereas positive numbers are used to indicate that additional information is required or is being provided by the driver. How these error and informational return codes are handled within a program is entirely application-specific. The ODBC API provides a function to retrieve standard ODBC error codes, DBMS-specific error codes, and error and informational text from the driver. This function, SQLError, has the following arguments:

- The environment handle in which the error occurred.
- The connection handle in which the error occurred.
- The statement handle in which the error occurred.
- A pointer to storage to receive a null-terminated string containing SQL state information. This will inform the application that data was truncated, among other things.
- A pointer to storage for a long integer that will receive the DBMS's native error code.
- A pointer to storage that will receive error text.
- A pointer to storage that will receive the length of error text, in bytes. This can be used to determine whether error text was truncated.

> **NOTE**
>
> The error code SQL_INVALID_HANDLE (-2), does not provide additional SQL state or error information. It indicates that an environment, connection, or statement handle was invalid. These errors are commonly the result of indirection or scope problems within the application.

The code example in Listing 51.8 displays and retrieves SQL state and/or error text and displays it to the user.

Listing 51.8. This Visual Basic function displays ODBC SQL states and error messages.

```
' include this prototype in the module:
Declare Function SQLError Lib "odbc.dll" (ByVal hEnv As Long,
            ByVal hDBc As Long, ByVal hStmt As Long,
            ByVal szSQLState As String, iNativeError As Long,
            ByVal szBuffer As String,
            ByVal iBufLen As Integer, iLenOut As Integer)
            As Integer

Sub ODBCError (ByVal hEnv As Long, ByVal hDBc As Long,
            ByVal hStmt As Long)
```

continues

Listing 51.8. continued

```
    Dim iError           As Integer
    Dim szSQLState       As String * 10
    Dim iNativeError     As Long
    Dim szErrorMsg       As String * 511
    Dim iMsgLength       As Integer
    Dim szODBCMsg        As String

    iError = SQLError(hEnv, hDBc, hStmt, szSQLState, iNativeError,
            szErrorMsg, SQL_MAX_MESSAGE_LENGTH - 1, iMsgLength)

    If (iError = 0) Then
     szODBCMsg = Left(szErrorMsg, iMsgLength)
     Beep
     MsgBox "ODBC Error: " & szODBCMsg
    Else
     Beep
     MsgBox "Undetermined ODBC Error."
    End If

End Sub
```

The error and informational data may be stored in the environment handle, the connection handle, or the statement handle, depending on the nature of the error or information. The application might supply NULL arguments for two of the three handles to retrieve information specific to the supplied handle. This error information is stored until the handle is reused.

Calling Stored Procedures and Functions

Support for stored procedures and functions is highly DBMS-specific. Oracle-stored procedures and functions are accessible through ODBC in much the same way as embedded SQL. In most cases, it is preferable to use stored procedures or functions to process inserts, updates, and deletes. This simplifies client-side development and allows for greater control over transactions by allowing database objects to handle errors, and to commit or rollback work, as needed.

Oracle-stored procedures and functions can be executed using either the prepared or direct execution methods, with the following SQL syntax:

```
procedures: {call proc_name('an example of direct execution', 'param2')}
functions:  {?=call proc_name('an example of prepared execution', ?, ?)}
```

Note that the entire statement must be enclosed in curly braces, and that when calling functions, a placeholder must be supplied for the return value. (Use prepared execution when calling functions.)

Listings 51.9 and 51.10 demonstrate the prepared and direct execution methods for calling Oracle procedures.

Listing 51.9. This C function inserts records into a table using an Oracle-stored procedure with prepared execution.

```c
int InsertCompanySP(
HENV     hEnv,           /* pre-allocated environment handle */
HDBC     hDBc,           /* pre-allocated connection handle  */
COMPANY *Companies,      /* pointer to an array of COMPANYs   */
int      iNumCompanies)  /* number of COMPANYs in the array  */
{
    RETCODE iError;
    int     i;
    HSTMT   hStmt;

    iError = SQLAllocStmt(hDBc, &hStmt);

    if (iError == SQL_SUCCESS)
        iError = SQLPrepare(hStmt,
                            "{call sp_insert_company(?, ?)}\0",
                            SQL_NTS);
    {
        if (iError == SQL_SUCCESS)
        {
            for (i = 0; i < iNumCompanies; I++)
            {
                SQLSetParam(hStmt, 1, SQL_C_CHAR, SQL_CHAR,
strlen(Companies[i].Company), 0,
                            Companies[i].Company, NULL);
                SQLSetParam(hStmt, 2, SQL_C_CHAR, SQL_C_CHAR,
                            strlen(Companies[i].Notes), 0,
                            Companies[i].Notes, NULL);

                iError = SQLExecute(hStmt);

                if (iError != SQL_SUCCESS)
                    break;
            }
        }

        iError = SQLFreeStmt(hStmt, SQL_DROP);
    }

    return(iError);
}
```

Listing 51.10. This Visual Basic function inserts records into a table using an Oracle-stored procedure with direct execution.

```vb
Function InsertCompanySP (ByVal hEnv As Long, ByVal hDBc As Long,
        Companies() As Company, ByVal iNumCompanies As Integer)
        As Integer

    Dim iError      As Integer
    Dim iTemp       As Integer
    Dim i           As Integer
```

continues

Listing 51.10. continued

```
Dim hStmt        As Long
Dim szSQL        As String
Dim szCompany    As String
Dim szNotes      As String

iError = SQLAllocStmt(hDBc, hStmt)

If (iError = SQL_SUCCESS) Then
    For i = 0 To (iNumCompanies - 1)
        szSQL = "{CALL sp_insert_company('"
        szSQL = szSQL & Companies(i).Company & "', '"
        szSQL = szSQL & Companies(i).Notes & "')}"

        iError = SQLExecDirect(hStmt, szSQL, SQL_NTS)

        If (iError <> SQL_SUCCESS) Then
            Call ODBCError(hEnv, hDBc, hStmt)
            Exit For
        End If
    Next I

    iTemp = SQLFreeStmt(hStmt, SQL_DROP)

End If


    InsertCompanySP = iError

End Function
```

> **NOTE**
>
> The application might not have to call SQLTransact when accessing stored procedures and functions. In most cases, it is the stored objects that should handle commits and rollbacks internally.

Currently, support for stored procedures and functions does not extend to packaged objects, even if they are declared publicly. In order to call a packaged procedure or function, an external stub must be created. ODBC can then access the packaged object through an external function, which calls into the package. This solution is clearly less than ideal, and provides somewhat of a deterrent to using packages with ODBC applications. This should not, however, prevent an application from using procedures and functions to handle transaction-based SQL. In terms of reliability and performance, procedures and functions are typically better suited to this task than embedded SQL when using ODBC.

Disconnecting and Freeing Resources

The application should free all ODBC resources and cleanly disconnect before exiting. First, all statement handles should be freed by calling SQLFreeStmt.

Next, the application should call SQLDisconnect, passing the active connection handle. Then, the application should call SQLFreeConnect, passing the connection handle as the argument. Finally, the application should use SQLFreeEnv to free all resources allocated for the environment handle.

The order in which these functions are called is very important. All statement handles for a connection should be freed prior to passing the connection handle to SQLDisconnect. Each connection handle for an environment should be disconnected and freed prior to passing the environment handle to SQLFreeEnv. Freeing allocated memory and disconnecting in the proper order ensures that the connection will not remain active on the server. Listing 51.11 illustrates these steps.

Listing 51.11. This C function disconnects from the data source and frees all resources allocated to the connection and environment handles.

```
int Disconnect(
HENV hEnv,
HDBC hDBc)
{
    int iRetVal;

    iRetVal = SQLDisconnect(hDBc);

    if (iRetVal != SQL_SUCCESS)
        ReportError(hEnv, hDBc, SQL_NULL_HSTMT);

    iRetVal = SQLFreeConnect(hDBc);

    if (iRetVal != SQL_SUCCESS)
        ReportError(hEnv, hDBc, SQL_NULL_HSTMT);

    iRetVal = SQLFreeEnv(hEnv);

    return(iRetVal);
}
```

The code example in Listing 51.11 assumes that all statement handles have been freed. SQL_DROP should be passed as the second parameter to SQLFreeStmt when an application is exiting to ensure that all resources are freed.

Debugging ODBC Applications

The ODBC API provides the developer with most of the tools needed to debug an ODBC application. The SQLError function, for example, is arguably more useful in debugging mode than in production code. The application can include debug code to display information from SQLError after every call to the ODBC API that results in a return value other than SQL_SUCESS. This is especially helpful in the initial phases of development, because it assists not only in locating programming bugs but also in determining what errors are likely to occur in a production environment. Steps should be taken to simplify the task of invalidating or removing debug code when it is no longer needed. An easy way to do this is to define a constant in the application and call it DEBUG_MODE, for example. The constant can be used to conditionally branch to debug code or to ignore it, depending on the value of the constant. By simply changing the value of the constant, the developer can then enable or disable debug code. This also simplifies the process of removing this code at a later date, by providing a single value to search for that will exist wherever debug code exists.

The ODBC API also gives the developer the ability to trace ODBC function calls and parameters. The application can call SQLSetConnectOption to enable tracing and to specify a trace file. Alternatively, the developer can enable tracing for all connections to a data source using the ODBC Administration applet. Refer to the Data Sources dialog in Figure 51.2. Clicking the Options button on this dialog brings up the ODBC Options dialog, which lets the user enable tracing for a data source and specify a log file. Tracing is simply logging ODBC function calls and arguments, providing a history of the application's interaction with ODBC.

Debugging time can be minimized by some investigation prior to design and development. Select a driver and determine what functions it supports before writing any code. When developing ODBC applications, never assume that a level 1 or level 2 extension will be supported by the driver. Purchase a utility (or write one yourself) that queries the driver for the functions that it supports. SQLGetFunctions can be used to accomplish this task. It accepts a connection handle, an integer constant specifying the function, and a pointer to storage to receive an integer value of TRUE (a nonzero value) if the function is supported, or FALSE (0) if it is not supported. This information is critical to the design of most applications. However, in some cases, it is desirable to use SQLGetFunctions at runtime to determine how the application will interact with the database.

Limitations of ODBC

One of the primary goals of the ODBC standard is to provide a DBMS-independent standard interface to relational databases. This, in turn, should enable the development of database-independent client applications. In theory, an application can be developed using embedded

SQL that will work regardless of the DBMS being accessed, whether it is Oracle, Sybase, DB2, or another DBMS. The primary limitation to this approach is that the standard ODBC SQL syntax reduces the language to the least common denominator. Outer join syntax, for example, is not currently supported by the ODBC standard.

In many cases, using ODBC precludes the use of the most powerful features of the database. When accessing Oracle through ODBC, packaged constructs are completely unavailable, and support for Oracle functions is awkward, at best. If outer joins are needed, they must be accomplished through the creation of views at design-time, which is a hindrance to applications requiring the construction of dynamic SQL.

Using ODBC might also demand a sacrifice in terms of performance. Although performance is not always sacrificed when using ODBC, most high-performance drivers are fairly expensive third-party products that are licensed on a per-workstation basis. Typically, a custom interface to the DBMS-specific network software can provide greater performance and flexibility. A custom interface to SQL*Net, however, would require additional time to design and develop. Because the ODBC standard is so widely supported and its API is relatively easy to use, minor deficiencies in performance can often be accepted in favor of shorter development cycles and more portable code.

Summary

Despite its limitations, ODBC is one of the most popular means of communicating with a database and has become the *de facto* standard for Microsoft Windows client development. Many of the Windows development tools provide interfaces that completely abstract the underlying API from the developer, making ODBC extremely easy to use. Regardless of the development tools used or the level of abstraction, a thorough understanding of the API is invaluable in making the most of an ODBC application. When greater control is required or when performance is an issue, there is no substitute for using the API directly.

Parallel Processing

52

by Advanced Information Systems, Inc.

In recent years, Multi-Processors (commonly referred to as MPs), Symmetrical Multi-Processors (SMPs), and Massively Parallel Processors (MPPs) have been sweeping the marketplace and gaining ground to offload vast amounts of data processing. This processing is performed in "parallel" among the available Central Processing Units (CPUs). In this chapter, I discuss how to choose, leverage, optimize, and convert to an Oracle parallel processing platform.

Understanding the Requirements for Parallel Processing

The following configurations describe which features, functions, and benefits are available through parallel processing:

Symmetrical Multiple Processors are usually a 1- to 49-processor system configuration having limited scalability. This is due to greater I/O per CPU as additional processors are added.

In *Parallel Processors*, the database query is divided into logical components that can be run in parallel on MP servers. Oracle7 Parallel Query uses this feature.

Massively Parallel Processors involve eight or more processors, as in the nCUBE 2 and 3 models with 65,536 parallel processors available.

Tightly coupled servers are MP servers in which all CPUs address shared memory or distributed memory addressing other processors. Tightly coupled servers provide very scalable operation without increased CPU I/O overhead.

Loosely coupled servers are MP servers that contain all CPUs in a multiple server configuration, such as a DEC VAX or ALPHA cluster.

If the system you develop performs as planned but is modified or used by more users than originally designed for, you can add an additional processor and RAM for about $10,000. This assumes, of course, that your file server selection has a multi-processor upgrade path.

MP file servers feature a preconfigured, fixed number of processors and cannot be expanded without an expense nearly equal to the original file server purchase price. The advantage of an MP system is that the fixed number of processors are optimized to run in parallel with minimal parallel processing CPU overhead.

Symmetrical Multi-Processors enable the file server to incorporate additional processors to be included as needed. Scalability does have its drawbacks. As more processors are added to the system, the law of diminishing returns applies. Each additional CPU will deliver less processing power available to the combined CPU parallel processing capability.

Massively Parallel Processors incorporate an initially expensive architecture that delivers cheaper overall performance. As more processors are added, performance increases without the loss of I/O associated with scalability in SMP systems.

Operating System Impact in Parallel Processing

Some operating systems are more scalable than others. As a system accumulates processors, additional tasks are required of the hardware, operating system, and Distributed Lock Manager (DLM) for that platform. The DLM facilitates processor availability for tasks to be scheduled between processors, on both local and remote clustered file server configurations.

The DEC Alpha 2100 is exemplary in demonstrating that a great file server is only as great as its chosen operating system.

A DEC Alpha 2100 file server model EV5/275 (MHz) running MS-NT will only achieve the best processing results with no more than three processors, and in fact will actually achieve slower overall results as additional processors are added!

That very same DEC Alpha file server model 2100 EV5/275 running at 275 MHz and running UNIX will continue to achieve the best processing results, regardless of how many processors are added to the system. In fact, the first four processors each add well over 90 percent additional throughput in a UNIX configuration.

This compares with only an additional 50 percent throughput benefit received for the second MS-NT processor added to the same exact system, operating systems being the only difference between these two examples.

New World Processing

Parallel processing was previously performed only by mainframes, which currently cost an average of $6 to 28 million to operate for five years versus any faster 32-bit or 64-bit, 30GB RAID5 SMP file server. Today, turnkey conversions can be done by AIS for less than $500,000, including fault-tolerant hardware, database software, application software, and a legacy conversion of the older application onto the new client/server platform.

The hardware costs for MP are approximately 1/32 that of the traditional mainframe hardware cost, while delivering very high numbers of transactions per second (TPS). Due to very high mainframe costs, price/performance ratios are not available, as illustrated by the lack of audited benchmarks from the mainframe arena.

Mainframe Benchmarks

The best public TPC benchmark of late is that of a $27,913,514.00, ES/9000 model 511 TPF mainframe running the TPF 3.1 database at 3,504.93 TPS/A v1.2. The test results report that this mainframe's total five-year system cost, including software, will equate to $7,964.00 per transaction (TPC/A).

This compares with MP industry price/performance trends of 147 to 713 TPC/A v1.2 for any similar UNIX platform. The best UNIX systems costs vary from $1,000.00 to $5,941.00 per TPC/A.

These tests, like all TPC benchmarks, also include a complete five-year system cost including maintenance and all software all totaling from between $20,000.00 to $4,239,200.00 complete.

Leveraging Parallel Processing Platforms

How does Oracle7 leverage these newer parallel processing platforms? The Oracle7 Enterprise Edition has some very "advanced" features. The major enhanced features lacking in the Oracle7 Workgroup Server that the Enterprise Edition leverages for parallel processing are the following options:

- Parallel Query Option
- Parallel Server Option
- Distributed Database Option
- Data Replication Option
- 64-bit Option

The *Parallel Query Option* distributes queries among the available processors to complete complex tasks much more quickly than a single CPU can process. Even a full table scan can be distributed among separate CPUs on the same file server with this feature. Oracle Parallel Query employs "Query Slaves" that actually provide the scheduling of these Parallel job streams. These Parallel features are developed by Oracle Corporation, in conjunction with the Parallel Platform designers from each of the hardware vendors, and they are transparent to the Oracle programmers and users! Oracle7.1 delivers the Parallel Query Option and leverages MP by providing sophisticated high-speed record latching. This distributes parts of queries among the available processors for significant throughput advantages. The Parallel Query option is also transparent to the DBA, as the Oracle7.1 software and host operating system automatically distribute these transactions among any MP, SMP, PP, or MPP system.

The *Parallel Server Option* creates a real-time copy of the Oracle instance and database on one or more file servers, or nodes on a network. This serves a dual purpose, as it can be used to do both of the following:

1. Balance the user load proportionally between separate file servers on a network
2. Enable an on- or off-site hot standby, real-time updated copy of the Oracle RDBMS

Balancing of the client/server user load proportionally between parallel server file servers and the associated parallel instances on a network can be achieved in three ways.

In the first method, as a PC windows client requests a connection from the client to the server, SQL*Net 2.2 is invoked and calls the /windows/oracle.ini variable:

```
LOCAL=TNS:your_connect_string or "alias"
```

The search path next defaults to your user's ora_home/network/admin directory to locate the user's tnsnames.ora file in search of your_connect_string or "alias." If half of the users have been defaulted to host1 and the other users were defaulted to host2, a proportional balance is achieved.

A second method of parallel load balancing is more difficult to accomplish. This balance is achieved at the TCP/IP or other protocol level by programming an automated switch sequence, triggered by a predetermined user limit.

When this high-water user connection mark is reached, users are shuttled to the next host specified in the program. If the primary host is unavailable, the secondary host is the recipient of all users requesting connections.

This fault-tolerant, fail-over mechanism can also be achieved by another method, enabling fault tolerance in an on- or off-site hot standby. This is accomplished through the parallel server's real-time updated copy of the Oracle RDBMS and is achieved through the tnsnames.ora file as well.

In the address list section of the tnsnames.ora file shown following, a second address entry specifies a redundant host name or Internet Protocol address (IP).

If the primary host database instance and SQL*Net listener are unavailable, then the second address connection is made to that second host's database listener, database, and associated database instance.

The Oracle "SID" or instance is the portion of the database cached in real memory, for that host database file server.

```
################
# Filename......: tnsnames.ora
# Name.........: LOCAL_REGION
# Date.........: 23-SEP-95 22:22:39
################
your_connect_string_is_this=
  (DESCRIPTION =
    (ADDRESS_LIST =
        (ADDRESS =
        (PROTOCOL = TCP)
          (Host = VENUS)
/*(The above host is the Primary host,*/
/*and is only used if the primary SID is available)*/
        (Port = 1521)
        )
        (ADDRESS =          <(These four lines are
        (PROTOCOL = TCP)    < the secondary host
        (Host = URANUS)     < description and are only used
        (Port = 1521)       < if the primary SID is unavailable)
        )
    )
    (CONNECT_DATA =
      (SID =ORAC)
```

```
/*(This should be a single instance name or "SID",*/
/*shared by all Parallel Server instances)*/
    )
  )
```

In the preceding scenario, all of the fault tolerance is transparent to the user. The user was never required to enter a connect string or to change a connect string.

If a tool requests that an Oracle connect string be entered by the user, the user can simply press Enter on the keyboard to substitute the connect string or alias from the manually set LOCAL=TNS:your_connect_string or "alias" line in the /windows/oracle.ini file.

This will then facilitate the user's connection to the first available Oracle database through that database's already running listener process.

The Oracle parallel server option always synchronizes transactions between the instances in memory and the database or databases. This assures transaction integrity in that all inserts, updates, and deletes committed on one parallel instance are immediately available to all users of any other parallel instance. These transactions can be applied to any parallel server instance on any other cluster or network node.

Parallel Server should not be confused with Parallel Processing, in that it can be used with the following:

■ Single or multiple processor configurations

■ Single file server configurations

■ Clusters of one or more file servers

Such a file server configuration should have at least 16MB of RAM for each Oracle instance, simultaneously required to be resident in memory.

The *Distributed Database Option* joins two or more remote databases as one database. The remote database location and/or server name are transparent to the users.

The *Data Replication Option* is useful when isolated information, from a laptop or local regional office, is to be duplicated and updated separately from the master database.

The Oracle7.2 *64-bit Option* allows for many unlimited and amazing Parallel Processing capabilities, including actual performance increases of up to 107 times faster than 32-bit systems, as well as the ability to leverage the following:

■ Tens of gigabytes of RAM for any Oracle instance

■ Tens of gigabytes of RAM for any Oracle data files that can be cached in memory

■ 32-kilobyte Oracle data blocks for faster parallel reads and writes

■ 64-bit executable code for Oracle7.2

■ 64-bit executable code for both Oracle Pro*C and Pro*COBOL

Comparing Parallel Processing to Mainframes

The following test results provided by the Oracle Corporation illustrate how these newer parallel processing platforms are faster, cheaper, and as fault-tolerant as any very expensive mainframe with terabytes of data.

Test Results

The tests shown in Table 52.1 were performed using maintenance releases 7.1, 7.2, and 7.3 of the Oracle7 server as a demonstration of the performance and scalability improvements engineered into these releases. Due to time constraints, not all of the tests could be run on releases 7.1 and 7.2. Some estimations and extrapolations based on available data were used to fill out the performance matrix.

Displaying time in minutes, the test results illustrate dramatic performance gains for all the major operations involved—summary creation, index builds, and complex queries. Release 7.2 provides a ten-fold improvement in summary creation performance over release 7.1. Index builds and complex query execution are about twice as fast. These performance gains are further extended with release 7.3: summary creation exhibits an amazing twenty-fold improvement over release 7.1. Complex query execution is five times faster and index creation delivers over a three-fold improvement.

Table 52.1. Performance comparison between releases 7.1, 7.2, and 7.3.

Operation	Release 7.1	Release 7.2 Results	Improvement over 7.1	Release 7.3 Results	Improvement over 7.1
Summary creation (6-D cube)	13,400.0**	1320.8	1015%	647.4	2070%
Single key index creation	967.7	398.6	243%	304.3	318%
Concatenated key index creation	1719.6	620.0	277%	389.9	441%
Complex query	149.1	75.4%	198%	29.9	498%

**This number is an estimate. The operation was not run to completion.

Oracle7 Server Scalable Parallel Architecture for Open Data Warehousing

Oracle's scalable parallel database architecture combines the best elements of traditional shared-nothing and shared-disk approaches to provide highly scalable database system performance for open data warehousing on all parallel hardware systems—from tightly coupled Symmetric Multi-Processor systems (SMP) to loosely coupled systems such as clusters and Massively Parallel systems (MPP). This chapter provides an outline of Oracle's parallel database architecture and illustrates the superiority of Oracle's "best-of-both-worlds" architecture over pure shared-nothing database systems in terms of performance, scalability, resource utilization, manageability, availability, and consistency with emerging trends in technology.

The increasing use of information as a key strategic weapon in business decision-making has led to an explosive growth in complex, data-intensive decision support applications in recent years. This growth has been further accelerated by the availability of cost-effective parallel processing systems from open system vendors. This section discusses the common architectural approaches that underlie parallel hardware and database systems.

Parallel Hardware Systems

Parallel hardware systems utilizing inexpensive commodity components have the potential to provide excellent price/performance advantages over traditional mainframe systems in data-intensive decision support applications. Tightly coupled Symmetric Multi-Processor systems (SMP) have been the most widely used parallel hardware systems. These systems utilize multiple processors that share common memory and disk resources and hence are also known as *shared-everything* systems. Primary advantages of SMP systems include simplicity of application development and ease of administration. These systems, however, do not provide any inherent fault-tolerance: the failure of a single critical component such as a CPU could bring the entire system down. Further, they are currently somewhat limited in terms of scalability and growth due to limitations in available system bus bandwidth and operating system software scalability.

Loosely coupled systems such as clusters and Massively Parallel Processing (MPP) systems eliminate some of the drawbacks of SMP systems, providing improved fault tolerance and easy incremental system growth. These systems are made up of multiple nodes, with each node consisting of a single processing unit—a single CPU or an SMP unit, with its own dedicated system memory. In terms of disk sharing, these systems come in a variety of flavors. At one extreme are "shared-nothing" systems where each set of disk devices has physical connectivity only to a single node; at the other end are "shared-disk" cluster systems with each node having direct physical access to all of the disks. There are also hybrid systems where each node has direct physical access to a subset of devices but has logical access, enabled through an operating system abstraction layer, to all disk devices. The level of physical connectivity determines the potential for fault tolerance available on these systems. On true shared-disk systems, for example, it is possible to implement database systems that provide access to all data as long as at least one node is available.

Loosely coupled systems, however, present greater challenges in terms of system administration and application development, as compared to SMP systems. One of the primary requirements for a parallel database system is to hide these complexities, presenting a logical unified view to the users, enabling them to transparently exploit all available resources on a loosely coupled system.

Traditionally, two distinct approaches—shared-nothing and shared-disk—have been used in the implementation of database systems on parallel hardware. Each approach, in its pure form, offers certain unique benefits and tradeoffs. This section provides a conceptual foundation for the central argument in this chapter: a hybrid architecture that combines the strengths of each approach is the most pragmatic real-world solution.

The Shared-Nothing Approach

In a pure shared-nothing architecture, database files are partitioned among the instances running on the nodes of a multi-computer system. As illustrated in Figure 52.1, each instance or node "owns" a subset of the data, and all access to this data is performed exclusively by the owning instance. In other words, a pure shared-nothing system uses a partitioned or restricted access scheme to divide the work among multiple processing nodes. Data ownership by nodes changes relatively infrequently—database reorganization and node failure are the typical reasons for change in ownership.

Parallel execution in a shared-nothing system is directly based upon the data partitioning scheme. Each partition is accessed in parallel by a single process or thread, with no provision for intrapartition parallelism. Conceptually, it is useful to think of a pure shared-nothing system as being very similar to a distributed database. A transaction executing on a given node has to send messages to other nodes that own the data being accessed and coordinate the work done on the other nodes, to perform the required read/write activity. Such message passing is commonly known as *function shipping*.

In principle, this is a very reasonable approach on shared-nothing parallel hardware: The approach is simple and elegant. It employs a software architecture that directly maps to the hardware system and has the potential to provide scalable performance on loosely coupled systems. Function shipping is an efficient execution strategy and typically provides significant performance gains over the alternative data shipping approach. However, as you will see in further detail later, the real-world applicability of a pure shared-nothing database architecture is seriously limited by certain drawbacks inherent to this scheme.

First, the shared-nothing approach is not appropriate for use on shared-everything SMP hardware. The requirement to physically partition data in order to derive the benefits of parallelism is clearly an artificial requirement in a shared-everything SMP system, where every processor has direct, equal access to all the data. Second, the rigid partitioning-based parallel execution strategy employed in the shared-nothing approach often leads to skewed resource utilization. The tight ownership model that prevents intrapartition parallel execution fails to utilize all available processing power in the presence of data or workload skew, delivering suboptimal use of available processing power.

FIGURE 52.1.

A shared-nothing database system.

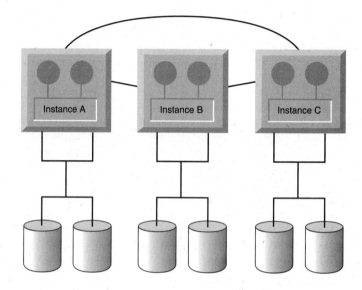

Third, the use of data partitioning as the exclusive basis for parallelism forces a trade-off between manageability and parallel execution performance, often introducing serious administrative complexities.

Finally, shared-nothing systems, due to their use of a rigid restricted access scheme, fail to fully exploit the potential for high fault-tolerance available in clustered systems.

The Shared-Disk Approach

This approach is based on the assumption that every processing node has equal access to all of the disks (data). In a pure shared-disk architecture, database files are logically shared among the nodes of a loosely coupled system with each instance having access to all the data. As illustrated in Figure 52.2, shared-disk access is accomplished either through direct hardware connectivity or by using an operating system abstraction layer that provides a single view of devices on all nodes. Therefore, a transaction running on any instance can directly read or modify any part of the database. Such systems require the use of interinstance communication to synchronize update activities performed from multiple instances.

FIGURE 52.2.

A shared-disk database system.

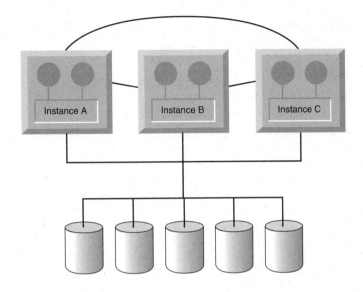

Pure shared-disk is a good approach on clustered systems where equal and direct access to all disks is typically available from every node. A single node variant of the shared-disk scheme also ideally maps to SMP systems. Shared-disk has the potential to offer excellent resource utilization because there is no concept of data ownership and every processing node can participate in accessing all data. Further, this approach provides unmatched levels of fault tolerance, with all data remaining accessible even with a single surviving node. However, on shared-nothing hardware systems with local affinity between processing nodes and disks, the assumption of direct data access is not valid. Logical shared access can usually be accomplished, but the exclusive use of such a scheme can result in unneeded internode data shipping, incurring significant performance penalties.

What the Real World Needs

Over the years, there has been much religious debate among academic researchers and industry analysts on what the ideal parallel database architecture is—shared-nothing or shared-disk. Although such debate still goes on, often producing interesting technical insights into the merits and drawbacks of either scheme, it's clear that no single scheme is without flaws. Given that, the authors believe that the most pragmatic real-world solution has to be a hybrid architecture that incorporates elements of each approach to provide the best of both worlds. Such an approach would provide the elegance and efficiency of pure shared-nothing systems, while avoiding their drawbacks in terms of resource utilization, manageability, and availability. At the same time, such a hybrid approach would also incorporate key attributes of pure shared-disk systems to deliver excellent resource utilization and fault tolerance.

Oracle7 Parallel Architecture: An Overview

The Oracle server was the first open relational database product to provide complete support for all parallel hardware architectures, with production availability on a variety of SMP systems for several years, and on loosely coupled cluster and MPP systems since 1990. The Oracle Parallel Server technology with its advanced parallel cache management facilities and the unique high performance, nonblocking concurrency mechanism is years ahead of any other commercial open systems product in performance, proven reliability, and unlimited scalability. Parallel query execution technology was introduced in Oracle7 Release 7.1 to serve as the basis for enabling data-intensive decision support applications on cost-effective open systems. Parallel execution capabilities were designed as core internal facilities designed to achieve highly scalable performance on all parallel hardware architectures. The initial release provided support for parallel execution of most operations involved in query execution including table scans, sorts, joins, aggregations, and ordering. In addition, this release included parallel execution of data loads, index creation, and recovery operations. Each subsequent release of the Oracle7 server has added significant functional and performance improvements to this initial offering. This section provides an outline of Oracle's server architecture and an overview of the dynamic parallel query execution technology.

Oracle Parallel Server Technology

The Oracle Parallel Server technology is at the heart of Oracle's server implementation on loosely coupled clustered and MPP systems. As shown in Figure 52.3, the parallel server utilizes a robust, fault-tolerant shared data access scheme and Oracle's proven, scalable parallel cache management technology to provide unmatched levels of availability and scalable performance on parallel hardware systems. This section outlines key elements of this technology with specific emphasis on decision support applications. The Oracle Parallel Server utilizes a shared data access mechanism that enables multiple instances of the database server, with an instance on each node of the loosely coupled system, to transparently share a common set of database files. The shared data access is direct on clustered systems where there is physical connectivity of every disk device to all nodes. On shared-nothing and hybrid hardware systems, the shared access is enabled through an efficient operating system abstraction layer. As you will see later in further detail, Oracle's parallel architecture utilizes an intelligent mix of efficient local data access and transparent shared access on these systems to provide a superior combination of performance, resource utilization, and fault tolerance.

Each server instance utilizes a dedicated buffer cache, with the consistency of data updates across the multiple caches ensured by Oracle's parallel cache management technology. Oracle's proven, scalable parallel cache management technology represents the result of years of joint development efforts with leading parallel hardware system vendors. Key components of this technology include an efficient interinstance communication mechanism and a distributed lock manager (DLM) subsystem.

FIGURE 52.3.
Oracle Parallel Server.

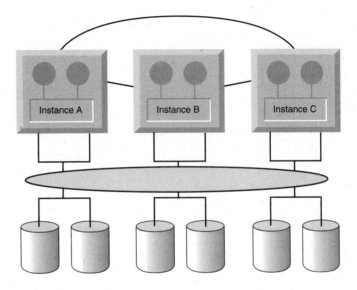

Parallel cache management plays a key role in providing scalable performance for on-line transaction processing (OLTP) applications characterized by highly concurrent update activities. In typical data warehouse systems, however, since the workload mostly consists of read-only access and bulk data additions and purges, parallel cache management doesn't play as much of a role. Oracle's unique nonblocking concurrency mechanism provides virtually unlimited concurrent data access to multiple readers and writers, practically eliminating contention and locking issues.

The shared data access scheme in Oracle's server architecture provides a logical single-system view of the data on all nodes, simplifying system administration issues. It also forms the foundation for providing superior fault tolerance—on most systems, Oracle's Parallel Server technology enables access to *all* data even with a single surviving node.

Oracle Parallel Query Technology

The term Parallel Query is somewhat incomplete because this technology encompasses a range of other data management operations such as data loads, index creation, summary creation and recovery, in addition to parallel query execution. Oracle's parallel technology is designed as a core internal capability of the server, providing superior performance and reliability without any compromises in the range of available server functionality. The key elements of this industry-leading technology are described in this chapter.

Dynamic Parallel Execution: Key Elements

This chapter also describes the basic building blocks of Oracle's dynamic parallel architecture. The key elements are consistent across all parallel hardware architectures—SMP, clustered, and MPP systems. As you will see later, there are some unique optimizations that leverage characteristics of loosely coupled hardware systems.

Parallel Operators

The basic unit of parallel execution is a *Data Flow Operator* (or simply operator). An operator is a higher-level task and often combines multiple relational subtasks into a composite parallel operation. For example, in a query like `select ename, empno from emp where salary > 50000`, application of the filter `SALARY > 50000` could be combined with the table scan into a single operator. Subtasks that can be executed in parallel include:

- Table scans
- Sorts
- Nested loop, sort-merge and hash joins
- Aggregation (`SUM`, `AVERAGE` and so on)
- Grouping (`GROUP BY`)
- Set operations such as `UNION`, `UNION ALL`
- Duplicate elimination (`DISTINCT`)
- Computation of user-defined functions
- Table population (`CREATE TABLE...AS SELECT`)
- Data loads
- Index builds
- Recovery

Query Servers

A set of processes known *as Query Servers* (sometimes called query slaves) execute each operator in parallel. Query servers are drawn from a configurable, system-wide pool of available servers. The user process where the query originates serves as the *Query Coordinator* and manages the tasks performed by multiple query servers. The coordinator also assembles and returns the result set.

Intraoperator and Interoperator Parallelism

As illustrated in Figure 52.4, parallel execution occurs at two distinct levels, *intraoperator parallelism* and *interoperator parallelism*. Intraoperator parallelism, sometimes called horizontal parallelism, is the execution of a single operation such as a table scan, sort, or join in parallel by multiple servers. Interoperator parallelism refers to the parallel execution of multiple distinct parallel operations concurrently. For example, while a set of query servers are scanning a table in parallel, another set of servers could be sorting the scanned rows in parallel. This is also known as *pipelined parallelism* or *vertical parallelism*.

FIGURE 52.4.

Parallel execution: building blocks.

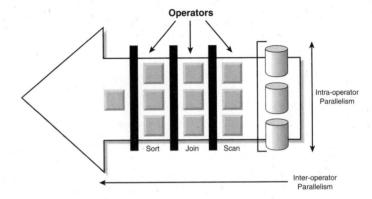

Table Queues: Dynamic Data Redistribution

It's useful to visualize the parallel execution in terms of an operator tree with directly connected parent-child nodes having a producer-consumer relationship. An efficient, dynamic interprocess communication mechanism called the *Table Queue* connects each producer-consumer pair and effectively redistributes the output from a set of producer servers to the next set of consumers. The redistribution happens dynamically and takes into account the optimal data partitioning requirement for a given operation. In the example of a table scan followed by a sort, producers generate output that is randomly partitioned, and the appropriate partitioning for a sort operation is by key value range. The table queue mechanism illustrated in Figure 52.5 takes rows retrieved by the table scan processes and transparently redistributes them, partitioned by key value ranges, to the sort servers.

Depending on the type of operation, the table queue mechanism dynamically chooses an appropriate redistribution method from the available partitioning schemes: *hash, key range, round robin,* or *broadcast.* In performing the data redistribution, the table queue mechanism automatically incorporates several intelligent optimizations to achieve workload balance among the query servers. In the key range partitioning case, for example, the determination of range values is based on a dynamic sampling of the incoming rows to achieve equal-sized partitions. The medium for interprocess communication among the query servers is shared memory on SMP systems and the high-speed interconnect for clustered and MPP systems.

FIGURE 52.5.

Table queues.

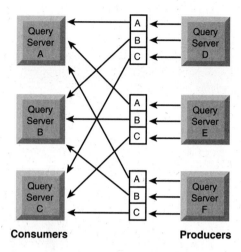

Consumers   **Producers**

Dynamic Table Partitioning

Parallel query execution typically begins with a parallel table scan operation as the first task. Oracle7 uses a dynamic table-partitioning scheme to automatically partition the table among the participating query servers. The intelligent performance and load-balancing optimizations incorporated in dynamic table partitioning underscore the superiority of Oracle's dynamic parallel architecture and its ability to deliver scalable, optimal performance without rigid physical data partitioning. The table being scanned is initially divided into logical partitions, one per available scan process. The initial partitioning takes physical location of data into consideration and minimizes disk contention. Further, in order to achieve optimal load balancing, each logical partition is subdivided into more granular chunks, and the query servers are assigned a chunk at a time to scan. If some query servers fall behind others in completing the scan, processes that have completed their work "steal" chunks of work from the busy servers, achieving improved throughput and optimal load balancing. As explained later, this strategy pays even richer dividends when combined with Oracle's shared-disk access scheme on clusters and MPP systems.

Oracle's dynamic table partitioning, coupled with intelligent redistribution of intermediate results using the table queue mechanism, enables customers to realize the benefits of parallel hardware immediately, without any need to perform expensive data reorganizations. Further, this approach delivers superior performance for a wide range of access patterns including ad hoc queries by knowledge workers. Although a static data partitioning approach could offer performance gains if the access patterns and data distributions are predictable and fixed, such a requirement is completely unrealistic in the real world. The frequent need to perform physical repartitioning of data—with changes in access patterns, additions in hardware, changes in data distributions, or growth in data volumes—imposes an undue administrative burden. This chapter presents a more detailed examination of this issue in the section "Internode Parallelism."

Flexible Parallelism

Each database table (or index) is assigned a degree of parallelism that's appropriate for operations on that object. The degree of parallelism is a user-defined attribute of the table, specified as a parameter at table creation time or assigned later using a simple SQL command. An appropriate degree of parallelism takes into account factors such as table size, available processors, and the number of disk devices that store the table data. If a degree of parallelism is not explicitly specified, the system computes an intelligent default value. Because table sizes and available processing resources change over time, Oracle's dynamic architecture also provides easy ways to change the degree of parallelism. Users can alter the parallelism using a direct SQL command or even override the value at run time using a query hint. It's useful to contrast this flexibility against the static partitioning-based approach where a physical repartitioning of the table is typically required to alter the degree of parallel execution.

Dynamic Parallel-Aware Query Optimization

Oracle's cost-based optimizer incorporates parallel execution considerations as a fundamental component in arriving at optimal query execution plans. As mentioned earlier, the optimizer dynamically computes intelligent heuristic defaults for parallelism based on the number of processors and the number of disk devices that store a given table. Evaluation of the costs of alternative access paths (table scan versus indexed access, for example) takes into account the degree of parallelism available for the operation, leading to execution plans optimized for parallel execution.

In addition to parallelism considerations, Oracle's cost-based optimizer includes a wealth of superior optimization techniques specifically targeted at common data warehouse operations. Star query optimization is a good example of this. Star queries involving a large "fact" table and multiple small "dimension" tables are intelligently optimized, delivering performance that matches special-purpose products from niche vendors. As a further example, parallel access of multiple underlying tables in a UNION ALL view incorporates several intelligent optimizations to deliver optimal performance.

Intelligent Performance Optimizations

In addition to dynamic parallel execution, Oracle's scalable parallel technology incorporates several efficient performance optimizations that specifically benefit typical data warehouse operations. Most of the parallel operations bypass the buffer cache, performing direct parallel database reads to deliver superior performance. Further, sorts, database loads, summary table creation, and index builds perform asynchronous, parallel direct writes to disk, achieving maximum throughput. These facilities effectively eliminate contention for the buffer cache between concurrent DSS operations and isolate DSS queries from concurrent OLTP activities on the system. Parallel table scans utilize an asynchronous read-ahead mechanism to achieve an over-lap between I/O and processing, delivering much higher throughput for queries involving large tables. Logging can be optionally disabled for bulk operations such as data loads, index builds, and summary creation using the CREATE TABLE...AS SELECT operation to achieve substantial improvements in performance.

Oracle Parallel Query on Loosely Coupled Systems

The basic architectural elements of Oracle's parallel technology remain consistent across all hardware systems. There are, however, some key optimizations that utilize Oracle's unique shared access technology to leverage distinct characteristics of loosely coupled systems and deliver superior scalability, resource utilization, and availability benefits on these systems.

Function Shipping

Oracle's parallel execution on loosely coupled systems extensively uses the function-shipping strategy to perform work on remote nodes. Query server processes located on remote nodes are sent efficient messages, often in the form of modified SQL subqueries, to indicate the work that needs to be done.

Loosely Coupled Systems

This may come as a surprise to many purists because function shipping is typically associated with shared-nothing database systems, and on systems where shared-disk access is available, data shipping is the typical approach. Oracle's parallel architecture, with its combination of key elements of both systems, makes intelligent use of function shipping when the data to be accessed is located at the remote node, to deliver efficient parallel execution eliminating un-needed internode data transfer over the interconnect.

Exploitation of Data Locality

Each node on a shared-nothing hardware system has direct hardware connectivity to a subset of disk devices, and it is more efficient to access these local devices from the "owning" node. Oracle's parallel query execution exploits this affinity of devices to nodes and delivers superior performance on these multi-computer systems. As with other elements of Oracle's dynamic parallel architecture, this strategy works transparently, without any need to perform value-based partitioning of data. The system dynamically detects the locality of data and makes intelligent use of it in two ways:

- Spawns query server processes on nodes where the data to be processed is located
- Assigns local data partitions to each slave, to eliminate or minimize internode data movement

Such dynamic exploitation of data locality maximizes local data access and minimizes suboptimal internode data transfer over the interconnect, delivering optimal performance on shared-nothing hardware systems.

Internode Parallelism

In principle, local data access is the preferred strategy on shared-nothing hardware systems; however, exclusive use of this approach, as in pure shared-nothing database architectures, leads to inefficient resource utilization. A number of factors can lead to this: First, data distribution across nodes typically get skewed over time, with additions and purges. Second, the data accessed by a number of queries may relate only to a subset of nodes. For example, if sales data is partitioned by month, a drill-down query on a specific calendar quarter involves only 25% of the nodes. In such situations, a pure partitioned execution strategy cannot leverage unutilized or underutilized processing power on other nodes, resulting in highly skewed resource utilization and suboptimal performance.

Oracle's intelligent combination of shared-nothing and shared-disk architectures makes efficient use of local access and shared access to avoid this problem. Initial work assignment to query servers is based on locality of data. In skewed cases, however, Oracle makes dynamic use of internode parallelism. Query servers located on remote nodes compensate for busy nodes by utilizing shared access, to deliver improved throughput and transparent utilization of all available processing power.

Superior Fault Tolerance

Oracle's implementation of the shared access scheme enables any node in a loosely coupled system to have direct logical access to all data and delivers unmatched levels of availability. In the worst case, even if only one node is available, all of the data is still accessible. Live instances recover transactions on failed instances, and the recovery is performed automatically without any additional administrative work. It's impossible to achieve such complete and transparent fault tolerance in a shared-nothing architecture. On these systems, there's at best a provision for supporting dual-ported disk systems resulting in a single backup node for each primary "owner" node. If both the primary and backup nodes fail, the subset of data owned by the primary node remains inaccessible.

The Oracle7 Advantage over Pure Shared-Nothing Systems

This section contrasts Oracle's scalable "best of both worlds" architecture against pure shared-nothing database systems, illustrating the superior real-world applicability of Oracle's approach.

Static Data Partitioning and Parallelism

Pure shared-nothing database systems base their parallel execution strategy *exclusively* on static data partitioning, resulting in a scheme that is fundamentally flawed. Let's explain why. Static data partitioning is a valuable data management facility that can improve the manageability and availability of very large objects in VLDB systems. The use of value-based partitioning as a Very Large Data Base (VLDB) administration facility has been around a long time, much before the advent of parallel processing. Partitioning is also useful for query optimization in some cases, as it eliminates the need to examine unneeded data.

Deriving parallel query execution exclusively from this administrative segregation of data, however, introduces substantial administrative complexities and severely limits the applicability of parallel processing. A rigid partitioning-based execution approach can provide optimal performance only if the query patterns can be predicted ahead of time. In real-world data warehouse environments, this is an unrealistic requirement because what's "interesting" to analyze is neither predictable nor fixed and is often data-dependent—the knowledge worker decides what to look at based on results of the current analysis. Even if a subset of access requirements can be predicted, because partitioning can be done only along one set of attributes, this approach optimizes performance only for a restricted subset of queries, limiting the applicability of parallel processing.

Frequent Need for Repartitioning

When data access requirements change over time, as they frequently do in real life, data has to be repartitioned to achieve acceptable performance levels. Further, repartitioning is also required with any of the following:

- Significant growth in data volumes
- Addition of processing nodes
- Shifts in data distribution patterns resulting in skewed partitions

Such frequent repartitioning of data adds substantial administrative costs and application downtime, limiting the practical applicability of such a scheme. Partitioning-based parallel execution is an inappropriate approach on shared-everything SMP systems. Some level of data partitioning may be desirable on these systems from a manageability point of view as data volumes grow. However, the need to partition all data, irrespective of the administrative needs, is an artificial requirement imposed solely based on the architectural limitation of pure shared-nothing database systems. Such a requirement introduces unneeded administrative complexities and prevents a vast majority of users on SMP systems from realizing the benefits of parallel technology. In short, the static parallel execution strategy requires frequent data reorganizations at substantial cost and downtime, just to achieve reasonable performance for a limited range of queries.

In contrast, Oracle's dynamic parallel execution strategy delivers the full potential of parallel processing for a much broader range of access patterns, including ad hoc queries, without any need for frequent, expensive repartitioning of data. The manageability benefits of data partitioning can be achieved today using a manual partitioning scheme involving multiple underlying physical tables combined using a UNION ALL view. Comprehensive support for static data partitioning will be available in the next version of the Oracle server. The key difference, however, is that Oracle's dynamic parallel execution strategy will provide all the benefits of data partitioning—improved VLDB manageability and optimization without incurring the costs of a strategy that's exclusively based on partitioning.

Leverage of Processing Power

The tight data ownership scheme that is central to the shared-nothing architecture prevents the exploitation of all available processing resources. There are many cases during normal operation where the available processing power of a pure shared-nothing system is limited to a subset of nodes. Data distribution across partitions typically tends to get skewed over time, with additions and purges. In such cases, the largest partition, or equivalently the slowest processing node, dominates the response time, resulting in suboptimal resource utilization. Even in cases where data is fairly uniformly spread across partitions, each query may not access all partitions. An obvious worst-case example is a query that does a full scan of a single partition— this will be exclusively processed by the owning node, resulting in serial execution, even on massively parallel hardware!

This fundamental limitation of pure shared-nothing systems is particularly significant in the following common situation. Data warehouse environments frequently maintain rolling windows of data partitioned by some time unit, say one month. For example, sales data from a fixed number of months may be kept in a table; new data is rolled in on a monthly basis while the oldest month's data is rolled out. Drill-down queries against such data typically involve a particular month or subset of months. For example, a query might generate a report of revenue and profit by product line for a particular fiscal quarter. In a pure shared-nothing system, the processing power available for this query would be restricted to just the nodes that own the three months' data, leveraging only a fraction of the full processing power of the system.

Some shared-nothing systems attempt to rectify their lack of intrapartition parallelism using a multilevel partitioning scheme, sometimes called "hybrid partitioning." In this scheme, data is initially distributed across all nodes using a hash function. At the next level, data within each node is partitioned by key range into a number of subpartitions. The idea is that the hash step will insure the participation of all nodes in processing a query because the distribution is somewhat random. Within each node, if a significant number of partitions can be eliminated based on the query predicate, each node will process only a subset of the range partitions, improving response time. This may seem like a good idea in principle until you look at the underlying administration issues. On an MPP system with 32 nodes, for example, if each hash partition is subdivided into 25 ranges, there will be a total of 800 partitions to create and manage! What's worse, as the partitions get skewed over time, as they often do, the administrator has to repartition all these 800 pieces all over again. This results in nothing short of an administrative nightmare. Furthermore, if these 800 partitions relate only to a single table there will likely be several thousand of these partitions to manage in a typical system.

Oracle's parallel architecture, with its intelligent combination of data locality and shared access strategies, is far less prone to these data skew problems. Initial partitioning of data is based on maximizing locality. In cases of data skew, however, idle or underutilized nodes can transparently compensate for busy nodes, utilizing shared-disk access, to deliver optimal performance.

Ease of Administration

The excessive dependence of shared-nothing systems on static data partitioning introduces substantial administrative complexities. Users have just one control—static data partitioning—for achieving two potentially conflicting objectives: manageability and parallel execution performance. What's desirable from a manageability and availability point of view may not yield acceptable performance and vice versa, forcing users to compromise one or the other. Further, the frequent need to perform expensive offline data repartitioning imposes further administrative burden, potentially rendering this approach impractical in a number of situations. The rigid data ownership model in shared-nothing systems also prevents incremental system growth—data has to be repartitioned before any additional processing resources can be utilized—negating one of the major benefits of parallel hardware systems. In contrast, Oracle's real-world architecture delivers the true potential of parallel processing with minimal administrative complexity.

Robust Scalability

In a pure shared-nothing architecture, the ideal speedup goal of processing a query in time (T/N) is seriously compromised by the failure of a single processor. In the simplest pure shared-nothing configuration, each processing unit masters a set of disks and no other processing unit has direct access to that set of disks. If the work of executing a query has truly been spread over the N processors, then the failure of a single processor stops the execution of the query for the duration of the outage because no other processing unit has access to the failed processor's set of disks.

To get around this problem, some shared-nothing implementations utilize dual-ported disks, and each processing unit serves as both a master to a particular set of disks and as a backup for another processor unit. If a processor fails, the associated backup does double duty, taking over the work of the failed processor as well as processing its own normal workload. Therein lies the rub. Because the backup now has 2/N of the total work to do, it will finish in 2T/N the time. The completion time for the query is really the completion time of the slowest processing unit, so the entire query will finish in 2T/N the time instead of T/N. In other words, during periods of outage of even a single processor, one gets only *half* the performance that one paid for. To make matters worse, the time that some processing unit in the system is down is roughly proportional to the number of processing units, so this problem actually gets worse as one adds processors—a kind of reverse scalability feature. Oracle's unrestricted access implementation does not have this problem. Because every processing unit has logical access to every disk, work associated with a failed processor can be spread among all the remaining processors, providing robust scalability and virtually no degradation in performance.

Emerging Trends in Technology

Oracle's parallel technology, with its ability to provide transparent shared data access, is consistent with emerging trends in hardware technology. The next generation of mass storage products in the open systems market will most likely be based on high-performance switched protocols such as Fiber Channel, capable of supporting 100M per second bidirectional bandwidth (200M/sec total) per connection. Fiber Channel is gaining considerable momentum in the mass storage world, and large-scale, shared-disk physical connectivity is likely to be available in the near future.

Arbitrated-loop Fiber Channel configurations connecting large numbers of processors to a shared set of disks are being developed even now. Switch-based Fiber Channel configurations will offer even more flexibility and scalability. The switched configuration will be proportional to the number of ports on the switch. This greatly enhanced physical connectivity can be transparently exploited by the unrestricted access solution provided by Oracle's parallel architecture. In fact, in the face of ever-increasing shared-disk physical connectivity, it will become increasingly difficult to defend rigid shared-nothing implementations in which each processor can only get to the vast majority of the data on the system via a networked request to another processor.

Another significant direction in storage technology is the availability of storage subsystems that present a single device appearance to the operating system, but internally use many disks and gigabytes of cache memory to hide device boundaries and mask failures. With a single logical device capable of storing hundreds of gigabytes and transfer rates of hundreds of megabytes per second, the pure shared-nothing limitation of access to the device by one instance only is a severe compromise in processing power. With Oracle's unrestricted access implementation, all the processors in the system can access all the disks in the logical device without going through a "master" instance, delivering scalable performance.

Parallel Processing Platform Hardware Configuration Requirements

In this section, I discuss a few aspects of the required hardware configuration for a parallel processing platform.

Fail-Safe Redundant Hosts

HP, Sun, and Digital 64-bit UNIX provide for an instantaneous redundant host. In the event of a system-wide failure, a "switchover" of the production UNIX servers disks and software can be transferred to a development host automatically. The HP Switch Over daemon sends a regularly scheduled signal or "heartbeat" and receives state-of-health diagnostic information in response to that signal, or absence of a signal to the standby host.

When the standby host determines that the messages have stopped, users are warned of a pending shutdown. HP Switch Over then initiates a takeover, locking the current host's disks, and rebooting as the current host. Heartbeat sends messages to notify the dead or distressed host that a switchover sequence has occurred and issues the appropriate operating system shutdown, ensuring that the lame machine notices the takeover and halts.

The DEC Alpha file servers 2100, 8200 and 8400, utilizing the model EV/5 processor deliver added redundancy through "CPU failover" and "memory failover." If a single CPU or RAM failure occurs during processing, the SMP file server continues uninterrupted processing! At the time of failure, a "system in distress" page is transmitted to service support personnel for immediate notification of the particular problem.

Cross or Remote Mounted Disk Drives

Remote storage devices should not be used in parallel processing because they must interface with at least the two (2) file servers. Any read/write activity is effectively doubled, between the disks of a remote mounted file system as they must interface with each disk's separate processor in the configuration.

Remote file systems must also interface with the network router, cable, connectors, concentrators, Adaptable User Interfaces (AUIs), host adapters, smart controller cards, and buses in the path connecting these two systems. Remote file systems effectively double seek time at a minimum, but they can also degrade network performance for the entire Local Area Networks involved.

Disk Drive Allocation

The number of physical disks mounted and available to the file system are critical to the performance of Oracle7 and related client/server applications. Performance bottlenecks can occur because there is access to only a single "RAID5 stripe" or a single input/output disk read/write "needle," regardless of the number of logical volumes per physical disk drive.

The physical and not logical volume devices are used to balance the I/O of the background Oracle processes across the disks.

Disk Partitioning

Physical disks may be "partitioned" or configured by a logical device manager in subunits that may allow a single disk drive to appear to be multiple disk drives, with different device names. The converse is also true as several disks may appear to be a single disk partition.

Before you install Oracle7, check with your operating system administrator for clarification of these physical, not the logical, device names. Also verify the necessary path, permissions, and storage space of the data files that you can create on each disk drive.

Maximizing Parallel Platform Database and Disk Performance Through Balancing the Oracle Processes

The system tablespace, rollback segments, control files, and redo logs are always active for every Oracle instance. If Archive mode is enabled, then transaction logging will "journal" all data base activity enabling a point-in-time recovery if needed, in conjunction with your full database backup. Archive mode should write to a duplexed tape and disk media. The fastest recovery will be directly from disk if this is possible.

These processes use specific files, which should be distributed across different disk drives for optimal database speed.

Be certain that all Oracle background and foreground processes have the same operating system process priority. Contention will arise as a high-priority process waits for a low-priority process, which may never swap back in.

Disk Optimization For Oracle7 and the Parallel Server Oracle7 Option

The optimum number of disks for the Oracle installation should at a minimum enable the separation of the table data on disk one and the index data on disk two, in any size.

With additional disk availability, the Oracle7 system offers tablespace on disk three, rollback segments on disk four, temporary tablespace on disk five, and the redo logs on disk six.

The triple-copied control files are always written to when major RDBMS events occur and are not a serious performance bottleneck. The control files should always be separated across multiple disks, whenever more than one disk drive is available by direct mount to the file system. This triple redundancy ensures rapid recovery in the event of a disk drive failure or accidental erasure.

Time zones and business application groups should influence the tablespace design so that a database maintenance window for one application does not interfere with the operation of 7/24 maximum availability systems.

Disk Storage Devices

The Oracle disk storage devices in Table 52.2 can be standard devices, mirrored devices, Write Once Read Many optical disc (WORM), Write Many Read Many optical disc (WMRM), Redundant Arrays of Independent Disks (RAID) and other media types. These disks should have relatively high read/write rate (8-9 milliseconds for standard disk drives) and should not be cross-mounted from other file system servers, except in the case of an out-of-file-space emergency.

Optical Storage

The media read and write rates for optical storage are significantly slower and therefore should not be used as high-performance file system devices for normal database query activity. These optical devices are very well suited for backups, long-term data archival, and are usually guaranteed for long-term readability of 50 years or more.

Table 52.2. Storage device pricing and performance.

Disk/Tape Storage Media Type	Storage Maximum Gigabytes	Average Access Time Milliseconds	Average Write Time Milliseconds	Media Device Driver Cost
Standard "Barracuda" Fast/Wide 20MB@Second	4GB	8 MS	8 MS	$1,400.00
Optical WORM 12 Inch	25GB	135 MS	68 MS	$7,000.00
Cybernetics 2500 Optical WMRM 5.25 Inch	1.3GB	19.8 MS	500 KBS	$3,495.00
Cybernetics CY-8505 8mm tape	25GB	67.5 S	12-90M@min.	$4,250.00
DEC TZ-80 tape cartridge	40GB	10 S	333M@min.	$5,500.00
Exabyte EXB-8505 8mm tape	5-10GB	67.5 S	10-35M@min.	$4,125.00
Mirrored Disks Fast/Wide 20MB@Second	4GB	4-9 MS/2 disks	4-9 MS/2 disks	$1,400.00

Disk/Tape Storage Media Type	Storage Maximum Gigabytes	Average Access Time Milliseconds	Average Write Time Milliseconds	Media Device Driver Cost
RAID 5 Array Fast/Wide 20MB@Second	4GB	12-16 MS	12-16 MS	$1,400.00
Microtek Floptical Compact Disks	120MB		60k @Sec	$5,000.00
SONY minidisk Read/write CD	120MB		600k @Sec	$1,000.00

RAID Versus the Speed of Disk Mirroring

Commonly referred to as fault tolerant disk systems, Redundant Arrays of Independent Disks (RAID) and "mirrored disk arrays" both use different RAID levels to provide redundant duplication of data disk storage devices.

In RAID5, when a single disk drive failure occurs, the redundant duplicate media spread across the remaining disks are used to recreate the data that was stored on the now unavailable disk drive. A "scratch pool" contains extra disk drives reserved for each RAID5 Array. In the event that failure occurs to any of the RAID5 Arrays, an extra disk from the scratch pool is temporarily added to redefine that RAID5 stripe.

This recovery of data should be considered complete only after a new disk is installed and mounted onto the file system.

Performance of common RAID, other than RAID Level 1 and 5, is significantly slower as the data from each drive is duplicated among an average of three to five other disk drives. This impacts not only the number of physical read/writes but degrades CPU and I/O performance across the processor bus as well.

The database implications here are twofold in that file writing is significantly slower due to duplication across three (3) to five (5) disks on average. Another common RAID drawback is that the real-time reads are only possible from the single master disk, and not from the redundant copy.

What are RAID Levels 0 - 5? Each RAID level offers a different approach to data redundancy and fast access to that data. Fault tolerance, read/write performance, and storage capacity are unique to each RAID level.

■ RAID Level 0: Striping of data across multiple disks to increase performance. This increased performance sacrifices fault tolerance, which RAID Level 0 completely lacks. RAID Level 0 does not dedicate any disks to error checking or disk mirroring. Storage capacity is maximized and the up-front cost is minimal.

■ RAID Level 1: Commonly referred to as *mirroring*. Fault tolerance is implemented by creating a twin for each data disk. Read performance is improved but write time maybe increased as data must be written twice. This RAID level requires double capacity as two gigabytes are required to store each gigabyte of data in fault-tolerant redundancy. This is the most expensive and one of the most popular forms of disk mirroring. Best for use as an operating system disk, commonly referred to as a "system disk" and/or an Oracle7 source code location.

■ RAID Level 2: Error correction is used to recover data instead of data duplication storage on extra disks.

■ RAID Level 3: Error correction is implemented at the drive controller hardware and at a parity or duplicate drive, for the most efficient use of large, similar blocks of data. Only one write is allowed to the disk array at one time.

■ RAID Level 4: Better performance and less fault tolerance than RAID Level 3. Similar in that reads from multiple drives occur simultaneously and the same storage efficiency as RAID Level 3.

■ RAID Level 5: Software striping of data and the backup copy across the disk array for the best performance for security, cost advantages and Oracle7 database servers. Boosts performance with simultaneous reads and writes. This is the best and most popular form of RAID fault tolerance.

Mirrored Disk Drives

RAID Levels 1 and 5 enable a noticeable performance increase while simultaneously providing a consistent data mirror, one for one, across each mirrored disk drive.

Performance is optimized by the operating system as queries for data across mirrored disks are split among the duplexed physical media. This optimizes the physical read/write ratio because when two (2) files are accessed from the same disk which has been mirrored, both disks are used to retrieve the data, thus speeding up reads, enabling faster throughput.

The data actually travels from the disks, through the host adapter and finally across the CPU bus for I/O.

Mirroring also allows for separation of a live system into two (2) segments, one of which remains active to the users. This momentarily "breaks" the mirror while data can be copied via any high-speed means to an archive disk or compressed tape for backup and recovery purposes.

The mirror is then "re-silvered" as it is re-attached and rolls forward to update any file server activity since the initial separation from the master disk drive.

This breaking of the mirror procedure momentarily eliminates the second disk mirror recovery procedure from your contingency plan and should therefore only be done after other alternative backups are verified.

Parallel Processor Types, Smart Controller Cards, and Bus I/O

If the processor is a 32-bit Intel i486 and no more than two processors are connected to a 64-bit bus via the host adapters, then no input/output contention will result, if the MHz rating of the bus is verified to be identical to, or greater than the CPU clock speed rating. This may also be refereed to as a "PCI" or "local" bus.

As other more powerful processors enter the marketplace, specific attention to the architecture, processor type, the number of processors per bus and their maximum throughput rates per clock tick cycle (the MHz rating) must be addressed.

When a single 64-bit processor is connected to a 64-bit bus, having the same clock speed or MHz rating, then no contention or delay of information processing results. If, however, two (2) such 64-bit processors share the same single 64-bit bus with the same clock speed, each individual processor must wait a full cycle while the other processor is active.

This also means that when both processors are active, each processor can only receive input/output half of the time, from the common bus peripheral devices such as disks, tape devices, or network host adapter interfaces.

It is therefore wise to verify that your expansion processor bus is rated "wide and fast" for 20MB@second throughput, or "fiber channel" 200M@second processor throughput. This will help to eliminate the parallel processor contention for the CPU bus and to allow for the speediest of computational zest.

If the Intel DX processor is a DX2, the processor internal clock speed is doubled or in the DX4, tripled. This is relative only to the internal CPU operations, NOT the input/output across the common bus. The MHz rating of the bus is actually the speed or bandwidth at which the information input/output travels.

- Reduced Instruction Set Chip: A Reduced Instruction Set Chip (RISC) can actually process efficiently many CPU operations per cycle more than the older Complex Instruction Set Computation (CISC), and RISC may also utilize Branch Prediction computation on supported CPUs. A common example includes the wildly popular 275 MHz 64-bit DEC Alpha processor. DEC currently has a 64-bit Alpha processor running at 1000 MHz.

- PowerPC: The PowerPC chip is half as thin as the Pentium and therefore more efficient in power consumption, electrical resistance, and computational speed.

PowerPC chips are also expected to be the next popular, true 64-bit processor introduced in late 1995. The PowerPC architecture is newer, more flexible, requires less overhead, and can process up to six simultaneous instructions per cycle versus the current two to three instructions of Intel x86 P-5 and P-6 high end processors. The high-end Intel x86 requires roughly twice the number of transistors per chip to maintain the backward compatibility of previous x86 CPUs.

■ Smart Controller Cards: Smart controller cards enable significant price/performance ratio increases among the smart card providers, and they are currently utilized only by the Oracle7 RDBMS. This is the result of Oracle's high-speed record latch and network management research. Smart cards offload computation from the main processor's CPU. A smart card is usually placed directly at the cable interface to the file server. In the AT&T Global Information Systems 3000 (formerly the NCR 3000) platform, smart cards attach to the host adapter, before the network wire and eliminate network protocol exchange between the network and the CPU. This is accomplished by means of a secondary processor available from the smart card. The resulting efficiency can be as large as a 50 percent performance throughput increase for a total investment of less than $5,000.00.

Making the Right Choice

With all of these MP, SMP and MPP platforms, how can you be certain make the right choice for your business applications today and tomorrow?

Transaction Processing Performance Council (TPC) Benchmarks

The Transaction Processing Performance Council benchmarks effectively illustrate:

■ Simulated banking application benchmarks on SMP via the TPC/A, B, and C

■ A level playing field of independently audited Price/Performance benchmarks

■ Forum open to challenge for 60 days by the entire competitive members

■ Resource for many other types of benchmarks

■ Resource for Performance Tuning Optimization

The best single resource from the TPC is probably the Complete Listing Of TPC Results and includes up-to-date listings of all TPC/A, B, C, D, and E benchmarks detailing the company sponsor, system, database, operating system tested, and complete five-year costs including all software and system maintenance support fees.

TPC/A: Online Transaction Processing (OLTP)test that scales upward to measure database update, disk I/O, transaction integrity. All costs are divided by the total system cost and measured in Transactions per Second(TPS), when driven from multiple terminals.

TPC/B: Current database stress test (not OLTP) detailing significant disk I/O, transaction integrity, all costs, moderate system and application execution time.

TPC/C: Simulated order entry of five complex, concurrent OLTP transactions; order delivery, payment record entry, status checks, and warehouse stock level environment test, including all costs, measured in Transactions Per Minute (TPM).

TPC/D: New decision support (DS) OLTP for large systems, processing 17 long running "real-world" queries against complex data structures. Available since Q-2 95.

TPC/E: New large business "Enterprise" database stress test for complex query processing on very large databases available Q-1, 1996.

TPC Quarterly reports contain executive summaries of the TPC results published in the quarter as well as a complete historical benchmark listing. Executive summaries are two-page summations of the lengthy Full Disclosure Reports. The summations describe major components, performance data, detailed pricing of the system/configurations, and their related diagrams. Supplementary information included relates to competitive system and database analysis topics.

Complete Full Disclosure Reports are an average of 100 pages but include detailed price breakdowns by components and the specific optimizations used to achieve the best performance results.

The TPC Price Performance ratio reports are available from within your organization, or you can telephone the TPC for reports and information directly in Sunnyvale, California, at (408) 295-8894.

Sample TPC Benchmarks

Following in Table 52.3 are a few sample TPC/A and TPC/C benchmarks. The TPC consists of 44 members from the hardware and software industry including:

- Amdahl, AT&T/GIS(NCR), Compaq, Cray Research, DEC, Fujitsu, HP, Sequent, Silicon Graphics, Inc. (SGI), and Sun
- CA/Ingres, IBM, Informix, Microsoft, nCUBE, Novell, Oracle, SCO, and SYBASE

TPC Results are subject to challenge by competitors and independently audited for 60 days prior to their publication. Benchmarks are summarized to include the complete five-year cost of the system including software with full support and administration costs. These figures are then expressed in total Transactions Per Second (TPS), (TPM), and the associated Price Performance Ratio.

Table 52.3. Sample TPC benchmarks.

Company	System	TPC/ARev	Throughput	$Price/perf	5 YR. Total Cost	RDBMS	O/S	Date
AT&T	NCR3655/ 48 CPU C/S	v 1.2	713.56 TPS/A	$5,941.	$4,239,200.00	Oracle7	MP/RASSVR4.2	10/93
Compaq	Prolinea2000 5864200	v 1.2	240.68TPS/A	$4,890.	$1,176,922.00	Oracle7.0.15	SCO UNIX 3.2.4	9/93
Compaq	system-pro/ XL5862100	v 1.2	242.23TPS/A	$5,130.	$1,242,662.00	Oracle7.0.15	SCO UNIX 3.2.4	8/93
Compaq	system-pro/ XL5862040	v 1.2	171.82TPS/A	$5,437.	$834,146.00	Oracle7.0.10	SCO UNIX 3.2.4	1/93
HP	9000T500 C/S	v 3.00	5070tpm/C	$530.00 @tpm/C	$2,872,151.00	Oracle7.3	HP-UX 10.10	7/95
HP	9000K410 C/S	v 3.00	3809tpm/C	$364.00 @tpm/C	$1,384,763.00	Oracle7.3	HP-UX 10.01	9/95
HP	9000H70 C/S	v 1.2	411.73TPS/A	$6,866.	$2,745,542.00	Oracle7.0.11	HP-UX 9.0	6/93
HP	9000H50 C/S	v 1.1	184.55TPS/A	$8,637.	$1,593,366.00	Oracle7.0.10	HP-UX 9.0	6/93
I.B.M.	ES/9000742 Fastpath	v 1.2	1427.07TPS/A	$13,348.	$19,175,741.0	IMSDB4.1 W RSR	MVS/ESA4.3	12/93
I.B.M.	RS/6000570 C/S	v 1.2	128.50TPS/A	$6,536.	$1,095,880.00	Oracle7	AIX3.2.3UNIX	12/93
Sequent	S2000/750 C/S	v 1.2	1002.37TPS/A	$9,313.	$9,335,113.00	Oracle7.0.12	DYNEXptkV 2.0.1	6/93

Historical IBM 3090 Model 600J performance is 25 TPS, per processor. At six processors, this equates to 150 TPS/A v1.2. These machines cost $6 million to operate for five years, including software, maintenance, and support, thus generating a price performance ratio of $40,000.00@Transaction. The figures shown in Table 52.3 reflect why the current trend is towards client/server and away from the mainframe.

Parallel Processing Platform Selection Criteria

Choosing your parallel processing platform requires specific selection criteria. Decisions you make regarding how you will evaluate the information and select the best current and future solution will have a long-term impact on your entire network user community.

When selecting a platform, consider your real-world experiences with your current file servers:

- Is your current query response time (TPS) and related performance fast enough?
- What is your current user community growth rate?
- How many concurrent and total users will you need to support in a few years' time?
- What will your current and future applications require in RAM, disk storage, and processor I/O?
- What are your concurrency requirements in RAM, disk storage, and processor I/O per user?
- Transaction type and percentages of: on-line, batch, select, insert, update, or delete?
- Is the ability to double throughput by adding another processor important?

When your data answering these questions is collected, it should illustrate which file servers you should consider. This should strategically allow for the inclusion of one or more additional Parallel Processors (PP), Symmetrical Multi-Processors (SMP), or Massively Parallel Processors (MPP) as an optional upgrade path for performance improvements if needed.

The logical design should be used to guide the platform design process by providing maximum throughput, ease of use, and ease of maintenance.

The platform and physical design information is then used to distribute tablespaces on opposite disks of the high volume and heavy load queries so as to minimize disk trashing of tablespace files and elimination of I/O contention.

The high-volume queries should access table and index data, spread across different disks so as to minimize disk contention between users and queries, referencing the proposed physical design.

Remember when calculating index size space estimates, indexes can be as large as tables, and frequently total 150 percent larger than actual table sizes, in megabytes.

Parallel Index Platform Design

Disk access is a major performance bottleneck. Server performance degrades as disk I/O occurs. An index on selective columns can greatly improve server performance as the index reduces disk I/O. All database servers support B-tree indexes. B-trees store key values and their physical storage addresses in a hierarchical tree of index pages.

Calculating Legacy Tablespace and Data File Sizes for the Parallel Platform

Tablespaces are composed of the physical data files on the disks where the data actually resides.

`Select * from sys.DB_FILES` is the maximum number of Oracle data files that can be opened per database on that operating system. `Select * from sys.DBA_DATA_FILES` lists the current data files, sizes, current status and paths used by that Oracle database.

Indexspaces are identical to a tablespace except for the index objects which should exclusively occupy this space. Because of the physical disk separation of tables and indexes, queries using the indexes and retrieving table data from non-indexed columns use two different disks, cutting in half the read/write time.

When a table is "striped," it uses multiple data files. These are optimally spread across multiple disk drives for the fastest table and index access possible.

Table Sizing and Types for Parallel Processing Platform Disk Design

When tables are created through the execution of Data Definition Language (DDL), storage parameters are given for the initial sizing and data file. This is the specific disk and full path of the objects creation and for the subsequent or future space allocation extension, when additional storage space will be required.

The initial parameter is the size in kilobytes or megabytes of the first contiguous extent. This is composed of Oracle blocks, in which the data is actually stored internally to the database. The normal block size is 2K minus about 50–100 bytes, which Oracle uses internally.

The available contiguous disk space must be as large as these "initial" values. A buffer of between 33 percent to 50 percent, additional RDBMS reserved disk space, is reasonable from a platform design standard. This can be queried from the Oracle view by using the following command:

```
Select * from sys.DBA_FREE_SPACE
```

When an existing table has two (2) or more extents, it should be reorganized for performance considerations and to avoid the famous `ORA-1547 Failed to allocate extent of size (number of extents needed) in tablespace (tablespace name)` error message. This indicates that your object cannot grow without the addition of a new data file for the tablespace and table or tablespace import with the `compress files=Y` export parameter option.

Before redesigning your tablespaces, be sure that your tablespaces having data files greater than one (1) can be unified on your proposed disk layout, *unless they are striped tablespaces.* This will ensure that your largest objects will fit into the new single extents. Also verify that percent free is zero (0), or you may be surprised that your contiguous free space is rapidly used up when new data requires additional extents.

Temporary Segment Parallel Processing Platform Design

A temporary segment is opened for each active user in the Oracle RDBMS. Optimally the temporary tablespace is a "striped " tablespace, or one in which the multiple data files associated with this tablespace are spread across multiple disks. The temporary tablespace and default tablespace are both ALTER USER modifiable parameters.

Parallel Processing Platform Backup Device Design

If archive mode is enabled, the archive destination path should point to a fast, removable media such as a WORM-CD, Cybernetics CY-8505 8mm tape device, or Digital Linear Tape device (DLT) featuring compression capable of storing up to 24GB per tape or 5 gigabytes uncompressed. A standard 2.2–5GB Exabyte 8mm tape drive may also be used, offering less capacity for the same price.

These three tape devices offer the capability to store from 8GB up to 40GB compressed onto a single tape or five (5) GB uncompressed per tape. This eliminates the need for attended backup tape changers and automated tape-changing hardware, which can fail. The cybernetics read/write rates vary up to 85MB per minute when used with an optimum SCSI II interface.

The fastest backup device available is the Digital Linear Tape device (DLT). The data backup or "transfer" rate is a speedy one gigabyte per three minutes! Cartridges are independently rated for over 40,000 cycles of tape writes. The DLT has a storage capacity of 20 to 40 gigabytes per cartridge. The DLT is also priced at less than $5,500.00, which is in the same price range as the other two tape devices.

Parallel Processing Platform Database Creation Requirements

The Oracle installer utility for Oracle7 now avoids the previous limit of 32 maximum data files and other limitations encountered when creating databases from the Oracle version 6 installation utility.

The utility is accessed initially by copying it from the installation media into a temporary location. Do this only after you have read the installation guide specifically written for your hardware platform and operating system version release. About 200MB may be required for the temp directory until you remove it, after your installation.

After loading the system variables and specifying directory locations for product locations, give special attention to not accepting the default locations and tablespace sizes for the system, rollback, and control file locations.

These database files should be spread across several different physical disk drives for performance optimization. If the on-line help facilities of many products are installed, the sizing of the tablespaces must increase to hold this data. Specifically the Oracle case tools and SQl*TextRetrieval will require at least a 25MB tablespace for their help examples when loaded.

New Data Types That Enhance Parallel Processing Platforms

The Blob and VARCHAR2 column data types are new to Oracle7 and should be used accordingly.

Oracle's *Media Server* uses the Blob to store video and audio text for real-time playback, fast forward, and rewind directly from an MP, SMP or MPP server as delivered to between 30,000 to 150,000 concurrent users over cellular, twisted pair, co-ax, and fiber-optic cabling.

Blob or "Binary Large Object" may be up to a 2GB long RAW field which should be used in a "striped" disk tablespace configuration. This will enable the maximum disk I/O performance.

Blob data types are used in the storage of large data objects, where searching and indexing would otherwise not be possible.

Oracle Callable Interfaces (OCI) can be required to read this data type as a bitstream using Oracle's Pro*C tool, from the file server.

VARCHAR2 data types are a variable-length character field used to avoid wasted column space for missing data in the storage of your records. VARCHAR2 should be used wherever possible, unless math is or will be done (requiring data validation) with the data being stored in this particular column. A 2-byte end-of-file marker is the cost of this feature, while any space savings below this is saved and available for other data storage uses.

Routine Parallel Platform Server Maintenance

Database errors are logged throughout the Oracle system by a configurable parameter in the initSID.ora file located in the $oracle_home/dbs directory.

The default path for the Oracle system errors that the user may have seen before contacting you for advice is in $oracle_home/rdbms/log. This path may be altered by including usr dump destination in your initSID.ora file.

The tkprof tool can be used to analyze these errors if they do not seem obvious to you, or they can be faxed to Oracle for their assistance and interpretation by calling (415) 506-1500 first and speaking to an analyst who will assist you in analyses and logging a TAR with the identification by you of your temporary order number or permanent Customer Service Information (CSI) number.

Parallel Processing Database and Tool Upgrades

When you are upgrading your file server Operating System, a new version of Oracle will most likely have to be installed to support this upgrade after the new OS is installed. Prior to this, always ensure that full database exports and backups are available, and that redundant copies of the new media are available if possible.

When upgrading the Oracle source code, be sure to select "Database upgrade" from the menu and *not* the "Install New Database" from the orainst menu. If you do select "Install New Database" by mistake and then you enter your existing Oracle SID name, your old instance and database will be initialized or purged of all data, user IDs, and objects and will therefore be useless except as a fresh database.

If you do want to create a user test-bed or staging area, you can use the orainst installer utility for new database SID creation from your existing source code and executables.

> **NOTE**
>
> Before any such maintenance or installation proceeds, be sure to have full database exports and verified backups available to you, and absolutely do not use an existing Oracle SID or any current database files from your file server. `Select * from DBA_DATA_FILES` will echo the current status of data files, for that database only.

SQL*Net versions installed on the server must match the client versions for connection between the client and the server, when using SQL*Net.

- SQL*Net 2.2 with the Multiple Protocol Interchange for Legacy Platforms: Allows the operation of several protocols on the network without collision across the network, or relative to the oracle SQL*Net process. Applications include the interoperability of TCP/IP, SPX/IPX, AppleTalk, and other protocols, simultaneously from disparate operating systems and to the same Oracle7 file server.

- SQL*Net 2.2: Features dead-user detection, for the automated logoff of inactive users who have been idle for a predetermined time period. Also allows you to utilize the networking Multiple Protocol Interchange (MPI), enabling TCP/IP and SPX to run simultaneously. This SQL*Net version enables multi-threaded server connections, via a single Client/Server process (without the additional overhead of a shadow process) as well.

You must also keep or install the other SQL*Net versions that your clients may use such as versions 1.1 for Apple Macs.

Parallel Processing Platform Free Space Calculations

The current Oracle7 Administration guide contains the sizing calculations for both free tablespace (`select * from SYS.DBA_FREE_SPACE`) and table size estimates. These include the reasons why not to use percent increase other than zero (0) in your Data Definition Language, except in high-availability systems where you may not have the option of adding a data file in an emergency. You should frequently monitor available disk space, data file free space, chained rows, and the number of extents.

To calculate Oracle block space used by an Oracle table or index, execute this query:

```
Select count(distinct(substr(rowid, 1, 8)¦¦substr (rowid, 15, 4)))
from tablename;
```

Multiply this total by your Oracle block size (usually 2048-8192 or 32KB), giving bytes of data and deducting the Pctfree value, if any.

As with Oracle version upgrades in the future, you may want to contact Oracle at (415) 506-1500 to verify that the printed material you are using in your manual is the best and most up-to-date resource for these calculations. As the architecture shifts, these manuals become outdated and are supplemented by definitive white papers on various subjects.

For more information regarding Parallel Platform Optimization, refer to the following sources:

- *ORACLE RDBMS Performance Tuning Guide Version 7.0*
- *Oracle7 Physical Database Design Guide*
- *Oracle7 Performance Tuning and Optimization Guide*

Summary

Traditionally, two distinct approaches—shared nothing and shared disk—have been used in the implementation of database systems on parallel hardware. Each approach in its pure form offers certain unique benefits and tradeoffs. This chapter illustrated a conceptual foundation for its central argument: a hybrid Oracle architecture that combines the strengths of each approach is the most pragmatic real-world solution.

The TPC benchmarks are an invaluable resource for the independent verification of realistic performance gains. Conversions include fault tolerant SMP or MPP configuration, in conjunction with application migration, reengineering, and new development.

Oracle's scalable parallel architecture combines the best elements of pure shared-disk and shared-nothing approaches to provide a proven real-world architecture that enables customers to realize the true potential of parallel processing. Oracle's unique approach optimally exploits the distinct characteristics of all parallel hardware architectures—SMP, clusters, and MPP systems—to deliver scalable performance with superior manageability and unmatched levels of availability. As President Clinton said recently, "There is no mainframe explanation for the PC (client/server) world in which we are now living."

Networking Oracle®

53

by Joe Greene

Welcome to the world of database networking. Some people come rushing to this world based upon promises that they have heard about magnificent performance or the capability to use their graphical user interfaces on personal computers for applications that access large corporate databases in a friendly and efficient manner. Others, however, are dragged into this world kicking and screaming. The architectures are so complex. You have to learn all those networking terms, and it takes forever for your support staff to get all those drivers loaded correctly so that you can access your databases. Finally, you have to rely on the network administrators in addition to the system administrators to keep the system up so that you can access your data.

The good news is that client/server and networking to access databases has moved beyond the point of radical, new technology and into the realm of the stable production environment. Sure, you have to pay some dues to learn the new terms and understand what hardware and software components you are using to get your information. I, for one, never want to go back to the days of the dumb terminal when it comes time to write a production application. Very few business users can be "wowed" by the traditional terminal interface where they have to learn to navigate through a series of menus or enter commands at the command line.

This chapter has an ambitious goal of providing you an understanding of networking as it relates to Oracle databases. Because many users are inexperienced in modern networking environments (using a Novell server to print your documents does not count), the terms serve as an initial stumbling block that you must overcome. The next layer of complexity comes from the fact that there are a large number of people out there designing network components. There are a few standards out there, but a number of vendors are competing with one another to set "the" standard. You need to be aware of the common products that are out there and how they work. Finally, Oracle itself presents a number of networking challenges. The challenge comes from Oracle's large customer base that has many different needs. As a result, Oracle offers a wide range of products that you might have to become familiar with, depending on what you need.

To approach these problems, I divided this chapter into the following sections:

- A quick introduction to some basic networking concepts.
- A discussion of the basic types of networking that you might encounter in your Oracle systems.
- Some coverage of the more common alternative database networking architectures.
- An overview of SQL*Net, Oracle's most basic networking product family.
- An introduction to some common middleware products (the software that enables your applications and databases to interface with your networks).
- An overview of how you can use gateways to connect Oracle to non-Oracle databases, such as IBM's DB2.

- A presentation of some sample database network configurations to give you a feel for some working environments.
- Finally, some tips on developing and implementing network database environments.

Because this is a challenging amount of material to cover in a limited number of pages, I should get started.

A Quick and Dirty Introduction to Networking

Although it might seem too basic to some of you, I thought that I would define a computer network as a collection of hardware and software that enables multiple computers to communicate with one another. Network engineering types might think of more precise or elegant definitions, but I think that this is good enough for our purposes here. Figure 53.1 is a basic drawing that illustrates this definition. The concept is quite simple. You have two or more computers that are connected together in a manner to exchange information. Later in this chapter, I will go through the details of different network transmission standards and all of those annoying details. However, for now, focus in on the basic concepts of computers and a network that somehow connects them together.

FIGURE 53.1.

Basic concepts behind a computer network.

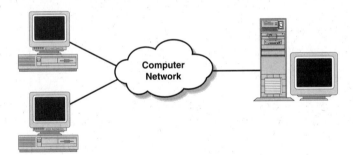

As mentioned in the introduction to this chapter, part of the problem in setting up networks to support databases is dealing with all the components, versions, standards, and so on that exist in the networking market. The network folks have designed a very useful tool to diagram this process. They use a stacking diagram that shows various layers of functionality and how they stack on one another to build a complete network connection. They typically use a seven-layer model, which details more of the networking environment and also supports a wide range of application uses. Although their model makes an interesting discussion, in the interest of efficiency, I have simplified the model to deal more closely with the database networking models that you will come across. This database seven-layer model is shown in Figure 53.2. Networking purists might argue that I sometimes combine layers of the traditional seven-layer model and split a layer into two layers. However, this is how Oracle and other vendors tend to bundle their products, therefore it is an easier way for a DBA or developer to view networking.

FIGURE 53.2.

Seven-layer database network stacking model.

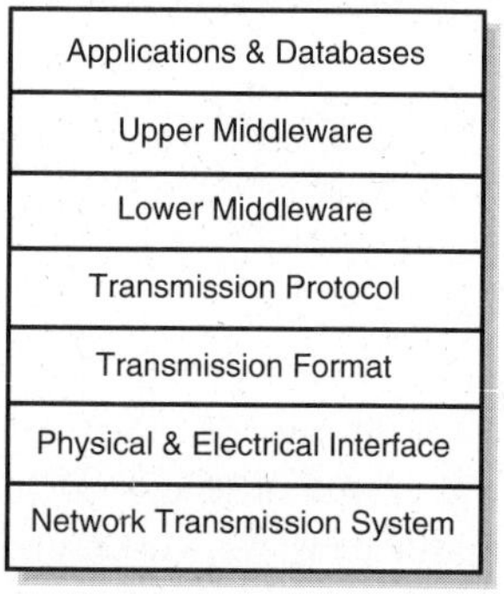

Applications & Databases
Upper Middleware
Lower Middleware
Transmission Protocol
Transmission Format
Physical & Electrical Interface
Network Transmission System

The lowest layer is the networking transmission system. Typically, your local computer networking staff arranges this for you. The transmission equipment is designed to transmit the signals between computers. It usually transmits only a limited range of transmission formats (types of signaling) and protocols (the addressing and packaging of the transmission). It also tends to limit the types of physical connections that you can use to tap into the network with your network interface cards. Because this part of the network is usually arranged for you, it can actually help narrow down the large number of possibilities that you have to consider; as a result, the transmission formats and protocols are an excellent place to start when designing your systems.

The second layer up provides the physical and electronic interface between your computer and the network transmission system. This layer consists of some cabling and a network interface card that plugs into your computer. With servers, you typically do not have a lot of choices for a network interface card (usually one or two cards per transmission protocol). With PCs, you have a large number of choices for the various transmission protocols. The most important thing to ensure is that the card you choose is compatible with your operating system (especially when you are using newer operating systems such as Windows NT and Windows 95).

The next layer to consider is the transmission format. This layer tracks when your computer can make a transmission on the network and ensures that the signals are correct so that other computers can detect them. The transmission format is typically the domain of the electronics engineers who worry about signal voltages and such details. There are three types of common transmission formats:

- Ethernet: This is perhaps the simplest and most common signaling format. With this format, everyone transmits their signals onto a wire whenever they want to, and the systems detect and resolve any conflicts that arise. Typical speed is 10 million bits per second (bps), which is limited to about 3 million bps as a sustained transmission rate. A 100 million bps version is starting to appear on the market.

- Token Ring: With this network transmission format, everyone transmits signals when it is "their turn." Token-Ring networks are popular in IBM environments with their speed of either 4 or 16 million bps.

- ATM (Asynchronous Transfer Mode): This is a newcomer on the market. It is not common in local area networks (LANs) yet, but many manufacturers are starting to design and sell adapters using this technology. ATM relies on relatively high-speed burst transmissions.

The fourth layer (the transmission protocol) is similar to the envelope in which you send a letter by mail. This layer assembles the data you're transmitting into packets that can be routed through the network. Some of the more common transmission formats include the following:

- TCP/IP (Transmission Control Protocol/Internet Protocol): This is the basis of the Internet that you have probably read about. It started with a U.S. Government research project and turned out to be a standard that people could rally around. TCP/IP is the most common format that I have come across for client/server computing and connecting to UNIX-based computers.

- IPX/SPX: These are the transmission protocols used in Novell networking environments. Their use is typically limited to communications between PCs and Novell servers.

- NetBEUI: This is a protocol that some IBM and Microsoft networking products use for basic communications between PCs and LAN servers (such as Microsoft Windows NT). You will probably only encounter this protocol if you are running the workgroups version of Oracle.

I've had trouble using NetBEUI for client/server communications. I recommend that you consider using TCP/IP for client/server applications.

- SNA (System Network Architecture): This is actually more of an architecture than a protocol. It is the main environment for IBM mainframe shops.

The fifth layer is where the database-unique processing begins; I call it lower middleware. Middleware is a term that you encounter often in database networking. It refers to any supporting software that you need to connect your application or database management system to the networking utilities on your computer. I made up the term "lower middleware" to refer to products such as Oracle's SQL*Net that transmit database requests in a predefined format (such as TCP/IP) to the networking software on your host computer.

The next layer is what I call upper middleware. These products are designed to enable a variety of applications to interface with lower middleware products to interface with a database on a remote computer. Upper middleware is how I qualify Microsoft's ODBC (Open Database

Connection) standard, which takes queries and transactions from products such as the Visual C compiler or the Microsoft Query product and formats them to interface with a specific lower middleware product such as SQL*Net. Some products, such as Oracle's SQL*Plus, already have a direct interface to the lower layer of middleware (SQL*Net) and therefore do not need a separate lower middleware software package.

Finally, at the top of my stacking model are the applications that most users really care about. Of course, on the server end is the database management system. On the client end is the financial accounting or sales forecasting system that the users interact with on a daily basis. As I discuss later in the chapter, you have the option of using the PC and network to emulate a dumb terminal. In this host/terminal scenario, the PC application that you run is a terminal emulator that connects directly to the network transmission utilities.

Why did I go through the previous discussion? One of the greatest challenges that I have faced in integrating computer systems is getting all the drivers, network interface cards, operating systems, middleware, and application packages to work with one another. Don't be too alarmed. They work very reliably once you purchase the right components. The trick is figuring out the right equipment and software and configuring them properly.

Figuring it out is where the database seven-layer model comes in handy. Each of the layers corresponds to a product that you have to purchase. Your trick is ensuring that whenever two layers touch one another, the products on either end are compatible. This compatibility has to be specific to your host computer environment (for example, a Hewlett-Packard H50 UNIX server or Packard Bell Force 101CD running Windows 95), and the exact versions of the products on either side must be compatible with one another (for example, SQL*Net TCP/IP Version 2.3 for Windows 95 and the Microsoft Windows 95 TCP/IP stack). Sales people tell you that the products work with a particular environment, but they might not know the "gotchas"— if you can only use a particular network interface card, for example. When you're picking products, I recommend that you draw out your database seven-layer stack and look at the product specifications to ensure that all components are compatible with one another.

Overview of Oracle Networking

How does Oracle fit into the networking picture? The good news is that Oracle provides a large number of networking options (unfortunately, for the systems folks and DBAs, that is also the bad news). Oracle started out as a host-based application. However, the company quickly recognized the advantages of splitting processing between the host computers and the increasingly intelligent workstations and PCs that were appearing on users' desks. This lead to client/ server products such as SQL*Net and PC development tools such as Oracle Forms. The client/ server environment evolved to include interfaces to non-Oracle development tools and databases through the neutral ODBC and OLE interfaces, which I discuss later in this chapter. Finally, databases have grown in number and size. With a single, huge database to process information, many organizations have elected to build a series of smaller databases that are connected to one another. This is where the Oracle SQL*Net, Distributed Options, and Gateway products come into play. I discuss each of these concepts in more detail in the next few sections. Figure 53.3 summarizes the Oracle networking environment.

FIGURE 53.3.

Oracle networking overview.

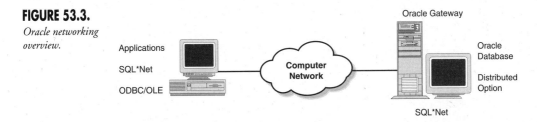

Before I leave this discussion, I want to point out something that I always considered a little bit odd. If you are working with the Oracle Workgroups Server products on a Microsoft Windows NT server, you actually use networking software to communicate from your regular Windows applications (such as SQL*Plus) that are running on the NT server to your Oracle database, which is designed to run in native NT mode. This happens because regular Windows applications run under an NT subsystem knows as Windows on Win32 (WOW). Oracle linked the 16-bit and 32-bit sides of the Windows NT system via SQL*Net. If you use Named Pipes as your communications protocol, you do not need to have a network interface card installed, but if you use TCP/IP as the protocol, you must have a network interface card. It's just something to remember if you are working in this environment.

Host/Terminal Connections

A good place to start is where Oracle started—with databases located on host computers that are accessed using terminals (or PCs that were acting as terminals). Figure 53.4 shows the basic configuration of the architecture; it has the blessing of being very simple. The host computer system provides facilities to connect terminals and supports one or more terminal types (such as DEC VT-100) to which it can send output and from which it can receive input. This type of connection usually has the following characteristics:

- The interface is usually capable of displaying only text and not graphics.

- You typically control the interface through a series of menus or command-line inputs.

- You do most of the data entry via forms that rely on function keys or tabbing to special fields that confirm you are ready to enter data.

- The host computer performs all of the processing, which includes the display of information, the business calculations, and the database management system processing.

- You usually write the applications using form-generation applications for user interaction and report-generation utilities for printed reports.

■ In many cases, the user interactive processing is supplemented with a series of batch reports that run at certain times of the day/week/month, which users read through to obtain the information that they need.

FIGURE 53.4.

Host/terminal networking.

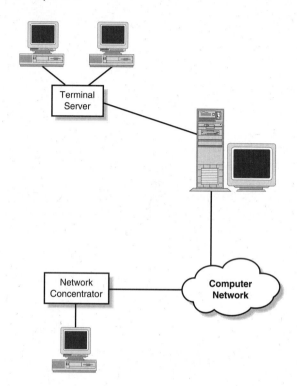

Client/Server Connections

Do you hate the buzzwords that float through the computer industry? Client/server must be one of the most frequently used (and misused) words in the computer industry. Once upper information systems management gets a buzzword in its head about the ultimate solution to all problems in the computer industry, you can bet every salesman out there is going to scramble to find a way to say that his product is an implementation of that buzzword. Client/server is no exception to that rule of buzzwords.

The host/terminal architecture dominated the industry for a number of years and its use continues today; however, it ran into some limitations. Some argue that the big host computer vendors became a little lazy and stopped turning out new equipment at a rapid pace. Others argue that as the processing load continued to grow, it became impossible to build computer processors that were powerful enough to keep up with demand. Still others argue that the large computer vendors never produced enough units to keep the cost per unit down.

Whichever reason you prefer (or even if you prefer to think that it was a little bit of all these reasons), the client/server architecture has grown over the last decade to become a very popular alternative to the traditional host/terminal world. Oh, a lot of shops still do not consider anything other than mainframes, COBOL, and terminals; however, because you are reading this book, you are probably not in this group. Now, I cover client/server in a little more detail.

Forming a definition is a good start to this discussion. Because I am not much of a theorist, I will stick to a simple definition. I define client/server architectures as systems where the computer processing load for a single application is distributed between multiple computers. In host/terminal computing, the terminal (or PC emulating a terminal) is only responsible for the presentation of the information. You can cite a number of examples that fit my definition which you might not want to call client/server, but it gives you the general idea. Figure 53.5 illustrates this general concept.

FIGURE 53.5.

Client/server networking.

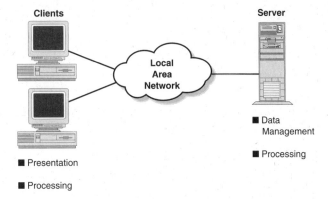

Clients

Server

Local
Area
Network

■ Data
  Management

■ Processing

■ Presentation

■ Processing

With a definition this broad, you could have a number of different distributions of labor that still qualify as client/server. Going back to my buzzword discussion, that is why you see a large number of different vendors with widely different products and architectures all claiming to be client/server. I guess that is part of free enterprise or something like that. What might be useful now are some sample distributions of labor that advertise themselves as client/server, as shown in Figure 53.6.

As you can see, there are a number of ways to split the application. Some of your choices in designing your architecture are limited by the tools you choose (or vice versa). You might want to split up your processing based on the relative capacity (or costs) of your standard server and client platforms. You might also find that your users' demands for graphics and response time influence your decisions. For example, if you have a group of users who demand excellent graphical interfaces and fast performance, you could buy a moderately powerful server and some high-end PCs. As another example, if you already have an overloaded but paid-for host computer and reasonably powerful PCs, you could extend the life span of the host by converting some of your applications to perform the database processing. You could perform some of the calculations on the host server and then perform the rest of the calculations on the client. The following are some general characteristics of most client/server environments to consider:

- You use graphical user interfaces (where the users can access information using a mouse to click a button on the screen or select an item from a scrollable list) to interact with the users.

- You have a wide range of tools and connectivity products to choose from. This can be a blessing in that you have the capability to preview a number of different products to see which one is best suited to your individual needs. It can also make the task of integrating products a bit more challenging.

- The capabilities of the client workstation become an important factor in the overall application performance. Because most organizations have PCs that vary somewhat in computing and memory capacity, you might find that you have to upgrade certain PCs in order to run your new client/server applications.

- The capacity of the network (especially wide area network links used to connect different facilities) can be an important factor in determining the overall performance of the applications.

FIGURE 53.6.

Sample distributions of labor in various applications.

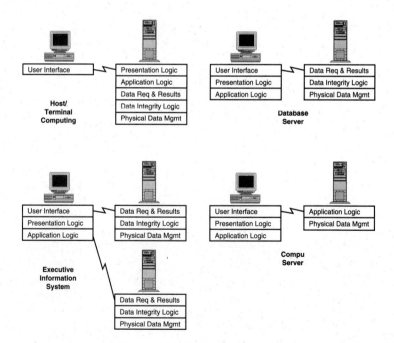

One final concept that you might need to consider is the difference between two-tier and three-tier client/server architectures. When client/server first started, you had just two machines (the client and the server). The client typically performed the display functions, and the server did most of the calculation work and database management. People liked the display capabilities of the PC but found that neither the PCs nor the server had sufficient processing capacity to perform complex calculations that might be necessary for detailed financial analysis or other such needs. These users did not want to move up to the more expensive larger computers (twice the processing capacity usually has much more than twice the price in the computer industry). Instead, developers came upon the idea of splitting the processing load for a given user and application among three different computers. The client machine still performed the user interface work; however, the other work was split between a database server and an application server. The database server focused on running the database management system, and the application server performed all the computations associated with the application. (See Figure 53.7.) The three-tier architecture is more complex to design and configure, but it can be the answer if you perform a lot of demanding computational work but do not want to invest in a single large computer.

FIGURE 53.7.

Two-tier and three-tier client/server architectures.

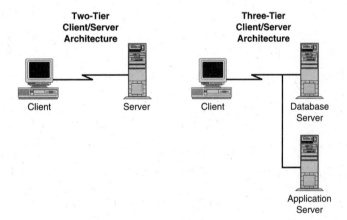

Two-Tier Client/Server Architecture — Client — Server

Three-Tier Client/Server Architecture — Client — Database Server — Application Server

Database-to-Database Connections

A logical extension of the concept of using multiple computers to perform the work of an application is the use of multiple servers to support the overall database processing capabilities for a large organization. For Oracle, these capabilities come in three phases. In the first phase, Oracle uses SQL*Net to enable users to access data in tables that were in a remote database through a database link. Figure 53.8 shows the general concept of the database link. To summarize the general concept, for example, I am telling Oracle to "get me all of the rows in table X, which is located in database Y, that meet my criteria." You issue a command (create database link), which creates a simple alias (such as marketing) for the database that the users refer to. The create database link command captures all the details of the connection (addresses, user ID and password to connect with, and so on) and stores them for use when the users request this connection. One of the drawbacks is that a database link connects you to the remote database with whatever user ID and password are specified in the create database link command. The user accesses the data with the privileges of this user ID and not the ID of the user who is issuing the query or sending the transaction (which could cause security problems).

FIGURE 53.8.

Database links.

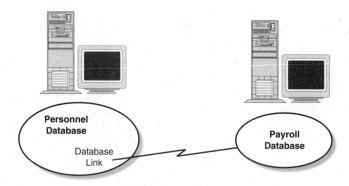

Overall though, this first phase was a good start on splitting up the database processing work load; however, other issues soon became apparent. The biggest issue was that remote locations usually had to rely on a relatively slow wide area network communications link to access a database located on a centralized server. Another factor was that programmers had to be aware of all the database links and put them into the SQL statements they issued.

The next generation of database-to-database connectivity came with Oracle's distributed database option (option means that you had to pay extra for it). With remote field offices that are connected to the central office by relatively slow communications lines, you could implement smaller servers in the field that get a nightly download of data from the central server. You would then write batch routines that ran at night, figured out which records needed to be downloaded, and so on. You could do this yourself, but it is much easier if the database management system takes care of this stuff for you. That is the idea behind the distributed database option.

There are two general features of such a system. First, you can access tables located on remote databases as easily as you access tables located on the disks that are attached to your local server. Second, if you have multiple copies of the data to speed up processing at remote sites, you can set up the system so that Oracle synchronizes the data between the systems. Actually, quite a bit of logic goes into ensuring that if you make a change in a particular record, it is applied to all the copies of the database—especially when some of the changes might take minutes or even hours to finish. It is much easier to put that burden on Oracle rather than code it into your application. There aren't a huge number of installations out there using this option, but it could be very useful in certain cases. Figure 53.9 illustrates the Oracle distributed database concepts.

FIGURE 53.9.
The Oracle Distributed Option.

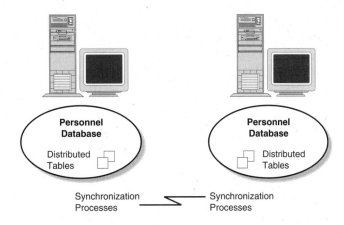

Assume you have linked multiple Oracle databases that are located on different servers to distribute the database processing load of your organization. What more can you ask for? You now have the ability to take advantage of the large number of PCs sitting on people's desks, you can have multiple servers (located wherever you need them in your wide area network) performing the database management tasks, and you can even use a three-tier client/server architecture to distribute complex computational loads to a different server. Well, there is one other possibility that Oracle sales representatives usually do not like to consider. What if you have a lot of data on DB2 that you do not want to convert to Oracle, or what if you have a subsidiary or business partner that has adopted VAX RDB as its standard database management system?

The answer to this question comes in the form of gateways. Oracle makes a series of gateways that link Oracle databases to DB2 and other major database products. It seems reasonable that Oracle will continue to work in this area to increase the number of gateways to other vendor's databases. The key to these gateways is that they are conceptually similar to the distributed option. All you (or your DBA and system administrator) have to do is install this gateway product and provide all the configuration information about where the data is stored, what format it is in, how you network into the database, and so on. The gateway software then takes care of the details whenever your applications issue a query or transaction that affect data in these remote databases. As with many of the networking products discussed in this chapter, the gateways are not for everyone, but they can be a big help to those who need them.

Just for the record, many of the other database vendors and third-party developers have gateways that connect to Oracle databases. They have seen the same market opportunities to sell software to organizations that are not planning to convert all their databases into Oracle systems. The key to picking the right gateway is to ensure that it supports the versions of the databases you are using and that it fits into your computer and network architecture. These gateways are relatively new products, and I would suggest checking with other customers who are using the products or perhaps even setting up a test system in your organization before you commit to purchasing the gateway as the ultimate solution to all your problems.

SQL*Net Version 1

Now that I have covered the general concepts of database networking, it is time to get into some specifics. A good place to start is with SQL*Net Version 1, which was the first product in the Oracle environment to support networking. Designed to support client/server computing and database links, SQL*Net Version 1 was a good start on this process and was fairly reliable. In fact, I did not start using SQL*Net Version 2 until recently, so that is some indication that SQL*Net Version 1 was not a bad product.

SQL*Net is a product that I classify as lower middleware. It does not alter the format of the query to comply with Oracle standards or handle the details of transferring the results into a format that the applications can handle. Instead, it sends and receives data in the format that it understands and lets other middleware or the applications themselves get that information into its format. Some applications are designed to interface directly with SQL*Net. Oracle's database management system, SQL*Plus, Oracle Forms, and its other development tools are all designed to interface directly with SQL*Net. You can develop applications using Oracle's precompilers and products such as Oracle Objects for OLE that interface directly with SQL*Net. Figure 53.10 shows this direct interface.

FIGURE 53.10.

*Products interfacing directly with SQL*Net.*

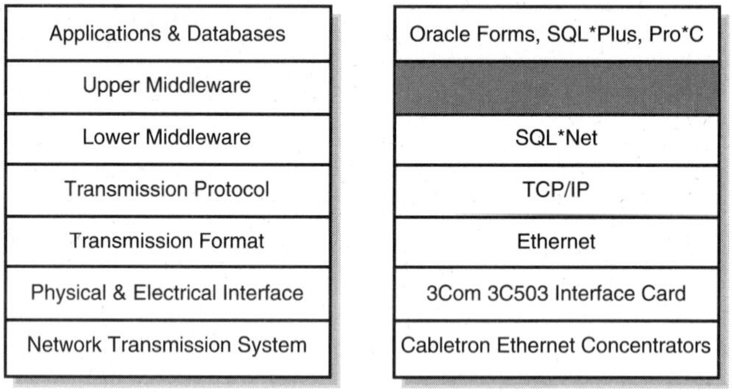

Applications & Databases	Oracle Forms, SQL*Plus, Pro*C
Upper Middleware	
Lower Middleware	SQL*Net
Transmission Protocol	TCP/IP
Transmission Format	Ethernet
Physical & Electrical Interface	3Com 3C503 Interface Card
Network Transmission System	Cabletron Ethernet Concentrators

You might have noticed in the last paragraph that the word Oracle preceded most of the products that I listed. Although there are third-party products that are designed to interface directly with SQL*Net (such big names as PowerBuilder), many other developers yearned for an "open" standard that would enable them to write one application that could interface with a number of different middleware packages and database management systems. This is how the products that I call upper middleware were born.

The basic concept is simple. Design a product that has a neutral, published interface from applications and then design a neutral interface and connection software for a variety of lower middleware transport protocols. Figure 53.11 illustrates this concept. One of the ways that you can tell a good idea in the computer industry is when every big company jumps on an issue and creates their own "industry standard" to implement the concept. Such is the case with what I call lower middleware.

FIGURE 53.11.

*Upper middleware interfacing with SQL*Net.*

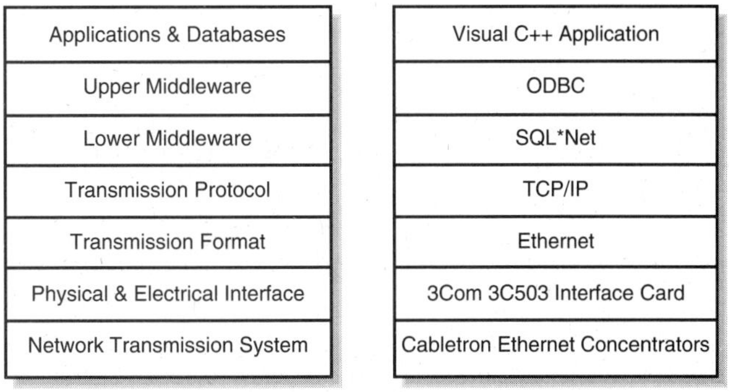

Applications & Databases	Visual C++ Application
Upper Middleware	ODBC
Lower Middleware	SQL*Net
Transmission Protocol	TCP/IP
Transmission Format	Ethernet
Physical & Electrical Interface	3Com 3C503 Interface Card
Network Transmission System	Cabletron Ethernet Concentrators

The biggest name in this market that I have encountered in my experience is Microsoft and the Open Database Connection (ODBC) standard. It has the advantage of accessing a large number of clients (PCs that run Microsoft Windows, Windows NT, or Windows 95). It also came out early in the client/server evolution process and so there are already a number of applications written with this standard. Finally, Microsoft provides a series of drivers and utilities with most of the operating systems delivered, so you can keep the cost of an installation down (you would be amazed how fast the cost of a client workstation can go up when you start buying a large number of "optional" packages).

This is not to say that Microsoft is the only upper middleware vendor on the market. There are a number of vendors such as Intersolv and Openlink that have worked to produce drivers that are faster than the standard ODBC drivers or that work with more database management systems. Once again, you are faced with a number of choices. One is a low cost solution; the others might provide improved performance. Still others, such as Openlink, merge the functionality of SQL*Net with an ODBC driver to reduce the number of middleware products that you need to install and maintain.

I have one final note to add about middleware. Just when you were confused enough with the various options related to ODBC, Microsoft throws in another wrinkle. They incorporated the concept of upper middleware into a structure that enables you to dynamically share data between applications and even launch one application from within another. This standard is called Object Linking and Embedding (OLE—you know there had to be an acronym for it). Anyway, I discuss the differences between ODBC and OLE later in this chapter. For now, you should understand SQL*Net as a lower middleware product and how it interfaces either directly to SQL*Net-ready applications such as SQL*Plus or the Oracle database management system and upper middleware products such as Microsoft's ODBC.

Next on the agenda is a discussion of how SQL*Net is implemented. Once again, there is more than one answer. Remember: part of the sales appeal of Oracle is that it works on a wide variety of computer systems and is designed to do many things. For this discussion on SQL*Net, I split the discussion of implementation into two separate discussions. The first discussion is about SQL*Net on computers (such as UNIX or VAX VMS) that run multiple processes at the same time. The other discussion covers SQL*Net on computers that are basically single tasking (such as Microsoft DOS and Windows 3.1).

On multitasking computers (those running multiple processes), Oracle SQL*Net Version 1 is implemented as a listener process. Listener is a good name for this process. It merely sits there in the background and listens for someone to send a signal into it. This signal could come from either the remote machine, in which case it picks up the signal from its interface to the network transmission protocol, or from the local application or database. When it is connected to the database, SQL*Net spawns (creates) a server process to handle the interface to the database management system and merely passes signals between this database interface process and the network drivers. Figure 53.12 illustrates the basics of this configuration.

FIGURE 53.12.

*SQL*Net Version 1 implemented as a server process.*

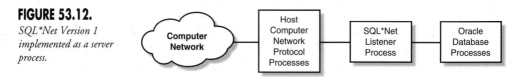

Microsoft Windows 3.1 and DOS do not support multiple background processes. As a result, Oracle had to adapt its SQL*Net Version 1 product to fit within this environment. The problem is that memory is usually in short supply on PC clients, so you do not want to waste memory space by permanently loading the SQL*Net drivers. To get around this problem, Oracle uses a Dynamic Link Library (DLL in computer-speak). The software is loaded into memory when needed to facilitate communication between the applications and the network protocol drivers. This can actually be more convenient because you do not have to worry about starting and stopping the background SQL*Net listener process under this architecture. Figure 53.13 illustrates the SQL*Net DLL concept under Microsoft Windows 3.1.

FIGURE 53.13.

*SQL*Net Version 1 implemented as a DLL.*

There is a lot that I could discuss regarding SQL*Net Version 1; however, because you might not even use this version of the software and it is usually transparent to developers and end users, I want to cover only one more topic: controlling and using the SQL*Net Version 1 listener process. As I mentioned earlier, if you are using SQL*Net under Microsoft Windows 3.1 and everything is set up correctly on your computer, you load the SQL*Net software automatically when needed. On computers where SQL*Net is a background process, you have to ensure that the background process is running before you use SQL*Net.

The good news is that Oracle provides relatively simple-to-use utilities to determine the status of this background process, start it, and stop it. The bad news is that you have to know the name of the process and the way to access it. To start off with, *process* is a term that works under UNIX. Under Windows NT, the more proper term is *service*. Novell refers to *Novell Loadable Modules* (NLMs). For the name of the process (service or whatever), you need to see what name your database administrator set up when installing the software. Which utility controls the background process is also important to know. Under Windows NT, you access the Services Utility under Control Panel to start up the service. Under UNIX, you use the tcpctl utility (with the start, stop, or status options) to work with the SQL*Net TCP/IP background process. The best advice that I can give you with the wide variety of configurations available is to check with your database administrator, system administrator, or whoever installed your SQL*Net software.

Finally, the topic that is most interesting to the average user is using SQL*Net Version 1 to access remote databases. This process is relatively simple; all you have to do is specify the database address in the manner appropriate to your application. The SQL*Net Version 1 address is composed of three parts. The first part tells SQL*Net which protocol you are using (T = TCP/IP, P = named pipes, and so on). The second part of the address shows which computer the desired database is on. In TCP/IP, for example, you can either use an alias defined in the hosts table (such as marketing) or the Internet address of the server (such as 10.15.20.25). Finally, you need to specify the SID (Oracle's system ID) for the database that you want. The SID is set up by the DBA when creating the new database, so that person has to tell you the name of the SID.

SQL*Net Version 1 enables you to create aliases for your remote databases. It also enables you to define default local and remote databases that are accessed when the user does not specify the desired database. The following is a sample call to the SQL*Plus utility that accesses the jdoe account in the MKT Oracle instance on the marketing server using the TCP/IP protocol:

```
$ sqlplus jdoe@t:marketing:MKT
```

I have one final note. If you are using an upper middleware product such as ODBC, you define the SQL*Net Version 1 address to the ODBC administrator and then use the ODBC alias when you reference the data source in your applications. Basically, your job is talking to ODBC. ODBC is then responsible for routing your request to the appropriate database.

SQL*Net Version 2

If you understand the basic concepts of SQL*Net Version 1, then you are well on your way to understanding SQL*Net Version 2. It is not really a revolution in the concept of how Oracle networks its products. It still interfaces directly with SQL*Plus and all the other Oracle tools (you do not even have to change any configuration files on those development products). It still interfaces to ODBC and OLE. The main differences between Version 1 and Version 2 are the following:

- In SQL*Net Version 2, the DBA has to prepare a series of files that contain all the connection information for the various data sources that are available. These data files associate a simple alias (such as main_sales) with all the information such as the SID, host computer, protocol to use for communication, and so on. All the users have to worry about, once they get copies of these files from the administrator on their computers, is what the aliases are and what information is stored in each of these databases.

- SQL*Net Version 2 can interface with a feature of the Oracle7 server known as the Multi-Threaded Server. In Version 1 of SQL*Net, you allocate a dedicated process for each user who connects to Oracle via SQL*Net. This process stays open until the user disconnects, which could be the end of the day for some users. This can become a problem when you have a large number of users accessing a system where they might be connected to their application all day even though they are not actively working with the database. The Multi-Threaded Server concept enables the SQL*Net users to share a series of server processes, each accessing the server process only when he has an active query or transaction.

- The later versions of SQL*Net Version 2 are much better at detecting when a user gets disconnected from Oracle without issuing a proper command to disconnect (for example, if they get bored and hit Ctrl-Alt-Delete in the middle of a long query). Under SQL*Net Version 1, this can cause a shadow process to hang around eating up large amounts of processor time (these processes run away and can take up the entire CPU). SQL*Net Version 2 has some time-out parameters that enable you to eliminate this problem.

- The names of the controlling processes are different between the two versions of SQL*Net so that you can easily tell which version is running.

- Finally, you really should use the Oracle network management tools to create the configuration files. You could edit the aliases in the old SQL*Net Version 1 files if you were ambitious (the default remote connection, and so on). However, unless you are really sure of what you are doing, use the Oracle utilities to make your network configuration files. They are somewhat complex in syntax and the names of the fields are not always obvious.

SQL*Net Version 2 is a sound product that provides the same basic services as SQL*Net Version 1. I caution you to allow adequate time to get SQL*Net set up properly. I have found that it always takes longer than you think it will to set up the SQL*Net configuration files correctly, start the background processes, and complete any upper middleware configurations such as ODBC. Even after you have done it several times, there seem to be a few quirks about each new type of server or each new network stack on the clients.

ODBC Versus OLE

Earlier in this chapter, I gave a brief introduction to ODBC and OLE, two standard upper middleware package standards created by Microsoft. There are other vendors who have created their own ODBC software packages because that is a utility that is separate from the basic operating system. I am not familiar with any users who have created their own version of OLE; however, Oracle has created Objects for OLE, which enables you to write software that uses OLE to interface with an Oracle database.

What are some of the differences between ODBC and OLE? The biggest, in my mind, is that Oracle supports OLE, and many of the other big database vendors do not. As a result, if you are writing an application that you want to sell to a broad audience with multiple database management systems, OLE might limit your options. Also, because ODBC is older, you might be able to find more third-party development software to support your development effort.

Most of the folks I have talked to indicate that they found OLE several times faster than ODBC. Some people on the ODBC side might counter that the initial Microsoft ODBC drivers were not as optimized as they could be and that you can increase ODBC performance by a good bit. Some of the OLE concepts (such as launching a small database application from within a word processor or spreadsheet) are very difficult to implement using ODBC. In summary, I see OLE as far more capable in the long run, and ODBC as more practical in many circumstances, at least for the next year or so.

Other Middleware Vendors

Another point I mentioned earlier is that there are other middleware vendors you might want to consider. Why? Perhaps you are working with an operating system such as Windows 95 right after it was released, and all the beta test drivers that you were shipped are buggy. You desperately want to get a product out the door, and you are searching for that one driver that will enable you to complete the porting of your software package to Windows 95. Also, you might be in a situation where you are writing an extremely demanding application, and you are pushing to optimize performance whenever possible. In this section, I present a brief overview of some of the middleware vendors on the market to give you a feel for some of the alternatives. After this book goes to press, another vendor might release a great product that could be the one that is right for you. You should perform the usual research steps (vendor search, magazine reviews, and so on) to see what products are available to you.

I'll start the product review with the products from Oracle shown in Figure 53.14. The basic middleware that Oracle provides is the SQL*Net product, which I classify as lower middleware. Oracle also offers its own set of ODBC drivers to compete in the upper middleware market. The Oracle ODBC drivers provide an interface to Oracle databases, so if you are trying to write applications for a wide variety of databases, you might still need to purchase additional ODBC drivers for those other databases. One thing to consider when working with new releases of Oracle is that the Oracle drivers might be more up to date than some of the third-party drivers, although the ODBC standard shields you from some of the internal changes that occur in the databases themselves. Oracle also markets its Objects for OLE product to serve as upper middleware for those who want to use OLE.

FIGURE 53.14.

Middleware products from Oracle.

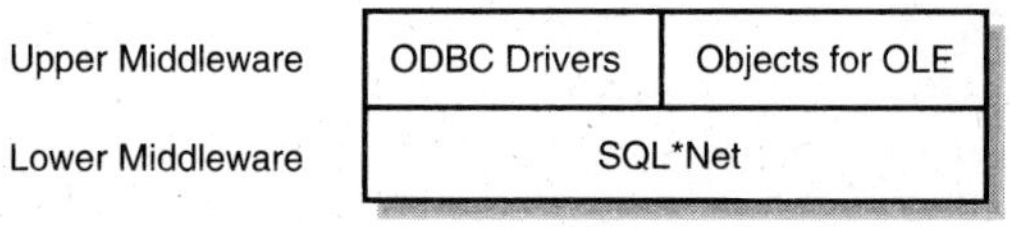

Upper Middleware	ODBC Drivers	Objects for OLE
Lower Middleware	SQL*Net	

Of course, Microsoft wrote both the ODBC and OLE upper middleware standards. The Microsoft development tools come with ODBC drivers and OLE support, in addition to development tools from other third-party vendors. These products compete with the Oracle ODBC drivers and Objects for OLE. Microsoft supports networking to its SQL*Server product as part of the operating system, so I guess you could call Microsoft's drivers lower middleware for a non-Oracle database.

Next on the list of representative vendors is Intersolv. What I have worked with is their ODBC drivers. They provide drivers for a range of databases, often before the database vendors come out with their releases. They also have the distinction of writing the drivers that are provided by some of the other database vendors. Intersolv owns the Q+E product line, which was one of the first tools that enabled you to connect spreadsheets such as Microsoft Excel to remote databases. Again, the main focus for Intersolv is the upper middleware ODBC market.

Last on this short survey of some of the vendors in the middleware market is a British firm called Openlink. They are somewhat unique in that they bundle together the functions of upper and lower middleware into a single package. You have to run their products on both the client and the server, but in return, you get to avoid installing and maintaining a number of lower middleware products. The basic architecture is shown in Figure 53.15.

FIGURE 53.15.

Openlink combined middleware concept.

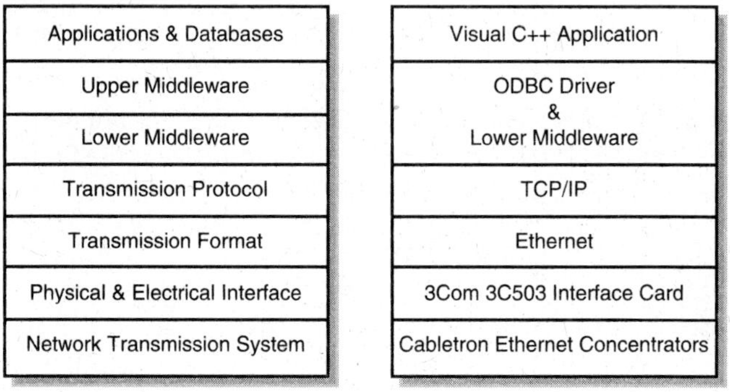

Applications & Databases	Visual C++ Application
Upper Middleware	ODBC Driver & Lower Middleware
Lower Middleware	
Transmission Protocol	TCP/IP
Transmission Format	Ethernet
Physical & Electrical Interface	3Com 3C503 Interface Card
Network Transmission System	Cabletron Ethernet Concentrators

Before closing this section, I want to mention that there are other standards out there competing in the middleware market. Several vendors in the UNIX and Apple worlds favor different standards that are similar to ODBC and OLE. Each touts the benefits of their framework over the others. If you spend a lot of time working in one of these environments, you might want to consider these competing standards. However, if you primarily use PCs as clients, ODBC and OLE are the two standards that you will encounter the most. I view it as though I am living with the standards set by the industry and not making them. If a standard is adopted by the rest of the computer industry, it does not matter how many wonderful features the competitors have; they will probably fade away due to lack of sales in a few years. The only difficulty that you face is figuring out where this fickle industry is headed.

Some Sample Configurations

So far in this chapter, I cover most of the networking topics that you probably need as a developer or user of a networked Oracle system. What is missing is that one single drawing which shows you all the pieces you need to buy for this networked Oracle system. I can't provide that drawing because, as I mentioned earlier, there are too many different options. You can now use Oracle development tools with non-Oracle databases and vice versa. What I thought would be useful here is a series of sample configurations that might give you some ideas about what working networked database configurations look like.

I have one big note of caution. You have to look at each type of system configuration on an individual basis. There are so many unusual reactions between different versions of the various products that you really should test things in your environment before you can be certain that it will work. There are things that you might not anticipate—for example, if none of the wide area network transmission equipment in your company is capable of transmitting the TCP/IP protocol or something really strange such as that. Anyway, enough said; just test everything out using demonstration software or limited quantities whenever possible before you commit to rewriting your entire application architecture using a given set of products.

With that traditional cautionary note out of the way, look at the first sample configuration. Because I started my discussion of network access to database with the host/terminal architecture, I thought that I would present an example of this environment. (See Figure 53.16.) Note that even though I use PCs to access the VAX Oracle database, they are emulating dumb, non-graphics terminals. The applications developed use the traditional, character-based interface where you hit F3 to commit your changes or F4 to exit out from where you are. Note that all the application development software and completed applications reside on the Oracle server (in this case a VAX) and that the linkages from the application to the database management system are already set up (you do not need to configure any links as you would in SQL*Net).

FIGURE 53.16.

Host/terminal example.

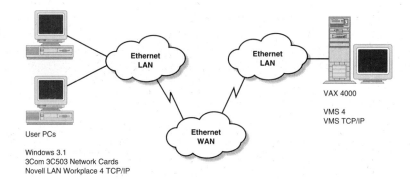

Next on my list of samples is a basic client/server system, illustrated in Figure 53.17. In this case, I show the Oracle tools set (which now goes by names such as Developer/2000 and Oracle Forms, but who knows what the marketing folks will call it next year) on PCs interfacing with an Oracle database on a UNIX server. Some key points to note about this architecture is that you do not have to use an upper middleware product on your clients (because these tools are all designed to interface directly with SQL*Net). Oracle tools have recently started to also support an ODBC interface. I guess Oracle wants to sell its development tools even to customers who use other database management systems.

FIGURE 53.17.

Oracle development tools interfacing with an Oracle database.

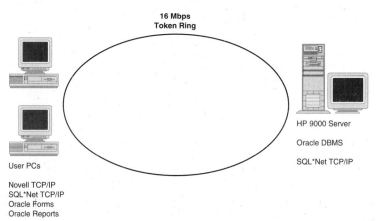

Next, I cover a system that uses upper middleware—in this case, ODBC—to interface with an Oracle database located on a UNIX server, as shown in Figure 53.18. This environment uses the Microsoft C++ compiler with a set of third-party ODBC drivers from Intersolv. The database is Oracle 7.1, located on a Sun UNIX server. One key point to note from this example is that you must ensure that your ODBC driver is compatible with the exact version of networking software that you are using (you might have trouble, for example, if you move your application to Windows 95). Also, when using a development tool such as C++, you must be sensitive to details such as the data types that the ODBC driver is returning to your application (it does not map to character, VARCHAR, and NUMBER, as in the Oracle database). This detail work can take up some time, so you might want to run some tests up front to figure out the calls and returns that you will be dealing with.

FIGURE 53.18.

Example of an ODBC environment.

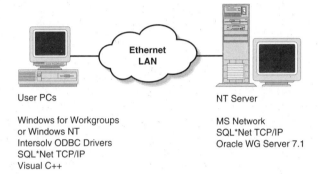

```
User PCs

Windows for Workgroups
or Windows NT
Intersolv ODBC Drivers
SQL*Net TCP/IP
Visual C++
```

```
NT Server

MS Network
SQL*Net TCP/IP
Oracle WG Server 7.1
```

Finally, I thought it'd be useful to include an example of a distributed database environment. I have not encountered a large number of these configurations, but that could change in the future as gateway and distributed database processing technology continues to improve. Figure 53.19 illustrates one such system. The basic concept behind this system is that the two databases (perhaps one is in Cleveland and the other is in Chicago) are linked together. Users interact with their local database and let the distributed option take care of ensuring that the remote database is updated. Delays in the transmission of the database between the systems do not delay the user's processing.

FIGURE 53.19.

Example of a distributed database environment.

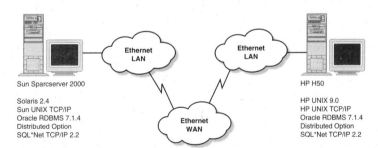

```
Sun Sparcserver 2000

Solaris 2.4
Sun UNIX TCP/IP
Oracle RDBMS 7.1.4
Distributed Option
SQL*Net TCP/IP 2.2
```

```
HP H50

HP UNIX 9.0
HP UNIX TCP/IP
Oracle RDBMS 7.1.4
Distributed Option
SQL*Net TCP/IP 2.2
```

Network Development Tips

Here, I summarize some of my experiences dealing with networked database environments into a series of tips. Think of this information as highly condensed examples. Anyway, I urge you to at least consider the following directions:

- I first recommend that you do not cheat and try to implement the production environment late in the development cycle. It is tempting to say that you will develop everything on a stand-alone workstation and then convert it to the client/server environment the week before testing (you can certainly get it working in a week, right?). Anyway, I like to spend the time getting the true working environment set up in the beginning for several reasons. First, you might find that some of your drivers and products are incompatible. You might have to troubleshoot and then order replacement products, which can take an amazing amount of time. Also, your developers need immediate feedback during development when they write software that is not optimized for the end-user environment. For example, imagine a piece of code that pulls down to the PC all the data from a very large table (with lots of long text fields) located on the server just to calculate the sum of a single number field. This code would be extremely slow over a busy network. The developer could use a built-in Oracle sum function and only have to return a few bytes of data with the result.

■ Now, I give you a recommendation where I do not always practice what I preach. I recommend that you do not deviate from common computer environments and tools. I like to live on the bleeding edge of technology, but that makes it extremely challenging to get those production applications out on time. Incompatibilities of drivers and tools with new operating systems such as Windows 95 requires that you have a fair amount of experience dealing with lower-level system details and a wide range of access to vendors. In an ideal world, you would have a lab environment where you could test and get new products working and then use them in your production and development environments.

■ Know about your network monitoring and testing utilities. Many errors, especially those in the client/server environment, translate into something similar to "There is something, somewhere that is not right." I hate those error messages but must live with them. What you then do is use some of the low-level testing utilities to go step by step through the system to see where the problem lies. For example, if I am setting up the C++/ODBC to UNIX database via TCP/IP environment and encounter a problem, I have to use several utilities to test the connection. I typically start by using the ping utility that is common to most TCP/IP environments to ensure that I have basic networking connectivity between the two computers. I then use Oracle Net Ping to see if my two SQL*Net processes are communicating with one another. Next, I use an easy ODBC access tool such as Microsoft Query to see if I set up my ODBC configuration correctly. Finally, I create a new Visual C++ application using the App Wizard to see if I could access the database from a basic C++ environment (if I get a table list when selecting the data source in App Wizard, it is a good sign that ODBC is set up correctly). Anyway, as you can see, you might have to use a number of products to see where your problem lies. What you are trying to do is find a simple tool that tests each of the interfaces in the network stack one at a time, starting at the bottom.

■ Another favorite tip of mine is that you should get familiar with the various vendor bulletin board systems, Web sites, FTP sites, and so on. Having a PC with a reasonably fast modem and an Internet connection can save you an enormous amount of time. In a few minutes' time, I have downloaded drivers from the U.K. that got the developers going—products that might have taken a week or more to get through the mail. Your problem could be as simple as needing a special patch from a specific vendor if you have a certain old model of PC.

- Have help lined up in advance when possible. This can take a number of forms. Perhaps you can have a local vendor or contractor who has done this before come in to help you set things up. You should also have support from the product vendors, at least during installation. It is very useful to keep all those books and purchase order copies in a file so that when you have problems, you can get the answers you need quickly.

- Bring in all your local experts from the start. This list of people might include network administrators, system administrators, database administrators, and others. If they participate in the process when you are ordering and setting up the configuration, they can often save you a fair amount of time and money. They can tell you little things such as "We are on Novell 3 now, but we will be upgrading to Novell 4 next week so you'd better be ready for it." Most information systems shops are so busy that it is often impossible for any one person to be aware of all the things going on. Get input from the individual experts early and often.

- Start with simple applications when moving to a new environment. You could try to make your first client/server application the mission-critical executive information system that the CEO and all the vice presidents use every day. If so, you have a lot more guts than I do. One example of a good first system to develop in a new environment is the system that tracks the time spent on various projects in the information systems group. This has several advantages. First, it is relatively simple so you don't have to spend a lot of time on it. Second, your fellow information systems staff will probably be a lot kinder if there are performance problems or bugs than your company executives would be. Finally, if the system has a lot of problems, you are not affecting the company's bottom line while you work out all the bugs. It is a good place to learn some of the "how-tos" and work with issues such as performance.

- Always leave yourself time for problem resolution with the environment itself. I have seen setup take only a day with simple environments that have been done before with only a few vendors involved, and I've also seen setup take weeks or months for cutting-edge technology. An assurance from your sales representative that everything will work is not something I would bet the project on. That sales representative might be completely truthful about never having had a problem setting up the software, but he might not have tried it in an environment like yours.

- Finally, go through the database stack model and spec sheets when planning the system. You have to get down to the detail level of things—such as Windows NT 3.51 on the server with the NT 3.51 TCP/IP stack interfacing to Version 2.2 of SQL*Net and so on. Whenever possible, get evaluation copies of the software and hardware to test before purchasing the products. Another alternative might be to contact others who have the same environment that you do to figure out what worked and did not work for them. It is tempting to move quickly through the planning steps to get a project going, but it can cost you a lot of troubleshooting time later if you miss some things.

This list of tips could continue; however, I think that these basic suggestions should get you through most of the hurdles. Do not take this as the voice of doom. I have always been able to get the database network environments I work with operational. Sometimes, it was a challenge to get things set up, especially in leading-edge environments; however, things usually worked well once the process was finished.

Summary

This chapter took on an ambitious project. To try and describe the wide range of networking options that are available in Oracle in the space of a single chapter is somewhat like trying to summarize *War and Peace* in a single paragraph. The technical details of the various Oracle products fill up many different books in their manual set with detailed configuration options and installations instructions. Obviously, with the wide range of products that Oracle provides and the number of different environments it supports, I could not even begin to look at all the options here. Instead, I chose to focus on providing an overview of database networking. The goal was to give you a feel for all the products that have to work together for that seemingly simple connection from your desktop to the database.

Along the way, I tried to provide some examples and share some of my experiences. This is a tough chapter to come up with detailed examples (the list of configuration options that I had to set on just one configuration would probably fill a chapter in itself). I did try to summarize some of the more common tricks that I have used in the section "Network Development Tips." As a final note, I urge you to consider giving yourself an adequate amount of time when setting up a networked database environment. It is easy to think that because everything is vendor-provided, all you have to do is open the boxes, load the software, and begin working. I found that it often takes days to get the settings of new drivers right and get all the kinks worked out of the architecture. Of course, if you already have dozens of similar installations and you are simply copying a working configuration, you might be able to get working right away. On the other hand, if you have a slightly (and I mean slightly) different configuration, you should leave yourself some time for testing and problem solving.

Oracle PowerBrowser

54

by Matthew Bennett

This chapter is about Oracle Corporation's latest Internet product, Oracle PowerBrowser. At the time of this writing, PowerBrowser is a beta product and might have some functionality changes. However, the information here will give you a glimpse of Oracle Corporation's plans for this product, its basic functionality, and an idea of how to use it.

What Is the World Wide Web?

Before going into the details of Oracle's PowerBrowser, it is important to get an understanding of what the World Wide Web (a.k.a. the Web or WWW) is and how it came to be. First will be a short history of the Web, including the Internet, and then a description of how the browser came to be. Rounding out this section will be an attempt to predict what is happening with the Web and where it will take us.

Short History of the Web

In the 1960s the United States government, through the efforts of the Advanced Research Projects Agency (ARPA), felt it would be important to link university computers and researchers to assist them in conducting basic research through the sharing of information. This project became known as the ARPAnet. Although only 107 hosts were added to the system between 1969 and 1977, the engineers in charge of the ARPAnet realized that the new communications network was going to grow into something larger than originally anticipated. On January 1, 1983, all of the ARPAnet was switched from NCP (with a possibility of 256 hosts) to TCP/IP (with a possibility of 4,294,967,296 hosts) and became what is now known as the Internet. The National Science Foundation (NSF) funded most of the early development of the Internet, but on April 30, 1995, the U.S. government released the Internet to commercial networks and service providers and shut down the National Science Foundation (NSF) backbone.

Before the World Wide Web, the Internet consisted mostly of electronic mail (e-mail), Usenet newsgroups, and FTP or file transfer sites. Tools were invented to help categorize what information could be found and where it was, but the Internet was not what you would call user-friendly. If you wanted to send e-mail to a close friend at another Internet site, the easiest way to get his or her e-mail address was to use the phone and call him or her directly (this may still be the case). If you needed a particular computer program or file, it was nearly impossible to find unless you knew exactly where it was.

In March, 1989, Tim Berners-Lee at the European Laboratory for Particle Physics (CERN) proposed a new set of protocols for Internet information distribution. This set of protocols became known as the World Wide Web protocols and was soon adopted by other organizations. A consortium of organizations was formed, and it became known as the W3 Consortium.

Birth of the Browsers

Soon after the WWW protocols were defined, the National Center for Supercomputing Applictions (NCSA) worked on creating an interface for them. The goal of the interface was to provide a graphical, easy-to-use application that would encourage others to develop and support the World Wide Web. One thing that greatly helped this cause was that NCSA developed its front-end (Mosaic) simultaneously on three different graphical user interfaces (GUIs): the X windowing system found on UNIX, the Macintosh user interface from Apple Computers, and the Windows interface from Microsoft. Its release in 1993 has made the WWW the most popular Internet service in use today.

Shortly after the release of Mosaic, James Clark and Marc Andreessen got together and formed Netscape Communications Corporation. Jim was one of the founders of the highly successful Silicon Graphics Incorporated, and Marc was one of the original authors of Mosaic. Together they set out to build a better browser than Mosaic. To help gain market share, they made their browser freely downloadable for people to try, thus setting the standard for other Web browsers. Today almost every browser on the market, including Oracle PowerBrowser, is freely available.

If the browsers are free, how does anyone make any money? In order to browse the WWW, you need to have servers sending information—and those are not free. In order to take advantage of all the neat features the Netscape browser has to offer, companies, individuals, and Web site providers must utilize the Netscape server. Also, Netscape has started charging a very small fee for its browser.

Another way that companies such as Microsoft are making money is through bundles. Microsoft can provide you with a free browser or server that runs on Windows NT in hopes that it will sell more copies of Windows NT.

Oracle Corporation hopes that after you have seen the power of PowerBrowser and how easily it interacts with the Oracle Relational Database Management System (RDBMS), you will become interested in purchasing Oracle databases.

Future Vision of the Web

The World Wide Web is about sharing information but is still in its infancy. As more companies compete in the WWW-tools and -applications business, you will see many neat and interesting enhancements made. You will also see some creative applications and uses for these products. Although only time will tell what really happens, here is where the future trends in Web technology seem to be heading both on the Internet and on stand-alone corporate networks.

On the Internet

Reading through the *Los Angeles Times*, it is not uncommon to see WWW addresses of the companies promoting products in advertisements. Whether you are looking for computer-related products or designer clothes, you can go to the Web to see information about the companies selling you those products and information about the products themselves. Soon, if you are happy with the products advertised, you will be able to purchase them through electronic means. This will allow you to purchase a Hong Kong tailored suit at the local Hong Kong price without having to leave Provo, Utah, or wherever you may be.

In addition to electronic commerce, you will be able to perform routine errands without having to leave your home. Several banks just announced that they are setting up banking services on the WWW. No longer will it require a trip to the bank to find out why your account balance is lower than your records indicate. Soon, you will be able to renew your driver's license, sign up for community events, watch first-run movies, and maybe even vote via the World Wide Web. One of the key technologies that will make this happen is coupling mature databases, such as the Oracle RDBMS, with Web servers. Managing these large amounts of data using current methods is just impossible.

In order for commerce to be completely enabled on the Web, vendors need to be able to perform secure transactions. Although Netscape supposedly has the ability to perform secure or encrypted transactions, two computer science students at the University of California, Berkeley, were able to crack the encryption method. After learning of the problem, Netscape Communications, Inc., immediately posted a new version of software that fixed the flaw the students used to crack the encryption method. Although many users still feel safe using the system, not everyone will feel good about doing financial transactions over the Web until they can be completely sure about the security of their transactions.

When completely secure transactions are possible on the Internet, a reliable method of storing those transactions will be necessary. Currently, those transactions are stored in relational databases. Rather than trying to recreate technology, companies will simply couple their Web applications with their RDBMs, as has already started happening.

Internal to Corporate Networks

Although I believe that it will take some time before the WWW evolves much past a larger version of what the online service providers currently have to offer, I do see some interesting things happening inside of corporations.

When I ran my own consulting company, I was in the business of putting together client/server applications. I generally worked with the smaller companies that did not have the means of investing in mainframe technology. With client/server computing, you leverage the desktop computer with the power of a smaller-than-mainframe–back-end server. This is a great idea on paper as far as capital costs, but it is much more complex than the mainframe solution. Not only do you have to worry about application programming, you have to worry about keeping two machines running rather than one, middleware that doesn't like your application or your network, early software that is so full of bugs it crawls, and so on.

I see Web technology replacing client/server computing in the very near future. Rather than having to worry about software on the client machine, simply install a Web browser. Rather than having to worry about middleware, just make sure the client and the server are running TCP/IP (the standard protocol on the Internet). Programming is reduced to writing HTML (which is discussed later in this chapter), which is often touted as being easier than any other computer language on the market.

I also see Web technology serving as an information system within the corporate environment. When you hire a new employee, rather than giving him or her a notebook with all the company policies and practices, point them to the internal Web server. If you need to find out what the structure of the company is, look on the corporate Web server for the company organizational chart. Not only will the information get to those who need it, but it will be a lot easier to keep updated.

In order for this to happen, Web browsers and servers are going to have to be able to talk to corporate databases such as Oracle, Sybase, Informix, or DB2. Although HTML is easy to learn, the need to talk to databases is going to mean extensions. Those extensions are going to need rapid application-development tools to facilitate building Web applications.

Browsers are also going to have to be able to do some of the data validation on the client machine rather than just on the server. Right now if you want to fill in a questionnaire on the Web, you do so and then press a Submit button. This sends all of the information back to the server for validation. If the server encounters an error, it sends the browser to a new page mentioning that it encountered an error. Enabling the browser to perform validation functions will streamline the user interface, allowing client/server-type applications to be developed.

Now that you have an idea of what the World Wide Web is, take a look at PowerBrowser and how it can help you in your quest to become Web-enabled.

PowerBrowser

In the next section of this chapter, you will be introduced to PowerBrowser and what it does. After listing the hardware and software requirements, installation instructions will be given.

What Is It?

Unlike Netscape or Mosaic, PowerBrowser is not just a WWW browser. It also has some features that make it more generally useful, such as a design-layout tool and the capability to be a personal Web server. Oracle has also added some extensions to HTML that it is calling DBML (database markup language). These extensions provide database access, the addition of a

BASIC scripting language, integration with the desktop using OLE, the capability of the browser to perform validation, and integration with the server-storing legacy data.

The way the current version works is that one program handles all three tasks (browsing, designing, and serving). When PowerBrowser is officially released, it is likely to be three separately executable programs, with the design and layout tool not officially being distributed. Oracle Corporation may ship an alpha version of it, then quickly follow it up with a more stable version.

PowerBrowser as a Web Browser

PowerBrowser is currently a Netscape 1.1–compatible browser. That means that all of the Netscape enhancements supported in version 1.1 are also supported by PowerBrowser. It also supports several new enhancements, such as the database markup language (DBML) and Network Loadable Objects (NLO), which allow enhancements to be made to the browser dynamically.

Oracle is aggressively pursuing home-video-on-demand technology and has thus added the ability to play MPEG-decoded movies embedded within an HTML page. Because of bandwidth limitations, compression technology has not yet made this reliable over the Internet, but it is possible over standard Ethernet—which most corporate networks run on.

PowerBrowser is a product currently under active development; by the time you read this, there will probably be several other enhancements. The best place to go for up-to-date information about the browser is Oracle Corporation's Web site at `http://www.oracle.com`.

PowerBrowser as a Web Design Layout Tool

When you first start learning to create HTML pages (covered shortly), it seems relatively easy and straightforward—but it is a whole lot like being blind and driving a car by feeling the bumps in the road. In order to see what you have created, you have to load the file into your browser. By using PowerBrowser's designer, you can see the HTML document as it is created.

PowerBrowser as a Web Server

Creating a bunch of HTML pages is not enough to set up a Web server. After the pages are created, you need some sort of program that forwards those pages when browsers ask for them. Most servers run on UNIX machines. However, sometimes there may only be one or two requests a day for a particular page. Rather than dedicate an expensive and difficult-to-maintain UNIX machine, you can use PowerBrowser running under Microsoft Windows (3.1 or 95).

Hardware Requirements

PowerBrowser currently only runs under Microsoft Windows 3.1 and Windows 95. There are versions planned for UNIX using the X windowing system and an Apple Macintosh.

Currently it is a small program; if you can run Windows, you can run PowerBrowser. It takes about 3 MB of disk space, which is quite small compared to most Windows programs.

Because PowerBrowser is meant to be used on the Internet, an Internet connection is desirable (but not necessary). This connection can be through some sort of modem or a network connection. You also have the option of running on your own local area network, separate from the Internet. If no network or Internet connections are available, PowerBrowser can still display HTML pages from your local hard disk. The help files included with PowerBrowser will just be HTML pages stored on the local disk.

Software Requirements

To run PowerBrowser, you need to have either Microsoft Windows 3.1 or Windows 95 loaded on your machine. No additional software is required (except DOS with Windows 3.1).

Should you want to connect to the Internet or corporate network through a network connection (for example, Ethernet), you will need a copy of TCP/IP software. It is included on the Windows 95 CD-ROM but needs to be purchased separately for Windows 3.1. Almost any WinSock-compatible TCP/IP software should work.

If you are using dial-up access, you will need a copy of serial line Internet protocol (SLIP) or point-to-point protocol (PPP). If you are using online services such as CompuServe or America Online, they generally include such programs with their browsers.

Installation

Installing PowerBrowser is a fairly simple process. If you are downloading it from the Internet, you currently have the option of saving the files on your hard disk, creating a single 1.44 MB disk or two 720 KB disks. (As the program gets larger, more disks may be required.) When you are downloading to two disks, you are prompted for the second disk.

After you have the installation disk (or disks), installation is as simple as running the self-extracting executable found on the disk. It asks you for the destination directory, then sets up a program group for you automatically.

The hardest part about installation is actually getting the TCP/IP software installed correctly. If you are sure that your networking software works fine, then PowerBrowser should not have any problems. If you do have problems, the best place to go for help is `http://www.oracle.com`. Unfortunately, this assumes that you have a Web and an Internet connection. You can also send e-mail to `torgo@us.oracle.com`.

After the software is installed, you need to configure your preferences. This is done by going into the Options menu and selecting the Preferences option. The first time you run this menu option, a Setup Wizard prompts you for information. You are given the chance of doing a Generic setup, an Oracle employee setup, or Portal Information Network Setup. Unless you are an Oracle employee, I suggest selecting the Generic setup. You are then prompted for your userid, your full name, and your e-mail address. After you fill in those fields, click the OK button.

The next time you go into the preferences, you will notice that there is no Setup Wizard and that most of the preference options are filled in.

Navigating with PowerBrowser

The first thing you are going to want to do with PowerBrowser is surf the World Wide Web. After you play around a bit, you will want to customize your environment so that you can find your favorite Web addresses quickly. The purpose of this section is to explain that and then show you what else PowerBrowser can do as a browser.

Overview of the PowerBrowser Browser

Figure 54.1 shows the PowerBrowser browser looking at my newly created skiing home page. Notice how it looks slightly different than other browsers you may have seen. On the left side of the screen, you notice an area containing bookmarks and an area containing a history of the places you have visited. Because you can have more than one Web site open at a time, Web sites are presented in their own child windows.

FIGURE 54.1.

The Oracle PowerBrowser browser.

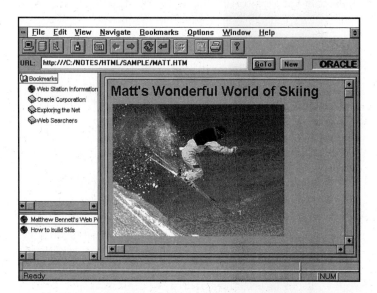

Going to Your Favorite Web Page

If you have not set up a bookmark with your own favorite Web site, you can specify the uniform resource locator (URL) address on the URL line, as shown in Figure 54.2.

FIGURE 54.2.

Specify the URL (uniform resource locator) address on the URL line to have PowerBrowser take you there.

URL

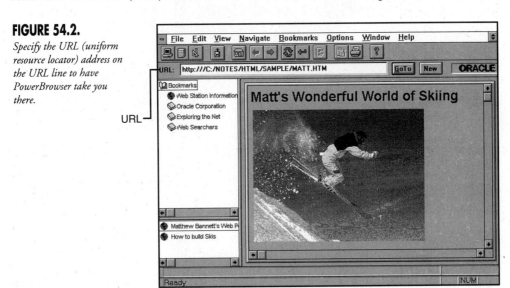

After you have entered the correct address, either press Enter or click the GoTo button. To tell you that PowerBrowser is actually transferring data, the Oracle logo in the upper-right part of the screen rotates. If the address cannot be found, an error message appears.

Viewing Multiple Web Sites at the Same Time

As mentioned above, you have the option of opening multiple Web sites at the same time. This can be done one of two ways. The easiest way is to click on the New button found next to the GoTo button on the URL line. This will open a new browser child window. You can then enter a new URL address in the new window and be in two places at once as shown in Figure 54.3.

How to Create and Use Bookmarks

The World Wide Web is a big place full of all sorts of interesting sites. When you are surfing the Web it is nice to be able to get back to your favorite sites without having to remember the URL addresses. (Trust me when I say they are easy to forget.) Figure 54.4 shows the bookmark section in PowerBrowser.

FIGURE 54.3.

PowerBrowser enables you to see two Web sites at the same time.

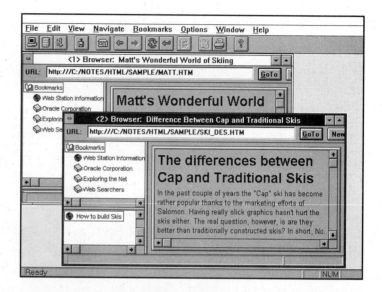

FIGURE 54.4.

Here are some of the bookmarks that come with PowerBrowser.

Bookmarks

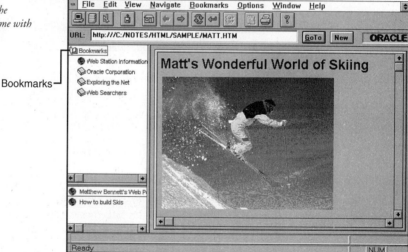

Notice how bookmarks are stored in separate books or bookmark folders. Rather than list all of your bookmarks together, you have the ability to classify them into separate categories. This makes it easier to find. Remember the Web is a big place, and you may have hundreds of favorite sites, not just a handful.

To add a folder, use the Add Folder menu option of the Bookmarks menu. You are presented with the dialog box shown in Figure 54.5. Provide the name of the folder that you would like to create. If you check Add as child of selected folder, the new folder will be inside the currently selected folder. This enables you to have folders containing other folders. Once you have given the folder a name, click the OK button.

FIGURE 54.5.

The dialog box used to create new bookmark folders.

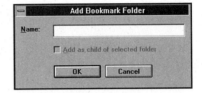

To add a bookmark to the currently selected folder, use the Add Bookmark menu option in the Bookmarks menu. The Edit Bookmark Details dialog box shown in Figure 54.6 should appear.

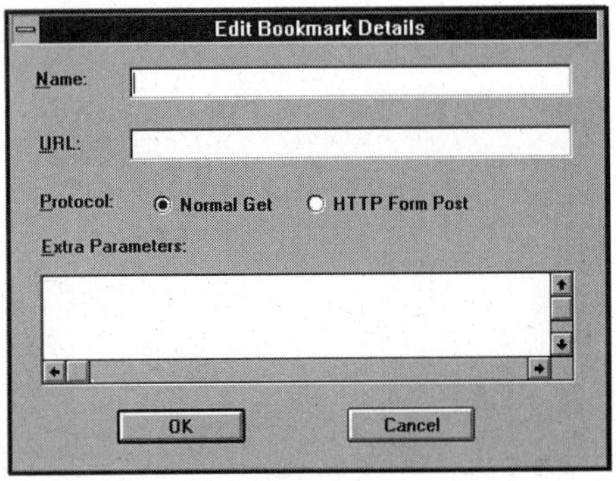

FIGURE 54.6.

The dialog box used to create new bookmarks.

Unlike adding a bookmark folder, adding a bookmark is slightly more involved. You are allowed to specify the name of the bookmark, which will appear in the bookmark subwindow on the left of your screen. Next, specify the URL address. I suggest making sure the URL address is valid by copying it from the URL line in the browser using Ctrl+C before opening the bookmark dialog box and then pasting it in the bookmark dialog box using Ctrl+V. If you require it, you can specify the protocol and any extra parameters.

In the current version, it is important to use the Save Bookmarks option in the Bookmarks menu before exiting PowerBrowser. Otherwise, the bookmarks created during your session will be forgotten.

After you start using bookmarks extensively, you are going to want to do more than just add them. Editing and deleting bookmarks and bookmark folders can all be done through the Bookmarks menu.

If you are migrating from Netscape and want to take all of your existing bookmarks with you, PowerBrowser has an option to migrate them; this obviates the need for you to recreate them. Simply select the Import Bookmarks option from the Bookmarks menu; this brings up a file dialog box, from which you can choose the file that contains your current Netscape bookmarks.

The History List

During any PowerBrowser browsing session, you may come across one or two sites that merit going back to. If you will be going back continually, it is best to create a bookmark. However, if you will only be going back once or twice, it is better to use the history list as shown in Figure 54.7.

FIGURE 54.7.

Use the history list shown here to go back to recently visited Web sites.

You do not need to manually add items to this list. PowerBrowser automatically keeps track of the Web pages you have recently accessed and lists them by page header on the left of your screen. To go back to a recently visited page, simply double-click on the name found in your history list. If the page is still in the cache or buffer, then it will load immediately. Otherwise, it will go out and reload that page for you.

After you are done with your history list, you have the option of clearing it out using the Clear option found on the Navigate menu.

In addition to being able to use the history list to revisit recent sites, you can also use it to audit where your browser has been. I am the father of three children, and naturally they like to use the Web. Although they are currently quite young and would never venture into questionable

Web sites, I have the option of auditing where they go without having to stand over their shoulder. I make sure to clear out the history list before they start and then make sure it has a sufficient number of entries when they are done. Just knowing that I can do this will hopefully keep them from learning how to make fertilizer bombs in junior high.

Navigating Within PowerBrowser

To help you navigate the Web, PowerBrowser has several options found on the toolbar as shown in Figure 54.8.

FIGURE 54.8.

The toolbar found at the top of the PowerBrowser window.

Toolbar

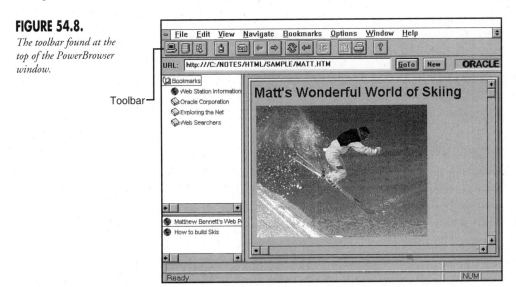

If you place the cursor over a toolbar button and wait, tool tips will appear letting you know its function. Notice that the first three toolbar buttons (going from left to right) have to do with which mode you are in (Browser, Server, or Designer).

The next button enables you to load an HTML page from your disk. This is great for testing an HTML page that you have created before placing it on a server. Following this button is the one that takes you to your favorite home page. I'm an Oracle fan, so mine naturally points to the Oracle Web page.

The next group of two buttons enables you to go forward or backward. If you have been navigating through the Web and need some information from a previous page, use the back arrow to go back to it. After you have the information, use the forward arrow to go ahead to where you were before you went back. The arrows should be grayed out or disabled when there are no pages to go back or forward to.

The buttons following are used to reload a page or go back a whole level. Because I access the Web using dial-up lines, there is sometimes garbage on the line and large graphics may be garbled. When this happens, I simply reload the page, and most of the time it comes through clean the second time.

Next is the Stop button. When loading a large HTML page or graphic, it is nice to be able to stop it using this button.

The last three buttons on the toolbar are used to copy, print, and get help. When you come across needed information in a Web page, it is nice to be able to print it.

Sending E-Mail Using the Browser

When browsing the Web, you often have the chance to send e-mail to administrators of Web sites. PowerBrowser allows you to send mail by clicking on the Send Mail option in the File menu. Be sure that you have configured PowerBrowser so that there is an SMTP server, or it will complain.

Customizing the Environment

I was recently at a conference with two of my coworkers, and we all had the same exact laptop computer with similar software. Throughout the course of the day, the laptops were continually being used, and it was amazing that, although one laptop may have been closer, each of us preferred to use our own. Why? Because each of us had configured our laptops to our liking. Although the developers of PowerBrowser have come up with some nice user interface features, not everybody will like them. It is nice to be able to configure PowerBrowser to your own liking.

Configuring PowerBrowser is fairly straightforward. The first configuration that you are going to want to do is making sure that all of your preferences are set up correctly. This can be done by going into the Preferences option of the Options menu. It will then bring up the Preferences dialog box shown in Figure 54.9.

Notice the tabs across the top. Five separate categories are listed: Proxies, User, Cache, Helpers, and Timeouts. When filling in the information for Proxies, it is best to talk to your system administrator to find out which values should be used. If you are the system administrator and don't know which values should be here, initially leaving them blank is probably the best thing to do. After you become more familiar with the Web and your network, it will become apparent which values you should use.

FIGURE 54.9.

The Preferences dialog box allows you to change certain preferences.

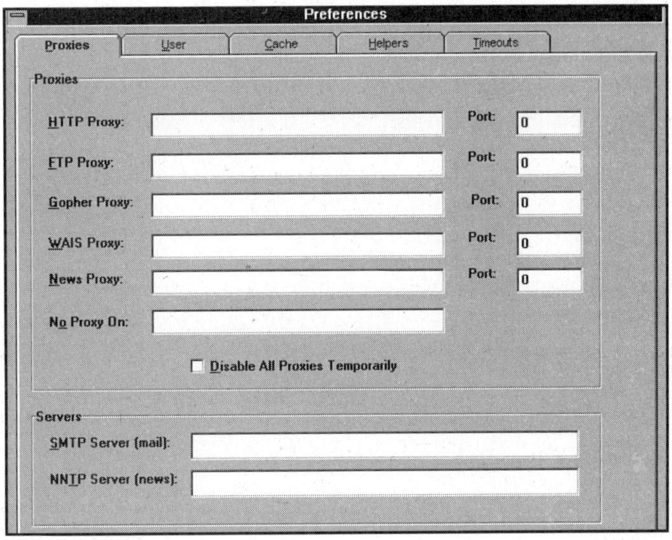

Setting the User Preferences

When installing PowerBrowser for the first time, you should have entered some of the basic user preferences. Figure 54.10 shows the user preference specification dialog box.

FIGURE 54.10.

This is where you specify user preferences for PowerBrowser.

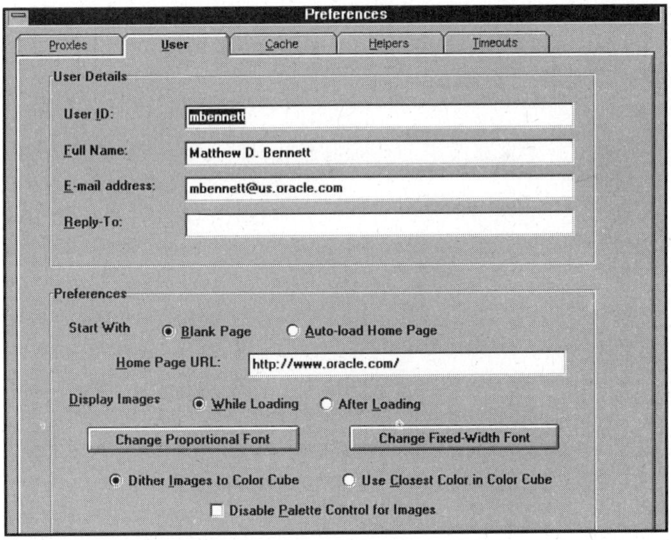

The User ID, Full Name, and E-mail address should already be filled in. If you need to change any of this information, this is the place to do it. The Reply-To line allows you to specify a second e-mail address, should you want replies to your original to go someplace other than your original e-mail address. When it is left blank, the Reply-To defaults to your previously specified e-mail address.

PowerBrowser has used the default options for the rest of the user preferences, but you may change them in this dialog box.

The Start with preferences determine what happens when PowerBrowser is initially started. The default is to not go to any page on the Web. The other option is to automatically load your home page. For those directly connected to the corporate network or the Internet, this is not a bad option. For those using dial-up lines (like me), it is nice to not have it connect to the home page immediately. Notice how there is a line where you can dynamically set your home page location.

The next set of options specifies the overall look of the HTML pages while you are looking at them. Notice that you have the option of looking at images while they are loading or only after they are done. You also have the option of changing your proportional and your fixed-width fonts. When you click on either of the buttons, the Windows font dialog box appears listing all of the fonts you have on your system. This requires that you load the desired fonts onto your system before you can use them in PowerBrowser.

The next three, and final, options specify color settings. You have the option of dithering colors to match those in your color palette or just choosing the closest on the palette. The default is to dither, and I recommend this setting. Finally, you have the option to disable the palette control for images.

Setting the Cache Preferences

In the first half of 1995, the Client/Server Systems Division (renamed the Web/Workgroup Systems Division) was responsible for putting on seminars throughout the United States. During the seminar, we demonstrated that you could use the Web to download trial versions of our software. Unfortunately we could not be guaranteed direct Internet connections at any of the seminar sites. This meant that we were required to use dial-up lines, and graphical images were drawn unbearably slowly. To keep the presentation interesting, the technical person responsible for the seminar would log onto the Net and run through all of the HTML pages that would be demonstrated before the presentation began. This had the effect of caching all of the images so that during the presentation, they were never downloaded. Unless you are doing something similar, you will probably never worry about the cache parameters in PowerBrowser.

The cache preferences screen is shown in Figure 54.11. The defaults should suffice for most users.

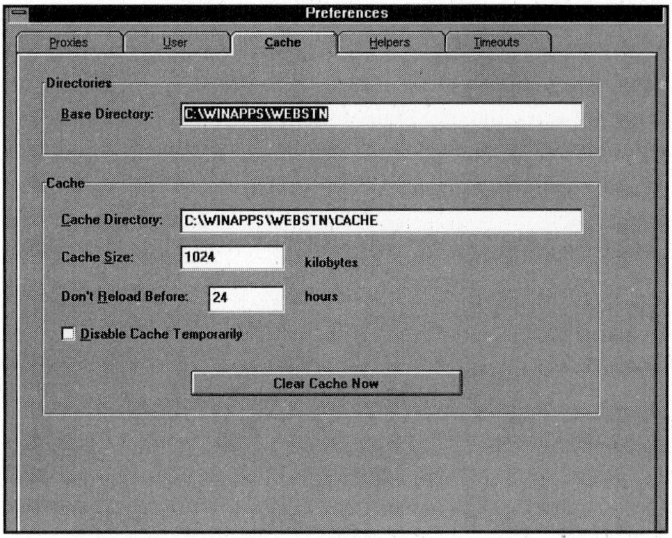

FIGURE 54.11.

The PowerBrowser cache preferences or parameters.

The first preference actually tells where the home directory for PowerBrowser is. Unless you manually move files around on your hard disk after installing PowerBrowser, you should not have to change this parameter.

In the cache preferences, you have the ability to specify the cache directory, and how large it is. A 1MB cache should be large enough for most users. If you are frequently going between large pages with lots of graphics on each page and don't want to reload pages all the time, then you may want to increase the size to something larger. When we were doing the seminars program, 8 MB was more than enough.

Next you have the option of specifying how often to reload pages and whether or not to temporarily disable the cache. The only time I have ever disabled the cache is when doing performance analysis on my own local network. Sometimes you want to get an average of how long it takes to load several pages, and so it is nice to be able to manually disable the cache. When browsing the Web for information, however, you will rarely have the need to turn it off.

Finally, you have the option of clearing out your cache immediately.

For most users, the cache preferences will rarely be altered. If you do need them changed, however, this is the area to do it.

Setting the Helpers Preferences

The Web is a dynamic place, making things possible today that weren't even thought about yesterday. Today it is common to see bitmaps and text at most Web sites; tomorrow we will be seeing video and animation. In order to see this new media, PowerBrowser has the capability to specify helper applications.

Helper applications make it possible to process media types that are not currently built into PowerBrowser. For instance, some browsers cannot natively display JPEG files. To get around this limitation, these browsers utilize a helper application that is not built into the browser but allows you to see the JPEG image. In PowerBrowser, the Helpers Preferences allow you to specify the helper applications that will be used to display or manipulate external media types.

The Helpers preferences dialog box is shown in Figure 54.12. As you can see, PowerBrowser comes with several media types already specified.

FIGURE 54.12.

The Helpers preferences dialog box.

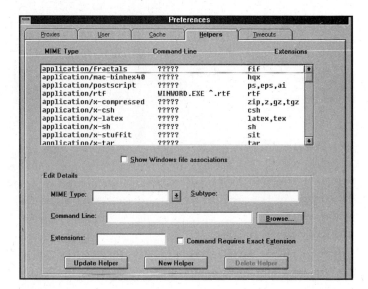

The list area found at the top shows all of the preset media types with their command-line execute statements and media-type suffixes. If you click on one of the lines, more detailed information is shown below it. Because most of the helper applications come set up already, you should not have to worry about doing so here.

Setting the Timeouts Preferences

The final set of preferences, shown in Figure 54.13, has to do with timeouts. Timeouts settings specify how long the application waits before it decides to give up trying to perform an operation.

FIGURE 54.13.

This is the Timeouts Preferences dialog box.

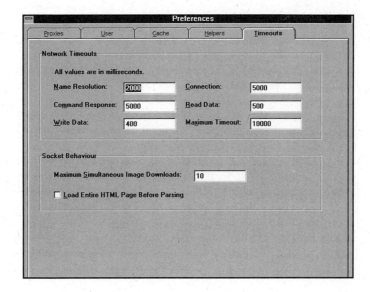

As stated, all time-out values are given in milliseconds (1,000 milliseconds = 1 second). Although the defaults may seem unusually long for most local networks, the Internet is much larger and requires it. The values that can be changed are

■ *Name Resolution.* This is the maximum amount of time allowed to translate the name of the Web site you are going to into a machine address.

■ *Connection.* This is the maximum amount of time allowed to connect to a Web site.

■ *Command Response.* This is the maximum amount of time allowed to respond to a command.

■ *Read Data.* This is the maximum amount of time allowed to start reading data from a Web site (an HTML page is data).

■ *Write Data.* This is the maximum amount of time allowed to start writing data to your own machine. (Notice how small the default value is.)

■ *Maximum Timeout.* This is the maximum amount of time allowed for any given event, not previously mentioned, to happen.

The default values should be adequate for most users. If you find that you are consistently getting time-out error messages on more than one Web site, you may wish to increase some of the parameters. Remember to check out several Web sites, however. It is not uncommon on the Internet to have one or two machines shut down for maintenance.

Where To Go for Help

If you get stuck using some of the PowerBrowser features, the first place to go for help is the online help. If, after going through there, you find that you still have questions, don't hesitate to mail us at torgo@us.oracle.com.

After you get your browser working correctly, the next question you may have is: Where do I go to find out about xyz? There are several good Web sites that act as lookup sites for URL addresses using keyword searches. My favorite is Yahoo, which can be found at http://www.yahoo.com.

Designing Web Pages

As with any software project, it is best to design what you are about to build before you go out and build it. The same is true with HTML documents. Even if you just sit down and sketch what the flow of the pages is going to be, you will save yourself countless hours of correcting mistakes.

After you have your design and are ready to build your Web pages, there are two ways that you can go: the hard way and the easy way. This is a teaching book and, naturally, it would not be as emotional an experience to learn the easy way first. After you get disgusted with the hard way, then I will show you how PowerBrowser's built-in design tools make Web-page creation simple and easy.

I will round out this section with a discussion of the database markup language extensions.

The Hard Way: With HTML

Hypertext Markup Language (HTML) is a subset of the more complete Standard Generalized Markup Language (SGML). It is used to describe the general format of a document. Although a language such as PostScript contains font and size information, HTML does not. Instead, it contains tags or format descriptions. It is then left to the viewing tool to choose the proper fonts and sizes. (See the section on setting user preferences to see how to customize the fonts for PowerBrowser.) Although most nonprogrammers may be scared away from HTML when they hear it is a language, it really is quite simple.

A Simple HTML Page

Perhaps you want to give the title name for your page and a short description of what can be found there. This can be done by entering the following into a text editor (the notepad included with Microsoft Windows can be used) and saving it to a file with the .HTM extension:

```
<title> Matt's Wonderful World of Skiing </title>
Matt's Wonderful World of Skiing
```

This produces the output shown in Figure 54.14. It is not the most exciting page you have ever seen, but then again it is only a start.

FIGURE 54.14.

This is the result of the simple HTML listing.

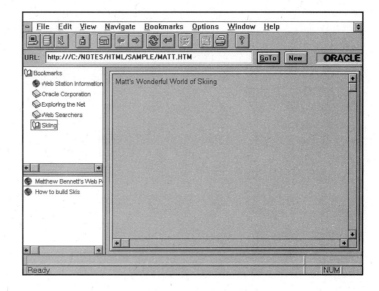

In HTML, there is often the tag that marks the beginning of the text to be formatted and a closing tag to mark the end. In this case, I used the <title> tag to set the appropriate title of my document. Any other text that is not encompassed in a format tag set is displayed as normal body text.

It would be nice to display "Matt's Wonderful World of Skiing" as something other than just plain body text. To display it as a header, you can surround it with the tag set <h1> ... </h1>. There are six levels of header tag sets. Thus you can choose from <h1> or <h2> ... to <h6>. Let's add a heading and some more text to the HTML listing just created.

```
<title> Matt's Wonderful World of Skiing </title>
<h1> Matt's Wonderful World of Skiing </h1>
For those that like to ski . . . this is the place to be.
```

The result is shown in Figure 54.15.

FIGURE 54.15.

The result of adding a heading to the simple HTML listing.

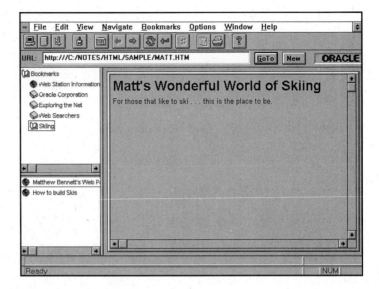

You will notice that with HTML, white space (tabs, spaces, and carriage returns, for example) has no meaning to the formatter. You could list a single word on each line and PowerBrowser will string them together to form sentences and paragraphs. However, sometimes you will want carriage returns to separate your paragraphs. This is done with the <p> tag. Just place <p> every time you wish to print a carriage return.

Character Formatting in HTML

Now that you understand some basics about HTML, let's get a little more creative. One of the most important differences between HTML and plain ASCII text is the ability to place emphasis on words by making them bold or italic.

To add bold typeface to words in the continuing example, simply place <b> ... </b> around the desired words.

```
<title> Matt's Wonderful World of Skiing </title>
<h1> Matt's Wonderful World of Skiing </h1>
For those that like to <b> ski </b> . . . this is the place to be.
```

Italic is very similar to bold; the tag set consists of <i> ... </i>.

```
<title> Matt's Wonderful World of Skiing </title>
<h1> Matt's Wonderful World of Skiing </h1>
For those that like to <b> ski </b> . . . this is the place to <i> be </i>.
```

Your HTML page should now look like the following:

FIGURE 54.16.

The simple HTML example with bold and italics added.

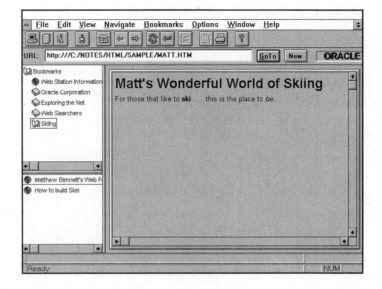

While the bold and italic typefonts are supposedly replacements for underlined text, it is still nice to be able to underline on occasion. A new standard that is emerging in HTML is to use the <u> ... </u> tag for underlining. PowerBrowser naturally supports it.

PowerBrowser also supports the ability to embed fixed-width fonts into documents. Because the typefont is different than the normal body text font and more closely resembles the old character-based displays of DOS, I like to use it when giving instructions on what to type into the computer. The tag set is <tt> ... </tt>, where the *tt* is short for typewriter text.

Embedding Images in HTML

Rather than bore you with more text formatting, let's move on to something more interesting, like displaying images in an HTML document.

PowerBrowser can display GIF and JPEG images within an HTML document. To display an inline image (an image next to text within an HTML document), use the tag <img src=*filename*>. Make sure you substitute the correct image filename in place of *filename*.

To place a picture of a man skiing in our HTML document, we would change the listing to the following:

```
<title> Matt's Wonderful World of Skiing </title>
<h1> Matt's Wonderful World of Skiing </h1>

<img src=manski.gif>

<p>
For those that like to <b> ski </b> . . . this is the place to <i> be </i>.
```

Notice how I added the paragraph tag. Without it, the text would appear to the right of the inline image. The resulting HTML page is shown in Figure 54.17.

FIGURE 54.17.

*This is the HTML page
with an inline image.*

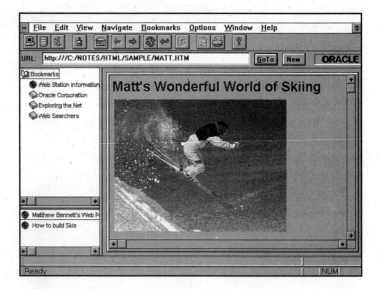

Indenting, Bullets, and Numbering in HTML

The next goal in creating my Web page is to have a listing of my favorite places to ski. To make the layout more pleasing, I would like to indent a bulleted list. This is done with the indenting tag `<ul> ... </ul>` and list tag `<li>`.

To present my favorite places to ski as a bulleted list, I would use the following:

```
<h2> Matt's favorite places to ski </h2>
<ul>
<li> Snowbird, <b> UT </b>
<li> Alta, <b> UT </b>
<li> Solitude, <b> UT </b>
<li> Mammoth Mountain, <b> CA </b>
<li> Vail, <b> CO </b>
<li> Squaw Valley, <b> CA </b>
</ul>
```

If I then wanted to add a numbered list of my all-time favorite skis, I would use the indenting tab `<ol> ... </ol>` with the list tag `<li>` as shown here.

```
<h2> Matt's all-time favorite skis (in order) </h2>
<ol>
<li> Research Dynamics, Puma
<li> K2, SLC
<li> Rossignol 4S
</ol>
```

The results of these two additions are shown in Figure 54.18.

FIGURE 54.18.

The Web page with a bulleted and a numbered list.

Notice that with both lists, the list-item tag (`<li>`) remains the same. Only the indenting tags change.

Hypertext Links in HTML

The next major feature of HTML is that of hypertext links. Not only do you have the option of going to another section of the current document, but you also have the ability to jump to other documents. In the preceding example, I listed my three all-time favorite skis. Rather than just list them, it would be nice to have a hypertext link further on in the document explaining the significance of each.

Providing links in the current document is done by assigning a label or destination and then providing the jump line. The label or destination is assigned with the tag: `<a name="destination"> ... </a>`. Because it is a unique destination, a unique destination name must be given in the opening section of the tag. There is an area for text and then the closing section of the destination tag.

Providing the jump-to link is done with the following tag: `<a href="#destination"> ... </a>`. Notice the use of the number symbol (#). Whatever appears between the opening and closing section of the tag is highlighted and serves as a place for the user to click to use the link.

In our example, links can be provided in the current file by adding jump-to and destination tags in the following manner:

```
<h2> Matt's all-time favorite skis (in order) </h2>
<ol>
<li> Research Dynamics, <a href="#PumaLink"> Puma </a>
<li> K2, <a href="#SLCLink"> SLC </a>
<li> Rossignol, <a href="#4SLink"> 4S </a>
</ol>

<a name="PumaLink"> Puma </a> <p>
When I was 14, I wanted . . .
<a name="SLCLink"> SLC — Traditional construction </a> <p>
I like a good traditional ski as opposed to a "cap" ski  . . .
<a name="4SLink"> 4S </a> <p>
A buddy of mine borrowed these  . . .
```

Because you do not want to make your HTML pages too large, you will often want your hypertext links to jump to places in other documents. This is done by adding the second HTML page filename to the `href` section of the jump-to tag: `<a href="file#destination"> ... </a>`. The destination file must have a destination tag.

You also have the option of creating hypertext links to Web pages on separate computers. In this case, replace the `file#destination` reference with the URL address.

I have not tried to give you an exhaustive HTML tutorial. Instead, my goal was to highlight its simplicity. You may create simple HTML pages.

Using the PowerBrowser Design Tool

If HTML is so easy, why is working with straight HTML considered the hard way? As with any new concept, the initial learning steps may be easy or hard. HTML just happens to have fairly simple initial learning steps. Once you get past simple formatting, however, HTML becomes much more complicated, and a good layout tool can aid you dramatically.

Currently, the PowerBrowser design tool is under construction and most likely will not ship with the first release of the production version. To give you an idea of what you can do, however, Figure 54.19 shows what it currently looks like.

Notice that in addition to text and images, you can place fields, buttons, checkboxes, and radio buttons on HTML pages (things I didn't cover in the HTML minitutorial). There is also something similar to a property sheet found on the left side of the screen. The combination of these features allows you to build client/server applications with Web technology similar to using Oracle Power Objects.

As with Power Objects, PowerBrowser uses the familiar drag-and-drop metaphor to get things done. After you place text areas on your pages, rather than having to type the text in by hand, simply drag the text file from your file manager and drop it into the text area. This enables you to prepare text using your favorite editor.

FIGURE 54.19.

PowerBrowser's current design tool.

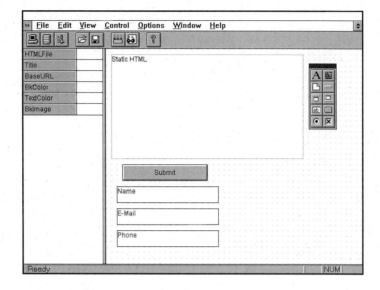

Using the Layout Wizards

In addition to the design tool, PowerBrowser contains layout wizards or templates. Rather than having to design Web pages from scratch without any help, you will have several layout styles to choose from. If you are building an electronic catalog Web page, you will be able to bring up the Layout Wizard for catalog Web pages. After specifying several important pieces of information (such as where the picture and description of your catalog items exist electronically), PowerBrowser automatically generates your HTML for you. You then have the option of going in and modifying it to your liking.

The only Layout Wizard that currently exists is one to generate a personal home page. Simply provide information about yourself, including a picture, and it generates a nice home page.

DBML Extension Overview

There are some rather large Web sites on the Internet. There are some larger ones, however, that are not accessible by the public Internet community because they reside within corporate networks. One such site that I have worked with currently has over 300 HTML pages. Making sure that those pages contain current information by editing the HTML is a nightmare. A better way to administrate is to pull information out of the database and dynamically create HTML pages from that.

Using a database with HTML requires that some extensions be added. Oracle's extensions are known as the Database Markup Language (DBML). These extensions allow for Oracle Basic (the same Basic engine supplied with Oracle Power Objects) to be embedded into HTML documents. New methods specific to PowerBrowser have been added, and the ones specific to Power Objects have been removed.

In addition to the ability to access databases and embed Basic within HTML documents, DBML also allows for tighter integration with the desktop using Microsoft's object linking and embedding (OLE).

Going over the DBML extensions in detail is beyond the scope of this chapter. As PowerBrowser is released, the best place to go for the DBML specification will be `http://www.oracle.com`.

PowerBrowser as a Server

In addition to being a browser and an HTML layout tool, PowerBrowser can also act as a personal server. Starting the personal server is as simple as clicking on the Personal Server button found on the toolbar, setting up the correct home page, and then clicking the Start Server button found on the toolbar.

Having the ability to serve Web pages from your personal machine solves several problems. First, you can edit your HTML pages locally, and you don't have to worry about copying them onto another machine. Second, you don't have to invest large amounts of time and money setting up a dedicated Web server running UNIX or Windows NT.

Summary

In this chapter, you learned how to use Oracle's PowerBrowser as a browser and how to create simple HTML documents. You had a preview to the design and layout tool as well as an overview of the DBML extensions to HTML. You also read about how to turn PowerBrowser into a personal Web server.

Most users of PowerBrowser will use it to replace their Mosaic or Netscape browser. As the world becomes more Web-enabled, it is hoped that the need for Web-authoring tools and personal servers will make PowerBrowser a very attractive solution.

It was my hope to give you a preview of a work-in-progress. By the time you read this in the book, PowerBrowser will have evolved to be even more powerful. Because no software product is ever complete, I welcome your comments (both on the software and on the content of this chapter). I can be reached via Internet e-mail at `mbennett@us.oracle.com` or on CompuServe at `75120,2747`.

The Oracle WebSystem and the World Wide Web Interface Kit

55

by Kenneth R. Zimmerman

IN THIS CHAPTER

As described in Chapter 54, "Oracle PowerBrowser," the World Wide Web is the Internet technology that provides universal access to file-based information. In February 1995, Oracle Corporation became the first major relational database management system (RDBMS) vendor to release technology enabling safe and reliable access to enterprise data from the World Wide Web (WWW). This technology, known as the WOW (Web-Oracle-Web) Gateway, is part of the Oracle WWW Interface Kit.

The World Wide Web Interface Kit is a set of software created independently around the world by developers attempting to solve the problem of incorporating database resident information with the WWW's file-based server technology. Each component in the WWW Interface Kit solved a particular problem in dealing with Web-RDBMS integration. The WOW Gateway, Oracle's own contribution to the kit, is the most universal and extensible of the solutions. A year after its introduction, practically an eon in the Web's time frame, it remains superior to other vendors' offerings.

The distribution of the World Wide Web Interface Kit to thousands of users internationally led Oracle to create a commercial superset of this technology. Oracle WebSystem was first demonstrated during International Oracle User Week in Philadelphia at the end of September 1995 as part of the PowerBrowser, then named WebStation, product launch. Consisting of three parts, the Oracle Web Listener, Oracle Web Agent, and the Oracle7 Server, WebSystem provides a single integrated solution to the problem of effective Web-RDBMS integration.

> **TIP**
>
> Complete information and trial versions of most of Oracle's technologies are on its home page. The Uniform Resource Locator (URL) for Oracle's home page is `http://www.oracle.com/`.

The Oracle World Wide Web Interface Kit

The WWW Interface Kit consists of several independently developed technologies along with one from Oracle, the WOW Gateway. The components are Common Gateway Interface (CGI) gateways, search engines, and a PL/SQL compiler. You can download the complete kit as a set or each individual component separately.

> **CAUTION**
>
> As Oracle moves to a single solution for Oracle/Web integration, it might not continue to carry the WWW Interface Kit. The kit is not displayed on Oracle's home page but is still available from `http://dozer.us.oracle.co:8080/ftp/sdk10/owik.tar.Z`.

Each component other than the WOW Gateway has a home URL, provided in the descriptions that follow.

HTTP Servers

All the components in the WWW Interface Kit depend on the presence of an HTTP server. An HTTP server is the software that listens for Web page requests and then provides the information. It is similar to other Internet services such as FTP and Telnet. The Oracle WebServer, described later in this chapter, is one such HTTP server. If you're using WebServer, however, the components of the WWW Interface Kit are less attractive in light of Oracle WebSystems' extensive features. In that case, use WebSystem exclusively.

> **TIP**
>
> Don't have a copy of WebServer yet? As with most of Oracle's server technologies, Oracle WebServer is available for free 90-day trial from Oracle's home page at `http://www.oracle.com/`.

The role of an HTTP server is to listen for Web page requests, resolve aliases and other redirections that might take place, and finally return the Web page to the requesting client. Another role of the HTTP server is to launch scripts as defined by a standard called the Common Gateway Interface (CGI).

Common Gateway Interface

When you request a page from a directory that is identified in the HTTP server's configuration file as containing scripts, the server runs the specified file and returns its contents as a Web page. For example, the standard NCSA HTTP server installation has a cgi-bin directory and a shell script called test-cgi. If you specify the URL `http://www.chatsoft.com/cgi-bin/test-cgi`, the test-cgi script runs. The following segment shows the contents of the test-cgi script:

```
#!/bin/sh
echo Content-type: text/plain
echo
echo CGI/1.0 test script report:
echo
echo argc is $#. argv is "$*".
echo

echo SERVER_SOFTWARE = $SERVER_SOFTWARE
echo SERVER_NAME = $SERVER_NAME
echo GATEWAY_INTERFACE = $GATEWAY_INTERFACE
echo SERVER_PROTOCOL = $SERVER_PROTOCOL
```

```
echo SERVER_PORT = $SERVER_PORT
echo REQUEST_METHOD = $REQUEST_METHOD
echo HTTP_ACCEPT = "$HTTP_ACCEPT"
echo PATH_INFO = "$PATH_INFO"
echo PATH_TRANSLATED = "$PATH_TRANSLATED"
echo SCRIPT_NAME = "$SCRIPT_NAME"
echo QUERY_STRING = "$QUERY_STRING"
echo REMOTE_HOST = $REMOTE_HOST
echo REMOTE_ADDR = $REMOTE_ADDR
echo REMOTE_USER = $REMOTE_USER
echo AUTH_TYPE = $AUTH_TYPE
echo CONTENT_TYPE = $CONTENT_TYPE
echo CONTENT_LENGTH = $CONTENT_LENGTH
```

You see that the first thing the script provides is the identifying line that precedes all Web pages:

```
Content-type: text/plain
```

You include this line because of another standard followed by Web browsers, the Multipurpose Internet Mail Extensions (MIME). When the Web browser sees the preceding line, it knows how to handle the rest of the transmitted file. Other examples of MIME types include the following:

`image/gif`	Graphic Interchange Format (GIF) images
`audio/x-wav`	X-wave format sound files
`application/zip`	Zip format compressed archives

Upon receipt of the `Content-type:` preamble, the Web browser launches the appropriate helper program to complete the request. In many cases, the helper program is built in to the Web browser. This is the case with most common MIME types as well as Oracle's own PowerBrowser Web client.

Forms

As dynamic as CGI programs might be, to be truly versatile there must be a means to respond to input. This is accomplished with forms. Forms are Web pages that contain fields which the user can enter and transmit to the server. Figure 55.1 from the Oracle WebServer shows one such form.

Forms can also contain other GUI elements besides fields. The following list shows some other graphical form elements:

- Buttons
- Checkboxes
- Radio buttons

The following segment is a portion of the HTML that creates the form shown in Figure 55.1:

```
<H1>
<IMG SRC="autotit.gif" alt="The Oracle Web Auto Dealer">
```

```
</H1>
<IMG SRC="image/nsx.gif"><P>
Welcome to the <STRONG>Oracle Auto Dealer</STRONG>!
Check out our exciting new collection of cars and vans! <BR>
<FORM METHOD="POST" ACTION="/cgi-bin/wow/auto.register">
Account: <INPUT TYPE="text" NAME="pCustid">
Password: <INPUT TYPE="password" NAME="pPassword">
<INPUT TYPE="submit" VALUE="Let's go shopping!"><BR>
</FORM>
```

FIGURE 55.1.

A simple Web form.

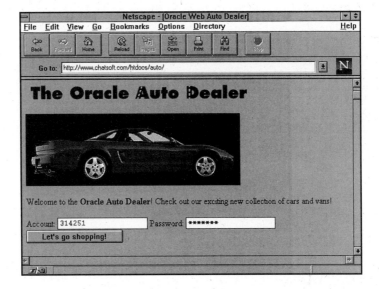

The HTML tags `<INPUT TYPE="text" ... >` and `<INPUT TYPE="password"...>` capture the user name and password. Using `TYPE="password"` means the user will see asterisks when he types instead of the password itself. `TYPE="submit"` indicates a button, and `VALUE=` specifies the name appearing on the button.

HTTP Port

As with other Internet services, HTTP is a well-known service. This means that applications expect to communicate with it through a known service or port number. In the case of HTTP servers, this number is usually 80 or 8080. Most Web browsers automatically issue the request to port 80, but a different port number might be specified in the browser's setup or in the URL itself as in `http://www.chatsoft.com:8080/`.

General Installation Recommendations

You can download the components of the World Wide Web Interface Kit individually or all at once. They are available as source code only or in precompiled binary form for Sun4 SunOS 4.1.3 systems.

> **TIP**
>
> Even if you are running SunOS 4.1.3 on a Sun4 machine, you should download the source code only and recompile. This ensures that the code runs properly on your system, and you can also modify it for your particular needs. Most importantly, it provides an opportunity for you to understand how CGI processing takes place.

Regardless of the path you take, you should heed the following recommendations from Oracle to make it easier to start using the various technologies.

1. Determine where you want to place the Interface Kit files.

2. Create a link to this location and call it /oraweb. For example, if you want to place the files in the /opt/oraweb directory, under UNIX, the following command creates the link to /oraweb:

   ```
   $ ln /opt/oraweb /oraweb
   ```

   If the /opt and the / (root directory) are on different file systems, you might have to use the -s option to the link command in the following way:

   ```
   $ ln -s /opt/oraweb /oraweb
   ```

3. If you're installing the entire source distribution, which is recommended, create a source directory under oraweb.

   ```
   $ mkdir /oraweb/sdk-src
   ```

4. If you are already running an HTTP server such as the NCSA HTTPd, you should create a link to the httpd directory under the oraweb directory.

Following are brief descriptions of each component in the World Wide Web Interface Kit.

WOW Gateway

The WOW Gateway is a PL/SQL-based gateway developed by Magnus Lönnroth of Oracle Corporation. This is the best product in the kit and the precursor to the Oracle Web Agent. It is covered in detail in the section "WOW Gateway," later in this chapter.

WORA

Constantin Ocrainets of Russia developed WORA, an Oracle table browser. WORA is a single-program Pro*C executable that functions as both the CGI gateway and server application. It connects to the Oracle7 server and uses the data dictionary system tables to extract information on tables, views, and columns.

WORA generates HTML forms from which users can specify and view a list of available tables, views, and columns, specify query conditions, and view the result set of the query. WORA does not allow updates, but source code is provided so the user can add this functionality. WORA functions quite well as a simple data browser.

WORA uses the GET method, one of two form processing methods specified in the CGI 1.0 standard. There are system limits on the number of parameters, their lengths, and the length of the query condition. The POST method is preferred but not implemented in WORA.

> **CAUTION**
>
> Most of the items in the World Wide Web Interface Kit rely on UNIX operating system features to compile and run; however, you can modify some to run on other operating systems that offer similar features.

The home URL for WORA is `http://weirdb.jinr.dubna.su/wora/wora.html`.

DECOUX

A post-processing gateway by Guy Decoux of France, DECOUX relies on several configuration files that specify which predefined query and action to perform. It is accessed via a Pro*C executable, and an Oraperl solution is also available. DECOUX relies on another CGI parameter called ISINDEX to perform its functions. ISINDEX is simply a GET tag that causes the browser to display a standard input box with a message prompting for key words. Unfortunately, it is subject to the same problems as any other GET method CGI program.

The home URL for DECOUX is `http://moulon.inra.fr`.

ORAYWWW

An Oraperl-based gateway and form builder by Arthur Yasinski of Canada, ORAYWWW facilitates the creation of HTML forms dynamically. The forms can allow queries only, or you can write them to update and delete data as well. Its strength is its capability to selectively specify both allowed user functions and the columns displayed.

The home URL for ORAYWWW is `http://www.nofc.forestry.ca:80/oraywww/`.

TSS Demo

TSS is a free-text indexing and search system with a PL/SQL front end by Peter Larsson of Sweden. TSS is a complicated system but is simple to get up and running. It uses several Oracle Call Interface (OCI) daemons to perform its functions of searching and indexing. The actual API for the software is in PL/SQL. The interaction required between Oracle and the operating system is performed using the DBMS_PIPE package. This provides the means of reading documents through a user-developed function.

For more information, contact Peter Larsson, `plarsson@astrakan.se`.

PL/SQL Compiler

pls.sun4 (or PL/Web) is a stand-alone PL/SQL compiler for the SunOS 4 operating system. It contains built-in extensions to PL/SQL to provide HTML processing. It provides a means for developers to produce PL/SQL applications without an Oracle7 database. It also provides the capability to interactively develop PL/SQL HTML applications, which requires use of HTML pages provided with the compiler. You can then save the code as source files on the server.

This compiler is available only for SunOS 4 and there are no other sites for it.

> **NOTE**
>
> A sure sign of the WWW Interface Kit's grassroots acceptance is in the Samples mailing list. Created and managed by Thomas Dunbar, Research & Graduate Studies, Virginia Tech, Samples, along with its companion Web site `http://gserver.grads.vt.edu/`, is dedicated to PL/SQL-based interfaces. Both are increasingly peppered with Web-based application queries including those for the WOW Gateway and Oracle WebSystem.
>
> To join the mailing list, fill out the HTML form found at `http://gserver.grads.vt.edu/subscribe_sample.html`.

WOW Gateway

In early 1994, Oracle became the first major RDBMS to release a gateway for the WWW. Called WOW for Web-to-Oracle-to-Web, it was released into the public domain and remains the best means of getting Oracle databases on the Internet for little or no cost. Commercial operations that require more robust and supported operation (WOW is an unsupported product) should use the Oracle WebServer, which is covered fully later in this chapter.

Traditionally, most gateways are coded in C, Perl, or shell scripts. WOW is remarkable in that it provides the capability to develop all Web applications in PL/SQL. This means that the same language that developers already use to write other Oracle applications can be harnessed to the power of the Internet and the World Wide Web. This is all done using traditional CGI call mechanisms so that the programs are called as if they were files in the CGI directory.

WOW consists of several components:

- WOW is a shell script provided in C-shell format but easily converted to Bourne or Korn shell to provide the same functions, namely setting environment variables related to the database connection.

- wowstub is an OCI program that converts POST data into calls to stored procedures with arguments passed correctly as entered, that is, with + replaced by space and so on.

- HTP is the hypertext package containing all procedures used by the WOW gateway.

- HTF is the hypertext package containing all functions used by the WOW gateway. The functions return values, whereas the procedures do not. The functions are required to check error conditions and alter behavior as needed.

A Simple Demonstration of WOW Using SQL*Plus

To grasp what WOW does, look at a simple example using SQL*Plus. PL/SQL until recently did not provide a means of exchanging data except through tables. In Oracle7, there are a number of packages that extend the facilities available to the language. One of these new packages is DBMS_OUTPUT. Within this package are several functions, including put_line(), which sends its arguments to a buffered stream. The following example illustrates its use.

```
DBMS_OUTPUT.PUT_LINE('Your total order comes to ' || TO_CHAR(total_order));
```

DBMS_OUTPUT specifies the package name, and put_line() specifies the particular function within that package. A single character string value or expression is required. This case uses an expression concatenating a character string and a total value, which is first converted from numeric to character string type.

In addition to DBMS_OUTPUT, you must have a program that knows to extract such buffered information. The likely choice is SQL*Plus. Whenever you call a PL/SQL stored procedure or an anonymous PL/SQL block, an inline program is executed. Provided that you'd previously issued the SET SERVEROUTPUT ON command, the output is sent to the standard output of the application upon completion of the block or procedure.

In fact, to appreciate how WOW works, you should see an example in SQL*Plus. For the purposes of this example, assume that the HTP and HTF packages were installed under a user ID called wowuser. A call to the bold procedure results in the following output with the appropriate HTML bracketing tags for boldface output:

```
$ sqlplus wowuser
enter password: *****
Connected.
SQL> SET SERVEROUTPUT ON
SQL> EXECUTE htp.bold('This is a test');
<B>This is a test</B>
PL/SQL procedure successfully completed.
SQL>
```

wowstub: The Agent Component

Of course, you don't want to have to invoke SQL*Plus every time you produce HTML, so instead, the wowstub program fills the need as the primary CGI interface program. wowstub itself does not perform the application functions but functions as a pipeline between the HTML server and the Oracle database. Be aware that the program need not be called wowstub; however, if you change the name, you must also change references to that program name. They are found in HTML files and in the WOW shell script.

When invoked, wowstub evaluates several environment variables and determines whether the GET or POST method is used. Additionally, it checks to see if the program was invoked in debug mode. Finally, it reads the parameters from standard input for POST or from the INFO environment variable for GET and ISINDEX requests and connects to the database using the name and password specified in the environment variables. It is very important that the gateway is installed such that the contents of the agent are not visible to unauthorized users. Otherwise, with the name and password in plain sight, wowstub and the data with which it interacts are compromised. Count on it!

The WOW gateway provides a database server-resident means of seamlessly tying business rules into Web forms processing. Web forms are the interactive Web pages that enable user interaction with the Web site. Unlike traditional, static Web pages, forms enable Web developers to create highly customized and interactive Web sites.

You can test a correctly configured server using Telnet. You can instruct Telnet, which traditionally connects to well-known port 23, to use the Web server's port 80 instead. The following example of this technique illustrates what happens during a Web page request. User entries are shown in bold. You must end the HEAD statement with two line feed or Ctrl+J characters.

```
# telnet www.chatsoft.com 80
Trying 555.137.257.36 ...
Connected to chatsoft.com
Escape character is '^]'.
HEAD / HTTP/1.0↵↵

HTTP/1.0 200 OK
Date: Thursday, 24 Aug 95 10:15:22 GMT
Allow: GET, HEAD
Server: Oracle Web Server/1.0.0.0.1
Content-Length: 1973
Content-type: text/html
Last-modified: Thursday, 17 Aug 95 8:12:23 GMT
URI: <index.html>
Connection closed by foreign host.
```

The WOW Shell Script

In order for the wowstub program to properly execute, you must have a wrapper program that takes care of setting up environment variables and any other functions to be performed each time the gateway is called. This is the purpose of the WOW shell script. As in the case with the wowstub program, you can change the name to something more appropriate with the application it performs. For the following examples, however, I use the name WOW.

Extending WOW Using PL/SQL

PL/SQL is Oracle Corporation's procedural SQL-based programming language. Based on ADA, PL/SQL offers object-oriented features to fully harness SQL's potential. Combining polymorphism and encapsulation with SQL data manipulation language (DML) statements, users can craft the most sophisticated of business rules and execute them efficiently within the Oracle7 engine. Additionally, you can use PL/SQL to develop the procedural code within Oracle's development applications, such as Forms, Graphics, and Reports. As such, Oracle developers need not learn a new language to process HTML.

In the WOW gateway, PL/SQL packages such as htp.bold and htp.italic are written in two pieces, the called procedure and a matching function. This is due to the inability to call a function without capturing the result, which is consistent with strongly checked languages such as ADA and with current solid code practices. Frequently, in less rigorous languages, errors arise from unchecked result codes and return values. You will notice that all of the functions conclude with a call to the print or p procedure. This places the output in the put buffer from which the application, wowstub in this case, extracts the results.

The following code segment shows the contents of the htf.bold function. You see how it merely encapsulates the passed string in the HTML tags for bolding; <B> and </B> and returns it to the calling htp.bold procedure. The htp.bold procedures always perform the htp.p procedure to place the text on the output buffer.

```
function bold    (ctext  in varchar2) return varchar2 is
begin return('<b>' || ctext || '</b>' ); end;
procedure bold   (ctext  in varchar2) is
begin p(htf.bold(ctext)); end;
```

When a certain feature is not available in WOW, you can add it either to the application or, better yet, to the HTP and HTF packages. An example of a common limitation will further illuminate this choice.

When developing HTML forms using WOW, you can specify input fields in the following forms:

```
procedure formField(cname in varchar2, nsize in integer);
procedure formField(cname in varchar2);
procedure formField(cname in varchar2, cvalue in varchar2);
```

All of the forms require the name of the field as the first argument. This is how values are tagged before passing through to the CGI program. Depending on whether the next argument is missing, an integer, or a varchar2 field, PL/SQL expects to set the field to a default width, the specified width, or the default width with an initial default value. What is missing is the capability to create a field with a specified width and an initial default value. To do this, you extend WOW by adding the following procedure prototype, function prototype, procedure, and function. All are required.

```
function formField(cname in varchar2, nsize in integer, cvalue in varchar2)
    return varchar2;
function formField(cname in varchar2, nsize in integer, cvalue in varchar2)
    return varchar2 is
begin
    return('<input type="text" name="' || cname || '" size="' ||
          to_char(nsize) || '" value="' ||
          cvalue || '">');
end;
procedure formField(cname in varchar2, nsize in integer, cvalue in varchar2);
procedure formField(cname in varchar2, nsize in integer, cvalue in varchar2) is
begin p(htf.formField(cname,nsize,cvalue)); end;
```

WOW's Limitations

As groundbreaking as WOW is, it is usually not appropriate for commercial utilization without extensive extensions to the feature set. Because WOW product support is not available from Oracle, feature extension is left up to the individual developer as the HTML standard evolves. Additionally, WOW requires manual setup for each Web server's implementation. Ideally, there should be a one-stop solution: Web server, gateway, agent. Oracle has such a product in the Oracle Web Server.

Oracle WebSystem

As the Internet became more accepted as an information conduit, many organizations established an Internet presence in an effort to be available to both customers and resources. The need to potentially service tens of millions users was an impediment to setting up a home on the WWW, which required flexible, secure, and reliable Web access and management. Developers needed a reliable solution to the problems of scalability, information partitioning, and life-cycle management. Such a need drove the development of the Oracle WebSystem (OWS). It provides integrated installation, management, and development tools along with its use of native language (PL/SQL) server-side processing to take advantage of extant business rules.

OWS Components

The Oracle WebSystem is actually three complementary products:

- Oracle HTTP Listener
- Oracle Web Agent
- Oracle7 Server

The Oracle Web Listener is an optimized HTTP server intended for use in high-traffic mission-critical environments. It is tuned for the requirements of highly interactive database originated processing and data sourcing. It provides information from flat files, the Oracle Web Agent, and other CGI/1.1-compliant applications.

The Oracle Web Agent is the successor to WOW itself. It is a highly improved production-quality version of the WOW, wowstub, and HTP/HTF packages. It has been greatly extended, secured, and optimized for use in the Oracle Web Server environment. The agent concept is also exploited in Oracle Mobile Agents. Because the agent is placed close to the source of information, functions for the remote client are performed far more quickly than through the multiple round trips required in a traditional client/server architecture. This is because the local agent has a higher speed connection than the remote browser, which is likely to be many hops away.

The Oracle7 Server is the same Oracle7 technology that corporations have relied on to reliably service worldwide applications. It provides desktop management capabilities in an eminently scalable relational database management system. For enterprises that want to use an existing Oracle7 server, the Oracle Web Server Option provides all the features without the additional Oracle7 server.

Comparison to WOW

WOW paved the way for OWS. It proved that the Web-agent-server path was reliable, flexible, and technically viable. It also demonstrated that support and vertical integration were necessary to make it commercially viable. OWS provides the following features that were missing from WOW:

- Vertical product integration—Using Oracle Installer technology, the management of the OWS products is integrated with other Oracle products. No longer is the management of Oracle/Internet technology a manual, homegrown job. Additionally, the agent technology is a registerable service in SQL*Net Version 2. This further facilitates the management of multiple Web-based applications through a known interface, the Oracle Network Manager.

- Product evolution—As HTTP, HTML, and other Internet standards progress, so will OWS. Already, OWS supports proposed HTML3 extensions including background GIFs and tables.

- Improved performance—Traditional HTTP servers expected to move files, not database-resident information. As such, their performance was based on getting the same information out many times. The best means for file serving was through multithreaded processing where each new connection invoked a new server process. The Oracle Web Listener accomplishes its improved throughput through a single process/single thread asynchronous engine. As such, time to service a request is significantly reduced, which increases response time, especially under heavy loads.

- Improved flexibility—As part of the Oracle Web Server, multiple languages are supportable simultaneously. This might not have been available under other servers, and it certainly wasn't available transparently for the WOW user.

■ Improved security—In addition to Secure Network Services (SNS), an option already available to WOW users running SNS, the Oracle Web Listener provides several additional securing mechanisms: Basic and Digest Authentication, IP-based restriction, domain-based restriction, file-based restriction, and, in later releases, encryption. Also, both Secure Sockets Layer (SSL) and Secure HTTP (S/HTTP) will be supported in future releases of Oracle Web Listener and PowerBrowser.

■ Client-side processing—Additionally, through PowerBrowser, WebSystem provides integrated client-side processing, enabling business-rule processing and sophisticated programmability at the front end as well.

WOW Conversion Issues

In order to extend the facilities in OWS and resolve some earlier architectural vagaries, the Oracle Web Agent packages contain many extended and renamed package components. In order to use existing WOW applications with the Oracle Web Server, you must accommodate the following differences.

■ The WOW PL/SQL packages, previously called HTP and HTF, have been consolidated into a single package called OWA.

■ The default signature procedure, wow.sig, is now owa_util.signature.

■ The WOW procedure, wow.showsource, is now called owa_util.showsource.

■ The WOW C program, wowstub, is now called owa.

■ To accommodate the use of existing WOW code, OWA_DEFAULT_SERVICE is provided. It enables the Web administrator to specify the default service owa will use if the URL provides an unknown service. You can think of services as applications or PL/SQL packages.

■ The following procedures and functions have been renamed. To accommodate these differences, change the names of the affected subprograms in your application.

WOW Name	OWA Name
url	anchor
gif	img
formUndo	formReset
item	listItem
ddef	dlistDef
dterm	dlistTerm

■ The use of the following procedures and functions might also require coding changes. The procedure formText is now called formTextarea. The procedure formText is now used for single-line text fields. Text areas are scrollable sections of n-rows by n-columns. In addition to the name change, the new formTextarea also accommodates initialization of the text area. To do this, issue a text outputting call between the formTextareaOpen and the TextareaClose statements.

```
...
htp.formTextareaOpen('comments',10,60);
htp.print('This text will appear in the comments field as
the default text.');
htp.formTextareaClose;
...
```

- As mentioned previously, the formField procedure required extension to set both its width and initial value. This still applies. However, there is also another required modification. In cases where only the initial value is provided, you should use the following form:

```
formText(cname, NULL, NULL, cvalue);
```

- Fixing a previous limitation, the formDo button has been renamed and extended. It is now called formSubmit in keeping with the HTML name for the object it represents, a submission button. What was previously missing was a means of setting the both the name associated with the name/value pair passed to WOW and the label displayed on the button. You can recode existing calls to formDo as follows:

```
formSubmit(NULL, label);
```

To fully utilize the feature and enable multiple buttons in a single form, you should instead use the following form:

```
formSubmit(cname, cvalue, cattributes);
```

WebSystem

WebSystem offers all the features of the WOW gateway and more. Commercial support, future enhancements, and tighter integration with other Oracle technologies including Oracle Applications through Oracle Internet Commerce are all a part of WebSystem's offerings.

WebSystem Installation

WebSystem even goes farther offering effectively one-button installation. Whether you're installing the full WebSystem package using Oracle Installer or WebServer Option for when you already have an Oracle7 database, the procedure is simple.

Prerequisites

Initially, WebSystem was released for the Sun Solaris 2.4 platform whose installation is shown here. The process is similar for all platforms.

Prior to installing WebSystem, you must do the following:

- Make certain ORACLE_HOME is set.

■ Make certain ORACLE_SID is set.

■ If installing only the WebServer Option, copy the oweb.tar.Z file to $ORACLE_HOME.

WebServer Option Installation

Following is the script of one installation:

```
# cd $ORACLE_HOME
# pwd
/export/home/oracle
# zcat oweb.tar | tar xvf -        # unpack the oweb.tar.Z
x owsins/ows/mesg/owsus.msb
x owsins/ows/mesg/owsus.msg
.
.
.
# cd owsins/ows/install
# pwd
/export/home/oracle/owsins/ows/install
# install.sh

Creating product area /export/home/oracle/ows

Copying the Web Server binaries to /export/home/oracle/bin

Please enter the port number you want to use as your administration server. Valid port
numbers range from 1 to 65535 [default 8888]:

Please enter hostname (including domain) name for your machine.

Example: oraweb.oracle.com: www.chatsoft.com
Please enter the name of the 'oracle' software owner: oracle
Please enter the name of the 'oracle dba' group: dba
Setting Oracle Web admin password to 'manager'
    Installation of the Oracle WebServer file set is complete.
You now need to ensure your ORACLE_HOME environment variable is set
    and run the following command as the oracle software owner to start
    the Administration Server:
        /export/home/oracle/bin/wlctl start 8888
    To complete installation of the Oracle WebServer, open the
    following URL location with your web browser:
        http://www.chatsoft.com:8888/ows-abin/register
    and follow directions as they appear on the pages.
    When you attempt to use the Administration Server you will
    be requested to authenticate youself by entering the username
    'admin' with password 'manager' in the appropriate login screen.
```

That's it! The installation of the software package is complete.

Starting Up the Web Listener

The following code segment shows how to start the Web Listener to complete the registration and setup process.

```
$ pwd
/export/home/oracle
$ bin/wlctl/start 8888

Oracle Web Listener, Version 1.01fc5
Copyright 1995 Oracle Corp.  All Rights Reserved.

Information: Listening on port 8888
Information: The server started successfully
Server now running as process 882
```

Once the Web Listener is running, you complete the rest of the process using a Web browser and the WebServer itself.

Setting Up the Web Agent

As indicated in the previous installation messages, connect to the WebServer using the URL `http://www.chatsoft.com:8888/ows-abin/register`. You see the screen in Figure 55.2.

FIGURE 55.2.

WebServer Registration form.

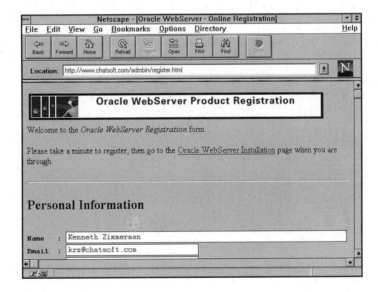

You must fill in every field. Once this form is completed and submitted, you see the screen shown in Figure 55.3.

At this point, follow the remaining tasks to complete the installation:

1. Configure an Oracle Web Agent service, OWA_DBA, for the Administration Server that you are currently using.

2. Configure your first Oracle Web Listener.

3. Configure a default Oracle Web Agent service, OWA_DEFAULT_SERVICE, for your first Oracle Web Listener that you configured in step 2.

FIGURE 55.3.

WebServer Installation form.

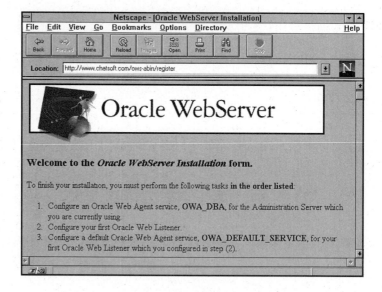

Figure 55.4 shows the fields and buttons that you use to set up the Agent service.

FIGURE 55.4.

Agent Setup Installation form.

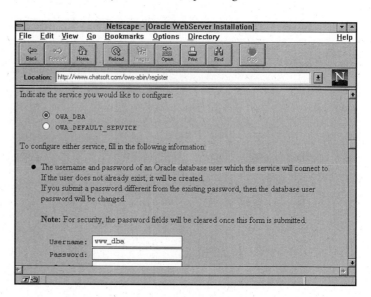

Finally, create the first Web Listener other than the Administrative Server by completing the form section below the WebServer Installation form section. It is shown in Figure 55.5.

FIGURE 55.5.

Creating an Oracle Web Listener.

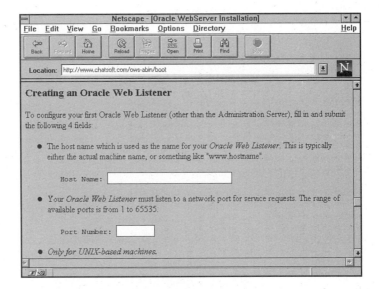

Learning More About WebSystem

Once the system is up and running, all of the product documentation is provided in the /doc/ directory of the WebServer directory. Figure 55.6 shows how to access this section using the URL http://www.chatsoft.com/doc/.

FIGURE 55.6.

WebSystem's online documentation.

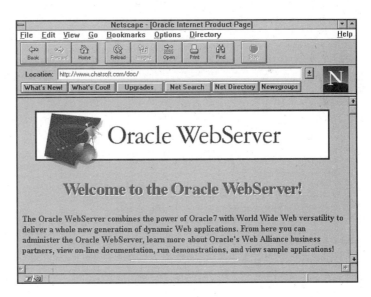

Summary

Oracle led the development of commercial Web/RDBMS integration. It freely released a set of technology, the WOW Gateway, which continues to be vital as a result of grassroots support. WebSystem now provides the commercial, high-performance secure gateway to enterprise data, which companies have increasingly needed. As you work with these technologies, keep in mind that they are all extensible. If you need additional features, build them in! All of the components are provided in source code so that you can improve them for your own needs. And, if you are stuck, check out the various Internet and commercial service provided forums covering Web/RDBMS technologies:

- Thomas Dunbar's site at `http://gserver.grads.vt.edu/`
- Oracle's home page at `http://www.oracle.com/`
- The Oracle Users forum on CompuServe
- `comp.databases.oracle` newsgroup
- `comp.infosystems.www` newsgroup

Oracle Packages

PART

Personal Oracle7™

56

Personal Oracle7 is a version of the Oracle7 database and it is currently available in the following editions:

- Personal Oracle7 for Windows 95
- Personal Oracle7 for Microsoft Windows
- Personal Oracle7 for OS/2
- Personal Oracle7 for Power Macintosh

Currently, you can download the 90-day free trial software from the Oracle World Wide Web server at `http://www.oracle.com`. Personal Oracle7 is bundled with a set of Oracle database administration tools or the Personal Oracle7 Navigator for Windows 95, Oracle backup and recovery tools, Oracle utilities, Oracle Objects for OLE, Oracle7 ODBC driver, and Oracle online documentation.

This chapter presents the overview of Personal Oracle7, the system requirements for installing Personal Oracle7, and how it differs from other Oracle packages. It also introduces you to the major components of Personal Oracle7.

Although Personal Oracle7 shares many features with the Oracle7 Server, which functions as a database server and supports a large number of clients, Personal Oracle7 is designed for a single user or developer. This chapter explains when using Personal Oracle7 is appropriate and how Personal Oracle7 meets your business and technical needs.

Overview of Personal Oracle7

Oracle7 runs on many operating systems and it scales well on a wide range of hardware platforms, including personal computers, Macintosh, workstations, midrange computers, and mainframe computers. Personal Oracle7 is a single-user database, and it is designed for users who want to use or to develop an Oracle7 database on Windows 95, Microsoft Windows, OS/2, or Power Macintosh. It supports up to 25 concurrent database sessions, but it is not designed to be a database server. The scalability of Oracle7 enables developers to port their applications developed on Personal Oracle7 to other operating systems on different hardware platforms.

Personal Oracle7 Components

Personal Oracle7 includes the Oracle7 database, Oracle database tools, Oracle utilities, SQL products, Oracle Objects for OLE, Oracle7 ODBC driver, Oracle networking software, SQL*Net version 1 and version 2, and online documentation. Personal Oracle7 for Windows 95 includes the Personal Oracle7 Navigator, which replaces a portion of the Oracle database tools, such as the Database Manager. The current major components of Personal Oracle7 are summarized in Table 56.1. For additional information about the Personal Oracle7 components, please refer to your *Personal Oracle7 Installation and User's Guide.*

Table 56.1. Personal Oracle7 Components.

Components	Descriptions	Personal Oracle7 for Windows 95	Personal Oracle7 for MS Windows	Personal Oracle7 for OS/2	Personal Oracle7 for Power Macintosh
Database					
Database	Oracle7 Database	Yes	Yes	Yes	No
Distributed Options	Database links, distributed queries and updates, read-only snapshots	Yes	Yes	Yes	No
Symmetric Replication	Updatable snapshots	Yes	NA	NA	Yes
Administration Tools					
Database Manager	Startup and shutdown with customized initialization parameters	NA	Yes	Yes	Yes
User Manager	Create and manage user accounts, roles, and privileges	NA	Yes	Yes	Yes
Object Manager	Create and manage database objects	NA	Yes	Yes	Yes
Session Manager	View and kill user sessions	NA	Yes	Yes	Yes
Database Expander	Expand the size of your database	NA	Yes	Yes	Yes

continues

Table 56.1. continued

Components	Descriptions	Personal Oracle7 for Windows 95	Personal Oracle7 for MS Windows	Personal Oracle7 for OS/2	Personal Oracle7 for Power Macintosh
Administration Tools					
Password Manager	Change the database password	NA	Yes	NA	Yes
Navigator	Database tool	Yes	NA	NA	NA
Backup and Recovery Tools					
Backup Manager	Back up your Oracle7 database	NA	Yes	NA	NA
Recovery Manager	Recover your Oracle7 database	NA	Yes	NA	NA
Utilities					
Export	Export your Oracle7 database to an export file	Yes	Yes	Yes	Yes
Import	Import data into your Oracle7 database from an export file	Yes	Yes	Yes	Yes
SQL*Loader	Load data from other data source into your Oracle7 database	Yes	Yes	Yes	Yes
SQL Products					
PL/SQL	Oracle procedural language extension to SQL	Yes	Yes	Yes	Yes

Components	Descriptions	*Personal Oracle7 for Windows 95*	*Personal Oracle7 for MS Windows*	*Personal Oracle7 for OS/2*	*Personal Oracle7 for Power Macintosh*
SQL*DBA	Administer the database, including areas that cannot be managed with the database administration tools	Yes	Yes	Yes	Yes
SQL*Plus	A command language interface enables you to execute SQL and PL/SQL commands and scripts	Yes	Yes	Yes	Yes
Networking Software					
SQL*Net	Oracle network interface to enable clients to connect to and access the Oracle7 database	Yes	Yes	Yes	Yes
Middleware					
Oracle Objects for OLE	Visual Basic Customer Control and a C++ class library	Yes	Yes	Yes	NA
Oracle7 ODBC Driver	Enables other database applications to work with Oracle7 database	Yes	Yes	Yes	NA

continues

Table 56.1. continued

Components	Descriptions	Personal Oracle7 for Windows 95	Personal Oracle7 for MS Windows	Personal Oracle7 for OS/2	Personal Oracle7 for Power Macintosh
		Middleware			
Online Documen-tation	Most of the documentation is available on-line and in help format	Yes	Yes	Yes	Yes

System Requirements

Before you install Personal Oracle7, make sure that your system meets the following minimum hardware and software requirements. Refer to your *Personal Oracle7 Installation and User's Guide* for additional information on how to determine your system requirements. This section also gives you several tips on installing and using Personal Oracle7.

Hardware Requirements

This section describes the minimum hardware requirements for installing and running Personal Oracle7.

- A 486-based (or higher) IBM, Compaq, 100 percent compatible PC, or a Power Macintosh computer.
- A minimum of 16MB of RAM; 32MB is recommended.

> **TIP**
>
> The ORA-9368 error message is usually caused by not having enough memory to run the Personal Oracle7 database.

- A minimum of 50MB of free disk space. Certain Personal Oracle7 installation options might require additional free disk space.
- Access to a CD-ROM drive (local or network) from your PC. A CD-ROM drive is not required if you download the software from the Web site.

■ A compatible network interface card (NIC) for Oracle products to communicate with each other over a network through SQL*Net. If you are not planning to connect to Oracle products over a network, you may not need the NIC.

Software Requirements

This section describes the minimum software requirements for installing and running Personal Oracle7.

■ Personal Oracle7 for Windows 95 requires Microsoft Windows 95.

Personal Oracle7 for Windows requires Microsoft Windows 3.1 or Windows for Workgroups 3.11.

Personal Oracle7 for OS/2 requires IBM OS/2 Version 2.1 or IBM OS/2 Warp Version 3.

Personal Oracle7 for Power Macintosh requires Macintosh operating system Version 7.5 or greater.

NOTE

Personal Oracle7 for Windows is not designed to run under OS/2 or Windows NT. Therefore, running Personal Oracle7 for Windows under a WinOS/2 session or Windows 3.1 emulation of Windows NT is not supported.

■ Personal Oracle7 for Windows requires Microsoft Win32, which is included on the Personal Oracle7 for Windows CD-ROM (both editions). Win32 is Microsoft's 32-bit extension to Microsoft Windows 3.1. Because Personal Oracle7 is a 32-bit database, you need to install Win32 first and make sure it is working properly before you install Personal Oracle7 for Windows.

CAUTION

If you experience the stack overflow error, the following steps might help you resolve it:

■ You might need to change STACKS=9,256 to STACKS=36,256 in the CONFIG.SYS file.

■ Certain display drivers, such as STBVISN.DRV, might not be compatible with Win32 and might cause stack overflow errors. Replacing the display driver might solve the problem.

■ Network transport protocol software (Named Pipes, SPX, TCP/IP, or AppleTalk), which is required to be supported by Oracle SQL*Net Version 1 or 2 if you are planning to connect to Oracle products through SQL*Net.

Database Administration Tools

This section introduces you to the database administration tools of the Personal Oracle7. These graphical database tools enable you to perform the common database administration tasks and to maintain and customize your database. For step-by-step instructions on how to use the database administration tools, please refer to your *Personal Oracle7 Installation and User's Guide* and the *Oracle Database Tools User's Guide*.

Database Manager

The Database Manager enables you to start or shut down the database, check the status of the database, customize the database configurations, and modify aliases for the database. Figure 56.1 shows the Oracle Database Manager dialog box.

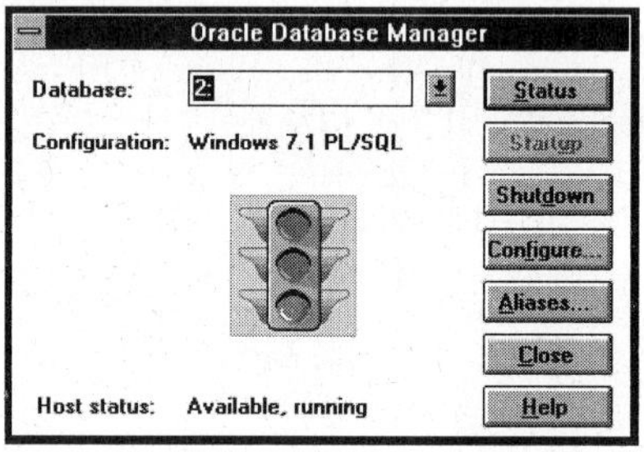

FIGURE 56.1.

The Oracle Database Manager dialog box.

Before you select any dialog element in the Database Manager, you want to make sure the Database dialog box contains a correct database name and the Configuration dialog box shows the appropriate configuration name for the database you have selected. The database name for the local Personal Oracle7 database is 2: (the number two followed by a colon). You can assign a database alias for it. You can also select a remote database name.

A configuration is equivalent to an initialization parameter file. Therefore, if you modify any initialization parameter using the Configure dialog box, then you need to make the same change in your initialization parameter file if you are going to use SQL*DBA to start or shut down your database. When you use the Configure dialog box to customize and set the initialization parameters, the changes are saved in VS10.INI. The Database Manager uses both the built-in (VSP10.INI) and user-defined (VS10.INI) configurations.

Database Password Manager for Windows

The Database Password Manager enables you to change the database password to protect your database. The database password is the same as the password for INTERNAL. The default database password is ORACLE in Personal Oracle7 for Windows. The initial database password in Personal Oracle7 for OS/2 is assigned by you during the installation.

CAUTION

Shut down the database before you use the Password Manager to change the database password. Otherwise, you will not be able to shut down the database from the Database Manager because the database will not accept any password. If your database is started up with an initialization parameter REMOTE_LOGIN_PASSWORDFILE=SHARED in the configuration, you can change the database password while the database is up.

TIP

In Personal Oracle7 for Windows, if you add DBA_AUTHORIZATION=BYPASS in \WINDOWS\ORACLE.INI and restart Windows, when you start the database in the Database Manager, it will not prompt you to input the database password. Similarly, for Personal Oracle7 for Windows 95, you can add DBA_AUTHORIZATION=PASS in the Windows 95 Registry.

The User Manager

The User Manager enables you to create and delete user accounts and roles, grant user and role privileges, and change a user's password.

When you create a new user using the User Manager, the default tablespace for the new user is USER_DATA and the temporary tablespace is TEMPORARY_DATA. If any one of the tablespaces does not exist, you will receive a warning dialog box. If you select OK to continue, the User Manager will use the SYSTEM tablespace. The workaround is to use SQL*DBA to create new users by specifying a default tablespace and a temporary tablespace in the CREATE USER statement for each new user.

The Object Manager

The Object Manager enables you to create and modify database objects, including tables, indexes, synonyms, database links, views, and snapshots. You can also use the Object Manager to grant object privileges to users or roles.

The Session Manager

The Session Manager enables you to view all the sessions, the session IDs, serial number, and the status of each connected session. The Session Manager also enables you to disconnect or terminate sessions.

The Database Expander

When the database is 75 percent full, you should expand the database. The Database Expander enables you to view the current free and used space in each tablespace. After you select a tablespace that you need to expand, you can input the size (in KB) you want to add and click the Expand button to expand the tablespace. In Personal Oracle7 for Windows, the Database Expander adds a new data file in the \ORAWIN\BIN directory. However, the original data files are stored in the \ORAWIN\DBS directory. For the Database Expander to add new data files in the \ORAWIN\DBS directory, you can change the working directory of the Database Expander to \ORAWIN\DBS in the Properties option of the Database Expander icon.

Personal Oracle7 Navigator for Windows 95

The Personal Oracle7 Navigator for Windows 95 enables you to access all of your projects, database connections, and database objects. It functions like the database administration tools and enables you to create, modify, and delete database objects. You can create a new project and administer the database using the Oracle7 Navigator menu bar or the Oracle7 Navigator toolbar. Figure 56.2 shows the Personal Oracle7 Navigator dialog box.

FIGURE 56.2.

The Personal Oracle7 Navigator dialog box.

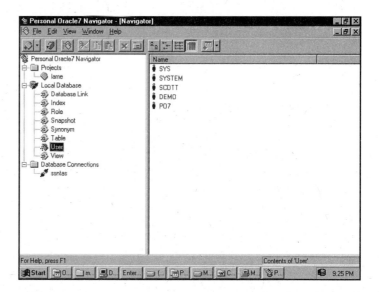

Database Backup and Recovery Tools

This section gives an overview of the Backup Manager and the Recovery Manager for Windows. For instructions on using these tools, refer to your *Personal Oracle7 Installation and User's Guide* and the *Oracle Database Tools User's Guide*.

The Backup Manager

The Backup Manager enables you to do an online (hot) backup of a selected tablespace and the control file and an offline (cold) backup of the entire database to a tape or selected directory. The Online - Selected Tablespace option is available only when the database is running and in ARCHIVELOG mode.

The Recovery Manager

After a database failure, you can use the Recovery Manager to recover your database. The Recovery Manager enables you to do Automatic Recovery, Restore from full database backup, Restore data file, and then do recovery, or Restore control file, and then do recovery.

The Export, Import, and SQL*Loader Utilities

This section describes the characteristics of the Database Exporter, Database Importer, and SQL*Loader utilities. It also provides several tips for using these utilities.

The Database Exporter and Database Importer

When you want to move data between Oracle databases, you can use the Database Exporter to export tables, users, or the full database to a transportable file. Then, you can use the Database Importer to read data from the transportable file back into an Oracle database. This transportable file can be used as a database backup. These export and import utilities are available for various platforms. That means the transportable file generated by the Database Exporter from the Windows environment could be used to import the data into an Oracle7 database in another platform.

SQL*Loader

The SQL*Loader utility enables you to load data from external files in ASCII format into Oracle database tables. Before using the SQL*Loader utility, you might need to create a SQL*Loader control file, which is used by the SQL*Loader utility to interpret the data file.

SQL Products

Personal Oracle7 includes the following SQL products:

- PL/SQL. Procedural Language/Structured Query Language is the procedural language extension to SQL.

- SQL*DBA. The SQL*DBA utility enables you to execute SQL scripts and perform database administration tasks. Certain database administration tasks can only be performed using the SQL*DBA utility. For example, to create a new database, you can use the SQL*DBA utility. Currently, the GUI implementation of SQL*DBA does not support the monitor functions, such as MONITOR SESSION.

> **NOTE**
>
> If you receive the ORA-01991 error while you are creating a new database using the SQL*DBA utility, you might need to change the setting of the REMOTE_LOGIN_PASSWORDFILE parameter in the configuration to SHARED. Its default setting is EXCLUSIVE.

- SQL*Plus. SQL*Plus is a command language interface that enables you to run SQL and PL/SQL scripts and commands.

The SQL products are discussed in detail in Chapters 5, 6, and 7.

Middleware

This section describes the additional components that are included with Personal Oracle7: Oracle Objects for OLE and Oracle7 ODBC driver.

Oracle Objects for OLE

Oracle Objects for OLE is a set of programmable objects (dynaset objects) that enables you to develop C++, Microsoft Visual Basic, and OLE 2 scripting-enabled applications to access the data of an Oracle database and the advanced Oracle7 features. It supports Borland C++ 4.0 or higher, Microsoft Visual C++ 1.5 or higher, Microsoft Visual Basic 3.0 or higher, Visual Basic for Applications, and any other Windows-based application that supports OLE 2 scripting. Part VIII of this book gives an overview of Oracle Objects for OLE and discusses the OLE Server and Data Control.

Oracle7 ODBC Driver

The Oracle7 ODBC driver is a program that can function as an interpreter between the ODBC interface and the native interface to an Oracle7 database. It enables the direct access between the ODBC-compliant database applications and the Oracle7 database. For example, the Oracle7 ODBC driver enables you to use Microsoft Access to retrieve and modify data from your Oracle7 database.

Before you use the Oracle7 ODBC driver, you might need to use the ODBC Administrator to configure it properly. The following steps illustrate how to configure the current Oracle7 ODBC driver:

1. Select the ODBC Administrator icon.
2. In the Data Source dialog box, select the Add button.
3. In the Add Data Source dialog box, select the appropriate Oracle database version from the Installed ODBC Driver list, and then select OK.
4. The Oracle7 ODBC Setup dialog box appears on the screen; enter the required information. Figure 56.3 shows the Oracle7 ODBC Setup dialog box.

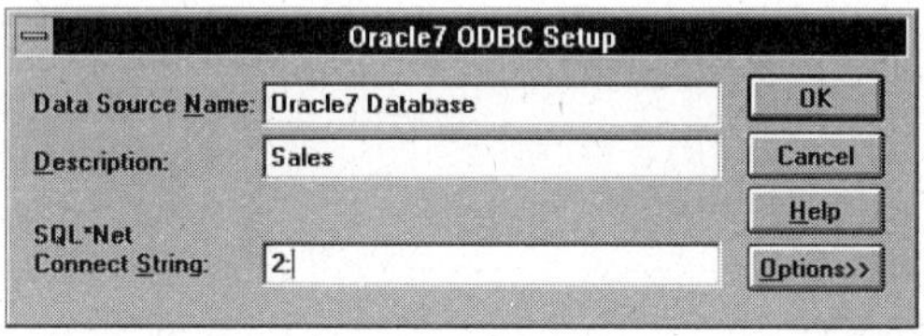

FIGURE 56.3.

The Oracle7 ODBC Setup dialog box.

When you access the local Personal Oracle7 database, you can use 2: as the SQL*Net connect string.

Personal Oracle7 Database Options and Networking Software

This section describes the database options that are available in Personal Oracle7. It includes the distributed options and Symmetric Replication option.

Distributed Options

The distributed options enable you to develop and deploy distributed databases. Personal Oracle7 enables you to create database links to access remote databases, create distributed queries to retrieve information from remote databases, do distributed updates to modify data in remote databases, and create read-only table snapshots to replicate data from remote databases.

The Symmetric Replication Option

The Symmetric Replication option supports "update anywhere," which means all copies of data at different sites can be updated and the updates are applied to all other copies. The update can be made at the data level or schema level. The Oracle7 Symmetric Replication option also supports both conflict avoidance and conflict detection and resolution. For more information on symmetric replication, refer to the *Oracle7 Server Distributed Systems, Volume II: Replicated Data*.

SQL*Net and Network Manager

SQL*Net is the Oracle network interface that enables the clients to connect to the Oracle database servers and enables the connectivity among the Oracle database servers in a distributed environment. The Network Manager is a GUI tool that enables you to create and modify your SQL*Net V2 configurations. Chapter 53 contains additional information about SQL*Net.

When To Use Personal Oracle7

Personal Oracle7 is preconfigured and easy to install, maintain, use, and manage with a set of GUI database tools. If you are an application developer and you develop applications for an Oracle7 database using Windows 95-based, Windows-based, or OS/2-based tools, you can install and run Personal Oracle7 on the same system. Personal Oracle7 is cost-effective because it delivers all the power and functionality of Oracle7 at a lower cost. Personal Oracle7 is appropriate for mobile, on-site, or remote users who require a local database on the same machine.

Summary

This chapter gave you an overview of Personal Oracle7, including system requirements, installation tips, a summary of the major components, and how Personal Oracle7 is different from the Oracle7 Server. The next two chapters introduce you to the Oracle7 Workgroup Server and the Oracle7 Server for the desktop platforms.

Workgroup/2000™

57

by Winnie In-Kuan Cheang

IN THIS CHAPTER

Oracle announced the Workgroup/2000™ suite of integrated client/server tools in January, 1995. The available product list in the Oracle Workgroup/2000 suite is growing. Information about the Oracle Workgroup/2000 suite is available on the Oracle World Wide Web server. Currently, you can download the 90-day free trial software from the Oracle World Wide Web server at `http://www.oracle.com`.

This chapter gives an overview of what is included in the Oracle Workgroup/2000 suite, the system requirements for Oracle Workgroup Server, and the differences between Oracle Workgroup Server and other Oracle packages. This chapter concentrates on the Oracle7 Workgroup Server, which is part of the Oracle Workgroup/2000 suite. It also discusses what tools and utilities are included and their major components. This chapter explains when it is appropriate to use the Oracle Workgroup Server and how it meets your business and technical needs.

Overview of the Oracle Workgroup/2000 Suite

The Oracle Workgroup/2000 suite is targeted for the workgroup client/server environment in which the users and developers have easy access and control of their database with integrated graphical tools and utilities. The following products are part of the Oracle Workgroup/2000 suite:

- Personal Oracle7
- Oracle7 Workgroup Server (for NetWare, Windows NT, OS/2, UnixWare, SCO, and Solaris x86)
- Oracle Objects for OLE
- Oracle Power Objects

Personal Oracle7 is presented in Chapter 56, "Personal Oracle7," Oracle Objects for OLE is discussed in detail in Part VIII of this book, and Part VII gives an in-depth look at Oracle Power Objects. This section gives an overview of the Oracle7 Workgroup Server.

How Oracle7 Workgroup Server Differs from Other Oracle Packages

The Oracle7 server supports large-scale and distributed database environments, whereas the Oracle7 Workgroup Server is designed for small- to medium-sized workgroups that require powerful client/server solutions with the advantages of easy installation, ease-of-use, and simplified database administration and management. The Oracle7 Workgroup Server is a full-functioning, multiuser Oracle7 server. It is designed to meet the needs of workgroups to access data within a personal computer local area network environment.

Certain Oracle7 features are currently not available in the Oracle7 Workgroup Server Version 7.1, such as the distributed options, data replication, two-phase commit, parallel options, symmetric data replication, and the parallel server option. Some of them are not implemented in the Oracle7 Workgroup Server because most of the independent workgroups do not require real-time access to the data from their distributed databases.

The Oracle7 Workgroup Server is based on the Oracle7 architecture. It is completely scaleable because it shares the same Oracle7 code base as the Oracle7 Server that runs on over 80 different hardware and operating system platforms, from desktop to mainframe. Therefore, when you scale your Oracle7 database and applications from one platform to another, it is transparent to the users.

The Oracle7 Workgroup Server is bundled with a set of graphical database administration tools to enable you to perform the common database administration tasks in a graphical user interface environment. An authorized administrator can easily manage and maintain the database with these tools without typing in any SQL command.

The Oracle7 Workgroup Server also comes with an initial or seed database that has been pre-configured for the workgroup environment. The initial database contains four tablespaces: SYSTEM, USER_DATA, TEMPORARY_DATA, and ROLLBACK_DATA. When you use the User Manager tool to create a new database user account, its default tablespace will be USER_DATA and its temporary tablespace will be TEMPORARY_DATA. The initial database defaults to NOARCHIVELOG mode. You can change it to ARCHIVELOG mode to archive redo log files.

The Oracle7 Workgroup Server is tightly integrated with the operating system (OS) to produce the optimal performance. The Oracle7 Workgroup Server supports symmetric multiprocessing (SMP), asynchronous I/O, and direct file system support on most of the Desktop and Intel UNIX platforms. It also supports OS registry on Windows NT and OS threads on the Windows NT, NetWare, and OS/2 platforms. Table 57.1 summarizes the current operating system integration support.

Table 57.1. Operating system integration support.

	Oracle7 Workgroup Server version 7.1 for			
Components	*Windows NT*	*NetWare*	*OS/2*	*UnixWare*
Symmetric multiprocessing	Yes	N/A	Yes	Yes
OS threads	Yes	Yes	Yes	N/A
Asynchronous I/O	Yes	Yes	N/A	Yes
Direct file system support	Yes	Yes	Yes	Yes
Integrated OS authentication	Yes	Yes	Yes	Yes
Native graphical administration tools	Yes	N/A	Yes	Yes
OS registry support	Yes	N/A	N/A	N/A

Oracle7 Workgroup Server Components

The Oracle7 Workgroup Server includes the Oracle7 database, Oracle database tools, Oracle utilities, SQL products, SQL*Net, Oracle Objects for OLE, Oracle7 ODBC driver, and online documentation. These Oracle7 Workgroup Server components can be categorized into the server or client software. The primary components of the Oracle7 Workgroup Server are summarized in Table 57.2. For a complete list of all components and their detailed descriptions, refer to your *Oracle7 Workgroup Server User's Guide.*

Table 57.2. Oracle7 Workgroup Server components.

	Oracle7 Workgroup Server version 7.1 for			
Components	*Windows NT*	*NetWare*	*OS/2*	*SCO, Solaris x86, UnixWare*
Server Software				
Oracle7 Workgroup Server	Yes	Yes	Yes	Yes
PL/SQL	Yes	Yes	Yes	Yes
SQL*DBA	Yes	Yes	Yes	Yes
SQL*Loader	Yes	Yes	Yes	Yes
Export	Yes	Yes	Yes	Yes
Import	Yes	Yes	Yes	Yes
SQL*Net V1 and/or V2				
Named Pipes	Yes	N/A	N/A	N/A
SPX	Yes	Yes	Yes	Yes
TCP/IP	Yes	Yes	Yes	Yes
LU6.2 (V2)	N/A	Yes	N/A	N/A
NETBIOS	N/A	N/A	Yes	N/A
Oracle Names Server	Yes	Yes	Yes	Yes
Oracle Network Manager	N/A	N/A	N/A	Yes
Oracle Database Tools				
Database Manager	N/A	N/A	Yes	Yes
Database Expander	N/A	N/A	Yes	Yes
Object Manager	N/A	N/A	Yes	Yes
Session Manager	N/A	N/A	Yes	Yes
User Manager	N/A	N/A	Yes	Yes

Components	Oracle7 Workgroup Server version 7.1 for			
	Windows NT	*NetWare*	*OS/2*	*SCO, Solaris x86, UnixWare*
Import	N/A	N/A	N/A	Yes
Export	N/A	N/A	N/A	Yes
Backup Manager	Yes	N/A	N/A	Yes
Recovery Manager	Yes	N/A	N/A	Yes
Database Password Manager	Yes	N/A	N/A	Yes
Start Oracle Networks	N/A	N/A	N/A	Yes
Stop Oracle Networks	N/A	N/A	N/A	Yes
Online Help	Yes	N/A	Yes	Yes
Maintenance Manager	N/A	N/A	N/A	Yes
Oracle Book Online Documentation	Yes	N/A	Yes	Yes
Client Software for Windows				
SQL*Net V1 and/or V2				
Named Pipes	Yes	N/A	N/A	N/A
SPX	Yes	Yes	Yes	Yes
TCP/IP	Yes	Yes	Yes	Yes
Oracle Network Manager	Yes	Yes	Yes	Yes
Oracle Database Tools				
Database Manager	Yes	Yes	Yes	Yes
Database Expander	Yes	Yes	Yes	Yes
Object Manager	Yes	Yes	Yes	Yes
Session Manager	Yes	Yes	Yes	Yes
User Manager	Yes	Yes	Yes	Yes
Import	Yes	Yes	Yes	Yes
Export	Yes	Yes	Yes	Yes
SQL*Loader	Yes	Yes	Yes	Yes
SQL*Plus	Yes	Yes	Yes	Yes
Oracle Objects for OLE	Yes	Yes	Yes	Yes
Oracle7 ODBC Driver	Yes	Yes	Yes	Yes

continues

Table 57.2. continued

Components	Oracle7 Workgroup Server version 7.1 for			
	Windows NT	*NetWare*	*OS/2*	*SCO, Solaris x86, UnixWare*
Oracle Book Online Documentation	Yes	Yes	Yes	Yes
Client Software for OS/2				
Oracle7 Utilities	N/A	Yes	Yes	N/A
Oracle Database Tools	N/A	N/A	Yes	N/A
SQL*Net V1 and/or V2				
SPX	N/A	Yes	Yes	N/A
TCP/IP	N/A	Yes	Yes	N/A
NETBIOS	N/A	N/A	Yes	N/A
SQL*VDM	N/A	Yes	Yes	N/A
Client Software for Intel UNIX, SQL*Net, Oracle Database Tools, and Oracle Book Online Documentation	N/A	N/A	N/A	Yes
Client Software for DOS				
Oracle7 Utilities	Yes	Yes	N/A	N/A
SQL*Net TCP/IP V1	Yes	Yes	N/A	N/A
SQL*Net SPX V1	N/A	Yes	N/A	N/A
SQL*Net Named Pipes V1	Yes	N/A	N/A	N/A

System Requirements

This section specifies the minimum hardware and software requirements to install the Oracle7 Workgroup Server. The hardware and software requirements depend on many factors, such as the size of the Oracle database System Global Area (SGA), the number of current client connections, and the applications installed on the system. You need to refer to your *Oracle7 Workgroup Server User's Guide* for detailed information on how to determine your system requirements. This section also provides several tips on installing and using the Oracle7 Workgroup Server.

Server Hardware Requirements

This section describes the minimum server hardware requirements for installing and running the Oracle7 Workgroup Server.

- A minimum of 386 (486 or higher is recommended) - based IBM, COMPAQ, or 100 percent compatible PC.
- A minimum of 16 MB of RAM; 32 MB is recommended. The minimum amount of RAM required depends primarily on the size of the Oracle database SGA, the number of concurrent user connections, the type of client/server transactions, and the applications installed on the server.

> **TIP**
>
> During the installation of the Oracle7 Workgroup Server for Intel UNIX, the relinking process requires swap space, which should be at least twice the size of the total physical memory installed in your server. For example, if you have 32 MB of RAM in your server, the swap space should be at least 64 MB.

> **TIP**
>
> Before you install the Oracle7 Workgroup Server for NetWare, you might want to make sure the NetWare operating system recognizes all the memory that you install on the server. You can issue the MEMORY command at the server console prompt to find out how much memory is recognized by NetWare.

- For Windows NT, NetWare, and OS/2: a minimum of 50 MB of free disk space.
- For Intel UNIX (UnixWare, Solaris x86, and SCO): a minimum of 200 MB of free disk space.

> **TIP**
>
> If the installation of the Oracle7 Workgroup Server for Intel UNIX fails because of lack of disk space, you might need to remove any partially installed products from the Oracle home directory. If you install the Oracle7 Workgroup Server from a temporary stage home directory, you might need to delete that directory and rebuild it. Remember that the Oracle Installer does not recognize any symbolic links in the Oracle home directory when the Oracle Installer calculates free disk space. If you are sure that you have enough free disk space to complete the installation, you can ignore the insufficient space warning from the Oracle Installer.

- Have access to a CD-ROM drive locally or remotely (through a network).
- A compatible network interface card (NIC) and the appropriate software.

Server Operating System Requirements

This section describes the minimum server operating system requirements for installing and running the Oracle7 Workgroup Server.

- Windows NT 3.1 or higher, NetWare 3.12 or higher, OS/2 2.1 or higher, UnixWare 2.0 or higher, Solaris x86 2.4 or higher, or SCO Open Server 3.0 or higher.

TIP

To avoid a possible server crash or abend problem, before you install the Oracle7 Workgroup Server for NetWare, you might need to apply the latest NetWare operating system patches from Novell. You might also need to install the latest disk driver(s) (.DSK) for your disk controller and the latest LAN (.LAN) driver(s) for the network interface card(s) (NIC) on your NetWare server. The *Novell Server Library NLM Updates* release notes for the Oracle7 Workgroup Server for NetWare list the required patch files from Novell.

TIP

When you are installing the Oracle7 Workgroup Server for Intel UNIX and it fails in the relinking phase, you might not have the make utility or the networking software libraries installed on your system. You can verify the make utility by following one of the steps below:

- UnixWare: Make sure that /usr/bin/make is linked to /opt/oracle/bin/make.
- SCO: Make sure that the make utility is installed under the /bin directory. The make utility is automatically installed with the SCO Development System installation.
- Solaris x86: Make sure that the make utility is in the /usr/ccs/bin directory.

TIP

For the Oracle7 Workgroup Server for Intel UNIX, the ORACLE_HOME, ORACLE_SID, ORACLE_TERM, PATH, SHELL, and DISPLAY environment should be set properly in the .profile or .login file.

Client System Requirements

This section describes the minimum client system requirements for installing and running the client system of the Oracle7 Workgroup Server.

- Windows: Windows 3.1 or higher, minimum of 4 MB of RAM; 8 MB is recommended, minimum of 30 MB of free disk space, and a CD-ROM drive.
- OS/2: OS/2 2.1 or higher, minimum of 4 MB of RAM; 8 MB is recommended, minimum of 30 MB of free disk space, and a CD-ROM drive.
- DOS: DOS 5.0 or higher, minimum of 4 MB of RAM; 8 MB is recommended, and minimum of 30 MB of free disk space.
- Intel UNIX: UnixWare 2.0 or higher, Solaris x86 2.4 or higher, or SCO Open Desktop 3.0 or higher, minimum of 4 MB of RAM; 8 MB is recommended, minimum of 100 MB of free disk space, and a CD-ROM drive.

Oracle7 Workgroup Server Tools and Utilities

The Oracle7 Workgroup Server tools and utilities are listed in Table 57.2. Most of the Oracle database user tools are discussed in Chapter 56. Some of them, such as Start Oracle, Stop Oracle, and the Maintenance Manager, are specific to the Intel UNIX servers. They are introduced in the following sections. This section also introduces the Network Manager for Windows. For a detailed description, refer to your *Oracle7 Workgroup Server User's Guide* and the *Oracle Database Tools User's Guide*.

In the Oracle7 Workgroup Server for the Intel UNIX, most of the database administration tools can be executed from the Oracle Admin toolbar. You can bring up the Oracle Admin toolbar from an xterm window by entering the following command at the operating system prompt:

```
$ otoolbar
```

The Oracle Admin toolbar contains the icons for most of the database tools, such as the Database Manager, Database Expander, Object Manager, User Manager, Backup Manager, and Start Oracle Networks.

Start Oracle Networks for Intel UNIX

You use the Start Oracle Networks to start up the SQL*Net listener on your Oracle7 Workgroup Server to accept SQL*Net client connections. You can execute this utility by clicking the Start Oracle Networks icon from the Oracle Admin toolbar. The processes start running in the background, and a minimized xterm window appears at the bottom of your screen. If you want to see what processes are running, you can maximize the xterm window at the bottom of your screen. The xterm window disappears when all its processes are completed.

After the Oracle7 Workgroup Server installation, it is not necessary to use Start Oracle Networks to start up the SQL*Net listener. You might need to use the Start Oracle Networks utility to activate the SQL*Net listener after you install a patch, reconfigure your networks, or after a system crash.

Stop Oracle Networks for Intel UNIX

The Stop Oracle Networks utility is for shutting down the SQL*Net listener. After the SQL*Net listener has been shut down, the database will not receive any SQL*Net client connections. You can execute this utility by clicking the Stop Oracle Networks icon from the Oracle Admin toolbar. The processes start running in the background and a minimized xterm window appears at the bottom of your screen. If you want to see what processes are running, you can maximize the xterm window at the bottom of your screen. The xterm window disappears when all Stop Oracle Networks processes are completed. It is appropriate to use the Stop Oracle Networks utility to shut down the SQL*Net listener before you reconfigure your networks and install a patch.

Maintenance Manager for Intel UNIX

The Maintenance Manager is used to install or remove patches for Oracle from your Oracle7 Workgroup Server. A patch may be in the form of a file (which can be downloaded from an online bulletin board), or a cartridge tape released by Oracle. There is no icon for the Oracle Maintenance Manager on the Oracle Admin toolbar. You can start the Maintenance Manager from an xterm window by entering the following command at the operating system prompt:

```
$ mainmgr
```

The Update button in the Maintenance Manager is used to install patches and the Rollback button is used to remove patches. You can install a patch from a file or from a tape depending on the format and media of the patch.

Network Manager for Windows

Before you start using SQL*Net Version 2, you might need to create or modify several configuration files, such as LISTENER.ORA and TNSNAMES.ORA. These files are not easy to create or modify manually because they need to follow certain syntax for different network protocols. The Network Manager for Windows is a graphical tool, and it enables you to create these configuration files by entering the necessary information on the screen. Before the

Network Manager generates the configuration files, it validates the information that you enter and warns you if it discovers any inconsistency. Figure 57.1 shows the Network Manager dialog box.

FIGURE 57.1.

The Oracle Network Manager dialog box.

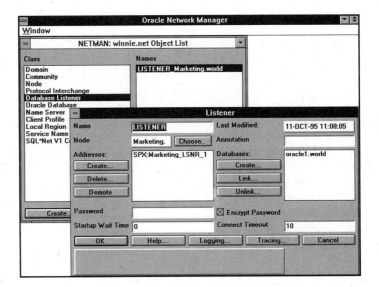

When To Use Oracle7 Workgroup Server

Because of the similarities among the Oracle7 Server, Oracle7 Workgroup Server, and Personal Oracle7, it is not obvious which product meets the needs of your client/server applications. This section suggests when it is appropriate to use the Oracle7 Workgroup Server and how Oracle7 Workgroup Server meets your business and technical needs.

The Oracle7 Workgroup Server is appropriate in the following situations:

- Network Protocol Support. In a small- to medium-size company, when all personal computers are connected together in a local area network using one or more of the following network protocols: Named Pipes, SPX/IPX, TCP/IP, IBM's APPC, and NETBIOS. If you want the power and functionality of the Oracle7 database, it is appropriate to use the Oracle7 Workgroup Server because it is designed and optimized in the workgroup environment, and it supports the common network protocol for the desktop and Intel UNIX platforms.

- Decision Support and Online Transaction Processing (OLTP). Oracle7 Workgroup Server brings the power of a multiuser Oracle7 database, and it integrates with a set of client/server tools to the desktop platform. Combining with the preconfigured initial database, the Oracle7 Workgroup Server is optimized for developing and deploying decision support and online transaction processing (OLTP) applications in the workgroup environment.

■ Independent Workgroup. In a large company, the Oracle7 Workgroup Server provides the flexibility, scalability, and openness for an independent workgroup in developing and deploying applications that do not require the distributed options. It offers flexibility to a workgroup by making the Oracle7 Workgroup Server available on all the major desktop and Intel UNIX platforms. The advantage of scalability enables you to port your Oracle applications and data to other systems and platforms transparently. It meets the needs of a workgroup that needs data to be migrated between Oracle databases. Openness means it is compliant with and supports the industry standards, such as ODBC and OLE.

■ Ease of Administration. The Oracle7 Workgroup Server includes a suite of graphical database administration tools to simplify the database administration tasks. For example, you can start a database by clicking a single Startup button in the Database Manager dialog box. This advantage meets the needs of an independent workgroup that does not have a database administrator with extensive database administration experience. With the Oracle7 Workgroup Server, a database administrator can use the User Manager to create a new database user account or use the Database Expander to expand the database without writing a single SQL statement.

■ Operating System Support. Oracle7 Workgroup Server is tightly integrated with the operating system. Table 57.1 shows the operating system integration support. Therefore, no matter which platform you select, the Oracle7 Workgroup Server is designed to take advantage of the operating system architecture. By providing the client tools, the Oracle Workgroup Server is also appropriate for a workgroup with client machines on various platforms, including Windows NT, Windows, OS/2, DOS, and Intel UNIX.

■ Minimize Training Time. The graphical user interface tools and utilities that come with the Oracle7 Workgroup Server provide ease-of-use and therefore reduce the training time. The server also increases the productivity of the users by making the look and feel of the graphical user interface tools and utilities uniform across the Windows NT, OS/2, Windows, and Intel UNIX clients. Therefore, the Oracle7 Workgroup Server is appropriate for users who do not have extensive database tools and utilities training and who are under time constraints to complete a workgroup project that is developed and deployed across all major desktop and Intel UNIX platforms.

Summary

This chapter discussed the Oracle7 Workgroup Server, the major server and client components of the Oracle7 Workgroup Server, and the system requirements. We have compared the Oracle7 Workgroup Server with other Oracle packages and explained when it is appropriate to use the Oracle7 Workgroup Server. The Oracle7 Server for the desktop platform is discussed in the next chapter.

Oracle7 Server™

58

by Winnie In-Kuan Cheang

IN THIS CHAPTER

The Oracle7 Server is one of the Oracle packages; it includes the Oracle7 database and client/server tools and utilities. Currently, it is available in the following editions:

- Oracle7 Server for Windows NT
- Oracle7 Server for NetWare
- Oracle7 Server for OS/2

This chapter presents the overview of Oracle7 Server and its major components. The Oracle7 Server is different from the Personal Oracle7 and the Oracle7 Workgroup Server. This chapter compares these three Oracle packages and discusses how Oracle7 Server differs from the other two Oracle packages. Each of the Oracle packages is tailored to meet specific client/server application development and deployment needs. This chapter explains when it is appropriate to use the Oracle7 Server and how it meets your business and technical needs.

Overview of the Oracle7 Server

The Oracle7 Server is a full-function Oracle7 database with integrated client/server tools and utilities. This section gives an overview of the Oracle7 Server and how it differs from other Oracle packages. It also discusses what components are included in the Oracle7 Server.

Oracle7 Server Components

The Oracle7 Server includes the multiuser Oracle7 database with the distributed options, Oracle database utilities, graphical tools, SQL products, SQL*Net, Secure Network Services, Oracle Objects for OLE, Oracle7 ODBC driver, and online documentation. The Oracle7 Server components are categorized into the server or client software. Table 58.1 summarizes the primary components of server software of the Oracle7 Server. For a complete list of all components and the detailed description, refer to your *Oracle7 Server User's Guide*.

Table 58.1. Oracle7 Server components.

| Components | Oracle7 Server Version 7.2 for | | |
	Windows NT	NetWare	OS/2
Server Software			
Oracle7 Server	Yes	Yes	Yes
PL/SQL	Yes	Yes	Yes
Server Options (purchased separately)			
Distributed Option	Yes	Yes	Yes
Parallel Query Option	Yes	Yes	Yes
		(for NetWare 4.1)	

Components	Oracle7 Server Version 7.2 for		
	Windows NT	*NetWare*	*OS/2*
Symmetric Replication Option or	Yes	Yes	Yes
Advanced Replication Option		(for NetWare 4.1)	
SQL*Plus	Yes	Yes	Yes
SQL*DBA	Yes	Yes	Yes
SQL*Loader	Yes	Yes	Yes
Export	Yes	Yes	Yes
Import	Yes	Yes	Yes
SQL*Net V1 and/or V2			
Named Pipes	Yes	N/A	Yes
SPX	Yes	Yes	Yes
TCP/IP	Yes	Yes	Yes
LU6.2 (V2)	N/A	Yes	N/A
AppleTalk	N/A	Yes	N/A
NetBIOS	N/A	N/A	Yes
Oracle Names	Yes	Yes	Yes
Server Manager	N/A	Yes	N/A
Instance Manager	Yes	N/A	N/A
Oracle Manager	N/A	Yes	N/A
Oracle Performance Monitor	Yes	N/A	N/A
Event Viewer	Yes	N/A	N/A
Oracle Database Tools			
Database Password Manager	Yes	Yes	N/A
Backup Manager	Yes	N/A	Yes
Recovery Manager	Yes	N/A	Yes
Database Expander	Yes	N/A	Yes
Oracle Book Online Documentation	Yes	N/A	Yes

The client software of the Oracle7 Server is basically the same as that of the Oracle7 Workgroup Server and is summarized in Table 58.2. In the Oracle7 Server Version 7.2 for NetWare, three of the additional client software are Oracle Snap-In for NetWare Administrator, SQL*Plus for Windows NT, and SQL*Plus for OS/2. The important new tools and utilities are explained later in this chapter.

System Requirements

This section specifies the minimum hardware and software requirements for installing the Oracle7 Server software. The hardware and software requirements depend on a number of major factors, such as the size of the Oracle database system global area (SGA), the number of concurrent client connections, and the applications installed on the system. You need to refer to your *Oracle7 Server User's Guide* for detailed information on how to determine your system requirements. This section also provides several tips on installing and using the Oracle7 Server.

Server Hardware Requirements

This section describes the minimum hardware requirements for installing and running the Oracle7 Server.

- A minimum of 486 (or higher) or Pentium-based IBM, Compaq, or 100 percent compatible PC.

- The minimum amount of RAM required depends primarily on the size of the Oracle database SGA, the number of concurrent user connections, the type of client/server transactions, and the applications installed on the server. The following memory requirements is only a starting point:

  For Windows NT: A minimum of 16 MB of RAM; 32 MB is recommended.

  For NetWare: A minimum of 20 MB of free RAM, which is in addition to the RAM required by the NetWare operating system for loading its NetWare loadable modules (NLMs) and for it to cache the File Allocation Table (FAT). Additional 10 MB of free RAM is required if you select to install the Symmetric Replication Option.

  For OS/2: A minimum of 16 MB of RAM; 32 MB is recommended.

TIP

Follow the next steps to determine the amount of free memory on your NetWare server before you install the Oracle7 Server:

1. At the server console prompt, load MONITOR.NLM.

2. Select "Resource Utilization" from the Monitor Screen and press Enter.

3. Note the Cache Buffers statistics in bytes and in percentage.

The total amount of free memory available on the server is the Cache Buffers in bytes. The Cache Buffers percentage indicates the percentage of free RAM on your server.

■ For Windows NT: A minimum of 65 MB of free disk space. An additional 35 MB of free disk space is needed if you select to install the online documentation onto the server.

For NetWare: A minimum of 30 MB of free disk space on the server for the Oracle7 Server for NetWare.

For OS/2: A minimum of 45 MB of free disk space.

■ A compatible network interface card (NIC) and its networking software supported by the server operating system.

■ A CD-ROM drive attached locally or remotely as a logical drive.

Server Operating System Requirements

This section describes the minimum server operating system requirements for installing and running the Oracle7 Server.

■ Windows NT 3.51 or higher, NetWare 3.12 or 4.1, or IBM OS/2 version 2.1 or higher.

Client System Requirements

The following system requirements are for installing the client software components of the Oracle7 Server on your client machine. Additional hardware and software might be required depending on your client machine's operating system and your network.

■ A minimum of 386 (or higher) or Pentium-based IBM, Compaq, or 100 percent compatible PC. A 486 (or higher) machine is recommended.

■ At least 4 MB of RAM; a minimum of 8 MB for Windows NT client.

■ Enough free disk space for the selected client installation procedure or software. For example, a minimum of 54 MB of free disk space is required for a typical installation of the client software of the Oracle7 Server for NetWare.

■ A compatible network interface card (NIC) and its networking software supported by the server and client operating system.

■ A CD-ROM driver attached locally or remotely as a logical drive.

Oracle7 Database Tools and Utilities

The Oracle7 Server includes a suite of client and server tools and utilities for administering and maintaining your Oracle7 database. They include the server-based Oracle7 utilities, such as SQL*DBA, SQL*Loader, Export, and Import. The graphical user interface database tools and utilities are also included. Most of them are discussed in the previous chapters. This section introduces a number of new tools and utilities included in the Oracle7 Server Version 7.2.

For a complete list of the database tools and utilities included in the Oracle7 Server package, refer to your *Oracle7 Server User's Guide*. For more information about these tools and utilities, refer to the *Oracle7 Server Utilities User's Guide*, the *Oracle7 Server User's Guide*, the *Oracle Database Tools User's Guide*, and the *Oracle Server Manager User's Guide*.

Instance Manager

The Instance Manager is included in the Oracle7 Server Version 7.2 for Windows NT. This graphical tool enables you to create, modify, and delete Oracle instances. You can only start or shut down an instance using Instance Manager while you are creating or deleting an instance. You can use SQL*DBA or Database Manager to start or shut down a database.

Oracle Performance Monitor

The Oracle Performance Monitor is included in the Oracle7 Server Version 7.2 for Windows NT. It is a useful tool in helping you to monitor the performance of your distributed databases. You can select one or more variables to monitor from the Performance Monitor. Figure 58.1 shows a Performance Monitor dialog box.

FIGURE 58.1.

An Oracle Performance Monitor dialog box.

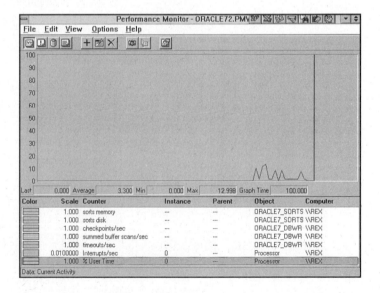

Event Viewer

The Oracle7 Server Version 7.2 for Windows NT also includes an Event Viewer. When errors and alert conditions appear on your databases, the Event Viewer will notify you. After you view a list of errors and alert conditions from the Event Viewer, you can print the list or save it to a file.

Server Manager

The Server Manager is a database tool that enables you to start, shut down, and administer your local and remote databases which are Oracle7 Version 7.0 or higher. In Oracle7 Server Version 7.2 for NetWare, you can activate the line mode interface Server Manager from the file server console or the graphical interface Server Manager from a Windows workstation. If you want to load the Server Manager from the NetWare server console prompt, enter the following command:

```
:LOAD  SVRMGR
```

The Server Manager enables you to have centralized database administration in a distributed database environment. There are three primary components in the graphical interface of the Server Manager: Administration Manager, SQL Worksheet, and System Monitors. Figure 58.2 shows the Oracle Server Manager for Windows dialog box. For descriptions on how to use Oracle Server Manager, refer to your *Oracle Server Manager User's Guide*.

FIGURE 58.2.

The Oracle Server Manager for Windows dialog box.

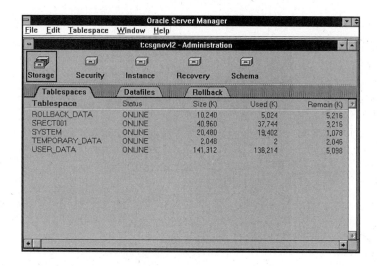

The Administration Manager component enables you to manage the database storage (tablespace, data files, and rollback segments), manage database security (users, roles, and profiles), manage instances and sessions, back up and recover a database, and view database schema objects, such as constraints, triggers, and snapshots.

The SQL Worksheet enables you to enter, edit, and execute SQL and PL/SQL statements and scripts. Its Command History dialog box stores the last 20 commands you have executed. You can retrieve an entire command or part of a command from the Command History dialog box.

The System Monitors enable you to gather and review database performance statistics. The source of the statistics in the System Monitors component is the Oracle dynamic performance tables. Users who want to use the System Monitors need to have access to these dynamic performance tables. By running the UTLMONTR.SQL script, you can grant access to these tables to all users.

Screen Mode Utilities for NetWare

The Oracle7 Server Version 7.2 for NetWare includes four new screen mode utilities for NetWare: Oracle Manager (NWDBMGR), Export (NWEXPORT), Import (NWIMPORT), and SQL*Loader (NWLOADER). Although the functions of the screen mode utilities and the line mode utilities are basically the same, the screen mode utilities are menu-driven and they provide online help and directory browsing in the native NetWare server environment.

The Oracle Manager for NetWare allows you to administer the current database instance, alter a tablespace to be offline or online, configure the Oracle7 Server, and to create a new database instance.

The Export utility for NetWare in screen mode enables you to select the export mode, browse and select a user or tables from a list of available objects to export, enable or disable the export of grants, rows, constraints, and indexes options, and to set other parameters, such as record length, buffer size, commit after each array, and generate log file. Figure 58.3 shows the screen mode export utility.

FIGURE 58.3.

The export utility for NetWare in screen mode.

SQL*Net Easy Configuration for NetWare

The SQL*Net Easy Configuration utility for NetWare allows you to configure the listener and database alias for the Oracle SPX Protocol Adapter, Oracle TCP/IP Protocol Adapter, and Oracle AppleTalk Protocol Adapter.

SQL*Plus for NetWare

Finally, SQL*Plus, an SQL-based language interface and end-user reporting tool, is available for NetWare. SQL*Plus for NetWare is included with the Oracle7 Server Version 7.2 for NetWare. You can start SQL*Plus for NetWare by entering the following command at the server console prompt:

```
:LOAD  SQLPLUS
```

SQL*Plus for Windows NT

SQL*Plus for Windows NT is a 32-bit application that enables you to run SQL and PL/SQL scripts in the Windows NT environment. SQL*Plus for Windows NT is included with the Oracle7 Server Version 7.2 for Windows NT.

How Oracle7 Server Differs from Other Oracle Packages

The Oracle7 Server is designed for developers and organizations that require distributed database systems to develop and deploy client/server applications in an enterprise-wide environment. This section highlights the differences between Oracle7 Server and other Oracle packages, including Personal Oracle7 and Oracle7 Workgroup Server.

The primary difference between the Oracle7 Server and Personal Oracle7 is that the Oracle7 Server is a multiuser database system, whereas the Personal Oracle7 is a single-user/developer database system. Although the Oracle7 Server and the Oracle7 Workgroup Server share many similarities, the Oracle7 Server is targeted at users who require real-time data access across distributed databases, whereas the Oracle7 Workgroup Server is targeted at users who need data to reside on a single server in a workgroup or small-to-medium sized business environment.

Operating System Integration Support

Similar to the Oracle7 Workgroup Server, the Oracle7 Server is also tightly integrated with the server operating system. However, the Oracle7 Server can function beyond a local area network environment because it supports the enterprise network environment. Table 58.2 shows three of the operating system integration supports.

Table 58.2. Operating system integration support.

| | Oracle7 Server Version 7.2 for | | |
	Windows NT	*NetWare 4.1*	*OS/2*
Symmetric Multiprocessing (SMP)	Yes	Yes	Yes
NetWare Directory Services (NDS)	N/A	Yes	N/A
Windows NT Services (Registry)	Yes	N/A	N/A

In Oracle7 Server for NetWare, the Symmetric Multiprocessing (SMP) support and NetWare Directory Services (NDS) support are available only with NetWare 4.1. Both SMP and NDS are not available in NetWare 3.12. The SMP support enables the processes and login threads to be distributed among the available CPUs to avoid high utilization on a single CPU. The Parallel Query Option requires the SMP support in NetWare 4.1.

Oracle7 Server Version 7.2 for NetWare supports NetWare Directory Services (NDS), which enables you to have central access to your network resources, including NetWare servers, users, printers, and databases in a distributed environment. Using the NetWare NWADMIN for Windows utility, the NDS support enables you as an Oracle database administrator to create an Oracle database instance as a new object in the directory tree. If you want to allow the NetWare 4.1 users and groups to be able to connect to the Oracle database instance through a single database user account, you can map the NetWare 4.1 users and groups to a database user account using NWADMIN. You can also allow a NDS group to inherit the privileges of a database role by mapping the NDS group to a database role.

The NDS support has the following requirements:

- The server operating system must be NetWare 4.1.
- The NetWare NWADMIN utility for Windows must be available on a workstation.
- SQL*Net Version 2.2 or above must be installed on both the server and client.
- The Oracle Snap-In for NetWare Administrator must be installed and available on a workstation.

Oracle7 Features

The Oracle7 Server is different from other Oracle packages in terms of the Oracle7 database features. Certain Oracle7 features are available for the Oracle7 Server, but they are not available for other Oracle7 packages, such as the parallel query option. Table 58.3 summarizes some of the Oracle7 features currently available for each Oracle package.

Table 58.3. Oracle7 new features available for the Oracle packages.

	Personal	*Oracle7*	*Oracle7*
Oracle7 Features	*Oracle7*	*Workgroup Server*	*Server*
Distributed Option	Yes	N/A	Yes
Parallel Query Option	N/A	N/A	Yes
SQL*Net	Yes	Yes	Yes
Parallel Server	N/A	N/A	N/A

When To Use Oracle7 Server

To select an Oracle package that meets your business needs and technical needs is not an easy task. You might need more than one Oracle package for your organization or business to develop and deploy your client/server applications. This section discusses when using the Oracle7 Server is appropriate and how it meets your business and technical needs.

- Distribution Option. In a distributed environment, you might have several databases located at various buildings or cities. The database users might require real-time access to multiple databases at different locations simultaneously. This operation might require distributed query and distributed updates against multiple databases. The distributed option provides these functions and is available as an option for the Oracle7 Server. If you want a multiuser Oracle7 server with the distributed option to run on a desktop platform, the Oracle7 Server will meet these requirements. For more information about the distributed option, refer to the *Oracle7 Server Concepts Manual*.

- Parallel Query Option. The parallel query option enables a SQL statement to be processed by multiple CPUs simultaneously to increase the database performance. The parallel query option is available as an option for the Oracle7 Server. If your server has multiple CPUs and it is running either Windows NT or a NetWare operating system that supports SMP, and you want to take advantage of the parallel query option, you can choose the Oracle7 Server rather than the Personal Oracle7 or the Oracle7 Workgroup Server. The parallel query option is not available for the Personal Oracle7 or the Oracle7 Workgroup Server. For detailed information about this option, refer to the *Oracle7 Server Concepts Manual*.

- Symmetric Replication Option or Advanced Replication Option. The symmetric replication option enables you to maintain and update multiple copies of data from all sites in different locations. Symmetric replication is a highly complicated process. For detailed description about this option, refer to the *Oracle7 Server Distributed System, Volume II: Replicated Data*.

Summary

This chapter compared the Oracle7 Server with the Personal Oracle7 and Oracle7 Workgroup Server. It also discussed the system requirements and the major features of the Oracle7 Server. In summary, the Oracle7 Server for the desktop platforms is the same as the Oracle7 Server that runs on UNIX, MVS, and other platforms, except for certain operating system specific features, such as the parallel server option.

PART

Appendixes

Using PowerBuilder

by Advanced Information Systems, Inc.

IN THIS CHAPTER

PowerSoft Corporation's PowerBuilder is a highly object-oriented visual development tool. It is primarily used for Microsoft Windows development, although it aspires to support other platforms. PowerBuilder ships with the desktop version of the Watcom SQL database engine, which (until the release of Personal Oracle7) was widely considered the best of the desktop databases.

The PowerBuilder object model is extended to its unusual development environment, which features separate "painters" for different types of objects. One of the more interesting features of the environment is the Library Painter, which provides a visual representation of the objects within each .PBL, or "pibble."

The primary focus of this appendix is PowerBuilder's support for the development of database applications. The closing sections of the appendix present a brief overview of some of the more significant features of PowerBuilder and briefly discuss the primary strengths and weaknesses of the product.

Connecting to the Database

Additional configuration is required to prepare an ODBC data source for use in PowerBuilder. The proprietary interface driver, PBOR7040.DLL, is required to connect to Oracle. Unfortunately, this driver does not ship with the desktop version of PowerBuilder. It is available with the Enterprise edition and PowerBuilder Team/ODBC, which also include a number of additional toolkits.

After installing SQL*Net and the PowerBuilder Oracle interface, install the Oracle ODBC driver and configure a data source using the ODBC Administration utility (typically installed as a Windows Control Panel applet). Next, you should create a PowerBuilder database profile, using the database painter. From the Database Painter, select Setup from the Connect option cascade of the File menu to open the Database Profile Setup dialog box as illustrated in Figure A.1.

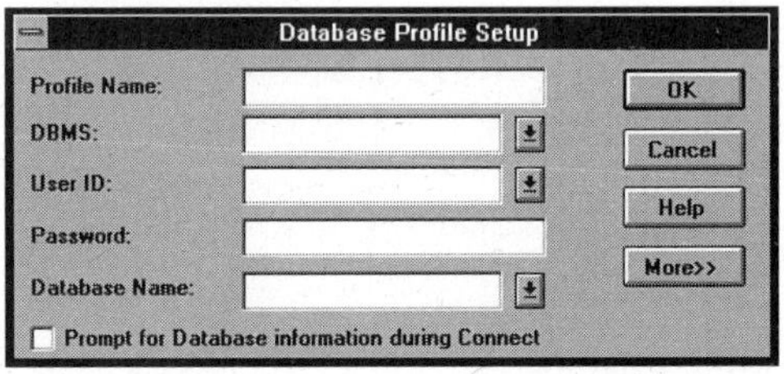

FIGURE A.1.

The Database Profile Setup dialog box is used to configure a PowerBuilder connection for Oracle.

In the Profile Name field, enter a description to be used for the Oracle profile. This value is simply used as a name for the profile. The DBMS field should be set to OR7 for version 7 of Oracle. The DBMS field is used by PowerBuilder to determine which proprietary interface driver to use. User ID, Password, and Database Name are not used for Oracle connections, and you can leave them blank. The check box in the lower left can be used to force PowerBuilder to prompt for connection information when using the Profile to connect to the database. If this box is not checked, PowerBuilder will not prompt for this information if it is supplied. This should be left blank so that the information can be supplied at run time using a login window, rather than the generic dialog box. Click on the More command button in the lower right-hand corner to display more options. The Server Name field requires a SQL*Net connect string for version 1 of SQL*Net, or a service name for SQL*Net version 2. For example, if TCP/IP is being used to connect to the database using SQL*Net version 1, the Server Name might be entered as

```
T:ORACLE_SERVER:ORACLE7
```

The Login ID and Login Password fields should not be supplied in most cases, as storing these values would be considered a security risk. These parameters are used for the Oracle ID and password, and they can be supplied at run time. DBPARM is used to store additional database-specific connection information. It can be left blank to connect to Oracle, but setting DBPARM to PBDMS=1 will allow PowerBuilder to use Oracle-stored procedures to return results to DataWindow objects. When you have entered the appropriate parameters, the Database Profile Setup dialog box might appear as shown in Figure A.2.

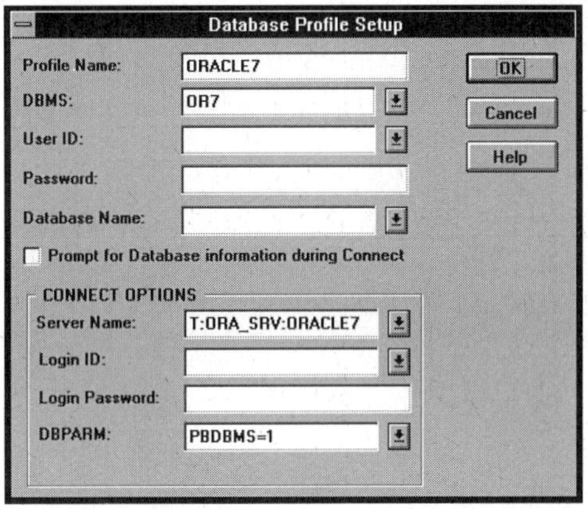

FIGURE A.2.

This Database Profile Setup dialog box is an example of the parameters required to connect to Oracle.

Additional preparation is required on the Oracle server to prepare Oracle for certain PowerBuilder features. The SQL script supplied with the Oracle interface, PBORCAT.SQL, should be run by the DBA. This creates objects in Oracle that will be accessed by PowerBuilder to provide additional features that would otherwise be inaccessible. For example, although Oracle-stored procedures were not specifically designed to return result sets, the objects created by PBORCAT.SQL enable PowerBuilder to retrieve results from Oracle using DataWindow objects. This feature and other issues regarding database connectivity and communication will be discussed in greater detail in the following sections.

Communicating with the Database

At design-time, you can use the Database Profile to connect to Oracle by selecting Prompt from the Connect option of the File menu of the database painter, and selecting the name of the Oracle profile from the drop-down list in the Data Sources dialog box.

At run-time, PowerBuilder uses a transaction object to connect to the data source. The default transaction object is named sqlca, and additional transaction objects can be used by declaring a variable of type transaction. Listing A.1 is an example of connecting to Oracle using a declared transaction object.

Listing A.1. This script sets transaction object values and connects to the database.

```
transaction sqlca_sps;

sqlca_sps = create transaction;

sqlca_sps.DBMS       = "OR7"
sqlca_sps.userid     = "scotty"
sqlca_sps.dbpass     = "tiger"
sqlca_sps.servername = "T:ORA_SRV:ORACLE7"
sqlca_sps.dbparm     = "PBDBMS=1"

connect using sqlca_sps;

if sqlca_sps.sqlcode <> 0 then
    MessageBox ("Database Error", sqlca_sps.sqlerrtext)
    HALT close
end if
```

Listing A.1 illustrates the use of two of the additional properties of the transaction object, sqlcode and sqlerrtext. If the sqlcode property is non-zero, this indicates that an error has occurred for the last database transaction in which the object was used. Sqlcode will contain 0 for success, -1 to indicate an error, or 100 if a SELECT statement retrieves no rows. Sqldbcode can be used to access the database vendor's error code. The sqlerrtext property provides information on the type of error that occurred from the RDBMS. In many applications, it will be acceptable to use the default global transaction object, SQLCA. However, if an application communicates with multiple databases or needs multiple connections with different parameter values, additional transaction objects must be declared. The transaction object is used for all communication with the database, including result sets retrieved through DataWindows.

The DataWindow is the primary means of retrieving result sets in PowerBuilder.

When the DataWindow painter is started, a Select DataWindow dialog box is presented. When the New command button is clicked, the data source and style for the new DataWindow must be selected. The style options include Free-Form (for data entry forms), Grid, Tabular, and Graph, among others. Of the data source options, SQL Select and Stored Procedure are the most significant.

When SQL Select is chosen as the data source, the user must first select the tables or views to be used in the SELECT statement. Next, columns must be chosen for the result set. Selected columns are displayed in the lower left side of the tabbed window within the DataWindow painter. The first tab is used to create the ORDER BY clause. Columns can be dragged from the left side to the right side of the window to be included in the ORDER BY, and a check box is used to indicate ascending or descending order. The next tab to the right is the WHERE clause definition.

Drop-down combos can be used to select the columns, comparison operators, and comparison values for each expression in the WHERE clause. The Logical drop-down is used to apply AND/OR logic to the next expression in the list. The Group tab is used to define a GROUP BY clause for SELECT statements containing aggregate functions. It operates on the same drag-and-drop principle as the Order tab. The Having tab is used to define a HAVING clause and operates in much the same way as the WHERE tab. The Compute tab is used to define functions and aggregate functions that can be added to the column list.

The last tab on the far right is used to display the SQL syntax that has been generated based on these selections. You can edit the syntax manually, if necessary. From the Options menu, select Convert to Syntax to invoke the editor. SQL Selects can be constructed in this manner instead of using the graphical interface, if desired. To toggle back to the graphical interface, select Convert to Graphics from the Options menu.

TIP

Right-clicking in the Where, Having, and Compute tabs displays a pop-up menu that can be used to provide drop-down lists of columns, functions, and arguments that can be used.

To create a UNION, select Create Union from the Objects menu. This will open a new Select Painter, and the unioned result can be defined in exactly the same manner. To specify DISTINCT, select this option from the Options menu.

The SQL used by the DataWindow can be parameterized to some degree, using the Retrieval Arguments option of the Objects menu. These arguments can be used as the comparison values in the WHERE or HAVING clauses and in computed columns. Arguments are passed to the DataWindow at run time using the Retrieve() function of the data window, as illustrated following:

```
dw_1.Retrieve(arg1, arg2);
```

In addition to parameterized SQL, the DataWindow object's SetSQLSelect() function can be used to modify the SQL statement at run-time. However, the columns of the result set must always match the output defined at design-time.

If a transaction object other than the default SQLCA will be used for the DataWindow, the transaction object should be specified using the `SetTransObject()` method. DataWindows are displayed by placing a DataWindow object on a window, specifying the name of the DataWindow, and making two function calls (assuming that the DataWindow will be using a transaction object that is already connected). The following code segment is used to display a DataWindow using a declared transaction object that is connected to the data source:

```
dw_1.SetTransObject(sqlca_sps);
dw_1.Retrieve(arg1);
```

The DataWindow will also use its own internal transaction object. Some attributes of this internal transaction object are accessible through the `DBErrorCode`, `DBErrorMessage`, and `SetTrans` functions. `DBErrorCode` and `DBErrorMessage` are used to get the native error code and text from the DataWindow's internal transaction object. `SetTrans` can be used to copy a transaction objects values to the internal DataWindow transaction object, as in the following example:

```
dw_1.SetTrans(sqlca_sps);
```

The difference between `SetTrans` and `SetTransObject` is that `SetTrans` supplies only connection information, and it allows the DataWindow to process all transaction logic (commits and rollbacks) internally. `SetTrans` should be used for read-only DataWindows.

Oracle-stored procedures were not designed to retrieve result sets. However, if the PBORCAT.SQL script is run in Oracle, a workaround for retrieving result sets to PowerBuilder is available. The script creates a procedure called `Put_Line`, which is used by other procedures to create SQL to be used for this purpose. Listing A.2 is an example of an Oracle-stored procedure that will return a result set to PowerBuilder.

Listing A.2. This script creates a stored procedure that can be used to return a result set to a PowerBuilder DataWindow.

```
CREATE OR REPLACE PROCEDURE get_emps IS
BEGIN
    PBDBMS.Put_Line('SELECT dept, last_name, first_name ');
    PBDBMS.Put_Line('FROM employees ');
    PBDBMS.Put_Line('ORDER BY dept, last_name, first_name');
END;
```

To use this function, select Stored Procedure as the data source in the DataWindow painter. After selecting the stored procedure name, the definition of the DataWindow proceeds normally.

When the DataWindow result set definition is complete, you can use the Layout Editor to change the appearance of the output. Depending on the style of the DataWindow, this will include the width of columns, fonts, border styles, line art and graphics, headers and footers, and numerous other elements.

In addition to SQL and stored procedures, DataWindows can use other DataWindows as a source, or non-DBMS sources such as DDE can be accessed. The options available for retrieving and displaying result sets using DataWindows are too numerous to discuss in full detail in this appendix. The preceding overview of DataWindows highlights the basics.

There are two alternatives to DataWindows that can be used to retrieve results in PowerBuilder. Cursors can be declared and used for multiple row result sets, and for single row results, a simple SELECT statement can be issued. Listing A.3 demonstrates the use of cursors to retrieve results in PowerBuilder scripts.

Listing A.3. This script declares a cursor and retrieves results, placing column data in PowerBuilder variables.

```
DECLARE order_det CURSOR FOR
    SELECT quantity, price
    FROM order_details
    WHERE order_no = :lb_order_no.Text;

    Integer iQuantity;
    Dec{2}  dPrice;
    Dec{2}  dTotal;

    OPEN order_det;

    Do While (SQLCA.sqlcode = 0)
        FETCH order_det INTO :iQuantity, :dPrice;
        dTotal = dTotal + (iQuantity * dPrice);
    Loop

    CLOSE order_det;

    st_total.Text = String(dTotal);
```

A single row result set can be retrieved using an embedded SELECT statement, as illustrated here:

```
SELECT order_date, status INTO :szDate, :szStatus
FROM view_orders
WHERE order_no = :lb_orders.Text
```

The same methods that are used to retrieve results can be used to perform transactions. DataWindows and cursors can be used for in-place UPDATES and DELETES and embedded SQL, in addition to DataWindows and cursors, can be used to insert, update, and delete individual records. Stored procedures in Oracle can be called from PowerBuilder to perform any of these operations, either in aggregate, or on individual records.

Columns that may be updated through a DataWindow must be defined in the DataWindow painter, unless the default behavior is acceptable. By default, if the DataWindow operates on a single table, all columns are updatable. If it operates on multiple tables or a view, no columns are updatable. This behavior can be modified by using the Update option from the Rows menu. Update syntax is defined using the dialog box displayed in Figure A.3.

FIGURE A.3.

This dialog box is used to define update and delete behavior for a DataWindow.

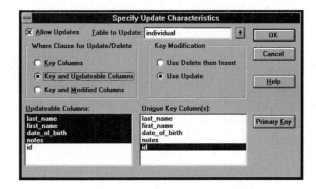

Most of the options should be self-explanatory. Of the available options, the Where Clause for Update/Delete and Key Modification radio button groups are particularly significant. In essence, the DataWindow uses an optimistic locking scheme, allowing other users to update records that are displayed in the DataWindow. The Where Clause is very important in determining how conflicting updates are handled. In most cases, Key and Updateable Columns should be selected in this group. When this option is selected, if the key and updateable columns in the table do not match the original values selected, the update will fail. When this occurs, the DataWindow should be refreshed, or some other mechanism should be designed to allow the user to view the modified record. The user can then make an informed decision before blindly overwriting changes made by another user. This prevents a "last change wins" scenario from occurring. In nearly all situations, the selection for Key Modification should be moot, because the primary key will not be in the list of updateable columns.

> **CAUTION**
>
> Modifying key values is very dangerous, as it can result in serious referential integrity problems. If a key value must be modified, the proper integrity constraints should be enforced by the database. In many environments, foreign key constraints are not enforced by the database for performance reasons. In these situations, the database relies on the application to enforce the primary key constraint, and it would be particularly dangerous to allow a key to be modified if it is referenced by another table.

The DataWindow provides `InsertRow()`, `Update()`, and `DeleteRow()` functions. It is important to note that if a DataWindow will be used for these operations, the `SetTransObject()` function should be used in order to maintain control over transaction processing.

In most cases, cursors are preferable for performing these operations on open result sets. Although the DataWindow is essentially an abstraction of a cursor, declaring a cursor will simplify the code for these operations and make it more readable and thus easier to maintain. For example, the cursor declared in Listing A.3 could be redeclared to perform updates based on user input as in Listing A.4.

Listing A.4. This script declares a cursor, retrieves results, and updates rows inplace.

```
DECLARE order_det CURSOR FOR
    SELECT order_no, item, price
    FROM order_details
    ORDER BY order_no, item_no;

    Long    iOrder;
    String  szItem;
    Dec{2}  dPrice;

    OPEN order_det;

    Do While (SQLCA.sqlcode = 0)
        FETCH order_det INTO :iOrder, :szItem, :dPrice;
        IF (szItem = lb_Item.Text) THEN
            UPDATE order_details SET price = DEC(:sle_new_price.Text)
                WHERE CURRENT OF order_det;
        END IF
    Loop

    CLOSE order_det;

    IF (SQLCA.sqlcode = 100) THEN
        SQLCA.Commit;
    ELSE
        SQLCA.Rollback;
    END IF
```

A much better approach than either DataWindows or cursors would be to use stored procedures to process the transactions on the server side. This would relieve the application of the burden of transaction control, and it would greatly reduce the network traffic produced by in-place cursor operations executed from the client application. Before an Oracle-stored procedure can be called from Oracle, it must be declared. The following code fragment declares and calls a stored procedure that performs the same operation as Listing A.4:

```
DECLARE PROCEDURE update_price FOR updt_price(:iItem, :dPrice);
EXECUTE update_price;
```

Note that in the previous example, update_price is a PowerBuilder alias for the Oracle procedure updt_price, and it is assumed that iItem and dPrice are PowerBuilder variables that are visible within this scope. In this case, no arguments need to be provided when EXECUTE update_price is called. These two lines of code replace about a dozen lines in Listing A.4 and enable the database to perform the entire operation. This could eliminate a considerable amount of network traffic, and it allows transaction control to be handled by the procedure, instead of the client application. The many advantages of using stored procedures make it difficult to justify any other means of applying transactions in Oracle.

However, an embedded SQL statement could be used to perform the update, as illustrated in the following:

```
UPDATE order_details SET price = :dPrice WHERE item_no = :iItem USING sqlca_sps;
IF (sqlca_sps.sqlcode = 0) THEN
    sqlca_sps.Commit;
ELSE
    sqlca_sps.Rollback;
END IF
```

The preceding example illustrates one possible argument for using embedded SQL in preference to stored procedures in that it is easier to read and understand, and it will work for other RDBMSs. The preceding fragment also demonstrates the USING clause, which identifies a transaction object other than the default SQLCA.

One of PowerBuilder's primary strengths is its variety of methods for communicating with the database. In this section, a select few of the basic concepts have been presented to illustrate the alternatives. As a result, some of the more advanced topics have been omitted, including discussions of the DynamicStagingArea and the DynamicDescriptionArea system variables, which are used to store additional database information for prepared SQL, as well as dynamic SQL parameter information. They are rarely referenced in code by most programmers, but it is important to know that they exist.

Summary

In addition to numerous methods for communicating with a database, PowerBuilder's object-oriented features are its primary strength. It supports inheritance, multiple inheritance, and polymorphism, and has a number of extremely useful predefined system objects in addition to the SQLCA. The Message object is arguably the most significant of these system objects. In conjunction with the ability to create user-defined events, the Message object allows for a very clean and efficient means of communicating data between objects that maps very well into the underlying Windows API. In addition to providing attributes to store variables with standard data types, user-defined objects and structures can be placed in a Message object, which can then be sent to another form or control.

The ability to pass data from instance to instance is particularly important in MDI applications, and sending messages is the best way to accomplish this task.

As mentioned in the introduction, the library painter is a unique and useful feature, as a reference if nothing else. It allows developers to browse the PowerBuilder class hierarchy, including all object attributes and functions. For sites that use PVCS, programmers can check source code in and out of revision control. With the Enterprise edition, PowerBuilder can also be used to generate C++ classes compatible with Watcom's C++ compiler.

Despite its many strengths, the PowerBuilder development environment can be somewhat frustrating. It is very modal, and every time a script is edited, it is recompiled, so all external references must be resolved. This adds additional complexity to team development. If one developer needs to reference objects that have been designed and are being coded by another developer, the only option is to export the objects requiring external references to text files, and editing them with a regular text editor. This, too, can present problems, because when the objects are imported back into the environment, the scripts are compiled, and once again, all external references must be resolved. Even when programming solo, a developer can be tripped up by a single statement, such as

```
open(w_mdi_child);
```

This statement does not work if `w_mdi_child` does not yet exist.

Although this constant compilation eliminates many of the bugs that crop up due to typographical and syntax errors in early phases of development, it slows the process considerably. When you are designing a PowerBuilder application, you should carefully think through a strategy for the order in which objects are constructed. Commenting out external references in the early phases of development may save time, as well.

Another disadvantage relates to the proprietary nature of the product. The database interfaces for many of the most popular RDBMSs are not shipped with the inexpensive desktop edition. Without the necessary interface, the only alternative is to use the ODBC API directly or a do-it-yourself proprietary interface (such as using Pro*C to interface with Oracle, for example). Either alternative eliminates the possibility of going quick and dirty with DataWindows. The proprietary scripting language, although it is a very good language, can be a drawback for shops making the transition from mainframe to client/server because of the additional learning curve. Most programmers have some experience with BASIC or Pascal, but they will not have any experience with PowerScript until they use PowerBuilder.

Despite these potential drawbacks, PowerBuilder is one of the best development tools available for Microsoft Windows. Its powerful object-oriented features and extensive support for database applications make it a solid candidate for any client/server project.

Using SQLWindows

B

by Advanced Information Systems, Inc.

IN THIS CHAPTER

SQLWindows is an object-oriented development tool for Microsoft Windows that is most easily distinguished from its competition by its unique programming interface. SQLWindows Application Language, or SAL, uses an outline structure that is unlike any tool of its kind. The application outline represents the hierarchy of constants, variables, and objects within the application by placing them at different levels of indentation within the outline structure. At each level, the outline can be expanded or collapsed, in order to view details or hide levels of detail when navigating to a particular section.

In addition to a unique language and programming structure, SQLWindows provides several means of communicating with an ODBC data source, both programmatically and through bound controls. This appendix focuses on these aspects of the product, including QuickObjects and the SAL programming interface to ODBC. In addition, a brief overview of the object-oriented features of SQLWindows is provided.

Connecting to the Database

SQLWindows can only connect using the Q+E drivers supplied with the product. These drivers should be installed with SQLWindows and the SQLBase desktop database engine. You can use Quest, the interactive querying, reporting, and data source configuration tool included with SQLWindows, to configure a new ODBC data source and ensure that it is accessible by SQLWindows.

After launching Quest, select ODBC from the Utilities menu. The dialog box displayed is the Data Sources dialog box of the ODBC administration program. You can use this dialog box to define a new data source in ODBC.INI, and data sources defined here will be available to all applications.

Next, add the data source to the Quest desktop by selecting Add from the Database option of the Utilities menu. The Add Database dialog box will present a list of defined ODBC data sources. Click on the name of the data source to be added, and enter a user ID and password in the appropriate fields. When adding an Oracle data source to the list of Quest databases, the dialog box might appear as in Figure B.1.

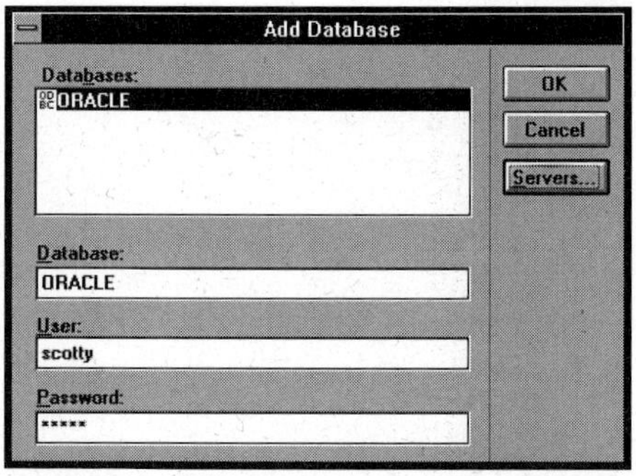

FIGURE B.1.

The Quest Add Database dialog box.

Click on OK to add the selected data source to Quest's list. You can use Quest to create and save queries and reports and to view catalog information, such as table definitions. Try viewing a small table to test the connection. If data can be accessed through Quest, it can be accessed through SQLWindows QuickObjects and SAL SQL functions as well.

Communicating with the Database

The easiest way to communicate with a database through SQLWindows is to use QuickObjects. There are three main categories of QuickObjects: visualizers, commanders, and the data source. Visualizers and commanders are data-aware controls that tie a window control to values stored in the database. A data source is used to connect to the database and provide data to bound controls. To place a data source on the form, click on the Quest icon on the tool palette, and select cQuickDatabase as the class. The object should appear on the form as in Figure B.2.

FIGURE B.2.

A cQuickDatabase object that will be used as a data source.

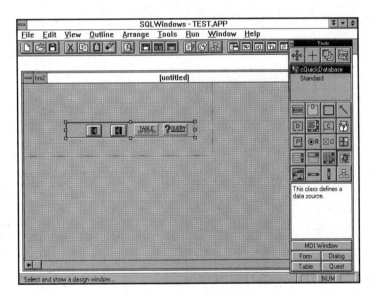

After placing the new data source on the form, click on table or query to choose the means by which it will be populated. If a query is selected, a new query can be defined, or a file containing the prewritten SQL can be identified. Alternatively, a cQuickTable object can be used as the data source. The primary difference between a cQuickTable and a cQuickDatabase object that is using a table as its data source is the default display format. A cQuickTable defaults to table display type, while a cQuickDatabase object defaults to the VCR button format, which displays a single record at a time.

SQLWindows refers to bound controls that display data as Visualizers. After defining the result set for the data source, Visualizers can be placed on the form and bound to columns in the data source. The simplest of the Visualizers is the data field. To create a bound data field, select the data field icon on the tool palette and select cQuickField as the class. When cQuickField is clicked in the class window of the tool palette, a drop-down list box appears in the lower portion of the tool palette. Select the name of the data source from the drop-down list, and in the list of columns below, select the name of the column to which the data field will be bound. Other controls can be used as Visualizers. Radio buttons or drop-down list boxes can be bound to description columns of lookup tables, check boxes can be bound to columns containing Boolean values, and list boxes and multi-line edits can be bound to columns to display data.

Commanders, in SQLWindows terminology, refer to pushbutton classes of QuickObjects that perform operations on a data source. To create a new Commander, click on the pushbutton icon on the tool palette, select the data source name from the drop-down list, and select from the list of Commander types. This creates an object of type cQuickCommander. These include First, Last, Next, Prev, and Retrieve. The first four are used to position the record pointer, and the last is used to fetch the row at the current record position.

The additional methods New, Apply, Delete, and Discard can be used to edit the record set. As is typically the case with bound controls, it is probably not advisable to use these methods when accessing a remote database through ODBC. The lack of control over the transaction and SQL that is prepared adds a considerable amount of risk to this method of applying transactions.

The SAL programming language provides functions for communicating with the database that are very similar to the underlying ODBC API. In addition, it provides numerous system variables and abstract data types to make the API easier to use. Connecting to the database, for example, requires that three system variables be set, followed by a single function call (SqlConnect). The system variables SqlDatabase, SqlUser, and SqlPassword must be set to the name of the ODBC data source, the user ID, and the password, respectively. SqlConnect takes a single argument, the buffer that will receive the new connection handle if the function succeeds. SqlConnect returns TRUE if it succeeds, FALSE if it fails. The example in Listing B.1 uses SAL to establish a database connection by taking values from a login form and an initialization file to connect to the data source.

Listing B.1. This code fragment uses SAL to connect to an ODBC data source.

```
Contents
    Pushbutton:pbOK
        Message Actions
            On SAM_Click
                iLen = SalGetProfileString("ORACLE TEST", "DSN",
                        "ORACLE", szTmpBuf, "TEST.INI")
                Set SqlDatabase = SalStrLeft(szTmpBuf, iLen)
                Set SqlUser = dfUser
                Set SqlPassword = dfPassword
                bSuccess = SqlConnect(hSQLMain)
                If (bSuccess = FALSE)
                    Call SalMessageBox("Unable To Connect.",
                        "Oracle Test", 0)

Window Variables
    Sql Handle: hSQLMain
    Boolean: bSuccess
```

Note that the parameter passed to `SqlConnect` is of type `SqlHandle`. This is an abstract data type used in SAL exclusively for database communications.

After connecting to the data source, SQL can be processed in a number of different ways. SAL provides methods for prepared and immediate execution of `SELECT` statements, as well as `INSERT`, `UPDATE`, and `DELETE`. The implementation of immediate execution in SAL is actually just a shortcut to using prepared execution. This point will be illustrated with the following examples. SQLWindows provides several alternative methods for retrieving a result set.

The most verbose of these options is to first call `SqlPrepare()`, followed by `SqlExecute()` and `SqlFetch()` to retrieve the first row. The code fragment in Listing B.2 illustrates the use of these methods.

Listing B.2. This example retrieves a result set.

```
Contents
    Pushbutton:pbRefresh
        Message Actions
            On SAM_Click
                Set szSQL = "SELECT Last_name, First_name
                    FROM TEMP INTO :szLast, :szFirst".
                Set bSuccess = SqlPrepare(hSQLMain, szSQL)
                If (bSuccess = TRUE)
                    Set bSuccess = SqlExecute(hSQLMain)
                If (bSuccess = TRUE)
                    Set bSuccess =  SqlFetchNext(hSQLMain, iRet)

Window Variables
    Sql Handle: hSQLMain
    Boolean: bSuccess
    String: szSQL
    Number: iRet
```

Note that the `SELECT` statement must provide parameters to receive column values.

If columns are not bound when the statement is prepared, the application will not be able to retrieve the values at run-time. The second parameter to `SqlFetchNext()` is of some interest as well. It is used to receive a code indicating the current state of the row that was just fetched. This code has four possible values:

- `FETCH_Delete`—indicates that the row has been deleted since the cursor was built
- `FETCH_EOF`—indicates that the end of the cursor has been reached
- `FETCH_Ok`—indicates that the record has not been modified
- `FETCH_Update`—indicates that the record has been modified since the cursor was created

This value may not be entirely accurate depending on the transaction isolation level. For example, if the transaction isolation level is set to read-only, this value would be either `FETCH_Ok`, or FETCH_EOF because the snapshot would not be refreshed after the cursor was created. In most database environments, transaction isolation should be set to read-only, if possible, as this reduces contention and improves performance. Unless an application has a specific need that requires in-place updates or similar cursor operations, this level of isolation should be acceptable.

A possible alternative to the methods demonstrated in Listing B.2 is to combine the SqlPrepare() and SqlExecute() function calls with a single call to SqlPrepareAndExecute(), as illustrated following:

```
Set bSuccess = SqlPrepareAndExecute(hSQLMain, szSQL)
If (bSuccess = TRUE)
    Set bSuccess =  SqlFetchNext(hSQLMain, iRet)
```

The operation can be simplified further with a call to SqlImmediate():

```
Set bSuccess = SqlImmediate(szSQL)
```

After making the call to SqlImmediate(), the first row is already bound to application variables. Subsequent calls to SqlFetchNext() will begin with the second row in the result set. Unfortunately, the first time SqlImmediate() is called, it calls SqlConnect() with a handle that it manages internally. For this reason, it can be somewhat slow the first time it is called. However, each subsequent time it calls only the remaining three functions, SqlPrepare(), SqlExecute(), and SqlFetchNext(). It can also be used with transaction SQL, in which case, it does not make the call to SqlFetchNext().

Transaction-based SQL can be processed using the same functions, in a very similar manner. Listing B.3 is an example of a transaction that inserts a record based on values in the data fields of a form.

Listing B.3. This code fragment inserts rows based on the values in the data fields of a form and demonstrates transaction control in SQLWindows.

```
Contents
    Pushbutton:pbRefresh
        Message Actions
            On SAM_Click
                Set szSQL1 = "SELECT individual_ids.nextval
                            INTO :iNewID FROM dual"
                Set bSuccess = SqlImmediate(szSQL1)
                Set szSQL2 = "INSERT INTO individual VALUES (
                        :iNewID, :dfLast, :dfFirst, :dfNotes)"
                Set szSQL3 = "INSERT INTO phone VALUES (
                        :iNewID, :dfType, :dfNumber)"
                If (bSuccess = TRUE)
                    Set bSuccess = SqlPrepareAndExecute(hSQLMain,
                            szSQL2)
```

```
            If (bSuccess = FALSE)
                Call SqlPrepareAndExecute(hSQLMain, 'ROLLBACK')
            Else
                Set bSuccess = SqlPrepareAndExecute(szSQL3)
            If (bSuccess = FALSE)
                Call SqlPrepareAndExecute(hSQLMain, 'ROLLBACK')
            Else
                Call SqlCommit(hSQLMain)

Window Variables
    Sql Handle: hSQLMain
    Boolean: bSuccess
    String: szSQL1
    String: szSQL2
    String: szSQL3
    Number: iRet
```

In the example, if either insert fails, the entire transaction is rolled back. Note the somewhat odd way in which commits and rollbacks are handled by SAL. SqlCommit() is a function, while no corresponding function exists for a rollback. The rollback must be accomplished through another call to SqlPrepareAndExecute().

Although SQLWindows has no functions specifically designed to support stored procedures, the ODBC syntax for Oracle can be used to execute a stored procedure using the methods previously described. For example, instead of the separate SqlPrepareAndExecute() statements in Listing B.3, a single statement could be used to execute a stored procedure, as illustrated following:

```
Set szSQL2 = "{call insert_indiv_phone(dfLast, :dfFirst, :dfNotes
        , :dfType, :dfNumber)}"
Set bSuccess = SqlPrepareAndExecute(hSQLMain, szSQL2)
```

This example assumes that the stored procedure is using the sequence to get the new ID, and it is handling commits and rollbacks internally.

The methods that have been described for communicating with the database from SQLWindows are a subset of a larger API. Additional functions include methods for scrolling cursors backwards, or to an absolute row position, naming transactions and cursors, and determining the number of rows in a result set before they are fetched.

Unfortunately, some of the more useful functions apply only to SQLBase connections. For example, the SqlError() and SqlGetErrorText() functions can be used to retrieve the error number, description, and remedy for the database error that occurred most recently. However, these values are not received from the driver, but read from a text file that ships with the product, containing only SQLBase error codes, messages, and remedies. Despite a few SQLBase-only features, the methods provided by SAL are fairly comprehensive, and they will prove adequate for most client/server development projects.

Summary

In addition to extensive support for database applications, the object-oriented features of SQLWindows are numerous, although somewhat unorthodox. It supports inheritance, multiple inheritance, and the ability to define classes based on visual and non-visual objects. One of the more interesting features of the SQLWindows model of inheritance is the concept of class variables. SAL distinguishes these from instance variables, which are treated as normal class members. No matter how many instances of an object are created, they share the same class variables. In other words, class variables are global to the class. This implementation can be somewhat useful. For example, a database connection class could have a global counter that stores the number of active connections. Unfortunately, this counter would be somewhat tedious to maintain, because for non-visual classes, constructors and destructors do not exist. The code that creates a new instance of a non-visual object is responsible for calling member functions used to initialize the instance. By the same token, the code that destroys a non-visual object is responsible for calling any clean-up routines.

In fact, the concept of constructors and destructors is not really a part of visual objects either. Visual objects simply have the ability to respond to the Windows messages WM_CREATE and WM_DESTROY, which are represented by SAL as SAM_Create and SAM_Destroy. By defining Message Actions to respond to these messages, the rough equivalents of constructors and destructors can be created.

Another feature of SAL that seems somewhat at odds with the object-oriented model is the fact that all data members and member functions are public (except for variables declared within functions). It would also seem that the programmer should be able to declare variables within Message Actions, which are the closest thing to private member functions within SAL. The fact that variables cannot be defined in event-handlers should be kept in mind when designing SQLWindows applications, so you can attempt to keep the number of instance variables (or window variables) to a reasonable level.

Despite a few shortcomings in the object model employed by SQLWindows, the SAL programming language has many powerful features. Perhaps the most useful of these is the ability to create and respond to user-defined messages. A message can be defined as a global constant in the User section and sent to forms and controls using the SALSendMessage() function. To respond to a user-defined message, a window or control need only add the message and code to handle the message in its Message Actions section. The way in which event-handlers are defined in SAL maps into the actual Windows message very well, which allows SQLWindows objects more flexibility in the messages it can respond to.

SAL also has very good support for common Windows APIs, including DDE, OLE, and (through QuickObjects) MAPI. You can also use QuickObjects to interface with Lotus Notes and NetWare mail, making it very easy to build messaging capabilities into SQLWindows applications. The outline editor and a few unorthodox features of SAL take some getting used to, but overall, SQLWindows is a serious client/server development tool. It is particularly well-suited to rapid prototyping, through the use of QuickObjects.

Using Visual Basic

C

by Advanced Information Systems, Inc.

IN THIS CHAPTER

Microsoft Visual Basic has become the most popular development tool for Windows applications. Its easy-to-use IDE, ANSI standard programming language, and extensive third-party product support have contributed largely to its success.

While Visual Basic lacks many of the object-oriented features of its competitors, the simplicity of the programming language and the development environment make it a frequent choice for rapid prototyping and client/server development. Third-party custom controls, many of which would take months to develop, can be added to a project instantly. Visual Basic provides connectivity to any ODBC data source, as well as support for other common Windows services, including OLE and DDE.

Third-Party Products That Decrease Development Time and Add Value

Among the most comprehensive third-party applications which can quickly jump-start your project is Rapid Application Foundation (RAF) from Advanced Information Systems. RAF is a structured approach to Rapid Application Development. RAF leverages several of the industry's best development products. These products, coupled with RAF, provide a robust development platform while preserving ease of programming. The RAF foundation offers a development path well suited for Rapid Application Development, while preserving ease of maintenance.

RAF includes a set of source code libraries consisting of predeveloped code and precoded form templates. The RAF libraries simplify the effort of building any application while providing robust features only found in professional software applications.

Immediate Benefits to RAF Users

RAF enables applications to be prototyped in minutes instead of weeks. The benefit begins as the RAF prototype is optimized with predeveloped foundation libraries, enabling development of world-class client/server applications in record time. Built-in functionality enables your prototype to immediately connect to all ODBC-compliant databases. Connections may be made directly through database procedures, ODBC, or other precoded techniques. Inter-form communication allows an unlimited number of screens, pop-up windows, notes, combo list boxes, charts, graphs, and spreadsheets to efficiently communicate between applications automatically.

Rapid Application Development

The RAF approach delivers rapid applications for the Windows environment, simplifying window creation through the use of precoded form templates. RAF provides a framework that unifies application coders into a maintainable programming model. RAF greatly minimizes the complexity of code maintenance and learning to develop under the Windows environment.

RAF Courses

Advanced Information Systems, Inc. provides on-site skills transfer courses. These courses offer classroom sessions, as well as project development. AIS trainers customize the lab exercises to directly build your in-house project applications. AIS can be reached at (800)327-9725.

The majority of this appendix focuses on Visual Basic's ODBC interface, which has relatively few features but is extremely easy to use. In addition, the final section includes a brief summary of the Visual Basic environment and language structure, as well as its strengths and weaknesses.

Connecting to the Database

No additional configuration is required to connect to an ODBC data source from Visual Basic. Any drivers and data sources installed and configured using the ODBC administration program are accessible. The Visual Basic Database object is used to establish connections through its OpenDatabase method. The OpenDatabase method takes four arguments, three of which apply only to local desktop databases:

- database name — an empty string for ODBC data sources
- open exclusive — Boolean, always set to False for ODBC data sources
- read only — Boolean, always set to False for ODBC data sources
- connect string — the ODBC connect string, includes "ODBC;", the data source name, user ID, password, and any additional database-specific parameters

To connect to Oracle, the connect string requires no special parameters. The code fragment in Listing C.1 uses values from a generic ODBC login form to build a connect string.

Listing C.1. The Database object is used to connect to the data source.

```
Dim dbOracle As Database
Dim szConnect As String

szConnect = "ODBC;DSN=" & lstDSNs.Text & ";"
szConnect = szConnect & "UID=" & txtID.Text & ";"
szConnect = szConnect & "PWD=" & txtPassword.Text & ";"

Set dbOracle = OpenDatabase("", False, False, szConnect)
```

The connect string constructed in Listing C.1 might look like:

```
"ODBC;DSN=ORACLE;UID=scotty;PWD=tiger;"
```

The methods of the Database object are used to retrieve results, apply SQL transactions, and call stored procedures. In most cases, the application should declare one Database object globally.

The primary means of retrieving results from an ODBC data source is the Snapshot object. The Snapshot object is created using the `CreateSnapshot` method of the Database object. The `CreateSnapshot` method takes two arguments: a SQL `SELECT` statement, and a numeric constant used to control processing of the SQL. Unless the application needs to be portable to different RDBMSs, this numeric constant should be set to `DB_SQLPASSTHROUGH`, (64), which sends the statement directly to the server for processing. This mode allows the developer to use the native syntax of the RDBMS, and prevents the local Microsoft Access engine from attempting to parse and process the SQL. The following code fragment provides a simple example of the use of the `CreateSnapshot` method:

```
Dim dsContacts   As Snapshot

Set dsContacts = dbOracle.CreateSnapshot("SELECT a.last_name, a.first_name,
                    ➥b.phone_nbr FROM individual a, phone b
                    ➥WHERE a.ID = b.IndividualID(+) ORDER BY 1, 2",
                    ➥DB_SQLPASSTHROUGH)
```

The example assumes that the Database object has already connected to the data source. Note that if `DB_SQLPASSTHROUGH` is not specified, a syntax error results because the local Access engine attempts to parse the SQL and does not recognize the outer join syntax.

After applying the SQL and creating the result set, there are numerous methods that can be applied to position the record pointer in the cursor. The `MoveFirst`, `MoveLast`, `MoveNext`, and `MovePrevious` methods are the most commonly used, and their purposes should be self-explanatory. Visual Basic provides the additional method `FindFirst` to position the record pointer at the first record matching specific criteria. For example, assuming that the record pointer is positioned at the first record, the following line would find the first individual with the last name Smith, based on the result set returned by the previous example:

```
dsContacts.FindFirst("last_name = 'Smith'")
```

The criteria supplied as the argument to FindFirst are syntactically equivalent to a WHERE clause in SQL. The additional methods FindNext, FindPrevious, and FindLast operate on the same basis.

After positioning the record pointer, an application can assign variables to result set column values using the Fields property of the Snapshot. The Fields collection is simply a representation of the columns in the result set. They can be accessed by name or by a zero-based index, starting with the left-most column. Listing C.2 demonstrates methods for assigning application variables to result set data.

Listing C.2. The Fields collection is used to access result set data.

```
Dim iRow As Long

iRow = 0
dsContacts.MoveFirst

While Not dsContacts.EOF
    ReDim Preserve szLast(iRow)  As String
    ReDim Preserve szFirst(iRow) As String
    ReDim Preserve szPhone(iRow) As String
    szLast(iRow) = dsContacts.Fields("last_name").Value
    szFirst(iRow) = dsContacts.Fields(1).Value
    szPhone(iRow) = dsContacts.Fields("phone_nbr").Value
    dsContacts.MoveNext
Wend

dsContacts.Close
```

CAUTION

When assigning values from the Fields collection to variables, the application should always check for null values, as below:

```
If (IsNull(dsContacts.Fields("last_name")) = False) Then
    szLast(iRow) = dsContacts.Fields("last_name").Value
End If
```

Assigning a null value to an application variable will produce a run-time error.

As evident from Listing C.2, the more readable form of accessing the Fields collection is to access them by name. When there are only a few columns in the result set, this point does not seem significant. However, if there are 20 or 30 columns in the result, it becomes very difficult to identify a column by index. Also, any changes to the SQL which created the result set may cause the indexes to reference different columns. While it may save a few keystrokes to use numeric indexes, in the interest of writing maintainable code, the Fields collection should be accessed by column name whenever possible.

When the columns of the result set are not static at design-time, the Count property of the Fields collection can be used to determine the number of columns, and the Name property (which applies to each individual field), can be used to create column headings.

> **TIP**
>
> A single Visual Basic object, such as a Database or Snapshot object, cannot be passed as a parameter to a function, but an array of objects can. When dealing with single object, it can be declared as a single element array so that it can be passed to functions and subroutines, and generic methods can be written to operate on these objects.

While Visual Basic also provides Dynaset, Table, and QueryDef objects for retrieving result sets, these objects are not commonly used to communicate with ODBC data sources. The primary difference between a Snapshot and the Dynaset and Table objects in ODBC environments is that the Snapshot creates a read-only result set, while the Dynaset and Table objects' result sets can be edited. However, these objects should not be used for database transactions, for reasons that will be discussed next.

The Dynaset is similar to the Snapshot, except that its result set is refreshed every time a change is made to one of its underlying tables. This is true only for local database files. With ODBC connections, the Dynaset object is, in essence, identical to the Snapshot object, except that the Dynaset can be used for in-place updates, deletes, and insertions.

While Table objects could be used by applications accessing ODBC data sources, it would be unacceptable to do so in most situations. Using the `OpenTable` method is not as readable as a `SELECT` statement in which the columns are clearly identified and referenced by name, and when accessing Oracle, the Table object is the equivalent of a Dynaset created with the SQL `SELECT * FROM` *table_name*. In both cases, the column list is expanded, and the statement is sent to the server using the API function `SQLExecDirect()`.

A QueryDef object is similar to a view that is created and stored by the application. The QueryDef object simply stores frequently used SQL so that it can be read from the database and executed as needed. QueryDefs cannot be created over ODBC connections. Views are a better alternative, because they are stored in the database with a bound access plan, and the SQL does not need to be executed from the client application.

The Visual Basic DataControl provides another option for retrieving a result set through ODBC. The DataControl is used to bind controls to result set columns. To retrieve a result set using a DataControl, its Connect property must be set to the full connect string, as previously described for the `OpenDatabase` method. This property can be set at run-time using a statement like the one below:

```
Data1.Connect=szConnect
```

This example assumes that `szConnect` was constructed as in Listing C.1. The RecordSource property of the DataControl is used to retrieve the result set. If this property is set at design-time, results will be retrieved as soon as the Connect property is assigned and a connection is established. If the Connect property is also assigned at design-time, results will be fetched when the object is instantiated. The RecordSource property can consist of a table name, view name, or a `SELECT` statement. The `DB_SQLPASSTHROUGH` option is not available to the DataControl, so if a `SELECT` statement is used as the RecordSource property, it may not contain an outer join or any other Oracle-specific syntax. In order to use a DataControl with a complex `SELECT` statement, a view should be created so the DataControl can simply use the view as the data source.

Controls can be bound to result set columns through the DataControl. A text box, for example, can be bound to a DataControl by setting its RecordSource property to the name of the DataControl and setting its DataField property to the name of the column in the result set that it should contain. When the result set is retrieved, the text box is then automatically populated with the value of the specified column at the current record position. Numerous third-party vendors provide custom controls that can be bound to result sets in this manner. The standard controls that can be bound to a result set through the DataControl are limited to text boxes, checkboxes, labels, images, and picture boxes.

The Recordset property of the DataControl is nearly identical to a Dynaset object. The `MoveFirst` method and other positioning methods apply to the Recordset property of the DataControl, as well as the `BOF` and `EOF` properties, and the Fields collection. Consequently, the DataControl's result set can be accessed programmatically, in addition to being accessed by bound controls. Using bound controls is generally not the best approach to developing client/server applications, however. The nature of bound controls requires that the cursor to which they are bound persists for the life of the bound controls. For most applications, it is preferable to read the data, populate the necessary controls programmatically, and close the cursor. Note that in Listing C.2, the Snapshot object is used to populate a Visual Basic array, and then it is immediately closed, thereby freeing the cursor on the server. In heavily used systems with a large number of clients, this can have a significant impact on performance.

While the DataControl can be used to perform inserts as well as in-place updates and deletions, it is strongly recommended to use these methods through ODBC. Unfortunately, when Visual Basic establishes an ODBC connection, the ODBC AutoCommit connection option is enabled, and Visual Basic does not provide a method to disable this option. As a result, transaction control is not possible. Even if the transaction involves only a single table and a single operation, the DataControl is a bad choice for applying transactions. The DataControl always updates every column. If there are unbound columns, these values must be set manually, which complicates the entire process. For example, if an application needs to supply a transaction timestamp with every update, there is no clean way to do this. The DataControl does not support passthrough mode, so the Oracle system variable, `sysdate`, cannot be supplied as a value. The application has to supply a time based on the local workstation's clock, which would not only require an assignment to a member of the Fields collection, it would almost certainly introduce inaccuracies. These same problems apply to the Dynaset and Table objects because they use the same methods for applying transactions.

There are three possible solutions to overcome the AutoCommit problem. One solution would be to use Oracle stored procedures exclusively for transaction processing. The ExecuteSQL method of the Database object can be used to call Oracle stored procedures, providing an easy and safe way to communicate transactions to the database. Using stored procedures also simplifies the development of the client application, by freeing it from the responsibility of generating dynamic SQL and controlling transactions. The ExecuteSQL method requires a single argument. The argument is a text string of the SQL to be executed. This method uses passthrough mode by default, so any SQL that can be evaluated by Oracle can be supplied, including the ODBC syntax for calling Oracle procedures. Listing C.3 demonstrates the use of the ExecuteSQL method to call an Oracle stored procedure.

Listing C.3. The ExecuteSQL method can be used to call Oracle stored procedures.

```
Dim iRows    As Integer
Dim szStmt   As String

szStmt = "{call insert_individual('" & txtLastName.Text & ", '"
szStmt = szStmt & txtFirstName.Text & ", '" & txtNotes.Text
szStmt = szStmt & ", '" & txtDateOfBirth.Text & "')}"

iRows = dbOracle.ExecuteSQL(szStmt)
```

The ExecuteSQL method returns the number of rows affected by the transaction, and this value can be tested to determine the success or failure of the operation.

Unfortunately, because Visual Basic does not support prepared execution of SQL statements, it cannot call Oracle stored procedures that use output parameters, or add parameters to the procedure call. The statement must be built dynamically, as in Listing C.3.

A second possible means of overcoming the AutoCommit problem is to use a third-party product, such as Oracle Objects for OLE. This product provides direct replacements for the Visual Basic objects and methods for communicating with Oracle databases. For example, the following code fragment establishes an Oracle session through VB that can be used for transaction control:

```
Dim Session   As Object
Dim dbOracle  As Object

Set Session = CreateObject("OracleInProcServer.XOraSession")
Set dbOracle = Session.OpenDatabase("ORACLE", "scotty/tiger", 0&)
```

The preceding example uses the Visual Basic generic (OLE) Object data type and the CreateObject function to request a new XOraSession object from Oracle's OLE server. The methods of the Session object can then be used to create other objects, and to manage transactions, using the `BeginTrans`, `CommitTrans`, and `Rollback` methods. A full discussion of the features of Oracle Objects for OLE is beyond the scope of this appendix. However, it is important to note that it can provide Visual Basic applications with the capability to control transactions, add parameters to SQL and procedure calls, and make use of output parameters when accessing Oracle databases, among other things.

The potential shortcoming of the previous two means of bypassing Visual Basic's AutoCommit behavior is that they are not portable. If a client application needs to access different RDBMSs, these solutions may not be feasible. A third approach to overcoming the AutoCommit problem is to use the ODBC API directly, which opens numerous possibilities, including the creation of a truly portable client application.

A small subset of the ODBC API can be used to provide transaction control in Visual Basic applications accessing ODBC data sources. The declarations in Listing C.4 should be placed in a module, and will provide access to all functions needed to connect, apply transactions through embedded SQL, and roll back or commit them, as needed.

Listing C.4. ODBC API declarations for Visual Basic.

```
Declare Function SQLAllocConnect Lib "odbc.dll" (
                ByVal hEnv As Long, hDBc As Long) As Integer
Declare Function SQLAllocEnv Lib "odbc.dll" (
                hEnv As Long) As Integer
Declare Function SQLAllocStmt Lib "odbc.dll" (
                ByVal hDBc As Long, hStmt As Long) As Integer
Declare Function SQLDisconnect Lib "odbc.dll" (
                ByVal hDBc As Long) As Integer
Declare Function SQLDriverConnect Lib "odbc.dll" (
                ByVal hDBc As Long, ByVal hWnd As Integer,
                ByVal szCSin As String, ByVal cbCSin As Integer,
                ByVal szCSOut As String, ByVal cbCSMax As Integer,
                cbCSOut As Integer, ByVal f As Integer) As Integer
Declare Function SQLExecDirect Lib "odbc.dll" (
                ByVal hStmt As Long, ByVal SQLString As String,
                ByVal SQLStringLen As Long) As Integer
Declare Function SQLFreeConnect Lib "odbc.dll" (
                ByVal hDBc As Long) As Integer
Declare Function SQLFreeEnv Lib "odbc.dll" (
                ByVal hEnv As Long) As Integer
Declare Function SQLFreeStmt Lib "odbc.dll" (ByVal hStmt As Long,
                ByVal EndOption As Integer) As Integer
Declare Function SQLSetConnectOption Lib "odbc.dll" (
                ByVal hDBc As Long, ByVal fOption As Integer,
                ByVal vParam As Long) As Integer
Declare Function SQLTransact Lib "odbc.dll" (
                ByVal hEnv As Long, ByVal hDBc As Long,
                ByVal fnType As Integer) As Integer

Global Const SQL_NTS = -3
Global Const SQL_DRIVER_NOPROMPT = 0
Global Const SQL_COMMIT = 0
```

continues

Listing C.4. continued

```
Global Const SQL_ROLLBACK = 1
Global Const SQL_MAX_MESSAGE_LENGTH = 512
Global Const SQL_AUTOCOMMIT = 102
Global Const SQL_DROP = 1
```

After establishing a connection for retrieving results with the OpenDatabase method, the application should establish a second connection to the database using the API functions—for applying transactions. After establishing this connection, SQLSetConnectOption() should be used to disable AutoCommit. Listing C.5 demonstrates how this might be accomplished.

Listing C.5. Establishing a database connection using the ODBC API.

```
Dim hEnv             As Long
Dim hDBc             As Long
Dim szConnectString  As String

Dim iError           As Integer
Dim hWnd             As Integer
Dim iLenCSOut        As Integer
Dim szCSOut          As String * 254

szConnectString = "ODBC;DSN=ORACLE;UID=scotty;PWD=tiger;"
hWnd = frmMDIFrame.hWnd

' Allocate environment
iError = SQLAllocEnv(hEnv)

' Allocate connection
iError = SQLAllocConnect(hEnv, hDBc)

' Load driver & connect to ODBC data source
iError = SQLDriverConnect(hDBc, hWnd, szConnectString, SQL_NTS,
        szCSOut, 254, iLenCSOut, SQL_DRIVER_NOPROMPT)

' Disable autocommit
iError = SQLSetConnectOption(hDB, SQL_AUTOCOMMIT, 0)
```

Obviously, in practice, the connect string would not be hard-coded and the return value of each function should be checked. The example in Listing C.5 is intended only to demonstrate the use of the ODBC API to establish a database connection.

Once a connection has been established, the application can apply transactions using SQLExecDirect() after allocating a statement handle with SQLAllocStmt(). SQLTransact() can then be used to commit or roll back a transaction based on the return value of SQLExecDirect(). After applying the transaction, the application should call SQLFreeStmt() to free the resources allocated to the statement handle. Listing C.6 provides an example of the calls to these functions.

Listing C.6. Applying a transaction using embedded SQL.

```
Dim hStmt          As Long

' Allocate a statement handle
iError = SQLAllocStmt(hDBc, hStmt)

For i = 0 To iStmts
    ' Apply SQL
    iError = SQLExecDirect(hStmt, szSQL(i), SQL_NTS)
    If iError Then
        ' Rollback
        iNextErr = SQLTransact(hEnv, hDB, SQL_ROLLBACK)
        Exit For
    End If
Next i

If (iError = 0) Then
    ' Commit
    iError = SQLTransact(hEnv, hDB, SQL_COMMIT)
End If

' Free the statement handle
iError = SQLFreeStmt(hStmt, SQL_DROP)
```

The example in Listing C.6 assumes that the environment and connection handle, hEnv and hDBc, are valid and connected to the data source, and that szSQL is an array of iStmts SQL statements. If any statement in the transaction fails, a rollback is issued and processing of the transaction is discontinued. If all statements are processed without errors, the entire transaction is committed. Regardless of whether the transaction is committed or rolled back, the application frees the statement handle.

When the application exits, it needs to disconnect from the data source and free all resources allocated to the environment and connection handles. This can be accomplished with three functions calls, as illustrated in the following lines:

```
iError = SQLDisconnect(hDB)
iError = SQLFreeConnect(hDB)
iError = SQLFreeEnv(hEnv)
```

The full capabilities of ODBC are far beyond the scope of this discussion, but many additional capabilities can be provided, and an application can be constructed in a manner that is completely database-independent using embedded SQL. However, if an application does not need to be portable to other database platforms, it may be easier to use stored procedures or a third-party product, such as Oracle Objects for OLE, to apply transactions from Visual Basic.

It is unfortunate that Visual Basic does not provide a means by which AutoCommit can be disabled for connections established internally. This is a limitation of the implementation of the Jet Database Engine that Visual Basic uses.

One of the most powerful (and potentially dangerous) features of Visual Basic is the means by which errors are trapped, using the `On Error` statement. This statement is well-used in Visual Basic programming because all untrapped run-time errors are fatal. The `On Error` statement is used to specify an error handler to which execution jumps if an error occurs. The error handler can be specified using `GoTo`, or `Resume Next` can be specified to allow program execution to continue normally. The system variables `Err` and `Error$` store a numeric code and a text description for the error that occurred most recently. The fact that only the most recent value is stored is what makes `On Error Resume Next` a somewhat dangerous way to trap and handle errors. It is very convenient to use, but the value of `Err` should be checked wherever an error requiring a specific action occurs.

A common mistake in Visual Basic programming is to misunderstand its array dimensions. Consider the following declaration, for example:

```
ReDim szStrings(2) As String
```

Most would assume that this declares an array of two strings. However, the previous statement actually allocates an array of three strings. The subscript in an array declaration sets the upper bound, not the number of elements in the array, so `szString(0)`, `szString(1)`, and `szString(2)` are all valid, based on the declaration. The base subscript can be changed to 1, using the `Option Base` statement:

```
Option Base 1
```

If this statement appears in the same module as the previous array declaration, the array would have only two elements, `szString(1)` and `szString(2)`. In this case, `szString(0)` would be an invalid reference.

Summary

The Visual Basic programming language is particularly easy to learn and use. Nearly all developers have some experience with BASIC, and many of the language constructs have been in place since the very first versions of what is now referred to as BASIC A.

Despite some idiosyncrasies, a lack of object-oriented features, and relatively weak database support, Visual Basic is an extremely useful development tool. Its shortcomings are offset by the simplicity of its IDE and language, and extensive third-party support. The uncluttered and completely non-modal IDE, a flexible ANSI-standard programming language, and a wide variety of prebuilt objects make Visual Basic an excellent choice for projects requiring rapid development.

Using Delphi

D

*by Advanced
Information
Systems, Inc.*

Borland's Delphi is one of the newest visual development tools for Microsoft Windows. It has positioned itself in the market as a high-performance alternative to Microsoft Visual Basic. What separates Delphi from its competition in this regard is its ability to compile stand-alone executables and DLLs, with no run-time libraries required.

Delphi provides full support of ODBC and numerous object classes for communicating with ODBC data sources. It ships with a single-user desktop version of Borland's InterBase Server and its ODBC-enabled ReportSmith querying and reporting tool. The client/server edition also ships native IDAPI drivers for Oracle, Sybase, and Informix, among others.

Object Pascal, the programming language used in Delphi development, supports many of the object-oriented features typically associated with C++, including public and private data members and functions, inheritance, and polymorphism. The language also supports a wide range of data types and advanced features, including true pointer types and structured exception handling.

Although Object Pascal and Delphi provide an abundance of noteworthy features, this appendix focuses primarily on Delphi's support for database applications. An overview of the more significant features of the language is included, as well as a brief discussion of the strengths and weaknesses of Delphi.

Configuring a Data Source

To make a data source available to Delphi, IDAPI.CFG must be edited using the BDE configuration utility. This utility can be accessed from the Tools menu in the IDE. When the utility is started, it displays currently configured data sources, some of which may be preconfigured IDAPI interfaces, depending on the options selected when Delphi was installed. The main window of the BDE configuration utility should appear as shown in Figure D.1.

FIGURE D.1.

The main window of the Delphi BDE configuration utility.

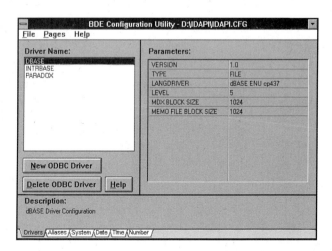

Delphi can interface with any ODBC data source configured and defined in ODBC.INI. To configure an existing ODBC data source for Delphi's use, click the New ODBC Driver command button. A simple dialog box displays and requires three basic items. The SQL Link Driver name is simply an identifier to be used by Delphi, and any unique name can be used. Using the Default ODBC Driver drop-down, select from the list of currently installed drivers. If the required driver does not appear in the list, it has not been correctly installed. ODBC drivers can be installed using ODBCADMN.EXE, a Microsoft utility that is typically provided by driver vendors. After selecting a driver, the Default Data Source Name drop-down will be populated with a list of the data sources defined for the selected driver. Figure D.2 provides an example of how this dialog box might look when configuring the Oracle7 ODBC driver.

FIGURE D.2.

The Add ODBC Driver dialog box can be used to set up the Oracle7 driver for use in Delphi.

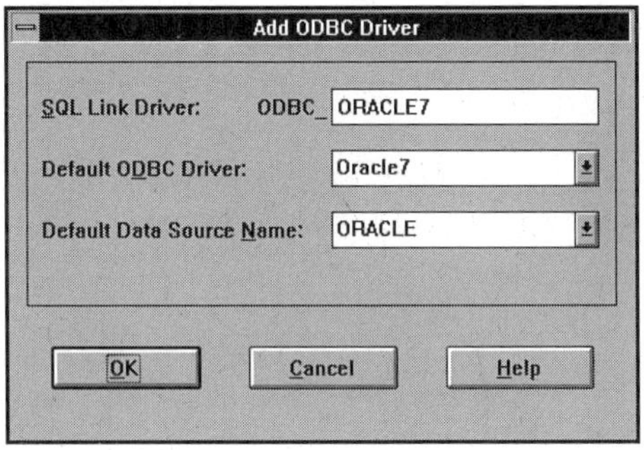

After selecting the default data source, click the OK button to add the driver. The newly added driver should now appear in the main window of the configuration utility, as shown in Figure D.3.

FIGURE D.3.

Parameters can be set from the main window of the configuration utility.

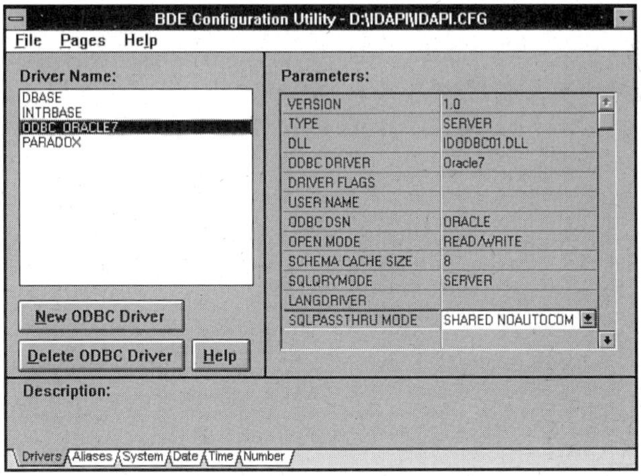

Of the available parameters, SQLQRYMODE and SQLPASSTHRU MODE are the most significant. Setting SQLQUERYMODE to SERVER causes Delphi to deliver all queries to the database server for processing. This prevents the local BDE from attempting to process the query from the desktop. The SQLPASSTHRU mode should be set to SHARED NOAUTOCOMMIT. This setting prevents transactions sent to the server from being committed automatically. The tabs across the bottom of the BDE configuration utility's main window allow the setting of additional parameters, including date, time, and numeric formats. These settings apply to the local database engine and should not need to be modified for ODBC connections.

The BDE configuration utility supports multiple configuration files. The changes can be saved in a new file, and the utility will optionally update WIN.INI to use the new file as the default. When adding a new data source, you may want to save the configuration file with a different name so that the old file can be used as a backup, in case other data sources were changed inadvertently. After the configuration file is saved, Delphi can access the new data source.

Communicating with the Database

Delphi supplies several classes that can be used to establish and maintain connections to the database, process transactions, and retrieve result sets. The most useful of these classes include:

- TSession—Used to manage database connections
- TDatabase—Used to establish a connection and control transactions
- TQuery—Subclass of TDataSet, used to retrieve results and apply transactions
- TStoredProc—Subclass of TDataSet, used to call stored procedures
- TDataSource—Used to bind data-aware controls to result sets and to link related result sets
- TField—Corresponds to a column in a result set

All of these objects are available on the Data Access tab of the toolbar.

Communication with the database is initiated by the TDatabase component. Before establishing a connection, the DriverName and DatabaseName properties must be set. These should correspond to the driver name (specified when the data source was set up through BDE Configuration) and a valid data source name for the specific driver. The application connects to the database by using the Open method, or by setting the Connected property to True.

> **TIP**
>
> Although all objects' properties and methods can be accessed through the object inspector, some objects and properties have special dialog boxes. For example, double-clicking the TDatabase component displays a dialog box that makes it easier to view and modify its properties.

If the Params property does not have all required parameters set, the TDatabase object displays a login form automatically, provided that the LoginPrompt is set to True. Connection parameters are set using the Params property, which is actually a TStrings object. Parameters are set using the Add method, as demonstrated in the following code fragment:

```
dbOra.Params.Add('SERVER NAME=ORACLE');
dbOra.Params.Add('USER NAME=scotty');
dbOra.Params.Add('PASSWORD=tiger');
dbOra.Connected := True;
```

The KeepConnected property, when set to True, keeps the connection open even when no result sets are open and no transactions are in progress. The TransIsolation property determines how records are read when they are currently involved in a transaction. Oracle supports tiReadCommitted, which allows only committed changes to be read, and tiRepeatableRead in read-only mode. The latter mode prevents Oracle from attempting to refresh the Snapshot for records that have already been read.

The TDatabase object is also used for transaction control (assuming that SQLPASSTHRU MODE was set to SHARED NOAUTOCOMMIT when the data source was configured). The StartTransaction, Commit, and Rollback methods should be used whenever SQL transactions are applied. The exception to this rule is when the application calls a stored procedure which handles commits and rollbacks internally.

In some cases, the behavior of the TDatabase object can be overridden by the TSession object. The TSessions object is particularly useful for applications that connect to more than one database or need more than one connection for asynchronous processing. The KeepConnections property of the TSessions object will override the KeepSessions property of individual TDatabase objects. The TSession object is always global and has additional methods for querying the BDE configuration files. It stores an array of connected TDatabase objects in its Databases property, and the number of connected TDatabase objects in its DatabaseCount property.

The TQuery object is the primary means for communicating with the database. It is used not only to retrieve results, but also to apply SQL transactions. The SQL property is a TStrings object used to store the SQL to be executed. An application can use a TQuery to build simple dynamic SQL very easily, using the Params property. Application variables can be substituted for literal values wherever they might appear. For example, the following statements can be used to generate a result set dynamically based on a value entered by a user in a TEdit object:

```
qryGetCusts.SQL.Add('SELECT * FROM CUSTOMERS WHERE LAST_NAME LIKE :LastName');
qryGetCusts.Params[0].AsString(txtLastName.Text);
```

This is particularly useful for data entry forms where records will be inserted frequently into the same table or view. The Params property is an array of TParams objects. They are referenced by subscripts and set using the AsString, AsInteger, AsFloat, or one of the other properties that store a value based on a data type.

When SQL is parameterized, it should be prepared only once. It can then be executed repeatedly with different parameters. The code fragment in Listing D.1 illustrates the use of the Prepare and ExecSQL Methods, as well as transaction control provided by the TDatabase object.

Listing D.1. Dynamic SQL and transaction processing in Delphi.

```
{this code is executed once}
qryAddCust.SQL.Add('INSERT INTO CUSTOMERS (LAST_NAME, FIRST_NAME) ');
qryAddCust.SQL.Add('VALUES (:Last, :First)');
qryAddCust.Prepare;

{this code can be executed many times}
dbOracle.StartTransaction;
qryAddCust.Params[0].AsString(txtLast.Text);
qryAddCust.Params[1].AsString(txtFirst.Text);
try
    qryAddCust.ExecSQL;
    dbOracle.Commit;
except
    dbOracle.Rollback;
end;
```

The ExecSQL method should be used only for statements that do not return a result set. For SELECT statements, the Open method should be used. After a result set has been returned from the database, the TQuery object will have an array of TFields objects, which can be accessed in much the same way as TParam objects. Listing D.2 demonstrates the methods used to retrieve result sets from a TQuery object.

> **TIP**
>
> The right mouse button has special uses for many objects. Right-clicking a TQuery object displays a pop-up menu that you can use to access two dialog boxes that are specific to designing a TQuery. You can use the Fields Editor and Define Parameters dialog boxes to build queries visually.

Listing D.2. Using the query object to retrieve results without bound controls.

```
qryGetCusts.Open;
while (qryGetCusts.EOF = False) do
begin
    lstFullName.Add(Concat(qryGetCusts.Fields[0].AsString, + ','
                          + qryGetCusts.Fields[0].AsString));
    qryGetCusts.MoveBy(1);
end;
qryGetCusts.Close;
qryGetCusts.SQL.Clear;
```

Several important properties and methods that apply to the TQuery are illustrated by Listing D.2. The EOF and BOF properties are Boolean values, set to true when the record pointer is positioned at end-of-file or at beginning-of-file, respectively. The properties AsString, AsInteger, and so on apply to the TFields objects in much the same way as they are applied to TParam objects, only they are typically used to read, rather than set values. MoveBy can be used to move the record pointer any number of records in the current direction, (which is forward by default). First, Last, Prior, and Next can also be used to position the record pointer. The Close method should always be called when the result set is no longer needed, and the Clear method of the SQL property should be used to clean up when an application sets this property dynamically at run-time.

There are several other important TQuery properties that are not demonstrated by the code example in Listing D.2. The RequestLive property can be used to create a cursor that is updatable and refreshes automatically. However, there are numerous restrictions that can prevent this property from being used. In most cases, this should be set to False even when it is supported because it is likely to increase network traffic and database contention. The UpdateMode property is applicable only to live result sets and is used to set the requirements for matching records on updates. When an application does not need scrollable cursors, the Unidirectional property should be set to True. This improves performance, particularly when scrollable cursors are not supported by the driver. In these cases, Delphi attempts to emulate a scrollable cursor, potentially causing it to read the entire result set before returning from the Open method.

One property that should not be overlooked is the Database property. This value must correspond to the Database property of a connected TDatabase object. The Database property should not be confused with the DataSource property, which is used to locate unbound parameters at run-time through a TDataSource object, which can be very useful in creating relationships between queries.

The TDataSource component is used to bind data-aware controls to result sets. Delphi includes a full complement of data-aware controls, including a grid, radio buttons, check boxes, lists, and drop-down combos. The DataSet property of the TDataSource object is used to specify the query or table that it will use to bind results to controls. The AutoEdit property is applicable only to live results sets. When set to True, this property forces the underlying result set into Edit mode when a bound control is modified. When communicating with remote database servers, using the AutoEdit property for updating records is generally unacceptable, because transaction control is lost.

Bound controls are most useful in displaying read-only result sets or when used in conjunction with a separate query to apply an update to an existing record. A record can be retrieved and displayed with minimal code using bound controls, but in order to use the transaction methods of the TDatabase component, code must be written to apply any updates using a separate query.

A TDataSource component does not have its own set of TField objects—it simply accesses an existing result set to supply information to bound controls. Controls are bound to a TDataSource through the DataSource and DataField properties. The DataSource must correspond to an existing TDataSource object's name, and the DataField property should correspond to a column in the underlying query or table. If these properties are set correctly, bound controls are populated automatically when the TQuery or TTable is opened and the TDataSource is enabled.

The simplest way to implement this technique requires no code at all. A TTable object can be placed on the form with its Database and TableName properties set and its Active property set to True. Next, a TDataSet object is placed on the form, and its DataSet property is set to the name of the TTable object. Finally, a data-aware TDBGrid is placed on the form, and its DataSource property is set to the name of the TDataSource object. At run-time, as soon as the application connects to the database, the table is read and the grid is populated. This simplicity is one of the great attractions to using bound controls.

However, the use of bound controls is a questionable technique, particularly in MDI applications. In order for bound controls to display data, the query or table object must remain open; this prevents the object from being used to apply other transactions or queries. If you have several MDI windows concurrently open with bound controls, using multiple TQuery or TTable objects can become very expensive in terms of workstation, network, and server resources. Although it requires more handwritten code, using a query to populate controls and closing the query immediately is a safer and more efficient approach.

A better use of the TDataSource object involves the creation of dynamic SQL. In addition to accessing data from TQuery and TTable objects, the TDataSource object can be used to provide parameters to TQueries at run-time. The DataSource property of the TQuery object is used to specify the name of a TDataSource to check when attempting to resolve unbound parameters. If the name of an unbound TQuery parameter matches a column name in a TDataSource data set, the value of the matching column at the current record position will be used as the parameter. For example, an accounts receivable system may need to display summary records of outstanding accounts and also provide transaction details as requested. This can be accomplished using two TQueries and a TDataSource that use information supplied at run-time. One TData query might provide the summary level information in a read-only data-aware grid, including the account number. Right-clicking on a particular account might be used as the mechanism to display a pop-up with the account details for the selected account. The SQL for the TQuery object used to retrieve the detail information might be defined at design-time as

```
SELECT DATE, DEBIT_AMT, CREDIT_AMT
FROM TRANSACTIONS WHERE ACCT_NO = :acct_no
ORDER BY DATE
```

A TDataSource object can be used to supply the parameter value to this query. The DataSet property of the TDataSource object should be set to the summary-level TQuery, which uses the SQL below:

```
SELECT ACCT_NO, ACCT_NAME, BALANCE
FROM ACCTS_REC
ORDER BY ACCTS_REC
```

The TQuery object should then set its DataSource property equal to the name of the TDataSource object. When the detail TQuery is opened, it will receive the value of ACCT_NO for the current summary record as the parameter to its SQL with no intervention at run-time. The TDataSource object is particularly useful in creating this kind of master-detail relationship.

Delphi also provides support for stored procedures through its implementation of the TStoredProc component. As with the other descendants of TResultSet, the TStoredProc object requires the name of a connected TDatabase object in its Database property. The name of the stored procedure in the database should be selected from the drop-down list provided for the StoredProcName property. The ParamBindMode is used to indicate how parameters will be bound at run-time, by name or by index. The Active property should be set to False unless the stored procedure will return a result set. If this is the case, setting the Active property to True will cause the stored procedure to fire.

The TStoredProc component is ideal for applying parametered transactions on data entry forms. Stored procedures are executed in much the same way as SQL transactions applied through TQuery objects. Listing D.3 provides an example of using a stored procedure to insert records from a simple data entry form.

Listing D.3. Demonstrating the use of the TStoredProc component.

```
{This code should only be executed once,
 perhaps in the form's constructor       }
spInsIndiv.Prepare;

{This code will be executed for each transaction}
spInsIndiv.ParamByName('Last').AsString := txtLast.Text;
spInsIndiv.ParamByName('First').AsString := txtFirst.Text;
spInsIndiv.ParamByName('DOB').AsString := txtDOB.Text;
spInsIndiv.ParamByName('Notes').AsString := txtNotes.Text;
try
    spInsIndiv.ExecProc;
    Application.MessageBox('A new record was added.',
                          'Oracle Unleashed', mb_OK)
except
    Application.MessageBox('Unable to add the current record.',
                          'Oracle Unleashed', mb_OK);
end;
```

Note that the method for executing a stored procedure, ExecProc, is different than the method used to execute a query. As with dynamic SQL queries, the procedure needs to be prepared before parameters are bound, but only once. Assigning values to parameters using the ParamByName method works in much the same way as accessing the array of TParams by index. Using ParamByName is probably a better choice because it results in more readable code.

TIP

The parameters to stored procedures can be viewed at design-time by right-clicking the TStoredProc object and selecting Define Parameters from the pop-up menu.

When calling stored procedures with output parameters, you must allocate sufficient space for variables that will be bound to the output parameters. This is a potential problem when using string variables. For example, the following lines of code will result in a general protection fault:

```
var
    PChar:  szOut;
begin
    spGetNotes.Prepare;
    spGetNotes.ParamByName('NotesOut').AsString := szOut;
```

The next code fragment should work, (assuming that the length of the string returned from the database will never exceed 255 bytes):

```
var
    String:  szOut[255];
begin
    spGetNotes.Prepare;
    spGetNotes.ParamByName('NotesOut').AsString := szOut;
```

When using stored procedures, explicit transaction control might not be necessary. In most cases, any commits or rollbacks should be handled within the stored procedure. This is the safest way to process transactions, and it simplifies the code that applies transactions from the client side.

The methods of communicating with the database described in this section are a small subset of all the options provided by Delphi. Additional database components include the TBatchMove object and the TReport object, which allows ReportSmith reports to be integrated with Delphi applications.

Summary

As mentioned in the introduction to this appendix, the object-oriented features, support for pointers and complex data types, and language structure provided by Object Pascal are among Delphi's greatest strengths.

In addition to the standard data types, Object Pascal allows the creation of any type of pointer, including pointers to user-defined classes and structures, (records, in Pascal terminology). Pointers are allowed within complex data types and class definitions, as well.

Class declarations in Object Pascal are very similar to C++ declarations. The ability to declare member data elements and private functions improves encapsulation and allows for information hiding. Also in the C++ tradition, Delphi's model of inheritance allows base class functions to be overridden by descendants, allowing polymorphic behavior in user-defined classes. Unfortunately, support for overloaded member functions seems to be lacking.

Another strong feature of Object Pascal is its support for structured exception handling. Listings D.1 and D.3 provide examples of the `try...except` blocks used to handle exceptions in Delphi. The `finally` keyword can be used to create a resource protection block that frees memory without handling the exception. The code listings in D.1 and D.3 do not actually handle the exceptions, either. Delphi provides a fairly comprehensive list of pre-defined exceptions that can be handled using the syntax:

```
on exception do statement
```

An exception instance is never destroyed until it is handled. User-defined exceptions can also be declared and thrown.

Delphi's weaknesses are few, considering that it is a first version of a fairly complicated development tool. Aside from the occasional UAE and some bugs in the security features of the local database server, Delphi seems to be a stable and solid product. The database objects, while easy to use, do seem to be geared more to desktop applications than client/server development, with heavy emphasis on bound controls. However, SQL Traces will show that it makes very efficient use of the ODBC API in certain situations. This is because it maps to the API more cleanly than most Windows development tool's ODBC layers, which typically don't provide methods for using prepared execution. The close relationship to ODBC is somewhat surprising considering that IDAPI drivers are shipped with the product. For developers that are already familiar with the ODBC API, this should make a switch to IDAPI nearly transparent.

Overall, Delphi goes a long way toward living up to its billing as "the RADical performance tool". The IDE is fairly intuitive, the object hierarchy well-designed, and the Object Pascal programming language is arguably the best among the desktop development tools. The easy-to-configure ODBC connectivity and support for stored procedures make it a good choice for developing client applications to interface with Oracle.

INDEX

Add to Your Sams Library Today with the Best Books for Programming, Operating Systems, and New Technologies

The easiest way to order is to pick up the phone and call

1-800-428-5331

between 9:00 a.m. and 5:00 p.m. EST.

For faster service please have your credit card available.

ISBN	Quantity	Description of Item	Unit Cost	Total Cost
0-672-30681-6		Oracle DBA Survival Guide (Book/CD-ROM)	$49.99	
0-672-30757-X		Developing Personal Oracle7 Applications (Book/CD-ROM)	$45.00	
0-672-30873-8		Essential Oracle7	$25.00	
0-672-30609-3		Teach Yourself ODBC Programming in 21 Days	$29.99	
0-672-30832-0		Teach Yourself Database Programming with Visual Basic 4 in 21 Days (Book/CD-ROM)	$39.99	
0-672-30789-8		Developing Client/Server Applications with Visual Basic 4 (Book/CD-ROM)	$49.99	
0-672-30833-9		PowerBuilder 4 Unleashed (Book/CD-ROM)	$49.99	
0-672-30837-1		Visual Basic 4 Unleashed (Book/CD-ROM)	$45.00	
0-672-30851-7		Teach Yourself Database Programming with Delphi (Book/CD-ROM)	$39.99	
0-672-30771-5		Essential Visual Basic 4	$25.00	
0-672-30511-9		Developing SQLWindows 5 Applications (Book/CD-ROM)	$45.00	
0-672-30613-1		Database Developer's Guide with Visual C++ (Book/CD-ROM)	$49.99	
		Shipping and Handling: See information below.		
		TOTAL		

❏ 3 ½" Disk

❏ 5 ¼" Disk

Shipping and Handling: $4.00 for the first book, and $1.75 for each additional book. Floppy disk: add $1.75 for shipping and handling. If you need to have it NOW, we can ship product to you in 24 hours for an additional charge of approximately $18.00, and you will receive your item overnight or in two days. Overseas shipping and handling adds $2.00 per book and $8.00 for up to three disks. Prices subject to change. Call for availability and pricing information on latest editions.

201 W. 103rd Street, Indianapolis, Indiana 46290

1-800-428-5331 — Orders   1-800-835-3202 — FAX   1-800-858-7674 — Customer Service

Book ISBN 0-672-30872-X